A World of Baby Names

A World of Baby Names

Revised and Updated

TERESA NORMAN

A PERIGEE BOOK

A Perigee Book
Published by The Berkley Publishing Group
A division of Penguin Group (USA) Inc.
375 Hudson Street
New York, New York 10014

Text design by Irving Perkins Associates
Cover design by Dale Fiorillo

First Perigee edition: February 1996

Revised and updated Perigee edition: July 2003

Revised and updated edition ISBN: 0-399-52894-6

Library of Congress Cataloging-in-Publication Data
Norman, Teresa.
A world of baby names / Teresa Norman.—Rev. and updated.
p. cm.
Includes bibliographical references (p.) and index.
ISBN 0-399-52894-6
1. Names, Personal—Dictionaries. I. Title.
CS2377.N67 2003
929.4'4'03—dc21
2003046015

Printed in the United States of America
10 9 8 7 6 5 4 3 2 1

To my mother, June Wray . . .
she has given me the precious gifts of life and love.

To my wonderful husband, John . . .
his steadfast love and support I treasure dearly.

And to my beloved children:
John Michael, Brian, Joseph, and Anne . . .
named before this book was written,
they are my inspiration.

Contents

Acknowledgments

THIS PROJECT was completed with the help and support of many people. A special thanks goes out to my mother, June Wray, to Christina Arbini, Silvia Butler, Esme Bird, Dasari Rao, You Bi, Sophia (Dao Ming) Ding, Yuliya Anatolievna Shilina, Mariya Yakovlevna Shilina, Thanh Binh Bui, and Thao Thu Hong for their contributions. I am indebted to them all.

Teresa Norman, 2003

Introduction

In 1992, 974,000 people legally immigrated to the United States from at least sixty-four different countries, bringing with them their languages, their cultures, and their names. But, like many of our immigrant great-grandparents, one of the first things many of them did was adopt an American name as a way to better assimilate into American society.

In an effort to reaffirm our cultural identity, we often begin by choosing ethnic names for our children. African-Americans are bestowing more African names upon their offspring than before; people of Irish ancestry are choosing Gaelic names; Native Americans are selecting names from their native languages; people who adopt children from foreign countries often seek out a name from the child's homeland. An ethnic name enables us to identify with a larger group sharing a common heritage.

A World of Baby Names contains names from more than sixty countries and many different languages and cultural groups, as well as biblical names, and astrological and mythological names. The book also includes information on naming customs and name lore as pertains to each country or cultural group.

I've always been fascinated by the study of names. For me, it goes beyond just learning the meaning of names and actually offers an interesting look at the history of many cultures: the way they lived; the languages and dialects they spoke; and the social customs and political influences that affected their lives. Thousands of years of civilization unfold through the study of names: the great intellectual triumphs of India and China a thousand years before the Europeans managed to crawl out of the Dark Ages; the spread of Christianity and Islam; golden ages of reason and learning; dark ages of ignorance, fear, and brutal conquest; and the search for freedom and new, uncharted territories. Every major historical event has affected the types of names found in different times and in different lands. In this book, I've tried to do more than just list thousands of names from around the world. I've tried to give the names historical and cultural context. I've tried to make learning about names as exciting for you as it is for me.

Whether you are searching for a special name for your precious child, helping a youngster to find the history and meaning of his or her name, or just browsing out of curiosity, I hope this book can be of service to you.

If you have a favored name you would like to share, or a cultural group or language you would like to see listed, I would be pleased to hear from you. You can write me through my publisher, Perigee Books.

Each entry in *A World of Baby Names* is alphabetized according to the English alphabet; thus, entries having initial letters with a diacritical mark, such as Åmund, are alphabetized as if they had none.

Many entries contain a cross-reference. When the cross-reference is, for example, "*See* MARY" or "*See* JOHN (Male Names)," Mary (or John) can be found in the same chapter. However, if the cross-reference is, for example, "*See* MARY (English Names)," Mary will be found in the chapter indicated.

Although pronunciations have been included in this book, it is important to be aware that many sounds spoken in other languages have no English equivalents. Also note that names are pronounced differently in different parts of many countries, as the name Sarah is in the U.S. Therefore, many pronunciations are approximate and at times, just the most common are used.

Abbreviations Used in This Text

Var: Variant forms or spellings, such as Catherine and Katherine

Short: Shortened forms, such as Brad from Bradley

Dim: Diminutive forms, such as Jeannette from Jeanne

Pet: Pet forms, such as Danny from Daniel

A World of Baby Names

Chapter One

African Names

Africa is home to hundreds of languages and more than a thousand ethnic groups. Though customs vary, the naming traditions of the major cultural groups discussed in this chapter are representative of those across the continent.

Children are revered throughout Africa and the birth of a child is an occasion for rejoicing. The naming ceremony is generally ritualistic and festive. It is cause for celebration to distinguish the child—to welcome him into the community and to congratulate the parents.

A person's name is considered his most valuable possession, for it is the only thing that can survive death. Great care is therefore taken in selecting a child's name, and many factors are considered before the name is chosen. Names such as the female Komuko (this one will not die) and the male Zimoko (thank you) reflect the sad fact of high infant mortality and the parents' fervent hope that their child will survive. Birth order, the day of the week on which the child is born, important events, physical characteristics, religion, and circumstances surrounding the child's birth are important considerations in choosing a name.

A Yoruba child is named on the seventh day after birth if it is female and on the ninth day if the baby is male. Twins and children born to Christian or Muslim parents are named on the eighth day. Three names are bestowed at the naming ceremony: the personal name (the *oruko*), the "praise" name (the *oriki*), and the kinship name (the *orile*).

Traditionally, the oruko name is based on circumstances surrounding the birth or the family's living situation at the time. Examples of these types of names include the male name Adebayo (he came in a joyful time) and the female Abidemi (born during the father's absence). Other examples of oruko names fall into the category called "born-with" names and include Taiwo (firstborn twin) and Kehinde (second of twins). These "twin" names apply to children of either sex.

The oriki typically expresses the hopes the parents have for the child's future, or in some cases, simply refers to a unique attribute of the child. The female name Abimbola (born to be rich) and the male Adunbi (born to be pleasant) are examples of these names.

Finally, the orile name denotes which kinship group the child comes from. This genealogical name is often ancient, traced back as far as possible to the earliest known ancestor. This is comparable to our family names, which are often patronymics.

A person's name is also of particular significance to the Ghanaian people. From the beginning, children are taught the importance of their names and to act properly and responsibly in order to bring honor to their names. If they are named after an important figure, it is their duty to emulate the life of that person.

Ghanaian names consist of two parts: the Akeradini, the name of the deity associated with the day upon which the child is born, and the Agyadini, the name given to the child by its father. The Akeradini is bestowed upon the child immediately after birth. It is considered a "born-with" name. Examples are the female Adwoa (born on Monday) and the male Kwasi (born on Sunday). Often the family combines the birthday name with the birth order name, creating a unique name for the child. The Agyadini is not given until the naming ceremony on the seventh day after birth. The name is chosen from distinguished members of the father's family.

The Ibo people of Nigeria are another group for whom a child's naming ceremony is of great importance. In general, an Ibo baby is named eight days after birth and the ceremony often begins with a spiritual diviner finding out which divinity reincarnated the child. Offerings are made to the spirit, who is regarded as the child's protector, and the child is given the name of the reincarnator. Several other names are also bestowed at the ceremony. A baby may be given a name indicative of its physical characteristics, the day on which it was born, or the parents' happiness at the birth of the child. The female Adamma (child of beauty) and the male Chijioke (God gives talent) are two such examples. The name chosen to be the primary name is the one that either expresses the parents' aspirations for the child's future or one that refers to the circumstances surrounding the child's birth.

The Abaluyia ethnic group of western Kenya generally bestow names upon their children immediately after birth. These children often have at least six names. Two names are from the father's family group; two from the mother's family group; one denoting the day of the week on which the child was born; one denoting the season. Other names can be given to describe family or regional circumstances or a physical characteristic of the child.

The Swahili people, one of Africa's largest cultural groups, are a mixture of African and Arab races. Their language, Kiswahili, has been heavily influenced by Islam and many Swahili names are easily recognizable as Kiswahilized Arabic names.

Immediately after birth, a Swahili child is given a childhood name (*jina la utotoni*) by an elderly relative. In those cases where no relative is available, the midwife chooses the name. The childhood name is descriptive of the child's physical characteristics, circumstances surrounding the birth, or the family's living situation. Seven days after the birth, a Swahili child is given an adult name (*jina la ukubwani*). Commonly a Muslim or Bible name, it is bestowed upon the child by his or her parents or paternal grandparents. If the child is firstborn and male, he is given the name of the paternal grandfather. If the firstborn child is female, she will be given the name of her paternal grandmother.

The presence of Islam in the countries of northern and eastern Africa has a direct influence on the choice of names in those countries. The peoples of the Sudan, Somalia, the Nigerian Hausa, and the Fulani are examples of groups with strong Islamic ties. Accordingly, most names bestowed upon their children are Muslim or Africanized Muslim names.

Great care should be taken to pronounce African names correctly. The wrong inflection of voice or accenting the wrong syllable will in many cases change the meaning of the name and will be considered by the bearer to be a personal insult.

African Male Names

Abayomi Oriki name meaning "born to bring me joy." Yoruba, Nigeria. (AH-BAH-YO-ME)

Abdalla Muslim name derived from the Arabic 'Abd-Allāh (servant of God). Arabic, N. Africa; Swahili, E. Africa. (AB-DAHL-LAH)

Abdu Muslim name derived from the Arabic 'Ābid (servant or worshiper of God). Arabic, N. Africa; Swahili, E. Africa. Var: Abdi. (AB-DOO)

Abeeku Akeradini name meaning "born on Wednesday." Fante, Ghana. (AH-BAY-KOO)

Abejide Oruko name meaning "born during winter." Yoruba, Nigeria. (AB-BEH-JEE-DEH)

ABIODUN Oruko name meaning "born at the time of war." Yoruba, Nigeria. (AH-BEE-O-DOON)

ABIOLA Oruko name meaning "born in honor, born during the new Yam festival." Yoruba, Nigeria. (AH-BEE-O-LAH)

ADDAE Agyadini name meaning "morning sun." Akan, Ghana. (AH-DAH-EH)

ADE Oriki name meaning "royal." Yoruba, Nigeria. (AH-DEH)

ADEBAYO Oruko name meaning "he came in a joyful time." Yoruba, Nigeria. (AH-DEH-BAH-YO)

ADEBEN Twelfth-born. Akan, Ghana. (AH-DEH-BEN)

ADEJOLA Oriki name meaning "the crown feeds on honors." Yoruba, Nigeria. (AH-DEH-JO-LAH)

ADESOLA The crown honored us. Yoruba, Nigeria. (AH-DEH-SO-LAH)

ADIKA Akeradini name meaning "the first child of a second husband." Ewe, Ghana. (AH-DEE-KAH)

ADIO Oriki name meaning "be righteous." Yoruba, Nigeria. (AH-DEE-O)

ADISA One who makes himself clear, one who makes his meaning clear. Yoruba, Nigeria. (AH-DEE-SAH)

ADOFO Agyadini name meaning "warrior." Akan, Ghana. (AH-DŌ-FO)

ADOM Help from God, God's blessing. Akan, Ghana. (AH-DOHM)

ADUNBI Oriki name meaning "born to be pleasant." Yoruba, Nigeria. (AH-DOON-BE)

ADUSA Akeradini name meaning "thirteenth-born." Akan, Ghana. (AH-DOO-SAH)

AHMED Muslim name derived from the Arabic *ahmad* (more commendable, praiseworthy). Arabic, N. Africa; Swahili, E. Africa. (AH-HMED)

AIYETORO Oriki name meaning "peace on earth." Yoruba, Nigeria. (AH-YEH-TŌ-RO)

AJANI He fights for possession. Yoruba, Nigeria. (AH-JAH-NEE)

AKANNI Our encounter brings possessions. Yoruba, Nigeria. (AH-KAHN-NEE)

AKIIKI Friend. Muneyankole, Uganda. (AH-KEE-EE-KEE)

AKINLABI Oruko name meaning "we have a boy." Yoruba, Nigeria. (AK-KEEN-LAH-BE)

AKINLANA Oriki name meaning "valor." Yoruba, Nigeria. (AH-KEEN-LAH-NAH)

AKINS Oriki name meaning "brave boy." Yoruba, Nigeria. (AH-KEENS)

AKONO It is my turn. Yoruba, Nigeria. (AH-KOH-NO)

AKUA Akeradini name meaning "born on Thursday." Fante, Ghana. (AH-KOO-AH)

AKWETEE Younger of twins. Ga, Ghana. (AH-KWAY-TEH)

ALI Muslim name derived from the Arabic *'ali* (noble, sublime, elevated, exalted). Arabic, N. Africa; Swahili, E. Africa. (AH-LEE)

AMADI He seemed destined to die at birth. This type of name is sometimes given to children in an effort to trick the spirits into passing over them and not take them back to the spirit world. Benin, Nigeria. (AH-MAH-DEE)

AMBONISYE God has rewarded me. Nyakyusa, Tanzania. (AM-BO-NEES-YEH)

ANANE Akeradini name meaning "fourth son." Akan, Ghana. (AH-NAH-NEH)

ANDWELE God brought me. Nyakyusa, Tanzania. (AHN-DWEH-LEH)

ANIWETA A spirit brought it. Ibo, Nigeria. (AH-NEE-WET-TAH)

ANUM Akeradini name meaning "fifth-born." Akan, Ghana. (AH-NOOM)

APARA A child that comes and goes. Yoruba, Nigeria. (AH-PAH-RAH)

ASHUR Muslim name derived from the name of the Islamic month of Ashur. Arabic, N. Africa; Swahili, E. Africa. (AH-SHOOR)

ASIM Derived from the Arabic *'āsim* (protector, guardian, defender). Arabic, N. Africa; Swahili, E. Africa. (AH-SEEM)

ASWAD Black. Arabic, N. Africa. (AHS-WAHD)

ATSU Akeradini name meaning "younger of twins." Ewe, Ghana. (AT-SOO)

ATU Akeradini name meaning "born on Saturday." Fante, Ghana. (AH-TOO)

AYIZE Let it come. Zulu, S. Africa. (AH-YEE-ZEH)

AYO Oriki name meaning "happiness." Yoruba, Nigeria. (AH-YO)

Azizi Derived from the Arabic *'azīz* (beloved, precious). Arabic, N. Africa; Swahili, E. Africa. (AH-ZEE-ZEE)

Babafemi My father loves me. Yoruba, Nigeria. (BAH-BAH-FEH-ME)

Badru Of Arabic origin derived from *badr* (full moon). Arabic, N. Africa; Swahili, E. Africa. (BAH-DROO)

Bakari Of noble promise. Swahili, E. Africa. (BAH-KAH-REE)

Baruti Teacher. Tswana, Botswana. (BAH-ROO-TEE)

Bem Peace. Tiv, Nigeria. (BEHM)

Betserai Help, assistance, aid. Shona, Zimbabwe. (BET-SEH-RAH-EE)

Bobo Akeradini name meaning "born on Tuesday." Fante, Ghana. (BO-BO)

Bomani Warrior. Ngoni, Malawi. (BO-MAH-NEE)

Boseda Born on Sunday. Tiv, Nigeria. (BO-SEH-DEH)

Chenzira Born on the road. Shona, Zimbabwe. (CHEN-SEE-RAH)

Chijioke Chi gives talent. *See* CHIKE. Ibo, Nigeria. (CHEE-JEE-O-KEH).

Chike Power of Chi. Chi is the name of an important Ibo personal god who is thought to remain with a person from the moment of conception until death. Ibo, Nigeria. (CHEE-KEH)

Chinelo Thought of Chi. *See* CHIKE. Ibo, Nigeria. (CHEE-NEH-LOH)

Chinese Chi is protecting, Chi is guarding. *See* CHIKE. Var: Cinese. Ibo, Nigeria. (CHEE-NEH-SEH)

Chinua Blessings of Chi. *See* CHIKE. Ibo, Nigeria. The name is borne by Nigerian writer and poet Chinua Achebe. (CHEE-NOO-AH)

Chioke Gift of Chi. *See* CHIKE. Ibo, Nigeria. (CHEE-O-KEH)

Chionesu Guiding light, protector. Shona, Zimbabwe. (CHEH-NEH-SOO)

Chisulo Steel. Yao, Malawi. (CHEE-SOO-LOH)

Chiumbo Small, small creation, small child. Mwera, Kenya. (CHEE-OOM-BO)

Dada Oriki name meaning "a child with curly hair." Yoruba, Nigeria. (DAH-DAH)

Dakarai Happiness. Shona, Zimbabwe. (DAH-KAH-RAH-EE)

Darweshi Saintly, devout. Swahili, E. Africa. (DAHR-WEH-SHE)

Daudi Africanized form of the Arabic Dawūd, a cognate of David, which is from the Hebrew *dāwīd* (beloved). Swahili, E. Africa. (DAH-OO-DEE)

Dawud Arabic form of the Hebrew David, a derivative of *dāwīd* (beloved). Arabic, N. Africa. (DAH-OOD)

Dulani Cutting. Ngoni, Malawi. (DOO-LAH-NEE)

Dumaka Help me with hands, lend me a helping hand. Ibo, Nigeria. (DOO-MAH-KAH)

Ebo Akeradini name meaning "born on Tuesday." Fante, Ghana. (EH-BO)

Ehioze I am above people's jealousy, jealousy is beneath me. Benin, Nigeria. (EH-HE-O-ZAY)

Enam God's gift. Ewe, Ghana. (EH-NAHM)

Fadil Derived from the Arabic *fāḍil* (generous), which is from *faḍala* (to surpass). Arabic, N. Africa. (FAH-DEEL)

Fakih Arabic name meaning "one who recites the Koran, an intellectual," from *fakara* (to meditate, to contemplate). Arabic, N. Africa. (FAH-KEE)

Faraji Derived from the Arabic *faraj* (remedy, cure, consolation). Arabic, N. Africa; Swahili, E. Africa. (FAH-RAH-JEE)

Fenyang Conqueror. Tswana, Botswana. (FEHN-YANG)

Fifi Akeradini name meaning "born on Friday." Fante, Ghana. (FEE-FEE)

Foluke Placed in God's hands. Yoruba, Nigeria. (FO-LOO-KEH)

Fulumirani A journey. Ngoni, Malawi. (FOO-LOO-ME-RAH-NEE)

Funsani Request, petition. Ngoni, Malawi. (FOON-SAH-NEE)

Gahiji The hunter. Rwanda, Rwanda. (GAH-HE-JEE)

Gamba Warrior. Shona, Zimbabwe. (GAM-BAH)

Garai To be settled, established. Shona, Rhodesia. (GAH-RAH-EE)

Gowon Rainmaker. Tiv, Nigeria. (GO-WAHN)

Gwandoya Met with misery. Luganda, Uganda. (GWAHN-DŌ-YAH)

GYASI Agyadini name meaning "wonderful." Akan, Ghana. (JAH-SEE)

HABIB Arabic name derived from *habib* (beloved, dear). Arabic, N. Africa. (HAH-BEEB)

HABIMANA God exists. Rwanda, Rwanda. Var: Habimama. (AH-BE-MAH-NAH)

HAJI Born during the hajj. The hajj is the pilgrimage to Mecca that every Muslim is expected to make at least once. The name is derived from the Arabic *hajj* (pilgrim). Swahili, E. Africa. (HAH-JEE)

HAKIZIMANA It is God who saves. Rwanda, Rwanda. (AH-KEE-ZEE-MAH-NAH)

HAMADI Praised. Muslim name derived from the Arabic *ḥamida* (to praise, to commend). Arabic, N. Africa; Swahili, E. Africa.

HAMIDI Praising, thankful. Muslim name derived from the Arabic *ḥāmid* (praising, thankful, commendable), which is from the root *ḥamida* (to praise, to commend). Swahili, E. Africa. (HAH-ME-DEE)

HAMISI Born on Thursday. Swahili, E. Africa. Var: Hanisi. (HAH-ME-SEE)

HANIF Muslim name derived from the Arabic *hanif* (true believer of Islam). Arabic, N. Africa. (HAH-NEEF)

HARITH Arabic name derived from *ḥaratha* (to be a good provider, capable). Arabic, N. Africa. (HAH-REETH)

HARUN Muslim name derived from the Arabic *harūn* (exalted, lofty, elevated). Arabic, N. Africa. (HAH-ROON)

HASANI Derived from the Arabic *ḥasan* (beautiful, handsome, good). Swahili, E. Africa. Var: Hassani, Husani. (HAH-SAH-NEE)

HASHIM Derived from the Arabic *hāshim* (destroying, crushing), which is from *hashama* (to crush, to smash). Arabic, N. Africa. *See* HĀSHIM (Muslim/Arabic Names). (HAH-SHEEM)

HONDO War. Shona, Zimbabwe. (HAHN-DŌ)

IBRAHIM Cognate of Abraham, which is derived from the Hebrew Avraham (father of a multitude, father of many). Hausa, Nigeria. (EE-BRA-HEEM)

IDI Born during the Idd festival. The Idd festival marks the end of Ramadan, the ninth month of the Islamic year, during which time Muslims fast from sunrise to sunset. Swahili, E. Africa. (EE-DEE)

IMAROGBE Child born to a good and caring family. Benin, Nigeria. (EE-MAH-RO-BEH)

IPYANA Grace. Nyakyusa, Tanzania. (EEP-YAH-NAH)

ISHAQ Cognate of the Hebrew Yitzchak (he will laugh), which is from *yitshāq* (laughter). The name is borne in the Bible by one of the three sons of Abraham and Sarah. Arabic, N. Africa. (EES-HAHK)

ISSA Salvation, protection. Swahili, E. Africa. (EE-SAH)

IYAPO Oruko name meaning "many trials, many difficult situations." Yoruba, Nigeria. (EE-YAH-PO)

JABARI Muslim name derived from the Arabic *jābir* (comforter, bringer of consolation). Swahili, E. Africa. (JAH-BAH-REE)

JABULANI Be happy, be joyful. Ndebele, Zimbabwe. (JAH-BOO-LAH-NEE)

JAFARI Derived from the Arabic *ja'far* (stream). Swahili, E. Africa. *See* JA'FAR (Muslim/Arabic Names). (JAH-FAH-REE)

JAHI Dignity. Swahili, E. Africa. (JAH-HEE)

JAJA Honored, commended. Ibo, Nigeria. (JAH-JAH)

JELA The father is in prison at the time of birth. Swahili, E. Africa. (JEH-LAH)

JELANI Mighty, strong. Ibo, Nigeria. (JEH-LAH-NEE)

JIBRI Arabic form of Gabriel, which is from the Hebrew *gavhrī'ēl* (God is my strength). Gabriel is one of the seven archangels of God, the herald of Good News. Arabic, N. Africa. (JEE-BREE)

JOJO Akeradini name meaning "born on Monday." Fante, Ghana. (JO-JO)

JUMA Born on Friday. Swahili, E. Africa. (JOO-MAH)

JUMAANE Born on Tuesday. Swahili, E. Africa. (JOO-MAH-NEH)

JUMOKE Oriki name meaning "everyone loves the child, the child is beloved." Yoruba, Nigeria. (JOO-MO-KEH)

KAFELE Worth dying for. Ngoni, Malawi. (KAH-FEH-LEH)

KAMANGENI He seems to be related. Ngoni, Malawi. (KAH-MAHN-GEH-NEE)

KAMAU Quiet warrior. Kikuyu, Kenya. (KAH-MAH-OO)

KAPENI Knife. Yao, Malawi. (KAH-PEH-NEE)

Kasiya Departure, embarkation. Ngoni, Malawi. (KAH-SEE-YAH)

Kayode He brought joy. Yoruba, Nigeria. (KAH-YO-DEH)

Kefentse Conqueror. Tswana, Botswana. (KEH-FENT-SEH)

Kehinde Oruko name meaning "second born of twins." Yoruba, Nigeria. (KEH-HEEN-DEH)

Kereenyaga Mysterious mountain, mountain of mystery. Kikuyu, Kenya. (KEH-REHN-YAH-GAH)

Khaldun Eternal. Arabic name derived from *khalada* (to last forever, to be eternal). Arabic, N. Africa. (KAHL-DOON)

Khalfani Born to rule, destined to lead. Swahili, E. Africa. (KAHL-FAH-NEE)

Khalid Derived from the Arabic *khālid* (eternal, undying), which is from *khalada* (to last forever, to be eternal). Arabic, N. Africa; Swahili, E. Africa. (KHAH-LEED)

Khamisi Born on Thursday. Swahili, E. Africa. Var: Khamidi. (KAH-ME-SEE)

Kifimbo A twig. The name refers to a very small, thin baby. Swahili, E. Africa. (KEE-FEEM-BO)

Kitwana Pledged to live. Swahili, E. Africa. (KEE-TWAH-NAH)

Kizza Born after twins. Luganda, Uganda. (KEEZ-SAH)

Kodwo Akeradini name meaning "born on Monday." Twi, Ghana. (KO-DWO)

Kofi Akeradini name meaning "born on Friday." Twi, Ghana. (KO-FEE)

Kojo Akeradini name meaning "born on Monday." Akan, Ghana. (KO-JO)

Kokayi Summon the people. Shona, Zimbabwe. (KO-KAY-YEE)

Kondo War. Swahili, E. Africa. (KON-DŌ)

Kondwani Joyful, full of happiness. Ngoni, Malawi. (KON-DWAH-NEE)

Kontar Akeradini name meaning "only child." Akan, Ghana. (KOHN-TAR)

Kopano Union. Tswana, Botswana. (KO-PAH-NO)

Kosoko No hoe to dig a grave. An example of a name given to a child to keep it from dying. Yoruba, Nigeria. (KO-SO-KO)

Kpodo Akeradini name meaning "first born of twins." Ewe, Ghana. (KPOH-DŌ)

Kudyauku Feast. Ngoni, Malawi. (KOO-YAH-OO-KOO)

Kufuo The father shared the pains of birth. Fante, Ghana. (KOO-FOO-O)

Kwabena Born on Tuesday. Akan, Ghana. (KWAH-BEH-NAH)

Kwakou Born on Wednesday. Ewe, Ghana. Var: Kwaku. (KWAH-KOO)

Kwasi Akeradini name meaning "born on Sunday." Akan, Ghana. Var: Kwesi. (KWAH-SEE)

Kwayera Dawn, sunrise. Ngoni, Malawi. (KWAH-YEH-RAH)

Lateef Derived from the Arabic *laṭīf* (gentle, kind, pleasant). Arabic, N. Africa. (LAH-TEEF)

Lebna Heart, soul, spirit. Amharic and Tigrinya, Ethiopia. (LUHB-NAH)

Lisimba Lion-torn, hurt by a lion. Yao, Malawi. (LEE-SEEM-BAH)

Lugono Sleep. Ngoni, Malawi. (LOO-YO-NO)

Lutalo Warrior. Luganda, Uganda. (LOO-TAH-LO)

Machupa One who likes to drink, he enjoys drinking. Swahili, E. Africa. (MAH-CHOO-PAH)

Madu People, man. Ibo, Nigeria. (MAH-DOO)

Madzimoyo Water of life. Ngoni, Malawi. (MAD-ZEE-MO-YO)

Malawa Flowers, blossoms. Yao, Malawi. (MAH-LAH-WAH)

Mandala Spectacles. Ngoni, Malawi. (MAHN-DAH-LAH)

Mandondo Drops. Ngoni, Malawi. (MAHN-DOHN-DŌ)

Masamba Leaves. Yao, Malawi. (MAH-SAHM-BAH)

Mashama You are surprised, taken by surprise. Shona, Zimbabwe. (MAH-SHAH-MAH)

Masud Fortunate. An Arabic name derived from *mas'ūd* (fortunate, lucky), which is from *sa'ida* (to be lucky). Arabic, N. Africa; Swahili, E. Africa. Var: Masoud. (MAH-SOOD)

Matsimela Roots. Sotho, Lesotho. (MAT-SEE-MEH-LAH)

Mawuli God exists, there is a God. A name often bestowed in thanks to God for the gift of a child. Ewe, Ghana. (MAH-WOO-LEE)

Mazi Sir. Ibo, Nigeria. (MAH-ZEE)

Mbwana Master. Swahili, E. Africa. (M-BWAH-NAH)

Mensah Akeradini name meaning "third-born son." Ewe, Ghana. (MEN-SAH)

Mhina Delightful, enjoyable. Swahili, E. Africa. (M-HEE-NAH)

Mlengalenga Heaven. Ngoni, Malawi. (M-LENG-GAH-LENG-GAH)

Mosi First-born. Swahili, E. Africa. (MO-SEE)

Mtima Heart. Ngoni, Malawi. (M-TEE-MAH)

Mudada The provider. Shona, Zimbabwe. (MOO-DAH-DAH)

Muḥammad Praiseworthy. The most popular of the Muslim names, Muḥammad is derived from the Arabic *muḥammad* (praiseworthy), which is from *hamida* (to praise). Arabic, N. Africa; Swahili, E. Africa. *See* MUḤAMMAD (Muslim/Arabic Names). (MOO-HAH-MAHD)

Munyiga An annoyer, one who bothers other people, a pest. Mukiga, Uganda. (MOON-YEE-GAH)

Musa Child. Swahili, E. Africa. (MOO-SAH)

Mvula Rain. Ngoni, Malawi. (M-VOO-LAH)

Mwai Good fortune, blessings, prosperity. Ngoni, Malawi. (MWAH-EE)

Mwamba Strong, powerful. Nyakyusa, Tanzania. (MWAHM-BAH)

Najja Born after. Muganda, Uganda. (NAHJ-JAH)

Nakisisa Child of the shadows. Muganda, Uganda. (NAH-KEE-SEE-SAH)

Nassor Victorious. Derived from the Arabic *nāṣir* (one who helps render victory, supporter). Arabic, N. Africa; Swahili, E. Africa. (NAH-SOR)

Ndale A trick. Ngoni, Malawi. (N-DAH-LEH)

Ndulu Dove. Ibo, Nigeria. (N-DOO-LOO)

Negasi He will be crowned, he will become royalty. Amharic and Tigrinya, Ethiopia. (NUH-GAH-SEE)

Ngolinga Crybaby, whiner. Yao, Malawi. (N-GO-LING-GAH)

Ngozi Blessings, good fortune. Ibo, Nigeria. (N-GO-ZEE)

Ngunda Dove. Yao, Malawi. (N-GOON-DAH)

Njau Young bull. Kikuyu, Kenya. (N-JOW)

Nwabudike The child is power, the son is the father's power. Ibo, Nigeria. (NWAH-BOO-DEH-KEH)

Obasi In honor of the Supreme God. Ibo, Nigeria. (O-BAH-SEE)

Obataiye Oriki name meaning "king of the world, world ruler." Yoruba, Nigeria. (AH-BAH-TAH-EE-YEH)

Obayana The king warms himself at the fire. Yoruba, Nigeria. (AH-BAH-YAH-NAH)

Obi Heart. Ibo, Nigeria. (O-BEE)

Obike A strong household, a concerned family. Ibo, Nigeria. (O-BEE-KAY)

Odion First born of twins. Ibo, Nigeria. (O-DEE-OHN)

Ogbonna The image of his father, he looks like his father. Ibo, Nigeria. (O-BO-NAH)

Ojore A man of war, soldier. Ateso, Uganda. (O-JO-REH)

Okechuku A gift of God. Ibo, Nigeria. Var: Okechukwu. (O-KEH-CHOO-KOO)

Okello Born after twins. Ateso, Uganda. (O-KEL-O)

Okpara First-born son. Ibo, Nigeria. (OAK-PAH-RAH)

Oladele Oriki name meaning "we are honored at home." Yoruba, Nigeria. (AH-LAH-DEH-LEH)

Olafemi Honor favors me, fortunate. Yoruba, Nigeria. (AH-LAH-FEH-MEE)

Olaniyan Surrounded by honor. Yoruba, Nigeria. (AH-LAH-NEE-YAHN)

Olubayo Highest joy, rejoicing. A name bestowed in reference to the great joy a child brings. Yoruba, Nigeria. (O-LO-BAH-YO)

Olufemi God loves me, beloved of God. Yoruba, Nigeria. (O-LOO-FEH-ME)

Olugbala God of the people. Yoruba, Nigeria. (O-LOO-BAH-LAH)

Olujimi Given by God. Yoruba, Nigeria. (O-LOO-JEE-ME)

Olumide God arrives. Yoruba, Nigeria. (O-LOO-ME-DEH)

Olumiji God awakens, my lord awakens. Yoruba, Nigeria. (O-LOO-ME-JEE)

Olushola Blessed by God, God has blessed me. Yoruba, Nigeria. (O-LOO-SHO-LAH)

Oluwa Our God, our Lord. Yoruba, Nigeria. (O-LOO-WAH)

Oluyemi Fulfillment from God, satisfied. Yoruba, Nigeria. (O-LOO-YEH-ME)

Omar Arabic name derived from *'amir* (flourishing, thriving), which is from *'amara* (to live long, to prosper). Arabic, N. Africa; Swahili, E. Africa. Var: Omari, Omavi. (O-MAR)

Onuwachi God's world, God's earth. Ibo, Nigeria. (O-NOO-WAH-CHEE)

Osakwe God agrees. Benin, Nigeria. (O-SAH-KWEH)

Osayimwese God made me complete. Benin, Nigeria. (O-SAH-EEM-WEH-SEH)

Osei Agyadini name meaning "noble, honorable." Fante, Ghana. (O-SEH-EE)

Othenio Born at night. Luu, Kenya. (O-THEE-NEE-O)

Paki Witness. Xhosa, S. Africa. (PAH-KEE)

Radhi Goodwill. Swahili, E. Africa. (RAHD-hee)

Rafiki Derived from the Arabic *rafiq* (friend, companion). Swahili, E. Africa. (RAH-FEE-KEE)

Rashidi Derived from the Arabic *rashīd* (rightly guided, of good council), which is from *rashada* (to follow the right course). Swahili, E. Africa. (RAH-SHEE-DEE)

Rhamadhani Born during the month of Ramadan. Ramadan is the name of the Islamic ninth month, during which time Muslims fast from sunrise to sunset. Swahili, E. Africa. (RAH-MAH-DAHN-HEE)

Rudo Love. Shona, Zimbabwe. (ROO-DOH)

Runako Handsome, good-looking. Shona, Zimbabwe. (ROO-NAH-KO)

Sadiki Faithful. Swahili, E. Africa. (SAH-DEE-KEE)

Saeed Happy, fortunate. Derived from the Arabic *sa'id* (lucky, happy, fortunate), which is from *sa'ida* (to be happy). Arabic, N. Africa; Swahili, E. Africa. (SAH-EED)

Salehe Good. Swahili, E. Africa. (SAH-LEH-HEE)

Salih Derived from the Arabic *ṣāliḥ* (virtuous, righteous, proper). Arabic, N. Africa. (SAH-LEE)

Salim Derived from the Arabic *salīm* (safe, secure). Arabic, N. Africa; Swahili, E. Africa. (SAH-LEEM)

Sefu Sword. Swahili, E. Africa. (SEH-FOO)

Sekani Laughter. Ngoni, Malawi. (SEH-KAH-NEE)

Sekayi Laughter. Shona, Zimbabwe. (SEH-KAH-YEE)

Sekou Learned. The name was borne by Sékou Touré (1922–84), the first head of state of independent Guinea. Guinea. (SEH-KOO)

Simba Lion. Swahili, E. Africa. (SEEM-BAH)

Sulaiman Arabic form of Solomon, which is derived from the Hebrew *shĕlōmōh* (peaceful). The name is borne in the Bible by an Israelite king noted for his great wisdom and ability to communicate with animals. Arabic, N. Africa. (SOO-LAH-EE-MAHN)

Tahir Derived from the Arabic *ṭāhir* (pure, chaste), which is from *tahura* (to be pure, to be clean). Arabic, N. Africa. (TAH-HEER)

Taiwo Oruko name meaning "first born twin." Yoruba, Nigeria. (TAH-EE-WO)

Talib Derived from the Arabic *tālib* (seeker, seeker of knowledge). Arabic, N. Africa. (TAH-LIB)

Tau Lion. Tswana, Botswana. (TAH-OO)

Thabiti A man, a true man. Mwera, Kenya. (THAH-BEE-TEE)

Thandiwe Beloved. Zulu, S. Africa. (TAHN-DEE-WEH)

Themba Hope. Xhosa, S. Africa. (TEHM-BAH)

Tsalani Goodbye, farewell. Ngoni, Malawi. (TSAH-LAH-NEE)

Tumaini Hope. Mwera, Kenya. (TOO-MAH-EE-NEE)

Uchechi The will of Chi, God's will. Ibo, Nigeria. (OO-CHAY-CHEE)

Umi Life. Yao, Malawi. (OO-ME)

Unika Light up, to shine. Lomwe, Malawi. (OO-NEE-KAH)

Useni Tell me. Yao, Malawi. (OO-SEH-NEE)

Wachiru Lawmaker's son. Kikuyu, Kenya. (WAH-CHEER-OO)

Walid Derived from the Arabic *walīd* (newborn), which is from *walada* (to give birth). Arabic, N. Africa. Var: Waleed. (WAH-LEED)

Wambua Born during the rainy season. Kamba, Kenya. (WAHM-BOO-AH)

Wanjohi Brewer. Kikuyu, Kenya. (WAHN-JO-HEE)

Wekesa Born during the harvest time. Lechya, Kenya. (WAY-KAY-SAH)

Yafeu Bold. Fante, Ghana. (YAH-FEH-O)

Yazid Derived from the Arabic *zayd* (increasing), which is from *zāda* (to increase, to become greater). Arabic, N. Africa; Swahili, E. Africa. (YAH-ZID)

Yonas Cognate of Jonah, which is derived from the Hebrew *yōnāh* (a dove). Ethiopia. (YOH-NAHS)

Yusuf Arabic cognate of Joseph, which is derived from the Hebrew *yōsēf* (may he add). Arabic, N. Africa; Swahili, E. Africa. Var: Yusef, Yussef. (YOO-SUF)

Zahur Flower. Derived from the Arabic *zāhir* (flourishing, blossoming). Swahili, E. Africa. (ZAH-HOOR)

Zesiro First born of twins. Buganda, Uganda. (ZEH-SEE-ROH)

Zikomo Thank you. Ngoni, Malawi. (ZEE-KO-MO)

Ziyad An increase. Derived from the Arabic *zāda* (to increase, to become greater). Arabic, N. Africa. (ZEE-YAHD)

Zuberi Strong. Swahili, E. Africa. (ZOO-BEH-REE)

African Female Names

Aba Akeradini name meaning "born on Thursday." Fante, Ghana. Var: Abba. (AH-BAH)

Ababuo A child that keeps coming back. Given to a child to dissuade the spirits from taking it back to the spirit world. Ewe, Ghana. (AH-BAH-BOO-OH)

Abagbe This child was wished for, we begged to have this one to lift up. Yoruba, Nigeria. (AH-BAH-BEH)

Abam Akeradini name meaning "second child after twins." Twi, Ghana. (AH-BAHM)

Abayomi Oriki name meaning "she brings joy, she brings happiness." Yoruba, Nigeria. (AH-BAH-YO-ME)

Abeba Flower. Ethiopia. (AH-BEH-BAH)

Abebi We asked for her. Yoruba, Nigeria. (AH-BAY-BEE)

Abeje We asked to have this child. Yoruba, Nigeria. (AH-BEH-JEH)

Abeke We asked for her to pet her. Yoruba, Nigeria. (AH-BEH-KEH)

Abena Akeradini name meaning "born on Tuesday." Fante, Ghana. Var: Abana, Abina. (AH-BEH-NAH)

Abeni We asked for her, and look, we got her! Yoruba, Nigeria. (AH-BEH-NEE)

Abeo She has come to bring happiness and great joy. Yoruba, Nigeria. (AH-BEH-O)

Abidemi Born during the father's absence. Yoruba, Nigeria. (AH-BEE-DEH-MEE)

Abikanile Listen. Yao, Malawi. (AH-BEE-KAH-NEE-LAH)

Abimbola Oriki name meaning "born to be wealthy." Yoruba, Nigeria. (AH-BEEM-BO-LAH)

Abiona Oruko name meaning "born on a journey." Yoruba, Nigeria. (AH-BEE-O-NAH)

Abrihet She shines with light. Tigrinya, Ethiopia. (AH-BREE-HET)

Acenith The name of an African goddess of love. (AS-SEN-NITH)

Ada First-born female. Ibo, Nigeria. (AH-DAH)

Adamma Child of beauty, beautiful child, queenly. Ibo, Nigeria. Var: Adama. (AH-DAHM-MAH)

Adanna She is her father's daughter. Ibo, Nigeria. (AH-DAHN-NAH)

Adebola Honor is hers. Yoruba, Nigeria. (AH-DEH-BO-LAH)

Adedagbo Happiness is a crown. Yoruba, Nigeria. (AH-DEH-DAH-BO)

Adeleke Crown brings happiness. Yoruba, Nigeria. (AH-DEH-LEH-KEH)

Adeola Crown brings honor. Yoruba, Nigeria. (AH-DEH-OH-LAH)

Adesimbo Noble birth. Yoruba, Nigeria. (AH-DEH-SEEM-BO)

Adesina This child opens the way (for more children). Often bestowed after a woman has had difficulty in conceiving a child, in the hopes that more children will follow. Yoruba, Nigeria. (AH-DAY-SEE-NAH)

Adia A gift from God, a present from God. Swahili, E. Africa. (AH-DEE-AH)

Adowa Born on Tuesday. Akan, Ghana. Var: Adjoa. (AH-DŌ-WAH)

Aduke Oriki name meaning "beloved, cherished." Yoruba, Nigeria. (AH-DOO-KEH)

Adzo Akeradini name meaning born on Monday. Fante, Ghana. Var: Adjoa, Adwoa. (AHD-ZO)

Afafa First child of second husband. Ewe, Ghana. (AH-FAH-FAH)

Afiya Health. Swahili, E. Africa. (AH-FEE-YAH)

Afryea Born during happy times. Ewe, Ghana. (AH-FRY-YAH)

Afua Akeradini name meaning "born on Friday." Ewe, Ghana. (AH-FOO-AH)

Aina Difficult birth, the birth had complications. Yoruba, Nigeria. (AH-EE-NAH)

Aisha Life. Derived from the Arabic 'Ā'isha (alive and well), which is from *'āsha* (to live). The name was borne by the Prophet Muhammad's third and favorite wife. *See* 'Ā'ISHA (Muslim/Arabic Names). Var: Asha, Ayisha. Arabic, N. Africa; Swahili, E. Africa. (AH-EE-SHAH)

Aiyetoro Peace on earth. Yoruba, Nigeria. (AH-YEH-TŌ-RO)

Akanke To want her is to love her, to see her is to love her. Yoruba, Nigeria. (AH-KAHN-KEH)

Akilah Arabic name meaning "intelligent, one who reasons." Arabic, N. Africa. (AH-KEE-LAH)

Akosua Born on Sunday. Ewe, Ghana. (AH-KO-SOO-AH)

Akua Born on Wednesday. Ewe, Ghana. (AH-KOO-AH)

Akwete First born of twins. Ga, Ghana. Var: Akwate, Akwetee. (AH-KWEH-TEH)

Akwokwo Younger of twins. Ga, Ghana. (AH-KWO-KWO)

Alaba Second child born after twins. Yoruba, Nigeria. (AL-LAH-BAH)

Alake One to be petted and fussed over. Yoruba, Nigeria. (AH-LAH-KEH)

Alile She weeps. Often bestowed upon a child born into misfortune. Yao, Malawi. Var: Alili. (AH-LEE-LEH)

Aluna Come here. Mwera, Kenya. Var: Aluma. (AH-LOO-NAH)

Ama Born on Saturday. Ewe, Ghana. (AH-MAH)

Amadi Rejoicing, celebrating. Ibo, Nigeria. (AH-MAH-DEE)

Aminah Faithful, honest. Derived from the Arabic *amīn* (trustworthy, faithful), which is from *amuna* (to be faithful, to be reliable). Arabic, N. Africa; Swahili, E. Africa. Var: Amina, Amineh. (AH-MEE-NAH)

Annakiya Sweet face. Hausa, Nigeria. (AH-NAH-KEE-YAH)

Anuli Joyous, delightful. Ibo, Nigeria. (AH-NOO-LEE)

Asabi She is superior, she is of choice birth. Yoruba, Nigeria. (AH-SAH-BEE)

Asha Life. Derived from the Arabic *'āsha* (to live). Arabic, N. Africa; Swahili, E. Africa. (AH-SHAH)

Ashura Born during the Islamic month of Ashur. Swahili, E. Africa. (AH-SHOO-RAH)

Asya Born during a time of grief. Swahili, E. Africa. (AHS-YAH)

Ayah Bright. Swahili, E. Africa. (AH-YAH)

Ayobami I am blessed with joy. Yoruba, Nigeria. (AH-YO-BAH-ME)

Ayobunmi Joy is given to me. Yoruba, Nigeria. (AH-YO-BOON-ME)

Ayodele Oriki name meaning "joy comes home, she brings joy to our home." Yoruba, Nigeria. (AH-YO-DEH-LEH)

Ayofemi Joy likes me. Yoruba, Nigeria. (AH-YO-FEH-ME)

Ayoka She brings joy to all. Yoruba, Nigeria. (AH-YO-KAH)

Ayoluwa The joy of our people. Yoruba, Nigeria. (AH-YO-LOO-WAH)

Ayoola Joy in wealth. Yoruba, Nigeria. (AH-YO-OO-LAH)

Aziza Derived from the Arabic *'azīza* (esteemed, precious, beloved). Arabic, N. Africa; Swahili, E. Africa. Var: Azizah. (AH-ZEE-ZAH)

Baako Akeradini name meaning "first-born." Akan, Ghana. (BAH-AH-KO)

Baba Akeradini name meaning "born on Thursday." Fante, Ghana. (BAH-BAH)

Baderinwa Worthy of respect. Yoruba, Nigeria. (BAH-DAY-REEN-WAH)

Bahati Fortunate, lucky. Swahili, E. Africa. (BAH-HAH-TEE)

Barika Derived from the Arabic *bari'a* (excelling, successful). Arabic, N. Africa. (BAH-REE-KAH)

Bayo Oriki name meaning "joy is found." Bestowed in reference to the great joy a child brings to the family. Yoruba, Nigeria. (BAH-YO)

Bejide Oruko name meaning "born during the rainy season." Yoruba, Nigeria. (BEH-JEE-DEH)

Bolade Oriki name meaning "honor arrives." Yoruba, Nigeria. (BO-LAH-DEH)

Bolanile The wealth of this house, she is our treasure. Yoruba, Nigeria. (BO-LAH-NEE-LAH)

Bunmi My gift. Yoruba, Nigeria. (BOON-ME)

Buseje Ask me. Yao, Malawi. (BOO-SEH-JEH)

Chaonaine It has seen me. Ngoni, Malawi. (CHAH-OH-NAH-EE-NAH)

Chausiku Born at night. Swahili, E. Africa. (CHAH-OO-SEE-KOO)

Chiku Chatterer. Swahili, E. Africa. (CHEE-KOO)

Chinue Blessings of Chi. Chi is the name of an important personal god who is thought to remain with a person from the moment of conception until death. Ibo, Nigeria. (CHEEN-WEH)

Chipo Gift. Shona, Zimbabwe. (CHEE-PO)

Chuki Born during a time of hatred. Swahili, E. Africa. (CHOO-KEE)

Dada Child born with curly hair. Yoruba, Nigeria. (DAH-DAH)

Dalila Gentle, tender. Swahili, E. Africa. Var: Dalia. (DAH-LEE-LAH)

Dalili Sign, omen. Swahili, E. Africa. (DAH-LEE-LEE)

Dayo Joy arrives, joy is here. Yoruba, Nigeria. (DAH-YO)

Desta Joy. Amharic, Ethiopia. (DEH-STAH)

Do First child after twins. Ewe, Ghana. (DŌ)

Dofi Second child after twins. Ewe, Ghana. (DŌ-FEE)

Doto Second of twins. Zaramo, Tanzania. (DŌ-TŌ)

Dziko The world. Nguni, S. Africa. (ZEE-KO)

Ebun Gift. Yoruba, Nigeria. (EH-BOON)

Efia Akeradini name meaning "born on Friday." Fante, Ghana. Var: Efva. (EH-FEE-AH)

Enomwoyi She is bestowed with grace and charm. Benin, Nigeria. (EH-NOM-WOH-YEE)

Enyonyam It is good for me. Ewe, Ghana. (EN-YO-NAM)

Eshe Life. Swahili, E. Africa. (EH-SHEH)

Esi Akeradini name meaning "born on Sunday." Fante, Ghana. (EH-SEE)

Esinam God heard me. Ewe, Ghana. (ESS-EE-NAM)

Fabayo A lucky birth brings joy. Yoruba, Nigeria. (FAH-BAH-YO)

Faizah Derived from the Arabic *fa'iz* (victor; winner), which is from *fāza* (to achieve; to win). Arabic, N. Africa. (FAH-EE-ZAH)

Fatima Derived from the Arabic *fāṭima* (she who weans an infant; she who abstains from forbidden things). The name was borne by Fāṭima bint-Muhammad (c. 606–32), the Prophet's favorite daughter and progenitor of the Fatimid dynasty. Arabic, N. Africa; Swahili, E. Africa. Var: Fatimah, Fatuma. (FAH-TEE-MAH)

Fayola Lucky, good fortune, blessed. Yoruba, Nigeria. (FAH-YO-LAH)

Femi Love me. Yoruba, Nigeria. (FEH-MEE)

Fola Honorable, respected. Yoruba, Nigeria. (FAW-LAH)

Folade Honor arrives, she brings honor. Yoruba, Nigeria. (FAW-LAH-DEH)

Folami Oriki name meaning "honor and respect me." Yoruba, Nigeria. (FAW-LAH-ME)

Folayan Walking with dignity, having a proud gait. Yoruba, Nigeria. (FAW-LAH-YAHN)

Foluke Placed in God's care. Yoruba, Nigeria. (FOH-LOO-KEH)

Fujo Born after the parents separated. Swahili, E. Africa. (FOO-JO)

Fukayna Knowledgeable, scholarly. Arabic, N. Africa. (FOO-KEH-EE-NAH)

Goitsemedime God knows. Tswana, Botswana. (COAT-SAY-MO-DEE-MEH)

Habiba Sweetheart, beloved. Derived from the Arabic *ḥabīb* (beloved), which is from *ḥabba* (to love). Arabic, N. Africa; Swahili, E. Africa. Var: Habibah. (HAH-BE-BAH)

Hadiya From the Arabic *hādi* (religious leader, guide). Arabic, N. Africa; Swahili, E. Africa. Var: Hadiyah. (HAH-DEE-YAH)

Hafsah Old Arabic name of uncertain meaning borne by Ḥafṣa bint-'Umar (d. 665), a wife of the Prophet Muḥammad and daughter of the second rightly guided caliph 'Umar ibn-al-Khaṭṭāb. She was chosen to safeguard the sole written copy of the Koran after the death of Muḥammad. Arabic, N. Africa. (HAF-SAH)

Halima Gentle, kind, patient. Arabic name borne by the nurse of the Prophet Muḥammad. She cared for him after the death of his mother when he was about six years old. Arabic, N. Africa; Swahili, E. Africa. Var: Halimah. (HAH-LEE-MAH)

Hanifa Derived from the Arabic *hanif* (true believer of Islam). Arabic, N. Africa. Var: Hanifah. (HAH-NEE-FAH)

Haqikah Truthful. Arabic, N. Africa. (HAH-KEE-KAH)

Hasana First-born twin. Hausa, Nigeria. (HAH-SAH-NAH)

Hasanati Good, beautiful. Derived from the Arabic *ḥasan* (beautiful, handsome, good), which is from *ḥasuna* (to be good). Swahili, E. Africa. (HAH-SAH-NAH-TEE)

Hasina Good, beautiful. Derived from the Arabic *ḥasan* (beautiful, handsome, good), which is from *ḥasuna* (to be good). Swahili, E. Africa. (HAH-SEE-NAH)

Hawa Longing. Swahili, E. Africa. (HAH-WAH)

Hembadoon The winner. Tiv, Nigeria. (HEM-BAH-DOON)

Husniya Excellence, beauty. Derived from the Arabic *ḥusn* (excellence, beauty, goodness), which is from *ḥasuna* (to be good). Arabic, N. Africa. Var: Husniyah. (HOO-SNEE-YAH)

Idowu Oruko name meaning "first child after twins." Yoruba, Nigeria. (EE-DŌ-WOO)

Ifama Everything is fine, all is well. Ibo, Nigeria. (EE-FAH-MAH)

Ife Love. Yoruba, Nigeria. (EE-FEH)

Ifetayo Love brings happiness and joy. Yoruba, Nigeria. (EE-FEH-TAH-YO)

Ikuseghan Peace is better than war. Benin, Nigeria. Var: Ikusegham. (EE-KOO-SEH-HAN)

Isoke A wonderful gift from God. Benin, Nigeria. (EE-SO-KEH)

Iverem Blessing, favor, good fortune. Tiv, Nigeria. (EE-VEH-REM)

Izegbe Long-awaited child. Benin, Nigeria. Var: Izebe. (EE-ZEH-BEH)

Jaha Dignity. Swahili, E. Africa. (JAH-HA)

Jamila Beautiful, elegant. From the Arabic *jamīl* (beautiful, graceful), which is from *jamula* (to be beautiful). Arabic, N. Africa; Swahili, E. Africa. Var: Jamilah. (JAH-ME-LAH)

Japera We are finished, now we offer thanks. Shona, Zimbabwe. (JAH-PEH-RAH)

Jendayi Give thanks. Shona, Zimbabwe. (JEN-DAH-YEE)

Jumapili Born on Sunday. Mwera, Kenya. (JOO-MAH-PEE-LEE)

Jumoke Oriki name meaning "loved by all, everyone loves the child." Yoruba, Nigeria. (JOO-MO-KEH)

Kagiso Peace. Tswana, Botswana. (KAH-GHEE-SO)

Kakra Akeradini name meaning "second of twins." Fante, Ghana. (KAH-KRAH)

Kamaria Like the moon. Swahili, E. Africa. Var: Kamania. (KAH-MAH-REE-AH)

Kanika Black cloth. Mwera, Kenya. (KAH-NEE-KAH)

Kehinde Oruko name meaning "second of twins." Yoruba, Nigeria. (KEH-HEEN-DEH)

Kesi Born when the father had difficulties. Swahili, E. Africa. (KAY-SEE)

Khadija Born prematurely. Derived from the Arabic *khadīja* (premature child). The name was borne by the first wife of the Prophet Muḥammad and mother of his children. *See* KHADĪJA (Muslim/Arabic Names). Arabic, N. Africa; Swahili, E. Africa. Var: Kadija. (KAH-DEE-JAH)

KIBIBI Little lady. Swahili, E. Africa. (KEE-BE-BE)

KIFIMBO A twig. The name refers to a very small, thin baby. Swahili, E. Africa. (KEE-FEEM-BO)

KISSA Born after twins. Luganda, Uganda. (KISS-SAH)

KOKO Born second. Adangbe, Ghana. (KO-KO)

KOKUMO Oriki name meaning "this one will not die." Yoruba, Nigeria. (KO-KOO-MO)

KUKUA Akeradini name meaning "born on Wednesday." Fante, Ghana. (KOO-KOO-HA)

KULIRAGA Weeping. Yao, Malawi. Var: Koliraga. (KOO-LEH-RAH-GAH)

KULWA First of twins. Zaramo, Tanzania. (KOOL-WAH)

KUNTO Third-born child. Twi, Ghana. (KOON-TŌ)

KYALAMBOKA God save me. Nyakyusa, Tanzania. (KEE-AL-LAM-BO-KAH)

LATEEFA Gentle, kind. Derived from the Arabic *laṭīf* (gentle). Arabic, N. Africa. Var: Lateefah. (LAH-TEE-FAH)

LEILA Derived from the Arabic *leila* (dark beauty, dark as night). Arabic, N. Africa; Swahili, E. Africa. Var: Laila, Layla, Leyla. (LAH-EE-LAH)

LINDA Wait. Xhosa, S. Africa. (LEEN-DAH)

LULU Precious, a pearl. Swahili, E. Africa. (LOO-LOO)

LUMUSI Born face-downward. Ewe, Ghana. (LOO-MOO-SEE)

MAIBA Grave. Shona, Zimbabwe. (MAH-EE-BAH)

MALAIKA Angel. Swahili, E. Africa. (MAH-LAH-EE-KAH)

MAMA Born on Saturday. Fante, Ghana. (MAH-MAH)

MANDISA Sweet. Xhosa, S. Africa. (MAN-DEE-SAH)

MARJANI Coral. Swahili, E. Africa. (MAHR-JAH-NEE)

MASHAVU Cheeks. Used in reference to a baby with chubby cheeks. Swahili, E. Africa. (MAH-SHAH-VOO)

MASIKA Born during the rainy season. Swahili, E. Africa. (MAH-SEE-KAH)

MASKINI Poor. Swahili, E. Africa. (MAH-SKEE-NEE)

MAUDISA Sweet one, she is sweet. Xhosa, S. Africa. (MAH-OO-DEE-SAH)

MAULIDI Born during the Islamic month of Maulidi. Swahili, E. Africa. (MAH-OO-LEE-DEE)

MAWIYAH The essence of life. Arabic, N. Africa. (MAH-WEE-YAH)

MAWUSI In the hands of God. Ewe, Ghana. (MAH-WOO-SEE)

MESI Water. Yao, Malawi. (MEH-SEE)

MONIFA I am lucky. Yoruba, Nigeria. (MO-NEE-FAH)

MOROWA Queen. Akan, Ghana. (MO-RO-WAH)

MOSI First-born. Swahili, E. Africa. (MO-SEE)

MUDIWA Beloved, dearest. Shona, Zimbabwe. (MOO-DEE-WAH)

MUMINAH True believer, pious. Arabic, N. Africa. (MOO-MEE-NAH)

MUNIRAH Enlightener. Arabic, N. Africa. (MOO-NEE-RAH)

MUTETELI Dainty. Rwanda, Rwanda. (MOO-TAY-TAH-LEE)

MWAJUMA Born on Friday. Swahili, E. Africa. (MWAH-JOO-MAH)

MWANAHAMISI Born on Thursday. Swahili, E. Africa. (MWAH-NAH-HAH-MEE-SEE)

MWANAJUMA Born on Friday. Swahili, E. Africa. (MWAH-NAH-JOO-MAH)

MWANAWA First-born. Zaramo, Tanzania. (MWAH-NAH-WAH)

NABULUNGI Beautiful one. Luganda, Uganda. (NAH-BOO-LONG-GHEE)

NAEEMAH Benevolent, contented, happy. From the Arabic *na'īm* (content, happy), which is from *na'ima* (to live comfortably, to be carefree). Arabic, N. Africa. (NAH-EE-MAH)

NAILAH One who succeeds. Derived from the Arabic *nā'il* (attainer), which is from *nāla* (to attain). Arabic, N. Africa. (NAH-EE-LAH)

NAKI First-born girl. Adangbe, Ghana. (NAH-KEE)

NAMONO Younger of twins. Luganda, Uganda. (NAH-MO-NO)

Nanyamka Gift of God. Ewe, Ghana. (NAH-YAHM-KAH)

Nathifa Clean, pure. Arabic, N. Africa. (NAH-THEE-FAH)

Nayo She is our joy. Yoruba, Nigeria. (NAH-YO)

Neema Born during good times, born during prosperous times. Swahili, E. Africa. (NEH-EH-MAH)

Nehanda Strong, powerful. Zezuru, Zimbabwe. (NEH-HAN-DEH)

Ngabile I have it. Nyakyusa, Tanzania. (N-GAH-BE-LEH)

Ngozi Blessing. Ibo, Nigeria. (N-GO-ZEE)

Njemile Upstanding, honorable. Yao, Malawi. (N-JEH-ME-LEH)

Nkosazana Princess. Xhosa, S. Africa. (N-KO-SAH-ZAH-NAH)

Nneka Her mother is important, her mother is supreme. Ibo, Nigeria. (N-NEH-KAH)

Nobantu Popular. Xhosa, S. Africa. (NO-BAHN-TOO)

Nomalanga Sunny. Zulu, S. Africa. (NO-MAH-LENG-GAH)

Nombeko Respect. Xhosa, S. Africa. (NOM-BEH-KO)

Nombese A wonderful child, a special child. Benin, Nigeria. (NOM-BEH-SEH)

Nomble Beauty. Xhosa, S. Africa. (NOM-BLEH)

Nomusa Merciful, compassionate. Ndebele, Zimbabwe. (NO-MOO-SAH)

Nonyameko Patience. Xhosa, S. Africa. (NONG-YA-MEH-KO)

Nourbese A wonderful child, a special child. Benin, Nigeria. (NOOR-BEH-SEH)

Nuru Light. Derived from the Arabic *nūr* (light), which is from *nawara* (to light up; to illuminate). Swahili, E. Africa. (NOO-ROO)

Obioma Kind. Ibo, Nigeria. (O-BE-O-MAH)

Ode Born along the road. Benin, Nigeria. (O-DEH)

Olabisi Joy is multiplied. Yoruba, Nigeria. (O-LAH-BE-SEE)

Olaniyi There's glory in prosperity. Yoruba, Nigeria. (O-LAH-NEE-YEE)

Olubayo Greatest joy, highest joy. Yoruba, Nigeria. (O-LOO-BAH-YO)

Olufemi God loves me. Yoruba, Nigeria. (O-LOO-FEH-ME)

Olufunmilayo God gives me joy and happiness. Yoruba, Nigeria. (O-LOO-FOON-ME-LAH-YO)

Oluremi God consoles me, God is consolation. Yoruba, Nigeria. (O-LOO-REH-ME)

Omolara Born at the right time. Benin, Nigeria. (O-MO-LAH-RAH)

Omorose Beautiful child, lovely child. Benin, Nigeria. (O-MO-RO-SEH)

Omusupe She is the most precious thing. Benin, Nigeria. (O-MO-SOO-PEH)

Oni Desired, wanted. Benin, Nigeria. (O-NEE)

Oni Born in a sacred place. Yoruba, Nigeria. (AW-NEE)

Oseye The happy one, the joyous one. Benin, Nigeria. (O-SEH-YEH)

Panya Mouse. Bestowed in reference to a tiny baby. Swahili, E. Africa. (PAHN-YAH)

Panyin Akeradini name meaning "first born of twins, elder twin." Fante, Ghana. (PAHN-YEEN)

Pasua Born by cesarean section. Swahili, E. Africa. (PAH-SOO-AH)

Pili Second-born. Swahili, E. Africa. (PEE-LEE)

Rabiah Arabic name derived from *rabi'ah* (spring). Arabic, N. Africa. (RAH-BE-AH)

Radhiya Agreeable, content. Derived from the Arabic *rida* (contentment, satisfaction). Swahili, E. Africa. (RAHD-HE-YAH)

Ramla Seer of the future, predictor of the future. Swahili, E. Africa. (RAHM-LAH)

Rashida Rightly guided, righteous. Derived from the Arabic *rashīd* (rightly guided, wise), which is from *rashada* (to follow the right course). Arabic, N. Africa; Swahili, E. Africa. Var: Raashida, Rachida, Rasheeda. (RAH-SHEE-DAH)

Raziya Agreeable, pleasant. Swahili, E. Africa. (RAH-ZEE-YAH)

Rehema Compassion, concern. Swahili, E. Africa. (REH-HEH-MAH)

Rufaro Happiness, joy. Shona, Zimbabwe. (roo-FAH-ro)

Rukiya Derived from the Arabic *ruqiy* (ascent, rising up, progress), which is from *raqiya* (to ascend, to rise up). Swahili, E. Africa. (ROO-KEE-YAH)

Saada Help. Swahili, E. Africa. (SAH-AH-DAH)

Sabah Morning. Derived from the Arabic *ṣabāḥ* (morning). Arabic, N. Africa. (SAH-BAH)

Safiyya Confidant, best friend. Derived from the Arabic *ṣafiyya* (confidant), which is from *ṣafa* (to be pure, to be select). Arabic, N. Africa; Swahili, E. Africa. Var: Safiya, Safiyeh, Safiyyah. (SAH-FEE-YAH)

Saidah Happy, fortunate. Derived from the Arabic *sa'id* (lucky, happy), which is from *sa'ida* (to be lucky; to be happy). Arabic, N. Africa. (SAH-EE-DAH)

Salama Safety, security. Swahili, E. Africa. Var: Salma. (SAH-LAH-MAH)

Salihah Virtuous, correct. Derived from the Arabic *sālih* (virtuous, righteous), which is from *ṣaluḥa* (to be righteous). Arabic, N. Africa. (SAH-LEE-HAH)

Salma Safe, healthy. Derived from the Arabic *sālima* (safe, healthy), which is from *salima* (to be safe). Swahili, E. Africa. Var: Selma. (SAHL-MAH)

Sanura Kitten-like. Swahili, E. Africa. (SAH-NOO-RAH)

Sauda Dark-complexioned. Swahili, E. Africa. (SAH-OO-DAH)

Sekelaga Rejoice, celebrate. Nyakyusa, Tanzania. (SEH-KEH-LAH-GAH)

Shani Wonderful, marvelous. Swahili, E. Africa. (SHAH-NEE)

Sharifa Honorable, distinguished, outstanding. Derived from the Arabic *sharīf* (honorable; eminent), which is from *sharafa* (to be distinguished). Arabic, N. Africa; Swahili, E. Africa. Var: Sharufa. (SHAH-REE-FAH)

Shukura Grateful. Swahili, E. Africa. Var: Shukuma. (SHOO-KOO-RAH)

Sibongile Thanks, appreciation. Ndebele, Zimbabwe. (SEE-BON-GEE-LEH)

Sigele Left. Ngoni, Malawi. (SEE-GEH-LEH)

Sisi Born on Sunday. Fante, Ghana. (SEE-SEE)

Siti Lady. Swahili, E. Africa. (SEE-TEE)

Subira Patience is rewarded. Swahili, E. Africa. (SOO-BE-RAH)

Suhailah Gentle, easy. Derived from the Arabic Suhayl, the name of the second-brightest star in the southern skies, which is also known as Canopus. Arabic, N. Africa. (SOO-HAH-EE-LAH)

Suma Ask. Nyakyusa, Tanzania. (SOO-MAH)

Tabia Talents, gifts. Swahili, E. Africa. (TAH-BE-AH)

Tahirah Pure. Derived from the Arabic *ṭāhir* (pure; chaste), which is from *ṭahura* (to be pure; to be clean). Arabic, N. Africa. (TAH-HEE-RAH)

Taiwo Oruko name meaning "first-born twin." Yoruba, Nigeria. (TAH-EE-WO)

Takiyah Piety, righteousness. Derived from the Arabic *tuqā* (piety; fear of God). (TAH-KEE-YAH)

Tale Green. Tswana, Botswana. (TAH-LEH)

Taliba Seeker of knowledge. Derived from the Arabic *taliba* (seeker of knowledge). Arabic, N. Africa. Var: Talibah. (TAH-LEE-BAH)

Tanisha Born on Monday. Hausa, Nigeria. (TAH-NEE-SHA)

Teleza Slippery. Ngoni, Malawi. (TAH-LEH-ZAH)

Thandiwe Loving one, affectionate. Xhosa, S. Africa. (TAN-DEE-WEH)

Thema Queen. Akan, Ghana. (TAY-MAH)

Themba Trusted, had faith in. Zulu, S. Africa. (TEHM-BAH)

Titilayo Happiness is eternal, eternally joyful. Yoruba, Nigeria. (TEE-TEE-LAH-YO)

Tulinagwe God is with us. Nyakyusa, Tanzania. (TOO-LEE-NAH-GWEH)

Tusajigwe We are blessed, we have been favored. Nyakyusa, Tanzania. (TOO-SAH-JEE-GWEH)

Uchenna God's will. Ibo, Nigeria. (OO-CHEEN-NAH)

Ulu Second-born female. Ibo, Nigeria. (OO-LOO).

Umayma Little mother. Derived from the Arabic *'umayma* (little mother). Arabic, N. Africa. (OO-MAH-EE-MAH)

Umm Mother. Derived from the Arabic *'um* (mother). Arabic, N. Africa. (OOM)

Urbi Princess. Benin, Nigeria. (OOR-BE)

URENNA Her father's pride. Ibo, Nigeria. (OO-REN-NAH)

UWIMANA Daughter of God. Rwanda, Rwanda. (OO-WEE-MAH-NAH)

WALIDAH Newborn. Arabic name derived from *walīd* (a newborn), which is from *walada* (to give birth). Arabic, N. Africa. (WAH-LEE-DAH)

WASEME Let them talk. Swahili, E. Africa. (WAH-SEH-MEH)

YAA Born on Thursday. Ewe, Ghana. (YAH-AH)

YAMINA Proper, of moral excellence. Derived from the Arabic *yamīna* (proper; of good morals). Arabic, N. Africa. Var: Yaminah. (YAH-ME-NAH)

YE Elder of twins, first born of twins. Ewe, Ghana. (YEH-EH)

YEJIDE She looks like her mother. Yoruba, Nigeria. (YEH-JEE-DEH)

ZAHRA Flower. Derived from the Arabic *zahra* (flower, blossom), which is from *zahara* (to blossom, to flower). Arabic, N. Africa; Swahili, E. Africa. Var: Zahara. (ZAH-RAH)

ZAINABU Derived from the Arabic *zaynab* (the name of a very fragrant plant). *See* ZAYNAB (Muslim/Arabic Names). Swahili, E. Africa. (ZAH-EE-NAH-BOO)

ZAKIYA Pure, righteous, pious. Derived from the Arabic *zakiy* (pure, righteous). Arabic, N. Africa; Swahili, E. Africa. (ZAH-KEE-YAH)

ZALIKA Well-born. Swahili, E. Africa. (ZAH-LEE-KAH)

ZAWADI Gift, present. Swahili, E. Africa. (ZAH-WAH-DEE)

ZESIRO First of twins, elder of twins. Luganda, Uganda. (ZEH-SEE-RO)

ZUBAIDAH A marigold flower. Derived from the Arabic *zubaidā* (a marigold). Arabic, N. Africa. (ZOO-BAH-EE-DAH)

ZUWENA Good. Swahili, E. Africa. Var: Zwena. (ZOO-WEH-NAH)

Chapter Two

African-American Names

Not surprisingly, the early history of African-American names was heavily influenced by the institution of slavery, and an example of this influence can be found in the bestowal of names. More often than not, it was the owners who named the slaves, nearly always giving them names that were foreign to their country of origin. Bible names, classical names, literary names, descriptive names, and occupational names were the categories most often chosen. In other cases, names were derived from white surnames.

In most cases, these early African-Americans were not given surnames. However, when two or more slaves had the same name, a second was added for identification purposes. These additions often came in the form of a parent's name or the name of the previous owner. It was also common to add a descriptive term, such as Big Jack or Young Sam.

While slaves were generally given short forms of names, freed blacks often chose names in their full form, finding them more dignified and a mark of the difference in their status. Common slave names, such as Sambo and Bett, were discarded in favor of classical, more elegant names and names that were somewhat different from the standard pool in use by whites. These were generally elaborations or variations of common names, and inventions coined by the individuals.

This predilection toward interesting names continues to this day. African-Americans began using coinages in the 19th century, and today this trend is on the increase. The prefixes *La-* and *Sha-* form the foundation of many invented names for both sexes. Variant forms of Sean and the female element *eesha* are also popular choices to build modern coinages around. Classical Latin names, such as Ulysses and Venus, continue to be well represented, and the influence of the Caribbean is manifest in the number of names found of Spanish and French origin.

Many African-Americans are leading the way to cultural revivalism and are becoming more Afrocentric in orientation. A part of this process is seen in the naming of their children. More African names are in use than ever before, and the adoption of Muslim names is on the increase as more people reach out to embrace the religion of Islam.

This chapter highlights some of the more popular names and modern coinages in use by the African-American community. If you are interested in names of African, Muslim, or Spanish origin, chapters one, nineteen, and thirty deal expressly with those names.

African-American Male Names

ANDRÉ French form of Andrew, a name derived from the Greek *andreios* (manly). Var: Ahndray, Andrae, Andray, Aundray. (AHN-DRAY)

ANTRON Modern coinage based on the name Anton, a form of Anthony. *See* ANTHONY (English Names). (AN-TRON)

AUGUSTUS Latin name derived from *augustus* (great, venerable). Short: Gus. (AU-GUS-TUS)

BAURICE Modern coinage based on the name Maurice (Moorish). *See* MAURICE. (BOAR-REES)

BRIDON Modern coinage of uncertain derivation. (BRI-DUN)

CHÉ Modern name of uncertain derivation. It is most likely the transferred use of a common Spanish nickname. (CHAY)

CHIKAE Perhaps from the Ibo (Nigeria) Chike (power of God). (CHEE-KAY)

CLEAVON Modern coinage of uncertain derivation. Var: Clevon, Kleavon, Klevon. (KLEE-VON)

CLEON Modern coinage perhaps formed as an elaborated form of Leon (lion) or as a variant form of the Greek Cleo (glory). (KLEON, KLEE-ON)

DAIQUAN Modern coinage of uncertain derivation. (DAY-KWAN)

DARIO A borrowing from the Italian, Dario is from the Greek Dareios, which is of uncertain derivation. *See* DARIO (Italian Names). (DAH-REE-O)

DA'RON Modern coinage that is possibly a variation of Darren. *See* DARREN (English Names). Var: Dar Ron, De'Ron, D'Ron. (DAH-RON)

DAYLON Modern coinage of uncertain derivation. (DAY-LON)

DE'LEWIS Modern coinage formed by adding the prefix *De-* to the name Lewis (famous in war). *See* LOUIS (French Names). Var: D'Lewis. (DEE-LOO-ISS)

DELON Modern coinage of uncertain derivation. Var: Deelon, De'Lon, De'Lonn, Delonn, D'Lon, D'Lonn. (DEE-LON, DEE-LON)

DEMETRIOS A borrowing from the Greek, Demetrios has the definition "of Demeter." *See* DEMETRIOS (Greek Names). Var: Demetrious, Dimetrious. (DEH-MEE-TREE-OS)

DENELL Modern coinage probably formed by adding the prefix *De-* to the element *nell*, which is found in names such as Cornell and Nelson. Denell is also bestowed as a female name. (DEH-NEL)

DENZELL Borrowing of a Cornish place-name of uncertain derivation. It gave rise to the surname Denzil in the 16th century. Var: Denzel. (DEN-ZEL)

DEVIN Derived from the Irish *dámh* (a poet). Var: Devan, Devon, Devyn. (DEH-VUN)

DE OLE Modern name combining the prefix *De-* with the name Ole, a Danish variant of Olaf (ancestor's relic). Var: Deole, D'Ole. (DEE-OL)

DION A borrowing from the French, Dion is from the Latin Dio, originally a short form of any of the various names of Greek origin that begin with the name element *Dios* (of Zeus). Var: Deion, Deon, De'On. (DEE-ON)

DOMINIC Derived from the Latin Dominicus (belonging to a lord), which is from *dominus* (a lord, a master). Var: Dominick, Dominik, Dominique. (DOM-IH-NIK)

DONMINIC Modern variation of Dominic (belonging to a lord). *See* DOMINIC. (DON-MIH-NIK)

DONYELL Modern coinage formed from the name Don and the suffix *-ell*. (DON-NEE-EL, DON-YEL)

EDWIN Derived from the Old English Eadwine, a compound name composed of the elements *ēad* (prosperity, riches) and *wine* (friend): hence, "wealthy friend." Var: Eddwyn, Eddwynn, Edwyn. Short: Ed. Pet: Eddie. (ED-WIN)

ELON Modern coinage of uncertain derivation. It is perhaps based on the French *élan* (spirited self-assurance, verve, vivaciousness). (EE-LON, Ā-LON)

ELROY Variant of Leroy, a modern coinage thought to be based on the French *le roi* (the king). Var: Elroi, El Roy. (EL-ROI)

GENTRY Derived from the Middle English *genterie* (of noble or high birth). Var: Jentree, Jentry. (JEN-TREE)

GERMAIN A borrowing from the French, Germain is from the Late Latin *germānus* (brother), which is derived from *germen* (a sprout, a bud, embryo). Var: Germaine, Jermain, Jermaine. (JER-MANE)

HAKEEM Derived from the Arabic *hakīm* (judicious). (HAH-KEEM)

IVORY Derived from *ivory*, which denotes the tusks of such animals as elephants and walruses. The use of the name by African-Americans is often in reference to the name of the West Africa country Ivory Coast. (Ī-VREE, Ī-VEH-REE)

JAIMAN Modern coinage of uncertain derivation. Var: Jaeman, Jayman. Short: Jae, Jai, Jay. Pet: Jaimie, Jaymie. (JAY-MUN)

JALAL From the Arabic Jalāl (greatness), a name derived from *jalla* (to be great). (JAH-LAHL)

JALEEL Derived perhaps from the Arabic Jalāl (greatness) or a coinage based on the Arabic Jamīl (beautiful, handsome). (JAH-LEEL)

JALEN Modern coinage perhaps based on the name Galen (calm, serene) or as a combination name formed by combining parents' names such as Jay and Helen. Var: Jailen, Jaylen. (JAY-LEN)

JAMAL Derived from the Arabic Jamāl, which is from *jamāl* (beauty). (JAH-MAHL)

JAMIL Derived from the Arabic Jamīl, which is from *jamīl* (beautiful, handsome), which is from *jamala* (to be beautiful). Var: Jameel. (JAH-MEEL)

JAMISON Transferred use of the English surname meaning "Jamie's son." *See* JAMIE (American Names). Var: Jamieson. Pet: Jamie. (JAY-MIS-SUN)

JARNAIL Modern coinage of uncertain derivation. (JAR-NAIL)

JASHON Modern coinage perhaps based on the name Jason (healer). *See* JASON (American Names). (JAY-SHON)

JA'SHON Modern coinage of uncertain derivation. It might be a variant form of Jashon or a combining of the prefix *Ja-* with Shon, an American variant of the Irish Sean (God is gracious). *See* SEAN (Irish Names). Var: Ja'Shaun, Ja'Shonn. (JAH-SHON)

JATHAN Modern coingage, perhaps based on the name Jason (healer). (JAY-THUN)

JEDEDISH Modern coinage of uncertain derivation. It could be a variation of Jedidiah (beloved of Jehovah). *See* JEDIDIAH (Biblical Names). Short: Jed. (JED-DEH-DEESH)

JEFFERSON Transferred use of the English surname, which originated as a patronymic meaning "son of Geoffrey, son of Jeffrey." *See* GEOFFREY (American Names). Short: Jeff. (JEF-FER-SUN)

JELANI An Ibo name meaning "mighty, strong." Var: Jalani, Jehlani. (JEH-LAH-NEE)

JERONE Modern coinage probably based on the name Jerome (holy name). *See* JEROME (American Names). (JEH-RONE)

JESSE Derived from the Hebrew Yishai, which is from *yīshai* (gift, wealth). *See* JESSE (Biblical Names). (JES-EE)

JEVIN Modern coinage perhaps based on the name Devin (a poet). *See* DEVIN (American Names). Var: Jevon. (JEH-VIN)

JONIGAN Modern elaboration of the name John (God is gracious). *See* JOHN (American Names). (JON-IH-GUN)

JUWAN Modern coinage of uncertain derivation. It was probably coined to impart an African or Muslim sound. (JOO-WAHN)

KADIN Modern coinage of uncertain derivation. It could represent a variant of the surname Kaden, which is of Germanic origin and derived from a place-name meaning "fen." (KAY-DIN)

KANZAN Of uncertain derivation. (KAN-ZAN)

KARIO Modern coinage perhaps based on the name Mario. (KAR-EE-O)

KEAZIAH Of uncertain derivation, Keaziah might be a modern coinage formed by combining elements from different names, or it might be a variant of the Hebrew female name Ketziah (cassia). *See* KETZIAH (Jewish/Hebrew Female Names). (KEE-ZĪ-AH)

KEENAN Anglicized form of the Irish Cianán (little Cian, little ancient one). Cianán is a diminutive form of Cian (ancient, in the past). Var: Keenen, Kenan, Kienan. (KEE-NUN)

KELVIN Transferred use of the surname that arose from the name of a Scottish river. Kelvin was first used as a personal name in England in the 1920s, perhaps in honor of Baron Kelvin (1824–1907), the British mathematician and physicist to whom the Kelvin scale of temperature is attributed. (KEL-VIN)

KENIDS Modern coinage of uncertain derivation. (KEE-NIDS)

KENYA A borrowing of the name of the country in east central Africa. The name is often bestowed as a symbol of ethnic pride. (KEN-YAH)

KÉSHA Modern coinage of uncertain derivation. (KEH-SHA)

KESHON Modern coinage perhaps based on the name Shon, an American variant of the Irish Sean (God is gracious). Var: Kesean, Ke Sean, Ke Shon. (KEE-SHON, KEE-SHON)

KHALID Derived from the Arabic *khālid* (eternal, undying). *See* KHĀLID (Muslim/Arabic Names). (KAH-LEED)

KI-JANA Modern coinage containing the element *jana*, a variant form of John (God is gracious). (KEE-JAH-NAH)

KING Derived from *king* (ruler, king). The name is often bestowed in honor of Rev. Dr. Martin Luther King, Jr. (1929–68). (KING)

KIVI Transferred use of a Finnish surname meaning "dweller by a stone." (KIH-VEE)

KOICE Modern coinage perhaps based on the name Royce (Roy's son). (KOICE)

KYAN Modern coinage of uncertain derivation. It is possibly influenced by the name Ryan. (KĪ-UN)

LAKISTA Modern coinage of uncertain derivation. (LAH-KIS-TAH)

LAMAR Derived from the French surname La Mar (dweller by a pool). (LAH-MAR)

LAMOND Transferred use of the English surname of Scandinavian origin. It is derived from the Old Norse *lög* (law) and *mann* (man): hence, "lawman, lawyer." Var: La Mond, La Monde, Lamont, Lammond. (LAH-MOND)

LAMONTE Derived from the Spanish *monte* (mountain). Var: Lamont. (LAH-MAHN-TAY)

LAPHONSO Modern variation of Alphonso (noble and ready). *See* ALPHONSE (French Names). Var: Lafonso, LaPhonso. (LAH-FON-SO)

LA ROY Modern coinage based on the name Leroy (king). (LAH-ROI)

LAURENCE Derived from the Latin Laurentius (man from Laurentum). Laurentum, the name of a small town in Italy, is probably derived from *laurus* (laurel). Var: Larenz, Laurenze, Lawrence, Lorenz. (LAU-RENS)

LA VONN Modern coinage combining the prefix *La-* and Vonn, a variant of the Irish Vaughn (small, little). Var: La Vaun, Lavon, La Voun. (LAH-VON)

L'AWAN Modern coinage of uncertain derivation. (LAH-WAHN)

LEE RON Modern combination name composed of the names Lee and Ron. *See* LEE *and* RON (American Names). (LEE-RON)

LEON Variant form of Leo (a lion). *See* LEO (Italian Names). (LEE-ON)

LEONDRA Modern coinage based on the name Leon (lion). (LEE-ON-DRAH)

LEROY Modern coinage based on the French *le roi* (the king). Var: Lee Roy, Le Roi, Le Roy. (LEE-ROI)

LE SONN Modern coinage of uncertain derivation. (LEE-SON)

LIONEL Transferred use of the English surname derived from *lion* (lion) and the French diminutive suffix *-el*: hence, "little lion." Var: Lionell, Lionnel, Lyonell. (LĪ-o-nel)

LUCAS Ecclesiastic Late Latin name thought to be a derivative of Lucius, which is from the root *lux* (light). Alternatively, some believe the name is derived from the Ecclesiastic Greek Loukas, a contraction of Loukanos (man from Lucania). (LOO-KUS)

LUTHER Derived from the Old High German *Hluodohari* (famous in war), a compound name composed from the elements *hluod* (famous) and *wīg* (war, strife). (LOO-THER)

MALCOLM Derived from the Gaelic Maolcolm (servant of St. Columba), a compound name composed of the elements *maol* (servant, votary) and Colm (Columba). *See* MALCOLM (Scottish Names). (MAL-KUM, MAL-KULM)

MANDELA Bestowed in honor of South African President Nelson Mandela. (MAN-DEL-LAH)

MARCUS Latin name of uncertain derivation. Most believe it has its root in Mars, the Roman mythological god of war, and give it the definition "war-like." Others, however, think it might be from *mas* (manly) or from the Greek *malakoz* (soft, tender). Short: Marc. (MAR-KUS)

MARQUIS Derived from the French *marquis*, which denotes a nobleman ranking above an earl and count and below a duke. (MAR-KEES)

MASIO Short form of Tomasio, which is a cognate of Thomas (a twin). The name is also bestowed as an independent given name. *See* THOMAS (English Names). Var: Macio. (MAH-SEE-O)

MAURICE French name derived from the Late Latin Mauritius (Moorish), which is from Maurus (a Moor). The Moors were a Muslim people of mixed Arab and Berber descent, and the name came to mean "dark" or "swarthy" in reference to their coloring. (MOR-REES)

Napoleon Compound name composed from the Greek elements *neapolis* (new city) and *leōn* (lion): hence, "lion of the new city." (NAH-PO-LEE-ON)

Nathan Derived from the Hebrew *nāthān* (gift). Short: Nate. (NAY-THUN)

Neville Transferred use of the surname originating as a Norman baronial name from several places in Normandy called Neuville or Neville, which are composed from the French elements *neuve* (new) and *ville* (town). Var: Neval, Nevil, Nevill, Nevyll. (NEH-VIL)

Odessa A borrowing of the name of a city in west-central Texas. (O-DEH-SAH)

Orlando Borrowed from the Spanish, Orlando is derived from the French Roland, which is from the Old High German Hruodland, a compounding of the elements *hruod* (fame) and *land* (land): hence, "fame of the land." Var: Arlando, Orlondo. Short: Lando. (OR-LAN-DŌ)

Parnell French diminutive form of Peter (a rock, a stone). *See* PETER (American Names). Var: Parnall, Pernell. (PAR-NEL)

Phoenix Derived from the Greek *phoinix* (phoenix, bright red). *See* PHOENIX (Mythology and Astrology Names). Var: Phenix. (FEE-NIKS)

Quadrees Modern coinage containing the element *quad* (four). Var: Kwadrees, Quadrhys. (KWAD-DREES)

Quentin From the Latin Quentīnus, a derivative of the Roman personal name Quintus, which is from the vocabulary word *quintus* (the fifth). The name was traditionally bestowed upon the fifth-born child. (KWEN-TIN)

Rashard Modern coinage quite possibly based on the French pronunciation of Richard (stern king). *See* RICHARD (English Names). (RAH-SHARD)

Rashon Modern coinage utilizing the element *shon* and probably influenced by Muslim names such as Rashad and Rashid. Var: Rachan, Rashaan, Rasham, Rashan, Rashawn, Reshaun, Reshawn. (RAH-SHON)

Raymond From the Old Norman French Raimund (wise protection), which is derived from the Germanic Raginmund, a compound name composed of the elements *ragin* (advice, judgment, counsel) and *mund* (hand, protection). Var: Raymonde, RayMonde, Raymondo, Raymund. Short: Ray, Raye. (RAY-MUND)

Roman Derived from the Latin *Romanus* (a Roman), which is from Roma, the name of the capital city of Italy. (RO-MAN)

Rondré Modern coinage which is very likely a combining of the names Ron (ruler of judgment) and André (manly). Var: Rondre, Ron Dre, Ron Dré. (RON-DRAY)

Roshaun Modern combination formed by the addition of the prefix *Ro-* to Shaun, an Anglicized form of the Irish Seán (God is gracious). *See* SEÁN (Irish Names). Var: RoShawn, Roshon. (RO-SHON)

Royce Transferred use of the surname meaning "Roy's son." *See* ROY (American Names). Var: Roice, Royse. (ROIS)

Sean Derived from Seán, an Irish cognate of John (God is gracious). *See* JOHN (American Names). Var: Shauen, Shaun, Shawn, Shon. (SHON)

Shante Modern coinage possibly of French influence. Var: Shantay, Shanté, Shantay, Shonte, Shonté. (SHAN-TAY)

Sharone Modern coinage based on the female name Sharon (a plain, a flat area). *See* SHARON (Female Names). Var: Sha Rone. (SHA-RONE)

Shawnel Modern coinage formed by the addition of the diminutive suffix *-el* to Shawn, an Anglicized form of the Irish Seán, a cognate of John (God is gracious). *See* JOHN (American Names). Var: Shawnell, Shawnelle. (SHAW-NEL)

Solomon Biblical name derived from the Hebrew *shĕlōmōh* (peaceful). *See* Solomon (Biblical Names). Var: Soliman, Solimon, Soloman. (SOL-O-MUN)

Stevon Modern variant of Stephen (a crown, garland). *See* STEPHEN (English Names). (STEE-VON, STEE-VON)

Tandie Modern coinage perhaps based on the Scottish surname Tandy, which arose as a pet form of Andrew (manly). (TAN-DEE)

Tanier Modern coinage of uncertain derivation. It could possibly be a variant of Tanner (a person who tans leather hides). (TAN-YER)

Tavares Transferred use of the Spanish surname meaning "descendant of the hermit, descendant of the retired man." (TAH-VAH-REZ)

Temple Transferred use of the surname derived from the Old English *tempel* (temple): hence, "dweller near the temple." (TEM-PL)

Terence From the Latin Terentius, an old Roman family name of uncertain derivation. It might be derived from *terenus* (soft, tender). Var: Terance, Terrance, Terrence. Pet: Terry. (TARE-ENS)

TERYL Modern coinage which is perhaps a blending of the names Terry and Daryl. Var: Tarell, Terrell. Pet: Terry. (TARE-IL)

TEVIN Modern coinage perhaps based on the name Kevin. (TEH-VIN)

THEO A short form of Theodore (God's gift), Theo is also bestowed as an independent given name. *See* THEODORE. (THEE-O)

THEODORE Derived from the Latin Theodorus, which is from the Greek Theodōros, a compounding of the elements *theos* (God) and *dōron* (a gift): hence, "God's gift." Var: Theodor. Short: Theo. Pet: Teddy. (THEE-O-DOR)

TITO Spanish form of the Greek Titos, an ancient name of uncertain derivation. Some believe it to be from the Greek *tīo* (to honor). Titus is the English cognate. (TEE-TŌ)

TREMAINE Transferred use of the Cornish surname derived from the place-name Tremaine (stone village). The name has the definition "from Tremaine." Var: Tremain, Tremayne. (TREH-MANE)

TREY Derived from the Middle English *trey* (three), which is ultimately from the Latin *tres* (three). The name was traditionally given to the third-born or the third-born son. Var: Tre. (TRAY)

TROY Transferred use of the surname originating from the place-name Troyes in Aube, Normandy. Alternatively, the name may be bestowed in reference to the name of the ancient Phrygian city in northwestern Asia Minor, which was the scene of the Trojan War. Var: Troi, Troixe, Troixes. (TROI)

TY Short form of any of the names beginning with the element *Ty-*. It is also occasionally bestowed as an independent given name. Var: Tye. (TĪ)

TYPHOON Derived from *typhoon* (a violent tropical cyclone), which is derived from the Chinese *tai-fung* (great wind). Short: Ty. (TĪ-FOON)

TYRONE Derived from the Greek Turannos (sovereign, king). Alternatively, Tyrone is the transferred use of an Irish place-name in county Ulster. It is of uncertain derivation. Short: Ty. (TĪ-RONE)

TYSON Transferred use of the English surname derived from the Old French *tison* (firebrand). Var: Tieson. Short: Tie, Ty. (TĪ-SUN)

TYUS Modern coinage of uncertain derivation. Short: Ty. (TĪ-US)

ULYSSES Latin form of the Greek Odysseus. The name is borne in mythology by the hero of the *Odyssey*. *See* ODYSSEUS (Mythology and Astrology Names). (YOO-LIS-SEEZ)

VALDEZ Transferred use of the Spanish surname originating from the German Baldo, which is derived from *bald* (bold). (VAHL-DEZ)

VELTRY Modern coinage of uncertain derivation. (VEL-TREE)

VERLIN Believed to be derived from the Latin Verginius (spring-like, flourishing), an old Roman family name that has its root in *ver* (spring). Var: Verle, Verlon. (VER-LIN)

VOSHON Modern coinage, perhaps a variant of Shon, an American form of the Irish Seán, a cognate of John (God is gracious). (VO-SHON)

WEBSTER Transferred use of the surname meaning "weaver." The name, which arose as an occupational name, is derived from the Old English *webbestre* (a female weaver). Var: Webbster. Short: Webb. (WEB-STER)

WENDICE Modern coinage of uncertain derivation. (WEN-DIS)

XAYVION Modern coinage possibly based on the Spanish Xavier (the new house). *See* JAVIER (Spanish Names). Var: Savion, Sayveon, Sayvion, Xavion, Xayveon, Zayvion. (ZAY-VEE-ON)

ZARION Modern coinage of uncertain derivation. (ZARE-REE-UN, ZAH-RI-UN)

ZEKE African name derived from the Bobangi *zēke* (to laugh, to laugh at). (ZEEK)

ZEPHYRUS Latin name derived from the Greek *zephyros* (the west wind). The name is borne in Greek mythology by the god of the west wind. (ZEF-ER-US)

ZEUS Greek name borne by the supreme god of the ancient Greek pantheon. The name is believed to be derived from the Indo-European root *deiwos* (God, deity). (ZOOSS)

African-American Female Names

AALIYAH Variant of the Hebrew Aliyah (to ascend). (AH-LEE-YAH)

AFRICA Borrowed from the name of the continent. Often bestowed upon African-American female children as a symbol of ethnic pride. Alternatively, Africa is used as an Anglicized form of the Irish Gaelic Aifric (pleasant). (AF-REE-KAH)

ANGELYNNE Combination name composed of the names Angel (messenger of God) and Lynne (lake). *See* ANGEL and LYNN (English Names). (AIN-jl-LIN)

ARIESA Modern coinage of uncertain derivation. (AH-REE-EH-SAH)

ATHENA Ancient name of uncertain etymology borne by the Greek mythological goddess of wisdom, skill, and warfare. Var: Athene. (ah-THEE-nah)

BERNITA Feminine form of Bernie, which is a pet form of Bernard (bold or strong as a bear). *See* BERNARD (English Male Names). (BER-NEE-TAH)

BEVERLEY Transferred use of the surname derived from the Old English elements *beofor* (beaver) and *lēac* (stream): hence, "dweller near the beaver stream." Var: Bever-Leigh, Beverlie, Beverly. Short: Bev. (BEV-ER-LEE)

BRANDY Derived from *brandy*, which denotes an alcoholic liquor distilled from wine or from fermented fruit juice. Var: Brandee, Brandey, Brandi, Brandie. (BRAN-DEE)

CACHAY Modern coinage probably based on the French *cachet* (genuine, authentic; superior, prestige, distinction). Var: Cashay, Kachay, Kashay. (KA-SHAY)

CANDACE Derived from the Latin *candidus* (white, pure, sincere). Var: Candice, Candyse, Kandace, Kandice. Pet: Candi, Candie, Candy, Kandi, Kandie, Kandy. (KAN-DUS)

CHALESE Modern coinage of uncertain derivation. (SHA-LEES)

CASSANDRA Derived from the Greek Kassandra, a name of uncertain etymology. Var: Kassandra. Short: Cass, Kass. Pet: Cassi, Cassie, Cassy, Kassi, Kassie, Kassy. (KAH-SAN-DRA)

CHANDA Modern coinage derived from the popular element *Chan-*. Var: Chandah. (CHAN-DAH, SHAN-DAH)

CHANDELLE Derived from the French *chandelle* (candle). Var: Chandell, Shandell, Shandelle. Short: Chan, Shan. (SHAHN-DEL)

CHANTAL French name derived from the Old Provençal *cantal* (stone, boulder). Var: Chantall, Chantel, Chantelle. Short: Chan. (SHAHN-TAHL)

CHANTERELLE French diminutive form of the Latin *cantharus* (drinking cup). The name is borrowed from that of a type of mushroom, prized for its shape and flavor. Var: Chantrelle. Short: Chan. (SHAN-TEH-REL, SHAN-TREL)

CHARLENE 20th-century coinage used as a feminine form of Charles (full-grown, a man, a freeman): hence, "a woman." Var: Charlayne, Cherlene, Cherline, Sharlayne, Sharleen, Sharlene. Pet: Charli, Charlie. (SHAR-LEEN)

CHARMAINE Derived from the Old French *charme* (a song, verse, chant). Var: Charmain, Charmayne. (SHAR-MANE)

CHARRON Modern variant of Sharon (a plain, a vast area). *See* SHARON. Var: Char Ron, Charrón. (SHAR-RON)

CHAZMIN Modern coinage probably influenced by the name Jasmin. (CHAZ-MIN)

CHEIRON Modern variant of Sharon (a plain, a vast area). *See* SHARON. (SHARE-UN)

CHERISE Modern coinage possibly based on the French *cerise* (cherry, cherry-flavored, deep red). Var: Cherice, Cherrise, Sherice, Sherise. (SHER-EES)

CHERYL 20th-century coinage perhaps formed by combining names such as Cherry and Beryl. Var: Cherelle, Cheril, Cherril, Cherrill, Charel, Sherill, Sherril, Sherryl, Sheryll. (SHARE-EL)

CINNAMON Borrowed from the name of a favored spice. The name is ultimately derived from the Hebrew *qinnāmon* (cinnamon). (SIN-AH-MUN)

COLANDA Modern coinage probably based on the name Yolanda. (KO-LON-DAH)

COZETTE Modern coinage perhaps based on *cozy* (comfortable, warm, snug). (KO-ZET)

DANEAN Modern coinage which possibly arose as the combining of elements from parents' or relatives' names. Var: DaNeen, D'Nean. (DAH-NEEN)

DANELL Modern coinage which is a possible variant of Danielle, a feminine form of Daniel (God is my judge). Var: Da'Nell, Danella. Pet: Dani, Danie. (DAH-NEL)

DARAH Modern coinage perhaps modeled after the name Sarah. (DAR-AH, DAH-RAH)

DARLONNA Modern name perhaps coined from elements of names such as Darlene and Donna. (DAR-LON-NAH)

DARSHELLE Modern coinage of uncertain derivation. (DAR-SHEL)

DAVENIA Modern coinage perhaps formed by combining names such as Dave and Eugenia (DAH-VEEN-EE-AH)

Delicia Derived from the Latin *deliciae* (delight). Var: Daleesha, Dalicia, Dalisia, Deleesha, Delesia, Delisia. (DEH-LEE-SHA)

Denell Modern coinage formed by the addition of the prefix *De-* to the name Nell, which is a short form of names containing *nell* as an element. Var: Denelle. (DEH-NEL)

Denise Feminine form of Dennis, which is an English cognate of the Greek Dionysios (a follower of the god Dionysos). Var: Daneece, Danice, Denice, Deniece, Deniese, Denyse, De Nyse. (DAH-NEES)

Désirée Borrowed from the French, Désirée is from the Latin Desiderāta, which is derived from *desiderata* (desired). Var: Desirae, Desiree, Dessirae, Dessiree, Deziree. (DEZ-IH-RAY)

Dessa Rae Modern combination name, perhaps influenced by Desiree (desired). (DES-SAH-RAY)

Dija A short form of Khadija (premature baby), Dija is also occasionally bestowed as an independent given name. *See* KHADIJA. (DEE-JAH)

Dondi Modern coinage of uncertain derivation. (DON-DEE)

Dyvette Modern coinage probably based on the French Yvette (little archer). *See* YVETTE (French Names). (DIH-VET)

Earlene Feminine form of Earl. *See* EARL (English Names). Var: Earline, Erlene, Erline, Irelene. (ER-LEEN)

Eartha Derived from *earth*, which denotes the planet on which we live. (ER-THA)

Ebony Derived from *ebony*, which denotes a hard, heavy, black wood. Var: Ebonii. (EH-BUN-EE)

Glennette Modern feminine form of Glenn, a Scottish name derived from the Gaelic *glenn* (mountain valley). (GLEN-NET)

Jackie A pet form of Jacqueline and its variants, Jackie is also bestowed as an independent given name, often as a feminine form of Jack. *See* JACK (American Male Names). Var: Jacki, Jacqua, Jacqué, Jacqui, Jacquie. (JAK-EE)

Jade Taken from the name of the hard, green or white jadeite or nephrite stone. The word came to the English via the French, from the Spanish *piedra de ijada* (stone of the side: from the belief that it could cure pains in the side). (JADE)

Jaleesa Modern coinage formed with the name Lisa, a short form of Elisabeth (God is my oath). Var: Ja Leesa, Ja Lisa. (JAH-LEE-SAH)

Jalinda Modern coinage formed with the name Linda. *See* LINDA (English Names). Var: Jalynda. (JAH-LIN-DAH)

Jamila Derived from the Arabic Jamīla, which is from *jamīl* (beautiful, graceful). Var: Jamilah. (JAH-MEE-LAH)

Jandellyn Modern coinage of uncertain derivation. (JAN-DEH-LIN)

Janet Diminutive form of Jane (God is gracious) which has been in use since the Middle Ages. Var: Ja'net, Janette, Jannette. Short: Jan. (JAN-ET)

Janice Modern variant of Jane (God is gracious). *See* JANE (American Names). Var: Janessa, Janiece, Janis, Jeanice, Jeneesa, Jenise. (JA-NIS, JAH-NEES)

Jasmine Taken from the name of the tropical plant having colorful, fragrant flowers used in perfumes and teas. The word is derived from the Persian *yāsamīn* (jasmine). Var: Jasmin. (JAZ-MIN)

Jaylene Modern coinage formed by combining the names Jay and the element *lene*. (JAY-LEEN)

Jenessa Modern coinage formed from the name Jen. Short: Jen, Nessa. Pet: Jenni, Jennie, Jenny. (JEH-NES-SAH)

Jonavá Modern coinage of uncertain derivation. (JON-AH-VAY)

Kacia Modern name of uncertain derivation. Var: Kaisha, Kasha, Kasia. (KAY-SHA)

Kaneesha Modern coinage of uncertain derivation. Var: Kaneisha. (KAH-NEE-SHA)

Kaniqua Modern coinage of uncertain derivation. Var: Kanikwa. (KAH-NEE-KWA)

Keisha Popular modern coinage of uncertain derivation. Var: Keesha, Keshah. (KEE-SHA)

Kendra Feminine form of the English Kendrick. *See* KENDRICK (English Male Names). Var: Kendrah. (KEN-DRA)

Kenya Borrowed from the name of the East African country. Often bestowed as a symbol of ethnic origin and pride. (KEN-YAH)

Kesia Of African origin meaning "favorite." Var: Keshia. (KEH-SHE-AH)

Khadija Derived from the Muslim name Khadīja, which is from the Arabic *khadīja* (premature baby). *See* KHADĪJA (Muslim/Arabic Names). Short: Dija. (KAH-DEE-JAH)

Kianna Modern coinage of uncertain derivation. (KEE-AH-NAH)

Kinshasha Borrowing of the name of the capital of Zaire. (KEEN-SHASH-AH)

Kisa Modern coinage of uncertain derivation. Var: Keesa, Kysa. (KEE-SAH)

Kneshia Modern coinage of uncertain derivation. It is probably modeled after the popular modern name Keisha. (NEE-SHAH, KAH-NEE-SHA)

K'Sea Modern fanciful variant of the name Casey. *See* CASEY (English Names). Var: Ksea. (KAY-SEE)

Kwaniesha Modern coinage of uncertain derivation. It appears to have been influenced by the name Keisha. (KWAH-NEE-SHAH)

L'Abana Modern coinage possibly based on the biblical name Abana (stony). Var: Labahna, Labana. (LAH-BAH-NAH)

La Chelle Modern coinage formed by the addition of the prefix *La-* to Chelle, a short form of Michelle (who is like God?). *See* MICHÈLE (French Names). (LAH-SHEL)

La Dawn Modern coinage combining the prefix *La-* with the name Dawn. *See* DAWN (American Names). Var: Ladawn, Ladawna, LaDawnah. (LAH-DAWN)

La Dean Modern feminine form of the name Dean. *See* DEAN (English Male Names). (LAH-DEEN)

La Delle Modern coinage used as a feminine form of Dell (dweller in the dell). *See* DELL (English Male Names). Var: La Dell, La Delle, Ladelle. (LAH-DEL)

La Donna Modern coinage combining the prefix *La-* with the name Donna. *See* DONNA (American Names). (LAH-DON-NAH)

Lahonda Modern coinage of uncertain derivation. (LAH-HON-DAH)

La Keisha Modern coinage formed by the addition of the prefix *La-* to the name Keisha. *See* KEISHA. Var: Lakeesha, La Keesha, Lakeisha, Lakisha, La Kisha, Lekeesha, Le Keesha, Lekisha, Le Kisha. (LAH-KEE-SHA)

La Neesha Modern coinage of uncertain derivation. Var: Laneesha, Laneeshah, Laneisha, La Neisha, Laneishah, La Neishah. (LAH-NEE-SHA)

Larshell Modern coinage of uncertain derivation. It might have originated as a combination of name elements from parents or other family members. (LAR-SHEL)

La Shauna Modern coinage formed by the addition of the prefix *La-* to the name Shauna. *See* SHAUNA (American Names). Var: La Shawn, La Shawna, La Shon, La Shonna, La Shonnah. (LAH-SHON-NAH, LAH-SHAUN-NAH)

La Shaunda Modern coinage combining the prefix *La-* with the name Shaunda. *See* SHAUNDA. Var: La Shawnda, La Shonda, La Shondah. (LAH-SHON-DAH, LAH-SHAUN-DAH)

La Tasha Modern coinage combining the prefix *La-* with the name Tasha, a Russian pet form of the name Natalie. *See* NATALIYA (Russian Names). Var: Latasha. Short: Tasha. (LAH-TAH-SHA)

Lavita Modern coinage derived from the Latin *vita* (life). Var: Laveeda. (LAH-VEE-TAH)

La Von Modern coinage probably based on the name Yvonne. (LAH-VON)

Leisha Modern coinage of uncertain derivation. It is probably modeled after the name Keisha. Var: Leesha, Leeshah, Leeshia, Leishah. (LEE-SHA)

Lenice Modern coinage probably modeled after the name Denice. Var: La Neece, Laniece, La Neese, Le Neese. (LEH-NEES)

Leticia Derived from the Latin *laetitia* (gladness, happiness). Var: Lateesha, Laticia, La Ticia, La Teesha, Latisha, La Tisha, Leteesha, Le Teesha. Short: Licia, Tisha. (LEH-TEE-SHA)

Libya Taken from the name of the North African country. The name can be bestowed as a symbol of national or ethnic pride. (LIB-EE-AH)

Lynnelle Modern coinage formed by the addition of the feminine suffix *-elle* to Lynn. *See* LYNN (English Names). Var: Lynnel. (LIN-NEL)

Mamie Originally a pet form of Margaret or Mary, Mamie is also bestowed as an independent given name. *See* MARGARET *and* MARY (English Names). Var: Mami. (MAY-MEE)

Me'Shell Modern elaboration of the name Michelle (who is like God?). *See* MICHÈLE (French Names). (ME-SHEL)

Mishaila Modern coinage based on the name Michelle (who is like God?). *See* MICHÈLE (French Names). (MIH-SHAY-LAH, MEE-SHAY-LAH)

Miskaela Modern coinage based on the name Michaela (who is like God?). *See* MICHAELA (American Names). Var: Meeskaela. (MIS-KAY-LAH, MEE-SKAY-LAH)

MONISHA Modern coinage of uncertain derivation, perhaps influenced by the name Monica. (MO-NEE-SHA)

NICHELE Modern coinage probably based on the name Michelle. Var: Na Chelle, Nichelle. (NIH-SHEL)

NIKEESHA Modern coinage of uncertain derivation. Var: Niceesha, Nickeesha, Nickisha, Nicquisha, Niquisha, Nykesha. (NIH-KEE-SHA)

ORLAIN Modern coinage of uncertain derivation. It might be based on or influenced by the name Arlene. (OR-LANE)

RACHEL Derived from the Hebrew *rāchēl* (ewe). *See* RACHEL (Biblical Names). Var: Rachael, Racheal. (RAY-CHEL)

RACHELL Elaborated form of Rachel (ewe). *See* RACHEL (Biblical Names). Var: Rachelle, Rochell, Rochelle. (RAH-SHEL, RO-SHEL)

RA' KEISHA Modern coinage using the name Keisha. (RAH-KEE-SHA)

RANDELLE Feminine form of Randall (wolf shield). *See* RANDALL (English Male Names). (RAN-DEL)

RANIELLE Modern coinage apparently modeled after the name Danielle. (RAN-YEL)

RHONDA Believed to be derived from the Welsh elements *rhon* (lance) and *da* (good). Var: Randa, Ronda, Rondah. (RON-DAH)

RICHELLE Feminine form of Richard (brave ruler), formed by the addition of the feminine suffix *-elle* to Rich. *See* RICHARD (English Male Names). (RIH-SHEL)

ROLANDA Feminine form of Roland (famous land). *See* ROLAND (English Male Names). Var: Ro Landa, Rolandah. (RO-LAN-DAH, RO-LAHN-DAH)

RONNA Feminine form of Ron, which is a short form of Ronald (ruler of judgment). *See* RONALD (English Male Names). Var: Roni, Ronnie. (RAH-NAH)

RONNELL Feminine form of Ron, which is a short form of Ronald (ruler of judgment). *See* RONALD (English Male Names). Var: Ronell, Ronelle, Ronnel. (RON-NEL)

SABRINEEKA Modern coinage of uncertain derivation. Var: Sebreneeka. (SAH-BRIH-NEE-KAH)

SARONNA Modern coinage perhaps based on the name Sharon (a plain, a flat area) or as an elaboration of Ronna, a feminine form of Ron, which is a shortened form of Ronald (ruler of judgment). (SAH-RO-NAH, SAH-RON-NAH)

SATORIA Modern coinage perhaps based on the name Victoria. (SAH-TOR-EE-AH)

SAVANNAH Derived from the Spanish *sabana* (a treeless plain). Var: Savanna. (SAH-VAN-NAH)

SHAKONDA Modern coinage of uncertain derivation. (SHA-KON-DAH)

SHALAINE Modern coinage. Var: Shalaina, Shalayna, Shalayne. (SHA-LAIN)

SHALEELA Modern coinage of uncertain derivation. Var: Shaleelah, Shalila, Shalilah. (SHA-LEE-LAH)

SHALONDA Modern coinage of uncertain derivation. (SHA-LON-DAH)

SHAMIKA Modern coinage of uncertain derivation. Var: Shameeka, Shameekah, Shamikah. (SHA-MEE-KAH)

SHAN Anglicized form of Siân, the Welsh cognate of Jane (God is gracious). *See* JANE (English Names). Pet: Shanee. (SHAN)

SHANDRA Modern coinage based on the name Sandra or Shan, or perhaps as a combination of both. *See* SANDRA (English Names) *and* SHAN. (SHAN-DRAH)

SHANIQUE Modern coinage of uncertain derivation. Var: Shaneeka, Shaneeke, Shanika, Shanikah, Shaniqua. (SHA-NEEK, SHA-NEE-KWA)

SHANIYA Modern coinage of uncertain derivation. (SHA-NEE-YAH)

SHANTAINA Modern coinage based on the popular element *shan*. Var: Shantainah, Shantayna, Shantaynah. (SHAN-TAY-NAH)

SHARAMA Modern coinage of uncertain derivation. Var: Sharamah, Shirama. (SHA-RAH-MAH)

SHARLON Modern coinage of uncertain derivation. It might be an elaboration of Sharon or a combination of names such as Sharon and Marlon. (SHAR-LON)

SHARON Hebrew name meaning "a plain, a flat area." In biblical times, Sharon was a fertile, coastal plain in Palestine where roses and oak trees grew in abundance. Var: Sharana, Sharen, Sharona, Sharonah, Sharonna, Sherran. (SHARE-UN)

SHAUNDA Modern coinage based on the name Shauna (God is gracious). Var: Shonda, Shondah, Shawnda, Shawndah. (SHON-DAH, SHAUN-DAH)

SHAVONDA Modern coinage of uncertain derivation. (SHA-VON-DAH)

Shawannah Modern coinage perhaps influenced by the names Shawna or Shoshannah. (SHA-WAH-NAH)

Shayleen Feminine form of Shay (seizing by the heel, supplanting). *See* SHAY (American Male Names). (SHAY-LEEN)

Shirell Modern coinage based on the name Cheryl. *See* CHERYL. (SHIR-REL)

Shuwani Modern coinage of uncertain derivation. (SHOO-WAH-NEE)

Simone A borrowing from the French, Simone is a feminine form of Simon (heard). *See* SIMON (English Males Names). Var: Symone. (SIH-MONE)

TaLisa Modern coinage most likely based on the name Lisa. Var: Talisa, Telisa. (TAH-LEE-SAH)

Tamika Modern coinage of uncertain derivation. Var: Tameeka. (TAH-MEE-KAH)

Tamrika Modern coinage of uncertain derivation. Var: Tamreeka. (TAM-REE-KAH)

T'anay Modern coinage of uncertain derivation. Var: Taneé. (TAH-NAY)

Tanisha Modern coinage of uncertain derivation. Var: Teneesha. (TAH-NEE-SHA)

Tarja Modern coinage of uncertain derivation. (TAR-EE-AH, TAR-JAH)

Tashanee Modern coinage of uncertain derivation. (TAH-SHAN-EE)

Tashina Modern coinage of uncertain derivation. Var: Tasheena, Tasheenah, Tashinah. (TAH-SHEE-NAH)

Tawny Derived from *tawny,* which denotes a soft, brownish-yellow or tan color. The word is derived from the Old French *tanné* (tanned). Var: Tawnee, Tawney. (TAW-NEE)

Terra Derived from *terra* (the earth). Var: Tera, Terah, Terrah. (TARE-AH)

Tiara Derived from *tiara* (a crown, coronet, headdress). (TEE-AR-AH)

Tisha Short form of various names containing the element *tisha, ticia.* It is also bestowed as an independent given name. Var: Ticia. Short: Tish. (TISH-AH)

Tishra Modern coinage based on the element *tish.* Var: Tishrah. (TISH-RAH)

Tyana Modern coinage of uncertain derivation, perhaps influenced by the name Deanna. (TEE-AH-NAH, TEE-AH-NAH)

Velinda Modern coinage influenced by the name Melinda. Var: Valinda. (VEH-LIN-DAH)

Vianna Modern coinage of uncertain derivation. (VEE-AN-NAH)

Whitney Transferred use of the surname derived from *Hwítan-íg* (Hwita's island). Hwita is an Anglo-Saxon personal name derived from *hwít* (white). Var: Whitnee. (WHIT-NEE)

Wyetta Feminine form of Wyatt (little Guy). *See* WYATT (American Male Names). (WĪ-ET-TAH)

Wynelle Elaboration of the name Wynn, a modern English name derived from the Welsh *gwyn* (white, fair, blessed). (WIN-NEL)

Wynette Variant form of Wynn, formed by the addition of the diminutive suffix *-ette. See* WYNNE. (WIN-NET)

Yolande Of uncertain etymology, some believe it to be a derivative of Violante (violet), a medieval French name derived from the Latin Viola (violet). Var: Ylonda, Yolanda, Yolandah, Yolonda. (YO-LAHN-DAH)

Yonkela Modern coinage of uncertain derivation. (YON-KEL-LAH)

Zeborah Modern coinage apparently influenced by the name Deborah. (ZEB-AH-RAH)

Zelfa Modern coinage of uncertain derivation. (ZEL-FAH)

Zhané Modern coinage of uncertain derivation. (ZHA-NAY)

Chapter Three

American Names

The United States is a mosaic of ethnic origins, and nowhere is this more keenly observed than in types of names used in this country. Currently, about forty-four separate ancestry groups are represented in the United States, and all have given their share of names to society.

Many of these names have been Americanized to fit the sounds of the English language, and in most cases diacritical marks, so important to other languages but unknown to our own, have been dropped. Because of the prejudice aimed at new arrivals, the Scottish and Irish often dropped the *Mac* and O prefixes from their names. Since many immigrants were illiterate and had no knowledge of the true spellings of their names, immigration officials usually spelled them as best as they could or even assigned different ones.

For boys, common Bible names have been popular for many years. Many that were considered old-fashioned just a short time ago, such as Jedidiah and Noah, are making a reappearance. Some of these are shortened into single-syllable "strong-sounding" names such as Jed from Jedidiah and Jake from Jacob.

It is interesting to note that a large number of male names, such as Bradford, Kirk, and Taylor, actually originated as English surnames. Another current naming trend points toward the use of topographical features and place-names, such as Ridge, Lake, Dakota, and Dallas. These types of names, as well as increased usage of foreign names, classical Latin names, and names from mythology, have led to a decrease in the bestowal of common Teutonic names, such as Walter and Albert.

For girls, the types of names being used today have also changed. One of the most significant trends is the use of surnames for female given names. Originally a southern tradition, the practice has spread throughout the country. Most often, it is the first-born daughter who is given the mother's maiden name as a first or middle name. However, names unrelated to those of the parents are also being used, and it is no longer considered unusual to find girls named Blair, Carter, or Madison.

With the exception of Rose, flower and related names such as Pansy and Violet have been exchanged for such names as Holly, Ivy, and Willow. Jewel names like Opal, Pearl, and Ruby are usurped by Amber, Jade, and Chalcedony.

Another fast-growing trend is the use of modern coinages. Quite often these names are formed by using elements from the names of parents or relatives, or they are based on popular name elements such as *Sha-* or *-ana*.

American Male Names

ADAM Derived from the Hebrew *adama* (red earth). *See* ADAM (Biblical Names). Var: Addam. (AD-UM)

AIDAN Anglicized form of the Irish Aodhan (little fiery one). The name was popularized by actor Aidan Quinn (b. 1959). (Ā D-UN)

ALAN Celtic name of uncertain derivation. *See* ALAN (English Names). Var: Alen, Allan, Allen, Allon, Allun, Alon, Alun. Short: Al. (AL-UN)

ALDEN Transferred use of the surname derived from the Old English Aldwine, a compounding of the elements *ald* (old) and *wine* (friend). (AHL-DEN)

ALEC Scottish form of Alex, a short form of Alexander (defender or helper of mankind). *See* ALEXANDER. (ALEK)

ALEX A short form of Alexander (defender or helper of mankind), Alex is also bestowed as an independent given name. *See* ALEXANDER. (AL-EKS)

ALEXANDER Derived from the Greek Alexandros (defender or helper of mankind), a compounding of the elements *alexein* (to defend, to help) and *andros* (man). Short: Al, Alec, Alex. Pet: Sandy. (AL-EK-ZAN-DER)

ANDREW English form of the Greek Andreas, a name derived from *andreios* (manly). *See* ANDREW (Biblical Names). Short: Drew. Pet: Andy. (AN-DREW)

ANTHONY Derived from the Latin Antonius, an old Roman family name of unknown etymology. "Priceless" and "of inestimable worth" are popular folk definitions of the name. Var: Anton, Antonio. Short: Toni, Tonio, Tony. (AN-THUH-NEE)

ARCHER Transferred use of the surname derived from *archer* (a bowman). (AR-CHER)

ARLAN Variant form of Erland (foreigner, stranger). *See* ERLEND. Var: Arland, Arlen. (AR-LAN)

ARNEL Transferred use of the surname derived from Arnold (eagle strength). *See* ARNOLD (English Names). Var: Arnell. (AR-NEL)

ASA Derived from the Hebrew *āsā* (a healer, a physician). (ACE-AH)

ASHTON Transferred use of the surname meaning "belonging to Ashton." The name originated from the English place-name, which is composed of the elements *æsc* (ash tree) and *tūn* (town, settlement, village, enclosure). (ASH-TUN)

AUSTIN Contracted form of Augustine (great, venerable). (AU-STIN)

AVERILL Transferred use of the English surname, which is of debated definition. Some believe it to mean "April." Others think the name is of Germanic origin and has the definition "wild boar battle." Var: Averille, Averrill, Averrille. (AVE-EH-RL)

BANNER Derived from *banner* (a flag, a standard, a banner). Alternatively, Banner is a shortened form of the Scottish surname Bannerman (a bearer of the banners). (BAN-NER)

BANNOCK Transferred use of the surname, which is believed to be derived from the Russian Banich (one who has been exiled or banished). Var: Banick. (BAN-NUK)

BARRY Anglicized form of the Irish Bearach (spearlike). (BARE-REE)

BAY Modern name derived from *bay* (an indentation in the shoreline of a lake or sea). (BAY)

BEAR Derived from *bear* (a bear, an animal of the Ursidae family). (BARE)

BEAU A borrowing from the French, Beau is derived from *beau* (pretty, a dandy, handsome). Var: Bo. (BO)

BECK Transferred use of the Scandinavian surname meaning "dweller near the brook." (BEK)

BECKETT Transferred use of the English surname meaning "dweller near the brook." Var: Beckitt. (BEK-ET)

BECKON Modern coinage of uncertain derivation. (BEK-UN)

BENJAMIN Derived from the Hebrew *binyāmīn* (son of the right hand). *See* BENJAMIN (Biblical Names). The name was borne by American statesman and inventor Benjamin Franklin (1706–90). Short: Ben. Pet: Benny. (BEN-JAH-MIN)

BENNETT Transferred use of the surname originating as a variant form of Benedict, a name derived from the Latin *benedictus* (blessed). Var: Bennet. Short: Ben. Pet: Benny. (BEN-NET)

BENTLEY Transferred use of the surname originating from the English place-name Bentley (clearing overgrown with bent grass). Var: Bently. Short: Ben. Pet: Benny. (BENT-LEE)

BENTON Transferred use of the surname originating from a Northumberland place-name meaning "a town or enclosure where bent grass grows." Short: Ben. Pet: Benny. (BENT-UN, BEN-TUN)

BERT A short form of any of the names containing *Bert* (bright) as an element, Bert is also bestowed as an independent given name. Var: Burt. (BERT)

BILL A short form of William (resolute protector), Bill is also bestowed as an independent given name. *See* WILLIAM. Pet: Billy. (BILL)

BIRCHALL Transferred use of the English surname composed from the Old English elements *birce* (birch) and *heall* (hall): hence, "dweller near the hall of birch trees." Var: Birchell, Burchall, Burchell. (BER-CHALL)

BISHOP Transferred use of the surname derived from *bishop* (a high-ranking member of the clergy). (BISH-UP)

BLAINE Transferred use of the Scottish surname meaning "the son of the disciple of Blaan [yellow] or Blane [the lean]." Var: Blayne. (BLANE)

BLAIR Transferred use of the Scottish surname meaning "dweller on the plain." Var: Blaire. (BLARE)

BLAISE Borrowed from the French, Blaise is of uncertain etymology. Some believe it is derived from the Latin Blaesus, which is from *blaesus* (deformed, stuttering). Var: Blaize, Blayze, Blaze.

BLAKE Transferred use of the surname, which is of two separate derivations. It originates both from the Old English *blæc* (black, dark-complexioned) and from the Old English *blāc* (bright, shining, pale, wan). The use of Blake as a given name stems from its prior use as a nickname for someone with either a very dark or a very light complexion. Var: Blaike. (BLAKE)

BOB A short form of Robert (bright with fame), Bob is also occasionally bestowed as an independent given name. Pet: Bobbie, Bobby. (BOB)

BOYD Transferred use of the surname derived from the Irish Gaelic *buidhe* (yellow) and from the surname Mac Giolla Buidhe (son of the one with yellow hair). Var: Boyde. (BOID)

BRAD A short form of any of the names containing *brad* as an element, Brad is also bestowed as an independent given name. (BRAD)

BRADEN Transferred use of the English surname meaning "from Bradden, a dweller near the broad valley." The name originates from several place-names meaning "broad valley." Var: Bradon, Braydan, Brayden, Braydon. (BRAY-DN)

BRADFORD Transferred use of the surname arising from English place-names composed of the Old English elements *brad* (broad) and *ford* (a ford, a place to cross a river). Short: Brad. (BRAD-FORD)

BRADLEY Transferred use of the surname originating from English place-names derived from the Old English elements *brad* (broad) and *lēah* (wood, clearing, meadow, enclosure): hence, "dweller at the broad meadow." Short: Brad. (BRAD-LEE)

BRADY Transferred use of the surname originating from separate derivations. It is derived from the Old English elements *brad* (broad) and *ēage* (eye): hence, "one with broad eyes." It is also from the Old English elements *brad* (broad) and *ēg* (island) or *gehæg* (enclosure): hence, "dweller on the broad island, dweller near the broad enclosure." Var: Bradey. (BRAY-DEE)

BRANDON Variant form of Branton, a surname that originated from English place-names composed of the Old English elements *brom* (broom, brushwood) and *dun* (hill): hence, "dweller near the brushwood hill." Alternatively, Brandon is a variant form of Brendan, an Anglicized form of the Irish Breandán (prince). *See* BREANDÁN (Irish Names). Var: Brendon. (BRAN-DUN)

BRANNON Transferred use of the surname, which is from the Irish Mac Brannan, the Anglicized form of the Gaelic Mac Branáin (son of Bran). Bran is a popular Gaelic name meaning "raven." (BRAN-NUN)

BRANT Transferred use of the surname, which is from the Old English *brand* (firebrand, sword) and the Old Norse *brandr* (firebrand, sword). Var: Brandt. (BRANT)

BRAZIER Transferred use of the surname originating as an occupational name derived from the Old English *brasier* (a brass founder, a worker of brass), which is from *brasian* (to make of brass). Var: Braisier, Braizier, Brasier. (BRAY-ZHUR)

BRENNAN Transferred use of the surname, which is from the Irish O Brennan, the Anglicized form of the Gaelic Ó Braonáin (descendant of Braoin). Braoin is a Gaelic name meaning "sorrow, sadness." Brennan is also an English surname and is evolved from the Old English Burnand (burned hand). The name makes reference to the medieval practice of burning the hands of those caught breaking the law. Var: Brennand, Brennen. (BREN-NAN)

BRENNER Transferred use of the English surname derived from the Old French *brenier* (keeper of the hounds) or from the Old Norse *brenna* (to burn, burner of charcoal, bricks, or lime). (BREN-NER)

Brent Transferred use of the English surname, which originates from two separate sources. Brent (the burnt) is an evolution of the Old English *beornan* (to burn) and was originally used as a nickname for a criminal who had been branded for his crimes. It is also derived from *brend* (burnt land) and is used as an English place-name; in this instance, Brent has the definition "dweller by the burnt land." (BRENT)

Brett Transferred use of the English surname derived from the Old French *Bret* (a Breton), an ethnic name for a native of Brittany. Var: Bret, Brit, Britt. (BREHT)

Brian A borrowing from the Irish, Brian is of uncertain etymology. It is generally thought to be of Celtic origin, but its meaning is disputed. Some believe it to be derived from the root *bri* (force, strength), *brîgh* (valor, strength), or *bruaich* (a hill, steep, high). It is also given the definition "kingly." Var: Briann, Briant, Brien, Brient, Brion, Bryan, Bryann, Bryon, Bryonn. Short: Bri. (BRĪ-UN)

Brice An English name originating as a surname taken to England by the French in the Middle Ages. It is believed to be of Celtic origin and might be derived from the element *bri* (force, strength) or *brîgh* (valor, strength). Var: Bryce. Short: Bri. (BRICE)

Brock Transferred use of the surname, which is of several derivations. It is from the Old English *brocc* (badger), from the Old French *broque*, *brocke* (a young deer), and from the Old English *brōc* (brook, stream). (BRAHK)

Brody Transferred use of the surname, which is of several derivations. It is a Scottish name meaning "from Brodie," which is a place-name believed to be derived from the Gaelic *broth* (a ditch). It is also an English surname derived from the Old English *brothie* (black) and an Anglicized Irish surname meaning "son of Bruaideadh." Bruaideadh is a Gaelic name meaning "fragment." Var: Brodie. (BRO-DEE)

Brook Derived from *brook* (a stream, a small creek). Var: Brooke. (BROOK)

Bryson Transferred use of the surname that originated as an Anglicization of the Gaelic Ó Muirgheasáin (descendant of Muirghearán). The name is an old Irish name beginning with the element *muir* (sea). Var: Briceson, Brycen, Brysen. (BRĪ-SEN)

Buchanan Transferred use of the Scottish surname meaning "belonging to Buchanan [Scotland]." It is believed to ultimately be a Pictish name with no connection to the Welsh *bychan* (small) or the Gaelic *bothan* (a hut), as many suppose. Short: Buck. (BYOO-KAN-NUN)

Buck Derived from *buck* (a male deer, a stag). Alternatively, Buck is used as a short form of Buchanan. (BUHK)

Burke Transferred use of the surname meaning "from Burgh [in Suffolk]" or "from Bourg [in France]." The names are derived from the Old English and Old French *burg* (a stronghold). Var: Berke, Burk. (BERK)

Burton Transferred use of the English surname that originated from a place-name derived from the Old English elements *burg* (a stronghold, fortress) and *tūn* (town, settlement, village, enclosure). Short: Burt. (BER-TUN)

Cade Transferred use of the English surname, which is of several derivations. *See* CADE (English Names). (KADE)

Calder Transferred use of the English surname derived from several river names, which are believed to be from the Gaelic elements *coille* (a wood) and *dur* (a stream) or from the Welsh *call* (a breaking or starting out) and *dwr* (water). (KAHL-DER)

Caldwell Transferred use of the English surname meaning "dweller at Caldwell." Caldwell is a Yorkshire place-name derived from the Old English elements *ceald* (cold) and *wiella* (well, spring). (KAHLD-WELL)

Cale Transferred use of the surname derived from the Gaelic *caol* (thin, slender). Var: Cayl, Kail, Kayl, Kayle. (KAIL)

Callister Derived from the Irish surname Mac Callister, a variant of Mac Alister (son of Alister), an Irish form of the Gaelic Mac Alastair. Alastair is the Gaelic form of Alexander (defender or helper of mankind). (KAL-LIH-STER)

Calum A borrowing from the Scottish, Calum is a Gaelic form of the Latin Columba (a dove). Var: Callum. (KAL-UM)

Calvin From the French surname Cauvin, a derivative of the Latin *calvinus* (little bald one), which has its root in *calvus* (bald). The name was originally bestowed in honor of French Protestant reformer John Calvin (1509–64). Var: Kalvin. (KAL-VIN)

Camas From *camas* (a delicate wild plant with edible bulbs and bluish flowers). It is derived from the Chinook Indian *chamas* (sweet). Var: Camus. Short: Cam. (KAM-MUS)

Cameron Transferred use of the Scottish surname that originated from the Gaelic nickname *cam sròn* (crooked nose). Var: Kameron. Short: Cam, Kam. (KAM-ER-UN)

CARL Derived from the Old English *ceorl* (freeman, peasant, man). In the Middle Ages, Carl was used as a nickname for a bondman, villain, or a person of low birth and rude manners. Alternatively, Carl is used as a short form of Carlton. *See* CARLTON. (KARL)

CARLTON Transferred use of the English surname that originated from place-names composed of the Old English elements *carl* (freeman, peasant, man) and *tūn* (town, settlement, village): hence, "settlement of freemen." Var: Carleton. Short: Carl. (KARL-TUN)

CARSON Transferred use of the surname meaning "Carr's son." The name Carr is of several derivations. It is from the Middle English and Scottish *car, carre* (marsh, mossy place), from the Welsh *caer* (a fort), and from the Gaelic *carr* (rock). (KAR-SUN)

CARTER Transferred use of the surname that originated in the Middle Ages as an occupational name for someone who used a cart to transport goods. (KAR-TER)

CASE Transferred use of the English surname of French origin, which has the definition "from Case, belonging to Case." It is derived from the Latin *casa* (a dwelling place, a dwelling). (KASE)

CASEY Transferred use of the Irish surname, which is from the Gaelic O'Cathasaigh (descendant of Cathasach), a derivative of *cathasach* (watchful, vigilant). Var: Kasey, K.C., Kayce. (KAY-SEE)

CHAD Believed to be a modern variant of the obsolete Old English Ceadda, a name of uncertain meaning. (CHAD)

CHADWICK Transferred use of the English surname meaning "Chad's place." It is derived from the name Chad and the Old English *wíc* (place). Short: Chad. (CHAD-WIK)

CHANNING Transferred use of the English surname, which is a variant of Canning. Canning (Cana's son) is composed of the obsolete and probably Teutonic name Cana and the Old English filial suffix *-ing*. (CHAN-NEEN)

CHASE Transferred use of the English surname meaning "dweller at the hunting ground," which is derived from the Old French *chacier, chasser* (to hunt, to chase). (CHASE)

CHRISTIAN Derived from the Late Latin *christiānus*, which is from the Greek *christianos* (a Christian, a follower of Christ). Var: Christion, Khristian, Kristian. Short: Chris, Khris, Kris. (KRIS-CHEN)

CHRISTOPHER Derived from the Ecclesiastic Late Latin Christophorus, which is from the Ecclesiastic Greek Christophoros (bearing Christ). The name is composed of the elements *Christos* (Christ) and *pherein* (to bear). Christopher Robin is the name of the little boy in A. A. Milne's children's classic *Winnie the Pooh*. Var: Kristoff, Kristopher. Short: Chris, Kris. Pet: Kit. (KRIS-TEH-FER)

CLANCY Derived from the Irish surname Clancy and Mac Clancy, which is from the Gaelic Mac Fhlannchaidh (son of Flannchadh). Flannchadh is believed by some to mean "ruddy warrior." Var: Clancey. (KLAN-SEE)

CLARK Transferred use of the surname derived from the Old English *clerec, clerc* (clerk). It originated as an occupational name for a clergyman cleric or a man in a religious order. Var: Clarke. (KLARK)

CLEVELAND Transferred use of the English surname meaning "from the cliff land," which is derived from the Old English elements *cleve* (cliff) and *land* (land). (KLEEV-LAND)

CLINT A short form of Clinton (settlement by the cliff), Clint is also bestowed as an independent given name. *See* CLINTON. (KLINT)

CLINTON Transferred use of the English surname believed to be derived from an English place-name formed by the Middle English elements *clint* (cliff, slope, bank of a river) and *tūn* (town, settlement, village): hence, "settlement by the cliff." Short: Clint. (KLIN-TUN)

CODY Derived from the Irish Gaelic surname Mac Óda (son of Odo), a name thought to date to the 13th century. Odo is an obsolete name meaning "wealthy." (KO-DEE)

COLBY Transferred use of the English surname, which is of Scandinavian origin and has the definition "from Colby, from Kol's settlement." It is derived from the Old Norse elements *kol* (coal-black) and *byr* (settlement). Alternatively, Colby is used as a short form of Colburn. *See* COLBURN. Var: Coleby. (KOL-BEE)

COLE Transferred use of the surname derived from the Old English *col* (coal). It originated as a nickname for someone who was coal-black, swarthy, or darkly complexioned. Cole is also used as a short form of any of the names beginning with the element *Col-*. (KOLE)

COLEMAN Transferred use of the English surname derived from the Old English elements *col* (coal) and *mann* (man), which originated as an occupational name for a charcoal burner or someone who dealt with coal. Var: Koleman. Short: Cole, Kole. (COAL-MUN)

COLIN A borrowing from the English, Colin originated as a medieval variant of the obsolete Colle, a short form of Nicholas (victory of the people). Alternatively, Colin is the Anglicized form of the Gaelic Cailean (dove). Var: Collan, Collin, Collun, Coln, Colun. (KAH-LIN, KO-LIN)

COLT Derived from *colt* (a young male horse). It is also used as a short form of Colter (keeper of the colt herd). *See* COLTER. (KOLT)

COLTER Transferred use of the English surname derived from the elements *colt* (a young male horse) and *herder* (one who cares for a herd): hence, "keeper of the colt herd." Short: Colt. (KOL-TER)

CONNOR Anglicized form of the Irish Gaelic Conchobhar, a compound name composed of the elements *conn* (wisdom, counsel, strength) or *con* (hound, dog) and *cobhair* (aid). "High will, desire" and "hound lover" are other definitions attributed to the name. Var: Conner. (KON-NER)

COOPER Transferred use of the English surname that originated as an occupational name for a cooper, a cask or barrel maker or seller. It is derived from the Middle English *couper* (a cask). Short: Coop. (KOO-PER)

CORBIN Transferred use of the English surname derived from the Old French *corbin* (a raven). Var: Corban, Corbyn. Pet: Corby. (KOR-BIN)

CORD A short form of Cordelle (rope), Cord is also bestowed as an independent given name. (KORD)

CORDELLE Derived from the French *cordelle* (rope). Var: Cordel, Cordell. Short: Cord. (KOR-DEL)

COREY A borrowing from the Irish, Corey is a name of more than one derivation. It is the transferred use of the surname derived from the Gaelic *coire* (a cauldron, a seething pool, a hollow): hence, "dweller in or near a hollow." Alternatively, it is an Anglicized form of the various surnames derived from *corra* (a spear). Var: Cori, Corie, Correy, Corry, Cory, Korey, Kory. (KOR-EE)

CORRIDON Transferred use of the Irish surname believed to be derived from the Gaelic *corra* (a spear). The name originated in the southern part of county Clare. Var: Corydon. (KOR-EE-DON)

CRAIG Transferred use of the Scottish surname derived from the Gaelic *creag* (rugged rocks, crag): hence, "dweller by the crag." Var: Craigg, Kraig, Kraigg. (KRAIG)

CRAMER Transferred use of the English surname that arose as an occupational name meaning "shopkeeper, peddler, stallkeeper." It is of Teutonic origin and is derived from the Dutch *kramer*, the German *krämer*, the Scottish *crame*, all of which mean "shopkeeper, goods." Var: Kramer. (KRAY-MER)

CULLEN A borrowing from the Irish, Cullen is the Anglicized form of the Irish surname Mac Cuilinn (son of Cuileann). Cuileann is an Irish name meaning "holly." Var: Cullan, Cullin. (KUL-LUN)

DACK Transferred use of the English surname originating from the Anglo-Saxon personal name Dæcca, which is believed to be from the Old Norse *dagr* (day) or the Old English *dæg* (day). (DAK)

DAKOTA Derived from the Siouan word *dakóta* (allies, to be thought of as friends). The name is borrowed from the name given to the tribes of northern Plains Indians, also known as Sioux and Lakota. (DAH-KO-TAH)

DALLAS Borrowed from the name of a Texas city named for U.S. Vice President G. M. Dallas (1792–1864). The surname, of Scottish origin meaning "belonging to Dallas, from Dallas," is derived from the Gaelic elements *dail* (a field) and *eas* (a waterfall): hence, "the waterfall field." (DAL-LUS)

DAMIAN Derived from the Greek Damianos, which is thought to be from *damān* (to tame). Var: Damon, Daymian, Daymon. (DAY-MEE-UN)

DANIEL Derived from the Hebrew *dānī'ēl* (God is my judge). The name is borne in the Bible by a Hebrew prophet whose faith kept him from harm in a den of hungry lions. Short: Dan. Pet: Danny. (DAN-YEL)

DARCY Transferred use of the English surname that originated as the baronial name D'Arcy (from Arcy, a place in La Manche, Normandy). Var: Darcey. (DAR-SEE)

DARRELL Transferred use of the English surname that originated as the French de Arel (from Airelle, a town in Calvados). Var: Darrall, Darrel, Darryl, Darylle, Darryll, Daryl. (DARE-UL)

DARREN Modern name of uncertain origin and meaning. It might have been coined as a variation of Darrell or as a combination of a child's parents' names, such as Darrell and Karen. Var: Darin, Darran, Darron, Darryn. (DARE-UN)

DAVID From the Hebrew *dāwīd* (beloved). The name is borne in the Bible by the second Israelite king. Short: Dave. Pet: Davey, Davie, Davy. (DAY-VID)

DAVIS Transferred use of the surname, which is a shortened form of Davison (Davy's son). Davy was a popular medieval pet form of David and was often bestowed independently from the original name. Short: Dave. Pet: Davey, Davie, Davy. (DAY-VIS)

DECLAN Borrowed from the Irish, Declan is the Anglicized form of Deaglán, which is of uncertain meaning. *See* DECLAN (Irish Names). Var: Decclan, Decklan, Decklen, Decklin, Decklyn, Deklan, Deklen, Deklin. (DEK-LIN)

DELANEY Transferred use of the Irish surname, which is from the Gaelic O'Dubhshláine. The first element of Dubhshláine is from the Gaelic *dubh* (black, dark), but the second is uncertain. Some believe it is the name of the river Slaney; others think it is a form of *slán* (healthy, whole). Var: Delany. (DAH-LANE-EE)

DEREK Derived from a short form of the obsolete Germanic Thiudoreiks, a compound name composed from the Old German elements *thiuda* (folk, people) and *reiks* (ruler, leader, king). The name was taken to England in the Middle Ages by Flemish cloth traders. Var: Darrek, Darrick, Dereck, Derreck, Derrick. (DARE-RIK)

DESTON Modern coinage perhaps used as a variation of Dustin. It could also be based on *destiny* (fate, what will happen to a person). *See* DUSTIN. (DES-TON)

DEVIN A borrowing from the Irish, Devin is derived from the Gaelic *dámh* (a poet). Var: Devan, Deven, Devon. (DEV-UN)

DEVLIN Borrowed from the Irish, Devlin is an Anglicized form of an Irish surname of several origins. *See* DEVLIN (Irish Names). Short: Dev. (DEV-LIN)

DIRK A contracted form of Derek (leader of the people), Dirk is now regarded as an independent given name. *See* DEREK. Var: Dirck. (DERK)

DOMINIC Derived from the Latin Dominicus (belonging to a lord), which is from *dominus* (a lord, a master). Var: Domenic, Dominick, Dominyck, Dominyk, Domonic, Domonick. Short: Dom, Nick. (DOM-IH-NIK)

DRAKE Transferred use of the English surname meaning "dweller at the sign of the drake; dweller at the sign of the dragon." (DRAKE)

DREW Originally a short form of Andrew (manly), Drew is now commonly bestowed as an independent given name. *See* ANDREW. (DROO)

DUANE Anglicized form of Dubhán (little dark one), a diminutive form of the Gaelic *dubh* (black, dark). Var: Dewayne, De Wayne, Dwain, Dwaine, Dwane, Dwayne, D'Wayne. (DUH-WANE, DOO-WANE)

DUGAN Transferred use of the surname, which is the Anglicized form of the Gaelic Dubhgán (little dark one), a compounding of the elements *dubh* (dark, black) and the diminutive suffix *-gán*. Var: Dugann. (DOO-GUN)

DURAN Derived from the Latin *durans* (enduring, durable, long-lasting). Var: Durand, Durant. (DER-RAN)

DUSTIN Transferred use of the surname, which is of uncertain origin. Some believe it to be an altered form of Thurston, which is derived from the Old Norse Thorstein (Thor's stone). *See* THORSTEIN (Scandinavian Names). Pet: Dusty. (DUS-TIN)

DYLAN A borrowing from the Welsh, Dylan is a name of uncertain derivation. Some believe it to be from an Old Celtic element meaning "sea." *See* DYLAN (Welsh Names). Var: Dillan, Dillon, Dillyn, Dyllan. (DIL-LUN)

EDISON Transferred use of the English surname meaning "Eadie's son, Edie's son." Eadie and Edie are obsolete Old English names derived from *ēad* (prosperity, wealth). Short: Ed. Pet: Eddie, Eddy. (ED-IH-SON)

ELI Derived from the Hebrew *'ēlī* (high, ascent). *See* ELI (Biblical Names). (EE-LĪ)

ELLIOT Transferred use of the surname that originated as a diminutive of the Old French Élie, a cognate of the Hebrew Elijah (Jehovah is God). *See* ELIJAH (Biblical Names). The name received a boost in popularity due to the central character in the popular movie *E.T.* Var: Eliot, Eliott, Elliott. (EL-LEE-ET)

ELLIS Transferred use of the surname originating from the personal name Elis, a Middle English variant of Elisha (God is salvation). *See* ELISHA (Biblical Names). (EL-LISS)

EMERY English variant of the Old French Aimeri, a name derived from the Old High German Amalrich (work ruler), which is a compounding of the elements *amal* (work) and *rich* (ruler, king). Var: Emeri, Emmery, Emory. (EM-EH-REE)

ERIC Derived from the Old Norse Eirìkr, a compounding of the elements *ei* (ever, always) and *ríkr* (ruler): hence, "eternal ruler." Var: Erick, Erik, Irricc. (ERR-RIK)

ERLEND A borrowing from the Scandinavian, Erlend is derived from the Old Norse *örlendr* (foreigner, stranger). Var: Erland. (ER-LEND)

ETHAN Ecclesiastic Late Latin name derived from the Hebrew *ēthān* (strength, firmness, long-lived). The name is borne in the Bible by a very wise man whom Solomon surpassed in wisdom. Var: Ethen. (EE-THUN)

EVAN Anglicized form of the Gaelic Eóghan (youth). Var: Even, Evun. (EH-VUN)

EVEREST Transferred use of the English surname meaning "Everett's son." Everett is an old variant of Evered, a name derived from the Old English Eoforheard (brave as a wild boar), which is a compounding of the elements *eofor* (a wild boar) and *heard* (strong, brave, hearty). Var: Everett, Everist, Everitt, Everritt. (EV-EH-REST)

FALLON Transferred use of the surname derived from the Irish O'Fallamhain (descendant of Fallamhan). Fallamhan is derived from the Gaelic *follamhnus* (superiority, mastery). Var: Fallan, Fallen, Fallin, Fallyn. (FAL-LIN)

FARRELL Anglicized form of the Irish Gaelic Fearghall (superior valor, man of valor), which is composed from the elements *fer* (superior, best) or *fear* (man) and *ghal* (valor). Var: Farell, Ferrall, Ferrell. (FARE-REL, FARE-UL)

FARRIN Transferred use of the English surname which is of uncertain derivation. It is possibly derived from the Old English elements *fæger* (handsome) and *hine* (servant) or *fearr* (bull) and *hine* (servant). Alternatively, the name is from the Irish O'Farachain (descendant of Faramund). Var: Farran, Farren, Farryn, Ferran, Ferren, Ferrin, Ferryn. (FARE-UN)

FINCH Derived from *finch* (a small songbird). (FINCH)

FLEET A short form of Fleetwood, Fleet is also bestowed as an independent given name. *See* FLEETWOOD. (FLEET)

FLEETWOOD Transferred use of the English surname derived from the place-name Fleetwood, which is derived from the Old English elements *fleót* (a creek) and *wudu* (wood): hence, "creek wood." Short: Fleet. (FLEET-WOOD)

FORREST Transferred use of the English surname, which arose in the 13th century in the form of de Foresta (of the forest): hence, "dweller or worker in the forest." Var: Forestt, Forrestt. (FOR-EST)

FOSTER Transferred use of the surname, which is of various origins. *See* FOSTER (English Names). (FOS-TER)

FOX Derived from *fox*, which denotes a small, wild member of the dog family with a bushy tail and pointed ears. The fox is traditionally thought of as being sly and crafty. (FOX)

FRASER A borrowing from the Scottish, Fraser is the transferred use of the surname, which is a corruption of the earlier Frisell (a Frisian, from the Frisian Islands in the North Sea). Var: Frasier, Frazer, Frazier. (FRAY-ZHER)

FREE Derived from *free* (liberated, without restraint). (FREE)

GABE A short form of Gabriel (God is my strength), Gabe is also bestowed as an independent given name. *See* GABRIEL. (GABE)

GABRIEL Derived from the Hebrew *gavhrī'ēl* (God is my strength). The name is borne in the Bible by one of the seven archangels, the herald of Good News who appeared to Mary to announce her pregnancy and the impending birth of the Christ child. Short: Gabe. (GABE-REE-EL)

GALEN Derived from the name Claudius Galenus (c. 130–200), a Greek physician and writer on medicine and philosophy to whom the system of medical practice Galenism is attributed. His surname is believed to be derived from *galēnē* (calm, serene). Var: Galenn. (GAY-LEN)

GARRETT Transferred use of the surname that evolved from Gerald (spear rule) and Gerard (brave with a spear). *See* GERALD *and* GERARD (English Names). Var: Garett, Garret, Garritt. Pet: Garry, Gary. (GARE-ET)

GARRISON Transferred use of the surname originating from the place-name Garriston in North Yorkshire. Alternatively, Garrison developed from the surname Garretson (son of Garret). Short: Garry, Gary. (GARE-RIH-SON)

GARTH Transferred use of the English surname derived from the Middle English *garth* (an enclosed yard or garden). The name originated as an occupational name for a person in charge of a garden or an enclosed yard or paddock. The name has recently been popularized by the fame of country singer Garth Brooks. (GARTH)

GARY From the Old English Garwig (spear of battle), a compound name composed from the elements *gar* (a spear) and *wig* (battle). Alternatively, Gary developed as a pet form of any of the various names beginning with the Germanic element *gar* (spear). Var: Garry. (GARE-EE)

GEOFFREY Derived from the Middle English Geffrey, which is from the Old French Geoffroi, a name thought to have evolved from several different Germanic names. *See* GEOFFREY (English Names). Var: Jeffery, Jeffrey, Jeffry. Short: Geoff, Jeff. (JOF-FREE, JEF-FREE)

GIDEON Derived from the Hebrew *gidh'ōn* (hewer, one who cuts down). The name is borne in the Bible by an Israelite judge who was a leader in the defeat of the Midianites. (GID-EE-UN)

GLEN Derived from the Gaelic *gleann* (mountain valley, a narrow, secluded valley). It is unclear whether the surname or the given name came first. Var: Glenn, Glyn, Glynn. (GLEN)

GRAHAM Transferred use of the surname originating from the place-name Grantham in Lincolnshire. The first element is uncertain, but the second is from the Old English *ham* (home, dwelling, manor). Var: Ghramm, Greame, Grahame. (GRAM, GRAY-UM)

GRANT Transferred use of the English surname derived from the Anglo-French *graund, graunt* (great) and the Old French *grand, grant* (great). The name Grant originated as a nickname for a large or tall person. (GRANT)

GRIFFIN A borrowing from the Welsh, Griffin is from Griffinus, a Latinate form of Griffith used in the Middle Ages. *See* GRIFFITH. (GRIF-FIN)

GRIFFITH A borrowing from the Welsh, Griffith is of debated origin. Some believe it to be an Anglicized form of Gruffydd, the Welsh form of the Roman Rufus (red, ruddy). Others think the name is derived from the Old Welsh Grippiud (prince). (GRIF-FITH)

GUTHRIE Transferred use of the Scottish surname and place-name derived from the Gaelic *gaothair* (windy place). The name was originally given to those who lived near Forfar. Alternatively, the name is from the Gaelic surname Mag Uchtre (son of Uchtre), which might be derived from the Gaelic *uchtlach* (child). Var: Guthrey. (GUTH-REE)

GUY A borrowing from the French, Guy is derived from the Old French *guie* (a guide, a leader). (GĪ)

HALE Transferred use of the English surname derived from the Old English *halh* (nook, recess, remote valley): hence, "dweller in the hale, dweller in the remote valley." (HALE)

HAVEN Modern coinage derived from *haven* (safe place, refuge). (HAY-VEN)

HAYES Transferred use of the surname derived from the Old English element *hege* (hedge, a hedged enclosure): hence, "dweller near the hedged enclosure." Var: Hays. (HAZE)

HEATH Derived from the Middle English *hethe*, which is from the Old English *hæð* (a heath, a moor). Var: Heathe. (HEETH)

HIATT Transferred use of the English surname meaning "dweller at the high gate," which is derived from Middle English *hy* (high) and *yate* (a gate, an opening). Var: Hyatt. (HĪ-AT)

HOLT Transferred use of the surname meaning "dweller at a wood, dweller near a wooded hill," which is of English and Scandinavian origin. It is derived from the Old English and Old Norse *holt* (a wood; a wooded hill). (HOLT)

HOYTE Transferred use of the surname of Scandinavian origin. It is believed to be derived from the Old Norse *hugu* (heart, mind, spirit). Var: Hoyce, Hoyt. (HOIT)

HUNT Transferred use of the surname derived from the Middle English *hunte* (a hunter, a huntsman). Alternatively, Hunt is used as a short form of Hunter (a huntsman). (HUNT)

HUNTER Transferred use of the surname derived from the Middle English *hunte* (a hunter, a huntsman). Short: Hunt. (HUN-TER)

IAN Scottish form of John (God is gracious). *See* JOHN. (EE-UN)

IKE Originally a pet form of Isaac (laughter), Ike is also bestowed as an independent given name. It rose in popularity in the U.S. due to its being the nickname of the 34th president, Dwight D. Eisenhower (1890–1969). His campaign slogan of "I like Ike" became household words in the 1950s. (IKE)

INGRAM Transferred use of the surname originating from the Germanic personal name Angilramnus or Ingilramnus, which are composed from the elements *angil* (angel) and *hraban* (raven). (ING-GRUM)

ISAAK Ecclesiastic Greek form of the Hebrew Yitzchak (he will laugh), which is derived from *yitshāq* (laughter). The name is borne in the Bible by one of the three patriarchs, the son of Abraham and Sarah and progenitor of the Hebrews. Var: Isaac. (Ī-ZAK)

JACK Originally a pet form of John (God is gracious) and Jackson (son of Jack), Jack is now often bestowed as an independent given name. *See* JOHN. Pet: Jackie, Jacky. (JAK)

JACKSON Transferred use of the surname that originated in 14th-century England as a patronymic meaning "son of Jack." Short: Jack. Pet: Jackie, Jacky. (JAK-SUN)

JACOB From the Ecclesiastic Late Latin Iacobus, which is from the Greek Iakōbos, a name derived from the Hebrew Yaakov. The name has its root in *ya'aqob* (seizing by the heel, supplanting). The name is borne in the Bible by the father of twelve sons, who became the progenitors of the twelve tribes of Israel. Pet: Jake. (JAY-KOB)

JAIDON Modern coinage of uncertain derivation. Var: Jaidan, Jaiden, Jaydan, Jayden, Jaydon, Jaydun. (JAY-DUN)

JAKE Originally a pet form of Jacob (seizing by the heel, supplanting), Jake is now popularly bestowed as an independent given name. *See* JACOB. (JAKE)

JALEN Modern coinage perhaps based on the name Galen (calm, serene) or formed by combining names such as Jay and Helen. (JAY-LEN)

JAMES From the Ecclesiastic Late Latin Iacomus, an evolution of Iacobus, which is from the Ecclesiastic Iakōbos, a cognate of the Hebrew Yaakov. The name has its root in *ya'aqob* (supplanting, seizing by the heel). Some say Iacomus arises from an error in the transcription of manuscripts from the Greek to the Latin by an early monk. Short: Jim. Pet: Jamie, Jimmy. (JAYMZ)

JAMIE A pet form of James and Jamison, Jamie is also occasionally bestowed as an independent given name. *See* JAMES *and* JAMISON. Var: Jamey. (JAY-MEE)

JAMISON Transferred use of the English surname meaning "Jamie's son." *See* JAMIE. Var: Jamieson. Pet: Jamie. (JAY-MIS-SUN)

JARED Greek cognate of the Hebrew Yered, a name derived from *yaredh* (descent). Var: Jarrod, Jerod, Jerrod. (JARE-ED)

JASON English cognate of the Latin and Greek Iāson (healer), a name derived from *iasthai* (to heal). Popularly bestowed in the U.S., the name Jason is borne in Greek mythology by a prince who led the Argonauts. Var: Jayson. (JAY-SON)

JAXSEN Modern coinage based on the name Jackson (son of Jack). See JACKSON. Short: Jax. (JAKS-UN)

JAY Originally a pet form of any of the names beginning with the letter *J*, it is now usually bestowed as an independent given name. (JAY)

JEDEDISH Modern coinage of uncertain derivation. It could be a variation of Jedidiah (beloved of Jehovah). *See* JEDIDIAH. Short: Jed. (JED-EH-DEESH)

JEDIDIAH Derived from the Hebrew Yedidiah (beloved of Jehovah). *See* JEDIDIAH (Biblical Names). Short: Jed. (JEH-DIH-DĪ-AH)

JEFFERSON Transferred use of the English surname originating as a patronymic meaning "son of Geoffrey, son of Jeffrey." *See* GEOFFREY. Short: Jeff. (JEF-FER-SUN)

JEREMY English vernacular form of Jeremiah (the Lord loosens, God will uplift), which dates to the 13th century. *See* JEREMIAH (Biblical Names). Var: Jeramy, Jeromy. Short: Jerr. Pet: Jerry. (JER-AH-MEE)

JEROME Derived from the Latin Hieronymus, a compound name composed from the elements *hieros* (holy) and *onyma* (name): hence, "holy name." *See* JEROME (English Names). Short: Jerr. Pet: Jerry. (JEH-ROME)

JERRAN Modern coinage of uncertain derivation. Var: Jerren, Jerrin, Jerryn. (JER-UN)

JERRY A pet form of any of the various names beginning with the element *Jer-*, Jerry is also bestowed as an independent given name. Var: Gerry. (JARE-REE)

JESSE Derived from the Hebrew Yishai, which is from *yīshai* (gift, wealth). *See* JESSE (Biblical Names). The name is borne by black leader Jesse Jackson. Short: Jess. (JES-EE)

JEVIN Modern coinage perhaps based on the name Devin (a poet). *See* DEVIN. Var: Jevon. (JEH-VIN)

JOHN Derived from the Middle Latin Johannes, which is from the Ecclesiastic Late Latin Joannes, which is from the Greek Iōannes. Iōannes is from the Hebrew Yehanan, a short form of Yehohanan, which is derived from *yehōhānān* (Yahweh is gracious). John is the most enduring of the biblical names and remains one of the most popular names bestowed in the United States. *See* JOHN (Biblical Names). Var: Jon. Pet: Johnnie, Johnny, Jonnie, Jonny. (JON)

JONATHAN Derived from the Hebrew Yonatan, a short form of Yehonatan, which is derived from *yehōnātān* (Yahweh has given). The name is borne in the Bible by the eldest son of King Saul. Short: Jon. Pet: Jonnie, Jonny. (JON-AH-THAN)

JORDAN Derived from the Hebrew Yarden (to flow down, descend). The name was originally used in the Middle Ages for a child baptized in holy water said to be from the river Jordan. Var: Jordon, Jordyn. Pet: Jory, Judd. (JOR-DUN)

JORY A pet form of Jordan (to flow down, descend), Jory is also bestowed as an independent given name. *See* JORDAN. (JOR-EE)

JOSEPH Ecclesiastic Late Latin form of the Ecclesiastic Greek Iōsēph, which is from the Hebrew Yosef, a name derived from *yōsēf* (he shall add, may God add). *See* JOSEPH (Biblical Names). Var: Joeseph. Short: Joe. Pet: Joey. (JO-SUF, JO-SEF)

JOSHUA Derived from the Hebrew Yehoshua, which is from *yehōshū'a* (Jehovah is help, God is salvation). The name is borne in the Bible by Moses' successor, who led the children of Israel into the Promised Land. Short: Josh. (JAH-SHOO-AH)

JOSIAH Derived from the Hebrew *yōshīyāh* (the Lord supports, the Lord saves, the Lord heals). Var: Josyah, Joziah. (JO-SĪ-AH, JO-ZĪ-AH)

JUDD Originally a Middle English pet form of Jordan (descending, flowing down), the modern use of Judd comes from the transferred use of the surname, which developed from the pet form. *See* JORDAN. (JUD)

JULY Borrowed from the name of the seventh month, which is derived from the Latin *Julius*, *mensis Julius* (the month of Julius). The month, named for Julius Caesar, received a boost in popularity from Larry McMurtry's Pulitzer Prize–winning epic *Lonesome Dove*. (JOO-LĪ, JOO-LĪ)

JUSTIN From the Latin Justīnus, which is derived from *justus* (lawful, right, just). (JUS-TIN)

KADIN Modern coinage of uncertain derivation. It could represent a variant of the surname Kaden, which is of Germanic origin and derived from a place-name meaning "fen." (KAY-DIN)

KALEN Modern coinage of uncertain derivation. Var: Kalin. (KAY-LIN)

KAYSON Modern coinage of uncertain derivation. It is perhaps based on the name Jason. (KAY-SUN)

KEENAN Anglicized form of the Irish Cianán (little Cian, little ancient one). Cianán is a diminutive form of Cian (ancient, in the past). Var: Kenan, Kienan. (KEE-NUN)

KELBY Transferred use of the English surname meaning "dweller at the farmstead by the stream." It is composed of the Old Norse elements *kelda* (a spring) and *býr* (a farmstead, an estate). (KELL-BEÝ)

KELLER Transferred use of the surname, which is an Anglicized form of the Irish Ó Céileachair (companion-dear). Alternatively, Keller is a German surname meaning "tavernkeeper, cellarer." It is derived from the Middle High German *kellære* (storekeeper, cellarer). (KEL-LER)

KELLY Anglicized form of the Irish Ceallagh, which is thought to be derived from *ceallach* (strife). The use of Kelly as a given name is most likely from the transferred use of the surname O'Kelly or Kelly, which is the second most common surname in Ireland. Var: Kelley. (KEL-LEE)

KELSEY Transferred use of the surname originating from the obsolete Old English Cēolsige, a compound name composed of the elements *cēol* (ship) and *sige* (victory). Var: Kelcey, Kelcy, Kelsy. (KEL-SEE)

KEMP Transferred use of the surname derived from the Old English *cempa* (fighter, warrior) and the Middle English *kempe* (athlete, wrestler). (KEMP)

KENDALL Transferred use of the English surname, which is of several derivations. *See* KENDALL (English Names). Var: Kendell. Short: Ken. (KEN-DAL)

KENNARD Transferred use of the English surname that evolved from the Anglo-Saxon Cenheard and Cyneheard. The first name is composed of the Old English elements *céne* (bold) and *heard* (hearty, strong, brave). The second is from the Old English *cyne* (royal) and *heard* (hearty, strong, brave). Var: Kinnard. Short: Ken. Pet: Kenny. (KEN-NARD)

KENNEDY Anglicized form of the Irish Cinnéidid (helmeted head, ugly head). The personal name gave rise to the famous surname. Short: Ken. Pet: Kenny. (KEH-NEH-DEE)

KENNETH Of Scottish origin, Kenneth is the Anglicized form of the Gaelic Cinaed and Cionaed (born of fire), and Coinneach and Caoineach (comely, handsome). Short: Ken. Pet: Kenny. (KEN-NETH)

KENT Transferred use of the surname arising from the name of the county of Kent. The name, of uncertain derivation, is perhaps from the Welsh *cant* (rim, edge, border) or from the Old Welsh *cant* (white, bright). (KENT)

KENYON Transferred use of the Irish surname that originated as an English place-name and was later used as an Anglicized form of the Gaelic Mac Coinín and Ceannfhionn. Coinín is derived from *coinín* (rabbit), and Ceannfhionn is composed of the elements *ceann* (head) and *fhionn* (white, fair). (KEN-YON)

KERMIT Anglicized form of the Irish Gaelic Diarmaid (without injunction, a freeman). The name is composed of the elements *di* (without) and *airmit* (injunction). (KER-MIT)

KERRY Anglicized form of the Irish Gaelic Ciardha, a name derived from *ciar* (black): hence, "black-haired one." (KER-REE)

KEVIN Anglicized form of the Irish Gaelic Caoimhín (little gentle one), a diminutive form of *caomh* (gentle, kind, noble, beautiful, lovable). Var: Kevan. Short: Kev. (KEH-VIN)

KIPP Transferred use of the surname derived from the Northern English *kip* (a pointed hill). Var: Kip. (KIP)

KIRK Transferred use of the surname derived from the Old Norse *kirkja* (church): hence, "dweller by the church." (KERK)

Kit A pet form of Christopher (bearing Christ), Kit is also bestowed as an independent given name. *See* CHRISTOPHER. (KIT)

Kivi Transferred use of a Finnish surname meaning "dweller by a stone." (KIH-VEE)

Kodiak Believed to be a native Russian name meaning "island." The name is borrowed from the Alaskan place-name belonging to an island off the southwest coast of the state. The name is also borne by a very large brown bear found on the island. (KO-DEE-AK)

Kyle Transferred use of the Scottish surname that originated from the region of the same name in southwestern Scotland. Kyle, a topographical term referring to a narrow, straight channel, is derived from the Gaelic *caol* (narrow, a sound, a strait). (KILE)

La Conner Transferred use of a place-name derived from the name Connor. *See* CONNOR. (LAH-KON-NER)

Lance Old French form of the Old High German Lanzo, a name derived from *lant* (land). The use of the name is advanced from the homonymous *lance* (a light spear, a lance). (LANSS)

Lane Transferred use of the surname derived from the Old English *lane* (a lane, a narrow country road). (LANE)

Lawyer Derived from *lawyer,* which denotes one who is trained in the law. (LAW-YER)

Leander Derived from the Greek Leiandros (lion man, like a lion). The name is composed of the elements *leōn* (lion) and *andros* (man). *See* LEANDER (Mythology and Astrology Names). (LEE-AN-DER)

Lee Transferred use of the surname derived from the Old English *lēah* (wood, clearing, meadow, enclosure): hence, "dweller in or near the wood or clearing." (LEE)

Leeson Transferred use of the surname derived from the Old English name Leceson (son of Lece). Lece is an Old French variant of Letitia, which is from the Latin *laetitia* (joy). Var: Leasen, Leason. (LEE-SON)

Leighton Transferred use of the surname derived from the Old English *lēac* (leek) and *tūn* (town, settlement). Var: Layten, Layton, Leyten, Leyton. (LAY-TUN)

Lennon From the Irish O' Lonáin (descendant of Lonán). Lonán is derived from the Gaelic *lon* (blackbird): hence, "little blackbird." Alternatively, the name is from the surname O'Leannáin (descendant of Leannán). Leannán is a Gaelic name meaning "little lover." Var: Lennan, Lennen. Short: Len. (LEN-NUN)

Lennox Transferred use of the English surname derived from a place-name in Dumbarton. The name is believed to be derived from the Gaelic *leamhanach* (elmtrees). Short: Len. Pet: Lenny. (LEN-NUKS)

Leo Late Latin name derived from *leo* (a lion). Leo is also used as a short form of any of the names using it as a beginning element. (LEE-O)

Leroy Modern coinage based on the French *le roi* (the king). Var: Lee Roy, Le Roi, Le Roy. (LEE-ROI)

Logan Transferred use of the Irish surname, which is from the Gaelic *lagán* (a little hollow), a diminutive form of *lag* (a hollow): hence, "dweller at a little hollow." (LO-GUN)

Lonnie A name of uncertain etymology, it might be a variant of Lenny (lion-hearted, brave as a lion) or a modern coinage made by combining elements from the names of parents or relatives. (LON-NEE)

Loren American variant of the German Lorenz, a cognate of Laurence, which is from the Latin Laurentius (man from Laurentum). Laurentum, the name of a town in Latium, is thought to be derived from *laurus* (laurel). Var: Lorin. (LOR-UN)

Lucas Ecclesiastic Late Latin name thought to be a derivative of Lucius, which is from the root *lux* (light). Alternatively, some believe the name is derived from the Ecclesiastic Greek Loukas, a contraction of Loukanos (man from Lucania). (LOO-KUS)

Lucky Derived from *lucky* (having good fortune, good luck). (LUK-EE)

Luke Middle English and Anglo-French form of Lucas. *See* LUCAS. The name is borne in the Bible by one of the four evangelists, the author of the third Gospel, Luke, and the Acts of the Apostles. (LUKE)

Lyle Transferred use of the English surname that evolved from the French De L'Isle (dweller on the isle). (LILE)

Mac Derived from the Gaelic *mac* (son). The name is also used as a short form of any of the names of which it is an element. Var: Mack. (MAK)

MacAllister Transferred use of the surname meaning "son of Alister." Alister is a Gaelic form of Alexander (defender or helper of mankind). *See* ALEXANDER. Var: Mac Alister, Macallister. Short: Mac. (MAH-KAL-ISS-TER)

MacKenzie Transferred use of the Irish surname, which is from the Gaelic MacCoinnigh (son of Coinneach). Coinneach is derived from *cainneach* (fair one, handsome). Var: Mackenzie, McKenzie. Short: Mac. (MAH-KEN-ZEE)

MALCOLM Derived from the Gaelic Maolcolm (servant of St. Columba), a compound name composed of the elements *maol* (servant, votary) and Colm (Columba). *See* MALCOLM (Scottish Names). (MAL-KUM, MAL-KULM)

MARIO Derived from the Latin Marius, an old Roman family name of uncertain derivation. (MAH-REE-O)

MARK English cognate of Marcus. *See* MARCUS (English Names). The name is borne in the Bible by one of the four Evangelists, the author of the second Gospel, Mark. Var: Marc. (MARK)

MARLAND Transferred use of the English surname meaning "dweller at the famous land." The name is composed from the Old English elements *mere* (fame, famous) and *land* (land). Var: Marlin, Marlon, Marlond, Marlondo. (MAR-LUND)

MARSHALL Transferred use of the surname originating from the Old French *mareschal*, which is from the Old High German *marahscalh*, a word composed from the elements *marah* (horse) and *scalh* (servant). The term arose as an occupational name for a groom. In the 13th century, the term was also indicative of a farrier and later was used to denote a high officer of state. Var: Marshal, Marshel, Marshell. (MAR-SHUL)

MASON Transferred use of the surname derived from *mason* (a person who builds with stone, brick, or concrete). The name arose as an occupational name in the 12th century. (MAY-SUN)

MATTHEW Evolution of the Middle English Matheu, which is ultimately derived from the Hebrew Matityah (gift of God). *See* MATTHEW (English Names). Short: Matt. (MATH-YOO)

MATTHIAS Ecclesiastic Greek name derived from the Hebrew *mattīthyāh* (gift of God). The name is borne in the Bible by the apostle chosen by lot to replace Judas Iscariot. (MAH-THĪ-US)

MAX A short form of Maxwell (dweller by Maccus' pool), Max is also bestowed as an independent given name. *See* MAXWELL. (MAX)

MAXWELL Transferred use of the Scottish surname originating from a place-name derived from the name Maccus (great) and the Old English *wella, wielle* (spring, pool). Short: Max. (MAX-WEL)

MICHAEL Derived from the Hebrew *mīkhā'ēl* (who is like God?). The name is borne in the Bible by one of the seven archangels. He is the one closest to God and is responsible for carrying out God's judgments. Var: Michaell, Michail. Short: Mike. Pet: Micky, Mikey. (MĪ-KL)

MILES Derived from the Old French Milon, which is from the Old High German Milo, a name of uncertain derivation. It might be from the German *mild* (mild, peaceful, calm) or from the Old Slavonic root *milu* (merciful). (MILES)

MITCHELL Transferred use of the surname derived from the personal name Michel, a variant of Michael (who is like God?) used in the Middle Ages. Var: Mitchel. (MICH-EL)

MORGAN From the Old Welsh Morcant, a compound name thought to be composed of the elements *môr* (sea) and *cant* (circle, completion) or *can* (white, bright). (MOR-GAN)

MUIR Transferred use of the Scottish surname meaning "dweller near the moor." It is derived from the Old English and Old Norse *mór* (moor, heath). Var: Muire. (MYOOR)

MURPHY A borrowing from the Irish and Scottish, Murphy is the Anglicized form of the Gaelic Murchadh (sea warrior). Murphy is the most common surname in Ireland. Var: Murphie. (MER-FEE)

MURRAY Transferred use of the surname, which is an Anglicized form of the Gaelic Murchadh (sea warrior). Var: Murrey. (MER-REE)

NATHAN Derived from the Hebrew *nāthān* (gift). Short: Nate. (NAY-THUN)

NED A pet form of Edward (wealthy protector), Ned is also bestowed as an independent given name. *See* EDWARD. (NED)

NEIL Anglicized form of the Gaelic Niall, which is of disputed meaning. Some believe it is from *niadh* (a champion); others think it is from *néall* (a cloud). Var: Neal, Neale, Neill. (NEEL)

NELSON Transferred use of the surname arising as a patronymic and a metronymic meaning "son of Neil" and "son of Nell." Short: Nel, Nels. (NEL-SUN)

NEVILLE Transferred use of the surname originating as a Norman baronial name from several places in Normandy called Neuville or Neville, which are composed from the French elements *neuve* (new) and *ville* (town). Var: Nevil, Nevile, Nevill. (NEH-VIL)

NEVIN Transferred use of the surname derived from the Gaelic Cnaimhin (little bone) and Giollanaebhin (servant of the disciple of the saint). Var: Neven. (NEH-VIN)

NICHOLAS Derived from the Greek Nikolaos (victory of the people), a compounding of the elements *nikē* (victory) and *laos* (the people). The name was borne by St. Nicholas, a 4th-century bishop of Myra, on whom our modern-day St. Nicholas, or Santa Claus, is based. Var: Nickolas, Nicolaas, Nikolas. Short: Nick, Nik. Pet: Nicky. (NIK-O-LUS)

NOAH Derived from the Hebrew *nōach* (rest, comfort). *See* NOAH (Biblical Names). (NO-AH)

OLSEN Transferred use of the Scandinavian surname meaning "Olaf's son." *See* OLAF (Scandinavian Names). Var: Olson. (OL-SUN)

ORVILLE Of debated origin, some believe it is derived from a Norman baronial name taken from a French place-name meaning "golden city." Others think it is merely an invention of the novelist Fanny Burney, who used it for the hero in her novel *Evelina* (1778). Var: Orval. (OR-VIL)

OWEN Of uncertain derivation, some believe it to be from the Welsh *oen* (lamb). Others feel it is from the Gaelic *êoghunn* (youth), and yet another suggestion is that it is the Welsh form of the Latin Eugenius (well-born, noble). (O-WEN)

PACEY Transferred use of the surname which is from the Old French *de Peissi, de Pacy* (from Pacy-sur-Eure). Var: Pacy. (PAY-SEE)

PARDEE Of uncertain derivation, Pardee might be a variant of the surname Pardey, which is derived from the French *par Dieu* (by God). (PAR-DEE)

PARISH Transferred use of the surname meaning "dweller near the parish." The name is derived from the Middle English *parische* (parish). Var: Parrish. (PARE-ISH)

PARK Derived from the vocabulary word *park* (an enclosed ground, a park). Alternatively, Park may be the transferred use of the surname, which is derived from the vocabulary word. Var: Parke. (PARK)

PARKER Transferred use of the surname that arose as an occupational name for one who worked in a park. The name is derived from the Middle English *parker* (a park keeper, a gamekeeper). (PAR-KER)

PARNELL French diminutive form of Peter (a rock, a stone). *See* PETER (English Names). Var: Parnall, Pernell. (PAR-NEL)

PATRICK Derived from the Latin *patricius* (a patrician). Short: Pat. (PAT-RIK)

PAYTON Transferred use of the English surname, which is from the place-name Payton in Devon. The name is thought to be derived from the obsolete Anglo-Saxon personal name Pægan and the Old English *tūn* (town, settlement, village). Var: Peyton. (PAY-TUN)

PEPPER Derived from *pepper,* which denotes any of the pungent spices obtained from pepper plants. (PEP-ER)

PERRY Transferred use of the surname meaning "dweller by the pear tree." It is derived from the Middle English *perye* (pear, pear tree). (PARE-REE)

PHILIP Derived from the Latin Philippus, which is from the Greek Philippos (lover of horses). The name is composed of the elements *philos* (loving) and *hippos* (a horse). Var: Philipp, Phillip, Phillipp. Short: Phil. (FIL-LIP)

PHOENIX Derived from the Greek *phoinix* (phoenix, bright red). *See* PHOENIX (Mythology and Astrology Names). Var: Phenix. (FEE-NIKS)

PIERCE A derivative of Piers, an Old French and Middle English form of Peter (a rock). The name was common in the Middle Ages and gave rise to several surnames. (PIERCE)

POWELL Patronymic derived from the Welsh apHowell (son of Howell). Howell is the Anglicized form of Hywel (eminent, prominent, conspicuous). (POW-EL)

PRESTON Transferred use of the surname meaning "from Preston." The name is derived from the English place-name composed of the Old English elements *préost* (priest) and *tūn* (town, settlement, village): hence, "the priest's village." (PRES-TUN)

QUENTIN From the Latin Quentīnus, a derivative of the Roman personal name Quintus, which is from *quintus* (the fifth). The name was traditionally bestowed upon the fifth-born child. (KWEN-TIN)

RAMSEY Transferred use of the Scottish surname derived from several different place-names. It is from the name Hræm's Island, which is derived from the Old English elements *hræm* (raven) and *ég, íg* (island); from Ram's Island, which is from the Old English *ramm* (a ram) and *ég, íg* (island); or from Ramm's Island, which derives its name from the Old Norse elements *rammr* (strong) and *ey* (island). Var: Ramsay. (RAM-ZEE)

RAND A short form of Randall (shield wolf), Rand is also bestowed as an independent given name. *See* RANDALL. (RAND)

RANDALL Transferred use of the English surname derived from Randolf (shield wolf), a name derived from the Scandinavian elements *rand, rönd* (the edge or rim of a shield) and *ulfr* (wolf). Var: Randal, Randel, Randle. Short: Rand. Pet: Randy. (RAN-DAL)

RANDY A pet form of Randall (shield wolf), Randy is also bestowed as an independent given name. *See* RANDALL. (RAN-DEE)

RAY Originally a short form of Raymond (wise protection), Ray is also bestowed as an independent given name. Var: Raye. (RAY)

RAYMOND From the Old Norman French Raimund (wise protection), which is derived from the Germanic Raginmund, a compound name composed of the elements *ragin* (advice, judgment, counsel) and *mund* (hand, protection). Var: Raymonde, RayMonde, Raymund. Short: Ray, Raye. (RAY-MUND)

READ Transferred use of the English surname derived from the Middle English *read, reade* (red), which is from the Old English *read* (red). The name originated as a nickname for someone with red hair or a red, ruddy complexion. Var: Reade, Reed. (REED)

REESE Anglicized form of the Welsh Rhys (ardor). Var: Reece, Rees. (REES)

REID Transferred use of the Scottish surname that originated as a nickname for someone with red hair or a red, ruddy complexion. The name is derived from the Scottish *reid* (red). (REED)

RIDER Transferred use of the English surname derived from the Old English *rīdere* (rider, knight, mounted warrior). (RIDE-ER)

RIDGE Modern name derived from *ridge* (a long, narrow crest of a range of hills or mountains). (RIJ)

RILEY Transferred use of the surname derived from the Old English elements *ryge* (rye) and *lēah* (wood, clearing, meadow, enclosure): hence, "dweller by the rye field." (RĪ-LEE)

RIVER Derived from *river* (a large creek, a river). (RIH-VER)

ROBERT Derived from the Old High German Hruodperht (bright with fame), a compounding of the elements *hruod* (fame) and *beraht* (bright). Short: Bob, Rob. Pet: Bobbie, Bobby, Robbie, Robby. (RAH-BERT, ROB-ERT)

ROBIN Originally a pet form of the name Robert (bright fame), Robin is now commonly used in reference to the bird of the same name. Short: Rob. Pet: Robbie, Robby.

ROCKY Derived from *rocky* (stony, full of rocks). Some believe, however, that the name is a variation of the English surname Rockley (dweller at the rocky lea), which is composed of the Old English elements *rocc* (a rock) and *lēah* (wood, clearing, meadow). (ROK-EE)

RONALD Scottish name derived from the Scandinavian Rögnvaldr (ruler of judgment), a compound name composed of the Old Norse elements *regin, rögn* (advice, judgment, decision) and *valdr* (ruler, power). Short: Ron. Pet: Ronnie, Ronny. (RON-ALD)

ROSS Transferred use of the Scottish surname derived from the Gaelic *ros* (a promontory or peninsula): hence, "dweller on the peninsula." Alternatively, the name originated as a nickname for a person with red hair or a ruddy complexion, in which case it is derived from the Gaelic *ruadh* (red). (ROS)

ROY Transferred use of the surname that originated as a descriptive nickname for a person with red hair or a ruddy complexion. It is derived from the Gaelic *ruadh* (red). (ROI)

ROYCE Transferred use of the surname meaning "Roy's son." *See* ROY. Var: Roice, Royse. (ROIS)

RUSH Transferred use of the English surname derived from the Anglo-French Rousse, which is from *rouse* (red). The name originated as a nickname for one with red hair or a ruddy complexion. (RUSH)

RUSTON Transferred use of the surname meaning "from Ruston." The name is taken from the English place-name meaning "Rust's estate." It is derived from the name Rust, an old variant of Russet (red-haired one), and the Old English *tūn* (town, settlement, village, enclosure). Var: Rustin. Short: Russ. Pet: Rusty. (RUS-TUN)

RUSTY A pet form of Ruston (from Ruston, from Rust's estate), Rusty is also bestowed as an independent given name. It is often bestowed in reference to *rusty*, as a nickname for one with red hair or a ruddy complexion. (RUS-TEE)

RYAN From the Irish surname O'Riain (descendant of Rian). Rian is an ancient Irish name believed to be a diminutive form of *rí* (king): hence, "little king." Var: Rian. (RĪ-AN)

RYE Derived from *rye*, which denotes a type of cereal grass, the seeds and grain of which are used in cooking, baking, and whiskey making. (RĪ)

SAGE Derived from *sage*, which denotes a type of plant regarded by many to have special healing and cleansing properties. (SAGE)

SAMUEL Ecclesiastic Late Latin form of the Ecclesiastic Greek Samouel, which is from the Hebrew Shmuel, a name derived from *shĕmūʾēl* (name of God, his name is God). Var: Sam. Pet: Sammy. (SAM-YOOL)

SANDY Derived from *sandy*, which is often used as a nickname for one with sandy-colored hair. Alternatively,

Sandy is used as a short form of Alexander (defender or helper of mankind). *See* ALEXANDER. (SAN-DEE)

SCOTT Transferred use of the surname derived from the Old English *Scottas*, originally "an Irishman" and later "a Scotchman, a Gael from Scotland." Pet: Scotty. (SKOT)

SCOUT Derived from *scout*, which denotes a person sent out to spy the land or to observe the movements of an enemy or adversary. (SKOUT)

SEAN Derived from Seán, an Irish cognate of John (God is gracious). *See* JOHN. Var: Shauen, Shaun, Shawn, Shon. (SHON)

SETH Derived from the Hebrew *sheth* (appointed). The name is borne in the Bible by the third son of Adam and Eve, born after the death of Abel at the hands of his brother, Cain. (SETH)

SHAD Short form of Shadrach, a Babylonian name of uncertain meaning. Some believe it means "Aku's command." The name is borne in the Bible by one of the three young Hebrew captives cast into a blazing furnace for refusing to worship the Babylonian gods. They were protected by God and emerged from the furnace unharmed. (SHAD)

SHANE Anglicized form of the Irish Seaghán, a variant form of Eóin, which is a Gaelic cognate of John (God is gracious). *See* JOHN. Var: Shaine, Shayne. (SHANE)

SHAW Transferred use of the surname derived from the Middle English *schagh, schawe, shawe* (wood, copse, grove), which is from the Old English *scaga, sceaga.* The name originally meant "dweller in or near a wood or grove." (SHAW)

SHAWNEL Modern coinage formed by the addition of the diminutive suffix *-el* to Shawn, an Anglicized form of the Irish Seán, a cognate of John (God is gracious). *See* JOHN. Var: Shawnell, Shawnelle. (SHAW-NEL)

SHAY A borrowing from the Irish, Shay is a pet form of Shamus, the Irish form of James (supplanting, seizing by the heel). It is also bestowed as an independent given name. *See* JAMES. Var: Shea, Shey. (SHAY)

SHELBY Transferred use of the surname derived from an English place-name meaning "a willow grove, a place where willows grow." (SHEL-BEE)

SHELTON Transferred use of the English surname derived from the place-name Shelton (town near the shelf or ledge). The name is composed of the Old English elements *scelf, scylfe* (a shelf, a ledge) and *tūn* (town, settlement, village, enclosure). (SHEL-TUN)

SHERMAN Transferred use of the surname, which is a variant of Shearman, an English surname that originated as an occupational name for a cutter of wool or cloth. The name is derived from the Middle English *schereman,* a combining of the elements *scheren* (to cut) and *man* (man). Short: Sherm. (SHER-MUN)

SKY A short form of Skylar, Sky is also occasionally bestowed as an independent given name. (SKY)

SKYLAR Modern coinage of uncertain derivation. It might be based on *sky* or perhaps on the name of the Isle of Skye, an island off the coast of Scotland. Short: Sky. (SKY-LAR)

SLOANE Transferred use of the surname, which is an Anglicized form of the Gaelic Slaughan (warrior, soldier). Var: Sloan. (SLONE)

SMOKEY Derived from *smoky* (having excessive smoke, having the color of smoke). The name was popularized by singer Smokey Robinson and by Smokey the Bear, a cartoon mascot used to prevent forest fires. (SMO-KEE)

SONNY Derived from *sonny,* a term used to address a young boy. (SUN-NEE)

SOREN A borrowing from the Danish, Soren is thought to be derived from the Latin Sevērinus, an old Roman family name derived from *sevērus* (severe, strict, stern). (SOR-EN)

SPENCER Transferred use of the English surname derived from the Anglo-French *espenser* and the Old French *despensier* (dispenser of provisions, a butler or steward who had control of the provisions of a household). Var: Spenser. (SPEN-SER)

STEPHEN From the Latin Stephanus, which is from the Greek Stephanos, a name derived from *stephanos* (a crown, a garland). The name is borne in the Bible by St. Stephen, one of the seven chosen to assist the Twelve Apostles, and the first Christian martyr. Var: Stefan, Stefen, Stefon, Stephan, Stephon, Stevan, Steven, Stevon. Short: Steve. Pet: Stevie. (STEE-VEN)

STERLING Transferred use of the surname, which is a variant of the English Starling. It is derived from the Old English *stærling* (a starling, a type of bird) and arose as a nickname in reference to the bird. Modern use of the name often equates it to *sterling* (silver; of excellent quality). (STER-LEEN, STER-LING)

STODDARD Transferred use of the English surname derived from the Old English elements *stód* (stud, a horse) and *heorde* (herd). The name arose as an occupational name for a keeper of horses. Var: Stoddart. (STAH-DARD)

Storm Modern name derived from *storm* (an atmospheric disturbance, high winds, etc.). (STORM)

Swaine Transferred use of the English surname of English and Scandinavian origin. It is derived from the Old English *swán* and the Old Norse *sueinn*. The name originally meant "a swine herder" but later had the general meaning "herdsman, servant." Var: Swain. (SWAINE)

Tae Modern coinage of uncertain derivation. Var: Tay, Taye. (TAY)

Talon Derived from *talon* (the sharp claw of a bird of prey). Var: Talyn. (TAL-UN)

Tandie Modern coinage perhaps based on the Scottish surname Tandy, which arose as a pet form of Andrew (manly). (TAN-DEE)

Tanier Modern coinage of uncertain derivation. It could possibly be a variant of Tanner (a person who tans leather hides). (TAN-YER)

Tanner Transferred use of the English and German surname that arose as an occupational name for a tanner, a person who tanned leather hides. Var: Tannar, Thanner. (TAN-NER)

Tannis Modern coinage of uncertain derivation. It is perhaps based on the name Tanner. (TAN-NIS)

Tannon Modern coinage of uncertain derivation. It could possibly be a variant of Tanner (a person who tans leather hides). (TAN-NUN)

Taylor Transferred use of the surname derived from the Anglo-French *taillour* (tailor), which is from the Old French *taillier* (to cut). The name arose as an occupational name. (TAY-LOR)

Teger Modern name of uncertain derivation. (TEH-GER)

Telfor Derived from the English surname Talfor (iron cutter). The name is derived from the French Taillefer, a compounding of the elements *tailler* (to cut) and *fer* (iron). It arose as an occupational name or a nickname for one who worked with iron. Var: Telfer. (TEL-FER)

Terence From the Latin Terentius, an old Roman family name of uncertain derivation. It might be derived from *terenus* (soft, tender). Var: Terance, Terrance, Terrence. Pet: Terry. (TARE-ENS)

Terry A pet form of Terence, Terry is also bestowed as an independent given name. *See* TERENCE. (TARE-REE)

Theo A short form of Theodore (God's gift), Theo is also bestowed as an independent given name. *See* THEODORE. (THEO)

Theodore Derived from the Latin Theodorus, which is from the Greek Theodōros, a compounding of the elements *theos* (God) and *dōron* (a gift): hence, "God's gift." Var: Theodor. Short: Theo. Pet: Teddy. (THEE-O-DOR)

Thomas Derived from the Aramaic *tě'ōma* (a twin). The name is borne in the Bible by an apostle who doubted the resurrection of Christ. It is from him that the label "doubting Thomas" came. Var: Thomass, Tomas. Short: Thom, Tom. Pet: Tommy. (TOM-AS)

Thurston From Þorsteinn (Thor's stone), an Old English name derived from the Old Norse elements *þórr* (Thor) and *steinn* (stone). Var: Thurstan, Thursten. (THUR-STUN)

Toby A pet form of Tobias (the Lord is good, God is good), Toby is commonly bestowed as an independent given name. *See* TOBIAS (English Names). Var: Tobey. (TŌ-BEE)

Todd Transferred use of the English surname derived from the Middle and dialectal English *tod, todde* (a fox). (TAHD)

Tonio A short form of Antonio, Tonio is also bestowed as an independent given name. *See* ANTHONY. (TŌ-NEE-O)

Tony A short form of Anthony, Tony is also bestowed as an independent given name. *See* ANTHONY. (TŌ-NEE)

Trace Modern name derived from *trace* (a mark left by the passage of something; a very small amount; to follow the trail of something). (TRACE)

Trail Modern name derived from *trail* (a path; to follow behind, to follow the tracks of something). (TRAIL)

Travis Transferred use of the surname derived from the Old French *traverse* (the act of passing through a gate or crossing a river or bridge). The name arose as an occupational name for someone who collected the toll from those passing the boundary of a town or lordship. Var: Travess, Treves, Trevis. (TRAV-ISS)

Trent Transferred use of the English surname meaning "dweller by the river Trent." The origin of the river name is uncertain and speculative. (TRENT)

Trevor Transferred use of the English surname meaning "belonging to Trevear." Trevear is a place-name in Cornwall meaning "the big farm, the big estate." It is derived from the Cornish and Welsh *tre* (a homestead, an estate) and *mear, mawr* (great, large). Alternatively, Trevor was used as an Anglicized form of the Irish Treabhar (discreet). Var: Trevar, Trever. Short: Trev. (TREV-OR)

TROUT Modern name derived from *trout* (a type of fish). (TROUT)

TULLY A borrowing from the Irish, Tully is an Anglicized form of Tuathal (people mighty). (TUL-LEE)

TUPPER Transferred use of the English surname derived from Tupp, a dialectal nickname meaning "ram," and the suffix *-er*. (TUP-PER)

TURK Modern name probably derived from the surname meaning "a Turk, one from Turkmen or Turkey." (TURK)

TYLER Transferred use of the surname derived from the Old French *tieuleor, tieulier* (tiler, tile maker) and the Middle English *tyler, tylere* (a brick, a tile). The name originated as an occupational name for a tile or brick maker or layer. Var: Tylar, Tylor. Short: Ty. (TĪ-LER)

TYSON Transferred use of the English surname derived from the Old French *tison* (firebrand). Var: Tieson. Short: Tie, Ty. (TĪ-SUN)

ULYSSES Latin form of the Greek Odysseus. The name is borne in mythology by the hero of the *Odyssey*. *See* ODYSSEUS (Mythology and Astrology Names). (YOO-LIS-SEEZ)

VAN Derived from the English surname Van. It is from the Middle English *vanne* and the Middle French *van*, words denoting a type of old winnowing machine. Alternatively, the name can be a borrowing of the Dutch Van, an element in family names meaning "of, from" and indicating place of origin. Var: Vann. (VAN)

VANCE Transferred use of the surname meaning "son of Van." The name is of Dutch and English origin. (VANCE)

VERLIN Believed to be derived from the Latin Verginius (spring-like, flourishing), an old Roman family name that has its root in *ver* (spring). Var: Verle, Verlon. (VER-LIN)

VINCENT French form of the Late Latin Vincentius (conquering), which is derived from *vincere* (to conquer). Var: Vince. Pet: Vinny. (VIN-SENT)

WADE Transferred use of the surname derived from the Old English *wada* (go), which is from the verb *wadan* (to go). Alternatively, the name arose from the Old English *gewæd, wæd* (ford, wading place) and was indicative of one who dwelled near a ford. (WADE)

WALKER Transferred use of the surname that arose as an occupational name for a cleaner, fuller, and thickener of cloth. The name is derived from the Middle English Walkere, which is from the Old English *wealcere* (a walker), the root of which is the Old English *wealcan* (to roll, turn, and full cloth). (WAH-KER, WALK-ER)

WARREN Transferred use of the surname meaning "dweller at or keeper of a game preserve." The name is derived from the Old French *warenne* (a warren, a game preserve). (WAH-REN, WAR-REN)

WAYNE Transferred use of the surname originating from the Old English *wægn, wæn* (wagon, cart). The name arose as an occupational name for a wagoner. (WANE)

WEBB Transferred use of the surname meaning "weaver." It is derived from the Old English *webba* (male weaver) and *webbe* (female weaver). (WEB)

WESKEN Modern coinage of uncertain derivation, possibly influenced by Weston "from Weston." (WES-KIN)

WESLEY Transferred use of the surname taken from the place-name Westley, derived from the Old English elements *west* (west) and *lēah* (wood, clearing, meadow). The surname has the definition "dweller near the western wood or clearing." Var: Wezley. Short: Wes. (WES-LEE, WEZ-LEE)

WILLIAM From the Old Norman French Willaume, which is from the Old High German Willehelm (resolute protector). The name is composed of the elements *willeo* (will, determination) and *helm* (helmet, protection). Short: Bill, Will. Pet: Billy, Willy. (WIL-YUM)

WOLF Derived from *wolf*, which denotes a wild, dog-like animal of the genus *Canis*. Var: Wolfe, Wulf, Wulfe. (WOLF, WULF)

WRAY Transferred use of the English surname, which is of Scandinavian origin and means "dweller in or near the corner or nook." The name is derived from the Old Norse *urá* (corner, nook). (RAY)

WYATT Transferred use of the English surname derived from the Anglo-French personal name Wyot and the French personal name Guyot, which is derived from the name Guy (a guide, a leader) and the diminutive suffix *-ot:* hence, "little Guy." (WĪ-AT)

YANCY Of American Indian origin, Yancy is said to be from the efforts of 17th-century Indians to pronounce the word *English*. It came out as *Yankee*, which led to the development of the name Yancy. Var: Yancey. (YAN-SEE)

YOUNG Transferred use of the surname derived from the Old English *geong* (young). (YUNG)

ZACHARY English cognate of Zacharias (God remembers). *See* ZACHARIAS (Biblical Names). Var: Zachery, Zachory, Zackary, Zackery, Zakary, Zakery. Short: Zack, Zak. (ZAK-ER-REE, ZAK-EH-REE)

Zack A short form of Zachary (remembrance of the Lord, God remembers), Zack is also bestowed as an independent given name. *See* ZACHARY. Var: Zak. (ZAK)

Zane A variant form of John (God is gracious). *See* JOHN. The name was borne by author Zane Grey (1875–1939). (ZANE)

Zebulun A Hebrew name believed to be derived from the Assyrian *zabālu* (to carry, exalt). The name is borne in the Bible by the tenth son of Jacob. He was the patriarch of the tribe bearing his name. Var: Zebulon. Short: Zeb. (ZEB-YOO-LON)

Zethus Of uncertain derivation, Zethus might be based on the name Zeus. (ZEE-THUS)

American Female Names

Abbey A short form of Abigail (father of exaltation). *See* ABIGAIL (English Names). Var: Abbie. (AB-BEE)

Abilene Borrowed from the name of a Texas city, Abilene is derived from the Hebrew *abilene* (a plain). In biblical times, Abilene was a district on the east slope of the Anti-Lebanon range in the Holy Land. Short: Abi. (AB-IH-LEEN)

Adaline A borrowing from the French, Adaline is a diminutive form of Adèle, a name derived from the Germanic element *adal* (noble). Short: Ada. Pet: Addi, Addie, Addy. (AD-AH-LINE)

Adrienne French feminine form of Adrien, which is from the Latin Adriānus (from the city of Adria) and Hadriānus (from the city of Hadria). Var: Adrian, Adriana, Adriann, Adrianna, Adrienn. Pet: Addi, Addie, Addy. (Ā D-REE-EN)

Alaina Variant form of Elaine, a French cognate of the Greek Helenē (light, torch, bright). Alternatively, Alaina is used as a Scottish feminine form of Alan. *See* ALANA (Scottish Names). Var: Alayna, Alena, Allaina, Allayna, Olena. (AH-LANE-AH)

Alcinda Modern coinage of uncertain derivation. It is perhaps based on the name Lucinda (light). (AHL-SIN-DAH)

Alexa Short form of Alexandra (defender or helper of mankind). Alexa is also an independent name derived from the Greek *alexein* (to defend, to help). Var: Elexa. Short: Alex. (AH-LEX-AH)

Alexandra Feminine form of Alexander (defender or helper of mankind). *See* ALEXANDER (Male Names). Var: Alexandrea, Alexandria. Short: Alex, Sandra. Pet: Alli, Allie, Sandi, Sandie, Sandy. (AL-EX-ZAN-DRAH)

Alexis Derived from the Greek *alexein* (to defend, to help). Short: Alex. (AH-LEX-ISS)

Alicia Latinate form of Alice (nobility), a name that evolved through a series of variants from the Germanic Adalheidis (noble one, nobility). *See* ALICE (English Names). Var: Alycia, Alyssa. Pet: Ali. (AH-LEE-SEE-AH, AH-LEE-SHA)

Alison Matronymic meaning "son of Alice." *See* ALICE (English Names). Var: Alisson, Allison, Allisson, Alyson. Short: Ali, Alli, Allie. Pet: Lissi, Lissie. (AL-LIH-SUN)

Alyssa Variant form of Alicia (nobility). *See* ALICIA. Alternatively, the name Alyssa can be derived from the name of the alyssum flower. Var: Alissa. (AH-LIS-SAH)

Amanda Derived from the Latin *amanda* (lovable, worthy to be loved). The name originated as a literary coinage of English playwright Colley Cibber (1671–1757). Var: Amandah, Ammanda. Short: Manda. Pet: Mandie, Mandy. (AH-MAN-DAH)

Amber Derived from *amber,* which denotes a translucent fossil resin used in jewelry making. It is derived from the Arabic *'anbar* (amber). (AM-BER)

Amberlee Modern combination name formed from the names Amber and Lee. The name may be modeled after Kimberley. *See* AMBER *and* LEE. Var: Amberleigh, Amberley, Amberlie. (*AM-ber-lee, am-ber-LEE*)

Amilee Combination name composed from the names Amy and Lee. *See* AMY *and* LEE. Var: Amilea. (Ā-ME-LEE)

Amy From the Middle English Amye, which is from the Old French Aimee (beloved), a name derived from the verb *aimer* (to love). Var: Aimee, Amee, Amia, Amie. (Ā-ME)

Andrea Feminine form of the Greek Andreas (manly), which is derived from andros (man): hence, "womanly, feminine." Var: Andria. Pet: Andee, Andie. (AN-DREE-AH)

Angela A Latinate form of Angel, a name derived from *angel* (divine messenger, a messenger of God), which has its root in the Greek *angelos* (messenger). Var: Angella, Anngele. Pet: Angie. (AN-JEH-LUH)

Angelica Derived from *angelic* (like an angel), which is derived from the Latin *angelicus* and the Greek *angelikos* (angelic). Var: Angelika. Pet: Angie. (AN-JEL-IH-KAH)

Anita Originally a Spanish pet form of Ana (gracious, full of grace), Anita is commonly bestowed in the English-speaking world as an independent given name. Var: Annita. (AH-NEE-TAH)

Anna Cognate of the Hebrew Hannah (gracious, full of grace and mercy), which is derived from *hannāh, chaanach* (grace, gracious, mercy). Var: Ann, Annah, Anne. Pet: Annie. (AN-NAH, AH-NAH)

Annalisa Combination name formed with the names Anna and Lisa. *See* ANNA *and* LISA. Var: Annaliza. (AN-NAH-LEE-SAH)

Anne French form of Anna (gracious, full of grace and mercy). In medieval Christian tradition, Anne was the name assigned to the mother of the Virgin Mary, as Joachim was assigned to her father. *See* ANNA. (AN)

April Borrowed from the name of the fourth calendar month, which is from the Latin *aprilis* (second, latter).The ancient Roman calendar began with the month of March, with April being the second month. (Ā-PRIL)

Arianne From the Latin Ariadne, which is derived from the Greek Ariadnē (the very holy one). The name is borne in Greek mythology by the Cretan king Minos' daughter, who gave Theseus a ball of string by which he found his way out of the labyrinth after killing the Minotaur. Var: Arianna, Arienna, Arienne. (AH-REE-AN)

Ariel A borrowing from the Hebrew masculine name Ariel, which is derived from *'arī'ēl* (lion of God). The use of the name for the central character in the popular children's movie *The Little Mermaid* popularized its use as a female name. Var: Ariele, Ariell, Arielle. (AR-EE-EL, AIR-EE-EL)

Arizona Transferred use of the name of the state, which is derived from the Papago Indian *arizonac* (little springs). (AIR-EH-ZO-NAH)

Arlene Modern coinage believed to be modeled after names such as Darlene and Marlene. Var: Arlana, Arlean, Arleen, Arleyne, Arline. (AR-LEEN)

Arnett Transferred use of the English surname meaning "little eagle." The name is derived from the element *arn* (eagle) and the diminutive suffix *-et*. Var: Arnet, Arnette. Pet: Nettie. (AR-NET)

Artia Feminine form of Art. *See* ART *and* ARTHUR (Welsh Male Names). Var: Artina. (AR-TEE, AR-TEE-AH)

Ashley Originated as a surname derived from the Old English elements *æsc* (ash trees) and *lēah* (wood, clearing, meadow, enclosure): hence, "dweller near the ash tree forest." Ashley was originally bestowed as a male name in England, but its use in Great Britain and the U.S. is now predominantly female. Var: Ashlee, Ashlie, Ashly. (ASH-LEE)

Asia A borrowing of the name of the continent. (A-ZHA)

Audrey Derived from the Old English Æthelthryth, a compounding of the elements *æthel* (noble) and *thryth* (might, strength): hence, "noble strength." Var: Audree, Audreina, Audry. (AUD-REE)

Aura Derived from the Latin *aura* (air). Var: Aurea. (AUR-AH)

Autumn Derived from *autumn*, which denotes the season of the year that comes between summer and winter. (AU-TUM)

Bailey Transferred use of the English surname, which originated from various sources. *See* BAILEY (English Male Names). Var: Bailee, Bailie, Baily. (BAY-LEE)

Baines Transferred use of the surname meaning "from Baines [in France]." The name is derived from the French *bain* (a bath). Alternatively, the name could be derived from the Scottish surname Bain, which is from the Gaelic *bán* (white, fair, pale). (BAINZ)

Bambi Derived from the Italian *bambina* (female baby). The name was popularized by the Disney movie *Bambi*. (BAM-BEE)

Barbara Latin name derived from *barbarus* (foreign, strange), a term applied to non-Romans or those deemed to be uncivilized. Var: Barbra. Short: Barb. Pet: Babs, Barbi, Barbie. (BAR-BAH-RAH)

Becca A short form of Rebecca (a noose), Becca is now popularly bestowed as an independent given name. *See* REBECCA. Var: Beccah, Bekka, Bekkah. Pet: Becki, Beckie, Becky, Bekki, Bekkie, Bekky. (BEH-KAH)

Belva Transferred use of a place-name derived from the Latin and meaning "beautiful view." Var: Belvah. (BEL-VAH)

BETH A short form of Elisabeth and Bethany, Beth is also commonly bestowed as an independent given name. *See* BETHANY *and* ELISABETH. (BETH)

BETHANY Derived from the Hebrew *Bet t'eina* (house of figs). The name is that of a town near Jerusalem at the foot of the Mount of Olives where Jesus stayed during Holy Week before his crucifixion. Short: Beth. (BETH-AH-NEE)

BETTY A pet form of Elisabeth (God is my oath), Betty is also bestowed as an independent given name. *See* ELISABETH. (BET-TEE)

BEVERLEY Transferred use of the surname derived from the Old English elements *beofor* (beaver) and *lēac* (stream): hence, "dweller near the beaver stream." Var: Bever-Leigh, Beverlie, Beverly. Short: Bev. (BEV-ER-LEE)

BLAINE Transferred use of the Celtic surname derived from the Gaelic *blian* (the groin; angular, thin, a hollow). (BLANE)

BLAIR Transferred use of the Scottish surname derived from place-names containing the Gaelic element *blár* (a plain, a level field): hence, "dweller on the plain." Var: Blaire. (BLARE)

BOBBIE A pet form of Roberta (bright and famous), Bobbie is also bestowed as an independent given name. *See* ROBERTA. Var: Bobbi. (BAH-BEE)

BONITA Derived from the Spanish *bonita* (beautiful). Var: Bunita. Short: Bun, Nita. Pet: Bonni, Bonnie, Bonny, Bunni, Bunnie, Bunny. (BAH-NEE-TAH, BO-NEE-TAH)

BONNIE Derived from the Lowland Scotch *bonnie* (beautiful, good-natured and cheerful). *See* BONNIE (Scottish Names). Alternatively, Bonnie is a pet form of Bonita (beautiful). *See* BONITA. Var: Bonni, Bonny. (BON-NEE)

BRANDY Derived from *brandy*, which denotes an alcoholic liquor distilled from wine or from fermented fruit juice. Var: Brandee, Brandey, Brandi, Brandie. (BRAN-DEE)

BREE A short form of names beginning with the element *Bri-* or *Bre-*, Bree is often bestowed as an independent given name. Var: Breea, Bria, Brie. (BREE)

BRENNA Of disputed origin and meaning, some believe it to be a feminine form of the Celtic Bren, which is from the root *bri* (strength, force). Alternatively, it might be derived from the Gaelic *bran* (raven). (BREN-NAH)

BREQLYNN Modern coinage of uncertain derivation. Var: Brecklyn, Brecklynn. (BREK-LIN)

BRETT Transferred use of the English surname derived from the Old French *Bret* (a Breton), an ethnic name for a native of Brittany. Var: Bret, Brette, Britt, Britte. (BRET)

BRIANNA Feminine form of Brian, a name believed to be of Celtic origin and having the definition "strength." *See* BRIAN (Male Names). Var: Breann, Breanna, Breanne, Briana, Brianne. Short: Bree. (BREE-AN-NUH)

BRICE A name that originated as a French surname and was taken to England in the Middle Ages. It is believed to be of Celtic origin and derived from the element *bri* (force, strength) or *brîgh* (valor, strength). (BRICE)

BRITTANY Derived from the name of the peninsula and the former province of northwestern France: hence, "from Brittany, a Breton." Var: Brittainy. Short: Britt. (BRIT-NEE)

BRONTË Originally bestowed in honor of three English sisters and novelists. Charlotte Brontë was the author of *Jane Eyre*. The name is derived from the Greek *brontē* (thunder). (BRON-TAY, BRON-TEE)

BROOKE Derived from the Middle English *brok* (a brook, a small stream, breaking forth). Var: Brook. (BROOK)

BRYLIEVA Modern coinage of uncertain derivation. (BRĪ-LEE-VAH, BRI-LAY-VAH)

BRYN A borrowing from the Welsh, Bryn is derived from *bryn* (hill). It is used as a masculine name in Wales. Var: Brin, Brinn, Brynn. (BRIN)

BUFFY A name that originated as a pet form of Elisabeth, probably from a child's attempt to pronounce Beth. (BUF-FEE)

BUNNY Derived from *bunny*, a diminutive form of the dialectal *bun* (a rabbit). Alternatively, Bunny is used as a pet form of the name Bonita (beautiful). *See* BONITA. Var: Bunni, Bunnie. (BUN-NEE)

CAIDYN Modern coinage of uncertain derivation. Var: Kaiden, Kaydyn. (KAY-DUN)

CALANDRA Compound name composed from the Greek elements *kalos* (beauty, beautiful) and *andros* (man): hence, "beautiful one." The name is also that given to a type of lark. Var: Calandrah, Kalandra, Kalandrah. Pet: Calla, Callie, Kallie. (KAH-LAHN-DRA)

CALEDONIA Derived from the Latin Calēdonia, the name given to the highlands in northern Scotland. Var:

Calledonia. Pet: Calla, Cali, Calie, Calli, Callie, Cally. (KAL-EH-DONE-YAH)

CALLA Pet form of any of the names beginning with the element *Cal-*. Alternatively, Calla is borrowed from a type of lily prized for its beauty. Var: Calah, Callah. Pet: Cali, Calie, Calli, Callie, Calley, Cally. (KAL-LAH)

CALLIE A pet form of any of the names beginning with the element *Cal-*, Callie is also bestowed as an independent given name. Var: Cali, Calie, Calli, Calley, Cally. (KAL-LEE)

CAMEO Derived from the vocabulary word *cameo* (a carving on gems or shells), which is from the Medieval Latin *cammaeus*. Var: Kameo. (KAM-E-O)

CAMERON Transferred use of the Scottish surname that originated from the Gaelic nickname *cam srón* (crooked nose). Var: Cameran, Cameryn, Camryn, Kameran, Kameron, Kameryn. Short: Cam, Kam. Pet: Cami, Kami. (KAM-ER-UN, KAM-RIN)

CAMI A short form of Camilla (virgin of unblemished character), Cami is also bestowed as an independent given name. *See* CAMILLA. Var: Camie. (KAM-EE)

CAMILLA Derived from the Latin *camilla* (virgin of unblemished character). Var: Camille. Short: Cami, Camie. Pet: Millie, Milly. (KAH-MIL-LAH)

CANADA Borrowed from the name of the country to the north of the U.S. It is from the Iroquois Indian *caneadea* (where the heavens rest upon the earth, horizon). (KAN-AH-DAH)

CANDACE Derived from the Latin *candidus* (white, pure, sincere). Var: Candice, Candyse, Kandace, Kandice. Pet: Candi, Candie, Candy, Kandi, Kandie, Kandy. (KAN-DUS)

CAREY Originally a pet form of Caroline (full-grown), Carey is now commonly bestowed as an independent given name and is often confused with the Irish Kerry (black-haired one). The name is now also used as a pet form of the various names beginning with the element *Car-*. Var: Carri, Carrie, Kari, Karrie. (KAR-REE)

CARISSA Italian elaboration of Cara (beloved, dear). Var: Carrissa. Short: Cari, Carie, Carri, Carrie, Rissa. (KAH-RIS-SAH)

CARLA Feminine form of Carl and Charles, both of which are derived from the Old English *ceorl* (man, freeman, peasant). Var: Karla. Pet: Carley, Carli, Carly, Karley, Karli, Karly. (KAR-LAH)

CARLANA Elaborated form of Carla. *See* CARLA. (KAR-LAN-AH)

CARLIE A pet form of Carla (a freeman, peasant, full-grown), Carlie is also bestowed as an independent given name. *See* CARLA. Var: Carleigh, Carley, Carli, Carly. (KAR-LEE)

CARMEN Spanish cognate of Carmel (vineyard, orchard). *See* CARMEN (Spanish Names). Var: Carman, Carmon. (KAR-MEN)

CAROL Feminine form of the Latin Carolus, which is a cognate of Charles (full-grown, a man, a freeman), and a short form of Caroline, another feminine form of Carolus. Alternatively, the name is derived from *carol* (joyous song, a carol). Var: Carole, Carrol, Carroll, Carryl, Caryl. (KARE-OL, KARE-UL)

CAROLINE Feminine form of the Latin Carolus, which is a cognate of Charles (full-grown, a man, a freeman). *See* CHARLES (English Male Names). Var: Carolyn, Karoline, Karolyn. Short: Carey, Cari, Carri, Carrie, Kari, Karrie. (KARE-O-LINE, KARE-O-LIN)

CARTER Transferred use of the English surname that originated in the Middle Ages as an occupational name for someone who used a cart to transport goods. (KAR-TER)

CASEY Variant form of Cassie, which is a pet form of Cassandra. *See* CASSANDRA. Var: Casi, Kasey, Kasi, Kayci, Kayse. (KAY-SEE)

CASSANDRA Derived from the Greek Kassandra, the mythological daughter of Priam and Hecuba who had the power of prophecy. Var: Casaundra, Kasandra, Kassandra, Kasaundra. Short: Cass, Kass, Sandra, Saundra. Pet: Cassi, Cassie, Cassy, Kassi, Kassie, Sandi, Sandie, Sandy. (KA-SAN-DRA)

CASSIDY Transferred use of the surname derived from the Irish surname O'Caiside, which is of uncertain meaning. One historian believes it is derived from the Gaelic element *cas* (a twisted lock of hair; ingenious, clever, sly) and the personal suffix *-idhe*: hence, "clever one, one with the twisted locks." Or from the Gaelic element *cais* (love, esteem) and the plenary suffix *-de*: hence, "full of love and esteem." Short: Cass. Pet: Cassi, Cassie, Cassy. (KAS-SIH-DEE)

CELESTE Derived from the French *céleste*, which is from the Latin *caelestis* (celestial, heavenly). Var: Celestia. (SEH-LEST)

CHANDA Modern coinage derived from the popular element *Chan-*. Var: Chandah. (CHANDA, SHANDA)

CHANDELLE Derived from the French *chandelle* (candle). Var: Chandell, Shandell, Shandelle. Short: Chan, Shan. (SHAHN-DEL)

CHANDLER Transferred use of the English surname that arose as an occupational name for a maker or dealer of candles. The name is derived from the Middle English *chaundler, candeler*. (CHAND-LER)

CHANDRA Sanskrit name that means "illustrious, eminent." Var: Chandrah. Short: Chan. (CHAN-DRAH)

CHANTAL French name derived from the Old Provençal *cantal* (stone; boulder). Var: Chantall, Chantel, Chantelle. Short: Chan. (SHAHN-TAHL)

CHAPLIN Transferred use of the surname derived from the Middle English and Old French *chapelain* (chantry priest, the priest was the priest who sang the daily mass). The name originated as an occupational name for a chantry priest or for those who worked for chantry priests. Var: Chapelin, Chapelyn, Chaplyn. (CHAP-LIN)

CHARISMA Modern name derived from *charisma* (an inspiring personality). (KAH-RIZ-MAH)

CHARISSA Derived from the Greek *kharis* (grace). Short: Rissa. (KAH-RIS-SAH)

CHARLENE 20th-century coinage used as a feminine form of Charles (full-grown, a man, a freeman): hence, "a woman." Var: Charlayne, Cherlene, Cherline, Sharlayne, Sharleen, Sharlene. Pet: Charli, Charlie. (SHAR-LEEN)

CHARNEY Transferred use of the English surname meaning "from Charney, from the island in the Charn River." (CHAR-NEE)

CHASTITY Derived from *chastity* (modesty, purity, virtuousness). (CHAS-TIH-TEE)

CHELSEA Borrowed from the name of a London borough on the northern bank of the Thames. Var: Chelsie. (CHEL-SEE)

CHER Short form of Cheryl and its variant forms. (SHARE)

CHERILYNN Combination name formed from the names Cheryl and Lynn. *See* CHERYL *and* LYNN. Var: Cherilin. (SHARE-EL-LIN)

CHERYL 20th-century coinage perhaps formed by combining names such as Cherry and Beryl. Var: Cherelle, Cheril, Cherril, Cherrill, Sharel, Sherill, Sherril, Sherryl, Sheryll. (SHARE-EL)

CHESNA Slavic name meaning "peaceful." Pet: Chessy. (CHEZ-NAH)

CHEYENNE Derived from the Dakota Indian *shaiyena* which is from *shaia* (to speak unintelligibly). The name is that of a tribe of Algonquian Indians, as well as a river and city name. Var: Shaienne, Shai'enne. (SHY-AN, SHY-EN)

CHRISTINA Derived from the Ecclesiastic Late Latin *christiānus*, which is from the Ecclesiastic Greek *christianos* (a Christian, a follower of Christ). Var: Christiene, Christine, Cristina, Khristina, Khristine, Kristina, Kristene. Short: Chris, Cris, Khris, Kris, Tina. Pet: Chrissi, Chrissie, Chrissy, Christi, Christie, Christy, Cristi, Cristie, Cristy, Khristi, Khristie, Khristy, Krissy, Kristi, Kristie, Kristy. (KRIS-TEE-NAH)

CIARA Irish name derived from *ciar* (black): hence, "black-haired one." In the U.S., Ciara is pronounced phonetically, rather than with its Gaelic pronunciation of *keer-ah*. (SEE-AR-AH)

CICELY Variant form of Cecilia (blind, dim-sighted). *See* CECILIA (English Names). (SIS-AH-LEE)

CINNABAR Borrowed from the name of the bright red mineral. The name is thought to be derived from the Persian *šangarf* (red lead, cinnabar). Var: Cynnabar. (SIN-AH-BAR)

CLARICE Elaboration of Clara, a name derived from the Latin *clārus* (bright, clear, famous). Var: Clarissa, Clarisse, Klarissa, Klarrissa, Klarrissia. (KLAH-REES)

COLLEEN Derived from the Irish *colleen* (a girl, a lass). The name is not used in Ireland and seems to have originated in the United States. Var: Collene, Kolleen, Kollene. (KOL-LEEN)

CORAL Derived from *coral*, which refers to the pinkish calcareous skeletons secreted by marine polyps and used in jewelry making. Var: Koral. (KOR-AL)

CORINNA Derived from the Greek Korinna, a derivative of Korē (maiden). Var: Corinne, Korinna, Korinne. Pet: Cori, Corrie, Kori. (KO-RIN-NAH)

COURTNEY Transferred use of the French surname meaning "from Courtenay [in northern France]." The name, originally bestowed upon both males and females, is now more commonly given to girls. (KORT-NEE)

COZETTE Modern coinage perhaps based on *cozy* (comfortable, warm, snug). (KO-ZET)

CRICKET Originally a pet name for Christine, Cricket is now usually bestowed as an independent given name, often in reference to the cricket insect. (KRIK-ET)

CROSBY Transferred use of the surname derived from the Old Norse *kross* (cross) and *býr* (farm): hence, "dweller at the farm near the cross." Alternatively, the name is from the Irish Mac and Chrosáin, which is from the Gaelic *crosán* (satirist). Var: Crosbi, Crosbie, Crozbie, Krosbie, Krozbie. (KROZ-BE)

Crystal 19th-century coinage derived from *crystal*, which denotes very clear, brilliant glass, or a clear, transparent quartz. Var: Cristal, Cristell, Crystell, Krystal. (KRIS-TEL)

Daisy Derived from the name of the daisy flower, which is derived from the Old English *dæges eage* (day's eye: in reference to its round yellow center resembling the sun). (DAY-ZEE)

Dana Transferred use of the surname, which is of uncertain origin. It might have arisen as a feminine form of Dan, a Hebrew name meaning "judge." The name was popularized by Richard Dana (1815–82), author of *Two Years Before the Mast*. Var: Dayna. (DAY-NAH)

Danacia Modern coinage of uncertain derivation. It possibly originated as a blending of the names of the parents or relatives of a child. (DAN-AH-SEE-AH)

Danae Derived from the Greek Danaē (the parched or dry one). The name is borne in Greek mythology by a daughter of Acrisius, and mother of Perseus by Zeus, who visited her in the form of a golden shower when she was shut in a tower by her father. Var: Danea, Denae, Dené. Pet: Dani, Danie. (DAH-NAY)

Danean Modern coinage that possibly arose as the combining of elements from parents' or relatives' names. Var: Dineen. Pet: Dani, Danie. (DAH-NEEN)

Danell Modern coinage that is a possible variant of Danielle, a feminine form of Daniel (God is my judge). Var: Da'Nell, Danella. Pet: Dani, Danie. (DAH-NEL)

Danette Modern feminine form of Dan, a name derived from the Hebrew *dān* (judge), or a short form of Daniel (God is my judge). Var: Dannette. Pet: Dani, Danie, Danni, Dannie. (DAH-NET)

Danielle Feminine form of Daniel (God is my judge). *See* DANIEL (Male Names). Var: Daniela, Daniella, Danniella, Dannielle. Pet: Dani, Danie. (DAN-YEL)

Darah Modern coinage perhaps modeled after the name Sarah. (DAR-AH, DAH-RAH)

Darby Anglicized form of the masculine Irish name Diarmaid (without injunction, a freeman). (DAR-BEE)

Darcy Transferred use of the surname originating as the baronial name D'Arcy (from Arcy, a place in La Manche, Normandy). Var: Darcey, Darcie, Darsee. (DAR-SEE)

Darenda Modern name of uncertain derivation. It might have been coined from name elements of parents or relatives of the child, or modeled after the name Brenda. Var: Derenda. (DAH-REN-DAH)

Darla Thought to have originated as a variant of Darlene (darling). *See* DARLENE. (DAR-LAH)

Darlene Modern coinage based on the endearment "darling." (DAR-LEEN)

Darlonna Modern name perhaps coined from elements of names such as Darlene and Donna. (DAR-LON-NAH)

Darren Modern name of uncertain origin and meaning. It might have been coined as a variation of Darrell or as a combination of a child's parents' names, such as Darrell and Karen. Var: Darin, Darryn, Deran, Derren, Derryn. (DARE-UN)

Darsell Modern coinage, perhaps influenced by the name Darcy (from Arcy). Var: Darcel, Darcell, Darcella, Darcelle, Darsele, Darsella, Darselle. (DAR-SEL)

Dawn Derived from *dawn*, which is from the Middle English *dauninge* (daybreak, dawn). (DAWN, DON)

Deandra Modern coinage formed by using the popular prefix *De-* and the name Andra (womanly). Var: De Andra. Short: Dee. (DEE-AN-DRAH)

Deanna Originally used as a variant of Diana (divine), Deanna is now commonly used as a feminine form of Dean or as a combination of the names Dee and Anna. *See* DEAN (English Male Names), ANNA, *and* DEE. Var: Deeanna. Short: Dee. (DEE-AH-NAH)

Deborah Derived from the Hebrew *devōrāh* (a bee, a swarm of bees). The name is borne in the Bible by a prophetess and judge who led the Israelites to victory over the Canaanites. Var: Debora, Debra. Short: Deb. Pet: Debbi, Debbie, Debby, Debi, Debie, Deby. (DEB-AH-RAH, DEH-BOR-AH)

Delaney Transferred use of the Irish surname derived from the Gaelic O'Dubhshláine, which is of uncertain meaning. *See* DELANEY (Male Names). Var: Delainea. Short: Laney, Lanie. (DAH-LANE-EE)

Delicia Derived from the Latin *deliciae* (delight). Var: Daleesha, Dalicia, Dalisia, Deleesha, Delesia, Delisia. (DEH-LEE-SHA)

Demi Derived from *demi* (half, not full-sized). The name was popularized by actress Demi Moore. (DEH-MEE)

Denell Modern coinage formed by the addition of the prefix *De-* to the name Nell, which is a short form of names containing *nell* as an element. Var: Denelle. (DEH-NEL)

DENISE Feminine form of Dennis, which is an English cognate of the Greek Dionysios (a follower of the god Dionysos). Var: Daneece, Danice, Denice, Deniece, Deniese, Denyse, De Nyse. (DAH-NEES)

DESTINY Derived from *destiny* (fate). (DES-TIH-NEE)

DEVON A borrowing of the Irish male name derived from the Gaelic *dámh* (a poet). Var: Devan, Devin, Devyn. (DEH-VUN)

DIANA Derived from the Latin Diviana, which is from *divus* (divine). The name is borne in Roman mythology by the virgin goddess of the moon and of hunting. Var: Diane, Dianna, Dianne, Dionne, Dyan, Dyana, Dyann, Dyanna, Dyanne. Short: Di. (DĪ-AN-NAH)

DIXIE Borrowed from the term that denotes the southern states of the U.S., especially those that made up the Confederacy. Dixie was popularized as a given name in the 19th century by an 1859 minstrel song by D. D. Emmett, which became a Confederate war song. Var: Dixy. (DIKS-EE)

DONNA Modern coinage used as a feminine form of Donald (world ruler) or as a name derived from the Italian *donna* (lady). Var: D'onna. (DON-NAH)

DONYA Modern coinage, perhaps an elaboration of the name Donna or a feminine form of the male name Don. *See* DONALD (English Male Names). Var: Dania. (DON-YAH)

DOREEN Variant form of Dora, a name composed from the Greek *dōron* (gift) and the Irish diminutive suffix *-een*. Var: Dorine. (DOR-EEN)

DREW Transferred use of the male Drew, a short form of Andrew (manly). The name was popularized as a female name by actress Drew Barrymore. (DROO)

EDEN Derived from the Hebrew *'ēdhen* (delight). The Garden of Eden was the name of the paradise where Adam and Eve lived before eating from the Tree of Knowledge. (EE-DEN)

EGYPT Borrowed from the northeastern African country of Egypt, which is famous for its Pyramids and its ancient culture. (EE-JIPT)

ELAINE Variant form of Helen, which is derived from the Greek Helenē, the root of which is *ēlē* (light, torch, bright). Elaine is popularly bestowed as a middle name. Var: Elaina. (EE-LANE)

ELISA A short form of Elisabeth (God is my oath), Elisa is also bestowed as an independent given name. *See* ELISABETH. Var: Elise, Eliza. (EL-LEE-SAH)

ELISABETH Derived from the Hebrew *elīsheba'* (God is my oath). The name is borne in the Bible by the mother of John the Baptist. Var: Elizabeth. Short: Beth, Elisa, Elise, Eliza, Lisa, Lisabeth, Liz, Liza, Lizabeth. Pet: Betsy, Betty, Ellie, Elsie, Lizzie, Lizzy. (EH-LIZ-AH-BETH, EE-LIZ-AH-BETH)

ELLEN Originally a variant form of Helen, Ellen is now also commonly used as a variant of Eleanor. Both names, however, are ultimately derived from the same Greek root, *ēlē* (light, torch, bright). Var: Ellyn. Pet: Ellie, Nel, Nellie, Nelly. (EL-LEN)

EMILY From the Latin Aemilia, a derivative of Aemilius, an old Roman family name believed to be derived from *aemulus* (trying to equal or excel, emulating, rival). Var: Emilee, Emili. Pet: Emi, Emie, Emmie, Emmy. (EM-IH-LEE)

EMMYLOU Combination name composed of the names Emmy and Lou. *See* EMILY *and* LOUIS (English Male Names). (EM-MEE-LOO)

ENFINITY Modern coinage based on *infinity* (endless, unending). (EN-FIN-IH-TEE)

ERICA Feminine form of Eric (eternal ruler). *See* ERIC (Male Names). Var: Erika. (ERR-IH-KAH)

ERIN Derived from the Gaelic Érinn, the dative case of Érie, which is the Irish name for Ireland. (ERR-IN)

FAITH Derived from *faith*, which denotes unquestioning belief and complete trust in God. The word has its root in the Latin *fides* (confidence, belief). (FAITH)

FALLON From the Irish surname O'Fallamhain (descendant of Fallamhan). Fallamhan is from the Gaelic *follamhnus* (supremacy). Var: Fallan, Fallyn. (FAL-LUN)

FAUNA Derived from *fauna*, which denotes the animals of a specified time or area. (FAU-NAH)

FAWN Derived from *fawn* (a baby deer). Var: Fawna, Fawnah, Fawniah. (FAWN)

FAYE Believed to be derived from the Middle English *faie* (fairy). It is more commonly bestowed as a middle name. (FAY)

FELICIA Derived from *felicity* (good fortune, happiness), which has its root in the Latin *felicitas* (happiness). (FEH-LEE-SHA)

GAIL Originally a short form of Abigail (father of exaltation), Gail is now commonly used as an independent given name. Var: Gayle. (GALE)

GENEVA Of disputed origin, Geneva might be a borrowing of the name of a city and lake in Switzerland, which is derived from the Old French *genevre* (juniper berry). Alternatively, it might have originated as a diminutive form of Genevieve. *See* GENEVIEVE (English Names) Var: Janiva. (JEN-EE-VAH, JEN-EE-VAH)

GEORGEANNE Combination name composed from the male name George and Anne. *See* GEORGE (Male Names) *and* ANNE. Var: Georgieanne (JORJ-AN; JORJ-EE-AN)

GEORGIA Latinate feminine form of George (earth-worker, farmer). *See* GEORGE (English Male Names). (JOR-JAH)

GERALDINE Feminine form of Gerald (spear ruler). *See* GERALD (English Male Names). Pet: Geri, Gerry. (JER-AL-DEEN)

GERALYN Modern combination name formed from the names Geri and Lynn. *See* GERI *and* LYNN. (JER-AH-LIN)

GERI A pet form of any of the names beginning with the element *Ger-*, Geri is also bestowed as an independent given name. Var: Gerry. (JER-EE)

GINA Originally a short form of Georgina (earth-worker, farmer), Gina is now used as an independent given name. Var: Geena. (JEE-NAH)

GINGER Originally a nickname for someone with red hair, Ginger is now sometimes used as a diminutive form of Virginia (spring-like, flourishing). Pet: Ginni, Ginnie, Ginny. (JIN-JER)

GINNY Pet form of various names containing the element *gin*. Var: Ginni, Ginnie. (JIN-NEE)

GISELLE German name derived from *gisil* (to owe, a pledge, a mutual obligation). It was a practice in the early Middle Ages for rival factions to offer a person, often a child, to each other as a pledge of peace. Var: Gisele. (JIH-ZEL)

GLORIA Derived from the Latin *glōria* (glory). The name was not used as a given name until the 20th century, when it was used for the name of a character in George Bernard Shaw's play *You Never Can Tell* (1898). (GLOR-EE-AH)

GLORIANA Elaborated form of Gloria (glory). *See* GLORIA. (GLOR-EE-AN-NAH)

GOLDIE Derived from *gold*, which denotes a precious metal used in jewelry making and currency. (GOLD-EE)

HALLEY Transferred use of the English surname meaning "dweller at the hall meadow." The name is derived from the Old English elements *heall* (hall, gathering place) and *lēah* (wood, meadow, clearing). Var: Hallie, Hally. (HAL-EE)

HARPER Transferred use of the surname derived from the Middle English *harp* (a harp), which arose as an occupational name for a harp player.

HAYDEN Transferred use of the English surname derived from several place-names. It is from the Old English elements *hēg* (hay) and *denu* (valley); *hēg* (hay) and *dun* (hill); and *hege* (hedge) and *dun* (hill). Alternatively, the name is from the Irish Gaelic ÓhÉideáin and ÓhÉidín (descendant of Eideán or Éidín). The names are derived from *éideadh* (clothing). Var: Haydan, Haydin, Haydun, Haydyn. (HAY-DUN)

HAYLEY Transferred use of a Northern English surname, which is a derivative of Hale or Hales (residing in a nook, recess, or remote valley). It has also been suggested that Hayley derives from the place-name Hailey, which is composed of the Old English elements *hēg* (hay) and *lēah* (wood, clearing, meadow). Var: Haley, Haylie. (HAY-LEE)

HEATHER Taken from the name of the plant having very small scale-like leaves and purplish-pink flowers. The word is derived from the Old English *haddyr* (heather, plants of the heath family). (HEH-THER)

HILARY Taken from the Latin Hilaria, which is derived from *hilaris* (cheerful, noisy, merry). Var: Hillary. (HIL-AH-REE)

HOLLIS Transferred use of the English surname meaning "dweller at the holly trees." It is derived from the Old English *holegn* (holly tree). (HAHL-ISS)

HOLLY Taken from the name of the holly tree, an evergreen whose stiff, glossy, sharp-pointed leaves and clusters of red berries are used in Christmas decorations. The name is derived from the Old English *holegn* (holly tree). Var: Hollee, Holli, Hollie. (HAHL-EE)

HOPE Derived from *hope*, which is derived from the Old English *hopa* (expectation, hope, wish). (HOPE)

HUNTER Transferred use of the surname derived from the Middle English *hunte* (a hunter, a sportsman). (HUN-TER)

INDIA Borrowed from the name of the country. (IN-DEE-AH)

IONIA Taken from the name of an ancient region in western Asia Minor colonized by the Greeks in the 11th century B.C. (Ī-O-NEE-AH)

Isabelle A spanish variant form of Elisabeth (God is my oath). *See* ISABELA (Spanish Names). Var: Isabell, Isabella. Short: Bell, Bella, Belle. Pet: Izzie. (IZ-AH-BEL)

Ivy Taken from the name of the plant, which is an evergreen climbing vine of the ginseng family. The word is derived from the Old English *ifig* (climber). (Ī-VEE)

Jackie A pet form of Jacqueline and its variants, Jackie is also bestowed as an independent given name, often as a feminine form of Jack. *See* JACK (Male Names). Var: Jacki, Jacqui, Jacquie. (JAK-EE)

Jacqueline A borrowing from the French, Jacqueline is a feminine form of Jacques, which is a cognate of James and Jacob (seizing by the heel, supplanting). *See* JACOB *and* JAMES (Male Names). Var: Jacklin, Jacklyn, Jaclyn, Jacquelyn, Jaquelyn. Pet: Jacki, Jackie, Jacqui, Jacquie. (JAK-WEH-LIN)

Jade Taken from the name of the hard, green or white jadeite or nephrite stone. The word came to the English via the French, from the Spanish *piedra de ijada* (stone of the side: from the belief that it could cure pains in the side). (JADE)

Jamie Feminine form of James (supplanting, seizing by the heel). *See* JAMES (Male Names). (JAY-MEE)

Janae Modern coinage probably based on the name Danae. Var: Janea, Jenae, Jenea, Jenee. (JAH-NAY)

Jane English cognate of the French Jehanne and Jeanne, which are feminine forms of Jean, a cognate of John (God is gracious). *See* JOHN (Male Names). The name was popularized by movies based on E. R. Burroughs' *Tarzan of the Apes*. Jane is the name of the woman who is captured by Tarzan. Var: Jayne. Pet: Janee, Janey, Janie, Jaynie. (JANE)

Janelle Modern coinage combining Jane with the feminine suffix *-elle*. Var: Janel, Janele, Janella, Jenelle, Jennell. Short: Jan, Jen. Pet: Jenni, Jennie, Jenny, Nelli, Nellie, Nelly. (JAH-NEL)

Janet Diminutive form of Jane (God is gracious) that has been in use since the Middle Ages. Var: Ja'net, Janette, Jannette. Short: Jan. (JAN-ET)

Janey A pet form of Jane (God is gracious), Janey is also bestowed as an independent given name. *See* JANE. Var: Janee, Janie, Jaynie. (JAY-NEE)

Janice Modern variant of Jane (God is gracious). *See* JANE. Var: Janessa, Janiece, Janis, Jeanice, Jeneesa, Jenise. (JA-NIS, JAH-NEES)

Jasmine Taken from the name of the tropical plant having colorful, fragrant flowers used in perfumes and teas. The word is derived from the Persian *yāsamīn* (jasmine). Var: Jasmin, Jasmyn, Jazmin, Jazmine, Jazmyn. (JAZ-MIN)

Jatana Modern coinage of uncertain derivation. (JAH-TAN-NAH)

Javonna Modern coinage of uncertain derivation. Var: Javona, Javonnah. (JAH-VON-NAH)

Jaylene Modern coinage formed by combining the names Jay and the element *lene*. (JAY-LEEN)

Jean English cognate of the French Jeanne, which is a feminine form of Jean (God is gracious), a cognate of John. Jean is a popular middle name. Pet: Jeanie, Jeannie. (JEEN)

Jeanette From the French Jeannette, a diminutive form of Jeanne (God is gracious). Var: Genette, Janette, Jenett, Jenette. Short: Jan, Jen, Jean. Pet: Jeannie, Jenni, Jennie, Jenny, Netti, Nettie. (JEH-NET)

Jenessa Modern coinage formed from the name Jen. Short: Jen, Nessa. Pet: Jenni, Jennie, Jenny. (JEH-NES-SAH)

Jennara Modern coinage possibly influenced by the name Gennaro (January, of Janus). See GENNARO (Italian Male Names). (JEH-NAR-RAH)

Jennifer Cornish derivation of Guinevere, which is from the Welsh Gwenhwyfar (fair lady). *See* GUINEVERE (English Names). Until the 20th century, Jennifer was largely a name common only to Cornwall. Var: Gennifer, Ginnifer, Jenifer, Jinnifer. Short: Jen. Pet: Genni, Gennie, Genny, Ginni, Ginnie, Ginny, Jenni, Jennie, Jenny, Jinni, Jinnie, Jinny. (JEN-IH-FER)

Jenny A pet form of various names beginning with the element *Jen-*, Jenny is also bestowed as an independent given name. Var: Jenna, Jenni, Jennie. Short: Jen. (JEN-NEE)

Jerri A feminine form of Jerry, a male pet form originating from any of the various names containing the element *Jer-*. Var: Jerrie. (JER-ree)

Jerrilynn Modern combination of the names Jerri and Lynn. *See* JERRI *and* LYNN. Var: Jerrilinn, Jerrilyn, Jerrylynn, Jerylynn. (JER-REE-LIN)

Jessica A name of uncertain origin and meaning. *See* JESSICA (English Names). Var: Jesica, Jesseca. Short: Jess. Pet: Jessi, Jessie. (JES-IH-KAH)

Jessie Originated as a pet form of Janet and Jean. Now, however, it is more commonly used as a feminine form of Jesse, which is derived from the Hebrew *yīshai* (gift), and as a pet form of Jessica. Var: Jessi, Jessy. Short: Jess. (JES-SEE)

JILL Originally a short form of Jillian, which is a variant of Julian (downy-bearded, youth), Jill is now commonly bestowed as an independent given name. *See* JULIAN (English Male Names). (JIL)

JOANNA Middle Latin feminine form of Joannes (God is gracious). *See* JOHN (Male Names). Var: Joann, Jo Ann, Jo Anna, Joanne, Jo Anne. (JO-AN-NAH)

JOCEILE Modern coinage made by combining name elements. Short: Jo. (JO-SEEL)

JOREEN Modern coinage of uncertain derivation. Var: Joreene. Pet: Jorie. (JOR-EEN)

JOSETTE Borrowed from the French, Josette is a diminutive form of Josée (God will add). See JOSÉE (French Names). Var: Joset, Jozette. Pet: Joey, Josee, Josie, Jozie. (JO-SET)

JOVANNA Possibly based on the Italian Giovanna (God is gracious) or Joviana (Jove, Jupiter). *See* GIOVANNA *and* JOVIANA (Italian Names). Var: Jovannah. Short: Jo, Vanna, Vannah. (JO-VAH-NAH)

JUNE Taken from the name of the sixth month, June was first bestowed as a given name in the 20th century. It is derived from the Latin Juno, the Roman mythological goddess of marriage and queen of the gods. (JOON)

JUNIPER Taken from the name of a small evergreen shrub bearing berries used in flavoring gin. (JOO-NIH-PER)

KAIYA Modern coinage of uncertain derivation. Var: Kaiah, Kaija, Kya. (KĪ-YA)

KAMI A pet form of Kamilla, Kami is also bestowed as an independent given name. *See* CAMILLA. (KAM-EE)

KANESSA Modern coinage based on Vanessa. *See* VANESSA (English Names). (KAH-NES-SAH)

KARAS Variant of the Greek Charis, which is derived from *charis* (grace, beauty, kindness). (KARE-US, KAR-US)

KAREN Danish form of Katherine, which is derived from the Greek Aikaterinē, the root of which is *katharos* (pure, unsullied). Var: Caren, Carin, Karena, Karin, Karrin, Karyn. (KARE-EN)

KATIE A pet form of Katherine (pure, unsullied), Katie is also bestowed as an independent given name. Var: Kady, Kati, Katey, Katy. (KAY-TEE)

KAY Originated as a pet form of any of the various names beginning with the letter K. Var: Kaye. (KAY)

KAYLEEN Modern coinage combining the name Kay with the name element *-leen*. *See* KAY. Var: Kaylene. (KAY-LEEN)

KAYLEY Transferred use of the Anglicized Irish surname, which is from the Gaelic Mac Caollaidhe (son of Caollaidhe) and O'Caollaidhe (descendant of Caollaidhe). The name is derived from *caol* (slender). Var: Kailee, Kaili, Kali, Kayla, Kaylea, Kaylee, Kayleigh. (KAY-LEE)

KAYLYNN Modern coinage combining the names Kay and Lynn. *See* LYNN *and* KAY. Var: Kailyn, Kailynn, Kaylin, Kaylinn. (KAY-LIN)

KEILYN Modern coinage of uncertain derivation. Var: Keelin, Keelyn, Keilinn, Keilynn, Keylinn, Keylyn, Keylynn. (KEY-LIN)

KELLY Transferred use of the Irish surname meaning "war, strife" or the transferred use of English place-names derived from the Cornish *celli* (wood, grove). *See* KELLY (English Names). Var: Kelee, Kelley, Kelli, Kellie. (KEL-EE)

KELSEY Derived from the obsolete Old English name Cēolsige, a compounding of the elements *cēol* (a ship) and *sige* (victory). (KEL-SEE)

KENDALL Transferred use of the English surname derived from a place-name in northwestern England. It has its root in the Old Norse *keld* (spring). Var: Kendal, Kendell. (KEN-DAL)

KENDRA Feminine form of the English Kendrick. *See* KENDRICK (English Male Names). Var: Kendrah. (KEN-DRA)

KENNA Feminine form of Ken, which is a short form of various names beginning with the element *Ken-*. (KEN-NAH)

KENNEDY Anglicized form of the Irish Cinnéidid (helmeted head, ugly head). Var: Kennedee, Kennidy. Pet: Dee, Kenny. (KEN-NIH-DEE)

KERRY Transferred use of an Irish place-name, which is now in common use as a girl's given name. Alternatively, Kerry is an Anglicized form of the Gaelic Ciardha (black-haired one). Var: Keri. (KARE-EE)

KIANNA Modern coinage likely influenced by the name Diana (divine). Var: Keeana, Kiana, Kianah. (KEE-AH-NAH, KEE-AN-NAH)

KIERCE Modern coinage of uncertain derivation. (KEERSS)

KILEY Transferred use of the Irish surname, which is a variant of O'Kiely. The name is from the Gaelic

O'Cadhla (descendant of Cadhla), which is from *cadhla* (graceful, beautiful). (KĪ-LEE)

KIM Originally a short form of Kimberely, Kim is also bestowed as an independent given name. *See* KIMBERELY (English Names). (KIM)

KIMBERLEY A name of debated origin. *See* KIMBERELY (English Names). Var: Kimberlee, Kimberly. Short: Kim. Pet: Kimmi, Kimmie, Kimmy. (KIM-BER-LEE)

KIRA A borrowing from the Greek, Kira is a feminine form of Kyros (a lord, a master). (KEER-AH)

KRISLYN Modern coinage formed from the names Kris and Lynn. *See* CHRISTINA *and* LYNN. (KRIS-LIN)

KYLA Feminine form of Kyle (a narrow channel). *See* KYLE (Male Names). Var: Kylie. (KĪ-LAH)

KYLE Transferred use of the Scottish surname that originated from the region of the same name in southwestern Scotland. Kyle, a topographical term referring to a narrow, straight channel, is derived from the Gaelic *caol* (narrow, a sound, a strait). (KILE)

LACY Transferred use of the English surname meaning "belonging to Lacy or Lassy." The name, derived from several French place-names, was brought to England by companions of William during the Norman Conquest. Var: Lacey. (LAY-SEE)

LA DAWN Modern coinage combining the popular prefix *La-* with the name Dawn. *See* DAWN. Var: Ladawn, Ladawna. (LAH-DAWN)

LANA Short form of Alana, which is a feminine form of Alan. The name is ultimately of uncertain meaning. *See* ALAN (English Male Names). (LAN-AH)

LANE Transferred use of the surname derived from the Old English *lane* (a lane, a narrow country road). (LANE)

LARISA A borrowing from the Russian, Larisa is a name of uncertain derivation. Some believe it to be derived from the name of the ancient city of Thessaly; others feel it might be derived from the Latin *hilaris* (cheerful). Var: Laressa, Larissa. (LAH-RIH-SAH, LAH-REE-SAH)

LARK Taken from the name of a type of small songbird, Lark is derived from the Middle English *larke, laverke* (lark). (LARK)

LA TASHA Modern coinage combining the prefix *La-* with the name Tasha, a Russian pet form of the name Natalie. *See* NATALIYA (Russian Names). Var: Latasha. Short: Tasha. (LAH-TAH-SHA)

LAURA Derived from the Latin *laurus* (laurel). In ancient Greece, the leaves from the laurel bush were woven into wreaths to crown the winners of various contests. Var: Lora. Pet: Lauri, Laurie, Lori, Lorie. (LAU-RAH, LOR-AH)

LAURALEE Modern combination name formed from the names Laura and Lee. *See* LAURA *and* LEE. Var: Lauralea, Lauraleigh, Loralee, Loralea, Loraleigh. (LAU-RAH-LEE, LOR-AH-LEE)

LAURALYNN Modern combination name formed from the names Laura and Lynn. *See* LAURA *and* LYNN. Var: Lauralin, Loralin, Loralynn. (LAU-RAH-LIN, LOR-AH-LIN)

LAUREL Derived from the Latin *laurus* (laurel). The word denotes a type of evergreen shrub having glossy, aromatic leaves. Var: Lauriel. (LAU-REL, LOR-EL)

LAUREN English cognate of the French Laurence, a feminine form of Laurent, which is derived from the Latin Laurentius (man from Laurentum, a town in Latium). (LAU-REN, LOR-EN)

LAURENE Modern elaboration of Laura. *See* LAURA. (LAU-REEN, LOR-REEN)

LAVITA Modern coinage derived from the Latin *vita* (life). Var: Laveeda. (LAH-VEE-TAH)

LA VON Modern coinage probably based on the name Yvonne. (LAH-VON)

LAWN Derived from *lawn*, which denotes a manicured grassy area, especially those around houses, or a very fine, sheer cloth of linen or cotton. (LAWN)

LAZETTE Modern coinage of uncertain derivation. Var: Laizette. (LAH-ZET, LAY-ZET)

LEAH Derived from the Hebrew *lā'āh* (weary, to tire) or from *lē'āh* (wild cow, gazelle). The name is borne in the Bible by Jacob's first wife and mother of seven of his twelve children. Leah is also used as an alternative spelling of Lee. *See* LEE. (LEE-AH)

LEANNE Modern combination of the names Lee and Anne. Alternatively, the name is used as a variant spelling of Lianne (sun). *See* ANNE, LEE, *and* LIANE. Var: Leanna, Leeann, Lee Ann, Lee Anna, Lee Anne, Leighann. (LEE-AN)

LEE Transferred use of the surname derived from the Old English *lēah* (wood, clearing, meadow, enclosure): hence, "dweller near the wood or clearing." In Middle English, the spelling evolved to *leigh* and *legh*. Var: Lea, Leah, Leigh. (LEE)

Leisha Modern coinage of uncertain derivation. It is probably modeled after the name Keisha. Var: Leesha, Leeshah, Leeshia, Leishah. (LEE-SHA)

Lenice Modern coinage probably modeled after the name Denice. Var: La Neece, Laniece, La Neese, Le Neese. (LEH-NEES)

Liana Derived from the French *liana* (to bind, to wrap around). (LEE-AH-NAH, LEE-AN-NAH)

Liane English short form of the French Éliane (sun). *See* ÉLIANE (French Names). Var: Leanne, Liana, Lianna, Lianne. (LEE-AN)

Libby Originally a pet form of Elisabeth, Libby is now commonly bestowed as an independent given name. Var: Libbie. (LIB-EE)

Lindsay Taken from the old Scottish surname de Lindsay (from Lindsay). Lindsay, once a part of the county of Lincolnshire in northeastern England, is derived from Lincoln, a shortened form of Lindum Colonia, the first part of which is thought to be from the Welsh *llyn* (lake) and the second from the Latin *colonia* (colony, settlement). Var: Lynsey. Short: Lindie, Lindy, Linni, Linnie, Linny. (LIN-ZAY)

Lindsey Taken from the Old English surname Lindesie (from Lindsey), which is derived from a place-name composed of the Old English elements *lind* (the linden tree) and *ey* (wetland). Var: Lynsey. Short: Lindie, Lindy, Linni, Linnie, Linny. (LIN-ZEE)

Linnea A borrowing from the Scandinavian, Linnea was originally bestowed in honor of the Swedish botanist Karl von Linné (1707–78), who gave his name to the Linnaean system of classifying plants and animals. Var: Linea, Linnae, Linnaea, Lynnea. Pet: Linni, Linnie, Linny, Lynni, Lynnie. (LIN-NAY)

Lisa Originally a short form of Elisabeth (God is my oath), Lisa is now commonly bestowed as an independent given name. *See* ELISABETH. Var: Leesa, Leeza, Leezah, Leisa, Lisa. (LEE-SAH)

Lorraine Transferred use of the English surname originating from the name of a province in eastern France, which is derived from the Latin Lotharingia (territory of the people of Lothar). Lothar, the name of the son of the Frankish king Clovis, is of Germanic origin and is derived from the elements *hluod* (famous) and *hari, heri* (army): hence, "famous army." In the U.S., the name became popular after troops passed through this area during World War II. Var: Laraine, Larraine, Loraine, Lorayne. Pet: Lari, Larie, Lori, Lorie, Lorri, Lorrie. (LOR-RANE, LAH-RANE)

Lynette A name of several derivations. *See* LYNETTE (English Names). Var: Lanette, Linette, Linnette, Lynett, Lynnett, Lynnette, Lynnitte. Pet: Lynnie. (LIN-NET)

Lynn Transferred use of a British place-name derived from the Welsh *llyn* (lake). It is also thought to have originated as a short form of Lynnette, a name of several derivations, or of Linda (beautiful, tender). Alternatively, Lynn is a short form of the various names containing the element *lyn* or *line*. Var: Lin, Linn, Linne, Lynne. Pet: Lynnie. (LIN)

Lynnelle Modern coinage formed by the addition of the feminine suffix *-elle* to Lynn. *See* LYNN. Var: Lynnel. Pet: Lynnie. (LIN-NEL)

MacKenzie Transferred use of the Irish surname, which is from the Gaelic MacCoinnigh (son of Coinneach). Coinneach is derived from *cainneach* (fair one; handsome). Var: Mackenzie, Mckenzie, McKenzie. (MAH-KEN-ZEE)

Madeleine French cognate of Magdalene (of Magdala, a town on the coast of the Sea of Galilee). *See* MAGDALENE (Biblical Names). Var: Madeline, Madelyn. Pet: Maddi, Maddie, Maddy. (MAD-EH-LIN, MAD-EH-LINE)

Madison Transferred use of the English surname meaning "Mad's son." Mad was a common pet form of Matthew (gift of God) during the Middle Ages. Madison may also be a matronymic derived from the name Maud, an old pet form of Mathilda (battle mighty): hence, "son of Maud." Var: Maddison. (MAD-IH-SON)

Maggie A pet form of Magnolia and Margaret, Maggie is also bestowed as an independent given name. *See* MARGARET (English Names) *and* MAGNOLIA. Var: Maggi, Maggy. (MAG-EE)

Magnolia Taken from the name of the trees or shrubs of the magnolia family which bear large, fragrant flowers. Pet: Maggi, Maggie, Maggy. (MAG-NO-LEE-AH)

Mallory Transferred use of the English surname of French origin. It is derived from the Old French *maloret, maloré* (the unfortunate one, the unlucky one). Var: Mallery, Mallori. (MAL-O-REE)

Mandy A short form of Amanda (lovable), Mandy is also bestowed as an independent given name. *See* AMANDA. Var: Mandi, Mandie. (MAN-DEE)

Marcenya Modern coinage of uncertain derivation. (MAR-SEN-YAH)

MARCIA Feminine form of the Latin Marcius, a variant of Marcus, which is of debated meaning. *See* MARCUS (English Male Names). Var: Marsha. (MAR-SHA)

MARE Derived from *mare,* which denotes a female horse. Alternatively, Mare is used as a short form of Mary. *See* MARY. (MARE)

MARIA Latinate form of Mary. *See* MARY. (MAH-REE-AH)

MARIANNE Originated as an extended spelling of Marian, a variant of Marion, which is a French diminutive form of Marie, a cognate of Mary. It is now used as a hybrid, combining the names Mary and Anne. *See* ANNE *and* MARY. Var: Mariann, Marianna, Mary Ann, Mary Anna, Mary Anne. (MARE-EE-AN)

MARIE French cognate of Mary. *See* MARY. Marie is popularly chosen as a middle name. Var: Maree. (MAH-REE)

MARIEL A borrowing from the French, Mariel is a diminutive form of Marie, which is commonly used as an independent given name. *See* MARY. Var: Marielle, Merrial, Merrielle. (MARE-EE-EL)

MARILYN Modern compound name composed of the names Mary and Lynn. *See* LYNN *and* MARY. Var: Maralyn, Marilynn. (MARE-EH-LIN)

MARISSA Modern elaboration of Maria, formed by adding the suffix *-isa, -issa,* as in names such as Clarissa. *See* MARY. Var: Marisa. (MAH-RIS-SAH)

MARLA Contracted form of Marlene, which is a German contraction of Mary Magdalene. *See* MAGDALENE (English Names) *and* MARY. (MAR-LAH)

MARY Derived from the Hebrew Miryām, a name of debated meaning. Many believe it to mean "sea of bitterness" or "sea of sorrow." However, some sources cite the alternative definitions of "rebellion," "wished-for child," and "mistress or lady of the sea." The name is borne in the Bible by the mother of Jesus, the son of God. Var: Mari. (MARE-EE)

MASON Transferred use of the surname derived from *mason* (a person who builds with stone, brick, or concrete). The name arose as an occupational name in England in the 12th century. (MAY-SON)

MAXY Feminine form of Max, a short form of any of the masculine names beginning with the element *Max-*. Var: Maxi, Maxie. (MAX-EE)

MAY Originated as a pet form of Mary and Margaret. Modern usage of the name is usually in reference to the name of the fifth month, which is derived from the Latin *Maius* (the month of Maia). In Greek mythology, Maia is the name of the goddess of increase. Var: Mae. (MAY)

MEGAN A borrowing from the Welsh, Megan is a pet form of Marged, the Welsh cognate of Margaret (a pearl). *See* MARGARET (English Names). Var: Meagan, Meagen, Meaghan, Meggin, Meghan. (MEH-GAN, MAY-GAN)

MELANIE Derived from the Greek Melaina, which is from the root *melas* (black, dark). Var: Melanee, Melany, Mellony, Melony. Short: Mel. (MEL-AH-NEE)

MELISSA Derived from the Greek *melissa* (a bee). *See* MELISSA (English Names). Var: Melisah, Mellissa. (MEH-LIS-SAH)

MERRY Derived from *merry* (cheerful, happy, lighthearted). (MER-EE)

MERRYANNE Popular combination of the names Merry and Anne, which is modeled after the earlier Maryanne. *See* ANNE *and* MERRY. Var: Merryann, Merry Ann, Merry Anne. (MER-REE-AN)

MICHAELA Feminine form of Michael (who is like God?). *See* MICHAEL (Male Names). Var: Mickaela, Mickhala, Mikaela. Pet: Micki, Mickie, Miki, Mikie. (MIH-KAY-LAH)

MICHELLE Feminine form of the French Michel, a cognate of Michael (who is like God?). *See* MICHAEL (Male Names). Var: Mechelle, Me'shell, Michele, Michella, Mischelle, Mishelle. Short: Chelle, Shell, Shelle. Pet: Missy, Shelly. (MIH-SHEL)

MISHAILA Modern coinage based on the name Michelle (who is like God?). *See* MICHELLE. (MIH-SHAY-LAH, MEE-SHAY-LAH)

MISKAELA Modern coinage based on the name Michaela (who is like God?). *See* MICHAELA. Var: Meeskaela. (MIS-KAY-LAH, MEE-SKAY-LAH)

MISTY Modern coinage derived from *misty* (foggy, misty). The name first became popular during the 1960s and 1970s. Var: Mistee, Misti, Mistie. (MIS-TEE)

MOLLY Originally a pet form of Mary, Molly is now bestowed as an independent given name. *See* MARY. Var: Mollie. (MAH-LEE)

MONACO Borrowed from the name of the principality located off the coast of France. Var: Monico. (MON-AH-KO)

MONICA Ancient name of uncertain etymology. *See* MONICA (English Names). Var: Monicah, Monika. Monyca, Monyka. (MON-IH-KAH)

MONTANA Borrowed from the name of the state in the northwestern U.S. It is derived from the Latin *montana* (mountainous). (MON-TAN-AH)

MORGAN From the Old Welsh Morcant, a compound name thought to be composed of the elements *môr* (sea) and *cant* (circle, completion) or *can* (white, bright). (MOR-GAN)

MORIAH Hebrew name meaning "Jehovah is my teacher, God is my teacher." It is a borrowing of the name of a mountain where Abraham prepared to sacrifice his son Isaac. Var: Mariah, Meria, Meriah, Meriya, Moriya. (MO-RĪ-AH, MAH-RĪ-AH, MER-Ī-AH)

NADINE Elaboration of Nadia, the French form of the Russian Nadya (hope). Var: Nadeen, Nadeene. (NAY-DEEN)

NANCY Originated as a pet form of Nan, which originated as a pet form of Ann (gracious, full of grace). *See* ANNE. Now, however, Nancy is regarded as an independent given name, with Nan as its short form. Var: Nancee. Short: Nan, Nance. (NAN-SEE)

NEIDA Modern coinage, perhaps based on Nita. *See* ANITA. Var: Needa, Neeta. (NEE-DAH)

NEVADA Borrowed from the name of the western state, which is derived from the Spanish *nevada* (snowy). (NEH-VA-DAH, NEH-VAH-DAH)

NICOLE A borrowing from the French, Nicole is a feminine form of Nicolas (victory of the people). *See* NICHOLAS (Male Names). Var: Niccole, Nickole, Nicol, Nikkole, Nikole. Pet: Nicci, Nici, Nicki, Nickie, Nicky, Niki, Nikie, Nikki, Nikkie, Nikky. (NIH-KOLE)

NIKITA Russian form of Nicole (victory of the people). *See* NICOLE. Var: Nickita, Nikeeta, Nikkita, Niquita. (NIH-KEE-TAH)

NINA A borrowing from the Russian, Nina is a diminutive form of Anne (gracious, full of grace, mercy). *See* ANNE. Alternatively, Nina is also a borrowing from the Spanish, where it is used as a pet form of several names, such as Cristina. (NEE-NAH)

NISSA Modern coinage of uncertain derivation. (NIS-SAH)

NOEL Derived from the French *noël* (Christmas). The name is traditionally used for a child born during the Christmas season. (NO-EL)

OCEANA Modern coinage derived from *ocean* (the sea, the outer sea). (O-SHE-AN-NAH)

OLIVIA Elaboration of Olive (olive tree). Short: Liv. Pet: Livvi, Livvie, Livvy. (O-LIV-EE-AH)

ONEIDA Derived from the Iroquois Oneiute (standing rock), the name denotes a member of the Oneida tribe, who originally lived near Oneida Lake in New York State. (O-NĪ-DAH)

PACIFICA A borrowing from the Spanish, Pacifica is derived from the Latin Pacificus (to pacify, to make peace), which is from the root *pax* (peace). (PAH-SIH-FEE-KAH)

PAIGE Transferred use of the English surname derived from the Anglo-French *page* (a page, a boy attendant). (PAGE)

PARADISE Modern name derived from *paradise* (heaven, a place of perfection and great beauty), which is from the Ecclesiastic Late Latin *paradisus* (heaven, abode of the blessed). (PARE-AH-DĪS)

PARISH Transferred use of the surname meaning "dweller near the parish." The name is derived from the Middle English *parische* (parish, a church district). Var: Parrish. (PARE-ISH)

PATRICIA Derived from the Latin *patricius* (a patrician, an aristocrat). Short: Pat, Tricia. Pet: Patti, Patty. (PAH-TRISH-AH)

PAULA Feminine form of Paul (small). *See* PAUL (English Male Names). (PAUL-AH, POL-AH)

PAULETTE Feminine diminutive form of Paul (small). *See* PAUL (English Male Names). (PAUL-ET, POL-ET)

PAYTON Transferred use of the English surname, which is from the place-name Payton in Devon. The name is thought to be derived from the obsolete Anglo-Saxon personal name Pægan and the Old English *tūn* (town, settlement, village). Var: Peyton. (PAY-TUN)

PEARL Derived from *pearl,* which denotes the milky-colored gem that is formed inside certain oysters. (PURL)

PENNY Originally a pet form of Penelope, Penny is also bestowed as an independent given name. Its use in the U.S. is reinforced by the word *penny*, which refers to the one-cent coin. *See* PENELOPE (English Names). Var: Pennie. (PEN-NEE)

PEPPER Derived from the name of the pungent spice. The name is indicative of a lively personality. (PEP-PER)

PHILENE Feminine form of Phil, the short form of Philip (lover of horses). *See* PHILIP (Male Names). Var: Philean. (FIL-LEEN)

PIPER Transferred use of the surname of English and Scandinavian origin derived from the Old English *pīpere* (piper, one who plays the pipe) and the Old Norse *pípari* (piper, one who plays the pipe). The name was popularized by the fame of actress Piper Laurie. Var: Pyper. (PĪ-PER)

PRAIRIE Derived from *prairie* (a plain, a large grassland). (PRARE-EE)

QUINN Derived from the Irish surname O'Quinn, which is from the Gaelic O'Cuinn (descendant of Conn). The name is derived from *conn* (wisdom, reason, intelligence). (KWIN)

RACHEL Derived from the Hebrew *rāchēl* (ewe). The name is borne in the Bible by the younger of the two wives of Jacob. *See* RACHEL (Biblical Names). Var: Rachael, Racheal, Rachell, Rachelle, Rochell, Rochelle. (RAY-CHEL)

RAE Feminine form of Ray, which originated as a short form of Raymond. *See* RAYMOND (Male Names). Rae is a popular choice for a middle name and as an element in combination names. Var: Raye. (RAY)

RAIN Derived from *rain*, which denotes the water that falls to the earth. Var: Raine. Pet: Rainnie. (RANE)

RANDELLE Feminine form of Randall (wolf shield). *See* RANDALL (Male Names). (RAN-DEL)

RANIELLE Modern coinage apparently modeled after the name Danielle. (RAN-YEL)

RAQUEL A borrowing from the Spanish, Raquel is a cognate of Rachel (ewe). *See* RACHEL. The name was made popular through the fame of actress Raquel Welch. Var: Raquell. (RAH-KEL)

RAVEN Derived from *raven*, which denotes a large, black bird of the crow family. (RAY-VEN)

RAVENNA Either an elaborated form of Raven or a borrowing of the name of a northern Italian commune in Emilia-Romagna. (RAH-VEN-NAH)

RAYANNE A combining of the names Ray and Anne. *See* RAY (Male Names) and ANNE. Var: Raiann, Raianne, Rayann, Rayanna. (RAY-AN)

REBA Originally a short form of Rebecca (noose), Reba is now commonly bestowed as an independent given name. *See* REBECCA. (REE-BAH)

REBECCA From the Ecclesiastic Late Latin and Ecclesiastic Greek Rhebekka, which is derived from the Hebrew *ribbqāh* (noose). Var: Rebeccah, Rebekka, Rebekkah. Short: Becca, Beccah, Bekka, Bekkah, Reba. Pet: Becki, Beckie, Becky. (REH-BEK-KAH)

RHEANNA Modern coinage probably based on the Welsh name Rhiannon. Var: Reann, Reanna, Reanne, Rheana, Rheanne. (REE-AN-NAH)

RHIANNON A borrowing from the Welsh, Rhiannon is an ancient Celtic name of uncertain derivation. Some believe it to be derived from the Old Celtic Rigantona (great queen). The name, which is borne in Celtic mythology by a goddess of fertility, was not used as a given name until the 20th century. Its popularity outside Wales is due in large part to the song "Rhiannon," by the rock group Fleetwood Mac. Var: Reannon, Rheannon. (REE-AN-NUN)

RHONDA Believed to be derived from the Welsh elements *rhon* (lance) and *da* (good). Var: Randa, Ronda, Rondah. (RON-DAH)

RICHELLE Feminine form of Richard (brave ruler), formed by the addition of the feminine suffix *-elle* to Rich. *See* RICHARD (English Male Names). (RIH-SHEL)

RIGEL Borrowed from the name of the brightest star in the constellation Orion, Rigel is derived from the Arabic *rijl* (foot). Var: Rijal, Rygel, Ryjal. (RĪ-JIL)

ROBERTA Feminine form of Robert (bright and famous). *See* ROBERT (Male Names). Pet: Bobbi, Bobbie. (RAH-BER-TAH, RO-BER-TAH)

RONI Feminine form of Ron, which is a short form of Ronald (ruler of judgment). *See* RONALD (Male Names). Var: Ronie, Ronni, Ronnie. (RAH-NEE)

RONNELL Feminine form of Ron, which is a short form of Ronald (ruler of judgment). *See* RONALD (Male Names). Var: Ronell, Ronelle, Ronnel. (RON-NEL)

ROSE Derived from *rose*, which denotes a beautiful, fragrant flower regarded as a symbol of love. *See* ROSE (English Names). Pet: Rosie. (ROZE)

ROSEANNE Combination name formed from the names Rose and Anne. *See* ANNE *and* ROSE. Var: Roseann, Rose Ann, Rose Anne. (ROZE-AN)

ROXANE From the Greek Roxanē, which is believed to be derived from the Persian Roschana (dawn of day). The name was borne by the Bactrian wife of Alexander the Great, which seems to substantiate the name's roots. Var: Roxann, Roxanna, Roxanne. Pet: Roxi, Roxie, Roxy. (RAHKS-AN)

ROYCE Transferred use of the surname meaning "Roy's son." *See* ROY (Male Names). (ROISS)

RYAN From the Irish surname O'Riain (descendant of Rian). Rian is an ancient Irish name believed to be a diminutive of *rí* (king): hence, "little king." Var: Rian, Rianne, Ryann, Ryanne. (RĪ-AN, RĪ-UN)

Sadie Originally a pet form of Sarah (princess), Sadie is also bestowed as an independent given name. *See* SARAH. (SAY-DEE)

Saffron Derived from *saffron*, which denotes the dried stigmas of the crocus flower used in flavoring and coloring foods. It also denotes a bright orange-yellow color such as that of the stigmas. (SAF-FRON)

Sage Derived from *sage*, which denotes a type of plant regarded by many to have special healing and cleansing properties. (SAGE)

Sahara Taken from the name of the great African desert which extends from the Atlantic to the Red Sea. The name is derived from the Arabic *sahrā* (desert). (SAH-HAR-AH, SAH-HARE-UH)

Sally Originally a pet form of Sarah (princess), Sally is now bestowed as an independent given name. *See* SARAH. (SAL-EE)

Samantha Feminine form of Samuel (name of God, his name is God) believed to have originated in the southern U.S. in the 19th century. *See* SAMUEL (Male Names). Short: Sam. Pet: Sammi, Sammie. (SAH-MAN-THA)

Sandra Short form of Alexandra or Cassandra, Sandra is now commonly bestowed as an independent given name. *See* ALEXANDRA *and* CASSANDRA. Var: Sandrah, Saundra, Saundrah. Pet: Sandi, Sandie, Sandy. (SAN-DRAH)

Sarah Derived from the Hebrew *sārāh* (princess). The name is borne in the Bible by the wife of the patriarch Abraham and mother of Isaac. Var: Sara. Pet: Sadie, Sally, Sari, Sarie. (SER-AH, SAH-RAH)

Savannah Derived from the Spanish *sabana* (a treeless plain). (SAH-VAN-NAH)

Scout Derived from *scout*, which denotes a person sent out to spy the land or to observe the movements of an enemy or adversary. (SKOUT)

Serena Derived from *serene* (calm, peaceful, tranquil), which is from the Latin *serenus* (clear, calm, exalted). Var: Sarena. (SAH-REE-NAH)

Serenity Derived from *serenity* (calmness, tranquillity). (SEH-REN-IH-TEE)

Shaina Feminine form of Shane (God is gracious). *See* SHANE (Male Names). Var: Shayna, Sheina. (SHAY-NAH)

Shalana Modern coinage of uncertain derivation. Var: Shalaina, Shalane. (SHA-LAN-AH)

Shaleen Modern coinage of uncertain derivation. Var: Shalene, Shaline, Sheleen, Shelene. (SHA-LEEN)

Shan Anglicized form of Siân, the Welsh cognate of Jane (God is gracious). *See* JANE. Pet: Shanee. (SHAN)

Shandra Modern coinage based on the name Sandra or Shan, or perhaps as a combination of both. *See* SANDRA *and* SHAN. (SHAN-DRAH)

Shanna Of various derivations, Shanna is either a variant form of Shannon, an elaborated form of Shan, or a short form of the Hebrew Shoshannah. *See* SHAN, SHANNON, *and* SHOSHANNAH. (SHAN-NAH)

Shannon Anglicized form of the Irish Seanán, which is a diminutive of *sean* (old, wise). Alternatively, Shannon can be a borrowing of the name of the longest river in Ireland. It is believed to be derived from the Gaelic *sean* (old) and *abhann* (river). Var: Shannen. Short: Shan. (SHAN-NUN)

Sharon Hebrew name meaning "a plain, a flat area." In biblical times, Sharon was a fertile, coastal plain in Palestine where roses and oak trees grew in abundance. Var: Sharen, Sharona, Sharonah, Sharonna, Sherran. (SHARE-UN)

Shasta Taken from the name of a mountain in northern California, it is of American Indian origin, but of uncertain meaning. (SHAS-TAH)

Shauna Feminine form of the Irish Shaun, a variant of Sean, which is an Irish cognate of John (God is gracious). *See* JOHN (Male Names). Var: Shawn, Shawna, Shonna. (SHAUN-AH)

Shaunda Modern coinage based on the name Shauna (God is gracious). Var: Shonda, Shondah, Shawnda, Shawndah. (SHON-DAH, SHAUN-DAH)

Shayleen Feminine form of Shay (seizing by the heel, supplanting). *See* SHAY (Male Names). (SHAY-LEEN)

Shelby Transferred use of the surname derived from an English place-name meaning "a willow grove, a place where willows grow." (SHEL-BEE)

Shelly Transferred use of the surname derived from the Old English Scelfleáh. The name is composed of the elements *scelf* (a shelf, a ledge) and *lēah* (wood, clearing, meadow): hence, "dweller on the clearing near the ledge." Var: Shellee, Shelley. Short: Shell, Shelle. (SHEL-LEE)

Sheridan Transferred use of the Irish surname meaning "grandson of Siridean." Siridean is an old Irish name meaning "peaceful." Var: Sherridan. (SHARE-IH-DUN)

SHERRY Taken from the name of the fortified Spanish wine, which takes its name from the city of Jerez (formerly Xeres). Alternatively, Sherry can be a reworking of the French *chérie* (darling). Var: Sha Ree, Sharree, Sharri, Sharry, Sheri, Sherrye. (SHARE-REE)

SHOSHANNAH A borrowing from the Hebrew, Shoshannah is derived from *shōshannāh* (a lily, a rose). Var: Shoshanna. Short: Shanna, Shannah. (SHO-SHAN-NAH, SHO-SHAH-NAH)

SIERRA Taken from the name of the Sierra mountain range which is derived from the Spanish *sierra* (mountain). (SEE-ERR-AH)

SKY Taken from *sky*, which denotes the upper atmosphere. Var: Skye. (SKY)

SONDYA Variant form of Sonya, the Russian pet form of Sofya (wisdom, skill). (SOND-YAH)

SONYA Russian pet form of Sofya, a cognate of the Greek Sophia (wisdom, skill). Var: Sonia, Sonja. (SON-YAH)

SPENCER Transferred use of the English surname derived from the Anglo-French *espenser* and the Old French *despensier* (dispenser of provisions, a butler or steward who had control of the provisions of a household). Var: Spenser. (SPEN-SER)

SPRING Taken from the name of the season between winter and summer, when the plants begin to grow again after lying dormant for the winter. Var: Springer. (SPRING)

STEPHANIE From the French Stéphanie, a cognate of the Greek Stephana, which is a feminine form of Stephanos (a crown, a garland). Var: Stefanee, Steffanie. Short: Steph. Pet: Fanni, Fannie, Stephi. (STEH-FAH-NEE)

STEVIE Feminine form of Steven (a crown, a garland). *See* STEPHEN (Male Names). (STEE-VEE)

STORMY Modern name derived from *stormy*, which denotes inclement weather. Var: Stormi, Stormie. (STOR-ME)

SUMMER Taken from the name of the warmest season of the year. (SUM-MER)

SUNNY Derived from *sunny*, which denotes a clear day filled with sunlight or a bright, happy personality. (SUN-NEE)

TALISA Modern coinage most likely based on the name Lisa. Var: Talisa, Telisa. (TAH-LEE-SAH)

TAMARA Derived from the Hebrew Tamar (date palm, a palm tree). Var: Tamarah, Tamera, Tammara, Tammarah, Tamra. Short: Tam. Pet: Tami, Tamie, Tammi, Tammie, Tammy. (TAM-RAH, TAM-ER-AH, TAH-MARE-AH)

TANADIA Modern coinage of uncertain derivation. (TAH-NAH-DEE-AH, TAH-NAY-DEE-AH)

TANYA Originally a Russian pet form of Tatiana, which is of uncertain derivation. *See* TATIANA (Russian Names). Var: Tania, Taunya, Tawnya. (TAHN-YAH, TAN-YAH)

TARA Transferred use of an Irish place-name belonging to a hill in central Ireland, which was an ancient seat of kingship. Tara (hill) was used by Margaret Mitchell for the name of a plantation in her epic *Gone with the Wind*, resulting in the use of it as a female given name. (TAR-AH, TER-AH)

TARALYNN Modern combination name composed of the names Tara and Lynn. *See* LYNN *and* TARA. Var: Taralin, Taralinn, Taralyn. (TER-AH-LIN)

TARJA Modern coinage of uncertain derivation. (TAR-EE-AH, TAR-JAH)

TARYN Modern coinage based on the name Tara (hill) or Karen (pure, unsullied). Var: Taren. (TARE-UN)

TAUNA Modern coinage, possibly influenced by Fauna or Taunya. (TAWN-AH)

TAWNY Derived from *tawny*, which denotes a soft, brownish-yellow or tan color. The word is derived from the Old French *tanné* (tanned). Var: Tawnee, Tawney. (TAW-NEE)

TERRA Derived from *terra* (the earth). Var: Tera, Terah, Terrah. (TARE-AH)

TERRIS Modern coinage of uncertain derivation. Var: Tarris, Tarrys, Terrys. (TER-RIS)

TERYL Modern coinage of uncertain derivation. (TARE-IL)

TIARA Derived from *tiara* (a crown, coronet, headdress). (TEE-AR-AH)

TIFFANY Transferred use of the surname derived from the Old French Tifaine (Epiphany), which is from the Ecclesiastic Late Latin Theophania (Ephiphany, manifestation of God). Var: Tiffanie. (TIF-AH-NEE)

TINA A short form of Christina (a Christian, a follower of Christ), Tina is also bestowed as an independent given name. *See* CHRISTINA. Var: Teena. (TEE-NAH)

TISHA A short form of various names containing the element *tisha, ticia,* it is also bestowed as an independent given name. Var: Ticia. Short: Tish. (TISH-AH)

TISHRA Modern coinage based on the element *tish.* Var: Tishrah. (TISH-RAH)

TIVIAN Modern coinage most likely influenced by the name Vivian. (TIV-EE-UN)

TRACY Transferred use of the surname derived from Tracy-Bocage or Tracy-sur-Mer, Norman baronial names from Calvados meaning "place of Thracius." Var: Traci, Tracie, Tracey. (TRAY-SEE)

TREASURE Derived from *treasure,* which denotes hidden riches, accumulated wealth, or something greatly valued. The word is from the Latin *thesaurus* and the Greek *thēsauros* (a store, a treasure). (TREH-ZURE)

TRICIA A short form of Patricia (a patrician, an aristocrat), Tricia is also bestowed as an independent given name. Var: Trisha. (TRIH-SHA)

TUESDAY Taken from the name of the third day of the week. It is derived from the Middle English *Twisdai,* which is from the Old English *Tiwes dæg* (Tiu's day). Tiu is the Old English name given to the ancient Indo-European sky-god. (TOOZ-DAY, TYOOZ-DAY)

TUPPER Transferred use of the English surname derived from Tupp, a dialectal nickname meaning "ram," and the suffix *-er.* (TUP-PER)

TYANA Modern coinage of uncertain derivation, which is perhaps influenced by the name Deanna. (TEE-AH-NAH, TEE-AH-NAH)

UNITY Derived from *unity* (oneness, harmony, united), which is from the Latin *unitas* (oneness). (YOO-NIH-TEE)

VALERIE A borrowing from the French, Valerie is from the Latin Valerius, an old Roman family name derived from *valere* (to be strong, healthy). Var: Valarie. Short: Val. (VAL-EH-REE)

VELVET Derived from *velvet,* which denotes a rich, luxurious fabric having a soft, thick pile. The word is derived from the Old French *veluotte,* which has its root in the Latin *villus* (shaggy hair). Var: Velva. (VEL-VET)

VENETIA A name of uncertain etymology. It has been used in England since the Middle Ages, and some believe it to be a Latin rendering of the Welsh Gwyneth (blessed, a state of bliss), or a variant feminine form of the Latin Benedictus (blessed). *See* GWYNETH (Welsh Names) *and* BENEDICT (English Male Names). The name corresponds to that of an ancient Roman province and a former region of northeastern Italy; thus it might be a borrowing of such. Var: Veneta. (VEN-EE-SHA)

VENICE Borrowed from the name of the Italian seaport. (VEN-ISS)

VIANNA Modern coinage of uncertain derivation. (VEE-AN-NAH)

VIENNA Borrowed from the name of the Austrian city. Var: Vienn. (VEE-EN-NAH)

VINETTE Feminine form of Vinny, the pet form of Vincent (conquering). *See* VINCENT (Male Names). (VIN-NET)

VIRGINIA Derived from the Latin Verginius (spring-like, flourishing), an old Roman family name which has its root in the Latin *ver* (spring). *See* VIRGINIA (English Names). Pet: Ginnie, Ginny. (VER-JIN-YAH, VER-JIN-EE-AH)

WALLACE Transferred use of the surname derived from the Old French *Waleis* (a Welshman, a foreigner). As a given name, Wallace was originally bestowed in honor of Sir William Wallace (1272?–?1305), a Scottish patriot and leader in the struggle against Edward I of England. Var: Wallis. (WAL-LUS)

WEDNESDAY Taken from the name of the fourth day of the week, derived from the Middle English *Wednes dei,* which is from the Old English *Wodnes dæg* (Woden's day). Woden is the name of the chief Germanic god, who is equated with the Norse god Odin. (WENZ-DAY)

WENDY Borrowed from the English, Wendy originated as a nickname of novelist J. M. Barrie. *See* WENDY (English Names). Var: Wendi, Wendie. (WEN-DEE)

WHITNEY Transferred use of the surname derived from *Hwítan-íg* (Hwita's island). Hwita is an Anglo-Saxon personal name derived from *hwít* (white). Var: Whitnee. (WHIT-NEE)

WILLOW Taken from the name of the tree, which is derived from the Middle English *wilwe* (willow). Willow trees are noted for their flexibility and graceful appearance, hence the adjective *willowy,* which means "gracefully slender and lithe," qualities seen as desirable feminine attributes. (WIL-LO)

WINDY Derived from *windy* (blustery, movement of air). (WIN-DEE)

WREN Derived from the Old English *wrenna, wrœnna* wren. (REN)

WYETTA Feminine form of Wyatt (little Guy). *See* WYATT (Male Names). (WĪ-ET-TAH)

WYNELLE Elaboration of the name Wynn (white, fair, blessed). *See* WYNNE. (WIN-NEL)

WYNETTE Variant form of Wynn, formed by the addition of the diminutive suffix *-ette*. *See* WYNNE. (WIN-NET)

WYNNE Modern English name derived from the Welsh *gwyn* (white, fair, blessed). Var: Wynn. (WIN)

YOLANDE Of uncertain etymology, some believe it to be a derivative of Violante (violet), a medieval French name derived from the Latin Viola (violet). Var: Ylonda, Yolanda, Yolandah, Yolonda. (YO-LAHN-DAH)

YVONNE A borrowing from the French, Yvonne is a feminine form of Yvon and Yves, names of Germanic origin and derived from the element *iv* (yew). *See* YVES (French Male Names). Var: Evonne. (EE-VON, YIH-VON)

ZHANÉ Modern coinage of uncertain derivation. (ZHA-NAY)

ZOE Derived from the Greek Zōē (life). (ZO-EE)

CHAPTER FOUR

Biblical Names

Children are a gift from God;
they are his reward.
Children born to a young man are like
sharp arrows to defend him.
Happy is the man who has his quiver
full of them.
Psalms 127:3–5

IN BIBLICAL times girls were valued mainly for their ability to work, whereas boys were valued because they carried on the family name. In fact, sons were so important that upon the birth of her first son, a woman changed her name to "mother of" followed by the son's name.

In the earliest times, before people believed that there was life after death, parents believed that upon death they lived on through their children. If there were no children, there was no future. If a man died without children, it was the duty of the nearest male relative to marry the deceased's wife. Upon the birth of their first son, the child was given the name of the mother's first husband and inherited his property.

In Old Testament times a child was named immediately after birth. The chosen name was always meaningful. It would describe the child's character, circumstances surrounding the birth, or the family's feelings toward God. Names derived from place-names were also used, as were those of plants and animals.

In New Testament times the baby was named eight days after the birth, and if the child was male, it was circumcised at the same time. Besides the naming ceremony, one or two other ceremonies also took place at this time. If the new baby was the first-born son, the parents were required to "buy it back." First-born sons were thought to belong to God in a special way, in reference to God passing over the Israelites' eldest sons when all the first-born sons in Egypt died. From then on, God declared that the first-born sons belonged to him (Exodus 13:13–15). Males of the first generation after the exodus from Egypt were redeemed (bought back) by dedicating the Levites for God's service, who then became the nation's priests and spiritual leaders. After that, each family was required to pay five silver pieces to the priest to redeem their first-born sons.

Another birth ceremony was carried out regardless of which child was born. This was the purification sacrifice performed by the mother. In order to worship God after childbirth, the woman had to become "clean" again, and to achieve this she was required to sacrifice first a pigeon and then a lamb. (Two pigeons were acceptable if the woman was too poor to afford a lamb.) In later years money could be put into the offering boxes in the temple to pay for the priest to perform the ceremony.

In the Christian tradition early followers mainly used Old Testament Hebrew names. The practice eventually changed in favor of New Testament names as the Christians began to protest Judaism. During the Reformation, in response to the growing discontent with the Catholic Church, many Protestant faiths turned again to Old Testament names. The Puritans in particular shunned New Testament names in favor of Old Testament names or those that denoted abstract virtues such as Faith, Hope, and Charity. As a symbol of their break with the Church of England and their rejection of established church practices, Puritan extremists took delight in choosing the oddest-sounding names they could find, even going so far as to use entire verses of Scripture for their children's names.

Because of the omnipresence of Christianity, the most widespread names in the world are those taken from the Bible. John, by far the most popular name chosen for male children, is found in every Western language, in more than a hundred forms. Mary and its variants are the overwhelming favorite for girls' names. Mary is the most frequently used female name in Catholic countries, and the variant Marie is also given to males as a middle name to put them under the special protection of the virgin mother of Jesus.

Biblical Male Names

AARON Derived from the Hebrew *aharōn* (the exalted one). Aaron was the elder brother and spokesman of Moses, who suffered from a speech impediment, as well as the first high priest of the Hebrews. (EXOD. 4) (ERR-RUN, AA-RUN)

ABEL Derived from the Hebrew *hebel* (breath). Abel, the second son of Adam and Eve, was a shepherd whose sacrifice of a lamb was more pleasing to God than the offering of fruits and vegetables by his elder brother, Cain. He was killed by Cain in a fit of jealous rage. (GEN. 4) (Ā-BULL)

ABIRAM Hebrew name meaning "the exalted one is father, father of height." Abiram, a son of Eliab, joined Korah's rebellion against Moses and Aaron and was henceforth swallowed up by an earthquake. (NUM. 16) (AH-BEE-RAM)

ABNER Derived from the Hebrew *'abnēr* (the father is a light, father is a lamp). Abner, a cousin of Saul and commander in chief of his army, introduced David to Saul after the victory over Goliath. (1 SAM. AND 2 SAM.) (AB-NER)

ABRAHAM Hebrew name meaning "father of many." Abraham's original name was Abram (exalted father). He was the son of Terah and patriarch of both the Hebrews and Arabs. He was the husband of Sarah and father of Ishmael and Isaac. (GEN. 12–25) (Ā-BRA-HAM)

ABRAM The father is exalted. Abram was the original name of Abraham. *See* ABRAHAM. (Ā-BRAM)

ADAM Derived from the Hebrew *adama* (red earth). Adam was the first man created by God and placed in the Garden of Eden. His first recorded act was to name the beasts of the field and the birds of the air. It was from Adam's rib that Eve, the first woman, was formed. (GEN. 1–5) (AD-UM)

ALEXANDER Derived from the Greek elements *alexein* (to defend, to help) and *andros* (man): hence, "defender or helper of mankind." The name is borne in the Bible by several characters, including a son of Simon of Cyrene who was forced to carry the cross of Jesus. (MARK 15:21) (AL-EX-AN-DER)

AMOS Derived from the Hebrew *'āmōs* (borne, a burden). Amos was one of the twelve minor prophets, a commoner who prophesied in the 8th century B.C. The book of Amos is attributed to him. (Ā-MOS)

ANANIAS Jehovah has given. The name is borne in the Bible by several characters, including a devout man who became Paul's instructor. (ACTS 9) (AH-NAH-NI-AHS)

ANDREW Derived from the Greek *andreios* (manly). The name is borne by one of the apostles. He was a fisherman, a brother of Simon Peter, a disciple of John the Baptist, and the first disciple of Jesus. (JOHN 6) (AN-DREW)

Asa Derived from the Hebrew *āsā* (healer, physician). The name was borne by the third king of Judah, who zealously demanded the true worship of God over idols. (1 Kings) (Ā-sah)

Azariah Whom Jehovah helps. The name is borne by several Old Testament characters, including a grandson of Zadok, who succeeded his grandfather as high priest. (1 Kings 4) (az-ah-RĪ-ah)

Barak Lightning. Barak was the son of Abinoam, who waged a successful war campaign against Jabin at the urging of the prophetess Deborah. (Judg. 4) (BAR-ak)

Barnabas Derived from the Aramaic *barnebhū'āh* (son of exhortation). Barnabas was an apostle and missionary companion of Paul. He sold all his possessions and gave the money to the apostles after Pentecost. (Acts 4) (BAR-nah-bus)

Bartholomew From the Greek Bartholomaios (son of Talmai). Talmai is an Aramaic name meaning "hill, mound, furrows." The name was borne by one of the Twelve Apostles, thought to be the same person as Nathanael. According to Christian tradition, he preached in Arabia or India and was crucified. (bar-THOL-o-mew)

Benaiah Jehovah has built. Benaiah was a warrior and captain of King David's bodyguard who rose to the rank of commander in chief under King Solomon. (2 Sam. 23) (beh-NAY-ah)

Benjamin From the Hebrew *binyāmīn* (son of the right hand). The name is borne by the youngest of Jacob's twelve sons, the patriarch of the tribe of Benjamin. (Gen. 35) (BEN-jah-min)

Cain Derived from the Hebrew *qaying* (smith, craftsman). Cain was the first-born son of Adam and Eve, a worker of the soil who killed his younger brother Abel in a fit of jealousy. He was banished and sent into exile and ended up settling in the "land of Nod." (Gen. 4) (kane)

Caleb Hebrew name meaning "a dog; faithful." It is borne in the Bible by a leader of the Israelites, one of those sent by Moses to scout out the land in the second year after the Exodus. He and Joshua were the only people over the age of twenty to enter the Promised Land. (Num. 13, 32) (KAY-leb)

Clement Derived from the Latin *clēmens* (mild, gentle, merciful). The name was borne by a Christian of Philippi and a friend of Paul's. (Phil. 4) (KLEH-ment)

Cornelius Believed to be derived from the Latin *cornu* (horn). It is borne in the Bible by a centurion, a devout man and the first Gentile converted by Peter. (Acts 10) (kor-NEE-lee-us)

Cyrus Derived from the Old Persian *kūrush*, which is of uncertain meaning. The name was borne by Cyrus the Great, founder of the Persian Empire and liberator of the Jews from their Babylonian captivity. (2 Chron. 36) (SĪ-rus)

Dan Judge. Dan was the fifth son of Jacob by Bilhah, Rachel's maidservant, and progenitor of the tribe named after him. (Gen. 30) (dan)

Daniel Derived from the Hebrew *dāni'ēl* (God is my judge). Daniel was one of the major Hebrew prophets, whose faith in God miraculously delivered him from a den of hungry lions. His story and prophecies are recorded in the Old Testament book of Daniel. (DAN-yehl)

Darius A name of uncertain meaning borne by three Persian kings, including Darius the Great (550?–?486 b.c.). (Ezra 4) (dah-RĪ-us)

Dathan Borne by a Ruebenite chieftain who joined Korah's rebellion against Moses and Aaron and was henceforth swallowed up in an earthquake. Dathan is thought to mean "fount." (Num. 16) (DAY-than)

David Derived from the Hebrew *dāwīd* (beloved). The name was borne by the eighth and youngest son of Jesse. He became the second and greatest of the Israelite kings. As a youth, he slew the giant Goliath with a rock and sling, as is recounted in the story of David and Goliath. (1 Sam. 16) (DAY-vid)

Demas Borne by a fellow missionary of Paul. (Col. 4) (DEM-ahs)

Demetrius Derived from the Greek Demetrios (of Demeter). The name is borne in the Bible by a silversmith who made a living crafting shrines and models of the temple of Diana. He started a riot after sales fell off as a result of the preaching of Paul (Acts 19). The name was also borne by a Christian of great merit (3 John 12). (deh-MEE-tree-us)

Eleazar Derived from the Hebrew *el'āzār* (God has helped). The name is borne in the Bible by the son of Aaron and his successor as high priest. (Num. 20) (ELL-ee-Ā-zar)

Eli Derived from the Hebrew *'ēlī* (high, ascent). Eli was high priest of Israel at a time when the Ark was at Shiloh, and a teacher of Samuel. (1 Sam. 3) (EE-lī)

Eliakim God will raise up. The name is borne in the Bible by several characters, including a son of Hilkiah who became governor of the palace of Hezekiah. (ISA. 22) (EE-LĪ-AH-KIM)

ELIAS Greek variant, used in the RSV New Testament, of the Hebrew Elijah (Jehovah is God). (EE-LĪ-AHS)

ELIEZER Hebrew name meaning "God of help." It was borne by several characters, including one of the two sons of Moses. (EXOD. 18) (EL-EE-EE-ZER)

ELIJAH Derived from the Hebrew *'ēlīyāhū* (Jehovah is God). The name was borne by a 9th-century B.C. prophet who, after many years of service, was taken up into heaven in a chariot of fire. (1 KINGS) (EE-LĪ-JAH)

ELISHA Derived from the Hebrew *elīshā'* (God is salvation). The name was borne by the disciple and successor of Elijah. (1 KINGS) (EE-LĪ-SHA)

ELKANAH God created. Elkanah was the name of several biblical characters, including the husband of Hannah and the father of Samuel. (1 SAM.) (ELL-KAY-NAH)

ENOCH Derived from the Hebrew hănōkh (dedicated). The name was borne by the eldest son of Cain and by a son of Jared and father of Methuselah. (GEN.) (EE-NOK)

EPHRAIM Derived from the Hebrew *ephrayim* (very fruitful). Ephraim was the second son of Joseph and Asenath and progenitor of the tribe named after him. (GEN. 41) (EE-FRAH-IM)

ERASTUS Derived from the Greek Erastos (lovely, beloved). The name is borne in the Bible by a Christian sent into Macedonia by Paul. (ACTS 19) (EH-RAS-TUS)

ESAU Derived from the Hebrew *'ēsāw* (hairy). The name is borne in the Bible by a son of Isaac and Rebekah who sold his birthright to Jacob, his younger twin brother. (GEN. 25) (EE-SAW)

EZEKIEL Derived from the Hebrew *yechesq'ēl* (God strengthens). The name is borne in the Bible by a 6th-century B.C. Hebrew prophet whose ministry lasted more than twenty-three years. His prophecies are recorded in the Old Testament book of Ezekiel. (EE-ZEEK-EE-ELL)

FESTUS A name of uncertain derivation borne by the procurator of Judea. It was through him that Paul made his famous appeal to Caesar. (ACTS 25) (FESS-TUSS)

GABRIEL Derived from the Hebrew *gavhrī'ēl* (God is my strength). The name is borne in the Bible by one of the seven archangels, the herald of Good News who appeared to Mary to announce her pregnancy and the impending birth of the Christ child. (LUKE 1) (GAY-BREE-ELL)

GALLIO A name some believe means "milky." It was borne by the elder brother of Seneca, the philosopher and tutor of Nero. Gallio, noted as being an amiable and affectionate man, was proconsul of Achaia under the reign of the emperor Claudius. He refused to listen to a group of Jews who were trying to have Paul arrested. (ACTS 18) (GAL-LEE-O)

GEDALIAH Hebrew name meaning "made great by Jehovah." The name is borne in the Bible by several characters, including the grandfather of the prophet Zephaniah. (ZEPH. 1) (GED-AH-LĪ-AH)

GERSHON Expulsion. Gershon was the eldest of Levi's three sons. (GEN. 46) (GER-SHON)

GIDEON Derived from the Hebrew *gidh'ōn* (hewer, one who cuts down). The name is borne in the Bible by an Israelite judge who was a leader in the defeat of the Midianites. Peace followed for forty years thereafter. Gideon is said to have had seventy sons. (GID-EE-UN)

HEZEKIAH Derived from the Hebrew *hizqīyāh* (Yahweh strengthens). The name is borne in the Bible by a king of Judah who reigned at the time of Isaiah. (2 KINGS 18) (HEZ-AH-KĪ-AH)

HIRAM Derived from the Hebrew *'ahīrām* (exalted brother). The name is borne by several characters, including a king of Tyre who entered into an allegiance with King David and later King Solomon. He assisted in the building of David's palace by sending workmen and cedar and fir trees. (2 SAM. 5) Var: Horam, Huram. (HĪ-RAM)

HOSEA Derived from the Hebrew *hōshēa'* (salvation). Hosea was the first of the minor prophets, and the only one from the northern kingdom whose writings have been preserved. His prophecies are recorded in the Old Testament book of Hosea. (HO-SEE-AH, HO-ZAY-AH)

HOSHEA Variant form of Joshua (deliverance, God is salvation). It is borne in the Bible by several characters, including the son of Nun, who was later known as Joshua. (NUM. 13) Var: Oshea. (HO-SHE-AH)

IRA Derived from the Hebrew *'īrā* (watchful). The name is borne in the Bible by a Jairite priest and confidential adviser of King David. (2 SAM. 20) (Ī-RAH)

ISAAC Derived from the Hebrew *yitshāq* (laughter). Isaac was the only son of Abraham by Sarah and the patriarch of the Hebrews. He was the husband of Rebekah and the father of Esau and Jacob. (GEN. 21) (Ī-ZAC, Ī-ZAYK)

ISAIAH Derived from the Hebrew *yĕsha 'yah* (Yahweh is salvation). The name was borne by an 8th-century B.C.

prophet considered to be the greatest of the three major prophets. His prophecies are recorded in the Old Testament book of Isaiah. (Ī-ZAY-AH)

ISHMAEL Derived from the Hebrew *yishmā'ēl* (God hears). The name is borne in the Bible by the son of Abraham and his concubine Hagar. After the birth of Isaac, Ishmael and Hagar were taken into the desert and abandoned. They were saved by God, and Ishmael became the patriarch of the Arab people. (GEN. 21) (ISH-MAY-EL)

ISRAEL Derived from the Hebrew *yisrā'ēl* (contender with God). The name was bestowed upon Jacob after his prayer struggle with the angel at Peniel. Israel is also the collective name of the twelve tribes descended from Jacob's twelve sons. (GEN. 32 AND JOSH. 3) (IZ-RAY-EL, IZ-RAY-EL)

JACOB Derived from the Hebrew *ya'aqob* (seizing by the heel, supplanting). The name was borne by the younger twin brother of Esau. He purchased not only his brother's birthright but also the blessing that enabled one to invoke the power of God. Jacob was the husband of Leah and Rachel, and the father of twelve sons, who became the patriarchs of the twelve tribes of Israel. (GEN. 25–49) (JAY-KEB, JAY-KOB)

JAIRUS Borne by the ruler of the synagogue at Capernaum, whose only daughter was restored to life by Jesus. (MARK 5) (JAY-RUSS)

JAMES Variant form of Jacob (seizing by the heel, supplanting). James was the elder brother of John, both of whom were among the Twelve Apostles. Many believe that his mother (Salome) and Mary were sisters, making James a cousin of Jesus. He was beheaded by Herod Agrippa, making him the first martyr among the apostles. The name was also borne by a brother of Jesus who actively opposed Christ's ministry. After Jesus' death, however, he played a leading role in the affairs of the early church and was known as a devout man. Jewish historian Josephus says he was martyred in A.D. 62 by the high priest. (JAYMZ)

JAPHETH Derived from the Hebrew *yepheth* (enlargement). The name is borne in the Bible by the youngest son of Noah, one of the eight saved in the ark. He and his two brothers were the progenitors of the many tribes that repopulated the earth following the Flood. (GEN. 9) (JAY-FETH)

JASON Derived from the Greek *iasthai* (to heal). The name is borne in the Bible by a kinsman of Paul who hosted Paul and Silas in Thessalonica. (ACTS 17) (JAY-SUN)

JEDAIAH Hebrew name meaning "invoker of Jehovah." It is borne by several Old Testament characters, including a priest of Jerusalem after the exile. (1 CHRON. 9) (JEH-DĪ-AH)

JEDIDIAH Beloved of Jehovah. The name was given by Nathan to the newly born Solomon as a token of the divine favor of God. (2 SAM. 12) (JED-IH-DĪ-AH)

JEREMIAH Derived from the Hebrew *yirmeyāhu* (the Lord loosens, God will uplift). The name is borne in the Bible by several characters, one of whom was a major prophet of the 7th and 6th centuries B.C. His prophecies and warnings of the future are recorded in the Old Testament book of Jeremiah. (JER-EH-MĪ-AH)

JESIMIEL God sets up. The name is borne in the Bible by a Simeonite prince. (1 CHRON. 4) (JEH-SIM-EE-EL)

JESSE Derived from the Hebrew *yīshai* (gift, wealth). The name is borne in the Bible by the father of eight sons, the youngest of whom became King David. (RUTH 4) (JES-SEE)

JESUS Greek form of Joshua (Jehovah is help, God is salvation). The name is borne in the Bible by Jesus Christ (4 B.C.?–?A.D. 29), the son of God and the Virgin Mary. He is regarded by Christians to be the fulfillment of the Old Testament prophecy of the promised Messiah. His ministry lasted for three years: the first in relative obscurity, the second in great public favor, and the third in opposition. He was crucified yet rose from the dead three days later. His teachings are recorded in the four Gospels, Matthew, Mark, Luke, and John. (JEE-ZUS)

JETHRO Derived from the Hebrew *yitro* (abundance, excellence). The name is borne in the Bible by a prince or priest of Midian, the father of Zipporah, the wife of Moses. (EXOD. 18) (JETH-RO)

JOASH Contraction of Jehoash (whom Jehovah bestowed). The name was borne by several biblical characters, including the father of Gideon. (JUDG. 6) Var: Jehoash. (JO-ASH)

JOEL Derived from the Hebrew *yō'ēl* (Jehovah is his God). The name was borne by several characters, including the second of the twelve minor prophets, thought to have lived in the 5th century B.C., whose prophecies are recorded in the Old Testament book of Joel. (JO-EL)

JOHANAN Hebrew name meaning "God is gracious." It is borne by several biblical characters, including one of the Gadite heroes who joined David in the desert of Judah. (1 CHRON. 12) (JO-HAY-NAN)

JOHN Ultimately derived from the Hebrew *yehōhānān* (God is gracious). The name was most notably borne by John the Apostle, a brother of James and possibly a cousin of Jesus. He authored four books of the New Testament. The name is also borne by John the Baptist, a kinsman and forerunner of Jesus. John is the most popular masculine biblical name, having more than a hundred forms in many different languages. (JON)

JONAH Derived from the Hebrew *yōnāh* (dove). The name was borne by a Hebrew prophet famous for being thrown overboard in a storm and being swallowed by a great fish for disobeying God. He was deposited unharmed upon the shore three days later. His personal history is recounted in the Old Testament book of Jonah. (JO-NAH)

JONATHAN Derived from the Hebrew *yehōnāthān* (Yahweh has given). The name is borne by several characters, including the eldest son of King Saul and a close friend of David's. (1 SAM. 20) (JON-AH-THAN)

JORDAN Derived from the Hebrew *yarden* (to flow down, descend). The name is that of the chief river of Palestine, in which Jesus was baptized. Jordan originated as a given name in the Middle Ages, being bestowed upon those baptized in holy water said to be taken from the Jordan River. (JOR-DAN)

JOSEPH Derived from the Hebrew *yōsēf* (may he add, God shall add). The name is borne in the Bible by a favorite son of Jacob and Rachel (GEN. 30), by the husband of the Virgin Mary and foster father of Jesus (MATT. 1), and by Joseph of Arimathea, a rich Jew and secret follower of Jesus, who helped take Jesus' body from the cross to prepare it for burial, and supposedly took the Holy Grail to England (JOHN 19). (JO-SEF)

JOSHUA Derived from the Hebrew *yehōshū'a* (Jehovah is help, God is salvation). The name is borne in the Bible by Moses' successor, who led the children of Israel into the Promised Land. His history is recorded in the Old Testament book of Joshua. (JOSH-YOO-AH)

JOSIAH Derived from the Hebrew *yōshīyāh* (the Lord supports, the Lord saves, the Lord heals). Josiah was a celebrated 7th-century B.C. king of Judah. (2 KINGS 22) (JO-SĪ-AH)

LABAN Derived from the Hebrew *lābhān* (white). The name is borne in the Bible by the father of Rachel and Leah. (GEN. 29) (LAY-BUN)

LEVI Derived from the Hebrew *lēwī* (joining, adhesion). The name is borne in the Bible by the third son of Jacob and Leah. He was progenitor of the tribe of Levi, which took on priestly duties for the twelve tribes. (GEN. 29) (LEE-VĪ)

LUKE A name of debated origin. *See* LUKE (English Names). It is borne in the Bible by one of the four evangelists, a physician and author of the New Testament books of Luke and the Acts of the Apostles. (LUKE)

MALACHI Derived from the Hebrew *mal'ākhī* (my messenger). The name was borne by the last of the minor prophets, the author of the last book of the Old Testament canon. He lived and prophesied in the 5th century B.C. (MAL-AH-KĪ)

MARK A name of debated derivation. *See* MARK (English Names). It is borne in the Bible by one of the four evangelists, whose Jewish name was John. Mark is the reputed author of the second Gospel, Mark. (MARK)

MATTHEW Derived from the Hebrew *mattūthyāh* (gift of God). The name is borne in the Bible by a disciple of Jesus and one of the Twelve Apostles. After being called to be a follower of Jesus, he changed his name from Levi to Matthew. He authored the first book of the New Testament, Matthew. (MATH-YOO)

MATTHIAS Derived from the Hebrew *mattūthyāh* (gift of God). Matthias was one of the Twelve Apostles, chosen by lot to replace Judas Iscariot. (MAH-THĪ-US)

MESHACH Derived from the Hebrew *mēshakh* (agile). The name was borne by one of the three Hebrew captives in training at the Babylonian court. They miraculously emerged unharmed from the blazing furnace in which they were cast. (DAN. 3) (ME-SHACK)

MICAH Derived from the Hebrew *mīkhāyah* (who is like God?). The name is borne in the Bible by several Old Testament characters, including an 8th-century B.C. prophet of Judah. His prophecies are found in the book of Micah. Var: Micaiah. (MĪ-KAH)

MICHAEL Derived from the Hebrew *mīkhā'ēl* (who is like God?). The name is borne in the Bible by several characters. It is most famously that of one of the archangels, the one closest to God, who has the responsibility of carrying out God's judgments. Michael is regarded as the leader of the heavenly host and is the patron saint of soldiers. (DAN. 10, REV. 12) (MĪ-KL, MĪ-KAY-EL)

MORDECAI Derived from the Hebrew *mordĕkhai*, which possibly means "a little man" or "worshiper of Marduk." The name is borne by the cousin and foster father of Esther. He saved the Jews from the destruction planned by Haman, an event celebrated by the Jewish feast of Purim. (ESTHER 2, 3) (MOR-DEH-KĪ, MOR-DEH-KAY-Ī)

Moses Derived from the Hebrew *mōsheh* (drawn out of the water), which is thought to be from the Egyptian *mes, mesu* (son, child). The name is borne in the Bible by the leader who brought the Israelites out of bondage in Egypt. He received the Ten Commandments on Mount Sinai and led his people to the borders of Canaan and the Promised Land. (Exod.) (MO-zez, MO-zes)

Nathan Derived from the Hebrew *nāthān* (gift). The name is borne in the Bible by a prophet who rebuked King David for the death of Uriah, which enabled the king to marry Bathsheba, Uriah's wife. (2 Sam. 12) (NAY-than)

Nathanael Derived from the Hebrew *nĕthan'ēl* (gift of God). The name is borne in the Bible by a disciple of Jesus, one of those to whom Christ appeared after the resurrection. He is believed to be the same character as Bartholomew. (John 21) Var: Nathaniel. (nah-THAN-yel)

Nehemiah Derived from the Hebrew *nechemyāh* (comforted by Jehovah). The name is borne in the Bible by a Hebrew leader of about the 5th century B.C. He was a patriot of the exile and governor of the city of Jerusalem, which he returned to physical and religious order. Nehemiah authored the book that bears his name. (nee-hem-Ī-ah)

Noah Derived from the Hebrew *nōach* (rest, comfort). The name is borne in the Bible by the patriarch commanded by God to build the ark, upon which he saved his family and two of each creature from the Great Flood. He is seen as the second progenitor of the human race. (Gen. 6) (NO-ah)

Paul Derived from the Latin *paulus* (small). Paul was the adopted name of Saul of Tarsus, a Jewish Roman citizen converted to Christianity by a vision of Christ which blinded him for several days. He became one of the great missionary apostles and authored several New Testament epistles. Paul is regarded as cofounder of the Christian Church. (pahl)

Peter Derived from the Latin *petrus* (a rock) and the Greek *petros* (a rock, a stone). The name is borne in the Bible by one of the Twelve Apostles. Originally called Simon, Peter was the brother of Andrew and a fisherman by trade. He was a great missionary and is regarded as cofounder and the first pope of the Christian Church. (PEE-ter)

Philemon Derived from the Greek *phīlēmon* (affectionate). The name is borne by an early Christian to whom the apostle Paul addressed an epistle. (fil-LEE-mon)

Phillip Derived from the Greek Phillipos (lover of horses). The name is borne in the Bible by one of the Twelve Apostles. (Matt. 10) (FIL-lip)

Reuben Derived from the Hebrew *rĕūbēn* (behold, a son!). Reuben was the eldest son of Jacob and Leah and patriarch of the tribe bearing his name. (Gen. 29) (ROO-ben)

Reuel Hebrew name meaning "friend of God." Reuel is a byname for Jethro, the father-in-law of Moses. (Exod. 2) (ROO-el, ree-OO-el)

Samson Derived from the Hebrew *shimshōn* (the sun). Samson was an Israelite judge whose great strength stemmed from his long hair, which as a Nazarite he was forbidden to cut. He was treacherously betrayed to the Philistines by his mistress, Delilah. (Judg. 13–16) Var: Sampson. (SAM-son)

Samuel Derived from the Hebrew *shĕmū'ēl* (name of God, heard of God). The name is borne in the Bible by a Hebrew judge and prophet who anointed Saul as the first king of Israel. (1 Sam. 1:20) (SAM-yool)

Saul Derived from the Hebrew *shā'ūl* (asked for, asked of God). The name is borne in the Bible by the first Israelite king. (1 Sam. 8–10) (sahl)

Seth Derived from the Hebrew *shēth* (appointed). The name is borne in the Bible by the third son of Adam and Eve, born after the death of Abel at the hands of Cain. (Gen. 4) (seth)

Shem Derived from the Hebrew *shēm* (name, renowned). The name is borne in the Bible by the eldest of Noah's three sons, progenitors of the human race after the Great Flood. (Gen. 5) (shem)

Shiloh Thought to mean "he who is to be sent." Shiloh is a word used in the Bible to denote the Messiah (Gen. 49), as well as the name of a town of Ephraim which became a sanctuary of the tribes of Israel after the Conquest (Judg. 21). (SHĪ-lo)

Silas Derived from the Aramaic *sh'îlâ* (asked for). The name is borne in the Bible by a prominent member of the early church at Jerusalem. He accompanied Paul on his second missionary journey. (Acts 16) (SĪ-lus)

Simeon Derived from the Hebrew *shim'ōn* (heard). The name is borne in the Bible by several characters, including a devout man who was visiting the temple when the infant Jesus was being presented before God. Upon seeing the Christ child, he uttered words of thanksgiving and prophecy which are now set in the canticle "Nunc Dimittis." (Luke 2) (SIM-ee-on, SIM-ee-un)

SIMON Derived from the Hebrew *shim'ōn* (heard). The name is borne in the Bible by several characters, including Simon of Cyrene, the man seized from the crowd during the procession of the crucifixion to carry the heavy cross after Jesus could no longer bear its weight. (MATT. 27) (SĪ-MON)

SOLOMON Derived from the Hebrew *shĕlōmōh* (peaceful). The name is borne in the Bible by the son and successor of King David, renowned for his wisdom and ability to communicate with animals. (1 KINGS 1–11) (SOL-O-MUN)

STEPHANAS Derived from the Greek *stephanos* (a crown, a garland). The name is borne in the Bible by a member of the church at Corinth. (1 COR. 16) (STEH-FAHN-US)

STEPHEN Derived from the Greek *stephanos* (a crown, a garland). The name is borne in the Bible by one of the seven deacons, a preacher of the Gospel who became the first Christian martyr. (ACTS 6) (STEE-VEN, STEH-FEN)

TERAH Of uncertain derivation, some believe it to mean "wild goat." It is borne in the Bible by the father of Abraham. (GEN. 11) (TER-AH)

THEOPHILUS Derived from the Greek *theos* (God) and *philos* (loving): hence, "beloved of God, lover of God." The name is borne in the Bible by a Christian to whom Luke addressed the Gospel of St. Luke and the Acts of the Apostles. (THEE-AH-FILL-US)

THOMAS Derived from the Aramaic *tĕ'ōma* (a twin). Thomas was one of the Twelve Apostles, some believe a brother of James and Matthew. He doubted the resurrection of Christ, an act giving rise to the title "doubting Thomas," used to indicate a skeptic or a chronic doubter. (MATT. 10) (TOM-AHS)

TIMOTHY Derived from the Greek *timē* (honor, respect) and *theos* (God): hence, "honoring God." The name is borne in the Bible by a young disciple and companion of Paul, to whom Paul addressed two epistles. (ACTS 16) (TIM-AH-THEE)

TITUS Derived from the Greek Titos, which is of uncertain derivation. Most believe it is from *tīo* (to honor). The name is borne in the Bible by a disciple and companion of Paul, to whom Paul addressed an epistle. (TĪ-TUS)

TOBIAH Derived from the Hebrew *tōbhīyāh* (the Lord is good, God is good). The name is borne in the Bible by an Ammonite who opposed the rebuilding of Jerusalem after the exile. (NEH. 2) (TO-BĪ-AH)

URIAH Derived from the Hebrew *ūrīyāh* (God is light). Uriah was a Hittite captain in David's army and husband of the beautiful Bathsheba. He was sent to the front lines to be killed so that King David could marry Bathsheba. (2 SAM. 11) (YOO-RĪ-AH)

ZACCHAEUS Ultimately derived from the Hebrew *zĕcharyah* (God remembers). The name is borne in the New Testament by a chief tax collector at Jericho. Of short stature, he climbed a tree to see Jesus, who spied him sitting there and spent the day at his house. (LUKE 19) (ZAK-KEE-AHS)

ZACHARIAH Derived from the Hebrew *zĕcharyah* (God remembers). The name is borne in the Bible by the grandfather of Hezekiah. (2 KINGS 18) (ZAK-AH-RĪ-AH)

ZACHARIAS Derived from the Hebrew *zĕcharyah* (God remembers). The name is borne in the Bible by a priest, the husband of Elisabeth and father of John the Baptist. The angel Gabriel announced the pregnancy of Elisabeth, who was past childbearing age, saying that the son would be the forerunner of the promised Messiah. Because Zacharias refused to believe the message, he was struck dumb until the baby was circumcised and named. (LUKE 1) (ZAK-AH-RĪ-AHS)

ZEBEDEE Derived from the Hebrew *zĕbhadyāh* (God has bestowed). Zebedee was a Galilean fisherman, the husband of Salome and father of the disciples James and John. (MATT. 4) (ZEB-AH-DEE)

ZEBULUN Believed to be derived from the Assyrian *zabālu* (to carry, to exalt). The name was borne by the tenth son of Jacob (the sixth of Jacob and Leah), who was patriarch of the tribe of Zebulun. (GEN. 30) (ZEH-BYOO-LUN)

ZECHARIAH Derived from the Hebrew *zĕcharyah* (God remembers). The name was borne by many biblical characters, including a 6th-century B.C. Hebrew prophet, the eleventh of the twelve minor prophets. He urged the rebuilding of the temple. His prophecies are recorded in the Old Testament book of Zechariah. (ZEK-AH-RĪ-AH)

ZEDEKIAH Righteousness of Jehovah. The name is borne in the Bible by the last king of Judah. (2 KINGS 23) (ZED-EH-KĪ-AH)

ZEPHANIAH Derived from the Hebrew *tsĕphanyāh* (the Lord has hidden). The name is borne in the Bible by a Hebrew prophet of the 7th century B.C., the ninth in order of the twelve minor prophets. His prophecies are recorded in the Old Testament book of Zephaniah. (ZEF-AH-NĪ-AH)

Biblical Female Names

ABANA Hebrew name meaning "stony." The name is borrowed from that of a river of Damascus mentioned by Naam. It is now called Barada (cool). (2 KINGS 5) Var: Abanah. (AH-BAH-NAH)

ABBIE A pet form of any of the names beginning with the element *abi*, Abbie is also bestowed as an independent given name. Var: Abby. (AB-BEE)

ABIGAIL Derived from the Hebrew *avīgayil* (father is rejoicing). The name is borne in the Bible by the wise and beautiful wife of Nabal, who later became the wife of King David. (1 SAM. 25) Pet: Abbie, Abby. (AB-IH-GAIL)

ABIHAIL Father of strength. Abihail is borne in the Bible by the sister-in-law of King David. (2 CHRON. 11) Pet: Abbie, Abby. (AB-IH-HAIL)

ABIJAH The Lord is father. The name is borne in the Bible by the mother of Ashur. (1 CHRON. 2) Var: Abiah. Pet: Abbie, Abby, Abi. (AH-BĪ-JAH)

ABISHAG Hebrew name meaning "wise, educated." The name was borne by a beautiful young woman who cared for David in his old age. (1 KINGS 1) Pet: Abbie, Abby. (AH-BIH-SHAG)

ADAH Adornment. Adah was the wife of Lamech and mother of Jabal and Jubal. (GEN. 4) Var: Ada. (Ā-DAH)

AHINOAM My brother is gracious. The name is borne in the Bible by a wife of King David. (1 SAM. 25) (AH-HIN-O-AHM)

AJALON Place of gazelles. The name is borrowed from that of a valley in Dan where the Israelites defeated the Amorites while the sun and moon stood still in answer to Joshua's prayer. (JOSH. 10) Var: Aijalon. (AY-JAH-LON)

AMANA Established. The name is borrowed from that of a mountain where the river Abana has its source. (AH-MAY-NAH)

ANNA Anglicized form of Hannah (gracious, full of grace, mercy). The name is borne in the Bible by the prophetess in the temple when the baby Jesus was presented. She declared him to be the Messiah. (LUKE 2) (AH-NAH)

APPHIA Hebrew name meaning "increasing." It is borne in the Bible by a Christian woman some believe to be the wife of Philemon. (PHILEM. 2) (AF-FEE-AH)

ASENATH Of debated etymology, some believe Asenath to be an Aramaic name meaning "thornbush." Others think it is possibly an Egyptian name meaning "gift of the sun-god." It was borne by the wife of Joseph and mother of Manasseh and Ephraim. (GEN. 41) (ASS-EH-NATH)

ATARAH A crown. Var: Atara. (AT-AH-RAH)

ATHALIA The Lord is exalted. Athalia is borne in the Bible by the daughter of King Ahab and Jezebel. She unfortunately inherited the character of her mother. (2 KINGS 8) (ATH-AH-LEE-AH)

AZUBAH Forsaken, deserted. The name is borne in the Bible by the wife of Caleb. (1 CHRON. 2) (AH-ZOO-BAH)

BATHSHEBA Hebrew name meaning "daughter of the oath, daughter of Sheba." It was borne by the beautiful wife of Uriah, the Hittite. After King David placed her husband on the front lines of battle to ensure his death, the king married Bathsheba. She was the mother of Solomon. Short: Sheba. (2 SAM. 11) (BATH-SHE-BAH)

BATHSHUA Daughter of riches, daughter of Shua. The name was borne by a wife of Judah. (1 CHRON. 2) (BATH-SHOO-AH)

BERENICE Derived from the Greek elements *pherein* (to bring) and *nikē* (victory): hence, "bringer of victory." The name is borne in the Bible by the eldest daughter of Herod Agrippa I, wife of her uncle Herod. (ACTS 25) Var: Bernice. (BER-AH-NEES)

BETH From *bēth* (house), the second letter of the Hebrew alphabet. The name eventually came to mean "a family." (GEN. 24) (BETH)

BETHANY House of dates or figs. The name is borrowed from that of a small village on the eastern slope of the Mount of Olives, ultimately associated with the last days of Jesus. (LUKE 24) (BETH-AH-NEE)

BETHEL Derived from the Hebrew *bēth'ēl* (house of God). The name is borrowed from that of an ancient and holy city south of Shiloh. (1 SAM. 30) (BETH-EL)

BEULAH Derived from the Hebrew *be'ūlāh* (married). Beulah was a name for Palestine, given to acknowledge that God will be married to his people and their land. (ISA. 62) (BYOO-LAH)

BILHAH Bashful, faltering. The name belonged to the handmaid Rachel gave to Jacob. She became the mother of Dan and Naphtali. (GEN. 30) (BIL-HAH)

BITHIAH Daughter of Jehovah. Bithiah was the name of a daughter of Pharaoh who became the wife of Mered. (1 CHRON. 4) (BITH-EE-AH)

BITHYNIA Of the Bithyni. The name is borrowed from that of a province in northwestern Asia Minor. Its major city, Nicaea, was the site of the celebrated Council of Nicaea, convened by the emperor Constantine. (BI-THEE-NEE-AH)

CALAH The name of one of the most ancient cities of Assyria, said to have been founded by Ashur. It is thought to mean "old age." (KAY-LAH)

CANDACE A name of uncertain derivation borne in the Bible by the queen of the Ethiopians. A eunuch belonging to her court was returning to Ethiopia from Jerusalem when, in the desert of Gaza, he was met by Philip the Evangelist and converted to Christianity. (ACTS 8) (KAN-DAS)

CASIPHIA Silver, white, shining. The name is borrowed from that of a settlement of exiled Levites in northern Babylonia. (EZRA 8) (KAS-IH-FĪ-AH)

CHARITY Derived from the Latin *caritas* (esteem, affection, valued). In Christian theology, charity represents the love of God for mankind or the love of man for one another. (1 COR. 3) (CHAIR-IH-TEE)

CHLOE Derived from the Greek *khloē* (blooming, verdant). The name is borne in the Bible by a woman mentioned in 1 Cor. 1:11. Some of her Christian slaves informed Paul of the dissension at Corinth. (KHLO-WEE)

CILICIA The name of a Roman province in southeastern Asia Minor. Its capital was Tarsus, the home of the apostle Paul. The name might be derived from *cilicium* (goat-hair cloth), for which the province was famous. (SILL-I-SEE-AH)

CLAUDIA Derived from the Latin *claudus* (halting, lame). The name is borne in the Bible by a Christian lady of Rome. (2 TIM. 4) (CLAW-DEE-AH)

DAMARIS Of uncertain derivation, some believe it to mean "heifer." It is borne in the Bible by a woman of Athens who was converted to Christianity by Paul. (ACTS 17) (DAH-MAR-ISS)

DEBORAH Derived from the Hebrew *debōrāh* (a bee). The name is borne in the Bible by Rebekah's nurse and by a great prophetess and judge who helped to organize an army and oversaw a decisive victory over the Canaanites. (JUDG. 4) (DEH-BOR-AH, DEH-BOR-AH)

DELILAH Derived from the Hebrew *delīlāh* (delicate). The name was borne by the Philistine mistress of Samson who discovered the secret of his great strength. She treacherously betrayed him to the Philistines. Samson and Delilah is a popular Bible story. (JUDG. 16) (DEE-LĪ-LAH)

DIANA Derived from the Latin *diviana* (divine). The name is that of the Roman mythological goddess of the moon and of hunting, who was popularly worshiped in New Testament times. (DĪ-AN-AH)

DINAH Derived from the Hebrew *dīnāh* (judged, vindicated). The name is borne in the Bible by a daughter of Jacob and Leah. (GEN. 30) (DĪ-NAH)

DORCAS Derived from the Greek *dorkas* (gazelle). The name was borne by a Christian woman of Joppa who devoted herself to works of charity. Through the prayers of Peter, she was raised from the dead, which led to many converting to Christianity. (ACTS 9) (DOR-KAS)

DOVE Derived from the Greek *taube* (dove), which is from the Indo-European root *dheubh* (smoky, misty). The dove is a frequently mentioned bird of the Bible. It is viewed as a symbol of peace and the Holy Spirit. (DUV)

DRUSILLA Feminine form of Drūsus, an old family of the Livian gens, which is of uncertain derivation. *See* DRUSILLA (Italian Names). The name is borne in the Bible by a daughter of Herod Agrippa I. She was the wife of Felix, procurator of Judea, and was present when Paul appeared before Felix at Caesarea. She and her young son perished in the eruption of Mount Vesuvius (A.D. 79). (ACTS 24) (DROO-SILL-AH)

EDEN Derived from the Hebrew *'ēdhen* (delight). The Garden of Eden was the name of the paradise where Adam and Eve were created and lived before eating from the Tree of Knowledge. (GEN. 3) (EE-DEN)

ELISABETH Derived from the Hebrew *elisheba'* (God is my oath). The name is borne in the Bible by the wife of Zacharias, a kinswoman of the Virgin Mary and mother of John the Baptist. That she should be the mother of the forerunner of Jesus was revealed to her by the archangel Gabriel. (LUKE 1) (EE-LIZ-AH-BETH)

ESTHER Of debated origin and meaning. *See* ESTHER (English Names). The name is borne in the Bible by the cousin and foster daughter of Mordecai. She became the wife and queen of the Persian king Ahasuerus. Through the wisdom of Mordecai and the boldness of Esther, the plotting of Haman to destroy the Jews was circumvented, an event celebrated by the Jewish feast of Purim. Esther's story is told in the Old Testament book that bears her name. (ESS-TER)

EUNICE Derived from the Greek Eunikē (good victory). The name is borne in the Bible by the mother of Timothy. She was thought to have been converted to

Christianity on Paul's first missionary journey. (ACTS 16) (YOO-NISS)

EVE Derived from the Hebrew *hawwāh* (life). The name is borne in the Bible by the first woman, said to have been created by God from one of Adam's ribs. Eve, the "mother of all the living," was the mother of Cain, Abel, and Seth. (GEN. 2) (EEV)

FAITH Derived from the Middle English *feith* (faith, belief). Faith is the unquestioning belief in God which does not require proof or evidence. (FAITH)

GABRIELA Feminine form of Gabriel (God is my strength), the name borne by one of the seven archangels. *See* GABRIEL (Male Names). (GAB-REE-ELL-LAH)

GRACE Derived from the Latin *gratia* (pleasing quality, favor, thanks). In Christian theology, grace is the unmerited love and favor of God toward mankind. (GRACE)

HANNAH Derived from the Hebrew *hannāh*, *chaanach* (gracious, full of grace, mercy). The name is borne in the Bible by the mother of Samuel. She was one of the two wives of Elkanah. (1 SAM.) (HAH-NAH)

HELAH Hebrew name meaning "rust." It is borne in the Bible by one of the two wives of Ashur. (1 CHRON. 4) (HEH-LAH)

HOPE From *hope* (desire, expectation, want). Faith, hope, and charity are the three main elements of the Christian character. (HOPE)

JAEL Hebrew name meaning "mountain goat." The name is borne in the Bible by the wife of Heber, the Kenite. After being defeated by Barak, the captain of the Canaanites' army fled and sought refuge with the tribe of Heber. Jael invited him into her tent and killed him with a tent peg as he lay sleeping. (JUDG. 4) (JAY-EL)

JANOAH Quiet, calm. The name is borrowed from that of a town on the border of Ephraim. (JOSH. 16) Var: Janohah. (JAH-NO-AH)

JECOLIAH The Lord has prevailed. Jecoliah was the mother of Uzziah, a king of Judah. (2 KINGS 15) Var: Jechiliah, Jecholiah. (JEH-KO-LĪ-AH)

JEDIDAH Hebrew name meaning "beloved." Jedidah was the wife of Amon and mother of Josiah. (2 KINGS 22) (JEH-DĪ-DAH)

JEMIMAH Derived from the Hebrew *yemīmāh* (a dove). The name is borne in the Bible by the first of Job's three daughters. (JOB 42) Var: Jemima. (JUH-MĪ-MAH)

JERIOTH Curtains. Jerioth was the name of the second wife of Caleb. (1 CHRON. 2) (JER-EE-ŌTH)

JERUSHAH Possessed, a possession. Jerushah was the name of the wife of Uzziah, a king of Judah, and mother of his son King Jotham. (2 KINGS 15) Var: Jerusha. (JEH-ROO-SHA)

JEZREEL God scatters, God sows. The name is borrowed from that of ancient biblical towns and the Valley of Jezreel, the scene of Gideon's decisive battle over the Midianites. (JUDG. 6) (JEZ-REE-EL, JEZ-REEL)

JOANNA Feminine form of Joanan, which is from the Hebrew Yochanan, a short form of *yehōchānān* (the Lord has been gracious). The name was borne by the wife of Chuza, King Herod's steward. She was among the women who visited Jesus' tomb after his death, only to discover it was empty. (LUKE 8) Var: Joannah. (JO-AH-NAH)

JORDAN Derived from the Hebrew *yarden* (descend, to flow down). The name is that of the chief river of Palestine. It was in this river that Jesus was baptized by John the Baptist. Jordan was originally bestowed upon children baptized in holy water said to be taken from the river. (JOR-DAN)

JOY A word used to denote great feelings of happiness, great pleasure, delight. According to Scripture, joy is an attribute of God and is one of the fruits of the spirit that are experienced despite circumstances. (JOY)

JUBILEE Derived from the Hebrew *yōbēl* (a ram's horn used as a trumpet to announce the sabbatical year). In Jewish history, the Jubilee was a year-long celebration occurring every fifty years, in which all bondsmen were freed from obligation, mortgaged lands were returned to the original owner and the land left fallow. (LEV. 25) (JOO-BEH-LEE)

JUDITH Anglicized form of the Hebrew Jehudith and Yehudit, feminine forms of Jehuda and Yehūdāh. These names, Anglicized as Judah, mean "he will be praised." Because Judah was the name of a kingdom in ancient Palestine, the name can also mean "from Judah." Judith is borne in the Bible by the daughter of Beeri the Hittite. She became one of the wives of Esau. (GEN. 26) (JOO-DITH)

JULIA Feminine form of Julius (downy-bearded, youth). *See* JULIA (English Names). In the Bible, Julia is the name of a Christian lady greeted by Paul. (ROM. 16) (JOO-LEE-AH)

KEILAH Citadel. Keilah is borrowed from the name of a biblical town of Judah delivered from the Philistines by David. (JOSH. 15) (KEE-Ī-LAH)

KEREN-HAPPUCH Horn of eye paint. The name is borne in the Bible by the youngest of the three daughters of Job, born after his years of affliction. The name makes reference to her beautiful eyes. (JOB 42) (KER-EN-HAH-PUCH)

KETURAH Incense. Keturah was the wife of Abraham, whom he probably married after Sarah's death. They had many children who were sent away into the east by Abraham. Sixteen progenitors of Arabian tribes are attributed to her. (GEN. 25) (KEH-TYOO-RAH)

KEZIAH Cassia. The name was borne by the second of Job's three daughters, born to him after his great affliction. (JOB 42) Var: Kezia. (KEH-ZI-AH, KEE-ZI-AH)

LEAH Derived from the Hebrew *lē'āh* (gazelle, wild cow) or from *lā'āh* (weary, to tire). The name is borne in the Bible by the eldest daughter of Laban and Jacob's first wife. Though her sister Rachel was Jacob's favorite wife, she nevertheless bore him seven children. (GEN. 29) (LEE-AH)

LILY General name used in the Bible for many varieties of flowers. Solomon believed the beauty and fragrance of the lily were allegorical to Christ, and even now the flower is symbolic of purity and perfection. (SONG OF SOL. 2) (LIL-EE)

LYCIA Ancient name of unknown meaning which was that of a country of southwestern Asia Minor, on the Mediterranean. Paul landed at two of its towns on his voyage to Rome. (LISH-EE-AH)

LYDIA A name of Greek origin belonging to an ancient and prosperous kingdom on the western coast of Asia Minor. Many of the early churches were founded in Lydia. Lydia was also the name of a woman from the Lydian town of Thyatira who sold purple-dyed garments at Philippi. She was Paul's first European convert. (LID-EE-AH)

MAGDALA A tower. Magdala was the name of a city on the western coast of the Sea of Galilee and was home to Mary Magdalene. (MATT. 15) (MAG-DAH-LAH)

MAGDALENE Of Magdala. The name was borne by Mary Magdalene, a woman Christ cured of seven demons. She thereafter became a follower of Jesus and was the first to see the empty tomb. (MATT. 27) (MAG-DAH-LEEN)

MAHALATH A lute, a lyre. The name is borne in the Bible by a daughter of Ishmael and wife of Esau. (GEN. 28) (MAH-HAH-LATH)

MARA Bitter. The name was taken by Naomi as an expression of her bitter sorrow and grief at the death of her husband and two sons. (RUTH 1) (MAR-AH)

MARAH Hebrew name meaning "bitter." In the Bible, Marah is the name of a fountain at the sixth station of the Israelites in the wilderness. The water was so bitter the people could not drink. Divinely directed, Moses cast a certain tree into the water which took away its bitterness. (EXOD. 15) (MAR-AH)

MARTHA Derived from the Aramaic *mārthā* (lady, mistress). The name is borne in the Bible by the sister of Lazarus and Mary of Bethany. (JOHN 11) (MAR-THA)

MARY Of debated origin and meaning. *See* MARY (English Names). The name is borne in the Bible by the virgin mother of Jesus, the son of God. Betrothed to be married to Joseph, Mary was notified of her pregnancy and the impending birth of the Christ child by the archangel Gabriel. She is thought to have been a part of Christ's following and was present when he was put upon the cross. After seeing the crucifixion of her son, Mary was taken into the home of John the Apostle to live. (MARE-REE)

MICHAIAH Borne by both males and females and derived from the Hebrew *mīkhāyah* (who is like God?). It is borne in the Bible by the queen-mother of King Abijah. (2 CHRON. 13) (MY-KAY-AH)

MICHAL Feminine form of Michael, which is derived from the Hebrew *mīkhā'ēl* (who is like God?). The name is borne in the Bible by the younger of Saul's two daughters. She became the wife of David and helped him escape from Saul, but later her father married her to another man. After David became king, he reclaimed her as his wife, but they eventually became alienated from one another. (1 SAM. 14) (MĪ-KL)

MIRIAM Derived from the Hebrew *miryām*, which is of debated meaning. *See* MARY (English Names). The name is borne in the Old Testament by the sister of Aaron and Moses. After the exodus of the Hebrew people from Egypt, she came to be known as a prophetess to the people. (EXOD. 6) (MIR-EE-UM)

NAAMAH Sweetness, the beautiful. Naamah was the name of the daughter of Lamech and Zillah (GEN. 4) and of one of the wives of King Solomon (1 KINGS 14). (NAY-AH-MAH)

NAOMI My joy, my delight. Naomi was the wife of Elimelech and mother of Mahlon and Chilion. Following the death of her husband and sons, she changed her name to Mara (bitterness) as an expression of her bitter sorrow and grief. Naomi was the mother-in-law of Ruth. (RUTH 1) (NAY-O-MEE)

Ophrah Hebrew name meaning "a fawn." It is borne in the Bible by a descendant of Judah. (1 Chron. 4) (O-prah)

Orpah Hebrew name meaning "a fawn, a forelock." It is borne in the Bible by the wife of Chilion. She was the daughter-in-law of Naomi. (Ruth 1) (OR-pah)

Persis Probably of Latin or Greek origin but of uncertain derivation. It is borne in the Bible by a Roman Christian recognized by Paul for her kindness and hard work for the early church. (Rom. 16) (PER-sis)

Phoebe Derived from the Greek Phoibē, which is a feminine form of Phoibos (bright one). The name is borne in the New Testament by a deaconess of the early church at the Corinthian port of Cenchrea. Some believe she was the bearer of Paul's epistle to the Romans. (Rom. 16) Var: Phebe. (FEE-bee)

Priscilla Diminutive form of Prisca, which is a feminine form of Priscus, an old Roman family name derived from the Latin *priscus* (ancient, old, primitive). The name is borne in the New Testament by the wife of Aquila, both of whom were early Christians. She is also called Prisca. (Acts 18) (prih-SIL-lah)

Rachel Derived from the Hebrew *rāchēl* (ewe). The name is borne in the Bible by the younger daughter of Laban. Jacob had to toil for fourteen years as well as marry Rachel's older sister, Leah, before Laban would agree to let Jacob and Rachel marry. She was the mother of Joseph and Benjamin. (RAY-chel)

Rebekah Derived from the Hebrew *ribbqāh* (noose), which is from *rabak* (to bind, to tie). The name is borne in the Bible by the wife of Isaac and mother of his twin sons, Esau and Jacob. (Gen. 22) (reh-BEH-kah)

Rhoda Derived from the Greek Rhodē (a rose). The name is borne in the Bible by a young lady in the house of Mary, the mother of John Mark. (Acts 12) (RO-dah)

Ruth Of uncertain etymology, most think it is derived from the Hebrew *ruth*, a possible contraction of *re'uth* (companion, friend). The name is borne in the Bible by the Moabite wife of Mahlon and daughter-in-law of Naomi. After the death of her husband and father-in-law, Ruth returned to Bethlehem with Naomi, where she married Boaz and gave birth to Obed, the grandfather of David. Her story is told in the Old Testament book of Ruth. (rooth)

Salome Derived from the Hebrew *shālōm* (peace). The name is borne in the Bible by the mother of the apostles James and John. Salome is believed to have been a kinswoman of the Virgin Mary and was present at the crucifixion and later witnessed the empty tomb. (Matt. 27) (SOL-ah-may, sah-LO-mee)

Sapphira Aramaic name meaning "beautiful." It is borne in the Bible by the wife of Ananias. They were both struck dead for lying. (Acts 5) (sah-FĪ-rah)

Sarah Derived from the Hebrew *sārāh* (princess). Sarah was the name of the half sister and wife of Abraham. Originally named Sarai, her name was changed to Sarah after Abraham was told of her pregnancy. Sarah was the mother of Isaac, the progenitor of the Hebrews. (Gen. 11) (SER-ah, SA-rah)

Susannah Derived from the Hebrew *shōshannāh* (a lily, a rose). The name is borne in the Bible by a woman falsely accused of adultery. Her story is told in the apocryphal book of Susannah and the Elders. In the New Testament, the name is borne by a woman who ministered to Jesus. (Luke 8) Var: Susanna. (soo-ZAN-nah)

Tabitha Derived from the Aramaic *tabhītha* (roe, gazelle). The name is borne in the Bible by a woman disciple of Joppa. She was miraculously brought back to life by Peter. (Acts 9) (TA-bi-tha)

Tamar Hebrew name meaning "palm, a date palm." The name is borne in the Bible by a daughter-in-law of Judah (Gen. 38) and by a daughter of King David (2 Sam. 13). (tah-MAR)

Tirzah Pleasantness. Tirzah was the youngest of Zelophehad's five daughters. (Num. 26) Var: Tirza. (TEER-zah)

Zeresh Gold, splendor. Zeresh was the wife of Haman. (Esther 5) Var: Zereth. (ZEE-resh)

Zilpah Of uncertain meaning, some believe it to mean "a dropping." Zilpah is borne in the Bible by Leah's handmaid who was given to Jacob. She became the mother of Gad and Asher. (Gen. 30) (ZIL-pah)

Zipporah A little bird, a female bird. The name is borne in the Bible by the daughter of Reuel. She was the wife of Moses and mother of Gershom and Eliezer. (Exod. 2) (ZIP-po-rah)

CHAPTER FIVE

Chinese Names

SURNAMES ARE believed to have originated in China about two thousand years ago, during the Han dynasty. However, there are some who think they go back much further. Either way, China has the oldest and most complex system of naming in the world.

For male children, "milk" names are bestowed at birth, "book" or "school" names when the child enters school, a "marriage" name at the time of his wedding, and another name when entering a business or profession. In addition, the child may also be given an "official" name if he enters government service, an "everyday" name for use among close friends, a surname, a generational name, and at some point, an "ornamental" name, which has great personal meaning.

Female children are named in much the same manner but do not receive "school" names or "official" names. Upon marriage, a woman keeps her surname yet often adds her husband's surname as a courtesy. At one time it was illegal for couples to marry if they had the same surname.

In China the majority of surnames are derived from a poem known as the *Pe-Kia-Sin*, "the families of a hundred houses." This poem is thought to have been written by the ancient emperor Yao (2357–2258 B.C.), one of the earliest mortal rulers.

The Chinese take great care in the selection of names. Infants are usually given a name having two elements. It is common for one of the elements to be used for each child in the family, whether male or female. More recently, however, the mainland government's enforced policy of one child per family has made this practice moot for most families.

The names of females are more elegant and graceful than those of males. Among the very superstitious, the "milk" names of male babies can be quite disgusting in the hopes that the evil spirits will be repulsed and stay away from the treasured male child.

Chinese Male Names

AÑ Peace. (AHN)

CHÀNG Smooth, unimpeded, free. (CHANG)

CHÉNG-GŌNG Succeed, success. (CHENG-GŌNG)

CŌNG Intelligent, smart. (TSUNG)

DÉSHÍ Virtuous man. (DE-UH-SHEE)

DŌNG East. (DŌNG)

ENLAI Appreciating, being appreciative of that which comes and goes. The name was borne by Premier Zhou Enlai (1898–1976). (EN-LĪ)

FĀ Growth, beginning. (FAH-AH)

FǍ Law, method, way. (FAH)

Fai Growth, beginning. (FAH-EE)

Feng (Fēng) Wind; custom. (FANG)

Gan (Gàn) Adventure. (GAHN)

Hao (Hǎo) The good. (HOW)

He-ping (Hé-píng) Peace. Var: He Ping. (HE-PING)

Huang (Huáng) Rich; emperor (HWANG)

Huang-fu (Huáng-Fú) Rich future. Var: Huang Fu (HWANG-FOO)

Hung Great. (HUNG)

Ji (Jì) Continuity, order. (JEE)

Jiao-long (Jiǎo-lōng) Dragon-like. Var: Jiao Long. (JEOW-LONG)

Jia (Jīa) Outstanding person, good. (JEE-EH)

Jin (Jīn) Gold. (JIN)

Jing (Jìng) Pure, clean. (JEEN)

Jing (Jīng) Capital, capital city; a short form of Beijing. (JING)

Jing-sheng (Jīng-shēng) Borne in the city, born in Beijing. The name is borne by China's most prominent dissident, Wei Jīng-shēng. (JING-SHEN)

Ju-long (Jù-lōng) Powerful, gigantic dragon. (JOO-LONG)

Kang (Kāng) Well-being, health. (KAHNG)

Keung Universe. (KEE-UNG)

Kong (Kōng) Empty, hollow, void. (KONG)

Kun (Kūn) Universe. (KWUNG)

Li (Lì) Chestnut; strength, might. (LEE)

Liang (Liáng) Good, excellent. (LEE-AHNG)

Li-liang (Lì-liáng) Excellent strength. Var: Li Liang. (LEE-LEE-AHNG)

Ming-hoa (Míng-hóa) Shining and elite. Var: Ming Hoa. (MING-HWAH)

On Peace. (ŌN)

Piao (Piào) Handsome, good-looking, pretty. (PEE-OW)

Qing-nian (Qīng-nián) The younger generation. Var: Qing Nian. (CHING-NEE-ENN)

Quon Bright. (KWAN)

Shaoqiang (Shàoqiáng) Strong and profound. Var: Shao Qiang, Shao-qiang. (SHAU-CHYANG)

Shen (Shēn) Spirit, deep thought. (SHEN)

Sheng (Shèng) Victory. (SHUNG)

Sheng-li (Shèng-lì) Very victorious. Var: Sheng Li. (SHUNG-LEE)

Shing Victory. (SHING)

Wang (Wàng) Hope, wish, desire. (WAHNG)

Xiao-ping (Xiǎoping) Small peace. The name was borne by Vice Premier Deng Xiaoping. (ZHOU-PING)

Xing-fu (Xìng-fú) Happiness. Var: Xing Fu. (ZHING-FOO)

Xi-wang (Xī-wàng) Hope, wish, desire. Var: Xi Wang (SHE-WAHNG)

Xun (Xùn) Fast, swift. (SHWING)

Yat-sen Borne by Dr. Sun Yat-sen, the inspiration behind the Wuchang Uprising, which led to China becoming a republic in 1912. (YAHT-SEN)

Yu (Yǔ) Universe. (YOO)

Yu (Yù) Bright, shining. (YOO)

Yuan (Yuán) Round, circular, spherical. (YWAHN)

Yun-qi (Yùn-qì) Fortune, luck. Var: Yun Qi (YING-SHEE, YING-CHEE)

Zhong (Zhōng) Middle brother, second brother. (SHŌNG, CHŌNG)

Zhu (Zhù) Wish, congratulate. (ZHOO)

Zhuang (Zhuàng) Strong, robust. (ZHOO-ANG)

Chinese Female Names

Ah-lam Like an orchid. (AH-LAHM)

An (Ān) Peace. (AHN)

Bao (Bǎo) Precious. (BOU)

Bao-yu (Bǎo-Yù) Precious jade. Var: Bao Yu.(BOU-YOO)

Bik Jade. (BIK)

Chang (Chàng) Free. (CHAWNG)

Chan-juan (Chán-jūan) The moon; graceful. Var: Chan Juan. (CHAN-JOO-AHN)

Chu-hua (Chú-hūa) Chrysanthemum. Var: Chu Hua. (CHOO-HWAH)

Chun (Chūn) Spring. (CHWEN)

Cong (Cōng) Intelligent. (KŌNG)

Dao-ming (Dào-Míng) Shining path. Var: Dao Ming. (DOW-MING)

Da-xia (Dà-xìa) Long summer. Var: Da Xia. (DAH-ZHYAH)

De (Dé) Virtue, morals. (DEH)

Fang (Fāng) Fragrant. (FAHNG)

Fang-hua (Fāng-hūa) Fragrant flower. Var: Fang Hua. (FAHNG-HWAH)

Fen (Fēn) Fragrant. (FUN)

Feng (Fèng) Phoenix. (FUNG)

Hua (Hūa) Flower. (HWAH)

Huan-yue (Hūan-yùe) Joyful, exuberant and happy. Var: Huan Yue (HWAHN-YOO-EH)

Hui-fang (Hùi-fāng) Fragrant, fine fragrance. Var: Hui Fang. (HWEH-FAHNG)

Hui-ying (Hùi-yǐng) Intelligent, clever. Var: Hui Ying. (HWAY-YING)

Jia-li (Jīa-lì) Good and beautiful. Var: Jia Li. (JAH-LEE)

Jiao (Jiǎo) Beautiful. (JEE-OW)

Jin (Jīn) Gold. (JEEN)

Jing Sparkling, crystal. (JING)

Juān (Juān) Beautiful. (JOO-AHN)

Lei (Lěi) Flower bud. (LAY)

Li (Lǐ) Plum. (LEE)

Li (Lì) Beautiful. (LEE)

Lian Graceful willow. (LEE-AHN)

Lien (Lién) Lotus. (LEE-EN)

Lien-hua (Líen-hūa) Lotus flower. (LEE-EN-HWAH)

Li-hua (Lí-hūa) Pear blossom. (LEE-HWAH)

Lili Of uncertain meaning, it is possibly based on the Western name of Lily. (LIL-LEE)

Ling (Líng) Delicate. (LING)

Lin Lin (Lín lín) A name that denotes the bright, cheerful sound of a bell. (LIN-LIN)

Mei (Měi) Beautiful. (MAY)

Mei-hua (Měi-hūa) Beautiful flower. (MAY-HWAH)

Mei-lien (Měi-líen) Beautiful lotus. (MAY-LEE-EN)

Mei-xing (Měi-xīng) Beautiful star. (MAY-SHING)

Mei-zhen (Měi-zhēn) Beautiful pearl. (MAY-CHUN)

Min (Mǐn) Quick, sensitive. (MIN)

Ming (Míng) Shining; tomorrow. (MING)

Niu (Nīu) Girl. (NEE-OO)

Yi (Yí) Gift; appearance; rite. (YEE)

Yin (Yín) Silver. (YING)

Yu (Yù) Jade. (YOO)

Yue (Yuè) Happy, pleased, delighted. (EE-YEH)

Xiao-niao (Xǐao-nǐao) Small bird. (ZHOU-NEE-OW)

Xiao-xing (Xǐao-xīng) Morning star. (ZHOU-ZHING)

Xin (Xìn) Elegant, beautiful. (SHING)

Zan (Zàn) Support, favor, praise. (TSAN, CHAN)

Zhin (Zhēn) Treasure. (CHENG)

Zhi (Zhì) Nature, character, quality. (CHU, CHR)

Zhong (Zhōng) Devoted, loyal, honest. (CHŌNG)

Zhuo (Zhuō) Outstanding, brilliant. (CHOO-O)

Zi (Zī) Grow, multiply. (TSEE)

CHAPTER SIX

Czech and Slovak Names

UNITED UNTIL the fall of communism, the Czech Republic and the Republic of Slovakia share a common naming heritage. The Czech and Slovak languages are very similar and are of the West Slavic branch of the Indo-European language tree. Czech and Slovak names, apart from biblical names and a few borrowed from other countries, have their roots in the Slavic, or Slavonic, language. The two most common elements in both male and female names are *slav* (glory) and *mír* (from *meri*, great, famous).

Generally, Czech names are phonetically spelled and the stress commonly falls on the first syllable. Surnames developed in common European fashion, with the majority of them being patronymics and those derived from nicknames and place-names.

Czech and Slovak Male Names

ALEXANDR Czech form of Alexander, a derivative of the Greek Alexandros (defender or helper of mankind), a compounding of the elements *alexein* (to defend, to help) and *andros* (man). Pet: Aleš, Olexa, Saša. (AH-LEHK-SAHN-DER)

ALEXEJ Czech form of Alexis, which is derived from the Greek *alexein* (to defend, to help). Pet: Aleš, Saša. (AH-LEX-EE)

ALOIS Czech form of Aloysius, a Latinized form of Aloys, a Provençal cognate of Louis (famous in war), which is from the Old High German Hluodowig, a compounding of the elements *hluod* (famous) and *wīg* (war, strife). Pet: Lojza. (AH-LO-EES)

AMBROZ Derived from the Greek Ambrosios (immortal). The name was borne by a 4th-century bishop of Milan, St. Ambrose, who is considered to be one of the four great Latin doctors of the church. Short: Brož. Pet: Brožek. (AHM-BROZ)

ANTONIN From the Latin Antonius, an old Roman family name of unknown etymology. The name is popular throughout Europe, due in large part to its connection with St. Anthony the Great, an Egyptian ascetic and the first Christian monk. "Priceless" and "of inestimable worth" are popular folk definitions of the name. Pet: Tonda, Toníček, Tonik, Tonin. (AHN-TŌ-NIN)

ARNOŠT Czech form of the German Ernst, which is from the Old High German Ernost and Ernust, names derived from *ernust* (earnest, resolute). (AHR-NOSHT)

BARNABÁ From the Late Latin and Greek Barnabas, which is derived from the Aramaic *barnebhū'āh* (son of exhortation). The name is borne in the Bible by a Christian apostle and missionary companion of St. Paul. (BAHR-NAH-BAH)

BARTOLOMĚJ Czech form of Bartholomew, which is derived from the Greek Bartholomaios (son of Talmai). Talmai is an Aramaic name meaning "hill, mound, furrows." The name is borne in the Bible by one of the Twelve Apostles of Christ. (BAHR-TOL-O-MEW)

BEDŘICH Czech form of Frederick, a cognate of the Germanic Friedrich (peace ruler), which is a derivative of the obsolete Fridurih, a compound name composed from the elements *frid* (peace) and *rik* (ruler, king). Pet: Béda, Bedříšek. Short: Ben. (BEH-DER-ZHEECH)

BENEŠ Czech form of Benedict, which is from the Latin Benedictus (blessed), which is from *benedicere* (to speak well of, to bless). Short: Ben. (BEN-ESH)

BLAŽEJ Derived from the Latin Blaesus, a derivative of *blaesus* (deformed, stuttering). (BLAH-ZHAY)

BOGDAN Compound name composed of the elements *bog* (God) and *dan* (gift): hence, "God's gift." Var: Bogudan. Short: Dan. (BŌG-DAHN).

BOGUMIL Compound name composed of the elements *bog* (God) and *mil* (love, grace, favor): hence, "God's love." Var: Bogmil. (BŌG-YOO-MEEL)

BOHDAN Czech form of Bogdan (God's gift). *See* BOGDAN. (BO-DAHN)

BOHUMIL Czech form of Bogumil (God's love). *See* Bogumil. Pet: Bohous. (BO-HOO-MEEL)

BOHUMÍR Compound name composed of the Slavonic elements *bog* (God) and *meri* (great, famous): hence, "God is great." (BO-HOO-MEER)

BOHUSLAV Compound name composed of the Slavonic elements *bog* (God) and *slav* (glory): hence, "God's glory." Pet: Bohous, Bohus. (BO-HOO-SLAHV)

BOJAN Derived from the old Slavonic element *boi* (battle). Pet: Bojánek, Bojek, Bojík. (BAH-JAHN)

BOLESLAV Compound name composed of the Slavonic elements *bole* (large, great) and *slav* (glory): hence, "great glory." Pet: Bolek. (BO-LEH-SLAHV)

BOŘIVOJ Compound name composed of the Slavonic elements *borit* (to fight) and *voi* (warrior): hence, "fighting warrior." Pet: Bořa, Bořek, Bořik. (BOR-EE-VOY)

BOŽIDAR Compound name composed of the elements *boži* (of God, divine) and *dar* (gift): hence, "divine gift, a gift of God." Pet: Boža, Božek. (BO-ZHEE-DAHR)

BRATISLAV Compound name composed of the Slavonic elements *brat* (brother) and *slav* (glory). (BRAH-TEE-SLAHV)

BŘETISLAV Compound name composed of the Slavonic elements *brech* (noise, din) and *slav* (glory). Pet: Břetík. (BREH-TEE-SLAHV)

BRONISLAV Compound name composed of the Slavonic elements *bron* (armor, protection) and *slav* (glory). Var: Branislav. Pet: Branek, Branik. (BRO-NEE-SLAHV)

BUDISLAV Compound name composed of the Slavonic elements *budit* (to awaken, to stir) and *slav* (glory). Pet: Buděk. (BOO-DEE-SLAHV)

CERNY Derived from *černý* (black). (SAIR-NEE)

ČESLAV Compound name composed of the Slavonic elements *chest* (honor) and *slav* (glory). Var: Ctislav. (CHEH-SLAHV)

CTIBOR Compound name composed of the Slavonic elements *chest* (honor) and *borit* (to fight): hence, "to fight with honor." Pet: Ctík. (STEE-BOR)

DALIBOR Compound name composed of the Slavonic elements *dal* (afar) and *borit* (to fight). Pet: Dal, Dalek, Libor. (DAH-LEE-BOR)

DANIEL Derived from the Hebrew *dānī'ēl* (God is my judge). *See* DANIEL (Biblical Names). Pet: Danek, Daneš, Danoušek. (DAN-YEL)

DAVID Derived from the Hebrew *dāwīd* (beloved). Pet: Davidek. (DAH-VEED)

DOBROMIL Compound name composed of the Slavonic elements *dobro* (good, kind) and *mil* (love, grace, favor). (DŌ-BRO-MEEL)

DOBROMÍR Compound name composed of the Slavonic elements *dobro* (good, kind) and *meri* (great, famous): hence, "good and famous." (DŌ-BRO-MEER)

DOBROSLAV Compound name composed of the elements *dobro* (good, kind) and *slav* (glory). (DŌ-BRO-SLAHV)

DUŠAN Derived from the element *dusha* (spirit, soul). Pet: Duša, Dušanek, Dušek. (DOO-SHAHN)

EDUARD Czech form of the English Edward, which is from the Old English Ēadweard (wealthy guardian), a compounding of the elements *ēad* (prosperity, fortune, riches) and *weard* (guardian, protector). Var: Edvard. Pet: Eda, Edík. (EH-DOO-AHRD)

EMIL Derived from the Latin Aemilius, an old Roman family name thought to be derived from *aemulus* (emulating, trying to equal or excel, rival). The name is borne by Olympic gold medal champion Emil Zatopek. (EH-MEEL)

EVŽEN Czech form of Eugene, a cognate of the Greek Eugenios, which is derived from *eugenēs* (well-born). Pet: Evža, Evženek, Evžík. (EHV-ZHEN)

FERDINAND Derived from the Spanish Ferdinando, a name of uncertain etymology. It is thought to be of Germanic origin and might be composed from the elements *frithu* (peace), *fardi* (journey), or *ferchvus* (youth, life) and *nanths* (courage), *nanthi* (venture, risk), or *nand* (ready, prepared). Short: Ferda. (FEHR-DEE-NAHND)

FILIP From the Latin Philippus, a derivative of the Greek Philippos (lover of horses), a compounding of the elements *philos* (loving) and *hippos* (a horse). Pet: Filek, Filípek, Filoušek. (FEE-LEEP)

FRANTIŠEK Derived from the Middle Latin Franciscus (a Frenchman), which is from Francus (a Frank, a freeman), which has its root in the Old French *franc* (free). Pet: Fanoušek, Fráňa, Franek, Franta, Frantík. (FRAHN-TEE-SHEK)

GABRIEL From the Hebrew Gavriel, which is derived from *gavhrī'ēl* (God is my strength). *See* GABRIEL (Biblical Names). Pet: Gába, Gabek, Riel. (GAH-BREE-EL)

GUSTAV A borrowing from the German, Gustav is a name of debated origin. Some believe it is from the Germanic Gotzstaf (divine staff), a compounding of the elements *gott* (God) and *staf* (staff). Others feel that it is derived from the Old Norse elements *Gautr* (the tribal name of the Goths) and *stafr* (staff): hence, "staff of the Goths." Pet: Gustik. (GOO-STAHV)

HAVEL Czech form of Paul, a derivative of the Latin Paulus, which originated as a Roman family name derived from *paulus* (small). *See* PAUL (Biblical Names). Pet: Háva, Havelek, Havlík. (HAH-VEL)

HNEDY Derived from *hne'dý* (brown). (HNEH-DEE)

HOLIC Derived from *holić* (barber). (HO-LEEK)

IGNÁC Czech form of the Latin Ignatius, a derivative of Egnatius, an old Roman family name of uncertain etymology. Some believe it to be of Etruscan origin. Others think it is from the Latin *ignis* (fire). Pet: Ignácek, Nácek, Nácicek. (EEG-NAHCH)

IVAN Czech cognate of John (God is gracious). Pet: Ivánek, Váňa, Váňuška. (EE-VAHN)

JACH Short form of any of the various Czech names beginning with the element *Ja-*. (YAHSH)

JÁCHYM Czech form of Joachim, a cognate of the Hebrew Jehoiakim, which is from Yehoyakim (God will establish). In medieval Christian tradition, Joachim was the name assigned to the father of the Virgin Mary, as Anne was assigned to her mother. Pet: Jach. (YAH-SHEEM)

JAKUB Czech cognate of Jacob, a name derived from the Ecclesiastic Late Latin Iacomus and Iacobus, derivatives of the Greek Iakōbos, which is from the Hebrew Yaakov. Yaakov is derived from *ya'aqob* (supplanting, seizing by the heel). Pet: Jach, Jakoubek, Kuba, Kubas, Kubeš, Kubiček. (YAH-KOOB)

JAN Czech form of John (God is gracious). *See* JOHAN. Pet: Honza, Honzik, Jach, Janeček, Janek, Janík, Jenda. (YAHN)

JAREK A pet form of any of the various names beginning with the Slavonic element *jaro* (spring), Jarek is also bestowed as an independent given name. Pet: Nonza, Honzík, Jaroušek. (YAH-REK)

JAROMIL Compound name composed of the Slavonic elements *jaro* (spring) and *milo* (love, grace, favor): hence, "lover of spring." Var: Jarmil. Pet: Jarda, Jarek, Jaroušek. (YAH-RO-MEEL)

JAROMÍR Compound name composed of the Slavonic elements *jaro* (spring) and *meri* (great, famous). Pet: Jarek, Jaroušek, Slávek. (YAHR-O-MEER)

JAROSLAV Compound name composed of the Slavonic elements *jaro* (spring) and *slav* (glory). Pet: Jarda, Jarek, Jaroušek, Slávek. (YAHR-O-SLAHV)

JINDŘICH Czech cognate of the German Heinrich (ruler of an enclosure, home ruler). The name is derived from the Old High German Haganrih, a compound name composed of the elements *hag* (an enclosure, a hedging-in) and *rihhi* (ruler), and from the Old High German Heimerich, a compounding of the elements *heim* (home, an estate) and *rik* (ruler, king). Pet: Jindra, Jindřík, Jindříšek, Jindroušek. (YEEN-DER-ZHEECH)

JIŘÍ Czech cognate of George, which is from the Greek Geōrgios (earthworker, farmer), a compounding of the elements *gē* (earth) and *ergein* (to work). Pet: Jíra, Jiran, Jiránek, Jiříček, Jiřík, Jirka, Jiroušek. (YEER-ZHEE)

JOHAN Czech form of John (God is gracious), which is from the Middle Latin Johannes, an evolution of the Ecclesiastic Late Latin Joannes. Joannes is from the Greek Iōannes, a derivative of the Hebrew Yehanan, a short form of Yehohanan, which is from *yehōhānān* (Yahweh is gracious). The name, borne by several important biblical characters, was also borne by many saints, twenty-three popes, and many kings throughout Europe. Pet: Hanek, Hanuš, Hanušek, Nušek. (YO-HAHN)

JOSEF Czech cognate of the Hebrew Yosef, a name derived from *yōsēf* (may he add). *See* JOSEPH (Biblical Names). Pet: Józa, Joža, Jožánek, Jozka, Jožka, Pepik. (YO-SUF)

JULIUS A borrowing from the Latin, Julius originated as an old Roman family name thought to be derived from Iulus (the first down on the chin, downy-bearded). As a person just beginning to develop facial hair is young, "youth" became an accepted meaning of the name. Pet: Julek. (YOO-LYOOS)

KAREL Czech cognate of Charles, a name derived from the Germanic *karl* (full-grown, a man). Pet: Kája, Kájíček, Kájik, Kájínek, Karlícek, Karlík, Karloušek. (KAH-REL)

KLIMENT Czech form of Clement, which is from the Late Latin Clēmens, a derivative of *clemens* (mild, gentle, merciful). (KLEE-MENT)

KONSTANTIN Czech form of Constantine, which is from the Latin Constantinus, a derivative of *constans* (steadfast, constant). The name was borne by Constantine the Great (280?–337), the first emperor of Rome to be converted to Christianity. (KON-STAHN-TEEN)

KOPEKY Derived from the Czech *kopec* (hill). (KO-PEH-KEE)

KORNEL From the Latin Cornelius, an old Roman family name of uncertain etymology. Some believe it is derived from *cornu* (horn). Pet: Kornek, Nelek. (KOR-NEHL)

KOVAR Derived from the Czech *kovář* (smith). (KO-VAHR)

KRYŠTOF Czech cognate of Christopher (bearing Christ), which is from the Ecclesiastic Late Latin Christophorus and the Ecclesiastic Greek Christophoros, a compounding of the elements *Christos* (Christ) and *pherein* (to bear). Pet: Kryša, Kryšek. (KREESH-TOF)

LEOŠ Czech form of the Late Latin Leo, a direct derivative of *leo* (lion). The name was borne by Czech composer Leoš Janaček (1854–1928). (LEH-ŌSH)

LEV Derived from the Czech *lev* (lion). (LEHV)

LIBOR Derived from the Latin Liberius, which is from the root *liber* (free). Pet: Libek, Liborek. (LEE-BOR)

LUBOMÍR Compound name composed of the Slavonic elements *lub* (love) and *meri* (great, famous). Var: Lubor, Lumír. Pet: Luba, Lubek, Lubík, Lubomírek, Luborek, Luboš, Lubošek. (LOO-BO-MEER)

LUDOMÍR Compound name composed of the Slavonic elements *lud* (people, folk, tribe) and *meri* (great, famous): hence, "famous people." Pet: Luděk. (LOO-DŌ-MEER)

LUDOSLAV Compound name composed of the Slavonic elements *lud* (people, folk, tribe) and *slav* (glory): hence, "glorious people." Pet: Luděk. (LOO-DŌ-SLAHV)

LUDVÍK Czech form of Ludwig (famous in war), a German name derived from the obsolete Hluodowig, a compound name composed of the elements *hluod* (famous) and *wīg* (war, strife). Pet: Lozja. (LOOD-VEEK)

LUKÁŠ Czech cognate of the Latin Lucas, a derivative of Lucius, which is from the root *lux* (light). Alternatively, some believe the name is derived from the Ecclesiastic Greek Loukas, a contraction of Loukanos (man from Lucania). Pet: Lukášek, Luki. (LOO-KAHSH)

MAREK Czech cognate of Mark, which is from the Latin Marcus, a name of uncertain derivation. Most believe it has its root in Mars, the name of the Roman mythological god of war, and give it the definition "warlike." Others, however, think it might be from *mas* (manly) or from the Greek *malakoz* (soft, tender). Pet: Mareček, Mareš, Mařík, Maroušek. (MAH-REK)

MARIAN From the Latin Mariānus (of Marius), which is from Marius, a derivative of Mars, the name of the Roman mythological god of war. As a result of similarity of form, the name eventually became associated with Maria, the name of the Blessed Virgin, and was often bestowed in her honor. The name is borne by Czech Prime Minister Marian Calfa. (MAH-REE-AHN)

MATĚJ Czech cognate of Matthew, which is from the Ecclesiastic Late Latin Matthaeus, a derivative of the Ecclesiastic Greek Matthaois and Matthias, contractions of Mattathias. The name is derived from the Hebrew Matityah, which has its root in *matīthyāh* (gift of God). Var: Matyáš. Pet: Máta, Matejek, Matějícek, Matějík, Matoušek, Matys, Matýsek. (MAH-TYOO)

MAXMILIÁN Czech form of Maximilian. *See* MAXIMILIAN (German Names). Short: Max. (MAX-MEEL-YAHN)

MEČISLAV Compound name, the first element of which is of uncertain derivation: from *miecz* (sword), the Old Polish *miecz* (man, father), or *mieszka* (bear). The second element is the Slavonic *slav* (glory). Pet: Meček, Mečík, Mečislavek. (MEH-CHEE-SLAHV)

METODĚJ Czech form of the Russian Mefodi, which is from the Greek Methodios (fellow traveler), a compounding of the elements *meta* (with) and *hodos* (road, path). The name was borne by the evangelist St. Methodius (d. 885), the first translator of the Bible into the Slavonic language. Pet: Metodek, Metoušek. (MEH-TŌ-DYEH)

Michal Czech form of Michael, which is from the Hebrew *mīkhā'ēl* (who is like God?). Var: Michel. Pet: Michálek, Miki, Míša. (MEE-KEL)

Mikoláš Czech cognate of Nicholas (victory of the people), which is from the Greek Nikolaos, a compounding of the elements *nikē* (victory) and *laos* (the people). Var: Mikuláš. Pet: Miki, Mikulášek. (MEE-KO-LAHSH)

Miloslav Compound name composed of the Slavonic elements *mil* (grace, favor, love) and *slav* (glory): hence, "lover of glory." Pet: Milda, Miloň, Miloš. Pet: Miki, Mikulášek. (MEE-LO-SLAHV)

Mirek A pet form of Miroslav (great glory), Mirek is also bestowed as an independent given name. *See* MIROSLAV. (MEE-REHK)

Miroslav Compound name composed of the Slavonic elements *meri* (great, famous) and *slav* (glory). Pet: Mirek, Slávek. (MEE-RO-SLAHV)

Oldřich Czech cognate of the German Ulrich (noble ruler), which is from the Old High German Udalrich, a compound name composed of the elements *uodal* (nobility, prosperity, fortune) and *rik* (ruler, power, king). Pet: Olda, Oldra, Oldřišek, Oleček, Olík, Olin, Oloušek. (OL-DREECH)

Olexa A pet form of Aleksander (defender or helper of mankind), Olexa is also bestowed as an independent given name. *See* ALEKSANDER. (O-LEKS-AH)

Ondřej Czech form of the Greek Andreas, a derivative of *andreios* (manly). The popularity of St. Andrew, one of the Twelve Apostles, led to the name and its cognates being firmly established throughout Europe. Pet: Ondra, Ondrášek, Ondřejek, Ondroušek, Ondrus. (OHN-DREE)

Oto Czech form of the German Otto, a name that originated as a short form of any of the various Germanic names containing the element *od* (wealth, riches, prosperity). Var: Ota. Pet: Otik. (O-TŌ)

Otokar From the German Ottokar, an evolution of the obsolete Odovacar, a compound name composed of the elements *od, ot* (prosperity, riches, fortune) and *wacar* (watchful, vigilant). Var: Otakar. Short: Ota, Oto. Pet: Otakárek, Otík. (O-TAH-KAHR)

Pavel Czech cognate of Paul, which is from the Latin Paulus, a name that originated as an old Roman family name derived from *paulus* (small). Pet: Pavliček, Pavlík, Pavloušek. (PAH-VEHL)

Petr Czech cognate of Peter, which is derived from the Ecclesiastic Latin Petrus and the Greek Petros, names derived from the vocabulary words *petrus* (a rock) and *petros* (a stone). Pet: Pét'a, Pet'ka, Petríček, Petrík, Petroušek, Petulka, Petunka. (PEH-TR)

Přemysl Czech form of the Latin Primus, which is directly derived from the vocabulary word meaning "first." Pet: Myslík, Přemek, Přemoušek. (PRAY-MEE-SIL)

Přibislav Compound name composed from the Slavonic elements *pribit* (to help, to be present) and *slav* (glory): hence, "helper of glory." Pet: Přiba, Přibík, Přibišek. (PREE-BIH-SLAHV)

Prokop From the Greek Prokopios (progressive), a compound name composed of the elements *pro* (before) and *kopios* (in great abundance, copious). The name was borne by a 4th-century Greek saint, the first to be martyred in Palestine under the reign of Diocletian. (PRAH-KOP)

Radek Czech form of Roderick (famous ruler), a name derived from the Latin Rodericus, which is from the Old High German Hrodrich, a compounding of the elements *hruod* (fame) and *rik* (king, ruler). Var: Radík. Pet: Radaček, Radan, Radko, Radoš, Radoušek. (RAH-DEHK)

Radomír Compound name composed of the Slavonic elements *rad* (glad) and *meri* (great, famous). Var: Radim, Radímír. Pet: Radeček, Radek, Radoušek, Mirek. (RAH-DEE-MEER)

Radoslav Compound name composed of the Slavonic elements *rad* (glad) and *slav* (glory). Pet: Radeček, Radek, Slávek. (RAH-DO-SLAHV)

Řehoř Czech cognate of Gregory, which is from the Greek Grēgorios (vigilant, a watchman), a name derived from the verb *egeirein* (to awaken). Pet: Hořek, Hořik, Řehák, Řehořek, Řehůrek. (REY-HOR)

Richard From the Old High German Richart (brave ruler), a compound name composed from the elements *rik, rīc* (power, ruler, king) and *hart* (strong, brave, hardy). Pet: Ríša. (REE-CHARD)

Roman From the Latin Rōmānus (a Roman), which is from Roma, the Latin and Italian name of Rome, the capital city of Italy. Pet: Románek. (RO-MAHN)

Rostislav Compound name composed of the Slavonic elements *rosts* (usurp, seize, appropriate) and *slav* (glory): hence, "seizer of glory." Pet: Rosta, Rostek, Rostíček, Rostík, Slávek. (RAH-STEE-SLAHV)

Rudolf A borrowing from the German, Rudolf is an evolution of the Old High German Hrodulf (famous wolf), a compounding of the elements *hruod* (fame) and *wulf* (wolf). (ROO-DAHLF)

SILNY Derived from the Czech *silný* (strong). (SEEL-NEE)

ŠIMON From the Ecclesiastic Late Latin Simon, which is from the Greek Simōn and Seimōn, cognates of the Hebrew Shimon. The name has its root in *shim'ōn* (heard). Pet: Šiek, Šimeček, Simůnek, Sionek. (SEE-MONE)

SLAVOMÍR Compound name composed of the Slavonic elements *slav* (glory) and *meri* (great, famous): hence, "great glory, glory is great." Pet: Sláva, Slávek. (SLAH-VO-MEER)

SOBĚSLAV Compound name composed of the Slavonic elements *sobi* (to usurp, to overtake) and *slav* (glory): hence, "usurper of glory." Pet: Slávek, Sobeš, Sobík. (SO-BYEH-SLAHV)

STANISLAV Compound name composed of the Slavonic elements *stan* (government) and *slav* (glory): hence, "glorious government." Pet: Slávek, Stáňa, Standa, Stanek, Stanícek, Staník, Stanouš, Stanoušek. (STAH-NEE-SLAHV)

ŠTĚPÁN Czech form of Stephen, a cognate of the Greek Stephanos, which is from *stephanos* (a crown, a garland). Pet: Štěpa, Štěpanek, Štěpek, Štěpík, Štěpka, Stepoušek. (SHTYEH-PAHN)

SVATOMÍR Compound name composed of the Slavonic elements *svyanto* (bright, holy) and *meri* (great, famous): hence, "holy and famous." (SVAH-TŌ-MEER)

SVATOPULK Compound name composed from the Slavonic elements *svyanto* (bright, holy) and *polk* (people, folk, race): hence, "holy people." (SVAH-TŌ-POOLK)

SVATOSLAV Compound name composed from the Slavonic elements *svyanto* (bright, holy) and *slav* (glory): hence, "holy glory." (SVAH-TŌ-SLAHV)

TECHOMÍR Compound name composed from the Slavonic elements *tech* (consolation) and *meri* (great, famous). (TEH-HO-MEER)

TECHOSLAV Compound name composed from the Slavonic elements *tech* (consolation) and *slav* (glory). (TEH-HO-SLAHV)

TOMÁŠ From the Ecclesiastic Greek Thōmas, which is derived from the Aramaic *tě'ōma* (a twin). Short: Tom. Pet: Toman, Tománek, Tomášek, Tomik, Tomoušek. (TŌ-MAHS)

URBAN From the Latin Urbānus (city dweller, urbanite), which is derived from *urbs* (a city). The name was borne by several saints and popes, which led to its widespread use across Europe. Pet: Ura, Urba, Urbek, Urek. (OOR-BAHN)

VALENTÝN Czech form of Valentine, which is from the Latin Valentīnus, a derivative of *valens* (to be healthy, strong). Pet: Valentýnek. (VAH-LEHN-TEEN)

VAVŘINEC Czech form of Laurence, which is from the Latin Laurentius (man from Laurentum). Laurentum, the name of a town in Latium, is thought to be derived from *laurus* (laurel). Short: Vavro. Pet: Vavřik, Vavřiniček. (VAH-VREE-NEK)

VELESLAV Compound name composed from the Slavonic elements *vele* (great) and *slav* (glory): hence, "great glory, glory is great." Pet: Vela, Velek, Veloušek. (VEH-LEH-SLAHV)

VĚNCESLAV Czech form of Wenceslas, a name composed of the elements *Wend*, a term denoting a member of the old Slavic people who now live in an enclave south of Berlin, and *slav* (glory): hence, "glory of the Wends." The variant form Václav is borne by Czech president Václav Havel (b. 1936). Var: Václav. Pet: Vasek, Věna, Věnek, Venoušek. (VYEHN-SEH-SLAHV)

VIKTOR Czech form of Victor, a Latin name derived from *victor* (conqueror, winner, victor). (VEEK-TOR)

VILÉM Czech cognate of the German Wilhelm, which is from the Old High German Willehelm (resolute protector), a compounding of the elements *willeo* (will, resolution) and *helm* (helmet, protection). Pet: Vileček, Vilek, Vilémek, Vilík, Viloušek. (VEE-LEHM)

VINCENC Czech form of Vincent (conquering), which is from the Late Latin Vincentius, a derivative of *vincere* (to conquer). Pet: Čenek, Vinca, Vincek, Vincenek. (VEEN-SENT)

VÍT Czech form of the Latin Vitus, a derivative of *vita* (life). Pet: Vitek. (VEET)

VLADIMÍR Compound name composed from the Slavonic elements *volod* (rule) and *meri* (great, famous): hence, "famous ruler." Short: Vlad. (VLAH-DEE-MEER)

VLADISLAV Compound name composed from the Slavonic elements *volod* (rule) and *slav* (glory): hence, "glorious rule." Var: Ladislav. Short: Vlad. (VLAH-DEE-SLAHV)

VOJTĚCH Popular compound name composed from the Slavonic elements *voi* (soldier, warrior) and *tech* (consolation, comfort, solace): hence, "soldier of consolation." Pet: Vojta, Vojtek, Vojtík, Vojtíšek. (VOY-TYEK)

ZBYHNĚV Czech cognate of the Polish Zbigniew (to do away with anger), a compounding of the elements *zbit* (to do away with, to be rid of) and *gniew* (anger). Pet: Zbyňa, Zbyněk, Zbyšek. (ZBEE-NYEHV)

ZDENĚK Czech form of the Latin Sidōnius (follower of St. Denis). Denis is derived from the Greek Dionysius (of Dionysos, the Greek mythological god of wine and revelry). Pet: Zdeněček, Zdeník, Zdenko, Zdenoušek, Zdíček. (ZDEH-NYEK)

ZDESLAV Compound name composed of the Slavonic elements *zde* (here, present) and *slav* (glory). Var: Zdislav. Pet: Zdík, Zdišek. (ZDEH-SLAHV)

ZELENY Derived from the Czech *zelený* (green). (ZEH-LEH-NEE)

ŽITOMÍR Compound name composed of the Slavonic elements *zhit* (to live) and *meri* (great, famous). Pet: Žitek, Zitoušek. (ZHEE-TŌ-MEER)

ŽIVAN Popular name derived from the Slavonic element *zhiv* (living, vigorous, alive). Pet: Živanek, Živek, Živko. (ZHEE-VAHN)

ZLATAN Derived from *zlato* (gold). Pet: Zlatek, Zlatíček, Zlatík, Zlatko, Zlatoušek. (ZLAH-TAHN)

Czech and Slovak Female Names

AGÁTA Czech form of the Greek Agathē, a name derived from *agathos* (good, kind). The name was borne by a famous 3rd-century saint, which led to its use across Europe. (AH-GAH-TAH)

ALENA A short form of Magdalena (of Magdala), Alena is also bestowed as an independent given name. *See* MAGDALENA. (AH-LAY-NAH)

ALEXANDRA Feminine form of the Greek Alexandros, a compound name derived from the elements *alexein* (to defend, to help) and *andros* (mankind). Pet: Saša. (AH-LEX-AHN-DRA)

ALŽBĚTA Czech form of Elizabeth, which is from the Hebrew *elisheba'* (God is my oath). Short: Běta. Pet: Alžbětka, Bětka, Betuška. (AHLZH-BYEH-TAH)

ANASTÁZIE From the Russian Anastasia, which is a feminine form of the Greek Anastasios (of the resurrection). Pet: Anastázka, Anka, Nast'a, Stázka, Stázička. (AH-NAH-STAH-ZEE)

ANDĚLA Czech form of Angela, a name derived from the Greek *angelos* (messenger, messenger of God). Var: Anděl. Pet: Andělka. (AHN-DYEH-LAH)

ANDREA Feminine form of the Greek Andreas, which is derived from *andreios* (manly). Pet: Andrejka. (AHN-DRAY-AH)

ANEŽKA Czech form of Agnes, which is from the Greek Hagnē, a derivative of *hagnos* (chaste, pure, sacred). The name is popular throughout Europe due to the fame of St. Agnese, a thirteen-year-old Roman martyred for her Christian beliefs during the reign of Diocletian. Pet: Aneša, Neška. (AH-NEHZH-KAH)

ANNA Cognate of the Hebrew Hannah, a derivative of *hannāh, chaanach* (grace, gracious, mercy). Pet: Anča, Andula, Andulka, Anička, Aninka, Anka, Anuška. (AH-NAH)

ANTONIE Feminine form of Antonin, a name derived from Antonius, an old Roman family name of unknown etymology. "Priceless" and "of inestimable worth" are popular folk definitions. Pet: Tonička, Tonka, Tony. (AHN-TŌ-NYEE)

BARBORA Czech cognate of Barbara (foreign woman), a Latin name derived from *barbarus* (foreign, strange), a term applied to non-Romans or those deemed to be uncivilized. Var: Varvara. Short: Bára, Bora, Vára. Pet: Barčinka, Baruna, Barunka, Baruška, Basia, Varina, Varinka, Varya, Varyuška. (BAHR-BOR-AH)

BÉATA Derived from the Greek *beatus* (blessed, happy). Pet: Béatka. (BAY-AH-TAH)

BEDŘIŠKA Feminine form of Bedřich, the Czech cognate of Frederick, a cognate of the Germanic Friedrich (peace ruler), which is a derivative of the obsolete Fridurih, a compound name composed from the elements *frid* (peace) and *rik* (ruler, king). (BEH-DREE-SHKAH)

BERTA A borrowing from the German, Berta is derived from *beraht* (bright, famous). Pet: Bertička, Bertinka. (BEHR-TAH)

BĚTA A short form of Alžběta, Běta is also bestowed as an independent given name. Pet: Bětka, Betuška. (BYEH-TAH)

BLANKA Czech cognate of the French Blanche, a name derived from *blanc* (white). Pet: Blanička. (BLAHN-KAH)

BOHDANA Feminine form of Bohdan (God's gift), a Czech cognate of Bogdan, a name composed of the

Slavonic elements *bog* (God) and *dan* (gift). Short: Bohda, Dana. (BO-DAH-NAH)

BOŽIDARA Feminine form of Božidar (divine gift, a gift of God), a compound name composed of the Slavonic elements *boži* (of God, divine) and *dar* (gift). Pet: Boža, Božena, Božka. (BO-ZHEE-DAH-RAH)

BŘETISLAVA Feminine form of Břetislav, a compounding of the Slavonic elements *brech* (noise, din) and *slav* (glory). Pet: Bretička, Břet'ka. (BREH-TEE-SLAH-VAH)

BRONISLAVA Feminine form of Bronislav (armor glory), a compound name composed of the Slavonic elements *bron* (armor, protection) and *slav* (glory). Var: Branislava. Pet: Braňa, Branka, Broňa, Bronička, Bronka. (BRO-NEE-SLAH-VAH)

CECÍLIE Feminine form of Cecil, which is derived from Caecilius, an old Roman family name that has its root in the Latin *caecus* (blind, dim-sighted). *See* CECILIA (Italian Names). Pet: Cecilka, Cílinka, Cilka. (SEH-SEE-LEE)

DALIBORA Feminine form of Dalibor (to fight afar), a compound name composed from the Slavonic elements *dal* (afar) and *borit* (to fight). Short: Dala. Pet: Dalena, Dalenka. (DAH-LEE-BOR-AH)

DANA Feminine form of the Hebrew Dan (he judged), a name borne in the Bible by one of Jacob's sons from whom the twelve tribes of Israel descended. Alternatively, Dana is used as a short form of Bohdana (God's gift). Pet: Danička, Danka, Danulka, Danuše, Danuška. (DAH-NAH)

DANIELA Feminine form of Daniel, which is derived from the Hebrew *dāni'ēl* (God is my judge). *See* DANIEL (Biblical Male Names). Pet: Dana, Danička, Danka, Danulka, Danuška. (DAH-NEE-EHL-LAH)

DANIKA Common to the Eastern Europeans, Danika is derived from an old Slavonic element meaning "morning star." Var: Danica. (DAH-NEE-KAH)

DARIE Feminine form of Darius, an old Latin name derived from the Greek Dareios, which is of uncertain origin and meaning. It is thought to ultimately be derived from Darayavahush, the name of an ancient Persian king. Pet: Darina, Darinka, Darka, Daruška. (DAH-REE)

DOBRILA Popular name derived from *dobro* (good, kind). (DŌ-BREE-LAH)

DOBROMILA Feminine form of Dobromil, a compound name composed from the Slavonic elements *dobro* (good, kind) and *mil* (love, grace, favor). Pet: Dobruška, Míla, Milka. (DŌ-BRO-MEE-LAH)

DOBROMÍRA Feminine form of Dobromír, a compound name composed from the Slavonic elements *dobro* (good, kind) and *meri* (great, famous). Pet: Mirka. (DŌ-BRO-MEER-AH)

DOBROSLAVA Feminine form of Dobroslav, a compounding of the Slavonic elements *dobro* (good, kind) and *slav* (glory). (DŌ-BRO-SLAH-VAH)

DRAHOMÍRA Compound name composed of the Slavonic elements *draho* (dear, beloved) and *meri* (great, famous). Short: Draha. Pet: Drahuše, Drahuška, Dráža, Mirha. (DRAH-HO-MEER-AH)

DUŠANA Feminine form of Dušan, a name derived from *dusha* (spirit, soul). Short: Duša. Pet: Dušanka, Dušička, Duška. (DOO-SHA-NAH)

EMÍLIE Derived from the Latin Aemilia, which is from Aemilius, an old Roman family name thought to be derived from *aemulus* (emulating, trying to equal or excel, rival). Pet: Ema, Emilka, Míla, Milka. (EH-MEE-LEE)

EVA Popular name derived from the Hebrew Chava (life). The name is borne in the Bible by the first woman created by God, "the mother of all the living." Pet: Evička, Evinka, Evka, Evulka, Evuška. (EH-VAH)

EVŽENIE Czech form of the Greek Eugenia, which is derived from *eugenēs* (well-born). Pet: Evža, Evženka, Evzicka. (EHV-ZHEH-NEE)

FRANTISKA Czech cognate of the Italian Francesca, the feminine form of Francesco, a cognate of Francis, which is from the Middle Latin Franciscus, a derivative of Francus (a Frank, a freeman). Pet: Fanka, Fany, Fanyka, Frána, Frantina. (FRAHN-TEES-KAH)

GABRIELA Feminine form of Gabriel, which is derived from the Hebrew *gavhrī'ēl* (God is my strength). *See* GABRIEL (Biblical Male Names). Pet: Gába, Gabi, Gabina, Gabinka, Gabra. (GAH-BREE-EL-LAH)

HANA A short form of Johana (God is gracious), Hana is also bestowed as an independent given name. *See* JOHANA. Pet: Hanička, Haninka, Hanka. (HAH-NAH)

HEDVIKA Popular Czech cognate of the German Hedwig, a derivative of the obsolete Haduwig, a compound name composed of the elements *hadu* (contention) and *wīg* (war, strife). Pet: Hedva, Hedvička. (HED-VEE-KAH)

IRENA From the Greek Eirēnē, which is derived from *eirēnē* (peace). Pet: Irča, Irenka. (EE-REH-NAH)

IVANA Popular name which is a feminine form of Ivan, a Czech cognate of John (God is gracious). *See* JOHANA. Pet: Ivan, Ivanka, Ivuška. (EE-VAH-NAH)

IVETA Czech cognate of the French Yvette, the feminine diminutive form of Yves (archer), a name of Germanic origin derived from the element *iv* (yew, the type of wood used in bow and arrow making). Pet: Iva, Ivetka, Ivka, Ivuška. (EE-VEH-TEH)

JANA Popular name which is a feminine form of Jan, a Czech cognate of John (God is gracious). *See* JOHN (Biblical Male Names). Pet: Janička, Janinka. (YAH-NAH)

JARKA Feminine form of Jarek, a name derived from *jaro* (spring). Pet: Jaruše, Jaruška. (YAHR-KAH)

JARMILA Feminine form of Jaromil (lover of spring), a compound name composed from the Slavonic elements *jaro* (spring) and *milo* (love, grace, favor). Pet: Jarča, Jarka, Jarunka, Jaruška. (YAHR-MEE-LAH)

JAROSLAVA Feminine form of Jaroslav (spring glory), a compounding of the Slavonic elements *jaro* (spring) and *slav* (glory). Pet: Jarča, Jarka, Jarunka, Jaručka, Slávka. (YAHR-RO-SLAH-VAH)

JINDŘIŠKA Feminine form of Jindřich, the Czech cognate of the German Heinrich (ruler of an enclosure, home ruler). The name is derived from the Old High German Haganrih, a compound name composed from the elements *hag* (an enclosure, a hedging-in) and *rihhi* (ruler), and from the Old High German Heimerich, a compounding of the elements *heim* (home, an estate) and *rik* (ruler, king). Pet: Jindra, Jindřina, Jindruška. (YEEN-DREESH-KAH)

JIŘINA Feminine form of Jiři, the Czech cognate of the Greek Geōrgios (earthworker, farmer), a compounding of the elements *gē* (earth) and *ergein* (to work). Pet: Jiřuška. (YEE-REE-NAH)

JOHANA Feminine form of Johan, a cognate of John (God is gracious). *See* JOHN (Biblical Male Names). Short: Hana, Jana. Pet: Hanka, Johanka. (YO-HAH-NAH)

JOLANTA Derived from the Italian Jolanda, which is from the French Yolande (violet), a name derived from the Latin *viola* (violet). Var: Jolana. Pet: Jola, Jolanka, Jolka. (YO-LAHN-TAH)

JUDITA Czech form of Judith, a cognate of the Hebrew Jehudith and Yehudit, feminine forms of Jehuda and Yehudhah. The names, Anglicized as Judah, mean "he will be praised." Because Judah was also the name of a kingdom in ancient Palestine, the name can also mean "from Judah." Pet: Dita, Jitka. (YOO-DEE-TAH)

JULIE A feminine form of the Latin Julius, an old Roman family name thought to be derived from Iulus (the first down on the chin, downy-bearded). Because a person just beginning to develop facial hair is young, the definition of this name and its related forms has evolved to "youth." Pet: Julča, Julinka, Julka. (YOO-LEE)

JUSTÝNA Derived from the Latin Justīnus, a name derived from *Justus* (just, lawful, fair). Pet: Justýnka. (YOO-STEE-NAH)

KAMILA Czech form of the Latin Camilla, which is derived from *camilla* (virgin of unblemished character). The name is borne in Roman mythology by a queen of the Volscians who fought in the army of the Trojan Aeneas. Pet: Kamilka. (KAH-MEE-LAH)

KARLA A borrowing from the German, Karla is a feminine form of Karl, a name derived from the Old Norse and Germanic *karl* (full-grown, a man, a freeman). (KAHR-LAH)

KAROLÍNA Popular feminine form of Karl (full-grown, a man, a freeman). Pet: Kája, Kájinka, Karla, Karlička, Karolínka. (KAH-RO-LEE-NAH)

KATEŘINA Czech cognate of the Greek Aikaterinē, a name derived from *katharos* (pure, unsullied). Pet: Kačenka, Kačka, Katka, Katuška. (KAH-TEH-REE-NAH)

KRASNA Derived from the Czech *krásný* (beautiful). Var: Krasara. (KRAHZ-NAH)

KVĚTA Popular name derived from *květ* (flower). Pet: Květka, Květušě, Květuška. (KVYEH-TAH)

LALA Popular name of Slavonic origin meaning "tulip." (LAH-LAH)

LIBĚNA Popular name derived from *lib* (love). Pet: Líba, Liběnka, Libuše, Libuška. (LEE-BYEH-NAH)

LIDA Czech form of the Greek Lydia (woman from Lydia, an ancient kingdom in western Asia Minor). Var: Lýdie. Pet: Lidka, Lidunka, Liduška. (LEE-DAH)

LUBA Derived from the Slavonic *lub* (love). Luba is also used as a short form of Lubomíra. *See* LUBOMÍRA. (LOO-BAH)

LUBOMÍRA Feminine form of Lubomír (great love), a compound name composed of the Slavonic elements *lub* (love) and *meri* (great, famous). Pet: Luba, Luběna, Lubina, Lubinka, Lubka, Luboška. (LOO-BO-MEE-RAH)

LUDMILA Compound name composed of the Slavonic elements *lud* (people, folk, tribe) and *mil* (grace, favor, love). Var: Lidmila. Pet: Lída, Lidka, Lidunka, Liduše, Liduška, Luduna. (LOOD-MEE-LAH)

MAGDALENA Derived from the Ecclesiastic Greek Magdalene (of Magdala, a town on the Sea of Galilee). Short: Alena, Magda. (MAHG-DAH-LEH-NAH)

Marcéla From the Latin Marcellus, a diminutive form of Marcus, which is of uncertain derivation. Most believe it has its root in Mars, the name of the Roman mythological god of war, and thus give it the definition "war-like." Others, however, think it might be from *mas* (manly) or from the Greek *malakoz* (soft, tender). Pet: Marcelka. (MAHR-SEH-LAH)

Maria Latin form of Mary, which is derived from the Hebrew Miryam (sea of bitterness, sea of sorrow). *See* MARY(English Names). Var: Marie. Pet: Majka, Mana, Marenka, Marika, Marinka, Maruška. (MAH-REE-AH)

Mariana Feminine form of Marian, which is from the Latin Mariānus (of Marius), a name derived from Mars, the name of the Roman mythological god of war. As a result of similarity of form, the name became associated with Maria, the name of the Blessed Virgin, and was often bestowed in her honor. Pet: Márinka, Maruška. (MAH-REE-AH-NAH)

Marika Pet form of Maria, Marika is also bestowed as an independent given name. *See* MARIA. (MAH-REE-KAH)

Markéta Czech form of Margaret, a cognate of the Greek Margarītēs, which is derived from *margaron* (a pearl). (MAHR-KEH-TAH)

Marta Czech form of Martha, a name derived from the Aramaic *mārthā* (lady, mistress). Pet: Martička. (MAHR-TAH)

Martina A popular name throughout Europe, Martina (war-like) is a feminine form of Martin, from the Latin name Martīnus, which is derived from mars, the name of the Roman mythological god of war. Pet: Martinka. (MAHR-TEE-NAH)

Matylda Czech cognate of Matilda, which is from the Old High German Mahthilde, a compound name composed of the elements *maht* (might, power) and *hiltia* (battle): hence, "powerful in battle." (MAH-TEEL-DAH)

Mečislava Feminine form of Mečislav, a compound name, the first element of which is uncertain. Some believe it to be from *miecz* (sword), the Old Polish *miecz* (man, father), or *mieszka* (bear). The second element is the Slavonic *slav* (glory). Pet: Mečina, Mečka. (MEH-CHEE-SLAH-VAH)

Milena Popular name derived from the element *mil* (love, grace, favor). Var: Milada, Miladena, Milana, Mladena. Short: Míla, Mlada. Pet: Miládka, Milenka, Milka, Miluše, Miluška, Mladka, Mladuška. (MEE-LAH-NAH)

Miloslava Feminine form of Miloslav (lover of glory), a compounding of the Slavonic elements *mil* (love, grace, favor) and *slav* (glory). Pet: Míla, Milka, Slávka. (MEE-LO-SLAH-VAH)

Mira A short form of any of the names containing the Slavonic element *meri* (great, famous), Mira is also commonly bestowed as an independent given name. Pet: Mirka. (MEE-RAH)

Miroslava Feminine form of Miroslav (great glory), a compounding of the Slavonic elements *meri* (great, famous) and *slav* (glory). Short: Mira. Pet: Mirka, Miruška, Slávka. (MEER-O-SLAH-VAH)

Monika Czech form of Monica, an ancient name of uncertain etymology. *See* MONICA (Greek Names). Pet: Monča, Monička. (MO-NEE-KAH)

Naděžda Czech cognate of the Russian Nadezhda (hope). Var: Naděja. Pet: Nad'a, Naděnka, Nad'ka. (NAH-DEHZH-DAH)

Neda Of Slavonic origin meaning "born on Sunday." Var: Nedda. (NEH-DAH)

Nikola Borrowed from the Greek, Nikola is a feminine form of Nikolaos (victory of the people), a compound name composed of the elements *nikē* (victory) and *laos* (people). Pet: Niki, Nikol, Nikolka. (NEE-KO-LAH)

Oldriška Feminine form of Oldřich, the Czech cognate of the German Ulrich (noble ruler). The name is derived from the Old High German Udalrich, a compounding of the elements *uodal* (nobility, prosperity, fortune) and *rik* (ruler, power, king). Pet: Olda, Oldra, Oldřina, Olina, Oluše, Riške. (OL-DREESH-KAH)

Olga A borrowing from the Russian, Olga is the feminine form of Oleg (holy), which is from the Scandinavian Helgi, a name derived from the Old Norse *heill* (hale, hardy; blessed, holy). Pet: Olina, Olinka. (OL-GAH)

Otýlie Derived from the French Ottilie, a derivative of Odile, which is from the Germanic Odila, a name derived from the element *od, ot* (prosperity, riches). Pet: Olylka. (O-TEE-LEE)

Pavla Feminine form of Pavel, a Czech form of Paul, which is derived from the Latin *paulus* (small). Pet: Pavlička, Pavlínka. (PAHV-LAH)

Petra Borrowed from the Greek, Petra is the feminine form of Petros, which is derived from *petros* (a rock, a stone). Pet: Petruška. (PEH-TRAH)

PŘIBISLAVA Feminine form of Přibislav (helper of glory), a compound name composed from the Slavonic elements *pribit* (to help, to be present) and *slav* (glory). Pet: Přiběna, Přibka, Přibuška. (PREE-BEE-SLAH-VAH)

RADINKA Of Slavonic origin meaning "lively." (RAH-DEEN-KAH)

RADOMÍRA Compound name composed of the Slavonic elements *rad* (glad) and *meri* (great, famous). Short: Rada. (RAH-DŌ-MEER-AH)

RADOSLAVA Compound name composed of the Slavonic elements *rad* (glad) and *slav* (glory): hence, "glad for glory." Short: Rada. (RAH-DŌ-SLAH-VAH)

RAINA Derived from the French Reina, which is from the Latin *regina* (queen). (RAH-EE-NAH)

RENÁTA From the Late Latin Renatus (reborn), which is derived from *renascor* (to be born again, to grow or rise again). The name was a common baptismal name signifying spiritual rebirth. Pet: Renátka, Renča. (REH-NAH-TAH)

ROMANA Feminine form of Roman, which is from the Late Latin Romanus (a Roman, an inhabitant of Rome). Pet: Romanka, Romča, Romi, Romka. (RO-MAH-NAH)

ROSTISLAVA Feminine form of Rostislav (seizer of glory), a compound name composed from the Slavonic elements *rosts* (usurp, seize, appropriate) and *slav* (glory). Pet: Rost'a, Rostina, Rostinka, Rostuška, Slávka. (ROS-TEE-SLAH-VAH)

RUT Czech cognate of Ruth, a name of uncertain etymology. Most believe it to be derived from the Hebrew *ruth,* a possible contraction of *re'uth* (companion, friend). (ROOT)

RŮŽENA Czech cognate of the Latin Rosa (a rose). Short: Růža. Pet: Růženka. (ROO-ZHAY-NAH)

SOBĚSLAVA Compound name composed from the Slavonic elements *sobi* (to usurp, to overtake) and *slav* (glory): hence, "usurper of glory." Pet: Soběna, Sobeška. (SO-BYEE-SLAH-VAH)

STANISLAVA Feminine form of Stanislav (glorious government), which is composed of the Slavonic elements *stan* (government) and *slav* (glory). Pet: Stáňa, Stánička, Stanuška. (STAH-NEE-SLAH-VAH)

STĚPÁNA Feminine form of Štěpán, a cognate of the Greek Stephanos, which is from *stephanos* (a crown, a garland). Pet: Stěpa, Stěpánka, Stěpka. (STYEH-PAH-NAH)

SVĚTLANA Derived from the Russian Svetlána (star). Pet: Světla, Světlanka, Světluše, Světluška. (SVYEHT-LAH-NAH)

TAT'ÁNA Feminine form of the Latin Tatiānus, a derivative of the old Roman family name Tatius, which is of uncertain origin. Short: Tána. Pet: Tánička. (TAHT-AH-NAH)

TEREZA Czech form of Teresa, which is thought to be derived from the Greek *therizein* (to reap, to gather in). Pet: Terezka, Terinka, Terka. (TEH-REH-ZAH)

VELESLAVA Feminine form of Veleslav (great glory), a compounding of the Slavonic elements *vele* (great) and *slav* (glory). Pet: Vela, Velina, Velinka, Velka, Veluška. (VEH-LEH-SLAH-VAH)

VĚRA Derived from the Russian Vjera (faith). Because the name coincides in form to the Latin *vera* (true), it is often believed to be derived from this, rather than the former. Pet: Věrka, Věrunka, Veruška. (VEH-RAH)

VERONIKA Czech form of Veronica, a name of debated origin and meaning. *See* VERONICA (German Names). Pet: Verča, Verunka. (VEH-RO-NEE-KAH)

VIKTORIE Czech form of Victoria, which is from the Latin *victoria* (victory). Pet: Viki, Viktorka. (VEEK-TOR-EE)

VIOLA Czech form of the French Viole, which is derived from the Latin *viola* (a violet). Pet: Violka. (VEE-O-LAH)

VLADIMÍRA Feminine form of Vladimír (famous ruler), a compounding of the Slavonic elements *volod* (rule) and *meri* (great, famous). Var: Vladmíra. (VLAH-DEE-MEE-RAH)

VLADISLAVA Feminine form of Vladislav (glorious rule), a compounding of the Slavonic elements *volod* (rule) and *slav* (glory). Var: Ladislava. Pet: Valeška. (VLAH-DEE-SLAH-VAH)

ZBYHNĚVA Feminine form of Zbyhněv (to do away with anger), a compound name composed from the elements *zbit* (to do away with, to be rid of) and *gniew* (anger). *See* ZBYHNĚV (Male Names). Pet: Zbyňa, Zbyša. (ZBEE-NYEE-VAH)

ZDEŇKA Feminine form of Zdeněk (follower of St. Denis). *See* ZDENĚK (Male Names). Var: Zdena, Zdenka. Pet: Zdenička, Zdenina, Zdeninka, Zdenuška. (ZDEHN-KAH)

ZDESLAVA Feminine form of Zdislav, a compounding of the Slavonic elements *zde* (here, present) and *slav* (glory). Var: Zdislava. Pet: Zdeša, Zdeška, Zdiša, Zdiška. (ZDEH-SLAH-VAH)

ZELENKA Derived from the Czech *zelený* (green). (ZEH-LAIN-KAH)

ŽITOMÍRA Feminine form of Žitomír, a compounding of the Slavonic elements *zhit* (to live) and *meri* (great, famous). Pet: Žitka, Žituše. (ZHEE-TO-MEER-AH)

ŽIVANKA Feminine form of Živan, which is from the Slavonic element *zhiv* (living, vigorous, alive). Short: Živka. Pet: Živuše, Živuška. (ZHEE-VAHN-KAH)

ZLATA Feminine form of Zlatan, which is derived from *zlato* (gold). Pet: Zlatina, Zlatinka, Zlatka, Zlatuše, Zlatuška, Zlatuna, Zlatunka. (ZLAH-TAH)

ŽOFIE Czech cognate of the Greek Sophia, a name directly derived from *sophia* (wisdom, skill). Pet: Žofinka, Žofka. (ZHO-FEE)

ZORA Popular name of Slavonic origin meaning "dawn." Var: Zorah, Zorana, Zorina. (ZOR-AH)

ZUZANA Czech form of Susannah, which is from the Hebrew Shoshana, a derivative of *shōshannāh* (a lily, a rose). Pet: Zuzanka, Zuzi, Zuzka. (ZOO-ZAH-NAH)

CHAPTER SEVEN

English Names

THE ANCIENT, unknown language of the aboriginal inhabitants of the British Isles was eventually superseded by the tongues of the Celtic immigrants from the mainland. And by the time of the Roman invasion in 55 B.C., the Celtic languages had become the native languages of the land. After the Romans set up government, the use of Latin was encouraged, and by the 3rd or 4th century, all but the lowest classes and those who lived in the far reaches spoke Latin and had adopted the Christian religion.

When the Romans vacated the island in the 5th century, a historical fog descended over the land. Little is known of this time except that barbaric Anglo-Saxon tribes invaded the area from the mainland. Two centuries later, all remnants of Roman civilization had been wiped out, the Anglo-Saxons held nearly all of the land, the Celtic-speaking Christian natives had been pushed far back into the hills, and Old English (Anglo-Saxon) was the dominant language.

Missionaries headed by St. Augustine were sent by Pope Gregory the Great in 597 to convert the Anglo-Saxons to Christianity, once again introducing Latin to the country. Toward the 8th century, the Danes ventured forth seeking adventure and new lands to conquer. Their influence lasted in different parts of the country for nearly three hundred years, during which time they adopted the Christian faith and Latin became the universal language of learning, the church, diplomacy, law, and to some extent, business. Later, after the death of Harthacanute in 1047, political ties were severed with Denmark, and Edward the Confessor was chosen as king.

Having been raised in France, Edward introduced the French culture and language to the land, and liberally bestowed lands and titles upon his friends and retainers, in effect paving the way for the Norman invasion.

The Norman Conquest in 1066 had a great effect on the English society and brought about a profound transformation in the English language. Although French became the official language of the government, the courts and law, the educated and the nobility, Old English was still spoken by the masses. As the two languages were used side by side, many Old English words were abandoned, French ones were added to the vocabulary, and countless others were modified. The English language of this period until the year 1475 is known as Middle English.

These events helped determine the types of names found in England today. Though the Roman names failed to remain viable, the Anglo-Saxons added a large number of names that have their roots in the Low German language group. The Scandinavians left a few personal names, but their contribution to place-names is far greater. After the Conquest, Norman and Breton names dominated the Saxon names until immigrants from the Low Countries reintroduced them in the Middle Ages.

The Reformation brought an influx of immigrants fleeing religious persecution from all across Europe. The names of these immigrants also added to English nomenclature, but it was the introduction of the Geneva Bible in 1560 that had the most profound effect on personal names in England. Biblical names became popular in the extreme, and the Puritans led the fervor by naming their children not only after biblical characters but also from portions of Scripture and other spiritual and moral utterances.

Aside from the rare exception, middle names were unused in England until late in the 18th century, at which time triple baptismal names were also occasionally used. Surnames came into use in the 12th century and were placed after the baptismal name, for they were of less importance. They originated principally as descriptive names based on appearance, residence, occupation, and family ties. Officially noted as hereditary in 1267, it wasn't until the 17th century that they achieved greater importance and registers began being indexed by surname rather than given name.

English Male Names

AARON Derived from the Hebrew *aharōn* (the exalted one). The name is borne in the Bible by the elder brother of Moses. Var: Aron, Arron. (AR-UN)

ABBOT Transferred use of the surname derived from the Old English *abbod* (the head of an abbey of monks), from the Latin *abbas*, which is from the Aramaic *abbā* (father). The name originated as an occupational name for an abbot or one who worked for an abbot. Var: Abbott. Short: Abe. (AB-BET)

ABRAHAM Derived from the Hebrew Avraham (father of many, father of a multitude). The name is borne in the Bible by the first patriarch and ancestor of the Hebrews and the Arabs. Abraham was little used as a given name in England until the 17th century, when the Puritans bestowed the name upon their male children. Short: Abe. (Ā-BRA-HAM)

ACTON Derived from the Old English Actun, a compound name derived from the elements *ac* (oak) and *tūn* (town, settlement, village): hence, "town by the oaks." (AK-TUN)

ADAM Derived from the Hebrew *adama* (red earth). The name is borne in the Bible by the first man created by God. According to biblical tradition, it was from Adam's rib that the first woman, Eve, was formed. (AD-UM)

ADDISON Transferred use of the surname derived from the Middle English Addisone (son of Addy). Var: Adison. (ADD-IH-SON)

ADRIAN English cognate of the Latin Adriānus (man from the city of Adria) and Hadriānus (man from the city of Hadria). The name was borne by Nicholas Breakspear (c. 1100–1159), the only English pope. He took the name Adrian IV. (Ā-REE-UN)

ALAN Celtic name of uncertain derivation. Alan was brought to England by the Normans during the Conquest. The name was borne by Alan, earl of Brittany, a follower of William the Conqueror. Var: Allan, Allen. Short: Al. (AL-UN)

ALBAN Derived from the Latin Albanus (from the Italian city of Alba). The name was borne by a British saint martyred in the 3rd or 4th century. (AHL-BUN, AL-BUN)

ALBERT Derived from the Old High German Adalbrecht, a compound name composed of the elements *adal* (noble) and *beraht* (bright, famous). Short: Al, Bert. Pet: Bertie. (AL-BERT)

ALEX Short form of Alexander (defender or helper of mankind). *See* ALEXANDER. Alex is also commonly bestowed as an independent given name. Var: Alec. Short: Al, Lex. (AL-EX)

ALEXANDER Popular name derived from the Greek Alexandros, a compound name composed of the elements *alexein* (to defend, to help) and *andros* (man): hence, "defender or helper of mankind." The name was borne by several early saints and martyrs which helped to establish the name's popularity. Short: Al, Alec, Alex, Lex. Pet: Sandy. (AL-EX-AN-DER)

ALFRED Derived from the Old English Ælfred, a compound name composed of the elements *ælf* (elf) and *ræd* (counsel). Elves were considered to be supernatural beings having special powers of seeing into the future; thus the name took on the meaning "wise counselor." Short: Al, Fred. Pet: Alfie. (AL-FRED)

ALTON Derived from the Old English Aldtun, which is composed of the elements *ald* (old) and *tūn* (town, settlement, village): hence, "old town." (AHL-TUN)

Alvar Derived from the Old English Ælfhere (elfin army), a compound name composed of the elements *ælf* (elf) and *here* (army, warrior). Short: Al. (AL-VAR)

Alvin Derived from the Old English Ælfwine (friend of the elves), a compound name composed of the elements *ælf* (elf) and *wine* (friend). Var: Alwyn, Aylwin. Short: Al, Alvy. Pet: Vinnie, Vinny. (AL-VIN)

Andrew English cognate of the Greek Andreas, derived from *andreios* (manly), which is from the root *anēr* (man). The name was borne by one of the Twelve Apostles of Christ, which originally induced the name's popularity. Contemporaneously, the name is borne by Prince Andrew, the duke of York (b. 1960), a son of Queen Elizabeth II and Prince Philip. Short: Drew. Pet: Andy. (AN-DREW)

Anthony English cognate of the old Roman family name Antonius, which is of uncertain origin and meaning. Popular throughout Europe, the name Anthony has been borne by many saints, the most notable being Anthony of Padua (1195–1231). Var: Anton, Antony. Short: Tony. (AN-THE-NEE)

Arnold Introduced to England by the Normans, Arnold (powerful as an eagle) is derived from the Germanic Arnwald, a compound name composed of the elements *arn* (eagle) and *wald* (power, strength). Short: Arn. Pet: Arnie, Arny. (AR-NOLD, AR-NLD)

Arthur Of Celtic origin but of unknown meaning. The name was borne by the legendary British king Arthur, leader of the knights of the Round Table, who supposedly lived in the 5th or 6th century. The name gained popularity from the great body of Arthurian legend that has remained of interest over the centuries. Short: Art. (AR-THER)

Ashley Originally a surname, Ashley is derived from the Old English elements *æsc* (ash trees) and *lēah* (wood, clearing, meadow), a name indicative of one who was a "dweller near the ash tree forest." As a given name, Ashley is now more commonly bestowed upon females than males. (ASH-LEE)

Aspen Taken from the name of the aspen tree, which is derived from the Old English *æspe*. The name is indicative of any of the kinds of poplar trees that have leaves which flutter in the slightest breeze. (AS-PEN, ASS-PEN)

Aston Originally a surname, Aston is derived from the Old English elements *east* (east) and *tūn* (town, settlement, village, enclosure): hence, "eastern town, eastern settlement." (ASS-TUN)

Aubrey Derived from the Germanic Alberic, which is composed from the elements *alb* (elf, supernatural being) and *ric* (ruler, king): hence, "elfin king." (AU-BREE)

Augustine English cognate of the Latin Augustinus, a diminutive form of Augustus, which is derived from *augustus* (great, venerable). The name was borne by the first archbishop of Canterbury (d. 613), a Roman monk sent to convert the English to Christianity. Short: Gus. (AU-GUS-TEEN)

Augustus A borrowing of the Latin Augustus, a name directly derived from *augustus* (great, venerable). Short: Gus. (AU-GUS-TUS)

Austin Contracted form of Augustine (great). *See* AUGUSTINE. Var: Austen, Austyn. (AU-STEN)

Avan Modern coinage of uncertain origin and meaning. (Ā-VUN)

Bailey Transferred use of the surname, which originated from various sources. It is from the Old French *baili* (administrator, manager), which is derived from *bailif* (an officer of justice, a warrant officer). It is also derived from the Middle English *bayle, baile* (the wall of the outer court of a feudal castle), which was indicative of one who worked at or near such a place. Alternatively, the name Bailey has been borrowed from a place-name in Lancashire which is from the Old English elements *beg* (berry) and *lēah* (wood, clearing, meadow). (BAY-LEE)

Barclay Transferred use of the Scottish surname, which is found as de Berchelai (from Berkeley) in the year 1086. Berkeley is derived from the Old English elements *beorc* (birch) and *lēah* (wood, clearing, meadow): hence, "the birch meadow." The name was taken to Scotland in 1165 by William de Berchelai, chamberlain of Scotland and patriarch of the powerful Scottish Barclays. Var: Berkley. Short: Clay. (BAR-KLAY)

Barnabas Borne in the Bible by the Christian apostle and missionary companion of Paul, the name Barnabas is derived from the Aramaic *barnebhū'āh* (son of exhortation). Its use as a given name in England dates to the 13th century. Var: Barnaby. Pet: Barney, Barny. (BAR-nah-bus)

Barrett Transferred use of the surname, which is of uncertain origin and meaning. Some believe it to be derived from the Old French *barat* (traffic, commerce), the meaning of which evolved to "trouble, contention, deception" in the 13th century. Pet: Barry. (BARE-ET)

Bartholomew From the Middle English Bartelmeus, a cognate of the Late Latin Bartholomaeus, which is from the Greek Bartholomaios (son of Talmai). Talmai is an Aramaic name meaning "hill, mound, furrows." The name is borne in the Bible by one of the Twelve Apostles of Christ. Short: Bart. (BAR-THOL-O-MEW)

Barton Transferred use of the surname originating as a place-name composed of the Old English elements *bere* (barley) and *tūn* (town, settlement, village, enclosure) and which was indicative of a place where barley was kept. Short: Bart. (BAR-TUN)

Basil From the Latin Basilius and the Greek Basileios, both of which are derived from *basileus* (kingly, royal). The name was borne by a 4th-century Greek theologian known as St. Basil the Great (c. 330–79). A bishop of Caesarea, he is considered to be one of the fathers of the Eastern Church. Short: Baz. (BAZ-IL)

Bastian A short form of Sebastian (man of Sebastia), Bastian is also in common use as an independent given name. *See* SEBASTIAN. (BAS-TEE-UN, BAHS-TEE-UN)

Baxter Transferred use of the surname Baxter, which originated as an occupational name in the Middle Ages and which is derived from the Old English *bæcestre* (baker). (BAX-TER)

Beau A borrowing of the French, Beau is directly derived from *beau* (handsome, a dandy). Its use as a given name dates to the early 19th century when it was borne by Beau Brummell (1778–1840), a friend of the prince regent, known for his fashionable dress and dandyish manner. However, it wasn't until the 20th century that the name became common, perhaps because of the character Beau Wilkes in the epic *Gone with the Wind*. (BO)

Benedict Derived from the Latin Benedictus (blessed), which is from *benedicere* (to speak well of, to bless). The name was borne by St. Benedict (c. 480–543), an Italian monk and founder of the Benedictine Order. He was responsible for the building of the great monastery at Monte Cassino, which remains the spiritual center of the Benedictines. Var: Bennett. Short: Ben. Pet: Benny. (BEN-EH-DIK, BEN-EH-DIKT)

Benjamin Derived from the Hebrew *binyāmīn* (son of the right hand, favorite son). The name is borne in the Bible by the youngest son of Jacob and Rachel, founder of one of the twelve tribes of Israel. Rachel died giving birth to Benjamin, and in the Middle Ages the name was commonly bestowed upon male children born into the same circumstances. Short: Ben. Pet: Benji, Benny. (BEN-JA-MIN)

Bennett Transferred use of the surname originating as a variant of Benedict (blessed). *See* BENEDICT. Var: Benet, Benett, Bennet. Short: Ben. Pet: Benny. (BEN-NET)

Bentley Transferred use of the surname derived from the Old English elements *beonot* (bent, stiff grass, heath) and *lēah* (wood, clearing, meadow). The surname was originally indicative of a "dweller by the grassy meadow or heath." Short: Ben. Pet: Benny. (BENT-LEE)

Bernard Derived from the Old High German Berinhard, a compound name composed from the elements *bero* (bear) and *hart* (bold, strong, hearty): hence, "bold or strong as a bear." The name was borne by St. Bernard of Menthon (923–1008), a French monk who founded hospices in the Swiss Alps, and by St. Bernard of Clairvaux (1090–1163), another French monk, who founded the Cistercian Order. Pet: Bernie. (BER-NARD)

Bertram Derived from the obsolete Old High German Berahtram (bright raven), a compound name composed from the elements *beraht* (bright, famous) and *hraban* (raven). The name, and its variant Bertrand, were introduced to England at the time of the Conquest. Var: Bertrand. Short: Bert. (BER-TRUM)

Bill 19th-century variant of Will, which is a short form of William (resolute protector). It is unclear why the first letter was altered from a *W* to a *B*; it could simply be the result of Bill evolving as a rhyming variant of Will. *See* WILLIAM. Pet: Billy. (BIL)

Blake Transferred use of the surname, which is of two separate derivations. It originates both from the Old English *blæc* (black, dark-complexioned) and *blāc* (bright, shining, pale, wan). The use of Blake as a given name stems from its prior use as a nickname for someone with either a very dark or a very light complexion. (BLAKE)

Brad A short form of both Bradford and Bradley, Brad is also bestowed as an independent given name. *See* BRADFORD *and* BRADLEY. (BRAD)

Bradford Transferred use of the surname that arose from English place-names composed of the Old English elements *brad* (broad) and *ford* (ford). The use of Bradford as a given name was uncommon before the 20th century. Short: Brad. (BRAD-FORD, BRAD-FERD)

Bradley Transferred use of the surname originating from English place-names derived from the Old English elements *brad* (broad) and *lēah* (wood, clearing, meadow). Bradley therefore takes the definition "dweller by the broad meadow or wood." Short: Brad. (BRAD-LEE)

Branton Transferred use of the surname originating from English place-names composed from the Old English elements *brom* (broom, brushwood) and *dun* (hill). The name was indicative of a "dweller by the brushwood hill." (BRAN-TUN)

Brent Transferred use of the surname, which originates from two separate sources. Brent (the burnt) is an evolution of the Old English *beornan* (to burn) and was originally used as a nickname for a criminal who had been branded for his crimes. However, it is also derived from *brend* (burnt land), a word used as an English place-name; in this case, Brent would mean "dweller by the burnt land." (BRENT)

Brett Transferred use of the English surname derived from the Old French *Bret* (a Breton), an ethnic name for a native of Brittany. The name was brought to England by the Norman Conquest of 1066. (BRET)

Brian Irish name of uncertain etymology. It is generally thought to be of Celtic origin, but its meaning is disputed. Some believe it to be derived from the root *bri* (force, strength), *brîgh* (valor, strength), or *bruaich* (a hill, steep, high). The name was introduced to different parts of England in the Middle Ages by Scandinavians from Ireland and by Bretons from Brittany. Var: Brien, Bryan. Short: Bri. (BRI-UN)

Brice Transferred use of the surname, brought to England by the French in the Middle Ages. Brice, believed to be of Celtic origin, can be derived from the root *bri* (force, strength) or *brîgh* (valor, strength). Var: Bryce. Short: Bri. (BRISE)

Brigham Transferred use of the surname derived from the Norfolk place-name Bridgham, which is from the Old English elements *brycg* (bridge) and *ham* (dwelling, home, manor): hence, "dwelling by the bridge." (BRIG-UM)

Bruce Transferred use of the surname originating from the French Brieuse (a locality in France). The name, which was introduced by the Normans, was firmly established in Scotland by Robert de Bruce (1274–1329), a Norman who ruled the country as Robert I from 1306 to 1329. (BROOS)

Bryant Transferred use of the surname derived from the given name Brian. *See* BRIAN. (BRI-ANT, BRI-UNT)

Burgess Transferred use of the surname derived from the Old French *burgeis* (inhabitant or freeman of a borough). The name was introduced to England in the 12th century. (BER-JUSS)

Burton Transferred use of the surname originating as an English place-name derived from the Old English elements *burg* (stronghold, fortress) and *tūn* (town, settlement, village, enclosure). (BER-TUN)

Byron Transferred use of the surname originating from a place-name derived from the Old English *æt byrum* (at the cowsheds). The use of Byron as a given name dates to its bestowal in honor of the English poet Lord Byron (1788–1824). (BY-RUN)

Cade Transferred use of the English surname, which has several different origins. Cade is derived from an Old English nickname for something or someone lumpy or rotund. It might also be from the Late Middle English *cade* (a young animal abandoned by its mother and raised by hand). Alternatively, Cade is derived from the Middle English *cade* (cask, barrel) and might have been either a nickname for someone with the physique of a barrel or an occupational name for a barrel maker. (KADE)

Caesar A borrowing of the Latin surname Caesar, used as the title of early Roman emperors. Its origin and meaning are uncertain. Some believe it is derived from *caedo* (to cut); others think it to be from *caesius* (blue-gray). Another suggestion is that it is derived from *caesaries* (hairy). Caesar was first used as a given name in the 16th century when it was brought to England by Cesare Adelmare (1558–1636), a Venetian physician to Queen Elizabeth. (SEE-ZER)

Calvin From the French surname Cauvin, a derivative of the Latin *calvinus* (little bald one), which has its root in *calvus* (bald). Calvin was originally bestowed as a given name in honor of John Calvin (1509–64), a French Protestant reformer. Short: Cal. (KAL-VIN)

Carl Derived from the Old English *ceorl* (a freeman, peasant, man). In the Middle Ages, Carl was used as a nickname for a bondman, villain, or a person of low birth and rude manners. (KARL)

Carlton Transferred use of the surname originating from English place-names composed of the Old English elements *carl* (freeman, peasant, man) and *tūn* (town, settlement, village, enclosure): hence, "settlement of freemen." Short: Carl. (KARL-TUN)

Carter Transferred use of the surname originating in the Middle Ages as an occupational name for someone who used a cart to transport goods. (KAR-TER)

Cary Transferred use of the surname originating from an English place-name derived from an old Celtic river name of uncertain meaning. Some believe it to be from the Gaelic *caraich* (to move, to stir) or *caraidh* (movement). Var: Carey. (KARE-EE)

Casey Transferred use of the Irish surname, which is from the Gaelic O'Cathasaigh (descendant of Cathasach), a derivative of *cathasach* (watchful, vigilant). (KAY-SEE)

Cassian From the Latin Cassiānus, a name derived from Cassius, an old Roman family name of uncertain meaning. It is possibly derived from the Latin *cassus* (hollow, empty). (KASS-EE-UN)

CECIL From the Latin Caecilius, an old Roman family name derived from *caecus* (blind, dim-sighted). The name, borne by a 3rd-century saint and companion of St. Cyprian, was common in England in the Middle Ages, after which it died out. The recent revival of Cecil as a given name stems from the transferred use of the surname derived from the Welsh Seissylt, which is believed to be from the Latin Sextilius, a derivative of *sextus* (sixth). (SEE-SIL)

CEDRIC An invention of Sir Walter Scott (1771–1832) for the character Cedric the Saxon in *Ivanhoe* (1819). He is believed to have based the name on Cerdic, a name of uncertain etymology borne by the traditional founder of the West Saxon kingdom. (SED-RIK, SEED-RIK)

CHAD Believed to be a modern variant of the obsolete Old English Ceadda, a name of uncertain meaning borne by a Lindisfarne monk who became bishop of the Mercians. (CHAD)

CHANDLER Transferred use of the surname originating in the Middle Ages as an occupational name for a maker or seller of candles. (CHAND-LER)

CHAPMAN Transferred use of the surname originating as an occupational name from the Old English *cēapmann, cēpemann* (merchant, trader), a compound word composed from the elements *cēapian* (to buy, to do business) and *mann* (man): hence, "merchant, businessman." (CHAP-MUN)

CHARLES A popular name throughout Europe and Great Britain, Charles is derived from the Germanic *karl* (full-grown, a man), which is a cognate of the Old English *ceorl* (a man, freeman, peasant). It is a royal name, being borne by ten kings of France as well as by kings of Hungary, Naples, Sardinia, and Württemberg. It was introduced to Great Britain by Mary, Queen of Scots (1542–87), who bestowed it upon her son, Charles James (1566–1625). His son and grandson both ruled as King Charles, furthering the name's popularity. Currently, the name is borne by Prince Charles (b. 1948), heir to the British throne. Pet: Charlie. (CHARLZ)

CHARLTON Transferred use of the surname taken from Old English place-names composed from the Old English elements *ceorl* (freeman, peasant, man) and *tūn* (town, settlement, village, enclosure): hence, "settlement of freemen." Pet: Charlie. (CHARL-TUN)

CHESTER Transferred use of the surname taken from the Old English place-name Ceastre, a contraction of Legacaestir, which is from the Latin *legionum castra* (camp of the legions). (CHES-TER)

CHRIS A short form of Christian (a Christian) and Christopher (bearing Christ), Chris is also commonly bestowed as an independent given name. *See* CHRISTIAN *and* CHRISTOPHER. (KRIS)

CHRISTIAN Derived from the Latin *christiānus* (a Christian, a follower of Christ), which is from the Greek *christianos* (a Christian). The name was used by writer John Bunyan (1628–88) for the main character in *Pilgrim's Progress*. Short: Chris. (KRIS-CHEN)

CHRISTOPHER An evolution of the Middle English Christofre, a name taken from the Ecclesiastic Late Latin Christophorus, which is derived from the Ecclesiastic Greek Christophoros, a compound name composed from the elements *Christos* (Christ) and *pherein* (to bear): hence, "bearing Christ." The name was borne by St. Christopher, a 3rd-century Christian martyr of Asia Minor who is the patron saint of travelers. Short: Chris, Kit. (KRIS-TŌ-FER, KRIS-TAH-FER)

CLARK Transferred use of the surname derived from the Old English *clerec, clerc* (clerk). It originated as an occupational name for a clergyman cleric or for a man in a religious order. (KLARK)

CLAUDE From the Latin Claudius, an old Roman family name derived from *claudus* (lame). Var: Claud. (KLOD)

CLAYTON Transferred use of the surname originating from a place-name derived from the Old English elements *claēg* (clay) and *tūn* (town, settlement, village, enclosure): hence, "settlement near the clay pit." Short: Clay. (KLAY-TUN)

CLEMENT From the Latin Clemens (mild, gentle, merciful), which is derived from the word of the same definition. Short: Clem. (KLEM-ENT)

CLIFF A short form of Clifford (ford at the cliff) and Clifton (settlement by the cliff), Cliff is also bestowed as an independent given name. *See* CLIFFORD *and* CLIFTON. (KLIF)

CLIFFORD Transferred use of the surname originating from a place-name derived from the Old English elements *clif* (cliff, slope, bank of a river) and *ford* (ford, river crossing): hence, "ford at the cliff." Short: Cliff. (KLIF-FERD)

CLIFTON Transferred use of the surname originating from a place-name for various old English towns. It is composed from the Old English elements *clif* (cliff, slope, bank of a river) and *tūn* (town, settlement, village, enclosure): hence, "settlement by the cliff." Short: Cliff. (KLIF-TUN)

CLINT A short form of Clinton (settlement by the cliff), Clint is also bestowed as an independent given name. *See* CLINTON. (KLINT)

CLINTON Transferred use of the surname believed to be derived from an English place-name formed by the Middle English elements *clint* (cliff, slope, bank of a river) and *tūn* (town, settlement, village, enclosure): hence, "settlement by the cliff." Short: Clint. (KLIN-TUN)

CLIVE Transferred use of the surname derived from the Old English *clif* (cliff, slope, bank of a river). The word is found in many English place-names, and Clive was probably first used for someone who lived near one of these places, or for someone who lived near a cliff or a riverbank. The use of Clive as a given name dates to the 18th century, when it was bestowed in honor of the baron of Plassey, Robert Clive (1725–74), the British soldier and statesman who established British control over India. (KLIVE)

CLYDE A borrowing of the name of the Scottish river Clyde, which is of uncertain etymology. (KLIDE)

COLE Transferred use of the surname derived from the Old English *col* (coal). It originated as a byname for someone who was coal-black, swarthy, or darkly complexioned. Cole is also used as a short form of Coleman (coalman) and Nicholas (victory of the people). *See* COLEMAN *and* NICHOLAS. (KOLE)

COLEMAN Transferred use of the surname derived from the Old English elements *col* (coal) and *mann* (man), which originated as an occupational name for a charcoal burner or someone who dealt with coal. Short: Cole. (KOLE-MUN)

COLIN Popular name originating as a medieval diminutive form of the obsolete Colle, a short form of Nicholas (victory of the people). Colin is now regarded as an independent given name. (KOL-IN)

CONRAD English cognate of the Germanic Konrad, which is derived from the Old High German Kuonrat, a compound name composed of the elements *kuon* (bold, wise) and *rat* (counsel). (KON-RAD)

COSMO From the Greek Kosmas, which is derived from *kosmos* (order, beauty). The name was borne by the brother of Damianos, both of whom were martyred in 303 under Diocletian. A cult arose about them, spreading westward and receiving much attention when the brothers' relics were supposedly found in Milan by St. Ambrose. (KOZ-MO)

CRAIG Transferred use of the Scottish surname derived from the Gaelic *creag* (rugged rocks, crag): hence, "dweller by the crag." (KRAGE)

CREIGHTON Transferred use of the surname that originally indicated a person from Chrichton, a town in southeastern Scotland, which derived its name from the Gaelic *crìoch* (border, boundary) and the Middle English *tune* (town, settlement, village): hence, "from Crichton, from the town near the border." (KRĪ-TUN)

CURTIS Derived from the French *curteis* (courteous). Curtis was originally used as both a given name and a surname. In the Middle Ages, it was used to indicate an educated man. Short: Curt. (KUR-TIS)

CYRIL From the Late Latin Cyrillus, a derivative of the Greek Kyrillos (lordly), which is derived from *kyrios* (a lord). The name was borne by St. Cyril (c. 376–444), a Christian theologian and archbishop of Alexandria, and by a Greek missionary to the Slavs, St. Cyril (827–69), to whom the Cyrillic alphabet is attributed. (SĪ-RIL, SEER-IL)

CYRUS Derived from the Greek Kyros, which might be derived from *kyrios* (lord). Alternatively, Kyros is used as a cognate of the Hebrew Koreish, a derivative of the Persian Kureish, which is from the ancient Kuru, a name believed to be from the Persian Khur (a name for the sun). Short: Cy. (SĪ-RUS)

DALE Transferred use of the surname, which is from the Old English *dael* (dale, hollow, valley). The name originated as en la Dale or de la Dale and was indicative of a person who lived "in the dale." (DALE)

DALEY Transferred use of the Irish surname, which is from the Gaelic O'Dálaigh (descendant of Dálach). Dálach is derived from *dáil* (assembly, gathering). Var: Daly. (DAY-LEE)

DAMIAN From the Greek Damianos, which is thought to be derived from *damān* (to tame). The name was borne by the brother of Kosmas, both of whom were martyred in 303 under Diocletian. A cult arose about them, spreading westward and receiving much attention when the brothers' relics were supposedly found in Milan by St. Ambrose. Var: Damon. (DAY-MEE-UN)

DANE Transferred use of the surname Dane (dweller in the valley), which is derived from the Old English *denu* (valley). (DANE)

DANIEL Derived from the Hebrew *dānī'ēl* (God is my judge). The name is borne in the Bible by a Hebrew prophet whose faith kept him alive in a den of lions. Daniel and the Lions' Den was a favorite story during the Middle Ages, which helped to promote the use of the name throughout Europe. Short: Dan. Pet: Danny. (DAN-YUL)

DANTÉ Borrowed from the French and Italian, Danté is a contracted form of Durante (enduring, lasting, steadfast), which is from the Latin *dūrans* (enduring). Var: Dantae, Dante, Dontae, Dontay, Donte, Donté. (DON-TAY)

DARBY Transferred use of the surname taken from the place-name Derby (deer settlement), which is derived from the Old Norse elements *diur* (deer) and *bý́r* (settlement, village). (DAR-BEE)

DARCY Transferred use of the surname originating as the baronial name D'Arcy (from Arcy, a place in La Manche, Normandy). (DAR-SEE)

DARIUS A borrowing from the Latin, Darius is an old name derived from the Greek Dareios, which is of uncertain origin. It is thought to ultimately be derived from Darayavahush, the name of an ancient Persian king. (DARE-EE-US)

DARRELL Transferred use of the surname originating as the French de Arel (from Airelle, a town in Calvados). Var: Darell, Darrel, Darryl, Darryll, Daryl. (DARE-UL)

DARREN Modern name of uncertain origin and meaning. It might have been coined as a variation of Darrell, or by combining a child's parents' names, such as Darrell and Karen. Var: Darin, Darrin. (DARE-UN)

DAVID Derived from the Hebrew *dāwīd* (beloved). It is borne in the Bible by the second and greatest of the Israelite kings. In the British Isles, the name was borne by St. David (also known as St. Dewi), a 6th-century Welsh bishop who is the patron saint of Wales, and by David I (c. 1084–1153), a king of Scotland who ruled from 1124 to 1153. Short: Dave. Pet: Davey, Davi, Davy. (DAY-VID)

DEAN Transferred use of the surname taken from various place-names composed of the Old English *denu* (valley). It originally was descriptive of one who lived in or near a valley. Another surname arose from the Middle English *deen* (dean) and the Old French *deien* (dean), an occupational name for the presiding official of a cathedral, collegiate church, university, or group. The names are now inextricable. Var: Deane. (DEEN)

DEL Originated as a colloquial pet form of Derek (leader of the people). *See* DEREK. Although it is still occasionally bestowed as an independent given name, Del is more often found as a name element in modern coinages. (DEL)

DELBERT Modern coinage formed by the compounding of the names Del and Bert. *See* BERT *and* DEL. Short: Del. (DEL-BERT)

DELL Transferred use of the surname derived from the Old English *dael* (dell, hollow, valley): hence, "dweller in the dell." (DEL)

DELROY Modern coinage formed by combining the names Del and Roy (red; king). *See* DEL *and* ROY. Short: Del. (DEL-ROY, DEL-ROY)

DENNIS From the French Denis, a name derived from the Greek Dionysius (of Dionysos, the Greek mythological god of wine and revelry). The name was borne by St. Denis, a 3rd-century evangelist who became the patron saint of France, thus establishing the name's continued popularity. In England, Dennis became common after the 12th century. Short: Den. Pet: Denny. (DEN-NIS)

DENTON Transferred use of the surname originating from English place-names composed of the Old English elements *denn* (den, lair, pasture, flattened place) or *denu* (valley) and *tūn* (town, settlement, village, enclosure): hence, "settlement near the den" or "settlement in the valley." (DEN-TUN)

DENZIL Transferred use of the Cornish surname originating in the 16th century from Denzell, a place in Cornwall. Var: Denzell, Denzelle, Denzill, Denzille. (DEN-ZIL)

DEREK Derived from a short form of the obsolete Germanic Thiudoreiks, a compound name composed from the Old German elements *thiuda* (folk, people) and *reiks* (ruler, leader, king). The name was brought to England in the Middle Ages by Flemish cloth traders. Var: Derick, Derrick. (DARE-IK, DARE-UK)

DESMOND A borrowing from the Irish, Desmond originated as a surname from the Irish place-name Deas-Mhumhna (South Munster) in the form of O'Deasmhumhnaigh (descendant of the Desmond man). Short: Des. (DEZ-MUND)

DIGBY Transferred use of the surname originating from a place-name in Lincolnshire, which is composed from the Old Norse elements *díki* (ditch) and *bý́r* (settlement, village): hence, "settlement by the ditch." (DIG-BEE)

DOMINIC Derived from the Latin Dominicus (belonging to the lord), which is from the word *dominus* (a lord, a master). The name was borne by St. Dominic (1170–1221), a Spanish priest and founder of the Dominican Order. Var: Dominick. Short: Dom. (DOM-IN-IK)

DONALD Anglicized form of the Gaelic Domhnall (world ruler), which is thought to be derived from the primitive Celtic Dubno-walo-s (mighty in the deep) or Dumno-valo-s (world mighty). Alternatively, some believe the name to be derived from the Gaelic *don* (brown). Short: Don. Pet: Donny. (DON-ULD)

DONTAVIS Modern coinage of uncertain origin and meaning. (DON-TAY-VIS)

DONTRELL Modern coinage of uncertain origin and meaning. (DON-TREL)

DOOLEY Transferred use of the surname, which is an Anglicized form of the Gaelic Ódubhlaoich (descendant of Dubhlaoch). Dubhlaoch has the definition "dark hero, dark-haired hero." Var: Dooly. (DOO-LEE)

DORIAN Invention of British writer Oscar Wilde (1854–1900), who chose the name for the central character in *The Portrait of Dorian Gray*. The name coincides with *Dorian* (a native of Doris, a mountainous region of Greece), which might have served as the inspiration for the name. (DORE-EE-UN)

DOUGLAS Transferred use of the surname derived from the Gaelic Dubhglas, a compounding of the elements *dubh* (black, dark) and *glas* (blue, green, gray). Dubhglas was a common Celtic river name, and the surname might have originated to denote one who lived near the river. Short: Doug. Pet: Dougie, Duggie. (DUG-LUS)

DOVER Transferred use of the surname which arose as a designation for one who lived in or near Dover, a seaport in southeastern England. (DŌ-VER)

DREW Originally a short form of Andrew (manly), Drew is commonly used as an independent given name. *See* ANDREW. (DROO)

DUANE Anglicized form of Dubhán (little dark one), a diminutive form of the Gaelic *dubh* (black, dark). Var: Dewayne, Dwane, Dwayne. (DOO-ANE, DUH-WANE, DWANE)

DUDLEY Transferred use of the surname originating from the place-name Dudda's Lea, which is composed from the obsolete Old English personal name Dudda and *lēah* (wood, clearing, meadow, enclosure). (DUD-LEE)

DUFF Transferred use of the surname, which is an Anglicized form of the Gaelic Ó Duibh (descendant of Dubh), a name derived from *dubh* (black, dark). Pet: Duffy. (DUF)

DUFFY Transferred use of the surname, which is an Anglicized form of the Gaelic Ó Dubhtaigh (descendant of Dubhtach), a name derived from *dubh* (black, dark). (DUF-EE)

DUKE Derived from *duke* (a prince who rules an independent duchy, or a noble man with the ranking just below that of a prince). Alternatively, Duke is used as a short form of Marmaduke (devotee of Maedóc). *See* MARMADUKE. (DOOK)

DUNSTAN Compound name derived from the Old English elements *dun* (dark) and *stān* (stone). The name was borne by St. Dunstan (c. 924–88), an English prelate and archbishop of Canterbury. (DUN-STUN)

DUSTIN Transferred use of the surname, which is of uncertain origin. Some believe it to be an altered form of Thurston, which is derived from the Old Norse Thorstein (Thor's stone). *See* THORSTEIN (Scandinavian Names). (DUS-TIN)

EAMON Gaelic form of Edmund (wealthy protector), which is in common use in England. *See* EDMUND. Var: Eamonn. (EH-MUN)

EARL Derived from *earl* (an earl, a nobleman), which is from the Old English *eorl* (nobleman, count). (URL)

EDGAR Derived from the Old English Eadgar, a name composed from the elements *ēad* (prosperity, fortune, riches) and *gar* (a spear): hence, "spear of prosperity." Short: Ed. Pet: Eddie, Eddy. (ED-GAR)

EDMUND Derived from the Old English Eadmund (wealthy protection), a compound name composed of the elements *ēad* (prosperity, fortune, riches) and *mund* (hand, protection). The name was borne by a 9th-century East Anglian king killed by invading Danes for refusing to share his Christian kingdom with them. He was revered as a martyr, and his cult quickly spread to the Continent. Short: Ed. Pet: Eddie, Eddy. (ED-MUND)

EDWARD Derived from the Old English Eadweard (wealthy or fortunate guardian), a compound name composed of the elements *ēad* (prosperity, fortune, riches) and *weard* (guardian, protector). Edward is a royal name, having been borne by three Anglo-Saxon kings and eight kings of England. Currently, the name is borne by Prince Edward (b. 1964), the youngest son of Queen Elizabeth II and Prince Philip. Short: Ed, Ned, Ted. Pet: Eddie. (ED-WARD)

EDWIN Derived from the obsolete Old English Eadwine, a compound name composed of the elements *ēad* (prosperity, fortune, riches) and *wine* (friend): hence, "wealthy friend." Short: Ed. Pet: Eddie, Eddy. (ED-WIN)

ELDON Transferred use of the surname originating in county Durham in the 14th century. It is believed to be derived from the personal name Ella (foreign, other) and *dun* (hill): hence, "Ella's hill." (ELL-DUN)

ELIAS A borrowing from the Greek, Elias is a cognate of the Hebrew Eliyahu, which is derived from *'ēlīyāhū* (Jehovah is God). The name is a variant of Elijah, the name borne in the Bible by a prophet of Israel in the 9th century B.C. (EE-LĪ-US)

ELLIOT Transferred use of the surname originating as a diminutive of the Old French Élie, a cognate of the Hebrew Elijah (Jehovah is God). *See* ELIJAH (Biblical Names). Var: Eliot, Eliott, Elliott. (EL-LEE-UT)

ELLIS Transferred use of the surname originating from the personal name Elis, a Middle English variant of the biblical names Elijah (Jehovah is God) and Elisha (God is salvation). *See* ELIJAH *and* ELISHA (Biblical Names). (EL-LIS)

ELMER Transferred use of the surname originating from the obsolete Old English Æthelmær, Æðelmær, a compound name composed of the elements *æthel, æðel* (noble) and *mær* (famous): hence, "noble and famous." (EL-MER)

ELROY Variant of Leroy, a modern coinage thought to be based on the French *le roi* (the king). (EL-ROY)

EMMET Transferred use of the surname originating as a pet form of the feminine Emma. Emma is derived from the Germanic Erma, a short form of any of the various female names beginning with the element *Erm-*. (EM-MET, EM-MUT)

ERIC Derived from the Old Norse Eiríkr (eternal ruler), a compound name composed of the elements *ei* (ever, always) and *ríkr* (ruler). The name was introduced to England before the Norman Conquest by Viking invaders and subsequent Scandinavian settlers. (ERR-ik)

ERNEST Cognate of the Germanic Ernst, which is from the Old High German Ernost and Ernust, names derived from *ernust* (earnest, resolute). The name was introduced to England in the 18th century following the coronation of George I (1660–1727), the "German King." Pet: Ernie. (ER-NUST)

ERROL Of debated etymology, some believe it is derived from a Scottish place-name of uncertain origin. Others think it is derived from the Latin *errare* (to wander). The name was borne by actor Errol Flynn (1909–59). Var: Erroll. (ERR-OL)

ESMOND Derived from the obsolete English name Ēastmund, a compound name composed of the elements *ēast* (beauty, grace) and *mund* (hand, protection): hence, "graceful protection" or "beautiful hand." (EZ-mund).

ETHAN A borrowing from the Ecclesiastic Late Latin, Ethan is derived from the Hebrew *ēthān* (strength, firmness, long-lived). The name is borne in the Bible by a very wise man whom Solomon surpassed in wisdom. (EE-THUN)

EUGENE A borrowing from the French, Eugene is derived from the Latin Eugenius, which is from *eugenēs* (well-born). Short: Gene. (YOO-JEEN)

EUSTACE From the Old French Eustache, which is derived from the Greek Eustachius and Eustakhios, two names of separate origin. Eustachius is derived from the elements *eu* (well, good, happy) and *stēnai* (to stand): hence, "steadfast." Eustakhios has its roots in *eu* (well, good, happy) and *stakhys* (grapes, harvest): hence, "happy in harvest." Eustace was introduced to England during the Norman Conquest. (YOO-STAS)

EVERARD Derived from the obsolete Eoforheard (strong as a wild boar), a compound name composed of the elements *eofor* (wild boar) and *heard* (hearty, strong, brave). Eoforheard had a cognate in the Old High German Eburhart, which evolved into the Modern German Eberhard and the French Everard. Thus, it is uncertain whether Everard was a natural evolution of Eoforheard, or whether Eoforheard was abandoned in favor of Everard at the time of the Conquest. (EV-EH-RARD)

EVERETT From the Dutch Evert and Everhart, which are derived, via the Old French Everart, from the Old High German Eburhart (strong as a wild boar), a compound name composed of the elements *ebur* (wild boar) and *harto* (strong, hearty). (EV-EH-RET)

FELIX Derived from the Latin *felix* (happy, lucky). Felix was the name of four popes and several early saints, one of whom was an apostle to East Anglia. (FEE-LIX)

FENTON Transferred use of the surname originating from several place-names derived from the Old English elements *fenn* (marsh, fen) and *tūn* (town, settlement, village, enclosure): hence, "settlement near the fen." (FEN-TUN)

FERDINAND From the Spanish Ferdinando, which is of uncertain origin and meaning. It is thought to be of Germanic origin composed from the elements *frithu* (peace), *fardi* (journey), or *ferchvus* (youth, life) and *nanths* (courage), *nanthi* (venture, risk), or *nand* (ready, prepared). Pet: Ferdie. (FER-DIH-NAND)

FIFE Transferred use of the surname originating from the place-name Fife, a region in eastern Scotland. Fife is thought to be named for Fib, a legendary Pictish hero who was one of the seven sons of Cruithne. Var: Fyfe. (FIFE)

FINNIAN Borrowed from the Irish, Finnian is an Anglicized form of the Gaelic Fionnán (little fair one), which is from *fionn* (fair). Var: Finian. Short: Fin, Finn. (FIN-EE-UN)

FINNIGAN Transferred use of the surname, which is an Anglicized form of the Gaelic Ó Fionnagáin (descendant of Fionnagán). Fionnagán is a diminutive form of *fionn* (fair): hence, "little fair one." Var: Finnegan, Finigan. Short: Fin, Finn. Pet: Finny. (FIN-EH-GAN)

FITZ Short form of Fitzgerald (son of Gerald), Fitz is also bestowed as an independent given name. (FITZ)

FITZGERALD Transferred use of the surname meaning "son of Gerald" (spear ruler), which was introduced to England by the Normans. *See* GERALD. Var: Fitz Gerald. Short: Fitz, Gerald. Pet: Gerry. (FITZ-JER-ALD)

FLETCHER Transferred use of the surname derived from the Old French *flechier* (arrow maker), which is from the root *flech* (an arrow). The name originated in the beginning of the 13th century as an occupational name for a maker or seller of arrows. Short: Fletch. (FLETCH-ER)

FLOYD Variant of the Welsh Lloyd (gray), which arose from English attempts to pronounce the Welsh *Ll*. *See* Lloyd. (FLOID)

FLYNN Transferred use of the surname, which is an Anglicized form of the Gaelic Ó Flainn (descendant of Flann). The name is derived from *flann* (red): hence, "red-haired one." (FLIN)

FORD Transferred use of the surname derived from the Old English *ford* (a shallow place in a river or stream which can be crossed by wading). The name originally denoted one who was a "dweller by the ford." (FORD)

FORREST Transferred use of the surname, which arose in the 13th century in the form of de Foresta (of the forest): hence, "dweller or worker in the forest." The word is derived from the Middle Latin *forestis* (unenclosed wood). Var: Forrestt. (FOR-EST)

FOSTER Transferred use of the surname, which is of various origins. Foster is thought to be derived from the Middle English *foster* (foster parent, nurse), from the Middle English *forester* (officer in charge of a forest or a forest worker), from the Middle English *forseter* (a maker of scissors, a shearer), and from the Middle English *furster, fuster* (a saddletree maker). (FOS-TER)

FRANCIS From Franceis, an Old French form of the Italian Francesco, which is from the Middle Latin Franciscus (a Frenchman). Franciscus is derived from Francus (a Frank, a freeman), which has its root in the Old French *franc* (free). Short: France, Frank. Pet: Frankie. (FRAN-SIS)

FRANK From the Old French *Franc* and the Germanic *Frank*, names referring to a member of the Germanic tribes that established the Frankish Empire, extending over what is now France, Germany, and Italy. The tribe is thought to have obtained their name from a type of spear or javelin (*franco*). Alternatively, Frank is used as a short form of Francis (a Frenchman, a freeman) and Franklin (a freeman). *See* FRANCIS *and* FRANKLIN. Pet: Frankie. (FRANK)

FRANKLIN Transferred use of the surname, which is from the Middle English *frankeleyn* (a freeman, a landowner of free but not noble birth). The word is derived from the French *franc* (free). Short: Frank. Pet: Frankie. (FRANK-LIN)

FRED A short form of Alfred (elf counselor) or Frederick (peace ruler), Fred is also commonly bestowed as an independent given name. *See* ALFRED *and* FREDERICK. Pet: Freddie, Freddy. (FRED)

FREDERICK Derived from the Germanic Friedrich (peace ruler), which is from the obsolete Fridurih, a compound name composed from the elements *frid* (peace) and *rik* (ruler, king). The name was brought to England in the 18th century when George I of Hanover became king of England. Short: Fred. Pet: Freddie, Freddy. (FRED-EH-RIK)

GALEN Derived from the name Claudius Galenus (c. 130–200), a Greek physician and writer on medicine and philosophy to whom the system of medical practice Galenism is attributed. The name Galenus is believed to be derived from *galēnē* (calm). (GAY-LEN)

GARETH Of uncertain origin and meaning, Gareth is first noted in Sir Thomas Malory's *Morte d'Arthur*, a collection of Arthurian tales, which were taken mostly from French sources. In this, Sir Gareth was the name used for Sir Gawain, a knight of the Round Table and nephew of King Arthur. It is unclear where Malory derived the name. Pet: Gary. (GARE-ETH)

GARFIELD Transferred use of the surname derived from the Old English elements *gāra* (a triangular piece of land) and *feld* (field, open country), which originated for someone who lived near a triangular field. (GAR-FEELD)

GARRET Transferred use of the surname that evolved from Gerald (spear rule, ruler with the spear) and Gerard (brave with the spear). *See* GERALD *and* GERARD. Var: Garrett. Pet: Gary, Garry. (GARE-ET)

GARRISON Transferred use of the surname originating from the place-name Garriston in North Yorkshire. Alternatively, Garrison developed from Garretson

(son of Garret). *See* GARRET. Pet: Gary, Garry. (GARE-RIH-SON)

GARTH Transferred use of the surname derived from the Middle English *garth* (an enclosed yard or garden). The name originated as an occupational name for a person in charge of a garden or an enclosed yard or paddock. (GARTH)

GARY From the Old English Garwig (spear of battle), a compound name composed of the elements *gar* (a spear) and *wig* (battle). Alternatively, Gary developed as a pet form of any of the various names beginning with the Germanic element *gar* (spear). Var: Garry. (GARE-EE)

GAVIN Of uncertain etymology, some believe Gavin to be from Gwalchmai, a Gaelic name derived from the elements *gwalch* (a hawk) and *maedd* (a blow, battle). In Arthurian legend, Gavin is a byname for Sir Gawain, a knight of the Round Table and nephew of King Arthur. (GAV-IN)

GENE Originally a short form of Eugene (well-born), Gene is commonly bestowed as an independent given name. *See* EUGENE. (JEEN)

GEOFFREY Derived from the Middle English Geffrey, which is from the Old French Geoffroi, a name thought to have evolved from several different Germanic names. Gaufrid, of the elements *govja* (a district) and *frithu* (peace); Walahfrid, from *valha* (traveler) and *frithu* (peace); and Gisfrid, from the elements *gis* (pledge) and *frithu* (peace), are thought to be the root names. In Britain the name was borne by Geoffrey of Monmouth (c. 1100–54), a Welsh bishop, historical chronicler, and preserver of Arthurian legend. Var: Jeffrey. Short: Geoff, Jeff. (JEF-REE)

GEORGE From the French Georges, a cognate of the Greek Geōrgios, which is derived from *geōrgos* (earthworker, farmer), a compounding of the elements *gē* (earth) and *ergein* (to work). The name George was uncommon in England until the Hanoverian George became king in 1714. The use of the name by the four succeeding kings firmly established its use and popularity. Pet: Geordie, Georgie. (JORJ)

GERALD Derived from the Germanic Gerwald, a compound name composed from the elements *ger* (a spear) and *wald* (rule): hence, "spear ruler, to rule with a spear." The name was introduced by the Normans, and though it was subsequently used by the English, it was never as common as Gerard, a name it was often confused with. The name died out in England by the end of the 13th century but was kept by the Irish. Toward the end of the 19th century, the name Gerald was reintroduced, and it has now become more popular than the enduring Gerard. Var: Jerrold. Short: Ged. Pet: Gerry, Jerry. (JARE-ULD)

GERARD Derived from the Old High German Gerhart (spear strength, brave with a spear), a compound name composed of the elements *ger* (a spear) and *hart* (hearty, brave, strong). Introduced to England by the Normans, Gerard has remained in steady use since the Middle Ages. Var: Gerrard, Jerrard. Pet: Ged, Gerrick, Gerry, Jerry. (JEH-RARD)

GERVAISE Of uncertain etymology, Gervaise is most likely a derivative of the Old German Gervas, the first element of which is *ger* (a spear) and the second of which is believed to be from the Celtic *vass* (servant): hence, "servant of the spear." The use of the name arose from the fame of St. Gervasius, a 1st-century martyr whose remains were found in Milan by St. Ambrose in 386. Var: Gervase. Pet: Gerry. (JER-VAZE)

GIDEON Derived from the Hebrew *gidh'ōn* (hewer, one who cuts down). The name is borne in the Bible by an Israelite judge who was a leader in the defeat of the Midianites. The name Gideon was favored by 17th-century Puritans. (GID-EE-UN)

GILBERT From the Old French Guillebert, a derivative of the Old High German Gisilberht, which is composed from the elements *gisil* (pledge) and *beraht* (bright, famous). The name was introduced by the Normans and became very popular, resulting in the formation of several surnames. Short: Gib, Gil. (GIL-BERT)

GILES From the Old French Gilles, a derivative of the Latin Aegidius, which is from the Greek *aigis* (a goatskin shield of Zeus, a protection). The name was borne by the semilegendary St. Giles, a 7th-century Athenian who had the power to work miracles and heal the crippled. He fled to southern Gaul and became a hermit to escape fame and the adoration of his fans. Nevertheless, he was popular throughout Europe, and his name was favored in the Middle Ages. Var: Gyles. (JILES)

GLEN Derived from the Gaelic *gleann* (mountain valley, a narrow, secluded valley). It is unclear whether the surname or the given name came first. Var: Glenn. (GLEN)

GODFREY From the Old French Godefrei, which is derived from the Germanic Godafrid, a compound name composed from the elements *god* (God) and *frid* (peace). The name was introduced to England by the Normans and became very popular in the Middle Ages, giving rise to several surnames. (GOD-FREE)

GODWIN An enduring name derived from the Old English Godewine (friend of God), which is composed of the elements *god* (God) and *wine* (friend). The name was borne by the earl of Wessex, the father of the last Saxon king, Harold II (c. 1022–66), and has given rise to several surnames. (GOD-WIN)

GOODWIN Transferred use of the surname originating from the obsolete Old English Gōdwine (good friend), a compound name composed of the elements *gōd* (good) and *wine* (friend). The name is often confused with Godwin (friend of God). (GOOD-WIN)

GORDON Transferred use of the Scottish surname believed to have originated from the place-name Gordon in Berwickshire. The place-name is of uncertain etymology. The use of Gordon as a given name dates to the 19th century, when it was bestowed in honor of the popular British general Charles Gordon (1833–85), called Chinese Gordon from his service in China, Egypt, and Sudan. (GOR-DUN)

GRAHAM Transferred use of the surname originating from the place-name Grantham in Lincolnshire. The first element is uncertain, but the second is from the Old English *ham* (home, dwelling, manor). The name was taken to Scotland in the 12th century by William de Graham, a Norman and founder of the famous Scottish clan. Var: Graeme, Grahame. (GRAM, GRAY-UM)

GRANT Transferred use of the surname derived from the Anglo-French *graund, graunt* (great) and the Old French *grand, grant* (great). The name Grant originated as a nickname for a large or tall person. (GRANT)

GRANVILLE Transferred use of the surname originating as a Norman baronial name from Seine-Inférieure in Normandy. The name is derived from the Old French elements *grand, grant* (great) and *ville* (town, city): hence, "great town" or "large town." (GRAN-VIL)

GREGORY From the Late Latin Gregorius, a cognate of the Greek Grēgorios (vigilant, a watchman), which is derived from the verb *egeirein* (to awaken). Gregory, a popular name among the early Christians, was borne by several early saints and many popes. In 1582 Pope Gregory XIII introduced the Gregorian calendar, a corrected form of the Julian calendar which is now used in most countries of the world. Short: Greg, Gregg. (GREG-OR-EE)

GRIFFIN Evolution of Griffinus, a Latinate form of Griffith that was used in the Middle Ages. *See* GRIFFITH (Welsh Names). Var: Griffun, Griffyn, Gryffin. (GRIH-FUN)

GUY A borrowing from the French, Guy is derived from the Old French *guie* (a guide, a leader). (GĪ)

HAL Originally a short form of Henry (home ruler), Hal is also bestowed as an independent given name. *See* HENRY. (HAL)

HALE Transferred use of the surname derived from the Old English *halh* (nook, recess, remote valley). The name was indicative of one who resided "in the hale," or "in the remote valley or recess." (HALE)

HALL Transferred use of the surname derived from the Old English *heall* (hall, that which is covered). The name originated as an occupational name for a person who worked at a manor home or hall. (HAHL)

HARDING Transferred use of the surname derived from the Old English personal name Hearding, which is a borrowing of the Old English *hearding* (bold man). (HAR-DING)

HAROLD Derived from the obsolete Old English Hereweald, a compound name composed of the elements *here* (army) and *weald* (ruler, power, control). Alternatively, the Scandinavians introduced the cognate Harald, which is composed of the Germanic elements *harja* (army) and *wald* (rule). The name was borne by King Harald I (d. 1040), also known as Harald Harefoot, and Harald II (1022–66), who was killed in the Battle of Hastings. The name died out in the early Middle Ages but was reintroduced in the 19th century with other Old English names. Pet: Harry. (HAR-ULD, HAR-ROLD)

HARRISON Transferred use of the surname originating in the Middle Ages as a patronymic meaning "son of Henry" or "son of Harry." Pet: Harry. (HAR-RIH-SON)

HARRY Originally an English cognate of the French Henri (home ruler, ruler of an enclosure), Harry is now usually regarded as a pet form of Henry instead of the legitimate original form, and is also used as a pet form of Harold and Harrison. (HAR-REE)

HARVEY Transferred use of the surname originating from the Old Breton Aeruiu or Hærviu (battleworthy), which are composed of the elements *hær* (battle) and *viu* (worthy). The name was introduced by the Bretons during the Conquest. Short: Harv, Harve. (HAR-VEE)

HAYES Transferred use of the surname derived from the Old English element *hege* (hedge, a hedged enclosure): hence, "dweller near the hedged enclosure." Var: Hays. (HAZE)

HENRY From the French Henri, from the German Heinrich, which is from the Old High German Haganrih (ruler of an enclosure), a compound name composed from the elements *hag* (an enclosure, a hedging-in) and *rihhi* (ruler), and from the Old High German Heimerich (home ruler), a compound name composed from the elements *heim* (home) and *rik* (ruler, king). The name, introduced by the Normans and borne by eight English kings, took the English vernacular form of Harry until the 17th century, when Henry became popular and Harry was used as the pet form. Prince Henry (b. 1984), the younger son of Prince Charles, is third in line to the throne. Pet: Hal, Hank, Harry. (HEN-REE)

HERBERT Derived from the Old English Herebeorht (bright army), a compound name composed of the elements *here* (army) and *beorht* (bright, fair, white). The name was not used much, and at the time of the Conquest was replaced by the Normans with the continental Germanic cognates Hariberht and Heriberht, which are composed of the elements *hari, heri* (army) and *beraht* (bright, famous). Short: Bert, Herb. Pet: Herbie. (HER-BERT)

HERMAN Introduced by the Normans, Herman is from the German Hermann, which is from the Old High German Hariman (army man, soldier), a compound name composed of the elements *hari* (army) and *man* (man). (HER-MUN)

HOWARD Transferred use of the surname, which may be of several different origins. It is believed to be derived from the Old French Huard, a derivative of the Old German Hugihard (heart brave), from the Old German Howart (high warden, chief warden), from the Old Norse Haward (high guardian, chief warden), and from the Old English Howeherde (ewe herd), which is composed from the elements *ēwe* (ewe) and *hierde* (herd). (HOW-ERD)

HUBERT Derived from the Germanic Huguberht, which is composed of the elements *hugu* (mind, heart, spirit) and *beraht* (bright, famous). Hubert was introduced by the Normans at the time of the Conquest, and later, settlers from the Low Countries helped to firmly establish the name. Short: Bert. (HYOO-BERT)

HUGH From the Old French Hue, which is from the Old High German Hugo, a derivative of *hugu* (heart, mind, spirit). Hugh was used to Anglicize the Gaelic names Aodh, Ùisdean, and Eóghan. Pet: Hughie. (HYOO)

HUMPHREY Transferred use of the surname originating from the Germanic Hunfrid, a compound name composed from the elements *hun* (strength, warrior) and *frid* (peace): hence, "warrior of peace." The name was brought to England by the Normans and replaced the earlier English Hunfrith, which was composed from the Old Norse *húnn* (bear cub) and the Old English *frith* (peace). Var: Humphry. (HUM-FREE)

IKE Originally a short form of Isaac (laughter), Ike is also bestowed as an independent given name. *See* ISAAC. (IKE)

INGRAM Transferred use of the surname originating from the Germanic personal name Angilramnus or Ingilramnus, which are composed from the elements *angil* (angel) and *hraban* (raven): hence, "angel-raven." (ING-GRUM)

IRA Derived from the Hebrew *'īrā* (watchful, the stallion). The name, borne in the Bible by Ira the Jairite, one of King David's priests, was used by 17th-century Puritans, who established it in England and America. (Ī-RAH)

ISAAC From the Ecclesiastic Greek Isaak, a derivative of the Hebrew *Yitzchak* (he will laugh), which is from *yitshāq* (laughter). The name is borne in the Bible by one of the three patriarchs, the son of Abraham and Sarah and father of Esau and Jacob. Pet: Ike. (Ī-ZIK)

IVOR Derived from the Scandinavian Ivar (bow warrior, archer). The name was introduced to England by Ivar the Boneless, who invaded East Anglia in retaliation for the death of his father. *See* IVAR (Scandinavian Names). (Ī-VER)

JACK Originally a pet form of John (God is gracious), Jack is now often bestowed as an independent given name. It evolved from the Middle English Jackin, which evolved from Jankin, a diminutive form of Jehan and Jan, which are Middle English forms of John. *See* JOHN. Pet: Jackie, Jacky. (JAK)

JACKSON Transferred use of the surname originating in the 14th century as a patronymic meaning "son of Jack." Short: Jack. Pet: Jackie, Jacky. (JAK-SUN)

JACOB From the Ecclesiastic Late Latin Iacobus, which is from the Greek Iakōbos, a name derived from the Hebrew Yaakov, which is from *ya'aqob* (seizing by the heel, supplanting). The name is borne in the Bible by a son of Isaac. Jacob was one of the three patriarchs and the father of twelve sons, who founded the tribes of Israel. Pet: Jake. (JAY-KUB)

JAKE Originally a pet form of Jacob (seizing by the heel, supplanting), Jake is also bestowed as an independent given name. *See* JACOB. (JAKE)

JAMES From the Ecclesiastic Late Latin Iacomus, an evolution of Iacobus, which is derived from the Greek Iakōbos. Iakōbos is from the Hebrew Yaakov, which is from *ya'aqob* (supplanting, seizing by the heel). James is a cognate of Jacob, though in most English-speaking countries it is regarded as a separate name. The name is borne in the Bible by the brother of Jesus. In Britain, James is a royal name, being borne by rulers of both England and Scotland. Short: Jim. Pet: Jimmy. (JAYMZ)

JAMIE Originally a pet form of James (supplanting, seizing by the heel), Jamie is commonly bestowed as an independent given name. *See* JAMES. Var: Jaimey, Jaimie, Jamey.

JAN Originated in the Middle Ages as a vernacular form of John (God is gracious). It is derived from the earlier forms Jehan and Johan, and its use was reinforced by the Scandinavian import Jan. *See* JAN (Scandinavian Names) *and* JOHN. (JAN)

JARVIS Transferred use of the surname originating from the Norman and Old German personal name Gervas, the first element of which is *ger* (spear) and the second of which is believed to be from the Celtic *vass* (servant): hence, "servant of the spear." *See* GERVAISE. (JAR-VIS)

JASON English cognate of the Latin and Greek Iāson (healer), which is derived from *iasthai* (to heal). The name is borne in Greek mythology by a prince who led the Argonauts and, with the help of the sorceress Medea, found the Golden Fleece. (JAY-SUN)

JASPER English form of Gaspar, a name of uncertain etymology which, along with Balthasar and Melchior, was assigned to the Three Wise Men, who brought gifts to the Christ child. The names are not found in the Bible and are thought to have been fixed in the 11th century. Gaspar might have been derived from the Persian *genashber* (treasure master), which is in keeping with his role of the bringer of precious gifts. (JAS-PER)

JAY Originally a pet form of any of the names beginning with the letter *J*, Jay is now commonly bestowed as an independent given name. (JAY)

JEFFERSON Transferred use of the surname originating as a patronymic meaning "son of Geoffrey, son of Jeffrey." *See* GEOFFREY *and* JEFFREY. Short: Jeff. (JEF-ER-SUN)

JEFFREY Variant spelling of Geoffrey which arose in the Middle Ages. *See* GEOFFREY. Var: Jeffery. Short: Jeff. (JEF-REE)

JEREMIAH From the Ecclesiastic Late Latin Jeremias, a cognate of the Ecclesiastic Greek Hieremias, which is from the Hebrew Yirmeyahu, a name derived from *yirmeyāh* (the Lord loosens, God will uplift). The name is borne in the Bible by a 6th- or 7th-century B.C. Hebrew prophet whose story and prophecies are recorded in the Old Testament book of Jeremiah. Pet: Jerry. (JER-EH-MĪ-AH)

JEREMY English vernacular form of Jeremiah (the Lord loosens, God will uplift), which dates to the 13th century. *See* JEREMIAH. Pet: Jem, Jerry. (JER-EH-MEE)

JEROME Derived from the Latin Hieronymus, a compound name composed from the elements *hieros* (holy) and *onyma* (name): hence, "holy name." The name was borne by St. Jerome (340–420), born Eusebius Hieronymus Sophronius in Pannonia, an ancient Roman province in central Europe. A monk and church scholar, St. Jerome was the author of the Vulgate (the translation of the Bible into Latin) and is regarded as one of the doctors of the church. Pet: Jerry. (JEH-ROME)

JERRY A pet form of any of the various names beginning with the element *Jer-*, Jerry is also bestowed as an independent given name. (JER-REE)

JESSE Derived from the Hebrew Yishai, which is from *yīshai* (gift, wealth). The name is borne in the Bible by the father of King David. Short: Jess. (JES-SEE)

JETHRO Derived from the Hebrew Yitro, which is from *yitro* (abundance, excellence). The name is borne in the Bible by the father of Zipporah, the wife of Moses. In Britain the name was borne by the noted agriculturalist Jethro Tull (1674–1741), whose name was adopted in 1968 by the British rock band Jethro Tull. (JETH-RO)

JOACHIM Derived from the Hebrew Jehoiakim, which is from Yehoyakim (God will establish). Jehoiakim is borne in the Bible by a king of Judah who was defeated by the Babylonians under King Nebuchadnezzar. In medieval Christian tradition, Joachim was the name assigned to the father of the Virgin Mary, as Anne was assigned to her mother. (JO-Ā-KIM, JO-Ā-KUM)

JOEL A borrowing from the Ecclesiastic Late Latin, Joel is from the Ecclesiastic Greek Iōēl, a name derived from the Hebrew Yoel, which is from *yō'ēl* (the Lord is God). The name is borne in the Bible by a minor Hebrew prophet (5th century B.C.?) whose prophecies and preachings are found in the Book of Joel. (JOLE, JO-WUL)

JOHN The most enduring of all the biblical names, John is derived from the Middle Latin Johannes, which is from the Ecclesiastic Late Latin Joannes, from the Ecclesiastic Greek Iōannes, a derivative of the Hebrew Yehanan, a short form of Yehohanan, which is from *yehōhānān* (Yahweh is gracious). The name, borne in the Bible by several important characters, was also borne by many saints, twenty-three popes, and many kings throughout Europe and England. First used by the Eastern Church, John was brought back to England after the first Crusades. It quickly became established, and during the last half of the 17th century, 28 percent of all males were baptized John. *See*

JOHN (Biblical Names). Var: Jon. Pet: Jack, Johnny, Johnnie. (JON)

JON A short form of Jonathan (God has given), Jon is also a Middle English vernacular form of John (God is gracious) and is commonly bestowed as a variant spelling of John quite independently of Jonathan. *See* JOHN *and* JONATHAN. Pet: Jonnie, Jonny. (JON)

JONATHAN From the Hebrew Yonatan, a short form of Yehonatan, which is derived from *yehōnātān* (Yahweh has given, God has given). The name is borne in the Bible by the eldest son of King Saul and a close friend of David's. Var: Johnathan, Jonathon. Short: Jon. Pet: Johnnie, Johnny, Jonnie, Jonny. (JON-AH-THUN)

JORDAN Derived from the Hebrew Yarden, which is from *yarden* (to flow down, descend). The name was originally used in the Middle Ages for a child who was baptized in holy water that was said to be from the river Jordan. Pet: Judd. (JOR-DUN)

JOSEPH A borrowing from the Ecclesiastic Late Latin, Joseph is from the Ecclesiastic Greek Iōsēph, which is from the Hebrew Yosef, a name derived from *yōsēf* (may he add). The name is borne in the Bible by the favorite son of Jacob, by the husband of the Virgin Mary, and by Joseph of Arimathea, a rich Jew who, according to medieval legend, brought the Holy Grail to Britain. Short: Joe. Pet: Joey. (JO-SUF)

JOSHUA Derived from the Hebrew Yehoshua, which is from *yehōshū'a* (Jehovah is help, God is salvation). The name is borne in the Bible by Moses' successor, who led the children of Israel into the Promised Land. Short: Josh. (JOSH-YOO-AH)

JOSIAH From the Hebrew Yoshiya, which is derived from *yōshīyāh* (the Lord supports, the Lord saves, the Lord heals). The name, borne in the Bible by a 7th-century B.C. king of Judah, was introduced into England after the Reformation. (JO-SĪ-AH)

JUDD Originally a Middle English pet form of Jordan (descending, to flow down), the modern use of Judd comes from the transferred use of the surname, which developed from the pet form. *See* JORDAN. (JUD)

JULIAN From the Latin Julianus, which is a derivative of Julius, an old Roman family name thought to be derived from Iulus (the first down on the chin, downy-bearded). Because a person just beginning to develop facial hair is young, "youth" became an accepted meaning of the name. (JOO-LEE-UN)

JUSTIN From the Latin Justīnus, which is derived from *justus* (lawful, right, just). The name was not used much in England before the 20th century. (JUS-TIN)

KEITH Transferred use of the Scottish surname originating from several place-names, which are of uncertain derivation. Keith might be formed from a Gaelic root meaning "the wind" or "wood." The use of Keith as a given name dates to the 19th century. (KEETH)

KELLY Anglicized form of the Irish Ceallagh, which is thought to be derived from *ceallach* (strife). The use of Kelly as a given name is most likely from the transferred use of the surname O'Kelly or Kelly (O'Ceallaigh), which is the second most common surname in Ireland. (KEL-LEE)

KELSEY Transferred use of the surname originating from the obsolete Old English Cēolsige, a compound name composed of the elements *cēol* (ship) and *sige* (victory). The name is bestowed upon males and females alike. Var: Kelsie, Kelsy. (KEL-SEE)

KELVIN Transferred use of the surname, which arose from the name of a Scottish river. Kelvin was first used as a personal name in the 1920s, perhaps in honor of Baron Kelvin (1824–1907), the British mathematician and physicist to whom the Kelvin scale of temperature is attributed. (KEL-VIN)

KEMP Transferred use of the surname derived from the Old English *cempa* (fighter, warrior) and the Middle English *kempe* (athlete, wrestler). (KEMP)

KENDALL Transferred use of the surname, which arose from the place-name Kendal in Westmorland, northwestern England. The town, which is in the valley of the river Kent, derives its name from the element *Kent* (the name of the river) and *dale* (valley): hence, "valley of the river Kent." Another source for the surname is the place-name Kendale in Humberside, northeastern England. In this case, the name is derived from the Old Norse element *keld* (spring) and the Old English *dale* (valley): hence, "valley of the spring." Var: Kendal. Short: Ken. (KEN-DUL)

KENDRICK Transferred use of the surname, which has several different roots. It is derived from the Old Welsh Cynwrig, an obsolete compound name composed of the elements *cyn* (high, chief) and *gwr, wr* (hero, man), or of *cyn* (high, chief) and *wrig* (hill, summit). As a Scottish surname, it is a short form of MacKendrick and MacKenrick, from the Gaelic MacEanraig (son of Henry). The English surname and its variant forms are derived from the Old English Cynerīc, a compounding of the elements *cyne* (royal) and *rīc* (power, rule). Var: Kenrick. Short: Ken. Pet: Kenny. (KEN-RIK)

KENELM Derived from the obsolete Old English Cenhelm and Cænhelm, compound names composed from the elements *cene* (bold, brave) and *helm* (helmet, protection). The name was borne by Cænhelm, a king of Mercia who was murdered in 819 and later venerated as St. Kenelm. Eight churches are dedicated to him throughout England. Short: Ken. Pet: Kenny. (KEN-ULM)

KENNETH Anglicized form of the Gaelic Cinaed and Cionaed (born of fire), and Coinneach and Caioneach (comely, handsome). The name, borne by Cinaed, Kenneth I MacAlpin (d. 860), the first king of Scotland, has continued to be perennially popular in Scotland and all of the English-speaking world. Short: Ken. Pet: Kenny. (KEN-NETH)

KENT Transferred use of the surname arising from the name of the county of Kent. The name, of uncertain derivation, is perhaps from the Welsh *cant* (rim, edge, border) or from the Old Welsh *cant* (white, bright). (KENT)

KENTON Transferred use of the surname originating from place-names derived from several sources. One such source is a combination of the name of the river Kenn, which is from the Gaelic *cain* (clear, bright, white), and the Old English *tūn* (town, settlement, village, enclosure): hence, "dweller from the village near the river Kenn." Another is derived from the obsolete Old English personal name Cēntūn, composed from the elements *cēne* (keen, bold) and *tūn* (town, settlement, village, enclosure): hence, "bold enclosure." And yet another source is the Old English Cynetūn (royal settlement), a compound name composed of the elements *cyne* (royal) and *tūn* (town, settlement, village, enclosure). Short: Ken. Pet: Kenny. (KEN-TUN)

KERR Transferred use of the surname derived from the Old Norse element *kjarr* (an overgrown wetland), which was originally indicative of someone who lived near such a place. (KER, KARE)

KEVIN Anglicized form of the Irish Caoimhín, Caomghin (handsome, comely birth), which is derived from *caomh* (comely, beloved, kind). Short: Kev. (KEH-VIN)

KIMBALL Transferred use of the surname derived from the Old Welsh Cynbel (war chief), a compound name composed of the elements *cyn* (chief) and *bel* (war), and from the Old English Cynebeald (royal and bold), a compound name composed of the elements *cyne* (royal) and *beald* (bold, brave). Short: Kim. (KIM-BUL)

KING A short form of Kingsley (king's wood), King is also bestowed as an independent given name based on *king* (monarch, king), which is derived from the Old English *cyning* (king, monarch). *See* KINGSLEY. (KING)

KINGSLEY Transferred use of the surname originating from the place-name Cyningeslēah, which is derived from the Old English elements *cyning* (king, monarch) and *lēah* (wood, clearing, meadow): hence, "king's wood." The name was indicative of a person who dwelled in or near the king's wood. Short: King. (KINGS-LEE)

KIPLING Transferred use of the surname originating from a place-name derived from the Northern English elements *kip* (a pointed hill) and *hlynn* (a torrent, a waterfall). The name was indicative of one who lived near a waterfall near the pointed hill. Short: Kip. (KIP-LING)

KIPP Transferred use of the surname derived from the Northern English *kip* (a pointed hill), which was indicative of one who dwelled near a pointed hill. Var: Kip, Kippar, Kipper. Pet: Kippie. (KIP)

KIRK Transferred use of the surname derived from the Old Norse *kirkja* (church), which was originally used for one who resided by a church: hence, "dweller by the church." (KIRK)

KYLE Transferred use of the Scottish surname originating from the region of the same name in southwestern Scotland. Kyle, a topographical term referring to a narrow, straight channel, is derived from the Gaelic *caol* (narrow, a sound, a strait). (KILE)

KYNASTON Transferred use of the surname originating from the Old English place-name Cynefriþestūn, "Cynefriþ's settlement." Cynefriþestūn is composed from the Old English personal name Cynefriþ (royal peace), a combining of the elements *cyne* (royal) and *friþ*, *frith* (peace), and *tūn* (town, settlement, village, enclosure). (KIN-NAH-STUN)

LAMBERT Of Germanic origin, Lambert is derived from the Old German Landobeorht, a compound name composed of the elements *land* (land) and *beorht* (bright, famous). The name was introduced to England in the Middle Ages by Flemish immigrants, who usually bestowed it in honor of St. Lambert, a 7th-century bishop of Maestricht. (LAM-BERT)

LANCE A borrowing from the Old French, Lance is from the Old High German Lanzo, which is derived from *lant* (land). The use of the name was advanced from the homonymous *lance* (a light spear, a lance). (LANS)

LAURENCE From the Latin Laurentius (man from Laurentum), which is from Laurentum, the name of a town in Latium, which is probably derived from *laurus* (laurel). The name was borne by St. Laurence the Deacon, who was martyred in Rome in 258. When ordered to hand over the church's treasures, he presented the sick and the poor. For this, he was roasted alive on a gridiron. 237 churches are dedicated to him in England. Var: Lawrence. Pet: Larry, Laurie. (LAW-RENS)

LEE Transferred use of the surname derived from the Old English *lēah* (wood, clearing, meadow). The name was indicative of a person who lived in or near a wood or clearing and thus takes the definition "dweller by the wood or clearing." (LEE)

LEIGHTON Transferred use of the surname originating from several place-names derived from the Old English elements *lēac* (leek) and *tūn* (town, settlement, village, enclosure). The surname might have arisen from a homestead where leeks were grown, or as an occupational name for a worker in a kitchen garden. Var: Layton. (LAY-TUN)

LELAND Transferred use of the surname derived from the Old English elements *lēah* (wood, clearing, meadow) or *læge* (fallow) and *land* (land, area). The name was indicative of one who lived near a clearing or a piece of fallow land. (LEE-LUND)

LEO A borrowing from the Late Latin, Leo is derived from *leo* (lion). The name, which was borne by thirteen popes, including Leo (I) the Great (400?–61), is also used as a short form of Leonard (lion-hearted). *See* LEONARD. (LEE-O)

LEON A variant form of Leo, a Late Latin name derived from *leo* (lion). *See* LEO. (LEE-ON)

LEONARD A borrowing from the Old French, Leonard is from the Old High German Lewenhart, a compound name composed from the elements *lewo* (lion) and *hart* (strong, brave, hearty): hence, "brave as a lion, lion-hearted." The name was introduced to England by the Normans but did not become popular until the 19th century. Var: Lennard. Short: Len, Leo. Pet: Lenny. (LEE-O-NARD, LEN-NERD)

LEROY Modern coinage thought to be based on the French *le roi* (the king). Var: LeRoy. (LEE-ROY)

LESLIE Transferred use of the Scottish surname taken from Lesslyn, a place-name in Aberdeenshire. The name might be derived from the Gaelic elements *lios* (enclosure, garden, fort) and *chuilinn* (a holly tree) or *liath* (gray): hence, "garden of hollies"or "the gray fort." The name, borne by a well-known Scottish clan, was not in common use as a personal name until late in the 19th century. Short: Les. (LES-LEE, LEZ-LEE)

LESTER Transferred use of the surname derived from the Middle English *lite, litte* (to dye). The name arose as an occupational name for a dyer. Alternatively, the surname was indicative of a person "from Leicester," a city in central England. Short: Les. (LES-TER)

LINCOLN Transferred use of the surname derived from the city of Lincoln in northeastern England. The name is found written in Latin in the 7th century as Lindum Colonia, which is probably a Latinate rendering of the Welsh *llyn* (lake, pool) and the Latin *colonia* (colony). Short: Linc, Link. (LINK-UN)

LINTON Transferred use of the surname originating from several place-names derived from the Old English elements *līn* (flax) or *lind* (linden, lime tree) and *tūn* (town, settlement, village, enclosure): hence, "enclosure for flax" or "settlement near the lime trees." (LIN-TUN)

LLOYD A borrowing from the Welsh, Lloyd is derived from *llwyd* (gray). The name arose as a nickname for someone with gray hair. (LOID)

LONNIE Of uncertain origin and meaning, Lonnie might be a variant of Lenny (lion-hearted, brave as a lion) or a modern coinage made by combining elements from the names of parents or relatives. *See* LEONARD. (LON-NEE)

LOUIS A borrowing from the French, Louis is derived from the Old French Loeis, which is from the Old High German Hluodowig, a compound name composed of the elements *hluod* (famous) and *wīg* (war, strife). Louis and its variant Lewis were also used to Anglicize the Gaelic names Laoiseach and Lughaidh. Var: Lewis. Short: Lew, Lou. Pet: Lewie, Louie. (LOO-ISS)

LOVELL Transferred use of the surname derived from the Anglo-French *lovel* (wolf cub), which is a diminutive form of *love* (wolf). (LUVL)

LUCAS Ecclesiastic Late Latin name thought to be a derivative of Lucius, which is from the root *lux* (light). Alternatively, some believe the name is derived from the Ecclesiastic Greek Loukas, a contraction of Loukanos (man from Lucania). Lucas has been a common name in England since the 13th century. (LOO-KUS)

LUKE Middle English and Anglo-French form of Lucas. *See* LUCAS. The name is borne in the Bible by one of the four evangelists, the author of the third Gospel, Luke, and the Acts of the Apostles. (LUKE)

LYLE Transferred use of the surname that evolved from the Anglo-French *de l'isle* (dweller on the isle). The name was brought to England by the Normans after the Conquest. (LILE)

LYNDON Transferred use of the surname originating from the place-name Lyndon in Leicestershire. The name is derived from the Old English elements *lind* (lime tree, linden) and *dun* (hill) and was indicative of a "dweller near the lime tree hill." Var: Lindon. (LIN-DUN)

MAGNUS A borrowing from the Latin, Magnus is derived from *magnus* (great, large). The name was brought to

England by the Scandinavians during the Middle Ages. (MAG-NUS)

MALCOLM Derived from the Gaelic Maolcolm (servant of St. Columba), a compound name composed of *maol* (servant) and the name *Colm* (Columba). St. Columba (521–97) was an Irish missionary who played a major role in converting Scotland and northern England to Christianity. (MAL-KUM)

MARC A short form of Marcus, Marc is also bestowed as a variant spelling of Mark. *See* MARCUS *and* MARK. (MARK)

MARCUS A borrowing from the Latin, Marcus is of uncertain derivation. Most believe it has its root in Mars, the name of the Roman mythological god of war, and thus give it the meaning "war-like." Others, however, think it to be from *mas* (manly) or from the Greek *malakoz* (soft, tender). Short: Marc. (MAR-KUS)

MARK English cognate of the Latin Marcus, a name of debated origin and meaning. *See* MARCUS. The name was borne in the Bible by one of the four evangelists, the author of the second Gospel. Mark was not a common name in England until the 19th century. Var: Marc. (MARK)

MARMADUKE A name of uncertain etymology, Marmaduke might be derived from the Irish Maelmaedóc (servant of Maedoc). Short: Duke. (MAR-MAH-DUKE)

MARSHALL Transferred use of the surname originating from the Old French *mareschal,* which is from the Old High German *marahscalh,* a word composed of the elements *marah* (horse) and *scalh* (servant). The term arose as an occupational name for a groom. In the 13th century the term was also indicative of a farrier and later was used to denote a high officer of state. (MAR-SHUL)

MARTIN From the Latin Martinus (of Mars, war-like), a derivative of Mars, the name of the Roman mythological god of war. The name was borne by St. Martin of Tours (c. 315–397). He is mainly remembered for splitting his cloak in two and giving half to a beggar. Var: Martyn. Pet: Marty. (MAR-TIN)

MARVIN A name that arose in the Middle Ages as a variant of the Welsh Mervyn (sea hill, eminent marrow). *See* MERVYN. Alternatively, it might be derived from the obsolete Merefin, a compound name composed of the element *mere* (lake, pond, sea) and the ethnic term *Finn* (a Finn, from Finland) or *fionn* (white, fair, clear). (MAR-VIN)

MASON Transferred use of the surname derived from *mason* (a person who builds with stone, brick, or concrete). The name arose as an occupational name in the 12th century. (MAY-SUN)

MATTHEW Evolution of the Middle English Matheu, which is from the Ecclesiastic Late Latin Matthaeus, a derivative of the Ecclesiastic Greek Matthaios and Matthias, contractions of Mattathias. The name is derived from the Hebrew Matityah, which has its root in *mattīthyāh* (gift of God). The name is borne in the Bible by one of the four evangelists, the author of the first Gospel. Short: Matt. Pet: Mattie. (MATH-YOO)

MAURICE A borrowing from the French, Maurice is from the Late Latin Mauritius (Moorish), which is derived from *Maurus* (a Moor). The Moors were a Muslim people of mixed Arab and Berber descent; thus the name came to mean "dark" or "swarthy" in reference to their coloring. Maurice was introduced to Britain by the Normans and underwent several variant spellings before returning to the original form. Var: Mauris, Moris, Morrice, Morris, Morys. Short: Mo. Pet: Maury. (MAU-REES, MOR-REES)

MAX A short form of Maximilian and Maxwell (the stream of Mack), Max is commonly bestowed as an independent given name. *See* MAXIMILIAN *and* MAXWELL. (MAX)

MAXIMILIAN This name arose as a blending of the Latin Maximus (greatest) and Aemiliānus by the Emperor Frederich III, who bestowed it upon his first-born son, Maximilian I (1459–1519), in honor of the two famous Roman generals. Maximus is directly derived from *maximus* (greatest), but the etymology of Aemiliānus is uncertain. Short: Max. (MAX-I-MIL-YUN)

MAXWELL Transferred use of the Scottish surname originating from a place-name derived from the name Maccus (great) and the Old English *wielle* (spring, pool) or *wella* (stream). The name was indicative of one who dwelled at Maccus' spring or the stream of Maccus. *See* MACCUS (Scottish Names). Short: Max. (MAX-WELL)

MAYNARD From the Anglo-French Mainard, which is derived from the Old High German Maganhard (mighty and brave), a compound name composed of the elements *magan* (power, strength, might) and *hart* (strong, hardy, brave). (MAY-NARD, MAY-NERD)

MELVIN Of uncertain etymology, Melvin might be an evolution of the obsolete Old English Mæthelwine, Mæðelwine, a compound name composed of the elements *mæthel, mæðel* (council, meeting) and *wine* (friend, protector): hence, "council protector." Var: Melvyn. Short: Mel. (MEL-VIN)

MERLIN English cognate of the Welsh Myrrdin, a name derived from the Primitive Celtic elements *mer, mori* (sea) and *dunom* (hill, fortress), therefore meaning "sea hill" or "sea fortress." The name was most famously borne in Arthurian legend by the magician helper and guide of King Arthur. Var: Merlyn. (MER-LIN)

MERRILL Transferred use of the surname derived from the female name Muriel (sea bright), an Anglicized form of the Irish Muirgheal. *See* MURIEL (Female Names) *and* MUIRGHEAL (Irish Female Names). (MER-RIL)

MERVYN Anglicized form of the Welsh Merfyn, which is derived from the Old Welsh elements *mer* (marrow, brains) or *môr* (sea) and *myn* (eminent, prominent, high, hill): hence, "sea hill" or "eminent marrow." Var: Mervin. (MER-VIN)

MICHAEL Derivative of the Hebrew *mīkhā'ēl* (who is like God?). The name is borne in the Bible by the archangel closest to God, the one responsible for carrying out God's judgments. Considered the leader of the heavenly host, Michael is regarded as the patron of soldiers. The name, one of the most successful of the biblical names, has cognates in many languages and is in popular use throughout Europe and abroad. Short: Mick, Mike. Pet: Micky, Mikey. (MĪ-KL)

MILES Brought to England by the Normans, Miles is from the Old French Milon, which is from the Old High German Milo, a name of uncertain derivation. *See* MILO. Var: Myles. (MĪ-LZ)

MILO Of Germanic origin, Milo is of uncertain derivation. It might be from the German *mild* (mild, peaceful, calm), which is derived from the Old German root *milan* (to mill, beat, crush, or rub until fine or tender). Alternatively, it might be from the Old Slavonic root *milu* (merciful). (MĪ-LO)

MILTON Transferred use of the surname arising from several English place-names originating from the Old English Mylentūn, which is composed of the elements *mylen* (mill) and *tūn* (town, settlement, village, enclosure), and from the Old English Middeltūn, which is from *middel* (middle) and *tūn* (town, settlement, village, enclosure). Short: Milt. Pet: Miltie. (MIL-TUN)

MITCHELL Transferred use of the surname derived from the personal name Michel, a variant form of Michael (who is like God?) used in the Middle Ages. *See* MICHAEL. Short: Mitch. (MIH-CHL)

MONROE Transferred use of the Scottish surname Munro, arising from the Gaelic elements *moine* (a morass, a marsh) and *ruadh* (red): hence, "dweller at the red morass." According to tradition, the ancestors of the Munros were said to be from a settlement near the river Roe in Ireland and thus took their name from *bun-Rotha* (mouth of the Roe) or *Rothach* (man from Roe). (MON-RO, MUN-RO)

MONTGOMERY Transferred use of the surname originating from a Norman baronial name derived from a place-name in Calvados, Normandy. The name, de Monte Goumeril, is composed of the Old French elements *mont* (hill) and the personal name Goumeril, a derivative of the Germanic Gomeric (man power). Short: Monty. (MONT-GOM-ER-REE, MONT-GUM-ER-EE)

MORTON Transferred use of the surname arising from a place-name derived from the Old English elements *mor* (a moor, a wasteland) and *tūn* (town, settlement, village, enclosure): hence, "from the settlement by the moor." Short: Mort. (MOR-TUN)

MYRON A borrowing from the Greek, Myron is derived from *myron* (myrrh, a fragrant resin used in making incense and perfume). The name was borne by a Greek sculptor of the 5th century B.C. and is said to have been taken up by early Christians because of the gift of myrrh made to the Christ child by the Three Wise Men. (MĪ-RUN)

NATHAN Derived from the Hebrew Natan, which is from *nāthān* (gift). The name was borne in the Bible by a prophet who rebuked David for the death of Uriah. Short: Nat, Nate. (NAY-THUN)

NATHANIEL From the Ecclesiastic Late Latin and Ecclesiastic Greek Nathanaēl, a derivative of the Hebrew Netanel, which is from *nĕthan'ēl* (gift of God). The name is borne in the Bible by one of the disciples of Christ, more commonly known as Bartholomew. Var: Nathanael. Short: Nat, Nate. (NA-THAN-YULL)

NED Pet form of Edward (wealthy guardian) in use since the 14th century. Ned is also bestowed as an independent given name. *See* EDWARD. (NED)

NEIL Anglicized form of the Gaelic Niall, which is of disputed meaning. Some believe it is derived from *niadh* (a champion); others think it is from *néall* (cloud). Until the 20th century, the use of Neil was confined mainly to Ireland and the border area between England and Scotland. Var: Neal. (NEEL)

NELSON Transferred use of the surname arising as a patronymic and a matronymic meaning "son of Neil" and "son of Nell." Short: Nel, Nels. (NEL-SUN)

NEVILLE Transferred use of the surname originating as a Norman baronial name from several places in Normandy called Neuville or Neville, which are composed from the French elements *neuve* (new) and *ville* (town). (NEH-VL)

Nicholas From the Old French Nicolas (victory of the people), which is from the Latin Nicolaus, a derivative of the Greek Nikolaos, a compound name composed of the elements *nikē* (victory) and *laos* (the people). The name was borne by St. Nicholas, a 4th-century bishop of Myra, who is regarded as the patron saint of Russia and Greece, and of children, sailors, and wolves. St. Nicholas is known to children as Santa Claus, the bringer of gifts at Christmastime. Var: Nicolas. Short: Nick. Pet: Nicky. (NIH-KO-LUS)

Nigel Evolution of the Scandinavian Njal, which originated from the Irish Niall, a name derived from the Gaelic *néall* (cloud) or *niadh* (champion). The Scandinavians took the name to Normandy, where it was Latinized as Nigellus. The Normans then introduced the name to England, where it became Nigel. (NĪ-JL)

Nolan Transferred use of the Irish surname derived from the Gaelic O'Nualláin (descendant of Nuallan), which is from *nuall* (shout). (NO-LUN)

Norman From the Old French Normant, derived from the Frankish *nortman*, which is composed of the elements *nort* (north) and *man* (man): hence, "northman, Norseman." The name was originally used to identify a member of the group of Scandinavians who occupied Normandy in the 10th century and, later, the native inhabitants of Normandy. Norman has a cognate in the Germanic Nordman, a compound name composed of the elements *nord* (north) and *man* (man), and it is this form that was used in England before the Norman invasion. Short: Norm. (NOR-MUN)

Norris Transferred use of the surname derived from the Anglo-French *norreis* (northerner) or from the Old French *norrice* (nurse). (NOR-RIS)

Oliver Derived from the French Olivier, which is generally considered to be from the Old French *olivier* (olive tree). Some believe it is of Germanic origin, however, and is thus probably from the Middle Low German Alfihar, a compound name composed of the elements *alf* (elf) and *hari* (army): hence, "elf army." Pet: Ollie. (AH-LIH-VER, O-LIH-VER)

Orson Derived from the French nickname Ourson (bear cub), which is from *ours* (a bear). (OR-SUN)

Orville Of debated origin, some believe Orville is derived from a Norman baronial name taken from a French place-name. Others believe it is merely an invention of the novelist Fanny Burney, used for the hero in her novel *Evelina* (1778). (OR-VL)

Osborn Evolution of the Old English Osbeorn (god bear, god warrior), a compound name composed of the elements *os* (a god) and *beorn* (bear, warrior). The name is found before the Norman Conquest and has a Scandinavian cognate in Asbjorn; thus the name might ultimately be of Scandinavian origin. Var: Osborne, Osbourne. Short: Oz. Pet: Ozzie. (OZ-BORN)

Oscar From the Old English Osgar (god spear), a compound name composed of the elements *os* (a god) and *gar* (spear). Alternatively, there is an Irish Oscar, which is derived from the Gaelic elements *os* (deer) and *cara* (friend). (OS-KER)

Osmond From the Old English Osmund (protected by the gods), a compound name composed of the elements *os* (a god) and *mund* (hand, protection). The name was also in use by the Normans before the Conquest and might have been derived from the corresponding Old Norse Asmundr, as the English form might have been influenced by Scandinavian immigrants to England. Var: Osmund. Short: Oz. Pet: Ozzie. (OZ-MUND)

Oswin Revival of the Old English Oswin (a friend of the gods), which is from the elements *os* (a god) and *wine* (friend). The name fell from use in the 14th century but was revived in the 19th. Short: Oz. Pet: Ozzie. (OZ-WIN)

Patrick Derived from the Latin *patricius* (a patrician). The name was adopted by St. Patrick (385?–?461), a missionary to and patron saint of Ireland. He was a Christian Briton and a Roman citizen whose original name was Sucat. Short: Pat. (PAH-TRIK, PA-TRIK)

Paul From the Latin Paulus, which originated as a Roman family name derived from *paulus* (small). The name was adopted in the Bible by a Jewish Roman citizen, Saul of Tarsus, who was converted to Christianity by a vision of Christ. Paul and St. Peter are regarded as the cofounders of the Christian Church. (PAHL, POLE)

Percy Transferred use of the surname originating as a Norman baronial name from place-names in Calvados and La Manche, Normandy. The name is from the Greek Perseus, which is derived from *pērtho* (to destroy). Short: Perce. (PER-SEE)

Perry Transferred use of the surname derived from the Middle English *pirige, pyrige* (pear tree). The name originated to indicate one who dwelled by a pear tree. (PARE-REE)

Peter From the Ecclesiastic Late Latin Petrus and the Greek Petros, names derived from *petra* (a rock) and *petros* (a stone). The name is borne in the Bible by one of the Twelve Apostles of Christ. Peter is considered to have been the first pope and cofounder of the Christian Church with Paul. The name is popular throughout Europe and abroad. Short: Pete. (PEE-TER)

PHILIP From the Latin Philippus, a derivative of the Greek Philippos, which is composed from the elements *philos* (loving) and *hippos* (horse): hence, "lover of horses." The name is borne in the Bible by one of the Twelve Apostles of Christ and is found on most of the family trees of European royalty. In England the name received a boost in popularity from Prince Philip (b. 1921), consort of Queen Elizabeth II. Var: Phillip. Short: Phil. Pet: Pip. (FIL-IP)

PIERCE Derivative of Piers, an Old French and Middle English form of Peter (rock). The name was common in the Middle Ages and gave rise to several surnames. *See* PIERS. Var: Pearce. (PEERS)

PIERS Brought to England by the Normans, Piers is an Old French cognate of Peter (rock). This form, and its variant Pierce, were in common use in England during the Middle Ages until the 18th century. *See* PETER. (PEERZ)

QUENTIN A borrowing from the French, Quentin is from the Latin Quentīnus, a derivative of the Roman personal name Quintus, which is from *quintus* (the fifth). The name was originally bestowed by Romans upon the fifth-born male child, a custom that the French and English adopted. Var: Quintin, Quinton. (KWIN-TUN)

QUINCY Transferred use of the surname originating as a Norman baronial name from the place-name Cuinchy in Pas-de-Calais, Normandy. The name is derived from Quince, a French form of the Latin Quintus (the fifth). *See* QUENTIN. (KWIN-SEE)

RAFE Variant spelling of Ralph (counsel wolf) based on the traditional pronunciation of the name. *See* RALPH. (RAFE)

RALPH From the Old Norse Raðulfr, Rathulfr, a compound name composed of the elements *rað*, *rath* (counsel) and *ulfr* (wolf). The name, introduced by the Scandinavians, was reinforced by the Normans, who brought in the Germanic cognate Radulf, which is from the elements *rād* (counsel) and *wulf* (wolf). The English developed their own cognate, Rædwulf, from the Old English elements *ræd* (counsel) and *wulf* (wolf). The name evolved into Rauf, Raff, and Rafe in the Middle Ages, Ralf in the 16th century, and Ralph in the 18th century. *Rāf* is the pronunciation in common use, but the pronunciation *ralf* can also be found. Var: Rafe, Ralf. (RAFE, RALF)

RANDALL Transferred use of the surname derived from Randolf (shield wolf), a personal name of Germanic origin introduced by both the Scandinavians in the form Randulfr and the Normans in the form Randolph. *See* RANDOLF. Var: Randal, Randell, Randle. Pet: Randy. (RAN-DL)

RANDOLF Derived from the Old Norse Randulfr, a name introduced by the Scandinavians, which is composed from the elements *rand*, *rönd* (the edge or rim of a shield) and *ulfr* (wolf): hence, "shield wolf." The use of the name was further reinforced by the Norman introduction of the Germanic cognate Randolph after the Conquest. Var: Randolph. Pet: Randy. (RAN-DOLF)

RANDY Originally a pet form of Randall or Randolf, Randy is also bestowed as an independent given name. *See* RANDALL *and* RANDOLF. (RAN-DEE)

RAY Originally a short form of Raymond (wise protection), Rayner (warrior of judgment), and Reynard (strong judgment), Ray is also bestowed as an independent given name. *See* RAYMOND, RAYNER, *and* REYNARD. (RAY)

RAYMOND From the Old Norman French Raimund (wise protection), which is derived from the Germanic Raginmund, a compound name composed of the elements *ragin* (advice, judgment, counsel) and *mund* (hand, protection). Short: Ray. (RAY-MUND)

RAYNER Introduced to England by the Normans, Rayner is from the Old German Raganher, a compound name composed from the elements *ragin* (advice, judgment, counsel) and *heri*, *hari* (army, warrior): hence, "warrior of judgment." Short: Ray. (RAY-NER)

READ Transferred use of the surname derived from the Middle English *read*, *reade* (red), which is from the Old English *read* (red). The name originated as a nickname for someone with red hair or with a red, ruddy complexion. (REED)

REES Anglicized form of the Welsh Rhys (ardor). *See* RHYS (Welsh Names). It also represents the transferred use of the surname derived from the personal name. (REES)

REGINALD From the Middle Latin Reginaldus, which is derived from the Old High German Raganald, Raginold, compound names composed from the elements *ragin* (advice, judgment, counsel) and *wald* (ruler). The name was introduced to England by the Normans. Var: Reynold. Short: Reg. Pet: Reggie. (REJ-IH-NULD)

REID Transferred use of the surname derived from the Scottish *reid* (red). The name arose as a nickname for someone with red hair or a red, ruddy complexion. *See also* READ. (REED)

REX 19th-century coinage derived from the Latin *rex* (king). (REX)

REYNARD From the Old French Renard, which is derived from the Old High German Reginhart, a compound name composed from the elements *ragin* (advice, judgment, counsel) and *hard* (strong, brave, hearty): hence, "strong judgment." The name was introduced to England by the Normans. Short: Ray. Pet: Renny. (REH-NARD)

RICHARD A borrowing from the Old French, Richard is derived from the Old High German Richart, a compound name composed from the elements *rik, rīc* (power, ruler) and *hard* (strong, brave, hardy): hence, "brave ruler." The name, introduced by the Normans, was borne by three kings of England. The first was Richard I (1157–99), called Richard the Lion-Hearted, the leader of the Third Crusade. Short: Rich, Rick. Pet: Richie, Ricky. (RIH-CHERD)

RILEY Transferred use of the surname derived from the Old English elements *ryge* (rye) and *lēah* (wood, clearing, meadow). The name was indicative of one who dwelled near a rye field. (RĪ-LEE)

ROBERT Introduced to England by the Normans, Robert is derived from the Old High German Hruodperht, a compound name composed of the elements *hruod* (fame) and *perht* (bright). The name was borne by Robert I (d. 1035), duke of Normandy and father of William the Conqueror, and by three kings of Scotland. Short: Bob, Rob. Pet: Bobby, Robby. (RAH-BERT)

RODERICK From the Middle Latin Rodericus, which is derived from the Old High German Hrodrich (famous ruler), a compound name composed from the elements *hruod* (fame) and *rik* (king, ruler). The name was introduced to England by the Scandinavians and later by the Normans but fell out of use during the Middle Ages until it was revived in the 19th century. Short: Rod. (ROD-EH-RIK)

RODNEY Originally the transferred use of the surname derived from the place-name Rodney Stoke. The derivation of Rodney is uncertain. Some believe it is from the Anglo-Saxon Rodan-ig (Roda's island). The word *stoke* is from the Old English *stōc* (dwelling, place, village). Rodney, in use as a given name since the 18th century, was originally bestowed in honor of the famous admiral Lord Rodney (1719–92). Short: Rod. (ROD-NEE)

ROGER Introduced to England by the Normans, Roger is derived from the Old High German Hrodger (spear fame), a compound name composed from the elements *hrōd, hruod* (fame) and *ger* (a spear). The form Roger replaced the English cognate Hrothgar. Var: Rodger. Short: Rodge. (ROJ-ER)

ROLAND A borrowing from the French, Roland is from the Old High German Hruodland, a compounding of the elements *hruod* (fame) and *land* (land): hence, "fame of the land" or "famous land." The name was introduced to England by the Normans. Var: Rowland. Pet: Roly. (RO-LUND)

ROLF A contraction of Rudolph (famous wolf), a Germanic name composed of the elements *hruod* (fame) and *wulf* (wolf). The name was introduced to England by the Normans. *See* RUDOLPH. (ROLF)

RONALD Introduced to Scotland by Scandinavian settlers in the form of Rögnvaldr (ruler of decision, judgment power), a compound name composed of the Old Norse elements *regin, rögn* (advice, judgment, decision) and *valdr* (ruler, power). Used primarily in Scotland and northern England during the Middle Ages, Ronald is now common throughout the English-speaking world. Short: Ron. Pet: Ronnie. (RON-ULD)

ROSCOE Transferred use of the surname derived from a place-name in Lancashire, on the northwestern coast of England. The name is derived from the Old Norse elements *rá* (a roe deer) and *skógr* (a wood). (ROS-KO)

ROY Derived from the Scottish Gaelic *ruadh* (red-haired, red). The name originated as a nickname for someone with red hair or a red, ruddy complexion, much as Read was used in England. Roy, now a common name throughout the English-speaking world, often takes the alternative definition "king" from the Old French *roy* (king) and is used as a name element in combination names such as Leroy (the king). (ROI)

RUSSELL Transferred use of the surname derived from the Old French *roussell* (red-haired), from *rous* (red). The name, which arose as a nickname for someone with red hair, was brought to England by the Normans. Short: Russ. (RUS-SL)

RUSTY Modern coinage from *rusty*, originally bestowed as a nickname for someone with reddish-brown hair. (RUS-TEE)

RYAN From the Irish surname O'Riain (descendant of Rian), an abbreviation of O'Maolriain (descendant of the servant of Rian). Rian is an ancient Irish name believed to be a diminutive form of *rí* (king): hence, "little king." (RĪ-UN)

SAM A short form of Samuel (name of God), Sam is also bestowed as an independent given name. *See* SAMUEL. Pet: Sammy. (SAM)

SAMSON A borrowing from the Ecclesiastic Late Latin, Samson is from the Ecclesiastic Greek Sampsōn, which is from the Hebrew Shimshon, a name derived from *shimshōn* (sun). The name is borne in the Bible by an Israelite judge known for his great strength. Var: Sampson. Short: Sam. Pet: Sammy. (SAM-SUN)

SAMUEL Ecclesiastic Late Latin form of the Ecclesiastic Greek Samouēl, which is from the Hebrew Shmuel, a name derived from *shĕmū'ēl* (name of God, his name is God). The name is borne in the Bible by a Hebrew judge and prophet who anointed Saul as the first king of Israel. Short: Sam. (SAM-YOOL)

SCOTT Transferred use of the surname derived from the Old English Scottas, originally "an Irishman" and, later, "a Gael from Scotland, a Scotchman." Pet: Scotty. (SKOT)

SEBASTIAN From the Latin Sebastiānus, a derivative of the Greek Sebastianos (a man of Sebastia, a town in Asia Minor). The name was borne by a 3rd-century Christian soldier of Rome (d. 288?), martyred under Diocletian by the arrows of his fellow soldiers. Short: Bastian, Seb. (SEH-BAHS-CHEN, SEH-BAHS-TEE-UN)

SETH From the Ecclesiastic Greek Sēth, a name from the Hebrew Shet, which is derived from *shēth* (appointed). The name is borne in the Bible by the third son of Adam and Eve, born after the death of his brother Abel. (SETH)

SEYMOUR Transferred use of the surname, which arose from a Norman baronial name taken from the place-name Saint Maur in Normandy. The name is derived from the Latin Maurus (a moor). (SEE-MOR)

SHANE Anglicized form of Seaghán, a variant of Eóin, which is a Gaelic form of John (God is gracious). *See* JOHN. (SHANE)

SHAUN Anglicized form of Seán, the Gaelic cognate of John (God is gracious). *See* JOHN. (SHAUN)

SHAW Transferred use of the surname derived from the Middle English *schagh, schawe, shawe* (wood, copse, grove), which is from the Old English *scaga, sceaga*. The name was used to indicate one who was a dweller in or near a wood or grove. (SHAW)

SHELDON Transferred use of the surname originating from several place-names, one of which had the original form Scelfdun, from the Old English elements *scelf, scylf(e)* (shelf, ledge, crag) and *dun* (a hill). (SHEL-DUN)

SHERMAN Transferred use of the surname derived from the Old English elements *scēarra* (shears) and *mann* (man).The name originated as an occupational name for a shearer of woolen cloth. Short: Sherm. (SHER-MUN)

SIDNEY Transferred use of the surname originating as a Norman baronial name taken from the place-name St. Denis in Normandy. Alternatively, the name arose independently in England and is derived from the Old English elements *sīd* (extensive, wide) and *ieg* (island in a river, riverside meadow). The name was indicative of one who dwelled on or near the wide, riverside meadow, or from the wide island. Short: Sid. (SID-NEE)

SILVESTER A borrowing from the Latin, Silvester is derived from *silvester* (of a wood or forest), which is from *silva* (wood). The name was borne by three popes, the first of whom is said to have baptized Constantine and cured him of leprosy. Var: Sylvester. Pet: Sly. (SIL-VES-TER)

SIMON A borrowing from the Ecclesiastic Late Latin, Simon is from the Ecclesiastic Greek Simōn and Seimōn, which are from the Hebrew Shimon, a derivative of *shim'ōn* (heard). The name is borne in the Bible by two of the apostles and a brother of Jesus, as well as several other New Testament characters. Simon was a very popular name in England during the Middle Ages but fell out of use after the Reformation. It has been taken up again as a given name but has not regained its previous popularity. (SĪ-MUN)

STANLEY Transferred use of the surname originating from several place-names derived from the Old English elements *stan* (stone) and *lēah* (wood, clearing, meadow): hence, "from Stanley" or "dweller near a stony clearing." Short: Stan. (STAN-LEE)

STEPHEN From the Latin Stephanus, which is from the Greek Stephanos, a derivative of *stephanos* (a crown, a garland). The name was borne in the Bible by St. Stephen. The first Christian martyr, he was one of the seven chosen to assist the Twelve Apostles. Var: Stephan, Steven. Short: Steve. (STEE-VEN, STEH-FUN)

STUART Transferred use of the surname, which is the French form of the English Stewart, a surname originating as an occupational name derived from the Old English *stiward, stiweard* (steward, keeper of the animal enclosure), a position that was in many cases a hereditary one, especially among noble or royal households. The name is borne by the Scottish royal family, said to be descended from a line of stewards from Brittany before the Conquest. The name was taken to Scotland by Mary, Queen of Scots, who was raised in France. Var: Stewart. Short: Stew, Stu. (STOO-ERT)

TAYLOR Transferred use of the surname derived from the Anglo-French *taillour* (tailor), which is from the Old French *taillier* (to cut). The name, which originated as an occupational name, was brought to England by the French in the 12th century. (TAY-LER)

TERENCE From the Latin Terentius, an old Roman family name of uncertain derivation. It might be derived from *terenus* (soft, tender). The name was borne by a Roman writer of comedies, Publius Terentius Afer (c. 190–159 B.C.), commonly known as Terence. Var: Terrance, Terrence. Short: Terry. (TER-UNS)

THADDEUS A borrowing from the Ecclesiastic Late Latin, Thaddeus is a derivative of the Ecclesiastic Greek Thaddaios, a name of uncertain derivation. Some believe it to be a variant of Theodōros (God's gift). Others feel it to be from an Aramaic word meaning "praised." The name is found in the Bible as a byname for Lebbaeus, an apostle of Christ. Short: Tad. (THAD-EE-US)

THEODORE From the Latin Theodorus, which is from the Greek Theodōros, a compound name composed of the elements *theos* (God) and *dōron* (gift): hence, "God's gift." Short: Theo. Pet: Ted, Teddy. (THEE-UH-DOR)

THOMAS From the Ecclesiastic Greek Thōmas, which is derived from the Aramaic *tĕ'ōma* (a twin). The name is borne in the Bible by an apostle who doubted the resurrection of Christ. It is from him that the label "doubting Thomas" came into being. Short: Thom, Tom. Pet: Tommy. (TOME-US, TOM-US)

TIMOTHY Derived from the French Timothée, which is from the Latin Timotheus, a derivative of the Greek Timotheos, a compound name derived from the elements *timē* (honor, respect) and *theos* (God). The name is borne in the Bible by a disciple and companion of the apostle Paul but was not used in England before the Reformation. Short: Tim. Pet: Timmy. (TIH-MU-THEE)

TOBIAS A borrowing from the Ecclesiastic Late Latin, Tobias is from the Ecclesiastic Greek Tōbias, which is from the Hebrew Tuviya, a name derived from *tōbhīyāh* (the Lord is good, God is good). Pet: Toby. (TŌ-BĪ-US)

TOBY Originally a pet form of Tobias (God is good), Toby is now commonly bestowed as an independent given name. *See* TOBIAS. (TŌ-BEE)

TODD Transferred use of the surname derived from the Middle and dialectal English *tod, todde* (a fox). (TOD)

TONY Originally a short form of Anthony, Tony is also bestowed as an independent given name. *See* ANTHONY. (TŌ-NEE)

TRAVIS Transferred use of the surname derived from the Old French *traverse* (the act of passing through a gate or crossing a river or bridge). The name arose as an occupational name for someone who collected the toll from those passing the boundary of a town or lordship. (TRAV-ISS)

TRISTRAM From the Old French Tristran, which is from the Gaelic Drystan, a name derived from *drest* (tumult, riot). The name was borne in medieval legend by a knight who was sent to Ireland by King Mark of Cornwall to bring Isolde back to be the king's bride. On the return trip, Tristram and Isolde accidentally drank a love potion intended for the king and fell in love. Tristram left to fight for King Howel of Brittany and, seriously wounded in battle, sent for Isolde. She arrived too late and died from grief next to Tristram's deathbed.The tale was the subject of many popular tragedies during the Middle Ages. Var: Tristan, Trystan, Trystram. (TRIS-TRUM)

TROY Transferred use of the surname originating from the place-name Troyes in Aube, Normandy. Alternatively, the name may be bestowed in reference to the name of the ancient Phrygian city in northwestern Asia Minor, which was the scene of the Trojan War. (TROI)

TYLER Transferred use of the surname derived from the Old French *tieuleor, tieulier* (tiler, tile maker) and the Middle English *tyler, tylere* (a brick, a tile). The name originated as an occupational name for a tile or brick maker or layer. Short: Ty. (TĪ-LER)

ULRIC Middle English evolution of the Old English Wulfrīc (wolf power), a compound name composed of the elements *wulf* (wolf) and *rīc* (power). Var: Ulrick. (UL-RIK)

VERNE Transferred use of the surname derived from atte Verne (at the ferns, dweller among the ferns). Predominantly a male name, Verne is also bestowed upon female children. (VERN)

VERNON Transferred use of the surname originating as a Norman baronial name from the place-name Vernon in Eure, Normandy. Vernon, a common French place-name, is derived from the Gaulish *vern-os* and the French *verne, vergne* (alder tree, alder grove). Short: Vern. (VER-NUN)

VICTOR A borrowing from the Latin, Victor is from *victor* (conqueror, winner). The name was borne by an early pope and several saints but was not used in England until the last half of the 19th century. Short: Vic. (VIK-TER)

VINCENT A borrowing from the Old French, Vincent is from the Late Latin Vincentius (conquering), which is derived from *vincere* (to conquer). The name was borne by St. Vincent de Paul (1580?–1660), a French priest who founded the Vincentian Order of the Sisters of Charity. Short: Vince. Pet: Vinnie, Vinny. (VIN-SENT)

VIRGIL From the Latin Vergilius, an old Roman family name of uncertain derivation. Some believe it to be from *ver* (spring) and give it the meaning "youthful, flourishing." Var: Vergil. (VER-JL)

WADE Transferred use of the surname derived from the Old English *wada* (go), from the verb *wadan* (to go). The name was borne in medieval legend by a fierce sea giant who was feared by the coastal tribes of the North Sea. Alternatively, the name arose from the Old English *gewæd, wæd* (ford, wading place) and was indicative of one who dwelled near a ford. (WADE)

WALLACE Transferred use of the surname derived from the Old French Waleis (a Welshman, a foreigner). As a given name, Wallace was originally bestowed in honor of Sir William Wallace (1272?–?1305), a Scottish patriot and leader in the struggle against Edward I of England. Pet: Wally. (WAH-LUS)

WALTER Introduced to England by the Normans, Walter is from the Old Norman French Waltier, which is from the Germanic Waldhere, a compound name composed from the elements *wald* (ruler) and *heri* (army): hence, "ruler of an army." Short: Walt. Pet: Wally. (WAL-TER)

WARD Transferred use of the surname derived from the Old English *weard, ward* (guard, watchman, keeper). The name arose as an occupational name for a warden or watchman. (WARD)

WARREN Transferred use of the surname meaning "dweller at or keeper of a game preserve." The name is derived from the Old French *warenne* (a warren, a game preserve). (WAH-RUN)

WAYNE Transferred use of the surname derived from the Old English *wægn, wæn* (wagon, cart). The name, which arose as an occupational name for a wagoner, was not used as a given name until the last half of the 20th century, when it was influenced by American actor John Wayne (1907–82). (WANE)

WELBY Transferred use of the surname originating from the place-name Welleby, which is derived from the Old Norse *uel* (well, spring) and *býr* (farm): hence, "dweller at the farm near the spring." (WEL-BEE)

WESLEY Transferred use of the surname taken from various English place-names called Westley. Westley is derived from the Old English elements *west* (west) and *lēah* (wood, clearing, meadow). The surname was indicative of one who dwelled at the western wood or clearing. The use of Wesley as a given name originates with its bestowal in honor of John (1703–91) and Charles (1707–88) Wesley, founders of the Methodist Church. Var: Westley, Wezley. Short: Wes. (WES-LEE, WEZ-LEE)

WILFRED Derived from the Old English Wilfrith (desire for peace), a compound name composed of the elements *willa* (a wish, a desire) and *frith* (peace). Var: Wilfrid. (WIL-FRID)

WILLARD Transferred use of the surname, which arose from the Old English personal name Wilheard (resolutely brave), a compound name composed of the elements *will* (will, determination) and *heard* (brave, hard, solid). Short: Will. (WIL-ERD)

WILLIAM From the Old Norman French Willaume, which is derived from the Old High German Willehelm, a compound name composed from the elements *willeo* (will, determination) and *helm* (protection, helmet): hence, "resolute protector." William is the most popular name introduced to England by the Normans. It was borne by William the Conqueror (1027?–87), who invaded England and defeated Harald at the Battle of Hastings, and by three other kings of England. Presently, the name is borne by Prince William (b. 1982), the eldest son of Prince Charles and Princess Diana. Short: Bill, Will, Wills. Pet: Billy, Willie, Willy. (WIL-YUM)

WINSTON Transferred use of the surname originating from an English place-name derived from the Old English elements *wine* (friend) and *tūn* (town, settlement, village, enclosure): hence, "friendly town." Winston was first used as a given name by the Churchill family, who bestowed it upon Winston Churchill (b. 1620) in honor of his mother, Sarah Winston. (WIN-STUN)

WOODROW Transferred use of the surname derived from the Old English elements *wudu* (a wood) and *ræw* (row, hedgerow). The name was indicative of one who dwelled at the hedgerow near the wood or in a row of houses near the wood. Pet: Woody. (WOOD-ROW)

WYSTAN Derived from the Old English Wigstan (battle stone), a compound name composed of the elements *wig* (battle, combat) and *stan* (stone). (WĪ-STUN)

YORICK Derived from Jorck, an old Danish form of George (earthworker, farmer). Shakespeare used the name for a court jester in his play *Hamlet*. (YOR-IK)

YORK Transferred use of the surname derived from the place-name York, a city in northeastern England. The name originated as Eburacum, a Roman rendering of an old Celtic name containing the element *ebur* (yew, yew tree). The name was later changed by Anglo-Saxon settlers to Eoforwic, which is derived from the Old English elements *eofor* (boar)and *wīc* (place, farm). Scandinavian settlers rendered the name Iorvík or Iork, which eventually became York. (YORK)

ZACHARIAH From the Ecclesiastic Late Latin and Ecclesiastic Greek Zacharias (remembrance of the Lord), which is from the Hebrew Zecharya, a derivative of *zĕcharyah* (God remembers, memory). Var: Zachary. Short: Zack, Zak. (ZAK-EH-RĪ-AH)

ZACHARY English cognate of the Ecclesiastic Late Latin and Ecclesiastic Greek Zacharias (God remembers, memory). *See* ZACHARIAH. Short: Zack, Zak. (ZAK-EH-REE)

ZEKE Originally a short form of Ezekiel (God strengthens), Zeke is also bestowed as an independent given name. *See* EZEKIEL (Biblical Names). (ZEEK)

English Female Names

ABIGAIL From the Hebrew Avigayil, which is derived from *avīgayil* (father of exaltation, father is rejoicing). The name was borne in the Bible by one of the wives of King David. The name also took on the meaning of "a lady's maid," due in part to its use as the name of a maid in the play *The Scornful Lady*, by Beaumont and Fletcher, in 1616. Pet: Abbie. (AB-IH-GALE)

ADELAIDE Variant of the Germanic Adelheid (nobility), a compound name composed of the elements *adal* (noble) and *heit* (kind, sort): hence, "nobility." The name was borne by the wife of King William IV. Short: Adele. Pet: Ada, Addie. (ADD-EH-LADE)

ADELE A name that originated as a shortened form of Adelheid and Adelaide (nobility) but is now bestowed as an independent given name. It was borne by the youngest daughter (c. 1062–1137) of William the Conqueror. Var: Adela. Short: Dell, Della. (AH-DEL)

ADRIA Feminine form of Adrian, which is from the Latin Adriānus (man from the city of Adria) and Hadriānus (man from the city of Hadria). (ADD-REE-AH)

ADRIANNE Feminine form of Adrian, which is derived from the Latin Adriānus (man from the city of Adria) and Hadriānus (man from the city of Hadria). Var: Adriann, Adrianna, Adriana. (Ā-DREE-UN, Ā-DREE-AN)

AGATHA Derived from the Greek Agathē, which is from *agathos* (good, kind). The name was popularized by the fame of a 3rd-century saint and martyr. *See* AGATA (Italian Names). Pet: Aggie. (AG-AH-THA)

AGNES Popular name throughout Europe, Agnes is derived from the Greek Hagnē, which is from *hagnos* (chaste, pure, sacred). The name was borne by a thirteen-year-old Roman martyred for her Christian beliefs during the reign of the Roman emperor Diocletian. *See* AGNESE (Italian Names). Pet: Aggie, Nessa, Nessie. (AG-NES)

ALANA Feminine form of Alan, an old name of Breton origin but of uncertain meaning. Some believe it to mean "handsome"; others promote the possibility that it is from a Celtic word meaning "rock." Var: Alanda, Alanna, Alannah. Short: Lana, Lanna, Lannah. (AH-LAN-NAH)

ALBERTA Feminine form of Albert, which is derived from the Old High German Adalbrecht, a compound name composed of the elements *adal* (noble) and *beraht* (bright, famous): hence, "bright through nobility" or "nobly bright." The name was borne by Princess Louise Alberta, the fourth daughter of Queen Victoria and Prince Albert. (AL-BER-TAH)

ALETHEA Derived from the Greek *alētheia* (truth). (AH-LEH-THEE-AH)

ALEXA A short form of Alexandra (defender or helper of mankind), Alexa is also bestowed as an independent given name and is thus derived from the Greek *alexein* (to defend, to help). *See* ALEXANDRA. Short: Alex, Lexa. Pet: Lexi, Lexy. (AH-LEX-AH)

ALEXANDRA Popular name derived from the Greek Alexandros, a male compound name composed of the elements *alexein* (to defend, to help) and *andros* (man). The name in its variant form Alexandrina was the first name of Queen Victoria. Var: Alexandrina. Short: Alex, Alexa, Alix, Lexa, Sandra. Pet: Andie, Lexi, Lexy, Sandi, Sandy. (AL-EX-AN-DRA)

ALEXIS Derived from the Greek *alexein* (to defend, to help). The name gained popularity, in part, by its use as the name of a character played by British actress Joan Collins in the popular television series *Dynasty*. Var: Alexia. Short: Alex. Pet: Lexi, Lexy. (AH-LEX-ISS)

ALICE Evolved through a series of variants of the Germanic Adalheidis, a compound name composed of the elements *adal* (noble) and *heid* (kind, sort): hence, "nobility." Adalheidis was contracted to Adalheid, which the French changed to Adélaïde, then contracted to Adaliz, and contracted yet again to Aaliz and Aliz. The English then changed the spelling to Aeleis, Alys, and eventually to Alice. The name was borne by the central character in Lewis Carroll's *Alice's Adventures in Wonderland* (1865) and *Through the Looking Glass* (1872). Var: Alys. Pet: Allie, Ally. (AL-LIS)

ALICIA Latinate form of Alice (nobility). *See* ALICE. Var: Alissa, Alyssa. Pet: Allie, Ally. (AH-LEE-SHA, AH-LEE-SEE-AH)

ALINDA Modern variant of Linda (beautiful, tender). *See* LINDA. (AH-LIN-DAH)

ALISON Matronymic meaning "son of Alice." Var: Allison. Pet: Allie, Ally. (AL-IH-SUN)

ALLEGRA Derived from the Latin *allegro* (cheerful, brisk, gay). (AH-LEG-RAH)

ALMA Derived from the Latin *almus* (nourishing, fostering). Alternatively, Alma may be a direct borrowing of the Spanish *alma* (soul). (AHL-MAH)

Alpha Derived from the first letter of the Greek alphabet, which is from the Hebrew *āleph* (ox, leader). The name, which denotes superiority or excellence, is also occasionally bestowed upon first-born daughters. Var: Alfa. (AL-FAH)

Althea Popular name derived from the Latin Althaea and the Greek Althaia, which is from *althainein* (to heal). The name was borne by the mythological mother of Meleager. *See* ALTHEA (Mythological Names). (AHL-THEE-AH)

Althena Modern coinage combining Althea (healer) and Athena (the Greek goddess of wisdom). *See* ALTHEA *and* ATHENA (Mythological Names). (AHL-THEE-NAH)

Alyssa A variant of Alicia (nobility), Alyssa is alternatively derived from the alyssum flower. *See* ALICIA. Var: Alissa. Short: Lissa, Lyssa. (AH-LIS-SAH)

Amanda A popular name derived from the Latin *amanda* (lovable, worthy to be loved), Amanda originated as a literary coinage of English playwright Colley Cibber (1671–1757). Short: Manda. Pet: Mandi, Mandy. (AH-MAN-DAH)

Amaranth Derived from *amaranth,* the name of a family of colorful plants and flowers, which is derived from the Greek *amarantos* (unfading). In legend, the amaranth is an imaginary flower that never fades and never dies. Var: Amarantha. (AM-AH-RANTH)

Amaryllis Of uncertain meaning, Amaryllis was the name borne by a shepherdess in the classical poems of Virgil and Theocritus. Alternatively, the name may be bestowed in reference to the genus name of a family of colorful flowering plants. Var: Amarilla, Amaryllа. Short: Marilla, Marylla. (AM-AH-RIL-LIS)

Amber Derived from the word *amber* (a translucent fossil resin used in jewelry making), which is from the Arabic *'anbar* (amber). (AM-BER)

Amelia An English variant of the Germanic Amalia, which is derived from *amal* (work). Alternatively, it may be a variant of Emilia (rival). *See* EMILY. (AH-MEE-LEE-AH, AH-MIL-YAH)

Amice Derived from the Middle English *amice* (a linen cloth worn by a priest at mass), which is from the Latin *amictus* (a cloak). Pet: Ami, Amy. (AM-ISS)

Amity Derived from the Middle English *amite* (friendship), which has its roots in the Latin *amicus* (friend). Var: Amita. Pet: Ami, Amy, Mitty. (AM-IH-TEE)

Amy Derived from the Middle English Amye, which is from the Old French Aimee (beloved), a name derived from the verb *aimer* (to love). The name is also used as a pet form of the various names that begin with the element *Ami-*. Var: Ami, Amie. (Ā-MEE)

Andra Feminine form of Andrew (manly), the English variant of the Greek Andreas, which is derived from the element *andros* (man). Pet: Andie. (AN-DRA)

Andrea English feminine form of the Greek Andreas, which is derived from the element *andros* (man). Pet: Andie. (AN-DREE-AH)

Andriana Coined by combining the names Andrea (womanly) and Anna (gracious, full of grace). There are several other possibilities as well, including the blending of Andra (womanly) and the Latin Arianna (holy). Var: Andrianna. Short: Anna. Pet: Andie. (AN-DREE-AN-NAH)

Andrine English feminine form of Andrew (manly), a cognate of the Greek Andreas, which is derived from the element *andros* (man). Pet: Andie. (AN-DREEN)

Angel Derived from *angel* (messenger of God, guiding spirit), which is ultimately derived from the Greek *angelos* (messenger, messenger of God). Var: Angela. Pet: Angie. (AIN-JL)

Angelica Derived from *angelic* (heavenly, like an angel), which is derived from the Latin *angelicus* (angelic) and the Greek *angelikos* (angelic). Pet: Angie. (AN-JEL-LIH-KAH)

Angelina Latinate variant of Angel or Angela. *See* ANGEL. (AN-JEH-LEE-NAH)

Anita Originally a Spanish pet form of Ana (gracious, full of grace), Anita is commonly bestowed in the English-speaking world as an independent given name. *See* ANNA. Short: Nita. (AH-NEE-TAH)

Anna A popular name throughout Europe and the British Isles, Anna is a Latinate variant of the French Anne, a cognate of the Hebrew Hannah (gracious, full of grace). *See* HANNAH. (AN-NAH)

Annabelle Combination name composed of the names Anna (gracious, full of grace) and Belle (beautiful). *See* ANNA *and* BELLA. Var: Annabel, Annabell, Annabella. (AN-NAH-BEL)

Anne Borrowed from the French, Anne is a cognate of the Hebrew Hannah (gracious, full of grace), which is from *hannāh, chaanach* (grace, gracious, mercy). In medieval Christian tradition, Anne was the name assigned to the mother of the Virgin Mary, as Joachim was assigned to her father. The name has remained popular in Britain and is borne by Princess Anne (b. 1950), daughter of Queen Elizabeth II and Prince Philip. Var: Ann, Anna. Pet: Annie. (AN)

ANNELLA English and Scottish elaboration of the name Anne (gracious, full of grace). *See* ANNE. (AH-NEL-LAH)

ANNETTE French pet form of Anne (gracious, full of grace), which is in common use in Great Britain. *See* ANNE. Var: Annetta. Pet: Annie. (AH-NET)

ANNIS Vernacular form of Agnes (chaste), which has been in use since medieval times. *See* AGNES. Var: Annice, Annys. Pet: Annie. (AN-ISS)

ANTONIA Feminine form of Anthony, a name derived from the old Roman family name Antonius, which is of uncertain origin and meaning. Some believe it to have originally been an Etruscan name. Short: Tonia. Pet: Toni, Tonie. (AN-TŌ-NEE-AH)

APRIL Derived from the name of the calendar month, which is derived from the Latin *aprilis* (second, latter). The ancient Roman calendar began with the month of March, with April being the second month. (Ā-PRIL)

ARLENE Modern name apparently modeled after names such as Darlene or Marlene. Var: Arleen, Arlena, Arlina, Arline, Arlyne. Short: Arla, Lena, Lina. (AR-LEEN)

ARLETTE Old name thought to be a French variant of the Germanic element *arn* (eagle). The name was borne by the mistress of Robert of Normandy. She was the mother of his son, William the Conqueror. (AR-LET)

ASHLEY This name, originally a surname, is derived from the Old English elements *æsc* (ash trees) and *lēah* (wood, clearing, meadow, enclosure) and was originally indicative of one who was a "dweller near the ash tree forest." (ASH-LEE)

AUDREY Derived from the Old English Æðelþryð, or Æthelthryth, a compound name composed of the elements *æðel, æthel* (noble) and *þryð, thryth* (might, strength): hence, "noble strength." Var: Audra, Audrie, Audrina, Audry. Pet: Audie, Audy. (AUD-REE, ODD-REE)

AUGUSTA Feminine form of the Latin Augustus, which is derived from *augustus* (great, venerable). (AH-GUS-TAH)

AURELIA Feminine form of the Latin Aurēlius (golden), a name derived from *aurum* (gold). Var: Aura Lee, Auralia, Auralie, Aurelie, Oralee, Oralie, Oralia. (O-REE-LEE-AH, OR-AH-LEE-AH)

AURORA Derived from the Latin *aurōra* (dawn). The name was borne by the Roman mythological goddess of dawn and by the princess in the popular fairy tale *Sleeping Beauty*. (O-ROR-AH)

AVA Of uncertain origin and meaning, Ava is thought to be a short form of the Germanic Aveza or Avia, which are also of uncertain meaning. (Ā-VAH)

AVELINE Introduced to England by the Normans, Aveline is thought to be a French diminutive form of the Germanic Avila, which is of uncertain meaning. (AH-VEH-LEEN, AH-VEH-LINE)

AVILA Of Germanic origin but of uncertain meaning, often bestowed in honor of St. Teresa of Avila (1515–82). (AH-VIL-AH, AH-VEE-LAH)

AVIS Brought to England by the Normans, Avis is a French form of the Germanic Aveza, a name of uncertain meaning. Because it coincidentally corresponds with the Latin *avis* (bird), it is often bestowed with this meaning in mind. Var: Avice. (Ā-VIS)

AZARIA Feminine form of the Hebrew Azariah (helped by God), the name of a biblical prophet. This is a relatively modern coinage. (AZ-AH-RĪ-AH, AH-ZAR-EE-AH)

BARBARA A borrowing from the Latin, Barbara (foreign woman) is derived from *barbarus* (foreign, strange), a term applied to non-Romans or those deemed to be uncivilized. Var: Barbra. Short: Barb. Pet: Babs, Barbie. (BAR-BAH-RAH, BARB-RAH)

BEATRIX Derived from the Latin *beatrix* (she who makes happy, she who brings happiness), which is from *beātus* (happy, blessed). The variant form Beatrice is borne by the daughter of Prince Andrew and Sarah Ferguson. Var: Beatrice. Short: Bea. Pet: Trixie. (BEE-AH-TRIX, BEE-AH-TRIX)

BECCA Originally a short form of Rebecca (noose, to tie or bind), Becca is now occasionally bestowed as an independent given name. *See* REBECCA. (BEKA)

BECKY A pet form of Rebecca (noose, to tie or bind), Becky is also commonly bestowed as an independent given name. *See* REBECCA. (BEH-KEE)

BELINDA Of uncertain origin and meaning, it has been suggested that the name is of Germanic origin, possibly a variant of Betlindis, which is thought to mean "snake" or "serpent." The name was chosen by Alexander Pope for his heroine of *The Rape of the Lock* (1712). (BEH-LIN-DAH)

BELLA Derived from the Latin *bella* (beautiful). The name is also used as a short form of any of the names containing the element *bella*. Var: Belle. (BEL-LAH)

BERENICE Derived from the Greek Berenikē, which is a variant of the older Pherenikē, a compound name composed of the elements *pherein* (to bring) and *nikē* (victory). Var: Bernice. (BER-EH-NEES, BER-NEES)

BERYL Derived from *beryl* (a type of pale green gemstone which includes emeralds and aquamarine). Beryl is derived from the Greek *bēryllos* (sea-green gem), which is from the Prakrit *veruliya* or the Dravidian *veluriya* (from the city of Vēlūr). Var: Beryla, Beryle. Pet: Berri, Berry. (BEH-RIL)

BESS A short form of Elizabeth (God is my oath), Bess is also commonly bestowed as an independent given name. It gained great popularity from its association with Queen Elizabeth I (1533–1603), who was known as Good Queen Bess. *See* ELIZABETH. Pet: Bessie, Bessy. (BES)

BETH Originally a short form of Elizabeth (God is my oath) and Bethany (house of figs), Beth is popularly bestowed as an independent given name and as an element in compound names such as Mary-Beth or Laura-Beth. (BETH)

BETHANY Derived from Bet t'eina, the name of the biblical town near Jerusalem, at the foot of the Mount of Olives, where Jesus stayed during Holy Week before his crucifixion. The name means "house of figs." Short: Beth. (BEH-THA-NEE)

BETTINA Latinate form of Betty, which is a pet form of Elizabeth (God is my oath). *See* ELIZABETH. (BEH-TEE-NAH)

BETTY A pet form of Elizabeth (God is my oath), Betty is also in common use as an independent given name. Var: Bettina. Short: Bet, Bett. (BEH-TEE)

BEVERLEY Transferred use of the surname derived from the Old English elements *beofor* (beaver) and *lēac* (stream): hence, "dweller near the beaver stream." Var: Beverlie, Beverly. Short: Bev. (BEV-ER-LEE)

BILLIE Feminine form of Billy, a pet form of William (resolute protector). *See* WILLIAM (Male Names). (BIL-LEE)

BIRDIE Derived from the Old English *bridd* (bird). (BER-DEE)

BLAINE Transferred use of the surname derived from the Gaelic *blian* (the groin, angular, thin, a hollow). Var: Blain, Blane, Blayne. (BLANE)

BLAIR Transferred use of the Scottish surname derived from place-names containing the Gaelic element *blár* (a plain, a level field): hence, "dweller on the plain." Var: Blaire. (BLARE)

BLANCHE Derived from the Old French *blanchir* (to make white), which is from *blanc* (white). The name, introduced to England by the Normans, can be coincidentally derived from the Middle English *blanchen* (to make white, to take color from). The name was originally used as a nickname for someone with pale blond hair and is now often mistakenly thought to mean "blond." (BLANCH)

BLISS Derived from the Old English *bliths* (bliss, joy). Var: Blisse, Blyss, Blysse. (BLIS)

BLOSSOM Derived from the Old English *blotsm*, *blotsma* (blossom, flower). The name is commonly used as an endearment for a young girl. (BLOS-SUM)

BLYTHE Derived from the Old English *blithe* (cheerful, gay). Var: Blithe. (BLĪTHE)

BOADICEA A name of disputed origin, meaning, and pronunciation, Boadicea is very possibly derived from the Old Welsh *bouda* (victory). It was borne by the 1st-century Briton who led 120,000 countrymen in a rebellion against Roman occupation in A.D. 60–61. Var: Boudica, Boudicca. (BO-AD-AH-SEE-AH)

BOBBIE Originally used as a pet form of Roberta (bright in fame), this name is also used as an independent given name. *See* ROBERTA. Var: Bobbi. (BO-BEE, BAH-BEE)

BONNIE Derived from the Scottish *bonnie* (pretty, pleasant), which is from the French *bon* (good). The name was borne in Margaret Mitchell's epic *Gone with the Wind* by the infant daughter of Scarlett O'Hara and Rhett Butler. Var: Bonny. (BAH-NEE)

BRENDA Of uncertain origin and meaning, Brenda is thought to be a Celtic name originating in the Shetland Islands and derived from *brandr* (the blade of a sword). Alternatively, it might be a feminine form of the obsolete Brandolf (sword wolf). (BREN-DAH)

BRENNA Of disputed origin and meaning, some believe it to be a feminine form of the Celtic Bren, from the root *bri* (strength, force). Alternatively, it might be derived from the Gaelic *bran* (raven). (BREN-NAH)

BRIANNE Feminine form of Brian, which is believed to be of Celtic origin and of the meaning "strength." *See* BRIAN (Male Names). Var: Brianna. (BREE-AN)

BRIDGET Anglicized form of the Gaelic Bríghid, which is believed to be derived from *brígh* (strength). *See*

BRIGHID (Irish Names). The name was borne by an ancient Celtic goddess, by St. Bridget of Kildare (451?–523), an Irish abbess and patron saint of Ireland, and by St. Birgitta (1302?–73), a Swedish nun and founder of the Order of the Brigittines. Short: Biddy, Bride, Bridie. (BRIJ-IT)

BROOKE Derived from the Middle English *brok* (a brook, a small stream, breaking forth). (BROOK)

BRYONY Derived from *bryony* (the name of a perennial vine with greenish flowers), which is from the Latin *bryonia* (to swell, to sprout). Var: Briony. (BRĪ-AH-NEE)

CAITLIN Borrowed from the Irish, Caitlin is a variant of Caitríona, the Gaelic form of Catherine (pure, unsullied). *See* CATHERINE. Var: Caitlyn, Catelin, Catelyn, Kaitlin, Kaitlyn, Katelin, Katelyn, Katelynn. (KATE-LIN)

CAMILLA Derived from the Latin *camilla* (virgin of unblemished character). Var: Camille. Short: Cami, Milla. Pet: Millie, Milly. (KAH-MIL-LAH)

CANDACE Derived from the Latin *candidus* (white, pure, sincere). Var: Candance, Candice, Candida, Candide, Candyce. Pet: Candy. (KAN-DUS)

CARA Derived from the Latin *cara* (beloved) or from the Irish Gaelic *cara* (friend). Alternatively, Cara is used as a short form of Caroline and Charlotte. *See* CAROLINE *and* CHARLOTTE. (KAR-AH)

CAREEN Modern name of uncertain origin and meaning. It could possibly be a variant form of Carina (keel of a ship) or of Carleen (a freeman). *See* CARINA *and* CAROLINE. (KAH-REEN)

CARINA Derived from the Latin *carina* (keel of a ship). Carina is the name of a southern constellation which contains the star Canopus, the second-brightest star in the heavens. (KAH-REE-NAH)

CARLA Popular feminine form of Carl and Charles, both of which are derived from the Old English *ceorl* (man, freeman, peasant). Var: Carley, Carlie, Carlin, Carly, Karla. (KAR-LAH)

CARMEL Derived from the Hebrew and meaning "vineyard" or "orchard." Mount Carmel is a mountain in northwestern Israel inhabited in early Christian times by a group of hermits who later became Carmelite monks in the Order of Our Lady of Mount Carmel. Var: Carmela, Karmel, Karmela. (KAR-MEL)

CAROL Feminine form of the Latin Carolus, which is a cognate of Charles (full-grown, a man) and a short form of Caroline, which is a feminine form of Carolus. The name is alternatively derived from the vocabulary word *carol* (joyous song, a carol). *See* CHARLES (Male Names). Var: Carole, Caryl. (KARE-RL)

CAROLINE Feminine form of the Latin Carolus, which is a cognate of Charles (full-grown, a man). *See* CHARLES (Male Names). Var: Carolina, Carolyn. Short: Carey, Caro, Carol, Carole, Carrie, Lynn. (KARE-O-LIN, KARE-O-LINE)

CASEY Variant of Cassie, which is a pet form of Cassandra. *See* CASSANDRA. Var: Casie, Kacey, Kacie, Kasey. (KAY-SEE)

CASSANDRA Derived from the Greek Kassandra, the mythological daughter of Priam and Hecuba who had the power of prophesy given to her by Apollo. Unfortunately, after she thwarted his advances, Apollo later decreed that no one should believe her. Var: Kassandra. Short: Cass, Sandra. Pet: Cassie. (KAH-SAN-DRA)

CASSIA Adopted from the cassia spice, a variety of cinnamon. The word is derived from the Greek *kasia* (a kind of cinnamon). Short: Cass, Cassi, Cassie. (KAS-SEE-AH)

CASSIDY Transferred use of the surname derived from the Irish surname O'Caiside (descendant of Caiside). Caiside is an old name believed to be derived from the Gaelic *cas* (a bent, curly, twisted lock; ingeniously clever) or from *cais* (love, esteem). Short: Cass, Cassi, Cassie. (KAS-SIH-DEE)

CATHERINE English cognate of the Greek Aikaterinē, which is derived from *katharos* (pure, unsullied). Catherine has remained a perennially popular name and has been borne by many saints and members of European nobility. Var: Catharine, Cathryn. Short: Cath. Pet: Cathy. (KATH-EH-RIN)

CECILIA Feminine form of Cecil, which is derived from Caecilius, an old Roman family name, which has its root in the Latin *caecus* (blind, dim-sighted). The name was borne by a 3rd-century Christian who founded a church in the Trastevere section of Rome. During the 6th century, a story of her life was written and she was henceforth venerated as a martyr. She is regarded as the patron saint of musicians. Var: Cecily, Cicely. Short: Celia. Pet: Cis, Cissie, Sessy, Sissie, Sissy. (SEH-SIL-YAH)

CELESTE English borrowing of the French Céleste, a derivative of *céleste* (celestial, heavenly), which is from the Latin *caelestis* (heavenly, celestial). (SEH-LEST)

CELIA Derived from the Latin Caelia, a feminine form of the old Roman family name Caelius, which is thought to be a derivative of the Latin *caelum* (heaven). Celia is also used as a short form of Cecilia (blind, dim-sighted). *See* CECILIA. (SEE-LEE-AH)

CHANTALE English cognate of the French Chantal, which is derived from the Old Provençal *cantal* (stone, boulder). Var: Chantelle. (SHAN-TAHL)

CHARIS Derived from the Greek *kharis* (grace). Var: Charissa. (KARE-ISS, KAR-ISS)

CHARITY Derived from *charity*, which denotes the love of God for mankind or the love of mankind for others. Charity is derived from the Latin *carus* (dear, valued). (CHARE-IH-TEE)

CHARLENE Coined in the 20th century, Charlene is a feminine form of Charles (full-grown, a man). *See* CHARLES (Male Names). Pet: Charlie. (SHAR-LEEN)

CHARLOTTE Feminine diminutive form of Charles (full-grown, a man), which originated in France but is just as commonly used in England. *See* CHARLES (Male Names). The name was borne by Queen Charlotte (1744–1818), wife of George III. Pet: Charlie, Lottie. (SHAR-LET)

CHARMAINE Derived from the Middle English and Old French *charme* (charm, chant), which is from the Latin *canere* (to sing). Var: Charmain. (SHAR-MANE)

CHARMIAN English cognate of the Greek Kharmion, which is derived from *kharma* (delight, joy). Var: Sharman. (SHAR-ME-UN)

CHERISH Derived from *cherish* (to show love, to treasure something or someone). (CHER-ISH)

CHERRY Originally used as an English form of the French *chérie* (darling), Cherry is now commonly thought to be in reference to the fruit. (CHER-REE)

CHERYL 20th-century coinage possibly made by combining Cherry and Beryl. Var: Cherelle. (CHER-RIL)

CHERYTH Modern variant of Cheryl or any of the other names containing the element *cher*. (CHER-ITH)

CHEVONNE Anglicized form of the Irish Siobhán, which is a Gaelic feminine form of Sean (John). *See* SIOBHÁN (Irish Names). (SHEH-VON)

CHLOE Derived from the Greek Khloē (blooming, verdant). The name was used as a summer epithet of Demeter, the Greek goddess of agriculture and fertility. (KLO-EE)

CHRISTA Latinate short form of Christine (a Christian, a follower of Christ) and any of the other names beginning with the element *Chris-*. *See* CHRISTINE. Christa is a common name in many European countries. Var: Krista. Short: Chris, Kris. Pet: Chrissie, Chrissy, Christie, Christy. (KRIS-TAH)

CHRISTABELLE Modern coinage made by combining the names Christa (a Christian) and Belle (beautiful). *See* BELLA *and* CHRISTA. Var: Christabel, Christabella. Short: Bella, Belle, Chris, Christa. (KRIS-TAH-BEL)

CHRISTIANA Feminine form of Christian, which is from the Greek *christianos* (a Christian, a follower of Christ). Var: Christianna. Short: Christi, Christie, Christy. (KRIS-TEE-AN-NAH, KRIS-CHEE-AN-NAH)

CHRISTINE Derived from the Latin Christiāna, which is from *christiānus*, a derivative of the Greek *christianos* (a Christian, a follower of Christ). Var: Christine, Kristeen, Kristine, Kristene. Short: Chris, Christa, Kris, Krista. Pet: Chrissie, Chrissy, Christi, Christie, Krissie, Krissy, Kristie, Kristy. (KRIS-TEEN)

CINDY A pet form of Cynthia or Lucinda, Cindy is now also popularly used as an independent given name in its own right. *See* CYNTHIA *and* LUCINDA. (SIN-DEE)

CLARA Derived from the Latin *clārus* (bright, clear, famous), Clara is a common name throughout Europe and the British Isles, its popularity once due in part to the fame of St. Clare of Assisi (c. 1193–1253), the Italian nun who founded the order of the Poor Clares. Var: Clare, Claire. Pet: Clarrie. (KLARE-AH)

CLARABELLE Compound name made by combining the names Clara (bright, clear, famous) and Belle (beautiful). *See* BELLA *and* CLARA. Var: Clarabel, Clarabella, Claribel, Claribelle, Claribella. (KLARE-AH-BEL)

CLARINDA Variant of Clara, made by combining Clara (bright, clear, famous) with the suffix *-inda*. Short: Linda. Pet: Clarrie. (KLAH-RIN-DAH)

CLARICE Elaboration of Clara, a name derived from the Latin *clārus* (bright, clear, famous). Var: Clarissa, Clarisse. (KLAH-REES)

CLAUDIA Derived from the Latin Claudius, an old Roman family name, which is from *claudus* (lame). (KLAU-DEE-AH, KLAH-DEE-AH)

CLEMENTINE Feminine form of Clement, which is derived from the Latin *clemens* (mild, gentle). Var: Clementina. Short: Tina. (KLEM-EN-TINE)

CLEO Derived from the Greek *kleos* (glory, fame). In Greek mythology, Clio is the name of the Muse of history. Var: Clio. (KLEO)

COLLEEN Derived from the Irish *colleen* (girl), which is from the Gaelic *cailín* (young girl). The name is used in England and the United States but is uncommon in Ireland. (KOL-LEEN)

CONNIE Originally a pet form of Constance (constancy), Connie is now commonly bestowed as an independent given name. (KON-NEE)

CONSTANCE English cognate of the French Constantia, which is derived from the Latin *constans* (standing together, constancy). The name was brought to England by the Normans. Pet: Connie. (KON-STANS)

CORA Derived from the Greek Korē, which is from *korē* (maiden). The name is borne in Roman mythology as a byname for Proserpina and in Greek mythology as a byname for Persephone. Pet: Cori, Corri, Corrie. (KO-RA)

CORAL Derived from *coral*, which refers to the calcareous skeletons secreted by marine polyps. This material is a pinkish color and is used in jewelry making. Pet: Cori, Corri, Corrie. (KO-RAL)

CORALIE Variation of Cora (maiden) or Coral. *See* CORA *and* CORAL. (KOR-A-LEE)

CORDELIA Of uncertain origin, Cordelia is thought to be from the Celtic name Creiryddlydd (daughter of the sea). The name is borne in Shakespeare's *King Lear* by Lear's youngest daughter, the only one who was faithful to him. Short: Delia, Lia. Pet: Cori, Corri, Corrie. (KOR-DEE-LEE-AH, KOR-DEEL-YAH)

CORINNA English cognate of the Greek Korinna, a derivative of Korē (maiden). The name was borne by a Greek poetess from Boeotia, who won a wreath of victory at Thebes, and whose works survive only in fragmentary form. Var: Corinne, Corrina, Corrine. Pet: Cori, Corri, Corrie. (KOR-RIN-NAH, KOR-REE-NAH)

COSIMA Feminine form of the Italian Cosmo, a derivative of the Greek Kosmas, which is from *kosmos* (universe, order, harmony). (KO-SEE-MAH)

COURTNEY Transferred use of the French surname meaning "from Courtenay [in northern France]." The name, originally bestowed upon both males and females, is now more commonly given to girls. Var: Courtenay. (KORT-NEE)

CRESSA Originally a short form of Cressida, Cressa is now commonly bestowed as an independent given name. *See* CRESSIDA. (KRES-SAH)

CRESSIDA Of unknown origin and meaning, Cressida was borne in medieval legend by a Trojan princess and daughter of Calchas, a priest who defected to the Romans. Cressida later is unfaithful to her Trojan lover, Troilus, and leaves him for the Greek Diomedes. Short: Cressa, Cressi. (KREH-SIH-DAH)

CRYSTAL 19th-century coinage derived from *crystal*, which denotes very clear, brilliant glass or a clear, transparent quartz. Var: Chrystal, Krystal. (KRIH-STAL)

CYNTHIA Popular name derived from the Latin and Greek Kynthia, a name for Artemus, the mythological goddess of the moon and hunting and twin sister of Apollo. The name has its root in *Kynthios* (from Kynthos, a mountain on the island of Delos). Pet: Cindy. (SIN-THEE-AH)

CYRA Feminine form of Cyrus, which is from the Greek Kyros, a name thought to be derived from *kyrios* (lord) or from the Persian *khur* (the sun). Var: Kyra. (SĪ-RAH, SERE-RAH, KĪ-RAH, KERE-RAH)

DAHLIA A borrowing of the name of the dahlia flower, which takes its name from the Swedish botanist Anders Dahl (1759–89). Var: Dalya. (DAHL-YAH)

DAISY Taken from the name of the daisy flower, which is derived from the Old English *dæges eage* (day's eye). (DAY-ZEE)

DANA Transferred use of the surname, which is of uncertain derivation. Alternatively, Dana can be used as a feminine form of Dan, a Hebrew name meaning "judge." (DAY-NAH)

DANIELLE Feminine form of Daniel, which is derived from the Hebrew *dānī'ēl* (God is my judge). Var: Daniella. Short: Dani. (DAN-YELL)

DARIA Feminine form of Darius, an old Latin name derived from the Greek Dareios, which is of uncertain origin. It is thought to ultimately be derived from Darayavahush, the name of an ancient Persian king. (DAR-EE-AH)

DARLENE Modern coinage based upon the endearment "darling." Var: Darlena. (DAR-LEEN)

DARRENE Feminine form of Darren, which is of uncertain origin and meaning. *See* DARREN (Male Names). (DAH-REEN)

DAVINA A borrowing from the Scottish, Davina is a feminine form of David, which is derived from the Hebrew *dāvīd* (beloved). Var: Davinia. (DAH-VEE-NAH, DAH-VIN-AH)

DAWN Derived from *dawn*, which is from the Middle English *dauninge* (daybreak, dawn). (DAUN)

DEANNA Originally a variant form of Diana (divine), this name is now often used as a feminine form of Dean. *See* DEAN (Male Names) *and* DIANA. Pet: Annie, Dee, Dee Dee. (DEE-AN-NAH)

Deborah Derived from the Hebrew *devōrāh* (a bee, a swarm of bees). The name is borne in the Bible by a prophetess and judge who led the Israelites to victory over the Canaanites. Var: Debora, Debra. Short: Deb. Pet: Debbi, Debbie, Debby, Debs. (DEH-BOR-AH, DEB-AH-RAH, DEB-RAH)

Dee Pet form of any of the various names beginning with the letter *D* or containing the elements *de*, *di*, or *dy*. Var: Dee Dee. (DEE)

Deirdre Of uncertain origin, Deirdre was the name borne by a legendary Irish princess who was betrothed to the king of Ulster, Conchobhar. She eloped, however, to Scotland with her lover, Naoise, who was then treacherously murdered by the king. Deirdre supposedly died of a broken heart. The name might be derived from the Old Irish Derdriu (young girl) or from the Celtic Diédrè (fear). Var: Deidra, Deirdra, Diedra, Diedre, Dierdre. Pet: Dee, Dee Dee. (DEER-DRA, DEE-DRA)

Delia Short form of Cordelia, Delia is also a feminine form of Delius, which is derived from the Latin *delius* (from the island of Delos). The name was used as a name for the Greek mythological goddess Artemis, whose supposed birthplace was on the island. Pet: Dee, Dee Dee. (DEE-LEE-AH, DEEL-YAH)

Delicia Derived from the Latin *deliciae* (delight). Var: Delice. Pet: Dee, Dee Dee. (DEE-LEE-SEE-AH, DEE-LEE-SHA)

Delilah Derived from the Hebrew *delīlāh* (delicate). Delilah was the name borne in the Bible by the mistress of Samson. Var: Delila. Short: Lila, Lilah. Pet: Dee. (DEE-LĪ-LAH, DIH-LĪ-LAH)

Della Modern coinage used as a feminine form of Dell, which is derived from the Old English *del* (a dell, a small valley or glen). Alternatively, Della is used as a short form of Adela (nobility). Short: Dell. (DEL-LAH)

Delores English cognate of the Spanish Dolores (sorrows). *See* DOLORES (Spanish Names). Var: Deloris. Pet: Dolly. (DEH-LOR-US)

Dena Bestowed as a feminine form of Dean (dean) or as a variant of Dina (judgment). *See* DEAN (Male Names) *and* DINAH. (DEE-NAH)

Denise Feminine form of Dennis, which is an English cognate of the Greek Dionysios (a follower of the god Dionysos). Var: Danice, Denice. (DEH-NEES)

Diana Derived from the Latin Diviana, which is from *divus* (divine). The name is borne in Roman mythology by the virgin goddess of the moon and of hunting. It has received a boost in popularity from Princess Diana. Var: Diane, Dianna, Dianne, Dionne, Dyan. Short: Di. (DĪ-AN-NAH)

Dinah Derived from the Hebrew *dīnāh* (judged). The name Dinah is borne in the Bible by a daughter of Jacob. Var: Dena, Dina. (DĪ-NAH)

Dionne Variant of Dianne (divine) or a feminine form of the French Dion, which is derived from Diōnis, a Greek name containing the element *dio* (Zeus). *See* DION (French Male Names). (DEE-ON)

Doe Originally a pet form of any of the various names beginning with the letter *D*, Doe is now often bestowed as an independent given name, perhaps in reference to *doe* (a female deer). Pet: Doey. (DŌ)

Dolly Pet form of Dorothy (gift of God) and Delores (sorrows), Dolly is now commonly bestowed as an independent given name. *See* DELORES *and* DOROTHEA. (DOL-LEE)

Donna Modern coinage used as a feminine form of Donald (world ruler) or as a borrowing from the Italian *donna* (lady). *See* DONALD (Male Names). (DON-NAH)

Dora A short form of any of the various names containing the Greek element *dōron* (gift), Dora is also commonly bestowed as an independent given name. Pet: Dori, Dorie, Dory. (DOR-AH)

Doreen Variant of Dora (gift), formed by adding the Irish diminutive suffix *-een*. *See* DORA. Var: Dorene, Dorine. Pet: Dori, Dorie, Dory. (DOR-EEN)

Doria Of disputed derivation, Doria might be a feminine form of Dorian or a variant of Dora (gift). Alternatively, it is possible that it originated as a variation of Doris (Dorian woman). *See* DORIAN (Male Names), DORA, *and* DORIS. Pet: Dori, Dorie, Dory. (DOR-EE-AH)

Dorinda Elaboration of Dora (gift), Dorinda was coined in the 18th century. *See* DORA. Short: Dori, Dorie, Dory. (DOR-IN-DAH)

Doris Derived from the Greek Dōris (Dorian woman). The Dorians were one of the four main tribes of ancient Greece who settled in the mountainous area also known as Doris. The name is borne in Greek mythology by a goddess of the sea. (DOR-ISS)

Dorothea A borrowing of the Greek Dōrothea, a compound name composed of the elements *dōron* (gift) and *theos* (God): hence, "gift of God." Dorothea and its variant forms are popular throughout Europe and the British Isles. Var: Dorothee, Dorothy, Dorthy. Pet:

Dollie, Dolly, Dora, Dori, Dorie, Dory, Dot, Dottie. (DOR-O-THEE-AH)

Earlene Feminine form of Earl, which originated as an aristocratic title and is derived from the Old English *eorl* (warrior, nobleman). Var: Earline, Erlene, Erline. (ER-LEEN)

Ebba Contracted form of the Old English name Eadburga (fortress of prosperity, wealthy protection), a compounding of the elements *ēad* (prosperity, fortune, riches) and *burg* (fortress). The name was borne by a 7th-century saint, Ebba the Elder (d. 638). A sister of Oswald, king of Northumbria, she founded a Benedictine abbey in Berwickshire. (EBB-BAH)

Ebony Taken from *ebony*, which denotes a hard, heavy, black wood. It is popularly bestowed by black parents as a symbol of ethnic pride. (EH-BEH-NEE)

Edith Derived from the Old English Ēadgyð, Eadgyth, a compound name composed of the elements *ēad* (prosperity, fortune, riches) and *gyð, gyth* (war, strife): hence, "prosperous in war." Var: Edyth, Edythe. Pet: Edie. (EE-DITH)

Edna Derived from the Hebrew *'ēdnāh* (rejuvenation, delight). Edna is found in the apocryphal book Tobit, as the name of the mother of Sarah and stepmother of Tobias. Var: Ednah. (ED-NAH)

Edwina Feminine form of Edwin, which is derived from Eadwine, an Old English compound name composed of the elements *ēad* (prosperity, fortune, riches) and *wine* (friend): hence, "prosperous friend." The name was borne by the wife of Earl Mountbatten, the former Edwina Ashley. (ED-WEE-NAH)

Eileen English variant of the French Aveline, a name derived from the Germanic Avila, which is thought to be a Latinate form of Aveza, a name ultimately of uncertain meaning. Alternatively, Eileen is an Anglicized form of the Irish Eibhlín, a cognate of Evelyn. *See* EVELYN. Var: Aileen, Aline, Ileene, Ilene. (Ī-LEEN)

Elaine Variant form of Helen (light). *See* HELEN. The name was borne in Arthurian legend by a woman of Astolat who loved Sir Lancelot. Var: Ilaine. (EE-LANE)

Eleanor Derived from Alienor, a Provençal form of the Greek Helenē, which is derived from the element *ēlē* (light, torch, bright). Var: Eleanora, Eleonora, Elinor, Ellenor. Short: Ellen. Pet: Ellie, Nell, Nellie, Nelly. (ELL-EH-NOR)

Elisa A short form of Elizabeth (God is my oath), Elisa is also bestowed as an independent given name. Short: Lisa. (EH-LEE-SAH)

Eliza Short form of Elizabeth (God is my oath) that is now commonly bestowed as an independent given name. *See* ELIZABETH. Eliza Dolittle was the name of the central character in George Bernard Shaw's play *Pygmalion* (1913), on which the popular musical and film *My Fair Lady* is based. (EE-LĪ-ZAH)

Elizabeth Derived from the Hebrew *elīsheba'* (God is my oath). The name is borne in the Bible by a kinswoman of the Virgin Mary and mother of John the Baptist. In England the name was borne by Queen Elizabeth I (1533–1603). The name continues its popularity by its association with the queen mother (b. 1900), the former Elizabeth Bowes-Lyon, and her daughter Queen Elizabeth II (b. 1926). Var: Elisabeth, Elspeth. Short: Beth, Elisa, Eliza, Lisa, Lisabeth, Lisbet, Liz, Liza, Lizabet. Pet: Bess, Bessie, Bessy, Betsy, Bettina, Betty, Ellie, Elsa, Elsie, Libbie, Libby, Lizzie, Lizzy. (EE-LIZ-AH-BETH)

Ella Brought to England by the Normans, Ella originated as a short form of any of the various names containing the Germanic element *ali* (foreign, other). Alternatively, Ella is now taken as a variant of Ellen (light). *See* ELLEN. (EL-LAH)

Ellen Originally a variant form of Helen, Ellen is now also commonly used as a variant of Eleanor. Both names, however, are ultimately derived from the same Greek root, *ēlē* (light, torch, bright). Pet: Ellie, Nell, Nellie, Nelly. (EL-LUN)

Ellie A pet form of any of the various names containing the element *el*, Ellie is also commonly bestowed as an independent given name. (EL-LEE)

Elsa Originally a pet form of Elizabeth, Elsa is now in common use as an independent given name and was popularized as the name of the affectionate lioness in the book and film *Born Free*. (EL-SAH)

Emeny Of uncertain origin and meaning, Emeny first came into use in medieval England. Var: Emonie, Imanie. Short: Em. Pet: Emmie, Emmy. (EM-EH-NEE)

Emerald Taken from *emerald*, which denotes the bright green variety of beryl used in jewelry making. Var: Emarald, Emmarald, Emmerald. Short: Em. Pet: Emmie, Emmy, Merl. (EM-MER-LD)

Emily English cognate of the Latin Aemilia, which is from Aemilius, an old Roman family name probably derived from *aemulus* (trying to equal or excel, rival). Var: Emilia. Short: Em. Pet: Emmie, Emmy. (EM-IH-LEE)

Emma Variant of the Germanic Erma, which originated as a short form of any of the various names containing the element *erm(en)* or *irm(en)* (strength). Short: Em. Pet: Emmie, Emmy. (EM-MAH)

EMMELINE Variant form of Emily, formed by adding the diminutive suffix *-ine:* hence, "little rival." *See* EMILY. Pet: Emmie, Emmy. (EM-MEH-LINE, EM-MEH-LEEN)

ENID Of uncertain origin and derivation, Enid might be derived from the Old Welsh *enaid* (soul), a word used as an endearment. In Arthurian legend, Enid was the virtuous and patient wife of Geraint, one of the knights of the Round Table. (EE-NID)

ERICA Feminine form of Eric, the English cognate of the Old Norse Eiríkr (honorable ruler). *See* ERIKA (Scandinavian Names). (ERR-I-KAH)

ERIN Derived from the Gaelic Érinn, the dative case of Érie, which is the Irish name for Ireland. Though Erin is popular in England and the U.S., it is not normally bestowed as a given name in Ireland. (ERR-IN)

ESMERALDA A borrowing of the Spanish name Esmeralda, which is taken from the word meaning "emerald." Esmeralda was the name of the Gypsy girl loved by the hunchback Quasimodo in Victor Hugo's novel *The Hunchback of Notre Dame* (1831). Var: Esmerelda. Pet: Esmie. (EZ-MER-ELL-DAH)

ESTELLE Common to England, Estelle is the French cognate of the Spanish Estella, which is derived from the Latin *stella* (star). Var: Estella. Short: Stella. (EH-STEL)

ESTHER Popular name of debated origin and meaning. Some believe it to be the Persian translation of the Hebrew name Hadassah (myrtle); others think it is derived from the Persian *stara* (star). It has also been suggested that it derived from the Babylonian Ishtar, the name of a goddess of love and fertility. The name is borne in the Bible by the Jewish wife of the Persian king Ahasuerus. (ESS-TER)

ETHEL Originally a short form of any of the various Old English compound names containing the element *æthel* (noble), Ethel is now an independent name in its own right. (EH-THUL)

EUDORA A borrowing from the Greek, Eudora is composed of the elements *eu* (well, good, fair) and *dōron* (gift): hence, "good gift." The name is borne in Greek mythology by one of the Nereids, the fifty sea-nymph daughters of Nereus. (YOO-DOR-AH)

EUGENIA A borrowing from the Greek, Eugenia is a feminine form of Eugenios, which is derived from *eugenēs* (well-born). *See* EUGENE (Male Names). The name is borne by the daughter of Prince Andrew and Sarah Ferguson. Var: Eugenie. Short: Genie. (YOO-GEEN-EE-AH)

EULALIA A borrowing from the Latin and the Greek, Eulalia is composed of the elements *eu* (well, good, fair) and *lalein* (to talk). (YOO-LĀ-LEE-AH)

EUNICE Derived from the Greek Eunikē, a compound name composed of the elements *eu* (well, good, fair) and *nikē* (victory). The name is borne in the Bible by the understanding mother of Timothy. (YOO-NIS)

EUPHEMIA Derived from the Greek Euphēmia, a compound name composed of the elements *eu* (well, good, fair) and *phēmē* (voice). The name was borne by a young virgin martyr of Chalcedon who so courageously withstood her torture that her fame spread both East and West. Euphemia was an especially popular name in England during the Victorian era. Pet: Effie, Eppie. (YOO-FEE-ME-AH)

EVANGELINE Coined from the Latin *evangelium* (good news, the Gospel). Pet: Angie, Evie. (EE-VAN-JEH-LEEN, EE-VAN-JEH-LINE)

EVE Derived from the Hebrew Chava (life), which is from *hawwāh* (life). The name is borne in the Bible by the first woman, "the mother of all the living," and hence is common throughout Europe and the British Isles. Var: Eva. Pet: Evie. (EEV)

EVELYN English variant of Aveline, a French diminutive form of the Germanic Avila, which is of ultimately uncertain derivation. *See* AVELINE. Var: Evelina, Eveline, Evelyne. Short: Lynn. Pet: Evie, Linni, Linnie. (EH-VEH-LIN)

EVETTE English form of the French Yvette (yew). *See* YVETTE (French Names). Alternatively, Evette is a modern creation coined by the addition of the French diminutive suffix *-ette* with the name Eve (life). *See* EVE. Pet: Evie. (EE-VET)

FAITH Derived from *faith,* which denotes unquestioning belief and complete trust in God. The word has its root in the Latin *fides* (confidence, belief). Faith, a very popular name among the 17th-century Puritans, continues to be an often-used name among modern Christians. (FAYTH)

FAY Thought to be derived from the Middle English *faie* (fairy), Fay achieved a measure of popularity during the 19th century. Today, it is more commonly bestowed as a middle name. Var: Fae, Faye. (FAY)

FELICIA Feminine form of Felix, which is derived from the Latin *felix* (lucky, happy). (FEH-LEE-SHA)

FELICITY Derived from *felicity,* which denotes happiness or good fortune. The name has its root in the Latin *felicitas* (happiness). (FEH-LIS-IH-TEE)

Fern Derived from *fern*, which denotes the nonflowering plant. The name is borne by the little girl who loved Wilbur the pig in E. B. White's classic *Charlotte's Web*. Var: Ferne. (FERN)

Fleur Derived from the Old French *fleur* (flower). Its use as a name in England began in the Middle Ages. It is rarely used as a given name in France, which prefers the names of saints and martyrs. Pet: Fleurette. (FLURE)

Floella Modern coinage made by combining the names Flo and Ella. *See* ELLA *and* FLORENCE. Short: Flo. (FLO-EL-LAH)

Flora Derived from the Latin *floris* (a flower). The name is borne in Roman mythology by the goddess of flowers and spring. Short: Flo. Pet: Florrie. (FLOR-AH)

Florence Medieval English form of the Latin Florentia, which is derived from *florens* (blooming, flourishing, prosperous). The name was made popular by Florence Nightingale (1820–1910), a nurse in the Crimean War who is regarded as the founder of modern nursing. Short: Flo. Pet: Florrie, Flossie. (FLOR-UNS)

Flower Directly derived from *flower*, which denotes a flower or a bloom. Flower has its root in the Latin *floris* (a flower). The name gained popularity during the 1960s and 1970s but has since declined in use. (FLOU-ER)

Frances French feminine form of Franceis (a Frank, from the Frankish Empire), which is also in common use in England. Short: Fran. Pet: Frankie, Frannie, Franny. (FRAN-SUS)

Francine Diminutive form of the French Françoise, which is derived from the Old French *françois* (French).This name is popularly bestowed in England as well as in France. Var: Franceen, Francene. Short: Fran. Pet: Frankie, Frannie, Franny. (FRAN-SEEN)

Frederica Feminine form of Frederick, which is derived from the Germanic Friedrich (peaceful ruler), a compound name composed of the elements *frithu* (peace) and *rik* (king, ruler). Pet: Freddie. (FRED-EH-REE-KAH)

Gabrielle Feminine form of Gabriel, which is derived from the Hebrew *gavhrī'ēl* (God is my strength). Gabriel is the name borne in the Bible by one of the seven archangels, the herald of Good News who appeared to Mary to announce her pregnancy and the impending birth of the Christ child. Var: Gabriela, Gabriella. Pet: Gaby. (GAB-REE-ELL)

Gail Originally a short form of the biblical Abigail (father of exaltation), it is now commonly used as an independent given name. *See* ABIGAIL. Var: Gale, Gayle. (GALE)

Gay Derived from *gay* (joyous, lighthearted). Popular in the early 20th century, Gay has recently declined in popularity due to its alternative modern meaning, "homosexual," and it is now more often found as a middle name. Var: Gae, Gaye. (GAY)

Gaynor Medieval variant of Guinevere (white, fair, blessed), which remains in common use. *See* GUINEVERE. (GAY-NER, GAY-NOR)

Gemma A borrowing from the Latin, Gemma is taken from *gemma* (precious stone, jewel).The name was borne by St. Gemma Galgani (1878–1903) and is often bestowed in her honor. Var: Jemma. (JEM-MAH)

Geneva Of disputed origin, Geneva might be a borrowing of the name of a city and lake in Switzerland, which is derived from the Old French *genevre* (juniper berry). Alternatively, it might have originated as a diminutive form of Genevieve. *See* GENEVIEVE. (GEN-EE-VAH)

Genevieve Derived from the Gaulish Genovefa, a name with Celtic roots but the meaning of which is uncertain. The first element is believed to be from *genos* (race, people, tribe); the second is possibly from an element meaning "woman." Its alteration in the translation from the Celtic to the French seems to be the cause of the confusion. Pet: Genni, Gennie, Genny. (JEN-EH-VEEV)

Genista Borrowed from the Latin name of the broom plant, *planta Genista*. Pet: Genni, Gennie, Genny. (JEH-NIS-TAH)

Georgia Latinate feminine form of George, which is ultimately derived from the Greek *geōrgos* (husbandman, earthworker, farmer). Pet: Gee Gee, Georgie. (JORJ-AH)

Georgina Feminine form of George, which is ultimately derived from the Greek *geōrgos* (husbandman, earthworker, farmer). Georgina originated in 18th-century Scotland and is now used with frequency in England and other European countries. Var: Georgene, Georgine. Short: Gina. Pet: Georgie. (JORJ-EE-NAH)

Geraldine Feminine derivative of Gerald (spear ruler), which is from the Old High German Gerwald, a compound name composed of the elements *ger* (spear) and *wald* (rule). Pet: Geri, Gerry. (JER-AL-DEEN)

Gertrude Derived from the Old High German Geretrudis, a compound name composed of the elements *ger* (spear) and *trut* (maiden, dear) or *þruþ* (strength). The name Gertrude was introduced to England in the late Middle Ages by German immigrants. Short: Gert. Pet: Gertie, Trudie, Trudy. (GER-TROOD)

GHISLAIN Fairly recent coinage of uncertain origin. It might be related to the French name Giselle (pledge). *See* GISELLE (French Names). Var: Ghislaine. (GEES-LANE)

GILLIAN Arose in the 16th century as a variant of Julian, a derivative of the old Roman family name Julius, which is thought to be derived from Iulus (the first down on the chin, downy-bearded, youth). *See* JULIA. Gillian was first bestowed upon males and females alike. Now, however, it is an exclusively female name. Var: Jillian. Short: Gill, Jill. Pet: Gilly, Jilly. (JIL-LEE-UN)

GINA Originally a short form of Georgina (earthworker), Gina is now used as an independent given name. *See* GEORGINA. (JEE-NAH)

GINGER Originally a nickname for someone with red hair, Ginger is now sometimes used as a diminutive form of Virginia (spring-like, flourishing). Pet: Ginnie, Ginny. (JIN-JER)

GLENNA Feminine form of the Scottish Glenn, which is derived from the Scottish Gaelic *glenn* (mountain valley). Var: Glenne. (GLEN-NAH)

GLENYS Modern coinage that originated in Wales and is probably derived from *glân* (pure, holy). There is some speculation, however, that it is an elaboration of Glenna (mountain valley). *See* GLENNA. Var: Glenice, Glennis, Glynis, Glynnis. (GLEN-ISS)

GLORIA Derived from the Latin *glōria* (glory), Gloria was not used as a given name until the 20th century, when George Bernard Shaw used it as the name of a character in his 1898 play *You Never Can Tell.* (GLOR-EE-AH)

GODIVA Derived from the Old English Godgifu, a compound name composed of the elements *god* (God) and *gifu* (gift): hence, "God's gift." The name was made famous by the 11th-century Lady Godiva, who, according to legend, on the dare of her husband rode naked through the streets of Coventry so that he would abolish a heavy tax imposed on the townspeople. (GUH-DĪ-VAH)

GRACE Inspired by *grace* (eloquence or beauty of form, kindness, mercy, favor), which is derived from the Latin *gratia* (favor, thanks). The name was made popular by 17th-century Puritans, who bestowed it in reference to God's favor and love toward mankind. Pet: Gracie. (GRACE)

GREER Transferred use of the surname originating in the Middle Ages from a contraction of Gregor, a cognate of the Latin Gregorius (watchful, vigilant). The name became popular as a female name in the 20th century from its association with actress Greer Garson (b. 1908), who was given her mother's maiden name. Var: Grier. (GREER)

GUINEVERE English cognate of the Welsh Gwenhwyfar (fair lady), a compound name composed from the elements *gwen, gwyn* (white, fair, blessed) and *hwyfar* (smooth, soft). The name was borne in Arthurian legend by the beautiful wife of King Arthur, who became the mistress of Sir Lancelot. Repentant for her unfaithfulness, Guinevere retired to the convent at Amberesbury. Var: Guinever, Gwenevere. Short: Gwen. (GWEN-IH-VEER)

GWEN A short form of any of the various names containing the Celtic element *gwen, gwyn* (white, fair, blessed), the name is also commonly bestowed as an independent given name. (GWEN)

GWENDOLYN English variant of the Welsh Gwendolen (fair-browed), a compound name composed of the elements *gwen, gwyn* (white, fair, blessed) and *dolen* (brows, eyebrows). Var: Gwendolin, Gwendoline, Gwendolynn. Short: Gwen, Wendoline, Wendolyn. Pet: Gwenda, Gwenna, Wenda, Wendie, Wendy. (GWEN-DŌ-LIN)

GWENYTH English variant of the Welsh Gwynaeth, a name derived from *gwen, gwyn* (white, fair, blessed). Short: Gwen. (GWEN-ITH)

HANNAH A popular name throughout Europe, Hannah is derived from the Hebrew *hannāh, chaanach* (gracious, full of grace, mercy). The name, borne in the Bible by the mother of the prophet Samuel, received a boost in popularity by the Puritans, who favored Bible names. (HAH-NAH, HAN-NAH)

HARRIET English form of the French Henriette, a feminine diminutive of Henri (ruler of an enclosure, home ruler). *See* HENRY (Male Names). Var: Harriette. Pet: Hattie. (HAR-REE-UT)

HAYLEY Transferred use of a Northern English surname derived from Hale or Hales (residing in a nook, recess, or remote valley). It has also been suggested that Hayley derives from the place-name Hailey, which is composed of the Old English elements *hēg* (hay) and *lēah* (wood, clearing, meadow). The name gained popularity through the fame of actress Hayley Mills. Var: Haley. (HAY-LEE)

HAZEL Taken from the name of the hazelnut tree, which is derived from the Old English *hæsel* (hazel). Alternatively, the name can also be derived from the Hebrew *hazā'ēl* (God sees). (HAY-ZL)

HEATHER A name borrowed from the plant, common to the British Isles, which has scale-like leaves and small purplish-pink flowers. The word is derived from the Old English *haddyr* (heather, plants of the heath family). (HEH-THER)

HEBE A borrowing from the Greek, Hebe is derived from *hēbē* (youth). The name is borne in Greek mythology by the goddess of youth, a daughter of Hera and Zeus. (HEE-BEE)

HELEN Cognate of the Greek Helenē, which is derived from the root *ēlē* (light, torch, bright). The name is borne in Greek legend by the beautiful wife of the king of Sparta. Her abduction by the Trojan prince Paris sparked off the Trojan War. Var: Helena, Helene. Pet: Nell, Nellie, Nelly. (HEL-UN)

HENRIETTA British form of the French name Henriette, a feminine diminutive of Henri, which is derived from the German Heinrich (ruler of an enclosure, home ruler). *See* HENRY (Male Names). Pet: Hattie, Hennie, Hettie. (HEN-REE-EH-TAH)

HESTHER Medieval variant of Esther, a name of debated origin. *See* ESTHER. Var: Hester. (HES-TER)

HILARY Taken from the Latin Hilaria, which is derived from *hilaris* (cheerful, noisy, merry). Hilary, bestowed upon both males and females, is now more commonly used as a female name. Var: Hillary. (HIL-AH-REE)

HILDA Latinized short form of any of the female compound names composed of the element *hildr* (battle). Now in common use as an independent given name, Hilda was brought to England by Scandinavian invaders before the Norman Conquest. The name was borne by a Northumbrian saint (614–80) who founded the abbey at Whitby. Var: Hylda. (HIL-DAH)

HOLLY Taken from the holly tree, an evergreen whose stiff, glossy, sharp-pointed leaves and clusters of red berries are used in Christmas decorations. The name is derived from the Old English *holegn* (to prick). Var: Hollie. (HOL-LEE)

HONEY Taken from *honey,* which denotes the thick, sweet substance that bees make from the nectar of flowers. The word is derived from the Old English *hunig* (honey) and has long been used as a term of endearment. It gained popularity as a given name from a character in Margaret Mitchell's novel *Gone with the Wind.* (HUH-NEE)

HONOUR Taken from *honour,* which is derived from the Latin *honor* (esteem, integrity, dignity). Var: Honor, Honoria. Short: Nora. (ON-UR)

HOPE Taken from *hope,* which is derived from the Old English *hopa* (expectation, hope). The name, first bestowed by the Puritans, continues to be popular. (HOPE)

IDA Of Germanic origin, Ida is derived from the element *īd* (work, labor). The name, introduced to England by the Normans, died out toward the end of the 14th century but was revived in the 19th century. (Ī-DAH)

IDONY Popular name first formed in the Middle Ages as an evolution of the Old Norse name Iðunnr, which is derived from the element *ið* (again). Var: Idonea, Iduna. (Ī-DUN-EE)

IMOGEN Of uncertain origin and meaning, Imogen was first recorded as the name of the heroine in Shakespeare's play *Cymbeline.* The name is thought to be a misprint of Raphael Holinshed's Innogen, a Celtic name supposedly derived from the Gaelic *inghean* (girl, maiden). Var: Imogene. (IM-EH-JEN)

INDIA Taken from the name of the subcontinent, India seems to have originally been bestowed in reference to familial ties with, and affection for, the country. (IN-DEE-AH)

IONA Taken from the name of a small island in the Hebrides, a group of islands off the west coast of Scotland. The derivation of the name is uncertain. Some believe it to be a misspelling of Ioua, an older name for the island. Its Gaelic name is *I,* from the Old Norse *ey* (island). Thus, it stands to reason that the name might be derived from this root. (Ī-O-NAH)

IONE 19th-century coinage thought to be either a variant of Iona or derived from Ionia, the name of an ancient region in western Asia Minor which was colonized by the Greeks in the 11th century B.C. *See* IONA. Var: Iony. Pet: Noni, Nonie. (Ī-O-NEE)

IRENE Derived from the Greek Eirēnē, which is from *eirēnē* (peace). The name is borne in Greek mythology by the goddess of peace, a daughter of Zeus and Themis. (Ī-REEN)

IRIS A name of two distinct derivations in use throughout Europe and the British Isles. In England, Iris is one of the flower names and is derived from the genus name *Iris.* Elsewhere in Europe, it is generally taken from Iris, the mythological Greek goddess of the rainbow. (Ī-RIS)

ISABELLE Originated as a Spanish variant of Elizabeth but is now also common to England. It was first made popular from its association with Queen Isabella (1296–1358), the wife of Edward II. Var: Isabel, Isabella, Isbel, Isbell, Isobel. Pet: Izzie, Izzy, Bell, Bella, Belle. (IZ-AH-BELL)

ISOLDE Of debated origin and meaning, Isolde might be derived from the Old High German Isold, a compound name composed of the elements *is* (ice) and *waltan* (to rule): hence, "ruler of the ice." Alternatively, it could be a variant of the Welsh Esyllt (beautiful, fair). The name is borne in medieval legend by an Irish princess who was betrothed to King Mark of Cornwall. Through a magic potion, she became the beloved of Tristram, who was married to another Isolde. Var: Iseult, Isolt, Yseult, Ysolt. (IH-SOLD-EH, IH-SOLD)

IVY Taken from the name of the plant, which is an evergreen climbing vine of the ginseng family. The word is derived from the Old English *ifig* (climber). Var: Ivey. (Ī-VEE)

JACQUELINE Borrowed from the French, Jacqueline is a feminine form of Jacques, which is a variant of James and Jacob. Both of these names are derived from the Hebrew *ja'aqob* (supplanted, seized by the heel). *See* JACQUES (French Male Names). Var: Jacklin, Jacklyn, Jacquelyn. Pet: Jackie, Jacky, Jacqui. (JAK-WEH-LIN)

JADE Taken from the name of the hard, green or white jadeite or nephrite stone. The word came to England, via the French, from the Spanish *piedra de ijada* (stone of the side: from the belief that it cured pains in the side). Var: Jaide, Jayde. (JADE)

JAMIE Feminine form of James, which is derived from the Hebrew *ja'aqob* (supplanted, seized by the heel). *See* JAMES (Male Names). Var: Jaime. (JAY-MEE)

JAN Short form of any of the various names containing the element *jan*. Alternatively, it is used as a feminine form of John, which is from the Hebrew *yehōhānān* (Yahweh is gracious). *See* JOHN (Male Names). Var: Jana, Janna. (JAN)

JANE English cognate of the French Jehanne and Jeanne, which are feminine forms of Jean, a cognate of John (God is gracious). *See* JOHN (Male Names). Jane, a perennially popular name, was the name of the central character in Charlotte Brontë's *Jane Eyre* (1847). Var: Jayne. Pet: Janey, Janie, Jayney, Jaynie. (JANE)

JANELLE Modern coinage of Jane (God is gracious), made by adding the feminine suffix *-elle*. *See* JANE. Var: Janella. Short: Jan. (JA-NEL)

JANET Diminutive form of Jane (God is gracious) in use since the Middle Ages. Var: Janette. Short: Jan. (JAN-ET)

JANICE Modern variant of Jane (God is gracious), made by adding the suffix *-ice*. *See* JANE. Var: Janis. Short: Jan. (JAN-ISS)

JANINE English variant of the French Jeannine, a feminine form of Jean (God is gracious). *See* JEAN. Var: Janina, Jeanine. (JA-NEEN)

JASMINE Taken from the name of the tropical plant having colorful, fragrant flowers used in perfumes and teas. The word is derived from the Persian *yāsamīn* (jasmine). Var: Jasmin, Jasmyn, Jazmin, Jazmine, Jazmyn. (JAZ-MIN)

JEAN English cognate of the French Jeanne, which is a feminine form of Jean (God is gracious). *See* JEAN (French Male Names) *or* JOHN (Male Names). Var: Jeana, Jeane. Pet: Jeanie, Jeannie. (JEEN)

JEANETTE From the French Jeannette, a diminutive form of Jeanne (God is gracious). *See* JEAN (French Male Names) *or* JOHN (Male Names). Var: Genette, Jennet. Pet: Jeanie, Jeannie, Jenni, Jennie, Jenny, Netti, Nettie, Netty. (JEH-NET)

JENNIFER Cornish derivation of Guinevere, which is from the Welsh Gwenhwyfar (fair lady). *See* GUINEVERE. Until the 20th century, Jennifer was largely a regional name. Now, however, it has become one of the most popular names in the English-speaking world. Short: Jenn. Pet: Jenni, Jennie, Jenny. (JEN-NIH-FER)

JENNY Originally a pet form of Jennifer (fair lady), Jenny is now also bestowed as an independent given name. Var: Jenni, Jennie. (JEN-NEE)

JESSICA Of uncertain derivation and meaning, Jessica might be an elaboration of Jessie, which was originally a pet form of Janet and Jean. Alternatively, it can be interpreted as an elaborated feminine form of Jesse, which is derived from the Hebrew *yīshai* (gift). *See* JESSE (Male Names), JANET, *and* JEAN. Short: Jess. Pet: Jessie. (JESS-IH-KAH)

JESSIE Originated as a pet form of the names Janet and Jean (God is gracious). Now, however, it is more commonly used as a feminine form of Jesse, which is derived from the Hebrew *yīshai* (gift), and as a pet form of Jessica. *See* JANET, JEAN, *and* JESSICA. Short: Jess. (JES-SEE)

JETTA Taken from *jet*, which denotes a hard, black, lustrous variety of lignite used in jewelry making. The word is derived from the Greek *gagatēs* (stone from Gagas, a town and river of Lycia in Asia Minor). (JET-TAH)

JILL Originally a short form of Jillian, which is a variant of Julian (downy-bearded, youth), Jill is now commonly bestowed as an independent given name. Pet: Jilli, Jillie, Jilly. (JIL)

JILLY Pet form of any of the various names containing the first element *Gill* or *Jill*. Var: Jilli, Jillie. (JIL-LEE)

JO A short form of the various female names containing the element *Jo*, it is also popularly used as an element in combination names such as Mary Jo and Jo Ellen. (JO)

JOAN Contracted form of the French Johanne, which is a feminine form of John (God is gracious). The name's most famous bearer is perhaps Joan of Ark (1412–31), the young French saint and heroine who claimed to be a soldier of God. Under her leadership, the French Army defeated the English at Orléans in 1429. She was eventually captured and sold to the English, who burned her at the stake for witchcraft in 1431. She was canonized in 1920. *See* JOHN (Male Names). Pet: Joani, Joanie, Joni. (JONE)

JOANNA Middle Latin feminine form of Joannes (God is gracious). The name is derived from the Greek Iōannēs, a derivative of the Hebrew Yehanan, which is a short form of Yehohanan, itself derived from *yehōhānān* (Yahweh is gracious). Var: Joanne. Short: Jo. (JO-AN-NAH)

JOCELYN A transferred use of the surname derived from the French Joscelin. Joscelin is derived from the obsolete Gautzelin, which finds its root in the Germanic tribal name *Gauts*. Jocelyn was originally bestowed upon male children, but now it is an exclusively female name. Var: Jocelin, Joceline, Josceline. Pet: Joss. (JOS-EH-LIN)

JODY Originally a pet form of Judy, itself a pet form of Judith, which is ultimately derived from the Hebrew Yehudit (praise). Jody is now bestowed as an independent given name. Var: Jodi, Jodie. (JO-DEE)

JOSEPHINE English form of the French Joséphine, a feminine form of Joseph, which is derived from the Hebrew *Yōsēf* (God will add, God will increase). Short: Jo. Pet: Josie. (JO-SEH-FEEN)

JOSIE Pet form of Josephine (God will add, God will increase), Josie is also used as an independent given name. *See* JOSEPHINE. (JO-SEE)

JOY Taken from *joy* (delight, great pleasure, joy), which is derived from the Middle English and Old French *joie* (joy). (JOY)

JOYCE Evolution of the obsolete Jocosa, which is derived from the Latin *jocosa* (merry, happy). Originally a male name, Joyce is now more commonly bestowed upon females. (JOICE)

JUDITH Cognate of the Hebrew Jehudith and Yehudit, which are feminine forms of Jehuda and Yehūdhāh. These names, Anglicized as Judah, mean "he will be praised." Because Judah was also the name of a kingdom in ancient Palestine, the name can also mean "from Judah." Pet: Judi, Judie, Judy. (JOO-DITH)

JUDY Originally a pet form of Judith (praised, woman from Judah), Judy is now commonly bestowed as an independent given name. *See* JUDITH. Var: Judi, Judie. (JOO-DEE)

JULIA Feminine form of the Latin Julius, an old Roman family name thought to be derived from Iulus (the first down on the chin, downy-bearded). Because a person just beginning to develop facial hair is young, the definition of this name and its related forms has evolved to "youth." (JOO-LEE-AH)

JULIANA Common throughout Europe, Juliana is the Latin feminine form of Julianus, which is a derivative of Julius (the first down on the chin, downy-bearded, youth). *See* JULIA. Var: Juliann, Julianna, Julianne. (JOO-LEE-AN-NAH)

JULIE French cognate of Julia (downy-bearded, youth), which has been in common use in the English-speaking world since the 1920s. *See* JULIA. (JOO-LEE)

JULIET English form of the French Juliette, which is a diminutive form of Julie (downy-bearded, youth). *See* JULIA. The name is borne by the heroine of Shakespeare's *Romeo and Juliet*, a famous tragedy about star-crossed lovers. (JOO-LEE-ET)

JUNE Taken from the name of the sixth month, June was first bestowed as a given name in the 20th century. The name is derived from the Latin Juno, the Roman mythological goddess of marriage and queen of the gods. (JOON)

JUSTINA Feminine form of Justin, which is derived from the Latin Justinus, which has its root in *justus* (rightful, proper, just). Var: Justine. (JUS-TEE-NAH)

KAREN Danish form of Katherine, a cognate of the Greek Aikaterinē, which is from *katharos* (pure, unsullied). A popular name, Karen has been used by the English only since the 1950s. (KARE-UN)

KATE A short form of Katherine (pure, unsullied) and its variants, Kate is also commonly bestowed as an independent given name. The name is borne by the shrewish woman in Shakespeare's ever-popular play *The Taming of the Shrew*. (KATE)

KATHERINE Cognate of the Greek Aikaterinē, which is derived from *katharos* (pure, unsullied). Katherine is a very popular name throughout Europe, and is common to European royalty. In England, it was borne by the first wife of Henry VIII, Katherine of Aragon (1485–1536).

Var: Catharine, Catherine, Cathryn, Katharine, Kathryn. Short: Cath, Kat, Kath. Pet: Cathy, Kate, Katie, Katy, Kay, Kit, Kitty. (KATH-EH-RIN)

Kathleen Anglicized form of the Irish Caitlín, which is a Gaelic form of Katherine (pure, unsullied), derived via the Old French Catheline. *See* KATHERINE. Var: Cathleen. Short: Cath, Kath. Pet: Cathy, Kathy, Kay. (KATH-LEEN)

Katie A pet form of any of the various names beginning with the element *Kat(h)*, Katie is also commonly bestowed as an independent given name. Var: Katy. (KAY-TEE)

Katrina Derived from the Dutch and German Katrine, a variant form of Katherine (pure, unsullied). *See* KATHERINE. Short: Kat, Trina. Pet: Katie, Katy. (KA-TREE-NAH)

Kay As a female name, Kay originated as a pet form of any of the various names beginning with the letter K. It is now commonly bestowed as an independent given name. As a male name, its root is found in the Latin *gai* (rejoiced). (KAY)

Kayley Transferred use of the Anglicized Irish surname, which is from the Gaelic MacCaollaidhe (son of Caollaidhe) and O'Caollaidhe (descended from Caollaidhe). Caollaidhe is an old male name derived from the element *caol* (slender). Var: Caleigh, Cayleigh, Cayley, Kaleigh, Kaley, Kali, Kayleigh, Kayla, Kayly. Short: Kay. (KAY-LEE)

Keeley Modern coinage that might be a transferred use of the Irish surname Keeley, which is a variant of Kayley, an Anglicized form of MacCaollaidhe and O'Caollaidhe. These names are derived from the Gaelic *caol* (slender). Var: Keeleigh, Keeli, Keely, Keighly. (KEE-LEE)

Kelly Transferred use of the Irish surname, Anglicized from O'Ceallaigh (descended from Ceallagh), which is derived from *ceallagh, ceallach* (strife, war). Alternatively, Kelly may be from local place-names derived from the Cornish *celli* (wood, grove). Originally a male name, Kelly is now also in use as a female name. Var: Kelley, Kelli, Kellie. (KEL-LEE)

Kelsey Derived from the obsolete Old English Cēolsige, a compound name composed of the elements *cēol* (ship) and *sige* (victory): hence, "victory ship." Originally a male name, Kelsey is now becoming popular as a female name. Var: Kelsi, Kelsie. (KEL-SEE)

Kendall Transferred use of the surname derived from a place-name in northwestern England, which has its root in the Old Norse *keld* (spring). Var: Kendal, Kendell. (KEN-DUL)

Kendra Feminine form of Kendrick, from the surname of several different origins. *See* KENDRICK (Male Names). (KEN-DRA)

Kerry Transferred use of an Irish place-name. Alternatively, Kerry can be an Anglicized form of the Gaelic Ciardha (black-haired one) and is also considered by many to be a pet form of Katherine (pure, unsullied). *See* CATHERINE. (KERR-EE)

Keziah English cognate of the Hebrew Ketziah, which is derived from *qesī'āh* (cassia, a kind of cinnamon). The name is borne in the Bible by the second of Job's three beautiful daughters. Var: Kezia. Pet: Kizzi, Kizzie, Kizzy. (KEE-ZĪ-AH)

Kiera Feminine form of Kieran, an Anglicized form of the Irish Ciarán, which is derived from the Gaelic *ciar* (black) and the diminutive suffix *-an:* hence, "little dark one." The name was originally bestowed upon those babies born with dark hair or a dark complexion. (KEER-AH)

Kim Originally a male name, a short form of Kimberely, which is of debated origin. *See* KIMBERELY. Kim is now common as an independent given name and is being bestowed upon females more often than upon males. Pet: Kimmie. (KIM)

Kimberely Of debated origin, Kimberely seems to be a borrowing of the name of the South African city and diamond-mining center. This Kimberely is thought to be derived from *kimberlite*, a kind of peridotite rock which contains diamonds. Others think it to be derived from Lord Kimberely, whose name is believed to be a compound name composed of an Old English personal name of unknown meaning and *lēah* (wood, clearing, meadow, enclosure). Kimberely originated as a male name but is now more common as a female name. Var: Kimberly, Kimberleigh. Short: Kim. Pet: Kimmie. (KIM-BER-LEE)

Kimbra Modern coinage probably derived from combining the names Kim and Debra (a bee). *See* DEBORAH *and* KIM. Short: Kim. Pet: Kimmie. (KIM-BRA)

Kyla Feminine form of Kyle, which originated as a Scottish surname and is derived from the Gaelic *caol* (narrow). *See* KYLE (Male Names). (KĪ-LAH)

Lana Short form of Alana, a name ultimately of uncertain meaning. *See* ALANA. Lana is now commonly bestowed as an independent given name. (LAN-AH)

Lark Taken from the name of the songbird, which is derived from the Middle English *larke, laverke* (lark). (LARK)

Laura Derived from the Latin *laurus* (laurel, an evergreen shrub or tree whose leaves were woven into wreaths by the ancient Greeks to crown victors in various contests). Originally an Italian name, Laura came into use in England in the 19th century, and is now popularly bestowed throughout the English-speaking world. Var: Lora. Pet: Laurie, Lori. (LAU-RAH, LOR-AH)

Laurel Taken from *laurel* (an evergreen shrub or tree). The name came into use in the 19th century, perhaps because of its similarity to Laura. *See* LAURA. Var: Lorelle. Pet: Laurie. (LAU-REL, LOR-EL)

Lauren English cognate of the French Laurence, a feminine form of Laurent, which is derived from the Latin Laurentius (man from Laurentum, a town in Latium). (LAU-REN, LOR-EN)

Lavinia Borne in Roman mythology by the daughter of King Latinus. She was the last wife of Aeneas and was considered to be the mother of the Roman people. The name is a feminine form of Latinus (from Latium, the area surrounding and including ancient Rome). Var: Lavina. (LAH-VIN-EE-AH)

Leah Derived from the Hebrew *lā'āh* (weary, to tire). The name is borne in the Bible by the eldest daughter of Laban and the first of Jacob's four wives. Var: Lea, Lia. (LEE, LEE-AH)

Leanne Modern name combining the names Lee (dweller by the wood or clearing) and Anne (gracious, full of grace). Alternatively, it is a variant spelling of Lianne (sun). *See* ANNE, LEE, *and* LIANE. (LEE-AN)

Lee Transferred use of the surname derived from the Old English *lēah* (wood, clearing, meadow), Lee has the meaning "dweller by the wood or clearing." In Middle English, the spelling of *lēah* evolved to *leigh, legh*. Lee is popularly used as a name element in combination names such as Kathy-Lee and Lee-Ann. Var: Lea, Leigh. (LEE)

Leila Derived from the Arabic *leila* (night, dark beauty) or the Persian *leila* (dark-haired). Its use in England began with George Byron's poem "The Giaour" (1813). Var: Leela, Leilah, Leilia, Lela, Lila, Lilah. (LEE-LAH, LAY-LAH)

Leona Feminine form of Leon, which is derived from the Latin *leo* (lion). Var: Liona. (LEE-O-NAH)

Leonora Short form of Eleonora (light, torch, bright), which is also bestowed as an independent given name. Var: Lenora, Lennora, Lennorah, Lenorah. (LEE-AH-NOR-AH)

Leslie Transferred use of the surname originating in Scotland from the place-name Lesslyn, which is said to be derived from *less lea* (smaller meadow, smaller clearing). Leslie is used as both a male and a female name, but the variant spelling Lesley is more commonly used for girls. Var: Lesley. (LES-LEE, LEZ-LEE)

Letitia Derived from the Latin *laetitia* (gladness, happiness). Letitia, a popular name during the Victorian era, is now becoming less common. Var: Laetitia, Lettice. Short: Tia. Pet: Lettie, Letty. (LEH-TEE-SHA)

Liane English short form of the French Éliane (sun). *See* ÉLIANE (French Names). Liane and its variant forms are popular throughout the English-speaking world. Var: Leanne, Liana, Lianna, Lianne. (LEE-AN)

Lilian Derived from the older Lilion, which is thought to be from the Latin *lilium* (lily). Var: Lillian. Pet: Lil, Lili, Lilli, Lillie, Lilly, Lily. (LIL-EE-UN)

Lilith From the Assyrian-Babylonian *lilītu* (of the night). In ancient Semitic folklore, the name was used for a female demon and vampire that lived in desolate areas. In medieval Jewish folklore, Lilith was the first wife of Adam, before Eve's creation. She was supposedly turned into a demon for refusing to obey Adam and became a night witch who menaced infants and small children. In spite of its negative attributes, Lilith remains a common name. Var: Lillith. Short: Lil. Pet: Lili, Lilli, Lillie, Lilly. (LIL-ITH)

Lilly Taken from the name of the plant having delicate, trumpet-shaped flowers regarded as a symbol of purity and perfection. The word is derived from the Middle English *lilie*, which is from the Old English and Latin *lilium* (lily). Alternatively, Lily is used as a pet form of both Lilian (lily) and Lilith (of the night). (LIL-EE)

Linda Of various derivations, Linda is formed from the Spanish *linda* (beautiful, pretty). It is also a short form of any of the Germanic compound names containing the element *lind* (tender, soft, weak). Alternatively, Linda is used as a short form of Belinda, which is a name of uncertain origin. *See* BELINDA. Var: Alinda. Pet: Lindie, Lindy. (LIN-DAH)

Linden Modern coinage possibly derived from the name of the tree, the flowers of which are used in herbal teas and preparations. Pet: Lindie, Lindy. (LIN-DUN)

Lindsay Taken from the old Scottish surname de Lindsay, meaning "from Lindsay," a part of the county of Lincolnshire in northeastern England. Lindsay is derived from Lincoln, a shortened form of Lindum Colonia, the first part of which is thought to be from the Welsh *llyn* (lake) and the second of which is from the Latin *colonia* (colony, settlement). The name, commonly used as both a male and a female name in Scotland, is more popular as a female name in England. Var: Lynsey. Short: Linds, Lyns. Pet: Lindie, Lindy, Linni, Linnie, Linny. (LINS-EE)

LINDSEY Taken from the old surname Lindesie, meaning "from Lindsey." In this instance, Lindsey is derived from the Old English elements *lind* (the linden tree) and *ey* (wetland). Var: Lynsey. Short: Linds, Lyns. Pet: Lindie, Lindy, Linni, Linnie, Linny. (LINS-EE)

LINNET A borrowing of the Old French name derived from *linette* (flax, flaxen-haired). The name may also be used in reference to the linnet, a small songbird of the Finch family which feeds on flaxseed. Var: Linnette, Lynette, Lynnette. Pet: Linni, Linnie, Linny. (LIN-ET)

LISA Short form of Elisabeth (God is my oath), which is commonly bestowed as an independent given name. *See* ELIZABETH. (LEE-SAH)

LISABETH Short form of Elisabeth (God is my oath), which is also used as an independent given name. *See* ELIZABETH. Var: Lizabeth. Short: Beth, Lisa, Liz, Liza. Pet: Lizzie, Lizzy. (LIZ-A-BETH)

LISHA Modern coinage influenced by the sound of names such as Felicia. (LEE-SHA)

LISSA Short form of Melissa (bee), Lissa is also used as an independent given name. *See* MELISSA. Alternatively, it is a variant spelling of Lyssa, a short form of Alyssa (nobility). *See* ALYSSA. (LIS-SAH)

LIZA Short form of Eliza and Elizabeth (God is my oath) commonly used as an independent given name. *See* ELIZABETH. Short: Liz. Pet: Lizzie, Lizzy. (LIZE-AH)

LOIS A borrowing of the Ecclesiastic Greek Lois, a name of uncertain meaning. It is borne in the Bible by the grandmother of Timothy, a companion of St. Paul. Its use in England began in the 16th century. (LO-ISS)

LOREEN Elaborated form of Lora, which is a variant of Laura (laurel). *See* LAURA. Var: Lorena, Lorene. Pet: Lori. (LOR-EEN)

LORETTA English cognate of the Italian Lauretta, a diminutive form of Laura (laurel). *See* LAURA. Pet: Lori. (LOR-ET-TAH)

LORI A pet form of any of the various names based on the name Laura (laurel), Lori is also used as an independent given name. *See* LAURA. (LOR-EE)

LORINDA Elaborated form of Lora (laurel), perhaps influenced by Linda (beautiful) or Dorinda (gift). *See* LAURA. Pet: Lori. (LOR-IN-DAH)

LORNA 19th-century coinage of English novelist R. D. Blackmore (1825–1900), borne by the heroine of his book *Lorna Doone* (1864). (LOR-NAH)

LORRAINE Transferred use of the surname originating from the name of a province in eastern France, which is derived from the Latin Lotharingia (territory of the people of Lothar). Lothar, the name of the son of the Frankish king Clovis, is of Germanic origin and is derived from the elements *hluod* (famous) and *hari*, *heri* (army): hence, "famous army." (LOR-RANE)

LOUELLA Modern coinage made by combining the names Louisa (famous in war) and Ella (foreign; light). *See* ELLA *and* LOUISA. Var: Luella. (LOO-EL-LAH)

LOUISA Feminine form of Louis (famous in war), which is from the Germanic Hluodowig, a compound name composed from the elements *hluod* (famous) and *wīg* (war, strife). Var: Louise. (LOO-EE-SAH)

LUCETTA Elaborated form of Lucy (light), made by the addition of the diminutive suffix *-etta*. *See* LUCY. Var: Lucette. (LOO-SET-AH)

LUCIA Feminine form of Lucius, which is derived from the Latin *lux* (light). The name was borne by St. Lucia of Syracuse, a 4th-century martyr whose popularity during the Middle Ages led to widespread use of the name. (LOO-SEE-AH)

LUCINDA Elaborated form of Lucia (light), produced by adding the suffix *-inda*. Lucinda originated as a literary name in Cervantes' *Don Quixote* (1605). Pet: Cindy, Lucy. (LOO-SIN-DAH)

LUCY English cognate of Lucia, which is derived from the Latin *lux* (light). Lucy is also used as a pet form of Lucinda. *See* LUCINDA. (LOO-SEE)

LYDIA Of Greek origin, Lydia (woman from Lydia, an ancient kingdom in western Asia Minor) is common throughout the English-speaking world. (LID-EE-AH)

LYNETTE Of several derivations. It is an English form of the Welsh Eluned (shapely) and a variant spelling of the Old French Linnet (flaxen-haired, flax). Alternatively, it is a modern variant of Lynn (lake), produced by the addition of the French feminine diminutive suffix *-ette*. *See* ELUNED (Welsh Names), LINNET, *and* LYNN. Var: Lynnette. Short: Lyn, Lynn. (LIN-ET)

LYNN Transferred use of a British place-name derived from the Welsh *llyn* (lake). It is also thought to have originated as a short form of Lynnette, a name of several derivations, or of Linda (beautiful, tender). *See* LINDA *and* LYNETTE. Alternatively, Lynn is used as a short form of any of the various names that contain the suffix *-lyn(n)* or *-line*. Var: Lyn. (LIN)

MADELEINE French cognate of Magdalene (of Magdala, a town on the Sea of Galilee), which is also in common use in England. *See* MAGDALENE. Var: Madelaine, Madeline, Madelyn, Madlyn, Madoline. Pet: Maddie, Maddy. (MAD-EH-LIN, MAD-EH-LINE)

MADISON Transferred use of the surname meaning "Mad's son." Mad was a common pet form of Matthew (gift of God) during the Middle Ages. Madison may also be a matronymic derived from the name Maud, an old pet form of Mathilda (battle mighty): hence, "son of Maud." Var: Maddison, Maddyson, Madyson. Pet: Maddie. (MAD-IH-SON)

MAHALIA A borrowing of the Aramaic name meaning "fatlings" (a calf, lamb, or kid). Var: Mehalia. (MAH-HAHL-EE-AH)

MALVINA Literary coinage by James Macpherson (1736–96), used in his Ossianic poems. It is believed to be derived from the Gaelic *maol-mhin* (smooth brow). (MAL-VEE-NAH)

MAMIE Originally a pet form of Margaret (pearl) or Mary, Mamie is now occasionally bestowed as an independent given name. *See* MARGARET *and* MARY. (MAY-MEE)

MARA Derived from the Hebrew *marah* (bitterness). The name is borne in the Bible by Naomi after the deaths of her husband and sons. (MAR-AH)

MARCIA Feminine form of the Latin Marcius, a variant of Marcus, which is derived from Mars, the Roman mythological god of war. Var: Marsha. Pet: Marcie, Marcy. (MAR-SHA)

MARGARET From the Greek Margarītēs, which is derived from *margaron* (a pearl). Margaret has been a popular name with European royalty. It was borne by Margaret of Anjou (1430–82), wife of Henry VI, by Margaret Tudor (1489–1541), sister of Henry VIII and wife of James IV of Scotland, and by Margaret Rose (b. 1930), daughter of George VI and his wife, Elizabeth. Var: Margary, Margeret, Margery, Marjorie, Marjory. Short: Marga, Marge. Pet: Madge, Maggie, Mamie, Margie, Marji, Marjie, Meggie, Peggy. (MAR-GAH-RET, MAR-GRET)

MARGERY Medieval variant of Margaret (pearl), which is still in common use. *See* MARGARET. Var: Margerie, Marjorie, Marjory. Pet: Margie, Marji, Marjie. (MAR-GER-REE)

MARGOT A borrowing of the French pet form of Marguerite, a cognate of Margaret (pearl). *See* MARGARET. Margot is now commonly used as an independent given name. (MAR-GO)

MARIA Latinate form of Mary, which is popular throughout Europe and the Christian world, and which is usually bestowed in honor of the mother of Jesus. *See* MARY. (MAH-REE-AH)

MARIABELLA Compound name composed of the names Maria and Bella (beautiful). The name, coined in the 17th century, continues to be in use. *See* BELLA *and* MARIA. Var: Maribel, Marybelle. (MAH-REE-AH-BEL-LAH)

MARIAM Shortened form of Mariamne, an early form of Mary first recorded by the 1st-century Jewish historian Flavius Josephus as the name of the wife of King Herod. *See* MARY. (MARE-EE-UM)

MARIAN Variant of Marion, which is a French diminutive form of Marie, a cognate of Mary. *See* MARY. The name is borne in English legend by Maid Marian, sweetheart of the popular 12th-century Robin Hood, who robbed the rich to help the poor. (MARE-EE-UN)

MARIANNE Originated as an extended spelling of Marian, a variant of Marion, which is a French diminutive form of Marie, a cognate of Mary. It is now used as a hybrid, combining the two popular names Mary and Anne (gracious, full of grace). *See* ANNE *and* MARY. Var: Mariann, Marianna, Maryann, Maryanne, Maryanna. (MARE-EE-AN)

MARIE French form of Mary, which has been in common use in England since the Middle Ages. Marie is popularly bestowed as a middle name and it is also quite often used as an element in combination names such as Anne-Marie. *See* MARY. (MAH-REE)

MARIELLA Latin diminutive form of Maria, in common use throughout Europe and the British Isles. Var: Mariel, Mariele, Marielle. (MARE-EE-EL-LAH)

MARILEE Modern compound name composed of the names Mary and Lee (wood, clearing). *See* LEE *and* MARY. Var: Marylee. (MARE-IH-LEE)

MARILYN Modern compound name composed of the names Mary and Lynn (lake). *See* LYNN *and* MARY. Var: Maralyn, Marilynn, Marylin. (MARE-IH-LIN)

MARINA Of debated origin and meaning, some believe it to be derived from the Latin Marius (of Mars, the Roman mythological god of war). Others think Marina is derived from the Latin *marinus* (of the sea). The name is borne by Princess Marina of Greece, who became the wife of Prince George in 1934, leading to the name's current revival. (MAH-REE-NAH)

MARION French diminutive form of Marie, which has been in common use in England since the Middle Ages. *See* MARIE *or* MARY. Var: Marian. (MARE-EE-UN)

MARISA Modern elaboration of Maria, formed by adding the suffix *-isa, -issa,* as in such names as Louisa (light) and Clarissa (famous, bright). *See* MARIA. Var: Marissa. (MAR-REE-SAH)

MARLA Contracted form of Marlene, which is a Germanic contraction of Maria Magdalene. *See* MAGDALENE *and* MARIA. Marla has also been bestowed as a feminine form of Marlon. *See* MARLAND (American Male Names). (MAR-LAH)

MARLENE German contraction of Maria Magdalene. *See* MAGDALENE *and* MARIA. The name was made popular through its connection to actress Marlene Dietrich (1901–92). Var: Marleen, Marlena. Pet: Marlie. (MAR-LEEN)

MARTHA Derived from the Aramaic Mārthā (lady, mistress). The name is borne in the Bible by the sister of Lazarus and Mary of Bethany. (MAR-THA)

MARTINA Feminine form of Martin, from the Latin name Martīnus, which is derived from Mars, the name of the Roman mythological god of war. Martina, a common name throughout Europe, received a boost in popularity through the fame of tennis star Martina Navratilova (b. 1956). Var: Martine. (MAR-TEE-NAH)

MARY Anglicized form of Maria, which is derived from the Hebrew Miryām (sea of bitterness, sea of sorrow). There is much debate over the meaning of the name, however. While "sea of bitterness or sorrow" seems to be the most probable, some sources give the alternative definitions of "rebellion," "wished-for child," and "mistress or lady of the sea." The name, borne in the Bible by the virgin mother of Jesus, has become one of the most enduringly popular names in the Christian world. (MARE-EE)

MAUD Anglicized Norman contraction of Matilda (powerful in battle) in use since the Middle Ages. *See* MATILDA. The name received a boost in popularity in the 19th century from Tennyson's use of it in his poem "Maud" (1855). Var: Maude. (MAUD, MAHD)

MAURA Of Celtic origin perhaps derived from *mohr* (great). Alternatively, Maura is a feminine form of the Latin Maurus (dark-skinned), which is from the Greek *mauritius* (of Moorish lineage, dark-skinned). (MAUR-AH, MOR-AH)

MAUREEN Anglicized form of Máirín, a pet form of Máire, which is the Irish cognate of Mary. *See* MARY. The name is common throughout the English-speaking world. Var: Maurene, Maurine. (MAUR-EEN, MOR-EEN)

MAVIS First used in the late 19th century, this name is taken from *mavis*, which denotes a small bird, the "song thrush." Short: Mave. (MAY-VIS)

MAXIE Originally a short form of Maxine (greatest), Maxie is occasionally bestowed as an independent given name. Var: Maxi. Short: Max. (MAX-EE)

MAXINE Modern feminine form of Max, a short form of Maximilian, which is a compound name composed from the Latin names Maximus (greatest) and Aemiliānus. *See* MAXIMILIAN (Male Names). Short: Max, Maxi, Maxie. (MAX-EEN)

MAY Originally used as a pet form of Mary and Margaret (pearl). *See* MARGARET *and* MARY. More recently, however, it is usually associated with the name of the month, which is derived from the Latin *Maius* (the month of Maia, the Greek mythological goddess of increase). May is often bestowed as a middle name, or used as a name element in combination names such as Anna-Mae or May-Lynn. The name was borne by the popular U.S. actress Mae West (1892–1980). Her shapely bustline led to her name being used for an inflatable life preserver vest for use by RAF aviators downed at sea during World War II. Var: Mae. (MAY)

MEGAN Pet form of the Marged, the Welsh cognate of Margaret (a pearl). *See* MARGARET. Var: Meagan, Meagen, Meggyn, Meghan. Pet: Meggie. (MEH-GAN, MEE-GAN)

MELANIE Derived from the Greek Melaina, which is from the root *melas* (black, dark). The name was made popular through its association with two 5th-century Roman saints, a grandmother and granddaughter remembered for their piety and good works for the poor. Var: Melany, Melony. Short: Mel. (MEL-AH-NEE)

MELINDA Modern coinage combining the name element *Mel* with the productive suffix *-inda*. *See* MEL. Alternatively, some believe Melinda is an elaboration of Linda (beautiful). *See* LINDA. Short: Mel. (MEH-LIN-DAH)

MELISSA Derived from the Greek *melissa* (a bee). The 16th century Italian poet Ariosto used the name for the good fairy who protected Bradamante and helped Ruggero escape from Atlante upon the hippogriff in the poem *Orlando Furioso*. Short: Lissa, Mel. (MEH-LIS-AH)

MELODY Taken directly from *melody* (melody, song), from the Greek *melōidia,* which is derived from the elements *melos* (song) and *aeidein* (to sing). Short: Mel. (MEL-O-DEE)

MERCY Taken from *mercy* (compassion, forgiveness, pity), which is derived from the Latin *merces* (payment, reward). The name was popular among the Puritans in the 16th and 17th centuries but is now less common. Var: Mercia. (MER-SEE)

MEREDITH Of debated meaning, some believe it to be derived from the Welsh elements *môr* (sea) and *differaf* (I protect): hence, "sea protector" or "protector of the sea." Others believe it is from the Welsh Maredudd, an obsolete name of which the second element is *idudd* (lord). Meredith originated as a surname, then was bestowed as a personal name upon male children. It is now more commonly used as a female name. (MARE-EH-DITH)

MERLA Feminine form of Merlin, a cognate of the Welsh Myrrdin, which is derived from the Celtic elements *mori* (sea) and *dunom* (hill, fortress): hence, "sea hill" or "fortress by the sea." *See* MERLIN (Male Names). Short: Merl. (MER-LAH)

MERLE From the French *merle* (blackbird), one of a small group of names derived from the names of birds. Var: Murle. Short: Merl. (MERL)

MERRIELLE Elaboration of Merry (cheerful, happy), formed by adding the feminine diminutive suffix *-elle*. *See* MERRY. Short: Merry. (MARE-REE-EL)

MERRY Taken from *merry* (cheerful, happy, lighthearted), which is derived from the Middle English *mery*. Merry was a popular name in the 19th century, no doubt due to its pleasant associations. Var: Meri, Merrie. (MARE-REE)

MERYL Modern feminine variant of Merrill, a name that originated as a surname derived from Muriel (bright sea). *See* MURIEL. The name's boost in popularity is perhaps due to the fame of actress Meryl Streep (b. 1949). Var: Meryle, Merryl. (MARE-IL)

MICHELLE French feminine form of Michael, which is derived from the Hebrew *mīkhā'ēl* (who is like God?). Michelle is in popular use throughout the English-speaking world. Short: Chelle, Shell. (MIH-SHEL)

MICKI Feminine form of Mick, a shortened form of Michael, which is derived from the Hebrew *mīkhā'ēl* (who is like God?). Var: Mickie, Mikki, Mikkie. (MIH-KEE)

MILDRED Derived from Mildðryð, Mildthryth, an obsolete Old English name composed of the elements *milde* (gentle, mild, generous) and *ðryð*, *thryth* (strength): hence, "gentle strength." The name was borne by a 7th-century saint and abbess, Mildthryth (d. 700), a daughter of a king of Mercia who, along with her sister St. Mildburh, was venerated during the Middle Ages for her acts of charity. Short: Mil. Pet: Millie, Milly. (MIL-DRED)

MILLICENT Derived from the obsolete Old High German Amalaswinth, a compound name composed of the elements *amal* (work) and *swinth* (strength). The name was brought to England by the Normans in the French forms Melisent and Melisende. Short: Mil. Pet: Millie, Milly. (MIL-LIH-SENT)

MIRABELLE Derived from the Latin *mīrābilis* (of great beauty, lovely). The name was common to both males and females in the later Middle Ages but is now exclusively a female name. Alternatively, the name coincides with that of a variety of European plum tree and the brandy that is made from the fruit. Accordingly, the name may be bestowed because of this association. (MIR-AH-BEL)

MIRANDA Coined by Shakespeare for the heroine of his play *The Tempest*. The name is derived from the Latin *mirandus* (wonderful, to be admired). Var: Marenda, Meranda. Short: Randa. Pet: Randi, Randie. (MER-AN-DAH)

MISTY Modern coinage from *misty* (misty, foggy). The name was quite popular in the 1960s and 1970s. Var: Misti, Mistie. (MIS-TEE)

MOIRA Anglicized form of Máire, the Irish cognate of Mary. *See* MARY. Moira, now common throughout Great Britain and Australia, is the form usually reserved in Scotland to indicate the Virgin Mary. Var: Moyra. (MOY-RAH)

MOLLY Originally a pet form of Mary, Molly is now bestowed as an independent given name in its own right. Var: Mollie. (MOL-LEE)

MONA Anglicized form of the Irish Muadhnait, a diminutive form of *muadh* (noble). Mona is now in common use in England. (MO-NAH)

MONICA Ancient yet still popular name of uncertain etymology. Monica was the name of the mother of St. Augustine, who was born in Numidia, an ancient country in northern Africa. Thus, the name might be of African origin. However, Monica is said to have been a citizen of Carthage, a city founded by the Phoenicians, so her name might be of Phoenician origin. Alternatively, some believe it to be from the Latin *moneo* (to advise). (MO-NEE-KAH, MAH-NEE-KAH)

MURIEL Anglicized form of the Irish Muirgheal and the Scottish Muireall, names composed from the Old

Celtic elements *muir* (sea) and *geal* (bright). Var: Meriel, Miriel, Murial. (MYOOR-EE-UL)

MYRA Coined by the poet Fulke Greville (1554–1628) for use in his love poems. Some believe it to be a variant of the Irish Moyra; an anagram of Mary; a borrowing of the name of a seaport in ancient Lycia; or from the Latin *myrrha* (myrrh). (MĪ-RAH)

MYRNA Anglicized form of the Irish Muirne (affection, beloved). *See* MUIRNE (Irish Names). Myrna is now in common use throughout the English-speaking world. Var: Morna. (MER-NAH)

NAN Originally a pet form or an anagram of Ann (gracious, full of grace). Nan is now generally used as a short form of Nancy, which also originated as a pet form of Nan but which is now regarded as an independent given name. *See* ANNA *and* NANCY. Var: Nana, Nanna. (NAN)

NANCY Originated as a pet form of Nan, which was originally a pet form of Ann (gracious, full of grace). *See* ANNA. Now, however, Nancy is regarded as an independent given name, with Nan as its short form. Short: Nan. (NAN-SEE)

NANETTE Diminutive form of Nan, a pet form of Ann and Nancy (gracious, full of grace). *See* ANNA *and* NANCY. Var: Nannette. (NAN-ET)

NATALIE From the Latin Natalia, a name derived from *diēs nātālis* (natal day, Christmas), which was originally given to children born on Christmas Day. Natalie and its variant forms are popular throughout Europe. (NAT-AH-LEE)

NERISSA Coined by Shakespeare for Portia's lady-in-waiting in the play *The Merchant of Venice*. Nerissa is believed to be from the Latin *nereis* (sea snail). Var: Nerisa. (NER-ISS-SAH)

NICOLE Borrowed from the French, Nicole is a feminine form of Nicolas, which is from the Greek Nikolaos, a compound name composed of the elements *nikē* (victory) and *laos* (the people): hence, "victory of the people." Var: Nicola. Pet: Nicolette, Nicki, Nikki. (NIH-KOLE)

NICOLETTE Originally a pet form of Nicole (victory of the people), Nicolette is now commonly bestowed as an independent given name. *See* NICOLE. Pet: Nicki, Nikki. (NIH-KO-LET)

NINA A borrowing of the Russian diminutive form of Anne (gracious, full of grace) and Antonia, Nina has been in use in England since the middle of the 19th century. *See* ANNE *and* ANTONIA. Var: Nena. (NEE-NAH)

NOEL A borrowing from the French, Noel is from *noël* (Christmas), which is derived from the Latin *nātālis* (natal). The name is commonly bestowed upon children born during the Christmas season. (NO-EL)

NONIE Originally a pet form of Ione and Nora (light), Nonie is also bestowed as an independent given name. *See* IONE *and* NORA. Var: Noni. (NO-NEE)

NORA Short form of any of the various names containing the element *-nora,* such as Eleanora, the name is also commonly bestowed as an independent given name. Var: Norah. Pet: Nonie, Norie. (NOR-AH)

NOREEN A borrowing from the Irish, Noreen is a diminutive form of Nora, which is a short form of any of the various names containing the element *-nora.* Var: Norene, Norina, Norine. Pet: Norie. (NOR-EEN)

NORMA Feminine form of Norman, from the Old High German Nordemann, which is composed of the elements *nord* (north) and *mann* (man): hence, "northman, man from the north." Alternatively, some believe Norma is derived from the Latin *norma* (normal, standard). (NOR-MAH)

OCTAVIA Cognate of the Italian Ottavia, a feminine form of Octavius, which is derived from the Latin *octavus* (eighth). Octavia was the name of the wife (d. 11 B.C.) of Mark Antony. (OK-TAY-VEE-AH)

OLIVE Evolution of the older and now unused Oliva, which was taken from the Latin *oliva* (a tree of the olive family). A branch from the olive tree has long been regarded as a symbol of peace. Pet: Livvi. (O-LIV, AH-LIV)

OLIVIA Elaboration of Olive (olive tree). *See* OLIVE. Olivia was used by Shakespeare as the name of the heiress in the play *Twelfth Night*. Short: Livia. Pet: Livvi. (O-LIV-EE-AH, AH-LIV-EE-AH)

OPAL Taken from *opal* (a semiprecious gemstone which reflects light in a dazzling display of colors), which is ultimately derived from the Sanskrit *upala* (precious stone, jewel). (O-PL)

OPHELIA Believed to have been coined by Sannazzaro in 1504 for the name of a character in his pastoral *Arcadia*. He is thought to have taken it from the Greek *ōphelia* (help, succor). The use of Ophelia in the English language seems to be a result of its being used for the name of Polonius' daughter, who was in love with Hamlet in Shakespeare's *Hamlet*. (O-FEE-LEE-AH)

ORIANA Of uncertain derivation and meaning, Oriana seems to have first been used as the name of a character in the medieval French romance *Amadis de Gaul*. Some believe Oriana to have been derived from the Latin *oriri* (to rise) or from the Old French *or* (gold). 16th-century madrigal poets applied the name to Queen Elizabeth, thus promoting its use in England. Var: Orianna. (OR-EE-AN-NAH)

Oriel Of debated etymology, some believe it to be derived from the Latin Aurēlius (golden). *See* AURELIA. Others think it is a borrowing of the name of Oriel College, which was taken from *oriel* (a bay window). (OR-EE-EL)

Pamela Coined by the English poet and statesman Sir Philip Sidney (1554–86) for the name of a character in his pastoral *Arcadia*. It seems to have been pure invention, for there are no other similar names on which it could have been based. The name was originally pronounced *pam-EE-lah*, and in the 18th century, *pah-MEL-lah*. It was not until the 20th century that the pronunciation evolved to *PAM-eh-lah* and the name became common. Var: Pamelia. Short: Pam. Pet: Pami, Pammi, Pammie, Pammy. (PAM-EH-LAH)

Patience Taken from *patience* (waiting without complaint, forbearance, calm endurance), which is derived from the Latin *pati* (to suffer). The name became popular among the Puritans and, though now less common, continues to be used. (PAY-SHENTZ)

Patricia Feminine form of Patrick, which is from the Latin *patricius* (a patrician, a noble aristocrat). The name became popular after its association with Princess Victoria Patricia Helena Elizabeth (b. 1886), who was known as Princess Patricia. Short: Pat, Tricia, Trisha. Pet: Patsy, Patti, Pattie, Patty. (PAH-TRISH-AH)

Paula Feminine form of Paul, which is derived from Paulus, a name originating as a Roman surname from the Latin *paulus* (small). (PAUL-AH, PAHL-AH)

Pauline A borrowing of the French feminine form of Paul, which is derived from Paulus, a Roman surname taken from the Latin *paulus* (small). (PAUL-EEN, PAHL-EEN)

Pearl Taken from *pearl*, the name of a type of gem which is found in certain mollusks and prized for its perfection. (PERL)

Peggy Modeled after Meggie, Peggy was originally a pet form of Margaret (pearl). It is now occasionally bestowed as an independent given name. *See* MARGARET. Short: Peg. (PEG-EE)

Penelope Derived from the Greek Pēnelopē, a name borne in Greek mythology by Odysseus' wife, who, for twenty years, patiently awaited his return. The etymology of the name is debated. Some believe it is derived from the Greek *penelops* (a kind of duck), since Penelope was said to have been exposed to die as an infant and was fed and protected by a duck. Others think it might be derived from *pēnē* (thread on a bobbin) and give it the definition "weaver, worker of the loom," for Penelope spent her evenings weaving and unweaving while she waited for her husband to return. Pet: Pennie, Penny. (PEN-EL-O-PEE)

Petra Feminine form of Peter, from the Late Latin Petrus, which is derived from *petros* (a stone) or *petra* (a rock). *See* PETER (Male Names). Short: Pet. (PET-RAH)

Petula Modern English coinage of uncertain derivation and meaning. Some believe it to be an elaboration of Pet, which is a short form of Petra as well as a term of endearment. Others believe it to be a fanciful invention based on the flower names petunia and tulip. The name is most notably borne by singer Petula Clark (b. 1932). (PEH-TYOO-LAH)

Philippa Feminine form of Philip, from the Greek Philippos, a name derived from the elements *philos* (loving) and *hippos* (horse): hence, "lover of horses." Philip was bestowed upon both male and female children until the 19th century, when Philippa became the standard feminine form. Var: Philipa, Phillipa, Phillippa. Short: Phil. Pet: Pippa, Pippi. (FIL-LIH-PAH)

Philomena Derived from the Greek Philomenēs (lover of strength), a name composed of the elements *philein* (to love) and *menos* (strength). The name Philomena was borne by a young 3rd-century Italian martyr whose bones were found in the catacomb of Priscilla in Rome in 1802. A cult rose up around her in the 19th century, but 20th-century scholars decided the remains were not those of the Philomena in the inscription, and technology found no evidence she was martyred. In 1961 her feast day was discontinued and her shrine dismantled. Short: Phil. (FIL-O-MEE-NAH)

Phoebe Feminine form of the Greek Phoibos (bright one), which is derived from *phoibos* (bright). Phoebe is found in Greek mythology as a name for Artemis, the goddess of the moon. In poetry, Phoebe is the moon personified. Var: Phebe. (FEE-BEE)

Phyllis A borrowing from the Greek, Phyllis is derived from *phyllon* (a leaf). The name is borne in Greek mythology by a girl who hanged herself for love and was transformed into an almond tree. Var: Phillis, Phylis. Short: Phil, Phyl. (FIL-ISS)

Pippa Originally a pet form of Philippa (lover of horses), Pippa is now in common use as an independent given name. *See* PHILIPPA. (PIP-AH)

Polly Variant of Molly, which is a pet form of Mary. *See* MARY. It is unclear how or why the changing of the M to a *P* came about, as it is with Meggy and Peggy. Some believe it to have been a simple case of Polly evolving as a rhyming variant. (POL-LEE)

Portia From the Latin Porcia, a feminine form of Porcius, an old Roman family name probably derived from *porcus* (a pig, a hog). The name Portia was borne by the heroine in Shakespeare's *The Merchant of Venice*. (POR-SHA)

Priscilla Diminutive form of the Latin Prisca, a feminine form of Priscus, which is a Roman surname derived from *priscus* (ancient, primitive). The name, popular among the 17th-century Puritans, is now most famously borne by actress Priscilla Presley. Short: Prisca. Pet: Prissy. (PRIH-SIL-AH)

Quanda Derived from the Old English *cwēn* (queen). (KWAN-DAH)

Queenie Derived from the Old English *cwēn* (queen), Queenie originated as an affectionate nickname for a child. It was not until the 19th century that its use as a given name began. Var: Queena. (KWEEN-EE)

Quenby Derived from the Old English *cwēn* (queen) and *bu, by* (settlement): hence, "queen's settlement." (KWEN-BEE)

Quilla Derived from the Middle English *quil* (quill, hollow stalk). (KWIL-LAH)

Quinn Transferred use of the surname derived from the Old English *cwēn* (queen). (KWIN)

Rachel From the Ecclesiastic Late Latin and the Ecclesiastic Greek Rāchēl, which is derived from the Hebrew *rāchēl* (ewe). The name is borne in the Bible by the younger of the two wives of Jacob, the mother of his sons, Joseph and Benjamin. Var: Rachael, Rachelle. Pet: Rae. (RAY-CHEL)

Rachelle Modern elaboration of Rachel (ewe), commonly thought to be French, but actually of English origin. *See* RACHEL. (RAH-SHEL)

Rae Feminine form of Ray, which is a short form of Raymond (wise protection). *See* RAYMOND (Male Names). Rae is also used as a short form of Rachel and as a name element in combination names such as Rae Ann. (RAY)

Raine Transferred use of the surname derived from the French *reine* (queen). The name is borne by Countess Raine Spencer, stepmother of the princess of Wales. (RANE)

Randi Feminine form of Randolph (wolf shield), a name of Germanic origin. *See* RANDOLF (Male Names). Randi is also used as a short form of Miranda (wonderful, to be admired). *See* MIRANDA. Var: Randie. (RAN-DEE)

Reanna Modern coinage that is possibly based on the Welsh Rhiannon (great queen) or is an altered form of Deanna (divine). *See* RHIANNON (Welsh Names) *and* DEANNA. Var: Reanne, Rheanna, Rheanne. (REE-AN-NAH)

Rebecca From the Ecclesiastic Late Latin and Ecclesiastic Greek Rhebekka, which is derived from the Hebrew *ribbqāh* (noose), from *rabak* (to bind, to tie). The name, borne in the Bible by the wife of Isaac, was not used in England until after the Reformation in the 16th century. Var: Rebekah. Short: Becca. Pet: Becky. (REH-BEH-KAH)

Regina A borrowing of the Latin Regina (queen), a feminine form of Rex (king), which has been in use since the Middle Ages. (REH-JEE-NAH, REH-JĪ-NAH)

Rexanne Compound name composed of the names Rex (king) and Anne (gracious, full of grace). *See* ANNE *and* REX (Male Names). Var: Rexana, Rexanna. (REX-AN)

Rexella Compound name composed of the names Rex (king) and Ella (light; foreign). *See* ELLA *and* REX (Male Names). Var: Rexelle. (REX-EL-LAH)

Rhoda From the Latin Rhode and the Greek Rhodē, which are derived from the Greek *rhodon* (a rose). (RO-DAH)

Rhonda Popular modern coinage believed to be derived from the Welsh elements *rhon* (lance) and *da* (good). Rhonda is common throughout the English-speaking world. (RON-DAH)

Rikki Feminine form of Ricky, which is a pet form of Richard (strong king). *See* RICHARD (Male Names). (RIH-KEE)

Rita A short form of the Spanish Margarita (pearl) or the Italian Margherita (pearl), Rita is commonly bestowed as an independent given name in the English-speaking world. *See* MARGARET. (REE-TAH)

Roberta Feminine form of Robert (bright fame), a French name brought to England by the Normans. *See* ROBERT (Male Names). Pet: Bobbie. (RO-BER-TAH)

Robin Originated as a pet form of the male name Robert (bright fame). *See* ROBERT. Now, however, Robin is commonly bestowed as a female name, usually in reference to the bird of the same name. Var: Robina, Robyn. (RO-BIN, RAH-BIN)

Rona Of uncertain derivation. Rona might be a feminine form of Ronald (wise ruler, powerful ruler) or a borrowing of the name of a Hebridean island. Rona is believed to have been coined in Scotland in the late 19th century. Var: Rhona. (RO-NAH)

Rosalie From the Latin *rosalia* (the annual ceremony of hanging garlands of roses on tombs), which is derived from *rosa* (rose). Rosalie was introduced to England from France in the 19th century. Pet: Rosie. (ROZ-AH-LEE)

Rosalind Introduced to England by the Normans, Rosalind is of Germanic origin. It is a derivative of the Old High German Roslindis, a compound name composed of the elements *hros* (horse) or *hrôs* (fame) and *lind* (gentle, tender, soft). The name was introduced to Spain by the Goths, where it evolved to Rosalinda. Consequently, folk etymology now attributes the name as being derived from the Spanish elements *rosa* (rose) and *linda* (beautiful). Var: Rosaleen, Rosalin, Rosalyn, Rosalynn, Roslyn, Roslynn. Short: Ros, Roz. Pet: Rosie. (ROZ-AH-LIN)

Rose Originally, Rose was a short form of any of the old Germanic names in use in England in the Middle Ages that contained the element *hros, ros* (horse). Flower names began being used in the 19th century, and now Rose is bestowed with reference to the flower. Pet: Rosie. (ROZE)

Roseanne Combination name formed from the names Rose (horse; rose) and Anne (gracious, full of grace). *See* ANNE *and* ROSE. Var: Rosanna, Rosanne, Roseann, Roseanna, Rozanne. Pet: Rosie. (ROZE-AN)

Roselle Elaboration of Rose (horse; rose), formed by the addition of the French feminine diminutive suffix *-elle*. *See* ROSE. Pet: Rosie. (RO-ZEL)

Rosemary Combination of the names Rose (horse; rose) and Mary. *See* MARY *and* ROSE. The name became popular at a time when flower names were coming into use, and it might therefore have originated as a borrowing of the name of the herb rosemary, which is derived from the Latin *ros marīnus* (dew of the sea). Pet: Rosie. (ROZ-MARE-EE)

Rowena Of uncertain origin and meaning, Rowena is thought to be derived from the obsolete Old English Hrōðwyn, Hrothwina, a compound name composed of the elements *hrōð, hroth* (fame) and *wine* (friend) or *wynn* (bliss, joy): hence, "famous friend" or "joyful fame." Alternatively, it might be a derivative of the Cymric Rhonwen, which is composed from the elements *rhon* (spear, lance) and *gwen, gwyn* (white, fair, blessed): hence, "white spear, blessed spear." Pet: Winnie. (RO-WEE-NAH)

Roxane From the Greek Roxanē, which is believed to be derived from the Persian Roschana (dawn of day). The name was borne by the Bactrian wife of Alexander the Great, which seems to substantiate the name's roots. Var: Roxanna, Roxanne. Pet: Roxie. (ROX-AN)

Ruby Taken from the name of the deep red gem. Ruby is derived from the Latin *rubeus* (reddish) via the Old French *rubi*. (ROO-BEE)

Ruth Of uncertain etymology, most believe Ruth to be derived from the Hebrew *rūth*, a possible contraction of *rē'ūth* (companion, friend). The name is borne in the Bible by a Moabite woman who was devoted to her mother-in-law. Her story is told in the Book of Ruth. (ROOTH)

Sabella Modern variant of Isabella (God is my oath). *See* ISABELLE. Short: Belle. (SAH-BEL-LAH)

Sabrina Of uncertain etymology, Sabrina is believed to be of Celtic origin, as it is borne in Celtic mythology by an illegitimate daughter of the Welsh King Locrine. The child was ordered drowned by the king's wife, Gwendolen, thus giving her name to the river in which the foul deed took place. Latin writings of the 1st century list the river's name as Sabrina, but it is now known as the Severn. (SAH-BREE-NAH)

Sally Originated as a pet form of Sarah (princess), but it is now bestowed as an independent given name. *See* SARAH. Short: Sal. (SAL-LEE)

Sandra A short form of Cassandra and Alexandra (defender or helper of mankind), Sandra is now commonly bestowed as an independent given name. *See* ALEXANDRA *and* CASSANDRA. Var: Sondra. Pet: Sandie. (SAN-DRAH)

Sarah Derived from the Hebrew *sārāh* (princess). The name is borne in the Bible by the wife of the patriarch Abraham and mother of Isaac. Sarah, a common Jewish name, was rarely used in England before the 16th-century Reformation. Var: Sara. Pet: Sally. (SARE-UH)

Sasha A borrowing of the Russian pet form of Alexandra (defender or helper of mankind), Sasha has been bestowed as an independent given name in England since it was introduced from France in the 20th century. *See* ALEXANDRA. (SAH-SHA)

Selda Derived from the Old English *selda* (companion). Alternatively, it is used as a variant spelling of Zelda, a Yiddish form of the German Salida (happiness, joy). *See* SALIDA (German Names). Var: Selde. (SEL-DAH)

SELENE From the Greek Selēnē, which is derived from *selēnē* (the moon). The name was borne by the Greek mythological goddess of the moon. Var: Selena, Selina. (SEH-LEEN)

SERAPHINA Derived from the Hebrew *sĕrāphīm* (burning ones), a name used in the Bible for the heavenly, winged angels surrounding the throne of God. Var: Serafina, Seraphine. Short: Fina. (SARE-AH-FEE-NAH)

SERENA Derived from *serene* (calm, peaceful, tranquil), which is from the Latin *serenus* (clear, calm, exalted). The name has been in use since the 13th century. (SEH-REE-NAH)

SHANEE Anglicized form of the Welsh Siani, which is a cognate of Jane (God is gracious). *See* JANE. (SHAN-EE)

SHANNAH Short form of the Hebrew Shoshannah, which is derived from *shoshan* (lily, rose). Var: Shanna, Shonna, Shonnah. (SHAN-NAH)

SHARON Derived from a biblical place-name meaning "a plain, a flat area." In biblical times, Sharon was a fertile, coastal plain in Palestine, extending from Mount Carmel to Jaffa, where roses and oak trees grew in abundance. Though the name was used by English Puritans, it wasn't until the middle of the 20th century that it became common. Var: Sharona, Sharron. (SHARE-UN)

SHEENA Anglicized form of Sìne, the Scottish Gaelic cognate of Jane (God is gracious). *See* JANE. (SHE-NAH)

SHEILA Anglicized form of Síle, the Irish Gaelic cognate of Cecilia (blind). *See* CECILIA. Var: Sheela, Shilla. (SHE-LAH)

SHELLEY Transferred use of the surname derived from Old English components meaning "clearing on or near a slope." Shelley was originally bestowed upon both male and female children. Now, however, it is exclusively a female name. Var: Shellie, Shelli, Shelly. Short: Shell. (SHEL-EE)

SHERRY From the name of the fortified Spanish wine, which takes its name from the city of Jerez (formerly Xeres). Alternatively, Sherry may be a reworking of the French *chérie* (darling). Var: Sherrie. (SHARE-EE)

SHIREEN A derivative of the Muslim Shirin, a name derived from the Persian *shirīn* (sweet, charming). (SHIR-EEN)

SHIRLEY Transferred use of the surname originating from the English place-name Shirley, which is derived from the Old English elements *scire* (shire) or *scīr* (bright, clear) and *lēah* (wood, clearing, meadow, enclosure). The name makes reference to the open space where the moot (an early English assembly of freemen which met to administer justice and discuss community issues) was held. Shirley was originally a male name, but its use in Charlotte Brontë's novel *Shirley* (1849) established it as a female name. Var: Sherley. Short: Shirl. (SHIR-LEE)

SIBYL Derived from the Latin and Greek Sibylla (a fortune-teller, prophetess). The sibyls, women of ancient Greece and Rome, were mouthpieces of the ancient oracles and seers into the future. In the Middle Ages, they were believed to be receptors of divine revelation; thus Sibyl came into use as a given name. Var: Sibylla, Sybil, Sybilla. (SIH-BL)

SILVER Taken from the name of the precious metal, which is derived from the Middle English *selver* and the Old English *seolfer*. (SIL-VER)

SILVIA Feminine form of Silvius (of the woods), a name derived from the Latin *silva* (wood). The name is borne in Roman mythology by Rhea Silvia, a vestal virgin who broke her vows and became the mother of Romulus and Remus. Var: Sylvia. (SIL-VEE-AH)

SLOAN Transferred use of the surname, an Anglicized form of the Irish Gaelic O'Sluagháin, which is derived from *sluagh* (a multitude of people, warriors). In England, Sloan is bestowed upon both male and female children. Var: Sloane. (SLONE)

SONYA Russian pet form of Sofya (wisdom) in common use in England since the 1920s. *See* SOPHIA. Var: Sonia, Sonja. (SONE-YAH, SON-YAH)

SOPHIA A borrowing from the Greek, Sophia is directly derived from *sophia* (wisdom, skill). The name has been in common use in England since the 17th century, when it was bestowed upon the infant daughter of James I. Currently, the fame of Italian actress Sophia Loren (b. 1934) has helped keep the name popular throughout Europe and Great Britain. Var: Sophie, Sophy. (SO-FEE-AH)

SORREL Modern coinage taken from the name of the plant also known as wood sorrel. The word is derived from the Middle English *sorel,* which is from the Old High German *sur* (sour) via the French *surele*. Var: Sorel, Sorell, Sorrell. (SOR-EL)

STACEY Derived from Stasia, a Russian pet form of Anastasia (resurrection). Stacey, believed to have originated in Ireland, is now common throughout the English-speaking world and is bestowed upon both male and female children. Var: Staci, Stacie, Stacy. (STAY-SEE)

STELLA A borrowing from the Latin, Stella is derived directly from *stella* (star). There is evidence that the name was used in England as far back as 1374, but it wasn't until the 16th century when Sir Philip Sidney used the name in his sonnets "Astrophel to Stella" that the name became commonly known. Stella is also used as a short form of Estelle. *See* ESTELLE. (STEL-LAH)

STEPHANIE A borrowing of the French Stéphanie, a cognate of the Latin Stephania, which is a variant of Stephana. Stephana is a feminine form of Stephanos, which is derived from the Greek *stephanos* (a crown, garland). Var: Steffany. Short: Steff, Steph. Pet: Steffi, Stevie. (STEH-FAN-EE)

SUSAN Anglicized form of the French Susanne, a cognate of the Ecclesiastic Late Latin Susanna (lily, rose). *See* SUSANNAH. Var: Suzan. Short: Sue. Pet: Susie, Suzie, Suzy. (SOO-ZAN)

SUSANNAH Derived from the Hebrew Shoshana, which is from *shōshannāh* (lily, rose). The name is borne in the Bible by a woman falsely accused of adultery. Her story is told in the apocryphal book of Susannah and the Elders. Var: Susanna, Susanne, Suzanna, Suzannah, Suzanne. Short: Sue. Pet: Susie, Suzie, Suzy. (SOO-ZAN-NAH)

TABITHA From the Ecclesiastic Greek Tabeitha, which is derived from the Aramaic *tabhītha* (roe, gazelle). The name is borne in the Bible by a woman who was brought back to life by St. Peter. (TAB-IH-THA)

TAMARA In common use throughout the English-speaking world, Tamara is a Russian cognate of the Hebrew Tamar (date palm, palm tree). Tamar is borne in the Bible by the daughter-in-law of Judah and mother of his twin sons, and by King David's daughter who was raped by Amnon, her half brother. Var: Tamra. Short: Tam. Pet: Tami, Tammie, Tammy. (TAM-AH-RAH, TAH-MARE-AH)

TAMSIN Contraction of Thomasina, a feminine form of Thomas (a twin), which is derived, via the Ecclesiastic Greek and Late Latin, from the Aramaic *tĕ'ōma* (a twin). *See* THOMASINA. Var: Tamzine. Short: Tam. Pet: Tami, Tammie, Tammy. (TAM-ZIN)

TANYA Originally a Russian pet form of Tatiana, which is of uncertain etymology, Tanya is in common use in the English-speaking world as an independent given name. *See* TATIANA (Russian Names). (TAN-YAH, TOHN-YAH)

TARA Transferred use of an Irish place-name belonging to a hill in central Ireland which was an ancient seat of kingship. Tara (hill) was used by Margaret Mitchell for the name of a plantation in her epic *Gone with the Wind*, resulting in the use of it as a female given name. (TAR-AH, TARE-AH)

TAWNY Taken from *tawny* (tan, brownish yellow), which is derived from the Old French *tanné* (tanned) via the Middle English *tauny*. The word denotes a soft, brownish-yellow or tan color. Var: Tawney. (TAWN-EE)

TEAL Taken from the name of the small, freshwater wild duck. The word is derived from the Middle English *tele*, which is akin to the Dutch *taling* (teal) and the Middle Low German *telink* (teal). Var: Teale. (TEEL)

TERRYL Modern elaboration of Terri. *See* TERRI. (TARE-IL)

TESSA Originally a pet form of Theresa, Tessa is now commonly bestowed as an independent given name. Short: Tess. (TEH-SAH)

THEA Short form of Theodora (God's gift), Thea is also used as an independent given name. *See* THEODORA. (THEE-AH)

THELMA Invention of author Marie Corelli for the name of the Norwegian heroine in her novel *Thelma* (1887). (THEL-MAH)

THEODORA Derived from the Greek Theodōra (God's gift), a compound name composed of the elements *theos* (God) and *dōron* (gift). The name was first used in England in the 17th century. Short: Dora, Thea. Pet: Dori, Dorie, Dory. (THEE-AH-DOR-AH)

THERESA Of uncertain etymology, Theresa is generally believed to be derived from the Greek *therizein* (to reap, to gather in). The first known bearer of the name was the Spanish wife of St. Paulinus, a 5th-century Roman bishop of Nola. Theresa was not used outside the Iberian Peninsula until the 16th century, when the fame of St. Teresa of Avila (1515–82) made the name popular among Roman Catholics throughout Europe. Var: Teresa, Treeza. Pet: Terri, Terrie, Tess, Tessa, Tracy. (TEH-REE-SAH)

THOMASINA Feminine form of Thomas, which is derived from the Aramaic *tĕ'ōma* (a twin). Var: Thomasine. (TOH-MAH-SEE-NAH, TAH-MAH-SEE-NAH)

TIA Short form of Letitia (gladness, happiness) or any of the various names ending in the element *-tia*. (TEE-AH)

TIFFANY Transferred use of the surname derived from the Old French Tifaine (Epiphany), which is from the

Ecclesiastic Late Latin Theophania (Epiphany, manifestation of God). (TIF-AH-NEE)

TINA Short form of Christina (a Christian), Tina is commonly bestowed as a given name in its own right. *See* CHRISTINE. (TEE-NAH)

TONI Originally a pet form of Antonia, a name of uncertain etymology. Alternatively, it may be used as a feminine spelling of Tony, a short form of Anthony. *See* ANTONIA. Var: Tonia, Tonie. (TŌ-NEE)

TRACY Transferred use of the surname derived from Tracy-Bocage or Tracy-sur-Mer, Norman baronial names from Calvados meaning "place of Thracius." Tracy, originally bestowed as a given name upon male children, is now predominantly a female name, perhaps since it is also used as a pet form of Theresa (harvester). *See* THERESA. Var: Tracey, Traci, Tracie. (TRAY-SEE)

TRICIA Short form of Patricia (a patrician), Tricia is now commonly bestowed as an independent given name. *See* PATRICIA. Var: Trisha. (TRISH-AH)

TRINA Originally a short form of Katrina (pure, unsullied), Trina is occasionally bestowed independently. Var: Treena. (TREE-NAH)

TRUDIE Originally a pet form of Gertrude (spear maiden), Trudy is now commonly bestowed as an independent given name. *See* GERTRUDE. Var: Trudy. (TROO-DEE)

UNITY Derived from *unity* (oneness, harmony, united), which is derived from the Latin *unitas* (oneness). Unity became popular in the 17th century, when names denoting moral or positive qualities came into vogue. (YOO-NIH-TEE)

URANIA From the Greek Ourania (the heavenly one), which is derived from *ouranos* (the sky, heaven). In Greek mythology, Urania was the Muse of astronomy. The use of the name in England seems to stem from16th-century poet Sir Philip Sidney's use of it in his poems addressed to "Urania." (YOOR-ANE-EE-AH)

URBANA Derived from the Latin Urbānus (from the city, city dweller), Urbana is a feminine form of Urban. Var: Urbanna. (UR-BAH-NAH)

URSULA A borrowing from Middle Latin, Ursula is a diminutive of the Latin *ursa* (she-bear). The name was borne by a legendary 4th-century saint, a Christian British princess said to have been martyred along with eleven thousand virgins by the Huns at Cologne. The story was very popular in the Middle Ages, which helped establish the name throughout England and Europe. Var: Ursala. (UR-SUH-LAH)

VALDA Modern elaboration of Val, a short form of Valerie (strong, healthy) and any of the other names that begin with the element *Val-*. Short: Val. (VAL-DAH)

VALERIE Imported from France in the 19th century, Valerie is from the Latin Valerius, an old Roman family name derived from *valere* (to be strong, healthy). Var: Valeria. Short: Val. (VAL-EH-REE)

VALETTA 20th-century elaboration of Val, formed by the addition of the feminine diminutive suffix *-etta*. *See* VAL. (VAH-LEH-TAH)

VANESSA An invention of satirist Jonathan Swift (1667–1745), Vanessa is a partial anagram of the name of his intimate friend Esther Vanhomrigh. Swift used the name in his *Cadenus and Vanessa*, which led to its use as a female given name. Var: Venessa. Short: Nessa. (VAH-NES-AH)

VENETIA Of uncertain etymology in use in England since the Middle Ages. Some believe the name to be a Latin rendering of the Welsh Gwyneth (blessed, a state of bliss) or a variant feminine form of the Latin Benedictus (blessed). *See* GWYNETH (Welsh Names) *and* BENEDICT (Male Names). The name corresponds to that of an ancient Roman province and a former region of northeastern Italy and thus might be a borrowing of such. (VEN-EE-SHA)

VERA Introduced in the late 19th century, Vera is from the Russian Vjera (faith). It coincides with the Latin *vera* (true), and the name is often believed to be derived from this, rather than the former. (VEER-AH)

VERENA Borrowed from the Swiss, Verena is a name of uncertain meaning. Some believe it to be from the Latin *verus* (true). It was borne by a 3rd-century saint who lived as a hermit near Zurich. Her cult is one of the oldest in Switzerland and has helped to keep the name popular. Var: Verina. (VER-EE-NAH)

VERITY Taken from *verity* (a truth, a reality), which is derived from the Latin *veritas* (truth) via the Old French *verite*. The name was popularized by the 17th-century Puritans. (VER-IH-TEE)

VERNA 19th-century coinage used as a feminine form of Vernon, which originated from the French baronial surname de Vernon (of Vernon). Alternatively, Verna is sometimes seen as a contracted form of Verena or Verona, both names of uncertain origin, or as a Latinized form of Verne (dweller among the ferns). *See* VERENA, VERNE (Male Names), *and* VERONA. (VER-NAH)

VERNE Transferred use of the surname which is derived from atte Verne (at the ferns, dweller among the ferns). Predominately a male name, Verne is also bestowed upon female children. Var: Verna. (VERN)

VERONA Modern name perhaps inspired by the name of the commune in northern Italy. It might also be a contracted form of Veronica (true image, bringer of victory). *See* VERONICA. (VER-O-NAH)

VERONICA Of debated origin and meaning, some believe it to be derived from the Late Latin *veraiconica*, the word given to a piece of cloth or garment with a representation of the face of Christ on it. *Veraiconica* is composed of the elements *verus* (true) and *iconicus* (of or belonging to an image). Alternatively, Veronica is thought to be a variant form of Berenice (bringer of victory), a derivative of the Greek Berenikē, which is a variant of the older name Pherenikē, a compound name composed from the elements *pherein* (to bring) and *nikē* (victory). Pet: Ronnie. (VEH-RON-EE-KAH)

VICTORIA Derived from the Latin *victoria* (victory). The name was generally unknown in England until the 19th century, when Edward, duke of Kent, married the German Maria Louisa Victoria of Saxe-Coburg (1786–1861). Their daughter, the future Queen Victoria (1819–1901), was christened Alexandrina Victoria, thus furthering recognition of the name. Pet: Tori, Torie, Tory, Vicki, Vickie, Vicky, Vikki. (VIK-TOR-EE-AH)

VIOLA Taken from the name of the flower, a large single-colored violet, which derived its name from the Latin *viola* (violet). The name was used by Shakespeare for the heroine in *Twelfth Night*. Short: Vi. (VEE-O-LAH, VĪ-O-LAH)

VIOLET From the Old French *violette*, a diminutive form of *viole*, which is derived from the Latin *viola* (a violet). The name has been in use since the Middle Ages but did not become common until the middle of the 19th century, when the use of flower names came into vogue. Short: Vi. (VĪ-O-LET)

VIRGINIA This name is mistakenly believed to be derived from the word *virgin*, a thought reinforced by the name of the state, so called in honor of Elizabeth I, the "virgin queen." In actuality, Virginia is derived from the Latin Verginius (spring-like, flourishing), an old Roman family name that has its root in the Latin *ver* (spring). Pet: Ginnie, Ginny. (VER-JIN-EE-AH, VER-JIN-YAH)

VIVIAN Cognate of the French Vivien (alive), a male name derived from the Latin Vivianus, which has its root in *vivus* (alive). Although in Great Britain it is occasionally bestowed upon females, the alternate spelling Vivien is the more common female form. In Arthurian legend, Vivian was the name of the Lady of the Lake, an enchantress who was the mistress of Merlin. Var: Viviana, Viviann, Vivianna, Vivianne, Vivien, Vyvyan. Short: Vi, Viv, Vivi. (VIV-EE-UN)

WANDA Of uncertain etymology, Wanda is generally believed to be of Germanic origin, perhaps from *vond* (wand, stem, young tree), or from *Wend*, a term denoting a member of the old Slavic people who now live in an enclave south of Berlin. The name was used in 1883 by author Ouida, who chose it for the heroine of her novel *Wanda*. (WAN-DAH)

WENDA Variant form of Wendy. Alternatively, Wenda is a short form of Gwendolyn (white-browed). *See* GWENDOLYN *and* WENDY. (WEN-DAH)

WENDY Originated as a nickname of novelist and playwright J. M. Barrie bestowed by Margaret Henley, the young daughter of English poet and editor W. E. Henley. She called Barrie her "Fwendy" (friendy), which evolved to "Fwendy-Wendy." Barrie first used the name in 1904 for a character in his *Peter Pan*, an ever-popular play which firmly established Wendy as a given name throughout the English-speaking world. Alternatively, Wendy is a modern pet form of Gwendolyn, most likely influenced by the previous name. *See* GWENDOLYN. Var: Wendi. (WEN-DEE)

WILLA Feminine form of William, which is a cognate of the Germanic Wilhelm (resolute protector). *See* WILLIAM (Male Names). (WIL-LAH)

WILLOW Taken from the name of the tree, which is derived from the Middle English *wilwe* (willow). Willow trees are noted for their flexibility and graceful appearance; hence the adjective *willowy* means "gracefully slender, lithe," qualities seen as desirable feminine attributes. (WIL-LOW)

WILMA In common use throughout the English-speaking world, Wilma originated as a contracted form of the German Wilhelmina, a feminine form of William (resolute protector). *See* WILLIAM (Male Names). (WIL-MAH)

WINIFRED Derived from the Welsh Gwenfrewi (blessed peace), a compound name composed of the elements *gwen* (white, fair, blessed) and *frewi* (peace, reconciliation). Short: Win. Pet: Winnie. (WIN-IH-FRED)

WYNNE Modern name derived from the Welsh *gwyn* (white, fair, blessed). Its coinage might have been influenced by Win, a popular short form of Winifred (blessed peace). *See* WINIFRED. Var: Wynn. (WIN)

XAVIERA Feminine form of Xavier, which represents a transferred use of a Spanish surname derived from the name of an estate in Navarre. *See* XAVIER (French Male Names). (ZAH-VEER-AH)

XENIA Derived from the Greek *xenia* (hospitality), which is from *xenos* (a guest, stranger). Xenia is an uncommon name, usually chosen by parents seeking something out of the ordinary. (ZEEN-EE-AH)

YASMIN A borrowing from the Arabic Yasmīn (jasmine), from the name of a bush bearing white, sweet-smelling flowers. (YAZ-MIN)

YOLANDE Of uncertain etymology, some believe it to be a derivative of Violante (violet), a medieval French name derived from the Latin *viola* (violet). Var: Yolanda. (YO-LAHN-DEH)

YSANNE Of uncertain origin, Ysanne might be composed of the element *ys*, as in Yseult, and Anne (gracious, full of grace). *See* ANNE. (EE-SAN)

YVETTE French feminine diminutive form of Yves (yew) in common use in England. *See* YVES (French Male Names). (EE-VET)

YVONNE A borrowing from the French, Yvonne is a feminine form of Yvon and Yves, names of Germanic origin derived from the element *iv* (yew). *See* YVES (French Male Names). (EE-VON)

ZANNA Short form of Suzanna (lily, rose), a name derived from the Hebrew Shoshannah (lily, rose). *See* SUSANNAH. Zanna is also bestowed as an independent given name. (ZAN-NAH)

ZARA Derived from the Arabic *zahra* (flower, blossom), which is from *zahara* (to blossom). The name received attention in 1981 when it was bestowed upon the second child of Princess Anne and Mark Philips. (ZAR-AH)

ZAYLIE Of uncertain etymology, some believe it to be a variant of Zelie, which itself is a variant of Celia (heaven). *See* CELIA. (ZAY-LEE)

ZELDA Of uncertain etymology, Zelda is thought by some to be a variant spelling of Selda, a name from the Old English *selda* (companion). Alternatively, Zelda is a Yiddish cognate of the German Salida (happiness, joy). *See* SALIDA (German Names). (ZEL-DAH)

ZELIE A borrowing from the French Zélie, a variant of Célie (leaven). *See* CELIA. (ZEE-LEE)

ZOË A borrowing from the Greek, Zoë is derived from *zōē* (life). Its use in England dates to the 19th century. (ZO-EE)

ZULA Derived from Zulu, an African tribal name for a pastoral people living in South Africa. The name Zula is used primarily by English blacks. (ZOO-LAH)

Chapter Eight

French Names

During the reign of Julius Caesar, the Roman expansion extended into Gaul, part of the area now known as France. After the fall of the Roman Empire, Germanic barbarian invasions were many and their influence on society was by no means insignificant. Toward the end of the early Middle Ages, Christianity became the primary religion in France, due in part to Charlemagne's practice of beheading those who did not wish to adopt the new religion.

These events in French history have a direct result on the types of names found in France today. Many have their roots in Latin and in the Old Germanic language. Predictably, biblical and saints' names are common.

In 1803, during the rule of Napoléon Bonaparte, a law was passed that required all French babies to be given French names spelled in a French way, such as those borne by important historical figures or by the various saints. This law was not enforced until 1957, at which time a list was developed of common French names and their French spellings. The list has since been liberalized to include optional spellings, the names of mythological figures, nature names, and a few popular foreign names. Even so, the public registrar can refuse to record the birth of a child if it does not bear a "proper" name.

French names consist of a first, middle, and last name. As in many other modern societies around the world, the first and middle names are often chosen merely because the parents like the way they sound, and not for aspirations the parents have for the child or for the meanings of the names.

It is quite common for French parents to use the name Marie as a middle name for their sons in order to put them under the special protection of the Virgin Mary. Similarly, Joseph is often added to female names.

Diminutive forms of names are commonly used, but unlike the English tendency to drop the last part or syllable from a name (Nicholas becomes Nick), the French often drop the first part of the name (Nicholas becomes Colas).

André, Jean, Pierre, and René are popular boys' names. Danielle, Francine, Marie, and Michèle are often chosen for girls.

French Male Names

ABEL A borrowing from the Latin and Greek, Abel is derived from the Hebrew *hebel* (breath). The name is borne in the Bible by the second son of Adam and Eve. Abel was the first murder victim, killed by his elder brother, Cain, in a fit of jealous rage. (AH-BEL)

ACHILLE From the Latin Achilles, a derivative of the Greek Achilleus, an ancient name of unknown etymology. The name was borne in Greek mythology by a leader of the Greek Army in the Trojan War. He was killed by Paris with an arrow that struck his heel, his only vulnerable spot. (AH-SHEEL)

ADALARD Derived from the Old German Adalhard, a compound name composed of the elements *adal* (noble) and *hard* (brave, strong, hearty): hence, "noble and strong." Var: Abelard, Alard, Allard. (AH-DAH-LAHR)

ADAM Derived from the Hebrew *adama* (red earth). The name is borne in the Bible by the first man created by God. According to biblical tradition, it was from Adam's rib that the first woman, Eve, was formed. (AH-DAHM)

ADRIEN French cognate of the Latin Adriānus (man from the city of Adria) and Hadriānus (man from the city of Hadria). (AH-DRYEHN)

AIMÉ Derived from *amee* (beloved), which is from the root *aimer* (to love). (Ā-MAY)

AIMERY Derived from the Old German Amalricus (work ruler), a compound name composed from the elements *amal* (work) and *ríc* (ruler, king). The name was taken to England by the Normans, where it underwent several variations in form. Var: Amaury. (Ā-MEH-REE)

ALAIN Variant of Alan, a Celtic name of uncertain etymology. The name was borne by an early Breton saint who was bishop of Quimper. Var: Allain. (AH-LANE)

ALBERT Derived from the Old High German Adalbrecht, a compound name composed from the elements *adal* (noble) and *beraht* (bright): hence, "bright through nobility." Var: Aubert. (AHL-BARE)

ALDRIC Derived from the German Adalrich, a compound name composed of the elements *adal, adel* (noble, nobility) and *rik, rīc* (ruler, king): hence, "noble ruler." Var: Aldrich, Aldrick, Audric. (AHL-DRIK)

ALEXANDRE From the Old French Alysaundre, Alexandre is the French cognate of the Greek Alexandros (defender or helper of mankind), a compound name composed from the elements *alexein* (to defend) and *andros* (mankind, man). Short: Alex, Sandre. (AH-LAYKS-AHN-DRAY)

ALFRED Derived from the Old English Ælfred (elf counsel), a compound name composed of the elements *ælf* (elf) and *ræd* (counsel). The name, taken up by the Norman French after the Conquest, is now in use throughout Europe. (AHL-FREY)

ALPHONSE Derived from the Old German Adalfuns, a compound name composed of the elements *adal* (noble) and *funs* (ready, prompt, apt). The name was borne by the French novelist Alphonse Daudet (1840–97). (AHL-FONS)

AMBROISE From the Old French Ambrose, a derivative of the Latin Ambrosius, which is from the Greek Ambrosios, a name derived from the word *ambrosios* (immortal). (AHN-BRWAZ)

AMÉDÉE Derived from the Latin Amadeus, a compound name composed of the elements *ama* (love) and *deus* (God): hence, "love of God." (AH-MAY-DAY)

ANATOLE From the Late Latin Anatolius, which is derived from the Greek *anatolē* (sunrise, daybreak, dawn). (AH-NAH-TOL)

ANDRÉ From the Old French Andrieu, which is from the Greek Andreas, a name derived from *andreios* (manly). André is a popular name and was borne by French painter André Derain (1880–1954). (AHN-DRAY)

ANSELME Of Germanic origin, Anselme (divine helmet, divine protection) is derived from the elements *ansi* (divinity, a god) and *helm* (helmet, protection). Var: Ansel, Ansell. (AHN-SELM)

ANTOINE Derived from the Latin Antonius, an old Roman family name of unknown etymology. The name is popular throughout Europe, due in large part to its connections with St. Anthony the Great, an Egyptian ascetic and the first Christian monk, whose relics were taken to Vienne, France, and who, with St. Anthony of Padua (1195–1231), worked miracles for the poor and the sick. (AHN-TWAHN)

ARISTIDE From the Greek Aristides, which is derived from *aristos* (best). The name was borne by Aristide Briannd (1862–1932), the French statesman who advocated a United States of Europe. (AHR-IH-STEED)

ARMAND From the German Hermann, which is from the Old High German Hariman, a compound name composed from the elements *heri* (army) and *man* (man): hence, "soldier, warrior." Var: Armond. (AHR-MON)

ARNAUD French form of Arnold, which is derived from the Old High German Aranold, an evolution of the older Germanic Arnwald, a compound name composed of the elements *arn* (eagle) and *wald* (ruler, power): hence, "eagle ruler, eagle power." (AHR-NOD)

ARNO Derived from the Germanic *arn* (eagle). (AR-NO)

AUBIN Derived from the Latin *albus* (white). (AU-BIN)

AUGUSTE From the Latin Augustus, which is derived from *augustus* (great, august, consecrated by the augurs). (O-GYOOST)

AUGUSTIN From the Latin Augustinus, a diminutive form of Augustus, which is derived from *august* (great, august, consecrated by the augurs). (O-GYOO-STAHN)

AURÈLE Derived from the Latin Aurēlius, an old Roman family name derived from *aurum* (gold). Var: Aurélien. (AU-RAY-LAY)

AURÉLIEN An alteration of Aurèle (golden) formed by the addition of the suffix *-ien*. *See* AURÈLE. (AU-RAY-LEE-EN)

BAILEY Derived from the Old French *baili* (administrator, manager), which is derived from *bailif* (an officer of justice, a warrant officer). (BAY-LEE)

BALDWIN From the Middle High German Baldewin, a compound name composed of the elements *bald* (bold) and *wini* (friend). The name was borne by Baldwin I (1058–1118), a Norman crusader and the first king of Jerusalem, as well as by four other crusader kings. Var: Baudoïn, Baudouin. (bau-DWEEN)

BAPTISTE From the Old French *baptiste*, which is derived from the Ecclesiastic Late Latin *baptista* (a baptist, one who baptizes). The name was traditionally bestowed in honor of John the Baptist and is now commonly used as part of the popular combination name Jean-Baptiste. (BAH-TEEST)

BARNABÉ From the Late Latin and Greek Barnabas, which is derived from the Aramaic *barnebhū'āh* (son of exhortation). (BAHR-NAH-BAY)

BARTHÉLEMY From the Late Latin Bartholomaeus and the Greek Bartholomaios, which is from the Aramaic, meaning "son of Talmai." Talmai is an Aramaic name meaning "hill, furrow." Var: Bartholomé. (BAHR-THEY-LEH-MEE)

BASILE From the Latin Basilius and the Greek Basileios (kingly, royal), names derived from *basileus* (king). (BAH-SEE-LAY)

BASTIEN A short form of Sébastien (man from Sebastia), Bastien is also commonly used as an independent given name. *See* SÉBASTIEN. (BAHS-TEE-EN)

BEAUFORT Compound name composed of the elements *beau* (handsome) and *fort* (strong). Short: Beau. (BO-FORT)

BELLAMY Derived from the Old French *bel amy* (fair friend, beautiful friend), which is from the Latin *bellus* (fair, beautiful) and *amicus* (friend). (BAY-LAH-MEE)

BENJAMIN From the Hebrew Binyamin, which is derived from *binyāmīn* (son of the right hand, favorite son). (BEN-ZHAH-MIN)

BENOÎT French cognate of Benedict, which is from the Latin Benedictus (blessed). (BEHN-WAH)

BERNARD From the Old High German Berinhard, a compound name composed from the elements *bero* (bear) and *hard* (strong, brave, hearty). The name was borne by St. Bernard of Clairvaux (1090?–1153), a French monk who founded the Cistercian Order and led the Knights of the Temple against the Turks, and by St. Bernard of Menthon (923–1008), a French monk who founded numerous hospices in the Swiss Alps. Var: Barnard, Bernardin, Bernon. (BARE-NAHR)

BERTRAM From the Old High German Berahtram, a variant of Berahthraban, a compound name composed of the elements *beraht* (bright) and *hraban* (raven). Var: Bertrand. (BARE-TRAHM)

BLAISE Of uncertain etymology, some believe it is derived from the Latin Blaesus, which is from *blaesus* (deformed, stuttering). The name was borne by Blaise Pascal (1623–62), a French mathematician, physicist, and philosopher. Var: Blaize. (BLEZ)

BRICE Derived from the Latin Britius, a name of uncertain etymology. (BRIS)

BRUNO A borrowing from the Old High German, Bruno is derived from *brun* (brown). (BROO-NO)

Byron Borrowed from the English, Byron originates from a place-name derived from the Old English *œt byrum* (at the cowsheds). (BY-RUN)

CAMILLE Bestowed upon both males and females, Camille is from the Latin Camillus, an old Roman family name of uncertain, probably Etruscan, origin. The name was borne by the Revolutionary journalist Camille Desmoulins (1760–94). (KAH-MEE-YEH)

CECIL From the Latin Caecilius, an old Roman family name derived from *caecus* (blind, dim-sighted). (SAY-SEEL)

CÉSAR From the Latin Caesar, a name of uncertain etymology. Some believe Caesar to be derived from *caedo* (to cut); others think it to be from *caesius* (blue-gray). Another suggestion is that it is derived from *caesaries* (hairy, with abundant hair). The name was borne by Gaius Julius Caesar (100?–44 B.C.), the Roman general and statesman who was dictator of the Roman Empire from 49 to 44 B.C. Caesar was subsequently used as the imperial title of the emperor of Rome from Augustus to Hadrian, and for the emperor of the Holy Roman Empire. It later evolved into a vocabulary word for an emperor or dictator. (SAY-ZAHR)

CHARLES A popular name throughout France, Charles is derived from the Germanic *karl* (full-grown, a man). It is a royal name, being borne by ten kings of France, including Charles VI (1368–1422), who was called the Well-Beloved. The name was also borne by St. Charles Borromeo, a nephew of Pope Pius IV. A bishop and cardinal, St. Charles (1538–84) established Sunday schools for the religious education of children and seminaries for the training of clergy. Pet: Charlot. (SHARL)

CHRISTIAN A popular name throughout France, Christian is derived from the Ecclesiastic Late Latin *christiānus* (a Christian, a follower of Christ), which is from the Greek *christianos* (a Christian). Var: Christien, Cretien. (KRIS-TYAHN)

CHRISTOPHE From the Ecclesiastic Late Latin Christophorus, which is derived from the Ecclesiastic Greek Christophoros, a compound name composed from the elements *Christos* (Christ) and *pherein* (to bear): hence, "bearing Christ." The name was borne by St. Christopher, a 3rd-century Christian martyr of Asia Minor who is the patron saint of travelers. (KREE-STOF)

CLAUDE Used by both males and females, Claude is from the Latin Claudius, an old Roman family name derived from *claudus* (lame). The name was borne by French painter Claude Lorrain (1600–82). (KLOD)

CLÉMENT From the Late Latin Clēmens (merciful), which is derived from *clemens* (mild, gentle, merciful). The name was borne by several saints, including Clement (d. A.D. 97), St. Peter's third successor and the first of the apostolic fathers, and Pope Clement VII (1478–1534), who excommunicated Henry VIII. (KLAY-MEHN)

COLOMBAIN From the Late Latin Columba, which is derived from *columba* (dove). The name was borne by several saints, including the Irish St. Columban (c. 540–615), a missionary of great influence on the Continent and founder of the monastery at Bobbio in northern Italy. (KO-LOM-BAHN)

CONSTANT From the Late Latin Constans, a name derived from *constans* (steadfast, constant). The use of Constant as a given name represents the transferred use of the surname, which is one of the most common in France. (KON-STAHN)

CONSTANTINE From the Latin Constantinus, which is derived from *constans* (steadfast, constant). Var: Constantin. (KON-STAHN-TEEN)

CORIN From the Latin Quirinus, which is derived from the Oscan *quiris* (a spear). Corin was originally bestowed in honor of St. Quirinus, a 4th-century bishop of Siscia who was martyred under Maximus. Var: Cyran. (KOR-IN)

CORNEILLE From the Latin Cornelius, an old Roman family name of uncertain etymology. Some believe it is derived from *cornu* (horn). The name was borne by a 3rd-century martyr whose relics were taken to France by Charles the Bald. (KOR-NEEL)

CURTIS Derived from the Old French *curteis* (courteous). Var: Curtice. (KOOR-TIS)

CYPRIEN From the Latin Cyprius, which is from the Greek *kyprios* (from Cyprus, a Cypriot). (SIP-RYEHN)

CYRILLE From the Late Latin Cyrillus, which is from the Greek Kyrillos (lordly), a derivative of *kyrios* (a lord). Var: Cyril. (SEER-IL)

DAMIEN From the Greek Damianos, which is thought to be derived from *damān* (to tame). The name was borne by the brother of Kosmas, both of whom were martyred in 303 under Diocletian. A cult arose about them, spreading westward and receiving much attention when the brothers' relics were supposedly found in Milan by St. Ambrose. Var: Damyon. (DAH-MYEN)

DANIEL Derived from the Hebrew *dāni'ēl* (God is my judge). The name is borne in the Bible by a Hebrew prophet whose faith kept him alive in a den of hungry lions. Daniel and the Lions' Den was a favorite story during the Middle Ages, which helped to promote the use of the name throughout Europe. (DAHN-YEL)

DAVID Derived from the Hebrew *dāwīd* (beloved). The name, a common surname and a popular given name in France, was borne by David d'Angers (1789–1856), a French sculptor who was born Pierre Jean David. Var: Davet, Davin. (DAH-VEED)

DELMAR Derived from the Spanish *del mar* (of the sea). Var: Delmer. (DEL-MAR)

DELPHIN From the Latin Delphinus (a dolphin) or alternatively, from Delphi, an ancient city on the slopes of Mount Parnassus in Greece. The name was borne by a 4th-century saint who was bishop of Bourdeaux. (DEL-FEEN)

DENIS From the Greek Dionysius (of Dionysos, the Greek mythological god of wine and revelry). The name was borne by St. Denis, a 3rd-century evangelist who became the patron saint of France, thus establishing the name's continued popularity. Var: Dennett, Dennis, Denys. (DEN-IS)

DIDIER From the Late Latin Dēsīderius, which is derived from *dēsīderium* (longing). The name was borne by several early saints, including 7th-century bishops of Auxerre, Cahors, and Vienne. (DEE-DYĀ)

DIMITRI From the Greek Dēmētrios (of Demeter), which is from Demeter, the Greek mythological goddess of agriculture and fertility. The name is composed of the elements *de* (the earth) and *mētēr* (mother). (DIH-MEE-TREE)

DION From the Latin Dio, originally a short form of any of the various names of Greek origin beginning with the name element *Dios-* (of Zeus). (DEE-ŌN)

DOMINIQUE From the Latin Dominicus (belonging to a lord), which is derived from *dominus* (a master). The name was borne by St. Dominic (1170–1221), a Spanish priest who founded the Dominican Order of Preachers. (DŌ-MIN-EEK)

DONATIEN From the Late Latin Dōnātus (given by God), which is derived from *donare* (to give, to donate). The name was borne by a 4th-century bishop of Casae Nigrae, who founded a North African Christian sect which held rigorous views on purity and sanctity. (DŌ-NAH-TYEHN)

EDGAR Derived from the Old English Eadgar (prosperity spear), a compound name composed from the elements *ēad* (prosperity, riches, fortune) and *gar* (a spear). (ED-GAHR)

EDMOND Derived from the Old English Eadmund (wealthy protection), a name composed of the elements *ēad* (prosperity, riches, fortune) and *mund* (hand, protection). The name was borne by a 9th-century East Anglian king killed by invading Danes for refusing to share his Christian kingdom with them. He was revered as a martyr, and his cult quickly spread to the Continent. (ED-MOND)

ÉDOUARD Of English origin, Édouard is derived from the Old English Eadweard, a compound name composed of the elements *ēad* (prosperity, riches, fortune) and *weard* (guardian, protector): hence, "wealthy protector." (Ā-DWAHR)

EGMONT Of Germanic origin, Egmont is derived from the elements *aug* (awe, fear) and *mond* (protection): hence, "awesome protection." In France, Egmont represents the transferred use of the surname. (EG-MONT)

ELOI A borrowing from the Spanish, Eloi is from the Latin Eligius (chosen), a name derived from *eligere* (to choose, to select). The name was borne by St. Eloi (c. 588–660). An artist with great talent for engraving and smithing, he gained sufficient wealth to found a monastery and a convent. He was appointed bishop of Noyon and Tournai by Dagobert I and is remembered for his generosity to the poor. (EE-LOY)

ÉMILE From the Latin Aemilius, an old Roman family name derived from *aemulus* (trying to equal or excel, rival). (Ā-MIL)

ÉMILIEN Derived from the Latin Aemiliānus, a derivative of Aemilius, an old Roman family name, which is from *aemulus* (trying to equal or excel, rival). Émilien was borne by several minor early saints, which influenced the popularity of the name. (Ā-MIL-YEN̄)

EMMANUEL From the Greek Emmanouēl, which is from the Hebrew Immanuel, a name derived from *'immānūēl* (God is with us). (EE-MAHN-YOO-EL)

ERIC Derived from the Old Norse Eiríkr (eternal ruler), a compound name composed of the elements *ei* (ever, always) and *ríkr* (ruler). (ER-IK)

ERNEST From the Germanic Ernst, which is from the Old High German Ernust and Ernost, names derived from *ernust* (earnest, resolute). (ER-NEST)

ESMÉ Derived from *esmé* (loved), the past participle of the verb *esmer* (to love). Alternatively, some believe the name to be a variant of Aimé (beloved). (EZ-MAY)

ESMOND A borrowing from the English, Esmond is derived from the Old English Ēastmund, a compound name composed of the elements *ēast* (beauty, grace) and *mund* (hand, protection): hence, "beautiful hand, graceful protection." (ES-MOND)

ÉTIENNE French cognate of Stephen, Étienne is from the Latin Stephanus, which is from the Greek Stephanos, a derivative of *stephanos* (garland, crown). The name was borne by the first Christian martyr, St. Stephen, one of the seven chosen to assist the Twelve Apostles, and by Étienne Boutroux (1845–1921), a philosopher often referred to as "the conscience of Europe." His doctoral thesis on the laws of nature was hailed as a turning point in the history of thought. (Ā-TYEN)

Eugène From the Latin Eugenius and the Greek Eugenios, which are derived from *eugenēs* (well-born, noble). (OU-ZHEN)

Eustache A derivative of the two Late Greek names Eustathius and Eustachius. Eustathius is derived from the elements *eu* (good, well) and *stēnai* (to stand), and Eustachius is from the elements *eu* (good, well) and *stachys* (grapes): hence, "fruitful." (OU-STAY-SHEH)

Évariste From the Late Greek Euarestos (well-pleasing, satisfying), a compound name composed from the elements *eu* (good, well) and *areskein* (to please, to satisfy). (Ā-VAH-REES-TAY)

Evrard From the English Everard (strong as a wild boar), a compound name composed of the elements *eofor* (a wild boar) and *heard* (hearty, strong, brave). Alternatively, Evrard may be from the Old High German Eburhart, which evolved into Eberhard and which is composed from *eber* (a wild boar) and *hart* (hearty, brave, strong). (EHV-RAHR)

Fabien From the Late Latin Fabiānus, which is from Fabius, an old Roman family name derived from *faba* (a bean). (FAH-BYEN)

Fabrice From Fabricius, an old Roman family name derived from the Latin *faber* (workman, craftsman). The name was originally bestowed in honor of Caius Fabricius Luscinus (d. 250 B.C.), a Roman statesman and military commander noted for his honesty and negotiating skills. (FAH-BREES)

Félix Derived from the Latin *felix* (lucky, happy). The name Félix was borne by four popes and many saints, sixty-seven of which are listed in the Roman Martyrology. (FAY-LEEKS)

Ferdinand From the Spanish Ferdinando, which is of uncertain origin and meaning. It is thought to be of Germanic origin, perhaps composed from the elements *frithu* (peace), *fardi* (journey), or *ferchvus* (youth, life) and *nanths* (courage), *nanthi* (venture, risk), or *nand* (ready, prepared). Var: Fernand. (FER-DEE-NAHN)

Firmin From the Latin Firminus, a derivative of Firmius, which is from *firmus* (firm, steadfast). Firmin was a popular name among early Christians and was borne by many early saints. (FIR-MIN)

Fletcher Transferred use of the surname derived from the Old French *flechier* (arrow maker), which is from the root *flech* (an arrow). The name originated in the beginning of the 13th century as an occupational name for a maker or seller of arrows. (FLECH-UR)

Florentin From the Latin Florentīnus, an elaboration of Florens, which is derived from *florens* (blossoming, flourishing). Var: Florent. (FLOR-EHN-TIN)

Florian From the Latin Flōriānus, an elaboration of Flōrus, an old Roman family name derived from *flōs* (flower). (FLOR-YEHN)

Fortuné Derived from the French *fortune* (fortune, chance). Var: Fortun, Fortune. (FOR-TYOO-NAY)

Francis From Franceis, an Old French form of the Italian Francesco, which is from the Middle Latin Franciscus (a Frenchman). Franciscus is derived from Francus (a Frank, a freeman), which has its root in the Old French *franc* (free). Var: Franchot. (FRAHN-SEES)

Franck From the Old French Franc and the Germanic Frank, names referring to a member of the Germanic tribes that established the Frankish Empire extending over what is now France, Germany, and Italy. The tribe is thought to have obtained its name from a type of spear or javelin called a *franco*. Alternatively, Frank is used as a short form of Francis (a Frenchman, a freeman). *See* FRANCIS. (FRAHNK)

François From the Old French *françois* (French). The name, borne by two kings of France, is often bestowed as a patriotic gesture. It is borne by former French President François Mitterrand (b. 1916). (FRAH-SWAH, FRAHN-SWAH)

Frédéric Derived from the Germanic Friedrich, which is from the obsolete Fridurih, a compound name composed from the elements *frid* (peace) and *rik* (ruler, king). Frederick is a royal name throughout Europe, being borne, among others, by nine kings of Denmark and seven kings of Prussia. (FRAY-DAY-RIK)

Gabriel From the Hebrew Gavriel, which is derived from *gavhrī'ēl* (God is my strength). The name is borne in the Bible by one of the seven archangels, the herald of Good News who appeared to Mary to announce her pregnancy and the impending birth of the Christ child. (GAH-BREE-EL)

Gaetan Derived from the name of the city of Gaeta, which was originally known as Caieta. The name is of uncertain derivation. (GAY-TAHN)

Gascon Of uncertain etymology. It is first recorded as that of the counts of Foix and Béarn. Some believe the name is a Germanic derivative of *gast* (guest, stranger). Others believe it is Basque in origin, and yet another explanation is that it is derived from the French *Gascon* (a native of Gascony, a region and former province in southwestern France), which is from the Latin *Vasco* (a Basque). Var: Gaston. (GAHS-TONE)

GASPAR Gaspar, along with Balthasar and Melchior, was a name assigned to the Three Wise Men, who brought gifts to the Christ child. The names are not found in the Bible and are thought to have been fixed in the 11th century. Of uncertain etymology, Gaspar might have been derived from the Persian *genashber* (treasure master), which is in keeping with his role of the bringer of precious gifts. Var: Gaspard, Jaspar, Jasper, Jesper. (GAHS-PAHR)

GAUTHIER French form of Walter (ruler of an army). *See* WALTER. Var: Gautier. (GAU-THYĀ)

GEOFFROI A name thought to have evolved from several different Germanic names. Gaufrid (peaceful district), of the elements *govja* (a district) and *frithu* (peace); Walahfrid (traveler of peace), from *valha* (traveler) and *frithu* (peace); and Gisfrid (pledge of peace), from *gis* (pledge) and *frithu* (peace), are thought to be the root names. Var: Geoffroy, Jeoffroi. (JOF-FREE)

GEORGES From the Greek Geōrgios, a derivative of *geōrgos* (earthworker, farmer), which is composed from the elements *gē* (earth) and *ergein* (to work). (ZORZH)

GÉRALD Derived from the Germanic Gerwald (spear ruler), a compound name composed from the elements *ger* (spear) and *walden* (to rule). The name was borne by St. Gerald of Aurillac (c. 855–909), who founded a monastery there in 890. Var: Géraud. (ZHAY-RAHL)

GÉRARD Derived from the Old High German Gerhart (brave with the spear), a compound name composed of the elements *ger* (spear) and *hart* (hearty, brave, strong). The name, borne by the popular French actor Gérard Depardieu, was also borne by many saints. (ZHAY-RAHR)

GERMAIN From the Late Latin Germānus (brother), which is derived from *germen* (a sprout, bud, embryo). The name was borne by several early saints including Germain of Paris (c. 496–576), a bishop who founded the monastery St.-Germain-des-Prés, in Paris, and who tried to bring an end to the brutality of the Frankish kings. Var: Germaine, Germane, Kerman. (ZHER-MEN, ZHER-MANE)

GILBERT Evolution of the Old French Guillebert, a derivative of the Old High German Gisilberht, which is composed of the elements *gisil* (pledge) and *beraht* (bright, famous). (ZHIL-BARE)

GILLES From the Latin Aegidius, which is from the Greek *aigis* (shield of Zeus, goatskin). The name was borne by St. Gilles, a 7th-century Athenian who had the power to work miracles and heal the crippled.He fled to southern Gaul and became a hermit to escape fame and the adoration of his fans. Nevertheless, he was one of the most popular saints in the later Middle Ages. (ZHEEL)

GRÉGOIRE From the Late Latin Gregorius, a cognate of the Greek Grēgorios (vigilant, a watchman), which is derived from the verb *egeirein* (to awaken). Var: Grégorie. (GREG-WAH)

GUILLAUME French form of the Old Norman French Willaume, which is derived from the Old High German Willehelm (resolute protector), a compound name composed from the elements *willeo* (will, determination) and *helm* (protection, helmet). (GEE-YOME)

GUY Derived from the Old French *guie* (a guide, a leader). (GEE)

HARCOURT A compound name composed of the elements *hari, heri* (army) and *court* (an enclosure): hence, "a fortified enclosure." (HAHR-CORT)

HENRI From the German Heinrich (ruler of an enclosure, home ruler), which is from the Old High German Haganrih, a compound name composed from the elements *hag* (an enclosure, a hedging-in) and *rihhi* (ruler), and from the Old High German Heimerich, a compound name composed from the elements *heim* (home) and *rik* (ruler, king). The name was borne by six kings of France, including Henri IV (1553–1610), one of the most beloved of the French kings. (AHN-REE)

HERBERT Derived from the Germanic Hariberht and Heriberht, which are composed of the elements *hari, heri* (army) and *beraht* (bright, famous): hence, "famous army." (HARE-BARE)

HERCULE From the Latin Hercules, which is from the Greek Hērakleēs, a name derived from the name Hera (the Greek mythological goddess, sister and wife of Zeus) and *kleos* (glory). The name is borne in Greek and Roman mythology by the son of Zeus and Alcmene, renowned for his amazing strength. (HARE-KYOOL)

HERVÉ From the Breton Herve, an evolution of the Old Breton Æruiu and Hærviu (battleworthy), which are composed of the elements *hær* (battle) and *viu* (worthy). (HARE-VAY)

HILAIRE Derived from the Latin Hilarius (cheerful), which is from *hilaris* (cheerful, glad). The name was originally bestowed in honor of St. Hilaire of Poitiers (c. 315–67), a bishop and theologian who was proclaimed a doctor of the church in 1851. (HEE-LARE)

Hippolyte From the Greek Hippolytus, which is derived from the elements *hippos* (horse) and *lyein* (to free, to loosen): hence, "to free or loosen horses." (EE-PO-LET)

Honoré Derived from the Late Latin Honorātus (honored), which is from *honor* (honor, repute, esteem). The name was borne by several early saints, including Honoratus of Arles (c. 350–429) who helped found the famous monastery of Lérins. (O-NO-RAY)

Hubert Derived from the Old High German Huguberht (bright in heart and spirit), which is composed of the elements *hugu* (mind, heart, spirit) and *beraht* (bright, famous). The name was borne by an 8th-century saint who was an active missionary in the forests of Ardenne. The patron saint of hunters and trappers in the Ardenne, Hubert is said to have witnessed a vision of the crucifix between the antlers of a stag. (HYOO-BARE)

Hugh From the Old French Hue, which is from the Old High German Hugo, a derivative of *hugu* (heart, mind, spirit). The name was borne by several saints and by Hugh Capet (938?–96), a king of France and founder of the Capetian dynasty. Var: Hugo, Hughes, Hughues. (HYOO)

Ignace From the Latin Ignatius, which is derived from Egnatius, an old Roman family name of uncertain etymology. Some believe it to be of Etruscan origin. Others derive it from the Latin *ignis* (fire). (EEG-NAHS)

Isaak A borrowing from the Ecclesiastic Greek, Isaak is from the Hebrew Yitzchak (he will laugh), which is from *yitshāq* (laughter). (EE-SAHK)

Isaïe From the Ecclesiastic Late Latin Isaias and the Ecclesiastic Greek Ēsaias, which are from the Hebrew Yeshayahu, a derivative of *yĕsha'yah* (God is salvation). (EE-SAY-EH)

Isidore From the Greek Isidōros, a compound name composed from Isis (the name of an Egyptian goddess) and the Greek *dōron* (gift): hence, "gift of Isis." The name was borne by Isidore of Seville (c. 560–636), a scholar and author who was declared a doctor of the church in 1722 by Pope Innocent XIII. (EE-SEE-DOR)

Jacques Popular name from the Ecclesiastic Late Latin Iacomus and Iacobus, derivatives of the Greek Iakōbos, which is from the Hebrew Yaakov, a derivative of *ya'aqob* (supplanting, seizing by the heel). Jacques is a cognate of the English James and Jacob, both of which are Anglicized forms of Yaakov. (ZHAHK)

Jean Perennially popular name, Jean is the French cognate of John, which is derived from the Middle Latin Johannes, an evolution of the Ecclesiastic Late Latin Joannes. Joannes is from the Greek Iōannes, a derivative of the Hebrew Yehanan, a short form of Yehohanan, which is from *yehōhānān* (Yahweh is gracious). The name, borne in the Bible by several important characters, was also borne by many saints, twenty-three popes, and many kings throughout Europe. Jean is commonly used in combination names, such as Jean-Luc. *See* JOHN (Biblical Names). Var: Jeannot, Jehan. (ZHAHN)

Jean-Baptiste Popular combination name composed from the names Jean (God is gracious) and Baptiste (baptist). The name is bestowed in honor of John the Baptist, the forerunner of Jesus, a prophet and preacher who urged people to turn away from their sins and be baptized. *See* BAPTISTE *and* JEAN. (ZHAHN-BAH-TEEST)

Jean-Christian Combination name composed of the names Jean (God is gracious) and Christian (a Christian). *See* CHRISTIAN *and* JEAN. (ZHAHN-KREES-TZHEN)

Jean-Claude Combination name composed of the names Jean (God is gracious) and Claude (lame). The name is borne by Olympic gold medal skier Jean-Claude Killy (b. 1943). *See* CLAUDE *and* JEAN. (ZHAHN-KLODE)

Jean-Luc Combination name composed of the names Jean (God is gracious) and Luc (Luke, man from Lucania). *See* JEAN *and* LUC. (ZHAHN-LUKE)

Jean-Marc Combination name composed of the names Jean (God is gracious) and Marc. *See* JEAN *and* MARC. (ZHAHN-MARK)

Jean-Michel Popular combination name composed of the names Jean (God is gracious) and Michel (who is like God?). *See* JEAN *and* MICHEL. (ZHAHN-MIH-SHEL)

Jean-Paul Popular combination name composed of the names Jean (God is gracious) and Paul (little). *See* JEAN *and* PAUL. (ZHAHN-POL)

Jean-Pierre Combination name composed of the names Jean (God is gracious) and Pierre (a rock). *See* JEAN *and* PIERRE. (ZHAHN-PYAIR)

Jérémie From the Ecclesiastic Late Latin Jeremias, a cognate of the Ecclesiastic Greek Hieremias, which is from the Hebrew Yirmeyahu, a name derived from *yirmeyāh* (the Lord loosens, God will uplift). (ZHAY-RAY-MEE)

Jérôme Derived from the Latin Hieronymus, a compound name composed from the elements *hieros* (holy) and *onyma* (name). The name was borne by St. Jerome

(340–420), born Eusebius Hieronymus Sophronius in Pannonia, an ancient Roman province in Central Europe. A monk and church scholar, St. Jerome was the author of the Vulgate (the translation of the Bible into Latin) and is regarded as one of the doctors of the church. (ZHAY-ROME)

Joël A borrowing from the Ecclesiastic Late Latin, Joël is from the Ecclesiastic Iōēl, a name derived from the Hebrew Yoel, which is from *yō'ēl* (the Lord is God). (ZHO-EL)

José A borrowing from the Spanish, José is a cognate of Joseph (may he add). *See* JOSEPH. (ZHO-ZAY)

Joseph A borrowing from the Ecclesiastic Late Latin, Joseph is from the Ecclesiastic Greek Iōsēph, which is from the Hebrew Yosef, a name derived from *yōsēf* (may he add). (ZHO-SEF)

Jourdain French cognate of Jordan, a borrowing of the name of the river in the Holy Land in which John the Baptist baptized Christ. The river's name is from the Hebrew *ha-yarden* (flowing down) and was originally bestowed upon those baptized in holy water that was said to be from the river. (ZHOR-DEN, ZHOR-DANE)

Jules Cognate of Julius, an old Roman family name thought to be derived from Iulus (the first down on the chin, downy-bearded). Because a person just beginning to develop facial hair is young, "youth" became an accepted meaning of the name. (ZHOOLZ)

Julien From the Latin Julianus, which is a derivative of Julius, an old Roman family name thought to be derived from Iulus (the first down on the chin, downy-bearded, youth). *See* JULES. Var: Julian, Jullien. (ZHOOL-YEHN)

Juste From the Old French Juste (just), which is from the Latin Justus, a direct derivation of *justus* (just, lawful, fair). Var: Just. (ZHOOST)

Justin From the Latin Justīnus, which is derived from *justus* (just, lawful, fair). (ZHOOS-TIN)

Karl Derived from the Germanic *karl* (a man, freeman, peasant). Var: Karel. (KARL)

Lambert Of Germanic origin, Lambert is derived from the Old German Landobeorht (bright land), a compound name composed of the elements *land* (land) and *beorht* (bright, famous). The name was borne by St. Lambert of Maastricht (c. 635–c. 705), a missionary bishop and martyr. (LAHM-BARE)

Lance From the Old High German Lanzo, which is derived from *lant* (land). The use of the name was advanced from the homonymous *lance* (a lance, a light spear). (LAHNS)

Lancelot Diminutive form of Lance (land). *See* LANCE. Var: Lancelin, Launcelot. Short: Lance. (LAHN-SEH-LOT)

Latimer Common first name and surname meaning "a translator of Latin." The name originally arose as an occupational name for a Latin translator. (LAH-TIH-MER)

Laurent From the Latin Laurentius (man from Laurentum), which is from Laurentum, the name of a town in Latium probably derived from *laurus* (laurel). (LO-RENT)

Léandre From the Latin Leander, which is from the Greek Leiandros (lion man), a compound name composed from the elements *leōn* (lion) and *andros* (a man). (LAY-AHN-DRAY)

Léo A borrowing from the Late Latin, Léo is derived from *leo* (lion). The name was borne by thirteen popes, including Leo I (the Great) (c. 400–61), who is remembered for his remarkable ability to lead the church through many years of crisis. (LAY-O)

Léon A variant of Léo (lion). *See* LÉO. The name was borne by French politician and journalist Léon Daudet (1867–1942). Var: Leone. (LAY-ŌN)

Léonard From the Old High German Lewenhart, a compound name composed from the elements *lewo* (lion) and *hart* (strong, brave, hearty): hence, "lion-hearted, brave as a lion." The name was borne by St. Léonard, of unknown date, who was greatly revered in the later Middle Ages. A hermit and founder of a monastery near Limoges in the 6th century, St. Léonard was considered the patron saint of prisoners by returning Crusaders. (LAY-O-NAHR)

Léonce French cognate of the Italian Leonzio, which is from the Late Latin Leontius, a derivation of Leo (lion). The name was borne by several early saints, including Leontius the Elder (d. c. 541), bishop of Bordeaux, who was succeeded by his brother Leontius the Younger (c. 510–c. 565). (LAY-ONS)

Léopold Of Germanic origin, Léopold is derived from the Old High German Liutbalt, a compound name composed from the elements *liut* (people) and *balt* (bold, strong): hence, "bold people." (LAY-O-POL)

Leroy Modern coinage thought to be based on the French *le roi* (the king). (LEE-ROY)

Lothair Derived from the Old High German Hludohari (famous warrior), a compound name composed from the elements *hluod* (famous) and *hari, heri* (army, warrior). (LO-THAIR)

LOUIS Derived from the Old French Loeis, which is from the Old High German Hluodowig (famous is war), a compound name composed from the elements *hluod* (famous) and *wīg* (war, strife). A very popular name, Louis has been borne by eighteen kings of France, including Louis XIV (1638–1715), whose reign encompassed a period of great power and flourishing French culture. (LWEE)

LOVELL Derived from the Anglo-French *lovel* (wolf cub), which is a diminutive form of *love* (wolf). Var: Louvel, Lowe, Lowell. (LUVL)

LUC From the Ecclesiastic Late Latin Lucas, a derivative of Lucius, which is from the root *lux* (light). Alternatively, some believe the name is derived from the Ecclesiastic Greek Loukas, which is a contraction of Loukanos (man from Lucania). (LUKE)

LUCIEN From the Latin Luciānus (of Lucius), a derivative of Lucius, which is from the root *lux* (light). (LEW-SEE-EN)

LYLE A borrowing from the English, Lyle originated from the French *de l'isle* (dweller on the isle), which was taken to England by the Normans. Var: Lisle. (LEEL)

MACAIRE From the Latin Macarius, a derivative of the Late Greek Makarios, which is from *makaros* (blessed). (MAH-KEHR)

MARC From the Latin Marcus, a name of uncertain derivation. Most believe it has its root in Mars, the name of the Roman mythological god of war. Others, however, think it is from *mas* (manly) or from the Greek *malakoz* (soft, tender). (MARK)

MARCEL From the Latin Marcellus, a diminutive form of Marcus, which is of uncertain derivation. *See* MARC. The name was borne by several early saints, including Marcellus the Righteous (d. c. 485), an abbot of the Eirenaion monastery near Constantinople, where the monks were organized in groups to sing praises to God around the clock. (MAR-SEL)

MARCELLIN From the Latin Marcellīnus, a diminutive variant of Marcus, which is a name of uncertain derivation. *See* MARC. (MAR-SEL-LIN)

MARIUS A borrowing from the Latin, Marius is an old Roman family name of uncertain derivation. Some believe it has its root in Mars, the name of the Roman mythological god of war, but others think it is derived from the Latin *mas* (manly). (MAHR-YOOS)

MARTIN From the Latin Martinus, a derivative of Mars, the name of the Roman mythological god of war. The name was borne by St. Martin of Tours (c. 315–97), an active missionary who is considered the father of monasticism in France. (MAHR-TAN)

MASON Derived from the Old French *maçon* (a mason, a builder of stone). Var: Masson. (MAH-SONE)

MATTHIEU The French cognate of Matthew, which is from the Ecclesiastic Late Latin Matthaeus, a derivative of the Ecclesiastic Greek Matthaios and Matthias, contractions of Mattathias. The name has its root in the Hebrew name Matityah, which is derived from *mattūthyāh* (gift of God). Var: Mathieu. (MATH-YOO)

MAXIME From the Latin Maximus, which is directly derived from *maximus* (greatest). Short: Max. (MAHKS-EEM)

MAXIMILIEN Arose as a blending of the Latin names Maximus and Aemiliānus by the Emperor Friedrich III, who bestowed it upon his first-born son, Maximilian I (1459–1519), in honor of the two famous Roman generals. Maximus is derived from the Latin *maximus* (greatest), but the etymology of Aemiliānus is uncertain. It is thought to be derived from the Latin *aemulus* (trying to equal or excel, rival). Short: Max. (MAHKS-IH-MIL-YEN)

MICHEL French cognate of Michael, a borrowing from the Ecclesiastic Late Latin, Greek, and Hebrew. Michael is derived from the Hebrew *mīkhā'ēl* (who is like God?). The name is borne in the Bible by the archangel closest to God, who is responsible for carrying out God's judgments. Considered the leader of the heavenly host, Michael is regarded as the patron of soldiers. The name is highly popular in France. (MEE-SHEL)

NARCISSE From the Latin Narcissus, which is derived from the Greek Narkissos, a name borne in Greek mythology by a handsome youth who was loved by the nymph Echo. Narcissus did not return her love, however, and Echo pined away until only her voice remained. After her death, Narcissus was made to fall in love with his own reflection in a pool, and there he remained, mesmerized until he turned into a flower. (NAHR-SEES)

NAZAIRE From the Late Latin Nazarius, which is derived from the place-name Nazareth, a town in Galilee in northern Israel where Jesus lived as a child. (NAH-ZAHR)

NICODÈME From the Greek Nikodēmos, a compound name composed of the elements *nikē* (victory) and *dēmos* (the people): hence, "victory of the people." (NEE-KO-DAYM)

Nicolas From the Latin Nicolaus, a derivative of the Greek Nikolaos (victory of the people), a compound name composed of the elements *nikē* (victory) and *laos* (the people). The name was borne by St. Nicolas, a 4th-century bishop of Myra who is regarded as the patron saint of Russia and Greece, and of children, sailors, and wolves. It is also from this St. Nicolas that the French *le Père Noël* is based. Var: Nicholas. Short: Colas. Pet: Nicollon. (NEE-KO-LAH)

Noë French cognate of Noah, from the Hebrew Noach, which is derived from *nōah* (rest, comfort, quiet). The name is borne in the Bible by the patriarch who built the ark to save his family and two of every creature from the Great Flood. (NO-AH)

Noël Evolution of the Old French Nouel, from *noel, nouel* (natal, Christmas), which is from the Latin *natālis diēs* (natal day, birthday) and *natālis diēs Domini* (natal day of the Lord, Christmas). The name is commonly bestowed upon children born during the Christmas season. (NO-EL)

Norman From the Old French Normant, derived from the Frankish *nortman*, which is composed of the elements *nort* (north) and *man* (man): hence, "northman, Norseman." The name was originally used to identify a member of the group of Scandinavians who occupied Normandy in the 10th century and, later, the native inhabitants of Normandy. Var: Normand. Short: Norm. (NOR-MAHN)

Octave From the Latin Octavius, which is derived from *octavus* (eighth). (OK-TAHV)

Olivier From the Old French *olivier* (olive tree). However, some believe it to be Germanic in origin and derived from the Middle Low German Alfihar (elf army), a compound name composed of the elements *alf* (elf) and *hari* (army). Var: Oliver. (O-LIV-EE-Ā)

Ourson Derived from the French *ourson* (bear cub), which is from *ours* (a bear). (OR-SUN)

Page Transferred use of the surname derived from the Anglo-French *page* (a page, a boy attendant). Var: Paige. Pet: Padgett, Paget. (PAGE)

Pascal From the Late Latin Paschālis (relating to Easter), a derivative of Pascha (Easter), which is from the Hebrew *pesach, pesah* (Passover). The name is often bestowed upon children born at Eastertime. Var: Pascale, Paschal, Pasquale. (PAHS-KAHL)

Patrice French cognate of Patrick, which is derived from the Latin *patricius* (a patrician). (PAH-TREES)

Paul From the Latin Paulus, which originated as a Roman family name derived from *paulus* (small). (POL)

Paulin From the Spanish Paulino, which is from the Late Latin Paulīnus, a derivative of Paulus (small). The name was borne by St. Paulinus (353–431), a bishop of Nola in Italy and a famous church poet. He was born at Bordeaux. (PO-LIN)

Perceval Derived from the Old French elements *perce* (pierce) and *val* (valley). Percival was the name of the knight in Arthurian legend who saw the Holy Grail. Var: Percival. Short: Percy. (PUR-SIH-VAHL)

Philibert Of Germanic origin, Philibert is derived from Filaberht (very bright, very famous), a compound name composed from the elements *fila* (much) and *beraht* (bright, famous). The name was borne by St. Philibert, a 7th-century founder of several monasteries and nunneries, and by Philibert de l'Orme (d. 1570), a French Renaissance architect. (FEE-LEE-BARE)

Philippe From the Latin Philippus, a derivative of the Greek Philippos, which is from the elements *philos* (loving) and *hippos* (horse): hence, "lover of horses." Philippe, found on most of the family trees of European royalty, was borne by six kings of France. Var: Philip, Philipe. (FEE-LEEP)

Philippe-Emmanuel Popular combination name composed of the names Philippe (lover of horses) and Emmanuel (God is with us). *See* EMMANUEL *and* PHILIPPE. (FEE-LEEP-EE-MAHN-YOO-EL)

Pierre French cognate of Peter, which is from the Ecclesiastic Late Latin Petrus and the Greek Petros, names derived from *petra* (a rock) and *petros* (a stone). Var: Perren, Perrin, Perryn. (PYAIR)

Prosper From the Latin Prosperus, which is derived from *prosperus* (favorable, prosperous). The name was borne by several early saints, including Prosper of Aquitane (c. 390–c. 455), a theologian known for his support of St. Augustine's teachings and for his chronicles of the world, from creation to the year 455. (PRO-SPARE)

Quentin Derived from the Latin Quintinus, which is from Quintus, an old Roman family name derived from the Latin *quintus* (the fifth). (KWIN-TN)

Quincy Transferred use of the surname originating as a Norman baronial name from the place-name Cuinchy in Pas-de-Calais, Normandy. The name is derived from Quince, a French form of the Latin Quintus (the fifth). Var: Quincey. (KWIN-SEE, KWIN-ZEE)

Rainier Derived from the Old German Raganher, a compound name composed from the elements *ragan* (counsel, advice) and *hari, heri* (army): hence, "wise army." (REH-NYĀ)

RAOUL A cognate of Ralph, Raoul is derived from the Germanic Radulf (wolf counsel), a compound name composed from the elements *rād* (counsel, advice) and *wulf* (wolf). Var: Raul. (RAH-OOL)

RAPHAEL A borrowing from the Ecclesiastic Late Latin, Raphael is from the Ecclesiastic Greek Rhaphaēl, which is from the Hebrew Refael, a name derived from *refā'ēl* (God has healed). The name is borne in the Bible by an archangel and messenger of God mentioned in the apocryphal books of Enoch and Tobit. (RAH-FĪ-EL)

RAYMOND Evolution of the Old Norman French Raimund, which is derived from the Germanic Raginmund, a compound name composed of the elements *ragin* (advice, counsel) and *mund* (hand, protection): hence, "wise protection." (RAY-MONE)

RÉGIS Transferred use of the French surname derived from the Latin *regis* (kingly). The name was borne by St. Jean-Françoise Régis of Narbonne (d. 1640), noted for devoting his energies to reforming prostitutes. (RAY-ZHEE)

RÉMY From the Latin Rēmigius, which is derived from *rēmigis* (oarsman). The name was borne by St. Rémy of Rheims (c. 438–c. 533), a bishop said to have baptized Clovis I, king of the Franks, on Christmas Day in 496. Var: Rémi. (RAY-MEE)

RENAUD Derived from the Old High German Raganald and Raginold, compound names composed from the elements *ragna, ragina* (advice, counsel, judgment) and *wald* (ruler): hence, "ruler of judgment." Var: Regnault, Reynaud. (RAY-NO)

RENÉ From the Late Latin Renātus, which is a direct derivative of *renātus* (reborn, born again). A perennially popular French name, René was, and in many cases still is, bestowed in celebration of the Christian's spiritual rebirth. The name was borne by the French philosopher and mathematician René Descartes (1596–1650). (REH-NAY)

RICHARD From the Old High German Richart (brave ruler), a compound name composed from the elements *rik, rīc* (power, ruler) and *hart* (strong, brave, hearty). (REE-SHAR)

RINALDO A borrowing from the Italian, Rinaldo is a cognate of Renaud (ruler of judgment). *See* RENAUD. (REE-NAHL-DŌ)

ROBERT Popular name derived from the Old High German Hruodperht, a compound name composed of the elements *hruod* (fame) and *perht* (bright): hence, "bright with fame." The name was borne by Robert I (d. 1035), duke of Normandy and father of William the Conqueror, and by many saints, including Robert Bellarmine (1542–1621), a theologian and scholar who is regarded as one of the doctors of the Catholic Church. (RO-BARE)

ROCH French cognate of the Italian Rocco, a name derived from the Germanic *hrok* (rest). The name was borne by a 14th-century French healer who was on pilgrimage to Rome when a plague broke out in northern Italy. St. Roch traveled from place to place nursing the sick and miraculously healing them, until he too fell victim to the plague and ended up being comforted by a dog. Upon his return to France, he was mistaken for an imposter and taken to prison, where he died. St. Roch is considered a patron saint of the sick. (RŌSH)

RODOLPHE Derived from the German Rudolf (wolf fame), which is an evolution of the Old High German Hrodulf, a compound name composed from the elements *hruod* (fame) and *wulf* (wolf). (RO-DŌLF-EH)

ROGER From the Old High German Hrodger (famous with the spear), a compound name composed of the elements *hrōd, hruod* (fame) and *ger* (a spear). (RO-ZHAY)

ROLAND From the Old High German Hruodland (famous land), a name composed from the elements *hruod* (fame) and *land* (land). The name was borne by a legendary vassal of Charlemagne, a brave and chivalrous hero who protected the rear guard of the Frankish Army as they retreated from Spain. His story is told in the *Chanson de Roland.* (ro-LAHN)

ROMAIN From the Latin Romanus (a Roman), which is derived from Roma (Rome). (RO-MAN)

ROUSSELL Derived from the Old French *roussell* (redhaired), which is from *rous* (red). Var: Rosselin, Rousell, Roussel, Russell. (ROO-SEL)

ROY Derived from the French *roi* (king). Var: Rey. (ROI)

ROYCE Transferred use of the surname meaning "Roy's son." (ROIS)

SACHA French cognate of the Russian Sasha, a pet form of Alexander (defender or helper of mankind). The name was introduced to France by the Ballet Russe, who performed in Paris from 1909 to 1920 under the leadership of Sergei Pavlovich Diaghilev. (SAH-SHAH)

SAMUEL Ecclesiastic Late Latin form of the Ecclesiastic Greek Samouēl, which is from the Hebrew Shmuel, a name derived from *shĕmū'ēl* (name of God, his name is God). (SAM-YOOL)

Sandre A short form of Alexandre (defender or helper of mankind), Sandre is also bestowed as an independent given name. *See* ALEXANDRE. (SAHN-DR)

Saül From the Ecclesiastic Late Latin Saul, a derivative of the Ecclesiastic Greek Saoul, which is from the Hebrew Shaul, a name derived from *shā'ūl* (asked of, borrowed). (SOL)

Sébastien From the Latin Sebastiānus, a derivative of the Greek Sebastianos (a man of Sebastia, a town in Asia Minor). Short: Bastien. (SAY-BAHS-TEE-EN)

Serge From the Russian Sergei, which is from the Latin Sergius, an old Roman family name of uncertain etymology. The name was borne by one of the most beloved of Russian saints (c. 1314–92), remembered for being kind, gentle, and humble. The name was introduced to France early in the 20th century at a time when the Ballet Russe was performing in Paris. (SER-GAY)

Séverin From the Latin Sevērīnus, which is from Sevērus, an old Roman family name derived from *sevērus* (severe, strict, stern). (SAY-VAY-RIN)

Seymour Transferred use of the surname, which arose from a Norman baronial name taken from the place-name Saint Maur in Normandy. The name is derived from the Latin Maurus (a moor). (SEE-MOR)

Sidney Transferred use of the surname originating as a Norman baronial name taken from the place-name St. Denis in Normandy. Var: Sydney. (SID-NEE)

Simon A borrowing from the Ecclesiastic Late Latin, Simon is from the Ecclesiastic Greek Simōn and Seimōn, which are from the Hebrew Shimon, a derivative of *shim'ōn* (heard). Var: Siméon. (SEE-MO)

Sorel Derived from the Old French *sorel* (reddish brown). The name was originally given to one with reddish hair. Var: Soren, Sorrell. (SOR-EL)

Spiro Derived from the Latin *spirare* (to breathe, to blow). (SPEE-RO)

Stéphane From the Latin Stephanus, which is from the Greek Stephanos, a derivative of *stephanos* (a crown, a garland). (STAY-FAHN)

Sylvain From the Latin Silvānus (of the woods), which is derived from *silva* (a wood). The name was borne by many saints, thus ensuring its use as a given name in France. Var: Silvain. (SEEL-VEN, SEEL-VANE)

Sylvestre From the Latin Silvester, which is from *silvester* (of a wood or forest), a derivative of *silva* (a wood). (SIL-VAY-STER)

Taillefer A compounding of the French elements *tailler* (to cut) and *fer* (iron). Taillefer arose as an occupational name or a nickname for one who worked with iron. Var: Telfer, Telfor, Telford, Telfour. (TEL-LEH-FEH)

Théodore From the Latin Theodorus, which is from the Greek Theodōros, a compound name composed of the elements *theos* (God) and *dōron* (gift): hence, "God's gift." (TAY-O-DOOR)

Théophile From the Greek Theophilus (beloved of God), a compound name composed of the elements *theos* (God) and *philos* (friend). (TAY-O-FEEL)

Thibault French cognate of Theobald, a Germanic name derived from the Old German Theudobald (bold and brave people), a compound name composed of the elements *theuda* (folk, people) and *bald* (bold, brave). Var: Thibaut. (TYEH-BOU)

Thierry French cognate of Theodoric, a Germanic name derived from the Gothic Thiudoreiks (ruler of the people), which is composed from *thiuda* (folk, people) and *reiks* (ruler, leader). (TYEH-REE)

Thomas From the Ecclesiastic Greek Thōmas, which is derived from the Aramaic *tě'ōma* (a twin). (TO-MAHS)

Timothée From the Latin Timotheus, a derivative of the Greek Timotheos, a compound name composed of the elements *timē* (honor, respect) and *theos* (God): hence, "honor and respect for God." (TEE-MO-THEY)

Toussaint Derived from the French *toussaint* (all saints). The name is commonly bestowed upon those born on or near All Saints' Day. (TOO-SAHN)

Tristan From the Old French Tristran, which is from the Celtic Drystan, a name derived from *drest* (tumult, riot). *See* TRISTRAM (English Names). (TREES-TAHN)

Troyes Transferred use of the surname originating from the place-name Troyes in Aube, Normandy. Var: Troy. (TRWAH)

Ulrich A borrowing from the German, Ulrich is derived from the Old German Udalrich, a compound name composed from the elements *uodal* (nobility, prosperity, fortune) and *rik* (ruler, power). The name was borne by St. Ulrich of Augsburg (890–973), the first saint whose canonization was decreed by a pope. (OOL-RISH)

Urbain From the Latin Urbānus (city dweller, urban), which is derived from *urbs* (a city). (OOR-BAHN)

Valentin From the Latin Valentīnus, which is derived from *valens* (to be healthy, strong). The name was borne by a 3rd-century Roman saint and martyr whose feast day,

February 14, coincides with that of a pagan festival marking the beginning of spring. (VAH-LEN-TIN)

VALÈRE From the Latin Valerius, an old Roman family name believed to be derived from *valere* (to be strong). (VAH-LARE-RAY)

VALÉRY Of Germanic origin, Valéry is from the Old German Walhrich, a compound name composed from the elements *walh* (foreign) and *ric* (ruler, power): hence, "foreign ruler." The name was borne by a 7th-century saint who founded the abbey of Lencome. (VAH-LARE-EE)

VALIANT Derived from the Old French *vaillant* (valiant, brave), which is from the Latin *valere* (to be strong). (vahl-YAHN)

VALLOIS Derived from the Old French Waleis (a Welshman, a foreigner). Var: Vallis. (VAHL-WAH)

VERNON Originated as a Norman baronial name from the place-name Vernon in Eure, Normandy. Vernon, a common French place-name, is derived from the Gaulish *vern-os* and the French *verne*, *vergne* (alder tree, alder grove). Short: Vern. (VURE-NO)

VERYL Derived from the Old French *verai* (true). Var: Verel, Verrall, Verrell, Verrill. (VAIRL)

VICTOR A borrowing from the Latin, Victor is from *victor* (conqueror, winner). The name was borne by an early pope and several saints. (VEEK-TOR)

VINCENT From the Late Latin Vincentius (conquering), which is derived from *vincere* (to conquer). The name was borne by St. Vincent de Paul (1580?–1660), a French priest who founded the Vincentian Order of the Sisters of Charity. (VEEN-SANE)

VIVIEN From the Latin Vivianus, a name derived from *vivus* (alive). St. Vivien of Saintes was a 5th-century bishop remembered for protecting his people during the Visigothic invasion of western France. (VEEV-YEH)

WYATT Derived from the Anglo-French Wyot and the French Guyot, names derived from *guie* (a guide, a leader). Var: Wiatt. (WY-UT)

XAVIER Transferred use of the Spanish surname derived from the place-name Xavier in Navarre. The name, which is believed to be derived from the Basque Etcheberria (the new house), was originally borne in honor of St. Francis Xavier (1506–52), a famous Spanish missionary to Japan and the East Indies and the patron saint of missionaries in foreign lands. Var: Javier. (ZAYV-YEH)

YANN Breton cognate of Jean, which is the French cognate of John (God is gracious). *See* JEAN. Pet: Yanni, Yannic, Yannick. (YAHN)

YVES Popular name of Germanic origin, Yves is derived from the element *iv* (yew, the type of wood used in bow making). (EEV)

YVON Of Germanic origin, Yvon is derived from the element *iv* (yew, the type of wood used in the making of bows and arrows). (EE-VO)

French Female Names

ABELIA A feminine form of Abel, which is derived from the Hebrew *hebel* (breath). *See* ABEL (Male Names). Var: Abella, Abelle. (AH-BEL-LEE-AH)

ADÉLAÏDE Derived from the Germanic Adalheid, a compound name composed of the elements *adal* (noble, nobility) and *heid* (kind, sort): hence, "noble one." Short: Adèle. (AH-DAY-LAID)

ADÈLE Short form of any of the various names containing the Germanic element *adal* (noble, nobility). The name was borne by the youngest daughter (c. 1062–1137) of William the Conqueror. She was the wife of Stephen of Blois, and because of her piety and goodness, came to be regarded as a saint. Var: Adele, Adelia, Adella, Adelle. Dim: Adelina, Adeline. (AH-DALE)

ADELINE A diminutive form of Adèle, Adeline is also commonly bestowed as an independent given name. Var: Adelina. (AH-DAY-LEEN)

ADRIENNE Feminine form of Adrien, which is from the Latin Adriānus (man from the city of Adria) and Hadriānus (man from the city of Hadria). (AH-DREE-EN)

AGATHE Derived from the Greek Agathē, which is from *agathos* (good, kind). The name was borne by a famous 3rd-century saint and martyr. *See* AGATA (Italian Names). (AH-GAH-TAH)

AGNÈS From the Greek Hagnē, which is derived from *hagnos* (chaste, pure). (AHN-YES)

AIDA Derived from the Old French *aide* (helper, aide, assistant). (Ā-DAH)

Aimée Derived from *amee* (beloved), which is from the root *aimer* (to love). Var: Aimè, Amee. (Ā-MEE)

Albertine Feminine form of Albert (noble and bright), a compound name composed of the Old High German elements *adal* (noble) and *beraht* (bright). Var: Albertina. (AHL-BER-TEEN)

Alette French variant of the Germanic Aleit, a contraction of Adalheid, a compound name composed of the elements *adal* (noble, nobility) and *heid* (kind, sort): hence, "noble one." (AH-LET)

Alexandra Derived from the Greek Alexandros (defender or helper of mankind), a compound name composed of the elements *alexein* (to defend) and *andros* (man).Var: Alexandrina, Alexandrine. Short: Sandra, Sandrine. (AH-LAYKS-ZAHN-DRAH)

Alexis Derived from the Greek *alexein* (to defend, to help). Var: Alexina, Alexine. (AH-LAYK-SIS)

Alice Evolved through a series of variants of the Germanic Adalheidis, a compound name composed of the elements *adal* (noble, nobility) and *heid* (kind, sort): hence, "noble one." Adalheidis was contracted to Adalheid, which the French changed to Adélaïde, then contracted to Adaliz, and contracted yet again to Aaliz, Aliz, and Alix. The English then changed the spelling to Aeleis, Alys, and eventually to Alice. Var: Alix, Aliz. (AH-LEES)

Aline Contracted form of Adeline, which is a diminutive form of Adèle (noble). *See* ADÈLE. (AH-LEEN)

Allegra Derived from the Latin *allegro* (cheerful, brisk, gay). (AH-LEH-GRA)

Amalie From the Germanic Amalia, a name derived from the element *amal* (work). Var: Amélie. (AH-MAH-LEE)

Amarante From the name of the flower, which is from the Latin Amarantus, a derivative of the Greek *amarantos* (unfading). In poetry, Amaranth is an imaginary flower that never fades and never dies. (AH-MAH-RAHN-TAY)

Amedée Derived from the Latin Amadeus, a compound name composed of the elements *ama* (love) and *deus* (God): hence, "love of God." Var: Amadee. (AH-MAH-DAY)

Amitée Derived from the French *amitié* (friendship), which has its root in the Latin *amicus* (friend). Var: Amitee. (AH-MIH-TAY)

Anaïs Provençal variant of Anne (gracious, full of grace). *See* ANNE. (AH-NAH-EES)

Andrée Feminine form of André, from the Old French Andrieu, which is from the Greek Andreas, a name derived from *andreios* (manly). (AHN-DRAY-AH)

Angèle From the Old French *angel* (angel), which is from the Latin *angelus*, a derivative of the Greek *angelos* (messenger, messenger of God). Var: Angelina, Angeline. Short: Ange. (AHN-ZHAY-LAY)

Angélique Derived from *angélique* (angelic), which is derived from the Latin *angelicus* and the Greek *angelikos*. (AHN-ZHAY-LEEK)

Anne Cognate of the Hebrew Hannah (gracious, full of grace), which is from *hannāh*, *chaanach* (grace, gracious, mercy). Pet: Annette. (AHN-NEH)

Anne-Elisabeth Combination name composed of the names Anne (gracious, full of grace) and Elisabeth (God is my oath). *See* ANNE *and* ELISABETH. (AHN-EH-LEE-SAH-BETH)

Anne-Marie Combination name composed of the names Anne (gracious, full of grace) and Marie. *See* ANNE *and* MARIE. (AHN-NEH-MAY-REE)

Annette A pet form of Anne (gracious, full of grace), Annette is also commonly used as an independent given name. *See* ANNE. (AHN-NET)

Antoinette Feminine diminutive form of Antoine, the French cognate of Anthony, which is from the Latin Antonius, an old Roman family name of unknown etymology. Short: Toinette. (AHN-TWAH-NET)

Apolline From the Latin Apollonia, which is from the Greek Apollonios, a derivative of Apollo, the name of the Greek mythological god of music, poetry, prophecy, and medicine. (AH-PO-LEEN)

Arianne From the Latin Ariadne, which is derived from the Greek Ariadnē (the very holy one). Var: Ariane. (AR-EE-AHN)

Asceline Thought to be a variant form of Adeline (noble). *See* ADELINE. Var: Aceline. (AHS-SEH-LEEN)

Aude From the Old German Alda, which is derived from the element *ald* (old). Var: Auda. (O-DEH)

Aure From the Latin *aura* (aura), which is derived from the Greek *aēr* (air). (O-REH)

Aurélie Feminine form of Aurèle, which is from the Latin Aurēlius, an old Roman family name derived from *aureus* (golden). (O-RAY-LEE)

Aurore Derived from the Latin *aurora* (dawn). The name is borne in Roman mythology by the goddess of dawn. Var: Aurora. (O-ROR-EH)

Aveline French diminutive form of the Germanic Avila, a name of uncertain meaning. The name was borne by the great-grandmother of William the Conqueror. Var: Avelaine, Eveline, Evelyne. (AHV-EH-LEEN)

Barbara A borrowing from the Latin, Barbara (foreign woman) is derived from *barbarus* (foreign, strange), a term applied to non-Romans or those deemed to be uncivilized. Short: Barbe. Pet: Babette. (BAHR-BAHR-AH)

Bastienne Feminine form of Bastien, which is a short form of Sébastien (man of Sebastia). *See* SÉBASTIEN (Male Names). (BAHS-TYEN-NEH)

Béatrice Derived from the Latin *beatrix* (she who makes happy, she who brings happiness), which is from *beātus* (happy, blessed). (BAY-AH-TREES)

Belle From the French *belle* (beautiful, fair). (BEL)

Bénédicte French feminine form of the English Benedict, which is from the Latin Benedictus (blessed). (BAY-NAY-DEEK-TEH)

Benoîte Feminine form of Benoît, which is a French cognate of Benedict (blessed). (BEN-WAHT)

Bernadette Feminine diminutive form of Bernard, which is from the Old High German Berinhard, a compound name composed from the elements *bern* (bear) and *hard* (hearty, strong, brave). The name is often bestowed in honor of the visionary St. Bernadette (1844–79). Born Marie-Bernarde Soubirous, she was a poor peasant girl who had eighteen visions of the Virgin Mary on the bank of the river Gave near Lourdes. Mary communicated with Bernadette and pointed out a forgotten spring of water which soon became a great pilgrimage shrine, where miracle cures were, and still are, sought. Short: Bernette, Nadette. (BARE-NAH-DET)

Bernardine Feminine form of Bernard (bold or strong as a bear), which is from the Old High German Berinhard, a compound name composed of the elements *bern* (bear) and *hard* (hearty, strong, brave). Var: Bernardina. (BARE-NAHR-DEEN)

Berthe From the German Bertha, originally a short form of various Old German compound names containing the element *beraht* (bright, famous). (BARE-THE)

Bibiane From the Latin Bibiana, a variant of Viviana, which is derived from *vivus* (alive). (BEE-BEE-AHN)

Blanche From the French *blanche* (white, blank). The name, originally used as a nickname for a blonde, took on the additional meaning of "pure" from the association of the color white and purity. Var: Blanch. (BLAHNCH)

Brigitte From the Irish Gaelic Bríghid, which is believed to be derived from *brígh* (strength). *See* BRÍGHID (Irish Names). (BRI-ZHEET)

Calandre French form of the Greek Kalandra, a compound name composed of the elements *kalos* (beautiful) and *andros* (man): hence, "beautiful one." Pet: Callie. (KAH-LAHN-DREH)

Camille Derived from the Latin *camilla* (virgin of unblemished character). Alternatively, it can be derived from Camillus, an old Roman family name of uncertain (possibly Etruscan) origin. The name was originally bestowed in honor of St. Camillus de Lellis (1550–1614), a soldier of fortune who changed his ways and founded the nursing order of the Servants of the Sick. (KAH-MEEL)

Caresse Derived from the French *caresse* (caress). (KAH-RESS)

Carla Feminine form of Carl, which is derived from the Old English *ceorl* (man, freeman, peasant). The name has a cognate in the German Karl, which is derived from the Germanic *karl* (man, freeman, peasant). (KAR-LAH)

Carole Short form of the Latin Carolus, which is a cognate of Charles (full-grown, a man), and a short form of Caroline, which is a feminine form of Carolus. The name is alternatively derived from the Old French *carole* (a joyous song, a carol). *See* CHARLES (Male Names). Var: Carola. (KAR-OL)

Caroline Feminine form of the Latin Carolus, which is a cognate of Charles (full-grown, a man). *See* CHARLES (Male Names). (KAR-O-LEEN)

Catherine From the Greek Aikaterinē, which is derived from *katharos* (pure, unsullied). Var: Katherine. Short: Rina. Pet: Katie. (KAT-REEN)

Cécile French cognate of the English Cecilia, a feminine form of Cecil, which is derived from Caecilius, an old Roman family name, which has its root in the Latin *caecus* (blind, dim-sighted). Var: Ceciliane. (SAY-SEEL)

Céleste Derived from *céleste* (celestial, heavenly), which is from the Latin *caelestis* (celestial, heavenly). Var: Celestine. (SAY-LEST)

Céline From the Latin Caelīna, which is from Caelius, an old Roman family name thought to be derived from *caelum* (heaven). Alternatively, Céline is a short form of Marcelline, a feminine form of Marcel, which is a derivative of Marcus. *See* MARCELLINE. Var: Célina. (SAY-LEEN)

Cendrine From the French Cendrillon (Cinderella), a name derived from *cendre* (ashes). (SEN-DREEN)

CERISE Derived from *cerise* (cherry, cherry-flavored). (SEH-REEZ)

CHANTAL Derived from a place-name in Saône-et-Loire, which is from the Old Provençal *càntal* (stone, boulder). The name is often bestowed in honor of St. Jeanne de Chantal. Born Jeanne Françoise Frémyot (1572–1641), she married Baron Christophe de Rabutin-Chantal and was widowed eight years later with four children. She became an associate of St. Francis de Sales, and together they founded a new order of nuns called the Order of the Visitation. She is remembered for her holiness, strength of character, and great administrative skill. (SHAHN-TAHL)

CHARLOTTE Feminine form of Charlot, which is a diminutive form of Charles (full-grown, a man). *See* CHARLES (Male Names). (SHAR-LET)

CHARMAINE Derived from the Old French *charme* (a song, verse, chant). (SHAR-MANE)

CHRISTELLE Alteration of Christine (a Christian), formed by replacing the suffix *-ine* with the suffix *-elle*. *See* CHRISTIANE. Var: Kristell, Kristelle. (KRIS-TEL)

CHRISTIANE From the Latin Christiāna, which is from the Ecclesiastic Late Latin *christiānus* (a Christian, a follower of Christ), a derivative of the Greek *christianos* (a Christian). Var: Christina, Christine, Kristina, Kristine. Short: Tina. (KRIS-TEE-AHN)

CLAIRE French cognate of Clara, which is derived from the Latin *clārus* (bright, clear, famous). Var: Clair, Clare. Dim: Clairette. (CLARE)

CLARICE From the Latin Claritia, which is derived from *clārus* (bright, clear, famous). Var: Clarisse. (KLAH-REES)

CLAUDE Used by both males and females, Claude is from the Latin Claudius, an old Roman family name derived from *claudus* (lame). The name was borne by several early saints and is common to the French royal families. Var: Claudine. (KLODE)

CLAUDETTE Variant form of Claude (lame), formed by the addition of the diminutive suffix *-ette*. *See* CLAUDE. (KLO-DET)

CLÉMENCE Feminine variant of the male Clément, a name derived from the Late Latin Clemens (merciful), which is from *clemens* (gentle, mild). (KLAY-MĀNS)

CLOTHILDE From the Old German Hlodhild (famous in battle), a compound name composed of the elements *hloda* (famous, renowned, loud) and *hildi* (battle). The name was borne by a daughter (c. 474–545) of the Burgundian king Chilperic who married the founder of the Frankish monarchy, Clovis I (c. 466–511) and converted him to Christianity. (KLO-TEELD)

COLETTE Short form of Nicolette, which is a diminutive form of Nicole (victory of the people). *See* NICOLE. The name, often used as an independent given name, was borne by St. Colette, a French nun who restored existing Poor Clare convents to their original strict rule and founded seventeen new ones. Var: Collette. (KO-LET)

COLOMBE From the Late Latin Columba (dove). The name was borne by several saints and martyrs, including Colomba of Córdova and Colombe of Sens. (KO-LŌMB)

CORINNE Derived from the Greek Korinna, which is a diminutive form of Korē (maiden), a byname of Proserpina in Roman mythology or of Persephone in Greek mythology. Dim: Coretta, Corette. (KO-RIN)

CYRILLE Borne by both males and females, Cyrille is from the Late Latin Cyrillus, which is from the Greek Kyrillos (lordly), a derivative of *kyrios* (a lord). (SIH-RIL)

DAISI French form of the English Daisy, a popular flower name derived from the Old English *dœges eage* (day's eye: in reference to its round yellow center resembling the sun). (DAY-ZEE)

DAMIANA Feminine form of Damien, the French cognate of the Greek Damianos, which is thought to be derived from *damān* (to tame). (DAH-MEE-AH-NAH)

DANIÈLE Feminine form of Daniel, which is derived from the Hebrew *dāni'ēl* (God is my judge). Var: Danielle. Pet: Dany. (DAHN-YEL)

DELPHINE From the Latin Delphīna (woman from Delphi). The name was borne by the 4th-century St. Delphinus of Bordeaux, a bishop from whom others, both male and female, took the name. (DEL-FEEN)

DENISE Feminine form of Denis, which is from the Greek Dionysius (of Dionysos, the Greek mythological god of wine and revelry). Var: Denice. (DEH-NEES)

DÉSIRÉE From the Latin Desiderāta, which is derived from *desiderata* (desired). Var: Desire. (DAY-ZIH-RAY)

DIAMANTA Derived from the French *diamant* (diamond). (DEE-AH-MAHN-TAH)

DIANE French cognate of Diana, a name derived from the Latin Diviana, which is from *divus* (divine). The name is borne in Roman mythology by the virgin goddess of the moon and of hunting. Var: Dianne. (DI-AN)

DOMINIQUE Bestowed upon both females and males, Dominique is from the Latin Dominicus (belonging to a lord), which is derived from *dominus* (a master, a lord). *See* DOMINIQUE (Male Names). (DO-MIN-EEK)

Dorothée Derived from the Greek Dōrothea, a compound name composed of the elements *dōron* (gift) and *theos* (God): hence, "gift of God." The name was borne by a 4th-century saint martyred under Diocletian. Sentenced to be beheaded, she was mocked by a lawyer named Theophilus, who asked her to send flowers and fruit from heaven. A child with a basket of roses and apples miraculously appeared and gave the basket to Theophilus, who was converted and martyred as well. (DOR-O-THAY)

Edith A borrowing from the English, Edith is from the Old English Ēadgyð, Eadgyth (prosperous in war), a compound name composed of the elements *ēad* (prosperity, fortune, riches) and *gyð, gyth* (war strife). The name is borne by former Prime Minister Edith Cresson (b. 1934). (EE-DITH)

Edmée Feminine form of Edmond (wealthy protection). *See* EDMOND (Male Names). (ED-MAY)

Edwige French cognate of the German Hedwig, which is derived from the obsolete Germanic Haduwig, a compound name composed from the elements *hadu* (contention, strife) and *wīg* (WAR). (ED-WEEG)

Elaine Variant form of Helen, a derivative of the Greek Helenē, which is from the element *ēlē* (light, torch, bright). (EH-LANE)

Eléonore Variant of the Greek Helenē, which is derived from the element *ēlē* (light, torch, bright). Var: Aliénor, Elinore. Short: Enora, Léonore. (EH-LAY-O-NOR)

Éliane From the Latin Aeliāna, which is from the family name Aeliānus (of the sun), a derivative of the Greek *hēlios* (sun). The name was borne by an early Christian martyr. (Ā-LEE-AHN)

Elisabeth Popular name derived from the Hebrew *elīsheba'* (God is my oath). The name, borne in the Bible by the mother of John the Baptist, was also borne by many saints, including Elisabeth Bichier des Âges (1773–1838), the founder of many small convents during the French Revolution. Short: Élise, Lise. Pet: Lisette. (Ā-LEES-AH-BETH)

Élise Short form of Elisabeth (God is my oath), Élise is also commonly bestowed as an independent given name. *See* ELISABETH. (Ā-LEES)

Éloise Of uncertain origin and meaning, some believe it is derived from the Old Germanic Helewidis, a compound name composed of the elements *haila* (hale, hearty, sound) and *vid* (wide). Others think it is a feminine form of Louis, which is from the Old High German Hluodowig, a compound name composed from the elements *hluda* (famous) and *wiga* (war): hence, "famous in war." The name was borne by the wife (d. 1164) of French theologian Peter Abelard (1079–1142), whose secret marriage was avenged by Éloise's uncle in the manner of Abelard being beaten and castrated. He became a monk and Éloise became the abbess of a nunnery. Var: Héloïse. (Ā-LO-EEZ)

Emeraude Derived from the French *émeraude* (emerald). Var: Esmeraude. (EH-MER-ODE)

Émilie From the Latin Aemilia, which is from Aemilius, an old Roman family name probably derived from *aemulus* (rival). The name was borne by St. Émilie de Rodat (1787–1852), founder of the Holy Family of Villefranche, and St. Émilie de Vialar (1797–1856), founder of several convents whose members are called Sisters of St. Joseph of the Apparition. Var: Émilianne, Émilienne. (Ā-MEE-LEE)

Emma Variant of the Germanic Erma, a name that originated as a short form of any of the various names containing the element *erm(en)* or *irm(en)*. (EM-MAH)

Emmeline Variant form of Émilie (rival), formed by adding the diminutive suffix–*ine*: hence, "little rival." *See* ÉMILIE. (EH-MEH-LEEN)

Emmanuelle Feminine form of Emmanuel, which is ultimately derived from the Hebrew *'immānūēl* (God is with us). *See* EMMANUEL (Male Names). (EE-MAHN-YOO-EL)

Esmée Feminine form of Esmé, which is derived from *esmé* (loved), the past participle of the verb *esmer* (to love). (EZ-MAY)

Estelle The French cognate of the Spanish Estella, which is derived from the Latin *stella* (star). (EH-STEL)

Esther Of debated origin and meaning, some believe it to be the Persian translation of the Hebrew name Hadassah (myrtle); others think it is derived from the Persian *stara* (star). It has also been suggested that it derives from the Babylonian Ishtar, the name of a goddess of love and fertility. Esther is borne in the Bible by the Jewish wife of the Persian king Ahasuerus. (ES-TER)

Étiennette Feminine form of Étienne, the French cognate of Stephen, which is from the Greek *stephanos* (garland, crown). *See* ÉTIENNE (Male Names). (Ā-TYEN-ET)

Eugénie Feminine form of Eugène, which is from the Latin Eugenius and the Greek Eugenios (well-born). See EUGÈNE (Male Names). Var: Eugenia. Short: Genia, Genie. (OU-ZHAY-NAY)

EULALIE From the Latin and Greek name Eulalia (fair in speech), which is composed from the elements *eu* (well, good) and *lalein* (to talk). (OU-LAL-EE)

EUPHÉMIE Derived from the Greek Euphēmia (of good voice, fair speech), a name composed of the elements *eu* (well, good, fair) and *phēmē* (voice). The name was borne by a young virgin martyr of Chalcedon who so courageously withstood her torture that her fame spread both East and West. (OU-FAY-MEE)

EVANGELINE From the Ecclesiastic Late Latin *evangelium* (good news), which is from the Greek *euangelos* (bringing good news). (EE-VAHN-ZHAH-LEEN)

EVE Derived from the Hebrew Chava (life), which is from *hawwāh* (life). The name is borne in the Bible by the first woman, "the mother of all the living," and hence is common throughout Europe. Var: Eva. (EEV)

FABIENNE Feminine form of Fabien, which is from the Late Latin Fabiānus, a derivative of Fabius, an old Roman family name derived from *faba* (bean). *See* FABIEN (Male Names). (FAH-BEE-EN)

FABIOLA Feminine diminutive form of Fabius, an old Roman family name derived from *faba* (bean). The name was borne by a 4th-century Roman saint who established the first hospice for the sick and needy at Porto. (FAH-BEE-O-LAH)

FAYE Thought to be derived from the Middle English *faie* (fairy), which is from the Old French *feie* (fairy). Var: Fae, Fay. Dim: Fayette. (FAY)

FÉLICIE Feminine form of Félix, which is derived from the Latin *felix* (lucky, happy). Var: Felicienne, Filicie. (FAY-LEE-SEE)

FÉLICITÉ Derived from the Late Latin Felicitas, a direct borrowing of *felicitas* (happiness, felicity), which is from *felix* (happy, lucky). (FAY-LEE-SEE-TAY)

FERNANDE Feminine form of Fernand, which is a variant of Ferdinand, a name of uncertain origin and meaning. *See* FERDINAND (Male Names). (FARE-NAHND)

FLEUR Derived from the Old French *fleur* (flower). (FLUR)

FLORE Cognate of Flora, which is derived from the Latin *floris* (a flower). The name was borne by a young Spanish woman martyred at Córdova in 851 during the persecution under the Moslem ruler Abd-ar-Rahman II. (FLOR)

FLORENCE From the Latin Florentia (a blooming), which is derived from *florens* (blooming, flourishing). (FLOR-ENZ)

FRANCE Short form of Frances and Françoise, France is also bestowed as an independent given name. *See* FRANCES *and* FRANÇOISE. (FRAHNS)

FRANCES Feminine form of Franceis, an Old French form of the Italian Franceso, which is from the Middle Latin Franciscus (a Frenchman). Franciscus is derived from Francus (a Frank, a freeman), which has its root in the Old French *franc* (free). Pet: Fanchon, Fanchone, Franchon, Franchone. (FRAHN-SAY)

FRANCINE A diminutive pet form of Françoise (French), Francine is commonly bestowed as an independent given name. *See* FRANÇOISE. (FRAHN-SEEN)

FRANÇOISE From the Old French François (French). Françoise is commonly found on the family tree of the French royal house of Bourbon-Orléans, and like the male form, François, is often bestowed as a patriotic gesture. Short: France. Pet: Fanchon, Fanchone, Franchon, Francine. (FRAHN-SWAHZ)

FRÉDÉRIQUE Feminine form of Frédéric, a derivative of the Germanic Friedrich (peace ruler), which is from the obsolete Fridurih, a compound name composed from the elements *frid* (peace) and *rik* (ruler, king). (FRAY-DAY-REE-KAY)

GABRIELLE Feminine form of Gabriel, which is from the Hebrew Gavriel, a name derived from *gavhrī'ēl* (God is my strength). Gabriel is borne in the Bible by one of the seven archangels, the herald of Good News who appeared to Mary to announce her pregnancy and the impending birth of the Christ child. Pet: Gaby. (GAH-BREE-EL)

GAETANE Feminine form of Gaetan, a name derived from the city of Gaeta. The name is of uncertain derivation. (GEE-TAHN)

GEMMA A borrowing from the Italian, Gemma is derived from the Latin *gemma* (gem, jewel). The name was borne by St. Gemma Galgani (1878–1903), a young woman who wished to be a Passionist nun but was unable to because of poor health. She endured the marks and pain of the stigmata for more than eighteen months and experienced numerous ecstasies and visions. (JEM-MAH)

GENEVIÈVE Derived from the Gaulish Genovefa, a name with Celtic roots but the meaning of which is uncertain. The first element is believed to be from *genos* (race, people, tribe); the second is possibly from an element meaning "woman." Its alteration in the translation from the Celtic to the French seems to be the cause for the confusion. The name is often bestowed in honor of the patron saint of Paris (420–500). In spite of much opposition and criticism, St. Geneviève was a nun who worked tirelessly for the people of Paris. During the

Frankish occupation, she heroically went in search of food, encouraged the people, and spoke up for the release of prisoners of war. Pet: Genny. (ZHEH-NEH-VYEHV)

GEORGETTE Feminine diminutive form of Georges, which is from the Greek Geōrgios, a derivative of geōrgos (earthworker, farmer), which is composed from the elements *gē* (earth) and *ergein* (to work). *See* Georges (Male Names). (ZHOR-ZHET)

GERMAINE Feminine form of Germain, which is from the Late Latin Germānus (brother), a name derived from *germen* (a sprout, bud, embryo). The name was borne by Germaine of Pibrac (c. 1579–1601), an unhealthy child with a withered hand who was martyred by her family and others. Accused of taking a loaf of bread to a beggar one winter day, she was made to open her apron, which was found to be full of spring flowers. Soon after, she was found dead in her sleeping place under the stairs. Miracles of healing are said to happen at her grave. Var: Germain, Germana. (ZHER-MAHN)

GHISLAINE Elaborated variant of Giselle, a name of Germanic origin derived from *gisil* (pledge). Var: Ghislain. (GEES-LANE)

GILBERTE Feminine form of Gilbert, which is an evolution of the Old French Guillebert, a derivative of the Old High German Gisilberht, which is a compound name composed of the elements *gisil* (pledge) and *beraht* (bright, famous). (ZHEEL-BARE-TEH)

GISELLE Of Germanic origin, Giselle is derived from *gisil* (pledge). The name was borne by a daughter of Charles the Simple. She was married to Rollo, the first duke of Normandy, as a pledge of amity between the Karlingen and the Normans in 911. (ZHEE-SEL)

HANNAH Derived from the Hebrew *chaanach* (gracious, full of grace, mercy). The name is borne in the Bible by the mother of the prophet Samuel. (HAH-NAH)

HARRIETTE English form of the French Henriette (home ruler). *See* HENRIETTE. Var: Harriet, Harrietta. (HAH-REE-ET)

HÉLÈNE From the Greek Helenē, which is derived from the element *ēlē* (light). The name was borne by the Christian mother (c. 248–327) of Constantine the Great. Her influence led to the toleration of Christianity, and she is credited with finding the True Cross buried in a hillock close to Calvary. (HAY-LEN)

HENRIETTE Feminine diminutive form of Henri, which is derived from the German Heinrich (ruler of an enclosure, home ruler). *See* HENRI (Male Names). (AHN-REE-ET)

HERMINE Feminine form of the German Hermann, a compound name composed of the Old German elements *hari, heri* (army) and *man* (man): hence, "soldier, army man." (ERR-MEEN)

HILAIRE Taken from the Latin Hilaria, which is derived from *hilaris* (cheerful, noisy, merry). (HEE-LAIR)

HONORIA Feminine form of the Late Latin Honorius, which is derived from *honor* (honor, esteem, integrity). Var: Honore, Honorine. (O-NO-REE-AH)

HORTENSE From the Latin Hortensia, a feminine form of the old Roman family name Hortensius (gardener), a derivation of *hortus* (a garden). (OR-TAINS)

HUGUETTE Feminine diminutive form of Hugh, an evolution of the Old French Hue, which is from the Old High German Hugo, a derivative of *hugu* (heart, mind, spirit). *See* HUGH (Male Names). Var: Huette. (HYOO-ET)

HYACINTHE Feminine form of the Latin Hyacinthus, a derivative of the Greek Hyakinthos (hyacinth, bluebell). The name was borne by several early saints, including the 3rd-century St. Hyacinth, a Roman martyr who was burned to death with her brother, Protus. (HEE-A-SEENT)

IDA Of Germanic origin, Ida is derived from the element *īd* (work, labor). (EE-DAH)

INÈS A borrowing from the Spanish, Inès is a cognate of Agnès (chaste, pure). *See* AGNÈS. (EE-NEHZ)

IRÉNÉE Derived from the Greek Eirēnē (peace). The name was borne in Greek mythology by the goddess of peace, who was a daughter of Zeus and Themis. (EE-RAY-NAY)

ISABELLE A borrowing from the Spanish, Isabelle originated as a variant of Elisabeth (God is my oath). The name, imported in the early Middle Ages, is commonly found on the family trees of French royalty. (EE-SAH-BEL)

JACINTE Variant of Hyacinthe (hyacinth, bluebell) based on Jacinta, the Spanish form of the name. *See* HYACINTHE. (ZHAH-SEENT)

JACQUELINE Feminine form of Jacques, which is a cognate of James and Jacob, both of which are derived from the Hebrew *ja'aqob* (supplanted, seized by the heel). Var: Jacquine. Dim: Jacquette. (ZHAHK-LEEN)

JANE A borrowing from the English, Jane is a cognate of the French Jeanne and Jehanne, which are feminine forms of Jean (God is gracious). *See* JEANNE. (ZHAYN)

JEANNE Feminine form of Jean, the French cognate of John (God is gracious). *See* JEAN (Male Names). Jeanne is one of the most popular of all the French female names. Dim: Ginette, Janique, Jeannette, Jeannine, Jeannique. (ZHAHN)

JEANNETTE A diminutive form of Jeanne (God is gracious), Jeannette is commonly bestowed as an independent given name. *See* JEANNE. Var: Ginette. (ZHAH-NET)

JEANNINE A diminutive form of Jeanne (God is gracious), Jeannine is also bestowed as an independent given name. *See* JEANNE. Var: Janine. (ZHAH-NEEN)

JESSAMINE Derived from the Middle French *jessemin* (jasmine). Var: Jessamina. (JEH-SAH-MEEN)

JOCELINE Derived from the Norman French Joscelin, a name derived from the obsolete Gautzelin, which finds its root in the Germanic tribal name *Gauts*. (ZHAHS-LEEN)

JOËLLE Feminine form of Joël, which, via the Ecclesiastic Late Latin, is from the Ecclesiastic Greek Iōēl, a name derived from the Hebrew Yoel, which is from *yō'ēl* (the Lord is God). Var: Joelliane. (ZHO-EL)

JOHANNE Feminine form of Johann, a German cognate of Jean (God is gracious). *See* JEAN (Male Names). Var: Joanna, Joanne. (ZHO-HAHN)

JORDANE Feminine form of Jordan, a borrowing of the name of the river in the Holy Land, which is from the Hebrew *ha-yarden* (flowing down). The river is that in which John the Baptist baptized Christ. Therefore, the name was originally bestowed upon those baptized in holy water that was said to be from the river. (ZHOR-DANE)

JOSÉE Feminine form of the Spanish José, a cognate of Joseph (may he add). *See* JOSÈPHE. Var: Josiane. (ZHO-ZAY)

JOSÈPHE Feminine form of Joseph, a borrowing from the Ecclesiastic Late Latin, which is from the Ecclesiastic Greek Iōsēph, which in turn is from the Hebrew Yosef, a name derived from *yōsēf* (may he add). The name is often used in conjunction with Marie in honor of Joseph and Mary, the parents of Jesus Christ. (ZHO-SAYF-EH)

JOSÉPHINE Variant of Josèphe (may he add) formed by the addition of the hypocoristic suffix *-ine*. The name was most famously borne by the first wife of Napoléon Bonaparte, the Empress Joséphine (1763–1814). She was previously married to vicomte Alexandre de Beauharnais, a French Army officer who was guillotined. For five years Joséphine presided over a glittering court until Napoléon had the marriage annulled because she had not provided him with a child. Pet: Fifi, Fifine, Josette. (ZHO-ZEH-FEEN)

JUDITH Cognate of the Hebrew Jehudith and Yehudit, which are feminine forms of Jehuda and Yehūdhāh. These names, Anglicized as Judah, mean "he will be praised." Because Judah was also the name of a kingdom in ancient Palestine, the name can also mean "from Judah." The name is borne in the Bible by a woman who saved her people from Nebuchadnezzar's invaders by gaining the confidence of the general Holofernes and cutting off his head while he was asleep. Her story is told in the apocryphal book of Judith. (ZHOO-DITH)

JULIE French cognate of Julia, a feminine form of the Latin Julius, an old Roman family name which is thought to be derived from Iulus (the first down on the chin, downy-bearded). Because a person just beginning to develop facial hair is young, the meaning of the name and its related forms has evolved to mean "youth." Dim: Juliette. (ZHOO-LEE)

JULIENNE Feminine form of Julien, which is from the Latin Julianus, a derivative of the old Roman family name Julius. *See* JULIE. (ZHOO-LEE-EN)

JULITTE Derived from the Latin Julitta, a name of uncertain origin. Some believe it to be a Late Latin form of Judith (he will be praised); others think it is a variant of Julia. The name was borne by a 4th-century woman martyred in Tarsus with her infant son, Quiricus. (ZHOO-LEET)

JUSTINE Feminine form of Justin, which is from the Latin Justīnus, a name derived from *justus* (just, lawful, fair). (ZHOO-STEEN)

KALLIROE Derived from the Greek Kallirrōē (beautiful stream), a compound name composed of the elements *kallos* (beauty) and *rōē* (stream). (KAH-LEE-RO)

LAURE French cognate of Laura, which is derived from the Latin *laurus* (laurel, an evergreen shrub or tree whose leaves were woven into wreaths by the ancient Greeks to crown victors in various contests). Var: Lauren, Laurene. Dim: Lauretta, Laurette. Pet: Laurelle, Laurie. (LOR)

LAURENCE Feminine form of Laurent, which is from the Latin Laurentius (man from Laurentum), a name derived from Laurentum, the name of a town in Latium, which is probably derived from *laurus* (laurel). *See* LAURENT (Male Names). Var: Laurentine. (LOR-EHNS)

LA VERNE Derived from the Latin *vernus* (belonging to spring). The name was typically given to one born during springtime. Var: La Vergne, Laverna, La Vernia. (LAH-VERN)

LÉA French cognate of Leah, which is derived from the Hebrew *lā'āh* (weary, to tire). The name was borne in the

Bible by the eldest daughter of Laban and the first of Jacob's four wives. (LAY-AH)

Léonie Derived from the Latin Leonia, the feminine form of Leonius, which is derived from *leo* (lion). (LAY-O-NEE)

Léonne Feminine form of Léon, the French cognate of Leo, which is derived directly from the Latin *leo* (lion). (LAY-ON)

Léonore Short form of Eléonore (light, bright), Léonore is also used as an independent given name. *See* ELÉONORE. (LAY-O-NORE)

Léontine Derived from the Latin Leontina, a feminine form of Leontius, which is derived from *leo* (lion). (LAY-ON-TEEN)

Liliane Variant of the English Lilian, which is believed to be derived from the Latin *lilium* (lily). (LEE-LEE-AHN)

Lorraine Transferred use of the surname originating from the name of a province in eastern France, which is derived from the Latin Lotharingia (territory of the people of Lothar). Lothar, the name of the son of the Frankish king Clovis, is of Germanic origin and is derived from the elements *hluod* (famous) and *hari, heri* (army): hence, "famous army." Var: Loraine. (LOR-REN)

Louise Feminine form of Louis (famous in war), which is from the Old High German Hluodowig, a compound name composed from the elements *hluod* (famous) and *wīg* (war, strife). The popular name was borne by St. Louise de Marillac (1591–1660), cofounder of the Daughters of Charity with St. Vincent de Paul. Var: Heloise, Louisiane. (LWEEZ)

Louise-Marie Combination name composed of the names Louise (famous in war) and Marie, the French cognate of Mary. *See* LOUISE *and* MARIE. (LWEEZ-MAH-REE)

Luce Feminine form of Luc, which is from the Ecclesiastic Late Latin Lucas, a derivative of Lucius, which is from the root *lux* (light). Alternatively, some believe the name is derived from the Ecclesiastic Greek Loukas, which is a contraction of Loukanos (man from Lucania). *See* LUC (Male Names). Dim: Lucette. (LEWS)

Lucia Feminine form of the Latin Lucius, which is derived from the root *lux* (light). Dim: Lucette. (LEW-SEE-AH)

Lucienne Feminine form of Lucien, which is from the Latin Luciānus (of Lucius), a derivative of Lucius, which is from the root *lux* (light). Short: Lucie. (LEW-SEE-EN)

Lucille Derived from the Latin Lucilla, which is a pet form of Lucia (light). *See* LUCIA. (LEW-SEEL)

Lucinde French form of Lucinda, an elaborated form of Lucia (light) which originated as a literary name in Cervantes' *Don Quixote* (1605). (LEW-SIND)

Lydie French cognate of the Greek Lydia (Lydian, woman from Lydia, an ancient kingdom in western Asia Minor). (LĪ-DEE)

Madeleine French cognate of Magdalene, which is derived from the Greek Magdalēnē (of Magdala, a town on the Sea of Galilee). The name is often bestowed in honor of the biblical Mary Magdalene, the woman Christ cured of seven demons. She was the first to see him after the resurrection and rushed to tell the apostles. Var: Madeline, Madelon. (MAD-EH-LEHN)

Magali Provençal name of uncertain etymology. Some believe it might be a variant form of Magdalena (of Magdala) or Margaret (a pearl). Var: Magalie. (MAH-GAL-EE)

Magnolia Taken from the name of the trees or shrubs of the magnolia family which bear large, fragrant flowers. (MAHG-NOL-YAH)

Manon Originally a pet form of Marie, Manon is also bestowed as an independent given name. *See* MARIE. (MAH-NŌN)

Marcelline Feminine form of Marcellin, which is from the Latin Marcellīnus, a diminutive variant of Marcus, which is a name of uncertain derivation. *See* MARC (Male Names). Var: Marcelina, Marceline, Marcellina. (MAHR-SAY-LEEN)

Marcille Feminine form of Marcel, which is from the Latin Marcellus, a diminutive form of Marcus, which is of uncertain derivation. *See* MARC (Male Names). (MAHR-SEEL)

Margot A pet form of Marguerite (a pearl), Margot is also bestowed as an independent given name. *See* MARGUERITE. Var: Margaux, Margo. (MAHR-GO)

Marguerite French cognate of Margaret, which is from the Greek Margarītēs, a name derived from *maragon* (a pearl). The name was borne by several saints, including Marguerite Marie (1647–90), a nun who experienced four visions of Christ. (MAHR-GYOOR-EET)

Maria Popular name throughout Europe, Maria is the Latin form of Mary, which is derived from the Hebrew Miryām (sea of bitterness or sorrow). There is much debate over the meaning of this name, however. While "sea of bitterness/sea of sorrow" seems to be the most probable, some sources cite the alternative definitions of "rebellion," "wished-for child," and "mistress or lady of the sea." (MAH-REE-AH)

MARIAMNE Variant form of Mariam, which is from the Hebrew Miryām (sea of bitterness or sorrow). The name was used by Jewish historian Flavius Josephus (A.D. 37–?95) as that of the wife of King Herod, but it is often bestowed in honor of the Virgin Mary. Var: Mariane, Marianne. (MAH-REE-AM-NEE)

MARIANNE Variant of Mariamne, which is derived from the Hebrew Miryām (sea of bitterness or sorrow). In addition to being a given name, Marianne is also the name of the symbolic figure of a woman dressed in French Revolutionary costume who is regarded as the personification of the French Republic. Var: Mariane. (MAH-REE-AHN)

MARIE French cognate of Mary, which is derived from the Hebrew Miryām (sea of bitterness or sorrow). *See* MARIA. The name, extremely popular in France, is often used as an element in combination names. It is also commonly bestowed upon males as a middle name in honor of the Virgin Mary, with the intention of bringing the bearer under her special protection. (MAH-REE)

MARIE-ANGE Combination name composed of the names Marie and Ange (angel). *See* ANGÈLE *and* MARIE. (MAH-REE-AHNZH)

MARIE-CLAIRE Combination name composed of the names Marie and Claire (bright, clear, famous). *See* CLAIRE *and* MARIE. (MAH-REE-CLARE)

MARIE-FRANCE Combination name composed of the names Marie and France (French). *See* FRANCE *and* MARIE. (MAH-REE-FRAHNS)

MARIE-JOSÉE Combination name composed of the names Marie and Josée (may he add). *See* JOSÉE *and* MARIE. The name is bestowed in honor of the Virgin Mary and her husband, Joseph. (MAH-REE-ZHO-ZAY)

MARIE-JOSÈPHE Combination name composed of the names Marie and Josèphe (may he add). *See* JOSÈPHE *and* MARIE. The name is bestowed in honor of the Virgin Mary and her husband, Joseph. (MAH-REE-ZHO-SEF-EH)

MARIELLE Diminutive form of Marie which is commonly bestowed as an independent given name. *See* MARIE. (MAH-REE-EL)

MARIE-LOUISE Combination name composed of the names Marie and Louise (famous in war). *See* LOUISE *and* MARIE. The name was borne by the second wife (1791–1847) of Napoléon Bonaparte. (MAH-REE-LWEEZ)

MARIE-NOËLLE Combination name composed of the names Marie and Noëlle (Christmas child). *See* MARIE *and* NOËLLE. The name is commonly bestowed upon children born during the Christmas season in special honor of the Virgin Mary and in commemoration of the birth of the Christ child. (MAH-REE-NO-EL)

MARIE-THÉRÈSE Combination name composed of the names Marie and Thérèse (harvester). *See* MARIE *and* THÉRÈSE. (MAH-REE-TAY-REHZ)

MARIE-ZÉPHYRINE Combination name composed of the names Marie and Zéphyrine (west wind). *See* MARIE *and* ZÉPHYRINE. (MAH-REE-ZAY-FREEN)

MARION Old French diminutive form of Marie in common use since the Middle Ages. *See* MARIE. Var: Marionne. (MAH-REE-ŌN)

MARJOLAINE Derived from *marjolaine*, the French name of the herb sweet marjoram. (MAHR-ZHO-LANE)

MARTHE Derived from the Aramaic Mārthā (lady, mistress). (MAHR-THE)

MARTINE Feminine form of Martin, which is from the Latin Martinus, a derivative of Mars, the name of the Roman mythological god of war. *See* MARTIN (Male Names). (MAHR-TEEN)

MARVELLE Derived from the Old French *merveille* (a wonder, a marvel). Var: Marveille, Marvel, Marvella. (MAHR-VEL)

MARYVONNE Combination name composed of the names Marie and Yvonne (yew). *See* MARIE *and* YVONNE. (MAH-REE-VON)

MATHILDE Derived from the Old High German Mahthilda, a compound name composed of the elements *maht* (might, praise) and *hiltia* (battle): hence, "powerful in battle." (MAH-TILD)

MAUDE Contracted form of Mathilde (powerful in battle), which has been in use since the Middle Ages. *See* MATHILDE. (MOD)

MAURA A feminine form of the Latin Maurus (dark-skinned), which is from the Greek *mauritius* (of Moorish lineage, dark-skinned). Var: Maurelle, Maurine. (MOR-AH)

MELISANDE Derived from the Greek *melissa* (a honey bee). (MEH-LEE-SAHND)

MELISENT Derived from the obsolete Old High German Amalaswinth, a compound name composed of the elements *amal* (work) and *swinth* (strength). Var: Melisent, Millicent, Millicente. (MAY-LEE-SEH)

MÉLODIE Derived from the French *mélodie* (melody, song). (MEH-LO-DEE)

MICHÈLE Popular name, Michèle is a feminine form of Michel, the French cognate of Michael, which is a borrowing from the Ecclesiastic Late Latin, Greek, and Hebrew. The name is derived from the Hebrew *mīkhā'ēl* (who is like God?). *See* MICHEL (Male Names). Var: Michelle. Dim: Micheline. (MEE-SHAY-LEH)

MICHELINE A diminutive form of Michèle and Michelle, Micheline is also bestowed as an independent given name. *See* MICHÈLE. (MEE-SHAY-LEEN)

MIGNON Derived from the French *mignon* (delicate, dainty), which is from the Old French *mignot* (dainty). (MEE-NYŌN)

MIRABELLE From the Latin *mīrābilis* (wondrous), which is derived from *mirari* (to wonder at). (MEER-AH-BEL)

MIREIO A Provençal name believed to be a variant form of Miriam, which is from the Hebrew Miryām (sea of bitterness or sorrow). *See* MARIA. Var: Mireille. (MEER-EE-O)

MONIQUE French cognate of Monica, an ancient yet still popular name of uncertain etymology. Monica was the name of the Numidian-born mother of St. Augustine, so the name might be of African origin. However, Monica is said to have been a citizen of Carthage, a city founded by the Phoenicians, so her name might be of Phoenician origin. Alternatively, some believe it to be from the Latin *moneo* (to advise). (MO-NEEK)

MURIEL A borrowing from the English, Muriel is an Anglicized form of the Irish Muirgheal and the Scottish Muireall, names composed of the Old Celtic elements *muir* (sea) and *geal* (bright): hence, "bright sea." (MYOOR-EE-EL)

MYRIAM French cognate of Miriam, which is from the Hebrew Miryām (sea of bitterness or sorrow). Var: Myriana. (MEER-EE-AHM)

NADIA French form of the Russian Nadya, a pet form of Nadezhda, which is directly derived from the word meaning "hope." The name was introduced to France early in the 20th century when the Ballet Russe was established in Paris. (NAHD-YAH)

NADINE Elaboration of Nadia, the French form of the Russian Nadya (hope). *See* NADIA. (NAH-DEEN)

NATALIE From the Latin Natalia, a name derived from *diēs nātālis* (natal day). The name is often bestowed upon children born on Christmas Day. Var: Nathalie. (NAH-TAH-LEE)

NICOLE Feminine form of Nicolas, which is from the Greek Nikolaos, a compound name composed of the elements *nikē* (victory) and *laos* (the people): hence, "victory of the people." Var: Nicola, Nicolle. Dim: Nicolette, Nicollette. Pet: Colette, Collette. (NEE-KOLE)

NICOLETTE Diminutive form of Nicole (victory of the people), which is also bestowed as an independent given name. *See* NICOLE. Var: Nicollette. Short: Colette, Collette. (NEE-KO-LET)

NINA A borrowing of the Russian diminutive form of Anne (gracious, full of grace) and Antonina. *See* ANNE *and* ANTOINETTE. Dim: Ninette. Pet: Ninon. (NEE-NAH)

NINON A pet form of Anne (gracious, full of grace) and Nina (gracious, full of grace), Ninon is also occasionally bestowed as an independent given name. (NEE-NŌN)

NOËLLE Feminine form of Noël, an evolution of the Old French Nouel, from *noel, nouel* (natal, Christmas), which is from the Latin *diēs nātālis* (natal day, birthday) and *nātālis diēs Domini* (natal day of the Lord, Christmas). The name is commonly bestowed upon children born during the Christmas season. Var: Noelle. (NO-EL-LEH)

NOÉMIE French cognate of Naomi, the Anglicized form of the Hebrew Naami, which is a variant of Naamah (pleasant, beautiful, delightful). (NO-Ā-MEE)

ODETTE Feminine diminutive form of the obsolete male name Oda, a short form of the various Germanic names beginning with the element *od* (prosperity, riches, fortune). Though the male name has dropped from use, Odette remains viable. (O-DET)

ODILE Derived from the Germanic Odila, which is derived from the element *od* (riches, prosperity, fortune). The name was borne by St. Odilia (d. c. 720), the founder of a nunnery at Odilienberg in the Vosges Mountains. She is considered the patron saint of Alsace in northeastern France. Var: Ottilie. Dim: Ottoline. (O-DEEL)

OLYMPE Derived from the Latin Olympia, a feminine form of Olympius, which is derived from Olympos, the name of a mountain in northern Greece believed to be the home of the gods. (O-LIM-PEH)

OPHELIE French cognate of Ophelia, a name believed to have been coined by Sannazzaro in 1504 for the name of a character in his pastoral *Arcadia*. He is thought to have taken the name from the Greek *ōphelia* (help, succor). (O-FEE-LEE)

ORIANE Of uncertain derivation and meaning, Oriane seems to have first been used as the name of a character in the medieval French romance *Amadis de Gaul.* Some believe Oriane to have been derived from the Latin *oriri* (to rise) or from the Old French *or* (gold). Var: Orianne. (O-REE-AHN)

ORNETTE French cognate of Ornetta, an altered form of the Italian Ornella, which is believed to be derived from the Tuscan word *ornello,* which denotes the flowering ash tree. (OR-NET)

PASCALE Feminine form of Pascal, which is from the Late Latin Paschālis (of or pertaining to Easter), a derivative of Pascha (Easter), which is from the Hebrew *pesach, pesah* (Passover). The name is often bestowed upon children born at Eastertime. Var: Pascala. (PAH-SKAHL)

PATRICE Borne by both males and females, Patrice is the French cognate of Patrick, which is derived from the Latin *patricius* (a patrician). *See* PATRICE (Male Names). (PAH-TREES)

PATRICIA A borrowing from the English, Patricia is a feminine form of Patrick, which is from the Latin *patricius* (a patrician, an aristocrat). Var: Patriciane. (PAH-TREE-SHA)

PAULE Feminine form of Paul, which is from the Latin Paulus, a Roman family name derived from *paulus* (small). Dim: Paulette. (POL-EH)

PAULINE From the Latin Paulina, a feminine form of the Late Latin Paulīnus, a derivative of the Roman family name Paulus, which is from *paulus* (small). (PO-LEEN)

PERRINE Feminine form of Perrin, an obsolete diminutive form of Pierre, which is the French cognate of Peter (a rock, a stone). While Perrin is not in current use, Perrine remains a viable name. *See* PIERRE (Male Names). (PER-REEN)

PHILIPPA Feminine form of Philippe (lover of horses), which is from the Latin Philippus, a derivative of the Greek Philippos, a compound name composed of the elements *philein* (to love) and *hippos* (horse). *See* PHILIPPE (Male Names). Var: Philippine. (FEE-LEEP-AH)

PHILOMÈNE French form of Philomena, a feminine form of the Latin Philomenus, which is from the Greek Philomenēs, a compound name composed of the elements *philein* (to love) and *menos* (strength): hence, "lover of strength." (FEE-LO-MAY-NEH)

PIERRETTE Feminine diminutive form of Pierre, the French cognate of Peter, which is from the Ecclesiastic Late Latin Petrus and the Greek Petros, names derived from *petra* (a rock) and *petros* (a stone). Var: Pieretta. (PYAIR-ET)

RACHEL From the Ecclesiastic Late Latin and the Ecclesiastic Greek Rhachēl, which is derived from the Hebrew *rāchēl* (ewe). Var: Rachelle. (RAH-SHEL)

RAYMONDE Feminine form of Raymond, an evolution of the Old Norman French Raimund, which is derived from the Germanic Raginmund, a compound name composed of the elements *ragin* (advice, counsel) and *mund* (hand, protection): hence, "wise protection." (RĪ-MON-DEH)

RÉBECCA From the Ecclesiastic Late Latin and Ecclesiastic Greek Rhebekka, which is derived from the Hebrew *ribbqāh* (noose), from *rabak* (to bind, to tie). (RAY-BEK-KAH)

RÉGINE Derived from the Latin Regina, which is from *rēgina* (queen), a feminine form of *rex* (king), which has been in use since the Middle Ages. (RAY-ZHEEN-EH)

REINE Derived from the Latin *rēgina* (queen). Var: Raina, Reina. (RĪ-NEH)

RENÉE Feminine form of René, from the Late Latin Renātus, which is a direct derivative of *renātus* (reborn, born again). A popular name, Renée is often bestowed in celebration of the Christian's spiritual rebirth. (REH-NAY-EH)

ROMAINE Feminine form of Romain, which is from the Latin Romanus (a Roman), a derivative of Roma (Rome). (RO-MEN, RO-MANE)

ROSALIE From the Latin *rosalia,* the annual ceremony of hanging garlands of roses on tombs. The word is derived from *rosa* (rose). (RO-SAH-LEE)

ROSE Originally, Rose was a short form of any of the various old Germanic names that contained the element *hros, ros* (horse), such as Roslindis. However, the name corresponds to that of the color and the popular flower, with which it is now identified. (ROS)

ROSE-MARIE Popular combination name composed of the names Rose (horse; rose) and Marie. *See* MARIE *and* ROSE. (ROS-MAH-REE)

ROXANE From the Greek Roxanē, which is believed to be derived from the Persian Roschana (dawn of day). The name was borne by the wife of Alexander the Great, which seems to substantiate the name's roots. Var: Roxanne. (ROKS-AHN)

SABINE Derived from the Latin Sabīna (Sabine woman). The Sabines were an ancient tribe who lived in the Apennines of central Italy and who were conquered by the Romans in the 3rd century B.C. (SAH-BEEN)

SALOMÉ Ecclesiastic Late Latin borrowing of the Greek Salōmē, which is from the Hebrew *shālōm* (peace). (SAH-LO-MAY)

SANDRA A short form of Alexandra (defender or helper of mankind), Sandra is also bestowed as an independent given name. *See* ALEXANDRA. (SAHN-DRAH)

SANDRINE A short form of Alexandrine (defender or helper of mankind), Sandrine is also bestowed as an independent given name. *See* ALEXANDRA. (SAHN-DREEN)

SARAH Derived from the Hebrew Sārāh (princess). (SAH-RAH)

SASHA A borrowing of the Russian pet form of Alexandra (defender or helper of mankind). The name was introduced into France during the first part of the 20th century when the Ballet Russe was established in Paris. (SAH-SHA)

SÉRAPHINE Derived from the Hebrew *sĕrāphīm* (burning ones), a name used in the Bible for the heavenly, winged angels surrounding the throne of God. Var: Séraphime. Pet: Phime, Phine. (SAY-RAH-FEEN)

SIMONE Feminine form of Simon, which is a borrowing from the Ecclesiastic Late Latin. The name is derived from the Hebrew Shimon, a derivative of *shim'ōn* (heard). *See* SIMON (Male Names). Pet: Sime, Simah. (SEE-MONE)

SOLANGE Derived from the Late Latin Sollemnia, which is from *sollemnis* (yearly, annual; solemn, religious). The name was borne by the 9th-century St. Solange of Bourges, a shepherdess murdered for resisting the advances of her master. (SO-LAHNZH)

SOPHIE From the Greek Sophia, a direct derivation of *sophia* (wisdom, skill), which is from *sophos* (wise). The name was borne by several early minor saints. (SO-FEE)

STÉPHANIE Cognate of the Latin Stephania, a variant of Stephana, which is a feminine form of Stephanus, a name derived from *stephanos* (a crown, a garland). Pet: Fanette. (STAY-FAH-NEE)

SUZANNE French cognate of Susannah, which is from the Hebrew Shoshanah, a name derived from *shōshannāh* (lily, rose). Var: Susanne. Pet: Suzette. (SOO-ZAHN)

SYBILLE Derived from the Latin Sibylla (a fortuneteller, a prophetess). The sibyls, women of ancient Greece and Rome, were mouthpieces of the ancient oracles and seers into the future. In the Middle Ages, they were believed to be receptors of divine revelation; thus Sibyl came into use as an acceptable given name. Var: Sibella. (SEE-BEEL)

SYLVIE Derived from the Latin Silvia, a feminine form of Silvius, which is derived from *silva* (wood). (SEEL-VEE)

THÉRÈSE French cognate of Theresa, a name of uncertain etymology. It is generally believed to be derived from the Greek *therizein* (to reap, to gather in). The first known bearer of the name was the Spanish wife of St. Paulinus, a 5th-century Roman bishop of Nola. Theresa was not used outside the Iberian Peninsula until the 16th century, when the fame of St. Teresa of Avila (1515–82) made the name popular among Roman Catholics throughout Europe. (TAY-REHZ)

VALÉRIE Derived from the Latin Valēria, the feminine form of Valērius, an old Roman family name derived from *valere* (to be strong, healthy). (VAH-LAY-REE)

VÉRONIQUE French cognate of Veronica, which is a name of debated origin and meaning. Some believe it to be derived from the Late Latin *veraiconica*, the word given to a piece of cloth or garment with a representation of the face of Christ on it. Veraiconica is composed from the elements *verus* (true) and *iconicus* (of or belonging to an image). Alternatively, Veronica is thought to be a variant of Berenice, a derivative of the Greek Berenikē, which is a variant of the older name Pherenikē, a compound name composed from the elements *pherein* (to bring) and *nikē* (victory). (VAY-RO-NEEK)

VICTORINE Derived from the French *victoire* (victory). Var: Victorina. (VEEK-TŌ-REEN)

VIGNETTE Derived from the French *vignette* (little vine), which is from *vigne* (a vine). Var: Vignetta. (VIN-YET)

VIOLE Derived from the Old French *viole*, which is from the Latin *viola* (a violet). Var: Violaine. (VEE-OLE)

VIOLETTE Derived from the Old French *violette*, a diminutive form of *viole*, which is from the Latin *viola* (a violet). (VEE-O-LET)

VIRGINIE Derived from Verginius (spring-like, flourishing), an old Roman family name, which has its roots in the Latin *ver* (spring). (VEER-ZHEE-NEE)

VIVIENNE Feminine form of Vivien, which is from the Latin Vivianus, a name derived from *vivus* (alive). Var: Vivean, Viviane, Viviann, Vivianne. Short: Vi, Viv, Vivi. (VEE-VEE-EN)

XAVIÈRE Feminine form of Xavier, which represents the transferred use of the Spanish surname derived from the place-name Xavier in Navarre. The name is believed to be derived from the Basque Etcheberria (the new house). *See* XAVIER (Male Names). (ZAYV-YER-EH)

YOLANDE Of uncertain etymology, some believe Yolande to be a derivative of Violante (violet), a medieval French name derived from the Latin Viola (violet). (YO-LAHND)

YVETTE Feminine diminutive form of Yves (archer), a name of Germanic origin derived from the element *iv* (yew, the type of wood used in bow and arrow making). *See* YVES (Male Names). (EE-VET)

YVONNE A popular name, Yvonne is a feminine form of Yvon (archer, yew) and a feminine diminutive form of Yves (archer, yew), names derived from the Germanic element *iv* (yew, the type of wood used in bow and arrow making). (EE-VON)

ZÉPHYRINE Derived from the Greek Zephyra, the feminine form of Zephyrus, which is derived from *zephyros* (the west wind). The name Zephyrus is borne in Greek mythology by the god of the west wind. (ZEH-FREEN)

ZOË A borrowing from the Greek, Zoë is derived from *zōē* (life). Var: Zoé, Zoelie, Zoelle. (ZO-EE)

Chapter Nine

German Names

The Germanic language evolved out of the old Indo-European tongue and continued to evolve over the centuries into twelve modern languages. This old language is a source of hundreds of names found in the nomenclature of many other countries, yet few foreign names found their way into German society until recently.

Early Germans preferred names that reflected their warfaring ways, and surnames and family names were unknown. Given names were usually compound and expressive of a specific idea. The root names were often derived from mythology, animals, terms relating to war and peace, nature, and social status.

When the trend developed to establish parentage by bestowing names made up from elements of those of the parents, many nonsensical names were coined and the meanings of the names were no longer that important. Before surnames were established, families quite often distinguished themselves by having the name of each member bear the same first syllable. As surnames developed, they were taken from traditional sources: places, occupational names, descriptive names, animals, and patronymics. The majority are derived from places.

Under Hitler's regime, the bestowal of names was strictly censored. A list of names was established and it was illegal to give a child a name that was not on the approved list. If a child was given two names, parents had to specify which was to be used on a daily basis. Nicknames were not allowed, with the exception of very popular ones, which were commonly bestowed as independent given names. Jewish people were made to adopt both first and last names that were specifically "Jewish sounding." Thankfully, these restrictions have since been dropped.

Modern naming trends show many old names from early German mythology are now going out of fashion. Names from the Low German dialects of northern Germany are becoming popular throughout the country, as are foreign names. Parents in the eastern areas are bestowing many Slavonic names upon their children, and in the western part of the country, names are heavily influenced by French. The continued influence of the Catholic Church in southern Germany helps keep many saints' names in common use.

German Male Names

Adal Derived from the Old High German *adal, adel* (noble, nobility). The name is also used as a short form of any of the various names containing *adal* as an element. Var: Adel. (AH-DAHL)

Adalrich Compound name composed from the elements *adal, adel* (noble, nobility) and *rik, rīc* (ruler, king): hence, "noble ruler." Var: Adelrich, Alaric, Alarich, Alarick, Alarik, Alerk, Alrik, Aurick, Aurik, Uadalrich, Ullric, Ulrich. Short: Adal, Adel. Pet: Udo, Uli, Uwe. (AH-DAHL-RISH)

Adam Derived from the Hebrew *adama* (red earth). The name is borne in the Bible by the first man created by God. According to biblical tradition, it was from Adam's rib that the first woman, Eve, was formed. (AH-DAHM)

Adelbert Derived from the Old High German Adalbrecht, a compound name composed of the elements *adal* (noble, nobility) and *beraht* (bright, famous): hence, "nobly bright, bright through nobility." Var: Adalbert. Short: Adal, Adel, Bert. (AH-DALE-BAIRT)

Adrian From the Latin Adriānus (man from the city of Adria) and Hadriānus (man from the city of Hadria). The name was borne by several popes of the Catholic Church. (AH-DREE-AHN)

Alex Short form of Alexander (defender or helper of mankind), Alex is also popularly bestowed as an independent given name. *See* ALEXANDER. (AH-LAYKS)

Alexander From the Greek Alexandros (defender or helper of mankind), a compound name composed of the elements *alexein* (to defend, to help) and *andros* (man). The name became popular through the fame of Alexander the Great (356–323 B.C.), the Macedonian king and military ruler who helped spread Greek culture across Asia Minor and to Egypt and India. Short: Alex. (AH-LAYK-SAHN-DARE)

Alexis Derived from the Greek *alexein* (to defend, to help). (AH-LAYKS-ISS)

Anicho Derived from the element *ano* (ancestor). (AH-NIH-KO)

Anton The German form of Anthony, which is derived from the Latin Antōnius, an old Roman family name of unknown etymology. The name is popular throughout Europe, due in large part to its connections with St. Anthony the Great, an Egyptian ascetic and the first Christian monk, and with St. Anthony of Padua (1195–1231), who worked miracles for the poor and the sick. Pet: Toni. (AHN-TONE)

Archibald Compound name derived from the Germanic elements *ercan* (genuine) and *bald* (bold, brave): hence, "genuinely bold." Short: Archi. (AHR-CHI-BAHLT)

Arend A borrowing from the Dutch, Arend (eagle power) is a cognate of Arnold. *See* ARNOLD. Var: Ahren, Aren. (AH-RAYNT)

Armin Derived from the Latin Arminius, which is a cognate of the Germanic Hermann (soldier, warrior). *See* HERMANN. Var: Armand. (AHR-MIN)

Arnd Contracted form of Arnold (eagle ruler). *See* ARNOLD. Var: Arndt. Pet: Arne. (AHRNT)

Arnold From the Old High German Aranold, an evolution of the older Germanic Arnwald, a compound name composed of the elements *arn* (eagle) and *wald* (ruler, power): hence, "eagle ruler, eagle power." Var: Arnald, Arnall, Arnaud, Arnell, Arnet, Arnett, Arnot, Arnott. (AHR-NOLT)

Artur Germanic cognate of Arthur, a name of Celtic origin but of unknown meaning. The name was borne by the legendary King Arthur of the Round Table. *See* ARTHUR (English Names). Short: Art. (AHR-TOOR)

August From the Latin Augustus, which is directly derived from *augustus* (great, venerable, consecrated by the augurs). (AU-GOOST)

Austin A borrowing from the English, Austin is a contracted form of Augustine (great), which is from the Latin Augustinus, a diminutive form of Augustus, which is derived from *augustus* (great, venerable, consecrated by the augurs). (AU-STIN)

Axel A borrowing from the Scandinavians, Axel is a cognate of the biblical Absalom, which is derived from the Hebrew *'abshālōm* (the father is peace). *See* ABSALOM (Biblical Names). Var: Aksel, Apsel. (AHKS-ALE)

Baldwin Derived from the Middle High German Baldewin (bold friend), a compound name composed of the elements *bald* (bold, brave) and *wini* (friend). Var: Balduin, Baldwyn. (BAHL-DWIN)

Barrett A borrowing from the English, Barrett is the transferred use of the surname, which is of uncertain origin and meaning. Some believe it to be derived from the Old French *barat* (traffic, commerce), the meaning of which evolved to "trouble, contention, deception" in the 13th century. Var: Barret. (BAHR-RATE)

BARTHOLOMAUS German cognate of the Late Latin Bartholomaeus, which is from the Aramaic Bartholomaios (son of Talmai). Talmai is an Aramaic name meaning "hill, mound, furrows." The name is borne in the Bible by one of the Twelve Apostles of Christ. Short: Bartel, Barthol, Bartold, Bertel. Pet: Mewes. (BAHR-TOL-O-MAUS)

BASTIEN A short form of Sebastien (man from Sebastia), Bastien is also bestowed as an independent given name. *See* SEBASTIEN. (BAHS-TEE-AHN)

BENEDIKTE Derived from the Latin Benedictus (blessed), which is from *benedicere* (to speak well of, to bless). Pet: Dix. (BAY-NAY-DIK-TAY)

BEREND Derived from the Old High German Berinhard, a compound name composed of the elements *bern* (bear) and *hard* (bold, hardy, brave, strong): hence, "strong as a bear, hardy as a bear." Var: Bernd. (BAY-RAYNT)

BERG Directly derived from *berg* (mountain). (BAIRK)

BERN Popular name derived from *bern* (bear). It is also used as a short form of Bernhard (bold as a bear). *See* BERNHARD. Var: Berne, Berrin. (BAIRN)

BERNHARD Derived from the Old High German Berinhard (bold as a bear), a compound name composed of the elements *bern* (bear) and *hard* (bold, hearty, brave, strong). Var: Barnard, Berend, Berinhard, Bernard, Bernardyn, Bernd, Bernon, Bernot. Short: Bern. (BAIRN-HAHRT)

BORIS A borrowing from the Russian, Boris is derived from *boris* (fight). The name is borne by tennis star Boris Becker. (BOR-ISS)

BRENDAN An ancient name of uncertain origin and meaning, Brendan is thought to be a Celtic name derived from *brandr* (the blade of a sword). Alternatively, it might be a derivative of the obsolete Brandolf (sword wolf). Var: Brandeis, Brendis. Short: Bren. (BRAIN-DAHN)

BRUNO From the German *bruno* (brown). The name was borne by St. Bruno of Cologne (1030–1101), a German monk and founder of the Carthusian Order. Var: Brunon. (BROO-NO)

CHRISTIAN Popular name derived from the Latin *christiānus*, which is from the Greek *christianos* (a Christian, a follower of Christ). Var: Krischan. (KRIS-TEE-AHN)

CHRISTOPH Derived from the Ecclesiastic Late Latin Christophorus and the Ecclesiastic Greek Christophoros, a compound name composed of the elements *Christos* (Christ) and *pherein* (to bear): hence, "bearing Christ." The name was borne by St. Christopher, a 3rd-century Christian martyr of Asia Minor who is the patron saint of travelers. Pet: Stoffel, Stoppel. (KRIS-TOF)

CLAUS Short form of Nicolaus (victory of the people), Claus is also popularly bestowed as an independent given name. *See* NICOLAUS. Var: Claas, Klaas, Klaus. (KLAUS)

DANIEL Derived from the Hebrew *dānī'ēl* (God is my judge). (DAHN-YEHL)

DAVID Derived from the Hebrew *dāvīd* (beloved). It is borne in the Bible by the second and greatest of the Israelite kings. (DAY-VID)

DENNIS Derived from the Greek Dionysius (of Dionysos, the Greek mythological god of wine and revelry). (DAY-NIS)

DEREK Short form of Theodoric, which is from the Late Latin Theodoricus, a name believed to be from the Germanic Thiudoreiks, a compound name composed from the Old German elements *thiuda* (folk, people) and *reiks* (ruler, leader, king): hence, "leader of the people." (DAY-RAKE)

DIETER A short form of Dieterich (ruler of the people), Dieter is also bestowed as an independent given name. *See* DIETRICH. (DEE-TER)

DIETRICH Variant of Derek, a short form of Theodoric, which is from the Late Latin Theodoricus, a name believed to be from the Gothic name Thiudoreiks, which is composed of the Old German elements *thiuda* (folk, people) and *reiks* (ruler, leader). Var: Dedrick, Dedrik, Derrich. Short: Dieter, Dietz, Dirk. (DEE-TRISH)

DIRK A borrowing from the Scandinavians, Dirk is a cognate of Derek (ruler of the people). *See* DEREK. (DIRK)

DOMINIK From the Latin Dominicus (belonging to a lord), which is derived from *dominus* (a master, a lord). (DOM-IH-NIK)

EBERHARD Derived from the Old High German Eburhart, a compound name composed of the elements *ebur* (a wild boar) and *hart* (hearty, hard, strong, brave): hence, "strong or brave as a wild boar." Var: Eberhardt, Eburhardt, Evrard. (Ā-BARE-HAHRT)

EDUARD German cognate of Edward, a name derived from the Old English Ēadweard (wealthy or fortunate guardian), a compound name composed of the elements *ēad* (prosperity, fortune, riches) and *weard* (guardian, protector). (Ā-DOO-AHRT)

EDWIN Borrowed from the English, Edwin is derived from the obsolete Old English Eadwine, a compound name composed of the elements *ēad* (prosperity, fortune, riches) and *wine* (friend): hence, "wealthy friend." Var: Edwyn. (Ā-DWIN)

EGINHARD Compound name composed of the elements *eg* (edge or point of a sword) and *hart* (hearty, hard, strong, brave): hence, "hard edge of the sword." Var: Einhard. Pet: Enno. (Ā-GIN-HAHRD)

EGON A name that arose in the Middle Ages and is derived from the element *eg* (edge or point of a sword). (E-GON)

ELLERY A borrowing from the English, Ellery (alder tree) is derived from the Old English *aler* (alder). (Ā-LAY-REE)

ELOI Borrowed from the Spanish, Eloi is from the Latin Eligius (chosen), a name derived from *eligere* (to choose, to select). (EE-LOY)

EMERY Derived from the Old High German Amalrich (work ruler), a compound name composed of the elements *amal* (work) and *rich* (ruler, king). Var: Amery, Emmerich, Emory. Pet: Emmo. (Ā-MAY-REE)

EMIL From the Latin Aemilius, an old Roman family name of uncertain derivation. Some believe it to be from the Latin *aemulus* (trying to equal or excel, rival). (Ā-MIL)

ERIK Popular name derived from the Old Norse Eirìkr (eternal ruler), a compounding of the elements *ei* (ever, always) and *rīkr* (ruler, king). However, there are some who believe the name comes to the Old Norse via the Germanic *ehre* (honor) and the Proto-Germanic *rīk* (king): hence, "honorable king." Var: Aric, Arick, Arrick, Erich. (Ā-RIK)

ERNUST From the Old High German *ernust* (earnest, resolute). Var: Earnest, Erno, Ernost, Ernst. (AIR-NUST)

EUGEN German cognate of Eugene, which is from the Latin Eugenius and the Greek Eugenios, names derived from *eugenēs* (well-born, noble). (OY-GEN)

FABIAN From the Latin Fabianus (of Fabius), which is derived from the Old Roman family name Fabius, a derivative of the Latin *faba* (a bean). (FAH-BEE-AHN)

FELIX Derived from the Latin *felix* (lucky, happy). Felix was the name of four popes and several early saints. (FAY-LIKS)

FLORIAN From the Latin Flōriānus, an elaboration of Florus, an old Roman family name derived from *flōs* (a flower). (FLOR-EE-AHN)

FOLKER Derived from the obsolete Old Norse Folkvardr, which is composed of the elements *folk* (people) and *varðr* (guard): hence, "people's guard." Var: Folkhard, Volker. Short: Folke, Folko, Fulko. (FOLKR)

FRANK Originated as a term referring to a member of the Germanic tribes that established the Frankish Empire extending over what is now France, Germany, and Italy. The tribe is believed to have obtained its name from a type of spear or javelin (*franco*). (FRAHNK)

FRANZ A short form of Franziskus (a Frenchman), Franz is also bestowed as an independent given name. *See* FRANZISKUS. (FRAHNTZ)

FRANZISKUS From the Middle Latin Franciscus (a Frenchman), which is from Francus (a Frank, a freeman), a name that has its root in the Old French *franc* (free). Var: Franciskus. Short: Franck, Franz. (FRAHN-ZIS-KOOS)

FRIEDERICH Derived from the Old High German Fridurih (ruler of peace), a compound name composed of the elements *frid* (peace) and *rik* (king, ruler). Var: Friedrich. Short: Fredi, Friedel, Fritz. (FREED-RISH)

FRIEDHELM Compound name composed of the elements *frid* (peace) and *helm* (helmet, protection): hence, "peace helmet." (FREED-HELM)

GABRIEL From the Hebrew Gavriel, which is derived from *gavhrī'ēl* (God is my strength). (GAH-BREE-EL)

GARRICK Derived from the Germanic element *gār* (spear). Alternatively, Garrick may be a variant of Gerrit, a Low German form of Gerhard (brave with the spear). *See* GERHARD. Var: Garek. Pet: Gary. (GAHR-RIK)

GEORG German cognate of George (earthworker, farmer), a name derived from the Greek Geōrgios, which is from *geōrgos*, a compounding of the elements *gē* (earth) and *ergein* (to work). The variant forms Jurgen and Jeorg are also in popular use. Var: Jeorg, Jurgen. (GAY-ORK)

GERALD From the Germanic Gerwald (spear ruler), a compound name composed from the elements *ger* (spear) and *walden* (to rule). (GAY-RAHL)

GERHARD Derived from the Old High German Gerhart, a compound name composed of the elements *ger* (spear) and *hart* (hearty, brave, strong): hence, "spear-brave, brave with the spear." Var: Garrick, Gerrit. Pet: Gary. (GARE-HAHRT)

GERLACH Compound name composed of the elements *ger* (spear) and *laic* (sport, play): hence, "spear sport." The name was borne by a 12th-century saint who was a hermit near Valkenberg. (GARE-LAHK)

GILBERT From the Old French Guillebert, a derivative of the Old High German Gisilberht (famous pledge), a compound name composed from the elements *gisil* (pledge) and *beraht* (bright, famous). (GEEL-BAIRT)

GISELBERT Derived from the Old High German Gisilberht, a compound name composed from the elements *gisil* (pledge) and *beraht* (bright, famous): hence, "famous pledge." (GEE-SEL-BAIRT)

GODFRIED Derived from the Germanic Godafrid, a compound name composed from the elements *god* (God) and *frid* (peace): hence, "peace of God." Var: Godfrey. (GOT-FREED)

GREGOR German cognate of Gregory, which is from the Late Latin Gregorius, a cognate of the Greek Grēgorios (vigilant, a watchman), which is derived from the verb *egeirein* (to awaken). The name was popular among early Christians and was borne by several saints and many popes. In 1582 Gregory XIII introduced the Gregorian calendar, a corrected form of the Julian calendar, which is now used in most countries of the world. Var: Grigor. (GRAY-GOR)

GÜNTHER Compound name composed from the Germanic elements *gund* (war, strife) and *har* (army). The name is borne in the *Nibelungenlied* by a king of Burgundy, the husband of Brunhild. (GOON-TER)

GUSTAF Derived from the Germanic Gotzstaf (divine staff), a compound name composed of the elements *gott* (God) and *staf* (staff). Alternatively, the name may be derived from the Old Norse elements *Gautr* (the tribal name of the Goths) and *stafr* (staff): hence, "staff of the Goths." Var: Gustav. (GOO-STAHF)

GUY A borrowing from the French, Guy is derived from the Old French *guie* (a guide, a leader). (GEE)

HAGAN Derived from the Old Norse Hákon (chosen descendant), a compound name composed of the elements *há* (high, chosen) and *konr* (son, descendant). (HAH-GAHN)

HALDEN German cognate of the Norwegian Halfdan (half Dane), which is from the Old Norse Hálfdanr, a compound name composed of the elements *hálfr* (half) and *Danr* (a Dane). (HAHL-DAN)

HANS Popular diminutive form of Johannes (God is gracious). *See* JOHANNES. Var: Han, Hann, Hanz. Pet: Hanno, Hanschen. (HAHNS)

HARALD Derived from the Old High German Hariwald (ruler of an army), a compounding of the elements *hari* (army) and *wald* (rule). (HAHR-AHLD)

HARTMANN Compound name composed of the Germanic elements *hart* (hearty, brave, strong) and *mann* (man): hence, "strong man." Var: Hardtman, Hartman. (HART-MUN)

HARTWIG Compound name composed of the Germanic elements *hart* (hearty, brave, strong) and *wīg* (war, strife): hence, "brave in war." (HAHRT-VIG)

HARVEY Derived from the Old Breton Aeruiu or Hærviu (battleworthy), which are composed of the elements *hœr* (battle) and *viu* (worthy). (HAHR-VEE)

HEINRICH Popular name derived from the Old High German Haganrih (ruler of an enclosure), a compound name composed from the elements *hag* (an enclosure, a hedging-in) and *rihhi* (ruler), and from the Old High German Heimerich (home ruler), a compound name composed from the elements *heim* (home) and *rik* (ruler, king). Var: Hinrich. Short: Hein, Heine. Pet: Harro, Heike, Heinecke, Heinz, Henke, Henning. (HINE-RISH)

HELMUT Popular compound name composed of the Germanic elements *helm* (helmet, protection) and *mout* (courage, bravery, spirit): hence, "courageous protector." Var: Helmuth, Helmutt. (HEL-MOOT)

HENDRIK A borrowing from the Scandinavians, Hendrick is a cognate of the German Heinrich (ruler of an enclosure, home ruler). *See* HEINRICH. (HEN-DRISH)

HERIBERT Derived from Heriberht and Hariberht, which are composed of the elements *hari*, *heri* (army) and *beraht* (bright, famous): hence, "bright army." (HARE-IH-BAIRT)

HERMANN Derived from the Old High German Hariman, a compound name composed of the elements *hari*, *heri* (army) and *man* (man): hence, "army man, soldier." (HARE-MAHN)

HORAZ German cognate of Horace, which is derived from the Latin Horatius, an old Roman family name of unknown etymology. (HOR-AHZ)

HUBERT Derived from the Old High German Huguberht (bright in spirit), a compound name composed of the elements *hugu* (heart, mind, spirit) and *beraht* (bright, famous). *See* HUBERT (French Names). (HOO-BERT)

HUGH From the Old French Hue, which is from the Old High German Hugo, a derivative of *hugu* (heart, mind, spirit). (HOO)

HUGO Common German name derived from the Old High German *hugu* (heart, mind, spirit). Var: Hugh. (HOO-GO)

HUNFRID Compound name composed from the Germanic elements *hun* (strength, warrior) and *frid* (peace): hence, "warrior of peace." Var: Humfried, Humphrey, Hunfried. (HOON-FREED)

ISAAK A borrowing from the Ecclesiastic Greek, Isaak is from the Hebrew Yitzchak (he will laugh), which is from *yitshāq* (laughter). (IH-SAHK)

JAKOB German cognate of Jacob, which is from the Ecclesiastic Late Latin Iacomus and Iacobus, derivatives of the Greek Iakōbos, which is from the Hebrew Yaakov, a derivative of *ya'aqob* (supplanting, seizing by the heel). (YAH-KOB)

JAN A borrowing from the Scandinavians, Jan is a popular cognate of John (God is gracious). *See* JOHANNES. Var: Jen, Jens. (YAHN)

JOHANN A short form of Johannes (God is gracious), Johann is commonly bestowed as an independent given name. *See* JOHANNES. Pet: Anno, Hanno. (YO-HAHN)

JOHANNES Middle Latin cognate of John (God is gracious), which is from the Ecclesiastic Late Latin Joannes and the Ecclesiastic Greek Iōannes, derivatives of the Hebrew *yōhānān*, a contraction of *yehōhānān* (Yahweh is gracious). Short: Hans, Johann. Pet: Hanschen. (YO-HAH-NESS)

JÖRG A borrowing from the Swiss, Jörg is a cognate of George (earthworker, farmer). *See* GEORG. (YUHRG)

JÖRN German form of the Danish Jørn, a variant of Jørgen, the Danish cognate of George (earthworker, farmer). *See* GEORG. (YUHRN)

JOSEF German form of the Ecclesiastic Late Latin Joseph, which is from the Ecclesiastic Greek Iōsēph, a derivative of the Hebrew Yosef, which is from *yōsēf* (may he add). (YO-SEF)

JULIAN From the Latin Julianus, which is a derivative of Julius, an old Roman family name thought to be derived from Iulus (the first down on the chin, downy-bearded). Because a person just beginning to develop facial hair is young, "youth" became an accepted meaning of the name. (YOO-LEE-AHN)

JUSTUS Directly derived from the Latin *justus* (just, lawful, fair). (YOO-STUS)

KARL Popular name derived from the Old Norse and Germanic *karl* (a man, freeman, peasant). (KARL)

KASPAR German form of Gaspar, a name of uncertain etymology which, along with Balthasar and Melchior, was assigned to the Three Wise Men, who brought gifts to the Christ child. The names are not found in the Bible and are thought to have been fixed in the 11th century. Gaspar might have been derived from the Persian *genashber* (treasure master), which is in keeping with his role of the bringer of precious gifts. (KAHS-PAHR)

KLEMENS From the Late Latin Clēmens (merciful), which is derived from *clemens* (mild, gentle, merciful). (KLAY-MANES)

KONRAD Popular name derived from the Old High German Kuonrat (wise counsel), a compound name composed of the elements *kuon* (bold, wise) and *rat* (counsel). Var: Conrad, Conradin, Conrado, Koenrad. Short: Koen. Pet: Cord, Cort, Konni, Kuno, Kurt. (KONE-RAHT)

KONSTANTIN Derived from the Latin Constantinus, which is from *constans* (steadfast, constant). (KONE-STAHNT-TEEN)

KURT A pet form of Konrad (wise counsel), Kurt is also popularly bestowed as an independent given name. *See* KONRAD. (KOORT)

LAMBERT Derived from the Old High German Landobeorht, a compound name composed of the elements *land* (land) and *beorht* (bright, famous). Var: Lambart, Lambrecht, Lambret, Lambrett. (LAM-BAIRT)

LEO A borrowing from the Late Latin, Leo is directly derived from *leo* (lion). Leo is also used as a short form of Leonhard (brave as a lion). *See* LEONHARD. (LEE-O)

LEONHARD From the Old French Leonard, a name derived from the Old High German Lewenhart, a compound name composed from the elements *lewo* (lion) and *hart* (strong, brave, hearty): hence, "brave as a lion, lion-hearted." (LEE-ON-HAHRT)

LEOPOLD Modern form of the Old High German Liutbalt (bold people), a compound name composed from the elements *liut* (people) and *balt* (bold, strong). Var: Leopoldo. (LEE-O-POLT)

LORENZ German cognate of Laurence, which is from the Latin Laurentius (man from Laurentum). Laurentum was the name of a town in Latium, which is probably derived from *laurus* (laurel). Var: Loritz. (LOR-ENZ)

LOTHAR Derived from the Old High German Hluodohari (famous warrior), a compound name derived from the elements *hluod* (famous) and *hari*, *heri* (army, warrior). Var: Loring, Lothair, Lotharing. (LO-THAHR)

Louis Derived from the Old French Loeis, which is from the Old High German Hluodowig (famous in war), a compound name composed from the elements *hluod* (famous) and *wīg* (war, strife). Var: Luis. (LOO-EES)

Ludwig Derived from the Old High German Hluodowig (famous in war), a compound name composed from the elements *hluod* (famous) and *wīg* (war, strife). Var: Ludovico, Ludwik. Pet: Luki, Lutz. (LOOD-VIG)

Lukas From the Ecclesiastic Late Latin Lucas, a derivative of Lucius, which is from the root *lux* (light). Alternatively, some believe the name is a contraction of Loukanos (man from Lucania). (LOO-KAHS)

Magnus Derived from the Latin *magnus* (great, large). (MAHG-NOOS)

Mallory Derived from the Old French *maloret, maloré* (the unfortunate one, the unlucky one). Var: Mallery. (MAL-LO-REE)

Manfred Derived from the Old German Maginfred (powerful peace), a compound name composed of the elements *magan* (power, ability, might) and *frid* (peace). Var: Manfried, Manfrit. (MAHN-FRED)

Marius A borrowing from the Latin, Marius is an old Roman family name of uncertain derivation. Some believe it has its root in Mars, the name of the Roman mythological god of war, but others think it is derived from the Latin *mas* (manly). (MAH-REE-OOS)

Markus From the Latin Marcus, a name of uncertain derivation. Most believe it has its root in Mars, the name of the Roman mythological god of war. Others, however, think it is from *mas* (manly) or from the Greek *malakoz* (soft, tender). Var: Markos. (MAHR-KOOS)

Martin From the Latin Martinus (of Mars, war-like), which is derived from Mars, the name of the Roman mythological god of war. The name became popular during the Middle Ages, due in part to the fame of the German theologian Martin Luther (1483–1546). (MAHR-TIN)

Matthaeus A borrowing from the Ecclesiastic Late Latin, Matthaeus is a derivative of the Ecclesiastic Greek Matthaios and Matthias, contractions of Mattathias. The name has its root in the Hebrew name Matityah, which is derived from *mattūthyāh* (gift of God). Var: Mathias, Matthaus, Matthes, Matthia, Matthias, Matthis. Short: Mathe, Mathi. Pet: Matz. (MAH-TAY-US)

Mauritius A borrowing from the Late Latin, Mauritius (Moorish) is derived from Maurus (a Moor). The Moors were a Muslim people of mixed Arab and Berber descent; thus the name came to mean "dark" or "swarthy" in reference to their coloring. Var: Mauritz, Moritz. (MAU-RIH-SHUS)

Max A short form of Maximilian, Max is also popularly bestowed as an independent given name. *See* MAXIMILIAN. (MAHKS)

Maximilian Arose as a blending of the Latin Maximus (greatest) and Aemiliānus by the Emperor Frederich III, who bestowed it upon his first-born son, Maximilian I (1459–1519), in honor of two famous Roman generals. Maximus is directly derived from *maximus* (greatest), but the etymology of Aemiliānus is uncertain. Short: Max. (MAHK-SIH-MIH-LEE-AHN)

Meinhard Derived from the Old High German Maginrad (strong counsel), a compounding of the elements *magin* (power, ability, might) and *rad* (counsel). Var: Maynard, Meinyard. Pet: Meinke, Meino. (MINE-RAHT)

Meinrad Derived from the Old High German Maginrad (strong counsel), a compounding of the elements *magin* (power, strength, might) and *rad* (counsel). Pet: Meinke, Meino. (MINE-RAHD)

Michael A derivative of the Hebrew *mīkhā'ēl* (who is like God?). The name is borne in the Bible by the archangel closest to God, the one responsible for carrying out God's judgments. Considered the leader of the heavenly host, Michael is regarded as the patron of soldiers. Var: Michel. Short: Micha. (ME-SHY-EEL)

Nicolaus A borrowing from the Latin, Nicolaus is from the Greek Nikolaos (victory of the people), a compound name composed of the elements *nikē* (victory) and *laos* (the people). Var: Niklaas, Nikolas, Nikolaus. Short: Claas, Claus, Klaas, Klaus. Pet: Nilo. (NIH-KO-LAUS)

Norbert Compound name composed of the elements *nord* (north) and *beraht* (bright): hence, "brightness of the north." (NOR-BAIRT)

Oliver Of debated origin, most believe Oliver is from the Old French *olivier* (olive tree). However, some believe it to be derived from the Middle Low German Alfihar (elf army), a compound name composed of the elements *alf* (elf) and *hari* (army). (O-LIH-VAIR)

Oskar German cognate of the English Oscar, which is from the Old English Osgar, a compound name composed of the elements *os* (a god) and *gar* (spear): hence, "spear of the gods." Var: Osker. (OS-KAHR)

Oswald A borrowing from the English, Oswald is derived from the Old English Osweald, a compound name composed of the elements *os* (a god) and *weald* (power): hence, "divine power." Var: Osvald, Oswaldo. (OS-VAHLD)

OTTO From the Old High German Otho and Odo, which are derived from *auda* (rich). The name was borne by Otto I (912–73), a king of Germany and emperor of the Holy Roman Empire. The older form Odo is also bestowed, but it is much less common. Var: Odo. (O-TŌ)

PATRICK Derived from the Latin *patricius* (a patrician, a nobleman). The name was made famous by St. Patrick (c. 385–461), a Christian Breton and Roman citizen who was a missionary to and patron saint of Ireland. (PAH-TRIK)

PAUL From the Latin Paulus, which originated as a Roman family name derived from *paulus* (small). (POL)

PAULIN Diminutive form of Paul (small): hence, "little Paul." *See* PAUL. (PO-LIN)

PAXTON Compound name composed of the Latin *pax* (peace) and *tūn* (town): hence, "town of peace." (PAHKS-TON)

PETER From the Ecclesiastic Late Latin Petrus and the Ecclesiastic Greek Petros, names derived from *petrus* (a rock) and *petros* (a stone). (PAY-TARE)

PHILIPP From the Latin Philippus, a derivative of the Greek Philippos, which is from the elements *philos* (loving) and *hippos* (a horse): hence, "lover of horses, loving a horse." The name is common across Europe and is found on most of the family trees of European royalty. (FIL-LIP)

RAIMUND Old Norman French name derived from the Frankish Raginmund, a compound name composed of the elements *ragin* (counsel, advice) and *mund* (hand, protection): hence, "wise protection." (RĪ-MOONT)

RAINER Derived from the Old German Raganher, a compound name composed from the elements *ragan* (counsel, advice) and *heri, hari* (army): hence, "wise army." Var: Reiner. (RĪ-NARE)

RALPH From the Old Norse Raðulfr, Rathulfr, a compound name composed of the elements *rað, rath* (counsel) and *ulfr* (wolf), and its German cognate Radulf, which is composed of the elements *rād* (counsel) and *wulf* (wolf). The name evolved into Rauf, Raff, and Rafe in the Middle Ages, Ralf in the 16th century, and Ralph in the 18th century. Var: Rafe. (RAHLF)

RANDOLF Derived from the Old Norse Randulfr, a compound name composed from the elements *rand, rönd* (the edge or rim of a shield) and *ulfr* (wolf): hence, "shield wolf." Var: Randolph. (RAHN-DOLF)

RAUL Derived from the Germanic Radulf (wolf counsel), a compound name composed of the elements *rād* (counsel, advice) and *wulf* (wolf). (RAH-OOL)

REINHARD Compound name derived from the Germanic Raginhart, which is composed of the elements *ragin* (counsel, advice) and *hart* (hearty, brave, strong): hence, "brave counsel." Var: Rainart, Rainhard, Reynard. Pet: Reineke, Renke, Renz. (RINE-HART)

RICHARD From the Old High German Richart (brave ruler), a compound name composed from the elements *rik, rīc* (power, king, ruler) and *hart* (hearty, brave, strong). Short: Rich, Rick, Rik. (RIH-CHAHRT)

ROBERT Popular name derived from the Old High German Hruodperht, a compound name composed of the elements *hruod* (fame) and *beraht* (bright): hence, "bright with fame." Var: Robar, Rubert, Rudbert, Rupert, Ruprecht. (RO-BAIRT)

ROCH German cognate of the Italian Rocco, a name derived from the Germanic *hrok* (rest). *See* ROCH (French Names). Var: Rochus. (ROK)

RODERICK From the Middle Latin Rodericus, which is derived from the Old High German Hrodrich (famous ruler), a compound name composed from the elements *hruod* (fame) and *rik* (king, ruler). Var: Roderich. Short: Rod. Pet: Roddy. (RO-DEH-RISH)

ROGER Popular name derived from the Old High German Hrodger (spear fame, famous with a spear), a compounding of the elements *hruod* (fame) and *gēr* (a spear). Var: Rotger, Rudiger. (RO-JER)

ROLAND A borrowing from the French, Roland is from the Old High German Hruodland (famous land), which is composed of the elements *hruod* (fame) and *land* (land). (RO-LAHNT)

ROLF Contracted form of Rudolf (wolf fame, famous wolf). *See* RUDOLF. (ROLF)

RUDIGER Derived from the Old High German Hruodiger (fame with a spear, spear fame), a compound name composed of the elements *hruod* (fame) and *gēr* (spear). Var: Rutger. Short: Rudi. (ROO-DIH-GER)

RUDOLF Evolution of the Old High German Hrodulf (wolf fame, famous wolf), a compound name composed from the elements *hruod* (fame) and *wulf* (wolf). The name was borne by Rudolf I of Hapsburg (1218–91), a German king and emperor of the Holy Roman Empire, and the founder of the Hapsburg dynasty. (ROO-DOLF)

RURIK A borrowing from the Russian, Rurik is a cognate of the German Roderick (famous king). *See* RODERICK. (ROO-RIK)

Sander A short form of Alexander (defender or helper of mankind), Sander is also bestowed as an independent given name. *See* ALEXANDER. (SAHN-DER)

Sebastien From the Latin Sebastiānus, a derivative of the Greek Sebastianos (a man of Sebastia, a town in Asia Minor). (SAY-BAHS-TIAN)

Severin From the Latin Sevērīnus which is from Sevērus, an old Roman family name derived from *sevērus* (severe, strict, stern). (SAY-VAY-RIN)

Siegfried Compound name composed from the Germanic elements *segu* (power, victory) and *frid* (peace): hence, "powerful peace, conquering peace." Var: Seifrid, Sigefrid, Sigfrid. Pet: Sicco, Sigo, Sikko. (SEEG-FREED)

Siegmund Compound name composed of the elements *sig* (victory) and *mund* (hand, protection): hence, "victorious protection." The name was borne by Sigmund Freud (1856–1939), the Austrian physician and neurologist who is considered the father of psychoanalysis. Var: Sigismund, Sigmund. (SEEG-MUND)

Sigurd A borrowing from the Scandinavians, Sigurd is from the obsolete Old Norse Sigvörðr (guardian of victory), a compound name composed of *sigr* (victory, conquest) and *vörðr* (guardian). (SIH-OORD)

Stanislav Of Slavonic origin, Stanislav is composed of the elements *stan* (government) and *slav* (glory): hence, "government is glory." Var: Stanislaus. Short: Stannes. (STAH-NIH-SLAHV)

Stefan German cognate of Stephen, which is from the Latin Stephanus, a derivative of the Greek Stephanos, which has its root in *stephanos* (a crown, a garland). Var: Steffen. Pet: Steffel. (STEH-FAHN)

Stein Derived from the German *stein* (stone). (SHTINE)

Sylvester From the Latin Silvester (of a wood or forest), a derivative of *silva* (a wood). The name was borne by three popes, the first of whom is said to have baptized Constantine and cured him of leprosy. (SEEL-VEH-STARE)

Theo A short form of Theobald (brave people) and Theodor (God's gift), Theo is also occasionally bestowed as an independent given name. *See* THEOBALD *and* THEODOR. (THEE-O)

Theobald Derived from the Old German Theudobald and Theodbald, compound names composed of the elements *thiuda* (folk, people) and *bald* (brave, bold): hence, "brave people." Short: Theo. (THEE-O-BAHLT)

Theodor Derived from the Latin Theodorus, which is from the Greek Theodōros, a compounding of the elements *theos* (God) and *dōron* (gift): hence, "gift of God." Var: Fedor, Pheodor. Short: Theo. (THEE-O-DOR)

Thomas From the Ecclesiastic Greek Thōmas, which is derived from the Aramaic *tě'ōma* (a twin). Var: Thoma. (TŌ-MAHS)

Tobias Ecclesiastic Late Latin name derived from the Ecclesiastic Greek Tōbias, which is from the Hebrew *tōbhīyāh* (the Lord is good). (TO-BEE-AHS)

Torsten A borrowing from the Scandinavians, Torsten is from the Old Norse Þórrsteinn, a compound name composed of the elements Þórr (Thor) and *steinn* (stone): hence, "Thor's stone." (TOR-STEN)

Traugott Compound name composed of the elements *traue* (trust) and *gott* (God): hence, "God's trust, trust in God." (TRAU-GOT)

Ulf A borrowing from the Scandinavians, Ulf (wolf) is derived from the Old Norse *úlfr* (wolf). (OOLF)

Ulrich Compound name composed of the elements *uodal* (nobility, prosperity, fortune) and *rik* (ruler, king): hence, "noble ruler" or "wealthy ruler." Pet: Uli, Ulz. (OOL-RIK)

Urban From the Latin Urbānus (city dweller, urban), which is derived from *urbs* (a city). The name was borne by several saints and popes. (OOR-BAHN)

Valentin From the Latin Valentīnus, which is derived from *valens* (to be healthy, strong). The name was borne by a 3rd-century Roman saint and martyr whose feast day, February 14, coincides with that of a pagan festival marking the beginning of spring. (VAH-LANE-TIN)

Veit Derived from the Latin Vitus, which is derived from *vita* (life). Var: Veicht. (VĪT)

Viktor Cognate of Victor, which is derived from the Latin *victor* (conqueror, winner). (VIK-TOR)

Vincens From the Late Latin Vincentius (conquering), which is derived from *vincere* (to conquer). Var: Vinzenz. (VIN-SAYNZ)

Vital German cognate of the Italian Vitale (vital, life-giving), which is from *vitalis* (vital), a word that has its root in *vita* (life). (VEE-TAHL)

Vitus A borrowing from the Latin, Vitus is derived from *vita* (life). (VEE-TOOS)

Walden Derived from the Old High German *waldan* (to rule). Pet: Welti. (VAHL-DEN)

Waldo Derived from the Old High German *waldan* (to rule). (VAHL-DŌ)

WALLACE A borrowing from the English, Wallace is the transferred use of the surname derived from the Old French Waldeis (a Welshman, a foreigner). Var: Wallach, Wallis, Walsh. (VAHL-LAS)

WALTER Derived from the Frankish Waldhere (ruler of the army), a compound name composed from the elements *waldan* (to rule) and *heri, hari* (army). Var: Valter, Walder, Waller, Walten, Walthari, Walton. (VAHL-TARE)

WARREN Derived from the Old French *warenne* (a warren, a game preserve). The name is indicative of one who was a dweller at or a keeper of a game preserve. Var: Waren. (VAH-REN)

WENDELL Of uncertain etymology, Wendell is generally believed to be derived from the Germanic *wenden* (to travel, to proceed on one's way), or from *Wend*, a term denoting a member of the old Slavic people who now live in an enclave south of Berlin. Var: Wendel. (VEN-dehl)

WERNER Derived from the Germanic Warenheri, a compound name composed of the elements *ware* (a defender, a guard) and *heri* (army): hence, "protecting army." Var: Verner, Warner, Wernhar. (VER-NER)

WILBERT Derived from the Old High German Willebert, a compound name composed of the elements *willeo* (will, resolution) and *beraht, berth* (bright, famous). Var: Wilbart, Wilburt, Wilpert, Wilbur. Short: Wil. Pet: Willi. (VIL-BERT)

WILFRED A borrowing from the English, Wilfred is derived from the Old English Wilfrith (desire for peace), a compound name composed of the elements *willa* (a wish, a desire) and *frith* (peace). Var: Wilfrid, Willifred. Short: Wil. Pet: Willi. (VIL-FRED)

WILHELM From the Old High German Willehelm (resolute protector), a compound name composed of the elements *willeo* (will, resolution) and *helm* (helmet, protection). Var: Williamon, Wilm. Short: Wil. Pet: Willi, Willy. (VIL-HEHLM)

WOLF Derived directly from the German *wolf* (a wolf). Wolf is also used as a short form of Wolfgang (traveling wolf). *See* WOLFGANG. Var: Wulf. (VULF)

WOLFGANG Compound name composed of the elements *wolf* (a wolf) and *gang* (going, walk, path): hence, "traveling wolf." The name was borne by a 10th-century bishop of Ratisbon. (VULF-GAHNG)

WOLFRIK Compound name composed of the elements *wolf* (a wolf) and *rik* (ruler, king). Var: Wolfric, Wolfrick, Wulfric, Wulfrick. Short: Wolf, Wulf. (VUL-FRIK)

German Female Names

ABIGAIL From the Hebrew Avigayil, which is derived from *avīgayil* (father of exaltation, father is rejoicing). Pet: Abbie. (AH-BIH-GAIL)

ADA A pet form of Adele (noble) and Adelaide (noble one), Ada is also a Germanic cognate of the biblical Adah (adornment). *See* ADAH (Biblical Names). (A-DAH)

ADALHEID Derived from the medieval Germanic Adalheidis, a compound name composed of the elements *adal* (noble) and *heid* (kind, sort): hence, "noble one." Var: Adelaide, Adelheid, Aleida, Aleit. Pet: Ada, Adda, Addie, Alke, Heidi. (AH-DAHL- HITE)

ADELAIDE Variant of Adalheid (noble one). *See* ADALHEID. The name was borne by the wife of King William IV. She was the daughter of the ruler of the German duchy of Saxe-Meiningen. The Australian city of Adelaide was named in her honor. Pet: Ada, Addie. (AH-DAH-LITE)

ADELE Short form of any of the various Germanic names containing the element *adal* (noble). The name was borne by a daughter of the Frankish king Dagobert II; she was revered as a saint. Pet: Ada. (AH-DEH-LEH)

ADRIA Feminine form of Adrian, which is derived from the Latin Adriānus (man from the city of Adria) and Hadriānus (man from the city of Hadria). Var: Adriana, Adrianna, Adrianne, Adrienne. (AH-DREE-AH)

AGATHE Derived from the Greek Agathē, which is from *agathos* (good, kind, honorable). *See* AGATA (Italian Names). Var: Agatha. Pet: Aggie. (AH-GAH-THEH)

AGNA A pet form of Agnethe (pure, chaste, holy), Agna is also bestowed as an independent given name. *See* AGNETHE. (AHG-NAH)

AGNETHE German cognate of Agnes, which is derived from the Greek Hagnē, a name derived from *hagnos* (chaste, pure, holy, sacred). *See* AGNESE (Italian Names). Pet: Agna. (AHG-NEH-TEH)

AGNES Latinized form of the Greek Hagnē (chaste, pure, sacred). *See* AGNETHE. (AHG-NEHS)

ALARICA Feminine form of Alaric (noble ruler). *See* ADALRICH (Male Names). Var: Alarice. (ALA-RIK-AH)

ALBERTA Feminine form of Albert, which is from the Old High German Adalbrecht (bright through nobility), a compound name composed from the elements *adal* (noble) and *beraht* (bright, famous). Var: Albertina, Albertine, Elberta, Elbertina, Elbertine. Short: Berta. (AHL-BAIR-TAH)

ALENA Originally a short form of Magdalena (of Magdala), Alena is commonly bestowed as an independent given name. *See* MAGDALENA. (AH-LAY-NAH)

ALEXA Short form of Alexandra (defender or helper of mankind), Alexa is also used as an independent given name. *See* ALEXANDRA. (AH-LEX-AH)

ALEXANDRA Popular name derived from the Greek Alexandros (defender or helper of mankind), a compound name composed of the elements *alexein* (to defend, to help) and *andros* (mankind, man). Short: Alexa. (AH-LAYK-SAHN-DRAH)

ALEXIA A borrowing from the Greek, Alexia is derived from the verb *alexein* (to defend, to help). Alexia is also used as a short form of Alexandra (defender or helper of mankind). *See* ALEXANDRA. Var: Alexis. (AH-LEX-EE-AH)

ALFREDA Feminine form of Alfred, which is derived from the Old English Ælfred, a compound name composed of the elements *ælf* (elf) and *ræd* (counsel): hence, "elf counselor." Var: Alfrida, Elfreda, Elfrida, Elfriede. Short: Freda, Frida, Frieda, Friede. Pet: Effi, Elfi. (AHL-FRAY-DAH)

ALICE An evolution of Adalheidis, a compound name composed of the elements *adal* (noble, nobility) and *heid* (kind, sort): hence, "noble one." Adalheidis was contracted to Adalheid, which the French changed to Adélaïde, then contracted to Adaliz, and contracted yet again to Aaliz, Aliz, and Alix. The English then changed the spelling to Aeleis, Alys, and eventually to Alice. Var: Ailis, Ailse, Alicia, Alison, Alisz, Aliz, Alys. Pet: Aili. (AHL-ISS)

ALKE Originally a pet form of Adalheid (noble one), Alke is also commonly bestowed as an independent given name. *See* ADALHEID. (AHL-KEH)

ALOISIA Feminine form of Alois, a German cognate of Aloysius, a name of unknown origin and meaning. It has been suggested that it is a Latin variant of the Old French Loeis (Louis). *See* LOUIS (French Male Names). Var: Aloysia. (AH-LO-WIS-AH)

AMALIA Derived from the Germanic *amal* (work). The name was borne by the Duchess of Saxe-Weimar, Anna Amalia (1739–1807). Var: Amalasand, Amalea, Amalie, Amelia, Amelie, Amilia. (AH-MAHL-EE-AH)

AMARA Derived from the Latin *amarantus* (unfading, eternal). Alternatively, Amara may be from the Latin *amārus* (bitter, sour). (AH-MAHR-AH)

ANASTASIA A borrowing from the Greek, Anastasia is a feminine form of Anastasios (of the resurrection), which is derived from *anastasis* (resurrection). Short: Ana, Nastasia, Stasia. (AH-NAH-STAH-SEE-AH)

ANGELIKA Derived from the Latin *angelicus* (heavenly, like an angel) and the Greek *angelikos* (angelic). Var: Angelike. Pet: Angie. (AHN-GAY-LEE-KAH)

ANITA A borrowing from the Spanish, Anita originated as a pet form of Ana (gracious, full of grace). It is now commonly regarded as an independent given name. (AH-NEE-TAH)

ANITRA Literary coinage invented by Norwegian playwright and poet Henrik Ibsen (1828–1906). Anitra was the name given to the Eastern princess in his work *Peer Gynt*. (AH-NEE-TRAH)

ANNA Popular Latinate cognate of the Hebrew Hannah, which is derived from *hannāh, chaanach* (gracious, full of grace, mercy). (AH-NAH)

ANNE Borrowed from the French, Anne is a cognate of the Hebrew Hannah, which is from *hannāh, chaanach* (gracious, full of grace, mercy). Pet: Anke, Annette, Antje. (AHN-NEH)

ANNELIESE Popular combination name composed of the names Anne (gracious, full of grace) and Liese, a pet form of Elisabeth (God is my oath). *See* ANNE *and* ELISABETH. Var: Annelise. (AH-NEH-LEES)

ANNEMARIE Popular combination name composed of the names Anne (gracious, full of grace) and Marie, a cognate of Mary. *See* ANNE *and* MARIA. (AH-NEH-MAH-REE)

ANNETTE Originally a pet form of Anne (gracious, full of grace), Annette is now commonly bestowed as an independent given name. *See* ANNE. (AH-NET-TEH)

ANSELMA Compound name composed of the elements *ansi* (a god) and *helm* (helmet, protection): hence, "divine helmet, divine protection." Var: Anselme. (AHN-SALE-MAH)

ANTONIA Popular throughout Europe, Antonia, a feminine form of Anthony, is derived from the old Roman family name Antonius, which is of uncertain derivation. Some believe it was originally an Etruscan name. Var: Antonie. (AHN-TŌ-NEE-AH)

ARABELLA Old name of uncertain etymology. Some believe it to be a Norman name derived from the element *arn* (eagle) or *arin* (a hearth). Others think it a variant of Annabel, another name of debated origin and meaning. *See* ANNABEL (Scottish names). Var: Arabel, Arabell. (AH-RAH-BEL-LAH)

ARMINA Feminine form of Armin (soldier, warrior), which is derived from the Old High German elements *hari, heri* (army) and *man* (man). (AR-MEE-NAH)

ASTA A borrowing from the Scandinavians, Asta is from the Old Norse Ásta, which is derived from *ást* (love). (AH-STAH)

ASTRID Popularly used in Germany, Astrid (beautiful goddess) is derived from Ássfriðr, an Old Norse compound name composed of the elements *áss* (a god) and *friðr* (beautiful, fair). (AH-STRID)

AVEZA Old Germanic name of uncertain meaning. It is perhaps a derivative of the Latin *avis* (bird). (AH-VAY-ZAH)

AVILA Medieval name of uncertain meaning. It is thought to be a variant of Aveza. *See* AVEZA. (AH-VEE-LAH)

BARBARA A borrowing from the Latin, Barbara (foreign woman) is derived from *barbarus* (foreign, strange), a term applied to non-Romans or those deemed to be uncivilized. Pet: Bärbel. (BAR-BAH-RAH)

BATHILDA Compound name composed from the elements *baten* (to bid, to command) and *hild* (battle, war): hence, "commanding battle maiden." (BAH-TIL-DAH)

BEATA Derived from the Latin *beatus* (blessed, happy). Var: Beate. (BAY-AH-TAH)

BEATRIX Derived from the Latin *beatrix* (she who makes happy, she who brings happiness), which is from *beātus* (blessed, happy). Var: Beatrice. Short: Bea, Beate. (BAY-AH-TRIKS)

BENEDIKTA Feminine form of Benedikte (blessed). *See* BENEDIKTE (Male Names). (BAY-NAY-DIK-TAH)

BENOÎTE A borrowing from the French, Benoîte (blessed) is the feminine form of Benoît, the French cognate of Benedikte. *See* BENEDIKTE (Male Names). (BAY-NOY-TEH)

BERNARDINE Feminine form of Bernard (bold as a bear), which is from the Old High German Berinhard, a compounding of the elements *bern* (bear) and *hart* (bold, strong, hearty). Var: Bernadina, Bernadine, Bernardina. Short: Berdina, Berdine, Nadine. (BARE-NAHR-DEE-NEH)

BERTHA Derived from the Old High German Berahta (bright one), which has its root in *beraht* (bright, famous). Var: Berta, Bertine. (BARE-THA)

BIRGIT A borrowing from the Scandinavians, Birgit is a cognate of the Irish Gaelic Bríghid, which is derived from the Gaelic *brígh* (strength). The name was made popular by St. Birgitta of Sweden (1302–73). A noblewoman and mother of eight children, she founded the Brigittine Order of nuns after her husband's death. Var: Brigitte. (BIR-GIT)

BRUNHILDE Cognate of the Scandinavian Brynhild, an ancient name composed of the Old Norse elements *brynja* (armor) and *hildr* (battle, fight): hence, "armored for battle." *See* BRYNHILD (Scandinavian Names). Var: Brunhild, Brünhilde, Brünnhilde. (BROON-HIL-DEH)

CARINA Derived from the Latin *carina* (keel of a ship). Carina is the name of a southern constellation which contains the star Canopus, the second-brightest star in the southern skies. (KAH-REE-NAH)

CARLA A borrowing from the English, Carla is the feminine form of Carl, which is derived from the Old English *ceorl* (man, freeman, peasant). Carla is a cognate of the Germanic Karla. Var: Carlin. (KAR-LAH)

CARMEN A borrowing from the Spanish, Carmen is a cognate of the Hebrew Carmel (vineyard, orchard). Mount Carmel is a mountain in northwestern Israel which was inhabited in early Christian times by a group of hermits who later became Carmelite monks in the Order of Our Lady of Mount Carmel. The name was originally used in reference to the Virgin Mary, Our Lady of Carmel. (KAR-MEN)

CECILIA Derived from the Latin Caecilia, a feminine form of Caecilius, an old Roman family name possibly derived from *caecus* (blind, dim-sighted). Var: Cäcilie. Short: Celia. Pet: Silke. (SEH-SEE-LEE-AH)

CELIA A short form of Cecilia (blind, dim-sighted), Celia is also commonly bestowed as an independent given name. *See* CECILIA. Pet: Silke. (SEE-LEE-AH)

CHARLOTTE A borrowing from the French, Charlotte is a feminine diminutive form of Charles (full-grown, a man). *See* CHARLES (French Male Names). (SHAR-LOT-TEH)

CHERYL Borrowed from the English, Cheryl is a 20th century coinage. Var: Charil, Charyl, Cherilyn, Sharilynn. (SHARE-IL)

Chloris A borrowing from the Greek, Chloris is derived from *chlōros* (pale green). The name was borne by the Greek mythological goddess of flowers. (KLOR-ISS)

Christa Latinate short form of Christiana (a Christian, a follower of Christ). Christa is also popularly bestowed as an independent given name. *See* CHRISTIANA. Pet: Christie. (KRIS-TAH)

Christiana A popular name, Christiana is a feminine form of Christian (a Christian, a follower of Christ), which is derived from the Greek *christianos* (a follower of Christ, a Christian). Var: Christiane. Short: Christa. Pet: Christie. (KRIS-TEE-AH-NAH)

Clara A common name throughout Europe, Clara is derived from the Latin *clārus* (bright, clear, famous). Var: Klara. (KLAH-RAH)

Claudette A borrowing from the French, Claudette is a diminutive form of Claudia (lame). *See* CLAUDIA. (KLAU-DEH-TEH)

Claudia Feminine form of the Latin Claudius, an old Roman family name derived from *claudus* (lame). The name is borne by German model Claudia Schiffer. (KLAU-DEE-AH)

Clementine Feminine form of Clement, a name derived from the Latin *clemens* (mild, gentle). (KLEH-MEN-TEE-NAH)

Clotilda Derived from the Old German Hlodhild, a compound name composed from the elements *hluod* (famous, renowned) and *hild* (battle, strife): hence, "famous in battle." Var: Clotilde. Short: Tilda. (KLO-TIL-DEH)

Conradina Feminine form of Conrad (wise counsel), a compound name composed of the elements *kuon* (bold, wise) and *rat* (counsel). Var: Conradine. (KON-RAH-DEE-NAH)

Constanze Feminine form of Constantine (constancy), which is from the Latin Constantinus, a name derived from *constans* (constant, steadfast, unchanging). Pet: Stanzi. (KON-STAHN-ZEH)

Cordula Of debated etymology, most believe it is derived from the Latin *cor* (heart). Others, however, believe it is actually of Celtic origin and think it is a derivative of Creirdyddlydd, a compound name composed of the Celtic elements *creir* (a jewel, a sacred relic) and Llud (the name of the goddess of the sea): hence, "jewel of the sea." (KOR-DOO-LAH)

Cornelia A borrowing from the Latin, Cornelia is the feminine form of Cornelius, an old Roman family name of unknown origin and meaning. Some believe it is derived from *cornu* (horn). (KOR-NAY-LEE-AH)

Corona Derived from the Latin *corona* (crown). (KO-RO-NAH)

Cosima Feminine form of Cosmo, which is from the Greek *kosmos* (universe, order, harmony). (KO-SEE-MAH)

Crescentia Derived from the Italian *crescenza* (growth), which is from the Latin *incrēmentum* (growth, increase). (KREH-SEN-TEE-AH)

Dagmar Of debated etymology, some believe Dagmar to be derived from the Germanic elements *dag* (day) and *mar* (splendid). Others think it is from the Old Scandinavian elements *dag* (day) and *mār* (maid). Var: Dagomar. (DAHG-MAHR)

Daniela Feminine form of Daniel, a name derived from the Hebrew *dāni'ēl* (God is my judge). *See* DANIEL (Male Names). (DAHN-YELL-AH)

Debra German form of Deborah, a name derived from the Hebrew *devōrāh* (a bee, a swarm of bees). Pet: Debbie, Debby. (DEH-BRAH, DAY-BRAH)

Diederike Feminine form of Dietrich (leader of the people). *See* DIETRICH (Male Names). Var: Didrika. (DEE-DREE-KEH)

Domino Derived from the Latin *dominus* (a master, a lord). (DŌ-MIH-NO)

Doris A borrowing from the Greek, Doris is derived from the Greek Dōris (Dorian woman). The Dorians were one of the four main tribes of ancient Greece who settled in the mountainous area also known as Doris. (DŌ-RIS)

Dorothea A borrowing from the Greek, Dorothea is a compound name composed of the elements *dōron* (gift) and *theos* (God): hence, "gift of God." Var: Dörte, Dörthe. (DOR-O-TEE-AH)

Ebba Feminine contracted form of the Old High German Eburhart (strong as a wild boar), a compounding of the elements *ebur* (wild boar) and *harto* (strong). (Ā-BAH)

Edith A borrowing from the English, Edith is derived from the Old English Eadgyth, Ēadgyð, a compound name composed of the elements *ēad* (prosperity, fortune, riches) and *gyth, gyð* (war, strife): hence, "prosperous in war." (Ā-DITH)

Effemy German form of the Greek Euphemia (fair speech), a compound name composed of the elements *eu* (well, good, fair) and *phēmē* (voice). Pet: Effi. (ĀF-FAY-MEE)

ELEONORE Derived from Alienor (light), a Provençal form of the Greek Helenē, which is derived from the element *ēlē* (light, torch, bright). (Ā-LAY-O-NO-REH)

ELISA Short form of Elisabeth (God is my oath), Elisa is also bestowed as an independent given name. *See* ELISABETH. Var: Elicia, Elise. (Ā-LEE-SAH)

ELISABETH Popular name derived from the Hebrew *elīsheba'* (God is my oath). Short: Elisa, Elise, Elsa, Elsbet, Elsbeth, Else, Ilsa, Liesa, Liesbeth, Liese, Lisa, Lisbeth, Lise. Pet: Betti, Bettina, Betty, Elli, Elsie, Ilyse, Lilli. (Ā-LIS-AH-BETH)

ELSA Short form of Elisabeth (God is my oath), Elsa is also bestowed as an independent given name. *See* ELISABETH. Var: Else, Elsha, Elsja. Pet: Elsie. (ĀL-SAH, EL-SAH)

EMELIE From the Latin Aemilia, which is from Aemilius, an old Roman family name probably derived from *aemulus* (emulating, trying to equal or excel, rival). Var: Emilie. (EH-MAY-LEE)

EMMA Variant of Erma, which is a short form of any of the various names beginning with the element *Erm-* (strength). (EM-MAH)

ERIKA Feminine form of Erik (eternal ruler). *See* ERIK (Male Names). Var: Erica. (ERR-EE-KAH)

ERMA Short form of any of the various names, many now obsolete, that begin with the element *Erm(en)*, *Irm(en)* (strength). Var: Emma, Irma. (ER-MAH)

ERMENTRAUD Compound name composed of Ermen (a name for the Germanic god of war) and *trut* (dear, maiden) or *þruþ* (strength). Var: Ermentrud, Ermintrude, Irmtraud, Irmtrud. (ER-MEN-TRAUT)

ERNA A borrowing from the Scandinavians, Erna is a name borne in Norse mythology by the wife of Jarl, the son of the god Heimdallr and the mortal Modir. The name is defined as "capable." (AIR-NAH)

ERNESTA Feminine form of Ernst (resolute), a name derived from the Old High German Ernost and Ernust, which are from *ernust* (resolute, earnest). Var: Ernestina, Ernestine. (AIR-NES-TAH)

ESTHER Of debated origin and meaning, some believe it to be the Persian translation of the Hebrew name Hadassah (myrtle); others think it is derived from the Persian *stara* (star). It has also been suggested that it is derived from the Babylonian Ishtar, the name of a goddess of love and fertility. The name is borne in the Bible by the Jewish wife of the Persian king Ahasuerus. (ES-TER)

ETHEL A borrowing from the English, Ethel originated as a short form of any of the various Old English compound names containing the element *æthel* (noble). Ethel is now regarded as an independent name in its own right. (Ā-TEL)

EUGENIE A borrowing from the Greek, Eugenie is a feminine form of Eugenios, which is derived from *eugenēs* (well-born). (YOO-JAY-NEE)

EVA Derived from the Hebrew Chava, which is from *hawwāh* (life). The name is borne in the Bible by the first woman, "the mother of all the living." (Ā-VAH)

EVELYN A borrowing from the English, Evelyn is a variant of Aveline, a French diminutive form of the Germanic Avila, which is of uncertain derivation. *See* AVILA. Var: Eveline. (EV-EH-LEEN)

FELICIE Feminine form of Felix, which is derived from the Latin *felix* (happy, lucky). Var: Felise. (FAY-LEE-SEE)

FERDINANDA Feminine form of Ferdinand, which is of uncertain origin and meaning. *See* FERDINAND (French Male Names). Var: Fernanda. (FARE-DIH-NAHN-DAH)

FLORA Derived from the Latin *floris* (a flower). The name is borne in Roman mythology by the goddess of flowers and spring. (FLOR-AH)

FLORENZ Derived from Florenze, the Italian cognate of Florence, which is from the Latin Florentia (a blooming), a name derived from the verb *florens* (to bloom). (FLOR-ENZ)

FRANZISKA German form of Francesca, the feminine form of Francesco, which is from the Middle Latin Franciscus, a derivative of Francus (a Frank, a freeman). Short: Fran, Franze, Ziska. Pet: Zissi. (FRAHN-ZEES-KAH)

FRIEDE Short form of Friedelinde (gentle peace) and Friederike (ruler of peace), Friede is now also bestowed as an independent given name. Var: Freda, Frida, Frieda. (FREE-DEH)

FRIEDELINDE Compound name composed from the Old High German elements *frid* (peace) and *lind* (gentle, soft): hence, "gentle peace." Short: Frieda, Friede. (FREE-DEH-LIN-DEH)

FRIEDERIKE Feminine form of Friedrich (ruler of peace). *See* FRIEDERICH (Male Names). Var: Federica, Frederica, Frederika, Fredrika. Short: Freda, Frida, Frieda, Friede, Rica. Pet: Fritzi, Ricca, Rikki. (FREE-DEH-RIK-EH)

Gabriele Feminine form of Gabriel (God is my strength). *See* GABRIEL (Male Names). (GAH-BREE-EH-LAH)

Galiena Of uncertain derivation, Galiena might be from Gallien, the name given to the land of Gaul. Var: Galiane. (GAH-LEE-EH-NAH)

Genovefa Gaulish name with Celtic roots, but the meaning of which is uncertain. The first element is believed to be from *genos* (race, people, tribe); the second is possibly from an element meaning "woman." Var: Genevieve, Genoveva, Genowefa. (JEH-NO-VEE-VAH)

Georgine Feminine form of George, a name ultimately derived from the Greek *geōrgos* (earthworker, farmer). (JOR-JEEN-EH)

Geralda Feminine form of Gerald (to rule with the spear). *See* GERALD (Male Names). Pet: Geri, Gerrie. (JAY-RAHL-DAH)

Geraldine Feminine form of Gerald (to rule with the spear). *See* GERALD (Male Names). Var: Geraldina. Pet: Geri, Gerrie. (JAY-RAHL-DEE-NEH)

Gerda A borrowing from the Scandinavians, Gerda is derived from the Old Norse Gerdr. The name is borne in Norse mythology by an exceptionally beautiful giantess who was the wife of Frey. Her name has been defined as "guarded, protected." Var: Garda, Gerde. Pet: Gerdie. (GARE-DAH)

Geri A pet form of Geralda and Geraldine, Geri is also bestowed as an independent given name. *See* GERALDA *and* GERALDINE. Var: Gerrie. (GARE-EE)

Gerlinde Compound name composed of the Germanic elements *ger* (spear) and *lind* (gentle, soft, tender). (GARE-LIN-DEH)

Gerta Originally a short form of Gertrude (spear maid), Gerta is now commonly used as an independent given name. *See* GERTRUDE. Short: Gert. Pet: Geertje, Geertke. (GARE-TAH)

Gertrude Derived from the Old High German Geretrudis, a compound name composed of the elements *ger* (spear) and *trut* (dear, maiden) or *þruþ* (strength): hence, "spear maiden" or "spear strength." Var: Gertrud, Gertruda. Short: Gert, Gerta. (GARE-TROOD)

Gilberta Feminine form of Gilbert (famous pledge). *See* GILBERT (Male Names). Var: Gilberte, Gilbertina, Gilbertine. Pet: Gillie, Gilly. (GIL-BARE-TAH)

Giselle Derived from the Germanic element *gisil* (to owe, a pledge, a mutual obligation). It was a practice in the early Middle Ages for rival factions to offer a person, often a child, to each other as a pledge of peace. Var: Ghisilaine. Gisela, Gisele, Gisella. (GEE-SEH-LAH)

Greta A short form of Margarethe (a pearl), Greta is also commonly bestowed as an independent given name. *See* MARGARETHE. Pet: Gretal, Gretel. (GREH-TAH)

Gretchen A popular pet form of Margarethe (a pearl), Gretchen is commonly bestowed as an independent given name. *See* MARGARETHE. (GREHT-CHEN)

Gretel Pet form of Greta and Margarethe (a pearl). *See* GRETA *and* MARGARETHE. The name became well known outside of Germany due to the popular children's fairy tale, "Hansel and Gretel." Var: Gretal. (GREH-TL)

Griselda Derived from the Germanic Griseldis, a compound name composed of the element *gries* (gravel, stone). Var: Griselle, Grizelda, Grizelle. Short: Selda, Zelda. (GRIH-SEL-DAH)

Gudrun A borrowing from the Scandinavians, Gudrun is an Old Norse name of debated origin. It is thought to be derived from *guð* (a god) and *rūn* (secret lore). Alternatively, it might be derived from Guthrūn, which is composed from the elements *guthr* (war, battle) and *runa* (close friend). *See* GUDRUN (Scandinavian Names). Var: Kudrun. (GUD-RUN)

Gustava Feminine form of Gustav (staff of the Goths). *See* GUSTAF (Male Names). Pet: Gussie, Gussy. (GOO-STAH-VAH)

Haldis Germanic name meaning "purposeful." Var: Halda, Haldisse. Pet: Haldi. (HAHL-DIS)

Hallie A pet form of Haralda (ruler of an army), Hallie and its variants are also bestowed as independent given names. *See* HARALDA. Var: Halley, Hally. (HA-LEE)

Hannah A popular name, Hannah is derived from the Hebrew *hannāh, chaanach* (gracious, full of grace, mercy). The name is borne in the Bible by the mother of the prophet Samuel. Var: Hanna. (HAH-NAH)

Haralda Feminine form of Harald (ruler of an army), which is composed of the elements *harja* (army) and *wald* (to rule). Var: Harilda. Pet: Halley, Hallie, Hally. (HAH-RAHL-DAH)

Harriet A borrowing from the English, Harriet (ruler of an enclosure, home ruler) is a cognate of the French Henriette, a feminine diminutive form of Henri, which is derived from the German Heinrich. *See* HEINRICH (Male Names). Var: Harietta, Hariette, Harrietta, Harriette. Pet: Hatti, Hattie, Hatty. (HAH-REE-ET)

HEDWIG Derived from the Germanic Haduwig, a compound name composed of the elements *hadu* (contention) and *wīg* (war, strife). Var: Hedva, Hedvika. (HED-VIG)

HEIDI A pet form of Adalheid (noble one) and Hildegard (battle protector), Heidi is also bestowed as an independent name. *See* ADALHEID *and* HILDEGARD. It became well known internationally from Johanna Spyri's famous story "Heidi." Var: Heida, Heide. (HĪ-DEE)

HELENE A borrowing from the Greek, Helene is derived from the root *ēlē* (light, torch, bright). *See* HELENĒ (Greek Names). (HEH-LEE-NEH)

HELGA A borrowing from the Scandinavians, Helga is derived from *heilagr* (prosperous, successful), which is from the Old Norse *heill* (hale, hardy, happy). The word *heill* later developed the meaning "blessed, holy." (HEL-GAH)

HENRIETTA A borrowing from the French, Henrietta is a diminutive form of Henri, the French cognate of Heinrich (ruler of an enclosure, home ruler). *See* HEINRICH (Male Names). Var: Hendrika, Henriette, Henrika. Short: Rietta. Pet: Hennie, Hettie. (HEN-REE-EH-TAH)

HILDA Derived from the element *hild* (battle, war). The name is also used as a short form of any of the various names containing *hild* as an element. (HIL-DAH)

HILDEGARD Compound name composed of the elements *hild* (battle, war) and *gard* (to protect): hence, "battle protector." Var: Hildagard, Hildagarde, Hildegarde. Short: Hilda, Hilde. Pet: Heidi, Hildie, Hildy. (HIL-DEH-GARD)

HUBERTA Feminine form of Hubert (bright in spirit), a compound name composed from the elements *hugu* (mind, spirit) and *beraht* (bright, famous). Short: Berta. Pet: Bertie, Berty. (HOO-BARE-TAH)

HUETTE Feminine diminutive form of Hugh, which is from the Old High German Hugo, a derivative of *hugu* (heart, mind, spirit). Var: Huetta. (HYOO-ET-TEH)

IDA Derived from the element *īd* (work, labor). (EE-DAH)

IDALIA Elaboration of Ida (worker, industrious), which is from *īd* (work, labor). Var: Idalie. (EE-DAHL-YAH)

IDETTE Diminutive form of Ida (worker, industrious) formed by the addition of the French diminutive suffix *-ette*. *See* IDA. (Ī-DEH-TEH)

IDONA Derived from the Scandinavian Idony (renewal), which is from the Old Norse Iðunnr, a name believed to be derived from *ið* (again). *See* IDONY (Scandinavian Names). Alternatively, Idona might be a variant of Ida (worker, industrious), which is derived from the Germanic element *īd* (work, labor). Var: Idonah, Idonna, Iduna. (Ī-DON-AH)

ILSE A pet form of Elisabeth (God is my oath), Ilse is also bestowed as an independent given name. *See* ELISABETH. (IL-SEH)

INGA A borrowing from the Scandinavians, Inga was originally a short form of the various names containing *Ing(e)* as a first element. It is now commonly bestowed as an independent given name. In Norse mythology, Ing was a name for the fertility-god Frey. Var: Inge. (ING-GAH)

INGRID A borrowing from the Scandinavians, Ingrid is a compound name composed of Ing (a name for the fertility-god Frey) and *friðr* (fair, beautiful): hence, "beautiful Ing." (ING-GRID)

IRENE Derived from the Greek Eirēnē, which is from *eirēnē* (peace). The name is borne in Greek mythology by the goddess of peace. Var: Eirene, Eirni. (IH-RAY-NEH)

IRMA Short form of any of the various names, many now obsolete, beginning with the element *Irm-*, which is from Irmin, the byname of the Germanic god of war. Irma is also commonly bestowed as an independent given name. Var: Irmina, Irmine. (ER-MAH)

ISOLDE Derived from the Old High German Isold, a compound name composed of the elements *is* (ice) and *waltan* (to rule): hence, "ruler of the ice." (EE-SOL-DEH)

JENNIFER A popular borrowing from the English, Jennifer is a Cornish derivation of Guinevere, which is from the Welsh Gwenhwyfar (fair lady), a compounding of the elements *gwen* (white, fair, blessed) and *hwyfar* (soft, smooth). Pet: Jenny. (JEN-NIH-FER)

JENNY Originally a pet form of Jennifer (fair lady), Jenny is also bestowed as an independent given name. *See* JENNIFER. (JEN-NEE)

JETTE Modern name derived from *jet*, which denotes a hard, black, lustrous variety of lignite used in jewelry making. The word is derived from the Greek *gagatēs* (stone from Gagas, a town and river of Lycia in Asia Minor). (YET-TEH)

JOHANNA Latinate feminine form of Johannes, which is a cognate of John (God is gracious). *See* JOHANNES (Male Names). Var: Johanne. Short: Jo. (YO-HAH-NAH)

JUDITH Cognate of the Hebrew Jehudith and Yehudit, which are feminine forms of Jehuda and Yehūdhāh. These names, Anglicized as Judah, mean "he will be praised." Because Judah was also the name of a kingdom in ancient Palestine, the name can also mean "from Judah." (YOO-DIT)

JULIA Feminine form of Julian (downy-bearded, youth), which is in popular use throughout Europe. *See* JULIAN (Male Names). Julia is also in use as a short form of Juliana, another feminine form of Julian. Var: Julie. (YOO-LEE-AH)

JULIANA Popular feminine form of Julian (downy-bearded, youth). *See* JULIAN (Male Names). Var: Juliane. Short: Julia, Liana, Liane. Pet: Julie. (YOO-LEE-AH-NAH)

KÄETHE German form of Kate, which is a pet form of Katherine, a name derived from the Greek Aikaterinē. The name has its root in *katharos* (pure, unsullied). Var: Kathe. Pet: Katchen, Käte. (KAY-TEH)

KAMILLA German cognate of the Italian Camilla, which is derived from the Latin *camilla* (virgin of unblemished character). Short: Milla. Pet: Millie. (KAH-MIL-YAH)

KAREN A borrowing from the Danes, Karen is a Danish form of Katharina (pure, unsullied). *See* KATHARINA. Var: Karin. (KAH-REN)

KARLA Feminine form of Karl, which is from the Old Norse and Germanic *karl* (man, freeman, peasant). The name is a cognate of Carla. (KAR-LAH)

KARLOTTE Feminine form of Karl (man, freeman, peasant), which is based on the French Charlotte. *See* KARLA. (KAHR-LOT-TEH)

KAROLA Short form of Karolina, which is a feminine form of Karl (man, freeman, peasant). *See* KAROLINE. Karola is also commonly bestowed as an independent given name. (KAHR-O-LAH)

KAROLINE Popular feminine form of Karl, which is from the Old Norse and Germanic *karl* (man, freeman, peasant). Var: Karolina. Short: Karola, Lina, Line. (KAH-RO-LEE-NEH)

KATHARINA Cognate of the Greek Aikaterinē, which is derived from *katharos* (pure, unsullied). Katharine is a popular name throughout Europe and is commonly found on the family trees of European royalty. Var: Katarina. Pet: Käethe, Katchen, Käte, Kathe, Katja. (KAH-TAH-REE-NAH)

KIRSTEN A borrowing from the Scandinavians, Kirsten is a cognate of Christiana (a Christian, a follower of Christ). *See* CHRISTIANA. (KIR-STEHN)

KORINNA A borrowing from the Greek, Korinna is a diminutive form of Korē (maiden): hence, "little maiden." Var: Corinna. (KO-RIN-NAH)

KRISTA Originally a short form of Kristen and Kristina (a Christian, a follower of Christ), Krista is also bestowed as an independent given name. *See* KRISTINA. Short: Kris. Pet: Kristie. (KRIS-TAH)

KRISTEN Popular Germanic variant of Kristina (a Christian, a follower of Christ). *See* KRISTINA. Short: Kris, Krista. Pet: Kristie. (KRIS-TEN)

KRISTIE Pet form of any of the various names beginning with the element *Kris-*. (KRIS-TEE)

KRISTINA Germanic cognate of the Late Latin Christiāna, the feminine form of Christiānus, which is derived from the Greek Christianos (a Christian, a follower of Christ). Short: Kris, Krista, Tina. Pet: Kristie. (KRIS-TEE-NAH)

LAURA A borrowing from the Italian, Laura is derived from the Latin *laurus* (laurel). Laurel is an evergreen tree or shrub whose leaves were woven into wreaths by the ancient Greeks to crown the victors in various contests. Var: Lore. (LAU-RAH)

LEONARDA Feminine form of Leonard, which is derived from the Old High German Lewenhart, a compound name composed of the elements *lewo* (lion) and *hart* (strong, brave, hearty): hence, "brave as a lion, lion-hearted." (LEE-O-NAHR-DAH)

LEOPOLDA Feminine form of Leopold (strong people), which is from the Old High German Liutbalt, a compound name composed of the elements *liut* (people) and *balt* (strong, bold). Var: Leopoldina, Leopoldine. Pet: Leoda, Leota, Leute. (LEE-O-POL-DAH)

LIANA A short form of Juliana (downy-bearded, youth), Liana is also bestowed as an independent given name. *See* JULIANA. Var: Liane. (LEE-AH-NAH)

LIESA Short form of Liesbeth (God is my oath), Liesa is also bestowed as an independent given name. *See* ELISABETH. (LEE-SAH)

LILIAN A borrowing from the English, Lilian is derived from the obsolete Lilion, which is thought to be from the Latin *lilium* (lily). Short: Lili. (LIL-EE-AHN)

LILLI A pet form of Elisabeth (God is my oath) and many of its variant forms, Lilli is also occasionally bestowed as an independent given name. (LIL-EE)

LINDA Of uncertain origin and meaning, Linda may be a short form of the Germanic Betlindis, a name thought to mean "snake" or "serpent." Var: Lind, Linde. Pet: Lindie. (LIN-DAH)

LISA A short form of Elisabeth (God is my oath) and many of its variant forms, Lisa is also popularly bestowed as an independent given name. *See* ELISABETH. (LEE-SAH)

LISBETH A short form of Elisabeth (God is my oath), Lisbeth is also bestowed as an independent given name. *See* ELISABETH. Var: Liesbeth. Short: Liesa, Lisa. Pet: Lilli. (LEES-BET)

LORELEI Derived from *Lurlei*, the name of the rock "ambush cliff," which is derived from the Middle High German *luren* (to watch) and *lei* (a cliff, a rock). The name was altered to Lorelei by Clemens Brentano, a German poet. In Germanic legend, Lorelei was a beautiful siren who sat upon a rock in the Rhine River and lured sailors to shipwreck and death. Var: Lura, Lurette, Lurleen, Lurline. (LOR-EH-LĪ)

LORRAINE Transferred use of the name of the province in eastern France, which is derived from the Latin Lotharingia (territory of the people of Lothar). Lothar, the name of the son of the Frankish king Clovis, is of Germanic origin and is derived from the elements *hluod* (famous) and *hari, heri* (army): hence, "famous army." Var: Loraine. (LOR-RAIN)

LOUISA Feminine form of Louis (famous in war), which is from the Germanic Hluodowig, a compound name composed from the elements *hluod* (famous) and *wīg* (war, strife). Var: Louisane, Louise, Louisa, Luise. (LOO-EE-SAH)

LUCIA A borrowing from the Italian, Lucia is a feminine form of Lucius, which is derived from the Latin *lux* (light). Var: Lucie. (LOO-SEE-AH)

LURETTE Diminutive form of Lura (watcher of the rock) formed by the addition of the French diminutive suffix *-ette*. *See* LORELEI. (LOOR-ET-TEH)

LYDIA A name of Greek origin derived from the name of an ancient kingdom in western Asia Minor: hence, "woman from Lydia." (LIH-DEE-AH)

MAGDA A short form of Magdalena (woman from Magdala), Magda is also commonly bestowed as an independent given name. *See* MAGDALENA. Pet: Maddie, Mady. (MAHG-DAH)

MAGDALENA Latinate form of Magdalene, which is from the Ecclesiastic Greek Magdalēnē (of Magdala, a town on the Sea of Galilee). Var: Madalene, Maddalen, Maddalena, Maddalene, Maddalyn, Malene. Short: Lena, Magda. (MAHG-DAH-LAY-NAH)

MARGARETHE Popular name derived from the Greek Margarītēs, which is from *margaron* (a pearl). The name is commonly found on the family trees of European royalty. Var: Margarete, Margit, Margot. Short: Greta, Grete, Marga, Meret. Pet: Gretal, Gretchen, Gretel. (MAHR-GAH-RAY-TEH)

MARIA A popular name in Germany, Maria is the Latin form of Mary, which is derived from the Hebrew Miryām (sea of bitterness or sorrow). There is much debate over the meaning of this name, however. While "sea of bitterness/sea of sorrow" seems to be the most probable, some sources cite the alternative definitions of "rebellion," "wished-for child," and "mistress or lady of the sea." The name is usually bestowed in honor of the Virgin Mary, the mother of Jesus Christ. Var: Maren, Marie. Pet: Maike, Maja, Mia, Mieze, Mitzi, Mizi. (MAH-REE-AH)

MARIE A borrowing from the French, Marie is a cognate of Maria. *See* MARIA. (MAH-REE)

MARIEL Derived from the French Mariella, which is a diminutive form of Marie. *See* MARIA. Var: Marike. (MAHR-EE-EL)

MARLIS Modern compound name composed of the names Maria and Elisabeth (God is my oath). *See* ELISABETH *and* MARIA. Var: Marlisa. (MAHR-LIS)

MARTHA Derived from the Aramaic *mārthā* (lady, mistress). The name is borne in the Bible by the sister of Lazarus and Mary of Bethany. (MAHR-THA)

MARTINA A popular name throughout Europe, Martina (war-like) is a feminine form of Martin, from the Latin name Martīnus, which is derived from Mars, the name of the Roman mythological god of war. (MAHR-TEE-NAH)

MATHILDA Derived from the Old High German Mahthilda (powerful in battle), a compound name composed of the elements *maht* (might, power) and *hiltia* (battle). Var: Matilda, Mathilde. Short: Tilda, Tilde. Pet: Mattie, Matty, Tillie, Tilly. (MAH-TIL-DAH)

MAUD Anglicized Norman contraction of Mathilda (powerful in battle), which has been in use since the Middle Ages. Var: Maude. (MAUD)

MELANIE A borrowing from the English, Melanie is from the Greek Melaina, which has its root in *melas* (black, dark). (MAY-LAH-NEE)

MIA A pet form of Maria, Mia is also bestowed as an independent given name. *See* MARIA. (MEE-AH)

MICHELLE A borrowing from the French, Michelle is a feminine form of Michael, which is derived from the Hebrew *mīkhā'ēl* (who is like God?). (MIH-SHEL)

MILLICENT Derived from the obsolete Old High German Amalswinth, a compound name composed of the elements *amal* (work) and *swinth* (strength): hence, "strong and industrious." Var: Melicent, Melisande, Melisenda, Mellicent, Milicent, Milissent. Pet: Milli, Millie, Milly. (MIL-LIH-SENT)

MINA A short form of Wilhelmina (resolute protector), Mina is also bestowed as an independent given name. *See* WILHELMINA. Var: Minna, Minne. Pet: Min, Mindy, Minnie, Minny. (MEE-NAH)

MINETTA Diminutive form of Mina, itself a short form of Wilhelmina (resolute protector). *See* WILHELMINA. Var: Minette. Pet: Minnie, Minny. (MIH-NEH-TAH)

MINNIE Pet form of any of the names containing *min-* as an element. Var: Minny. (MIN-NEE)

MIRJAM German cognate of Miriam, which is derived from the Hebrew *miryām* (sea of bitterness or sorrow). (MIR-YAHM)

MONIKA German cognate of Monica, an ancient yet still popular name of uncertain etymology. *See* MONICA (English Names). Var: Monike. (MO-NEE-KAH)

NADINE A short form of Bernadine (bold as a bear), Nadine is popularly bestowed as an independent given name. *See* BERNARDINE. Var: Nadina, Nadetta, Nadette. (NAH-DEEN)

NASTASIA A short form of Anastasia (resurrection), Nastasia is also bestowed as an independent given name. *See* ANASTASIA. (NAH-STAH-SEE-AH)

NICOLE A borrowing from the French, Nicole is a feminine form of Nicholas, which is from the Greek Nikolaos (victory of the people), a compounding of the elements *nikē* (victory) and *laos* (the people). (NIH-KOLE)

NITSA A pet form of Irene (peace), Nitsa is also bestowed as an independent given name. *See* IRENE. (NIT-SAH)

NORBERTA Feminine form of Norbert, a compound name composed of the elements *nord* (north) and *beraht* (bright, famous): hence, "brightness of the north." Var: Norberte. (NOR-BARE-TAH)

ODETTE Diminutive form of Odila (wealthy, prosperous) formed by the addition of the French diminutive suffix *-ette*. Var: Odetta. (O-DEH-TEH)

ODILA Derived from the element *od* (riches, prosperity, fortune). The name was borne by St. Odilia (d.c. 720), the founder of a nunnery at Odilienberg in the Vosges Mountains. Var: Odelia, Odelina, Odella, Odellia, Odiana, Odiane, Odile, Odilia, Ordella. (o-DEE-lah)

OLGA A borrowing from the Russian, Olga is the feminine form of Oleg (holy), which is from the Scandinavian Helgi, a name derived from the Old Norse *heill* (hale, hardy; blessed, holy). (OL-GAH)

OTTHILD Compound name composed of the Germanic elements *od* (riches, prosperity, fortune) and *hild* (battle, war): hence, "prosperous battle." Alternatively, the name is also used as a variant form of Odila (wealthy, prosperous). *See* ODILA. Var: Otila, Ottilia, Ottilie, Ottillia. Short: Oti, Otti. Pet: Tillie, Tilly. (O-TILD)

PATRICIA Feminine form of Patrick, which is from the Latin *patricius* (a patrician, an aristocrat, noble). Short: Pat, Tracia. Pet: Pattie, Patty. (PAH-TREE-SEE-AH)

PAULA Feminine form of Paul, which is from Paulus, a Roman surname derived from *paulus* (small). *See* PAUL (Male Names). (POL-AH)

PAULINE A borrowing from the French, Pauline is a feminine form of Paul (small). *See* PAUL (Male Names). Var: Paulina. (PO-LEE-NAH)

PETRA A borrowing from the Greek, Petra is a feminine form of Petros (a stone), a cognate of Peter. *See* PETER (Male Names). (PEH-TRAH)

PETRONILLA A borrowing from the Latin, Petronilla is a feminine diminutive form of the Roman family name Petrōnius, which is of uncertain derivation. The name Petronilla was borne by a 1st-century martyr, and early Christians came to associate it with Peter (a rock). *See* PETER (Male Names) Var: Petronille. (PAY-TRO-NIL-LAH)

RACHEL Derived from the Hebrew *rāchēl* (ewe). *See* RACHEL (Biblical Names). (RAY-CHEL)

RAGNHILD A borrowing from the Scandinavians, Ragnhild is a compound name composed of the Old Norse elements *regin* (advice, counsel, decision) and *hildr* (battle): hence, "battle counselor." Var: Ragnild, Reinheld, Renilda, Renilde. (RAHG-NILD)

RAINA Derived from the French Reina, which is from the Latin *regina* (queen). Var: Rayna. (RĪ-NAH)

REBEKKA From the Ecclesiastic Late Latin and Ecclesiastic Greek Rhebekka, which is derived from the Hebrew *ribbqāh* (noose), from *rabak* (to bind, to tie). (REH-BEH-KAH)

RENATE Feminine form of the Late Latin Renātus (reborn), which is derived from *renascor* (to be born again, to grow or rise again). Var: Renata. (REH-NAH-TAH)

RICARDA A borrowing from the Italian, Ricarda is the feminine form of Ricardo, the Italian cognate of Richard (strong king). *See* RICHARD (Male Names). Var: Riccarda. Short: Rica, Ricca. (REE-KAHR-DAH)

RITA Short form of the Spanish Margarita (a pearl) or the Italian Margherita (a pearl), which are cognates of Margarethe. Rita is also commonly bestowed as an independent given name. *See* MARGARETHE. (REE-TAH)

RODERICA Feminine form of Roderick (famous king). *See* RODERICK (Male Names). Var: Rodericka, Roderika. Short: Rica, Ricka. Pet: Rickie. (ROD-REE-KAH)

ROLANDA Feminine form of Roland (famous land), which is derived from the Old High German Hruodland, a compounding of the elements *hruod* (fame) and *land* (land). Var: Rolande. (RO-LAHN-DAH)

ROSALINDE Derived from the Old High German Roslindis, a compound name composed of the elements *hros* (a horse) or *hrôs* (fame) and *lind* (gentle, tender, soft). The name was introduced to Spain by the Goths, where it evolved to Rosalinda. Consequently, folk etymology now attributes the name as being derived from the Spanish elements *rosa* (rose) and *linda* (beautiful). Var: Rosalind. (ROS-AH-LIN-DEH)

ROSAMOND Derived from the Old High German Hrosmund, a compound name composed of the elements *hros* (a horse) or *hrôs* (fame) and *mund* (hand, protection). Var: Rosamund, Rosamunda, Rosemonde, Rozomonda, Rozomund. Short: Rosa. (ROSE-AH-MUND)

RUTH Of uncertain etymology, most believe it to be derived from the Hebrew *rūth*, a possible contraction of *re'uth* (companion, friend). (ROOTH)

SABINE Derived from the Latin Sabīna (Sabine woman). The Sabines were an ancient tribe who lived in the Apennines of central Italy and who were conquered by the Romans in the 3rd century B.C. Short: Bina. Pet: Binchen (SAH-BEE-NAH)

SANDRA A short form of Alexandra (defender or helper of mankind), Sandra is now commonly bestowed as an independent given name. *See* ALEXANDRA. (SAHN-DRAH)

SARA Derived from the Hebrew Sārāh (princess). The name is borne in the Bible by the wife of the patriarch Abraham and mother of his son, Isaac. (SAH-RAH)

SELDA A short form of Griselda (gravel, stone), Selda is also occasionally bestowed as an independent given name. *See* GRISELDA. Var: Zelda. (SEL-DAH)

SIDONIE Feminine form of the Latin Sidonius (of Sidon). Sidon was the chief city of ancient Phoenicia, now the site of the modern seaport of Saida in Lebanon. Var: Sidonia, Sidony. (SID-O-NEE)

SIEGFRIDA Feminine form of Siegfried, a compound name composed of the Germanic elements *segu* (power, victory) and *frid* (peace, protection): hence, "powerful peace," "powerful protection," or "peaceful victory." Var: Sigfreda. Short: Freda, Frida. (SEEG-FREE-DAH)

SIGRID A borrowing from the Scandinavians, Sigrid is derived from the Old Norse Sigfríðr, a compound name composed of the elements *sigr* (victory) and *friðr* (fair, beautiful): hence, "beautiful victory." Var: Siegrid. (SEEG-REED)

SILVIA Feminine form of the Latin Silvius, a name derived from *silva* (wood). Var: Sylvia. (SIL-VEE-AH)

SOLVEIG Norwegian name composed of the Old Norse elements *salr* (house, hall) and *veig* (strength): hence, "house of strength." Var: Solvig. (SOL-VAIG)

SOPHIA A borrowing from the Greek, Sophia is directly derived from *sophia* (wisdom, skill). Var: Sofie, Sophie. (SO-FEE-AH)

STEFANIE A popular name in Germany, Stefanie is from the French Stéphanie, a cognate of the Latin Stephania, which is a variant of Stephana. Stephana is a feminine form of Stephanas, which is derived from the Greek *stephanos* (a crown, a garland). Pet: Steffi. (SHTEH-FAH-NEE)

STEFFI A pet form of Stefanie (a crown, a garland), Steffi is also bestowed as an independent given name. *See* STEFANIE. (SHTEH-FEE)

SUSANNA German form of Susannah, which is from the Hebrew Shoshana, a derivative of *shōshannāh* (a lily, a rose). Var: Susanne, Suzanne. (SOO-SAHN-NAH)

SWANHILDA Adopted from the Saxons, Swanhilda is composed of the elements *swan* (swan) and *hild* (battle): hence, "battle swan." Var: Sunhild. Short: Hilda. (SVAHN-HIL-TAH)

SYBILLA Derived from the Latin and Greek Sibylla (a fortune-teller, prophetess). The sibyls, women of ancient Greece and Rome, were mouthpieces of the ancient oracles and seers into the future. In the Middle Ages, they were believed to be receptors of divine revelation; thus Sibyl came into use as an accepted given name. (SI-BIL-LAH)

TILDA Short form of any of the names containing *tilda* as an element. (TIL-DAH)

TRUDIE A pet form of Gertrude (spear strength, spear maiden), Trudie is also bestowed as an independent given name. *See* GERTRUDE. Var: Truda, Trudchen, Trude, Trudy. (TROO-DEE)

ULLA Derived from the Old Norse *ullr* (will, determination). (oo-lah)

ULRIKE Feminine form of Ulrich (noble ruler), a compound name composed of the elements *uodal* (riches, prosperity, fortune) and *rik* (ruler, king). Var: Ulrica, Ulrika. Short: Rica, Rika. Pet: Uli. (OOL-REE-KEH)

URSULA A borrowing from the Middle Latin, Ursula is a diminutive form of the Latin *ursa* (she-bear). The name was borne by a legendary 4th-century saint, a Christian British princess said to have been martyred along with eleven thousand virgins by the Huns at Cologne. The story was very popular in the Middle Ages, which helped establish the name throughout Europe. (OOR-SOO-LAH)

VALERIE A borrowing from the French, Valerie is from the Latin Valerius, an old Roman family name derived from *valere* (to be strong, healthy). (VAH-LAY-REE)

VERA Derived from the Russian Vjera (faith). Because it coincides in form to the Latin *vera* (true), the name is often believed to be derived from this, rather than the former. (VER-AH)

VERENA A Swiss name of uncertain meaning, some believe it to be from the Latin *verus* (true). It was borne by a 3rd-century saint who lived as a hermit near Zurich. Her cult is one of the oldest in Switzerland and has helped to keep the name popular. Var: Verina. (VEH-RAY-NAH)

VERONIKA German form of Veronica, a name of debated origin and meaning. Some believe it to be derived from the Late Latin *veraiconica*, the word given to a piece of cloth or garment with a representation of the face of Christ on it. *Veraiconica* is composed from the elements *verus* (true) and *iconicus* (of or belonging to an image). Alternatively, Veronica is thought to be a variant form of Berenice (bringer of victory), a derivative of the Greek Berenike, which is a variant of the older name Pherenike, a compounding of the elements *pherein* (to bring) and *nikē* (victory). (VEH-RO-NEE-KAH)

VIKTORIA German form of Victoria, which is from the Latin *victoria* (victory). The name is often found on the family trees of German royalty. Pet: Vicky. (VIK-TOR-EE-AH)

VIRGINIE A borrowing from the French, Virginie is often mistakenly believed to be derived from the word *virgin*. In actuality, it is derived from Verginius (spring-like, flourishing), an old Roman family name that has its roots in the Latin *ver* (spring). (VIR-JIN-EE)

VIVIANE A borrowing from the French, Viviane is from the Latin Vivianus, a name derived from *vivus* (alive). (VIV-EE-AH-NEH)

WANDA Of uncertain etymology, Wanda is generally believed to be of Germanic origin, perhaps from *vond* (wand, stem, young tree), or from *Wend*, a term denoting a member of the old Slavic people who now live in an enclave south of Berlin. Var: Vanda, Vande, Wenda. Pet: Wendi, Wendie, Wendy. (VAN-DAH)

WENDY A pet form of Wanda, Wendy is also bestowed as an independent given name. *See* WANDA. It is identical in form to the English Wendy, but the origins of the name are different. Var: Wendi, Wendie. (VEN-DEE)

WIEBKE A borrowing from the Scandinavians, Wiebke originated as a pet form of the medieval name Wibe, a contraction of the Germanic Wigburg, which was composed of *wīg* (war) and *burg* (castle, fortress). Var: Vibeka, Vibeke. (VIB-KEH)

WILFREDA Compound name composed of the elements *willeo* (will, desire, resolution) and *frid* (peace): hence, "resolute peace." Pet: Freddie, Freddy, Willie, Willy. (VEEL-FRAY-DAH)

WILHELMINA Feminine form of Wilhelm (resolute protector), a compound name composed of the elements *willeo* (will, desire, resolution) and *helm* (helmet, protection). Var: Wilhelmine, Willamina. Short: Mina, Mine, Willa, Wilma. Pet: Willie, Willy. (VEEL-HEL-MEE-NAH)

WILLA A short form of Wilhelmina (resolute protector), Willa is also bestowed as an independent given name. *See* WILHELMINA. Pet: Willie, Willy. (VEEL-LAH)

WILLIE Pet form of any of the names containing *wil* as an element. Var: Willy. (VEE-LEE)

WILMA A short form of Wilhelmina (resolute protector), Wilma is also bestowed as an independent given name. *See* WILHELMINA. (VIL-MAH)

WINIFRED A borrowing from the English, Winifred is derived from the Welsh Gwenfrewi, a compound name composed of the elements *gwen* (white, fair, blessed) and *frewi* (reconciliation, peace). Var: Winnifred, Winifrid, Winifride. Pet: Winnie, Winny. (VIN-EE-FRED)

YVETTE A borrowing from the French, Yvette is a feminine diminutive form of Yves (archer), which is derived from the Germanic element *iv* (yew). Yew is the type of wood used by fletchers for bow and arrow making. (EE-VET)

YVONNE A borrowing from the French, Yvonne is a popular feminine form of Yvon (archer) and a feminine diminutive form of Yves (archer), names derived from the Germanic element *iv* (yew, the type of wood used in the making of bows and arrows). (EE-VON)

Chapter Ten

Greek Names

The impressive cultures of ancient Mesopotamia, Egypt, and the Aegean came together in the formation of the great Greek civilization. Throughout the ages, various groups exerted influence upon the Greeks. Among them were the Mycenaeans, the aggressive Dorians from the north, the Phoenicians, and the philosophical Ionians.

From 1400 B.C. to 500 B.C., the Greek civilization went from great heights which prodded the advancement of man in Europe, to obscurity after the Dorians invaded, and back to becoming an important cultural and economic force. In the 3rd century B.C., under the leadership of Alexander the Great, Greece made its farthest reaches abroad and became a leader in influencing the shape of the modern world. Yet by 196 B.C., the country again suffered from strife and officially came under the protection of Rome.

The event of Christ's crucifixion and resurrection made a profound impact on Grecian society. The common tongue of the Mediterranean area at that time was Greek, and it was in that language that the four apostles wrote the Gospels and set out to spread the Good News. By the time of the deaths of St. Peter and St. Paul in A.D. 67, and in spite of daunting persecution, they had succeeded in converting a significant number of people to the new Christian religion.

The ascension to the throne by Constantine the Great was the early Christians' answer to prayer. His Edict of Milan put an end to persecution and granted religious freedom, a move that secured lasting reverence of him by the Greek people. Indeed, to this day, he is considered the true founding father of the Greek Orthodox Church and is often referred to as the thirteenth apostle.

This loyalty to the church is pervasive throughout Grecian society and has a measurable effect on the naming of children. Whereas the language gave many names to other tongues, Greek children are usually named after revered saints of the Greek Orthodox Church.

Traditional naming patterns are still held in many parts of the country. The first male is named after the paternal grandfather, the first female after the paternal grandmother. The second male and female children are named after their maternal grandparents. Subsequent children may bear names of other family members, or one from outside of the family, but they are not usually named after their father or mother. This traditional way of naming has ensured the popularity of many names.

Greek children are generally bestowed with one name at baptism, ten days after birth. The middle name is the father's first name in the genitive case, which no doubt helps distinguish between cousins who bear the same names: those of their grandparents. The family name of a male child is that of the father, but the surname of female children is that of the father in the genitive case. Upon marriage, women change their middle name to their husband's first name and assume his surname in the genitive case.

Genealogies were of great importance to the ancient Greeks, and each family group had one special ancestor to whom they paid tribute and referred themselves back to as a means of marking their lineage. Later, surnames developed much as they did in Europe. Occupational, descriptive, and place names came into use as last names, but patronymics were still more common, usually ending in a suffix meaning "son," such as *-poulos*, *-ou*, and *-akis*.

The high regard Greeks hold for their priests is also apparent in surnames that developed from the word *papa* (priest) prefixed to the priest's first name, as in the name of Greek Premier Andreas Papandreou (son of Priest Andreas).

Unlike many other European languages, which have undergone a profound change, the Greek language has retained great continuity over the ages, an amazing fact when viewed in regards to the countless invasions, strife, and internal turbulence the country has experienced, along with the amazing cultural and creative leaps it has taken. And as the language remains constant, so does the stability of Greek names.

Greek Male Names

ABEL Derived from the Hebrew *hebel* (breath). The name is borne in the Bible by the second son of Adam and Eve. Var: Avel. (AH-BEHL)

ACHERON A name meaning "river of woe," which is derived from the Greek *achos* (pain). In Greek and Roman mythology, Acheron is the name of the river in Hades across which the dead are ferried. (AH-KSER-ON, AH-KEHR-ON)

ACHILLIOS Derived from Achilleus, an ancient name of unknown etymology borne in Greek mythology by the leader and warrior of the Trojan War. He was killed by an arrow that struck his heel, his only vulnerable spot. (AH-KSIL-LEE-OS, AH-KEE-LEE-OS)

ADŌNIS A name of unknown etymology borne in Greek mythology by a handsome young man loved by Aphrodite, hence its accepted translation of "handsome, very good-looking" and its use as a noun indicating any exceptionally handsome young man. (AH-DŌ-NIS)

AËTIOS A name meaning "of or pertaining to an eagle," which is from *aetos* (eagle). (AH-EH-TEE-OS)

AGAPIOS Derived from *agapē* (love), the name is indicative of God's love for mankind. (AH-GAH-PEE-OS)

AGATHIAS Derived from *agathos* (good). (AH-GAH-THEE-AHS)

AIAKOS A name of unknown origin and meaning borne in Greek mythology by a son of Zeus. *See* AEACUS (Mythology and Astrology Names). (AH-EE-AH-KOS)

AIGEUS Derived from Aegidius, which is from *aigis* (the goatskin shield of Zeus, a protection). Var: Giles. (EE-JUS)

AINEIAS Derived from *ainein* (to praise). The name is borne in Greek mythology by the son of Anchises and Venus. He wandered about for years after escaping from the ruined city of Troy. Var: Aeneas, Eneas. (AH-EE-NEE-AHS)

AÏOLOS Classical name meaning "the changeable one." *See* AEOLUS (Mythology and Astrology Names). (A-EE-O-LOS)

AKTAIŌN A name meaning "an inhabitant of Akte [the ancient name of Attica]." *See* ACTAEON (Mythology and Astrology Names). (AHK-TAY-ŌN)

ALASTAIR A Gaelic form of Alexander (defender of mankind). *See* ALEXANDROS. Var: Alasdair, Alastor. (AH-LAH-STAIR)

ALEXANDROS Compound name composed of the elements *alexein* (to defend, to help) and *andros* (man): hence, "defender or helper of mankind." The name was borne by Alexander the Great (356–323 B.C.), a Macedonian king and military conqueror who helped spread the Greek culture across Asia Minor to Egypt and India. Var: Aleksandr, Aleksandur, Alexander, Alexandras. Short: Alek, Alekos, Alex, Alexei, Alexios, Alexis, Sander, Sandros. (AH-LEKS-AHN-DROS)

ALEXIOS Popular name derived from the verb *alexein* (to defend, to help): hence, "defender, helper." Alternatively, Alexios is used as a short form of Alexandros (defender or helper of mankind). *See* ALEXANDROS. Var: Alekos, Alexei, Alexis. (AH-LEHKS-EE-OS)

ALTAIR Derived from the Arabic *al tā'ir* (the bird). The Altair is the name of the brightest star in the constellation Aquila. (AHL-TAIR)

Ambrosios Derived from *ambrosios* (immortal). Var: Ambrocio, Ambrose, Ambrus. (AHM-BRO-SEE-OS)

Anaklētos A name meaning "called forth, invoked," Anaklētos originated as a form of divine address. Var: Anacletus. Short: Cletus, Klētos. (AH-NAH-KLEE-TOS)

Anastasios Derived from *anastasis* (resurrection). Var: Anastagio, Anastasio, Anastasius, Anasztaz. Short: Anstace. (AH-NAH-STAH-SEE-OS)

Anatolios Derived from *anatolē* (sunrise, daybreak, dawn). Var: Anatol, Anatole, Anatoli, Anatolio. (AH-NAH-TŌ-LEE-OS)

Andreas Popular name derived from *andreios* (manly). Var: Aindreas, Aindriu, Ander, Andor, Andras, Andres, Andrew, Andries, Androu. (AHN-DREY-AHS)

Angelo Derived from *angelos* (messenger). In New Testament Greek, the word took on the meaning "divine messenger, messenger of God." Var: Angel, Angell, Anzioleto, Anziolo. (AHN-JEH-LO, AHN-YEH-LO)

Aniketos Compound name composed of the elements *a* (not) and *nikān* (to conquer): hence, "unconquered." (AH-NEE-KEE-TOS)

Anso Derived from Anselmo (divine protection), the Italian cognate of the Germanic Anselme, a name composed of the elements *ansi* (divinity, a god) and *helm* (helmet, protection). (AHN-SO)

Antaīos From *antaios* (an adversary, the one who is opposite). *See* ANTAEUS (Mythology and Astrology Names). (AHN-TAY-OS)

Anthony Derived from Antonius, an old Roman family name of uncertain origin and meaning. Var: Andonios, Anton, Antonios, Antony. Short: Tonios, Tony. (AHN-THO-NEE)

Apollo Derived from Apollōn, an ancient name of unknown etymology borne in Greek mythology by the god of music, poetry, prophecy, and medicine. The name is indicative of physical perfection. Var: Apolo. Short: Polo. (AH-POL-LO)

Apostolos Derived from *apostolos* (an apostle, a person sent forth on a special mission). (AH-PO-STO-LOS)

Appollonios A derivative of Apollo, the name of the Greek god of music, poetry, prophecy, and medicine. (AH-POL-LO-NEE-OS)

Archimedes Compound name composed of the elements *archi* (chief, first, head) and *mēdesthai* (to ponder, to meditate upon): hence, "to first think about or meditate upon." The name was borne by a well-known Greek mathematician and inventor (c. 287–215 B.C.). (AHR-KEE-MEH-DES)

Argos Derived from *argos* (bright). The name is borne in Greek mythology by a giant with a hundred eyes who was ordered by Hera to watch Io. He was killed by Hermes and his eyes were put in the tail feathers of the peacock. Var: Argus. (AHR-GOS)

Ari Short form of any of the names beginning with the element *Ari-*. (AH-REE)

Aristides Derived from *aristos* (best). The name was borne by Aristides the Just (c. 530–468 B.C.), an Athenian general and statesman. Var: Aristeides, Aristid. Short: Ari. (AH-REE-STEE-DEHS)

Aristokles Compound name composed of the elements *aristos* (best) and *kleo* (fame): hence, "most famous." Short: Ari. (AH-REE-STO-KLEHS)

Aristotelis Compound name composed of the elements *aristos* (best) and *totalis* (total): hence, "totally the best." The name in its variant form, Aristotle, was borne by the famous Greek philosopher (384–322 B.C.) who is noted for his works on logic, ethics, politics, and metaphysics. Var: Aristotle. Short: Ari, Telis. (AH-REE-STO-TEH-LEES)

Arkhippos Compound name composed of the elements *arkhē* (ruler) and *hippos* (horse). The name was borne by St. Arkhippos, one of the earliest Christian converts. (AHR-KHEEP-POS)

Arsenios A name meaning "male, virile, masculine." Var: Arsene, Arsenio. (AHR-SEHN-EE-OS)

Athanasios Derived from the Greek *athanasia* (immortality, eternal existence). Short: Thanasis, Thanos. (AH-THA-NAS-EE-OS)

Augustine Derived from the Latin Augustinus, a diminutive form of Augustus, which is from *augustus* (great, venerable). The name was borne by St. Augustine (354–430), an early church father who was born in Numidia and became the bishop of Hippo in northern Africa. (AH-OO-GOO-STEEN)

Baltsaros Greek form of Balthasar, a name of uncertain etymology which tradition assigned to one of the three magi who visited the Christ child, the others being Gaspar and Melchior. Some believe the name is derived from the Chaldean Belteshazzar (Bel's prince) or from the Persian Beltshazzar (prince of splendor). Others think the name was merely an invention with an Eastern sound to it. (BAHLT-SAH-ROS)

Baptiste Derived from the Ecclesiastic Late Latin *baptista* (a baptist, one who baptizes). (BAP-TEEST)

Baruch Derived from the Hebrew *baruch* (blessed). (BAH-ROOK)

Basil A short form of Basileios (kingly), Basil is also bestowed as an independent given name. *See* BASILEIOS. (BAH-SEEL)

Basileios Derived from *basileus* (king). The name was borne by a 4th-century Greek theologian known as St. Basil the Great (c. 330–79). A bishop of Caesarea, he is regarded as one of the fathers of the Eastern Church. Var: Vasileios, Vasilios, Vasilis. Short: Basil, Vasos. (BAH-SEE-LEH-I-OSS)

Bastien Short form of Sebastianos (a man of Sebastia). *See* SEBASTIANOS. Short: Baste. (BAHS-TYEN)

Benedictos From the Latin Benedictus (blessed), a name derived from *benedicere* (to speak well of, to bless). *See* BENEDICT (Italian Names). Var: Benedict, Venedictos. (BEH-NEH-DEEK-TOS)

Carolos Greek cognate of Charles, which is derived from the Middle Latin Carolus (full-grown, a man). (KAH-RO-LOS)

Caesare From the Latin Caesar, a name of uncertain etymology. *See* CESARE (Italian Names). Var: Caseareo, Cesare. (SAY-ZAHR)

Christiano Derived from *christianos* (a Christian, a follower of Christ), which is from *christos* (the anointed). Var: Christian. Short: Chris. (KREES-TEE-AH-NO)

Christophoros Compound name composed of the Ecclesiastic Greek elements *Christos* (Christ) and *pherein* (to bear): hence, "bearing Christ." The name was borne by a 3rd-century martyr of Asia Minor who is the patron saint of travelers. Var: Kristofr, Kristor. Short: Chris. (KREES-TŌ-FOR-OS)

Christos Derived from *christos* (the anointed), which is from *chriein* (to anoint). Christos is the name given to Jesus of Nazareth (c. 4 B.C.–c. A.D. 29), who is regarded by Christians to be the fulfillment of the Messianic prophecy in the Old Testament, and the founder of the Christian religion. Var: Kristo, Kristos. (KREES-TOS)

Claudios Derived from the Latin Claudius, an old Roman family name derived from *claudus* (lame). (KLAH-OO-DEE-OS)

Cletus A short form of Anacletus (called forth, invoked), Cletus is also bestowed as an independent given name. *See* ANAKLĒTOS. (KLEH-TUS)

Constantinos From the Latin Constantinus, which is derived from *constans* (steadfast, constant). Constantine II (b. 1940) is the name of the former king of the Hellenes, exiled in 1967 following the "Colonel's Coup" of December 13. The name is also borne by Konstantinos Karamanlis, president of Greece. Var: Constantine, Konstandinos, Konstantinos. Short: Costa, Kastas, Kostas, Kostis. (KON-STAHN-TEE-OS)

Damaskenos A name meaning "of Damascus," the name of an ancient city which is now the capital of Syria. Var: Damaskinos. Short: Damasko. (DAH-MAH-SKEH-NOS)

Damianos Ancient name believed to be derived from *damān* (to tame). Var: Damae, Damen, Damian, Damon. (DAH-MEE-AH-NOS)

Dareios Ancient name of uncertain origin. It is thought to ultimately be derived from Darayavahush, the name of an ancient Persian king. (DAH-REH-EE-OS)

David From the Hebrew *dāwīd* (beloved). The name is borne in the Bible by the second and greatest of the Israelite kings. (DAH-VEED)

Demetri A short form of Demetrios (of Demeter), Demetri is also bestowed as an independent given name. *See* DEMETRIOS. (DEH-MEH-TREE)

Demetrios A name meaning "of Demeter." Demeter is an ancient name of unknown etymology borne by the Greek mythological goddess of agriculture and fertility. Var: Demetrius, Dhimitrios. Short: Demetri, Mitros. Pet: Mitsos. (DEH-MEH-TREE-OS)

Denys Derived from Dionysius (of Dionysos, the Greek mythological god of wine and revelry). *See* DIONYSIOS. (DEH-NYEHS)

Dion Short form of Dionysios (of Dionysos), Dion is also bestowed as an independent given name. *See* DIONYSIOS. (DEE-ON)

Dionysios A name meaning "of Dionysos." Dionysos is an ancient name of unknown etymology borne by the Greek mythological god of wine and revelry. Var: Dionysius, Dionysus. Short: Denes, Dion. Pet: Dunixi. (DEE-O-NYES-EE-OS)

Dorian Derived from the Greek *Dōrios*, one of the four main tribes of ancient Greece who settled in the mountainous area known as Doris. Var: Doran. (DOR-EE-AN)

Eleutherios Derived from *eleutheria* (liberty, freedom). Var: Eleftherios. (EH-LOO-THEH-REE-OS)

Elias Greek cognate of the Hebrew Eliyahu, which is derived from *'ēlīyāhū* (Jehovah is God). Var: Illias. (EH-LEE-AHS)

Elijah Anglicized form of the Hebrew Eliyahu (Jehovah is God), a name borne in the biblical Old Testament by a 9th-century B.C. prophet of Israel. Elias is the Greek cognate. (EH-LEE-YAH)

Elpidios Derived from *elpis* (hope). The name was borne by a 4th-century saint who spent twenty-five years living in a cave as a hermit. (EHL-PEE-DEE-OS)

Emmanouēl Greek cognate of the Hebrew Immanuel, a name derived from *'immānūēl* (God is with us). The name was used in the Old Testament by the prophet Isaiah in reference to the promised Messiah, and in the New Testament as another name for Jesus Christ. Var: Emmanuel. (EHM-MAH-NO-OO-EL)

Erasmios Derived from the verb *eran* (to love), Erasmios is defined as "lovely." Var: Erasmus. Short: Rasmus. (EH-RAHS-MEE-OS)

Ercole Cognate of the Greek Hērakleēs. *See* HĒRAKLEĒS. (ER-KOL)

Ēsaias Greek cognate of the Hebrew Yeshaya, which is from *yĕsha'yah* (God is salvation). (EE-SAH-EE-AHS)

Eugenios Derived from *eugenēs* (well-born, noble). Var: Eugen, Eugene, Eugenio. Short: Eugen. (YOO-HEH-NEE-OS)

Euphemios Compound name composed of the elements *eu* (well, good, fine) and *phēmē* (voice): hence, "fair speech, of good voice." (YOO-FEH-MEE-OS)

Eusebios Late Greek compound name composed of the elements *eu* (well, good) and *sebein* (to worship, to venerate). The name was borne by the Greek ecclesiastical historian Eusebius Pamphili (264?–340) and by Eusebius Hieronymus Sophronius (340?–420), known to us as St. Jerome, a Pannonian monk, church scholar, and author of the Vulgate. Var: Eusebius. (YOO-SEH-BEE-OS)

Eustachius Compound name composed of the elements *eu* (well, good) and *stachys* (grapes): hence, "fruitful." Var: Eustace, Eustache, Eustakhios, Eustis. (YOO-STAH-KEE-US)

Farris A cognate of Petros (a rock). *See* PETROS. (FAR-RIS)

Felix A borrowing from the Latin, Felix is derived from *felix* (lucky, happy). (FEH-LEEKS)

Flavian From the Latin Flāvius, an old Roman family name derived from *flāvus* (fair, blond, golden, tawny). (FLAH-VEE-AHN)

Galenus Derived from *galēnē* (calm). The name was born by Claudius Galenus (c. 130—200), a Greek physician and writer on medicine and philosophy to whom the system of medical practice Galenism is attributed. Var: Galen. (GAH-LEH-NUS)

Geōrgios Derived from *geōrgos* (earthworker, farmer), which is composed from the elements *gē* (earth) and *ergein* (to work). Var: Georg, Georges, Iorgos. (HYOR-HYEE-OS)

Gregor Short form of Grēgorios (vigilant, a watchman), Gregor is also bestowed as an independent given name. *See* GRĒGORIOS. (GREH-GOR)

Grēgorios Old name meaning "vigilant, a watchman," which is derived from the verb *egeirein* (to awaken, to watch). The name was borne by the brother of St. Basil, St. Grēgorios of Nyssa (331?–?95), a Greek theologian and bishop in Cappadocia. Var: Gregoire, Gregorie. Short: Gregor. (GREE-GOR-EE-OS)

Hali Derived from *hali* (the sea). (HAH-LEE)

Hērakleēs Compound name composed from Hēra (the name of the mythological queen of the gods) and *kleos* (fame, glory): hence, "glory of Hera, divine glory." The name is borne in Greek and Roman mythology by the son of Zeus and Alemene who was renowned for his amazing strength. Var: Herakles, Hercules. (HARE-AH-KLEES)

Hesperos The name of the evening star, which is believed to be derived from the Indo-European *wesperos* (evening). (HEH-SPER-OS)

Hieremias Ecclesiastic Greek name derived from the Hebrew *yirmeyāh* (the Lord loosens, the Lord will uplift). Hieremias is a cognate of Jeremiah. (HEER-EH-MEE-AHS)

Hieronymos Compound name composed of the elements *hieros* (holy) and *onyma* (name). Hieronymos (holy name) is a cognate of Jerome. Var: Hieronim. (HEER-ON-EE-MOS)

Hilarion Derived from the Latin Hilarius (cheerful), which is from *hilaris* (cheerful, glad). Var: Ilarion. (HEE-LAH-REE-ON)

Hippocrates Derived from the Greek element *hippos* (a horse). The name was borne by an ancient Greek physician (c. 460–370 B.C.) known to the modern world as the father of medicine. (HEE-PO-KRAH-TEHS)

Hippolytos Compound name composed of the elements *hippos* (a horse) and *lyein* (to loosen, to free): hence, "freer or loosener of horses." Var: Hipolit, Hippolytus. (HEE-POL-EE-TOS)

Homeros Derived from *homēros* (a pledge, a hostage). The name was borne by the epic poet of the 9th century B.C. who wrote the *Iliad* and the *Odyssey*. (HO-MEH-ROS)

Iakobos Derived from the Hebrew *ja'aqob* (seizing by the heel, supplanting). Iakobos is a cognate of Jacob, the name borne in the Bible by a son of Isaac and patriarch of the founders of the twelve tribes of Israel. Var: Iakovos. (YAH-KO-BOS)

IĀSON Direct derivation of *iāson* (healer). *See* JASON. (YAH-SON)

IEZEKIĒL Greek cognate of the Hebrew Yechezkel (God will strengthen). (YEH-ZEH-KEE-EL)

IGNATIOS From the Latin Ignatius, which is derived from Egnatius, an old Roman family name of uncertain etymology. Some believe it to be of Etruscan origin. Others derive it from the Latin *ignis* (fire). (EEG-NAH-TEE-OS)

IOANNES Ecclesiastic Greek cognate of John (God is gracious), which is derived from the Hebrew *yōhānān*, a contraction of *yehōhānān* (Yahweh is gracious). Var: Giankos, Giannes, Ioannikios, Ioannis, Jannes, Joannoulos, Yannis, Yannakis. Pet: Nannos, Yanni. (YO-AHN-NEHS)

IŌSĒPH Derived from the Hebrew Yosef, which is from *yōsēf* (may he add). The name is a cognate of Joseph. *See* JOSEPH (Biblical Names). (YO-SEF)

ISAAK Derived from the Hebrew Yitzchak (he will laugh), which is from *yitshāq* (laughter). Var: Isaakios. (EE-SAHK)

ISIDOROS Compound name composed of Isis, the name of the Egyptian goddess of fertility, and *dōron* (gift): hence, "gift of Isis." Var: Isadorios, Isidor, Isidore. (EE-SEE-DOR-OS)

JARED Greek cognate of the Hebrew Yered, a name derived from *yeredh* (descent). (YAH-RED, JAH-RED)

JASON A borrowing from the Latin, Jason is derived from the Greek Iāson, which is from *iāson* (healer). The name is borne in Greek mythology by a prince who led the Argonauts on a quest to find the Golden Fleece. (YAH-SON, JAH-SON)

JOACHEIM Derived from the Hebrew Jehoiakim, which is from Yehoyakim (God will establish). (YO-AH-KEEM, JO-AH-KEEM)

JULIAN From the Latin Julianus, which is a derivative of Julius, and old Roman family name thought to be derived from Iulus (the first down on the chin, downy-bearded). Because a person just beginning to develop facial hair is young, "youth" became an accepted meaning of the name. (YOO-LEE-AN)

KALOGEROS Compound name composed of the elements *kalos* (beautiful, fair) and *geras* (old age): hence, "fair old age." (KAH-LO-HEH-ROS)

KLEMENIS From the Latin Clemens (mild, gentle, merciful), which is derived from the word of the same definition. (KLEH-MEH-NEES)

KOSMAS Derived from *kosmos* (universe, order, harmony). Var: Kosmy. (KOS-MAHS)

KYPRIOS From Cyprus, a Cypriot. (KEEP-REE-OS)

KYRILLOS Derived from *kyrillos* (lordly), which is from *kyrios* (a lord). The name was borne by a 9th-century Greek prelate and missionary to the Slavs, to whom the Cyrillic alphabet is attributed. Short: Kiril, Kyros. (KEE-REEL-LOS)

LAURENTIOS From the Latin Laurentius (man from Laurentum), which is from Laurentum, the name of a town in Latium, which is probably derived from *laurus* (laurel). *See* LORENZO (Italian Names). (LAH-OO-REHN-TEE-OS)

LEIANDROS Compound name composed from the elements *leōn* (lion) and *andros* (a man, mankind): hence, "lion man, lion-like." *See* LEANDER (Mythology and Astrology Names). Var: Leander, Leandros. (LEE-AHN-DROS)

LEO Late Latin name derived from *leo* (lion). Alternatively, Leo is used as a short form of Leontios (lion). (LEH-O)

LEONTIOS Derivative of the Late Latin Leon, which is from *leo* (lion). Short: Leo. (LEH-ON-TEE-OS)

LOUKANOS Old name meaning "man from Lucania." Lucania was an ancient district in southern Italy now known as Basilicata. Var: Lukianos. Short: Loukas. (LOO-KAH-NOS)

LOUKAS Contracted form of Loukanos (man from Lucania). *See* LOUKANOS. (LO-OO-KAHS)

LUCAS Ecclesiastic Late Latin name thought to be a derivative of Lucius, which is from the root *lux* (light). Alternatively, some believe the name is derived from the Ecclesiastic Greek Loukas, a contraction of Loukanos (man from Lucania). Var: Lucais, Lukas. (LOO-KAHS)

LUCIAN Derived from the Latin Luciānus (of Lucius), which is from the root *lux* (light). (LOO-SEE-AHN)

LYSANDROS Combination name composed from the elements *lysis* (freeing, loosening) and *andros* (man, mankind): hence, "liberator, freer of mankind." The name was borne by a celebrated Spartan naval and military commander who conquered the Athenians. Var: Lysander. Short: Sander, Sandros. (LY-SAHN-DROS)

MAKAR Short form of Makarios (blessed), Makar is also bestowed as an independent given name. *See* MAKARIOS. (MAH-KAHR)

Makarios Derived from *makaros* (blessed). The name was borne by many saints, which helped to keep the name common. Short: Makar. (MAH-KAH-REE-OS)

Marinos Derived from the Latin *marinus* (of the sea), which has its root in *mare* (the sea). (MAH-REE-NOS)

Markos Greek form of the Latin Marcus, a name of uncertain derivation. Most believe it has its root in Mars, the name of the Roman mythological god of war, and thus give it the meaning "war-like." Others, however, think it is from *mas* (manly) or from the Greek *malakoz* (soft, tender). Short: Mark. (MAHR-KOS)

Martinos From the Latin Martinus (of Mars, warlike), a derivative of Mars, the name of the Roman mythological god of war. (MAHR-TEE-NOS)

Mattathias Derived from the Hebrew Matityah, which has its root in *mattīthyāh* (gift of God). (MAHT-TAH-THEE-AHS)

Matthias Contracted form of Mattathias (gift of God). The name is in more common use than the longer form. *See* MATTATHIAS. Var: Matthaios. (MAHT-THEE-AHS)

Maximos From the Latin Maximus, which is a direct use of *maximus* (greatest). (MAHKS-EE-MOS)

Methodios A name meaning "fellow traveler," which is composed of the Greek elements *meta* (with) and *hodos* (road, path). The name was borne by St. Methodius (d. c. 885), the first translator of the Bible into the Slavonic language. (MEH-THO-DEE-OS)

Mikhail A derivative of the Hebrew *mīkhā'ēl* (who is like God?). The name is borne in the Bible by the archangel closest to God, the one responsible for carrying out God's judgments. Considered the leader of the heavenly host, he is regarded as the patron of soldiers. Var: Mahail, Maichail, Michael, Mikhalis. Pet: Makis, Mikhos. (MEE-KAH-EEL)

Milo Of uncertain derivation. It might be from the German *mild* (mild, peaceful, calm), or it might be from the Old Slavonic root *milu* (merciful). Var: Miles, Myles. (MĪ-LO)

Milos Derived from the name of a Greek island in the Aegean Sea. Alternatively, Milos is a Greek form of Milosz, a Polish name derived from the element *mil* (grace, favor). (MEE-LOS)

Moris Greek form of the Latin Maurus (a Moor). The Moors were a Muslim people of mixed Arab and Berber descent; thus the name came to mean "dark" or "swarthy" in reference to their coloring. Var: Maur, Maurice. (MO-REES)

Mōsēs Ecclesiastic Greek name, which is from the Hebrew *mōsheh* (drawn out of the water) and from the Egyptian *mes, mesu* (son, child). Var: Moses, Moyses. (MO-SEHS)

Myron Direct derivative of *myron* (myrrh, a fragrant resin used in making incense and perfume). The name was borne by a Greek sculptor of the 5th century B.C. and is said to have been taken up by early Christians because of the gift of myrrh made to the Christ child by the Wise Men. (MEE-RON)

Nathanaēl Derived from the Hebrew Netalel, which is from *nĕthan'ēl* (gift of God). (NAH-THAN-AH-EL)

Nektarios Derived from *nektarios* (of nectar), which is from *nektar* (nectar). In Greek mythology, nectar was the drink of the gods, which imparted immortality. Var: Nectarios. (NEHK-TAH-REE-OS)

Nēstor Derived from *nēstor* (the one going or departing). *See* NESTOR (Mythology and Astrology Names). (NEHS-TOR)

Nikita A borrowing from the Russian, Nikita is a cognate of the Greek Aniketos (unconquered). *See* ANIKETOS. (NEE-KEE-TAH)

Nikodemos Compound name composed from the elements *nikē* (victory) and *dēmos* (people, population): hence, "victory of the people." Var: Nicodemus. Short: Nico, Niko. (NEE-KO-DEH-MOS)

Nikolaos Compound name composed of the elements *nikē* (victory) and *laos* (the people): hence, "victory of the people." The name was borne by St. Nikolaos, a 4th-century bishop of Myra who is regarded as the patron saint of Greece and Russia, and of children, sailors, and wolves. Nicholas is the name of the second son (b. 1969) of the deposed King Constantine II and Queen Anne-Marie. Var: Nicholas, Nikolos. Short: Nico, Niko, Nikos, Nilos. (NEE-KO-LAH-OS)

Nikomedes Compound name composed from the elements *nikē* (victory) and *mēdesthai* (to ponder, to meditate upon): hence, "to ponder victory." Short: Niko, Nikos. (NEE-KO-MEH-DEHS)

Nikos Popular short form of any of the various names beginning with the element *Niko-*. (NEE-KOS)

Nikostratos Compound name composed of the elements *nikē* (victory) and *stratos* (army): hence, "victorious army." Short: Niko, Nikos. (NEE-KO-STRAH-TOS)

Orestes Derived from the Greek *oros* (mountain). *See* ORESTES (Mythology and Astrology Names). Var: Oreste. (O-REH-STEHS)

ORION Of uncertain etymology borne in Greek mythology by a celebrated hunter who was beloved by Diana. After he was accidentally killed, he was transformed and placed into the heavens as a constellation. (O-REE-ON)

PARIS Of uncertain etymology. In Greek legend, it was Paris' kidnapping of Helen, the wife of the Spartan king Menelaus, which sparked the Trojan War. (PAHR-ISS)

PARTHENIOS A name meaning "of or like a virgin," Parthenios is derived from *parthenos* (a virgin). (PAHR-THEN-EE-OS)

PAUL From the Latin Paulus, which originated as a Roman family name derived from *paulus* (small). The name is borne by the crown prince of Greece (b. 1967), the eldest son of the deposed King Constantine II and Queen Anne-Marie. *See also* PAUL (Biblical Names). (PAH-OOL)

PAULOS From the Latin Paulus, a Roman family name derived from *paulus* (small). Var: Pavlos. (PAH-OO-LOS)

PELAGIOS A name meaning "of or belonging to the sea," Pelagios is derived from *pelagos* (the sea). (PEH-LAH-HEE-OS)

PERICLES Derived from the Greek *peri* (around, surrounding) and *kleos* (fame, glory): hence, "far-famed." (PEH-REE-KLEHS)

PETROS Direct derivative of *petros* (a stone). Var: Panos, Peder, Perrin, Peter, Petr, Piaras, Pieter, Pietr. (PEH-TROS)

PHILANDROS Compound name composed of the elements *philos* (loving) and *andros* (man): hence, "lover of mankind." Var: Philander. Short: Phil. (FIL-AHN-DROS)

PHILOMENOS Compound name composed of the elements *philos* (loving) and *menos* (strength): hence, "lover of strength." Var: Philomenēs, Philemon. (FIL-O-MEEN-OS)

PHILIP Derived from the earlier Greek Philippos (lover of horses), the name Philip is borne by the youngest child of the deposed King Constantine II and Queen Anne-Marie. *See* PHILIPPOS. Var: Filip, Filippo, Filips, Fulop, Philippe. Pet: Flip, Lippi, Lippio, Pippo. (FEE-LEEP)

PHILIPPOS Popular compound name composed of the elements *philos* (loving) and *hippos* (a horse). (FEE-LEE-POS)

POLYVIOS Compound name derived from *poly* (many) and *vios* (views): hence, "many views." (PO-LIV-EE-US)

PROKOPIOS Compound name composed of the elements *pro* (before) and *kopios* (in great abundance, copious): hence, "progressive." The name was borne by a 4th-century Greek saint, the first to be martyred in Palestine under the reign of Diocletian. Var: Procopius. (PRO-KO-PEE-OS)

REUBEN Derived from the Hebrew *rĕ'ūbēn* (behold, a son!). Var: Rouvin. (ROO-BEHN)

RHAPHAĒL A cognate of the Hebrew Refael, a derivative of *refāēl* (God has healed). (RAH-FAH-EHL)

ROMANOS Derived from the Latin Romanus (a Roman), which is from Roma, the name of the capital city of Italy. (RO-MAH-NOS)

SAMOUEL Greek cognate of the Hebrew Shmuel, a name derived from *shĕmū'ēl* (name of God, his name is God). (SAH-MO-WEL)

SAMPSŌN Greek cognate of the Hebrew Shimshon, a name derived from *shimshōn* (sun). (SAHMP-SON)

SANDER A short form of Alexander (defender or helper of mankind) and Lysander (freer of mankind), Sander is also bestowed as an independent given name. *See* ALEXANDROS *and* LYSANDROS. (SAHN-DEHR)

SANDROS A short form of Alexandros (defender or helper of mankind) and Lysandros (freer of mankind), Sandros is also bestowed as an independent given name. *See* ALEXANDROS *and* LYSANDROS. (SAHN-DROS)

SAOUL Cognate of the Hebrew Shaul, which is from *shāūl* (asked of, borrowed). (SAH-O-WEL)

SEBASTIANOS A name meaning "a man of Sebastia." Sebastia was the name of Samaria after the time of Herod the Great (73?–4 B.C.). Var: Sebastian. (SEH-BAH-STEE-AH-NOS)

SERAPHIM From the Ecclesiastic Late Latin *seraphim* (burning ones, the angels surrounding the throne of God), which is from the Hebrew *sĕrāphīm*, a word believed to be derived from *sāraph* (to burn). (SEH-RAH-FEEM)

SERGIOS From the Latin Sergius, an old Roman family name of uncertain etymology. (SEHR-YOS)

SĒTH Greek cognate of the Hebrew Shet, a derivative of *shēth* (appointed). The name is borne in the Bible by the third son of Adam and Eve, born after the death of his brother, Abel. (SETH)

SILAS Ecclesiastic Greek name derived from the Aramaic *sh'îlâ* (asked for). (SEE-LAHS)

Silvanos From the Latin Silvānus (of the woods), which is derived from *silva* (a wood). Silvanus was a Roman mythological god of the woods and fields. (SEEL-VAH-NOS)

Simon Ecclesiastic Greek name derived from the Hebrew Shimon, a derivative of *shim'ōn* (heard). Var: Seimon. (SEE-MON)

Socrates Popular name of uncertain derivation. It was borne by an ancient Greek philosopher and teacher (c. 470–399 B.C.). (SO-KRAH-TEHS)

Solomōn Hebrew name derived from *shĕlōmōh* (peaceful), which is from *shālōm* (peace). (SO-LO-MON)

Soterios Popular name derived from *sōtērios* (a savior, a deliverer). (SO-TEH-REE-OS)

Spiridon A popular name among the Ionian Islands, Spiridon is a name of debated derivation. Some believe it is derived from the Greek *spyrīz* (a round basket). Others think it is a diminutive form of the Latin *spiritus* (spirit, soul). The name was borne by a 4th-century Cypriot saint who was a hermit before becoming a bishop and playing a major role at the Nicene Council in 325. Var: Spyridon. (SPEE-REE-DON)

Stephanos Popular name derived from *stephanos* (a crown, a garland, that which surrounds). Var: Istivan, Stefan, Stefanos, Stephanas. (STEH-FAH-NOS)

Symeōn Derived from the Hebrew *shim'ōn* (heard). (SYEH-MEH-ON)

Telesphoros Compound name composed from the elements *telos* (an end, a completion) and *pherein* (to bear, to bring): hence, "bearing the end, to bring about the end." Telesphoros originated as the name used for the ancient Greek personification of Justice and later as the name of a god of health. (TEH-LEHS-FOR-OS)

Thaddaios Ecclesiastic Greek name of uncertain derivation. Some believe it to be a variant of Theodōros (God's gift). Others feel it is from an Aramaic word meaning "praised." (THAD-DAH-EE-OS)

Theodoros Compound name composed of the elements *theos* (God) and *dōron* (gift): hence, "God's gift." Var: Fedor, Feodor. Short: Theo. (THEH-O-DOR-OS)

Theodosios Compound name composed of the elements *theos* (God) and *dosis* (a gift, a giving): hence, "a gift of God, God-given." Short: Theo. (THEH-O-DŌ-SEE-OS)

Theophilos Compound name composed of the elements *theos* (God) and *philos* (loving): hence, "beloved of God." (THEH-O-FEE-LOS)

Thomas Ecclesiastic Greek name derived from the Aramaic *tĕ'ōma* (a twin). (THO-MAHS)

Timotheos Compound name composed of the elements *timē* (honor, respect) and *theos* (God): hence, "honor God, respect God." (TEE-MO-THEH-OS)

Titos Ancient name of uncertain derivation. Some believe it to be from the Greek *tīo* (to honor). (TEE-TOS)

Tychōn A name meaning "hitting the mark." It was borne by a 5th-century bishop of Amathus in Cyprus who is known for his work in suppressing the cult of Aphrodite. (TEE-HONE, TEE-CHON)

Ulysses Latin cognate of the Greek Odysseus (hater), which is from the root *dys* (hate). Odysseus was the name of the hero of the Odyssey. He was the king of Ithaca and a Greek leader in the Trojan War. (YOO-LIS-SES)

Vernados Greek cognate of the German Bernard, which is derived from the Old High German Berinhard (strong as a bear), a compound name composed of the elements *bero* (bear) and *hard* (hearty, strong, brave). (VEHR-NAH-DOS)

Verniamin Greek cognate of Benjamin, a name derived from the Hebrew *binyāmīn* (son of the right hand). *See* BENJAMIN (Biblical Names). (VEHR-NEE-AH-MEEN)

Zachaios Greek cognate of Zacchaeus, which is derived from the Ecclesiastic Greek Zacharias (remembrance of the Lord), a name derived from the Hebrew *zĕcharyah* (God remembers). *See* ZACCHAEUS (Biblical Names). Var: Zacheus. (ZAH-KAH-EE-OS)

Zeno Evolution of the earlier Zenoe, which is believed to be derived from Zeus, the name of the supreme deity in Greek mythology. The name was borne by Zeno of Citium (c. 334–261 B.C.), a Greek philosopher and founder of Stoicism. Var: Zenon. (ZEE-NO)

Zenobios Compound name composed of the elements *zēn* (of Zeus) and *bios* (life): hence, "the life of Zeus." (ZEE-NO-BEE-OS)

Zoltan Derived from *zōē (life)*. Var: Zoltar. (ZOL-TAHN)

Greek Female Names

ACACIA A borrowing from the name of the acacia tree. It is derived from the Greek *akakia* (a thorny tree), which is from *akē* (a point, a thorn). Var: Akakia. Pet: Cacia, Cacie, Kakia, Kakie. (AH-KAH-KEE-AH)

ADARA Hebrew name which is the feminine form of Adar (noble, exalted). Var: Adar, Adra. (AH-DAH-RAH)

ADONIA Feminine form of Adōnis, a name suggestive of a very handsome person. *See* ADŌNIS (Male Names). Var: Adona. (AH-DŌ-NEE-AH)

AEGEA Feminine form of Aegeus (a protection, a shield), the name of a Greek mythological king of Athens who killed himself when he thought his son was dead. (EE-YEH-AH, EE-JEE-AH)

AEOLA Feminine form of Aeolus, a name of uncertain derivation, which was borne by the Greek mythological god of the winds. (EE-O-LAH)

AGALIA Derived from the Greek *agalia* (brightness, joy, gaiety). (AH-YAH-LEE-AH)

AGATHĒ Popular name derived from *agathos* (good, kind, honorable). *See* AGATA (Italian Names). Var: Agata, Agatha. Pet: Aggie, Aggy. (AH-YAH-THEH)

AIKATERINĒ Derived from the Greek *katharos* (pure, unsullied). Var: Ecaterina, Ekaterina. (AY-KAH-TEH-REE-NEE, AY-KAH-TEH-RĪ-NEE)

AKANTHA Derived from the Greek *akantha* (thorn), which is from *akē* (a point, a thorn). Var: Acantha. (AH-KAHN-THA)

AKILINA A borrowing from the Russian, Akilina is derived from the Late Latin Aquilina, a diminutive form of *aquila* (eagle): hence, "little eagle." (AH-KEE-LEE-NAH)

ALALA Of uncertain derivation borne in Greek mythology by the goddess of war, the sister of Mars; thus it takes the definition "war-like." (AH-LAH-LAH)

ALDORA Compound name composed of the elements *ala* (a wing) and *dōron* (gift): hence, "a winged gift." (AHL-DOR-AH)

ALETHEA Derived from *alētheia* (truth). Var: Alethia, Alithea. Short: Thea. (AH-LEH-THEH-AH)

ALEXA Derived from the verb *alexein* (to defend, to help). Alexa (defender or helper) is also used as a short form of Alexandra (defender or helper of mankind). *See* ALEXANDRA. The variant Alexia is borne by the eldest daughter (b. 1965) of King Constantine and Queen Anne-Marie. Var: Aleka, Alexia, Alexina, Alexine, Alexis. Short: Alex, Lexa. Pet: Lexi. (AH-LEHKS-AH)

ALEXANDRA Feminine form of Alexandros (defender or helper of mankind), a compounding of the elements *alexein* (to defend, to help) and *andros* (man). Var: Alesandra, Alessandra, Alexandina, Alezandra, Alezondra. Short: Alesa, Alex, Alexa, Dina, Sandra, Zandra, Zondra. Pet: Lexi, Sandy. (AH-LEHKS-AHN-DRAH)

ALICE A borrowing from the English, Alice evolved through a series of variants of the German Adalheidis (nobility). *See* ALICE (English Names). (AH-LEES)

ALICIA Latinate form of Alice (nobility). *See* ALICE. (AH-LEES-EE-AH)

ALIDA A borrowing from the Hungarian, Alida is a cognate of the German Adelaide (nobility), a compound name derived from the elements *adal* (noble) and *heit* (kind, sort). Alternatively, Alida may represent a borrowing of the name of a city in Asia Minor. Var: Aleda, Alita. Short: Lida, Lita. (AH-LEE-DAH)

ALPHA Derived from the first letter of the Greek alphabet, which is from the Hebrew *āleph* (ox, leader). The name denotes superiority or excellence. Var: Alfa. (AHL-FAH)

ALTHAIA From the Greek *althaia* (healer), which is from *althainein* (to heal). Var: Althaea, Altheda, Altheta, Althia. Short: Thea, Theda, Theta. (AHL-THEE-AH)

AMARA Derived from the Greek *amarantos* (unfading, immortal). Alternatively, Amara may be from the Latin *amārus* (bitter, sour). (AH-MAH-RAH)

AMARANTHA Derived from the Greek *amarantos* (unfading, immortal). Var: Amaranda, Amarande, Amaranth, Amaranthe. (AH-MAR-AHN-THA)

AMBROSIA Derived from the Greek *ambrotos* (immortal). The name is borrowed from Greek and Roman mythology, where it represents the food of the gods. (AHM-BRO-SEE-AH)

AMBROSINA Diminutive form of Ambrosia (immortal). *See* AMBROSIA. Var: Ambrosine. Short: Brosina. (AHM-BRO-SEE-NAH)

ANASTASIA Feminine form of Anastasios (of the resurrection), which is derived from *anastasis* (resurrection). Var: Anastasie. Short: Ana, Anasta, Stacie, Stasia. (AH-NAH-STAH-SEE-AH)

ANATOLIA Feminine form of Anatolios, a name derived from *anatolē* (sunrise, dawn). Var: Anatola. Short: Ana. (AH-NAH-TŌ-LEE-AH)

ANDREA Feminine form of Andreas (manly), the Greek form of Andrew. The name is derived from *andreios* (manly), which is from *andros* (man); thus Andrea takes the definition "womanly, feminine." Var: Andrianna. Short: Anna. (AHN-DREE-AH)

ANDROMEDĒ Compound name composed of the elements *andros* (man) and *medesthai* (to ponder, to meditate upon): hence, "ponderer, meditator." The name is borne in Greek mythology by the wife of Perseus. She was an Ethiopian princess whom he rescued from a sea monster and later married. Andromeda is the name of a constellation that contains the brightest of the spiral nebulas. Var: Andromeda. Short: Meda. (AHN-DRO-MEH-DEE)

ANEMŌNĒ Directly derived from *anemōnē* (windflower), which is derived from *anemos* (wind). (AH-NEH-MO-NEE)

ANGELE Derived from *angelos* (messenger). In New Testament Greek, the word evolved to mean "messenger of God, an angel." Var: Angela. Pet: Angie, Angy. (AHN-YEH-LEH)

ANGELIKI Derived from the Latin *angelicus* (angelic), which has its root in the Greek *angelos* (messenger, a messenger of God). Pet: Angie, Angy. (AHN-YAH-LEE-KEE)

ANGIE Pet form of any of the various names containing *angel* as an element. Var: Angy. (AHN-YEE)

ANNA Derived from the Hebrew Hannah, which is from *hannāh, chaanach* (gracious, full of grace, mercy). Anna is also used as a short form of any of the various names containing it as an element. (AH-NAH)

ANTHEIA Derived from *antheios* (flowery). The name was used for Hera, the queen of the gods and the goddess of women and marriage. Var: Anthea, Anthia. Short: Antha, Thea. (AHN-THEE-AH)

ANTONIA Feminine form of Anthony, a name derived from Antonius, an old Roman family name of uncertain origin and meaning. Some believe it to have originally been an Etruscan name. "Priceless" and "inestimable worth" are popular folk definitions of the name. (AHN-TŌ-NEE-AH)

APHRODITĒ Classical name derived from *aphros* (foam). It was borne in Greek mythology by the goddess of love and beauty. (AH-FRO-DEE-TEE)

APOLLINE Feminine form of Apollonios (of Apollo), which is derived from Apollōn, the name of the Greek mythological god of music, poetry, medicine, and prophecy. Var: Apollina. (AH-POL-LEE-NEH)

ARETE Derived from Arēs, the name of the Greek mythological god of war, the son of Zeus and Hera. Var: Areta, Aretha. (AH-REH-TEH)

ARIADNE Derived from the elements *ari* (very, much) and *adnos* (holy). Ariadne (very holy one, devout) is a name borne in Greek mythology by King Minos' daughter, who gave a thread to Theseus, which enabled him to escape from the labyrinth. Var: Ariadna, Ariana, Ariane, Arianne. Short: Aria. (AH-REE-AHD-NEH)

ARTEMIS Of unknown etymology borne in Greek mythology by the goddess of the moon and hunting. Var: Artemia. (AHR-TEH-MEES)

ARTEMISIA A borrowing of the name of the plant artemisia. The name is derived from Artemis, the name of the mythological goddess of the moon and hunting. (AHR-TEH-MEE-SEE-AH)

ASPASIA Derived from *aspasia* (welcome). The name was borne by a clever, influential 5th-century B.C. woman of Athens, a mistress of Pericles. Short: Aspa, Aspia. (AH-SPAH-SEE-AH)

ASTER Derived from the Greek *astēr* (a star). Var: Asta, Astra, Astrea. (AH-STEHR)

ATALANTE A name from Greek mythology, Atalante is of uncertain derivation. It might be from Atlas (bearing, tolerating, strength), the name of a mythological Titan who was made to support the heavens on his shoulders. *See* ATALANTE (Mythology and Astrology Names). Var: Atalanta, Atlanta. (AH-TAH-LAHN-TEH)

ATHANASIA Derived from the Greek *athanasia* (immortal), which is composed from the elements *a* (not) and *thanatos* (death). (AH-THA-NAH-SEE-AH)

ATHĒNĒ Ancient name of unknown etymology borne in Greek mythology by the goddess of wisdom, skill, and warfare. Var: Athena. (AH-THEE-NEE)

BAPTISTA A borrowing from the Latin, Baptista is derived from the Ecclesiastic Late Latin *baptista*, which is from the Greek *baptistēs* (a baptizer). The name is usually bestowed in honor of John the Baptist, the man who baptized Jesus Christ. (BAHP-TEES-TAH)

BARBARA A borrowing from the Latin, Barbara (foreign woman) is derived from *barbarus* (foreign, strange), a term applied to non-Romans or those deemed to be uncivilized. Short: Barb. Pet: Barbie, Barby. (BAHR-BAHR-AH)

BASILA Feminine form of Basileios (kingly). See BASILEIOS (Male Names). Var: Basilea, Basilia. (BAH-SEE-LAH)

BERDINE Of Germanic origin, Berdine (bright maiden) is derived from *beraht* (bright, famous). Var: Berdina. (BEHR-DEE-NEH)

BERENIKĒ Evolution of the older Pherenikē (bringer of victory), a compound name composed of the elements *pherein* (to bring) and *nikē* (victory). Var: Berenice, Bernice. Short: Berna. (BEH-REH-NEE-KEE)

CALIDA Latin form of the Greek Kalidas (most beautiful), which is from *kalos* (beautiful). Pet: Calla, Calli. (KAH-LEE-DAH)

CANDACE Derived from the Latin *candidus* (white, pure, sincere). Var: Candice, Candis. Pet: Candie. (KAHN-DAHS)

CASSIA From the Greek *kasia* (a kind of cinnamon). Short: Cass. Pet: Cassie. (KAHS-SEE-AH)

CHARIS Derived from the Greek *charis* (grace, beauty, kindness), which is from the verb *chairein* (to rejoice at). Var: Charissa. (KAH-REES)

CHARISSA Elaborated form of Charis (grace, beauty, kindness). *See* CHARIS. (KAH-REE-SAH)

CHLORIS Derived from *chlōros* (pale green). The name was borne by the mythological goddess of flowers. Var: Chloras, Chlorise, Chlorisse, Cloris. (KLO-REES)

CHRISTA A short form of Christina (a Christian) and any of its variant forms, Christa is also bestowed as an independent given name. (KREES-TAH)

CHRISTI A short form of Christina (a Christian) and any of its variant forms, Christi is also bestowed as an independent given name. Var: Christie. (KREES-TEE)

CHRISTIANE Feminine form of Christiano (a Christian), which is derived from *christianos* (a follower of Christ, a Christian). Short: Christa, Christi, Christie. (KREES-TEE-AH-NEH)

CHRISTINA Popular name derived from *christianos* (a follower of Christ, a Christian). Var: Christine, Kristen, Krista, Kristine. Short: Christa, Christi, Christie. (KREES-TEE-NAH)

CLEMATIA Derived from the Greek *klēma* (a vine, a twig). (KLEH-MAH-TEE-AH)

CLEO A short form of Cleopatra (of a famous father), Cleo is also bestowed as an independent given name. *See* CLEOPATRA. Alternatively, Cleo is a variant form of Clio (fame, glory). *See* CLIO. (KLEH-O)

CLIO Derived from *kleos* (glory, fame). The name is borne in Greek mythology by the Muse of history. Var: Cleo. (KLEE-O)

CLYTIE From the Greek *klytīe* (the splendid one). The name is borne in Roman mythology by a water nymph who was a daughter of Oceanus. She fell in love with the sun-god Apollo and was transformed into the heliotrope. Var: Clyte, Clytia. (KLI-TEE-EH)

COSIMA Feminine form of Cosmo, which is from *kosmos* (universe, world, order). Var: Cosma. (KO-SEE-MAH)

CRESSIDA Of unknown origin and meaning. It was borne in medieval legend by a Trojan princess and daughter of Calchas, the priest who defected to the Romans. Cressida left her Trojan lover, Troilus, for the Greek Diomedes. "Golden" is a popular folk definition of the name. Var: Cresida. Short: Cressa. (KREHS-SEE-DAH)

CYMA Derived from the Greek *kyma* (a wave, something swollen), which is from *kyein* (to be pregnant). The name is representative of something flourishing. Var: Syma. (KYEH-MAH)

CYNARA Of uncertain etymology, some believe it is based on the name of the Aegean island of Zenara. Var: Zinara. (KYEH-NAH-RAH)

CYPRIA Based on the name of the Mediterranean island of Cyprus. It is of uncertain etymology. Var: Cipria, Cipriana, Cypra, Cypris. (KYEH-PREE-AH)

CYRA Feminine form of Cyrus, a cognate of the Greek Kyros, which is believed to be derived from *kyrios* (a lord, a master) or from the Persian *khur* (the sun). (KYEH-RAH)

CYTHEREA A name from Greek mythology, Cytherea was a title assigned to Venus, the goddess of love and beauty. The name is taken from the island of Cythera, her supposed birthplace. Var: Cythera, Cytheria. (KYEH-THEH-REH-AH)

DAMALIS Popular name derived from *damalis* (calf). Var: Damala, Damalas, Damali, Damalla. (DAH-MAH-LEES)

DAMARIS Derived from *damān* (tame, gentle): hence, "gentle girl." Var: Damara, Damarra. Short: Mara, Mari, Maris. (DAH-MAH-REES)

DAMIA Derived from the Greek *damāo* (taming). The name was borne by the goddess of the forces of nature.(DAH-MEE-AH)

Daphne Derived from the Greek *daphnē* (a laurel or bay tree). The name is borne in Greek mythology by a nymph who escaped from Apollo by turning into a laurel tree. Var: Daphna, Daphney. (DAHF-NEH)

Darice Feminine form of Darius, an old Latin name derived from the Greek Dareios, which is of uncertain origin. It is thought to ultimately be derived from Darayavahush, the name of an ancient Persian king. Var: Daria, Darise, Darrice. Short: Dari. (DAH-REE-SEH)

Deianira From Greek mythology, Deianira was the daughter of Alathaea and Oeneus, the second wife of Heracles, whom she accidentally killed by giving him a cloak soaked with Nessus' poisoned blood. Var: Deianeira. (DEE-YAH-NI-RAH)

Delia Feminine form of Delius (of Delos). Delos, a small Aegean island, is the legendary birthplace of Artemis and Apollo. (DEH-LEE-AH)

Delphine Inspired by the name of the delphinium flower, Delphine is derived from the Greek *delphin* (a dolphin). Var: Delfina, Delfine, Delfinia, Delphina, Delphinia. (DEHL-FEE-NEH)

Delta Derived from the Greek *delta* (the fourth letter of the Greek alphabet). The name is typically given to the fourth child. (DEL-TAH)

Demetria Derived from Dēmētēr, the name of the Greek mythological goddess of fertility and agriculture. Var: Demetra, Demitria, Dimitra, Dimitria. (DEH-MEH-TREE-AH)

Denise A borrowing from the French, Denise is a feminine form of Denis, the French cognate of the Greek Dionysios (a follower of the god Dionysos). Var: Denice. (DEH-NEE-SEH)

Diantha Derived from the name of the flower dianthus, which is from the Greek elements *dios* (divine) and *anthos* (a flower): hence, "divine flower." Var: Dianthe, Dianthia. (DEE-AHN-THA, DĪ-AHN-THA)

Didō Borne in Roman mythology by the legendary founder and queen of Carthage. She fell in love with Aeneas and killed herself when he left her. The name is of uncertain etymology. (DEE-DŌ, DĪ-DŌ)

Dionne Feminine form of Dion, a short form of Diōnis (divine) and Dionysios (of Dionysos). Var: Diona, Dione, Dionis. (DEE-ŌN-NEH, DĪ-ŌN-NEH)

Dominica Feminine form of Dominic (belonging to a lord), a name derived from the Latin *dominus* (a lord, a master). (DO-MEE-NEE-KAH)

Dora A short form of any of the various names containing the Greek element *dōron* (gift), Dora is also bestowed as an independent given name. (DŌ-RAH)

Dorinda A borrowing from the English, Dorinda is an 18th-century elaboration of Dora (gift). *See* DORA. (DŌ-REEN-DAH)

Doris A name meaning "Dorian woman." The Dorians, one of the four main tribes of ancient Greece, settled in the mountainous area known as Doris. The name is borne in Greek mythology by a goddess of the sea and therefore has taken on the additional definition "of the sea." Var: Dorea, Doria, Dorice, Dorise, Dorisse, Dorris, Dorrise. (DŌ-REES)

Dorkas Derived from *dorkas* (a gazelle). Var: Dorca, Dorcas, Dorcea, Dorcia. (DOR-KAHS)

Dorothea Compound name composed from the Greek elements *dōron* (gift) and *theos* (God): hence, "gift of God." Var: Dorthea. (DOR-O-THEH-AH)

Drusilla Feminine diminutive form of Drūsus, an old Roman family name of the Livian gens, which is of uncertain derivation. Drūsus is said to have been first used by a man who assumed the name after slaying the Gallic general Drausus, whose name is believed to be derived from a Celtic element meaning "strong." Var: Drucilla. Short: Dru. (DROO-SEEL-LAH)

Ēchō Derived from *ēchō* (an echo). The name is borne in Greek mythology by a nymph whose unrequited love for Narcissus caused her to pine away until only her voice remained. (EE-KO)

Eirēnē Derived from *eirēnē* (peace). The name is borne in Greek mythology by the goddess of peace, a daughter of Zeus and Themis. Var: Irena, Irene, Irina, Irini, Irinia, Iryna, Irynia. (Ī-REE-NEE)

Elaine A borrowing from the English, Elaine is a variant form of Helen, a name derived from the Greek Helenē, the root of which is *ēlē* (light, torch, bright). Var: Elena, Eleni. (EH-LANE-EH)

Eleftheria Feminine form of Eleutherios, which is derived from *eleutheria* (liberty, freedom). (EH-LEHF-THEH-REE-AH)

Ēlektra A name meaning "the shining one," Ēlektra is derived from the Greek *ēlektōr* (shining). The name is borne in Greek mythology by a daughter of Agamemnon and Clytemnestra. She persuaded her brother Orestes to kill their mother and their mother's lover in revenge for the murder of their father. Var: Electra. EE-LEK-TRAH)

ELENA A borrowing from the Italian, Elena is a cognate of the Greek Helenē (light, torch, bright). (EH-LEH-NAH)

ELISABETH Derived from the Hebrew *elīsheba'* (God is my oath). Var: Elisabet. Short: Elisia, Elissa. (EE-LIZ-AH-BETH)

ELLENA Elaboration of the English Ellen, a variant of Helen, which is a cognate of the Greek Helenē (light, torch, bright). Pet: Eleni, Elenitsa, Nitsa. (EL-LEHN-AH)

ELLICE Feminine form of Elias (Jehovah is God). *See* ELIAS (Male Names). Var: Ellise. (EHL-LEES)

ELMA Feminine form of Elmo, a name derived from the Germanic *helm* (helmet, protection). (EHL-MAH)

ELPIDA Feminine form of Elpidios, a name derived from *elpis* (hope). Var: Elpide. (EHL-PEE-DAH)

ERIANTHE Compound name composed from *erān* (to love) and *anthos* (a flower): hence, "lover of flowers." Var: Eriantha, Erianthia. (EH-REE-AHN-THEH)

ESMERALDA Borrowed from the Spanish, Esmeralda is directly derived from *esmeralda* (emerald). Var: Esmerelda. (EZ-MER-AHL-DAH)

EUDORA Compound name composed of the Greek elements *eu* (good, well, fine) and *dōron* (gift): hence, "good gift." The name is borne in Greek mythology by one of the Nereids, the fifty sea-nymph daughters of Nereus. Short: Dora, Euda. (YOO-DOR-AH)

EUDOSIA Compound name composed of the Greek elements *eu* (good, well, fine) and *dōsis* (a giving, a gift): hence, "good gift." Var: Eudocia, Eudokia, Eudoxia. (YOO-DŌ-SEE-AH)

EUGENIA Feminine form of Eugenios, a name derived from *eugenēs* (well-born). Var: Evgenia. (YOO-HEHN-EE-AH)

EULALIA Compound name composed of the elements *eu* (well, good, fair) and *lalein* (to talk): hence, "well-spoken." Var: Eulalie. Short: Eula. (YOO-LAH-LEE-AH)

EUNIKĒ Compound name composed of the elements *eu* (well, good, fair) and *nikē* (victory): hence, "good victory." The name is borne in the Bible by the mother of Timothy. Var: Eunice. (YOO-NEE-KEE)

EUPHEMIA Compound name composed of the elements *eu* (well, good, fair) and *phēmē* (voice): hence, "fair of voice, fair speech." The name was borne by a young virgin martyr of the ancient Greek city of Chalcedon who so courageously withstood her torture that her fame spread both East and West. Var: Euphemie. Pet: Ephie. (YOO-FEH-MEE-AH, YOO-FEE-MEE-AH)

EUPHENIA Derived from the Greek *euphōnia* (sweet-voiced, musical). (YOO-FEH-NEE-AH, YOO-FEE-NEE-AH)

EUSTELLA Compound name composed of the elements *eu* (well, good, fair) and the Latin *stella* (star): hence, "fair star." (YOO-STEHL-LAH)

EVA From the Hebrew Chava, a derivative of *hawwāh* (life). The name is borne in the Bible by the first woman, "the mother of all the living." She is said to have been created from one of Adam's ribs. (EH-VAH)

EVADNE Derived from the element *eu* (good, well, fair): hence, "well-pleasing one." (EH-VAHD-NEH)

EVANGELIA Latinate form of Evangeline (bringer of good news). *See* EVANGELINE. Short: Lia. Pet: Litsa. (EH-VAHN-YEH-LEE-AH)

EVANGELINE A borrowing from the French, Evangeline (bringer of good news) is derived from the Ecclesiastic Late Latin *evangelium* (good news), which is from the Greek *euangelos* (bringing good news). Var: Evangela, Evania. (EH-VAHN-YEH-LEE-NEH)

EVANTHE Compound name composed of the Greek elements *eu* (well, good, fair) and *anthos* (a flower): hence, "fair flower." Var: Evanth. (EH-VAHN-THEH)

FILIA Derived from the Latin *filia* (daughter). The name is also respresentative of filial love and devotion. (FEE-LEE-AH)

GAIA Derived from the Greek *gē* (earth). In Greek mythology, Gaia, mother of the Titans, is the earth personified as a goddess. Var: Gaea, Kaia. (JEE-AH)

GALATEA Borne in Greek mythology by a statue brought to life by Aphrodite after its creator, Pygmalion, fell in love with it. The name is derived from the Greek *gala* (milk, ivory-colored), which might be descriptive of the marble used for the sculpture. (YAH-LAH-TEH-AH)

GEORGIA Feminine form of Georgios, a name derived from *geōrgos* (earthworker, farmer), which is composed of the elements *gē* (earth) and *ergein* (to work). Var: Georgiana, Georgine. (YOR-HEE-AH)

GIANCINTE Derived from the Greek *hyakinthos* (hyacinth, bluebell). Var: Giacinta, Giacinte, Giancinta, Jacinta, Jacinte, Jacinthe. (JEE-AH-SIN-TEH)

GILLIAN A borrowing from the English, Gillian arose in the 16th century as a variant of Julian. Julian is from the old Roman family name Julius, which is thought to be derived from Iulus (the first down on the chin, downy-bearded). Since one first growing facial hair is young, the name has taken the definition "youth, youthful." Gillian was originally bestowed upon both males and females. Now, however, it is an exclusively female name. Var: Giliana, Giliane. Short: Gill. Pet: Gillie. (YEEL-LEE-AHN)

HAGNĒ Derived from the Greek *hagnos* (chaste, pure). *See* AGNESE (Italian Names). Var: Agna, Agne, Agnes. (HAHG-NEE)

HALCYONE Derived from the Greek *alkyōn* (kingfisher), which is from *hals* (sea). Halcyone was the name given to a legendary bird said to have a calming effect on the seas during winter storms. The name has taken on the descriptive definition of *halcyon* (calm, tranquil, happy). Var: Alcyone. (HAHL-SYEH-ŌN-EH)

HARMONIA Derived from the Greek *harmos* (a fitting). In Greek mythology, Harmonia, the daughter of Aphrodite and Ares, was the personification of harmony and order. (HAHR-MO-NEE-AH)

HELENĒ Popular name derived from the root *ēlē* (light, torch, bright). Helenē is the name borne in Greek legend by the beautiful wife of King Menelaus of Sparta. Her abduction by the Trojan prince Paris sparked off the Trojan War. The name became popular throughout the Christian world due to the fame of St. Helena (248–327), the mother of Constantine the Great. Her influence led to the toleration of Christianity and she is credited with finding the True Cross buried in a hillock close to Calvary. Var: Helena. Short: Lena. (HEH-LEH-NEE)

HELIA Feminine form of Helios, a name derived from *hēlios* (the sun). (HEH-LEE-AH, HEE-LEE-AH)

HERA Derived from the Greek *hērōs* (protector, watchman). The name Hera (protectress) is borne in Greek mythology by the sister and wife of Zeus. She was the queen of the gods and the goddess of women and marriage. (HEH-RAH)

HERMIONE Feminine form of Hermes, a name of uncertain derivation borne by the Greek mythological messenger god. Hermione is borne in Greek legend by the daughter of King Menelaus of Sparta and his wife, Helenē of Troy. (HEHR-MEE-O-NEH, HEHR-MĪ-O-NEE)

HESPER Derived from the Greek *hesperos* (the evening star). Var: Hespera, Hesperia. (HEHS-PEHR)

HYACINTH Derived from the Greek *hyakinthos* (hyacinth, bluebell). Var: Hyacinthe. (HĪ-AH-SINTH)

IANTHE A borrowing of the name of the purple or violet-colored flower derived from the Greek elements *ion* (violet) and *anthos* (a flower). Var: Iantha, Ianthina. (YAHN-THEH)

IDALIA Borrowed from the German, Idalia is derived from *īd* (work, labor). (Ī-DAH-LEE-AH)

IO Borne in Greek mythology by a young maiden who was loved by Zeus. She was turned into a heifer, either by Zeus to protect her or by a jealous Hera. She regained human form after she was driven to Egypt by Argus. (I-O)

IOANNA Feminine form of Iōannes, the Greek form of the Hebrew *yōhānān*, a contraction of *yehōhānān* (Yahweh is gracious). The name is a cognate of Jane, the feminine form of John. (YO-AHN-NAH)

IONA A borrowing of the name of a purple gem derived from the Greek *ion* (violet). Var: Ione, Ionia. (I-O-NAH)

IPHIGENEIA A name meaning "of royal birth," which is borne in Greek mythology by a daughter of Agamemnon. He offered her as a sacrifice to Artemis. In some versions, Iphigeneia is saved by the gods. Var: Iphigenia. (EE-FEE-HEN-EE-AH, IH-FEH-HEH-NĪ-AH)

IRIS Derived from the Greek *iris* (a rainbow). The name was borne by the mythological goddess of the rainbow, the messenger of the gods in the *Iliad*. Var: Irisa. (EE-REES)

ISADORA Feminine form of Isidoros (gift of Isis), a compound name composed of the name of the Egyptian goddess of fertility, Isis, and the element *dōron* (gift). Var: Isadore. Short: Dora. Pet: Dory. (EE-SAH-DOR-AH)

ISAURA Derived from Isaurus (belonging to Isauria, an Isaurian). Isauria was the name of an ancient Asian country between Cilicia and Pamphylia. Var: Isaure. Short: Aura. (EE-SAUR-AH)

JOCASTA Evolution of the older Iokastē, a name of uncertain derivation. In Greek mythology, Jocasta was the name of a queen who unwittingly married her own son, Oedipus, and had children by him. She killed herself after discovering the truth. (YO-KAH-STAH)

JUNIA Feminine form of Junius, an old Roman family name derived from Juno, the name of the Roman mythological queen of the gods. (YOO-NEE-AH)

JUSTINA A borrowing from the Latin, Justina is a feminine form of Justin, a derivative of Justinus, which is from *justus* (lawful, rightful, proper, just). (YOO-STEE-NAH)

KALANDRA Compound name composed of the elements *kalos* (beautiful) and *andros* (man): hence, "beautiful one." Var: Calandra. Pet: Calla, Calli, Kalla, Kalli. (KAH-LAHN-DRAH)

KALANTHA Compound name composed of the elements *kalos* (beautiful) and *anthos* (a flower): hence, "beautiful flower." Var: Calantha. Pet: Calla, Calli, Kalla, Kalli. (KAH-LAHN-THA)

KALIDAS Meaning "most beautiful," Kalidas is derived from *kallos* (beauty, beautiful). Short: Kali. (KAH-LEE-DAHS)

KALIGENIA Compound name composed of the elements *kallos* (beauty, beautiful) and *genēs* (born): hence, "born beautiful, beautiful daughter." Var: Kalligenia. Short: Kali. (KAH-LEE-HEN-EE-AH, KAH-LEE-HEN-Ī-AH)

KALLIOPE Compound name composed of the Greek elements *kallos* (beauty, beautiful) and *ops* (voice): hence, "beautiful voice." The name Kalliope is borne in Greek mythology by the Muse of epic poetry and eloquence. Var: Calliope. Short: Callia, Kali, Kalli. (KAHL-LEE-O-PEH, KAHL-LI-O-PEH)

KALLIRRŌĒ Compound name composed of the elements *kallos* (beauty, beautiful) and *rōē* (stream): hence, "beautiful stream." Short: Kali, Kalli. (KAHL-LEE-RO-EE)

KALLISTŌ A name meaning "she that is most beautiful," which is derived from *kallos* (beauty, beautiful). *See* CALLISTO (Italian Names). Var: Calista, Callista. Short: Kali, Kalli. (KAHL-LEES-TŌ)

KALONICE Compound name composed from the Greek elements *kallos* (beauty, beautiful) and *nikē* (victory): hence, "beautiful victory." (KAH-LO-NEE-KEH)

KALYCA Derived from the Greek *kalyx* (pod, bud, outer covering of a flower). The name takes the poetic definition of "rosebud." Var: Kalika. Short: Kali, Kaly. (KAH-LEE-KAH)

KASSANDRA Borne in Greek mythology by the daughter of Priana and Hecuba who had the power of prophecy given to her by Apollo in order to win her love. When she rejected him, Apollo decreed that no one should believe her visions of the future. Var: Casandra, Cassandra, Cassandre. Short: Cass, Kass. Pet: Cassie, Kassie. (KAH-SAHN-DRAH)

KATHERINE Popular variant of Aikaterinē (pure, unsullied). *See* AIKATERINĒ. Var: Kathèrina, Katheryn, Kathryn. Pet: Katy. (KAH-THEH-REE-NEH)

KHLOĒ Popular name derived from the Greek *khloē* (blooming, verdant). The name was used by the Greek poet Longus (3rd century A.D.) for the heroine in his pastoral romance *Daphnis and Khloe*. Var: Chloe, Cloe. (KLO-EE)

KLEOPATRA Compound name composed of the elements *kleos* (glory) and *patēr* (father): hence, "of a famous father." The name was made famous by the queen of Egypt (69?—30 B.C.), the mistress of Julius Caesar and Mark Anthony. Var: Cleopatra. Short: Cleo, Kleo. (KLEE-O-PAH-TRA)

KORĒ Popular name derived from *korē* (maiden). In Greek mythology, Korē is a name for Persephone. Var: Cora, Kora, Koren. Pet: Cori, Kori. (KOR-EE)

KORINNA Diminutive form of Korē (maiden): hence, "little maiden." The name was borne by a Greek poetess from Boeotia who won a wreath of victory at Thebes. Sadly, her works survive only in fragmentary form. Var: Corinna, Corinne, Corrina, Corrine. Pet: Cori, Corrie, Kori. (KO-REEN-NAH)

KYNTHIA Popular name derived from Kynthios (from Kynthos, a mountain on the island of Delos). The name is found in Greek mythology as the byname of Artemis, the goddess of the moon and hunting, and twin sister of Apollo. Var: Cinthia, Cynthia. (KEEN-THEE-AH)

LALAGE Derived from the Greek *lalage* (talkative, prattler, chatterer). Pet: Lalia. (LAH-LAH-YEH)

LANA Of uncertain derivation, Lana might be from the Latin *lana* (wool). (LAH-NAH)

LARISSA A borrowing from the Russian, Larissa is a name of uncertain derivation. Some think it is from the name of an ancient city of Thessaly. Another suggestion is that it has its root in the Latin *hilaris* (cheerful). Var: Larisse. (LAH-REES-SAH)

LEANDRA Feminine form of Leander (lion man). *See* LEIANDROS (Male Names). (LEH-AHN-DRAH)

LEDA A name of uncertain derivation borne in Greek mythology by a Spartan queen and wife of Tyndareus. Leda was the mother of Clytemnestra, Helenē of Troy, and Castor and Pollux. (LEH-DAH, LEE-DAH)

LELIA Contracted variant of Eulalia (well-spoken). *See* EULALIA. (LEH-LEE-AH)

LENA A short form of Helena (light) and any of the other names ending in the element *-lena*, Lena is also bestowed as an independent given name. (LEH-NAH, LEE-NAH)

LIA A short form of Evangelia (bringer of good news), Lia is also bestowed as an independent given name. *See* EVANGELIA. (LEE-AH)

LIDA A short form of Alida (nobility), Lida is also occasionally bestowed as an independent given name. *See* ALIDA. (LEE-DAH)

LIGIA Shortened feminine form of the Latin Eligius, which is derived from *eligere* (to choose, to elect, to select). (LEE-YEE-AH)

Lilika Elaboration of Lily, a name taken from the plant having delicate, trumpet-shaped flowers. It is regarded as a symbol of purity and perfection. The name is derived from the Latin *lilium* (lily). (LEE-LEE-KAH)

Lucia Popular feminine form of Lucius, a name derived from the Latin *lux* (light, torch, bright). The name was borne by St. Lucia of Syracuse, a 4th-century martyr whose popularity during the Middle Ages led to widespread use of the name. "Bringer of light" is a poetic definition of the name. (LOO-SEE-AH)

Lydia A name meaning "woman from Lydia," Lydia is taken from the name of an ancient kingdom in western Asia Minor. Var: Lidia. Pet: Liddie, Lydie. (LEE-DEE-AH)

Lyris Derived from the Greek *lyra* (a lyre). The lyre was a small harp used by the ancient Greeks. (LYEHR-EES)

Lysandra Feminine form of Lysandros, a compound name composed of the elements *lysis* (freeing, loosening) and *andros* (man, mankind): hence, "liberator, freer of mankind." Short: Sandra. Pet: Sandy. (LĪ-SAHN-DRAH)

Madeline A borrowing from the French, Madeline is a cognate of the Greek Magdalēnē (of Magdala, a town near the Sea of Galilee). *See* MADGALĒNĒ. Short: Mada. (MAH-DEH-LEEN-EH)

Magdalēnē Ecclesiastic Greek name meaning "of Magdala." Magdala was the name of a town near the Sea of Galilee. Short: Lena. (MAH-DAH-LEE-NEE)

Maia Of uncertain derivation and meaning. Maia is borne in Greek mythology by the loveliest of the Pleiades, the mother of Hermes by Zeus. The month of May is named in her honor. (MAY-AH, MY-AH)

Margarītēs Popular name derived from *margaron* (a pearl). Pet: Gryta. (MAHR-HAHR-Ī-TEES)

Maria Latinate form of Mary, which is derived from the Hebrew Miryām, a name of debated meaning. While "sea of bitterness" or "sea of sorrow" seems to be the most probable, some sources cite the alternative definitions of "rebellion," "wished-for child," and "mistress or lady of the sea." (MAH-REE-AH)

Marianne Originated as an extended spelling of Marian, a variant of Marion, which is a French diminutive form of Marie. It is now used as a hybrid, combining the names Maria and Anna. *See* ANNA *and* MARIA. Var: Marianna. (MAH-REE-AHN-NEH)

Marina Derived from the Latin *marinus* (of the sea), the root of which is *mare* (the sea). (MAH-REE-NAH)

Martha Derived from the Aramaic *mārthā* (lady, mistress). The name is borne in the Bible by the sister of Lazarus and Mary of Bethany. (MAHR-THA)

Melaina Derived from the root *melas* (black, dark). Var: Melania, Melanie. (MEH-LAH-EE-NAH, MEL-Ī-NAH)

Melantha Compound name composed of the Greek elements *melas* (black, dark) and *anthos* (a flower): hence, "dark flower." Var: Melantho. (MEH-LAHN-THA)

Melina Feminine form of *melinos* (quince-yellow), which is from *mēlon* (quince, apple). (MEH-LEE-NAH)

Melissa Derived from the Greek *melissa* (a honeybee), which is from *meli* (honey). Var: Meleta, Melisse, Melitta, Melleta, Mellisa. (MEH-LIS-SAH)

Melodie Derived from *melōidia* (melody), which is from the elements *melos* (song) and *aeidein* (to sing). Var: Melody. (MEH-LO-DEE)

Mona Derived from the Greek *mono* (single, alone). (MO-NAH)

Monica Ancient name of uncertain etymology. Monica was the name of the mother of St. Augustine, who was born in Numidia, an ancient country in northern Africa. Thus, the name might be of African origin. However, Monica is said to have been a citizen of Carthage, a city founded by the Phoenicians, so her name might be of Phoenician origin. Alternatively, some believe it to be from the Latin *moneo* (to advise). Var: Monika, Moniqua, Monique. (MO-NEE-KAH)

Myrtle Derived from the Greek *myrtos* (myrtle, plants from the genus *Myrtus*). Var: Myrtia, Myrtice, Myrtis, Myrtisa, Myrta. (MER-TL)

Nani Variant form of Anna (grace, gracious, mercy). *See* ANNA. (NAH-NEE)

Neoma Compound name composed from the Greek elements *neos* (new) and *mēnē* (moon): hence, "new moon." Var: Neomah. (NEH-O-MAH)

Nerissa A borrowing from the English, Nerissa is a name coined by Shakespeare for Portia's lady-in-waiting in the play *The Merchant of Venice*. It is believed to be influenced by the Latin Nereis (sea snail). Var: Nerice, Nerita. (NEH-REES-SAH)

Nikē Derived from *nikē* (victory). The name is borne in Greek mythology by the winged goddess of victory. (NEE-KEE, NI-KEE)

Nikola Feminine form of Nikolaos (victory of the people), a compound name composed of the elements *nikē* (victory) and *laos* (the people). Var: Nikole, Nikolia. Pet: Nikoleta, Nikki, Niki. (NEE-KO-LAH)

NIKOLETA Originally a pet form of Nikola (victory of the people), Nikoleta is now commonly bestowed as an independent given name. *See* NIKOLA. (NEE-KO-LEH-TAH)

NIOBĒ A name from Greek mythology, Niobē was a queen of Thebes and daughter of Tatalus. Her continual weeping for her slain children turned her into a stone from which tears continued to flow. The name is of uncertain derivation. (NEE-O-BEE, NĪ-O-BEE)

NYSA A common Greek name meaning "goal." Var: Nyssa, Nysse. (NYEH-SAH)

OBELIA Derived from the Greek *obeliskos* (a pointed pillar). Var: Obelie. (O-BEE-LEE-YAH)

ODELE Derived from the Greek *ōidē* (song), which is from *aeidein* (to sing). Var: Odella. (O-DEH-LEH)

OLYMPIA Feminine form of Olympios (of Olympus). Olympus, a mountain in northern Greece, was the home of the gods in Greek mythology. Var: Olympe. Short: Lympia, Pia. (O-LYEEM-PEE-AH)

OPHELIA Derived from the Greek *ōphelia* (a help, a helper). Shakespeare used the name in *Hamlet* for the daughter of Polonius who was in love with Hamlet. Var: Ophelie. Short: Phelia. (O-FEH-LEE-AH)

ORTHIA Derived from *orthos* (straight). The name is found in Greek mythology as a name for the goddess Artemis. (OR-THEE-AH)

OURANIA Classical name meaning "the heavenly one." It is borne in Greek mythology by the Muse of astronomy. Var: Urania. (OOR-AH-NEE-AH)

PALLAS A name borne in Greek mythology as a name for Athēnē, the goddess of wisdom. The name has therefore taken the definition of "wisdom." (PAHL-LAHS)

PANDORA Compound name composed from the Greek elements *pan* (all, every) and *dōron* (a gift): hence, "all-gifted." The name is borne in Greek mythology by the first mortal woman. Out of curiosity, she opened a box letting out all human ills. In some versions of the story, she let out all human blessings, leaving only hope. (PAHN-DOR-AH)

PANGIOTA Compound name composed from the elements *pan* (all, every) and *hieros* (holy): hence, "all-holy." Var: Panagiota. (PAHN-HEE-O-TAH)

PANTHEA Compound name composed of the Greek elements *pan* (all, every) and *theos* (God): hence, "of all the gods." Short: Thea. (PAHN-THEE-AH)

PARTHENIE Derived from the Greek *parthenos* (a virgin, a maiden). Var: Parthena, Parthenia. (PAHR-THEH-NEE)

PASHA Derived from the Ecclesiastic Greek *pascha* (Passover). The name is typically given to one born during the Easter season. Var: Pesha. (PAH-SHAH)

PAULA Feminine form of Paul, which is from Paulus, an old Roman family name derived from the Latin *paulus* (small). *See* PAUL (Male Names). (PAH-OO-LAH)

PELAGIA Derived from the Greek *pelagos* (the sea). (PEH-LAH-HEE-AH)

PĒNELOPĒ Popular name of uncertain origin borne in Greek mythology by Odysseus' wife, who for twenty years patiently awaited his return. Some believe the name is derived from the Greek *penelops* (a kind of duck), since Penelope was said to have been exposed to die as an infant and was fed and protected by a duck. Others think it might be derived from *pēnē* (thread on a bobbin) and give it the definition "weaver, worker of the loom," for Penelope spent her time weaving and unweaving while she waited for her husband to return. (PEE-NEH-LO-PEE)

PENTHEA Derived from the Greek *pente* (five). The name is typically given to child born fifth. Var: Penthia. (PEN-THEE-AH)

PERSEPHONE Borne in Greek mythology by the goddess of spring, the daughter of Zeus and Demeter. She was abducted by Hades to be his wife in the underworld. Var: Persephonie. (PEHR-SEH-FO-NEH)

PETRA Feminine form of Petros, a name derived from *petros* (a stone). Var: Perrine, Petrina, Petrine, Petronella, Petronelle. (PEH-TRA)

PETRINA Feminine form of Petros, the Greek cognate of Peter (a rock, a stone). *See* PETROS (Male Names). (PEH-TREE-NAH)

PHAIDRA From Greek mythology, Phaidra was the daughter of Minor and the wife of Theseus. The name is of uncertain derivation. Var: Phaedra. (FAY-DRAH)

PHILANA Compound name composed of the elements *philos* (loving) and *andros* (man): hence, "lover of mankind." Var: Philene, Philina, Phillina. (FEE-LAH-NAH)

PHILANTHA Compound name composed of the elements *philos* (loving) and *anthos* (flower): hence, "lover of flowers." (FEE-LAHN-THAH)

PHILIPPA Feminine form of Philippos (lover of horses), a compound name composed of the elements *philos* (loving) and *hippos* (a horse). Var: Filipina, Philippe, Phillipa, Phillippe. Pet: Pippa. (FEE-LEEP-PAH)

Philomela Compound name composed of the Greek elements *philos* (loving) and *melos* (song): hence, "lover of songs." The name is borne in Greek mythology by an Athenian princess who was raped by her brother-in-law Tereus. Philomela was transformed by the gods into a nightingale; her sister Procne into a swallow; and Tereus into a hawk. (FEE-LO-MEH-LAH)

Philomena Derived from Philomenēs (lover of strength), a compound name composed of the elements *philos* (loving) and *menos* (strength). Var: Filomena, Filomenia. (FEE-LO-MEH-NAH)

Philothea Compound name composed of the Greek elements *philos* (loving) and *theos* (God): hence, "lover of God." (FEE-LO-THEH-AH)

Phoebe Feminine form of Phoibos (bright one), which is derived from *phoibos* (bright). The name Phoebe is found in Greek mythology as a name of Artemis, the goddess of the moon. In poetry, Phoebe is the moon personified. Var: Phebe. (FEE-BEE)

Phoenix Derived from the Greek *phoinix* (dark red, blood-red). The phoenix was a mythical bird that lived for hundreds of years before consuming itself in fire and rising anew from the ashes to begin another long life. The bird is a symbol of immortality. (FEE-NEEKS)

Phyllis Popular name derived from the Greek *phyllon* (a leaf). The name is borne in Greek mythology by a girl who hanged herself for love, and was then transformed into an almond tree. Var: Philis, Phillis, Phillisse, Phylis, Phylisse. (FEEL-LEES)

Pia Short form of Olympia (of Olympus), Pia is also popularly bestowed as an independent given name. *See* OLYMPIA. (PEE-AH)

Rena A short form of Irena (peace), Rena is also bestowed as an independent given name. *See* EIRĒNĒ. Var: Rina. (REH-NAH)

Rhea Derived from the Greek *rhoia* (flowing). Var: Rea. (REH-AH)

Rhode Derived from the Greek *rhodon* (a rose). Var: Rhoda, Rhodia. (RO-DEH)

Ritsa A borrowing from the Russian, Ritsa is a pet form of Aleksandra (defender or helper of mankind). *See* ALEXANDRA. (REET-SAH)

Roxanē Greek name believed to be derived from the Persian Roschana (dawn of day). The name was borne by the Bactrian wife of Alexander the Great, which seems to substantiate the name's roots. (ROKS-AH-NEE)

Salōmē Ecclesiastic Greek name derived from the Hebrew *shālōm* (peace). Salome was the traditional name of the daughter of Herodias whose dancing so pleased Herod that he granted her request for the head of John the Baptist. (SAH-LO-MEE)

Sapphira Derived from the Ecclesiastic Greek Sappheirē (beautiful). Var: Sapphire. (SAH-FEE-RAH)

Selene Derived from the Greek *selēnē* (the moon). The name is borne in Greek mythology by the goddess of the moon. Var: Celena, Selena, Selia, Selina. (SEH-LEH-NEH, SEH-LEE-NEE)

Semelē Borne in Greek mythology by the mother of Dionysus. When she saw Zeus in all his glory, she was consumed in a fury of lightning. Var: Semele, Semelle. (SEH-MEH-LEE)

Sibyl Derived from the Greek *sibylla* (a prophetess, a fortune-teller). The sibyls, women of ancient Greece and Rome, were mouthpieces of the ancient oracles and seers into the future. In the Middle Ages they were believed to be receptors of divine revelation; thus Sibyl came into use as a given name. Var: Sibella, Sibley, Sibyll, Sibylla, Sybil, Sybilla, Sybyl. (SEE-BEEL)

Sofronia Derived from the Greek *sophia* (wisdom, skill), the root of which is *sophos* (wise). Var: Sophronia. (SO-FRO-NEE-AH)

Sophia Derived from the Greek *sophia* (wisdom, skill), which is from *sophos* (wise). Var: Sofia, Sophie. Pet: Sofi. (SO-FEE-AH)

Stacie A short form of Anastasia (of the resurrection), Stacie is also bestowed as an independent given name. *See* ANASTASIA. Var: Stacey, Stacy, Stasia, Steise. (STAY-SEE)

Stephana Feminine form of Stephanos, a name derived from the Greek *stephanos* (a crown, a garland). Var: Stefana, Stefania, Stefina, Stefinia, Stephania, Stephanie. (STEH-FAH-NAH)

Tabitha Derived from the Ecclesiastic Greek Tabeitha, a name derived from the Aramaic *tabhītha* (a roe deer, a gazelle). (TAH-BEE-THA)

Tatiana A borrowing from the Russian, Tatiana is the feminine form of the Latin Tatiānus, a derivative of the old Roman family name Tatius, which is of uncertain origin. The name Tatius was borne by a king of the Sabines who ruled jointly with Romulus. (TAH-TEE-AH-NAH)

TESSA Derived from the Greek *tessares* (four). The name was traditionally bestowed upon the fourth daughter. (TES-SAH)

THADDEA Feminine form of Thaddeus, a derivative of the Greek Thaddaios, which is of uncertain derivation. *See* THADDAIOS (Male Names). (THAD-DEH-AH)

THAIS Of uncertain derivation. Thais was borne by a 4th-century B.C. Athenian courtesan who accompanied Alexander the Great on his Asiatic campaign. (THA-EES)

THALASSA Derived from the Greek *thalassa* (sea). (THA-LAHS-SAH)

THALEIA Derived from the Greek *thallein* (to flourish, to bloom). The name is borne in Greek mythology by the Muse of comedy and pastoral poetry. Var: Talia, Thalia. (THA-LEH-EE-AH)

THEA A short form of Alethea (truth) or Anthea (flowery), Thea is also commonly bestowed as an independent given name. *See* ALETHEA *and* ANTHEIA. Alternatively, Thea may be viewed as a feminine form of Theo, which is derived from the Greek *theos* (God): hence, "goddess." Var: Theolan, Thia, (THEE-AH)

THEKLA Feminine form of Theokles (divine fame), which is from the elements *theos* (God) and *kleos* (glory, fame). The name was borne by the first virgin martyr, a disciple of St. Paul at Inconium. She was exposed to the lions at Antioch, but they supposedly crouched at her feet instead of attacking her. Var: Tecla, Tekla, Thecla. (THEK-LAH)

THEODORA Feminine form of Theodore (God's gift), a compounding of the elements *theos* (God) and *dōron* (gift). The name is borne by the youngest daughter of the deposed King Constantine II and Queen Anne-Marie. Var: Fedora, Feodora, Teodora. Short: Dora, Tedra. (THEH-O-DOR-AH)

THEODOSIA Feminine form of Theodosios (a gift of God, God-given), a compound name composed from the elements *theos* (God) and *dosis* (a giving, a gift). (THEH-O-DOS-EE-AH)

THEONE Derived from the Greek *theos* (God): hence, "godly." Var: Theona, Theonie. (THEH-O-NEH)

THEOPHANIA Derived from *theophaneia* (divine manifestation, a manifestation of God). The word is composed of the elements *theos* (God) and *phainein* (to appear). Var: Theophaneia. (THEH-O-FAH-NEE-AH)

THEOPHILIA Compound name composed of the elements *theos* (God) and *philein* (to love): hence, "loved by God." (THEH-O-FEE-LEE-AH)

THERESA Of uncertain etymology, Theresa is generally believed to be derived from the Greek *therizein* (to reap, to gather in). The first known bearer of the name was the Spanish wife of St. Paulinus, a 5th-century Roman bishop of Nola. Theresa was not used outside the Iberian Peninsula until the 16th century, when the fame of St. Teresa of Avila (1515–82) made the name popular among Roman Catholics throughout Europe. Var: Teresa, Terese, Therese, Tresa. Pet: Resi, Rezi, Terry, Tess, Tessie, Tracey. (TEH-REH-ZAH)

THETIS Of uncertain derivation, Thetis is a name borne in Greek mythology by one of the Nereids who was the mother of Achilles. (THEH-TEES)

TIFFANY A borrowing from the English, Tiffany represents the transferred use of the surname derived from the Old French Tifaine (Epiphany), which is from the Late Latin Theophania (Epiphany, manifestation of God). Var: Tefany, Tiffeny, Tiphanie.(TEEF-FAH-NEE)

TIMOTHEA Feminine form of Timotheos (honor God, respect God), a compounding of the elements *timē* (honor, respect) and *theos* (God). (TEE-MO-THEH-AH)

URANIA Derived from the Greek Ourania (heavenly one). In Greek mythology, Urania was the Muse of Astronomy. (YOO-RAY-NEE-AH)

URSA Derived from the Latin *ursa* (she-bear). Var: Ursel, Ursula. (OOR-SAH)

VANESSA A borrowing from the English, Vanessa is an invention of satirist Jonathan Swift (1667–1745). It is a partial anagram of the name of his intimate friend Esther Vanhomrigh. Swift used the name in his *Cadenus and Vanessa,* which led to its use as a female given name. Short: Nessa. (VAH-NEHS-SAH)

VARVARA A borrowing from the Russian, Varvara is a cognate of Barbara (foreign woman). *See* BARBARA. Var: Vavara, Vavra. Short: Vara. (VAHR-VAHR-AH)

VERONIKA Of uncertain origin and meaning. Some believe it to be derived from the Late Latin *veraiconica*, the word given to a piece of cloth or garment with a representation of Christ on it. *Veraiconica* is composed from the elements *verus* (true) and *iconicus* (of or belonging to an image). Alternatively, Veronika is thought to be a variant form of Berenike, which is a variant of the older name Pherenike, a compounding of the elements *pherein* (to bring) and *nikē* (victory). Var: Varonica. (VAH-RO-NEE-KAH)

XANTHE Derived from the Greek *xanthos* (yellow, golden). Var: Xantha, Xanthia. (KSAHN-THEH)

Xenia Derived from the Greek *xenia* (hospitality), which is from *xenos* (a guest, a stranger). Var: Zena, Zene, Zenia, Zenobia. (KSEH-NEE-AH)

Xylia Derived from the Greek *xylon* (wood), Xylia has the definition "of the forest." Var: Xyla, Xylina, Xylona. (KSEE-LEE-AH)

Zenaida A name meaning "pertaining to Zeus," which is from *zēn* (of Zeus). Var: Zenaide.

Zenobia Feminine form of Zēnobios (the life of Zeus), a compounding of the elements *zēn* (of Zeus) and *bios* (life). The name was borne by a 3rd-century queen of Palmyra noted for her beauty and intelligence as well as her ruthlessness with her foes. (ZEH-NO-BEE-AH)

Zephyra Feminine form of Zephyrus, a derivative of *zephros* (the west wind). The name Zephyrus is borne in Greek mythology by the god of the west wind. Var: Zefiryn, Zephira, Zephire, Zyphire.

Zōē Popular name derived directly from *zōē* (life). Var: Zoe, Zoelie, Zoelle, Zoia, Zoya. (ZO-EE)

CHAPTER ELEVEN

Hawaiian Names

THE HAWAIIAN isles were colonized between A.D. 300 and 600 by Polynesians sailing from other Pacific islands. Native traditions, culture, and the Hawaiian language remained pure and vital until the 1778 arrival of British Captain James Cook precipitated the coming of English-speaking missionaries.

As Hawaiian was only an oral language, the missionaries set out to make it a written one as well. Their immediate goal was to establish schools and translate the Bible and other religious material. Missionary influence also markedly affected island culture. Traditional feasts and rituals were discouraged as pagan, and converting the Hawaiian people to Christianity was carried out with zeal.

In 1860 King Kamehameha IV signed into law the Act to Regulate Names, which mandated that all citizens of the Kingdom of Hawaii follow the standard European system of naming.

Until this time, traditional naming practices were of great cultural importance. One's name was a force unto itself and was considered to be one's greatest possession. Once a name was spoken aloud, it assumed its own existence and had the power to help or harm its bearer.

Therefore, the choice of a name was a serious matter, and not only involved the parents but the extended family as well. There were several ways a name was chosen. First, a "night" or "dream" name could be put forth by the family's ancestor god through the dreams of family members. Second, the name could be heard spoken by the ancestor god in a supernatural voice. Third, the name could be given in a sign directed from the ancestor god. Any name chosen by the ancestor god had to be used. Failing to do so would result in illness and even death to the newborn.

Other types of names were given as well. There were secret names that were very sacred and never spoken aloud, everyday names that were often shortened forms of much longer names, names that were commemorative of special events, places, or personal achievements, and ancestral names through which one's lineage was traced. As in many other traditional societies, names were also given to children to trick evil spirits into staying away. These were called "reviling" names. They were invariably ugly or disgusting so as to make the evil spirits think the child was as repulsive as its name and consequently leave it alone.

Traditionally, there was no system of marriage and there were no surnames. After the Act to Regulate Names was passed, all citizens were made to assume a Christian first name, the resulting selection often a Bible name. Because many of the sounds of the English language are not pronounced in Hawaiian, the names were "Hawaiianized." Vowels were placed between consonants and added to the ends of the names, and the letters of the English alphabet not found in Hawaiian were replaced by Hawaiian ones, as in the table below. Daniel was changed to Kaniela, Jason to Iakona, Clarice became Kalalika, and so on.

English	*Hawaiian*
B, F, P	P
C, D, G, J, K, Q, S, T, X, Z	K
H	H
N	N
L, R	L
V, W	W
Y	I

Such names are not considered truly Hawaiian by those who study and work to preserve native culture. They are included here because the fact remains that they are now in common use in Hawaii.

After a Christian name was chosen, a person's native name was usually used as a surname, often in shortened form. Marriages were also performed and the woman was required to assume her husband's new surname, as were all children born to the couple. Many satisfied the legal requirement of giving their child a Christian first name, but also added a traditional Hawaiian name as a middle name.

In 1967 the Act to Regulate Names was changed, and the requirement that the first name be Christian was dropped. Hawaiians were once again free to bestow names in the traditional manner, yet the trend to do so is not proceeding as fast as many had hoped. Hawaiian names are still generally reserved for middle-name status.

Many names are unique, and parents may choose a name by consulting a Hawaiian dictionary and using care to keep the diacritical marks in place. Failure to do so can change the meaning of a wonderful name into a very undesirable one. Hawaiian words and names are generally stressed on the next to the last syllable. All vowels marked with macrons are also stressed and are somewhat longer in sound than other vowels. A glottal stop is marked by the symbol ‘, and is similar to the break between the English oh-oh.

Hawaiian names are beautiful and melodic. They can have several different meanings, and interestingly, they are also unisex. Some of the names in this chapter have been categorized as male and female with a thought to traditional Western ideas of masculine and feminine qualities.

Hawaiian Male Names

Ā‘ĀLONA Hawaiian form of Aaron, a name derived from the Hebrew *aharōn* (the exalted one). The name is borne in the Bible by the elder brother of Moses. Var: Aarona. (AH-AH-LO-NAH)

AHIMELEKA Hawaiian form of Ahimelech, a name borne in the Bible by a priest who gave David the shewbread and Goliath's sword. (AH-HEE-MEH-LEH-KAH)

AKAMU Cognate of Adam, which is from the Hebrew *adama* (red earth). The name is borne in the Bible by the first man created by God. According to biblical tradition, it was from Adam's rib that the first woman, Eve, was formed. Var: Adamu. (AH-KAH-MOO)

AKELA Hawaiian form of Asher (blessed, fortunate, happy), a name borne in the Bible by the eighth son of Jacob. Asher was the progenitor of the tribe of Israel. Var: Asera. (AH-KEH-LAH)

AKELIELA Hawaiian form of Adriel, a Hebrew name of debated meaning. Some believe it means "God's flock." Another source cites "God is my majesty." Var: Aderiela. (AH-KEH-LEE-EH-LAH)

AKILIANO Hawaiian form of Adrian, which is from the Latin Adriānus (man from the city of Adria) and Hadriānus (man from the city of Hadria). Var: Adiriano. (AH-KEE-LEE-AH-NO)

AKONI‘IA Hawaiian form of Adonijah (the Lord is my God).The name is borne in the Bible by the fourth son of King David. Var: Adoniia. (AH-DŌN-EE-EE-AH)

ALAKA‘I Hawaiian name meaning "guide, leader, conductor." (AH-LAH-KAH-EE)

ALEKA Cognate of Alex, which is a short form of Alexander (defender or helper of mankind). *See* ALEKANEKELO. Var: Alika. (AH-LEH-KAH)

ALEKANEKELO Hawaiian form of Alexander (defender or helper of mankind), a cognate of the Greek Alexandros, which is composed of the elements *alexein* (to defend, to help) and *andros* (man). Var: Alekanedero. Short: Aleka, Alika. (AH-LEH-KAH-NEH-KEH-LO)

ALEKONA Hawaiianized form of Alton, a name derived from the Old English Aldtun (old town), a compounding of the elements *ald* (old) and *tūn* (town, settlement, village). Var: Aletona. (AH-LEH-KO-NAH)

ALEMANA Hawaiian form of the French Armand, a cognate of the German Hermann (soldier, warrior), which is from the Old High German Hariman, a compounding of the elements *heri* (army) and *man* (man). Var: Aremana, Amana. (AH-LEH-MAH-NAH)

ALEPANA Hawaiian form of Alban, a name derived from the Latin Albanus (from the Italian city of Alba). Var: Alebana. (AH-LEH-PAH-NAH)

ALEPELEKE Hawaiian cognate of Alfred (elf counsel), a name derived from the Old English Ælfred, a compounding of the elements *ælf* (elf) and *ræd* (counsel). Elves were considered to be supernatural beings having special powers of seeing into the future; thus the name took on the meaning "wise counselor." Var: Alapai, Aleferede. (AH-LEH-PEH-LEH-KEH)

ALEWINA Hawaiianized form of Alvin (friend of the elves), which is from the Old English Ælfwine, a compounding of the elements *ælf* (elf) and *wine* (friend). Var: Alevina. (AH-LEH-VEE-NAH)

ALI'IMALU Compound name composed from the Hawaiian elements *ali'i* (chief, king, noble, royal) and *malu* (peaceful, stillness, protection): hence, "peaceful ruler." (AL-EE-EE-MAH-LOO)

ALOHALANI Compound name meaning "merciful, compassionate," which is composed of the elements *aloha* (love, mercy, compassion) and *lani* (sky, heaven, heavenly, spiritual). (AH-LO-HAH-LAH-NEE)

'ALOHILANI Compound name composed of the elements *'alohi* (bright, brightness) and *lani* (noble, highborn, aristocratic): hence, "nobly bright." (AH-LO-HEE-LAH-NEE)

ALOIKI Hawaiian form of Aloysius, a Latinized form of Aloys, a Provençal cognate of Louis (famous in war). Louis is from the Old High German Hluodowig, a compounding of the elements *hluod* (famous) and *wīg* (war, strife). Var: Aloisi. (AH-LO-EE-KEE)

AMOKA Hawaiian form of the Hebrew Amos (to be burdened or troubled). The name is borne in the Bible by a minor prophet whose prophecies are recorded in the Book of Amos. Var: Amosa. (AH-MO-KAH)

ANAKALĒ Hawaiian form of André, a French cognate of Andrew. *See* ANEKELEA. Var: Anadarē. (AN-AH-KAH-LAY)

ANAKONI Hawaiian form of Anthony, a derivative of the Latin Antonius, an old Roman family name of unknown etymology. "Priceless" and "of inestimable worth" are popular folk definitions of the name. Var: Anatoni. Short: Akoni, Atoni. (AN-AH-KO-NEE)

ANEKELEA Hawaiian form of Andrew, a cognate of the Greek Andreas, which is from *andreios* (manly). The name is borne in the Bible by the first of the Twelve Apostles of Christ. Var: Anederea. (AH-NEH-KEH-LEH-AH)

ĀNUENUE AKUA Compound name composed of the elements *ānuenue* (rainbow) and *akua* (God, spirit): hence, "God's rainbow." (AH-NOO-EH-NOO-EH-AH-KOO-AH)

APEKALOMA Hawaiian form of Absalom, a name derived from the Hebrew *'abshālōm* (the father is peace). The name is borne in the Bible by the favorite son of David, killed after rebelling against his father. Var: Abesaloma. (AH-PEH-KAH-LO-MAH)

APELA Hawaiian form of Abel, a name derived from the Hebrew *hebel* (breath). The name is borne in the Bible by the second son of Adam and Eve. Abel was the first murder victim, killed by his elder brother, Cain, in a fit of jealous rage. Var: Abela. (AH-PEH-LAH)

APELAHAMA Hawaiianized form of Abraham, a derivative of the Hebrew Avraham (father of many, father of a multitude). The name is borne in the Bible by the first patriarch and ancestor of both the Hebrews and the Arabs. Var: Aberahama. (AH-PEH-LAH-HAH-MAH)

APELAMA Hawaiian form of Abram, a contracted form of Abraham (father of a multitude, father of many). Abram was the name Abraham bore for ninety-nine years until it was changed to Abraham, and his wife's from Sarai to Sarah. Var: Aberama, Abiram, Apilama. (AH-PEH-LAH-MAH)

APIA Hawaiian form of Abiah, an Anglicized form of the Hebrew Abijah (whose father God is). The name is borne in the Old Testament by several characters. Var: Abia. (AH-PEE-AH)

APIKAI Hawaiian form of Abishai, which is from the Aramaic Avishai (my father is my gift, God is my gift). Var: Abisai. (AH-PEE-KAH-EE)

APOLO Hawaiian form of Apollo, which is derived from the Greek Apollōn, an ancient name of unknown etymology borne in Greek mythology by the god of music, poetry, prophecy, and medicine. The name is indicative of physical perfection. (AH-PO-LO)

Aukake Hawaiian form of August, which is derived from the Latin *august* (great, august, venerable). Var: Augate. (AH-OO-KAH-KEH)

Aukukeko Hawaiian form of Augustus, a derivative of the Latin *august* (great, august, venerable). Var: Auguseto. (AH-OO-KOO-KAY-KO)

Aukukino Hawaiian form of Augustine, a diminutive form of Augustus, which is derived from the Latin *august* (great, august, venerable). Var: Augutino. (AH-OO-KOO-KEE-NO)

Aulelio Hawaiian form of Aurelius, an old Roman family name derived from the Latin *aurum* (gold). The name was borne by Marcus Aurelius Antonius (121–80), Roman emperor and Stoic philosopher. Var: Aurelio. (AH-OO-LEH-LEE-O)

Ekana Hawaiianized form of Ethan, an Ecclesiastic Late Latin name derived from the Hebrew *ēthān* (strength, firmness, long-lived). The name is borne in the Bible by a very wise man whom Solomon surpassed in wisdom. Var: Etana. (EH-KAH-NAH)

Ekeka Hawaiian form of Edgar (prosperity spear), a name derived from the Old English Ēadgar, a compounding of the elements *ēad* (prosperity, riches, fortune) and *gar* (a spear). Var: Edega. (EH-KEH-KAH)

Ekekiela Hawaiian form of Ezekiel, which is from the Greek Iezekiēl, a derivative of the Hebrew *yechezq'ēl* (God strengthens). The name is borne in the Bible by a Hebrew prophet of the 6th century B.C. His prophecies are recorded in the Old Testament book of Ezekiel. Var: Ezekiela. (EH-KEH-KEE-EL-AH)

Ekela Hawaiian form of the Hebrew Ezra, which is derived from *ezrā* (help). The name is borne in the Bible by a Hebrew prophet and religious reformer of the 5th century B.C. His story is told in the Old Testament book of Ezra. Var: Ezera. (EH-KEH-LAH)

Ekemona Hawaiian form of Edmond (wealthy protection), a name derived from the Old English Ēadmund, a compounding of the elements *ēad* (prosperity, riches, fortune) and *mund* (hand, protection). Var: Edemona, Edumona, Ekumena. (EH-KEH-MO-NAH)

Ekewaka Hawaiianized form of Edward (wealthy protector), a name derived from the Old English Ēadweard, a compounding of the elements *ēad* (prosperity, riches, fortune) and *weard* (guardian, protector).Var: Edewada, Ekualo. (EH-KEH-WAH-KAH, Ā-KAY-VAH-KAH)

Eleneki Hawaiian form of Ernest, a cognate of the German Ernst, which is derived from the Old High German Ernost and Ernust, names derived from *ernust* (earnest, resolute). Var: Ereneti. Short: Eneki, Eneti. (EH-LEH-NEH-KEE)

Elia Hawaiian form of Elijah, an Anglicized form of the Hebrew Eliyahu (the Lord is my God). The name is borne in the Bible by one of the earliest of the Hebrew prophets. (EH-LEE-AH)

Elikai Hawaiian form of the Hebrew Elisha (my God is salvation). The name is borne in the Bible by an early Hebrew prophet who was a disciple of Elijah. Var: Elisai. (EH-LEE-KAH-EE)

Enoka Hawaiian form of Enoch, an Anglicized form of the Hebrew Chanoch (dedicated, educated). The name is borne in the Bible by the eldest son of Cain, the first-born son of Adam and Eve who was banished after killing his brother. (EH-NO-KAH)

Enosa Hawaiian form of the Hebrew Enosh (man). The name is borne in the Bible by a son of Seth, the third son of Adam and Eve. (EH-NO-SAH)

Epelaima Hawaiian form of Ephraim, a variant of the Hebrew Efrayim (fruitful). The name is borne in the Bible by the second son of Joseph, a son of Jacob. Var: Eperaima. (EH-PEH-LAH-EE-MAH)

Epena Hawaiian form of Eben, a Hebrew name derived from *even* (stone). Var: Ebena. (EH-PEH-NAH)

Eukakio Hawaiian form of Eustace, an English cognate of the Old French Eustache (steadfast; happy in harvest). *See* EUSTACE (English Names). Var: Eutakio. (EH-OO-KAH-KEE-O)

Eukepio Hawaiian form of the Late Greek Eusebios, a compound name composed of the elements *eu* (well, good) and *sebein* (to worship, to venerate). Var: Eusebio. (EH-OO-KEH-PEE-O)

Hailama Hawaiian form of Hiram, a name derived from the Hebrew *hirām*, *chiram* (lofty, exalted, exalted brother). Var: Hairama, Hilama, Hirama. (HAH-EE-LAH-MAH)

Hānauhou Hawaiian name meaning "rebirth, baptism." (HAH-NAH-OO-HO-OO)

Hānauhoulani Compound name composed of the elements *hānauhou* (rebirth, baptism) and *lani* (sky, heaven, heavenly, spiritual, divine): hence, "spiritual rebirth." (HAH-NAH-OO-HO-OO-LAH-NEE)

Halola Hawaiian form of Harold (ruler of the army), a name derived from the Old English Hereweald, a compounding of the elements *here* (army) and *weald* (ruler, power, control). Var: Harola. (HAH-LO-LAH)

Haoa Hawaiian form of Howard, a name that originated as a surname from several derivations. *See* HOWARD (English Names). (HAH-O-AH)

Hekekā Hawaiian form of the Latin Hector (steadfast), a cognate of the Greek Hektōr (holding fast), which is derived from *echein* (to hold, to have). Var: Heketa. (HEH-KEH-KAH)

Helemano Hawaiian form of Herman, a name derived from the Old High German Hariman (soldier, army man), a compounding of the elements *hari* (army) and *man* (man). Var: Heremano. (HEH-LEH-MAH-NO)

Heleuma Hawaiian name meaning "anchor, stone anchor." (HEH-LEH-OO-MAH)

Hemolelekeakua Compound name composed of the Hawaiian elements *hemolele* (perfection, perfect), *ke* (one, the one, the one in question), and *akua* (God, spirit): hence, "God is perfection." (HEH-MO-LEH-LEH-KEH-AH-KOO-AH)

Heneli Hawaiian form of Henry, the English cognate of the German Heinrich (home ruler, ruler of an enclosure). *See* HEINRICH (German Names). Var: Hanalē, Henelē, Heneri. (HEH-NEH-LEE)

Hiuwe Hawaiianized form of Hugh, a cognate of the Old High German Hugo, which is derived from *hugu* (heart, mind, spirit). Var: Hiu. (HEE-OO-WEH)

Hoaalohakūpa'a Compound name composed of the elements *hoa aloha* (friend) and *kūpa'a* (loyal, steadfast, faithful): hence, "loyal friend." Var: Kahoaalohakūpa'a. (HO-AH-AH-LO-HAH-KOO-PAH-AH)

Hokea The Anglicized form of the Hebrew Hosheia, which is from *hōshēa'* (salvation). The name is borne in the Bible by an 8th-century B.C. prophet whose prophecies are told in the Old Testament book of Hosea. Var: Hosea. (HO-KEH-AH)

Holakio Hawaiian form of the Italian Horatio, which is from Horatius, an old Roman family name of unknown etymology. (HO-LAH-KEE-O)

Holeka Hawaiian form of Horace, the English cognate of the Italian Horatio, a name derived from the old Roman family name Horatius, which is of uncertain derivation. Var: Horesa. (HO-LEH-KAH)

Huanu Hawaiian form of Juan, the Spanish cognate of John (God is gracious), which is ultimately derived from the Hebrew *yehōhānān* (Yahweh is gracious). (HOO-AH-NOO)

Huko Hawaiian form of the German Hugo, a derivative of *hugu* (heart, mind, spirit). (HOO-KO)

Hūlama Compound name composed of the Hawaiian elements *hū* (swelling, rising) and *lama* (light): hence, "swelling light." The name refers to one who is intelligent and smart. (HOO-LAH-MAH)

Iakepa Hawaiian form of Jasper, the English form of Gaspar, a name of uncertain etymology which, along with Balthasar and Melchior, was assigned to the Three Wise Men, who brought gifts to the Christ child. The names are not found in the Bible and are thought to have been fixed in the 11th century. Gaspar might have been derived from the Persian *genashber* (treasure master), which is in keeping with his role of the bringer of precious gifts. Var: Iasepa, Kakapa, Kasapa. (EE-AH-KEH-PAH)

Iakona Hawaiian form of Jason, the English cognate of the Greek Iāson (healer), which is from *iasthai* (to heal). The name is borne in Greek mythology by a prince who led the Argonauts in the quest to find the Golden Fleece. Var: Iasona. (EE-AH-KO-NAH)

Ialeka Hawaiian form of Jared, which is from the Hebrew *yeredh* (descent). The name is borne in the Bible by the patriarch who was fifth from Adam.Var: Iareda. (EE-AH-LEH-KAH)

Ieke Hawaiian form of Jesse, a cognate of the Hebrew Yishai, which is derived from *yīshai* (gift, wealth). The name is borne in the Bible by the father of King David. Var: Iese. (EE-EH-KEH)

Ielemia Hawaiian form of Jeremiah, a name derived from the Ecclesiastic Greek Hieremias, which is a cognate of the Hebrew Yirmeyahu, a derivative of *yirmeyāh* (the Lord loosens, God will uplift). The name is borne in the Bible by a 6th- or 7th-century B.C. Hebrew prophet whose story and prophecies are recorded in the Old Testament book of Jeremiah.Var: Ieremia. (EE-EH-LEH-MEE-AH)

Ika'aka Hawaiian form of Isaac, a cognate of the Hebrew Yitzchak (he will laugh), which is from *yitshāq* (laughter). The name is borne in the Bible by the son of Abraham and Sarah, the patriarch of the Hebrews. Var: Aikake, Isaaka. (EE-KAH-AH-KAH)

Ikaia Hawaiian form of Isaiah, a cognate of the Greek Ēsaias, which is from the Hebrew Yeshaya (God is salvation). The name is borne in the Bible by an 8th-century B.C. Hebrew prophet. Var: Isaia. (EE-KAH-EE-AH)

Ikaikalani Compound name meaning "divine strength," composed of the Hawaiian elements *ikaika* (strength, force, energy) and *lani* (sky, heaven, heavenly, spiritual, divine). (EE-KAH-EE-KAH-LAH-NEE)

Ikenaki Hawaiian form of the Latin Ignatius, a derivative of Egnatius, an old Roman family name of uncertain etymology. Some believe it to be of Etruscan origin.

Others believe it is derived from the Latin *ignis* (fire). (EE-KEH-NAH-KEE)

INOKENE Hawaiian form of Innocent, a name borne by thirteen popes, which is derived from the Latin *innocens* (innocent). (EE-NO-KEH-NEH)

IO'ELA Hawaiian form of Joel, a cognate of the Ecclesiastic Greek Iōēl, which is from the Hebrew Yoel, a derivative of *yō'ēl* (the Lord is God). The name is borne in the Bible by a minor Hebrew prophet. (EE-O-EH-LAH)

IOKEPA Hawaiian form of the Ecclesiastic Late Latin Joseph, which is from the Ecclesiastic Greek Iōsēph, a name derived from the Hebrew *yōsēf* (may he add, may God add). The name is borne in the Bible by the favorite son of Jacob, by the husband of the Virgin Mary, and by Joseph of Arimathea. Var: Iokewe, Iosepa. Short: Keō. (EE-O-KEH-PAH)

IOKIA Hawaiian form of Josiah, the English cognate of the Hebrew Yoshiya, which is derived from *yōshīyāh* (the Lord supports, the Lord saves, the Lord heals). (EE-O-KEE-AH)

IŌKINA Hawaiian form of Joachim, a cognate of the Hebrew Jehoiakim and Yehoyakim (God will establish). In medieval times, the name was assigned to the father of the Virgin Mary, as Anne was assigned to her mother. Var: Wākina. (EE-O-KEE-NAH)

IOKUA Hawaiian form of Joshua, a cognate of the Hebrew Yehoshua, which is from *yehōshū'a* (Jehovah is help, God is salvation). The name is borne in the Bible by Moses' successor, who led the children of Israel into the Promised Land. (EE-O-KOO-AH)

IONA Hawaiian form of Jonah, the English cognate of the Ecclesiastic Late Latin Jonas and the Ecclesiastic Greek Īonas, which are from the Hebrew Yonah (dove). The name is borne in the Bible by a Hebrew prophet who was thrown overboard during a storm after he had disobeyed God. He was swallowed by a huge fish but was cast unharmed upon the shore three days later. (EE-O-NAH)

IONAKANA Hawaiian form of Jonathan, the English cognate of the Hebrew Yonatan, a short form of Yehonatan, which is derived from *yehōnātān* (Yahweh has given, God has given). The name is borne in the Bible by the eldest son of King Saul and a close friend of David's. Var: Ionatana. (EE-O-NAH-KAH-NAH)

IUKEKINI Hawaiian form of Justin, a name derived from the Latin Justīnus, which is from *justus* (lawful, right, just). (EE-OO-KEH-KEE-NEE)

IUKINI Hawaiianized form of Eugene, a cognate of the Greek Eugenios, which is from *eugenēs* (well-born, noble). Var: Iugini. (EE-OO-KEE-NEE)

IULIO Hawaiian form of Julius, an old Roman family name thought to be derived from Iulus (the first down on the chin, downy-bearded). Because a person first beginning to develop facial hair is young, "youth" became an accepted meaning of the name. (EE-OO-LEE-O)

KAHA'AHEO Compound name composed of the elements *ka* (one, the one, the one in question) and *ha'aheo* (proud, to cherish with pride). (KAH-HAH-AH-HEH-O)

KAHAIĀOKAPONIA Compound name meaning "follower of the anointed one," composed of the elements *ka* (one, the one, the one in question), *hai* (offering, sacrifice, follower), *ā* (to), *o* (of), and *poni* (anoint). (KAH-HAH-EE-AH-O-KAH-PO-NEE-AH)

KAHAKUOKAHALE Compound name composed of the elements *ka* (one, the one), *haku* (lord, master, employer, owner), and *hale* (house, building, home): hence, "ruler of the home." (KAH-HAH-KOO-O-KAH-HAH-LEH)

KAHANU Compounding of the elements *ka* (one, the one, the one in question) and *hanu* (breath, to breathe, smell, respirate): hence, "the one who breathes." (KAH-HAH-NOO)

KAHAWAI Derived from *kahawai* (stream, brook, river). (KAH-HAH-WAH-EE)

KĀHEKA Derived from *kāheka* (pool, basin). (KAH-HEH-KAH)

KĀHEKA'ALOHI Compound name meaning "shining pool," which is composed of the elements *kāheka* (pool, basin) and *'alohi* (shining, brilliant, gleaming). (KAH-HEH-KAH-AH-LO-HEE)

KAHELEMEAKUA Compound name composed of the elements *ka* (one, the one), *hele* (walk), *me* (with), and *akua* (God, spirit): hence, "the one who walks with God." (KAH-HEH-LEH-MEH-AH-KOO-AH)

KAHUA Derived from the Hawaiian *kahua* (fortress, camp, base, site). (KAH-HOO-AH)

KAIHE Compound name meaning "spear," which is derived from the elements *ka* (one, the one, the one in question) and *ihe* (spear, javelin, dart). (KAH-EE-HEH)

KAIHEKOA Compound name meaning "the one who is brave with the spear." The name is composed of the elements *ka* (one, the one), *ihe* (spear, javelin, dart), and *koa* (brave). (KAH-EE-HEH-KO-AH)

KA'IKE'ĀPONA Compound name composed of the Hawaiian elements *ka* (one, the one), *'ike* (knowledge), and *ʻāpona* (embracing): hence, "the one embracing knowledge." (KAH-EE-KEH-AH-PO-NAH)

Kaʻilinemo Compound name meaning "the one with smooth skin," composed of the elements *ka* (one, the one), *ʻili* (skin), and *nemo* (smooth). (KAH-EE-LEE-NEH-MO)

Kaikala Hawaiian form of the Latin Caesar, a name of uncertain etymology. Some believe Caesar to be derived from *caedo* (to cut); others think it to be from *caesius* (blue-gray). Another suggestion is that it is derived from *caesaries* (hairy, with abundant hair). Var: Kaisara. (KAH-EE-KAH-LAH)

Kakaio Hawaiian form of Thaddeus, a cognate of the Greek Thaddaios, which is of uncertain derivation. Some believe it to be a variant of Theodōros (God's gift). Others feel it is from an Aramaic word meaning "praised." The name is borne in the Bible as a name of Lebbaeus, an apostle of Christ. Var: Tadaio. (KAH-KAH-EE-O)

Kakaio Hawaiian form of Zacchaeus, a derivative of the Ecclesiastic Greek Zacharias (remembrance of the Lord), a name derived from the Hebrew *zĕcharyah* (God remembers). Var: Zakaio. (KAH-KAH-EE-O)

Kakalia Hawaiianized form of Zacharias (remembrance of the Lord), a name derived from the Hebrew *zĕcharyah* (God remembers). Var: Zakaria. (KAH-KAH-LEE-AH)

Kakana Hawaiian form of Tarzan, the name of the jungle-raised hero of stories by E. R. Burroughs. The name is indicative of virility, strength, and manliness. (KAH-KAH-NAH)

Kakelaka Hawaiian form of the Hebrew Shadrach, a name of Babylonian origin but of uncertain meaning. The name is borne in the Bible by one of three captives who were cast into a blazing furnace but emerged from the flames unharmed. (KAH-KEH-LAH-KAH)

Kakumulani Compound name composed of the Hawaiian elements *ka* (one, the one), *kumu* (base, bottom, foundation), and *lani* (sky, heaven, heavenly, divine, spiritual): hence, "horizon, the base of the sky." (KAH-KOO-MOO-LAH-NEE)

Kalā Composed of the Hawaiian elements *ka* (one, the one) and *lā* (sun): hence, "the sun." (KAH-LAH)

Kalaila Hawaiian form of Clyde, a name derived from an old Scottish river name, which is of uncertain derivation. Var: Kalaida. (KAH-LAH-EE-LAH)

Kalauka Hawaiian form of Claude, a cognate of the Latin Claudius, an old Roman family name derived from *claudus* (lame). Var: Kalauda. (KAH-LAH-OO-KAH)

Kalawina Hawaiian form of Calvin, a name derived from the Latin *calvinus* (little bald one), which has its root in *calvus* (bald). Var: Kalavina. (KAH-LAH-VEE-NAH)

Kaleʻa Derived from the Hawaiian elements *ka* (one, the one) and *leʻa* (joy, pleasure, happiness, delight). (KAH-LEH-AH)

Kaleo Compounding of the elements *ka* (one, the one) and *leo* (voice, sound, tune, tone). (KAH-LEH-O)

Kaleolani Compound name meaning "heavenly voice," which is derived from the elements *ka* (one, the one), *leo* (voice, sound, tune, tone), and *lani* (sky, heaven, heavenly, divine). (KAH-LAY-O-LAH-NEE)

Kalepa Hawaiian form of Caleb, a cognate of the Hebrew Kaleb (dog). The name, which is indicative of faithfulness, is borne in the Bible by a leader of the Israelites. Var: Kaleba. (KAH-LEH-PAH)

Kalikiano Hawaiian form of Christian, a name derived from the Latin *christiānus* and the Greek *christianos* (a Christian, a follower of Christ). (KAH-LEE-KEE-AH-NO)

Kalikohemolele Compound name meaning "perfect bud, perfect child," which is composed from the Hawaiian elements *ka* (one, the one), *liko* (leaf bud, newly opened leaf; figuratively, a child, youth), and *hemolele* (perfect, virtue, perfection). (KAH-LEE-KO-HEH-MO-LEH-LEH)

Kalino Compounding of the Hawaiian elements *ka* (one, the one) and *lino* (bright, shiny, dazzling, brilliant): hence, "bright one." (KAH-LEE-NO)

Kalipekona Hawaiian form of Clifton, the transferred use of the English surname originating from the place-names of various old English towns. It is composed from the Old English elements *clif* (cliff, slope, bank of a river) and *tūn* (town, settlement, village, enclosure). Var: Kalifetona. (KAH-LEE-PAH-KO-NAH)

Kāliu Hawaiian form of the Latin Darius, an old name derived from the Greek Dareios, which is of uncertain origin. It is thought to ultimately be derived from Darayavahush, the name of an ancient Persian king. Var: Dariu. (KAH-LEE-OO)

Kalolo Hawaiian form of Charles, which is derived from the Germanic *karl* (full-grown, a man), a cognate of the Old English *ceorl* (a man, freeman, peasant). Var: Kale, Karolo. (KAH-LO-LO)

KAMAHA Derived from the elements *ka* (one, the one) and *maha* (rest, repose, freedom from pain, at ease): hence, "the one who is at rest." (KAH-MAH-HAH)

KAMAKAKOA Compound name composed of the elements *ka* (one, the one), *maka* (eye), and *koa* (brave, fearless, bravery): hence, "the brave eye." The name is indicative of one who is bold, unafraid, and brave.(KAH-MAH-KAH-KO-AH)

KAMAKANI Compounding of the elements *ka* (one, the one) and *makani* (wind, breeze): hence, "the wind, the breeze." (KAH-MAH-KAH-NEE)

KAMALIELA Hawaiian form of the Hebrew Gamaliel (God is my reward). The name is borne in the Bible by a leader of the tribe of Manasseh. (KAH-MAH-LEE-EH-LAH)

KAMALUHIAKAPU Compound name composed of the Hawaiian elements *ka* (one, the one), *maluhia* (peace, quiet, serenity), and *kapu* (sacred): hence, "sacred peace." (KAH-MAH-LOO-HEE-AH-KAH-POO)

KAMEKONA Hawaiianized form of Samson, a cognate of the Hebrew Shimshon, a name derived from *shimshōn* (sun). The name is borne in the Bible by an Israelite judge known for his great strength. Var: Samesona. (KAH-MEH-KO-NAH)

KAMOKU Compounding of the Hawaiian elements *ka* (one, the one) and *moku* (island, district, severed portion): hence, "the island." (KAH-MO-KOO)

KAMUELA Hawaiian form of Samuel, a cognate of the Hebrew Shmuel, a name derived from *shĕmū'ēl* (name of God, his name is God). The name is borne in the Bible by a Hebrew judge and prophet who anointed Saul as the first king of Israel. Var: Samuela. (KAH-MOO-EH-LAH)

KANA Hawaiian form of the Hebrew Dan (a judge). The name is borne in the Bible by the fifth son of Jacob. Alternatively, Dan is used as a short form of Daniel (God is my judge). Var: Dana, Dano. (KAH-NAH)

KANA'I Derived from the elements *ka* (one, the one) and *na'i* (to conquer, to take by force, conqueror): hence, "conqueror, victor." (KAH-NAH-EE)

KANAKANUI Compound name meaning "person of great size and power," composed of the elements *kanaka* (human being, man, person) and *nui* (big, large, great, powerful). (KAH-NAH-KAH-NOO-EE)

KANALĒ Hawaiian form of Stanley (dweller near a stony clearing), a name originating as a surname derived from several old English place-names. *See* STANLEY (English Names). Var: Sanale. (KAH-NAH-LEH)

KĀNEHO'OMALU Compound name meaning "man of peace," which is composed of the elements *kāne* (man) and *ho'omalu* (to make peace between warring parties). (KAH-NEH-HO-O-MAH-LOO)

KANIELA Hawaiian form of the Hebrew Daniel, a name derived from *dāni'ēl* (God is my judge). The name is borne in the Bible by a Hebrew prophet whose faith kept him alive in a den of lions. Var: Daniela. (KAH-NEE-EH-LAH)

KANOA Compounding of the elements *ka* (one, the one) and *noa* (freed from taboo). (KAH-NO-AH)

KAPALAOA Compound name composed of the elements *ka* (one, the one) and *palaoa* (ivory, sperm whale). (KAH-PAH-LAH-O-AH)

KAPALEKANAKA Compound name composed of the elements *ka* (one, the one), *pale* (defend, ward off, protect, guard), and *kanaka* (human being, man, mankind): hence, "defender of mankind." (KAH-PAH-LEH-KAH-NAH-KAH)

KAPALI Compounding of the elements *ka* (one, the one) and *pali* (cliff). (KAH-PAH-LEE)

KAPELIELA Hawaiianized form of Gabriel, a cognate of the Hebrew Gavriel, which is derived from *gavhrī'ēl* (God is my strength). The name is borne in the Bible by one of the seven archangels, the herald of Good News who appeared to the Virgin Mary to announce her pregnancy and the impending birth of the Christ child. Var: Gaberiela. (KAH-PEH-LEE-EH-LAH)

KAPONO Compounding of the elements *ka* (one, the one) and *pono* (moral, righteous, proper). (KAH-PO-NO)

KAULANA Derived from the Hawaiian *kaulana* (famous, celebrated, renowned). (KAH-OO-LAH-NAH)

KAULO Hawaiian form of Saul, a cognate of the Hebrew Shaul, which is from *shā'ūl* (asked of, borrowed). The name is borne in the Bible by the first king of Israel. Var: Saulo. KAH-OO-LO)

KĀWIKA Hawaiian form of the Hebrew David, which is derived from *dāvīd* (beloved). The name is borne in the Bible by the second and greatest of the Israelite kings. Var: Davida, Kewiki. (KAH-VEE-KAH)

KAWĪKANI Compounding of the elements *ka* (one, the one) and *wīkani* (strong): hence, "the strong one." (KAH-WEE-KAH-NEE)

KEAHILANI Compound name composed of the elements *ke* (one, the one), *ahi* (fire), and *lani* (sky, heaven, heavenly, spiritual): hence, "spiritual fire" or "fire in the sky." (KEH-AH-HEE-LAH-NEE)

KEAKA Hawaiian form of Jack, a pet form of John (God is gracious). *See* KEONI. (KEH-AH-KAH)

KEALA'ALOHI Compounding of the elements *ke* (one, the one), *ala* (path), and *'alohi* (shining, brilliant): hence, "shining path." The name is indicative of the parents' desire for a bright future for their child. (KEH-AH-LAH-AH-LO-HEE)

KEALAMAULOA Compound name composed of the elements *ke* (one, the one), *ala* (path), and *mau loa* (eternal, continuing): hence, "eternal path." (KEH-AH-LAH-MAH-OO-LO-AH)

KEIKEMAMAKE Compound name meaning "wished-for child, longed-for child," which is composed of the elements *keike* (child) and *mamake* (long for, desire). (KEH-EE-KEH-MAH-MAH-KEH)

KEKA Hawaiian form of Seth, a cognate of the Hebrew Shet, which is derived from *shēth* (appointed). The name is borne in the Bible by the third son of Adam and Eve, born after the death of his brother Abel. Var: Seta. (KEH-KAH)

KEKILA Hawaiian form of Cecil, a cognate of the Latin Caecilius, an old Roman family name derived from *caecus* (blind, dim-sighted). Var: Kikila. (KEH-KEE-LAH)

KEKOANUI Compound name composed of the Hawaiian elements *ke* (one, the one), *koa* (warrior), and *nui* (great, mighty, large): hence, "mighty warrior." (KEH-KO-AH-NOO-EE)

KELALA Hawaiianized form of Gerald (spear ruler), a name derived from the Germanic Gerwald, a compound name composed of the elements *ger* (a spear) and *wald* (rule). (KEH-LAH-LAH)

KELEKOLIO Hawaiianized form of Gregory, a cognate of the Greek Grēgorios (vigilant, a watchman), which is from the verb *egeirein* (to awaken). Short: Keli. (KEH-LEH-KO-LEE-O)

KELEMENETE Hawaiianized form of Clement, a cognate of the Latin Clemens, which is derived from *clemens* (mild, gentle, merciful). Var: Kelemeneke. (KEH-LEH-MEH-NEH-TEH)

KELI Hawaiian form of Greg, a short form of Gregory (vigilant, a watchman). Accordingly, Keli is used as a short form of Kelekolio, the Hawaiianized form of Gregory. *See* KELEKOLIO. (KEH-LEE)

KELI'I Derived from the Hawaiian *keli'i* (rich, noble, powerful, royalty). (KEH-LEE-EE)

KEMIKILIO Hawaiian form of Demetrius, which is from the Greek Demetrios (of Demeter). Demeter is an ancient name of unknown etymology borne by the Greek mythological goddess of agriculture and fertility. Var: Demitirio. (KAY-MEE-KEE-LEE-O)

KENEKE Hawaiianized form of Kenneth, an Anglicized form of the Gaelic Cinaed and Cionaed (born of fire), and Coinneach and Caioneach (comely, handsome). Var: Kenete, Keneki, Keneti. (KEH-NEH-KEH)

KENIKA Hawaiian form of Dennis, a cognate of the Greek Dionysios (of Dionysos). Dionysos is an ancient name of unknown etymology borne by the Greek mythological god of wine and revelry. (KEH-NEE-KAH)

KEŌ Hawaiian form of Joe, a short form of Joseph (may he add, may God add). *See* IOKEPA. (KEH-O)

KEOKI Hawaiianized form of George (earthworker, farmer), a cognate of the Greek Geōrgios, a compounding of the elements *gē* (earth) and *ergein* (to work). (KEH-O-KEE)

KEOLA Compounding of the elements *ke* (one, the one) and *ola* (life, health, living): hence, "life, the one who is alive." (KEH-O-LAH)

KEOLAMAULOA Compound name meaning "salvation," which is derived from *ke* (one, the one), *ola* (life), *mau* (constant, continuation, steady, always), and *loa* (distance, length, far). *Ola mau loa* is the Hawaiian term for "salvation." (KEH-O-LAH-MAH-OO-LO-AH)

KEONI Popular Hawaiian form of John (God is gracious), a name derived from the Middle Latin Johannes, which is from the Ecclesiastic Late Latin Joannes, a derivative of the Ecclesiastic Greek Iōannes, a cognate of the Hebrew Yehanan. Yehanan is a short form of Yehohanan, which is from *yehōhānān* (Yahweh is gracious). John, the most enduring of the biblical names, is borne in the Bible by several important characters, including John the Baptist, a cousin and forerunner of Christ. (KEH-O-NEE)

KEPAKIANO Hawaiianized form of Sebastian, a cognate of the Greek Sebastianos (a man of Sebastia, a town in Asia Minor). Short: Pakiana. (KEH-PAH-KEE-AH-NO)

KEPANO Hawaiianized form of Stephen, which is from the Latin Stephanus, a derivative of the Greek Stephanos, which is from *stephanos* (a crown, a garland). The name is borne in the Bible by St. Stephen. The first Christian martyr, he was one of the seven chosen to assist the Twelve Apostles. Var: Kekepana, Setepana, Tepano. (KEH-PAH-NO)

KEWINI Hawaiianized form of Kevin, the Anglicized form of the Irish Caoimhín and Caomghin (handsome, comely birth). (KEH-WEE-NEE)

KIKEONA Hawaiianized form of Gideon, a name derived from the Hebrew *gidh'ōn* (hewer, one who cuts down). The name is borne in the Bible by an Israelite judge who was a leader in the defeat of the Midianites. Var: Kileona. (KEE-KEH-O-NAH)

KIKINĒ Hawaiianized form of Sidney, a name that originated as a surname from more than one source. *See* SIDNEY (English Names). Var: Kikanē. (KEE-KEE-NAY)

KILIKIKOPA Hawaiianized form of Christopher (bearing Christ), a cognate of the Greek Christophoros, a compound name composed of the elements *Christos* (Christ) and *pherein* (to bear). Var: Kirisitopa. (KEE-LEE-KEE-KO-PAH)

KILILA Hawaiian form of Cyril, a cognate of the Greek Kyrillos (lordly), which is derived from *kyrios* (a lord). Var: Kirila. (KEE-LEE-LAH)

KILIPEKA Hawaiianized form of Gilbert (famous pledge), a name derived from the Old High German Gisilberht, a compounding of the elements *gisil* (pledge) and *beraht* (bright, famous). Var: Kilipaki. (KEE-LEE-PEH-KAH)

KILOHANA Derived from the Hawaiian *kilohana,* a word that refers to the outside, decorated sheet of tapa in the traditional *ku'inakapa* (bedclothes). The word has the extended meanings "best, superior, excellent." (KEE-LO-HAH-NAH)

KIMEONA Hawaiianized form of Simeon, a cognate of the Hebrew Shimon, which is derived from *shim'on* (heard). (KEE-MEH-O-NAH)

KIMO Popular Hawaiian form of James and its short form of Jim. James is from the Ecclesiastic Late Latin Iacomus, an evolution of Iacobus, which is derived from the Greek Iakōbos. Iakōbos is a cognate of the Hebrew Yaakov, which is derived from *ya'aqob* (supplanting; seizing by the heel). (KEE-MO)

KIMOKEO Hawaiian form of Timothy (honor God), a cognate of the Greek Timotheos, which is composed of the elements *timē* (honor, respect) and *theos* (God). Var: Timoteo. (KEE-MO-KEH-O)

KIMONA Hawaiianized form of Simon, a cognate of the Hebrew Shimon, which is derived from *shim'on* (heard). (KEE-MO-NAH)

KIONIKIO Hawaiian form of the Greek Dionysios (of Dionysos). Dionysos is the name of the Greek mythological god of wine and revelry. Var: Dionisio. (KEE-O-NEE-KEE-O)

KIPILIANO Hawaiian form of the Italian Cipriano which is from the Latin Cypriānus, a name refering to a person from the island of Cyprus. Var: Kipiriano. (KEE-PEE-LEE-AH-NO)

KOAMALU Compound name composed of the elements *koa* (bravery, courage, fearlessness) and *malu* (peace, protection, peacefulness, stillness): hence, "peaceful courage." (KO-AH-MAH-LOO)

KOMA Hawaiian form of Tom, a short form of Thomas (a twin). Thus, Koma is used as a short form of Komaki, the Hawaiianized form of Thomas. (KO-MAH)

KOMAKI Hawaiianized form of Thomas, a name derived from the Aramaic *tĕ'ōma* (a twin). The name is borne in the Bible by an apostle who doubted the resurrection of Christ. It is from him that the expression "doubting Thomas" arose. Var: Kamaki. Short: Koma, Toma. (KO-MAH-KEE)

KOMINIKO Hawaiian form of the Spanish Domingo, which is from the Latin Dominicus (belonging to a lord), a derivative of *dominus* (a lord, a master). Var: Dominigo. (KO-MEE-NEE-KO)

KONA Hawaiianized form of Don, a short form of Donald (world ruler). *See* DONALD (English Names). Var: Dona. (KO-NAH)

KŌNANE Derived from *kōnane* (bright moonlight). (KO-NAH-NEH))

KOUKAKALA Hawaiianized form of Douglas, a name that originated as a surname derived from the Gaelic Dubhglas, a compounding of the elements *dubh* (black, dark) and *glas* (blue, green, gray). Var: Dougalasa. (KO-OO-KAH-KAH-LAH)

KUAIKA Hawaiian form of Dwight, a name that originated as a surname and is thought to be from the Old Dutch *wit* (white, blond). Var: Duaita. (KOO-AH-EE-KAH)

KŪKĀNE Compounding of the elements *kū* (resembling, like, in a state of) and *kāne* (male, man, masculine): hence, "manly." (KOO-KAH-NEH)

KULAMAU'U Compound name composed of the elements *kula* (plain, field, open country, pasture) and *mau'u,* the general name used for different types of grasses and rushes. The word *kulamau'u* refers to a meadow. (KOO-LAH-MAH-OO-OO)

KULIANO Hawaiianized form of Julian, a cognate of the Latin Julianus, which is a derivative of Julius, an old Roman family name believed to be derived from Iulus (downy-bearded, the first down on the chin). Because a person just beginning to develop facial hair is young, "youth" became an accepted meaning of the name. (KOO-LEE-AH-NO)

KŪPA'ALANI Compound name meaning "divine resoluteness," which is derived from *kūpa'a* (steadfast, firm, resolute, loyal) and *lani* (sky, heaven, heavenly, divine, spiritual). (KOO-PAH-AH-LAH-NEE)

LA'AKEA Compound name composed of the elements *la'a* (sacred, holy, consecrated) and *kea* (light): hence, "light sacredness." The word makes reference to sacred light or sacred things. (LAH-AH-KEH-AH)

LAHAHANA Compound name composed of the elements *la* (sun) and *hahana* (heat): hence, "heat of the sun, the sun's warmth." (LAH-HAH-HAH-NAH)

LAIONELA Hawaiianized form of the French Lionel, a diminutive form of *lion* (lion). (LAH-EE-O-NEH-LAH)

LANI Popular name derived from *lani* (sky, heaven, heavenly, spiritual, divine). Lani is also a commonly used element in compound names and is thus used as a short form of such. (LAH-NEE)

LAPA'ELA Hawaiianized form of Raphael, a cognate of the Greek Rhaphaēl, which is from the Hebrew Refael, a name derived from *refāēl* (God has healed). The name is borne in the Bible by an archangel and messenger of God. Var: Lapa'ele. (LAH-PAH-EH-LAH)

LĪHAU Derived from the Hawaiian *līhau*, a word that denotes a gentle, cool rain. Such a rain was believed to be lucky for fishermen. The word has the alternate definitions of "moist, fresh, and cool" and "fresh as the dewladen air." (LEE-HAH-OO)

LŌKELA Hawaiian form of Roger (spear fame), a name derived from the Old High German Hrodger, which is composed from the elements *hruod* (fame) and *ger* (a spear). (LO-KEH-LAH)

LOKENĒ Hawaiianized form of Rodney, a name originating as a surname from the place-name Rodney Stoke. *See* RODNEY (English Names). (LO-KEH-NAY)

LOPAKA Hawaiianized form of Robert (bright fame), a name derived from the Old High German Hruodperht, which is a compounding of the elements *hruod* (fame) and *beraht* (bright, famous). (LO-PAH-KAH)

LUKA Hawaiianized form of Luke, a Middle English and Anglo-French form of Lucas, which is a derivative of Lucius. The name has its root in *lux* (light). Alternatively, some believe the name is a contraction of Loukanos (man from Lucania). The name is borne in the Bible by one of the four evangelists and author of the third Gospel, Luke. (LOO-KAH)

MAIKA'IKEAKUA Compound name meaning "God is good." The name is composed of the elements *maika'i* (good), *ke* (one, the one), and *akua* (God, spirit). (MAH-EE-KAH-EE-KEH-AH-KOO-AH)

MAKAIO Hawaiianized form of Matthew, a cognate of the Greek Matthaios and Matthias, which are contractions of Mattathias, a cognate of the Hebrew Matityah, which has its root in *mattīthyāh* (gift of God). The name is borne in the Bible by one of the four evangelists and author of the first Gospel, Matthew. Var: Mataio. (MAH-KAH-EE-O)

MAKANAAKUA Compound name composed of the Hawaiian elements *makana* (gift, present, reward) and *akua* (God, spirit, divine): hence, "reward of God, God's reward." (MAH-KAH-NAH-AH-KOO-AH)

MAKANAOKEAKUA Compound name composed of the elements *makana* (gift, present, reward), *o* (of), *ke* (one, the one), and *akua* (God, spirit): hence, "a gift of God." (MAH-KAH-NAH-O-KEH-AH-KOO-AH)

MAKANI Derived from *makani* (wind, a breeze). (MAH-KAH-NEE)

MAKIMO Hawaiian form of the Latin Maximus, a name derived from *maximus* (greatest). (MAH-KEE-MO)

MALAKI Hawaiian form of the Hebrew Malachi (my messenger, my servant). The name is borne in the Bible by the last of the Hebrew prophets. (MAH-LAH-KEE)

MALAKOMA Hawaiian form of Malcolm, a name derived from the Gaelic Maolcolm (servant of St. Columba), a compound name composed of *maol* (servant) and the name Colm (Columba). *See* MALCOLM (English Names). (MAH-LAH-KO-MAH)

MALEKO Hawaiian form of Mark, a cognate of Marcus, which is of uncertain derivation. Most believe it has its root in Mars, the name of the Roman mythological god of war. Others, however, think it might be from *mas* (manly) or from the Greek *malakoz* (soft, tender). The name is borne in the Bible by one of the four evangelists and author of the second Gospel, Mark. (MAH-LEH-KO)

MALUHIA Derived from the Hawaiian *maluhia* (peace, quiet, serenity). (MAH-LOO-HEE-AH)

MALUHIALANI Compound name composed of the elements *maluhia* (peace, quiet, serenity) and *lani* (sky, heaven, heavenly, spiritual, divine): hence, "divinely peaceful." (MAH-LOO-HEE-AH-LAH-NEE)

MALULANI Compound name composed of the elements *malu* (protection, shade, shelter, peace) and *lani* (sky, heaven, heavenly, spiritual, divine): hence, "divine protection." (MAH-LOO-LAH-NEE)

Maluokeakua Compound name composed from the elements *malu* (peace, protection, shade, shelter), *ke* (one, the one), and *akua* (God, spirit): hence, "God's peace." (MAH-LOO-O-KEH-AH-KOO-AH)

Manu Derived from the Hawaiian *manu* (bird). (MAH-NOO)

Manukū Derived from the Hawaiian *manu* (bird) and *kū* (resembling, like, in a state of): hence, "birdlike, like a bird." (MAH-NOO-KOO)

Manumakali'i Compound name composed of the Hawaiian elements *manu* (bird) and *makali'i* (tiny, very small): hence, "a tiny bird." (MAH-NOO-MAH-KAH-LEE-EE)

Mataio Hawaiianized form of Matthew, a cognate of the Greek Matthaios and Matthias, which are contractions of Mattathias, a cognate of the Hebrew Matityah, which has its root in *mattūthyāh* (gift of God). The name is borne in the Bible by one of the four evangelists and author of the first Gospel, Matthew. Var: Makaio. (MAH-TAH-EE-O)

Mikala Hawaiian form of the Hebrew Michael (who is like God?). The name is borne in the Bible by the archangel closest to God, the one responsible for carrying out God's judgments. Considered the leader of the heavenly host, Michael is regarded as the patron of soldiers. Var: Mika'ek. (MEE-KAH-LAH)

Nahele Derived from the Hawaiian *nahele* (forest, grove, wilderness). (NAH-HEH-LEH)

Nalunani Compound name composed of the elements *nalu* (wave, surf) and *nani* (beauty, beautiful): hence, "beautiful surf." (NAH-LOO-NAH-NEE)

Napana Hawaiian form of Nathan, a name derived from the Hebrew Natan, which is from *nāthān* (gift). The name is borne in the Bible by a prophet who rebuked David for the death of Uriah. Var: Natana. (NAH-PAH-NAH)

Nemo Derived from the Hawaiian *nemo* (smooth, smoothly polished). (NEH-MO)

Nihopalaoa Compound name composed of the elements *niho* (tooth) and *palaoa* (sperm whale, ivory): hence, "whale tooth." A whale tooth pendant was a traditional symbol of royalty. (NEE-HO-PAH-LAH-O-AH)

Nikolao Hawaiian form of Nicholas (victory of the people), a cognate of the Greek Nikolaos, which is a compound name composed of the elements *nikē* (victory) and *laos* (people). Var: Nikolo. (NEE-KO-LAH-O)

Noelani Compound name composed of the elements *noe* (mist, rain) and *lani* (sky, heaven, heavenly, spiritual, divine): hence, "heavenly mist." (NO-EH-LAH-NEE)

Nohea Derived from the Hawaiian *nohea* (handsome, comely, of fine appearance). (NO-HEH-AH)

Nohokai Compound name meaning "dweller on the seashore," which is composed of the elements *noho* (to live, to dwell) and *kai* (the sea). (NO-HO-KAH-EE)

Olakeakua Compound name composed of the elements *ola* (life, health, living), *ke* (one, the one), and *akua* (God, spirit): hence, "God lives." (O-LAH-KEH-AH-KOO-AH)

Oliwa Hawaiianized form of Oliver, a name of debated origin. Most believe it to be from the Old French *olivier* (olive tree). Others think it is of Germanic origin and believe it to be derived from the Middle Low German Alfihar (elf army), a compound name composed of the elements *alf* (elf) and *hari* (army). (O-LEE-WAH)

Pa'ahana Derived from the Hawaiian *pa'ahana* (industrious, busy). (PAH-AH-HAH-NAH)

Pakelika Hawaiianized form of Patrick, which is derived from the Latin *patricius* (a patrician, a nobleman). (PAH-KEH-LEE-KAH)

Pakiana Short form of Kepakiano, the Hawaiianized form of Sebastian (man from Sebastia). Pakiana is the Hawaiian form of Bastian. *See* KEPAKIANO. (PAH-KEE-AH-NAH)

Pakile A borrowing from the French, Basile is from the Latin Basilius and the Greek Basileios (kingly, royal), names derived from *basileus* (king). Var: Bakile. (PAH-KEE-LEH)

Palakiko Hawaiian form of Francis, which is ultimately derived from the Old French *franc* (free). *See* FRANCIS (English Names). Var: Farakiko. (PAH-LAH-KEE-KO)

Palani Hawaiian form of Frank, which is from the Old French Franc and the Germanic Frank, names referring to a member of the Germanic tribes that established the Frankish Empire extending over what is now France, Germany, and Italy. The tribe is thought to have obtained its name from a type of spear or javelin (*franco*). Palani is also a short form of Pelanekelina. *See* PELANEKELINA. Var: Farani. (PAH-LAH-NEE)

Palekolomaio Hawaiian form of Bartholomew, a cognate of the Late Latin Bartholomaeus and the Greek Bartholomaios. The name is a patronymic of Aramaic origin meaning "son of Talmai." Talmai is an Aramaic name meaning "hill, mound, furrows." The name is borne in the

Bible by one of the Twelve Apostles of Christ. Var: Baretolomaio. (PAH-LEH-KO-LO-MAH-EE-O)

PALENAPA Hawaiian form of Barnabas, a name derived from the Aramaic *barnebhū'āh* (son of exhortation). Var: Barenaba. (PAH-LEH-NAH-PAH)

PAPIANO Hawaiian form of Fabian, a name derived from the Latin Fabianus (of Fabius), a derivative of the old Roman family name Fabius, which has its root in *faba* (a bean). Var: Fabiano. (FAH-BEE-AH-NO)

PAULO Hawaiian form of Paul which is from the Latin Paulus, an old Roman family name derived from *paulus* (small). The name was adopted in the Bible by a Jew and Roman citizen, Saul of Tarsus, who was converted to Christianity by a vision of Christ. St. Paul and St. Peter are regarded as the cofounders of the Christian Church. (PAH-OO-LO)

PEKELO Hawaiianized form of Peter, a name derived from the Ecclesiastic Late Latin Petrus and the Ecclesiastic Greek Petros, names derived from *petrus* (a rock) and *petros* (a stone). The name is borne in the Bible by one of the Twelve Apostles of Christ. St. Peter and St. Paul are regarded as the cofounders of the Christian Church. Var: Petero. Short: Peka. (PEH-KEH-LO)

PELANEKELINA Hawaiianized form of Franklin, a name originating as a surname from the Middle English *frankeleyn* (a freeman, a landowner of free but not noble birth). The word is derived from the Old French *franc* (free). Var: Feranekelina. Short: Farani, Palani. (PEH-LAH-NEH-KEH-LEE-NAH)

PELEKE Hawaiian form of Fred, a short form of Alfred (elf counsel, wise counselor). *See* ALEPELEKE. Var: Ferede. (PEH-LEH-KEH)

PELEKI Hawaiianized form of Percy, a name originating as a surname from a Norman baronial name taken from place-names in Calvados and La Manche, Normandy. The name is from the Greek Perseus, which is derived from *pērtho* (to destroy). (PEH-LEH-KEE)

PELEKINAKO Hawaiian form of Ferdinand, an English cognate of the Spanish Ferdinando, which is of uncertain origin and meaning. It is thought to be of Germanic origin, composed from the elements *frithu* (peace), *fardi* (journey), or *ferchvus* (youth, life) and *nanths* (courage), *nanthi* (venture, risk), or *nand* (ready, prepared). Var: Feredinado. (PEH-LEH-KEE-NAH-KO)

PELIKE Hawaiian form of the Latin Felix, a name derived from *felix* (happy, lucky). Var: Felike. (PEH-LEE-KEH)

PENEKIKO Hawaiian form of Benedict, which is from the Latin Benedictus (blessed). Var: Benedito. Short: Beni, Peni. (PEH-NEH-KEE-KO)

PENI Hawaiian form of Ben, a short form of any of the various names beginning with the element *Ben-*. Accordingly, Beni is the short form of the Hawaiian variants of those names. Var: Beni. (PEH-NEE)

PENI'AMINA Hawaiian form of Benjamin, a cognate of the Hebrew Binyamin, which is derived from *binyāmīn* (son of the right hand, favorite son). The name is borne in the Bible by the youngest of Jacob's twelve sons. He was the progenitor of the tribe of Benjamin. Var: Beniamina. Short: Beni, Peni. (PEH-NEE-AH-MEE-NAH)

PILA Hawaiian form of Bill, a short form of William (resolute protector). *See* WILLIAM (English Names). (PEE-LAH)

PILIPO Hawaiianized form of Phillip (lover of horses), a cognate of the Greek Philippos, which is composed from the elements *philos* (loving) and *hippos* (a horse). (PEE-LEE-PO)

POLOIKA Hawaiian form of Floyd, a variant of the Welsh Lloyd (gray), which arose from English attempts to pronounce the Welsh *ll*. Var: Foloida. (PO-LO-EE-KAH)

PONIPAKE Hawaiian form of Boniface (auspicious, fortunate, of good fate), which is from the Late Latin Bonifatius, a compounding of the elements *bona* (good, fair) and *ventura* (luck, fortune). Var: Bonifake. (PO-NEE-PAH-KEH)

PULUKE Hawaiian form of Bruce, a name originating as a surname from the French Brieuse (a locality in France). Var: Buruse. (POO-LOO-KEH)

PULUNO Hawaiian form of the German Bruno, a name derived from *brun* (brown). Var: Buruno. (BOO-ROO-NO)

PŪNĀWAI Derived from the Hawaiian *pūnāwi* (water, spring). (POO-NAH-WAH-EE)

ULEKI Hawaiian form of Ulysses, a Latin form of the Greek Odysseus (hater), which is from the root *dys* (hate). The name is borne in mythology by a king of Ithaca who was a Greek leader of the Trojan War and the hero of the *Odyssey*. Var: Ulesi. (OO-LEH-KEE)

WALAKA Hawaiianized form of Walter (ruler of the army), which is from the Old Norman French Waltier, a derivative of the Germanic Waldhere, a compound name composed of the elements *wald* (ruler) and *heri* (army). Var: Walata. (WAH-LAH-KAH, VAH-LAH-KAH)

WALELIANO Hawaiianized form of Valerian, which is from the Latin Valerianus (of Valerius). Valerius is an old Roman family name derived from *valere* (to be strong, to be healthy). (WAH-LEH-LEE-AH-NO, VAH-LEH-LEE-AH-NO)

WALENA Hawaiian form of Warren, the transferred use of the surname meaning "dweller at or keeper of a game preserve." The name is derived from the Old French *warenne* (a warren, a game preserve). (WAH-LEH-NAH, VAH-LEH-NAH)

WALENEKINO Hawaiianized form of Valentine, which is from the Latin Valentīnus, a derivative of *valens* (to be strong, to be healthy). The name was borne by a 3rd-century Roman saint and martyr whose feast day, February 14, coincides with that of a pagan festival marking the beginning of spring. Var: Walakino, Walekino. (WAH-LEH-NEH-KEE-NO, VAH-LEH-NEH-KEE-NO)

WIKOLI Hawaiianized form of the Latin Victor, a name directly derived from *victor* (conqueror, winner, victor). Var: Vitori. (VEE-KO-LEE)

WINIKENEKE Hawaiianized form of Vincent, which is from the Latin Vincentius (conquering), a derivative of *vincere* (to conquer). Var: Vinikeneke. (VEE-NEE-KEH-NEH-KEH)

Hawaiian Female Names

AGATA Hawaiian form of Agatha, a name derived from the Greek Agathē, which is from *agathos* (good, kind). The name was borne by a 3rd-century saint and martyr. Var: Akaka. (AH-GAH-TAH)

AGENETI Hawaiian form of Agnes, a cognate of the Greek Hagnē, which is derived from *hagnos* (pure, chaste). The name was borne by a thirteen-year-old Roman martyred for her Christian beliefs during the reign of Diocletian. Var: Akeneki. (AH-GEH-NEH-TEE)

AHONUI Derived from the Hawaiian *ahonui* (patient, enduring, patience), the literal translation of which is "great breath." (AH-HO-NOO-EE)

AHULANI Compound name meaning "heavenly shrine," which is composed of the elements *ahu* (altar, shrine, heap, pile) and *lani* (sky, heaven, heavenly, divine). Short: Lani. (AH-HOO-LAH-NEE)

'ĀINAKEA Compound name composed of the elements *'āina* (land, earth) and *kea* (white, clear, fair). (AH-EE-NAH-KEH-AH)

'ĀINALANI Compound name composed of the elements *'āina* (land, earth) and *lani* (sky, heaven, heavenly, spiritual): hence, "heavenly land." Short: Lani. (AH-EE-NAH-LAH-NEE)

'ĀINANANI Compound name composed of the elements *'āina* (land, earth) and *nani* (beauty, beautiful): hence, "beautiful land, land of beauty." Short: Nani. (AH-EE-NAH-NAH-NEE)

AIRINA Hawaiianized form of Irene, a cognate of the Greek Eirēnē, which is from *eirēnē* (peace). (AH-EE-REE-NAH)

AKA Hawaiian form of Ada, a name originating as a pet form of Adele and Adelaide, both of which mean "noble, nobility." (AH-KAH)

AKAHELE Derived from the Hawaiian *akahele* (careful, cautious). (AH-KAH-HEH-LEH)

AKALA Hawaiian form of Agatha, a name derived from the Greek Agathē, which is from *agathos* (good, kind). The name was borne by a 3rd-century saint and martyr. Var: Agata. (AH-KAH-LAH)

'ĀKALA Derived from the Hawaiian *'ākala* (raspberries, pink). (AH-KAH-LAH)

AKAMAI Derived from the Hawaiian *akamai* (wisdom). (AH-KAH-MAH-EE)

AKA'ULA Derived from the Hawaiian *aka'ula* (red sunset), a compounding of the elements *aka* (shadow) and *'ula* (red, scarlet). (AH-KAH-OO-LAH)

AKEAKAMAI Compound name composed of the elements *ake* (to desire, to yearn for) and *akamai* (wisdom): hence, "yearning for wisdom." (AH-KEH-AH-KAH-MAH-EE)

AKELAIKA Hawaiian form of Adelaide, a derivative of the Germanic Adalheid, which is composed of the elements *adal* (noble, nobility) and *heid* (kind, sort). Var: Adelaida. (AH-KEH-LAH-EE-KAH)

AKELINA Hawaiian form of the French Adeline, a diminutive form of Adèle, a French name that originated as a short form of any of the various old Germanic names beginning with the element *adal* (noble, nobility). Var: Adalina. (AH-KEH-LEE-NAH)

AKENAKA Hawaiian form of Asenath, an Aramaic name meaning "thornbush." The name is borne in the

Bible by the wife of Joseph and mother of Ephraim and Manasseh. Var: Asenata. (AH-KEH-NAH-KAH)

AKENEKI Hawaiian form of Agnes, a cognate of the Greek Hagnē, which is derived from *hagnos* (pure, chaste). The name was borne by a thirteen-year-old Roman martyred for her Christian beliefs during the reign of Diocletian. Var: Ageneti. (AH-KEH-NEH-KEE)

'ALA Derived from the Hawaiian *'ala* (fragrant, perfumed), the figurative meaning of which is "chiefly, esteemed, venerated." (AH-LAH)

ALANA Derived from *alana* (awakening, rising up, coming forward). (AH-LAH-NAH)

'ĀLANA Derived from the Hawaiian *'ālana* (offering; light, buoyant). (AH-LAH-NAH)

ALAPELA Hawaiian form of Arabella, an old Scottish name of uncertain etymology. Some believe it to have originally been a Norman name derived from the element *arn* (eagle) or *arin* (a hearth). Others think it a variant of Anabel, another name of uncertain origin and meaning. See ANNABEL (Scottish Names). Var: Arabela. (AH-LAH-PEH-LAH)

ALAULA Derived from *alaula* (light of dawn, sunrise or sunset glow). The word is derived from the elements *ala* (path, road, trail) and *ula* (flame). (AH-LAH-OO-LAH)

ALEKA Hawaiian form of Alice (nobility), a name that evolved through a series of variants of the Germanic Adalheidis (noble one). *See* ALIVE (English Names). Var: Alesa, Alika, Alisa. (AH-LEH-KAH)

ALEKANEKALIA Hawaiian form of Alexandrina, a feminine form of Alexander (defender or helper of mankind), which is composed from the Greek elements *alexein* (to defend, to help) and *andros* (man). Var: Alekanederina. (AH-LEH-KAH-NEH-KAH-LEE-AH)

ALEKIA Hawaiian form of Alethea, a name derived from the Greek *alētheia* (truth). Var: Aletea, Aletia. (AH-LEH-KEE-AH)

ALEMA Hawaiian form of Alma, a name derived from the Latin *almus* (nourishing, fostering), as well as from the Spanish *alma* (soul). (AH-LEH-MAH)

ALEPEKA Hawaiian form of Alberta (bright through nobility), the feminine form of Albert. *See* ALBERT (English Male Names). Var: Alebeta. (AH-LEH-PEH-KAH)

ALESA Hawaiianized form of Alica (nobility), a name that evolved from a series of variants of the Germanic Adalheidis (noble one). *See* ALICE (English Names). Var: Aleka, Alika, Alisa. (AH-LEH-SAH)

ALETIA Hawaiian form of Alethea, a name derived from the Greek *alētheia* (truth). Var: Alekia, Aletea. (AH-LEH-TEE-AH)

ALOHALANI Compound name composed of the elements *aloha* (love, to be loved, to love) and *lani* (sky, heaven, heavenly, spiritual, divine): hence, "divine love." Short: Lani. (AH-LO-HAH-LAH-NEE)

ALOHANANI Compound name composed of the elements *aloha* (love, to be loved, to love) and *nani* (beauty, beautiful): hence, "beautiful love." Short: Nani. (AH-LO-HAH-NAH-NEE)

'ALOHI Derived from the Hawaiian *'alohi* (to shine, to sparkle, bright, brilliant). (AH-LO-HEE)

'ALOHILANI Compound name composed from the elements *'alohi* (to shine, to sparkle, bright, brilliant) and *lani* (sky, heaven, heavenly, spiritual, divine): hence, "heavenly brilliance." Short: Lani. (AH-LO-HEE-LAH-NEE)

'ALOHINANI Compound name composed from the elements *'alohi* (to shine, to sparkle, bright, brilliant) and *nani* (beauty, beautiful): hence, "beautiful brightness." Short: Nani. (AH-LO-HEE-NAH-NEE)

'ĀLUNA Derived from the Hawaiian *'āluna* (descent). (AH-LOO-NAH)

AMELIA A borrowing from the English, Amelia is a variant of the Germanic Amalia, a name derived from *amal* (work). (AH-MEH-LEE-AH)

ANA Hawaiian form of Anna, a Latinate cognate of the Hebrew Hannah (gracious, full of grace, mercy). The variant form Anne was assigned during the Middle Ages to the mother of the Virgin Mary, as Joachim was assigned to her father. Var: Ane. (AH-NAH)

ANAKAKIA Hawaiian form of Anastasia, a name derived from the Greek *anastasis* (resurrection). Var: Anatasia. (AH-NAH-KAH-KEE-AH)

ANAKALIA Hawaiian form of Andrea, the feminine form of the Greek Andreas, which is derived from the element *andros* (man). Var: Anadaria. (AH-NAH-KAH-LEE-AH)

ANAKONIA Hawaiian form of Antonia, a feminine form of Anthony, which is of uncertain origin and meaning. "Priceless" and "of inestimable worth" are popular folk definitions. Var: Anatonia. (AH-NAH-KO-NEE-AH)

ANEKA Hawaiian form of Annette, a diminutive form of Anne (gracious, full of grace, mercy). *See* ANA. Var: Aneta. (AH-NEH-KAH)

Anela Hawaiian form of Angela, a name derived from *angel* (messenger of God, guiding spirit), which is ultimately from the Greek *angelos* (messenger). (AH-NAY-LAH)

Aniani Derived from the Hawaiian *aniani* (mirror, glass; clear; to blow softly). (AH-NEE-AH-NEE)

Anita Originally a Spanish pet form of Ana (gracious, full of grace, mercy), Anita is commonly bestowed in the English-speaking world as an independent given name. Var: Anika. (AH-NEE-TAH)

Anikala Hawaiianized form of Anitra, a literary coinage of Norwegian playwright and poet Henrik Ibsen (1828–1906). Anitra was the name given to the Eastern princess in his work *Peer Gynt*. Var: Anitara. (AH-NEE-TAH-RAH)

'Ano'i Derived from the Hawaiian *'ano'i* (beloved, desired, desire). (AH-NO-EE)

Ānuenue Derived from the Hawaiian *ānuenue* (rainbow). (AH-NOO-EH-NOO-EH)

Anuhea From the Hawaiian *anuhea* (cool; softly fragrant). (AH-NOO-HEH-AH)

Aolani Compound name composed of the elements *ao* (light, daylight, to dawn) and *lani* (sky, heaven, heavenly, spiritual, divine). There are several poetic definitions that can be derived from these elements; for example: "spiritual light, heavenly dawn." Short: Lani. (AH-O-LAH-NEE)

Aonani Compound name composed of the elements *ao* (light, daylight, to dawn) and *nani* (beauty, beautiful): hence, "beautiful light." Short: Nani. (AH-O-NAH-NEE)

'Apelila Hawaiianized form of April, which is derived from the name of the calendar month. April is from the Latin *aprilis* (second, latter). The ancient Roman calendar began with the month of March, with April being the second month. Var: 'Aperila. Short: Lila. (AH-PEH-REE-LAH)

Apī Hawaiian cognate of Abbie, a short form of Abegail (father of exaltation, father is rejoicing). Thus, Apī is a short form of Apika'ila, a Hawaiianized form of such. See ABEGAILA. (AH-PEE)

Apika'ila Hawaiian form of Abigail, a cognate of the Hebrew Avigayil, which is derived from *avīgayil* (father of exaltation, father is rejoicing). The name is borne in the Bible by one of the wives of King David. Var: Abegaila, Abigaila. Pet: Abbie, Apī. (AH-PEE-KAH-EE-LAH)

'Āpona Derived from the Hawaiian *'āpona* (embracing). (AH-PO-NAH)

Arabela Hawaiianized form of Arabella, an old Scottish name of uncertain etymology. Some believe it to have originally been a Norman name derived from the element *arn* (eagle) or *arin* (a hearth). Others think it a variant of Annabel, another name of uncertain origin and meaning. *See* ANNABEL (Scottish Names). Var: Alapela. (AH-RAH-BEH-LAH)

Asenata Hawaiianized form of Asenath, an Aramaic name meaning "thornbush." The name is borne in the Bible by the wife of Joseph and mother of Ephraim and Manasseh. Var: Akenaka. (AH-SEH-NAH-TAH)

Aukaka Hawaiianized form of Augusta, a feminine form of the Latin Augustus, which is from *august* (great, venerable). Var: Augata, Augusera. (AH-OO-GOO-KAH-KAH)

Aukele Hawaiianized form of Audrey (noble strength), a name derived from the Old English Ædelþryð, Æthelthryth, a compound name composed of the elements *æðel, æthel* (noble) and *þryð, thryth* (might, strength). Var: Audere. (AH-OO-KEH-LEH)

'Auina Derived from the Hawaiian *'auina* (bending, sloping, declining). Var: Auwina. (AH-OO-EE-NAH)

Aurelia A borrowing from the Latin, Aurelia is a feminine form of Aurēlius (golden), a name derived from *aurum* (gold). Var: Aulelia. Short: Lia. (AH-OO-REH-LEE-AH)

Bateseba Hawaiianized form of Bathsheba, an Anglicized form of the Hebrew Bat-Sheva (daughter of an oath). The name is borne in the Bible by a wife of King David and mother of Solomon. (BAH-TEH-SEH-BAH)

'E'epa Derived from the Hawaiian *'e'epa* (extraordinary, a person with miraculous or supernatural powers). (EH-EH-PAH)

Ekekela Hawaiian form of Esther, a name of debated origin. *See* ESTHER (English Names). Var: Eseta, Esetera. (EH-KEH-KEH-LAH)

Ekela Hawaiian form of Ethel, a name that originated as a short form of any of the various Old English names containing the element *œthel* (noble). Var: Etela. (EH-KEH-LAH)

'Ele Derived from the Hawaiian *'ele* (black). (EH-LEH)

'Ele'ele Derived from the Hawaiian *'ele'ele* (black, dark, the black color of Hawaiian eyes). (EH-LEH-EH-LEH)

'ELELE Derived from the Hawaiian *'elele* (messenger, delegate). (EH-LEH-LEH)

'ELEU From the Hawaiian *'eleu* (lively, active, vivacious). (EH-LEH-OO)

ELENOLA Hawaiian form of Eleanor, a name derived from Alienor, a Provençal form of the Greek Helenē, which is from the root *ēlē* (light, torch, bright). Var: Elenoa, Elenora, Elianora. Short: Nora. (EH-LEE-NO-LAH)

ELIKA Hawaiian form of the Scandinavian Erika, a feminine form of Erik (eternal ruler). *See* ERIKA (Scandinavian Names). (EH-LEE-KAH)

ELIKAPEKA Hawaiian form of Elizabeth, a name derived from the Hebrew *elīsheba'* (God is my oath). Var: Elisabeta. Short: Elekia, Elesi, Elisa, Kapeka, Laika. (EH-LEE-SAH-BEH-TAH)

EME Hawaiianized form of Amy, a derivative of the Middle English Amye, which is from the Old French Aimee (beloved), a name derived from the verb *aimer* (to love). Var: Ema. (EH-MEH)

EMELĒ Hawaiian form of Emily, an English cognate of the Latin Aemilia, a feminine form of Aemilius, an old Roman family name derived from *aemulus* (emulating, trying to equal or excel, rival). Var: Emalia, Emelia. Short: Lia. (EH-MEH-LAY)

EMELINA Hawaiian form of Emmeline, a variant of Emily formed by the addition of the diminutive suffix *-ine*. *See* EMELĒ. Var: Emalaina. (EH-MEH-LEE-NAH)

'ENA Derived from the Hawaiian *'ena* (red-hot, glowing, fiery). The figurative meaning of the word is "raging, fierce," a definition connoting intensity, determination, and strength. (EH-NAH)

'ENAKAI Compound name composed of the elements *'ena* (red-hot, glowing, fiery; fierce, raging) and *kai* (sea). (EH-NAH-KAH-EE)

ESETERA Hawaiianized form of Esther, a name of debated derivation. *See* ESTHER (English Names). The name is borne in the Bible by the Jewish wife of the Persian king Ahasuerus. Var: Ekekela, Eseta. (EH-SEH-TEH-RAH)

ETELA Hawaiianized form of Ethel, a name that originated as a short form of any of the various Old English names containing the element *æthel* (noble). Var: Ekela. (EH-TEH-LAH)

EUNIKA Hawaiian form of Eunice, an English cognate of the Greek Eunikē (fair victory), a compound name composed of the elements *eu* (good, well, fair) and *nikē* (victory). Var: Iunia. (EH-OO-NEE-KAH)

EWA Derived from the Hebrew Chava, which is from *hawwāh* (life). Var: Eva, Īwa. (EH-VAH)

EWALINA Hawaiian form of Evelyn, an English variant of Aveline, a French diminutive form of the Germanic Avila, which is ultimately of uncertain derivation. Var: Evalina. (EH-WAH-LEE-NAH)

EWANEKELINA Hawaiian form of Evangeline, a name coined from the Latin *evangelium* (good news, the gospel). Var: Euanelia, Evanegelina. (EH-WAH-NEH-KEH-LEE-NAH)

HA'IKŪ Derived from the name of a flower that was seen as a symbol of royalty. (HAH-EE-KOO)

HAKUMELE Compound name composed of the Hawaiian elements *haku* (lord, master) and *mele* (song, chant, poem): hence, "poet, composer, a master of songs, chants and poetry." (HAH-KOO-MEH-LEH)

HALEAKUA Compounding of the Hawaiian elements *hale* (house) and *akua* (God, goddess, spirit): hence, "house of God." (HAH-LEH-AH-KOO-AH)

HALIAKA Hawaiianized form of Harriet, an English form of the French Henriette, a feminine diminutive form of Henri (ruler of an enclosure, home ruler). *See* HENRY (French Male Names). Var: Hariaka, Hariata. (HAH-REE-AH-TAH)

HALOLANI Derived from the Hawaiian *halolani* (to move quietly, to move like a bird, to move like a soaring bird). The word is made up of the elements *halo* (motion of the hands or fins in swimming, the motion of rubbing) and *lani* (sky, heaven, heavenly, spiritual). (HAH-LO-LAH-NEE)

HANI Derived from the Hawaiian *hani* (light-footed, to move softly or gently, to touch). (HAH-NEE)

HAUKEA Derived from the Hawaiian *hau kea* (white snow, snow), a compounding of the elements *hau* (snow, cool, a cool breeze, icy) and *kea* (white, clear). (HAH-OO-KEH-AH)

HAULANI Compound name composed of *hau*, a prefix added to names of goddesses and common feminine names, and *lani* (sky, heaven, heavenly; royalty, aristocratic, majesty). Short: Lani. (HAH-OO-LAH-NEE)

HAUNANI Compound name composed of the prefix *hau* and *nani* (beauty, beautiful). Short: Nani. (HAH-OO-NAH-NEE)

HAU'OLI Derived from the Hawaiian *hau'oli* (joy, happiness, happy, glad, joyful). (HAH-OO-O-LEE)

HI'ILANI A compounding of the elements *hi'i* (to hold, to carry in the arms, to carry a child) and *lani* (sky, heaven, heavenly, spiritual, ruler, majesty): hence, "held in the arms of heaven." Short: Lani. (HEE-EE-LAH-NEE)

HILALIA Hawaiianized form of Hilary, a name derived from the Latin Hilaria, which is from *hilaris* (cheerful, noisy, merry). Short: Lia. (HEE-LAH-LEE-AH)

HIPAKEIKI Derived from the Hawaiian *hipa keiki* (a lamb), a compounding of the elements *hipa* (sheep) and *keiki* (child, offspring, kid, calf, colt). (HEE-PAH-KEH-EE-KEE)

HIWAHIWAKEIKI Compound name composed of the elements *hiwahiwa* (precious, beloved, esteemed) and *keiki* (child): hence, "beloved child, precious child." (HEE-WAH-HEE-WAH-KEH-EE-KEE)

HOAKA Derived from the Hawaiian *hoaka* (brightness, shiny, to glitter). (HO-AH-KAH)

HOALOHALANI Compounding of the elements *hoaloha* (friend, beloved companion) and *lani* (sky, heaven, heavenly, spiritual, divine, majesty, ruler): hence, "divine friend, majestic friend." Short: Lani. (HO-AH-LO-HAH-LAH-NEE)

HOALOHANANI Compounding of the elements *hoaloha* (friend, beloved companion) and *nani* (beauty, beautiful): hence, "beautiful friend." Short: Nani. (HO-AH-LO-HAH-NAH-NEE)

HŌKŪAO Derived from the Hawaiian *hōkūao* (morning star), a word composed of the elements *hōkū* (star) and *ao* (light, daylight, dawn). (HO-KOO-AH-O)

HŌKŪAONANI Compound name composed of the elements *hōkūao* (morning star) and *nani* (beauty, beautiful): hence, "beautiful morning star." Short: Nani. (HO-KOO-AH-O-NAH-NEE)

HŌKŪ'ALOHI Compound name composed from the elements *hōkū* (star) and *'alohi* (shining, bright, to sparkle): hence, "shining star." (HO-KOO-AH-LO-HEE)

HŌKŪLANI Compound name composed of the elements *hōkū* (star) and *lani* (sky, heaven, heavenly): hence, "heavenly star." Short: Lani. (HO-KOO-LAH-NEE)

HOLOMAKANI Derived from the Hawaiian *holomakani* (breezy, airy, windy), the literal translation of which is "wind running." Short: Kani, Makani. (HO-LO-MAH-KAH-NEE)

HONEKAKALA Derived from the Hawaiian *honekakala* (honeysuckle). (HO-NEH-KAH-KAH-LAH)

HO'OLANA Derived from the Hawaiian *ho'olana* (cheerful, hopeful, to cheer up). (HO-O-LAH-NAH)

HUALI From the Hawaiian *huali* (bright, polished, gleaming; pure, unsullied, morally pure). (HOO-AH-LEE)

IANEKE Hawaiianized form of Janet, a diminutive form of Jane, which is a feminine form of John (God is gracious). *See* KEONI (Male Names). Var: Ianete. (EE-AH-NEH-KEH)

IENIPA Hawaiianized form of Jennifer, a Cornish variant of Guinevere, which is from the Welsh Gwenhwyfar (fair lady). *See* GWENHWYFAR (Welsh Names). (EE-EH-NEE-PAH)

IKAPELA Hawaiian form of Isabella, a Spanish form of Elisabeth (God is my oath). Var: Isabela. (EE-KAH-PEH-LAH)

ILEINA Hawaiian form of Elaine, an English variant of Helen, which is derived from the Greek Helenē, the root of which is *ēlē* (light, torch, bright). (EE-LEH-EE-NAH)

IŌ'ANA Hawaiianized form of Joanna, the Middle Latin feminine form of Joannes (God is gracious), a name ultimately derived from the Hebrew *yehōhānān* (Yahweh is gracious). Var: Koana. (EE-O-AH-NAH)

IOKE Hawaiian form of Joyce, an evolution of the obsolete Jocosa, which is derived from the Latin *jocosa* (merry, happy). The name originated as a male name, but is now considered to be a female name. (EE-O-KEH)

IOKEPINA Hawaiian form of Josephine, a feminine form of Joseph, which is from the Hebrew Yōsēf (may God add, God will increase). Var: Iokepine, Iosepine. (EE-O-KEH-PEE-NAH)

IOLANA Hawaiian form of Yolanda, a name of uncertain etymology. Some believe it to be a derivative of Violante (violet), a medieval French name derived from the Latin Viola (violet). (EE-O-LAH-NAH)

'IOLANA Derived from the Hawaiian *'iolana* (to soar, to soar through the air as a bird). (EE-O-LAH-NAH)

IUKIKA Hawaiian form of Judith, a cognate of the Hebrew Jehudith and Yehudit (he will be praised). Alternatively, the name can also mean "from Judah." *See* JUDITH (English Names). Var: Iudita. (EE-OO-KEE-KAH)

IUKIKINA Hawaiian form of Justine, a feminine form of Justin, which is derived from the Latin Justinus, a name that has its root in *Justus* (rightful, proper, just). Var: Iusitina. (EE-OO-KEE-KEE-NAH)

IUKINIA Hawaiian form of Eugenia, a feminine form of the Greek Eugenios, which is derived from *eugenēs* (well-born, noble). Var: Iugina, Iuginia, Iukina. (EE-OO-KEE-NEE-AH)

IULALIA Hawaiian form of Eulalia (fair speech), a Latin and Greek name derived from the elements *eu* (good, well, fair) and *lalein* (to talk). Var: Ulalia. (EE-OO-LAH-LEE-AH)

IULIA Hawaiian form of Julia, a feminine form of the Latin Julius, an old Roman family name derived from Iulus (the first down on the chin, downy-bearded). Because a person just beginning to develop facial hair is young, "youth" became an accepted definition of the name. Var: Kulia. (EE-OO-LEE-AH)

IULIANA Hawaiian form of Julianna, an elaborate form of Julia (downy-bearded, youth). *See* IULIA. Var: Kuliana. (EE-OO-LEE-AH-NAH)

IUNE Hawaiian form of June, the name of the sixth month which is derived from the Latin Juno, the Roman mythological goddess of marriage and queen of the gods. (EE-OO-NEH)

IUSITINA Hawaiian form of Justine, a feminine form of Justin, which is from the Latin Justinus, a name that has its root in *justus* (rightful, proper, just). Var: Iukikina. (EE-OO-SEE-TEE-NAH)

KA'AONA Derived from the name of a Hawaiian month (June 7 to July 6). Traditionally, children born during this time were thought to be lovable, attractive, and friendly. (KAH-AH-O-NAH)

KAHŌKŪ Compounding of the elements *ka* (one, the one, the one in question) and *hōkū* (star). (KAH-HO-KOO)

KAIA Derived from the Hawaiian *kai* (the sea). (KAH-EE-AH)

KAILANI Compound name composed of the elements *kai* (the sea) and *lani* (SKY)

KAIMĀLIE Compound name composed of the elements *kai* (sea, sea water) and *mālie* (calm, still, gentle): hence, "calm seas." (KAH-EE-MAH-LEE-EH)

KAKALINA Hawaiian form of Catherine, a cognate of the Greek Aikaterinē, which is derived from *katharos* (pure, unsullied). Var: Kakarina, Katalina, Katarina. (KAH-KAH-LEE-NAH)

KAKIELEKEA Compound name composed of the elements *ka* (one, the one), *kiele* (gardenia), and *kea* (white, clear): hence, "the white gardenia." (KAH-KEE-EH-LEH-KEH-AH)

KALA Hawaiian form of Sarah, a name derived from the Hebrew *sārāh* (princess). Var: Kalai, Kela, Sara, Sarai. (KAH-LAH)

KALALA Hawaiianized form of Clara, a name derived from the Latin *clārus* (bright, clear, famous). Var: Kalara. (KAH-LAH-LAH)

KALALIKA Hawaiianized form of Clarice, an elaborated form of Clara, which is from the Latin *clārus* (bright, clear, famous). Var: Kalarisa. (KAH-LAH-LEE-KAH)

KALAMA Compound name composed of the elements *ka* (one, the one) and *lama* (light, torch, lamp). The name is suggestive of enlightenment. (KAH-LAH-MAH)

KALAMELA Hawaiianized form of the Spanish Carmen, a name derived from the Hebrew Carmel (vineyard, orchard). The name was originally bestowed in reference to the Virgin Mary, "Our Lady of Carmel." (KAH-LAH-MEH-LAH)

KALANA Hawaiianized form of Sharon, a name derived from the biblical place-name meaning "a plain, a flat area." In biblical times, Sharon was a fertile, coastal plain in Palestine where roses and oak trees grew in abundance. (KAH-LAH-NAH)

KALANI Compounding of the elements *ka* (one, the one) and *lani* (sky, heaven, heavenly, spiritual; highborn, aristocratic, noble). Short: Lani. (KAH-LAH-NEE)

KALAUKIA Hawaiianized form of Claudia, a name derived from the Latin Claudius, an old Roman family name derived from *claudus* (lame). Var: Kalaudia, Kelaudia, Kelaukia. (KAH-LAH-OO-KEE-AH)

KALAUKINA Hawaiianized form of Claudine, an elaboration of Claudia, which is from the Latin *claudus* (lame).Var: Kalaudina. (KAH-LAH-OO-KEE-NAH)

KĀLE Hawaiian form of Sally, a name originating as a pet form of Sarah (princess). Sally is now regarded as an independent given name. Var: Sale. (KAH-LEH)

KALENA Hawaiian form of Karen, which is the Dutch form of Katherine, a name ultimately derived from the Greek *katharos* (pure, unsullied). (KAH-LEH-NAH)

KALIKA Derived from the Hawaiian word for "silk." (KAH-LEE-KAH)

KALILINOE Compound name composed of the elements *ka* (one, the one) and *lilinoe* (fine mist, gentle rain, drizzle). (KAH-LEE-LEE-NO-EH)

KALINI Hawaiian form of Karen, a Danish form of Katherine, which is from the Greek Aikaterinē, a name derived from *katharos* (pure, unsullied). (KAH-LEE-NEE)

Kalino Compound name composed of the elements *ka* (one, the one) and *lino* (bright, shiny, brilliant, dazzling). (KAH-LEE-NO)

Kaliona Compound name composed of the elements *ka* (one, the one) and *liona* (lion). (KAH-LEE-O-NAH)

Kalola Hawaiian form of Carol, a feminine form of the Latin Carolus, a cognate of Charles (full-grown, a man). Alternatively, Carol is derived from *carol* (a joyous song, a carol). Var: Karola. (KAH-LO-LAH)

Kalolaina Hawaiian form of Caroline, a French feminine form of the Latin Carolus, a cognate of Charles (full-grown, a man). Var: Kalalaina, Kalolina, Karalaina, Karolaina, Kealalaina. (KAH-LO-LAH-EE-NAH)

Kaloka Hawaiian form of Carlotta, an Italian feminine form of Carlo (full-grown, a man). Var: Kalota. (KAH-LO-KAH)

Kaloke Hawaiian form of the French Charlotte, a feminine form of Charlot, which is a diminutive form of Charles (full-grown, a man). Var: Halaki, Harati, Kalote. (KAH-LO-KEH)

Kalolina Hawaiian form of Caroline, a French feminine form of the Latin Carolus, a cognate of Charles (full-grown, a man). Var: Kalalaina, Kalolaina, Karalaina, Karolaina, Kealalaina. (KAH-LO-LEE-NAH)

Kalome Hawaiian form of Salome, an Ecclesiastic Greek name derived from the Hebrew *shālōm* (peace). (KAH-LO-MEH)

Kamāla A compound name composed of the Hawaiian elements *ka* (one, the one) and *māla* (garden, plantation). (KAH-MAH-LAH)

Kameli Compounding of the elements *ka* (one, the one) and *meli* (bee, honeybee, honey). (KAH-MEH-LEE)

Kamelia Hawaiian form of the Spanish Carmelia, a name derived from the Hebrew Carmel (vineyard, orchard). Mount Carmel is a mountain in northwestern Israel which was inhabited in early Christian times by a group of hermits who later became Carmelite monks in the Order of Our Lady of Mount Carmel. The name was originally bestowed in honor of the Virgin Mary, "Our Lady of Carmel." Var: Komela. (KAH-MEH-LEE-AH)

Kamoana Compounding of the Hawaiian elements *ka* (one, the one) and *moana* (ocean, open sea). (KAH-MO-AH-NAH)

Kanani Compounding of the Hawaiian elements *ka* (one, the one) and *nani* (beauty, beautiful). Short: Nani. (KAH-NAH-NEE)

Kapika Hawaiian form of Tabitha, a name derived from the Aramaic *tabhītha* (roe, gazelle). The name is borne in the Bible by a woman who was brought back to life by St. Peter. Var: Tabita. (KAH-PEE-KAH)

Kaponianani Compound name meaning "beautiful anointed one," which is composed of the elements *ka* (one, the one), *poni* (to anoint, to consecrate, to crown), and *nani* (beauty, beautiful). Short: Nani. (KAH-PO-NEE-AH-NAH-NEE)

Kapua Compound name composed of the elements *ka* (one, the one) and *pua* (flower, blossom). (KAH-POO-AH)

Kapua'ula Compound name composed of the elements *ka* (one, the one), *pua* (flower, blossom), and *'ula* (red, scarlet): hence, "the red flower." (KAH-POO-AH-OO-LAH)

Kaulana Derived from the Hawaiian *kaulana* (famous, renowned). (KAH-OO-LAH-NAH)

Kauluwehi Compound name composed of the elements *ka* (one, the one) and *uluwehi* (lush, luxuriant growth of vegetation, richly verdant). (KAH-OO-LOO-WAY-HEE)

Kawaimomona Compound name meaning "sweet water," which is composed of the elements *ka* (one, the one), *wai* (water, fresh water), and *momona* (sweet). (KAH-WAH-EE-MO-MO-NAH)

Kawena Compounding of the elements *ka* (one, the one) and *wena* (glow, the glow of sunrise or sunset, the glow of a fire). (KAH-WEH-NAH)

Kawena'ula Compound name composed of the elements *ka* (one, the one), *wena* (glow, the glow of sunrise or sunset), and *'ula* (red, scarlet): hence, "red glow." (KAH-WEH-NAH-OO-LAH)

Kea Short form of any of the names containing *kea* as an element. (KEH-AH)

Kealani Compound name composed of the elements *kea* (white, clear) and *lani* (sky, heaven, heavenly, spiritual): hence, "clear sky." Short: Kea, Lani. (KEH-AH-LAH-NEE)

Kealoha Compounding of the elements *ke* (one, the one) and *aloha* (love, loved one, beloved, friend). Short: Kea. (KEH-AH-LO-HAH)

Ke'alohi Compounding of the elements *ke* (one, the one) and *'alohi* (shining). (KEH-AH-LO-HEE)

Keeaola Compound name meaning "breath of life," which is composed of the elements *ke* (one, the one), *ea* (life, breath, spirit), and *ola* (life, health). (KEH-EH-AH-O-LAH)

KEIKIKALANI Compound name composed of the elements *keiki* (child), *ka* (one, the one), and *lani* (sky, heaven, heavenly, spiritual, majesty): hence, "heavenly child." (KEH-EE-KEE-KAH-LAH-NEE)

KEKE Hawaiian form of Kate, a short form of Katherine, a cognate of the Greek Aikaterinē which is derived from *katharos* (pure, unsullied). Var: Kete. (KEH-KEH)

KEKEPANIA Hawaiian form of Stephanie, a cognate of the Latin Stephania, which is a variant of Stephana. Stephana is a feminine form of Stephanos, which is derived from the Greek *stephanos* (a crown, garland). Var: Setepania. (KEH-KEH-PAH-NEE-AH)

KEKILIA Hawaiianized form of Cecilia, a feminine form of Cecil, which is from the Latin Caecilius, an old Roman family name derived from *caecus* (blind, dim-sighted). Var: Kekila, Kikilia, Sesilia, Sisilia. (KEH-KEE-LEE-AH)

KELA Hawaiian form of Della, a feminine form of Dell, which is derived from the Old English *del* (a dell, a small valley or glen). Var: Dela. (KEH-LAH)

KELALANI Compound name composed of the elements *kela* (excelling, exceeding, far-reaching) and *lani* (sky, heaven, heavenly, spiritual, divine): hence, "the sky far above." The name can be indicative of spiritual growth. Var: Lani. (KEH-LAH-LAH-NEE)

KELEKA Hawaiianized form of Teresa, a name of uncertain etymology. It is generally believed to be derived from the Greek *therizein* (to reap, to gather in). Var: Kelekia. (KEH-LEH-KAH)

KELEKINA Hawaiian form of Celestina, an elaborated form of Celeste, a borrowing from the French, which is derived from *céleste*, which has its root in the Latin *caelestis* (celestial, heavenly). Var: Keletina. (KEH-LEH-KEE-NAH)

KELIA Hawaiian form of Delia, a short form of Cordelia, which is a name of uncertain derivation. *See* CORDELIA (English Names). Var: Delia. (KEH-LEE-AH)

KELINA Hawaiian form of Selene, a name derived from the Greek *selēnē* (the moon). The name was borne by the Greek mythological goddess of the moon. Var: Selina. (KEH-LEE-NAH)

KEOHI Derived from the Hawaiian elements *ke* (one, the one) and *ohi* (maiden, young lady just entering womanhood). (KEH-O-HEE)

KENIKE Hawaiian form of Denise, a feminine form of Dennis, which is an English cognate of the Greek Dionysios (a follower of the god Dionysos). Var: Denise. (KEH-NEE-KEH)

KEOLA Compounding of the Hawaiian elements *ke* (one, the one) and *ola* (life, health). (KEH-O-LAH)

KEOLAKUPAIANAHA Compound name meaning "wonderful life, miraculous life," which is composed of the elements *ke* (one, the one), *ola* (life, health), and *kupaianaha* (miraculous, wonderful). Short: Keola. (KEH-O-LAH-KOO-PAH-EE-AH-NAH-HAH)

KEOKINA Hawaiian form of Georgina, a feminine form of George, the English cognate of the Greek Geōrgios (earthworker, farmer), a compounding of the elements *gē* (earth) and *ergein* (to work). Var: Geogiana, Geogina, Keokiana. (KEH-O-KEE-NAH)

KIANA Hawaiian form of Diana, which is from the Latin *divus* (divine). Var: Diana. (KEE-AH-NAH)

KIELEKEA Compounding of the Hawaiian elements *kiele* (gardenia) and *kea* (white): hence, "white gardenia." (KEE-EH-LEH-KEH-AH)

KILIA Hawaiian form of Celia, a name derived from the Latin Caelia, a feminine form of the old Roman family name Caelius, which is thought to be a derivative of the Latin *caelum* (heaven). Celia is also used as a short form of Cecilia (blind, dim-sighted). (KEE-LEE-AH)

KILIKINA Hawaiian form of Christine, a name ultimately derived from the Greek *christianos* (a Christian, a follower of Christ). Var: Kirikina, Kiritina. (KEE-LEE-KEE-NAH)

KILIWA Hawaiian form of Sylvia, a feminine form of the Latin Silvius (of the woods), a name derived from *silva* (wood). Var: Silivia. (KEE-LEE-WAH)

KIMI Hawaiian form of Kim, a name originating as a short form of Kimberley, which is of debated origin. *See* KIMBERELY (English Names). (KEE-MEE)

KINA Hawaiian form of the Hebrew Dinah, a name derived from *dīnāh* (judged). Var: Dina. (KEE-NAH)

KINIKIA Hawaiian form of Cynthia, a cognate of the Latin and Greek Kynthia, a name of Artemis, the mythological goddess of the moon and hunting. The name has its root in Kynthios (from Kynthos, a mountain on the island of Delos). Var: Kinitia, Sinitia. (KEE-NEE-TEE-AH)

KIPILA Hawaiian form of Sibyl, a name derived from the Latin and Greek Sibylla (a fortune-teller, prophetess). The sibyls were women of ancient Greece and

Rome who were mouthpieces of the ancient oracles and seers into the future. Var: Kepila, Sebila, Sibila. (KEE-PEE-LAH)

KODELIA Hawaiian form of Cordelia, a name of uncertain derivation. It is believed to be from the Celtic Creiryddlydd (daughter of the sea). Var: Kokelia. Short: Lia. (KO-DEH-LEE-AH)

KOKELIA Hawaiian form of Cordelia, a name of uncertain derivation. It is believed to be from the Celtic Creiryddlydd (daughter of the sea). Var: Kodelia. Short: Lia. (KO-KEH-LEE-AH)

KOLEKA Hawaiian form of the Hebrew Dorcas (a gazelle). Var: Doreka. (KO-LEH-KAH)

KOLENELIA Hawaiian form of Cornelia, a feminine form of the Latin Cornelius, an old Roman family name of uncertain etymology. Some believe it to be from *cornu* (corn). Var: Korenelia. Short: Lia. (KO-LEH-NEH-LEE-AH)

KOLIKA Hawaiian form of Doris, a Greek name meaning "Dorian woman." The Dorians were one of the four main tribes of ancient Greece who settled in the mountainous area known as Doris. Var: Dorisa. (KO-LEE-KAH)

KOLINA Hawaiian form of Corinne, an English cognate of the Greek Korinna, a derivative of *korē* (maiden). Var: Korina. (KO-LEE-NAH)

KŌLINA Hawaiian form of Doreen, a variant of Dora (gift), formed by the addition of the Irish diminutive suffix–*een*. Var: Dorina. (KO-LEE-NAH)

KOLOE Hawaiian form of Chloe, an English cognate of the Greek Khloē (blooming, verdant). The name was used as a summer epithet of Demeter, the Greek goddess of agriculture and fertility. (KO-LO-EH)

KOLOKEA Hawaiian form of Dorothea (gift of God), which is derived from the Greek elements *dōron* (gift) and *theos* (God). Var: Dorotea, Kōleka. (KO-LO-KEH-AH)

KOLOLIA Hawaiian form of Gloria, a name derived from the Latin *glōria* (glory). Var: Goloria. (KO-LO-LEE-AH)

KONIA Hawaiian form of Sonya, a Russian pet form of Sofya (wisdom, skill). Var: Sonia. (KO-NEE-AH)

KOPEA Hawaiian form of Sophia, a Greek name derived from *Sophia* (wisdom, skill). Var: Kopaea, Sofaea, Sofia, Sopia. (KO-PEH-AH)

KŪALIʻI Compound name composed of the elements *kū* (like, resembling) and *aliʻi* (chieftess, queen, royalty). (KOO-AH-LEE-EE)

KUAULI Compound name from the elements *kua* (back) and *uli* (green). "Lush vegetation, verdant" is the figurative definition. (KOO-AH-OO-LEE)

KUKANA Hawaiian form of Susannah, a name derived from the Hebrew Shoshana, which is from *shōshannāh* (a lily, a rose). The name is borne in the Bible by a woman falsely accused of adultery. Her story is told in the apocryphal book of Susannah and the Elders. Var: Susana. Short: Kuke, Suke, Suse. (KOO-KAH-NAH)

KŪLANI Compound name composed of the elements *kū* (like, resembling; to stand, anchor, to stay, to reach, to rise up) and *lani* (sky, heaven, heavenly, spiritual; majesty). A number of poetic definitions can be derived from these elements, such as "heavenly" or "anchored in heaven." Var: Lani. (KOO-LAH-NEE)

KŪNANI Compounding of the elements *kū* (resembling, like) and *nani* (beauty, beautiful). Short: Nani. (KOO-NAH-NEE)

LĀHELA Hawaiian form of Rachel, a name derived from the Hebrew *rāchēl* (EWE). Var: Rahela. (LAH-HEH-LAH)

LALA Hawaiian form of Laura, a name derived from the Latin *laurus* (laurel). Var: Lara. (LAH-LAH)

LANA Short form of any of the names containing *lana* as an element. (LAH-NAH)

LANAKILA Derived from the Hawaiian *lanakila* (victory, conquest, to triumph). Short: Lana. (LAH-NAH-KEE-LAH)

LANI Derived from the popular Hawaiian word *lani* (sky, heaven, heavenly, spiritual, divine; majesty, noble). It is also used as a short form of any of the compound names containing *lani* as an element. (LAH-NEE)

LEILANI Compound name composed of the elements *lani* (sky, heaven, heavenly, spiritual; majesty) and *lei* (a wreath of flowers and leaves, garland): hence, "heavenly lei." Short: Lani. (LEH-EE-LAH-NEE)

LEINANI Compound name composed of the elements *lei* (a wreath of flowers and leaves, garland) and *nani* (beauty, beautiful): hence, "beautiful lei." Short: Nani. (LEH-EE-NAH-NEE)

LEOLANI Derived from the Hawaiian *leolani* (high, tall, lofty). Short: Lani. (LEH-O-LAH-NEE)

LEONANI Compound name composed of the elements *leo* (voice) and *nani* (beauty, beautiful): hence, "beautiful voice." Short: Nani. (LEH-O-NAH-NEE)

LEPEKA Hawaiian form of Rebecca, a name ultimately derived from the Hebrew *ribbqāh* (noose), which is from *rabak* (to bind, to tie). The name is borne in the Bible by the wife of Isaac. Var: Rebeka. (LEH-PEH-KAH)

LIA Short form of any of the names containing *lia* as an element. (LEE-AH)

LINA Short form of any of the names containing *lina* as an element. (LEE-NAH)

LOKA Hawaiian form of the Spanish Rosa, which is from *rosa* (red, a rose). (LO-KAH)

LŌKĀLIA Hawaiian form of Rosalia, which is derived from the Latin *rosalia* (the annual ceremony of hanging garlands of roses on tombs). (LO-KAH-LEE-AH)

LOKAPELE Hawaiian form of Rosabelle, a compounding of the names Rosa (red, a rose) and Belle (beautiful). Var: Lokapela, Rosabela. (LO-KAH-PEH-LEH)

LOKE Hawaiian form of Rhoda, a name derived from the Latin Rhode and the Greek Rhodē, which are from the Greek *rhodon* (a rose). Var: Roda, Rode. (LO-KEH)

LOKEMELE Hawaiian form of Rosemary, a combination of the names Rose and Mary. The name became popular in England at a time when flower names came into vogue, and it might therefore have originated as a borrowing of the name of the herb rosemary, which is derived from the Latin *ros marinus* (dew of the sea). Var: Rosemere. (LO-KEH-MEH-LEH)

LOKOMAIKA'I Derived from the Hawaiian *lokomaika'i* (generosity, benevolence, kindness). (LO-KO-MAH-EE-KAH-EE)

LOKOMAIKA'INANI Compound name composed of the elements *lokomaika'i* (generosity, benevolence, kindness) and *nani* (beauty, beautiful). Short: Nani. (LO-KO-MAH-EE-KAH-EE-NAH-NEE)

LOPEKA Hawaiian form of Roberta, a feminine form of Robert (bright fame). *See* LOPAKA (Male Names). Var: Robeta. (LO-PEH-KAH)

LUPE Hawaiian form of Ruby, a name taken from that of a deep red gem. Ruby is derived from the Latin *rubeus* (reddish) via the Old French *rubi*. Var: Rube. (LOO-PEH)

MADELINA Hawaiian form of Madeline, a cognate of the Ecclesiastic Greek Magdalēnē (of Magdala, a town on the Sea of Galilee). Var: Makelina. Short: Lina. (MAH-DEH-LEE-NAH)

MAIKA'I Derived from the Hawaiian *maika'i* (good, well, fine, handsome). (MAH-EE-KAH-EE)

MAILA Hawaiian form of Myra, a name coined by poet Fulke Greville (1554–1628) for use in his love poems. Some believe it to be a variant of the Irish Moyra; an anagram of Mary; a borrowing of the name of a seaport in ancient Lycia; or a deriviation of the Latin *myrrha* (myrrh). Var: Maira. (MAH-EE-RAH)

MAKA'ALOHI Compound name composed of the Hawaiian elements *maka* (eye, face) and *'alohi* (shining, to sparkle, bright): hence, "shining eyes." (MAH-KAH-AH-LO-HEE)

MAKALEKA Hawaiian form of Margaret, a cognate of the Greek Margarītēs, which is derived from *margaron* (a pearl). Var: Makalika. (MAH-KAH-LAY-KAH)

MAKANAAKUA Compound name composed of the elements *makana* (gift, present) and *akua* (God, goddess, spirit): hence, "gift of God." Short: Makana. (MAH-KAH-NAH-AH-KOO-AH)

MAKANAMAIKA'I Compound name composed of the elements *makana* (gift, present) and *maika'i* (good, well, fine): hence, "good gift." Short: Makana. (MAH-KAH-NAH-MAH-EE-KAH-EE)

MĀKELA Hawaiian form of Marcella, the feminine form of the Latin Marcellus, a diminutive form of Marcus, which is of uncertain derivation. *See* MALEKO (Male Names). Var: Masela. (MAH-KEH-LAH)

MAKELINA Hawaiian form of Madeline, a cognate of the Ecclesiastic Greek Magdalēnē (of Magdala, a town on the Sea of Galilee). Var: Madelina. Short: Lina. (MAH-KEH-LEE-NAH)

MĀLA Derived from *māla* (garden, plantation). (MAH-LAH)

MALAEA Hawaiian form of Mary and Maria, names derived from the Hebrew Miryām, which is of debated meaning. Many believe it to mean "sea of bitterness" or "sea of sorrow." However, some sources cite the alternative definition of "rebellion," "wished for child," and "mistress or lady of the sea." The name, borne in the Bible by the virgin mother of Jesus, has become one of the most enduringly popular names in the Christian world. Var: Malia, Maraea, Mele, Mere. (MAH-LAH-EH-AH)

MALAKA Hawaiian form of Martha, a name derived from the Aramaic *mārthā* (lady, mistress). The name is borne in the Bible by the sister of Lazarus and Mary of Bethany. Var: Maleka, Marata, Mareka. (MAH-LAH-KAH)

MALAKINA Hawaiian form of Martina, a feminine form of Martin (war-like), a name derived from Mars, the Roman mythological god of war. Var: Maratina. (MAH-LAH-KEE-NAH)

Mālalani Compounding of the elements *māla* (garden, plantation) and *lani* (sky, heaven, heavenly, spiritual, divine; majesty): hence, "heavenly garden." Short: Lani. (MAH-LAH-LAH-NEE)

Maliaka Hawaiian form of Marietta, an Italian diminutive form of Maria. *See* MALAEA. Var: Mariata, Meliaka, Meriata. (MAH-LEE-AH-KAH)

Maliana Hawaiian form of Marianne and Marian, both of which originated as variants of Marion, a French diminutive form of Marie, a cognate of Mary. *See* MALAEA. Var: Mariana, Meleana, Mereana. (MAH-LEE-AH-NAH)

Maluhia Derived from the Hawaiian *maluhia* (peace, serenity, calmness, quiet). (MAH-LOO-HEE-AH)

Manaali'i Compounding of the elements *mana* (strength, supernatural power) and *ali'i* (chieftess, queen, royalty, noble): hence, "noble strength." (MAH-NAH-AH-LEE-EE)

Manalani Compound name composed of the elements *mana* (strength, supernatural power) and *lani* (sky, heaven, heavenly, spiritual, divine; majesty): hence, "divine power." Short: Lani. (MAH-NAH-LAH-NEE)

Mana'o'i'o Derived from the Hawaiian *mana'o'i'o* (faith, hope, confidence, belief). (MAH-NAH-O-EE-O)

Mana'olana Derived from the Hawaiian *mana'olana* (hope, confidence, to have faith in something). The literal translation is "floating thought." Short: Lana. (MAH-NAH-O-LAH-NAH)

Mana'olanakeiki Compound name composed of the elements *mana'olana* (hope, confidence, faith) and *keiki* (child): hence, "child of hope." (MAH-NAH-O-LAH-NAH-KEH-EE-KEE)

Manawale'a Derived from the Hawaiian *manawale'a* (a generous heart, benevolent, charitable). (MAH-NAH-WAH-LEH-AH)

Māpuana Derived from the Hawaiian *māpuana* (fragrance, fragrant air, windblown fragrance). (MAH-POO-AH-NAH)

Mei Hawaiian form of May, a name originally used as a pet form of Margaret and Mary. More recently, however, it is usually associated with the name of the fifth month, which is derived from the Latin *Maius* (the month of Maia, the Greek mythological goddess of increase).Var: Mahina. (MEH-EE)

Meli Derived from the Hawaiian *meli* (bee, honeybee). (MEH-LEE)

Melelina Hawaiian form of Marilyn, a modern name composed of the names Mary and Lynn (lake) Var: Merelina. Short: Lina. (MEH-LEH-LEE-NAH)

Melika Hawaiian form of Melissa, a name derived from the Greek *melissa* (a bee). The 16th-century poet Ariosto used the name for the good fairy who protected Bradamante and helped Ruggero escape from Atlante upon the hippogriff in the poem *Orlando Furioso*. Var: Melisa. (MEH-LEE-KAH)

Mikala Hawaiian form of Michelle, the French feminine form of Michael, a name derived from the Hebrew *mīkhā'ēl* (who is like God?). (MEE-KAH-LAH)

Mikilana Derived from the Hawaiian name of the Chinese rice flower, an attractive shrub having shiny leaves and fragrant blossoms. Var: Misilana. Short: Lana. (MEE-KEE-LAH-NAH)

Milena Hawaiian form of Myrna, an Anglicized form of the Irish Muirne (affection, beloved). Var: Mirena. (MEE-LEH-NAH)

Mili Short form of any of the names containing *mili* as an element. (MEE-LEE)

Miliama Hawaiian form of Miriam, a Hebrew name of debated meaning. *See* MALAEA. Var: Miriama. (MEE-LEE-AH-MAH)

Mililani Derived from the Hawaiian *mililani* (to praise, to glorify, to exalt, to give thanks). Short: Lani, Mili. (MEE-LEE-LAH-NEE)

Milimili Derived from the Hawaiian *milimili* (toy; beloved). Short: Mili. (MEE-LEE-MEE-LEE)

Milikena Hawaiian form of Millicent, a name derived from the obsolete Old High German Amalswinth (work strength), a compounding of the elements *amal* (work) and *swinth* (strength). Var: Milisena. Short: Mili. (MEE-LEE-KEH-NAH)

Miulana From the Hawaiian name of tall, attractive trees from the Himalayas which are related to the magnolia. (MEE-OO-LAH-NAH)

Moana Derived from the Hawaiian *moana* (ocean, open sea). (MO-AH-NAH)

Moananani Compound name composed of the elements *moana* (ocean, open sea) and *nani* (beauty, beautiful): hence, "beautiful sea." Short: Nani. (MO-AH-NAH-NAH-NEE)

Moani Derived from the Hawaiian *moani* (gentle breeze, a light, fragrant breeze). (MO-AH-NEE)

MOHALA Derived from the Hawaiian *mohala* (blossoming, flowering, opening up). (MO-HAH-LAH)

NAI'A Derived from the Hawaiian *nai'a* (dolphin, porpoise). (NAH-EE-AH)

NALUKEA Compound name composed of the elements *nalu* (wave, surf) and *kea* (white, clear): hence, "white wave." (NAH-LOO-KEH-AH)

NĀNĀLĀ Derived from the Hawaiian *nānālā* (sunflower), the literal translation of which is "sun gazer." (NAH-NAH-LAH)

NANEKA Hawaiian form of Nanette, a diminutive form of Nan, which is a pet form of Ann and a short form of Nancy. *See* NANEKI. Var: Naneta. Short: Nan. (NAH-NEH-KAH)

NANEKI Hawaiian form of Nancy, a name that originated as a pet form of Nan, which was originally a pet form of Ann (gracious, full of grace, mercy). Now, however, Nancy is regarded as an independent given name, with Nan as its short form. Short: Nan. (NAH-NEH-KEE)

NANI Derived from the Hawaiian *nani* (beauty, beautiful). Nani is also used as a short form of any of the compound names using it as an element. (NAH-NEE)

NANIAHIAHI Compound name composed of the elements *nani* (beauty, beautiful) and *ahiahi* (evening, to become evening): hence, "evening beauty." Short: Nani. (NAH-NEE-AH-HEE-AH-HEE)

NOELANI Compound name composed of the elements *noe* (mist, vapor) and *lani* (sky, heaven, heavenly): hence, "heavenly mist." Short: Lani. (NO-EH-LAH-NEE)

PAKELIKIA Hawaiian form of Patricia, the feminine form of Patrick, a name derived from the Latin *patricius* (a patrician, an aristocrat). Var: Paterekia. (PAH-KEH-LEE-KEE-AH)

PALAKIKA Hawaiian form of Frances, a French feminine form of Franceis (a Frank, from the Frankish Empire). Var: Farakika. (PAH-LAH-KEE-KAH)

PALAPALA Hawaiian form of Barbara (foreign woman), a Latin name derived from *barbarus* (foreign, strange), a term applied to non-Romans or those deemed to be uncivilized. Var: Barabara. (PAH-LAH-PAH-LAH)

PEAKALIKA Hawaiian form of Beatrice, a variant of the Latin Beatrix (she who makes happy, she who brings happiness), which is derived from *beātus* (happy, blessed). Var: Beatarisa, Biatirisa, Piakilika. (PEH-AH-KAH-LEE-KAH)

PELEKA Hawaiian form of the German Bertha, a name that originated as a short form of various Old German compound names containing the element *beraht* (bright, famous). Var: Bereta. Pet: Beke. (PEH-LEH-KAH)

PELEKILA Hawaiian form of Priscilla, a diminutive form of the Latin Prisca, a feminine form of Priscus, which is a Roman surname derived from *priscus* (ancient, primitive). Var: Peresekila, Peresila, Perisila. (PEH-LEH-KEE-LAH)

PELENAKINO Hawaiian form of Bernadette and Bernardine, feminine forms of Bernard (bold or strong as a bear), which is from the Old High German Berinhard, a compounding of the elements *bern* (bear) and *hard* (hearty, strong, brave, bold). Var: Berenadeta, Berenadino. (PEH-LEH-NAH-KEE-NO)

PELIKA Hawaiian form of Freda, a name that originated as a short form of any of the various old names containing the element *frid* (peace) or pryđ (strength). Var: Ferida. (PEH-LEE-KAH)

PELULIO Hawaiian form of Beryl, a name derived from the name of the pale green gemstone which includes emeralds and aquamarine. Beryl is derived from the Greek *bēryllos* (a sea-green gem), which is from the Prakrit *veruliya* and the Dravidian *veluriya* (from the city of Vēlur). Var: Berulo. (PEH-LOO-LEE-O)

PILIKI Hawaiian form of the Greek Phyllis, a name derived from *phyllon* (a leaf). The name is borne in Greek mythology by a girl who hanged herself for love and was transformed into an almond tree. (PEE-LEE-KEE)

PILIKIKA Hawaiian form of Bridget, an Anglicized form of the Gaelic Bríghid, a name believed to be derived from *brígh* (strength). See BRÍGHID (Irish Names). Var: Birigita. (PEE-LEE-KEE-KAH)

PILIPA Hawaiian form of Philippa, a feminine form of Philip, which is from the Greek Philipos (lover of horses), a compounding of the elements *philos* (loving) and *hippos* (horse). (PEE-LEE-PAH)

PINEKI Derived from *pineki*, the Hawaiian word for "peanut." (PEE-NEH-KEE)

POLEKE Hawaiian form of Paulette, a feminine diminutive form of Paul, a name derived from the old Roman family name Paulus (small). Var: Polete. (PO-LEH-TEH)

POLINA Hawaiian form of Pauline, a feminine diminutive form of Paul (small). (PO-LEE-NAH)

POLOLA Hawaiian form of Flora, a name derived from the Latin *floris* (a flower). The name is borne in Roman mythology by the goddess of flowers and spring. Var: Felora, Folora. (PO-LO-LAH)

POLOLENA Hawaiian form of Florence, a medieval English form of the Latin Florentia, which is derived from *florens* (blooming, flourishing, prosperous). Var: Felorena. (PO-LO-LEH-NAH)

PŌMAIKAʻI Derived from the Hawaiian *pōmaikaʻi* (lucky, fortunate, blessed). (PO-MAH-EE-KAH-EE)

PUA Derived from the Hawaiian *pua* (flower, blossom). Pua is also used as a short form of any of the names containing it as an element. (POO-AH)

PUAKAI Compounding of the Hawaiian elements *pua* (flower, blossom) and *kai* (sea, ocean): hence, "ocean flower." Short: Pua. (POO-AH-KAH-EE)

PUAKEA Compound name composed of the Hawaiian elements *pua* (flower, blossom) and *kea* (white, clear): hence, "white flower." Short: Pua. (POO-AH-KEH-AH)

PUALANI Compound name composed of the elements *pua* (flower, blossom) and *lani* (sky, heaven, heavenly, spiritual, divine; majesty, royal). Many poetic definitions can be derived from these elements, such as "heavenly flower" and "royal blossom." Short: Lani, Pua. (POO-AH-LAH-NEE)

PUANANI Compounding of the popular elements *pua* (flower, blossom) and *nani* (beauty, beautiful): hence, "beautiful flower, flower of beauty." Short: Nani, Pua. (POO-AH-NAH-NEE)

RUTA Hawaiian form of Ruth, a name of uncertain etymology. Most believe it to be derived from the Hebrew *ruth*, a possible contraction of *reʻuth* (companion, friend). The name is borne in the Bible by a Moabite woman who was devoted to her mother-in-law. Her story is told in the Book of Ruth. (ROO-TAH)

WALANIKA Hawaiian form of Veronica, a name of debated origin and meaning. *See* VERONICA (English Names). Var: Varonika, Walonika, Welonika. (WAH-LAH-NEE-KAH)

WANAʻAO Derived from the Hawaiian *wanaʻao* (dawn, sunrise, to dawn). (VAH-NAH-AH-O, WAH-NAH-AH-O)

WANAʻAONANI Compound name composed of the Hawaiian elements *wanaʻao* (dawn, sunrise, to dawn) and *nani* (beauty, beautiful): hence, "beautiful dawn." Short: Nani. (VAH-NAH-AH-O-NAH-NEE, WAH-NAH-AH-O-NAH-NEE)

WANAKA Hawaiian form of Wanda, a name of uncertain etymology. It is generally believed to be of Germanic origin, perhaps from *vond* (wand, stem) or from *Wend*, a term denoting a member of the old Slavic people who live in an enclave south of Berlin. (VAH-NAH-KAH, WAH-NAH-KAH)

WANIKA Hawaiian form of the Spanish Juanita, a diminutive form of Juana, which is the feminine form of Juan, the Spanish cognate of John (God is gracious). Var: Wanita. (WAH-NEE-KAH)

WELENA Hawaiian form of Verna, a 19th-century English coinage used as a feminine form of Vernon, a name that originated from the French baronial surname de Vernon (of Vernon). Var: Verena. (WEH-LEH-NAH)

WIKOLIA Hawaiian form of Victoria, a name derived from the Latin *Victoria* (victory). Var: Vitoria. (WEE-KO-LEE-AH)

WILA Hawaiian form of Vera, an English cognate of the Russian Vjera (faith). Var: Vira. (WEE-LAH)

CHAPTER TWELVE

Hindu/Indian Names

SINCE ANCIENT times, Hindu children have been given as many as three names, one of which is secret and unspoken. At least one of the names, preferably the everyday name, should be taken from the names of the gods, who are manifestations of the One God. In Hindu belief, God is manifest in all things, and the names of all things are the names of God. Thus, many names are derived from common words. To these root words are also added various popular suffixes. There are some five dozen terminations for male names, but only around ten suffixes for female names.

Most of the other Hindu and Sanskrit names that do not reflect the names of gods or have a religious meaning fall into several other categories: nature names, personal or abstract qualities, occupational names, and names from common words.

A child born after the death of a sibling may be given a name designed to keep evil spirits away. Such a name is invariably disgusting, in the hopes that the spirits will believe that the child, too, is repellent and stay away from it.

In some parts of India, it is common practice to mention a person's caste with his name, so as to distinguish between people of the same name. Some castes state the father's name first, and some castes add a surname for designation.

Hindu/Indian Male Names

AADI Derived from the Sanskrit *aadi* (first, beginning, initial). (AH-DEE)

AAKAV Shape, form. (AH-KAHV)

AAKESH Lord of the sky. (AH-KESH, AH-KAYSH)

AAKIL Intelligent, smart. (AH-KIL)

AALOK Light of God, divine light. (AH-LOK)

AAMIN Grace of God, divine grace. (AH-MIN)

AANAN Face, countenance. (AH-NAN)

AANDALEEB A borrowing of the native name of the bulbul bird. (AHN-DAH-LEEB)

AATMADEVA God of the soul. (AHT-MAH-DAY-VAH)

AATMIK Sanskrit name meaning "the soul." (AHT-MIK)

ABBAS Of Arabic origin derived from *'abbās* (austere). (AB-BAS)

ABDUL Of Arabic origin, this name is composed from *'abd* (servant of) and *al* (the): hence, "the servant." Abdul is used most commonly as the first element in compound names. (AB-DUL)

ABDULLAH Of Arabic origin, Abdullah is composed of the elements *'abd* (servant of) and *Allāh* (God): hence, "servant of Allah." Var: Abdulla. (AB-DUL-LAH)

ABHIRAJA Sanskrit compound name meaning "great king," which is composed of the elements *abhi* (great, eminent) and *raja* (king, ruler). (AB-HEE-RAH-JAH)

ADAMYA Sanskrit name meaning "formidable, difficult, stern." (AH-DAM-YAH)

ADHEESHA Emperor, king. (AD-HEE-SHA)

ADHIDEVA Compound name meaning "supreme god." (AD-HEE-DAY-VAH)

ADITYA The sun. Var: Aaditya. (AH-DIH-TEE-AH)

AGASTYA Of uncertain meaning borne by the patron saint of southern India. In the 6th or 7th century B.C. he led the movement of his people to the south, crossing the Vindhaya Mountains. He is said to have been the first teacher of literature and science in the south, and was a key figure in the development of Tamil language and literature. (AH-GAHS-TEE-AH)

AHARNISH Day and night. (AH-HAR-NISH)

AHSAN Gratitude, thankfulness. (AH-SAHN)

AILESH Popular name meaning "king of the earth, ruler of all." (Ā-LESH)

AJANABH A mountain. Ajanabh is a name of Vishnu. (AJ-AN-AHB)

AJIT Derived from the Sanskrit *a* (not) and *jitu* (conquered): hence, "unconquered; invincible." Ajit is another name form of Shiva and Vishnu. (AH-JEET)

AKALANKA Uncolored, stainless. The name was borne by the Jain logician Akalanka Bhatta (711–75). He lived during the reign of Krishnaraja and authored *Rajavatika.* (AK-AH-LAN-KAH)

AKBAR Of uncertain meaning, Akbar was the name borne by a Muslim king known as Akbar the Great (1542–1605). He was responsible for abolishing the pilgrim tax and the poll tax, and for establishing a liberal religious policy under which all religions were respected. These measures helped in the unification and expansion of his empire. He is also remembered for his patronage to the arts and literature and for his contribution to public works. (AK-BAR)

AKHIL King. (AHK-HEEL)

AKHILENDRA Compound name meaning "king of the universe, lord of the universe." (AK-HEE-LEN-DRAH)

AKILESH King of all, lord of all. (AK-EE-LESH)

AKSHAN Eye. (AK-SHAN)

AKSHAY Sanskrit name meaning "eternal, immortal, indestructable." (AK-SHAY)

AMAL Clean, pure, unsullied. (AH-MAHL)

AMALESH Derived from *amal* (clean, pure, unsullied). (AH-MAH-LESH)

AMAR Sanskrit name meaning "immortal." (AH-MAHR)

AMIL Derived from *amil* (unobtainable, inaccessible). (AH-MIL)

AMUL Priceless, of inestimable worth. (AH-MUL)

ANADI Sanskrit name meaning "God, omnipotent, the one with no beginning and no end." Var: Anaadi. (AN-AH-DEE)

ANAND Popular name derived from *ānanda* (joy, delight). (AH-NAND)

ANANTA An Indian name meaning "infinite," Ananta is also a name of the god Vishnu. (AH-NAN-TAH)

ANANYA Sanskrit name meaning "unique." (AH-NAHN-YAH)

ANDAL Of uncertain meaning borne by the Vaishnavite sage and poet of the 8th or 9th century. (AHN-DAHL)

ANIL Air, wind. (AH-NIL)

ANJAY Unconquerable. (AHN-JAY)

ANJUM Popular name meaning "token." (AHN-JOOM)

ANKUR Bud, bloom, sprout. (AHN-KUR)

ANSHU Popular name meaning "sunbeam, a ray of the sun." Var: Anshul. (AHN-SHOO)

ARJUN Derived from the Sanskrit *arjuna* (white, the color of milk). (AR-JOON)

ARSHAD Sanskrit name meaning "pious, devout." (AR-SHAHD)

ARUN Popular name derived from the Sanskrit *aruna* (rust-colored, reddish, reddish brown). (AH-ROON)

ARVIND Derived from the Sanskrit *arvind* (red lotus). Var: Aravinda, Arvinda, Aurobindo. (AR-VEEND)

ARYABHATA Borne by the 5th-century Indian astronomer and author of the *Aryabhatiyum,* in which he proposed his theories of astronomy. He maintained that the earth is round and was the first astronomer to deduce that the motion of the heavens was a result of the earth rotating on its axis. (AR-YAB-HAH-TAH)

ASEEM Popular name meaning "infinite, endless, eternity." (AH-SEEM)

Ashoka Sanskrit name meaning "without sorrow." Var: Ashok. (AH-SHO-KAH)

Ashvaghosha The sound of the horse. The name was borne by a 2nd-century philosopher who promoted his philosophy called *Tahat*. He was also an accomplished author and playwright and a composer of beautiful music. The name is composed of the elements *ash* (horse) and *ghosh* (announcer). (ASH-VAH-GO-SHA)

Atyaananda Compound name meaning "intense joy." (AT-YAH-AH-NAHN-DAH)

Avanindra Compound name meaning "lord of the earth." (AH-VAN-IN-DRA)

Avikar Derived from the Sanskrit *avikar* (faultless, perfection). (AH-VEE-KAR)

Baasu Wealthy. (BAH-SOO)

Babar Popular name derived from the Turkish *bābar* (lion). Babar was a name of Zahir ud-Din Muhammad (c. 1482–1530), the first Mogul ruler of India, whose forces defeated those of the sultan of Delhi in 1526. Var: Baber. (BAH-BAR)

Badar Derived from the Arabic Badr, which is from *badr* (full moon). (BA-DAR)

Bala Derived from the Sanskrit *bāla* (child, youth). The name is also used as a popular element in compound names. Var: Balen, Balu, Balun. (BAY-LAH)

Balabhadra Compound name composed of the Sanskrit elements *bala* (strength) and *bhadra* (auspicious, fortunate). Balabhadra is a name of Baldev, the elder brother of Krishna. Pet: Balu. (BAH-LAH-BAHD-RAH)

Balakrishna Compound name composed of the Sanskrit element *bāla* (young) and Krishna (the name of the Hindu deity). (BAY-LAH-KRISH-NAH)

Baldev From the Sanskrit elements *bala* (strength) and *deva* (a god): hence, "god of strength." The name was borne by the elder brother of Krishna, also known as Balarama and Balabhadra, who is considered the seventh incarnation of Vishnu. Vishnu took two of his hairs, a black one and a white one. Krishna was formed from the black hair and Baldev from the white. (BAL-DAYV)

Balraj Compound name composed of the Sanskrit elements *bala* (strength) and *raja* (king): hence, "king of strength." (BAH-LAH-RAJ)

Balu Derived from the Sanskrit *bāla* (child, youth). Balu is used both as an independent given name and as a short form of any of the various names beginning with the element *bāla*. (BAY-LOO)

Basant Spring. (BAH-SANT)

Bhakati Devotion. (BAH-KAH-TEE)

Bhanu The sun. (BAH-NOO)

Bharat From the Sanskrit *bharata* (being maintained). The name was borne by the son of King Dushyanta, who was the patriarch of the Pandavas and the Kauravas, which fought each other in the *Mahabharata* war. The name was also borne by the younger brother of Rama, who ruled the kingdom in Rama's name until his brother returned from exile, and by an ancient sage from whom the country of India got its name of Bharat. (BAH-RAHT)

Bhaskara Derived from the Sanskrit *bhās* (light) and *kara* (making): hence, "making light, shining, the sun." The name was borne by the astronomer and mathematician Bhaskaracharya (1114–?), Bhaskara the Teacher. He authored the *Siddhanta Shiromani*, a great work dealing with arithmetic, algebra, and astronomy. His accuracy and accomplishments are a marvel to the modern world. Var: Bhaskar. (BAS-KAH-RAH)

Bhasvan Lustrous. Derived from the Sanskrit *bhās* (light). (BAS-VAHN)

Bhaswar Lustrous. Derived from the Sanskrit *bhās* (light). (BAS-WAHR)

Bhavnish Sanskrit name meaning "king." (BAHV-NISH)

Bhoja Borne by a king (995–1055) and military leader known for having also been an accomplished scholar, poet, and builder. During Bhoja's reign, many temples and a college for Sanskrit studies were built, and it was he who conceived of turning the Vindhya hills into a green paradise. This was accomplished by damming the Betwa Valley to create the lake Bhoja Pal, now known as Bhopal. (BOH-JA)

Bishvajit Compound name meaning "conqueror of the universe." (BISH-VAH-JIT)

Brahma Derived from the Sanskrit *brahman* (worship, prayer). Brahma is the name of the creator of the universe, the chief member of the trinity of Brahma, Vishnu, and Siva, and the eternal and supreme essence and spirit of the universe. In Indian history, the name was borne by Brahmagupta (598–668), a mathematician and astronomer. He developed the concept of zero, was the first mathematician to use second-order differences, and the first to use algebra to solve astronomy problems. (BRAH-MAH)

Chaitanya Consciousness. The name was borne by one of the greatest of the Vaishnavite saints (1486–1533). He preached a philosophy of love and devotion to Krishna, and maintained that those, along with song and dance, would produce a state of ecstasy in which the personal influence of God could be attained. The chant "Hare Krishna, Hare Krishna" and *namasamkirtana* (the chanting of names) are attributed to Chaitanya. (CHĪ-TAN-YAH)

CHAND Derived from the Sanskrit *candra* (the moon, shining). Chand is used as a short form of any of the various names containing this element as well as an independent given name. Var: Chanda. (CHAND)

CHANDAK Moonlight. Derived from the Sanskrit *candra* (the moon, shining). Short: Chand. (CHAN-DAK)

CHANDAN Derived from the Sanskrit *candana* (the sandalwood tree). The wood is made into a paste which is used to make a mark on the forehead of Hindu worshipers. (CHAN-DAN)

CHANDRA Derived from the Sanskrit *candra* (the moon, shining). The name was borne by a son of Krishna. Var: Chander. Short: Chand, Chanda. (CHAN-DRAH)

CHANDRABHA Luster of moonlight. Derived from the Sanskrit *candra* (the moon, shining). (CHAN-DRAB-AH)

CHANDRAK Moonlight. Derived from the Sanskrit *candra* (the moon, shining). (CHAN-DRAK)

CHANDRAKANT Compound name composed of the Sanskrit elements *candra* (the moon, shining) and *kānta* (beloved): hence, "beloved of the moon." Short: Chand, Chanda. In Indian mythology, the Chandrakant (the Moonstone) is a gemstone supposedly formed by a congelation of moonlight and said to have a cooling and settling effect on the body. (CHAN-DRAH-KANT)

CHANDRAN Moonlight. Derived from the Sanskrit *candra* (the moon, shining). (CHAND-RAN)

CHANDRARAJ Compound name composed of the Sanskrit elements *candra* (the moon, shining) and *raja* (king): hence, "king of the moon." (CHAN-DRAH-RAJ)

CHANDRESH Compound name composed of the elements *candra* (the moon, shining) and *īśa* (ruler, king): hence, "ruler of the moon." (CHAN-DRESH)

CHARAKA Wanderer. The name was borne by a physician of the 2nd century B.C. who revised the *Agnivesha Samhita*, which came to be known as the *Charaka Samhita*, a compilation of medical information which defines the causes and symptoms of disease. It is an in-depth work, covering the subjects of anatomy, etiology, physiology, pathology, treatment, objectives, the influences of age and season, physicians, the use of medicines and appliances, procedure and sequence, conception, birth, and physical deformities. He advocated having a sound body and mind, proper prenatal care, and a good diet. (CHAR-AH-KAH)

CHARUDATTA Derived from the Sanskrit *charu* (beautiful). (CHAR-OO-DAH-TAH)

CHARVAKA Derived from the Sanskrit *charu* (beautiful). The name was borne by the radical materialist philosopher who proposed that when the body dies, so does the soul. His philosophy promoted an atheistic, permissive, and perhaps lascivious lifestyle. (CHAR-VAH-KAH)

CHINTAK Thoughtful, thinking. (CHIN-TAK)

CHIRANJIV Long-lived, one who has a long life. (CHEE-RAN-JIV)

CHIRAYU Long-lived, a long life. (CHEE-RAY-OO)

DAIVAT Strength, power. (DAY-VAT)

DAIVIK Godly, divine. (DAY-VIK)

DALJEET Conqueror of a troop. (DAHL-JEET)

DAMODAR Compound name meaning "rope around the belly." It is composed of the elements *dāma* (rope) and *udara* (belly). The name arose from a tale of Krishna as a child. His foster mother tied him to a large vessel to keep him out of mischief, but he dragged it around with superhuman strength until it was caught between two trees and uprooted them. (DAM-O-DAR)

DANVEER Generous. Derived from the Sanskrit *dāna* (gift). (DAN-VEER)

DARSHAN Vision. Derived from the Sanskrit *darsha* (to see, to perceive). (DAR-SHAHN)

DAUD Derived from the Arabic Dawūd, a cognate of the Hebrew David, which is derived from *dāvīd* (beloved). (DAH-OOD)

DAYANAND Compound name composed of the elements *dayā* (compassion) and *anand* (joy, delight): hence, "one who takes delight in being compassionate." (DAY-AN-AND)

DAYARAM Compound name composed of the elements *dayā* (compassion) and *rama* (pleasing). The name is indicative of Rama's compassion for others. *See* RAMA. (DAY-AH-RAHM)

DESHAD Derived from *desh* (nation, country). (DEH-SHAHD)

DESHAL National. Derived from *desh* (nation, country). (DEH-SHAL)

DESHAN Derived from *desh* (nation, country). (DEH-SHAN)

DEVAK Divine, god-like. From the Sanskrit root *deva* (a god). (DAYV-AK)

DEVAL Divine, god-like; temple. From the Sanskrit root *deva* (a god). (DAYV-AHL)

DEVANAND Compound name composed of the Sanskrit elements *deva* (a god) and *anand* (joy, delight): hence, "joy of the gods." (DAYV-AH-NAND)

DEVDAN Derived from the Sanskrit Devadāna (gift of the gods), which is from the elements *deva* (a god) and *dāna* (gift). Var: Debdan, Deodan. (DAYV-DANE)

DEVDAS Derived from the Sanskrit elements *deva* (a god) and *dāsa* (servant, slave): hence, "servant of the gods." (DAYV-DAS)

DEVEN Derived from the Sanskrit *deva* (a god). The name is a name of the god Indra. (DAYV-EN)

DEVENDRA Compounding of the element *deva* (a god) and Indra, the name of the god of the atmosphere and sky, the lord of the sky-gods. (DAYV-EN-DRAH)

DEVMANI Compound name derived from the elements *deva* (a god) and *mani* (jewel): hence, "jewel of the gods." (DAYV-MAH-NEE)

DEVRAJ Compounding of the elements *deva* (a god) and *raja* (king, ruler): hence, "king of the gods." (DAYV-RAJ)

DHAVAL Derived from *dhavala* (white, pure white). (DAH-VAHL)

DHAVLEN Derived from *dhavala* (white, pure white). (DAHV-LEN)

DHAVLESH Compounding of the elements *dhavala* (white, pure white) and *īśa* (lord, god): hence, "god of white." Dhavlesh is a name of Shiva. (DAHV-LESH)

DHIMANI From the Sanskrit meaning "intellectual." Var: Dheemant, Dhimant. (DEE-MAH-NEE)

DILIP Of uncertain derivation, some think Dilip is from the Sanskrit elements *dilī* (Delhi, the name of a territory and city in northern India) and *pa* (protecting, guarding): hence, "protector of Delhi." The name was borne by many kings in classical texts. (DIL-IP)

DINENDRA Compound name composed of the Sanskrit elements *dina* (day) and Indra, a name element referring to the god of the sky and atmosphere: hence, "lord of the day." (DIN-EN-DRAH)

DINESH Compound name composed of the Sanskrit elements *dina* (day) and *īśa* (lord): hence, "lord of the day." *Dinesh* is also used as a vocabulary word denoting the sun. (DIH-NESH)

DIPAK Derived from the Sanskrit *dīpa* (light, lamp) and *-ka*, which is both a diminutive suffix and a suffix indicating a type or characteristic: hence, "little lamp" or "like a lamp; shining, bright." Dipak is a name of Kama, the god of love. Var: Deepak. (DEE-PAK)

DIVYENDU The moon. (DIV-YEN-DOO)

EHAN Expected. (Ā-HAN)

EKAANTA Solitude, seclusion. (Ā-KAHN-TAH)

ESMAIL Hindu form of Ishmael, which is derived from the Hebrew *yishmā'ēl* (God hears). (EES-MAY-EL)

EVAN Equal, even. Var: Evak. (Ā-VAN)

FAHIM Derived from the Arabic *fahīm* (intelligent, learned), which is from *fahima* (to understand). (FAH-HEEM)

FAKHRUDDIN Derived from the Arabic Fakhr-al-Dīn (glory of the faith), a compounding of the elements *fakhr* (glory, pride), *al* (the), and *dīn* (religion, faith). (FAHK-ROOD-DIN)

FALAK Sky, the heavens. (FAL-AK)

FALAN Popular name meaning "to be fruitful, to be productive." Var: Faleen, Falit. (FAL-AN)

FAREED Derived from the Arabic *farīd* (unique), which is from the verb *farada* (to be unique). (FAH-REED)

FARUQ Derived from the Arabic *farūq* (a person who distinguishes right from wrong and truth from falsehood). Var: Farook, Farooq. (FAH-ROOK)

FIRDOS Derived from the Arabic *firdaws* (paradise). The name was borne by the Persian poet and historian Firdausi (c. 940–1020). He wrote the *Shah Namah* (Book of Kings), a voluminous work about the history of Persia before the arrival of the Arabs. Var: Firdaus, Firdose, Firdoze. (FIR-DOS)

FIROZ Derived from the Arabic *firoz* (victorious). Var: Feroz, Feroze, Firuz. (FEE-ROZ)

GANESH Compounding of the Sanskrit elements *gana* (multitude, throng) and *īśa* (lord): hence, "lord of the multitude." The name is borne by the Hindu god of wisdom, who is depicted with the head of an elephant and the body of a short, fat man. (GAH-NESH)

GARJANA A shout, a loud cry. (GAR-JAH-NAH)

GAURAV Pride. (GAU-RAV)

GAUTAMA Descendant of Gotama. *See* GOTAM. The name was borne by a famous logician, the author of the *Nyaya Sutra*, who lived before the time of Buddha. He was the son of Rahukana and the husband of Ahalya. Var: Gautam. (GAU-TAH-MAH)

GHOSHAL Announcer. Var: Ghochil. (GO-SHAHL)

GIRISH Lord of the mountain. Girish is a name of Shiva, so given because of his dwelling place in the Himalayan Mountains. (GIR-ISH)

GOBIND Variant form of Govind (one who finds cows). The name was borne by Gobind Rai (1666–1708), the son of Guru Tegh Bahadur, the ninth guru of the Sikhs. After his father was martyred at the hands of the Mogul emperor Aurangzeb in 1675, Gobind Rai succeeded his father, becoming the tenth guru of the Sikhs. He became known as Guru Gobind Singh, a leader who managed to unite his people and give them hope and promise for the future. Var: Gobinda. (GO-BIND)

GOPAL Derived from the Sanskrit *go* (cow) and *pala* (protector): hence, "protector of cows." Gopal is another name of Krishna. (GO-PAHL)

GOTAM Compound name composed of the Sanskrit elements *go* (cow) and *-tama*, a suffix denoting superiority: hence, "the finest cow." The name was borne by several historical figures, including the founder of the Nyana system of philosophy. (GO-TAHM)

GOVIND One who finds cows. Composed of the Sanskrit elements *go* (cow) and *-vinda* (finding). It is a name of Krishna. Var: Govinda. (GO-VIND)

GULSHAN Popular name meaning "garden." (GUL-SHAHN)

GUNADHYA Rich in virtues. The name was borne by a 1st-century B.C. writer, the author of the *Brihatkatha* (Great Romance), a collection of stories and fables written in Paishachi, the common man's language. Var: Gunaadhya. (GUN-AD-HYAH)

GURUDATTA Compound name composed of the elements *guru* (guru, spiritual adviser or teacher) and *dāna* (gift): hence, "gift of the guru." (GOO-ROO-DAH-TAH)

GYAN Derived from the Sanskrit *gyan* (knowledge). Var: Gyani. (GĪ-AN)

GYANDEV Compounding of the elements *gyan* (knowledge) and *deva* (a god): hence, "god of knowledge." (GĪ-AN-DEV)

HAFEEZ Derived from the Arabic *hāfiz* (guardian). (HAH-FEEZ)

HAIDAR Popular name derived from the Arabic *haidar* (lion). Var: Haider, Haydar, Hayder, Hyder. (HĪ-DAR)

HALA Borne by the 2nd-century poet and author of *Sattasati*, which is also known as *Gatha Saptasati*, a major work of love verses written in Prakit. (HAH-LAH)

HAMID Derived from the Arabic *hāmid* (praising, thankful), which is from *hamida* (to praise, to commend). (HAH-MEED)

HANS Derived from the Sanskrit *hans* (swan). In addition to being an independent given name, Hans is used as a short form of any of the various names formed with this element. (HANS)

HANSRAJ Compound name composed of the Sanskrit elements *hans* (swan) and *raja* (king): hence, "king of the swans." Short: Hans. (HANS-RAJ)

HARI Derived from the Sanskrit *hari*, a word of many definitions. It denotes a color of yellow, green or brown, a monkey, the sun, the wind, and several other things. It is most commonly used as a name of Vishnu, Krishna, and Shiva. (HAH-REE)

HARINDER Derived from the Sanskrit Hari (a name of Vishnu) and Indra (the name of the chief diety of the sky). (HAH-RIN-DER)

HARISH Compounding of the Sanskrit Hari (a name of Vishnu) and *īśa* (lord): hence, "lord Vishnu." Var: Haresh. (HAR-ISH)

HARJEET Victorious. (HAR-JEET)

HARSHAD Giver of joy, giver of happiness. Harshad is derived from *harsha* (joy, delight). (HAR-SHAD)

HARSHAL Joyful, happy. From the Sanskrit *harsha* (joy, delight). Var: Harshil, Harshul. (HAR-SHAL)

HARUN Derived from the Arabic *harūn* (exalted, lofty). The name was borne by the caliph of Baghdad Harūn al-Rashid (786–809), who was responsible for bringing in Hindu physicians to organize hospitals and medical schools in Baghdad. Var: Haroun. (HAH-ROON)

HASAN Derived from the Arabic *hasan* (beautiful, handsome, good). Var: Hasin. (HAH-SAHN)

HASTIN Elephant. (HAHS-TIN)

HEMACHANDRA Compound name composed of the elements *hema* (gold) and *chandra* (the moon, shining): hence, "the golden moon." The name was borne by Hemachandra Suri (1089–1172), a Jain monk and author of *Trisati Salaka Purusha Charita* (The Lives of 63 Great Men). (HEM-AH-CHAND-RAH)

HIMESH A name of Shiva, Himesh means "king of the snow." (HIH-MESH)

Ibrahim Derived from the Arabic Ibrāhīm, a cognate of the Hebrew Avraham (father of many, father of a multitude). He was the father of Ishmail, whose descendants are the Arabs. Abraham and Ishmail built the sacred Kaaba temple at Mecca which contains a black stone supposedly given to Abraham by the angel Gabriel. Var: Ebrahim. (IB-RAY-HEEM)

Iishim Spring, springtime. (EE-SHIM)

Indra Of uncertain derivation borne by the god of the atmosphere and sky, the lord of the sky-gods. Indra is more commonly used as an element in compound names. (IN-DRAH)

Indrajit Compound name composed of Indra, the name of the chief deity of the sky, and *-jit,* a suffix derived from *ji* (to conquer): hence, "the conqueror of Indra." The name is borne in the *Ramayana* by the son of Ravana, the demon king. (IN-DRAH-JIT)

Indrayan Derived from Indra, the name of the chief deity of the sky and atmosphere. The name is also that of a river. (IN-DRAH-YAN)

Isha Derived from the Sanskrit *īśa* (lord), a word that is also used as a common element in compound names. (ISH-AH)

Ishaan Meaning "the sun," Ishaan is also the name of one of the compass directions. Var: Ishan. (ISH-AHN)

Ishara An indication. (ISH-A-RAH)

Israj Compound name composed of the elements *īśa* (lord) and *raja* (king): hence, "king of the gods." (IS-RAJ)

Jabbar Derived from the Arabic *jābir* (comforter, bringer of consolation). (JAB-BAR)

Jafar Derived from the Arabic *ja'far* (stream). *See* JA'FAR (Arabic Names). Var: Jaffer. (JAH-FAR)

Jagannath Compound name composed from the Sanskrit elements *jagat* (world) and *nāntha* (lord): hence, "lord of the world." Jagannath, a name used for several of the gods, was borne by the father of Chaitanya, a Vaishnavite saint. (JAG-AN-NATH)

Jagdish Derived from the Sanskrit *jagat* (world) and *īśa* (lord): hence, "lord of the world." (JAHG-DEESH)

Jagjit Derived from the Sanskrit *jagajjit* (conqueror of the world). (JAG-JIT)

Jahan Derived from the Sanskrit *jahān* (the world). (JAH-HAHN)

Jahangir Derived from the Sanskrit *jahān* (the world) and *gir* (holder): hence, "holder of the world." (JAH-HAHN-GEER)

Jaidev Compound name composed of the elements *jaya* (victory) and *deva* (a god): hence, "victory of god." (JAY-DAYV)

Jaimini Derived from the Sanskrit *jaya* (victory). It was borne by a philosopher who was a pupil of Vyasa. Jaimini authored the *Mimansa Sutra* and promoted his philosophy called the *Purva Mimansa.* (JAY-MIH-NEE)

Jainendra Compound name composed of *jaya* (victory) and Indra, the name of the lord of the sky-gods: hence, "victory of Indra." Var: Jinendra. (JAY-NEN-DRAH)

Jairaj Compound name composed of the elements *jaya* (victory) and *raja* (lord): hence, "victory of the lord." (JAY-RAJ)

Jaladhi Ocean. (JAL-AD-HEE)

Jalal Derived from the Arabic *jalāl* (greatness). Var: Jalil. (JAH-LAL)

Janak Derived from the Sanskrit *jānaka* (descendant of Janaka). (JANE-AK)

Janesh Compound name composed from the elements *jān* (life, being) and *īśa* (lord): hence, "lord of the people." (JANE-ESH)

Jawaharlal Derived from the Sanskrit *jaya* (victory). The name was borne by the first prime minister of India, Jawaharlal Nehru (1889–1964). He became a follower of Gandhi and entered into Indian politics. Nehru took the mantle of leadership from Gandhi after a Hindu zealot gunned Mohatma down in 1948. He led his country with a philosophy of goodwill and harmony, a policy that led to India's being taken advantage of by several countries. After cultivating a friendship with China and supporting them before the United Nations, Jawaharlal Nehru was bitterly betrayed when China invaded India and forced the Indian Army to retreat. Disheartened and humiliated, Nehru died in 1964 after a brief illness. (JAH-WAH-HAR-LAL)

Jay Derived from the Sanskrit *jaya* (victory), Jay is also commonly used as an element in compound names. It was borne by a 12th-century poet, Jayadeva, who authored the *Gitagovindam,* a masterpiece in which Govinda (Krishna) is extolled through songs. Var: Jai. (JAY)

Jayakrishna Compound name composed from *jaya* (victory) and Krishna, the name of one of the most popular of the Hindu deities: hence, "victorious Krishna." (JAY-AH-KREESH-NAH)

Jayant Derived from the Sanskrit *jayanta* (victorious). (JAY-YANT)

JAYWANT Derived from the Sanskrit *jayavant* (possessing victory). (JAY-WANT)

JITENDRA "Conqueror of Indra." Jitendra is a compounding of the elements *jita* (conquered) and Indra, the chief sky-god. Var: Jeetendra, Jitender. (JIH-TANE-DRAH)

JIVAN Life. (JIH-VAN)

JOHAR Jewel. (JO-HAR)

JVALANT Sanskrit name meaning "bright, shiny." Var: Jwalant. (JVAH-LANT)

KABIR Borne by an Indian spiritual leader (1440–1519) who opposed casteism and preached universal equality and brotherhood. He worked at unifying Islam and Hinduism in an effort to bring about social and religious harmony. (KAH-BIR)

KADIR Derived from the Arabic *qadir* (capable). Al-Qādir (the Capable) is one of the ninety-nine attributes of Allāh. (KAY-DIR)

KALHANA Borne by a 12th-century historian and poet who authored the *Rajatarangini*, a narrative poem that relates the history of Kashmir. (KAL-HAH-NAH)

KALIDASA Compound name meaning "servant of the goddess Kali." It is composed of *kālī* (the black one) and *dāsa* (servant, slave). The name was borne by one of India's preeminent poets and dramatists, whose work is known for its perfection. According to legend, Kalidasa was very dense and it was through the grace of the goddess Kali that he received the gift of skillful writing. Var: Kalidas. (KAY-LEE-DAS-SAH)

KALINGA A bird. (KAH-LIN-GAH)

KALU Borne by the father of Nanak, the founder of the Sikh religion. (KAH-LOO)

KAMAL Derived from the Sanskrit *kamala* (lotus). (KAH-MAL)

KAMBAN Tamil name borne by a 12th-century poet who authored the Tamil *Ramayanam*, which is also known as the *Kamba Ramayanam*. (KAM-BAN)

KAMIL Derived from the Arabic *kāmil* (perfect), which is from *kamula* (to be perfect). (KAY-MIL)

KANU A name of Krishna, Kanu means "beautiful." (KAH-NOO)

KAPILA Derived from the Sanskrit *kapila* (monkey, monkey-colored). The name was borne by an ancient philosopher, the author of the *Samkhya* philosophy. Var: Kapil. (KAH-PIL-AH)

KARAN Derived from the Sanskrit *karna* (ear). (KAR-AHN)

KARDAMA Borne by the father of Kapila, the philosopher and author of the *Samkhya* philosophy. (KAR-DAH-MAH)

KARIM Derived from the Arabic *karīm* (noble, generous). The word also denotes jewels or precious stones, so the name can also mean something precious or valuable. Var: Kareem. (KAH-REEM)

KARNAK An auricle of the heart. (KAR-NAK)

KARNIK In control. (KAR-NIK)

KASI Derived from the Sanskrit *kāśi* (shining). (KAY-SEE)

KAVI Derived from the Sanskrit *kavi* (poet). (KAV-EE)

KAVINDRA Compound name composed of *kavi* (poet) and Indra, the name of the chief sky-god: hence, "lord of the poets." (KAV-IN-DRAH)

KESAVA A name of Vishnu meaning "hairy." His hair was composed of the rays of the sun. (KEH-SAH-VAH)

KHALID Derived from the Arabic *khālid* (eternal, undying). Var: Khaleed. (KAH-LEED)

KHALIL Derived from the Arabic *khalīl* (best friend, confidant). Var: Kaleel. (KAH-LEEL)

KHARAVELA Borne by the third king of the Cheta dynasty of Kalinga. He is remembered for expanding his empire's borders, his public works, and his respect of and tolerance for his people. (KAR-AH-VAY-LAH)

KHWAJA Muslim name derived from the Persian *khwaja* (lord, master). The name was borne by Khwaja Moinuddin Chishti (12th century), considered by many to be the greatest Sufi saint of India. (KWAH-JAH)

KIRAN Derived from the Sanskrit *kirana* (a ray of light). (KIR-AN)

KRISHNA Derived from the Sanskrit *krsna* (black, dark). The name is borne by one of the greatest of the Hindu gods. Because of a prophecy that a son of King Vasudeva would kill King Kamsa, Vasudeva's first six sons were murdered. The seventh child was miraculously transferred from the womb of Devaki to another woman, thus saving the child's life. After Krishna was born, he was secretly given to a cowherd's family in exchange for a female child. Later, King Kamsa seized the female baby, leaving Krishna in safety. He revealed himself as the incarnation of the supreme god on the eve of the *Mahabharata* war. Var: Kannan, Kishen, Kistna. (KRISH-NAH)

KUMAR Derived from the Sanskrit *kumāra* (boy, son). (KOO-MAR)

LAHAR A small wave. (LAH-HAR)

LAKSHMAN Prosperous, auspicious. Derived from *lakṣmana* (having auspicious marks). The name was borne by a loyal half brother of Rama, the embodiment of brotherly love. (LAK-SHMAHN)

LAKSHMIDAS Derived from Lakshmi (the name of Vishnu), the goddess of beauty, abundance, and prosperity and *dāsa* (servant, slave): hence, "a servant of the goddess Lakshmi." (LAK-SHMEE-DAS)

LATIF Derived from the Arabic *latīf* (kind, gentle). Var: Lateef. (LAH-TEEF)

LAVANAA Luster, shine. (LAH-VAN-AH)

LAVESH A small particle. (LAH-VESH)

LOCHAN Eyes. (LO-CHAN)

MAALIN One wearing a garland. (MAH-LIN)

MADHAV Derived from the Sanskrit *mādhava* (vernal, youthful, fresh). It was borne by Madhvacharya (1199–1278), one of the three main Vedantic philosophers. He is famous for his philosophy, *Dvaita* (dualism), in which he maintained that time, space, matter, and soul are subordinate to and dependent upon God. He urged Harihara I to found the Vijayanagar empire and served as prime minister to Harihara annd Bukka. Var: Madhava. (MAD-HAHV)

MAHADEV Compound name composed of the elements *mahā* (great) and *deva* (a god): hence, "the great god." (MAH-HAH-DAYV)

MAHARAJ Compound name composed of the elements *mahā* (great) and *raja* (king): hence, "great king." (MAH-HAH-RAJ)

MAHAVIRA Compound name composed of the elements *mahā* (great) and *vīra* (hero): hence, "the great hero." Mahavir is a common name for several of the gods. Var: Mahavir. (MAH-HAH-VEE-RAH)

MAHENDRA Compound name composed of the elements *mahā* (great) and Indra, the name of the chief god of the sky and atmosphere: hence, "great Indra." (MAH-HEN-DRAH)

MAHESH Compound name composed of the Sanskrit *mahā* (great) and *īśa* (ruler): hence, "great ruler." Mahesh is a name of Shiva. (MAH-HESH)

MAHIN Derived from the Sanskrit element *mahā* (great). (MAH-HIN)

MAHMOUD Derived from the Arabic *mahmūd* (praiseworthy). Var: Mahmood, Mehmood, Mehmoud, Mehmud. (MAH-MOOD)

MAJID Derived from the Arabic *mājid* (glorious, illustrious). Var: Majeed. (MAH-JEED)

MALIK Popular name meaning "king." Var: Mallik. (MAL-LIK)

MANSOOR Derived from the Arabic *mansūr* (victorious). (MAN-SOOR)

MANU Man. It is one of the names of Vishnu. The name was borne by the author of the *Manusmriti*, the ethical code and social hierarchy that guided Indian society for centuries. (MAH-NOO)

MILAN Meeting, union. (MIH-LAN)

MOHAJIT Derived from the Sanskrit *mohana* (attractive, bewitching). (MO-HAH-JIT)

MOHAN Derived from the Sanskrit *mohana* (attractive, one who attracts, bewitching). It is a name of Krishna. (MO-HAHN)

MOHANDAS Compounding of the Sanskrit elements *mohana* (attractive, one who attracts, bewitching) and *dāsa* (servant, slave): hence, "servant of Mohan." The name was borne by Indian leader Mohandas Karamchand Gandhi (1869–1948), also known as Mahatma Gandhi. Foremost, he was a man of peace, and is remembered for his deep concern for the underprivileged masses and for his protest against untouchability. He set up many programs for education and rural reconstruction, and set out to improve hygiene and living conditions for the poor. He was leader of the Indian National Congress and worked for Indian independence, being jailed many times for organizing *satyagraha* (passive resistance) movements and initiating civil disobedience. He was shot and killed in 1948 by a Hindu zealot who was upset by Gandhi's tolerance for Muslims. (MO-HAHN-DAS)

MOHANSHU Derived from the Sanskrit *mohana* (attractive). (MO-HAHN-SHOO)

NADIM Derived from the Arabic *nadīm* (drinking companion, friend). Var: Nadeem. (NAH-DEEM)

NAGARJUNA Borne by a philosopher, metaphysician, and author who lived in the 2nd century. Nagarjuna was instrumental in spreading Buddhism throughout India, and the famous Nagarjunakonda monasteries are named in his honor. (NAH-GAR-JOO-NAH)

NALIN Lotus. (NAH-LIN)

NANAK Borne by the founder of the Sikh faith. Nanak (1469–1539) was spiritually inclined from a young age, preferring the contemplation of philosophy to more practical pursuits. His religion promoted belief in and total surrender to one omnipotent god, purity of mind and body, equality of mankind, and good works. (NAN-AK)

NANDAN Derived from *nanda* (joy, delight, happiness). Var: Nandin. (NAN-DAN)

NARAYANA Derived from the Sanskrit *nara* (male, a man), Narayana is a name of Vishnu. Var: Narayan. (NAH-RAY-AH-NAH)

NAREN The best among men. Derived from the Sanskrit *nara* (male, a man). (NAR-EN)

NARENDRA Derived from the Sanskrit *nara* (man) and Indra, the name of the chief god of the sky. (NAH-REHN-DRA)

NARESH Compound name composed of the elements *nara* (male, a man) and *īśa* (ruler): hence "ruler of men." (NAH-RESH)

NAVEED Derived from the Persian *naveed* (good wishes, glad tidings). (NAH-VEED)

NEEL Blue, sapphire blue. Neel was the name of a monkey chief in Rama's army. (NEEL)

NEELENDRA Compound name composed of the elements *neel* (blue, sapphire blue) and Indra, the name of the chief sky-god. The name has the definition "lord of the oceans." (NEE-LEN-DRAH)

NEELMANI Compound name composed of the elements *neel* (blue, sapphire blue) and *mani* (jewel): hence, "a blue sapphire." (NEEL-MAH-NEE)

NIAZ Derived from the Persian *niāz* (offering, a gift). (NEE-AZ)

NIRVAN Derived from the Sanskrit *nirvāna* (a blowing out). The name is indicative of the supreme bliss achieved from the extinction of the human existence and the absorption of the soul into the supreme spirit. It is also indicative of a state or place of extreme bliss and peace. (NIR-VAHN)

NISHAD Taken from the name of the seventh note of an octave. (NIH-SHAD)

NOOR Derived from the Arabic *nūr* (light, illumination). (NOOR)

NUREN Radiance. Derived from the Arabic *nūr* (light, illumination). (NOOR-EN)

OMANAND Compound name composed of *om*, a sacred syllable used in meditation, and *anand* (joy): hence, "joy of om." (OM-AH-NAND)

PANINI Derived from the old family name Panis. Panini was a grammarian who developed a complete grammatical system which was incorporated into the Sanskrit language. (PAN-EE-NEE)

PARVAIZ Derived from the Persian *parvaiz* (fortunate, auspicious, happy, excellent). Var: Parvez, Parviz, Parwiz. (PAR-VAZE)

PATANJALI One fallen in the palm. The name was borne by the 2nd-century B.C. creator of *Yoga*. He explained his system in the *Yog Sutra*. (PAH-TAHN-JAH-LEE)

PRABHAT Derived from *prabhā* (light), Prabhat has the definition "dawn, morning light." (PRAB-HAT)

PRADEEP Derived from *pradīpa* (light). (PRA-DEEP)

PRADOSH Derived from the Sanskrit *pradośa* (light). The name is indicative of nightfall or twilight. (PRA-DOSH)

PRAKASH Derived from the Sanskrit *prakāśa* (light). (PRA-KASH)

PRAMOD Derived from the Sanskrit *pramoda* (joy, delight). (PRA-MOD)

PRASAD Derived from *prasāda* (brightness, brilliance). (PRA-SAHD)

PRATAP Derived from the Sanskrit *pratāpa* (heat, splendor, power, majesty). The name was borne by Maharana Pratap (1540–97), the ruler of Mewar, who is remembered for refusing to yield his kingdom to Akbar the Great. He became a master of guerrilla warfare and was successful in holding back Akbar's invaders. (PRA-TAP)

PRAVIN Derived from *pravīna* (skillful, able). (PRA-VIN)

PREM Derived from the Sanskrit *prema* (love, affection). (PREM)

RAFIQ Derived from the Arabic *rafiq* (friend, companion). Var: Rafee, Rafi, Rafieq, Rafik. (RAH-FEEK)

RAHIM Derived from the Arabic *rahīm* (compassionate, sympathetic). Al-Rahīm (the Compassionate One) is one of the attributes of Allāh. Var: Raheem. (RAH-HEEM)

RAJAB Derived from the Arabic *rajaba* (to glorify). Rajab is the name of the seventh month of the Arabic calendar. (RA-JAB)

RAJENDRA Compound name composed from the Sanskrit elements *rāja* (king) and Indra, the chief god of the atmosphere, whose name connotes strength and might: hence, "mighty king" or "Indra the king." The name was borne by an 11th-century king, Rajendra Chola, known for being both a competent ruler and a master builder.

Under his leadership his empire was greatly enlarged by conquering and annexing many territories. His buildings and public works were characterized by their grandeur. Var: Rajender, Rajinder. (RAH-JEN-DRAH)

RAJESH Compound name derived from the Sanskrit *rāja* (king) and *īśa* (ruler): hence, "the king is ruler, king of kings." (RAH-JESH)

RAJIV Derived from the Sanskrit *rājīva* (striped). The name was borne by Indian Prime Minister Rajiv Gandhi (1944–91), son of Indira Gandhi. He was assassinated during an election campaign to regain his position. (RAH-JEEV)

RAJNISH Compound name composed of the elements *rajanī* (night) and *īśa* (ruler): hence, "ruler of the night." The name is indicative of the moon. Var: Rajneesh. (RAJ-NISH, RAJ-NEESH)

RAM Derived from the Sanskrit *rāma* (pleasing). The name was borne by Ram Mohan Roy (1772–1833), the driving force behind the Indian National Movement. He advocated a return to traditional Hindu values and worship, denouncing the practices of polygamy, female infanticide, and *sati* as evil. He was also known for promoting the study of English and the Western world to bring India into the modern world community. (RAHM)

RAMA Derived from the Sanskrit *rāma* (pleasing). The name was borne by the Hindu's greatest, most revered king. The son of King Dasratha and the husband of Sita, he is remembered for never failing to do his duty and for his concern for his people. Revered as the seventh incarnation of Vishnu, Rama is one of the most popular of the Hindu deities. (RAH-MAH)

RAMAKRISHNA Compound name composed from the Sanskrit *rāma* (pleasing) and Krishna, the name of a popular Hindu deity: hence, "pleasing to Krishna." The name was borne by spiritual leader Ramakrishna Paramahansa (1836–86). He is famous for his devotion to attaining Enlightenment. As a young man, his passion for spiritual matters was frowned upon by his family and he was married at the age of twenty-three to Sharda Devi, a child of five. However, Ramakrishna remained absorbed in spiritual matters and spent time learning under many great spiritual leaders, and in time attained his own group of devotees. He revered his wife to the point of worshiping her as the divine mother, and called her the Holy Mother. He preached tolerance, brotherhood, equality for men and women, and an active quest for spiritual realization and Enlightenment. (RAH-MAH-KRISH-NAH)

RAMANANDA Compound name composed from the Sanskrit *rāma* (pleasing) and *ānanda* (happiness, joy): hence, "happiness and joy are pleasing." The name was borne by a great spiritual leader (1400–70) who preached his philosophy of one personal god (Rama) in Hindi, the common language of the people. He maintained that by being devoted to and worshiping Rama, one could attain salvation after death. His belief in equality for all and his opposition to casteism led to a loosening of the rigid social system. Short: Rama. (RAH-MAH-NAN-DAH)

RAMNATH Compound name composed of Rama, a popular Hindu deity, and *nātha* (lord): hence, "Rama is lord." (RAHM-NATH)

RANJIT Derived from the Sanskrit *ranjita* (affected, delighted, charmed). The name was borne by Prince Ranjit Singh (1780–1839), who unified the Punjab and brought it under his rule. Though he did not prepare anyone to succeed him, he is remembered for being generous, kind, and competent. (RAHN-JEET)

RASHID Derived from the Arabic *rashīd* (rightly guided). Var: Rasheed. (RAH-SHEED)

RATAN Derived from the Sanskrit *ratna* (jewel). (RAH-TAN)

RAVI Derived from the Sanskrit *ravi* (the sun). Ravi is a name for the god of the sun. (RAV-EE)

RAVINDRA Compound name composed of the elements *ravi* (the sun) and Indra, the chief god of the atmosphere, whose name denotes strength: hence, "the mighty sun." (RAV-IN-DRAH)

RAZA Derived from the Arabic *riza* (contentment, satisfaction). (RA-ZA)

ROHAN Derived from the Sanskrit *rohana* (ascending, rising). (RO-HAN)

ROSHAN Derived from the Persian *roshana* (dawn of day, light). (RO-SHAN)

SAARIK Borrowed from the name of a type of thrush. (SAH-RIK)

SABIR Derived from the Arabic *sābir* (enduring, patient). (SAH-BIR)

SACHDEV Compound name composed of the elements *satya* (truth) and *deva* (a god): hence, "god's truth." (SACH-DAYV)

SAHAJ Natural. (SAH-HAJ)

SAHIL Guide, leader. (SAH-HIL)

SAIYID Derived from the Arabic *sa'īd* (lucky, happy). Var: Saeed, Syed. (SĪ-YID, SĪ-EED)

SAJAN Beloved, dear. (SAH-JAN)

SAJJAN Good, gentle, kind. (SAJ-JAN)

Sami Derived from the Arabic *sāmi* (elevated, exalted). (SAH-MEE)

Sanjay Popular name derived from the Sanskrit *samjaya* (triumphant, victorious). The name was borne by Sanjay Gandhi (1948–80), a son of Indira Gandhi. (SAHN-JAY)

Sanjiv Popular name derived from the Sanskrit *samjiva* (reviving). Var: Sanjeev. (SAHN-JEEV)

Sarik Borrowed from the name of a type of myna bird. (SAR-IK)

Sekar Derived from the Sanskrit *śekhara* (peak, summit, top of the head). Var: Shekhar. (SHE-KAR)

Shafiq Derived from the Arabic *shafiq* (sympathetic, compassionate). (SHA-FEEK)

Shahzad Derived from the Persian *shahzād* (prince, a king's son). (SHAH-ZAHD)

Shakil Derived from the Arabic *shakīl* (handsome, well-developed). Var: Shakeel. (SHA-KEEL)

Shakir Derived from the Arabic *shākir* (thankful). (SHA-KIR)

Shandar Popular name meaning "proud." (SHAN-DAR)

Shankara Compound name composed from the Sanskrit *śam* (auspicious, lucky) and *kara* (making): hence, "to bring about good luck and happiness." Śamkara is a name for the gods Rudra, Shiva, and Skanda. The name Shankara was borne by a great man of religion and philosophy, Shankaracharya (788–820). He is responsible for bolstering Hinduism and for being a strong opponent of Buddhism. He established a center of religion in each of the four corners of India, which are still active today, reorganized the monastic orders, and converted many of the Buddhist and Mimansaka scholastic teachers to Hinduism. Var: Sankar, Sankara, Shankar. (SHAN-KAR-AH)

Sharif Derived from the Arabic *sharīf* (honorable, eminent). Var: Shareef. (SHA-REEF)

Shiva Derived from the Sanskrit *śiva* (auspicious, fortunate, benign). This name is bestowed in honor of Shiva, considered by many to be the first great person in India whose feats and good works elevated him to the heights of Deity, having control over creation, preservation, and destruction. He is worshiped throughout India and is the focus of numerous myths and legends. The Tandava style of dancing is said to be his creation. The name Shiva is also used as a common element in compound names. Var: Sheo, Shiv, Sib, Siva. (SHEE-VAH)

Shivaji Derived from the name of the Hindu god Shiva and *-ji* (an honorable suffix). The name was borne by the founder (1627–80) of the Maratha confederacy, which succeeded in holding back Mogul advancement in the south. He is known for having been a great strategist and for successfully employing guerrilla tactics. (SHEE-VAH-JEE)

Shobhan Derived from the Sanskrit *śobhanā* (handsome, splendid, brilliant). (SHOB-HAHN)

Shyam Derived from the Sanskrit *śyāma* (black, dark). The name is indicative of dark, Indian beauty. Var: Sam, Sham. (SHY-AM)

Sohan Attractive, handsome, charming. (SO-HAN)

Sohil Attractive, handsome, beautiful. (SO-HIL)

Subhash Derived from the Sanskrit prefix *su-* (good) and *bhāsā* (speech): hence, "well-spoken, eloquent." The name was borne by political leader Subhash Chandra Bose (1897–1945), who was vehemently opposed to British rule in India and believed that force would be the only way to gain Indian independence. He formed the Indian National Army and fought against the Allied forces during World War II. (SOO-BHASH)

Sudas Compound name composed of the prefix *su-* (good) and *dāsa* (servant, slave): hence, "a good servant." According to historical accounts, Sudas was the grandson of the great Bharata Divodas. He led the indigenous people during the Battle of Ten Kings (one of the earliest events recorded in Indian history), which brought about the integration of the Aryan and non-Aryan races on the Gangetic plains of India. Var: Sudaas. (SOO-DAHS)

Sudhir Compounding of the prefix *su-* (good) and *dhīra* (wise): hence, "sagacious, very wise." (SOO-DEER)

Suhail Derived from the Arabic *suhayl,* the name referring to the second-brightest star in the southern skies. (SOO-HAIL)

Sujay Compounding of the prefix *su-* (good) and *jaya* (victory): hence, "good victory." (SOO-JAY)

Sujit Compounding of the prefix *su-* (good) and the suffix *-jit* (conquering): hence, "good conquering, victory." (SOO-JIT)

Suman Compounding of the prefix *su-* (good) and *manas* (mind): hence, "intelligent, smart, wise." (SOO-MAHN)

Sumantra Compounding of the prefix *su-* (good) and *mantra* (advice): hence, "giver of good advice." (SOO-MAHN-TRAH)

Sundara Derived from the Sanskrit *sundara* (beautiful). Var: Sundar, Sunder. (SUN-DAH-RAH)

SUNDARAMA Compound name composed of the elements *sundara* (beautiful) and Rama, a popular Hindu deity: hence, "beautiful Rama." (SUN-DAH-RAH-MAH)

SUNIL Combining of the prefix *su-* (good) and *nīla* (dark blue): hence, "very dark blue." (SOO-NEEL)

SURAJ Combining of the prefix *su-* (good) and *raja* (king, ruler). The name is indicative of the sun. (SOO-RAJ)

SUSHOBAN Combining of the prefix *su-* (good) and *śobhanā* (beautiful, handsome, splendid): hence, "very handsome." (SOO-SHO-BAHN)

SUSRUTA Of debated origin and meaning, some believe it to be a variant of the Arabic Suqrat, but this is not substantiated. Others think it is an Indian name meaning "well-heard" or "having a good reputation." The name was borne by a 2nd-century B.C. surgeon, thought to be India's greatest surgeon outside recent history. He authored the *Susruta Samhita*, which is a vast source of surgical knowledge and instruction. Var: Sushrut, Sushruta. (SOO-SROO-TAH)

SYON Sanskrit name meaning "beautiful, auspicious, fortunate, happy." (SĪ-ON)

TAHIR Derived from the Arabic *tāhir* (pure, chaste). (TAH-HEER)

TAJ Sanskrit name meaning "crown." (TAHJ)

TANAY Son. (TAN-AY)

TARA From the Sanskrit *tāra* (shining). (TAH-RAH)

TARIK Derived from the Arabic *tāriq* (one who knocks at the door). Var: Taril, Tarin. (TAH-RIK)

TARUN Derived from the Sanskrit *taruna* (young, youth). (TAH-ROON)

TEJ Popular name meaning "gloriousness, magnificence." Tej is also used as a short form of Tejomay. (TEJ)

TEJOMAY Popular name meaning "glorious, magnificent, shining." Short: Tej. (TEJ-O-MAY)

TIPU Derived from *tipu* (tiger). The name was borne by Tipu Sultan (1750–99), ruler of Mysore. He is remembered for his adamant refusal to submit to the British or enter into any sort of allegiance with them. He was fiercely determined to keep Mysore independent and spent nearly thirty years fighting to keep it so. His response to the barbaric acts of the invaders by actions just as cruel gave him the reputation of being a tyrannical despot. (TEE-POO)

TIRU Derived from *tiru* (saintly, worshipful, devout). (TIR-OO)

TIRUVALLUVAR Compound name composed of the elements *tiru* (saintly, worshipful, devout) and Valluvar (the name of a village). The name was borne by a 5th-century poet who is most famous for his work the *Kural*. (TIR-OO-VAL-LYOO-VAR)

TORIL Popular name meaning "temperament, disposition." Var: Toral. (TOR-IL)

TULSI Derived from the Sanskrit *tulasī* (holy basil). Basil is an herb used during the worship of Vishnu, for it is said to be sacred to him. One story claims that it was produced from the hair of the goddess Tulasi; another says it was created during the churning of the oceans during the god's and demon's quest for the nectar of immortality. The name was borne by the poet and spiritual leader Tulsidas (1523–1624), the author of the *Ramcharitmanas*. To this day it is a sacred text, and is thought of by many to be a blueprint for proper behavior and a perfect family life. (TOOL-SEE)

UDAY To rise, to make an appearance. (OO-DAY)

UDAYAN Rising, making an appearance. (OO-DAY-AN)

UJALA Light, bright, shining. Var: Ujaala. (OO-JAHL-AH)

UMAR Derived from the Arabic *'āmir* (flourishing, thriving). (OO-MAR)

UMED Hope, desire, wish. (OO-MED)

URVIL Ocean, the sea. (UR-VIL)

UTTAM Derived from the Sanskrit *uttama* (superior, best, highest). (OO-TAHM)

VALMIKI Derived from the Sanskrit *valmika* (anthill). The name was borne by the great poet and author of the first book of poetry in Sanskrit, *Ramayana*. (VAL-MEE-KEE)

VANDAN Salvation. (VAN-DAN)

VARDHAMMA Growing, increasing. The name was borne by the son of Siddhartha, a chief of Kundapura, Vardhamma Mahavira (c. 599–526 B.C.). At the age of twenty-eight, he forsook the world, including his wife and daughter, and spent the next twelve years as a naked ascetic. He became the head of an order of ascetics in Magadha and Anga, and a leader of the Jain religion, which promoted a highly moral, nonmaterialistic lifestyle. Var: Vardhaman. (VARD-HAM-MAH)

VAREN Best, superior. (VAR-EN)

VARESH Composed of the elements *vara* (best, superior) and *īśa* (a god): hence, "the best god." (VAR-ESH)

VARIL Water. (VAR-IL)

Varun Lord of the sea, god of water. The name Varun also denotes the planet Neptune. Var: Varin, Varoon. (VAR-OON)

Vasant From the Sanskrit *vasanta* (spring, springtime). (VAH-SAHNT)

Vasu From the Sanskrit *vasu* (bright, the sun; good; wealthy). The name is also a name of Krishna. (VAH-SOO)

Vatsyayana Borne by the 6th-century author of the *Kama Sutra*, an in-depth encyclopedia of erotica. (VAT-SĪ-Ī-YAH-NAH)

Vijay Derived from the Sanskrit *vijaya* (victory). Var: Bijay, Vijen, Vijun. (VIH-JAY)

Vijayendra Compound name composed of the elements *vijaya* (victory) and Indra, the name of the chief god of the atmosphere, whose name denotes strength: hence, "victorious Indra" or "strong victory." Var: Vijendra. (VIH-JAY-EN-DRAH)

Vilok To see. (VIH-LOK)

Vimal Derived from the Sanskrit *vimala* (clean, pure, unsullied). (VIH-MAHL)

Vivek Derived from the Sanskrit *vivek* (wisdom, right judgment). The name is also used as a short form of Vivekananda (joy in wisdom). *See* VIVEKANANDA. (VIV-EK)

Vivekananda Compound name composed of the elements *vivek* (wisdom, right judgment) and *ānanda* (happiness, joy): hence, "wisdom brings joy." The name was borne by Narendra Nath Datta (1863–1902), a religious teacher who preached social responsibility and a universal, but diverse, religion. He was a disciple of Ramakrishna and, along with Shurda Devi, continued the teaching of Ramakrishna upon the master's death. He founded the Ramakrishna Mission at Belur in 1892, and in 1893 addressed the Parliament of Religions in the United States. Var: Vivekanand. Short: Vivek. (VIH-VEH-KAN-AN-DAH)

Yamal A twin, one of a pair. (YAH-MAHL)

Yamin Night. (YAH-MIN)

Yash Fame, glory. (YASH)

Yashaskar Compound name composed of the elements *yash* (fame, glory) and *kara* (maker): hence, "maker of fame, making one famous." (YASH-AS-KAR)

Yuri Lily. (YOO-REE)

Zafar Derived from the Arabic *zafar* (victory). (ZAH-FAR)

Zahir Derived from the Arabic *zāhir* (shining, flourishing). Var: Zaheer. (ZAH-HEER)

Ziya Derived from the Arabic *ziyā* (splendor, light). Var: Zia. (ZEE-YAH)

Hindu/Indian Female Names

Aanandini Always happy. Derived from *ānanda* (happiness, joy). (AH-NAN-DEE-NEE)

Abha Derived from the Sanskrit *ābhā* (light, splendor).Var: Aabha, Aabhaa, Abhaa. (AHB-HAH)

Achala Constant, unceasing. Var: Achalaa. (AH-CHA-LAH)

Adhika More, excess, extra. (AD-HEE-KAH)

Adhita Scholar. (AD-HEE-TAH)

Ahalya A name borne by the wife of the great logician Gautama. According to legend, the beautiful Ahalya attracted the unwanted attention of Indra, one of Gautama's disciples. Early one morning, Indra waited for Gautama to leave, then, posing as Gautama, went in and slept with Ahalya. Gautama returned, found the two together, and cursed them both. Ahalya turned to stone but was brought back to life by Rama during his exile. (AH-HAHL-YAH)

Ahilya Borne by the revered ruler Maharani Ahilya Bai (1725–95). She is known for having been a capable, compassionate ruler who brought prosperity to her people. Honorable, pious, benevolent, and generous, she was beloved by all. (AH-HIL-YAH)

Aisha Derived from the Arabic *'ā'isha* (alive and well), which is from *'āsha* (to live). The name was borne by the Prophet Muḥammad's favorite wife and is popular throughout the Muslim world. *See* 'Ā'ISHA (Arabic Names). Var: Aayusha, Aayushi, Ayesha. (Ā-EE-SHA)

Ajalaa The earth. (AH-JAL-AH)

Ajeya Formed by combining the elements *a* (not) and *jita* (conquered): hence, "unconquerable." (AH-JAY-AH)

Akhila Whole, complete, all. (AK-HEE-LAH)

Alisha Protected by God. (AH-LEE-SHA)

Alka Of uncertain derivation. "Youth" is a popular definition. (AL-KAH)

Amala Derived from the Arabic *amal* (hope) or from the Sanskrit *amal* (clean, pure). Var: Amalaa. (AM-AH-LAH)

Amarjaa Derived from *amrta* (immortal). (AM-AR-JAH)

Amber The sky, the horizon. Var: Ambar. (AM-BER)

Ambika Another manifestation of the goddess Parvati, the wife of the god Shiva. As Ambika, she is known as the Progenitor. (AM-BEE-KAH)

Amee Nectar of the gods, nectar of immortality. (AM-EE)

Amisha Popular name meaning "honest, forthright." (AM-EE-SHA, AM-IH-SHA)

Amita Combining of the elements *a* (not) and *mita* (measure): hence, "immeasurable, infinite." Var: Amiti. (AH-MEE-TAH, AH-MIH-TAH)

Amoli Precious, of inestimable worth. (AH-MO-LEE)

Anala Fire, fiery. Var: Analaa. (AH-NAH-LAH)

Ananda Derived from the Sanskrit *ānanda* (happiness, joy, bliss, delight). Ananda is also used as a common element in compound names. (AH-NAN-DAH)

Anandita Derived from the Sanskrit *ānanda* (happiness, joy), Anandita has the definition "bringer of joy and happiness." (AH-NAN-DEE-TAH)

Anganaa Popular name meaning "beautiful woman, lovely." (AN-GAN-AH)

Angee Having good limbs. (AN-GEE)

Anila Air, wind. The masculine form Anil is a name of Vayu, the wind-god. (AN-EE-LAH, AH-NIL-AH)

Anima Derived from the Sanskrit *animan* (minuteness, infinitely small). The name connotes petiteness. (AH-NIH-MAH)

Anisha Derived from *īśa* (lord). (AN-ISH-AH)

Anita Grace, mercy. (AN-IH-TAH, AN-EE-TAH)

Anju Popular name meaning "to honor, to shine." (AN-JOO)

Anuka Desirous. (AN-OO-KAH)

Anupa Incomparable, unique. Var: Anupaa. (AN-OO-PAH)

Anupriyaa Incomparable, unique. (AN-OO-PREE-YAH)

Anura Knowledge. (AN-OO-RAH)

Anusheela Devoted follower, devotee. (AN-OO-SHEE-LAH)

Apsara Celestial maiden. (AP-SAH-RAH)

Aradhana Dedication. (AR-AD-HAN-AH)

Arpana One who has been dedicated. (AR-PAH-NAH)

Aruna Derived from the Sanskrit *aruna* (rust-colored, reddish brown, the color of dawn). The masculine form Arun is the dawn personified. (AR-OO-NAH)

Arunika Derived from the Sanskrit *aruna* (reddish brown, the color of dawn). The name has the definition "the glow of dawn, the glow of sunrise." (AR-OO-NEE-KAH)

Arunima The red glow of dawn, the red glow of sunrise. Derived from *aruna* (reddish brown, the color of dawn). (AR-OO-NEE-MAH)

Arvindaa Derived from *aravinda* (lotus). (AR-VIN-DAH)

Asha Derived from the Sanskrit *āśā* (wish, desire, hope). (AHSH-AH)

Ashni A flash of lightning. (AHSH-NEE)

Asmee Popular name meaning "high self-esteem, self-confident." (AHS-MEE)

Avani Popular name derived from *avana* (earth). (AH-VAN-EE)

Aziza Derived from the Arabic *'azīza* (esteemed, precious, beloved, friend). (AH-ZEE-ZAH)

Azra A virgin. (AHZ-RAH)

Bahaar Spring, springtime. (BAH-HAHR)

Bakul Borrowed from the name of a mythological flower. Var: Bakula. (BAH-KOOL)

Banhi Fire, fiery. (BAHN-HEE)

Banita Woman. (BAHN-EE-TAH)

Bano A borrowing from the Persian, Bano is derived from *bāno* (lady, bride). (BAH-NO)

Beeja Origin, source. Var: Beej. (BEE-JAH)

Bela Directly derived from a word with several different meanings. "Wave," "time," and "limit" are examples. The word is also indicative of a type of flower and violin. (BEL-AH)

Bhamini Beautiful woman. (BAH-MEE-NEE)

Bhanumati Shining like the sun, bright. Derived from *bhanu* (the sun). (BAH-NOO-MAH-TEE)

Bharati Derived from the Sanskrit *bharata* (being maintained). *See* BHARAT (Male Names). (BAH-RAH-TEE)

Bhavika Devoted, dedicated. (BAH-VEE-KAH)

Bhuma The earth. (BOO-MAH)

Bhumika Derived from *bhuma* (the earth). (BOO-MEE-KAH)

Bibi A borrowing from the Persian, Bibi is derived from *bībī* (lady, mistress of the house). (BEE-BEE)

Binali Borrowed from the name of a musical instrument. (BIH-NAH-LEE)

Chahna Love, light, illumination. (CHAH-NAH)

Chaitali Energetic, having maximum energy. (CHĪ-TAH-LEE)

Chameli Borrowed from the Indian name of the jasmine flower. (CHA-MAY-LEE)

Chandaa Derived from the Sanskrit *candra* (the moon, shining). (CHAN-DAH)

Chandani Moonlight. Derived from *candra* (the moon, shining). (CHAN-DAH-NEE)

Chandni Moonlight. Derived from *candra* (the moon, shining). (CHAND-NEE)

Chandra Derived from the Sanskrit *candra* (the moon, shining). Var: Chandree, Chandrika. (CHAND-RAH)

Chandrakanta Compound name composed of the elements *candra* (moon) and *kānta* (beloved): hence, "beloved of the moon." Chandrakanta is the name given to the wife of the moon. (CHAND-RAH-KAHN-TAH)

Chandrima Moonlight. Derived from *candra* (the moon, shining). Var: Chandrimaa. (CHAND-REE-MAH)

Chandrjaa A moonbeam. Derived from *candra* (the moon, shining). (CHAN-DER-JAH)

Channa Popular name meaning "chickpea." (CHAHN-NAH)

Charita Having a good character, personable. (CHAR-EE-TAH)

Charu Derived from the Sanskrit *charu* (beautiful, lovely). (CHAR-OO)

Charumati Compound name composed of *charu* (beautiful, lovely) and *mati* (mind): hence, "one with wisdom and intelligence." (CHAR-OO-MAH-TEE)

Damayanti Subduing men through womanly attributes. Derived from the Sanskrit *damayanti* (subduing). (DAH-MAH-YAN-TEE)

Darpitaa Proud. (DAR-PIH-TAH)

Darsha To see, to perceive, to have vision. Var: Darshika, Darshina, Darshini, Darshna. (DAR-SHA)

Dayaa Derived from *dayā* (compassion). (DAH-YAH)

Dayanita Tender, compassionate. Derived from *dayā* (compassion). (DAH-YAH-NEE-TAH)

Devahuti Derived from *deva* (a god), this name was borne by the mother of Kapila, the ancient philosopher who promoted his philosophy, *Samkhya.* (DAY-VAH-HOO-TEE)

Devaki Black. Devaki was the mother of Krishna. *See* KRISHNA (Male Names). (DAY-VAH-KEE)

Deval Divine, god-like. Derived from *deva* (a god). (DAY-VAHL)

Devanee Divine, god-like. Derived from *deva* (a god). (DAY-VAH-NEE)

Devi Divine. Derived from the Sanskrit *deva* (a god). The name is borne by the primary Hindu goddess, the wife of Shiva. She has both a mild and a fierce aspect and has several different names for each. Var: Devee. (DAY-VEE)

Devika Derived from *deva* (a god) and the diminutive suffix *-ka:* hence, "little goddess." (DAY-VEE-KAH)

Dhanadaa Bestower of wealth. (DAH-NAH-DAH)

Dhara The earth. (DAH-RAH)

Dharinee The earth, a support. (DAH-RIH-NEE, DAH-REE-NEE)

Dharitri The earth. Var: Dharti. (DAH-RIH-TREE, DAH-REE-TREE)

Dhavala White, pure white. (DAH-VAH-LAH)

Divya Radiant, brilliant, resplendent. (DIV-YAH)

Draupadi Borne by the wife of Pandavas. She was one of the great women in the epic *Mahabharata.* (DRAU-PAH-DEE)

Drisana Borne by the daughter of the sun, Drisa. (DREE-SAH-NAH)

Dularee Beloved daughter, cherished daughter. (DOO-LAH-REE)

Durga Unattainable. Durga is a name of the goddess Devi in her fierce form. (DURE-GAH)

Ehani Desire, hope, wish, expectation. Var: Ehina. (EE-HAH-NEE, EH-HAH-NEE)

Ela Intelligent woman. (EE-LAH, EH-LAH)

Elakshi A woman with intelligent eyes. (EE-LAHK-SHEE, EH-LAHK-SHEE)

Eli Intelligent woman. Var: Elee. (EE-LEE, EH-LEE)

Elina Intelligent woman. Var: Elita. (EE-LEE-NAH, EH-LEE-NAH)

Erina Speech. (EE-REE-NAH, EH-REE-NAH)

Erisha Speech. (EE-REE-SHA, EH-REE-SHA)

Eshana Search, desire, want, wish. (EE-SHAH-NAH, EH-SHAH-NAH)

Eva A borrowing from the Latin, Eva is from the Hebrew Chava, a derivative of *hawwāh* (life). The name is borne in the Bible by the first woman created by God. She was supposedly formed from one of Adam's ribs while he slept. (EE-VAH)

Evani Elaborated form of Eva (life). *See* EVA. Var: Evina, Evira, Ivani. (EE-VAH-NEE)

Fulande Created from a flower. (FOO-LAHN-DEH)

Fulangi Created from a flower. (FOO-LAHN-GEE)

Gambhira Dignified, noble. (GAM-BEER-AH)

Garima Importance, significance. (GAH-REE-MAH)

Gauri Derived from *gaurī* (white, fair, light-colored), Gauri is a name of the goddess Parvati, the wife of Shiva. As Gauri, she is known as the Brilliant. Var: Gori, Gowri. (GAU-REE)

Gita Derived from the Sanskrit *gīta* (song). Var: Geeta. (GEE-TAH)

Gitanjali Compound name meaning "an offering of songs." (GEE-TAHN-JAH-LEE)

Gitika Compounding of the name Gita (song) and the diminutive suffix *-ka:* hence, "little song." Var: Geetika. (GEE-TEE-KAH)

Gyanda Knowledgeable. (GĪ-YAN-DAH)

Habiba A borrowing from the Arabic, Habiba is derived from *habīb* (dear, beloved), which is from *habba* (to love). Var: Habibah. (HAH-BEE-BAH)

Haimi Golden. (HĪ-MEE)

Halima Derived from the Arabic *halima* (gentle, patient). Var: Haleema, Halimah. (HAH-LEE-MAH)

Hamida Derived from the Arabic *hamid* (thankful, praising), which is from the root *hamida* (to praise). Var: Hameeda. (HAH-MEE-DAH)

Hanifa Derived from the Arabic *hanif* (true believer of Islam). Var: Haneefa. (HAH-NEE-FAH)

Hanita Divine grace. (HAN-EE-TAH)

Hansa Derived from *hans* (swan). (HAN-SAH)

Hansika Compound name meaning "beautiful swan, beautiful little swan." (HAN-SEE-KAH)

Hansila Derived from *hans* (swan). (HAN-SEE-LAH)

Harita Derived from the Sanskrit *hari*, a word of many definitions. It denotes a color of yellow, green, or brown, a monkey, the sun, the wind, and several other things. (HAR-EE-TAH)

Harsha Derived from *harsha* (joy, delight). (HAR-SHA)

Harshida Giver of joy, giver of happiness. Derived from *harsha* (joy, delight). (HAR-SHEE-DAH)

Harshika Joyful. Derived from *harsha* (joy, delight). Var: Harshina. (HAR-SHEE-KAH)

Hasika Laughter. (HAH-SEE-KAH)

Hasina Derived from the Arabic *hasan* (beautiful, good). (HAH-SEE-NAH)

Hemali Coated with gold. Derived from the Sanskrit *hema* (gold). (HEH-MAH-LEE)

Himani Covered with snow. Var: Heemani. (HEE-MAH-NEE)

Hiral Bright, shining. (HEE-RAHL)

Ichchani Borne by Ichchanidevi, one of the three queens of King Prithviraja (1163–92). (ICH-CHAHN-EE)

Idaa Earth (IH-DAH)

Ila Earth. (IH-LAH)

Ilesha Compound name composed of the elements *il* (earth) and *īśa* (lord): hence, "lord of the earth." (IL-ESH-AH)

Indira Derived from the Sanskrit *indirā* (beauty, splendor). The name was borne by Indira Gandhi (1917–84), prime minister of India (1966–77 and 1980–84). Resentment over many policies put in place under her leadership led to her assassination in 1984 by two of her Sikh bodyguards. (IN-DEER-AH)

Indranee Wife of Indra. Indra is the name of the chief god of the sky and atmosphere. (IN-DRAH-NEE)

INDRAYANI Wife of Indra. (IN-DRAH-YAH-NEE)

INDU Moon. (IN-DOO)

ISHA One who looks after, one who protects. Derived from the Sanskrit *īśa* (lord). (ISH-AH, EESH-AH)

ISHANA Desire. Var: Ishani. (ISH-AH-NAH, EESH-AH-NAH)

JAAMINI Night. (JAH-MEE-NEE)

JALAJAA A lotus. (JA-LAH-JAH)

JALANEELI Moss. (JA-LAH-NEE-LEE)

JALINI A water dweller. (JA-LEE-NEE)

JALITAA Lotus. (JA-LEE-TAH)

JAMILA Derived from the Arabic *jamīla* (beautiful, graceful). Var: Jameela. (JAH-MEE-LAH)

JANAKI Descendant of Janaka. It is a name of Sita, the daughter of King Janaka and wife of Rama. (JA-NAH-KEE)

JANIKAA A mother. (JA-NEE-KAH)

JANY Fire, fiery. (JAH-NEE)

JARITA Mother. Alternatively, Jarita was the name given to a legendary bird. (JA-REE-TAH)

JASMIN From the Arabic *yasmīn* (jasmine, a fragrant plant). (JAS-MEEN)

JASWINDER Derived from *jasu* (the name of Indra's thunderbolt) and Indra, the name of the god of the sky and atmosphere. (JAS-WIN-DER)

JAYA Derived from the Sanskrit *jaya* (victory). Jaya is also a name of the goddess Durga. (JAY-AH)

JAYAMALA Compound name composed of *jaya* (victory) and *mala* (garland): hence, "garland of victory." (JAY-AH-MAH-LAH)

JAYANTI Derived from *jayanta* (victorious). It is a name of Durga. Var: Jayantika. (JAY-AN-TEE)

JAYASHREE Compound name composed of the Sanskrit *jaya* (victory) and Shree, a variant of Sri, which is a name of Lakshmi, the goddess of beauty. The name has the definition "goddess of victory." (JAY-AH-SHREE)

JAYNA Derived from the Sanskrit *jaya* (victory). Var: Jayne. (JAY-NAH)

JAYTI Derived from the Sanskrit *jaya* (victory). (JAY-TEE)

JAYVANTI Derived from the Sanskrit *jaya* (victory). (JAY-VAN-TEE)

JENA Popular name meaning "patience." (JAY-NAH)

JIJABAI Borne by the mother of Shivaji (1627–80), the founder of the Maratha confederacy. (JEE-JAH-BĪ)

JINNAT Heaven. (JEEN-NAHT)

JIVANTA To give life, to create. (JEE-VAHN-TAH)

JODHA Borne by a daughter of Raya Biharimal of Amer. In 1562 she was wed to Akbar the Great and had one son, Jahangir. (JODE-HAH)

JUHI Borrowed from the name of a flower. (JOO-HEE)

JYOTI From *jyotis* (light, the light of dawn, fire, lightning; the sun, the moon). (JĪ-O-TEE)

JYOTSANA Moonlight. Derived from *jyotis* (light, fire, lightning; the sun, the moon). (JĪ-ŌT-SAH-NAH)

KAAMILEE Full of desire. (KAH-MEE-LEE)

KAANAN Forest. (KAH-NAN)

KAASU Light, shine, luster. (KAH-SOO)

KAILASH Borrowed from the name of a mountain in the Himalayas said to be the paradise of Shiva. It is of uncertain meaning. (KĪ-LASH)

KALA Derived from the Sanskrit *kālī* (the black one). (KAH-LAH)

KALI Derived from the Sanskrit *kālī* (the black one). The name is borne by the wife of Shiva in her fierce form, Ma Kali (Black Mother). She dances the cosmic dance, which unfolds on the plane of the human soul, and is responsible for destroying those aspects of one's character that stand in the way of finding one's true identity. Var: Kalee, Kallee. (KAH-LEE)

KALIKA A borrowing from the Greek, Kalika is derived from *kalyx* (pod, bud, outer covering of a flower). (KAH-LEE-KAH)

KALINDA Borrowed from the name of the mythical Kalinda Mountains. (KAH-LEEN-DA)

KALINDI Borrowed from the name of a river. (KAH-LEEN-DEE)

KALITA Known. (KAH-LEE-TA)

KALLOLEE Full of joy, happiness, and delight. (KAH-LO-LEE)

KALPANA Fantasy. Derived from the Sanskrit *kalpanā*. (KAHL-PAH-NAH)

KALYANI Derived from the Sanskrit *kalyāna* (beautiful, lovely; auspicious). Kalyani is a name of the goddess Durga in her mild form. (KAHL-YAH-NEE)

KAMALA Derived from the Sanskrit *kamala* (pale red, lotus). It is a name of the goddesses Lakshmi and Durga. (KAH-MAH-LA)

KAMALIKA Derived from the Sanskrit *kamala* (pale red, lotus). (KAH-MAH-LEE-KA)

KAMANIKA Beautiful. (KAH-MAH-NEE-KA)

KAMANIYA Beautiful. (KAH-MAH-NEE-YA)

KAMILA Derived from the Arabic *kāmil* (perfect). Var: Kameela. (KAH-MEE-LAH)

KAMLA Borne by the wife of Jawaharlal Nehru, the first prime minister of India. (KAM-LA)

KANA An atom, infinitely small. (KAH-NA)

KANIKA An atom, a small particle, infinitely small. (KAH-NEE-KA)

KANJANAA God of love. (KAN-JAN-AH)

KANTA Derived from *kānta* (beautiful, desired, wanted). (KAHN-TA)

KANTI Derived from *kānti* (beauty, loveliness). (KAHN-TEE)

KANTIMATI Derived from *kānti* (beauty, loveliness). The name was borne by the mother of the philosopher Ramanuja. (KAHN-TEE-MAH-TEE)

KANYA Virgin, young girl. Kanya is a name of the goddess Sakti. Var: Kanyaa. (KAHN-YA)

KARMA Derived from the Sanskrit *karma* (deed, act, fate, destiny). (KAR-MA)

KARPURA Borne by Karpuradevi, a Kalchuri princess who became the wife of Someswara, the king of Sapadalaksha. She was the mother of Prithviraja (1162–92), who ascended the throne in 1178 following the death of his father. (KAR-POOR-AH)

KARUNA Mercy, compassion. (KAH-ROO-NAH)

KASTURBA Musk. The name Kasturba was borne by the wife of Mahatma Gandhi. *See* MOHANDAS (Male Names). As his constant companion, she shared his troubles and supported him in all he did. Such was their devotion to one another that upon her death in 1944, Gandhi observed a three-week fast. (KAS-TOOR-BAH)

KATYAYANI A name of the goddess Parvati. It was borne by one of the wives of the great sage and philosopher Yajnavalkya. His other wife was Maiteryi. (KAT-YAH-YAH-NEE)

KAUSALYA Derived from the Sanskrit *kausalya* (belonging to the Kosala people). The name was borne by the wife of King Dasaratha and mother of Rama, one of the most popular of the Hindu deities. Var: Kaushali, Kaushalya. (KAU-SAL-YAH)

KERANI Sacred bells. (KAY-RAH-NEE)

KESAVA Having fine hair. (KAY-SAH-VAH)

KHALIDA Derived from the Arabic *khālid* (immortal, eternal). Var: Kaleeda. (KAH-LEE-DAH)

KIMAYA Divine, godly. (KEE-MAY-AH)

KIRAN Derived from the Sanskrit *kirana* (a ray of light). Var: Kirina. (KEE-RAHN)

KIRI Borrowed from the name of the amaranth flower. Var: Kirsi. (KEE-REE)

KISHORI Young girl, filly. Kishori is derived from the Sanskrit *kiśora*. (KEE-SHOR-EE)

KOHINOOR Derived from the Persian *kohinoor* (mountain of light). (KO-HEE-NOOR)

KOMAL Popular name meaning "delicate." Var: Komala. (KO-MAHL)

KUMARI Daughter, young girl. Kumari is the feminine form of the Sanskrit *kumāra* (boy, son). (KOO-MAH-REE)

KUSHALI Clever girl, adept. (KOO-SHAH-LEE)

KUSUM Popular name meaning "flower." (KOO-SOOM)

LAJILI Modest. Var: Lajita. (LAH-JEE-LEE)

LAJNI Shy, hesitant. (LAJ-NEE)

LAKSHA White rose. (LAK-SHA)

LAKSHANA Symbol, sign. (LAK-SHA-NA)

LAKSHMI Derived from the Sanskrit *laksmī* (sign, mark), the name Lakshmi denotes a good sign. It is borne by the wife of the god Vishnu. She is the goddess of beauty, abundance, prosperity, harmony, and good fortune. She is also known as Sri. Var: Laxmi. (LAK-SHMEE)

LALIKA A beautiful woman. (LAH-LEE-KA)

LALITA Derived from the Sanskrit *lalita* (playful, charming). Lalita is a name of the goddess Durga. (LAH-LEE-TA)

LATA Beautiful vine. (LAH-TAH)

LEENA Devoted, dedicated, consecrated. (LEE-NA)

LILA Derived from the Sanskrit *lilā* (play, divine play). Var: Leela. (LEE-LAH)

LILAVATI Free will of god. The name was borne by the daughter of 12th-century mathematician Bhaskaracharya. He name one of his systems of mathematics after her. (LEE-LAH-VAH-TEE)

Madhavi Feminine form of Madhav, which is derived from the Sanskrit *mādhava* (vernal, young, spring-like). Madhavi is a name of the goddess Lakshmi and the goddess Durga. (MAHD-HAH-VEE)

Madhu Derived from the Sanskrit *madhu* (sweet, honey; beautiful). Madhu is the name of the first month of the Indian year, which begins during the Gregorian calendar months of March and April. (MAHD-HOO)

Madhulekha Sweet girl, beautiful girl. The name is derived from the Sanskrit *madhu* (sweet, honey; beautiful). (MAHD-HOO-LAY-KAH)

Madhur From the Sanskrit *madhura* (sweet, pleasant). (MAHD-HOOR)

Mahi The earth. (MAH-HEE)

Mahika The earth. (MAH-HEE-KAH)

Mahima Greatness. Derived from the Sanskrit *mahā* (great). (MAH-HEE-MAH)

Maiteryi Borne by one of the wives of the great sage and philosopher Yajnavalkya. Katyayani was the name of his other wife. (MĪ-TAY-REE-EE)

Malati Derived from the Sanskrit *mālāti* (the jasmine flower). The word has the alternative definitions of "night" and "moonlight." (MAH-LAH-TEE)

Mali Gardener. (MAH-LEE)

Manikarnika Compound name composed from *mani* (jewel) and *karnik* (in control). The word *mani* is also used to indicate the penis, and as a name, it is considered to be somewhat magical, making it a popular element in compound names. Manikarnika was the name given to Rani Lakshmi Bai (1835–58) upon her birth. She was married in 1842 to Raja Gangadhar Rao, who changed her name. She is remembered for her bravery and her determined fight to regain the lands taken from her by the British upon the death of her husband. A skilled military leader and stateswoman, she gathered together a force of 15,000 men to fight for independence. Rani Lakshmi Bai was killed in battle on June 17, 1858. (MAH-NEE-KAR-NEE-KA)

Manjika Sweet sounding. (MAN-JEE-KA)

Manjulika Sweet. (MAN-JOO-LEE-KA)

Maraalika Small swan. (MAR-AH-LEE-KA)

Margi Direction. (MAR-GEE)

Mauli Crown, hair. (MAU-LEE)

Maya Illusion, fantasy. (MAY-AH)

Meena Derived from the Sanskrit *mīna* (fish; precious stone). The name is borne in Indian mythology by a daughter of Usha, the goddess of the dawn, and by a daughter of Kubera, the god of wealth and riches. Var: Meenal, Minal, Minali, Minisha. (MEE-NA)

Mehal Rain. (MAY-HAHL)

Mehjibin A borrowing from the Persian, Mehjibin (woman with a face as beautiful as the moon) is from the elements *mah* (moon) and *jibīn* (the temple, the side of the face). (MAY-JEE-BEEN)

Mehli Rain. (MAY-LEE)

Mili To meet. (MEE-LEE)

Mira Wealthy. The name was borne by one of India's greatest female saints, Mira Bai (1498–1547). Embittered by a series of deaths in her family, she spent most of her time pursuing the *bhakti* (devotion) of Krishna and writing poetry. Var: Meera, Miraata. (MEE-RA)

Mohana Feminine form of Mohan, which is derived from the Sanskrit *mohana* (enchanting, leading astray). The name is borne by one of the attendants of the god Vishnu. (MO-HAH-NAH)

Mohini Derived from the Sanskrit *muh* (to enchant, to lead astray). Mohini is the name the god Vishnu used when he disguised himself as a beautiful woman in order to interrupt Shiva's meditation. (MO-HEE-NEE)

Mona Alone, single, quiet. (MO-NAH)

Monika Derived from *mona* (alone, single, quiet) and the diminutive suffix *-ka:* hence, "little quiet one." (MO-NEE-KAH)

Nadira A borrowing from the Arabic, Nadira is derived from *nādir* (rare, precious), which is from *nadara* (to be rare). (NAH-DEER-AH)

Nahida Derived from the Arabic *nāhida* (a young girl with swelling breasts), which is from *nahada* (having round, swelling breasts). Var: Nahid. (NAH-HEE-DAH)

Nandana Derived from the Sanskrit *nanda* (joy, happiness). Var: Nandini, Nandita. (NAN-DAN-A)

Naresha Feminine form of Naresh (lord of men, ruler of men), a name composed from the elements *nara* (man) and *īśa* (lord, ruler). (NAH-RAY-SHA)

Naseem Morning breeze. (NAH-SEEM)

Nasrin Derived from the Persian *nasrīn* (wild rose). Var: Nasreen. (NAS-REEN)

Nayana Having beautiful eyes, lovely eyes. (NAY-YAH-NA)

NEHA Affectionate, loving. Var: Nehali, Nehi. (NAY-HA)

NIMA Popular name borrowed from that of the margosa tree. Var: Neema, Neemah. (NEE-MA)

NIMESHA Momentary, quick. It is indicative of an action that takes place in an instant. Var: Naimishi. Pet: Nimmi. (NEE-MAY-SHA)

NINA Popular name meaning "beautiful eyes, having lovely eyes." Var: Neena, Neenah. (NEE-NAH)

NIRANJANA Night of the full moon. Niranjana is a name of the goddesses Parvati and Durga. (NEE-RAN-JAN-AH)

NISHA Night. Var: Nishi. (NEE-SHA)

NITA Gracious, courteous. Var: Neeta, Nitali. (NEE-TAH)

NOOR From the Arabic *nūr* (light), which is from *nawara* (to illuminate). Var: Noora. (NOOR)

OJASVEE Luster, sheen, vitality. Var: Ojasvita. (O-JAS-VEE)

OMANA A woman. (O-MAH-NAH)

PAAVANA Clean, pure, unsullied. (PAH-VAH-NAH)

PAAVANI Borrowed from the name of the Ganges River, which flows from the Himalayas to the Bay of Bengal. The river is sacred and is seen as the "great purifier." (PAH-VAH-NEE)

PADMA Derived from the Sanskrit *padmā* (lotus). The word is also indicative of the chakras, the six points along the spine which are centers of psychic energy. Var: Padmini. (PAD-MA)

PADMASUNDARA Compound name composed of the elements *padmā* (lotus) and *sundara* (beautiful, attractive, lovely): hence, "beautiful lotus." (PAD-MA-SOON-DAH-RA)

PADMAVATI Derived from the Sanskrit *padmā* (lotus) and the possessive suffix *-vati* (resembling, having): hence, "lotus-like." Padmavati, a name of the goddess Lakshmi, was borne by a wife of the 3rd-century B.C. king Asoka of the Maurya dynasty. Short: Padma. (PAD-MA-VAH-TEE)

PANNA Emerald. (PAN-NA)

PARVANI Full moon, festival, celebration. Var: Parvina. (PAR-VAH-NEE)

PARVATI Popular name derived from the Sanskrit *pārvatī* (of the mountain). Parvati (daughter of the mountain) is a name of the goddess Devi in her mild form. (PAR-VAH-TEE)

PARVIN A borrowing from the Persian, Parvin is derived from *parvīn* (the Pleiades, star, one of the twenty-eight stations of the moon). Var: Parveen. (PAR-VEEN)

PAVANA Of the wind. Var: Pavani. (PAH-VAH-NAH)

PRAGYATA Wisdom, knowledge. (PRAG-YAH-TAH)

PRARTHANA Prayer. (PRAR-THA-NAH)

PRATIBHA Derived from the Sanskrit *pratibhā* (light, intelligence, understanding). (PRAH-TEEB-HAH)

PREMA Derived from the Sanskrit *prema* (love, affection). Prema is used as an element in many popular Indian names. (PRAY-MAH)

PREMLATA From the Sanskrit *premalatā* (a small creeping plant), used metaphorically as a symbol of love. (PRAME-LAH-TAH)

PRIYA Popular name derived from the Sanskrit *priyā* (beloved, dear, cherished; beautiful, lovely). Var: Priyal, Priyam, Priyanka, Priyasha, Priyata, Priyati. (PREE-YAH)

PROTIMA Borne by Protima Gauri Bedi, founder of Nrityagram (Village of Dance), a city devoted to the teaching of the seven classical Indian dances, two martial dance forms, Sanskrit, history, and Indian literature. (PRO-TEE-MAH)

PURNIMA Night of the full moon, day of the full moon. Derived from the Sanskrit *pūrnimā.* (POOR-NEE-MAH)

RADHA Popular name derived from the Sanskrit *rādhā* (success, prosperity, affection). The name is borne by a cowherd who is the beloved of Krishna. Their story is found in Jayadeva's poem the *Gita Govinda*. (RAHD-HAH)

RAJALAKSHMI Compound name composed from the elements *rāja* (king, sovereign) and Lakshmi, the name of the goddess of fortune. Pet: Raji. (RAH-JAH-LAK-SHMEE)

RAJANI Derived from the Sanskrit *rajanī* (the dark one, the night). Rajani is a name of the goddess Durga, the wife of Shiva. Var: Rajana, Rajni. (RAH-JAN-EE)

RAJATA Derived from the Sanskrit *rāja* (king, sovereign). (RAH-JAH-TAH)

RAJI Originally a short form of any of the various names containing the element *rāja* (king, sovereign), Raji is also bestowed as an independent given name. (RAH-JEE)

Rajnandini Compound name composed of the elements *rāj* (kingdom) and *nandini* (daughter): hence, "princess." (RAH-JNAN-DEE-NEE)

Ramaa Beautiful. Derived from the Sanskrit Ramā, a name of the goddess Lakshmi. Var: Ramya. (RAH-MAH)

Ramana Beautiful, a woman. Derived from the Sanskrit Ramā, a name of the goddess Lakshmi. Var: Ramani. (RAH-MAH-NAH)

Ramona Guardian, protector. (RAH-MO-NA)

Rana Derived from the Arabic *rana* (a beautiful object which catches the eye). (RAH-NAH)

Rani Derived from the Sanskrit *rani* (queen, sovereign). (RAH-NEE)

Ranita Tinkling. (RAH-NEE-TA)

Ranjana Pleasing, to worship, to adore. (RAN-JAH-NAH)

Ranya A borrowing from the Arabic, Ranya is derived from *ranya* (gazing at someone). (RAHN-YAH)

Rashida A borrowing from the Arabic, Rashida is derived from *rashīd* (rightly guided), which is from the verb *rashada* (to follow the right course). Var: Rasheeda. (RAH-SHEE-DAH)

Rati Popular name derived from the Sanskrit *rati* (rest, pleasure). Rati is the name borne by the wife of Kama, the god of love. (RA-TEE)

Ravija Born of the sun. Derived from the Sanskrit *ravi* (the sun). (RA-VEE-JA)

Riju Pure, innocent, untainted. (REE-JOO)

Rita Right, proper. (REE-TA)

Ritika Moving, flowing, running. (REE-TEE-KA)

Rohana Derived from the Sanskrit *rohana* (ascending, rising).

Roschan Derived from the Persian *roshan* (dawn of day, sunrise, light, shining). Var: Rochana, Rochani, Roschana, Roshan, Roshana, Roshni. (RO-SHAHN)

Roshanara A borrowing from the Persian, Roshanara is derived from *roshanārā* (light of the assembly). The name, indicative of great beauty, was borne by the youngest daughter of Shah Jahan (1592–1666). Upon her death, she was buried in his garden, which he named in her honor, the Garden of Roshan Ara. (RO-SHAN-AR-AH)

Ruchika Beautiful, attractive, lovely. (ROO-CHEE-KA)

Rukmini Derived from the Sanskrit *rukminī* (adorned with gold). Rukmini was the name borne by the daughter of King Bhishmaka who, in spite of her betrothal to King Sisupala, was the secret lover of Krishna and mother of his son Pradyumna. (ROOK-MEE-NEE)

Rupal Derived from *rūpa* (beauty, form). Var: Rupala, Rupali. (ROO-PAHL)

Rupinder Compound name composed of the elements *rūpa* (beauty, form) and Indra (the name of the chief god of the atmosphere, which is indicative of strength or excess): hence, "most beautiful." (ROO-PIN-DER)

Saba Derived from the Arabic *sabāh* (morning). (SAH-BAH)

Sachi Speech, eloquence. The name is borne by the mother of Chaitanya, a Vaishnavite saint. (SAH-CHEE)

Safia Derived from the Arabic *safiyya* (best friend, confidant). (SAH-FEE-YAH)

Salena The moon. (SAH-LAY-NAH)

Salma A borrowing from the Arabic, Salma is believed to be derived from *sālima* (safe, unharmed). Var: Salima. (SAHL-MAH)

Samina Happy. Var: Sameena, Sameenah. (SAH-MEE-NAH)

Sana Popular name meaning "praise, worship, prayer." (SAH-NAH)

Sananda Derived from *ānanda* (happiness, joy). (SAH-NAN-DA)

Sandyha Derived from the Sanskrit *sandhyā* (twilight). The name is borne by the personification of twilight, a daughter of the god Brahma. (SAN-DĪ-HAH)

Sanjana Gentle, tolerant. (SAN-JAH-NAH)

Santavana Hope. (SAN-TA-VAH-NAH)

Sanyogita Borne by one of the three queens of the Chauhan king Prithviraja (1162–92). (SAN-YO-GEE-TAH)

Sara A borrowing from the Arabic, Sara is from the Hebrew Sarah, a derivative of *sārāh* (princess; noble). (SAH-RAH)

Sarala Derived from the Sanskrit *sarala* (straight). (SAH-RAH-LAH)

Saraswati Derived from the Sanskrit *saras* (fluid, lake) and the possessive suffix *-vati* (having, resembling): hence, "having water, possessing a lake." (SAR-AHS-WAH-TEE)

Sarita A river, to flow. (SAH-REE-TAH)

SAROJA Derived from the Sanskrit *saras* (fluid, lake) and the suffix *-ja* (born): hence, "born in a lake." Saroja has the alternative definition "lotus." Var: Saroj. (SAH-RO-JA)

SAROJINI Derived from the Sanskrit *saroja* (lotus) and the possessive suffix *-ini:* hence, "having lotuses." The name was borne by Sarojini Naidu (1879–1949), the first woman president of the Indian National Congress. (SAH-RO-JEE-NEE)

SATYARUPA Derived from Satya (truth) and Rupa (beautiful, shapely), which is indicative of truth personified as a woman. The name was borne by the wife of Manu, the author of the *Manusmriti*, the code of ethics and social hierarchy by which Indian society lived for centuries. Var: Satarupa. (SAT-YAH-ROO-PA)

SAVITRI Derived from the Sanskrit *sāvitrī* (of the sun-god Savitr). The name is borne in the *Mahabharata* by the loyal wife of King Satyavan. After Satyavan's death, Savitri tirelessly lobbied the king of the underworld for Satyavan's life to be restored, which it finally was. Thus, Savitri has come to signify love and devotion. (SAH-VEE-TREE)

SHAHINA Tender, soft. (SHA-HEE-NA)

SHAHNAZ A borrowing from the Persian, Shahnaz is a compound name composed from *shāh* (king) and *nāz* (pride, glory). The name is indicative of one so beautiful she would be a king's pride and joy. (SHAH-NAZ)

SHAILA A name indicative of a small mountain. It is a name of the goddess Parvati. (SHĪ-LA)

SHAKUNTALA Derived from the Sanskrit *śakunta* (a bird). The name was borne in Indian mythology by the wife of King Dushyanta and mother of his son Bharata, from whom the country of India got its name of Bharat. (SHA-KOON-TAH-LAH)

SHAMEENA Popular name meaning "beautiful." (SHA-MEE-NAH)

SHANASA Praise, wish. (SHA-NAH-SAH)

SHANATA Derived from the Sanskrit *śānta* (pacified, calm). (SHA-NAH-TAH)

SHANTA Derived from the Sanskrit *śānta* (pacified, calm, controlled). The name is borne in the *Mahabharata* by the daughter of King Dasaratha and wife of the sage Rsyasrnga. Var: Shanti. (SHAN-TAH)

SHARADA Derived from the Sanskrit *śārada* (mature). Sharada is a name of the goddess Durga. (SHA-RAH-DAH)

SHARANEE Protector, guardian. Var: Sharanya. (SHA-RAH-NEE)

SHARDA Variant of Sharada, which is from the Sanskrit *śārada* (mature, ripe). The name was borne by Sharda Devi, the wife of spiritual leader Ramakrishna. At the age of five, she was wed to Ramakrishna in an unsuccessful effort to draw his attention away from religious involvement. Ramakrishna taught her spiritual matters and the *samadhi* (self-realization), and in time, actually worshiped her as the divine mother. Sharda Devi was known as the Holy Mother, and along with the devotee Vivekananda, carried on Ramakrishna's message after his death. (SHAR-DAH)

SHARNA Protection, guardian. (SHAR-NAH)

SHASHI Hindu name meaning "moonbeam." It was borne by one of the three queens of the Chauhan king Prithviraja (1162–92). (SHAH-SHEE)

SHASHIBALA Popular compound name composed of the elements *shasha* (moon, moonbeam) and *bala* (young girl): hence, "moon girl." (SHAH-SHEE-BAH-LAH)

SHASHINI Derived from the Sanskrit element *shahsa* (moon) and the possessive suffix *-ini:* hence, "having the moon, of the moon." (SHAH-SHEE-NEE)

SHEELA Derived from the Sanskrit *śīla* (kind, gentle, character, conduct), which is one of the six perfections to strive for. Var: Sheeli, Sheila. (SHEE-LAH)

SHIRIN Popular name derived from the Persian *shirīn* (charming, agreeable, sweet). Var: Shirina. (SHEE-REEN)

SHOBHA Derived from the Sanskrit *śobha* (splendor, beauty). (SHOB-HAH)

SHOBHANA Derived from the Sanskrit *śobhanā* (beautiful, splendid, brilliant). The name is borne in the *Mahabharata* by one of the Pleiades. Var: Shobhini. (SHOB-HAH-NAH)

SHONA Red, crimson, scarlet. (SHO-NAH)

SHRILEKHA Well-written, lustrous essay. (SHREE-LAY-KAH)

SHYAMA Derived from the Sanskrit *śyāma* (black, dark, beauty). The name is borne in Indian mythology by a daughter of Meru, the mountain at the center of the universe. She is seen as an incarnation of the Ganges River. It is also a name of the goddess Durga and the name of a goddess of the Jain religion. (SHĪ-YAH-MAH)

SHYLA One of the names of the goddess Parvati. (SHĪ-LAH)

SITA Derived from the Sanskrit *sītā* (furrow). The name is borne by the goddess of agriculture and the harvest, who is seen as an incarnation of the goddess

Lakshmi. Sita was married to Rama after he bent the great bow of Shiva, but was abducted by the evil king Ravana and taken to his island kingdom. She was rescued by Rama, but because the public doubted her virtue, she sacrificed herself by fire to prove her purity. She was restored to life by the fire-god Agni, but Rama yielded to public pressure and banished her. She lived in a hermitage with her twin sons until Rama accidentally found her. She gave him the children and was consumed by the earth, her spiritual mother. Sita is worshiped along with Rama. Var: Seeta, Seetha. (SEE-TAH)

SONA Gold. (SO-NAH)

SONAL Golden. Derived from *sona* (gold). Var: Sonala, Sonali, Sonika, Sonita. (SO-NAHL)

SRI Derived from the Sanskrit *śrī* (prosperity, power, beauty, luster). The name is borne by the goddess of prosperity, good fortune, and beauty. Also known as Lakshmi, she is the wife of Vishnu. Var: Shree, Shri. (SHREE)

SUDARSHANA Beautiful, handsome. Composed of the prefix *su-* (good) and *darshan* (vision). (SOO-DAR-SHAH-NAH)

SUHAILA Derived from the Arabic Suhayla, a popular name derived from *suhayl* (Canopus, the second-brightest star in the southern skies). (SOO-HAY-LAH)

SUJATA Composed of the prefix *su-* (good) and *jāta* (born): hence, "well-born, noble." (SOO-JAH-TAH)

SULAKHNA Borne by the young wife of Nanak, the founder of the Sikh faith. (SOO-LAK-NAH)

SUNAYANA Having beautiful eyes. Var: Sunayani. (SOO-NAY-YAH-NAH)

SUNDARI Attractive, beautiful, good-looking. Var: Sundara. (SOON-DAH-REE)

SUNITA Courteous, gracious, well-mannered. (SOO-NEE-TAH)

SUPRIYA Beloved. (SOO-PREE-YAH)

SURAGANA Divine, godly. Derived from the Sanskrit *sura* (god). (SOO-RAG-NAH)

SURINA A goddess. Derived from *sura* (god). (SOO-REE-NAH)

SUSHANTI Peace, quiet. (SOO-SHAHN-TEE)

SUSHILA Derived from the Sanskrit prefix *su* (good) and *śīla* (conduct): hence, "good conduct, proper." Var: Susheela. (SOO-SHE-LAH)

SUSHOBHANA Composed of the prefix *su-* (good) and *śobhanā* (beautiful, splendid, brilliant): hence, "very beautiful." (SOO-SHO-BAH-NAH)

SWARUP Borne by the mother of Jawaharlal Nehru, India's first prime minister. (SWAH-ROOP)

SYONA Beautiful, fortunate, happy. (SĪ-YO-NAH)

TAMANNA Desire, want, need. (TAH-MAN-NAH)

TAMAS Night, darkness. Var: Tamasa, Tamasi, Tamasvini. (TAM-AS)

TAMI The dark half of the moon. (TAM-EE)

TAMOHARA The sun. (TAM-O-HAR-AH)

TANAYA Daughter. Var: Tanuja. (TAN-AY-AH)

TANNISHTHA Dedicated, consecrated, devoted. (TAN-NISH-THA)

TANVI Young woman. (TAN-VEE)

TAPASYA Austerity, stern, severe. (TAP-AS-YAH)

TARA Derived from the Sanskrit *tārā* (star, planet, heavenly body). Tara is a name of the goddess Durga; the name of the wife of Brihaspati and mother of Budha the sun-god; the name of the wife of Buddha; the name of a Buddhist goddess; and the name of a goddess in the Jain religion. (TAH-RAH)

TARAL Flowing. (TAH-RAHL)

TARANI A beam of light. Var: Tarini. (TAH-RAH-NEE)

TARIKA Star, planet. (TAH-REE-KAH)

TARLA Fluid, flowing; brilliant, dazzling. (TAR-LAH)

TARUNIKA Young girl. (TAH-ROO-NEE-KAH)

TOSHALA One who satisfies. (TŌ-SHAH-LAH)

TRIPTA Satisfied, satiated. The name was borne by the mother of Nanak, the founder of the Sikh religion. (TRIP-TAH)

TUHINA Snow. (TOO-HEE-NAH)

UJALA Light. Var: Ujjala. (OOJ-AH-LAH)

UJILA Pure, bright, light. (OOJ-EE-LAH)

UJVALA Light, bright, beautiful. (OOJ-VAH-LAH)

UMA Popular name derived from *umā* (flax, turmeric). Uma is a name of the goddess Parvati. (OO-MAH)

UMALI Generous. (OO-MAH-LEE)

UMEEKA One of the names of the goddess Parvati. (OO-MEE-KAH)

UPALA Sandy shore. (OO-PAH-LAH)

USHA Popular name derived from the Sanskrit *usā* (dawn). Usha is the name given to the personification of dawn as the daughter of heaven and the sister of night. Var: Ushas. (OO-SHAH)

USHMIL Warmhearted. Var: Ushmila. (OOSH-MEEL)

VACHYA Expressed. (VACH-YAH)

VANAJA A girl of the forest. (VAN-AH-JAH)

VANALIKA Borrowed from the name of a sunflower. (VAN-AH-LEE-KAH)

VANDANI Worship, praise. Var: Vandana. (VAN-DAN-EE)

VANI Voice, sound. Vani is a name of the goddess Sarasvati. (VAN-EE)

VANIKA A little forest, a little wood. (VAN-EE-KAH)

VARANA A river. (VAH-RAH-NAH)

VARSHA A shower of rain. Var: Varisha. (VAR-SHAH)

VASUNDHARA The earth. (VAS-OON-DAH-RAH)

VEERA Brave, powerful, strong. (VEE-RAH)

VIDYA Education. (VEED-YAH)

VIJAYA Derived from the Sanskrit *vijaya* (victory). (VEE-JAY-YAH)

VIMALA Pure, attractive. (VEE-MAH-LAH)

VYOMA Sky. (VĪ-O-MAH)

VYOMIKA Of the sky. Vyomika is derived from *vyoma* (sky). (VĪ-O-MEE-KAH)

YAMINI Night, darkness. (YAH-MEE-NEE)

YASHILA Prosperous, successful. (YAH-SHEE-LAH)

YASHNA Prayer. Var: Yashnah. (YAHSH-NAH)

YASHODHANA Rich with prosperity and success. (YAH-SHŌD-HAH-NAH)

YASHODHARA Famous. The name was borne by the wife of Gautam Buddha. (YAH-SHŌD-HAR-AH)

YASHWINA Successful. (YASH-WEE-NAH)

YASMIN A borrowing from the Arabic, Yasmin is derived from *yāsamīn* (jasmine). Var: Yasmina, Yasminah. (YAS-MEEN)

YOSHA Woman. (YO-SHAH)

ZAHRA A borrowing from the Arabic, Zahra is derived from *zahra* (flower, blossom). (ZAH-RAH)

ZAINAB Derived from the Arabic *zaynab,* which is a borrowing of the name of a fragrant plant. The name was borne by a daughter of the Prophet Muḥammad, by two of his wives, and by one of his granddaughters. (ZAY-NAB)

ZAKIYYA A borrowing from the Arabic, Zakiyya is derived from *zakiy* (pure, clean, chaste), which is from *zaka* (to be pure, to be righteous). Var: Zakia, Zakiah, Zakiyyah. (ZAH-KEE-YAH)

ZARINA A borrowing from the Persian, Zarina is derived from *zarina* (golden, a golden vessel). (ZAH-REE-NAH)

ZUBAIDA Derived from the Arabic *zubaidā* (marigold). The name was borne by the wife (d. 831) of Harun al-Rashid, the fifth Abbasid caliph. The building of the city of Tabriz in 806 is attributed to her. Var: Zubeda. (ZOO-BAY-DAH)

CHAPTER THIRTEEN

Hungarian Names

THE EMERGENCE of Hungary as a major European power in the 19th century, and its alliance with Austria, has had a lasting effect on the bestowal of names. In addition to traditional Hungarian names, those with Germanic, Slavonic, and Latin roots are also now in common use. With the fall of communism, religion is once again freely practiced and Christian influence ensures the continued bestowal of saints' names. Anna, Maria, and Zsuzsánna are quite popular, as are István, János, and Miklós.

Unlike other European countries, Hungarians place the surname first.

Hungarian Male Names

ÁBEL Derived from the Hebrew *hebel* (breath). The name is borne in the Bible by the second son of Adam and Eve. (AH-BELL)

ÁBRAHAM Derived from the Hebrew Avraham (father of many, father of a multitude). The name is borne in the Bible by the first patriarch and ancestor of the Arabs and the Jews. (AHB-RAHM)

ÁDAM Derived from the Hebrew *adama* (red earth). The name is borne in the Bible by the first man created by God. (AH-DEM)

ADELBERT A borrowing from the German, Adelbert is derived from the Old High German Adalbrecht, a compound name composed from the elements *adal* (noble, nobility) and *beraht* (bright, famous): hence, "nobly bright, bright through nobility." Var: Albert. Short: Adel. Pet: Béla. (AH-DEL-BEHRT)

ADORJÁN Hungarian cognate of Adrian, a name derived from the Latin Adriānus (man from the city of Adria) and Hadriānus (man from the city of Hadria). Pet: Adi. (AH-DOR-YAHN)

ÁGOSTON Hungarian form of Augustinus, a diminutive form of the Latin Augustus, which is from *augustus* (great, venerable, consecrated by the augurs). (AH-GOSH-TON)

ALEXANDRE Hungarian form of the Greek Alexandros (defender or helper of mankind), which is composed from the elements *alexein* (to defend, to help) and *andros* (man). Short: Sándor. Pet: Sanyi. (AL-LEX-ZAHN-DREH)

ALFRÉD A borrowing from the English, Alfréd (elf counsel) is derived from the Old English Ælfred, a compound name composed from the elements *ælf* (elf) and *ræd* (counsel). Pet: Fredi. (AL-FREHD)

AMBRUS Hungarian cognate of the Greek Ambrosios, a name derived from *ambrosios* (immortal). (AHM-BRUS)

ANASZTÁZ Hungarian cognate of the Greek Anastasios, which is derived from *anastasis* (resurrection). (AH-NAHZH-SHTAZH)

ANDRAS Hungarian form of the Greek Andreas, which is derived from *andreios* (manly). Var: Andor, Andris, Endre. Pet: Andi, Bandi. (AHN-DRAHS)

ANTAL Hungarian form of Anthony, a name derived from Antonius, an old Roman family name of uncertain origin and meaning. "Priceless" and "of inestimable worth" are popular folk definitions of the name. Pet: Tonese, Toni. (AHN-TAHL)

ARISZTID Hungarian form of the Greek Aristides, a name derived from *aristos* (best). (AHR-eesh-teed)

ARON Hungarian form of Aaron, which is derived from the Hebrew *aharōn* (the exalted one). The name is borne in the Bible by the older brother of Moses. (AH-RUN)

ÁRPÁD Hungarian name meaning "seed." Árpád (?—907A.D.) was a Magyar leader and national hero of Hungary. (AHR-PAHD)

ARTUR Variant form of Arthur, a name of Celtic origin but of unknown meaning. *See* ARTHUR (English Names). (AHR-TOOR)

ATALIK Derived from the Tartar *ata* (paternal, father-like). (AT-TA-LEEK)

ATTILA Derived from the Latin family name Attilius, of uncertain etymology. Some believe it to be derived from the Tartar *ata* (paternal, father-like). (AH-TEE-LAH)

BALÁS Hungarian form of Blaise, a French name believed to be derived from the Latin *blaesus* (deformed, stuttering, a babbler). Var: Balász, Ballas. (BAH-LAHSH)

BÁLINT Hungarian name meaning "strong and healthy." Var: Baline. (BAH-LEENT)

BARNA Hungarian form of Barnabas, a name derived from the Aramaic *barnebhū'āh* (son of exhortation). The name is borne in the Bible by a Christian apostle and missionary companion of Paul. (BAR-NAH)

BARTALAN Hungarian form of Bartholomew, a name derived from the Late Latin Bartholomaeus, which is from Bartholomaios (son of Talmai). Talmai is an Aramaic name meaning "hill, mound, furrows." Var: Barta. Pet: Berti. (BAR-TEH-LAHN)

BÉLA Short form of Adelbert (nobly bright), Béla is also popularly bestowed as an independent given name. *See* ADELBERT. The name was borne by communist leader Béla Kun (1886–1939). (BAY-LEH)

BENEDIK Derived from the Latin Benedictus (blessed), which is from *benedicere* (to speak well of, to bless). The name was borne by St. Benedict (c. 480–543), an Italian monk and founder of the Benedictine Order. Var: Benedek. Short: Benek. Pet: Bence, Benci, Benke. (BEHN-NAH-DEEK)

BENJAMIN From the Hebrew Binyamin, which is derived from *binyāmīn* (son of the right hand, favorite son). The name is borne in the Bible by the youngest of Jacob's twelve sons. (BEHN-YAH-MEEN)

BERNÄT Hungarian form of Bernard, a name derived from the Old High German Berinhard (bold or strong as a bear), a compounding of the elements *bero* (bear) and *hard* (strong, brave, hearty). The name was borne by St. Bernard of Menthon (923–1008), a French monk who founded numerous hospices in the Swiss Alps. (BEHR-NOT)

BERTÓK Hungarian form of Bertram (bright raven), a derivative of the Old High German Berahtram, which is a variant of Berahthraban. The name is composed of the elements *beraht* (bright, famous) and *hraban* (raven). (BEHR-TOK)

BETHLEM Hungarian form of Bethlehem, a Hebrew name derived from *bēth lehem* (house of bread). Bethlehem, an ancient town of Judea, Palestine, was the birthplace of Jesus. The area is now part of western Jordan. (BETH-LEHM)

BOLDIZSÁR Hungarian form of Balthasar, a name medieval Christian tradition assigned to one of the three Wise Men who brought gifts to the Christ child. Some believe the name is derived from Belshazzar (Bel's prince) or from the Chaldean Beltshazzar (prince of splendor). Others think the name was merely an invention with an Eastern sound to it. Var: Boldisar. (BOLE-DEE-ZHAHR)

BORIS A borrowing from the Russian, Boris is derived from *boris* (fight). (BORE-EES)

DÁNIEL Derived from the Hebrew *dānī'ēl* (God is my helper). The name is borne in the Bible by a Hebrew prophet whose faith kept him alive in a den of hungry lions. Daniel and the Lions' Den was a favorite story during the Middle Ages, which helped to promote the use of the name across Europe. Var: Daneil. Pet: Dani. (DAN-EE-ELL)

DÁVID Derived from the Hebrew *dāvīd* (beloved). The name is borne in the Bible by the second and greatest of the Israelite kings. (DAY-VEED)

DEMETER Hungarian form of Demetri, a short form of the Greek Demetrios (of Demeter). Demeter is an ancient name of unknown etymology which was borne by the Greek mythological goddess of agriculture and fertility. Var: Dometer, Domotor. (DAY-MAY-TER)

DÉNES Hungarian form of the French Denes, a cognate of the Greek Denys, which is derived from Dionysius (of Dionysos). Dionysos is the name of the Greek mythological god of wine and revelry. Var: Dennes, Dienes. (DAY-NEHSH)

Dezső Hungarian form of the Latin Desiderius, which is derived from *dēsīderium* (desire, longing). (DEZH-O)

Ditrik Derived from the German Dietrich, a variant of Derek, which is a short form of Theodoric (ruler of the people). The name is from the Latin Theodoricus, which is believed to be derived from the Germanic Thiudoreiks, a compounding of the elements *thiuda* (folk, people) and *reiks* (ruler, leader, king). (DEE-TREEK)

Domokos Hungarian form of Dominic, a name derived from the Latin Dominicus (belonging to a lord), which is from *dominus* (a lord, a master). Var: Domonkos. Short: Dome, Domo. Pet: Dedo. (DŌ-MO-KOSH)

Donát Hungarian form of the Italian Donato, which is derived from the Late Latin Dōnātus (given by God). (DŌ-NAHT)

Dorján Hungarian form of Dorian, the name of one of the four main tribes of ancient Greece who settled in the mountainous area known as Doris. (DORE-YAWN)

Edgard Hungarian form of Edgar (spear of prosperity), an evolution of the Old English Ēadgar, which is composed of the elements *ēad* (prosperity, fortune, riches) and *gar* (a spear). (ED-GARD)

Edvard Hungarian form of Edward, an evolution of the Old English Ēadweard (wealthy protector), which is composed of the elements *ēad* (prosperity, fortune, riches) and *weard* (guardian, protector). (ED-VARD)

Elek Derived from the Greek Alexios, which is from the verb *alexein* (to defend, to help). Pet: Eli, Lekszi. (EL-LEK)

Elemér Hungarian form of Elmer, a name derived from the Old English Æthelmær (noble and famous), which is a compounding of the elements *æthel* (noble) and *mære* (famous). (EL-LEH-MEHR)

Elias A borrowing from the Greek, Elias is a cognate of the Hebrew Eliyahu, which is derived from *'ēlīyāhū* (Jehovah is God). Var: Illes. (EL-LEE-AHSH)

Emánuel Cognate of the Hebrew Immanuel, a name derived from *'immānūēl* (God is with us). The name was used in the biblical Old Testament by the prophet Isaiah in reference to the promised Messiah, and in the New Testament as another name for Jesus Christ. Pet: Mano. (EM-MAN-OO-EL)

Emil From the Latin Aemilius, an old Roman family name believed to be derived from *aemulus* (emulating, trying to equal or excel, rival). (EE-MEEL)

Erneszt Hungarian form of the German Ernest, an evolution of the Old High German Ernust and Ernost (earnest). Pet: Ernö. (EHR-NEZSHT)

Ernijó Derived from the Greek Eirenaios (peaceful), which is from *eirēnē* (peace). The name was borne by a father of the Eastern Church. (EHR-NEE-YO)

Ervin Hungarian cognate of the German Erwin, an evolution of the Old High German Herwin (friend of the army), which is a compounding of the elements *heri* (army) and *wine* (friend). (EHR-VIN)

Ferdinánd From the Spanish Ferdinando, which is of uncertain origin and meaning. *See* FERDINANDO (Spanish Names). Pet: Ferdi, Nandor. (FEHR-DEE-NAHND)

Ferenc Hungarian form of Francis, which is ultimately derived from the French *franc* (free). *See* FRANCIS (English Names). Var: Ferencz. Pet: Ferke, Ferko. (FEHR-ENK)

Filep Hungarian form of the Greek Philippos (lover of horses), which is composed from the elements *philos* (loving) and *hippos* (horses). The name is borne in the Bible by one of the Twelve Apostles of Christ. Var: Fülip, Fülöp. (FEE-LEP)

Fridrik Hungarian form of the German Friedrich (peace ruler). The name is derived from the obsolete Fridurih, a compounding of the elements *frid* (peace) and *rik* (ruler, king). Var: Fredek. (FREE-DREEK)

Gabriel From the Hebrew Gavriel, which is derived from *gavhrī'ēl* (God is my strength). The name is borne in the Bible by one of the seven archangels, the herald of Good News who appeared to Mary to announce her pregnancy and the impending birth of the Christ child. Pet: Gabi, Gábor. (GAB-RYEL)

Gáspár A name assigned to one of the Three Wise Men, who brought gifts to the Christ child, the others being Balthasar and Melchior. The names are not found in the Bible and are thought to have been fixed in the 11th century. Of uncertain etymology, Gaspar may have been derived from the Persian *genashber* (treasure master), which is in keeping with his role of the bringer of precious gifts. Pet: Gazsi. (GAHSH-PAHR)

Gellért Hungarian form of Gerard, a name derived from the Old High German Gerhart (brave with the spear). It is a compounding of the elements *ger* (a spear) and *hart* (hearty, brave, strong). Var: Geller. (GEL-EHRT)

Gergeli Hungarian cognate of Gregory (a watchman), which is from the Greek Grēgorios, a name derived from the verb *egeirein* (to awaken). Var: Gergelj, Gergely. Pet: Gergo, Gero. (GEHR-GELL-LEE)

GOTTFRID A borrowing from the German, Gottfrid is derived from the earlier Godafrid, a compounding of the elements *god* (God) and *frid* (peace): hence, "God's peace." (GOT-FREED)

GUSZTÁV From the German Gustav and the Swedish Gustaf, names of debated derivation. Some believe they are from the Germanic Gotzstaf (divine staff), a compounding of the elements *gott* (God) and *staf* (staff). Others feel they are derived from the Old Norse elements *Gautr* (the tribal name of the Goths) and *stafr* (staff): hence, "staff of the Goths." (GOOS-TAHV)

GYÖRGY Hungarian cognate of the Greek Geōrgios (earthworker, farmer), which is composed of the elements *gē* (earth) and *ergein* (to work). Var: Gyoergy. Pet: Gyuri, Gyurka. (DOR-DEE, DYOR-DEE)

GYULA Hungarian form of Julian, which is from the Latin Julianus, a derivative of Julius. Julius is an old Roman family name thought to be derived from Iulus (the first down on the chin, downy-bearded). Because a person just beginning to develop facial hair is young, "youth" became an accepted definition of the name. Var: Gyala. Pet: Gyuszi. (DOO-LAH, DYOO-LAH)

HAROLD Cognate of the Germanic Harald, a name composed from the elements *harja* (army) and *wald* (rule): hence, "ruler of an army." (HARR-OLD)

HENRIK Hungarian cognate of the German Heinrich (home ruler, ruler of an enclosure). *See* HEINRICH (German Names). (HEHN-REEK)

HERBERT A borrowing from the German, Herbert (bright army) is derived from the Old High German Heriberht and Hariberht, compoundings of the elements *heri, hari* (army) and *beraht* (bright, famous). (HEHR-BEHRT)

IGNÁC From the Latin Ignatius, which is derived from Egnatius, an old Roman family name of uncertain derivation. Some believe it to be from the Latin *ignis* (fire). Pet: Neci. (EEG-NACH)

IMRE Of debated origin. Some think it is of Germanic origin and derived from the element *irm(en)* (strength). Others believe it is a Hungarian form of the Germanic Emeric, which is thought to be a variant of Heinrich (home ruler, ruler of an enclosure). (EEM-REH)

INCE Derived from the Latin Innocent, which has its root in *innocens* (innocent). The name was borne by thirteen popes. (EEN-TSEH)

ISTVÁN Hungarian cognate of Stephen, which is from the Greek Stephanos, a name derived from *stephanos* (a crown, a garland). Pet: Pista, Pisti. (EESHT-VAN)

JAKOV Hungarian form of Jacob, which is from the Ecclesiastic Late Latin Iacomus and Iacobus, derivatives of the Greek Iakōbos, which is from the Hebrew Yaakov. The name has its root in *ya'aqob* (supplanting, seizing by the heel). The name is borne in the Bible by the father of twelve sons who founded the twelve tribes of Israel. Var: Jakab. (YAH-KAHV)

JÁNOS Hungarian cognate of John (God is gracious). The name is ultimately derived from the Hebrew *yehōhānān* (Yahweh is gracious). Pet: Janckzi, Jancsi, Jani, Jankia, Janko. (YAH-NOSH)

JENÖ Hungarian form of Eugene, which is from the Greek Eugenios, a derivative of *eugenēs* (well-born, noble). Pet: Jenci. (YEH-NO)

JÓZSEF Hungarian form of the Ecclesiastic Late Latin Joseph, which is from the Ecclesiastic Greek Iōsēph, a cognate of the Hebrew Yosef, which is derived from *yōsēf* (may he add). Var: Joszef. Pet: Joska, Joski, Jozsi. (YO-ZHEF)

JOZSUA Hungarian form of Joshua, a cognate of the Hebrew Yehoshua, which is derived from *yehōshū'a* (Jehovah is help, God is salvation). (YO-ZHOO-AH)

KÁLMÁN From the German Colman, a derivative of the Latin Columba (dove). (KAHL-MAN)

KARL A borrowing from the German, Karl is derived from the Old Norse and Germanic *karl* (a man, freeman, peasant). (KARL)

KÁROLY Hungarian cognate of Charles, a name derived from the Germanic *karl* (a man, freeman, peasant). Pet: Karcsi, Kari. (KAH-RO-LY)

KAZMÉR Derived from the Slavonic Kazimeriz, a compounding of the elements *kazić* (to destroy, to corrupt) and *meri* (great, famous): hence, "famous destroyer." (KAHZ-MEER)

KLEMENT From the Late Latin Clēmens, which is derived from *clemens* (mild, gentle, merciful). Var: Kelemen, Kellemen, Klemen. (KLEH-MEHNT)

KOLOMAN Believed to be derived from the elements *kol* (council) and *man* (man): hence, "councilman." (KO-LOW-MAN)

KONRÁD A borrowing from the German, Konrád is from the Old High German Kuonrat, a compound name composed of the elements *kuon* (bold, wise) and *rat* (counsel): hence, "wise counsel." Pet: Kurt. (KON-RAHD)

KORNÉL From the Latin Cornelius, an old Roman family name of uncertain etymology. Some believe it to be derived from the Latin *cornu* (horn). (KOR-NELL)

KRISTÓF Hungarian form of Christopher (bearing Christ), a cognate of the Greek Christophoros, which is a compounding of the elements *Christos* (Christ) and *pherein* (to bear). The name was borne by St. Christopher, a 3rd-century Christian martyr of Asia Minor who is the patron saint of travelers. (KREESH-TOF)

LADISLAS From the Slavonic Vladislav, a compound name composed from the elements *volod* (rule) and *slav* (glory): hence, "glorious rule." Var: László. Pet: Laci, Lacko, Laczko, Lazlo. (LAHD-ISS-LAHS)

LAJOS Hungarian form of Louis, a name derived from the Old High German Hluodowig (famous in war), a compounding of the elements *hluod* (famous) and *wīg* (war, strife). (LAH-YOHS)

LORENCZ Hungarian form of Laurence, which is from the Latin Laurentius (man from Laurentum). Laurentum, the name of a town in Latium, is probably derived from *laurus* (laurel). Var: Loránt, Loreca, Lorenc, Lörinc, Lorinez. Pet: Lenci. (LOR-REHNCH)

LUKACZ Hungarian form of Lucas, a Latin derivative of Lucius, which is from the root *lux* (light). Var: Lúkács. (LOO-KAHCH)

MARKUS Derived from the Latin Marcus, a name of uncertain derivation. Most believe it has its root in Mars, the name of the Roman mythological god of war. Others, however, think it is from *mas* (manly) or from the Greek *malakoz* (soft, tender). The name is borne in the Bible by one of the four evangelists, the author of the second Gospel, Mark. Pet: Marci. (MAR-KUS)

MARTONI Hungarian form of Martin (war-like), which is from the Latin Martinus, a derivative of Mars, the name of the Roman mythological god of war. Var: Márton. (MAHR-TOH-NEE)

MÁTYÁS Hungarian form of Matthias, a contraction of the Greek Mattathias, a cognate of the Hebrew Matityah, which has its root in *mattīthyāh* (gift of God). Pet: Máté. (MAH-TYASH)

MIHÁLY Hungarian form of Michael, a Hebrew name derived from *mīkhā'ēl* (who is like God?). The name is borne in the Bible by the archangel closest to God, the one responsible for carrying out God's judgments. Pet: Mika, Misi, Miska. (MEE-HAHL-LEE)

MIKLÓS Hungarian form of the Greek Nikolaos (victory of the people), a compound name composed from the elements *nikē* (victory) and *laos* (the people). (MEEK-LOSH)

MIKSA Hungarian cognate of the Latin Maximus, a name directly derived from *maximus* (greatest). (MEEK-SHA)

MORICZ Hungarian cognate of Maurice, a name derived from the Latin Mauritius (Moorish), a derivative of Maurus (a Moor). The name also came to mean "dark" or "swarthy" in reference to the coloring of the Moors. Pet: Mór. (MOR-EETSH)

MÓZES Hungarian form of the Ecclesiastic Greek Mōsēs, which is from the Hebrew Moshe, a derivative of *mōsheh* (drawn out of the water) and the Egyptian *mes*, *mesu* (son, child). The name is borne in the Bible by the leader who brought the Israelites out of bondage in Egypt. He received the Ten Commandments on Mount Sinai and led his people to the borders of Canaan and the Promised Land. Var: Mozses. (MO-ZHESH)

ÖDÖN Hungarian cognate of Edmund, a name derived from the Old English Ēadmund (wealthy protection), a compounding of the elements *ēad* (prosperity, fortune, riches) and *mund* (hand, protection). Pet: Ödi. (OO-DUN)

ORBÁN Hungarian form of Urban, a name derived from the Latin Urbānus (city dweller, urban), which has its root in *urbs* (a city). (OR-BAHN)

OSZKAR Hungarian form of Oscar, a name derived from the Old English Osgar (god spear), which is a compounding of the elements *os* (a god) and *gar* (a spear). (ŌSH-KAR)

OTTO From the Old High German Otho and Odo, which are derived from *auda* (rich). The name was borne by Otto I (912–73), a German king and emperor of the Holy Roman Empire. (Ō-TŌ)

PÁL Hungarian form of Paul, a name derived from Paulus, an old Roman family name derived from the Latin *paulus* (small). The name was adopted in the Bible by Saul of Tarsus upon his conversion to Christianity. Pet: Páli, Palko. (PAHL)

PÉTER Derived from the Ecclesiastic Late Latin Petrus and the Ecclesiastic Greek Petros, names derived from *petra* (a rock) and *petros* (a stone). The name is borne in the Bible by one of the Twelve Apostles of Christ. St. Peter is regarded as the first pope of the Catholic Church. Pet: Peterka, Peti. (PEH-TER)

PISTA A pet form of István, the Hungarian cognate of Stephen, Pista is also bestowed as an independent given name. *See* ISTVÁN. Pet: Pisti. (PEE-STAH)

REINHARD A borrowing from the German, Reinhart is an evolution of the older Raginhart, a compounding of the elements *ragin* (counsel, advice) and *hart* (hearty, brave, strong): hence, "brave counsel." (RINE-HARD)

RIKÁRD Hungarian cognate of Richard, an evolution of the Old High German Richart (brave ruler), which is a compounding of the elements *rik* (power, king, ruler) and *hart* (hearty, brave, strong). (REE-KARD)

RÓBERT Derived from the Old High German Hruodperht, a compound name composed from the elements *hruod* (fame, famous) and *beraht* (bright): hence, "bright with fame." Pet: Robi. (RO-BEHRT)

RUDOLF Derived from the Old High German Hrodulf (wolf fame, famous wolf), a compound name composed from the elements *hruod* (fame, famous) and *wulf* (wolf). Pet: Rudi. (ROO-DOLF)

SALAMAN Hungarian form of Solomon, a Hebrew name derived from *shĕlōmōh* (peaceful). Var: Salamon. (SHAH-LAH-MUN)

SÁMUEL Hungarian form of Samuel, a cognate of the Hebrew Shmuel, which is derived from *shĕmū'ēl* (name of God, his name is God). The name is borne in the Bible by a Hebrew judge and prophet who anointed Saul as the first king of Israel. Pet: Sami, Samu. (SHAHM-YOOL)

SÁNDOR A short form of Alexandre (defender or helper of mankind), Sándor is also popularly bestowed as an independent given name. *See* ALEXANDRE. Pet: Sanyi. (SHAHN-DOR)

SEBESTYEN Hungarian form of Sebastian, a derivative of the Greek Sebastianos (a man of Sebastia). Sebastia was the name of Samaria after the time of Herod the Great (73?–4 B.C.). Pet: Sebo. (SHEH-BAHSH-TEHN)

SIMON Derived from the Hebrew Shimon, which is from *shim'ōn* (heard). The name is borne in the Bible by two of the Twelve Apostles and a brother of Jesus, as well as several other New Testament characters. (SHEE-MON)

TÁBOR Derived from *tábor* (camp). (TAH-BOR)

TAMÁS Hungarian cognate of Thomas, an Ecclesiastic Greek name derived from the Aramaic *tĕ'ōma* (a twin). The name is borne in the Bible by an apostle who doubted the resurrection of Christ. Pet: Tomi. (TAH-MAHSH)

TOBIAS Ecclesiastic Late Latin name derived from the Ecclesiastic Greek Tōbias, which is from the Hebrew *tōbhīyāh* (the Lord is good). (TŌ-BEE-AHSH)

TWDOR Hungarian form of Theodor, a derivative of the Latin Theodorus, which is from the Greek Theodōros (gift of God). The name is composed from the elements *theos* (God) and *dōron* (a gift). Var: Tivadar, Todor. (TWOO-DORE)

VIDA Derived from the Latin *vitus* (life). (VEE-DAH)

VIKTOR Hungarian form of Victor, a name derived from the Latin *victor* (winner, conqueror, victor). Var: Vidor. (VEEK-TOHR)

VILHELM Hungarian cognate of the German Wilhelm (resolute protector), a name derived from the Old High German Willehelm, which is a compounding of the elements *willeo* (will, desire) and *helm* (helmet, protection). Var: Vilmos. Pet: Vili. (VIL-HELM)

VINCENZE From the Late Latin Vincentius (conquering), which is derived from *vincere* (to conquer). Short: Vincze. Pet: Vinci. (VEEN-CHENZEH)

WALTER Derived from the Frankish Waldhere (ruler of an army), a compound name composed of the elements *waldan* (to rule) and *heri, hari* (army). (WAL-TER)

ZOLTÁN Of Greek origin, derived from *zōē* (life). (ZOLE-TAHN)

ZSIGMOND Hungarian form of the German Siegmund (victorious protection). The name is a compounding of the elements *sig* (victory) and *mund* (hand, protection). Var: Zsigmund. Pet: Zsiga, Zsigi. (ZHIG-MUND)

Hungarian Female Names

ÁGATHA Derived from the Greek Agathē, which is from *agathos* (good, kind, honorable). The name was borne by a famous 3rd-century saint. *See* AGATA (Italian Names). Var: Ágota, Ágotha. Pet: Agi. (AHG-AH-THA)

ÁGNES Hungarian form of Agnes, a Latinized form of the Greek Hagnē, a name derived from *hagnos* (chaste, pure, sacred, holy). The name was borne by a thirteen-year-old Roman martyred for her Christian beliefs during the reign of Diocletian. (AHG-NESH)

ALBERTA Feminine form of Albert (bright through nobility). *See* ADELBERT (Male Names). Short: Berta. (AHL-BEHR-TAH)

ALEXANDRA Feminine form of Alexandre (defender or helper of mankind). *See* ALEXANDRE (Male Names). Short: Alexa. (AH-LEHK-SAHN-DRAH)

ALIDA Hungarian form of the German Aleida, a variant form of Adalheid (noble one). The name is derived from the Old High German Adalheidis, a compounding of the elements *adal* (noble) and *heid* (kind, sort). (AH-LEE-DAH)

ALISZ Hungarian form of Alice, a name ultimately derived from the Old High German Adalheidis (noble one). *See* ALICE (English Names). Var: Aliz. (AH-LEEZH)

AMÁLIA A borrowing from the German, Amália is derived from the element *amal* (work): hence, "industrious." Pet: Mali, Malika. (AH-MAH-LEE-AH)

ANASTASIA A borrowing from the Greek, Anastasia is a feminine form of Anastasios (of the resurrection), which is derived from *anastasis* (resurrection). Var: Anasztaizia. (AH-NAHSH-TAH-SHEE-AH)

ANGYALKA Hungarian form of Angelica, which is derived from the Latin *angelicus* (angelic, like an angel). (AHN-DAHL-KAH, AHN-DYAHL-KAH)

ANIKÓ Pet form of Anna (gracious, full of grace, mercy), Anikó is also popularly bestowed as an independent given name. *See* ANNA. Pet: Anci, Annuska, Nina. (AHN-NEE-KO)

ANNA Cognate of the Hebrew Hannah, which is derived from *hannāh, chaanach* (gracious, full of grace; mercy). The name was assigned in medieval times to the mother of the Virgin Mary, as Joachim was assigned to her father. Pet: Anikó, Annuska, Anyu, Nancsi, Nin, Ninacska, Nusa, Nusi, Panna, Panni. (AH-NAH)

AURELIA Feminine form of the Latin Aurēlius (golden), which has its root in *aurum* (gold). Pet: Aranka, Aranyu. (OR-RELL-EE-AH)

BERTA A borrowing from the German, Berta is derived from *beraht* (bright, famous). It is also commonly used as a short form of Alberta (bright through nobility). Pet: Bertuska. *See* ALBERTA. (BEHRT-TAH)

BORBÁLA Hungarian form of Barbara (foreign woman), a name derived from the Latin *barbarus* (foreign, strange). Pet: Boriska, Borsca. (BOR-BAHL-LAH)

CILI Hungarian form of Cecilia, a name derived from the Latin Caecilia, which is the feminine form of Caecilius, an old Roman family name derived from *caecus* (blind, dim-sighted). (TSEE-LIH)

CZENZI Derived from the Latin Cresentia, which is from the root *crescere* (to grow, to increase). (ZHEN-ZHEE)

DOROTHYA Hungarian cognate of the Greek Dorothea (gift of God), a compounding of the elements *dōron* (gift) and *theos* (God). Var: Doroltya, Dorottya. Short: Dora. Pet: Dorika. (DOR-AH-TEE-YAH)

EDITH A borrowing from the English, Edith is derived from the Old English Ēadgyth (prosperous in war), a compound name composed from the elements *ēad* (prosperity, fortune, riches) and *gyth* (war, strife). Var: Edit. Pet: Duci. (EE-DITH)

ELIZA A short form of Elizabeta (God is my oath), Eliza is also bestowed as an independent given name. *See* ERZSÉBET. (EE-LEE-ZHA)

ERIKA A borrowing from the German, Erika is a feminine form of Erik (eternal ruler). *See* ERIK (German Male Names). (EHR-REE-KAH)

ERNESZTINA Feminine form of Erneszt (earnest). *See* ERNESZT (Male Names). Short: Erna. (EHR-NEZH-SHTEE-NAH)

ERZSÉBET Hungarian cognate of Elizabeth, a name derived from the Hebrew *elīsheba'* (God is my oath). The name is borne in the Bible by the mother of John the Baptist. Var: Elizabeta, Erzébet, Orzsébet. Short: Eliza, Liza. Pet: Beti, Boske, Bözsi, Erszok, Erzsi, Liszka, Orse, Oriske, Zsa Zsa. (EHR-ZHEH-BET)

ESZTER Hungarian form of Esther, a name of debated origin and meaning. Some believe it to be the Persian translation of the Hebrew Hadassah (myrtle); others think it is derived from the Persian *stara* (star). It has also been suggested that it is derived from the Babylonian Ishtar, the name of a goddess of love and fertility. The name is borne in the Bible by the Jewish wife of King Ahasuerus. Var: Ester. Pet: Eszti. (EHZH-TER)

ETEL Hungarian cognate of Ethel, an English name that originated as a short form of any of the various Old English names containing the element *æthel* (noble). Pet: Etilka. (EH-TEL)

ÉVA Derived from the Hebrew Chava, which is from *hawwāh* (life). The name is borne in the Bible by the first woman, "the mother of all the living." She is said to have been created from one of Adam's ribs. The name is borne by Hungarian-born actress Eva Gabor. Pet: Evike, Evacska. (Ā-VAH)

FELÍCIA Feminine form of Felix, which is derived from the Latin *felix* (happy, lucky). (FAY-LEE-CHA)

FLORA Derived from the Latin *floris* (a flower). The name is borne in Roman mythology by the goddess of flowers and spring. Pet: Florka. (FLOR-AH)

FRANCZISKA Hungarian form of Francesca, the feminine form of Francesco, which is from the Middle Latin Franciscus, a derivative of Francus (a Frank, a freeman). Var: Franciska. Pet: Franci. (FRAHN-TSEESH-KAH)

FREDERICA A borrowing from the Italian, Frederica is a feminine form of Frederick (peace ruler, ruler of peace). *See* FRIDRIK (Male Names). Pet: Frici, Frida. (FRED-EH-REE-KAH)

FRIDA A pet form of Frederica (peace ruler), Frida is also bestowed as an independent given name. *See* FREDERICA. (FREE-DAH)

GABRIELL Feminine form of Gabriel (God is my strength). *See* GABRIEL (Male Names). (GAB-RYELL)

GERTRUD Derived from the Old High German Geretrudis, a compound name composed of the elements *ger* (spear) and *trut* (dear, maiden) or *þruþ* (strength). (GEHR-TRUD)

GITA Derived from the Greek Margarītēs, which is from *margaron* (a pearl). (GEE-TAH)

GIZELLA Hungarian form of the German Giselle (a pledge), which is derived from *gisil* (to owe, a pledge, a mutual obligation). It was a practice in the early Middle Ages for rival factions to offer a person, often a child, to each other as a mutual pledge of peace. Pet: Gizi, Gizike. (GEE-ZELLA)

GYÖRGYI Feminine form of György, the Hungarian cognate of George (earthworker, a farmer). *See* GYÖRGY (Male Names). Györgyi is equivalent to Georgina. (DYOR-DYEE)

HAJNA Hungarian form of Hannah, a Hebrew name derived from *hannāh*, *chaanach* (gracious, full of grace, mercy). The name is borne in the Bible by the mother of the prophet Samuel. (HAH-NAH)

HAJNAL Hungarian name meaning "dawn." (HAH-NAHL)

HEDVIGA Hungarian form of the German Hedwig, a name derived from the Old High German Haduwig, which is a compounding of the elements *hadu* (contention) and *wīg* (war, strife). (HEHD-VEE-GAH)

IDA A borrowing from the German, Ida is derived from the element *īd* (work, labor). (EE-DAH)

ILDIKÓ Of Germanic origin meaning "warrior." (EEL-DYEE-KO)

ILONA Hungarian form of the Greek Helenē, a name derived from the root *ēlē* (light, torch, bright). Var: Onella. Pet: Ica, Ili, Ilka, Ilonka, Iluska. (EE-LO-NAH)

IRÉN Hungarian form of Irene, a cognate of the Greek Eirēnē (peace). The name was borne by the Greek mythological goddess of peace. Pet: Irenke. (EE-REHN)

IRMA A borrowing from the German, Irma originated as a short form of any of the various names, many now obsolete, beginning with the element *irm(en)* (strength), which is from Irmen, the name of the Germanic god of war. Pet: Irmuska. (EER-MAH)

IZABELLA Hungarian form of the Spanish Isabella, a variant form of Elizabeth (God is my oath). Short: Bella. (EE-ZHA-BEHL-LAH)

JAKOVA Feminine form of Jakov (supplanting, seizing by the heel). *See* JAKOV (Male Names). (YAH-KAHV-AH)

JOHANNA Latinate feminine form of Johannes, which is a cognate of John (God is gracious). *See* JOHN (English Male Names) Pet: Janka. (YO-HAHN-AH)

JOLÁN Hungarian name meaning "country." Pet: Jolanka, Joli. (YO-LAHN)

JOZSEFA Feminine form of József (may he add, God shall add). *See* JÓZSEF (Male Names). Var: Jozefa. Short: Jozsa. (YO-ZHEH-FAH)

JUDIT Hungarian form of Judith, a cognate of the Hebrew Jehudith and Yehudit, feminine forms of Jehuda and Yehūdhāh. These names, Anglicized as Judah, mean "he will be praised." Because Judah was also the name of a kingdom in ancient Palestine, the name can also mean "from Judah." Pet: Jucika, Juczi, Jutka, Juthe. (YOO-DEET)

JULI Hungarian form of Julia, a feminine form of Julius (downy-bearded, the first down on the chin, youth). *See* GYULA (Male Names). Pet: Julcsa, Julinka, Julis, Juliska. (YOO-LEE)

JULIANJA Hungarian form of Juliana, an elaborated form of Julia (youth). *See* GYULA (Male Names). Var: Julianna. Pet: Julcsa, Julinka, Juliska. (YOO-LEE-AH-NYAH)

KAMILLA From the Italian Camilla, a name derived from the Latin *camilla* (virgin of unblemished character). (KAH-MEE-LAH)

KAROLINA Feminine form of Károly, the Hungarian cognate of Charles. *See* KÁROLY (Male Names). Var: Karola. (KAH-RO-LEE-NAH)

KATARINA Hungarian cognate of the Greek Aikaterinē, a name derived from *katharos* (pure, unsullied). Var:

Katalin. Pet: Kali, Kata, Katica, Katicza, Katinka, Katoka, Kató. (KAH-TAH-REE-NAH)

KLÁRA Hungarian form of Clara, a name derived from the Latin *clārus* (bright, clear, famous). Pet: Klari, Kláríka. (KLAH-RAH)

KLÁRISZA Hungarian form of Clarissa, a name derived from the Latin Claritia, which is from *clārus* (bright, clear, famous). Pet: Klari. (KLAH-REE-ZHA)

KLOTILD Hungarian form of the German Clotilda, a name derived from the Old German Hlodhild, a compound name composed from the elements *hluod* (famous, renowned) and *hild* (battle, strife): hence, "famous in battle." (KLO-TEELD)

KONSTANCZIA Hungarian form of Constance, a feminine form of Constantine (constancy), which is from the Latin *constans* (constant, steadfast, unchanging). Short: Stanczia. (KONN-SHTAHN-ZHEE-AH)

KORNELIA Derived from the Latin Cornelia, a feminine form of Cornelius, an old Roman family name thought by some to be derived from *cornu* (horn). (KOR-NEE-LEE-AH)

KRISZTINA Hungarian cognate of Christina, a name derived from the Ecclesiastic Late Latin *christiānus* and the Ecclesiastic Greek *christianos* (a follower of Christ, a Christian). Short: Kriska, Kriszta. (KREEZH-TEE-NAH)

LILIKE Hungarian form of Lily, a name derived from the Latin *lilium* (a lily). The lily has long been seen as a symbol of purity and perfection. (LEE-LEE-KAH)

LIZA Short form of Elizabeta (God is my oath), Liza is also bestowed as an independent given name. *See* ERZSÉBET. Pet: Liszka. (LEE-ZHA)

LUCZA Hungarian form of Lucia, a feminine form of the Latin Lucius, which is derived from the root *lux* (light). (LOO-ZHA)

LUJZA Hungarian form of Louisa, a Latinate feminine form of Louis (famous in war). *See* LOUISE (English Names). Pet: Lujzi, Lujzika. (LOO-EE-ZHA)

MAGDOLNA Hungarian form of Magdalena, a Latinate form of the Ecclesiastic Greek Magdalēnē (woman from Magdala, a town near the Sea of Galilee). The name is borne in the Bible by Mary Magdalene, a woman Christ cured of seven demons. (MAH-DOL-NYA)

MARGARTA Hungarian cognate of the Greek Margarītēs, which is from *margaron* (a pearl). Var: Margit. Pet: Gitta, Margo, Rita. (MAHR-GAHR-TAH)

MARIA Latinate form of Mary, which is derived from the Hebrew Miryām, a name of debated meaning. Most believe it means "sea of bitterness" or "sea of sorrow." However, alternative definitions include "rebellion," "wished-for child," and "mistress or lady of the sea." The name is borne in the Bible by the Virgin Mary, the mother of Jesus Christ. Var: Mara, Marja. Pet: Marcsa, Mari, Marika, Mariska, Marka. (MAHR-YAH)

MÁRTA Hungarian form of Martha, which is derived from the Aramaic *mārthā* (lady, mistress). Pet: Martuska. (MAHR-TAH)

MATHILD Derived from the German Mathilda, a name derived from the Old High German Mahthilda (powerful in battle). The name is composed from the elements *maht* (might, power) and *hiltia* (battle). (MAH-TEELD)

MONIKA Hungarian cognate of Monica, an ancient yet still popular name of uncertain etymology. *See* MONICA (English Names). (MON-EE-KAH)

NATÁLIA A borrowing from the Latin, Natalia is derived from *diēs nātālis* (natal day, Christmas). The name is traditionally bestowed upon children born on Christmas Day. (NAH-TAHL-EE-AH)

OLGA A borrowing from the Russian, Olga is a feminine form of Oleg (holy), which is from the Scandinavian Helgi, a name derived from the Old Norse *heill* (hale, hardy; blessed, holy). Pet: Olgacska. (OHL-GAH)

ORSOLYA Hungarian form of the Latin Ursula, a name derived from *ursa* (she-bear). (OR-SHOL-YAH)

PAULA Feminine form of Paul, which is from Paulus, a name that originated as an old Roman family name derived from the Latin *paulus* (small). Pet: Palika, Paliki. (PAW-LAH)

PIROSKA Hungarian form of the Latin Priscilla, a feminine diminutive form of Priscus, which is an old Roman family name derived from *priscus* (ancient, primitive). Pet: Piri. (PEE-RO-SHKA)

REBEKA Hungarian form of the Ecclesiastic Greek Rhebekka, a name derived from the Hebrew *ribbqāh* (noose). The name is borne in the Bible by the wife of Isaac. (REH-BEH-KAH)

RÉZ Hungarian name meaning "redheaded, having red or copper-colored hair." (REHZ)

ROZSA Hungarian name meaning "rose." Pet: Rozsi. (RO-ZHA)

SARA Derived from the Hebrew Sarah, which is from *sārāh* (princess). The name is borne in the Bible by the wife of Abraham and mother of Isaac. Pet: Sári, Sarika, Sasa. (SHAH-RAH)

SOFIA Hungarian form of the Greek Sophia, a direct derivative of *sophia* (wisdom, skill). Var: Zsofe, Zsofia. (ZHO-FEE-AH)

TEREZIA Of uncertain derivation, most believe it to be derived from the Greek *therizein* (to reap, to gather in) and give it the definition "harvester." *See* TERESA (Spanish Names). Var: Teréza, Threzsi. Short: Terez. Pet: Rezi, Teca, Teri, Terus, Treszka. (TEH-REHZ-YAH)

TZIGANA Hungarian name meaning "gypsy." Var: Czigany, Tzigane, Zigana. (ZEE-GAH-NAH)

VERA Latin name derived from *verus* (true). (VEE-RAH)

VICA Hungarian cognate of Vita, a Latin name derived from *vitus* (life). Var: Vicuka, Vicus, Vicuska. (VEE-KAH)

VIKTORIA Hungarian cognate of the Latin Victoria, a name directly derived from *victoria* (victory). (VEEK-TOR-YAH)

VIVA Derived from the Latin *vivus* (alive). Pet: Vicuska. (VEE-VAH)

ZSA ZSA A pet form of Erzsébet (God is my oath), Zsa Zsa is also bestowed as an independent given name. *See* ERZSÉBET. The name is borne by Hungarian-born actress Zsa Zsa Gabor. (ZHAH-ZHAH)

ZSUZSÁNNA Derived from the Hebrew Shoshana, which is from *shōshannāh* (a lily, a rose). The name is borne in the New Testament by a woman who followed and cared for Jesus. Pet: Suzsi, Zsuzsi, Zsuzsika, Zsuzska, Zsuzsu. (ZHOO-SHAH-NAH)

CHAPTER FOURTEEN

Irish Names

THE ANCIENT cultural influences of the Celts and the Druids, as well as the later rule by the Vikings, Normans, and the English have all had a great influence on Irish society, and these events in history have produced many interesting names that have their roots in Gaelic, Old Norse, French, Old English, and other languages.

Surnames became hereditary during the reign of King Brian Boru in the tenth century, making Ireland the first European country after the fall of the Roman Empire to adopt hereditary family names. Most family names are patronymics that indicate descendancy from an early ancestor or, in some cases, from the father.

The O prefix in Irish surnames, such as O Murchadha, stands for the Gaelic word *ua,* which means "grandson of" or "descendant of." The Gaelic prefix for a girl is *Ni,* which means "daughter of," as in Ni Murchadha.

The words *giolla* or *gille* (follower of, servant of) and *maol* or *mael* (follower of, servant of) were often attached to saints' names. *O, Mac, Fitz,* and *Ni* also prefixed these names, creating combinations such as Mac Giolla Críost (son of the follower of Christ).

As the citizenry of Ireland converted to Christianity, they also learned to read and write. It was at this time that they began to record their pedigrees in writing, which until then were recited and often went far back to ancient kings and chieftains.

English domination and oppression had a great effect on Irish names. Early in the fifteenth century, all Irishmen living in the counties of Dublin, Louth, Kildare, and Meath were ordered by Edward IV to take an English surname. Many people adopted English surnames or translated their Gaelic surnames into English to avoid the penalty of forfeiture of all their yearly goods.

Because of persecution and domination, English names came into great use and Gaelic spellings of names were Anglicized. In recent years, in response to the activities of the Gaelic League, more people are choosing to bestow Gaelic names upon their children. Aoibheann, Éadaion, and Siobhán are popular girls' names. For boys, Aodhán, Cathaoir, and Lughaidh are popular.

Irish Male Names

ABBÁN Diminutive form of *abb* (an abbot): hence, "little abbot." The name was borne by a 6th-century saint from Leinster. Abban is the Anglicized form of the name. (Ā-BAHN)

ABRACHAM Gaelic form of Abraham (father of a multitude), a name introduced to Ireland by the Anglo-Normans. *See* ABRAHAM. Var: Ábraham. (Ā-BRAH-HAHM)

ABRAHAM Derived from the Hebrew Avraham (father of many, father of a multitude). The name is borne in the Bible by the first patriarch and ancestor of the Hebrews and the Arabs. Abracham and Ábraham are Gaelic forms. In Ireland, the name was borne by writer Abraham (Bram) Stoker, the author of *Dracula*. Short: Bram. (Ā-BRA-HAM)

ACHAIUS Classical Latin name used to Anglicize the Gaelic Eochaidh (horseman). *See* EOCHAIDH. (AH-KEE-US)

ADAMNAN Anglicized form of Adhamhnán (little Adam). *See* ADHAMHNÁN. Var: Adanodan, Awnan, Ounam. (AD-AM-NAN)

ÁDHAMH Gaelic form of Adam, a name derived from the Hebrew *adama* (red earth). The name is borne in the Bible by the first man created by God. (Ā-THUHV)

ADHAMHNÁN Diminutive form of Ádhamh, the Gaelic form of Adam: hence, "little Adam." The name was borne by St. Adhamhnán (c. 624–704), an Irish saint and biographer of St. Columba. He is believed to have been the first person to write of sightings of the Loch Ness Monster. (Ā-THUHV-NAHN)

AEDUS Latinized form of the Gaelic Aodh (fire). *See* AODH. (EE-DUS)

AENEAS Derived from the Greek Aineias (to praise), this name is used to Anglicize the names Aengus and Aonghus (one, choice) and Éigneachán (little death). *See* AENGUS *and* ÉIGNEACHÁN. Var: Eneas. (EE-NEE-US)

AENGUS A borrowing from the Scottish, Aengus is an Anglicized form of the Gaelic Aonghus (one, choice, preeminent). (EEN-GUS)

ÁGUISTÍN Gaelic form of Augustine, a name derived from the Latin Augustinus, a diminutive of Augustus, which is directly derived from *augustus* (great, venerable). Var: Abhuistín, Agaistin, Ághuistín, Aibhistín, Oistín. (AW-GOOY-STEEN)

AIDAN Anglicized form of Aodhán (little fiery one). The name was borne by a 7th-century saint who was bishop of Lindisfarne. *See* AODHÁN. Var: Aedan, Aiden, Edan. (Ā-DN)

AILBHE Old Gaelic name of uncertain derivation. The name was borne by a 6th-century Irish saint who is the patron saint of the Diocese of Emly. In Irish mythology, the name is borne by a hound belonging to Mac Dathó, a legendary king of Leinster. The name was Anglicized as Albert (noble and bright). (AL-VYEH)

AILILL Old Gaelic name meaning "sprite." Ailill is a name borne in Irish myth by a legendary king of Connaught and husband to Queen Meadhbh. (Ā-LIL)

AILÍN Gaelic form of Alan, a Celtic name of uncertain derivation. *See* ALAN. (Ā-LIN)

AINDRÉAS Gaelic form of Andrew (manly), a name introduced to Ireland by the Anglo-Normans. Andrew is derived from the Greek Andreas, which is from *andreios* (manly). Var: Aindrias, Aindriú. (AHN-DREE-AHS)

AINMIRE Old name believed to mean "great lord." The name was borne by a 6th-century king of Tara. (AHN-MEER)

ALAIOS Gaelic form of Aloysius, a Latinized form of Aloys, which is a Provençal cognate of Louis (famous in war), which is from the Old High German Hluodowig, a compounding of the elements *hluod* (famous) and *wīg* (war, strife). Var: Alabhaois. (Ā-LEESH)

ALAN Celtic name of uncertain derivation. Some connect the name to the Welsh Alawyn (harmony). Others suggest it is from the Gaelic *alainn* (bright, fair, handsome), *ail* (noble), *aile* (other), or from a diminutive form of *alp*, an old Celtic word meaning "rock." Ailín is the Gaelic form. Var: Allan, Allen. (AL-LEN)

ALASTAR Gaelic form of Alexander (defender or helper of mankind). *See* ALEXANDER. Var: Alasdair, Alastrann, Alastrom. (AL-AH-STAR)

ALBANY Derived from the Latin *albus* (white), Albany is used to Anglicize the Gaelic Fionn (white, fair). *See* FIONN. Var: Alban. (AHL-BAH-NEE)

ALEXANDER Derived from the Greek Alexandros (defender or helper of mankind), a compounding of the elements *alexein* (to defend, to help) and *andros* (man). (AL-EX-AN-DER)

ALISTAIR Anglicized form of Alastar, which is a Gaelic form of Alexander (defender or helper of mankind). *See* ALEXANDER. Var: Allister. (AL-ISS-TER)

ALSANDER Irish form of Alexander (defender or helper of mankind). *See* ALEXANDER. (AL-SAN-DAIR)

ANÉAS Gaelic form of Aeneas (to praise), a name brought to Ireland to Anglicize several Gaelic names. *See* AENEAS. Var: Aneas. (AH-NEE-AHS)

ANGUS A borrowing from the Scots, Angus is the popular Scottish cognate of Aengus (one, choice, preeminent). *See* AENGUS. Short: Gus. (ĀN-GUS)

ANLON Anglicized form of Anluan (great champion). *See* ANLUAN. (AN-LON)

ANLUAN Compound name composed of the Gaelic elements *an* (great) and *luan* (a champion, a hero). Anlon is the Anglicized form. (AN-LON)

ANTAINE Irish form of Anthony, an English cognate of Antonius, an old Roman family name of uncertain etymology. Var: Anntoin, Antoin, Antoine. (AN-TANE)

AODH Ancient yet still common name derived from the Old Irish Aed (fire), which is from the Celtic Aidus (fire). The name is Anglicized as Hugh. Var: Aodha, Aoidh. Pet: Aodhaigh. (EH)

AODHAGÁN Diminutive form of Aodh (fire): hence, "little fiery one, little ardent one." The name is Anglicized as Egan. Var: Aodhgan. (EH-GAHN)

AODHAIGH Pet form of Aodh (fire), which is Anglicized as Hughey. (EH-EE)

AODHÁN Popular diminutive form of Aodh (fire): hence, "little fiery one." The name is Anglicized as Aedan, Aidan, Aiden, and Edan. (EH-THAHN)

AODHFIN Compound name composed of the Gaelic elements *aodh* (fire) and *fionn* (white, fair): hence, "white fire." Var: Aodhfionn. (EH-FIN)

ARALT Irish form of Harold (leader of the army), an English name that replaced Haraldr, a name of the same meaning introduced by Norse invaders. *See* HAROLD. (AR-AHLT)

ARDAL Anglicized form of Árdghal (high valor). Var: Artegal, Arthgallo. (AR-DAHL)

ÁRDGHAL Old name meaning "high valor." It has been Anglicized as Ardal, Artegal, and Arthgallo. (AR-DAHL)

ART Ancient yet still popular Gaelic name derived from the Celtic Arto-s (a stone, a bear). Art has been Anglicized as Arthur, though the names are not related. (ART)

ARTHUR Of Celtic origin but of unknown meaning. The name was borne by the legendary British king Arthur, leader of the knights of the Round Table, who supposedly lived in the 5th or 6th century. The Gaelic form Artúr has been used in Ireland since at least the 7th century. (AR-THER)

ARTÚR Gaelic form of Arthur, a Celtic name of unknown meaning. *See* ARTHUR. Var: Artuir. (AR-TUR)

BAIRD Derived from *bard* (a poet, a singer of epic poems, a minstrel). (BAIRD)

BANAN Derived from the Irish *ban* (white). (BAWN-AN)

BANBHAN Diminutive form of *banbh* (piglet): hence, "little piglet." (BAWN-VAHN)

BAOTHGHALACH Compound name composed of the Gaelic elements *baoth* (foolish, vain) and *galach* (valorous). Baothghalach has been Anglicized as Behellagh, Beolagh, Boetius, and Bowes. (BEH-HEL-LAHK)

BARCLAY Transferred use of the Scottish surname derived from Berkeley, an English place-name derived from the Old English elements *beorc* (birch) and *lēah* (wood, clearing, meadow). The name has been used in Ireland to Anglicize Parthálan, the Gaelic cognate of Bartholomew. Var: Berkley. (BAR-KLAY)

BARRA Pet form of Fionnbhárr (fair head). *See* FIONNBHÁRR. (BAR-RAH)

BARRY Anglicized form of Bearach (spear-like), Barry is also used as a pet form of Finbar (fair head). *See* BEARACH *and* FINBAR. (BARE-REE)

BART A short form of Bartholomew (son of Talmai), Bart is also bestowed as an independent given name. (BART)

BARTHOLOMEW From the Middle English Bartelmeus, a cognate of the Late Latin Bartholomaeus, which is from the Aramaic Bartholomaios (son of Talmai). Talmai is an Aramaic name meaning "hill, mound, furrows." The name is borne in the Bible by one of the Twelve Apostles of Christ. Parthálan is the Gaelic form. Short: Bart. (BAR-THOL-O-MEW)

BARTLEY Variant form of Bartholomew (son of Talmai). *See* BARTHOLOMEW. Beartlaí is the Gaelic form. (BART-LEE)

BEACÁN Diminutive form of *beag* (small): hence, "little one, wee one." The name was borne by a 6th-century saint, founder of a monastery in Westmeath. Becan is the Anglicized form. (BEH-KAWN)

BEAG Derived from the Gaelic *beag* (small). Bec is the Anglicized form of Beag. (BEK)

BEANÓN Gaelic form of Benignus, a Latin name derived from *benignus* (good, well-born). Benen is the Anglicized form. Var: Beinean, Beineón, Binean. (BEH-NON)

BEARACH Derived from the Gaelic *bear* (a spear, javelin, lance): hence, "spear-like." The name, which was borne by a 6th-century saint, has been Anglicized as Barry. (BAHR-AHK)

BEARCHÁN Diminutive form of Bearach (a spear): hence, "little spear." The name, which has been Anglicized as Bercan, was borne by five Irish saints. *See* BEARACH. (BAHR-KAHN)

BEARTLAÍ Gaelic form of Bartley, a variant of Bartholomew (son of Talmai). *See* BARTHOLOMEW. (BAHR-LEE)

BEC Anglicized form of the Gaelic Beag (small). (BEK)

BECAN Anglicized form of the Gaelic Beacán (little one). (BEH-KAHN)

BEHELLAGH Anglicized form of Baothghalach (foolishly valorous). *See* BAOTHGHALACH. (BEH-HEL-LAHK)

BENEDICT Derived from the Latin Benedictus (blessed), which is from *benedicere* (to speak well of, to bless). The name was borne by St. Benedict (c. 480–543), an Italian monk and founder of the Benedictine Order. Benedict is regarded as an equivalent of the native Maolbheannachta (hoper for blessing). (BEN-EH-DIKT)

BENEN Anglicized form of Beanón, the Gaelic form of the Latin name Benignus (good, well-born). (BEN-EN)

BEOLAGH Anglicized form of Baothghalach (foolishly valorous). *See* BAOTHGHALACH. Var: Behellagh, Behillagh, Boetius, Bowes. (BEE-O-LAH)

BERCAN Anglicized form of Bearchán (little spear). *See* BEARCHÁN. Var: Bercnan, Bergin. (BER-KAN)

BLAINE Transferred use of the Celtic surname derived from the Gaelic *blian* (the groin; angular, thin, a hollow). Var: Blain. (BLANE)

BLAIR Transferred use of the Scottish surname derived from place-names containing the Gaelic element *blár* (a plain, a level field): hence, "dweller on the plain." Var: Blaire. (BLARE)

BRADY Transferred use of the surname originating from separate derivations. It is derived from the Old English elements *brad* (broad) and *ēage* (eye): hence, "one with broad eyes." It is also from the Old English elements *brad* (broad) and *ēg* (island) or *gehæg* (enclosure): hence, "dweller on the broad island; dweller near the broad enclosure." Var: Bradey. (BRAY-DEE)

BRAN Popular name derived from the Gaelic *bran* (raven). The name was borne by an old Celtic deity. (BRAN)

BRANDAN Of uncertain derivation, Brandan might be derived from the Gaelic *bran* (raven), or it might be a variant of Breandán (prince). *See* BREANDÁN. (BRAN-DAN)

BRANDUBH Compound name composed of the Gaelic elements *bran* (raven) and *dubh* (black, dark): hence, "black raven." Branduff is the Anglicized form. (BRAN-DUH)

BRANDUFF Anglicized form of Brandubh (black raven). *See* BRANDUBH. (BRAN-DUF)

BRASIL Anglicized form of the Gaelic Breasal (war, strife, battle). *See* BREASAL. Var: Brazil, Bresal. (BRA-SIL)

BREANDÁN Evolution of the older Bréanainn (prince). The name, which was borne by several Irish saints, has been Anglicized as Brendan and Brennan. Var: Breanndán. (BREHN-DAN)

BREASAL Evolution of the Old Irish Bressal, which is believed to be derived from the Celtic *brestelo-s* (war, strife, battle). The name has been Anglicized as Brasil, Brazil, Bresal, and Basil. (BREH-SAHL)

BRENDAN Anglicized form of Breandán (prince). *See* BREANDÁN. Var: Brennan. (BREN-DAN)

BRET A borrowing from the English, Bret is derived from the Old French *Bret* (a Breton), an ethnic name for a native of Brittany. Var: Brett, Britt. (BRET)

BRIAN Popular name of uncertain etymology. It is generally thought to be of Celtic origin, but its meaning is disputed. Some believe it to be derived from the root *bri* (force, strength), *brígh* (valor, strength), or *bruaich* (a hill, steep, high). The name was most famously borne by King Brian Boru (926?–1014), whose repeat victories over battles with the Danes crushed their attempts at the conquest of Ireland. He was finally killed on Good Friday in 1014 during the decisive Great Battle of Clontarf. Var: Bryan, Bryon. (BRI-AN)

BRODY Transferred use of the Anglicized surname meaning "son of Bruaideadh." Bruaideadh is a Gaelic name meaning "fragment." (BRO-DEE)

BRÓN Derived from the Gaelic *brón* (sorrow). The name was Anglicized as Brone. (BRONE)

BRONE Anglicized form of Brón (sorrow). (BRONE)

BUADHACH Derived from the Gaelic *buaidh* (victory). The name Buadhach (victor, conqueror) has been Anglicized as Buagh and Victor. Var: Buach. (BOO-AHK)

BUAGH Anglicized form of Buadhach (victor, conqueror). *See* BUADHACH. (BOO-AHK)

CADHLA Gaelic name meaning "handsome." (CAW-LAH)

CAFFAR Anglicized form of Cathbharr (helmet). (KAF-FAR)

CAHAL Anglicized form of Cathal (battle mighty). *See* CATHAL. (KAW-HAL)

CAHIR Anglicized form of Cathaoir (warrior). *See* CATHAOIR. (KAW-HEER)

CAIRBRE Evolution of the Old Irish *coirbre* (charioteer). The name is Anglicized as Carbry. (KAR-BRUH)

CALBHACH Derived from *calbhach* (bald). The name has been Anglicized as Calvagh, Callough, and Charles. (KAHL-AHK)

CALLAGHAN Anglicized form of Ceallachán (small strife). *See* CEALLACHÁN. (KAL-AH-HAN)

CALLOUGH Anglicized spelling of Calbhach (bald). *See* Calbhach. (KAL-LUH)

CANICE Anglicized form of Coinneach (fair, comely, handsome). *See* COINNEACH. (KAN-EES)

CAOIMHÍN Derived from the diminutive form of *caomh* (gentle, kind, noble, beautiful, lovable): hence, "little gentle one," etc. The name has been Anglicized as Kevin and Kevan. Var: Caoimhghin. (KWEE-VIN)

CAOLÁN Diminutive form of the Gaelic *caol* (slender). The name, which was borne by seven Irish saints, has been Anglicized as Kealan and Kelan. (KWEE-LAHN)

CAR Short form of any of the various names beginning with the element *Car-*. (KAR)

CARBRY Anglicized form of Cairbre (charioteer). Short: Car. (KAR-BREE)

CARLIN Transferred use of the surname, which is an Anglicized form of O'Cearbhalláin (descendant of Cearbhallán). Cearbhallán is a diminutive form of Cearbhall (champion, warrior); therefore Carlin has the definition "little champion." Short: Car. Pet: Carlie, Carling, Carly. (KAR-LIN)

CARLUS Irish form of Charles (full-grown, a man). *See* CHARLES. (KAR-LUS)

CARLY Pet form of any of the various names containing the element *car*. Var: Carlie. (KAR-LEE)

CARNEY Transferred use of the surname, which is an Anglicized form of the Irish surnames O'Catharnaigh (descendant of Catharnach) and O'Cearnaigh (descendant of Cearnach). Catharnach is defined as "war-like" and Cearnach means "victorious." Var: Karney, Kearney. Short: Car. (KAR-NEE)

CARROLL Derived from the Latin Carolus, a cognate of Charles (full-grown, a man). *See* CHARLES. The name was used to Anglicize the Gaelic Cearbhall (champion, warrior). Pet: Carlie, Carly. (KARE-ROL)

CÁRTHACH Derived from the Old Irish *carthach* (loving), which is believed to have its root in the Celtic *karatako-s* (loving). The name, which was borne by a 7th-century Irish saint, was Anglicized as Cartagh, Carthage, and Carthy. (KAWR-TAHK)

CARTHAGE Anglicized form of Cárthach (loving). *See* CÁRTHACH. Var: Cartagh, Carthy. (KAR-THAJ)

CASSIDY Transferred use of the surname, which is an Anglicized form of O'Caiside (descendant of Caiside). Caiside is an old name believed to be derived from *cas* (a bent, curly, twisted lock; ingenious, clever) or from *cais* (love, esteem). (KAS-SIH-DEE)

CATHAL Old name believed to be derived from the Celtic Katu-valo-s (battle mighty). The name has been Anglicized as Charles. Var: Cahal. (KAH-HAL)

CATHAOIR Old name derived from the Old Irish Cathfer, which is believed to be from the Celtic Katu-viro-s (battle man, warrior). The name was Anglicized as Cahir and Charles. Var: Cathair. (KAH-HEER)

CEALLACH Old name derived from *ceallach* (war, strife). The name has been Anglicized as Kellagh. Var: Keallach. Pet: Cillian. (KEL-AHK)

CEALLACHÁN Diminutive form of *ceallach* (strife). The name, which is Anglicized as Callaghan, was borne by a 10th-century king of Munster from whom the surname descended. (KEL-LUH-KAHN)

CEARBHALL Gaelic name meaning "champion, warrior." (KAHR-EH-VAHL)

CECIL A borrowing from the English, Cecil is from the Latin Caecilius, an old Roman family name derived from *caecus* (blind, dim-sighted). Siseal is the Gaelic form. (SEE-SIL)

CEDRIC A borrowing from the English, Cedric is an invention of Sir Walter Scott (1771–1832) for the character Cedric the Saxon in *Ivanhoe* (1819). He is believed to have based the name on Cerdic, a name of uncertain etymology borne by the traditional founder of the West Saxon kingdom. The name has been given the definition "chieftain." (SED-RIK)

CHARLES A borrowing from the Scottish and English, Charles is derived from the Germanic *karl* (full-grown, a man), which is a cognate of the Old English *ceorl* (a man, freeman, peasant). The name was introduced to Great Britain by Mary, Queen of Scots (1542–87), who bestowed it upon her son, Charles James. His son and grandson both ruled as King Charles, furthering the name's popularity in the British Isles. The name has been used in Ireland to Anglicize many Gaelic names. Séarlas and Séarlus are the Gaelic forms. (CHARLZ)

CHRISTIAN English translation of the Gaelic Giolla Chríost (servant of Christ). Christian is derived from the Ecclesiastic Late Latin Christiānus, which is from the Greek Christianos (a Christian, a follower of Christ). (KRIS-CHEN)

CHRISTOPHER A 16th-century borrowing from the English, Christopher is derived from the Ecclesiastic Late Latin Christophorus, which is from the Ecclesiastic Greek Cristophoros, a compounding of the elements *Christos* (Christ) and *pherein* (to bear): hence, "bearing Christ." The name was borne by St. Christopher, a 3rd-century Christian martyr of Asia Minor who is the patron saint of travelers. (KRIS-TO-FER)

CIAN Old Irish name derived from *cian* (ancient, in the past). The name was borne by the son of Olioll Olun, a king of Munster, and by the son-in-law of King Brian Boru. Kean and Kian are Anglicized spellings. (KEEN)

CIANÁN Diminutive form of Cian (ancient, in the past). The name Cianán (little Cian) was borne by three Irish saints. Kenan and Kienan are Anglicized forms. (KEE-NAHN)

CIARÁN Popular name which is a diminutive form of *ciar* (black): hence, "little black-haired one." Kearn, Kern, Kerne, and Kieran are Anglicized forms of Ciarán. (KEER-AHN)

CIARDHA Derived from *ciar* (black): hence, "black-haired one." The name is Anglicized as Kerry. (KEER-EE)

CIARRAI Derived from *ciar* (black). Ciarrai is Anglicized as Kerry. (KEH-EHR-EE)

CILLIAN Pet form of Ceallach (war, strife). The name was borne by a 7th-century Irish missionary who was martyred in Germany. Var: Cillín, Killian. (KEEL-YAN)

CINNÉIDID Compound name composed from the Gaelic elements *ceann* (a head) and *éide* (armor) or *éidigh* (ugly): hence, "helmeted head" or "ugly head." The name, which was borne by the father of King Brian Boru, is Anglicized as Kennedy. Var: Cinnéide, Cinnéidigh. (KIN-NEH-DEE)

COILEÁN Derived from the Gaelic *coileán* (whelp, pup, cub). The name is Anglicized as Colin. Var: Cuileán. (KUH-LIN)

COINNEACH Derived from the Gaelic *cainneach* (fair one, handsome). The name, which was borne by the patron saint of Kilkenny, has been Anglicized as Canice and Kenny. (KUH-NUHK)

COIREALL Old name of uncertain derivation and meaning. The name has been Anglicized as Kerril and Cyril. (KOR-EE-AHL)

COLE Popular Anglicized form of Comhghall (co-pledge, fellow hostage). *See* COMHGHALL. (KOLE)

COLIN A popular borrowing from the English, Colin originated as a medieval diminutive of the obsolete Colle, a short form of Nicholas (victory of the people). Colin is now regarded as an independent given name and has also been used in Ireland to Anglicize the Gaelic Coileán (pup, cub, whelp). *See* COILEÁN. (KOL-IN)

COLM Irish form of the Late Latin Columba (dove), a name borne by a famous Irish saint. *See* COLUMBA. Var: Colum. (KOLUM)

COLMÁN Diminutive form of Colm (dove): hence, "dovelet, little dove." The name, which was borne by many Irish saints, is still very popular today. Colman is the Anglicized form. (KOL-MAHN)

COLUMBA A borrowing from the Latin, derived from *columba* (dove). The name was borne by St. Columba (c. 521–97), a famous Irish missionary of great influence in both Ireland and Scotland. He founded several monastery schools in Ireland before founding a monastery on the Isle of Iona, which he used as a base for his work in converting the Scots to Christianity. (KO-LUM-BAH)

COMÁN Derived from the Gaelic *comán* (little bent one), a diminutive form of *cam* (bent, crooked). Var: Coman. (CO-MAHN)

COMHGHALL Derived from the Old Irish Comgell (co-pledge, co-hostage). Pledges were people, often children, traded between two warring factions as pledges of peace. The name has been Anglicized as Cole. (KO-AHL)

COMHGHAN Derived from the Old Irish Comgan (co-birth, twin). The name has been Anglicized as Cowan. Var: Comdhan. (KO-GAHN, KO-EN)

CONAIRE Ancient name of uncertain derivation and meaning. It has been Anglicized as Conary, Connery, Conrey, Conroy, and Conry. (KO-NER-EE)

CONALL Old name believed to be derived from the Celtic *kuno-valo-s* (high-mighty). The name, which was borne by at least eight Irish saints, was also borne by one of the most famous warriors of Ulster. Var: Connell. (KON-AHL)

CONÁN Of debated derivation and meaning, some believe Conán to be a diminutive form of *cú* (hound, dog): hence, "small hound." Others suggest that it is derived from *conn* (wisdom, counsel, strength). Conan is the Anglicized spelling. Var: Conant. (KO-NAHN)

CONCHOBHAR Old compound name derived from *conn* (wisdom, counsel, strength) or *con* (hound, dog) and *cobhair* (aid). "High will, desire" and "hound lover" are other definitions attributed to the name. Conchobhar has been Anglicized as Connor, Conor, and Cornelius. Var: Concobhar, Conquhare. (KON-KO-VAHR)

CONLEY Anglicized form of Connlaogh (chaste fire). *See* CONNLAODH. (KON-LEE)

CONN Derived from the Old Irish Cond, which is believed to be from the Celtic *kondo-s* (sense, reason, wisdom, high). (KON)

CONNERY Anglicized form of Conaire, an ancient name of uncertain derivation and meaning. Var: Conary, Conrey, Conroy, Conry. (KO-NER-EE)

CONNLAODH Compound name composed of the Gaelic elements *connla* (chaste, prudent) and *aodh* (fire). The name has been Anglicized as Conley. Var: Connlaoi, Connlaoth. (KON-LEH, KON-LEE)

CONOR Anglicized form of Conchobhar, a name of debated meaning. *See* CONCHOBHAR. Var: Connor. Pet: Conny. (KON-OR)

CONWAY Transferred use of the surname derived from the Gaelic Cúmhaighe, a compound name composed of the elements *cú* (hound, dog) and *mhaighe* (a plain): hence, "hound of the plain." (KON-WAY)

COREY Of various derivations, Corey is the transferred use of the surname derived from the Gaelic *coire* (a cauldron, a hollow): hence, "dweller in or near a hollow." Alternatively, it is an Anglicized form of the various surnames derived from *corra* (spear). Var: Cori, Corrie, Corry, Cory. (KOR-EE)

COWAN Anglicized form of Comhghan (twin). *See* COMHGHAN. Alternatively, Cowan represents the transferred use of the surname Cowan (dweller at a hollow), which is derived from the Gaelic *cabhan*, *cobhan* (a hollow). Var: Cowen, Cowyn. (KO-WAN)

CRÍOSTÓIR Gaelic form of Christopher (bearing Christ). *See* CHRISTOPHER. (KRIS-TER)

CUINN Derived from the surname MacCuinn (son of Conn). Conn is an old Gaelic name meaning "sense, reason, wisdom; a freeman." Var: Quinn. (KWIN)

CULLEN Transferred use of the surname, which is an Anglicized form of the Irish MacCuilinn (son of Cuileann). Cuileann is an Irish name meaning "holly." Var: Cullan, Cullin. Pet: Cully. (KUL-LEN)

CURRAN Popular name derived from the Old Irish *cur* (hero, champion). (KER-RAN)

CYRIL Derived from the Late Latin Cyrillus, a derivative of the Greek Kyrillos (lordly). The name has been used to Anglicize the Gaelic Coireall. (SEER-IL)

DAHY Anglicized form of Dáithí (nimbleness, surefootedness, swiftness). *See* DÁITHÍ. (DAH-HEE)

DÁIBHIDH Gaelic form of David (beloved). *See* DAVID. Var: Dáibhid. Short: Dáth. Pet: Dáith, Dáithi, Dáithín. (DEH-VID)

DAINÉAL Irish form of Daniel (God is my judge). *See* DANIEL. Var: Dainial. (DEHN-EL)

DÁITHÍ Old name meaning "swiftness, speed, surefootedness." Alternatively, Dáithí is used as a pet form of Dáibhidh. *See* DÁIBHIDH. The name has been Anglicized as Dahy, David, and Davy. (DAH-HEE)

DÁIVI Gaelic form of Davy, which is a pet form of David (beloved). *See* DAVID. (DAH-VEE)

DAMAN Irish form of Damien (tame), which is from the Greek Damianos, a derivative of *damān* (to tame). (DAY-MAN)

DANIEL Derived from the Hebrew *dāni'ēl* (God is my judge). The name is borne in the Bible by a Hebrew prophet whose faith kept him alive in a den of lions. Dainéal and Dainial are Irish forms of Daniel. (DAN-YEL)

DARBY Anglicized form of Diarmaid (without injunction, a freeman). *See* DIARMAID. (DAR-BEE)

DARCY Transferred use of the French surname, which originated from the place-name Arcy: hence, "of Arcy." The surname was taken to Ireland in the 14th century, whereupon it came into use as a given name. (DAR-SEE)

DARRAGH Derived from the surnames O'Dara and O'Darach, short forms of O'Dubhdarach (descendant of Dubhdarach). Dubhdarach is a compound name composed from *dubh* (black, dark) and *dair* (oak): hence, "dark oak, black of the oak." Var: Darrah. (DAR-RAH)

DAVID Derived from the Hebrew *dāvīd* (beloved). It is borne in the Bible by the second and greatest of the Israelite kings. Dáibhidh and Dúibhidh are Gaelic forms. (DAY-VID)

DEASÚN Gaelic form of Desmond (South Munster). *See* DESMOND. (DEH-SOON)

DECLAN Anglicized form of Deaglán, which is of uncertain meaning. The name was borne by a 6th-century saint who was baptized by St. Colman. Var: Deklan. (DEK-LIN)

DELANEY Transferred use of the Irish surname derived from the Gaelic O'Dubhshláine, which is of uncertain meaning. (DEH-LAY-NEE)

DEMPSEY Transferred use of the surname, which is an Anglicization of O'Díomasaigh (descendant of Díomarach). Díomarach is a Gaelic name meaning "proud." (DEMP-SEE)

DENIS A borrowing from the French, Denis is derived from the Greek Dionysius (of Dionysos, the Greek mythological god of wine and revelry). The name has been used in Ireland to Anglicize the Gaelic Donnchadh (brown warrior; strong warrior). *See* DONNCHADH. Var: Dennis, Denys. (DEN-NIS)

DEREK A borrowing from the English, Derek is derived from a short form of the obsolete Germanic Thiudoreiks (ruler of the people), a compounding of the elements *thiuda* (folk, people) and *reiks* (ruler, leader). (DER-EK)

DERMOT Anglicized form of Diarmaid (without injunction, a freeman). *See* DIARMAID. Var: Dermod. (DER-MOT)

DERRY Transferred use of the surname meaning "son of Doireidh." The name Doireidh means "red-haired." (DARE-REE)

DESMOND Transferred use of the surname O'Deasmhumhnaigh, which originated from the Irish place-name Deas-Mhumhna (South Munster). (DEZ-MOND)

DEVIN Anglicized form of the old Gaelic name Dámh (poet). Short: Dev. (DEV-IN)

DEVLIN Transferred use of the Anglicized surname, which has several origins. It means "descendant of the plasterer or dauber; one who comes from Dublin [dark pool]; grandson of Doibhilin." Short: Dev. (DEV-LIN)

DIARMAID Derived from Diarmait (without injunction, a freeman), a compound name composed of the elements *di* (without) and *airmit* (injunction). The name has been Anglicized as Dermot, Darby, Jeremiah, Jerry, and Jerome. (JEER-MID)

DOIMINIC Irish form of Dominic (belonging to a lord). *See* DOMINIC. (DOY-MIN-IK)

DOMINIC Derived from the Latin Dominicus (belonging to a lord), which is from the word *dominus* (a lord, a master). Doiminic is the Gaelic form. Var: Dominick. (DOM-IN-IK)

DONAGH Anglicized form of Donnchadh (brown warrior). *See* DONNCHADH. Var: Donaghy, Donogh, Donough. (DUN-UH)

DONAHUE Anglicized form of Donnchadh (brown warrior). *See* DONNCHADH. (DON-AH-HYOO)

DONAL Anglicized form of Dónal, an Irish variant of Domhnall (world mighty). *See* DOMHNALL (Scottish Names). Var: Donall. (DON-AHL)

DÓNAL Irish variant of Domhnall (world mighty). *See* DOMHNALL (Scottish Names). The name has been Anglicized as Donal, Donald, and Donall. (DŌN-AHL)

DONALD A borrowing from the Scottish, Donald is an Anglicized form of the Gaelic Domhnall (world mighty, world ruler). *See* DOMHNALL (Scottish Names). Alternatively, there are some who believe Donald to be derived from the Gaelic *donn* (brown). (DON-LD)

DONN Derived from the Gaelic *donn* (brown). (DUN)

DONNÁN Diminutive form of the Gaelic *donn* (brown). The name Donnán (little brown-haired one) has been borne by four Irish saints. Donnan is the Anglicized form. (DUN-NAHN)

DONNCHADH Very old name derived from the Old Irish Donnchad and Dunchad, names that are believed to be derived from the Celtic Donno-catu-s (brown warrior) and Duno-catu-s (strong warrior) respectively. The name has been Anglicized as Denis, Donagh, Donohue, and Duncan. (DUN-NEH-KAH)

DONNELLY Transferred use of the surname, which is an Anglicized form of O'Donnghaile (descendant of Donnghal). Donnghal is a compound name composed of the elements *donn* (brown) and *ghal* (valor). (DON-NEH-LEE)

DONOVAN Transferred use of the surname, which is an Anglicized form of O'Donnabháin (descendant of Donndubhán). Donndubhán is a compound name composed from *donn* (brown) and a diminutive form of *dubh* (black, dark): hence, "dark brown or dark-haired." (DON-AH-VAN)

DOUGLAS Transferred use of the surname, which is the Anglicized form of Dubhglas, a Gaelic name derived from the elements *dubh* (black, dark) and *glas* (blue, green, gray). Dubhglas was a common Celtic river name, and the surname might have originated to denote one who lived near a river. (DUG-LUS)

DOWAN Anglicized form of Dubhán, a diminutive form of *dubh* (black, dark). (DŌ-WAN)

Dubh Derived from the Gaelic *dubh* (black, dark): hence, "black-haired, dark-haired." The name is Anglicized as Duff. (DUV)

Dubhán Derived from a diminutive form of *dubh* (black, dark): hence, "little black-haired one." The name has been Anglicized as Dowan. (DUV-AHN)

Dubhglas Compound name composed of the Gaelic elements *dubh* (black, dark) and *glas* (blue, green, gray). Besides being a personal name, Dubhglas was a common Celtic river name. Var: Dúghlas. (DUHV-GLAHS)

Duff Anglicized form of Dubh (black-haired). *See* DUBH. (DUF)

Dwyer Transferred use of the Irish surname, which is an Anglicized form of O'Duibhidhir (descendant of Dubheidir). Dubheidir is a compound name composed of the elements *dubh* (black, dark) and *eidir* (sense, wisdom). (DWYER)

Ea Anglicized form of the Gaelic Aodh (fire). *See* AODH. Var: Eth. (EH)

Eachann Evolution of Eachdhonn, a compound name composed of the elements *each* (horse, steed) and *dhonn* (lord): hence, "horse lord, master of horses." The name has been Anglicized as Hector. (AH-HAHN)

Eadbhard Irish form of Edward (wealthy or fortunate guardian). *See* EDWARD. Var: Éadbárd. (AHD-WAHRD)

Éamonn Irish form of Edmund (wealthy protection). *See* EDMUND (English Names). Eamon is also used as an Irish form of Edward (wealthy or fortunate guardian). *See* EDWARD. The name was borne by Eamon De Valera (1882–1975), prime minister and later president of Ireland. Var: Éamon, Eamon, Eamonn. (EH-MON)

Earnán Diminutive form of Earna (experience, wisdom, knowledge). The name is Anglicized as Ernan and Ernest. (AHR-NAWN)

Edward Introduced to Ireland by the Anglo-Normans, Edward is derived from the Old English Ēadweard, a compounding of the elements *ēad* (riches, prosperity, fortune) and *weard* (guardian, protector). Eadbhard is the traditional Irish form of Edward, but Éamonn is now also used as an equivalent. (ED-WARD)

Egan Anglicized form of Aodhagán (little fiery one). *See* AODHAGÁN. Var: Eagon, Egon. (EE-GAHN)

Éigneachán An old name thought to mean "force person." Éigneachán has been Anglicized as Aeneas and Ignatius. Var: Eigneachán, Ighneachán. (EHG-NAH-KHAHN)

Éimhín Diminutive form of the Gaelic *eimh* (swift). The name has been Anglicized as Evan, Evin, and Ewan. (EH-VEEN)

Éinrí Gaelic form of Henry (home ruler, ruler of an enclosure). *See* HENRY (English Names). Var: Anraí, Hannraoi, Hanraoi. (EN-REE)

Emmet Transferred use of the surname, which is a matronymic derived from the German feminine name Emma (strength). *See* EMMA (German Female Names). (EM-MET)

Eochaidh Derived from the Gaelic *each* (horse). Eochaidh (horseman) has been Anglicized as Achaius, Aghy, Atty, and Oghie. (O-KEE)

Eoghan Old name meaning "well-born, noble." Eoghan has been translated into English as Eugene and Owen. (YO-WUHN)

Eóin Popular Irish form of John (God is gracious). *See* JOHN. Eoin and Owen are Anglicized forms. (O-EN)

Ernan Anglicized form of Earnán (little experienced one). *See* EARNÁN. (ER-NAN)

Ernest Cognate of the Germanic Ernst, which is from the Old High German Ernust and Ernost, names derived from *ernust* (earnest, resolute). The name has been used in Ireland to Anglicize the Gaelic Earnán (little experienced one). (ER-NEST)

Eugene A borrowing from the French, Eugene is derived from the Latin Eugenius, which is from *eugenēs* (well-born). Eugene is used in Ireland to Anglicize the Gaelic Eoghan (well-born). (YOO-JEEN)

Euston Anglicized form of Úistean, an Irish diminutive form of Hugh (heart, mind, soul). (YOO-STON)

Evan Anglicized form of Éimhín (little swift one). Var: Ewan, Evin. Short: Ev. (EV-AN)

Fachnan Anglicized form of Fachtna, an old name of uncertain derivation. Var: Faughnan. (FAHK-NAN)

Fachtna Old name of uncertain derivation. Fachtna has been Anglicized as Fachnan and Faughnan. (FAHK-NAH)

Faolán Diminutive form of *faol* (a wolf). The name Faolán (little wolf) was borne by fourteen Irish saints. Felan and Phelan are the Anglicized forms. (FEH-LAHN)

Fardoragh Anglicized form of Feardorcha (a dark-complexioned man). *See* FEARDORCHA. (FAHR-DOR-AGH)

Feagh Anglicized form of Fiach (raven). (FEE-AGH)

FEARADHACH Derived from the Gaelic *fearadhach* (masculine, manly). The name has been Anglicized as Ferdinand. (FAHR-AH-THEHK)

FEARDORCHA Compound name composed of the elements *fear* (a man) and *dorcha* (dark): hence, "a dark-complexioned man." The name has been Anglicized as Fardoragh, Frederick, and Ferdinand. (FAHR-DOR-AHK)

FEARGHALL Derived from the Gaelic *fear* (a man) or *fer* (better, best, superior) and *ghal* (valor). (FAHR-GAHL)

FEARGHUS Gaelic form of the Old Irish Fergus, a compound name composed of the elements *fer* (better, best, superior) or *fear* (a man) and *guss* (vigor, strength). (FAHR-GUS)

FEHIN Anglicized form of Feichín (little raven). Var: Fechin. (FEH-HIN)

FEICHÍN Diminutive form of *fiach* (raven): hence, "little raven." The name was borne by five Irish saints and is Anglicized as Fechin, Fehin, and Festus. (FEH-CHIN)

FEIDHLIM Short form of Feidhlimidh (the ever good), which is used as an independent given name. Feidhlim was Anglicized as Felim, Phelim, Felix, and Philip. (FEH-LIM)

FEIDHLIMIDH Very old name meaning "the ever good." It was borne by six Irish saints and has been Anglicized as Felimy, Phelimy, Felix, and Philip. (FEE-LIM-EE)

FELAN Anglicized form of Faolán (little wolf). *See* FAOLÁN. Var: Phelan. (FEH-LAN)

FELIM Anglicized form of Feidhlim (the ever good). Var: Phelim. (FEH-LIM)

FELIMY Anglicized form of Feidhlimidh (the ever good). Var: Phelimy. (FEH-LIH-MEE)

FEORAS Irish cognate of Piers, a Norman form of Peter (rock), which is derived from the Ecclesiastic Late Latin Petrus and the Greek Petros, names derived from *petrus* (a rock) and *petros* (a stone). The name has been Anglicized as Pierce, Farris, and Ferris. (FEE-UH-RUS)

FERGAL Anglicized form of the Gaelic Fearghall (manly, valor). *See* FEARGHALL. Var: Forgael. (FER-GAHL)

FERGUS Old Irish compound name composed of the elements *fer* (best, better, superior) or *fear* (a man) and *guss* (vigor, strength). The name is borne in Irish legend by Fergus MacRoích, a huge warrior prince of Ulster who was victorious in the battle between his men and the men of Connaught. (FER-GUS)

FERRIS Anglicized form of Feoras, an Irish cognate of the Norman Piers, itself a cognate of Peter (a rock, a stone). *See* FEORAS. Var: Farris. (FER-RIS)

FESTUS A name used to Anglicize Fachnan and Feichín (little raven). (FES-TUS)

FIACH Derived from the Gaelic *fíach* (raven). The name was Anglicized as Feagh. (FEE-UHK)

FIACHRA Derived from the Gaelic *fíach* (raven). The name was borne by the 7th-century St. Fiachra the Solitary, an Irish monk who founded a famous monastery in Breuil, France. His shrine is a place of pilgrimage from where many miracles are said to have occurred. (FEE-UHK-RAH)

FINAN Anglicized form of Fionán (little fair one). Var: Fionan. (FIN-AN)

FINBAR Popular Anglicized form of Fionnbhárr (fair-haired). *See* FIONNBHÁRR. Pet: Barry. (FIN-BAHR)

FINEEN Anglicized form of Finghin (fair at birth). *See* FINGHIN. Var: Finneen, Finnin. (FIN-EEN)

FINGAL A borrowing from the Scottish, Fingal is an elaborated form of the Irish Finn (fair). The name was used by poet James Macpherson in his Ossianic poems. (FIN-GAHL)

FINGHIN Old name derived from the element *fionn* (fair) and *gein* (birth): hence, "fair at birth." The name has been Anglicized as Fineen and Finnin. Var: Finín. (FIN-JIN)

FINN Popular Anglicized form of Fionn (fair, white, clear). The name was borne by the legendary Finn MacCool, the father of the famous poet Ossian and the supposed builder of the Giants' Causeway on the Antrim coast. Finn MacCool is the popular subject of many Irish legends and stories, which portray him as both a giant and a man of normal stature. His Gaelic name is Fionn MacCumhal. Var: Fynn. (FIN)

FINNIAN Diminutive form of *fionn* (fair): hence, "little fair one." The name was borne by several Irish saints, namely the 6th-century St. Finnian of Moville. Var: Finian. (FIN-EE-AN)

FINTAN Anglicized form of Fionntán (little fair one). (FIN-TAN)

FIONÁN Diminutive form of *fionn* (fair): hence, "little fair one." The name, which was borne by many Irish saints, has been Anglicized as Finan and Fionan. (FINN-NAHN)

FIONN Derived from the Gaelic *fionn* (fair). Finn is the Anglicized form. The name was borne by the legendary

Fionn MacCumhal, better known as Finn MacCool. *See* FINN. (FIN)

FIONNBHÁRR Compound name composed of the Gaelic elements *fionn* (fair, white, clear) and *barr* (a head): hence, "fair-haired." Pet: Barra. (FIN-VER)

FIONNTÁN Diminutive form of *fionn* (fair, white, clear): hence, "little fair one." The name has been Anglicized as Fintan. (FIN-TAHN)

FLANN Old name derived from *flann* (red): hence, "red-haired" or "having a ruddy complexion." The name was once Anglicized as Florence. Var: Flainn. (FLAN)

FLANNÁN Diminutive form of Flann (red): hence, "little red-haired one, little ruddy one." Flannan is the Anglicized spelling. (FLAN-AHN)

FORBES Transferred use of the surname, which is thought to be derived from the Old Gaelic *forba* (a field). (FORBZ)

GABRIEL From the Hebrew Gavriel, which is derived from *gavhrī'ēl* (God is my strength). The name is borne in the Bible by one of the seven archangels, the herald of Good News who appeared to Mary to announce her pregnancy and the impending birth of the Christ child. Gaibrial is the Gaelic form. (GABE-REE-UL)

GAIBRIAL Gaelic form of Gabriel (God is my strength). *See* GABRIEL. (GABE-REE-AHL)

GALEN A borrowing from the English, Galen is derived from the name Claudius Galenus (c. 130–200), a Greek physician and writer on medicine and philosophy to whom the system of medical practice Galenism is attributed. The name is believed to be derived from *galēnē* (calm). (GAY-LEN)

GANNON Transferred use of the surname meaning "descendant of the fair-haired man." Pet: Gannie. (GAN-NUN)

GARBHÁN Diminutive form of *garbh* (rough): hence, "little rough one." The name was Anglicized as Garvan. (GAHR-VAHN)

GARRETT Transferred use of the surname, which evolved from Gerald (spear rule) and Gerard (brave with a spear). *See* GERALD *and* GERARD. Gearoíd is the Gaelic form. Var: Garret. (GAR-RET)

GARVAN Anglicized form of Garbhán (little rough one). (GAR-VAN)

GEARALT Gaelic form of Gerald (spear rule), a name introduced to Ireland by the Anglo-Normans. *See* GERALD. (GEHR-AHLT)

GEARÁRD Gaelic form of Gerard (brave with a spear), a name introduced to Ireland by the Anglo-Normans. *See* GERARD. Var: Giorárd. (GEHR-RAHRD)

GEARÓID Gaelic form of Garrett (spear rule; brave with a spear). *See* GARRETT. Var: Gioróid. (GEHR-ED)

GEOFFREY A borrowing from the English, the name Geoffrey has evolved from several different names. *See* GEOFFREY (English Names). Seathrún is the common Gaelic form of Geoffrey, which was also used to Anglicize Séafra and Seafraid (God's peace). Var: Jeffrey. (JEF-FREE)

GEORGE A borrowing from the English in the 18th century, George is from the French Georges, which is derived from the Greek Geōrgios, a compound name composed from *gē* (earth) and *ergein* (to work): hence, "earthworker, farmer." Seoirse is the Gaelic form. (JORJ)

GERALD Introduced by the Anglo-Normans, Gerald is derived from the German *Gerwald*, a compounding of the elements *gēr* (a spear) and *wald* (rule, power, might): hence, "spear might, to rule with a spear." Gearalt is the Gaelic form of the name. (JEHR-ALD)

GERARD Introduced by the Anglo-Normans, Gerard is derived from the Old High German Gerhard (spear brave, brave with a spear), a compounding of the elements *gēr* (a spear) and *hart* (hearty, brave, strong). Gearárd is the common Gaelic form. (JER-RAHRD)

GIL Short form of any of the various names beginning with the element *Gil-*. (GIL)

GILBERT From the Old French Guillebert (famous pledge), a derivation of the Old High German Gisilberht, a compounding of the elements *gisil* (pledge) and *beraht* (bright, famous). The name was introduced by the Anglo-Normans. Gilibeirt is the Gaelic form. Short: Gil. Pet: Gibbon. (GIL-BERT)

GILCHRIST Anglicized form of the Irish Giolla Chríost (servant of Christ). Short: Gil. Pet: Gilley. (GIL-KRIST)

GILDEA Anglicized form of Giolla Dhé (servant of God). Short: Gil. Pet: Gilley. (GIL-DAY-AH)

GILIBEIRT Gaelic form of Gilbert (famous pledge). *See* GILBERT. Pet: Giobún. (GIL-LEE-BERT)

GILL Anglicized form of Giolla (servant). (GIL)

GILLESPIE Anglicized form of Giolla Easpuig (bishop's servant). Short: Gil. Pet: Gilley. (GIL-LES-PEE)

GILLEY Pet form of various names beginning with the element *Gil-*. (GIL-LEE)

Gilmore Transferred use of the Anglicized surname, which is from Giolle Máire (servant of Mary). Short: Gil. Pet: Gilley. (GIL-MOR)

Giolla Chríost Combination name composed of the name element Giolla (servant of) and *Chríost* (Christ): hence, "servant of Christ." The name has been Anglicized as Gilchrist. (GIL-AH-KREEST)

Giolla Dhé Combination name composed of the name element Giolla (servant of) and *dhé* (God): hence, "servant of God." Gildea is the Anglicized form. (GIL-LAH-DEH)

Giolla Easpuig Combination name composed of the name element Giolla (servant of) and *easpuig* (bishop): hence, "bishop's servant." Gillespie is the Anglicized form. Var: Giolla Easpaig. (GIL-LAH-EHS-PEE)

Glaisne Old name of uncertain derivation, common to Ulster. Var: Glasny. (GLAS-NEE)

Glenn Derived from the Gaelic *gleann* (mountain valley, a narrow, secluded valley). It is unclear whether the given name or the surname came first. Var: Glen, Glyn. (GLEN)

Godfrey From the Old French Godefrei, which is derived from the German Godafrid, a compound name composed from the elements *god* (God) and *frid* (peace): hence, "God's peace." The name was introduced by the Anglo-Normans and was used to Anglicize its Irish equivalent, Gofraidh (God's peace). *See* GOFRAIDH. (GOD-FREE)

Gofraidh Irish form of the Old Norse Guthfrithr, Guðfriðr, a compounding of the elements *guth, guð* (God) and *frithr, friðr* (peace). Gofraidh is an Irish equivalent to the French Godfrey. *See* GODFREY. Var: Gothfraidh, Gothraidh, Séafra, Seafraid. (GO-FREE)

Gordon Transferred use of the Scottish surname believed to have originated from the place-name Gordon in Berwickshire. The place-name is of uncertain etymology. The use of Gordon as a given name dates to the 19th century. (GOR-DON)

Grady Transferred use of the surname, which is an Anglicized form of O'Grádaigh (descendant of Gráda). Gráda is derived from the Irish *gráda* (noble, illustrious). Var: Gradey. (GRAY-DEE)

Gréagóir Gaelic form of Gregory (vigilant, watchful). *See* GREGORY. Var: Grioghar. (GREG-OR)

Gregory Introduced to Ireland by the Anglo-Normans, Gregory is from the Late Latin Gregorius and the Greek Grēgorios (vigilant, a watchman), which is derived from the verb *egeirein* (to awaken). Gréagóir and Grioghar are Gaelic forms. (GREG-OR-REE)

Guy A borrowing from the French, Guy is derived from the Old French *guie* (a guide, a leader). (GĪ)

Harold Introduced by the Anglo-Normans, Harold is derived from the obsolete Old English Hereweald, a compounding of the elements *here* (army) and *weald* (rule, power, control): hence, "leader of the army." The name replaced the Scandinavian cognate Haraldr, which was introduced by the Norsemen. Aralt is the Irish form. (HAHR-OLD)

Hewney Anglicized form of the Gaelic Uaithne (green). Var: Aney, Owney, Oynie. (HEW-NEE)

Hogan Transferred use of the Anglicized surname, which is from O'Ógáin (descendant of Ógán). Ógán is a diminutive form of *óg* (youth). (HO-GAN)

Hugh A borrowing from the English, Hugh is from the Old French Hue, which is from the Old High German Hugo, a derivative of *hugu* (heart, mind, soul). Hugh has been used in Ireland to Anglicize Aodh (fire). (HYOO)

Hurley Transferred use of the surname, which is the Anglicized form of O'Urthaile (descendant of Urthaile). Urthaile is an old name of uncertain derivation. Var: Hurlee. (HER-LEE)

Ian Irish form of Iain, the Scottish Gaelic form of John (God is gracious). *See* JOHN. Ion is the Irish Gaelic form of Ian. (EE-UN)

Iarfhlaith Old name said to mean "tributary lord." Jarlath is the Anglicized form of the name, which was borne by the patron saint of Tuam. (YAHR-LATH)

Innis Transferred use of the Scottish surname, which is derived from the name of a barony in the former county of Moray in northeastern Scotland. Innis is the Gaelic word for "island." (IN-NIS)

Íomhar Gaelic form of Ivor (bow warriors, archers), a name introduced to Ireland by the Norsemen. *See* IVOR. (YO-VER)

Ion Irish Gaelic form of Ian, a cognate of John (God is gracious). *See* JOHN. (YON)

Ionatán Gaelic form of Jonathan (God has given). *See* JONATHAN. (YON-AH-TAHN)

Ióseph Gaelic form of Joseph (may he add). *See* JOSEPH. Var: Iósep, Seósamh, Seósap, Seósaph. (YO-SEF)

IVOR Derived from the Old Norse Ivarr, a compound name composed from the elements *ýr* (yew, bow) and *herr* (army, warriors): hence, "archers, bow warriors." Íomhar is the Gaelic form of the name, which was introduced by the Norsemen. (Ī-VOR)

JAMES A popular name in Ireland, James is from the Ecclesiastic Late Latin Iacomus, an evolution of the Greek Iakōbos, which is from the Hebrew Yaakov. This name has its root in *ya'aqob* (supplanting, seizing by the heel). Some say Iacomus arises from an error in the transcription of manuscripts from the Greek to the Latin by an early monk. Séamus is the equally popular Gaelic form. *See* SÉAMUS. Pet: Jamie. (JAYMZ)

JAMIE A pet form of James (supplanting, seizing by the heel), Jamie is also occasionally bestowed as an independent given name. *See* JAMES. (JAY-MEE)

JARLATH Anglicized form of Iarfhlaith, an old name of uncertain derivation. (JAR-LATH)

JASON A borrowing from the English, Jason is a cognate of the Latin and Greek Iāson (healer), which is from *iasthai* (to heal). The name is borne in Greek mythology by a prince who led the Argonauts and found the Golden Fleece. (JAY-SON)

JOHN The most enduring of all the biblical names, John is derived from the Middle Latin Johannes, which is from the Ecclesiastic Late Latin Joannes, from the Ecclesiastic Greek Iōannes, a derivative of the Hebrew Yehanan, a short form of Yehohanan, which is from *yehōhānān* (Yahweh is gracious). The name, borne in the Bible by several important characters, was also borne by many saints, twenty-three popes, and many kings throughout Europe and England. First used by the Eastern Church, John was brought back to the British Isles after the First Crusade. The name, with its many Irish forms, is one of the most popular in Ireland. Eoin, Ian, Ion, Seaghán, Sean, Seón, Shane, Shawn, and Shaun are Irish forms. (JON)

JONATHAN A borrowing from the English, Jonathan is from the Hebrew Yonatan, a short form of Yehonatan, which is derived from *yehōnātān* (Yahweh has given). The name is borne in the Bible by the eldest son of King Saul. In Ireland, the name was borne by the satirist Jonathan Swift (1667–1745). Ionatán is the Gaelic form. (JON-AH-THAN)

JOSEPH Ecclesiastic Late Latin name derived from the Greek Iōsēph, which is from the Hebrew Yosef, a direct derivation of *yōsēf* (may he add). The name is borne in the Bible by the favorite son of Jacob, by the husband of the Virgin Mary, and by Joseph of Arimathea, a rich Jew who, according to medieval legend, brought the Holy Grail to Britain. Iósep, Ióseph, and Seosamh are Gaelic forms. (JO-SEF)

KANE Transferred use of the surname, which is an Anglicized form of O'Catháin (descendant of Cathán). Cathán is a diminutive form of any of the names beginning with the element *Cath-*. Var: Kaine, Kayne. (KANE)

KEALAN Anglicized form of the Gaelic Caolán (slender). Var: Kelan. (KEE-LAHN)

KEEFFE Transferred use of the surname, which is the Anglicized form of O'Caoimh (descendant of Caomh). The name Caomh is derived from the Gaelic *caomh* (gentle, noble, beautiful, lovable). Var: Keefe. (KEEF)

KEEGAN Transferred use of the Anglicized surname, which is from MacAodhagáin (son of Aodhagán). The name Aodhagán is a diminutive form of Aodh (fire): hence, "little fire." Var: Kegan. (KEE-GAN)

KEIR A short form of Keiran (little black-haired one), Keir is also occasionally bestowed as an independent given name. *See* KEIRAN. (KEER)

KEIRAN Anglicized form of Ciarán (little black-haired one). *See* CIARÁN. Var: Kearn, Kern, Kerne. Short: Keir. (KEER-AN)

KELLAGH Anglicized form of the Gaelic Ceallach (war, strife). (KEL-LAGH)

KENNEDY Anglicized form of Cinnéidid (helmeted head, ugly head). *See* CINNÉIDID. The personal name gave rise to the famous surname. (KEN-NEH-DEE)

KERILL Anglicized form of Coireall, an ancient name of uncertain etymology. *See* COIREALL. (KER-IL)

KEVIN Popular Anglicized form of Caoimhín (little gentle one). *See* CAOIMHÍN. Var: Kevan. (KEH-VIN)

KIRWIN Transferred use of the surname, which is an Anglicized form of O'Ciardubháin (descendant of Ciardubhán). The name Ciardubhán is from the diminutive form of *ciardubh* (jet-black, dark black): hence, "little jet-black-haired one." Var: Kerwin. (KER-WIN)

KYLE Transferred use of the Scottish surname, which originated from the region of the same name in southwestern Scotland. Kyle, a topographical term referring to a narrow, straight channel, is derived from the Gaelic *caol* (a narrow, a sound, a strait). (KILE)

LABHRÁS Gaelic form of Laurence and Lawrence (man from Laurentum). *See* LAURENCE. Var: Labhras, Lubhrás. (LAU-RAHSH)

LACHTNA Old name derived from the Gaelic *lachtna* (gray, dun). The name, which was borne by the great-grandfather of King Brian Boru, was Anglicized as Lucius. (LUHK-NAH)

LANTY Anglicized form of Leachlainn (servant of St. Secundus). *See* LEACHLAINN. (LAN-TEE)

LAOGHAIRE Derived from the Gaelic *laoghaire* (calf keeper, calf herder). The name was borne by a king of Tara who supposedly had a confrontation with St. Patrick. Laoghaire gave rise to the surname Leary. (LEH-REE)

LAOISEACH Derived from Laoighis (belonging to Leix). Leix is the name of an Irish county. The name was Anglicized as Lewis, Louis, Lucius, and Lysagh. Var: Laoighseach. (LOO-EESH)

LASAIRIAN Derived from the diminutive form of *lasair* (a flame). The name was borne by four Irish saints. Laserian is the Anglicized form. Var: Laisrian. (LAY-SUH-REE-UN)

LAUGHLIN Anglicized form of Leachlainn, Lochlainn, and Lochlann. (LAUF-LIN)

LAURENCE A borrowing from the English, Laurence is from the Latin Laurentius (man from Laurentum). Laurentum, the name of a town in Latium, is probably derived from *laurus* (laurel). Labhrás and Lubhrás are Gaelic forms. Var: Lawrence. (LAU-RENS)

LEACHLAINN A short form of Maeleachlainn (servant of St. Secundis), Leachlainn is also bestowed as an independent given name. *See* MAELEACHLAINN. The name has been Anglicized as Lanty and Laughlin. (LEHK-LEN)

LEO A borrowing from the Late Latin, Leo is derived from *leo* (lion). The name was borne by thirteen popes, including Leo (I) the Great (400?–61). In Ireland, the name was first borne in honor of Pope Leo XIII (1810–1903), who ascended to the papacy in 1873. Leon is the Irish form. (LEE-O)

LEON Irish form of Leo (lion). *See* LEO. (LEE-ON)

LEWY Phonetic Anglicized form of Lughaidh, an ancient name of uncertain meaning. (LEW-EE)

LIAM Short form of Uilliam, the Irish cognate of William (resolute protector). *See* UILLIAM. Liam is also bestowed as an independent given name. (LEE-UM)

LOCHLAINN Popular name that originated from Lochlainn (Lakeland, Fiordland), the name the Irish used to denote the native land of the Norse invaders. The name was Anglicized as Loughlin and Laughlin. Var: Lochlain, Lochlann. (LOHK-LAN)

LOGAN Transferred use of the surname, which is from the Gaelic *lagán* (a little hollow), a diminutive form of *lag* (a hollow): hence, "dweller at a little hollow." (LO-GUN)

LOMÁN Derived from the diminutive form of *lom* (bare): hence, "little bare one." The name was borne by four Irish saints, including a follower of St. Patrick. (LO-MAN)

LORCÁN Derived from the diminutive form of *lorc* (fierce): hence, "little fierce one." The name was borne by St. Lorcan O'Toole (d. 1180), patron saint of Dublin. Lorcan is the Anglicized spelling. (LOR-KAN)

LUCAN A borrowing from the Latin, Lucan is derived from Lucanus, an old family name derived from Lucianus, a derivative of Lucius, which is from the root *lux* (light). The name was borne by the Roman poet Lucan (A.D. 39–65), whose Latin name was Marcus Annaeus Lucanus. Lúcán is the Gaelic form. (LOO-KAN)

LUCAS A borrowing from the English, Lucas is an Ecclesiastic Late Latin name derived from Lucius, the root of which is *lux* (light). Alternatively, some believe the name is derived from the Ecclesiastic Greek Loukas, a contraction of Loukanos (man from Lucania). Lúcás and Labhcás are Gaelic forms. (LOO-KAHS)

LÚCÁS Gaelic form of Lucas and Luke. *See* LUCAS *and* LUKE. Var: Labhcás. (LOO-KASH)

LUCIUS A borrowing from the Latin, Lucius is derived from the root *lux* (light) or from the Ecclesiastic Greek Loukas, a contraction of Loukanos (man from Lucania). Lucania was the name of a district in southern Italy. The name has been used in Ireland to Anglicize Lachtna and Laoiseach. (LOO-SHUS)

LUGHAIDH Ancient name of uncertain derivation. It is borne in Irish legend by Lugaidh mac Con-Rui, the son of Cú Roí mac Dairi. Lewy, Lewis, Louis, and Aloysius have been used to Anglicize the name. (LOO-EE)

LUKE Middle English and Anglo-French form of Lucas (light; man from Lucania). *See* LUCAS. The name is borne in the Bible by one of the four evangelists, a doctor and author of the third Gospel, Luke, and the Acts of the Apostles. Lúcás is the Gaelic form. (LUKE)

LYSAGH Anglicized form of Laoighseach and Laoiseach (belonging to Leix). *See* LAOISEACH. (LĪ-SAH)

MAELEACHLAINN Compound name meaning "servant of St. Secundinus." St. Secundinus was a follower of St. Patrick. The name was Anglicized as Malachy, Melaghlin, Miles, Milo, and Myles. Var: Maelsheachlainn. Short: Leachlainn. (MAL-UH-KLEHN)

MAGHNUS Gaelic form of Magnus (great). *See* MAGNUS. Var: Manus. (MAHK-NUS)

MAGNUS A borrowing from the Latin, Magnus is derived from *magnus* (great). The name was introduced to Ireland by the Norsemen. Maghnus is the Gaelic form. (MAG-NUS)

MAGUIRE Transferred use of the surname, which is the Anglicized form of Mag Uidhir (son of Odhar). Odhar is an old personal name meaning "pale, dun-colored." (MAH-GWIRE)

MAHON Anglicized form of Mathghamhain (a bear). *See* MATHGHAMHAIN. (MA-HOON, MA-HONE)

MAINCHIN Derived from the diminutive form of *manach* (a monk): hence, "little monk." The name was borne by several saints, including the patron saint of Limerick. Munchin is the Anglicized form. (MAN-KEEN)

MÁIRTÍN Gaelic form of Martin (war-like). *See* MARTIN. Var: Mártan. (MAHR-TEEN)

MAIT Short form of Maitiú, the Irish cognate of Matthew (gift of God). Mait is the Gaelic equivalent of Matt. (MUT)

MAITIAS Gaelic form of Matthias (gift of God). *See* MATTHIAS. (MUH-THĪ-UHS)

MAITÍN Diminutive form of Maitiú, the Irish cognate of Matthew (gift of God). *See* MATTHEW. (MUH-THIN)

MAITIÚ Irish cognate of Matthew (gift of God). *See* MATTHEW. Var: Matha. Short: Mait. (MUH-THYOO)

MALCOLM A borrowing from the Scottish, Malcolm is the Anglicized form of the Gaelic Maolcholm (servant of St. Columba). (MAL-KOM)

MANNIX Anglicized form of Mainchin (little monk). *See* MAINCHIN. (MAN-NIX)

MAOLBHEANNACHTA Very old name meaning "hoper for blessing, one desirous of the blessing." The name was Anglicized as Benedict. (MAHL-VAHN-NAHK-TAH)

MAOLCHOLM Old name meaning "servant of St. Columba." The name is Anglicized as Malcolm. Var: Maolcholuim, Maolcolm. (MAL-KOLM)

MAOLMÓRDHA Very old name meaning "majestic chief." It was Anglicized as Miles and Myles. (MAHL-MOR-EE-AH)

MARTIN From the Latin Martīnus, a derivative of Mars, the name of the Roman mythological god of war. The name was borne by St. Martin of Tours (315?–?397). He is mainly remembered for splitting his cloak in two and giving half to a beggar. He is also said to have been related to St. Patrick. Máirtín and Mártan are Gaelic forms. (MAR-TIN)

MATHGHAMHAIN Old name meaning "a bear." The name, which was borne by a brother of King Brian Boru, has been Anglicized as Mahon and Matthew. (MAH-YAHM-HAN)

MATTHEW Evolution of the Middle English Matheu, which is from the Ecclesiastic Late Latin Matthaeus, a derivative of the Ecclesiastic Greek Matthaios and Matthias, contractions of Mattathias. The name has its root in the Hebrew Matityah, which is derived from *mattīthyāh* (gift of God). The name is borne in the Bible by one of the four evangelists, the author of the first Gospel, Matthew. In Ireland, Matthew was used to Anglicize Mathghamhan (a bear). Short: Matt. (MATH-YOO)

MATTHIAS A borrowing from the Greek, Matthias is a contracted form of Mattathias, which is from the Hebrew Matityah, a derivative of *mattīthyāh* (gift of God). Maitias is the Gaelic form. (MAH-THĪ-AHS)

MEALLÁN Derived from the diminutive form of *meall* (pleasant): hence, "little pleasant one." Meldan and Mellan are Anglicized forms of the name, which was borne by four Irish saints. (MEHL-LAHN)

MELLAN Anglicized form of Meallán (little pleasant one). Var: Meldan. (MEL-LAN)

MICHAEL A derivative of the Hebrew *mīkhā'ēl* (who is like God?). The name is borne in the Bible by the archangel closest to God, the one responsible for carrying out God's judgments. Considered the leader of the heavenly host, Michael is regarded as the patron of soldiers. The name, one of the most successful of the biblical names, is in popular use in Ireland. Mícheál and Micheál are Gaelic forms. (MĪ-KL)

MÍCHEÁL Gaelic form of Michael (who is like God?). *See* MICHAEL. Var: Micheál. (MEE-HAHL)

MILES A borrowing from the English, Miles is from the Old French Milon, which is from the Old High German Milo, a name of uncertain derivation. *See* MILO (English Names). The name was used in Ireland to Anglicize the Gaelic Maolmórdha (majestic chief). Var: Myles. (MĪLZ)

MORGAN A borrowing from the Welsh, Morgan is thought to be derived from the elements *môr* (sea) and *can* (white, bright) or *cant* (circle, completion). The name has been used to Anglicize Murchadh (sea warrior). (MOR-GUN)

Muireadhach Derived from *muir* (sea), Muireadhach (seaman, sailor) has been Anglicized as Murry. (MUR-EH-THEHK)

Muirgheas Compound name composed from the elements *muir* (sea) and *gus* (choice): hence, "sea choice." The name was Anglicized as Maurice. (MUR-YAHS)

Munchin Anglicized form of Mainchín (little monk). *See* MAINCHÍN. (MUN-CHIN)

Murchadh Ancient name thought to be derived from the Celtic Mori-catu-s (sea warrior). The name has been Anglicized as Murrough and Morgan. (MUR-KAH)

Murrough Anglicized form of Murchadh (sea warrior). *See* MURCHADH. (MUR-RO)

Naomhán Derived from the diminutive form of *naomh* (holy): hence, "little holy one." Nevan is the Anglicized form. (NAU-AHN)

Neil Anglicized form of Niall, a name of debated etymology. *See* NIALL. Var: Neal, Neale, Neill, Nyle. (NEEL)

Nevan Anglicized form of Naomhán (little holy one). (NEH-VAN)

Niadh Derived from *niadh* (a champion). (NEE-UH)

Niall An ancient name of debated etymology, some suggest that it is derived from *niadh* (a champion); others think it is from *neall* (cloud). The name was borne by Niall of the Nine Hostages. Neal, Neil, and Nyle are Anglicized forms. Var: Néill. (NEE-AL)

Nicholas A borrowing from the English, Nicholas is from the Old French Nicolas (victory of the people), which is from the Latin Nicolaus, a derivative of the Greek Nikolaos, a compounding of the elements *nikē* (victory) and *laos* (the people). Nioclás is the Gaelic form. Var: Nicolas. Short: Nicol. (NIH-KO-LAS)

Nicol A short form of Nicholas (victory of the people), Nicol is also occasionally bestowed as an independent given name. *See* NICHOLAS. Niocol is its Gaelic cognate. (NIH-KOL)

Nioclás Gaelic form of Nicholas (victory of the people). *See* NICHOLAS. Short: Niocol. (NEE-KLAHS)

Niocol A short form of Nioclás (victory of the people), Niocol is sometimes bestowed as an independent given name. Nicol is its English cognate. (NEE-KOL)

Nolan Transferred use of the surname, which is an Anglicized form of O'Nuallacháin (descendant of Uallachán). Uallachán is a diminutive form of *uallach* (proud): hence, "little proud one." The name is also used as the Anglicized form of O'Nualláin (descendant of Nuallán). Nuallán is from a diminutive form of *nuall* (noble, famous): hence, "little noble one." Var: Noland. (NO-LAN)

Odhrán Diminutive form of *odhar* (pale green). Odran and Oran are the Anglicized forms. (O-RAHN)

Oghe Anglicized form of the Gaelic Eochaidh (horseman). Var: Oghie, Oho. (O-HE)

Oisín Diminutive form of *os* (a deer): hence, "a fawn, a little deer." The name was borne by a famous Fenian poet, the son of Fionn MacCumhail (Finn MacCool). The name has been Anglicized as Ossian and Ossin. (O-SEEN)

Oran Anglicized form of Odhrán (little pale green one). *See* ODHRÁN. Var: Odran. (O-RAN)

Oscar Derived from the Gaelic *oscar* (champion; warrior). The name was borne by the grandson of Fionn MacCumhail (Finn MacCool). (OS-KAR)

Ossian Anglicized form of Oisín (fawn). *See* OISÍN. Var: Ossin. (O-SEE-AN)

Owen Anglicized form of Eoghan (well-born). (O-WEN)

Paddy Popular pet form of Patrick. Padhra is the Gaelic form. (PAD-EE)

Pádraig Irish form of Patrick (a patrician, noble). *See* PATRICK. Var: Pádraic, Pádhraic, Padhraig. Pet: Padhra, Páid, Paidi, Páidín, Parra. (PAH-DREEK)

Parlan Anglicized form of Parthalán, the Gaelic form of Bartholomew (son of Talmai). *See* BARTHOLOMEW *and* PARTHALON. (PAR-LAN)

Parthalon Gaelic form of Bartholomew (son of Talmai). *See* BARTHOLOMEW. Parlan is the Anglicized form of the name. Var: Párthalán, Parthalán, Parthalón, Párthlán, Pártnan. (PAR-HAH-LAHN)

Patrick Derived from the Latin *patricius* (a patrician, an aristocrat). The name was adopted by St. Patrick (c. 385–461), a missionary to and the patron saint of Ireland. He was a Christian Breton and a Roman citizen whose original name was Sucat. Var: Patric. Short: Pat. Pet: Paddy. (PAT-REEK)

Paul From the Latin Paulus, which originated as a Roman family name derived from *paulus* (small). The name was adopted in the Bible by a Jew and Roman citizen, Saul of Tarsus, who was converted to Christianity by a vision of Christ. St. Paul and St. Peter are regarded as cofounders of the Christian Church. Pól is the Gaelic form of Paul. (POL)

Peadar Modern Gaelic form of Peter (a rock). *See* PETER. Var: Peadair. (PAA-DER)

Peter A borrowing from the English, Peter is from the Ecclesiastic Late Latin Petrus and the Greek Petros, names derived from *petrus* (a rock) and *petros* (a stone). The name was borne in the Bible by one of the Twelve Apostles of Christ. Peter is considered to be the first pope, and a cofounder of the Christian Church with St. Paul. Peadair and Peadar are Gaelic forms. (PEE-TER)

Philip Introduced by the Anglo-Normans, Philip is from the Latin Philippus, a derivative of the Greek Philippos (lover of horses), a compounding of the elements *philos* (loving) and *hippos* (a horse). The name is borne in the Bible by one of the Twelve Apostles of Christ. Pilib, Filib, and Filip are Gaelic forms. Short: Phil. (FIL-IP)

Piaras Gaelic cognate of Piers, the Old French cognate of Peter (a rock, a stone), a name introduced to Ireland by the Anglo-Normans. Piaras is also a cognate of Pierce, the English form of Piers. *See* PETER. Piaras was the form of Peter in common use until relatively recently, when the form Peadar evolved. (PEE-AH-RAHS)

Pierce A borrowing from the English, Pierce is the English form of Piers, an Old French form of Peter (a rock, a stone). Piaras is the Gaelic form. Var: Perce. (PEERSS)

Piers Introduced to Ireland by the Anglo-Normans, Piers is an Old French cognate of Peter (a rock, a stone). *See* PETER. Piaras is the Gaelic form of Piers. (PEERZ)

Pilib Gaelic form of Philip (lover of horses). *See* PHILIP. Var: Filib, Filip. (FIL-IP)

Pól Gaelic form of Paul (small). *See* PAUL. (POL)

Quinn Transferred use of the Anglicized surname, which is from O'Cuinn (descendant of Conn). Conn is a direct derivative of *conn* (wisdom, intelligence, reason; a freeman). (KWIN)

Rádhulbh Gaelic form of Ralph (wolf counsel), a name introduced by the Anglo-Norman settlers. *See* RALPH. (RAW-YULF)

Raghnall Gaelic form of several names introduced by the Norsemen and later by the Anglo-Normans. Rognvaldr (powerful judgment) was brought to Ireland by the Norsemen. *See* RAGNVALD (Scandinavian Names). Reginald and Reynold were brought by the Anglo-Normans. *See* REGINALD and REYNOLD (English Names). The name was also Anglicized as Randal and Ronald. (RAN-AL)

Ralph A name meaning "wolf counsel," which was introduced to Ireland by the Anglo-Normans. *See* Ralph (English Names). Rádhulbh is the Gaelic form. (RAFE, RALF)

Randall Transferred use of the English surname derived from Randolf (shield wolf), a personal name introduced to England by both the Scandinavians in the form Randulfr and by the Normans in the form Randolph. The name was also used in Ireland to Anglicize Raghnall. Var: Randal. (RAN-DAL)

Raymond Introduced by the Anglo-Normans, Raymond is from the Old Norman French Raimund, which is derived from the Germanic Raginmund, a compound name composed of the elements *ragin* (advice, judgment, counsel) and *mund* (hand, protection): hence, "wise protection." Réamonn is the Gaelic form. Short: Ray. (RAY-MOND)

Réamonn Gaelic form of Raymond (wise protection). *See* RAYMOND. (RYEH-MOND)

Richard A name introduced by the Anglo-Normans, Richard is derived from the Old High German Richart, a compounding of the elements *rik, rīc,* (power, ruler) and *hard* (strong, brave, hearty): hence, "brave ruler." Riocárd and Risteárd are the Gaelic forms. Var: Rickard. (RICH-ARD)

Riocárd Gaelic form of Richard (brave ruler). *See* RICHARD. Var: Riocard. (REE-KARD)

Risteárd Gaelic form of Richard (brave ruler), influenced by the French pronunciation of the name. *See* RICHARD. (REESH-TYARD)

Robert Introduced by the Anglo-Norman settlers, Robert is derived from the Old High German Hruodperht, a compound name composed of the elements *hruod* (fame) and *beraht* (bright): hence, "bright fame." Roibeárd and its many variants are the Gaelic forms of Robert. *See* ROIBEÁRD. Short: Rob. Pet: Robin. (ROB-ERT)

Robin A pet form of Robert, Robin is also occasionally bestowed as an independent given name. Roibin is the Irish equivalent. (RO-BIN)

Roderick Introduced by the Norsemen in the form Rothrekr, Roderick is from the Middle Latin Rodericus, which is derived from the Old High German Hrodrich, a compounding of the elements *hruod* (fame) and *rik* (king, ruler): hence, "famous king, famous ruler." The name has been used in Ireland to Anglicize Ruairí (red, rust-colored). Ruaidhrí is the Gaelic form. Pet: Roddy. (ROD-ER-RIK)

ROIBEÁRD Gaelic form of Robert (bright fame). *See* ROBERT. Var: Ribeard, Ribeart, Ribirt, Riobárd, Riobart, Roibeard. (RO-BAHRD)

ROIBIN Gaelic form of Robin, a pet form of Robert (bright fame). *See* ROBERT. (RO-BIN)

RÓNÁN Very old name derived from the diminutive form of *rón* (a seal): hence, "little seal." The name was borne by twelve saints as well as by an ancient king of Leinster who was deceived into killing his first-born son. Ronan is the Anglicized spelling. (RO-NAHN)

RORY Anglicized form of Ruairí (red, rust-colored). *See* RUAIRÍ. The name was borne by Rory O'Conor, the last high king of Ireland, who reigned from 1166 to 1170. (ROR-REE)

ROWAN Popular Anglicized form of Ruadhán (little red-haired one). *See* RUADHÁN. (RO-AN)

ROY A borrowing from the Scottish, Roy represents the transferred use of the surname originating as a descriptive nickname for a person with red hair or a ruddy complexion. It is derived from the Gaelic *ruadh* (red). (ROY)

RUADHÁN Diminutive form of *ruadh* (red): hence, "little red-haired one." The name was Anglicized as Rowan. (ROO-AN)

RUAIDHRÍ Gaelic form of the name Roderick (famous king), which was introduced by the Norsemen in the form Rothrekr. *See* RODERICK. The name was also Anglicized as Rory and Roger. (RWEE-EE-REE)

RUAIRÍ Irish name derived from the Gaelic *ruadh* (red, rust-colored). The name has been Anglicized as Rory. Var: Ruaraidh. (RWEE-EE)

RYAN Transferred use of the Anglicized surname, which is from O'Riain (descendant of Rian) and O'Riaghain (descendant of Riaghan). Rian and Riaghan are ancient names believed to be diminutive forms of *rí* (king): hence, "little king." (RĪ-AN)

SAEBHREATHACH Compound name composed of the Gaelic elements *saor* (noble) and *breathach* (judge): hence, "noble judge." The name was Anglicized as Justin. (SAH-VRAH-HUHK)

SAMUEL Ecclesiastic Late Latin form of the Ecclesiastic Greek Samouēl, a name derived from *shĕmū'ēl* (name of God, his name is God). The name is borne in the Bible by a Hebrew judge and prophet who anointed Saul as the first king of Israel. The name was also used in Ireland to Anglicize Somhairle (summer sailor). *See* SOMHAIRLE. Short: Sam. Pet: Sammy. (SAM-YOOL)

SCULLY Transferred use of the surname, which is an Anglicized form of O'Scolaidhe (descendant of Scolaidhe) and O'Scolaighe (descendant of Scolaighe). Scolaidh and Scolaighe are old personal names meaning "crier, town crier." There are some who believe the names mean "student" and are derived from the Old Irish *scol* (school). (SKULL-EE)

SÉAFRA Variant of Gothfraidh, which is an Irish cognate of Godfrey (God's peace). The name has been Anglicized as Geoffrey. Var: Seafraid, Séartha, Séathra. (SHE-AH-FRA)

SEAGHÁN Variant of Seán, a popular Irish form of John (God is gracious). The name is Anglicized as Shane. *See* SEÁN. (SHANE)

SEAMUS Anglicized spelling of Séamus, the Irish cognate of James (supplanting, seizing by the heel). Var: Shamus. Pet: Shay. (SHAY-MUS)

SÉAMUS Gaelic form of James (supplanting, seizing by the heel). Seamus and Shamus are the popular Anglicized forms. *See* JAMES. (SHAY-MUS)

SEAN Anglicized spelling of Seán, an Irish cognate of John (God is gracious). *See* SEÁN. Var: Shaun, Shawn. (SHAWN)

SEÁN The highly popular Irish form of John (God is gracious). *See* JOHN. The name is derived from the Old French Jehan and the French Jean, cognates of John, which were introduced to Ireland by Anglo-Norman settlers. Sean, Shane, Shaun, and Shawn are Anglicized forms. Var: Seaghán, Seón. (SHAWN)

SEANÁN Derived from the diminutive form of *sean* (old, wise). The name was borne by many Irish saints. Senan, Sinan, and Sinon are Anglicized forms. (SHAY-NAHN)

SÉARLAS Gaelic form of Charles (full-grown, a man). *See* CHARLES. Var: Séarlus. (SHAHR-LAS)

SÉATHRÚN Common Gaelic form of Geoffrey. *See* GEOFFREY. Var: Searthún, Seathrún. (SHAY-THROON)

SEOIRSE Gaelic form of George (earthworker, farmer), an importation from England in the 18th century. *See* GEORGE. Var: Seórsa. (SEE-AHR-SHA)

SEOSAMH Variant form of Ióseph, a Gaelic form of Joseph (may he add). *See* JOSEPH. Var: Seósap, Seósaph. (SHO-SAHV)

SHANE Popular Anglicized form of Seathán and Seaghán and also of Seán, Irish forms of John (God is gracious). *See* JOHN. (SHANE)

SHAY Pet form of Shamus, the Irish form of James (supplanting, seizing by the heel). Shay is also bestowed as an independent given name. *See* JAMES. (SHAY)

SHEARY Irish form of Geoffrey. *See* GEOFFREY. (SHAHR-EE)

SIADHAL Ancient name derived from *siadhail* (sloth). The name was borne by two Irish saints and was Anglicized as Shiel. Var: Siaghal. (SEED-HEL)

SIMON Ecclesiastic Late Latin form of the Greek Simōn and Seimōn, names derived from the Hebrew Shimon, which is from *shim'ōn* (heard). The name is borne in the Bible by two of the Twelve Apostles and a brother of Jesus, as well as several other New Testament characters. Síomón, Síomonn, and Síomún are the Gaelic forms. In Ireland Simon was also used to Anglicize Suibhne (well-going, pleasant). (SĪ-MON)

SÍOMÓN Gaelic form of Simon (heard). *See* SIMON. Var: Siómonn, Síomún. (SHE-MONE)

SISEAL Irish form of Cecil (blind). *See* CECIL. (SEE-SIL)

SIVNEY Anglicized form of Suibhne (well-going). *See* SUIBHNE. (SIV-NEE)

SOMHAIRLE Irish form of Sumerlidi, the Old Norse name for summer sailors or Vikings. It was during the summer months that the Vikings embarked on their raids upon the Irish and the Scots. The name was Anglicized as Sorley, and later as Samuel and Charles.

SORLEY Original Anglicized form of Somhairle (summer sailor). *See* SOMHAIRLE. (SOR-LEE)

STANLEY Transferred use of the English surname originating from several place-names derived from the Old English elements *stan* (stone) and *lēah* (wood, clearing, meadow). The name was originally indicative of one who dwelled near a stony, rocky clearing. Short: Stan. (STAN-LEE)

STEAFÁN Popular Gaelic form of Stephen (a crown, a garland). *See* STEPHEN. Var: Steimhin, Stiabhán, Stiabhna, Stiana, Stibhin, Stiofán. (STEF-AHN)

STEPHEN From the Latin Stephanus, which is from the Greek Stephanos, a derivative of *stephanos* (a crown, a garland). The name was borne by St. Stephen, the first Christian martyr, who was one of the seven chosen to assist the Twelve Apostles. Var: Steven. Short: Steve. (STEE-VEN)

STEVE A short form of Steven (a crown, a garland), Steve is also bestowed as an independent given name. *See* STEPHEN. (STEEV)

SUIBHNE Old name derived from *suibhne* (well-going, pleasant). The name was Anglicized as Sivney and sometimes as Simon. (SIV-NEE)

TADHG Very old name derived from the Gaelic *tadhg* (poet, philosopher). Teige and Teague are the Anglicized forms of the name, which was also occasionally Anglicized as Timothy and Thaddeaus. (TAYG)

TAIDHGÍN Diminutive form of Tadhg (poet, philosopher): hence, "little poet, little philosopher." The name was Anglicized as Tim. (TEE-GIN)

TÉADÓIR Gaelic form of Theodore (God's gift). *See* THEODORE. (TEH-DOR)

TEIGE Anglicized form of Tadhg (poet, philosopher). *See* TADHG. Var: Teague. (TEEG)

TERENCE A borrowing from the English, Terence is from the Latin Terentius, an old Roman family name of uncertain derivation. It might be derived from *terenus* (soft, tender). The name was used to Anglicize Toirdealbhach (shaped like Thor). *See* TOIRDEALBHACH. Pet: Terry. (TARE-RENS)

THADDEAUS Latin name from the Ecclesiastic Greek Thaddaios, a name of uncertain derivation. Some believe it to be a variant of Theodōros (God's gift). Others feel it might be from an Aramaic word meaning "praised." The name is found in the Bible as a name of Lebbaeus, an apostle of Christ. Thaddeaus was used in Ireland to Anglicize Tadhg. Var: Thaddeus. Short: Thade. Pet: Thady. (THAD-DEE-US)

THEODORE From the Latin Theodorus, which is from the Greek Theodōros (God's gift), a compounding of the elements *theos* (God) and *dōron* (gift): hence, "God's gift." Téadóir is the Gaelic form. (THEE-O-DOR)

THOM A short form of Thomas (a twin), Thom is also bestowed as an independent given name. *See* THOMAS. Var: Tom. (TOM)

THOMAS From the Ecclesiastic Greek Thōmas, a derivative of the Aramaic *tĕ'ōma* (a twin). The name is borne in the Bible by an apostle who doubted the resurrection of Christ. Tomás is the Irish form. Short: Thom, Tom. Pet: Tommy. (TOM-AHS)

TIAMHDHA Irish form of Timothy (honor God, respect God). *See* TIMOTHY. (TIM-HEH)

TIARNACH Anglicized form of Tighearnach (lordly). *See* TIGHEARNACH. (TEE-AHR-NAHK)

TIERNAN Anglicized spelling of Tiarnán and Tighearnán (little lord). *See* TIGHEARNÁN. (TEER-NAN)

TIERNEY Anglicized form of Tighearnach (lordly). *See* TIGHEARNACH. (TEER-NEE)

TIGHEARNACH Derived from *tighearna* (a lord). The name Tighearnach (lordly) was borne by four Irish saints and has been Anglicized as Tierney. (TEER-NAHK)

TIGHEARNÁN Derived from the diminutive form of *tighearna* (a lord): hence, "little lord." Tiernan is the Anglicized spelling. Var: Tiarnán. (TEER-NAHN)

TIMOTHY Derived from the French Timotheé, which is from the Latin Timotheus, a derivative of the Greek Timotheos (honor God, respect God), a compounding of the elements *timē* (honor, respect) and *theos* (God). The name is borne in the Bible by a disciple and companion of the apostle Paul but was not used in England or Ireland before the Reformation. Timothy was also used in Ireland to Anglicize Tadhg and Tomaltach. Tiomoid is the Gaelic form of Timothy. Short: Tim. (TIM-O-THEE)

TIOMOID Irish form of Timothy (honor God, respect God). *See* TIMOTHY. (TEE-MODE)

TOAL Anglicized form of Tuathal (people mighty). *See* TUATHAL. (TŌ-AHL)

TOIRDEALBHACH Old Irish name meaning "shaped like Thor" (the Norse mythological god of thunder and strength). Turlough and Tirloch are Anglicized spellings of the name, which was also Anglicized as Charles and Terence. (TOR-DEH-LAHK)

TOMÁISÍN Diminutive form of Tomás, the Irish form of Thomas (a twin): hence, "little Thomas." Tommy is the Anglicized form. (TAH-MAH-SEEN)

TOMÁS Common Irish form of Thomas (a twin). *See* THOMAS. (TAH-MAHS)

TUATHAL Ancient name derived from the Celtic Touto-valo-s (people mighty). The name has been Anglicized as Toal and Tully. (TOO-HAHL)

TULLY Anglicized form of Tuathal (people mighty). *See* TUATHAL. (TULL-EE)

TURLOUGH Common Anglicized form of Toirdealbhach (shaped like Thor). *See* TOIRDEALBHACH. Var: Tirloch. (TER-LO)

TYRONE Transferred use of a place-name in county Ulster, which is of uncertain derivation. (TĪ-RONE)

UAITHNE Old name derived from *uaithne* (green). It was Anglicized as Hewney, Oney, Owney, and Oynie as well as Anthony. (OON-YEH)

UALTAR Gaelic form of Walter (ruler of an army), a name introduced by the Anglo-Normans. *See* WALTER. Var: Uaitéir, Ualtéir. (WAL-TAR)

UILLEÓG Diminutive form of Uilliam, the Irish cognate of William: hence, "little William." The name was Anglicized as Ulick and Ulysses. Var: Uilleac, Uillioc. (IH-LIG)

UILLIAM Common Irish form of William (resolute protector), a name introduced by the Anglo-Normans. *See* WILLIAM. Short: Liam. (UHL-YAHM)

UINSEANN Gaelic form of Vincent (conquering), a name introduced by Anglo-Norman settlers. *See* VINCENT. Var: Uinsionn. (WIN-SHEN)

ÚISTEAN Irish diminutive form of Hugh (heart, mind, soul). The name was Anglicized as Euston. (OOSH-CHEN)

ULICK Anglicized form of Uilleac and Uilleóg (little William). *See* UILLEÓG. (OO-LIK)

VAUGHN Transferred use of the surname derived from the Welsh *fychan*, a variant of *bychan* (small, little). (VON)

VINCENT A borrowing from the Old French, Vincent is from the Late Latin Vincentius (conquering), which is derived from *vincere* (to conquer). The name was made popular by St. Vincent de Paul (1580?–1660), a French priest who founded the Vincentian Order of the Sisters of Charity. Uinseann and Uinsionn are the Gaelic forms. (VIN-SENT)

WALTER Introduced by the Anglo-Normans, Walter is from the Old French Waltier, which is from the Germanic Waldheri (ruler of an army), a compounding of the elements *wald* (rule) and *heri* (army). Ualtar, Ualteir, and Uailtéir are the Gaelic forms. Short: Walt. (WAHL-TER)

WILLIAM Introduced by the Anglo-Normans, William is from the Old Norman French Willaume, a derivative of the Old High German Willehelm, a compounding of the elements *willeo* (will, resolution) and *helm* (helmet, protection): hence, "resolute protector." Uilliam is the common Gaelic form. Short: Liam, Will. (WIL-YAHM)

Irish Female Names

Abaigeal Irish Gaelic form of Abigail (father of exaltation). *See* ABIGAIL. Short: Abaigh. (AB-IH-GEHL)

Abbey A short form of Abigail (father of exaltation), Abbey is also bestowed as an independent given name. *See* ABIGAIL. Var: Abbie. (AB-BEE)

Abigail From the Hebrew Avigayil, which is derived from *avīgayil* (father of exaltation, father is rejoicing). The name is borne in the Bible by one of the wives of King David. Abaigeal is the Gaelic form of Abigail. Pet: Abbey, Abbie. (AB-IH-GALE)

Affrica Latinized form of Aifric (pleasant). *See* AIFRIC. The name was borne by the 12th-century bride of Olaus the Swarthy, King of Man. Var: Afric, Africa. (AF-RIH-KAH)

Aghna Irish variant of Agnes (chaste, pure). *See* AGNES. (EH-NUH)

Agnes Derived from the Greek Hagnē, which is from *hagnos* (chaste, pure, sacred). The name was borne by a thirteen-year-old Roman martyred for her Christian beliefs during the reign of Diocletian. *See* AGNESE (Italian Names). Aignéis is a Gaelic form and Aghna is an Irish form of the name. Alternatively, Agnes has been used to Anglicize the Gaelic Mór (great). Pet: Aggie. (AG-NES)

Aideen Anglicized form of Étáin, an old Gaelic name of uncertain meaning. *See* ÉTÁIN. (Ā-DEEN)

Aifric Gaelic name meaning "pleasant," Aifric was borne by two abbesses of Kildare in the 8th and 9th centuries. Afric and Africa are Anglicized forms of the name. (Ā-FRIK)

Aignéis Gaelic form of Agnes (chaste, pure, sacred). *See* AGNES. (ĀG-NEESH)

Ailbhe A common name of uncertain derivation, some believe it to be derived from the Latin *albus* (white). Ailbhe has been Anglicized as Alvy, Elva, and Olive. Var: Oilbhe. (AL-VYUH)

Ailís Gaelic form of Alice (nobility). *See* ALICE. Var: Ailis, Ailíse, Ailse. Pet: Ailidh. (Ā-LISH)

Aimilíona Gaelic form of Amelina, a diminutive form of Amelia (industrious), which was introduced to Ireland by the Anglo-Normans. (Ā-MIL-EE-NUH)

Áine Gaelic name meaning "joy, praise; fasting." The name was borne by a granddaughter of the Irish King Lear as well as by the queen of the fairies of South Munster. Cnoc Áine, the Hill of Áine, was her dwelling place. The name has been Anglicized as Anna and Hannah. (AN-YUH)

Aingeal Gaelic form of Angela (angel, messenger of God). *See* ANGELA. (ĀN-GEL)

Aisling Derived from *aisling* (dream, vision, daydream). The name has been Anglicized as Esther. Var: Aislinn, Ashling, Isleen. (ASH-LING)

Alana Derived from the Gaelic *a leanbh* (O child), Alana is also used as a feminine form of Alan, a name of uncertain derivation. Var: Alannah. (AH-LAN-AH)

Alastrina Feminine form of Alistar, the Irish form of Alexander (defender or helper of mankind). Alastríona is the Gaelic form of Alastrina. (AL-AH-STREE-NAH)

Alastríona Gaelic form of Alexandra and Alexandrina (defender of mankind). *See* ALEXANDRA. (AL-AH-STREE-NAH)

Alexandra Feminine form of Alexander (defender or helper of mankind). *See* ALEXANDER (Male Names). Alastríona is a Gaelic form. Var: Alexandrina. (AL-EX-AN-DRAH)

Alice A borrowing from the English, Alice is derived from the Germanic Adalheidis, a compound name composed of the elements *adal* (noble) and *heid* (kind, sort): hence, "noble one, nobility." *See* ALICE (English Names). Ailis and Ailís are Gaelic forms of Alice. (AL-ISS)

Alicia Latinate form of Alice (nobility). Ailíse and Ailse are Gaelic forms. (AH-LEE-SHA)

Alma Old Irish name of uncertain derivation. Some translate the name as "all good," believing it to be derived from the Latin *almus* (good, loving). The name received a boost in popularity in 1854 following the Battle of Alma in the Crimean War. The battle was fought at the river Alma, the name of which is thought to be of Celtic origin. (AHL-MAH)

Amanda Popular name coined by the English playwright Colley Cibber (1671–1757). It is derived from the Latin *amanda* (lovable, worthy to be loved). Pet: Mandy. (AH-MAN-DAH)

Amelia Introduced to Ireland by the Anglo-Normans, Amelia is a variant of the Germanic Amalia, which is derived from *amal* (work). The name may also be a variant form of Emilia (rival). *See* EMILY. (AH-MEEL-YAH)

Amelina Diminutive form of Amelia (industrious). *See* AMELIA. Aimilíona is the Gaelic form. (AM-EH-LEE-NAH)

Angela Latinate form of Angel (messenger of God, guiding spirit), which is from the Greek *angelos* (messenger). Aingeal is the Gaelic form. Pet: Angie. (AN-JEH-LAH)

Anita A borrowing from the Spanish, Anita is a diminutive form of Anna (gracious, full of grace). *See* ANNA. (AH-NEE-TAH)

Anna Latinate variant of Anne, which is a cognate of the Hebrew Hannāh (grace, full of grace, mercy). *See* ANNE. The name was used in Ireland to Anglicize the Gaelic Áine (joy, praise; fasting). Ánna is the Gaelic form. (AN-NAH)

Anne Borrowed from the French, Anne is a cognate of the Hebrew Hannāh, which is from *hannāh*, *chaanach* (grace, gracious, mercy). In medieval Christian tradition, Anne was the name assigned to the mother of the Virgin Mary, as Joachim was assigned to her father. The name was used to Anglicize the Gaelic Áine. Var: Ann, Anna. Pet: Annie. (AN)

Annette A borrowing from the French, Annette is a pet form of Anne (gracious, full of grace, mercy) in common Irish use. *See* ANNE. (AN-NET)

Annie Originally a pet form of Anne (gracious, full of grace, mercy), Annie is also bestowed as an independent given name in Ireland and has been used to Anglicize the Gaelic Eithne (kernel). *See* EITHNE. (AN-NEE)

Aoibh Derived from *aoibh* (beauty). Aoibh is also used as a short form of Aoibheann (beautiful). (EEV)

Aoibheann Very old name derived from the Gaelic *aoibheann* (fair form, beautiful), which is from the root *aoibh* (beauty). The name was borne by the mother of the 6th-century St. Enda. Its variant Aoibhinn is borne in legend by the queen of the fairies in Thomond. Aoibheann has been Anglicized as Eavan. Var: Aibfinnia, Aoibhinn. Short: Aoibh. (EEV-UHN)

Aoife Ancient Irish name of uncertain derivation. Some believe it is from the Gaelic *aoibh* (beauty). Others think it to be a Gaelic form of Eva, which has also been used to Anglicize Aoife. In Ossianic poetry, Aoiffe is the name of the wife of Cuchullin. Var: Aoiffe. (EE-FYEH)

Ashling Anglicized form of the Gaelic Aisling (dream, vision, daydream). *See* AISLING. (ASH-LING)

Augusteen Feminine form of Augustine, which is from the Latin Augustinus, a diminutive form of Augustus, which is derived from *augustus* (great, venerable, consecrated by the augurs). (AU-GUS-TEEN)

Aveline Introduced by the Anglo-Normans, Aveline is thought to be a French diminutive form of the Germanic Avila, which is of uncertain derivation. (AV-EH-LEEN)

Avril A borrowing from the French, Avril represents the French spelling of the month of April. (Ā-VRIL)

Báirbre Gaelic form of Barbara (foreign woman). *See* BARBARA. Var: Bairbre. Pet: Baibín. (BAHR-BRAH)

Barbara A borrowing from the Latin, Barbara (foreign woman) is derived from *barbarus* (foreign, strange). The name was borne by an early Christian martyr who became one of the most popular saints in the Catholic Calendar. Báirbre is the Gaelic form. Short: Barb. Pet: Barbie. (BAHR-BAH-RAH)

Barran Diminutive form of *barra* (top, summit). The name (little top) was borne by a popular Irish saint. (BAHR-RAN)

Beatha Derived from *beatha* (life, livelihood). Var: Betha. (BEH-THA)

Bébhinn Ancient name meaning "sweet, melodious lady." It was borne by the mother and a daughter of Brian Boru (926?–1014), the most famous of the Irish high kings. Bevin is an Anglicized form of Bébhinn, which has also been Anglicized as Vivian and Vevina. (BEH-VIN)

Bernadette A borrowing from the French, Bernadette is a feminine form of Bernard (strong as a bear), formed by the addition of the diminutive suffix *-ette*. The name was borne by St. Bernadette of Lourdes (1844–79). *See* BERNADETTE (French Names). (BER-NAH-DET)

Berneen Irish feminine form of Bernard (strong as a bear), a name derived from the Old High German Berinhard, a compounding of the elements *bern* (bear) and *hart* (bold, strong, hearty). (BER-NEEN)

Beth A short form of Elizabeth (God is my oath), Beth is also bestowed as an independent given name. *See* ELIZABETH. (BETH)

Bevin Anglicized form of the Gaelic Bébhinn (sweet, melodious lady). *See* BÉBHINN. (BEH-VIN)

Bidelia Elaborate variant of Biddy, a pet form of Bridget (strength). *See* BRIDGET. Bidelia is used as an independent given name. (BIH-DEE-LYAH)

Bidina An elaborate variant of Biddy, a pet form of Bridget (strength). *See* BRIDGET. Bidina is used as an independent given name. (BIH-DEE-NAH)

Blath Derived from *blath* (flower). (BLAH)

Bláthnaid Ancient name derived from *blath* (flower). The name is translated as Florence (a blooming). Var: Bláithín, Bláthnait. Short: Blath. (BLA-NAH)

Breeda Anglicized form of Bríghid (strength). *See* BRÍGHID. (BREE-DAH)

Brenda Of uncertain origin and meaning, Brenda is thought to be a Celtic name originating in the Shetland Islands and derived from *brandr* (the blade of a sword). Alternatively, it might be a feminine form of the obsolete Brandolf (sword wolf). It is commonly used in Ireland as a feminine form of Brendan (prince). *See* BRENDAN (Male Names). (BREN-DAH)

Briana Feminine form of Brian, a popular name of debated meaning. *See* BRIAN (Male Names). Var: Brianna, Brina, Bryna. (BRĪ-ANA, BREE-ANA)

Bride Anglicized form of Bríghid (strength), the name borne in Irish mythology by the goddess of wisdom, poetry, and song. *See* BRÍGHID. (BRIDE)

Bridget Anglicized form of the Gaelic Bríghid (strength). *See* BRÍGHID. Pet: Biddy. (BRID-JET)

Bríghid Ancient name believed to be derived from the Gaelic *brígh* (strength). The name is borne in Irish mythology by the daughter of the fire-god, the goddess of wisdom, poetry, and song. It was also borne by St. Bríghid of Kildare (d. 510), a patron saint of Ireland. Out of reverence for the saint, the name was not in common use until the 17th century. Breeda, Bride, Bridget, and Brigid are Anglicized forms of Bríghid. Var: Bríd. Pet: Brídín. (BRIDE)

Caitríona Gaelic form of Catherine (pure, unsullied). Var: Caitlín, Caitrín, Catraoine, Catriona. Short: Cáit. Pet: Caiti, Cáitín. (KA-TREE-NAH)

Caoilfhionn Compound name composed of the elements *caol* (slender) and *fionn* (fair, white, clear). The name was Anglicized as Keelin and Latinized as Coelfinnia. (KEE-LIN)

Carla Feminine form of Carl, which is a cognate of Charles (full-grown, a man, a freeman). *See* CHARLES (Male Names). Var: Carleen. (KAR-LAH)

Catherine A borrowing from the English, Catherine is a cognate of the Greek Aikaterinē, which is derived from *katharos* (pure, unsullied). Caitrín and Caitríona are Gaelic forms. Var: Catharina, Catharine, Cathryn, Katherine, Kathryn. Short: Cath, Kate, Kath. Pet: Cathy, Kathy, Katie, Katty, Kay. (KATH-EH-RIN)

Cathleen Anglicized form of the Irish Caitlín, a Gaelic form of Catherine (pure, unsullied) derived via the Old French Catheline. *See* CATHERINE. Var: Kathleen. Short: Cath, Kath. Pet: Cathy, Kathy, Kay. (KATH-LEEN)

Cecilia Brought to Ireland by the Anglo-Normans, Cecilia is derived from Caecilius, an old Roman family name, which has its root in the Latin *caecus* (blind, dim-sighted). Sile and Sisile are Gaelic forms. Var: Cecily. Short: Celia. (SIH-SIL-YAH)

Charlotte Feminine diminutive form of Charles (full-grown, a man, freeman), which originated in France. Séarlait is the Gaelic form. *See* CHARLES (Male Names). Var: Charlot. (SHAR-LOT)

Chevonne Anglicized form of Siobhán, which is a feminine form of Sean (God is gracious). *See* SIOBHÁN. (SHEH-VON)

Christian From the Latin Christiānus (a Christian, a follower of Christ), a derivative of the Greek *christianos* (a Christian). The name was brought to Ireland by the Anglo-Normans and is used by both males and females in Ireland. (KRIS-CHEN)

Christina Derived from the Latin Christiāna, which is from *christiānus*, a derivative of the Greek *christianos* (a Christian, a follower of Christ). Chrístíona and Cristín are Gaelic forms. Var: Christine. Short: Chris, Christi, Tina. Pet: Christie, Christy. (KRIS-TEE-NAH)

Ciannait Feminine diminutive form of Cian (ancient). *See* CIAN (Male Names). Keenat and Kinnat are Anglicized forms. Ciannata is a Latinate form. (KEEN-AHT)

Ciara Popular name derived from *ciar* (black, dark): hence, "black-haired one." Var: Ceara. (KEER-AH)

Clare Derived from the Latin *clārus* (bright, clear, famous). The name was borne by St. Clare of Assisi (c. 1194–1255), the founder of the Order of Poor Ladies, now known as the Poor Clares. Clár is the Gaelic form. (KLARE)

Clíodhna Gaelic name of uncertain meaning. Var: Clídna, Clíona. (KLEE-OY-NAH)

Coelfinnia Latinate form of the Gaelic Caoilfhionn (slender and fair). *See* CAOILFHIONN. (KO-EL-FIN-NEE-AH)

Colette A borrowing from the French, Colette is a short form of Nicolette, a pet form of Nicole (victory of the people). *See* COLETTE (French Names). (KO-LET)

CONCHOBARRE Feminine form of Conchobhar, an ancient Irish name of debated meaning. *See* CONCHOBHAR (Male Names). (KON-KO-VAH-REH)

CORDELIA Of uncertain origin, Cordelia is thought to be from the Celtic Creiryddlydd (daughter or jewel of the sea). The name is borne in Shakespeare's *King Lear* by Lear's youngest daughter, the only one who was faithful to him. (KOR-DEE-LEE-AH, KOR-DEEL-YAH)

CRÍSTÍONA Gaelic form of Christina (a Christian, a follower of Christ), a name introduced to Ireland by the Anglo-Normans. *See* CHRISTINA. Var: Cristín. (KRIS-TEE-NAH)

DAMHNAIT Old name perhaps derived from *damh* (a poet). The name, borne by two Irish saints, is Anglicized as Devnet and Dymphna. (DEV-NAHT)

DANA Feminine form of Daniel (God is my judge). *See* DANIEL (Male Names). (DAN-AH, DANE-AH)

DAWN A recent borrowing from the English, Dawn is derived from *dawn* (daybreak, dawn). (DAWN)

DEBORAH Derived from the Hebrew *devōrāh* (a bee, a swarm of bees). The name is borne in the Bible by a prophetess and judge who led the Israelites to victory over the Canaanites. The name was introduced by the English and is used to Anglicize the Gaelic Gobinet (a mouth, a beak). Short: Deb. Pet: Debby. (DEB-OR-AH, DEH-BOR-AH)

DECLA Feminine form of Declan, the Anglicized form of the Gaelic Deaglán, which is of uncertain derivation. (DEHK-LAH)

DEIRBHILE Gaelic name meaning "poet's daughter." It has been Anglicized as Dervila and Dervla. (DEER-VIL-EH)

DEIRDRE A popular name of uncertain origin, Deirdre was the name of a legendary Irish princess who was betrothed to the king of Ulster, Conchobhar. She eloped, however, to Scotland with her lover Naoise, who was then treacherously murdered by the king. Deirdre supposedly died of a broken heart. The name might be derived from the Old Irish Derdriu (young girl) or from the Celtic Diédrè (fear). (DEE-DRAH)

DERVILA Anglicized form of the Gaelic Deirbhile (poet's daughter). Var: Dervla. (DER-VEE-LAH)

DEVNET Anglicized form of Damhnait (a poet). *See* DAMHNAIT. (DEV-NET)

DOIREANN Old Gaelic name meaning "sullen." Dorren is an Irish variant, Dorren and Dorothy were used to Anglicize it, and Dorinnia is a Latinate form. (DOR-EN)

DOMINICA Feminine form of Dominic (of the lord). The name was borne by an early Irish saint who was martyred in Germany. *See* DOMINIC (Male Names). (DŌ-MIN-EE-KAH)

DONELLE Feminine form of Donal (world ruler). *See* DONAL (Male Names). Var: Donla. (DON-EL)

DOREEN Variant form of Dora (gift) made by adding the Irish diminutive suffix *-een*. *See* DORA (English Names). Doreen was also used to Anglicize the Gaelic Doireann (sullen). *See* DOIREANN. Var: Dorean. (DOR-EEN)

DORINNIA Latinate form of the Gaelic Doireann (sullen). *See* DOIREANN. (DOR-IN-NEE-AH)

DORREN Irish form of the Gaelic Doireann (sullen). *See* DOIREANN. (DOR-REN)

DOWNETT Anglicized form of the Gaelic Damhnait (a poet). *See* DAMHNAIT. Var: Downet. (DOW-NET)

DYMPHNA Anglicized form of the Gaelic Damhnait (a poet). Var: Dympna. (DIMF-NAH)

ÉABHA Gaelic form of Eva (life). *See* EVA. (EH-VAH)

ÉADAOIN Evolution of Étáin, a name borne in Irish mythology by a sun-goddess. The name was Anglicized as Edwina. (EH-DEEN)

EALGA From *ealga* (noble), this name is taken from *Innis Ealga* (the Noble Isle), a phrase that is representative of Ireland. (EHL-GAH)

EAVAN Popular Anglicized form of the Gaelic Aoibheann (beautiful, fair form). *See* AOIBHEANN. (EE-VAHN)

EDANA Feminine form of Aidan, an Anglicized form of the Gaelic Aodhan (little fire). *See* AIDAN (Male Names). (EE-DAH-NAH)

EIBHLÍN Gaelic form of Eileen, which is of uncertain meaning. *See* EILEEN. Var: Eibhilin. (EH-EE-LEEN)

EILEANÓR Gaelic form of Eleanora (light, torch). *See* ELEANOR. Var: Eileanóra. Pet: Léan. (EL-LEH-NOR)

EILEEN Anglicized form of the Gaelic Eibhlín, a cognate of Evelyn, which is an English variant of Aveline. Aveline is a French diminutive form of the Germanic Avila, which is thought to be a Latinate form of Aveza, a name ultimately of uncertain meaning. Var: Aileen. Pet: Eily. (Ī-LEEN)

EILÍS Gaelic form of Elizabeth (God is my oath). *See* ELIZABETH. Var: Eilíse. (EH-LEESH)

Eimhear Old Gaelic name of uncertain derivation. It might be derived from *eimh* (swift). Emer is the common Irish form of Eimhear. (EM-ER)

Eimile Gaelic form of Emily (rival). *See* EMILY. (EM-IH-LEE)

Eireen Irish form of Irene (peace). *See* IRENE. (Ī-REEN)

Eistir Gaelic form of Esther, a name of debated etymology. *See* ESTHER. (EH-STER)

Eithne Popular Gaelic name derived from *eithne* (kernel). The name was borne by St. Eithne, a daughter of the 4th- and 5th-century king Laoghane. She was one of St. Patrick's first converts to Christianity. The name was Anglicized as Ena, Ethna, Etna, Etney, and Annie. Ethenia and Ethnea are Latinate forms. (EH-NEH)

Elaine Variant form of Helen, from the Greek Helenē, which is derived from the element *ēlē* (light, torch, bright). The name was borne in Arthurian legend by a woman of Astolat who loved Sir Lancelot. Var: Elan. (EE-LANE)

Elan Irish variant of Elaine (light, torch, bright). *See* ELAINE. (EE-LAN)

Eleanor English form of Alienor, a Provençal form of the Greek Helenē, which is from *ēlē* (light, torch, bright). Eileanór and Eileanóra are Gaelic forms. Var: Eleanora. (EL-EH-NOR)

Elisa A short form of Elisabeth (God is my oath), Elisa is also bestowed as an independent given name. *See* ELIZABETH. (EE-LEE-SAH)

Eliza A short form of Elizabeth (God is my oath), Eliza is also bestowed as an independent given name. *See* ELIZABETH. (EE-LIZE-AH)

Elizabeth Derived from the Hebrew *elīsheba'* (God is my oath). The name is borne in the Bible by the mother of John the Baptist. Elizabeth first came to Ireland in the Spanish form Isabel, but the form Elizabeth came into wide use during the Middle Ages due to the popularity of St. Elizabeth of Hungary (1207–31). Eilís and Eilíse are Gaelic forms. Var: Elisabeth, Elspeth. Short: Beth, Elisa, Eliza, Elsa, Lisa. Pet: Elsie, Lilibet, Liz, Lizzie. (EE-LIZ-AH-BETH)

Elva Anglicized form of Ailbhe, a Gaelic name of uncertain derivation. *See* AILBHE. Var: Alvy. (EL-VAH)

Emer Irish form of Eimhear, an old Gaelic name, which might be from *eimh* (swift). The name was borne by the wife of the Irish mythological hero Cuchulainn. (EM-ER)

Emily Cognate of the Latin Aemilia, which is from Aemilius, an old Roman family name probably derived from *aemulus* (emulating, trying to equal or excel, rival). Eimile is the Gaelic form. (EM-IH-LEE)

Emma Popular variant of the Germanic Erma, a name that originated as a short form of any of the various names containing the element *erm(en)* or *irm(en)* (strength). (EM-MAH)

Ena Anglicized form of the Irish Gaelic Eithne (kernel). *See* EITHNE. Var: Enya. (EH-NAH)

Ennis A borrowing of the name of the main town of county Clare in western Ireland. Inis is the Gaelic form. (EN-NIS)

Enya Variant of Ena, an Irish form of Eithne (kernel). *See* EITHNE. The name is borne by the popular Irish musician and composer Enya. (EN-YAH)

Esther A borrowing from the English, Esther is a name of debated origin and meaning. *See* ESTHER (English Names). Eistir is the Gaelic form. (ES-TER)

Étáin Old name borne in Irish mythology by a sun-goddess who was the lover of Midir, a fairy man. Aideen and Etain are Anglicized forms. (Ā-TAHN)

Ethenia Latinate form of the popular Gaelic name Eithne (kernel). *See* EITHNE. Var: Ethnea. (EH-THEE-NEE-AH)

Ethna Anglicized form of Eithne (kernel), a popular Gaelic name. Var: Etna, Etney. (ETH-NAH)

Eva Latinate form of Eve (life). *See* EVE. In Ireland, Eva was also used to Anglicize Aoife, an old name believed to be derived from *aoibh* (beauty). Éabha is the Gaelic form of Eva. (EE-VAH)

Eve Derived from the Hebrew Chava, which is from *hawwāh* (life). The name is borne in the Bible by the first woman created by God. Var: Eva. (EEV)

Eveleen Diminutive of Eve (life), formed by the addition of the Irish diminutive suffix *-een*. *See* EVE. The name is borne in the Bible by the first woman created by God. (EEV-LEEN)

Faoiltiarna Compound name composed of the elements *faol* (wolf) and *tiarna* (lord): hence, "wolf lord, lord of the wolves." Whiltierna is a modern spelling. (FOL-TEE-AR-NAH)

Feidhelm Ancient name of uncertain derivation. The name was borne by a daughter of King Laoghair of Tara who, along with her sister Eithne, was one of St. Patrick's first converts. The name is Anglicized as Fidelma. (FEE-DELM)

FIDELMA Anglicized form of Feidhelm, an old Irish name of uncertain derivation. Var: Fedelma. Short: Delma. (FIH-DEL-MAH)

FINA Anglicized form of the Gaelic Fíona (fair, white, clear). *See* FÍONA. Var: Finna. (FEE-NAH)

FINELLA Variant of Finola, an Anglicized form of Fionnghuala (white shoulders). *See* FIONNGHUALA. Var: Fenella. (FIH-NEL-LAH)

FINOLA Anglicized form of Fionnghuala (white shoulders). Var: Fenella, Finella. (FIH-NO-LAH)

FÍONA Derived from *fionn* (fair, white, clear). Fina is an Anglicized form. Var: Fiona. (FEE-NUH)

FIONNGHUALA Compound name composed of the Gaelic elements *fionn* (fair, white, clear) and *guala* (a shoulder): hence, "white shoulders." The name was Anglicized as Finola and Penelope. Var: Fionnuala. Short: Nuala. (FIN-NOO-LAH)

FLORA A borrowing from the English, Flora is derived from the Latin *floris* (a flower). The name was used in Ireland as an equivalent of Blath (flower). (FLOR-AH)

GEMMA A borrowing from the Italian, Gemma is derived from the Latin *gemma* (gem, jewel). The name is often bestowed in honor of St. Gemma Galgani (1878–1903). *See* GEMMA (French Names). (JEM-MAH)

GERTRUDE Derived from the Old High German Geretrudis, a compound name composed of the elements *gēr* (spear) and *trut* (dear, maiden) or *þruþ* (strength). The name was used in Ireland to Anglicize the Gaelic Gráinne. (GER-TROOD)

GILLIAN Feminine form of Julian, which is derived from the old Roman family name Julius, a name thought to be derived from Iulus (the first down on the chin, downy-bearded, youth). (JIL-LEE-UN)

GLORIA Derived from the Latin *glōria* (glory), Gloria was not in use as a given name until the 20th century, when Irish dramatist George Bernard Shaw used it as the name of a character in his 1898 play *You Never Can Tell*. (GLOR-EE-AH)

GOBINET Irish variant of the Gaelic Gobnait (a mouth, a beak). *See* GOBNAIT. Var: Gobnat, Gobnet, Gubnet. Pet: Gubby. (GOB-NET)

GOBNAIT Gaelic name derived from *gob* (a mouth, a beak). The name was borne by an Irish saint who is the patroness of Ballyvourney. Gobinet, Gobnat, Gobnet, and Gubnet are Irish variants of the name, which has also been Anglicized as Deborah and Abigail. Gobnata is a Latinate form. (GOB-NET)

GOBNATA Latinate form of Gobnat, an Irish variant of the Gaelic Gobnait (a mouth, a beak). *See* GOBNAIT. (GOB-NAH-TAH)

GRACE A borrowing from the English, Grace is from *grace* (favor, kindness, mercy, elegance or beauty of form), which is from the Latin *gratia* (favor, thanks). The name, which was made popular by the 17th-century Puritans, is used to Anglicize the Gaelic Gráinne (grain-goddess). (GRACE)

GRÁINNE Old name meaning "grain-goddess." Grania is the popular Irish form of the name, which has also been Anglicized as Gertrude and Grace. *See* GRANIA. (GRO-NYUH)

GRANIA Latinate form of Gráinne (grain-goddess). The name is borne in Irish legend by the betrothed of the hero Finn MacCool, who eloped with Dermot, one of Finn's followers. It was also borne by the 16th-century queen of the Western Isles, Grania Mhaol Ni Mhaolmhaigh, who was known to the English as Grace O'Malley. Var: Granna. (GRAH-NYAH)

HELEN A cognate of the Greek Helenē, which is derived from the root *ēlē* (light, torch, bright). The name was borne by St. Helena (c. 255–330), the Christian mother of Constantine the Great. Her influence led to the toleration of Christianity, and she is credited with finding the True Cross buried in a hillock close to Calvary. Léan and Léana are Gaelic forms. Var: Helena. Pet: Nellie. (HEL-EN)

HISOLDA Irish variant of Iseult, a name of debated etymology. *See* ISEULT. (HIH-SOL-DAH)

HONOR A name introduced to Ireland by the Anglo-Normans, Honor is derived from the Latin *honor* (esteem, integrity, dignity, honor). Ohnicio is an Irish form. Var: Honora, Honoria. (ON-OR)

ÍDE Derived from the Old Irish *itu* (thirst). Var: Ida, Ide, Ita. (EE-DEH)

INA Anglicized form of Aghna, the Irish form of Agnes (chaste, pure, holy). *See* AGNES. (IN-AH)

INIS Gaelic form of Ennis, a borrowing of the name of the county seat in county Clare. (IN-ISS)

IRENE A borrowing from the English, Irene is derived from the Greek Eirēnē (peace). The name is borne in Greek mythology by the goddess of peace. Eireen is an Irish form. (Ī-REEN)

Isabel Originated as a Spanish variant of Elizabeth (God is my oath). *See* ELIZABETH. The name was introduced to England by the French and spread from there to Ireland. Isibéal is the Gaelic form. Var: Isabella. (IZ-AH-BEL)

Iseult Of debated origin and meaning. Iseult might be derived from the Old High German Isold, a compound name composed of the elements *is* (ice) and *waltan* (to rule): hence, "ruler of the ice." Alternatively, it could be a variant of the Welsh Esyllt (beautiful, fair). The name is borne in medieval legend by an Irish princess who was betrothed to King Mark of Cornwall. Tristram was sent to get her, and, mistakenly drinking from a love potion that was meant for the king, they fell in love with each other. Var: Hisolda, Isolda, Isolde, Yseult, Ysolte. (EE-SOLT)

Isibéal Gaelic form of Isabel (God is my oath), a Spanish form of Elizabeth. *See* ELIZABETH *and* ISABEL. Var: Sibéal. (ISH-AH-BEL)

Iúile Gaelic form of Julia (downy-bearded, youth). *See* JULIA. (YOOL-EH)

Jan Feminine form of John (God is gracious). *See* JOHN (Male Names). Jan is also used as a short form of any of the various names beginning with the element *Jan-*. (JAN)

Jana Feminine form of John (God is gracious). *See* JOHN (Male Names). Short: Jan. (JAN-AH)

Jane A borrowing from the English, Jane is a cognate of the French Jehanne and Jeanne, feminine forms of Jean, which is a cognate of John (God is gracious). *See* JOHN (Male Names). Sinéad is the popular Gaelic form of Jane. (JANE)

Janet Diminutive form of Jane (God is gracious). *See* JANE. Sinéidin is the Gaelic form. (JAN-ET)

Jean A borrowing from the English and the Scottish, Jean is a cognate of the French Jeanne, a feminine form of Jean, a cognate of John (God is gracious). *See* JOHN (Male Names). Síne is the Gaelic form. (JEEN)

Joan A name introduced by the Anglo-Normans, Joan is a contracted form of the French Johanne, a feminine form of John (God is gracious). The name was made popular from the fame of Joan of Ark (1412–31). *See* JOAN (English Names). Var: Joanna, Joanne. (JONE)

Joanna Latinate form of Joan (God is gracious). *See* JOAN. (JO-AH-NAH)

Josephine A borrowing from the English and French, Josephine is a feminine form of Joseph, which is derived from the Hebrew *yōsēf* (God will add, God will increase). *See* JOSEPH (Male Names). The name was also used in Ireland to Anglicize the Gaelic Siobháinín. Seósaimhthín is the Gaelic form of Josephine. (JO-SEH-FEEN)

Julia Feminine form of the Latin Julius, an old Roman family name thought to be derived from Iulus (the first down on the chin, downy-bearded). Because a person just beginning to develop facial hair is young, "youth" became an accepted definition. Iúile is the Gaelic form. (JOO-LEE-AH)

Julie A borrowing from the French, Julie is a cognate of Julia (downy-bearded, youth), which has been in common use since the 1920s. *See* JULIA. (JOO-LEE)

Juliet A borrowing from the English, Juliet is from the French Juliette, a diminutive form of Julie (downy-bearded, youth). The name is borne by the heroine of Shakespeare's *Romeo and Juliet*, a tragedy about star-crossed lovers. (JOO-LEE-ET)

Karen A popular name in Ireland, Karen is the Danish form of Katherine, a cognate of the Greek Aikaterinē, which is derived from *katharos* (pure, unsullied). (KARE-EN)

Kate A pet form of Katherine, Kate is also bestowed as an independent given name. *See* CATHERINE. (KATE)

Kathy A pet form of Katherine and Kathleen (pure, unsullied), Kathy is also bestowed as an independent given name. *See* CATHERINE *and* CATHLEEN. (KA-THEE)

Katie A pet form of Katherine and Kathleen (pure, unsullied), Katie is also bestowed as an independent given name. *See* CATHERINE *and* CATHLEEN. (KAY-TEE)

Kay A pet form of Katherine and Kathleen, Kay is also bestowed as an independent given name. *See* CATHERINE *and* CATHLEEN. (KAY)

Keelin Anglicized form of Caoilfhionn (slender, fair). *See* CAOILFHIONN. (KEE-LIN)

Kelly Transferred use of the Anglicized surname derived from O'Ceallaigh (descendant of Ceallagh). Ceallagh is derived from *ceallagh, ceallach* (war, strife). Alternatively, the name might derive from various Scottish place-names that are from the Cornish *celli* (wood, grove). (KEL-LEE)

Kerry Transferred use of the Irish place-name. Alternatively, Kerry is an Anglicized form of the Gaelic Ciardha (black-haired one) and is also considered by many to be a pet form of Katherine (pure, unsullied). *See* CATHERINE. (KER-REE)

LABHAOISE Gaelic form of Louisa and Louise (famous in war). *See* LOUISE. (LAU-EE-SHAH)

LAURA A borrowing from the English, Laura is derived from the Latin *laurus* (laurel, an evergreen shrub or tree whose leaves were woven into wreaths by the ancient Greeks to crown victors in various contests). Originally an Italian name, Laura came into use in England in the 19th century and is now popularly bestowed throughout the English-speaking world. (LAU-RAH, LOR-AH)

LELIA Latinate form of Lily. *See* LILY. (LEH-LEE-AH)

LETITIA A borrowing from the English, Letitia is derived from the Latin *laetitia* (gladness, happiness, joy). The name came into vogue during the Victorian era. Var: Laetitia. (LEH-TEE-SHA)

LILE Gaelic form of Lily, a borrowing of the name of the plant. *See* LILY. (LIL-EE)

LILY Taken from the name of the plant having delicate, trumpet-shaped flowers, which are regarded as a symbol of purity and perfection. The word is derived from the Latin *lilium* (lily). (LIL-EE)

LISA A short form of Elisabeth (God is my oath), Lisa is also bestowed as an independent given name. *See* ELIZABETH. (LEE-SAH)

LORNA 19th-century coinage of English novelist R. D. Blackmore, borne by the heroine of his novel *Lorna Doone* (1869). (LOR-NAH)

LORRAINE Transferred use of the surname originating from the name of a province in eastern France, which is derived from the Latin Lotharingia (territory of the people of Lothar). Lothar, the name of the son of the Frankish King Clovis, is of Germanic origin and is derived from the elements *hluod* (famous) and *hari, heri* (army). (LOR-RANE)

LOUISE Feminine form of Louis, which is from the Germanic Hluodowig, a compound name composed from the elements *hluod* (famous) and *wīg* (war, strife). Labhaoise is the Gaelic form. Var: Louisa. (LOO-EEZ)

LUCY Feminine form of Lucius, which is derived from the Latin *lux* (light). The name has been used to Anglicize the Gaelic Luighseach. (LOO-SEE)

LUIGHSEACH Feminine form of Lughaidh, an old Irish name of uncertain derivation, which has been Anglicized as Louis and Lewis. Luighseach is Anglicized as Lucy. (LOO-SEH)

MÁDA Gaelic form of Maude (powerful in battle). *See* MAUDE. (MEH-DEH)

MADAILÉIN Gaelic form of Madeline (of Magdala). *See* MADELINE. Var: Máighdlín. (MAD-EH-LEHN)

MADELINE Irish cognate of Magdalene, which is derived from the Greek Magdalēnē (of Magdala, a town on the Sea of Galilee). The name was originally bestowed in honor of the biblical Mary Magdalene, a woman Christ cured of seven demons. Madailéin and Máighdlín are Gaelic forms. (MAD-EH-LEN)

MAEVE Anglicized form of Meadhbh, a name of uncertain meaning. *See* MEADHBH. Var: Meave. (MAYV)

MAGGIE Pet form of Margaret (a pearl). Maggie is also bestowed as an independent given name. *See* MARGARET. (MAG-GEE)

MAILLE Pet form of Máire. *See* MÁIRE. Maille is the equivalent of the English Molly, which is its Anglicized form. Var: Maili. (MEHL-LEH)

MÁILSE Pet form of Máire. Molly is used to Anglicize the name. *See* MÁIRE. Var: Máilsi, Máilti. (MEHL-SHEH)

MÁIRE Popular Gaelic form of Mary. The name and its English form of Mary were little used before the 17th century out of reverence for the Virgin Mary, and indeed the variant Muire is still reserved for the exclusive use of the mother of Christ. Moira is an Anglicized form. Var: Mears. Pet: Maili, Máille, Máilse, Máilsi, Máilti. (MAUR-YAH)

MÁIRGHRÉAD Gaelic form of Margaret (a pearl). *See* MARGARET. Var: Máiréad, Maireád. (MAUR-EED)

MÁIRÍA Gaelic form of Maria, which is a Latinate form of Mary. *See* MARY. (MAUR-EE-AH)

MÁIRÍN Diminutive form of Máire. The name is Anglicized as Maureen. *See* MAUREEN. (MAUR-EEN)

MAIRONA Diminutive form of Máire, the Gaelic form of Mary. *See* MARY. (MEH-RONA)

MAIRSILE Gaelic form of Marcella. *See* MARCELLA. (MAHR-SEEL)

MALLAIDH Gaelic form of Molly, a name that originated as a pet form of Mary. *See* MARY. (MAL-LEE)

MANDY A pet form of Amanda (lovable), Mandy is also occasionally bestowed as an independent given name. *See* AMANDA. (MAN-DEE)

MARCELLA A borrowing from the French, Marcella is a feminine diminutive form of Marcel, which is from the Latin Marcellus, a diminutive form of Marcus, which is of uncertain origin and meaning. *See* MARK (English Male Names). Mairsil and Mairsile are the Gaelic forms. (MAR-SEL-LAH)

Margaret Introduced to Ireland by the Anglo-Normans, Margaret is from the Greek *margarītēs*, which is derived from *margaron* (a pearl). Máirghreád and Mairéad are Gaelic forms. Pet: Maggie, Meg, Meggie, Peg, Peggy. (MAR-GAH-RET, MARG-RET)

Maria Latinate form of Mary. *See* MARY. Máiría is the Gaelic form. (MAH-REE-AH)

Marie A borrowing from the French, Marie is the French cognate of Mary. *See* MARY. (MAH-REE)

Márta Irish Gaelic form of Martha (lady, mistress). *See* MARTHA. (MAHR-TAH)

Martha Derived from the Aramaic *mārthā* (lady, mistress). The name is borne in the Bible by the sister of Lazarus and Mary of Bethany. Márta is the Gaelic form of the name, which has also been used to Anglicize Mór (great). (MAR-THA)

Martina Feminine form of Martin (war-like), a derivative of the Latin Martīnus, which is from Mars, the name of the Roman mythological god of war. (MAR-TEE-NAH)

Mary Anglicized form of Maria, which is derived from the Hebrew Miryām (sea of bitterness, sea of sorrow). There is much debate over the meaning of the name, however. While "sea of bitterness or sorrow" seems to be the most probable, some sources give the alternative definitions of "rebellion," "wished-for child," and "mistress or lady of the sea." The name, borne in the Bible by the virgin mother of Jesus, has become one of the most enduringly popular names in the Christian world. Máire is the Gaelic form of Mary. Pet: Molly, Polly. (MARE-REE)

Maude Introduced to Ireland by the Anglo-Normans, Maud is a contraction of Matilda (powerful in battle) in use since the Middle Ages. Máda is the Gaelic form. (MAUD, MOD)

Maura Of Celtic origin, perhaps derived from *mohr* (great). Alternatively, Maura is a feminine form of the Latin *maurus* (dark-skinned), which is derived from the Greek *mauritius* (of Moorish lineage). (MAUR-AH, MOR-AH)

Maureen Anglicized form of Máirín, a pet form of Máire, the Gaelic form of Mary. *See* MARY. Var: Maurine. (MAU-REEN, MO-REEN)

Maurya Irish phonetic variant of Máire, the Gaelic form of Mary. *See* MÁIRE *and* MARY. (MAUR-YAH)

Meadhbh Old Irish name of uncertain meaning. Some believe the name is from *meadhail* (joy) or from *mór* (great, large). Another suggestion is that it is from the Welsh *medd* (mead) and give it the definition "intoxicating one." The name was borne by a 1st-century queen of Connacht who fought against the hero Cuchulain. Maeve is the Anglicized form. (MAYV)

Meeda Anglicized form of Míde (my Íde). *See* MÍDE. (MEE-DAH)

Michelle A borrowing from the French, Michelle is a feminine form of Michael, a name derived from the Hebrew *mīkhā'ēl* (who is like God?). Var: Michele. (MIH-SHEL)

Míde Variant of Íde (thirst), formed by the addition of *mo* (my) as a term of endearment. *See* ÍDE. Meeda is the Anglicized form. (MEE-DAH)

Moina Anglicized form of Muadhnait (little noble one). *See* MUADHNAIT. Var: Moyna. (MOI-NAH)

Moira Anglicized form of Máire, which is the Gaelic form of Mary. *See* MÁIRE *and* MARY. Var: Moyra. (MOI-RAH)

Móirín Diminutive form of the Gaelic Mór (great). The name has been Anglicized as Moreen. (MOR-EEN)

Molly Originally a pet form of Mary, Molly is now commonly bestowed as an independent given name. *See* MARY. Máille, Máilse, Máilti, Maili, and Mallaidh are Gaelic forms. (MAHL-LEE)

Monat Anglicized form of Muadhnait, a diminutive of *muadh* (noble): hence, "little noble one." Var: Mona. (MO-NAHT)

Moncha Gaelic form of Monica, a name of uncertain etymology. *See* MONICA. (MON-CHA)

Monica Introduced by the English, Monica is an ancient name of uncertain etymology. The name was borne by the mother of St. Augustine, who was born in Numidia, an ancient country in northern Africa. Thus, the name might be of African origin. However, Monica is said to have been a citizen of Carthage, a city founded by the Phoenicians, so her name might be of Phoenician origin. Alternatively, some believe it to be from the Latin *moneo* (to advise). Moncha is the Gaelic form. (MON-IH-KAH)

Mór Ancient name derived from *mór* (great, large). More, Agnes, Martha, and Mary have been used to Anglicize the name. Var: Móire. (MOR)

More Anglicized form of the Gaelic Mór (great, large). (MOR)

Moreen Anglicized form of Móirín, a diminutive form of Mór (great, large): hence, "little great one." (MOR-EEN)

Morrin Anglicized form of Múireann (long-haired). *See* MÚIREANN. (MOR-RIN)

Muadhnait Diminutive form of *muadh* (noble): hence, "little noble one." Moina, Mona, Monat, and Moyna are Anglicized forms. Var: Muadhnata, Muadhnatan. (MOOY-NAHT)

Mugain Derived from *mogh* (slave). The name was borne by an Irish mythological goddess. (MUH-GIN)

Múireann Ancient Irish name meaning "long-haired, of the long hair." Morrin is the Anglicized form and Murinnia is the Latinate form. Var: Muireann, Muirinn, Murainn. (MOO-EER-AHN)

Muirgheal Compound name composed of the Gaelic elements *muir* (sea) and *geal* (bright, fair): hence, "sea bright, fair one of the sea." The name is Anglicized as Muriel. (MUR-YAHL)

Muirne Gaelic name meaning "beloved, affection." Morna and Myrna are Anglicized forms. (MUR-NEH)

Muriel Anglicized form of the Gaelic Muirgheal (sea bright, fair one of the sea). *See* MUIRGHEAL. (MYOOR-EE-EL)

Myrna Anglicized form of Muirne (affection, beloved). *See* MUIRNE. Var: Merna, Morna. (MER-NAH)

Nainsí Gaelic form of Nancy (gracious, full of grace, mercy). *See* NANCY. Var: Nainseadh. (NAN-SEE)

Nancy Nancy originated as a pet form of Nan, which was originally a pet form of Ann (gracious, full of grace, mercy). *See* ANNE. Now, however, Nancy is regarded as an independent given name, with Nan as its short form. Nainsí and Nainseadh are Gaelic forms. Short: Nan. (NAN-SEE)

Nelda Feminine form of Niall, a name of debated derivation. *See* NIALL (Male Names). (NEL-DAH)

Nessa Originally a pet form of Agnes (chaste, pure), Nessa is now also bestowed as an independent given name. *See* AGNES. (NES-SAH)

Niamh Gaelic name derived from *niamh* (bright). (NEHM)

Nicola Latinate feminine form of Nicholas, which is from the Greek Nikolaos, a compounding of the elements *nikē* (victory) and *laos* (the people): hence, "victory of the people." (NIH-KO-LAH)

Noelle From the French Noël, which is from *noël* (Christmas), a vocabulary word derived from the Latin *nātālis* (natal). The name is traditionally bestowed upon children born during the Christmas season. Nollaig is the Gaelic form. (NO-EL)

Noirin Gaelic form of Noreen, a diminutive form of Nora, which is a short form of Honora (honor) and Eleanora (light). (NOR-EEN)

Nollaig Gaelic form of Noelle (Christmas). *See* NOELLE. (NO-LAHG)

Nora A short form of Eleanora (light) and Honora (honor), Nora is commonly bestowed as an independent given name. *See* ELEANOR *and* HONOR. Nóra is the Gaelic form. Var: Norah. Pet: Nonie. (NOR-AH)

Nóra Gaelic form of Nora, a name that originated as a short form of Eleanor and Honora. Pet: Nóinín. (NOR-AH)

Noreen Irish diminutive form of Nora formed by the addition of the diminutive suffix *-een*. *See* NORA. Nóirín is the Gaelic form. (NOR-EEN)

Norlene Elaboration of Nora. *See* NORA. (NOR-LEEN)

Odharnait Derived from the diminutive form of *odhar* (green, olive-colored): hence, "little green one." The name was Anglicized as Orna and Ornat. (OR-NAT, OR-NAH)

Ohnicio Irish form of Honor (honor). *See* HONOR. (O-NEE-CEE-O)

Órfhlaith Old name meaning "golden lady." Orlaith, Orla, and Orlagh are Anglicized forms. Var: Orflath. (OR-EH-LATH)

Orla Anglicized form of Órfhlaith (golden lady). Var: Orlagh. (OR-LAH)

Orlaith Anglicized form of Órfhlaith (golden lady). (OR-LAITH)

Ornat Anglicized form of Odharnait (little green one). *See* ODHARNAIT. Var: Orna. (OR-NAT)

Pádraigín Gaelic form of Patricia (a patrician, an aristocrat). *See* PATRICIA. Pet: Paddy. (PAH-DREEK-IN)

Paili Irish form of Polly, a pet form of Mary. *See* MARY. Var: Pails. (PAHL-EE)

Patricia Popular feminine form of Patrick, which is from the Latin *patricius* (a patrician, an aristocrat, noble). *See* PATRICK (Male Names). Pádraigín is the Gaelic form. Short: Pat. Pet: Paddy, Patty. (PAH-TRISH-AH)

Pauline A borrowing from the French and English, Pauline is a feminine form of Paul (small). *See* PAUL

(Male Names). Póilín is the Gaelic form. (PAU-LEEN, PO-LEEN)

PEG A pet form of Margaret (a pearl), Peg evolved as a rhyming variant of Meg, another pet form of Margaret. *See* MARGARET. Peig is the Gaelic form. (PEHG)

PEGGY A pet form of Margaret (a pearl), Peggy evolved as a rhyming variant of Meggy, another pet form of Margaret. *See* MARGARET. Peigi is the Gaelic form. (PEH-GEE)

POLLY A pet form of Mary, Polly is also bestowed as an independent given name. *See* MARY. The Gaelic form is Paili. (PAH-LEE, POL-LEE)

RACHEL From the Ecclesiastic Late Latin and the Ecclesiastic Greek Rhachēl, which is derived from the Hebrew *rāchēl* (ewe). The name is borne in the Bible by the younger of the two wives of Jacob and mother of Joseph and Benjamin. Ráichéal is the Gaelic form. (RAY-CHEL)

RÁICHÉAL Gaelic form of Rachel (ewe). *See* RACHEL. (RAY-CHEL)

RATHNAIT Feminine diminutive form of Rath, which is derived from *rath* (grace, prosperity): hence, "little prosperous one." The name has been Anglicized as Renny. Var: Ranait. (RAH-NEH)

REGINA Derived from the Latin *regina* (queen), a feminine form of *rex* (king). The name has been in use since the Middle Ages. It has been used in Ireland as an equivalent of Riona and its Gaelic form, Rioghnach. *See* RÍOGHNACH. (REH-JEE-NAH, REH-JĪ-NAH)

RENNY Anglicized form of the Gaelic Rathnait (little prosperous one). *See* RATHNAIT. (REN-NEE)

RÍOGHNACH Gaelic name derived from *rioghan* (queen): hence, "queenly." The name was borne by the 6th-century St. Ríoghnach, sister of St. Finnian of Clonard. Riona is the Anglicized form of the name, which was also translated as Regina. (REE-NAH, REE-O-NAH)

RIONA Popular Anglicized form of Rioghnach (queenly). *See* RÍOGHNACH. (REE-O-NAH)

RÓIS Gaelic form of Rose. *See* ROSE. Var: Róise. (RŌSH)

RÓISÍN Irish form of Rosaleen, which is a diminutive form of Rose (horse; a rose). *See* ROSE. (RO-SHEEN)

ROSALEEN Diminutive form of Rose (a horse; a rose) formed by the addition of the Irish diminutive suffix *-een*. *See* ROSE. Róisín is the Gaelic form. (ROZE-AH-LEEN)

ROSE Originally a short form of any of the old Germanic names containing the element *hros*, *ros* (horse), such as Rosalind. Modern use of the name is now influenced by flower names, which began to be bestowed upon children in the 19th century. Róis and Róise are Gaelic forms. Pet: Rosie. (ROZE)

RÚT Gaelic form of Ruth. *See* RUTH. (ROOT)

RUTH Of uncertain etymology, some believe Ruth to be derived from the Hebrew *rūth*, a possible contraction of *rē'uth* (companion, friend). The name is borne in the Bible by a Moabite woman who was devoted to her mother-in-law. Her story is told in the Old Testament book of Ruth. Rút is the Gaelic form of the name. (ROOTH)

SABIA Anglicized form of Sive and the Gaelic Sadhbh (goodness). *See* SADHBH. (SAY-BEE-AH)

SABINA Derived from the Latin Sabīna (Sabine woman). The Sabines were an ancient tribe who lived in the Apennines of central Italy. The name, which was borne by three early saints and martyrs, was also used to Anglicize Saidhbhín (goodness) and Síle, a Gaelic form of Cecilia. *See* SAIDHBHÍN. (SAH-BEE-NAH, SAH-BĪ-NAH)

SADHBH Very old name meaning "goodness." Sadhbh has been Anglicized as Sabia, Sophia, Sarah, and Sally. Var: Sabha, Sadbha, Sadhbha, Saidhbhe, Sive. (SAYV)

SAIDHBHÍN Diminutive form of Sadhbh (goodness). The name was Anglicized as Sabina. (SEE-VIN)

SALLY Originally a pet form of Sarah, Sally is commonly bestowed as an independent given name. *See* SARAH. In Ireland, the name was also used to Anglicize the Gaelic Sadhbh, Síle, and Sorcha. (SAL-LEE)

SAMHAOIR Old name of uncertain derivation. It might be a variant of Samhairle, the Irish form of Sumerlidi, an Old Norse name for summer sailors or Vikings. The name is also an old river name and is found in Irish legend as the name of the daughter of Finn MacCool. (SAH-MEHR)

SANDRA A short form of Alexandra (defender or helper of mankind), Sandra is also bestowed as an independent given name. *See* ALEXANDRA. (SAN-DRAH)

SARAH Derived from the Hebrew *sārāh* (princess). The name is borne in the Bible by the wife of the patriarch Abraham and mother of Isaac. Sarah was also used in Ireland to Anglicize Sadhbh, Saraid, Sive, and Sorcha. (SAH-RAH)

SARAID Derived from *saraid* (excellent). The name has been Anglicized as Sarah. (SAH-RAH)

SÉARLAIT Gaelic form of Charlotte, a feminine diminutive form of Charles (full-grown, a man, freeman). *See* CHARLES (Male Names). (SHAR-LAT)

SEÓSAIMHTHÍN Gaelic form of Josephine, a feminine diminutive form of Joseph (may he add), which is borrowed from the French. *See* JOSEPHINE. (SHO-SAH-VEEN)

SHAUNA Feminine form of Shaun, a variant of Sean, which is an Irish cognate of John (God is gracious). *See* JOHN (Male Names). (SHAWN-AH)

SHEENA Anglicized form of Síne, the Gaelic cognate of Jean, a feminine form of John (God is gracious). *See* JEAN. (SHE-NAH)

SHEILA Anglicized form of Síle, an Irish form of Cecilia (blind, dim-sighted). Var: Sheela, Sheelagh, Selia. (SHE-LAH)

SHELLEY Transferred use of the English surname originating from the place-name Scelf-lēah, a compounding of the elements *scelf, scylfe* (shelf, ledge, slope) and *lēah* (wood, clearing, meadow): hence, "clearing on or near a slope." The name was originally bestowed upon both male and female children. Now, however, it is exclusively a female name. (SHEL-LEE)

SHONA Anglicized form of Síne, the Gaelic cognate of Jean, a feminine form of John (God is gracious). *See* JOHN (Male Names). (SHONA)

SIANY Anglicized form of the Gaelic Sláine (health). (SEE-AH-NEE)

SÍLE Gaelic form of Cecilia and Cecily (blind, dim-sighted). The name is Anglicized as Sheila, Selia, and Sally. (SHE-LEH)

SÍNE Gaelic form of Jean, which is a feminine form of John (God is gracious). *See* JEAN. The name is Anglicized as Sheena and Shona. (SHE-NEH)

SINÉAD Popular Gaelic form of Jane, a feminine form of John (God is gracious). *See* JANE. The name is borne by Irish actress Sinéad Cusack and singer Sinéad O'Connor. Var: Sinead, Sineaid. (SHIH-NADE)

SIOBHÁINÍN Diminutive form of Siobhán, the Gaelic form of Joan (God is gracious). *See* JOAN. The name has been Anglicized as Josephine. Var: Siubháinín. (ZHUH-VAHN-NIN)

SIOBHÁN Popular Gaelic form of Joan, a feminine form of John (God is gracious). *See* JOAN. The name was Anglicized as Chevonne and Judith. Var: Siubhán. (ZHUH-VAHN)

SISILE Gaelic form of Cecilia and Cecily (blind, dim-sighted). *See* CECILIA. (SIH-SIL-EE)

SIVE Irish form of Sadhbh (goodness). *See* SADHBH. The name was Anglicized as Sabia, Sarah, and Sophia. (SHE-VEH)

SLÁINE Old name meaning "health." Siany and Slanie are Anglicized forms. Slania is a Latinate form. (SLAH-NAH)

SLANIA Latinate form of Sláine, a Gaelic name meaning "health." (SLAHN-YAH, SLAHN-EE-AH)

SLANIE Anglicized form of Sláine, a Gaelic name meaning "health." (SLAH-NEE)

SOPHIA A borrowing from the English, Sophia is derived from the Greek *sophia* (wisdom, skill). The name has been in use in England since the 17th century, when it was bestowed upon the infant daughter of James I in 1607. The name is also used in Ireland to Anglicize Sadhbh and Sive. (SO-FEE-AH)

SORCHA Old name meaning "bright, clear." It was Anglicized as Sarah and Sally. (SOR-EH-KAH)

SUSAN Brought to Ireland by the Anglo-Normans, Susan is from the French Susanne, a cognate of the Late Latin Susanna, which is derived from the Hebrew *shōshannāh* (lily, rose). Súsanna and Sósanna are Gaelic forms. Var: Suzanne. Pet: Susie. (SOO-ZAHN)

SÚSANNA Gaelic form of Susan (lily, rose). *See* SUSAN. Var: Sósanna. Pet: Siúi, Sósaidh. (SOO-SAH-NAH)

TANITH Derived from the Old Irish *tan* (an estate). (TAN-ITH)

TARA Transferred use of the Irish place-name belonging to a hill in central Ireland which was an ancient seat of kingship. Tara (hill) was used by Margaret Mitchell for the name of a plantation in her epic *Gone with the Wind* (1937), which resulted in the use of it as a female given name. Teamhair is the Gaelic form. (TAR-AH)

TEAMHAIR Gaelic form of Tara (hill). *See* TARA. (TAW-HER)

TERESA Of uncertain etymology, Teresa is generally believed to be derived from the Greek *therizein* (to reap, to gather in). The first known bearer of the name was the Spanish wife of St. Paulinus, a 5th-century Roman bishop of Nola. Teresa was not used outside the Iberian Peninsula until the 16th century, when the fame of St. Teresa of Avila (1515–82) made the name popular among Roman Catholics throughout Europe. Toiréasa is a Gaelic form of the name, which is also used as a variant of the Irish Treasa and Treise (strength). Var: Tracy. (TEH-REE-SAH)

TIGRIS Derived from the Latin *tigris* (tiger). According to Irish tradition, Tigris was the name of a sister of St. Patrick. (TIH-GRIS)

TINA A short form of Christina (a Christian, a follower of Christ), Tina is also bestowed as an independent given name. *See* CHRISTINA. (TEE-NAH)

TOIRÉASA Gaelic form of Teresa, a name of uncertain etymology. *See* TERESA. (TŌ-REH-SAH)

TREISE Irish name meaning "strength." Var: Teresa, Treasa. (TREE-SEH)

ÚNA Old name of debated meaning. Some believe it is from an old word meaning "famine" or "hunger." Others believe it might be derived from the Old Irish *uan* (lamb). The name was Anglicized as Oona, Oonagh, and Ownah as well as Winifred and Unity. Var: Una. (OO-NAH)

UNITY Derived from the English *unity* (oneness, harmony, united), which is derived from the Latin *unitas* (oneness). Unity, made popular in the 17th century, has been used to Anglicize the Gaelic Una. *See* ÚNA. (YOO-NIH-TEE)

VALERIE A borrowing from the French, Valerie is from the Latin Valerius, an old Roman family name derived from *valere* (to be strong, healthy). (VAL-EH-REE)

VANESSA An invention of Irish satirist Jonathan Swift (1667–1745), Vanessa is a partial anagram of his intimate friend Ester Vanhomrigh. Swift used the name in his *Cadenus and Vanessa*, which led to its use as a female given name. (VAH-NES-SAH)

VEVINA Anglicized form of the Gaelic Bébhinn (sweet lady). *See* BÉBHINN. Vevina was a name used by Scottish poet James Macpherson (1736–96) in his Ossianic poetry. (VEH-VEE-NAH)

VIVIAN A borrowing from the English, Vivian is a cognate of the French Vivienne (alive). *See* VIVIENNE. The name has been used in Ireland to Anglicize the Gaelic Bébhinn (sweet lady). (VIV-EE-AHN)

VIVIENNE A borrowing from the French, Vivienne is a feminine form of Vivien (alive), which is derived from the Latin Vivianus, a name that has its root in *vivus* (alive). (VIV-EE-EN)

WINIFRED Derived from the Welsh Gwenfrewi, a compound name composed of the elements *gwen* (white, fair, blessed) and *frewi* (peace, reconciliation). The name was used to Anglicize the Gaelic Úna. Short: Win. Pet: Winnie. (WIN-IH-FRED)

YVONNE A borrowing from the French and English, Yvonne is a feminine form of Yvon and Yves (archer), names of Germanic origin derived from the element *iv* (yew). (EE-VON)

ZAIRA Invention of Irish writer C. R. Maturin, who used the name in his 1818 novel *Women; or, Pour et Contre*. (ZARE-AH)

Chapter Fifteen

Italian Names

The country of Italy has a rich and ancient history with influences from cultures and regions as varied as Spain, Gaul, Germany, ancient Greece, and northern Africa, but in spite of the large number of different peoples that have migrated to Italy, only two groups besides the Romans have had any lasting effect on Italian nomenclature—the Greeks and the Germans. Though the immigrants usually abandoned their native languages in favor of Latin, these groups retained and continued to use Teutonic and Greek names. Thus, a large number of present-day Italian names have their roots in these languages.

Many infants are traditionally named after relatives, living or dead. This custom was well established in the late Middle Ages, and given names were often handed down in rigid order. The name of the paternal grandfather was bestowed upon the first male child; the second male was given the name of his maternal grandfather; the father's name belonged to the third son; a fourth son took the name of his paternal great-grandfather. The first daughter took the name of the paternal grandmother; the second, that of the maternal grandmother; the third, the name of the mother; the fourth daughter was given the name of the paternal great-grandmother. Additional children were given the names of paternal and maternal granduncles and grandaunts.

Today, although the old system of naming is still quite common throughout Italy and remains the norm in many parts of the country, it is not followed as rigidly as in the past. Instead, many parents choose to bestow the name of their choice upon their children.

Those who decide to break from tradition and give their child a name other than that of a family member often turn to the Catholic Calendar of Saints for a suitable name. Saints' names are also used without regard to the calendar, especially if the chosen saint is among those that are especially admired.

The cult of the Virgin Mary is still popular in Italy, and many female children are named Maria or are given one of the numerous designations of the Virgin, such as Annunziata, Concetta, and Dolores. These names are also used in masculine form and are bestowed upon male infants in honor of the Virgin and to bring them under her protection. Italians were the first to use Maria as a masculine middle name—a practice that is now common throughout Europe.

In addition to religious names, the Italian people are fond of using the names of popular rulers of all countries for their children. This practice extends to using the names of important artists, authors, fictional characters, military leaders, movie stars, and honored scientists. In common with many other societies, names derived from personal characteristics and nature names are also popular.

Surnames came into use and became hereditary in Venice in the tenth or eleventh century. Over the course of eight hundred years they became established throughout the country. The first surnames evolved from personal names and descriptive nicknames, many of which were quite unflattering, such as Nasuto (large nose) or Gallina (chicken, timid). Patronymics, matronymics, and names based on occupation or place of origin form the bulk of the rest of the surnames.

Italian Male Names

ABBONDIO From the Late Latin Abundius, which is derived from *abundans* (abundant, abounding). (AB-BON-DEE-O)

ABRAMO Derived from the Hebrew Abram, a variant form of Avram (father is exalted), the original name of the biblical patriarch Abraham. *See* Abraham (Biblical Names). (Ā-BRAH-MO)

ACHILLEO Derived from the Greek Achillios, which is from the earlier Achilleus, an ancient name of unknown etymology. The name is borne in Greek mythology by the leader and warrior of the Trojan War. He was killed by the Trojan prince Paris with an arrow that struck his heel, his only vulnerable spot. Achilles is the hero of Homer's *Iliad.* (AH-KEE-LEE-O)

ADAMO Italian form of Adam, which is derived from the Hebrew *adama* (red earth). The name is borne in the Bible by the first man created by God. According to biblical tradition, it was from Adam's rib that the first woman, Eve, was formed. (AH-DAH-MO)

ADRIAN From the Latin Adriānus (man from the city of Adria) and Hadriānus (man from the city of Hadria). Var: Adriano. (AD-REE-AHN)

AENEAS Derived from the Greek Aineias, an ancient name derived from the Greek *ainein* (to praise). The name is borne in Greek and Roman mythology by the hero of Virgil's epic *Aeneid.* Aeneas, the Trojan son of Anchises and Venus, wandered for years after escaping from the ruined city of Troy. Var: Enea. (AH-NAY-US)

ALBERTO Italian cognate of Albert (bright through nobility), which is derived from the Old High German Adalbrecht, a compound name composed from the elements *adal* (noble) and *beraht* (bright). (AHL-BARE-TŌ)

ALDO Popular name of Germanic origin believed to be derived from the element *ald* (old). (AHL-DŌ)

ALESSANDRO Italian cognate of the Greek Alexandros (defender or helper of mankind), a compound name composed from the elements *alexein* (to defend, to help) and *andros* (man, mankind). The name became popular throughout Europe through the fame of Alexander the Great (456–323 B.C.), the Macedonian king and military ruler who helped spread the Greek culture across Asia Minor and to Egypt and India. Short: Alessio, Sandro. (AH-LEH-SAHN-DRO)

ALESSIO A short form of Alessandro (defender or helper of mankind), Alessio is also bestowed as an independent given name. *See* ALESSANDRO. (AH-LES-SEE-O).

ALFONSO Italian cognate of Alphonse, which is derived from the Old Germanic Adalfuns, a compound name composed of the elements *adal* (noble) and *funs* (ready, eager, prompt, apt). Pet: Alfio. (AHL-FON-SO)

AMATO Derived from Amāta (beloved, darling), the name of the wife of King Latinus, which is derived from *amātio* (a loving). Latinus was a king of the Laurentians who entertained Aeneas and gave his daughter, Lavinia, to him in marriage. (AH-MAH-TŌ)

AMBROGIO Italian form of the Late Latin Ambrosius, which is from the Greek Ambrosios, a name derived from *ambrosios* (immortal). The name was borne by a 4th-century saint who was bishop of Milan, and is considered to be one of the four great Latin doctors of the church. Short: Brogio. (AHM-BRO-GEE-O)

AMEDEO Derived from the Latin Amadeus, a compound name composed of the elements *ama* (love) and *deus* (God): hence, "love of God." (AH-MAH-DAY-O)

AMERIGO Italian variant of Enrico (ruler of an enclosure, home ruler). *See* ENRICO. The name was borne by the navigator and explorer Amerigo Vespucci (1454–1512). (AH-MAY-REE-GO)

ANACLETO From the Late Latin Anaclētus (called for, invoked), which is derived from the Greek Anaklētos, a name that originated as a divine name. Short: Cleto. (AH-NAH-KLEE-TŌ)

ANASTAGIO Derived from the Late Latin Anastasius (of the resurrection), which is from the Greek Anastasios, a derivative of *anastasis* (resurrection). (AH-NAH-STAH-GEE-O)

Anatolio From the Late Latin Anatolius, a name derived from the Greek *anatolē* (sunrise, daybreak, dawn). (AH-NAH-TŌ-LEE-O)

Andrea Popular name derived from the Greek Andreas, which is from *andreios* (manly). (AHN-DRAY-AH)

Angelo Derived from the Latin *angelus* (divine messenger, angel), which is from the Greek *angelos* (messenger). (AHN-GEH-LO)

Anselmo A name of Germanic origin, Anselmo (divine helmet, divine protection) is from the elements *ansi* (divinity, a god) and *helm* (helmet, protection). (AHN-SEL-MO)

Antioco Derived from the Greek Antiochos (stubborn, resistant), a compound name composed of the elements *anti* (against) and *ekhein* (to have). The name was borne by the father of the Macedonian general Seleucus, who in 300 B.C. named the city of Antioch in his father's honor. (AHN-TEE-O-KO)

Antonio Derived from the Latin Antōnius, an old Roman family name of unknown etymology. The name was often bestowed in honor of St. Anthony of Padua (1195–1231), a Franciscan friar who worked miracles for the poor and the sick. Short: Tonio. (AHN-TŌ-NEE-O)

Apollinare Derived from Apollo, the name of the god of music, poetry, prophecy, and medicine. (AH-POL-LIH-NAH-RAY)

Armino Italian form of the German Armin, which is derived from the Latin Arminius, a cognate of the Germanic Hermann (soldier, warrior). *See* HERMANN (German Names). Var: Armanno. (AR-MEE-NO)

Arnaud A cognate of the German Arnold (eagle ruler), Arnaud is from the Old High German Aranold, an evolution of the older Germanic Arnwald, a compound name composed of the elements *arn* (eagle) and *wald* (ruler, power). (AR-NAUD)

Arnoldo From the German Arnold, which is from the Old High German Aranold, an evolution of the older Arnwald, a compound name composed of the elements *arn* (eagle) and *wald* (ruler, power): hence, "eagle power." Var: Arnaldo. (AR-NOL-DŌ)

Arrigo Italian variant of Enrico (ruler of an enclosure, home ruler). *See* ENRICO. Var: Arrighetto. (AH-REE-GO)

Arturo Italian cognate of Arthur, a name of Celtic origin but of unknown meaning. *See* ARTHUR (English Names). Short: Art. (AHR-TOO-RO)

Attilio From the Latin family name Attilius, which is of uncertain etymology. Some believe it to be derived from the element *ata* (father, paternal). (AH-TEE-LEE-O)

Augustine Italian form of the Latin Augustinus, a diminutive form of Augustus, which is derived from *augustus* (great, venerable, consecrated by the augurs). The name was borne by St. Augustine (354–430), an early church father who was born in Numidia and became the bishop of Hippo in northern Africa. (AU-GOO-STEEN)

Augusto From the Latin Augustus, which is derived from *augustus* (great, venerable, consecrated by the augurs). (AU-GOO-STO)

Aurelio Derived from the Latin Aurēlius, an old Roman family name derived from *aurum* (gold). The name was borne by Marcus Aurelius Antonius (121–80), a Roman emperor and Stoic philosopher, as well as by several saints. (AU-RAY-LEE-O)

Baldassare Italian cognate of Balthasar, a name medieval Christian tradition assigned to one of the Three Wise Men, who brought gifts to the Christ child. Some believe the name is derived from the Chaldean Belshazzar (Bel's prince) or from the Persian Beltshazzar (prince of splendor). Others think the name might have merely been an invention with an Eastern sound to it. The name is borne in the Bible by the ruler of Babylon who had the prophet Daniel translate the strange writing that appeared on the wall of his dining hall. Var: Baltassare. (BAHL-DAH-SAH-RAY)

Bartolomeo From the Late Latin Bartholomaeus, which is from the Greek Bartholomaios (son of Talmai). Talmai is an Aramaic name meaning "hill, mound, furrows." The name is borne in the Bible by one of the Twelve Apostles of Christ. Var: Bartolommeo. Short: Bàrtolo, Meo. (BAR-TOL-O-MAY-O)

Basilio From the Latin Basilius and the Greek Basileios (kingly, royal), names derived from *basileus* (king). The name was borne by a 4th-century Greek theologian known as St. Basil the Great (c. 330–79). A bishop of Caesarea, he is regarded as one of the fathers of the Eastern Church. (BAH-SEE-LEE-O)

Battista Derived from the Ecclesiastic Late Latin *baptista* (a baptist, one who baptizes). The name was traditionally bestowed in honor of the biblical John the Baptist, a kinsman and forerunner of Christ. (BAH-TEES-TAH)

Benedetto Italian form of Benedict, which is derived from the Latin Benedictus, a direct derivative of *benedictus* (blessed). (BEN-NEH-DAY-TŌ)

BENEDICT Derived from the Latin Benedictus, which is directly derived from *benedictus* (blessed). The name was borne by St. Benedict of Nursii (c. 480–543), an Italian monk and founder of the Benedictine Order at Monte Cassino. (BEN-Ā-DIKT)

BENIGNO From the Late Latin Benignus (good, kind, well-born), which is derived from *benignus* (well-born), a compound of *bene* (well, good, favorably) and *genus* (birth). (BEN-NEEG-NO)

BENJAMINO Italian cognate of Benjamin, which is from the Hebrew Binyamin, a name derived from *binyāmīn* (son of the right hand). The name is borne in the Bible by the youngest of Jacob's twelve sons. Var: Beniamino. (BEN-JAH-MEE-NO)

BENVENUTO Compound name composed of the elements *bene* (well, good, favorably) and *venuto* (came, arrived): hence, "welcome." The name is often bestowed by parents who are overjoyed at the birth of their child. (BEN-VAY-NOO-TŌ)

BERNARDO From the Old High German Berinhard (strong as a bear), a compound name composed from the elements *bern* (bear) and *hard* (hearty, strong, brave). (BARE-NAHR-DŌ)

BIAGIO Italian form of the Latin Blasius (a babbler), which is believed to be derived from *blatio* (to babble, to prate). Var: Biasio, Baccio. (BEE-AH-GEE-O).

BONAVENTURA Compound name composed of the elements *bona* (good, fair) and *ventura* (luck, fortune): hence, "good fortune, good luck." (BO-NAH-VANE-TYOO-RAH)

BONIFACIO Derived from the Late Latin Bonifatius, a compound name composed from the elements *bonum* (good, profit, bonus) and *fatum* (fate): hence, "of good fate, auspicious." (BO-NIH-FAH-SEE-O)

BRIZIO Italian cognate of the French Brice, a name derived from the Latin Britius, which is of uncertain etymology. Alternatively, Brizio is used as a short form of Fabrizio (craftsman). *See* FABRIZIO. (BREET-ZEE-O)

BRUNO A borrowing from the Germans, Bruno is derived from the Old High German *brun* (brown). (BROO-NO)

CALOGERO Derived from the Latin Calogerus, which is from the Greek Kalogeros (fair old age), a compound name composed of the elements *kalos* (fair, good) and *giras* (old age). The name was borne by St. Calogerus, a 5th-century Sicilian hermit. (KAL-O-GAY-RO)

CALVINO Italian form of Calvin, a derivative of the Latin *calvinus* (little bald one). (KAHL-VEE-NO)

CAMILLO Masculine form of Camilla, a name directly derived from the Latin *camilla* (virgin of unblemished character). *See* CAMILLA (Female Names). (KAH-MEE-LO)

CARLO Popular Italian cognate of Charles, which is from the Middle Latin Carolus (full-grown, a man). Var: Carlino. (KAR-LO)

CARMINE Masculine form of Carmela (vineyard, orchard). The name is often bestowed to bring the child under the special protection of the Virgin Mary, "Our Lady of Carmel." *See* CARMELA (Female Names). (KAR-MINE)

CECILIO From the Latin Caecilius, an old Roman family name derived from *caecus* (blind, dim-sighted). The name was borne by a 3rd-century saint who was a friend and companion of St. Cyprian. (SAY-SEE-LEE-O)

CELSO From the Latin family name Celsus, which is derived from *celsus* (high, lofty, elevated). (SEL-SO)

CESARE From the Latin Caesar, a name of uncertain etymology. Some believe Caesar to be derived from *caedo* (to cut); others think it to be from *caesius* (blue-gray). Another suggestion is that it is derived from *caesaries* (hairy, with abundant hair). The name was borne by Gaius Julius Caesar (100?–44 B.C.), the Roman general and statesman who was dictator of the Roman Empire from 49 to 44 B.C. Caesar was subsequently used as the imperial title of the emperor of Rome from Augustus to Hadrian, and for the emperor of the Holy Roman Empire. It later evolved into a vocabulary word for an emperor or dictator. Var: Caseareo. (SAY-SAH-RAY)

CIPRIANO Derived from the Latin Cypriānus (a Cyprian), a name referring to a person from the island of Cyprus. (SEE-PREE-AH-NO)

CIRIACO From the Latin Cyriācus, which is from the Greek Kyriakos, a derivative of *kyrios* (a lord). (SEE-REE-AH-KO)

CIRO Italian form of the Latin Cyrus, which is from the Greek Kyros, a derivative of *kyrios* (a lord). (SEE-RO)

CLAUDIO From the Latin Claudius, an old Roman family name derived from *claudus* (lame). The name was borne by two Roman emperors, Claudius I (10 B.C.–A.D. 54) and Claudius II (214–70). (KLAU-DEE-O)

CLEMENTE From the Late Latin Clēmens (merciful), which is derived from *clemens* (mild, gentle, merciful). (KLAY-MANE-TAY)

COLUMBANO From the Late Latin Columbānus, a derivative of *columba* (dove, pigeon, gray bird). The name was borne by St. Columban (c. 540–615), an Italian monk and missionary who founded a monastery in 614 at Bobbio in northern Italy. (KO-LOOM-BAH-NO)

CORRADO Italian form of Conrad, the English cognate of the German Konrad (wise counsel), which is from the Old High German Kuonrat, a compounding of the elements *kuon* (bold, wise) and *rat* (counsel). Var: Corradino. (KO-RAH-DO)

COSMO Italian cognate of the Greek Kosmas, which is derived from *kosmos* (universe, order, harmony). Var: Cosimo. (KOS-MO)

CRISTOFORO From the Ecclesiastic Late Latin Christophorus, which is from the Ecclesiastic Greek Christophoros, a compound name composed from the elements *Christos* (Christ) and *pherein* (to bear): hence, "bearing Christ." The name was borne by St. Christopher, a 3rd-century Christian martyr of Asia Minor who is the patron saint of travelers. (KREES-TŌ-FO-RO)

DANIELE From the Hebrew *dānī'ēl* (God is my judge). The name is borne in the Bible by a Hebrew prophet whose faith kept him alive in a den of lions. Daniel and the Lions' Den was a favorite story during the Middle Ages, which helped to promote the use of the name throughout Europe. (DAN-YELL)

DANTE A contracted form of Durante (enduring, lasting, steadfast), which is from the Latin *dūrans*, the present participle of *dūrāre* (to last, to continue, to endure). The name was borne by the Italian poet, born Durante Alighieri (1265–1321), who wrote *The Divine Comedy*. (DAHN-TAY)

DARIO From the Latin Darius, an old name derived from the Greek Dareios, which is of uncertain origin. It is thought to ultimately be derived from Darayavahush, the name of an ancient Persian king. (DAH-REE-O)

DOMINICO From the Latin Dominicus (belonging to a lord), which is derived from *dominus* (a lord, a master). The name was borne by St. Dominic (1170–1221), a Spanish priest who founded the Dominican Order of Preachers. Var: Domenico. (DŌ-MEE-NEE-KO)

DONATO From the Late Latin Dōnātus (given by God), which is derived from *donare* (to give, to donate). The name was borne by Donato di Niccolò di Betto Bardi (1386?–1466), the Italian sculptor more commonly known as Donatello. (DŌ-NAH-TŌ)

EDMONDO Italian cognate of Edmund, which is from the Old English Ēadmund (wealthy protection), a name composed of the elements *ēad* (prosperity, riches, fortune) and *mund* (hand, protection). (ED-MON-DŌ)

EDUARDO Italian cognate of Edward (wealthy protector), an English name derived from the Old English Ēadweard, a compounding of the elements *ēad* (prosperity, riches, fortune) and *weard* (guardian, protector). Var: Edoardo. (ED-WAHR-DŌ)

EFISIO From the Latin Ephesius (an Ephesian), which is derived from Ephesus, an ancient Ionian city that once boasted a famous temple to Diana which was considered to be one of the Seven Wonders of the World. The name was borne by a 4th-century saint martyred under the reign of Diocletian. (Ā-FEE-SEE-O)

EIGIDIO From the Greek Aegidius (shield-bearer), which is derived from *aegis, aigis* (the goatskin shield of Zeus, a protection). The Aegis was carried by Zeus and his daughter Athena, and occasionally by Apollo. (EE-GEE-DEE-O)

ELPIDIO From the Late Latin Elpidius, which is from the Greek Elpidios, a name derived from *elpis* (hope). The name was borne by a 4th-century saint who spent twenty-five years living in a cave as a hermit. (EL-PEE-DEE-O)

EMANUELE Derived from the Greek Emmanouēl, which is from the Hebrew *'immānūēl* (God is with us). In the Bible, Emmanuel is the name of the promised Messiah. (EE-MAHN-YOO-ELL)

EMILIO Derived from the Latin Aemilius, an old Roman family name probably derived from *aemulus* (emulating, trying to equal or excel, rival). (Ā-MEE-LEE-O)

ENRICO Italian cognate of Henry, which is from the German Heinrich (home ruler, ruler of an enclosure). *See* HEINRICH (German Names). The name was borne by Enrico Fermi (1901–54), an Italian physicist who won the Nobel Prize in 1938. Short: Rico. (ĀN-REE-KO)

ENZO Short form of any of the various names ending in the element *-enzo*. (ĀN-ZO)

ERCOLE Italian form of the Latin Hercules, which is from the Greek Hērakleēs, a compound name composed from Hēra (the name of the mythological queen of the gods) and *kleos* (glory): hence, "glory of Hera, divine glory." The name Hercules is borne in Greek and Roman mythology by the son of Zeus and Alemene, renowned for his amazing strength. (ERR-KOLE)

ERMANNO From the German Hermann, which is from the Old High German Hariman, a compound name composed of the elements *hari* (army) and *man* (man): hence, "army man, warrior, soldier." (ERR-MAH-NO)

Ernesto From the German Ernst, which is from the Old High German Ernust and Ernost, names derived from *ernust* (earnest, resolute). (ERR-NAY-STO)

Ettore Hebrew cognate of the Latin Hector (steadfast), which is from the Greek Hektōr (holding fast), a name derived from *echein* (to hold, to have). (Ā-TOR-RAY)

Eugenio From the Latin Eugenius and the Greek Eugenios, names derived from *eugenēs* (well-born, noble). The name was borne by four popes and several early saints, including Eugenius of Carthage (d. 505). Short: Gino. (YOO-GEEN-EE-O)

Ezio From the Late Latin Aetius, an old Roman family name of unknown meaning. The name may also be derived from the Greek Aëtios, which is from *aetos* (eagle). (Ā-ZEE-O)

Fabian From the Latin Fabianus (of Fabius), which is derived from the old Roman family name Fabius, a derivative of the Latin *faba* (a bean). Var: Fabiano. (FAH-BEE-AN)

Fabio From Fabius, an old Roman family name derived from the Latin *faba* (a bean). The name is borne by the famous model and actor Fabio. (FAH-BEE-O)

Fabrizio From Fabricius, an old Roman family name derived from the Latin *faber* (workman, craftsman). Short: Brizio. (FAH-BREET-ZEE-O)

Fausto Derived from the Latin Faustus, which is from *fauste* (propitious, lucky, fortunate). (FAU-STO)

Fedele From the Late Latin Fidelis, a direct derivation of *fidēlis* (faithful, trusty, sincere). (FEE-DAY-LAY)

Federico Italian cognate of Frederick, which is from the German Friedrich (ruler of peace). *See* FRIEDRICH (German Names). Var: Federigo. Short: Rico. (FAY-DAY-REE-KO)

Felice Derived from the Latin *felix* (happy, lucky). Var: Felicio. (FAY-LEES)

Filiberto From the Germanic Filibert (very famous), a compound name composed of the elements *fil* (much) and *beraht* (bright, famous). Var: Philibert. (FEE-LEE-BARE-TŌ)

Filippo From the Latin Philippus, a derivative of the Greek Philippos, a compounding of the elements *philos* (loving) and *hippos* (horse): hence, "lover of horses." The name is borne in the Bible by one of the Twelve Apostles of Christ. Pet: Pippo. (FEE-LEE-PO)

Fiorenzo Italian form of Florence, which is from the Latin Florentius, a name derived from *florens* (to bloom, to flourish). Short: Fio. (FEE-O-RANE-ZO)

Flavio From the Latin Flavius, which originated as an old Roman family name derived from *flāvus* (fair, blond, golden, tawny). (FLAH-VEE-O)

Fortunato From the Late Latin Fortūnātus, a direct derivation of *fortūnātus* (fortunate, prosperous, lucky). (FOR-TYOO-NAH-TŌ)

Francesco From the Middle Latin Franciscus (a Frenchman), which is from Francus (a Frank, a freeman), a name that has its root in the Old French *franc* (free). Short: Franco. (FRAHN-CHES-KO)

Franco From the Old French Franc and the Germanic Frank, names referring to a member of the Germanic tribes that established the Frankish Empire, extending over what is now France, Germany, and Italy. The tribe is thought to have obtained its name from a type of spear or javelin (*franco*). Alternatively, Franco is used as a short form of Francesco (a Frenchman, a freeman). *See* FRANCESCO. (FRAHN-KO)

Gabriele From the Hebrew Gavriel, which is derived from *gavhrī'ēl* (God is my strength). The name is borne in the Bible by one of the seven archangels, the herald of Good News who appeared to Mary to announce her pregnancy and the impending birth of the Christ child. (GAB-REE-ELL)

Gaetano Derived from the name of the city of Gaeta, which was originally known as Caieta. The name is of uncertain derivation. (GĪ-TAH-NO)

Gaspare One of the names assigned to the biblical Three Wise Men, who brought gifts to the Christ child. The names are not found in the Bible, and are thought to have been fixed in the 11th century. Of uncertain etymology, Gaspare might have been derived from the Persian *genashber* (treasure master), which is in keeping with his role of the bringer of precious gifts. (GAS-PAH-RAY)

Gavino Believed to be derived from the Late Latin Gabīnus (of Gabium, a city in Latium). (GAH-VEE-NO)

Gennaro Derived from *Januārius*, the Latin name of January, the first month of the year, which is dedicated to Janus, an ancient Italian sun-god. The name was often bestowed in honor of the 3rd-century St. Januarius, the patron saint of Naples. (JEN-NAH-RO)

Georgio From the Greek Geōrgios, a derivative of *geōrgos* (earthworker, farmer), which is composed of the elements *gē* (earth) and *ergein* (to work). Var: Giorgio. (JEE-OR-JEE-O)

GERARDO From the Old High German Gerhart, a compound name composed of the elements *ger* (a spear) and *hart* (hearty, brave, strong): hence, "brave with a spear." Var: Gherardo. (JEH-RAR-DO)

GEREMIA Italian form of Jeremiah, which is from the Ecclesiastic Late Latin Jeremias, a cognate of the Ecclesiastic Greek Hieremias, which is from the Hebrew Yirmeyahu, a derivative of *yirmeyāh* (the Lord loosens, God will uplift). The name is borne in the Bible by a 6th- or 7th-century B.C. Hebrew prophet whose story and prophecies are recorded in the Old Testament book of Jeremiah. (JER-AH-MEE-AH)

GIACOBBE Italian cognate of Jacob, which is from the Ecclesiastic Late Latin Iacobus and the Greek Iakōbos, derivatives of the Hebrew Yaakov, which is from *ja'aqob* (seizing by the heel, supplanting). The name is borne in the Bible by a son of Isaac. Jacob was one of the three patriarchs and the father of twelve sons who founded the tribes of Israel. (GEE-AH-KO-BEH)

GIACOMO Italian cognate of James, which is from the Ecclesiastic Late Latin Iacomus, an evolution of Iacobus, which is derived from the Greek Iakōbos. Iakōbos is from the Hebrew Yaakov, which is from *ya'aqob* (supplanting, seizing by the heel). The form Iacomus is believed to have come about through an error in the transliteration of old manuscripts by an early Italian monk. (GEE-AH-KO-MO)

GIAMBATTISTA Combination name composed of the names Gianni (God is gracious) and Battista (baptist). The name is bestowed in honor of John the Baptist. *See* BATTISTA *and* GIANNI. (GEE-AHM-BAH-TEES-TAH)

GIAN Short form of Giovanni (God is gracious) and any of the other names containing the element *Gian*. It is also bestowed as an independent given name. *See* GIOVANNI. (GEE-AHN)

GIANCARLO Combination name composed of the names Gian (God is gracious) and Carlo (full-grown, a man). *See* CARLO *and* GIAN. (GEE-AHN-KAR-LO)

GIANNI A short form of Giovanni (God is gracious), Gianni is also bestowed as an independent given name. *See* GIOVANNI. Short: Gian. Pet: Giannino, Nino. (GEE-AH-NEE)

GILBERTO From the French Gilbert, an evolution of the Old French Guillebert, a derivative of the Old High German Gisilberht, which is composed from the elements *gisil* (pledge) and *beraht* (bright, famous). (GEEL-BARE-TŌ)

GINO A short form of Eugenio (noble, well-born), Gino is also popularly bestowed as an independent given name. *See* EUGENIO. (GEE-NO)

GIOVANNI Italian cognate of John (God is gracious), which is derived from the Middle Latin Johannes, an evolution of the Ecclesiastic Late Latin Joannes and the Ecclesiastic Greek Iōannes, derivatives of the Hebrew Yehanan, a short form of Yehohanan, which is from *yehōhānān* (Yahweh is gracious). The name is borne in the Bible by several important characters, including John the Baptist, a kinsman and forerunner of Christ. Var: Giannino, Gianozzo, Giovanoli. Short: Gian, Gianni. (JEE-O-VAH-NEE)

GIRALDO Italian cognate of Gerald (spear ruler, to rule with a spear), a name derived from the Germanic Gerwald, a compound name composed of the elements *ger* (a spear) and *wald* (rule). (GIR-AHL-DŌ)

GIULIANO Italian form of Julian, which is from the Latin Julianus, a derivative of Julius, an old Roman family name thought to be derived from Iulus (the first down on the chin, downy-bearded). Because a person just beginning to develop facial hair is young, "youth" became an accepted meaning of the name. (JYOO-LEE-AH-NO)

GIULIO Cognate of Julius, an old Roman family name thought to be derived from Iulus (the first down on the chin, downy-bearded, youth). *See* GIULIANO. (JYOO-LEE-O)

GIUSEPPE Italian cognate of Joseph, an Ecclesiastic Late Latin form of the Ecclesiastic Greek Iōsēph, which is from the Hebrew Yosef, a name derived from *yōsēf* (may he add). The name is borne in the Bible by the favorite son of Jacob and by the husband of the Virgin Mary. Pet: Beppe, Beppo. (JYOO-SEH-PEE)

GIUSTINO Italian cognate of Justin, which is from the Latin Justinus, a name derived from *justus* (lawful, rightful, just). Short: Giusto. (JYOO-STEE-NO).

GOFFREDO From the Old French Godefrei, which is derived from the Germanic Godafrid, a compound name composed from the elements *god* (God) and *frid* (peace): hence, "peace of God." Var: Godofredo. (GO-FRAY-DO)

GRAZIANO Derived from the Latin Gratiānus, which is from Gratius, a name derived from *gratus* (pleasing, beloved, dear). (GRAHT-ZEE-AH-NO)

GREGORIO From the Late Latin Gregorius, a cognate of the Greek Grēgorios (vigilant, a watchman), which is derived from the verb *egeirein* (to awaken). Gregory, a popular name among early Christians, was borne by several early saints and many popes. In 1582 Pope Gregory XIII introduced the Gregorian calendar, a corrected form of the Julian calendar which is now used in most countries of the world. (GRAY-GOR-REE-O)

GUALTIERO Italian form of Walter, which is from the Old Norman French Waltier, a derivative of the Germanic Waldhere, a compound name composed from the elements *wald* (ruler) and *heri* (army): hence, "ruler of an army." Var: Galtero. (GAHL-TAY-RO)

GUGLIELMO Italian cognate of William, which is from the Old High German Willehelm, a compound name composed from the elements *willeo* (will, determination) and *helm* (protection, helmet): hence, "resolute protector." The name was borne by Guglielmo Ferrero (1871–1942), an Italian historian and sociologist. (GOO-GLEE-EL-MO)

GUIDO Derived from *guida* (guide, a leader). The name was borne by Guido d'Arezzo (c. 995–1050), an Italian monk and musical theorist. (GWEE-DŌ)

GUSTAVO From the Latin Gustavus, which is from the German Gustav and the Swedish Gustaf (staff of the Goths). *See* GUSTAV (German Names). (GOO-STAH-VO)

IGNAZIO From the Latin Ignatius, which is derived from Egnatius, an old Roman family name of uncertain etymology. Some believe it to be of Etruscan origin. Others derive it from the Latin *ignis* (fire). The name was borne by several saints, including St. Ignatius of Loyola (1491–1556), a Spanish priest and founder of the Society of Jesus—the Jesuits. (EEG-NAT-ZEE-O)

ILARIO Derived from the Latin Hilarius, which is from *hilaris* (cheerful, glad). (EE-LAH-REE-O)

INNOCENZIO Italian cognate of Innocent, a name borne by thirteen popes, which is derived from the Latin *innocens* (innocent). (EE-NO-SANE-ZEE-O)

IPPOLITO Italian form of the Greek Hippolytos, a compound name composed of the elements *hippos* (a horse) and *lyein* (to loosen, to free): hence, "to free or loosen horses." (EE-POL-LEE-TŌ)

LAZZARO From the Ecclesiastic Late Latin Lazarus and the Ecclesiastic Greek Lazaros, names derived from the Hebrew *el'āzār* (God has helped). The name is borne in the Bible by Martha's brother whom Christ raised from the dead, and by a diseased beggar Christ used in his parable of the rich man and the beggar. (LAZ-ZAH-RO)

LEO Late Latin name derived from *leo* (lion). Alternatively, Leo is a short form of Leon (lion) and Leonardo (strong or brave as a lion). (LEE-O)

LEON Late Latin name derived from *leo* (lion). Var: Leone. Short: Leo. (LEE-ŌN)

LEONARDO From the Old High German Lewenhart, a compound name composed from the elements *lewo* (lion) and *hart* (strong, brave, hearty): hence, "strong as a lion, lion-hearted." The name was borne by Italian painter, sculptor, architect, engineer, and scientist Leonardo da Vinci (1452–1519). Short: Leo. (LEE-O-NAHR-DŌ)

LORENZO Italian cognate of Laurence, which is from the Latin Laurentius (man from Laurentum). Laurentum, the name of a small town in Latium, is probably derived from *laurus* (laurel). The name was borne by several saints, including St. Laurence the Deacon, who was martyred in Rome in 258. When ordered to hand over the church's treasures, he presented the sick and the poor. In retaliation, he was roasted alive on a gridiron. Short: Renzo. (LO-RANE-ZO)

LUCAN Derived from Lucanus (of Lucania), an old Roman family name. (LOO-KAN)

LUCIANO From the Latin Luciānus (of Lucius), a derivative of Lucius, which is from the root *lux* (light). Short: Lucio. (LOO-CHEE-AH-NO)

LUIGI Italian cognate of Louis, a name derived from the Old French Loeis, which is from the Old High German Hluodowig, a compound name composed from the elements *hluod* (famous) and *wīg* (war, strife): hence, "famous in war." Var: Luigino. (LOO-EE-JEE)

MANFREDO Italian cognate of Manfred, which is derived from the Germanic Maginfred, a compound name composed of the elements *magan* (might, strength, ability) and *fred, frid* (peace): hence, "mighty peace." (MAHN-FRAY-DŌ)

MARCELLO From the Latin Marcellus, a diminutive form of Marcus, which is of uncertain derivation. *See* MARCO. The name was borne by several early saints, including Marcellus the Righteous (d. c. 485), an abbot of the Eirenaion monastery near Constantinople where the monks were organized in groups to sing praises to God around the clock. (MAHR-SAY-LO)

MARCO Popular Italian name derived from the Latin Marcus, a name of uncertain derivation. Most believe it has its root in Mars, the name of the Roman mythological god of war. Others, however, think it is from *mas* (manly) or from the Greek *malakoz* (soft, tender). The name is borne in the Bible by one of the four evangelists and author of the second Gospel, Mark. (MAHR-KO)

MARIANO From the Latin Mariānus (of Marius), which is from Marius, an old Roman family name of uncertain derivation. Some believe it has its root in Mars, the name of the Roman mythological god of war, but others think it to be derived from the Latin *mas* (manly). As a result of similarity of form, the name eventually became associated with Maria, the name of the virgin mother of Jesus, and is often bestowed in her honor. (MAH-REE-AH-NO)

MARINO Derived from the Latin *marinus* (of the sea), which has its root in *mare* (the sea). (MAH-REE-NO)

MARIO Popular name derived from the Latin Marius, an old Roman family name of uncertain derivation. *See* MARIANO. (MAH-REE-O)

MARTINO From the Latin Martinus, a derivative of Mars, the name of the Roman mythological god of war. The name was borne by several saints, including St. Martin I (d. 655), a pope who was martyred under the Byzantine emperor Constans II. (MAHR-TEE-NO)

MASSIMILIANO Italian cognate of Maximilian, a blending of the Latin names Maximus and Aemiliānus used by the Emperor Friedrich III, who bestowed it upon his first-born son, Maximilian I (1459–1519), in honor of the two famous Roman generals. Maximus is derived from the Latin *maximus* (greatest), but the etymology of Aemiliānus is uncertain. Some believe it to be from the Latin *aemulus* (trying to equal or excel, rival). Short: Massimo. (MAHS-SEE-MEE-LEE-AH-NO)

MASSIMO From the Latin Maximus, which is derived directly from *maximus* (greatest). Massimo is also used as a short form of Massimiliano. *See* MASSIMILIANO. (MAHS-SEE-MO)

MATTEO Italian cognate of Matthew, which is from the Ecclesiastic Late Latin Matthaeus, a derivative of the Ecclesiastic Greek Matthaios and Matthias, contractions of Mattathias. The name has its root in the Hebrew name Matityah, which is derived from *mattūthyāh* (gift of God). The name is borne in the Bible by one of the four evangelists and author of the first Gospel, Matthew. (MAH-TAY-O)

MAURIZIO Italian cognate of Maurice, which is from the Late Latin Mauritius (Moorish), a derivative of Maurus (a Moor). The Moors were a Muslim people of mixed Arab and Berber descent; the name came to mean "dark" or "swarthy" in reference to their coloring. (MAU-REET-ZEE-O)

MICHELANGELO Combination name composed of the names Michele (who is like God?) and Angelo (angel, messenger of God). *See* ANGELO *and* MICHELE. The name, which refers to the biblical archangel Michael, was borne by Michelangelo Buonarroti (1475–1564), the famous Italian sculptor, painter, architect, and poet. (MEE-KEL-AHN-JEH-LO)

MICHELE Derivative of the Hebrew *mīkhā'ēl* (who is like God?). The name is borne in the Bible by the archangel closest to God, the one responsible for carrying out God's judgments. Considered the leader of the heavenly host, Michael is regarded as the patron of soldiers. Var: Michel. (MEE-KAY-LAY)

NALDO Short form of any of the various names ending in *-naldo*. (NAHL-DŌ)

NAZARIO Derived from the Late Latin Nazarius (of Nazareth, the name of the village where Jesus Christ was raised). (NAH-ZAH-REE-O)

NESTORE From the Greek Nestor, which is from *nēstor* (the one going or departing). *See* NESTOR (Greek Names). (NAY-STOR-AY)

NICCOLO Italian form of the Latin Nicolaus (victory of the people), which is from the Greek Nikolaos, a compound name composed from the elements *nikē* (victory) and *laos* (the people). Var: Niccolò, Nicolò. Short: Nico. (NEE-KO-LO)

NICO Short form of any of the various names beginning with *Nico-*. (NEE-KO)

NICODEMO Derived from the Greek Nikodemos, a compound name composed from the elements *nikē* (victory) and *dēmos* (people, population): hence, "victory of the people." The name is borne in the Bible by a Pharisee, a member of the Sanhedrin who spoke up for Jesus when the Pharisees wanted him arrested. Short: Nico. (NEE-KO-DAY-MO)

NICOMEDO From the Greek Nikomedes, a compound name composed of the elements *nikē* (victory) and *mēdesthai* (to ponder, to meditate upon): hence, "to ponder victory." Short: Nico. (NEE-KO-MAY-DŌ)

NICOSTRATO From the Greek Nikostratos, a compound name composed of the elements *nikē* (victory) and *stratos* (army): hence, "victorious army." The name was borne by a 4th-century Roman soldier martyred under Diocletian with a group of fellow soldiers. Short: Nico. (NEE-KO-STRAH-TŌ)

NUNZIO Derived from the Italian *nunzio* (messenger), which is from the Latin *nuntius* (messenger). Var: Nuncio. (NOON-ZEE-O)

ORAZIO Italian form of Horace, which is from the Latin Horātius, an old Roman family name of uncertain derivation. (O-RAHT-ZEE-O)

ORLANDO Italian cognate of Roland, which is from the Old High German Hruodland, a compound name composed of the elements *hruod* (fame) and *land* (land): hence, "fame of the land." (OR-LAHN-DŌ)

Ottavio From the Latin Octavius, which is derived from *octavus* (eighth). Var: Octavio. (O-TAH-VEE-O)

Paolo Italian cognate of Paul, which is from the Latin Paulus, a Roman family name derived from *paulus* (small). The name was adopted in the Bible by a Jewish Roman citizen, Saul of Tarsus, who was converted to Christianity by a vision of Christ. Paul and St. Peter are regarded as cofounders of the Christian Church. (PAO-LO)

Pasquale From the Late Latin Paschālis (of Easter), a derivative of *Pascha* (Easter), which is from the Hebrew *pesach, pesah* (Passover). The name is often bestowed upon children born at Eastertime. (PAHS-KWAH-LAY)

Patrizio From the Latin Patricius, which is directly derived from *patricius* (a patrician, a nobleman). (PAH-TREET-ZEE-O)

Pietro Italian cognate of Peter, which is from the Ecclesiastic Late Latin Petrus and the Ecclesiastic Greek Petros, names derived from *petra* (a rock) and *petros* (a stone). The name is borne in the Bible by one of the Twelve Apostles of Christ. Peter is considered to have been the first pope and cofounder of the Christian Church. Var: Pero, Piero. (PEE-Ā-TRO).

Pio Derived from *pio* (pious, devout, obedient), which is from the Latin *pius* (pious, devout). (PEE-O)

Placido Derived from the Late Latin Placidus, a direct derivation of *placidus* (gentle, quiet, calm, placid). The name is borne by tenor Plácido Domingo (b. 1941). (PLAH-SEE-DŌ)

Prospero From the Latin Prosperus, which is derived from *prosperus* (favorable, fortunate, prosperous). (PRO-SPAY-RO)

Quirino Derived from the Latin Quirīnus (a spearman, a warrior). The name is found in Roman mythology as the name of Romulus after his deification. (KWEE-REE-NO)

Rafaele From the Ecclesiastic Late Latin Raphael and the Ecclesiastic Greek Rhaphaēl, which are from the Hebrew Refael, a name derived from *refā'ēl* (God has healed). The name was borne by the famous painter and architect, born Rafaello Santi (1483–1520). Var: Rafaello, Raffaello. (RAH-FĪ-ELL)

Raimondo From the Old Norman French Raimund, a name derived from the Germanic Raginmund, a compound name composed of the elements *ragin* (advice, counsel) and *mund* (hand, protection): hence, "wise protection." (RAY-MON-DŌ)

Raniero Italian cognate of Rainier, a name derived from the Old German Raganher, a compounding of the elements *ragan* (counsel, advice) and *hari, heri* (army): hence, "wise army." (RAHN-Ā-RO)

Renato From the Late Latin Renātus, which is a direct derivative of *renātus* (reborn, born again). The name is often chosen as a baptismal name in celebration of spiritual rebirth. (RAY-NAH-TŌ)

Riccardo Italian cognate of Richard, which is from the Old High German Richart, a compound name composed of the elements *rik* (king, ruler) and *hart* (strong, brave, hearty): hence, "brave ruler." Var: Ricardo, Ricciardo. Short: Ricco. (REE-KAR-DŌ)

Rico Short form of any of the various names containing *rico* as an element. (REE-KO)

Rinaldo Cognate of the French Renaud (ruler of judgment), which is derived from the Old High German Raganald and Raginold, compound names composed of the elements *ragna, ragina* (advice, counsel, judgment) and *wald* (ruler). (REE-NAHL-DO)

Roberto Italian cognate of Robert, which is derived from the Old High German Hruodperht, a compound name composed of the elements *hruod* (fame) and *beraht* (bright): hence, "bright with fame." (RO-BARE-TŌ)

Romano Derived from the Latin Romanus (a Roman), which is from Roma (the Italian name of the capital city of Italy). (RO-MAH-NO)

Romeo From the Late Latin Rōmaeus (a pilgrim to Rome), which is from Roma (Rome). The name was made famous by Shakespeare when he used it in his tragedy about star-crossed lovers, *Romeo and Juliet*. (RO-MAY-O)

Romolo From the Latin Rōmulus (the one belonging to Roma). The name Rōmulus was borne by the twin brother of Remus; they are the legendary cofounders of Rome. (RO-MO-LO)

Rufino From the Latin family name Rufinus, which is derived from Rufus (red, ruddy), a name that originated as a nickname for one with red hair or a ruddy complexion. Var: Ruffino. (ROO-FEE-NO)

Ruggero Italian cognate of Roger (famous with a spear), which is from the Old High German Hrodger, a compounding of the elements *hruod* (fame) and *ger* (a spear). Var: Rogero, Ruggiero. (ROO-GAY-RO)

Salvatore Directly derived from the Italian *salvatore* (rescuer, deliverer, savior). Short: Sal. (SAHL-VAH-TOR-Ā)

SANSONE From the Ecclesiastic Late Latin Samson, which is from the Ecclesiastic Greek Sampsōn, a derivative of the Hebrew Shimshon, which is from *shimsōn* (sun). The name is borne in the Bible by an Israelite judge known for his great strength. (SAN-SO-NAY)

SANTO Derived from the Latin *sanctus* (holy). (SAHN-TŌ)

SATURNINO From the Latin Sāturninus (of or belonging to Saturn, a Saturnian), which is derived from Saturnus, a name borne in Roman mythology by the most ancient king of Latium, who came to Italy during the reign of Janus and then became honored as the god of agriculture, vegetation, and civilization. (SAH-TOOR-NEE-NO)

SEBASTIANO From the Latin Sebastiānus, a derivative of the Greek Sebastianos (a man of Sebastia, a town in Asia Minor). The name was borne by a 3rd-century Christian soldier of Rome (d. 288?) martyred under Diocletian by the arrows of his fellow soldiers. (SAY-BAHS-TEE-AH-NO)

SERAFINO From the Ecclesiastic Late Latin Seraphim (burning ones, the angels surrounding the throne of God), which is derived from the Hebrew *sĕrāphīm* (seraphim, angels), a derivative of *sāraph* (to burn). (SAY-RAH-FEE-NO)

SERGIO From the Latin Sergius, an old Roman family name of uncertain etymology. (SARE-JEE-O)

SESTO From the Latin Sextus (sixth). The name is traditionally bestowed upon the sixth-born male child. Var: Sisto. (SAY-STO)

SEVERINO From Severīnus, a Latin family name derived from the old Roman family name Sevērus, which is from *sevērus* (severe, stern, serious). (SAY-VAY-REE-NO)

SEVERO From the old Roman family name Sevērus, which is directly derived from the Latin *sevērus* (severe, strict, stern). (SAY-VAY-RO)

SIGISMONDO Italian form of Sigmund, which is derived from the German Siegmund and the Old Norse Sigmundr, names derived from the Germanic elements *sig* (victory, conquest) and *mund* (hand, protection): hence, "victorious protection." (SEE-GEES-MON-DŌ).

SILVANO From the Latin Silvānus (of the woods), which is derived from *silva* (a wood). Silvanus was a Roman mythological god of the woods and fields. (SEEL-VAH-NO)

SILVESTRO From the Latin Silvester, which is from *silvester* (of a wood or forest), a derivative of *silva* (a wood). The name was borne by three popes, the first of whom is said to have baptized Constantine and cured him of leprosy. (SEEL-VAY-STRO)

SILVIO From the Latin *silva* (a forest, a wood). (SEEL-VEE-O)

SIMON Ecclesiastic Late Latin and Greek form of the Hebrew Shimon, a name derived from *shim'on* (heard). The name is borne in the Bible by two of the Twelve Apostles and a brother of Jesus, as well as several other New Testament characters. (SEE-MONE)

STEFANO From the Latin Stephanus, which is from the Greek Stephanos, a derivative of *stephanos* (a crown, a garland). The name was borne by St. Stephen, the first Christian martyr, who was one of the seven chosen to assist the Twelve Apostles. (STAY-FAH-NO)

TADDEO Italian cognate of Thaddeus, an Ecclesiastic Late Latin name derived from the Ecclesiastic Greek Thaddaios, which is of uncertain derivation. Some believe it to be a variant of Theodōros (God's gift). Others feel it is from an Aramaic word meaning "praised." The name is found in the Bible as a name of Lebbaeus, an apostle of Christ. (TAD-DAY-O)

TANCREDO From the Germanic Tancred, a compound name composed of the elements *thank* (thought) and *rād* (counsel): hence, "thoughtful counsel." The use of the name in Italy is probably due to the fame of Tancred (1078?–1112), the Norman leader of the First Crusade. (TAN-CRAY-DŌ)

TEODOSIO From the Latin Theodosius, which is from the Greek Theodosios, a compound name composed of the elements *theos* (God) and *dōsis* (a gift, a giving): hence, "God-given, a gift of God." (TAY-O-DŌ-SEE-O)

TEOFILO From the Latin Theophilus, which is from the Greek Theophilos, a compound name composed of the elements *theos* (God) and *philos* (loving): hence, "beloved of God, a lover of God." (TAY-O-FEE-LO)

TIBERIO Meaning "of the Tiber," Tiberio is derived from the name of the Tiber River in central Italy. (TEE-BAY-REE-O)

TITO Derived from the Greek Titos, which is of uncertain derivation. Some believe it to be derived from the Greek *tīo* (to honor). (TEE-TŌ)

TITUS The Latin form of Tito, a name of uncertain derivation. The name was borne by the Roman emperor Titus Flavius Sabinus Vespasianus (A.D. 39?–81). (TĪ-TUS)

TOBIA From the Ecclesiastic Late Latin Tobias, which is from the Greek Tōbias, a name derived from the Hebrew *ṭōbhīyāh* (the Lord is good). (TŌ-BEE-AH)

TOMASSO From the Ecclesiastic Greek Thōmas, which is derived from the Aramaic *tě'ōma* (a twin). The name is borne in the Bible by an apostle who doubted the resurrection of Christ. Short: Maso. (TŌ-MAH-SO).

UBERTO Italian cognate of Hubert, a derivative of the Old High German Huguberht (bright in heart and spirit), which is composed of the elements *hugu* (heart, mind, spirit) and *beraht* (bright, famous). (OO-BARE-TŌ)

UGO Italian form of the Germanic Hugo, which is derived from *hugu* (heart, mind, spirit). (OO-GO)

ULISSE Italian form of the Latin Ulysses, a cognate of the Greek Odysseus (hater), which is from the root *dys* (hate). Odysseus was the name of the hero of the *Odyssey*. He was a king of Ithaca and a Greek leader in the Trojan War. (OO-LIS-SAY)

UMBERTO Italian form of the Germanic Humbert, a compound name composed of the elements *hun* (bear cub) and *beraht* (bright, famous). The name was borne by the ancestor of the Royal House of Savoy, Umberto delle Bianchemani, and more recently by the last Italian king. Umberto II (1904–83) succeeded to the throne in 1946 following his father's abdication, but reigned only two months. He left the country when the Italian people chose to form a republic in June of 1946. (OOM-BARE-TŌ)

VALENTINO From the Latin Valentīnus, which is derived from *valens* (to be healthy, strong). The name was borne by a 3rd-century Roman saint and martyr whose feast day, February 14, coincides with that of a pagan festival marking the beginning of spring. (VAH-LANE-TEE-NO)

VALERIO From the Latin Valerius, an old Roman family name believed to be derived from *valere* (to be strong). (VAH-LAY-REE-O)

VINCENZO From the Late Latin Vincentius (conquering), which is derived from *vincere* (to conquer). Var: Vincenzio. Short: Vinnie, Vinny. (VIN-CHEN-ZO)

VITALE Derived from the Italian *vitale* (vital, life-giving), which is from *vitalis* (vital), the root of which is *vita* (life). (VEE-TAH-LAY)

VITO Derived from *vita* (life). Alternatively, Vito is a short form of Vittorio (victory). *See* VITTORIO. (VEE-TŌ)

VITTORIO From the Italian *vittoria* (victory), which is from the Latin *victōria* (victory). The name was borne by the Italian king Vittorio Emanuele III (1873–1952). He abdicated in favor of his son Umberto, who reigned only two months before the people chose to form a republic. Short: Vito. (VEE-TOR-REE-O)

Italian Female Names

ADALGISA Compound name of Germanic origin, which is composed of the elements *adal* (noble) and *gisil* (pledge). Bellini used Adalgisa as the name of a Celtic priestess in his opera *Norma* (1831), which led to its current revival as a given name. (AH-DAHL-GEE-SAH)

ADDOLORATA Derived from the Italian *addolorato* (grieved, sorrowful, sorry). Addolorata is an example of a name derived from one of the designations of the Virgin Mary, "Madonna Addolorata" (Our Lady of Sorrows). (AD-DOL-LO-RAH-TAH)

ADRIANA Feminine form of Adriano (man from Adria or Hadria, a town in northern Italy). *See* ADRIAN (Male Names). Var: Adreana. (AD-REE-AH-NAH)

AEGLE Ancient name derived from the Latin Aeglē (radiance, brightness, splendor). (EEG-LAY)

AEMILIA From Aemilius, an old Roman family name probably derived from *aemulus* (emulating, trying to equal or excel, rival). Aemilia is often mistakenly believed to be related to the Germanic Amelia (work), but there is no connection. (EE-MEE-LEE-AH)

AGATA Italian form of the Greek Agathē, which is derived from *agathos* (good, kind, honorable). The name became popular through the fame of St. Agata, a young Christian martyr of the 3rd century. After spurning the advances of the Roman consul Quintinianus, she was ultimately tortured and her breasts were cut off before she was killed. She is often pictured carrying her two breasts on a plate, and because they were mistaken for bells, she became the patron saint of the bell ringers. (AH-GAH-TAH)

AGNELLA Derived from the Greek *hagnos* (chaste, pure, sacred). Var: Agnola. (AHG-NAY-LAH)

AGNESE Popular name derived from the Greek Hagnē, which is from *hagnos* (chaste, pure, sacred). The name was borne by St. Agnese, a thirteen-year-old Roman of the 3rd century who, after consecrating her virginity to Christ, refused marriage and would not sacrifice to pagan idols. She was stripped and sent to a brothel. After an attempt to burn her alive failed, she was killed by being stabbed in the throat with a sword. Agnese is similar in form to the Latin *agna* (lamb), which led to the lamb being adopted as her attribute. Var: Agnesca, Agnete. (AHG-NAY-SAY)

AIDA A name of uncertain derivation used by Verdi for the title character of his opera *Aida* (1871). (Ī-EE-DAH)

ALBA Derived from the Italian *alba* (dawn, daybreak), which is from the Latin *albus* (white). Alternatively, it may be from Alba, the "mother city" of Rome, which was built by Ascanius, the son of Aeneas, between the Alban lake and Mons Albanus. In this instance, Alba is derived from the Latin *albus* (white). (AHL-BAH)

ALBERTA Feminine form of Alberto (bright through nobility), which is from the Old High German Adalbrecht, a compounding of the elements *adal* (noble, nobility) and *beraht* (bright). Short: Berta. (AHL-BARE-TAH)

ALBINA From the Latin Albinus, which is from Albus, an old Roman family name derived from *albus* (white). The name was borne by a 3rd-century martyr whose relics are preserved at Campania. Var: Albinia. (AHL-BEE-NAH)

ALESSA A short form of Alessandra (defender or helper of mankind), Alessa is also bestowed as an independent given name. *See* ALESSANDRA. (AH-LAY-SAH)

ALESSANDRA Feminine form of Alessandro, the Italian cognate of Alexander (defender or helper of mankind), a compound name composed of the Greek elements *alexein* (to defend, to help) and *andros* (man, mankind). Short: Alessa, Alessia, Sandra. (AH-LAY-SAHN-DRA)

ALESSIA Italian form of the Greek Alexia, which is derived from the verb *alexein* (to defend, to help). Alessia is also used as a short form of Alessandra (defender or helper of mankind). *See* ALESSANDRA. (AH-LAY-SEE-AH)

ALLEGRA Derived from the Italian *allegro* (merry, cheerful, gay). (AH-LAY-GRA)

ALONZA Feminine form of Alonzo, a variant form of Alfonso, which is from the Old German Adalfuns, a compound name composed of the elements *adal* (noble) and *funs* (ready, prompt, apt). (AHL-ON-ZAH)

ALTHAEA Latin name derived from the Greek Althaia (healer), which is from *althainein* (to heal). (AHL-THEE-AH)

AMALIA Derived from the Germanic element *amal* (work). Var: Amalea. (AH-MAHL-EE-AH)

AMARA Derived from the Latin *amarantus* (unfading, immortal). Alternatively, Amara may be from the Latin *amārus* (bitter, sour). Short: Mara. (AH-MAHR-AH)

ANDREANA Feminine form of Andrea, which is from the Latin and Greek Andreas, names derived from the Greek *andreios* (manly), which has its root in *andros* (man). (AHN-DRAY-AH-NAH)

ANGELA Derived from the Greek *angelos* (messenger). In New Testament Greek, the word evolved to mean "divine messenger of God." Var: Angelia. (AHN-JAY-LAH)

ANITA Originally a Spanish pet form of Ana (gracious, full of grace). *See* ANNA. (AH-NEE-TAH)

ANNA Derived from the Hebrew Hannah, which is from *hannāh*, *chaanach* (gracious, full of grace, mercy). In medieval Christian tradition, Anne was the name assigned to the mother of the Virgin Mary, as Joachim was assigned to her father. Anna is also used as a short form of any of the various names containing it as an element. (AH-NAH)

ANNAMARIA Combination name composed of the names Anna (gracious, full of grace, mercy) and Maria (the name of the Virgin Mary). *See* ANNA *and* MARIA. (AH-NAH-MAH-REE-AH)

ANNUNZIATA Derived from the Italian *annunzio* (announcement, notice). The name is used in reference to the Annunciation, the time when the angel Gabriel announced to Mary God's favor upon her and the impending birth of the Christ child. The festival of the Annunciation, also known as Lady Day, is held in Italy on March 25, nine months before Christmas. Var: Annunciata. Short: Nunzia. (AH-NOON-ZEE-AH-TAH)

ANTONIA Feminine form of Antonio, which is from Antonius, an old Roman family name of uncertain origin and meaning. Some believe it to have originally been an Etruscan name. Short: Anta. (AHN-TŌ-NEE-AH)

ASSUMPTA Derived from the Latin *assumptio* (the Assumption). The Assumption was the taking of the body and soul of the Virgin Mary into heaven after her death. (AH-SOOM-TAH)

ASSUNTA From the Italian *assunto* (assumed, raised). The name is derived from the designation of the Virgin Mary, "Maria Assunta" (Our Lady of the Assumption). (AHS-SOON-TAH)

AUGUSTA Latin name which is the feminine form of Augustus, a derivative of *augustus* (great, venerable, consecrated by the augurs). (AU-GOOS-TAH)

AURELIA Feminine form of the Latin Aurēlius (golden), a name derived from *aurum* (gold). (AU-RAY-LEE-AH)

AURORA Derived from the Latin *aurōra* (dawn, daybreak, sunrise). The name was borne by the Roman mythological goddess of the dawn. (AU-ROR-AH)

BALBINA Feminine form of the Latin Balbus (stammerer), which is from *balbus* (stammering, stuttering). The name originated as a nickname for one who stuttered. (BAHL-BEE-NAH)

BAMBI A short form of the Italian Bambina (baby girl, a young girl), Bambi is also bestowed as an independent given name. (BAM-BEE)

BAMBINA Derived directly from the Italian *bambina* (a baby girl, a young girl). Short: Bambi. (BAM-BEE-NAH)

BAPTISTE Derived from the Ecclesiastic Late Latin *baptista* (a baptizer), which is from the Greek *baptistēs* (a baptizer). The name is usually bestowed in honor of John the Baptist, the one who baptized Jesus Christ. (BAP-TEES-TAY)

BARBARA Derived from the Latin *barbarus* (foreign, strange), a term applied to non-Romans or those deemed to be uncivilized. Short: Barb. (BAR-BAR-AH)

BEATA Feminine form of the Late Latin Beātus (blessed), which is directly derived from *beatus* (happy, blessed). (BAY-AH-TAH)

BEATRICE From the Latin *beatrix* (she who makes happy, she who brings happiness), which is from *beātus* (happy, blessed). Pet: Bice. (BEE-AH-TREES)

BELLA A short form of Isabella (God is my oath), Bella is also commonly bestowed as an independent given name derived from the adjective *bella* (pretty, charming, lovely, beautiful). *See* ISABELLA. (BAY-LAH)

BENEDETTA Derived from the Latin *benedictus* (blessed). (BANE-NAY-DAY-TAH)

BENIGNA Derived from the Latin *benignus* (good, wellborn), which is from the elements *bene* (good, well) and *genus* (birth). (BAY-NEEG-NAH)

BERTA Italian form of the German Bertha (bright one), a name derived from *beraht* (bright, shining). Alternatively, Berta is a short form of Alberta (bright through nobility). *See* ALBERTA. (BARE-TAH)

BIANCA Derived from the Italian *bianca* (white, fair). (BEE-AHN-KAH)

BIONDA Derived from *bionda* (black). (BEE-AHN-DAH)

BONA Directly derived from the Latin *bona* (good, fair). (BO-NAH)

BRIGIDA Italian cognate of the Irish Bríghid, which is believed to be derived from the Gaelic *brígh* (strength). The name was made popular in Italy by the fame of St. Birgitta (1302?–72), the patron saint of Sweden. A noblewoman and mother of eight children, she founded the Order of the Brigittines after her husband's death, and traveled to Rome, where she attempted to reform religious life. (BREE-GEE-DAH)

BRUNA Feminine form of Bruno (brown). *See* BRUNO (Male Names). (BROO-NAH)

BRUNELLA Elaboration of Bruna, which is a feminine form of Bruno (brown). *See* BRUNO (Male Names). Short: Nella. (BROO-NAY-LAH)

CALIDA Derived from the Greek Kalidas (most beautiful), which is from *kalos* (beautiful). (KAH-LEE-DAH)

CALLIFAE A borrowing from the name of the town of Callifae in lower Italy. (KAL-LEE-FAY)

CALLIGENIA From the Greek Kaligenia (beautiful daughter, daughter of beauty), a compound name composed of the elements *kalos* (beautiful) and *genēs* (born). (KAL-LEE-GEE-NEE-AH)

CALLIRRHOE Derived from the Greek Kallirrōē (beautiful stream), a compound name composed of the elements *kallos* (beauty) and *rōē* (stream). Var: Callirhoe, Calliroe. (KAL-LEE-RO)

CALLISTO Derived from the Greek Kallistō (she that is most beautiful), which is from *kallos* (beauty). The name is borne in Roman mythology by a nymph, a daughter of the Arcadian king Lycaon, and mother of Arcas. Beloved by Jupiter, she was transformed into a she-bear by Juno and then placed among the constellations. (KAH-LEES-TŌ)

CAMILLA Derived from the Latin *camilla* (virgin of unblemished character). The name is borne in Roman mythology by a queen of the Volscians who fought in the army of the Trojan Aeneas. Var: Camille. Short: Cami. (KAH-MEE-LAH)

CAPRICE Derived from the Italian *capriccio* (whim, fancifulness; a shivering). (KAH-PREES)

Cara Derived from the Italian *cara* (beloved, dear), which is from the Latin *carus* (beloved, dear). Var: Kara. (KAR-AH)

Carina Diminutive form of Cara (beloved, dear). *See* CARA. Var: Carinna. Short: Cari. (KAR-EE-NAH)

Carissa Elaboration of Cara (beloved, dear). *See* CARA. Short: Cari. (KAR-EE-SAH)

Carla Popular feminine form of Carlo (full-grown, a man), which is an Italian cognate of Charles. *See* CARLO (Male Names). (KAR-LAH)

Carlotta Feminine diminutive form of Carlo (full-grown, a man). *See* CARLO (Male Names). (KAR-LO-TAH)

Carmela Derived from the Hebrew, meaning "vineyard" or "orchard." Mount Carmel is a mountain in northwestern Israel which was inhabited in early Christian times by a group of hermits who later became Carmelite monks in the Order of Our Lady of Mount Carmel. The name is used in reference to the Virgin Mary, "Our Lady of Carmel." (KAR-MAY-LAH)

Carmeline Diminutive form of Carmela (vineyard, orchard). *See* CARMELA. (KAR-MAY-LEE-NEH)

Carolina Feminine form of the Latin Carolus (full-grown, a man), which is a cognate of Carlo. *See* CARLO (Male Names). Short: Caro. (KAR-O-LEE-NAH)

Catarina Popular name derived from the Greek Aikaterinē, which is from *katharos* (pure, unsullied). Var: Caterina. Short: Cat. (CAT-AH-REE-NAH)

Cecilia Feminine form of Cecil, which is derived from Caecilius, an old Roman family name, which has its root in the Latin *caecus* (blind, dim-sighted). The name was borne by a 3rd-century Christian who founded a church in the Trastevere section of Rome. During the 6th century, a story of her life was written and she was henceforth venerated as a martyr. She is regarded as the patron saint of musicians. (SAY-SEE-LEE-AH)

Celia Derived from the Latin Caelia, a feminine form of Caelius, an old Roman family name thought to be a derivative of the Latin *caelum* (heaven). (SEE-LEE-AH)

Celina Diminutive form of Celia (heaven). *See* CELIA. Var: Celinka. (SAY-LEE-NAH)

Chiara Italian form of Clara and Clare, names derived from the Latin *clārus* (bright, clear, famous). Var: Ciara (CHEE-AH-RAH)

Cinzia Italian cognate of the Greek Kynthia, a name derived from Kynthios (from Kynthos, the name of a mountain on the island of Delos). *See* KYNTHIA (Greek Names). (SIN-ZEE-AH)

Clara Popular name derived from the Latin *clārus* (bright, clear, famous). The name was often bestowed in honor of St. Clare of Assisi (c. 1194–1255), who, under the direction of St. Francis of Assisi, founded the Order of Poor Ladies, now known as the Poor Clares. (KLAH-RAH)

Clarice Derived from the Latin Claritia, which is from *clārus* (bright, clear, famous). Var: Clariss, Clarissa. (KLAH-REES)

Claudia Derived from the Latin Claudius, an old Roman family name, which is from *claudus* (lame). (KLAU-DEE-AH)

Clelia Derived from the Latin Cloelia, which is of uncertain derivation. The name was borne by an early Roman maiden who, hostage to the Etruscan invader Lars Porsenna, escaped with several companions and swam the Tiber River back to Rome. (KLAY-LEE-AH)

Clytie From the Greek Klytīe (the splendid one). The name is borne in Roman mythology by a water nymph who was a daughter of Oceanus. She fell in love with the sun-god Apollo and was transformed into the heliotrope. Var: Clytia. (KLĪ-TEE)

Colomba Derived from the Latin *columba* (dove, pigeon, gray bird). (KO-LOM-BAH)

Colombina Diminutive form of Colomba, which is derived from the Latin *columba* (dove, pigeon, gray bird). (KO-LOM-BEE-NAH)

Concetta A name used in honor of the Virgin Mary, "Maria Concetta," a title referring to the Immaculate Conception. Var: Conchetta. (KON-CHAY-TAH)

Consilia Derived from the Latin Consilium (counsel), Consilia is usually bestowed in honor of the Virgin Mary, "Our Lady of Good Counsel." (KONE-SEE-LEE-AH)

Consolata Derived from the Latin *consolatio* (consolation). The name is bestowed in honor of the Virgin Mary, "Maria Consolata," in reference to her role as comforter in times of trouble or distress. (KON-SO-LAH-TAH)

Constantina Feminine form of Constantine, from the Latin Constantinus, which is derived from *constans* (constant, unchanging). Var: Constantina, Constanza. (KONE-STAHN-TEE-NAH)

Cornelia Feminine form of the Latin Cornelius, an old Roman family name of uncertain etymology. Some believe it is derived from *cornu* (horn). (KOR-NAY-LEE-AH)

Cosima Feminine form of Cosmo, an Italian cognate of the Greek Kosmas, which is from *kosmos* (universe, order, harmony). (KO-SEE-MAH)

Cristina Derived from the Ecclesiastic Late Latin *christiānus*, which is from the Greek *christianos* (a Christian). Short: Tina. (KREES-TEE-NAH)

Daniela Feminine form of Daniele, which is derived from the Hebrew *dānī'ēl* (God is my judge). *See* DANIELE (Male Names). (DAHN-YALE-AH)

Daria Feminine form of Darius, an old Latin name derived from the Greek Dareios, which is of uncertain origin. It is thought to ultimately be derived from Darayavahush, the name of an ancient Persian king. (DAH-REE-AH)

Delfina From the Latin Delphīna (woman from Delphi). Alternatively, Delfina may be derived from the name of the delphinium flower, which is from the Greek *delphin* (a dolphin). (DEL-FEE-NAH)

Diana Derived from the Latin Diviana, which is from *divus* (divine). The name is borne in Roman mythology by the virgin goddess of the moon and of hunting. *See* DIANA (Mythology and Astrology Names). (DEE-AH-NAH)

Dominica Feminine form of Dominic, a derivative of the Latin Dominicus (belonging to a lord), which is from *dominus* (a lord, a master). (DŌ-MEE-NEE-KAH)

Domitilla Diminutive form of Domitius, an old Roman family name derived from *domus* (house, home, abode). Domitilla is often bestowed in honor of the 2nd-century saint Flavia Domitilla, a great-niece of the Roman emperor Domitian (A.D. 51–96). (DŌ-MEE-TEE-LAH)

Donata Feminine form of Donato (given by God), which is derived from the Latin *donatio* (donation, a gift). (DŌ-NAH-TAH)

Donatella Feminine form of Donatello, which is derived from the Latin *donatio* (donation, a gift). (DŌ-NAH-TAY-LAH)

Dorotea Italian cognate of the Greek Dōrothea, a compound name composed from the elements *dōron* (gift) and *theos* (God): hence, "gift of God." *See* DOROTHÉE (French Names). (DŌ-RO-TAY-AH)

Drusilla Derived from Drūsus, an old family name of the Livian gens, which is of uncertain derivation. Drūsus is said to have been first used by a man who assumed the name after slaying the Gallic general Drausus, whose name is believed to be from a Celtic element meaning "strong." The name Drusilla is borne in history by the daughter of Herod Agrippa. (DROO-SEE-LAH)

Edvige Italian cognate of the German Hedwig (war, strife), a compound name composed of the elements *hadu* (contention) and *wīg* (war, strife). Var: Edrige, Edvig. Pet: Edda. (ED-VEE-GAH)

Elda Modern Italian name of uncertain derivation and meaning. Some believe it to be a variant form of the Germanic Hilda (battle protector). *See* HILDA (German Names). (EL-DAH)

Elena Italian cognate of the Greek Helenē, which is derived from the element *ēlē* (light, torch, bright). (EL-LAY-NAH)

Eleonora Derived from Alienor, a Provençal form of the Greek Helenē, which is derived from the element *ēlē* (light, torch, bright). Short: Nora, Leonora. (EL-LAY-O-NO-RAH)

Elettra Italian form of the Latin Electra, which is from the Greek Elektra (shining one). *See* ELECTRA (Mythology and Astrology Names). (EL-LAY-TRAH)

Eliana From the Late Latin Aeliāna, the feminine form of the Latin family name Aeliānus (of the sun), which is derived from the Greek *hēlios* (sun). (EL-LEE-AH-NAH)

Elisa A short form of Elisabetta (God is my oath), Elisa is also bestowed as an independent given name. *See* ELISABETTA. (EL-LEE-SAH)

Elisabetta Popular name derived from the Hebrew *elīsheba'* (God is my oath). The name is borne in the Bible by a kinswoman of the Virgin Mary and mother of John the Baptist. Short: Betta, Elisa. Pet: Betty. (EL-EE-SAH-BAY-TAH)

Emerenzia Derived from the Latin *meritus* (merit). (EM-MAY-RANE-ZEE-AH)

Enrica Feminine form of Enrico, the Italian cognate of Henry (home ruler, ruler of an enclosure). *See* ENRICO (Male Names). Var: Enrika. Short: Rica, Rika. (EN-REE-KAH)

Eufemia Derived from the Greek Euphēmia, a compound name composed of the elements *eu* (good, well, fair) and *phēmē* (voice): hence, "fair speech." The name was borne by a young virgin martyr of Chalcedon in Greece who so courageously withstood her torture that her fame spread both East and West. (YOO-FAY-MEE-AH)

EUGENIA A borrowing from the Greek, Eugenia is derived from *eugenēs* (well-born, noble). Short: Gina. (YOO-JAY-NEE-AH)

EULALIA A borrowing from the Greek, Eulalia is a compound name composed of the element *eu* (well, good, fair) and the verb *lalein* (to talk): hence, "well-spoken." (YOO-LAY-LEE-AH)

EVA Derived from the Hebrew Chava (life), which is from *hawwāh* (life). The name is borne in the Bible by the first woman, "the mother of all the living." (Ā-VAH)

EVANGELIA Latinate form of the French Evangeline (bringer of good news), a name derived from the Ecclesiastic Late Latin *evangelium*, which is from the Greek *evangelos* (bringing good news). (Ā-VAHN-JAY-LEE-AH)

EVANGELINA Italian cognate of the French Evangeline (bringer of good news). *See* EVANGELIA. Short: Lina. (EE-VAHN-JAY-LEE-NAH)

FABIA The feminine form of Fabio, which is from the old Roman family name Fabius, a derivative of the Latin *faba* (a bean). (FAH-BEE-AH)

FABIANA Elaborated form of Fabia (a bean). *See* FABIA. (FAH-BEE-AH-NAH)

FABIOLA Elaboration of Fabia (a bean). *See* FABIA. The name was borne by St. Fabiola, a Roman widow who founded the first hospital in Rome to address the needs of those making pilgrimages to the Vatican. (FAH-BEE-O-LAH)

FAUSTA Derived from the Latin *fauste* (favorably, fortunately, lucky). (FAU-STAH)

FAUSTINA Elaboration of Fausta (lucky), which is derived from *fauste* (favorably, fortunately, lucky). (FAU-STEE-NAH)

FELICIA Feminine form of Felix, which is derived from the Latin *felix* (happy, lucky). (FAY-LEE-SEE-AH)

FELÌCITA From the Late Latin Felicitas, which is directly derived from *fēlīcitas* (happiness, felicity, good fortune). (FAY-LEE-SEE-TAH)

FIAMMETTA Derived from *fiamma* (flame, fire) and the diminutive suffix *-etta*: hence, "little fiery one." (FEE-AH-MAY-TAH)

FIDELIA Derived from the Latin *fidelis* (faithful, trusty), which is from the root *fides* (faith). (FEE-DAY-LEE-AH)

FILOMENA Derived from the Greek Philomena, a compound name composed of the elements *philein* (to love) and *menos* (strength): hence, "lover of strength." (FEE-LO-MAY-NAH)

FIORELLA Derived from *fiore* (flower). (FEE-O-RAY-LAH)

FLAVIA From the old Roman family name Flavius, which is derived from the Latin *flavus* (yellow). (FLAH-VEE-AH)

FLORENTINA Latinate feminine form of Florentīnus, which is derived from *florens* (blooming, flourishing). (FLOR-ANE-TEE-NAH)

FLORENZA Italian cognate of Florence, which is from the Latin Florentia (a blooming), a name derived from *florens* (blooming, flourishing, prosperous). Var: Fiorenza. (FLOR-RANE-ZAH)

FORTUNA Derived from the Latin *fortuna* (chance, fate, fortune). The name was borne by the Roman mythological goddess of good fortune and happiness. (FOR-TYOO-NAH)

FORTUNATA Feminine form of the Late Latin Fortūnātus, a direct derivation of *fortūnātus* (fortunate, prosperous, lucky). (FOR-TYOO-NAH-TAH)

FRANCA Feminine form of Franco (a Frank, a Frenchman), which is from the Late Latin Francus (a Frank, a freeman). (FRAHN-KAH)

FRANCESCA Feminine form of Francesco, the Italian cognate of Francis, which is from the Middle Latin Franciscus, a derivative of Francus (a Frank, a freeman). The name was borne by the 13th-century Francesca da Rimini, the beautiful daughter of the count of Ravenna, Giovanni da Polenta. In return for military support, Francesca's father betrothed her to the ugly and malformed lord of Rimini, Giovanni Malatesta. Paolo, Malatesta's handsome younger brother, acted as proxy in the marriage and he and Francesca soon fell in love. They were discovered and put to death in 1289 by Malatesta. Dante recorded the tragedy of Francesca da Rimini in his work *Inferno*. (FRAHN-CHASE-KAH)

FREDERICA Feminine form of Federico, the Italian cognate of Frederick (peace ruler, ruler of peace). *See* FEDERICO (Male Names). (FRAY-DAY-REE-KAH)

FULVIA From the old Roman family name Fulvius, which is derived from the Latin fulvus (tawny, brownish yellow). (FOOL-VEE-AH)

GABRIELA Feminine form of Gabriele, which is derived from the Hebrew *gavhrī'ēl* (God is my strength). *See* GABRIELE (Male Names). Var: Gabriella. (GAH-BREE-Ā-LAH)

GAETANE Feminine form of Gaetano (of Gaeta), a name derived from the name of the city of Gaeta, which was originally called Caieta. The name is of unknown derivation. Var: Gaetana. (GĪ-TAH-NEH)

GELSOMINA Inspired by the plant *gelsemium*, the name of which is from the Italian *gelsomino* (jessamine), which is derived from the Persian *yāsamīn* (jasmine). (JEL-SO-MEE-NAH)

GEMMA Derived from the Latin *gemma* (a swelling, a bud, a precious stone). (JEM-MAH)

GENEVRA Derived from the Old French *genevra* (juniper berry), which is from the Latin *juniperus* (juniper). Var: Genoveffa, Ginevra. (JAY-NAVE-RAH)

GHITA A short form of Margherita (a pearl), Ghita is also bestowed as an independent given name. *See* MARGHERITA. (GEE-TAH)

GIACINTA From the Latin *hyacinthus* (hyacinth), which is derived from the Greek *hyakinthos* (wild hyacinth, blue larkspur, a blue gem). (JEE-AH-SEEN-TAH)

GIAN Short form of any of the various names beginning with the element *Gian-*. Var: Giann. (JEE-AHN)

GIANNA Popular contracted form of Giovanna (God is gracious). *See* GIOVANNA. Short: Gian, Giann. Pet: Giannetta, Giannina. (JEE-AH-NAH)

GINA Originally a short form of Eugene (well-born) and Luigina (famous in war), Gina is now commonly bestowed as an independent given name. *See* EUGENIA *and* LUIGINA. (JEE-NAH)

GINEVRA Italian cognate of Jennifer, a Cornish derivation of Guinevere, which is from the Welsh Gwenhwyfar (fair lady), a compounding of the elements *gwen* (white, fair, blessed) and *hwyfar* (smooth, soft). *See* GUINEVERE (English Names). (GEE-NAVE-RAH)

GIOCONDA Derived from the Latin *jucunde* (pleasure, delight). (JEE-O-KON-DAH)

GIOVANNA Feminine form of Giovanni, the Italian cognate of John (God is gracious). *See* GIOVANNI (Male Names). Var: Gianina, Gianna, Giannina. Short: Anna, Gian, Giann. (JEE-O-VAH-NAH)

GIUDITTA Italian cognate of Judith (praised, woman from Judah), which is a cognate of the Hebrew Jehudith and Yehudit, feminine forms of Jehuda and Yehūdhāh (he will be praised). These names have been Anglicized as Judah, and since Judah was the name of a kingdom in ancient Palestine, the name has also come to mean "from Judah." (JYOO-DIT-TAH)

GIULIA Italian cognate of Julia (downy-bearded, youth). *See* JULIA. (JYOO-LEE-AH)

GIULIETTA A diminutive form of Giulia (downy-bearded, youth). *See* JULIA. (JYOO-LEE-ET-TAH)

GIUSEPPINA Feminine form of Giuseppe, the Italian cognate of Joseph (may he add, God will add). *See* GIUSEPPE (Male Names). (JYOO-SEP-PEE-NAH)

GRAZIA Derived from the Italian *grazia* (grace, favor, thanks), which is from the Latin *gratia* (grace, favor, thanks). (GRAHT-ZEE-AH)

GRAZIELLA Diminutive form of Grazia (grace, favor, thanks). *See* GRAZIA. (GRAHT-ZEE-Ā-LAH)

GULIELMA Feminine form of Guglielmo, the Italian cognate of William (resolute protector). *See* GUGLIELMO (Male Names). Var: Guillelmina. Short: Mina, Minna. (GOO-LEE-ALE-MAH)

IMELDA Derived from the Germanic Irmenhild, a compound name composed of the elements *irmen* (entire, all) and *hild* (battle): hence, "entire battle." (EE-MAYL-DAH)

IMMACOLATA Derived from the Latin *immaculatus* (immaculate). The name is bestowed in honor of the Virgin Mary, "Maria Immacolata," in reference to the Immaculate Conception. (EE-MAH-KO-LAH-TAH)

IRENE Derived from the Greek Eirēnē, which is from *eirēnē* (peace). (EE-RAY-NAY)

ISABELLA A borrowing from the Spanish, Isabella is a variant of Elizabeth (God is my oath), which is derived from the Hebrew *elīsheba'* (God is my oath). *See* ELISABETTA. Var: Isabela. Short: Bella. (EES-AH-BAY-LAH)

JOLANDA Italian form of the French Yolande (violet), which is derived from the Latin *viola* (violet). The name was bestowed upon the first-born of King Victor Emmanuel III in 1901, which initiated its revival in Italy. (JO-LAHN-DAH)

JULIA Feminine form of the Latin Julius, an old Roman family name thought to be derived from Iulus (the first down on the chin, downy-bearded). Because a person just beginning to develop facial hair is young, "youth" has become an accepted definition of this name and its related forms. (JOO-LEE-AH)

JULIANA A popular name, Juliana is the Latin feminine form of Julianus, from the old Roman family name Julius, which is believed to be derived from Iulus (downy-bearded, youth). *See* JULIA. (JOO-LEE-AH-NAH)

JULIET A borrowing from the English, Juliet is from the French Juliette, a diminutive form of Julia. *See*

JULIA. The name is borne by the heroine of Shakespeare's *Romeo and Juliet*. (JOO-LEE-ET)

Laura Derived from the Latin *laurus* (laurel). Laurel is an evergreen shrub or tree whose leaves were woven into wreaths by the ancient Greeks to crown victors in various contests. (LAU-RAH)

Laurenza Feminine form of Lorenzo, the Italian cognate of Laurence, a name derived from the Latin Laurentius (man from Laurentum). Laurentum, the name of a town in Latium, is probably derived from *laurus* (laurel). (LAU-RANE-ZAH)

Lauretta Diminutive form of Laura (laurel). *See* LAURA. (LAU-RAY-TAH)

Leonora A short form of Eleonora (light, torch, bright), Leonora is now more commonly bestowed as an independent given name. *See* ELEONORA. Short: Nora. (LAY-O-NOR-AH)

Letizia Italian form of Letitia, which is derived from the Latin *laetitia* (gladness, happiness, joy). (LAY-TEET-ZEE-AH, LAY-TEET-ZHAH)

Lia A short form of Evangelia (bringer of good news), Lia is also commonly bestowed as an independent given name. *See* EVANGELIA. (LEE-AH)

Liliana Italian form of Lillian, which is derived from the Latin *lilium* (LILY). The lily is regarded as a symbol of purity and innocence. (LEE-LEE-AH-NAH)

Lina Originally a short form of Evangelina (bringer of good news), Lina is also bestowed as an independent given name. *See* EVANGELINA. (LEE-NAH)

Luana Modern coinage composed of the elements *Lu-* and *-ana*, first used in the 1932 film *The Bird of Paradise*, seen in Italy under the title *Luana, la vergine sacra*. (LOO-AH-NAH)

Lucia Feminine form of Lucius, which is derived from the Latin *lux* (light). The name was borne by St. Lucia of Syracuse, a 4th-century martyr whose popularity during the Middle Ages led to widespread use of the name. Var: Luca. (LOO-CHEE-AH)

Luciana Elaboration of Lucia (light). *See* LUCIA. (LOO-CHEE-AH-NAH)

Luigina Feminine form of Luigi, the Italian cognate of Louis (famous in war). *See* LUIGI. (LOO-EE-JEE-NAH)

Luisa A borrowing from the Spanish, Luisa is a feminine form of Luis, which is a cognate of Louis (famous in war). *See* LUIGI (Male Names). (LOO-EE-SAH)

Maddalena Derived from the Ecclesiastic Greek Magdalēnē (of Magdala, a town on the Sea of Galilee). The name is borne in the Bible by Mary Magdalene, a woman Christ cured of seven demons. (MAD-DAH-LAY-NAH)

Mafalda Italian form of Matilda, which is derived from the Old High German Mahthilda, a compound name composed of the elements *maht* (might, power) and *hiltia* (battle): hence, "powerful in battle." The name was borne by the second daughter (1902–44) of King Victor Emmanuel III. (MAH-FAHL-DAH)

Manuela Feminine form of Manuel, a name derived from the Greek Emmanouēl, which is from the Hebrew *'immānūēl* (God is with us). (MAHN-WELL-LAH)

Marcella Feminine form of the Latin Marcellus, a diminutive form of Marcus, which is of uncertain derivation. *See* MARCO (Male Names). The name was borne by St. Marcella (325–410), a wealthy Roman matron who organized a religious study at her home after the death of her husband. After Alaric the Goth invaded Rome, she was tortured to death in an effort to make her disclose the whereabouts of her wealth. (MAR-SAY-LAH)

Marcia Feminine form of the Latin Marcius, a variant of Marcus, which is a name of uncertain derivation. *See* MARCO (Male Names). (MAR-SEE-AH, MAR-CHEE-AH)

Margherita From the Greek Margarītēs, a name derived from *margaron* (a pearl). Short: Ghita, Rita. (MAR-GER-EE-TAH)

Maria A highly popular name, Maria is the Latin form of Mary, which is derived from the Hebrew Miryām (sea of bitterness or sorrow). There is much debate over the meaning of this name, however. While "sea of bitterness/sea of sorrow" seems to be the most probable, some sources cite the alternative definitions of "rebellion," "wished-for child," and "mistress or lady of the sea." The name is bestowed in honor of the Virgin Mary, the mother of Jesus Christ. Var: Mara, Marea. (MAH-REE-AH)

Mariana Feminine form of the Latin Mariānus, a derivative of Marius, which is an old Roman family name of uncertain derivation. Some believe the name has its root in Mars, the Roman mythological god of war, but others think it is derived from the Latin *mas* (manly). Early Christians associated the name with Maria, the Latin name of the Virgin Mary, and thus it enjoyed widespread use. (mah-ree-AH-nah)

Mariella Diminutive form of Maria, the Italian form of the name of the Virgin Mary. *See* MARIA. (MAH-REE-EL-LAH)

Marietta Diminutive form of Maria. *See* MARIA. (MAH-REE-ET-TAH)

Marina Derived from the Latin *marinus* (of the sea), which has its root in *mare* (the sea). (MAH-REE-NAH)

Marta Eastern European form of Martha, an Aramaic name derived from *mārthā* (lady, mistress). The name is borne in the Bible by the sister of Lazarus and Mary of Bethany. (MAR-TAH)

Martina Feminine form of Martin, from the Latin name Martīnus, which is derived from Mars, the name of the Roman mythological god of war. Short: Tina. (MAR-TEE-NAH)

Massima Derived from the Latin *maximus* (the greatest). (MAS-SEE-MAH)

Mathilde A borrowing from the German, Mathilde is from the Old High German Mahthilda, a compound name composed of the elements *maht* (might, power) and *hiltia* (battle): hence, "powerful in battle." Var: Matilda. Short: Tilda. Pet: Tillie, Tilly. (MAH-TIL-DEH)

Maura Feminine form of the Latin Maurus (a Moor). The Moors were a Muslim people of mixed Arab and Berber descent; the name came to mean "dark" or "swarthy" in reference to their coloring. (MAU-RAH)

Melania Derived from the Greek Melaina, which is from the root *melas* (black, dark). The name was made popular through its association with two 5th-century Roman saints, a grandmother and granddaughter remembered for their piety and good works for the poor. (MAY-LAH-NEE-AH)

Mercede Derived from the Italian *mercede* (reward, recompense, payment). (MARE-SAY-DAY)

Michaela Feminine form of Michael, which is derived from the Hebrew *mīkhā'ēl* (who is like God?). *See* MICHELE (Male Names). (MEE-KAY-LAH)

Niccola Feminine form of Niccolo (victory of the people), the Italian cognate of Nicholas. *See* NICCOLO (Male Names). (NEE-KO-LAH)

Nicia Feminine form of Niccolo, the Italian cognate of Nicholas (victory of the people). *See* NICCOLO (Male Names). (NIH-SEE-AH, NIH-CHEE-AH)

Nora A short form of Eleonora (light, torch, bright), Nora is also bestowed as an independent given name. *See* ELEONORA. (NOR-AH)

Nunzia Derived from the Italian *nunzio* (messenger), which is from the Latin *nuntius* (messenger). Alternatively, Nunzia is used as a short form of Annunziata. (NUN-ZEE-AH)

Olimpia Derived from the Greek Olympia, which is a feminine form of Olympios (of Olympus). Olympus is a mountain in northern Greece which was the home of the gods in Greek mythology. Short: Pia. (O-LIM-PEE-AH)

Oriana Of uncertain derivation and meaning, Oriana seems to have first been used as the name of a character in the medieval French romance *Amadis de Gaul.* Some believe Oriana to have been derived from the Latin *oriri* (to rise) or from the Old French *or* (gold). (O-REE-AH-NAH)

Ortensia Derived from the Latin Hortensia, a feminine form of the old Roman family name Hortensius (gardener), which is derived from *hortensius* (of a gardener), a derivative of *hortus* (a garden). (OR-TANE-SEE-AH)

Ottavia Feminine form of Octavius, which is derived from the Latin *octavus* (eighth). The name was borne by the wife of the Roman general Mark Antony. (O-TAH-VEE-AH)

Paola Feminine form of Paolo, the Italian cognate of Paul, which is from the Latin Paulus, a name originating as a Roman surname derived from *paulus* (small). *See* PAOLO (Male Names). (PAO-LAH)

Patrizia Feminine form of Patrizio, which is from the Latin *patricius* (a patrician, an aristocrat, noble). (PAH-TREET-ZEE-AH)

Paulina Latin name which is the feminine form of the Late Latin Paulīnus, a derivative of the Roman family name Paulus, which is from *paulus* (small). (PAU-LEE-NAH)

Philippa A borrowing from the Greek, Philippa is the feminine form of Philippos (lover of horses), which is from the elements *philos* (loving) and *hippos* (horse). Pet: Pippa. (FIL-LIP-PAH)

Pia A short form of Olimpia (of Olympus), Pia is also commonly bestowed as an independent given name. *See* OLIMPIA. (PEE-AH)

Rachel From the Ecclesiastic Late Latin and Ecclesiastic Greek Rhachēl, which is derived from the Hebrew *rāchēl* (ewe). The name is borne in the Bible by the younger of the two wives of Jacob. She was the mother of two of his sons, Joseph and Benjamin. Var: Rachele. (RAY-CHEL)

Rebecca From the Ecclesiastic Late Latin and Ecclesiastic Greek Rhebekka, which is derived from the

Hebrew *ribbqāh* (noose), from *rabak* (to bind, to tie). The name is borne in the Bible by the wife of Isaac and the mother of his sons Jacob and Esau. (RAY-BAY-KAH)

Regina Latin name directly derived from *rēgina* (queen), a feminine form of *rex* (king). Regina has been in use as a given name since the Middle Ages. (RAY-JEE-NAH)

Renata Feminine form of the Late Latin Renātus (reborn), which is derived from *renascor* (to be born again, to grow or rise again). The name is a common baptismal name signifying spiritual rebirth. (RAY-NAH-TAH)

Riccarda Feminine form of Riccardo, the Italian cognate of Richard (strong king). *See* RICCARDO (Male Names). Short: Rica, Ricca. (REE-KAR-DAH)

Rosa Popular name derived from the Latin *rosa* (a rose). (RO-SAH)

Rosabella Combination name composed of the names Rosa (rose) and Bella (pretty, charming, lovely, beautiful). (RO-SAH-BAY-LAH)

Rosalba Elaborated form of Rosa (a rose). (ROS-AHL-BAH)

Rosalia Derived from the Latin *rosalia* (the annual ceremony of hanging garlands of roses on tombs), which is from *rosa* (a rose). (RO-SAH-LEE-AH)

Rosamaria Popular combination name combining the names Rosa (a rose) and Maria (the name of the virgin mother of Jesus). *See* MARIA *and* ROSA. (RO-SAH-MAH-REE-AH)

Rosana Elaborated form of Rosa (a rose). (RO-SAH-NAH)

Rosetta Diminutive form of Rosa (a rose). Var: Roseta. (RO-SAY-TAH)

Rosina Elaborated form of Rosa (a rose). (RO-SEE-NAH)

Rufina Derived from the Latin *rufus* (reddish, red), Rufina originated as a nickname for one with red hair. (ROO-FEE-NAH)

Ruth Of uncertain etymology, some believe Ruth to be derived from the Hebrew *rūth*, a possible contraction of *rē'uth* (companion, friend). The name is borne in the Bible by a Moabite woman who was devoted to her mother-in-law. Her story is told in the Old Testament book of Ruth. (ROOTH)

Sabrina Of uncertain etymology, Sabrina is believed to be of Celtic origin, as it is borne in Celtic mythology by an illegitimate daughter of the Welsh king Locrine. *See* SABRINA (Welsh Names). (SAH-BREE-NAH)

Sancia Popular name derived from the Ecclesiastic Late Latin *sanctus* (a saint, holy). (SAHN-CHEE-AH)

Sandra A short form of Alessandra (defender or helper of mankind), Sandra is also bestowed as an independent given name. *See* ALESSANDRA. (SAHN-DRAH)

Santuzza Feminine diminutive form of the name Santo (holy, saintly), which is derived from the Latin *sanctus* (holy). (SAHN-TOO-ZAH)

Sara Derived from the Hebrew *sārāh* (princess). The name is borne in the Bible by the wife of the patriarch Abraham and mother of Isaac. (SAH-RAH)

Sebastiana Feminine form of Sebastiano (man of Sebastia). *See* SEBASTIANO (Male Names). Short: Bastiana. (SAY-BAHS-TEE-AH-NAH)

Serafina Derived from the Hebrew *sĕrāphīm* (burning ones), which is from *sāraph* (to burn). The name is used in the Bible for the heavenly winged angels surrounding the throne of God. Short: Fina. (SAY-RAH-FEE-NAH)

Serena Derived from the Latin *serenus* (clear, calm, serene, exalted). (SAY-RAY-NAH)

Severina Feminine form of Severino (stern, serious). *See* SEVERINO (Male Names). (SAY-VAY-REE-NAH)

Sigismonda Feminine form of Sigismondo, the Italian cognate of Sigmund, a compound name composed of the Germanic elements *sig* (victory, conquest) and *mund* (hand, protection): hence, "victorious protection." (SEE-GEES-MON-DAH)

Silvana Derived from the Middle Latin *silvanus* (sylvan, of the woods or forest), which is from the Latin *silva* (a wood). (SEEL-VAH-NAH)

Silvia Derived from the Latin *silva* (a wood). (SEEL-VEE-AH)

Simona Feminine form of Simon (heard). *See* SIMON (Male Names). (SEE-MO-NAH)

Sophia A borrowing from the Greek, Sophia is derived directly from *sophia* (wisdom, skill). The name is borne by Italian actress Sophia Loren (b. 1934). (SO-FEE-AH)

Speranza Derived from the Italian *speranza* (hope, expectation, confidence, trust). (SPAY-RAHN-ZAH)

Stefania Italian form of the Latin Stephania, which is a feminine form of Stephanus, a name derived from *stephanos* (a crown, a garland). (STAY-FAH-NEE-AH)

SUSANA Derived from the Hebrew Shoshana, which is from *shōshannāh* (a lily, a rose). The name is borne in the Bible by a woman, falsely accused of adultery, who was the wife of Joachim. Her story is told in the apocryphal book of Susannah and the Elders. (SOO-SAH-NAH)

SUZETTA Diminutive form of Susana (a lily, a rose). *See* SUSANA. (SOO-ZAY-TAH)

TAMAR A borrowing from the Hebrew Tamar (date palm, palm tree). The name Tamar is borne in the Bible by the daughter-in-law of Judah and the mother of his twin sons, and by a daughter of King David who was raped by Amnon, her half brother. (TAH-MAR)

TATIANA A borrowing from the Russian, Tatiana is a feminine form of the Latin Tatiānus, which is believed to be derived from Tatius, a name of uncertain origin which was borne by a king of the Sabines who ruled jointly with Romulus. (TAH-TEE-AH-NAH)

TEODORA From the Greek Theodōra (gift of God), a compound name composed of the elements *theos* (God) and *dōron* (a gift). Short: Dora. (TAY-O-DOR-AH)

TESS A pet form of Therese, Tess is also bestowed as an independent given name. *See* THERESE. Pet: Tessi. (TESS)

THEKLA A borrowing from the Greek, Thekla is derived from Theokleia, a compound name composed of the elements *theos* (God) and *kleos* (glory): hence, "divine glory." The name was borne by the first virgin martyr, who is said to have been a disciple of St. Paul. Var: Tecla. (TEK-LAH)

THERESE Of uncertain etymology, Therese is generally believed to be derived from the Greek *therizein* (to reap, to gather in). The first known bearer of the name was the Spanish wife of St. Paulinus, a 5th-century Roman bishop of Nola. Theresa was not used outside the Iberian Peninsula until the 16th century, when the fame of St. Teresa of Avila (1515–82) made the name popular among Roman Catholics throughout Europe. Var: Teresa. Pet: Resi, Tess, Tessi. (TEH-RAY-SAH)

TIBERIA Feminine form of Tiberio (of the Tiber), a name taken from that of the Tiber River. (TEE-BAY-REE-AH)

TILDA A short form of Matilda (brave in battle), Tilda is also occasionally bestowed as an independent given name. *See* MATHILDE. Pet: Tillie, Tilly. (TEEL-DAH)

ULLA A borrowing from the Scandinavians, Ulla is derived from the Old Norse *ullr* (will, determination). (OO-LAH)

VALENTINA Feminine form of Valentine, from the Latin Valentinus, which is derived from *valens* (strong, vigorous, powerful). Short: Tina. (VAH-LANE-TEE-NAH)

VIOLETTA From the Old French *violette*, a diminutive form of *viole*, which is derived from the Latin *viola* (a violet). (VEE-O-LAY-TAH)

VIRGINIA Derived from the Latin Verginius (spring-like, flourishing), an old Roman family name, which has its root in *ver* (spring). (VER-JEE-NEE-AH)

VITTORIA Derived from the Italian *vittoria* (victory), which is from the Latin *victoria* (victory). (VIT-TOR-EE-AH)

VIVIANA From the Latin Vivianus, which has its root in *vivus* (alive). Var: Bibiana, Bibiane. (VEE-VEE-AH-NAH)

ZOLA Derived from the Italian *zolla* (a dirt clod, a ball of earth). (ZO-LAH)

Chapter Sixteen

Japanese Names

Originally, Japanese family names were used only by nobility, the military class, and those to whom the emperor granted the privilege. About fourteen hundred characters are used as first elements, to which about one hundred other characters, usually relating to topographical or landscape features, were added as final elements. Several clan names were also in use, but only by hereditary right or by special privilege.

After 1868 and the abolishment of feudalism, the policy changed and all people were allowed a family name. Today, most of the surnames are derived from nature, but some are derived from occupations.

Traditionally, male children are given a short, simple name in a ceremony six days following their birth. At the age of fifteen or sixteen, another ceremony is held and a formal name is given by which he will be known to all outside his family. In general, male names infer excellence, strength, and good luck. Number names are also common, some of which relate to birth order, long life, and good omens.

While most female names are derived from words that have straightforward meanings, such as Jin (tenderness, gentleness), others have hidden meanings. For example, many names are derived from nature, but instead of having a literal meaning, these names are usually symbols of sought-after virtues or admirable qualities. The name Matsuko (pine tree child) is not bestowed upon a child because the parents like pine trees. Rather, it is symbolic of the parents' wish for their child to live a long life.

Japanese Male Names

Akemi Dawn of beauty. (AH-KEH-MEE)

Akihiko Bright boy. (AH-KEE-HEE-KO)

Akio Bright boy. (AH-KEE-O)

Akira Intelligent, smart. (AH-KEE-RA)

Botan Borrowed from the name of the peony flower, the flower of the month of June. It is indicative of long life. (BAH-TAHN)

Chōkichi Long-lasting good luck. (CHO-KEE-CHEE)

Eiji Second-born son. (EE-JEE)

Gohachiro Five eight male. The name can be bestowed on the thirteenth child. (GO-HAH-CHEE-RO)

Gorō Fifth son. (GO-RO)

Hachiuma Eight horses. (HAH-CHEE-OO-MAH)

Harō Wild boar's first son. (HAH-RO)

Harue Born in the spring. Derived from *haru* (spring). (HAH-ROO-EH)

Hideaki Wise, discerning. (HEE-DEH-AH-KEE)

Hideo Excellent male. (HEE-DEH-O)

Hirohito A name borne by the present emperor, His Imperial Majesty Hirohito. He is the 124th emperor of the Imperial Dynasty, a line that has remained unbroken since the first emperor of Japan, Jinmu, ascended the throne more than 2,600 years ago. (HEE-RO-HEE-TŌ)

Hiromasa Composed from elements meaning "wise" and "straightforward." (HEE-RO-MAH-SA)

Hiroshi Generous. (HEE-RO-SHEE)

Hisoka Reserved, reticent. (HEE-SO-KA)

Hitoshi Derived from *hito* (one). (HEE-TŌ-SHEE)

Hosyu Derived from *hosyu* (conservativeness). (HO-SYU)

Huyu Winter. (HOO-YOO)

Ichirō First-born son. (EE-CHEE-RO)

Isas Worthy, meritorious. (EE-SAS)

Isi Rock. (EE-SEE)

Isoroku Fifty-six. (EE-SO-RO-KOO)

Jiro Second-born male. (JEE-RO)

Jun Obedient. (JUN)

Kamenosuke Turtle's helper. (KAH-MEN-O-SOO-KEH)

Kane Golden. (KA-NEH)

Kanji Popular name derived from the Japanese *kan* (tin). (KAHN-JEE)

Katsutoshi To win cleverly. (KAHT-SOO-TŌ-SHEE)

Kazuo First-born son. Derived from *kazu* (number). (KAH-ZOO)

Ken The same. (KEN)

Kenji Second son. (KEN-JEE)

Kin Golden. (KEEN)

Kiyoshi Quiet. (KEE-YO-SHI)

Koji Child, little. (KO-JEE)

Kumakichi Fortunate bear. (KOO-MAH-KEE-CHEE)

Makoto Sincerity, honesty. (MAH-KO-TŌ)

Masahiro Composed from elements meaning "straightforward" and "wise." (MAH-SAH-HEE-RO)

Masao Righteous, holy. (MAH-SAH-O)

Masato Justice. (MAH-SAH-TŌ)

Nagataka Everlasting filial duty. (NAH-GAH-TAH-KAH)

Naoko Straight, honest. (NAH-O-KO)

Ogano Little deer field. (O-GAH-NO)

Ozuru Big stork. (O-ZOO-ROO)

Saburo Third-born male. (SAH-BOO-RO)

Shiro Fourth-born son. (SHEE-RO)

Shūzō Third-born son. (SHOO-ZO)

Taizo Third-born son. (TAH-EE-ZO)

Takeshi Bamboo tree, unbending. (TAH-KEH-SHEE)

Taro First-born male. (TAH-RO)

Tobikuma Flying cloud. (TŌ-BEE-KOO-MAH)

Tokutaro Virtue first male. (TŌ-KOO-TAH-RO)

Tomi Rich, prosperous. (TŌ-MEE)

Torao Tiger man. (TŌ-RAH-O)

Toshihiro Composed from elements meaning "intelligent" and "wise." (TŌ-SHEE-HEE-RO)

Yasahiro Composed from elements meaning "tranquil" and "wise." (YAH-SAH-HEE-RO)

Yasuo Tranquil, calm. (YAH-SOO-O)

Yemon Guarding the gate. Derived from *mon* (gate). (YEH-MONE)

Yukio Snow boy. Derived from *yuki* (snow). (YOO-KEE-O)

Zinan Second son. (ZEE-NAN)

Japanese Female Names

Ai Derived from *ai* (love). (AH-EE)

Aiko Derived from *ai* (love) and *ko* (child): hence, "child of love, love child." (AH-EE-KO)

Akahana Derived from the elements *aka* (red, bright) and *hana* (flower): hence, "red or bright flower." Var: Akina. (AH-KAH-HAH-NAH)

AKAKO Derived from the Japanese *aka* (red). (AH-KAH-KO)

AKASUKI Composed from the elements *aka* (red) and *suki* (fond of): hence, "fond of red." (AH-KAH-SOO-KEE)

AKI Born in the autumn. Derived from *aki* (autumn). (AH-KEE)

ANZU Apricot. (AHN-ZOO)

AOI Hollyhock. (AH-OY)

ASA Derived from *asa* (morning), this name can have the definition "born in the morning." (AH-SAH)

ASAKO Child born in the morning. (AH-SAH-KO)

AYAKO Child of damask. (AH-YAH-KO)

AYAMĒ Derived from *ayamē* (iris). (AH-YAH-MEH)

AYAMEKO Derived from *ayamē* (iris) and *ko* (child): hence, "child of the iris." (AH-YAH-MEH-KO)

AYUMI Pace, walk. (AH-YOO-MEE)

AZAMI The flower of a thistle. (AH-ZAH-MEE)

BACHIKO Happy child. (BAH-CHEE-KO)

CHIKA Wisdom, intelligence. (CHEEKA)

CHIKAKO Child of wisdom. (CHEE-KAH-KO)

CHIYO A thousand generations. (CHEE-YO)

CHIYOKO Child of a thousand generations. (CHEE-YO-KO)

CHIZU A thousand storks. (CHEE-ZOO)

CHIZUKO Child of a thousand storks. (CHEE-ZOO-KO).

CHO Derived from *cho* (dawn), this name can mean "born at dawn." (CHO)

CHOKO Child of the dawn, born at dawn. (CHO-KO)

CHOYO A generation of dawns. (CHO-YO)

DAI Stand, base. (DAH-EE)

ETSU Delight. (ET-SOO)

ETSUKO Child of delight. (ET-SOO-KO)

ETSUYO A generation of delight. (ET-SOO-YO)

FUJIKO Child of the wisteria. (FOO-JEE-KO)

FUYU Derived from *fuyu* (winter), this name can mean "born in winter." (FOO-YOO)

FUYUKO Child of the winter. (FOO-YOO-KO)

GEN Spring, origin, source. (JEN)

GIN Derived from *gin* (silver). (JIN)

HAMA Shore, beach. (HAH-MAH)

HAMAKO Child of the shore. (HAH-MAH-KO)

HANA Bloom, blossom, flower. (HAH-NAH)

HANAE Tree branch blossom. (HAH-NAH-EH)

HANAKO Flower child. (HAH-NAH-KO)

HARU Born in spring. Derived from *haru* (spring). (HAH-ROO)

HARUE Tree branch spring. (HAH-ROO-EH)

HARUKO Spring child. (HAH-ROO-KO)

HATSU First born. (HAHT-SOO)

HAYA Quick, nimble. (HAH-YAH)

HIDÉ Excellent, superior. (HEE-DAY)

HIDEYO Excellent generation. (HEE-DEH-YO)

HIROKO Magnanimous, generous. (HEAR-O-KO)

HISA Enduring, lasting, sustaining. (HEE-SAH)

HISAE Enduring tree branch. (HEE-SAH-EH)

HISAKO Enduring child. (HEE-SAH-KO)

HISANO Long plain. (HEE-SAH-NO)

HISAYO Sustaining generation. (HEE-SAH-YO)

HOSHI Star. (HO-SHEE)

HOSHIKO Child of the star. (HO-SHEE-KO)

HOSHIYO Generation of the star. (HO-SHEE-YO)

IKU Nourishing, sustaining. (EE-KOO)

IKUKO Sustaining child. (EE-KOO-KO)

IMA Present, now. (EE-MAH)

IMAE Present generation. (EE-MAH-EH)

IMAKO Present child. (EE-MAH-KO)

INÉ Rice. The name connotes a nurturing character. (EE-NAY)

ISAMU Vigorous, robust, energetic. (EE-SAH-MOO)

ISHI Stone. The name connotes a firm, dependable, enduring character. (EE-SHEE)

ISHIKO Child of stone. (EE-SHEE-KO)

ITO Thread. (EE-TŌ)

IWA Rock. Like the name Ishi, Iwa denotes strength of character. (EE-WAH)

Jin Tenderness, gentleness. (JEEN)

Jun Obedience. (JUN)

Junko Child of obedience. (JUN-KO)

Kagami Mirror. (KAH-GAH-MEE)

Kai Forgiveness. (KAH-EE)

Kaiko Child of forgiveness. (KAH-EE-KO)

Kaiyo Generation child. (KAH-EE-YO)

Kamé Tortoise. The name denotes a long life. (KAH-MEH)

Kameko Tortoise child. (KAH-MEH-KO)

Kameyo Tortoise generation. (KAH-MEH-YO)

Kaminari Derived from the Japanese *kaminari* (thunder). (KAH-MEE-NAH-REE)

Kane Doubly accomplished. (KAH-NEE)

Kaneko Doubly accomplished child. (KAH-NEH-KO)

Kaoru Fragrance. (KAH-O-ROO)

Katsu Victorious. (KAHT-SOO)

Katsuko Victorious child. (KAHT-SOO-KO)

Kazu First; obedient, disciplined. (KAH-ZOO)

Kazuko Obedient child. (KAH-ZOO-KO)

Kei Popular name meaning "reverence, rapture, awe." (KEH-EE)

Keiko Child of reverence. (KEH-EE-KO)

Kichi Fortunate, lucky. Var: Kicki. (KEE-CHEE)

Kiku Crysanthemum branch. The crysanthemum is the flower assigned to the month of November. (KEE-KOO)

Kikue Tree branch crysanthemum. (KEE-KOO-EH)

Kikuko Crysanthemum branch child. (KEE-KOO-KO)

Kimi Without equal. (KIMMIE)

Kimie Tree branch without equal, inlet without equal. (KIM-MEE-EH)

Kimiko Child without equal. (KEE-MEE-KO)

Kimiyo Generation child. (KEE-MEE-YO)

Kin Derived from *kin* (gold). (KIN)

Kinu Derived from *kinu* (silk). (KEE-NOO)

Kinuko Child of silk. (KEE-NOO-KO)

Kinuyo Silk generation. (KEE-NOO-YO)

Kishi Beach, seashore. (KEE-SHEE)

Kishiko Child of the seashore. (KEE-SHEE-KO)

Kiwa Born on a border. (KEE-WAH)

Kiwako Child born on a border. (KEE-WAH-KO)

Kiwayo Generation on a border. (KEE-WAH-YO)

Kiyo Happy generations. The name connotes a scandal-free life or a life of purity. (KEE-YO)

Kiyoko Child of happy generations. (KEE-YO-KO)

Kiyoshi Bright, shining, clear. (KEE-YO-SHEE)

Ko Filial duty, daughterly devotion, child. (KO)

Kohana Compound name composed of the elements *ko* (little, child) and *hana* (flower): hence, "little flower." (KO-HAH-NAH)

Koko Here. (KO-KO)

Koma Derived from the elements *ko* (little, child) and *uma* (horse): hence, "foal, pony." It is also used as a traditional term of endearment. (KO-MAH)

Komako Pony child. (KO-MAH-KO)

Komé Rice. The name is indicative of a nurturing, dependable character. (KO-MEH)

Komeko Rice child. (KO-MEH-KO)

Koneko Derived from the Japanese *ko-neko* (kitten), which is from *neko* (cat). (KO-NEH-KO)

Koto Harp. (KO-TŌ)

Kukiko Snow child. (KOO-KEE-KO)

Kumi Popular name meaning "braid." (KOO-MEE)

Kumiko Child with braids. (KOO-MEE-KO)

Kumiyo Braid generation. (KOO-MEE-YO)

Kuni Born in the country. (KOO-NEE)

Kuniko Child born in the country. (KOO-NEE-KO)

Kyoko Mirror. (KEE-YO-KO)

Leiko Arrogant. (LEH-EE-KO)

Machi Ten thousand thousand. The name is indicative of the parents' desire for a long life for their child. (MAH-CHEE)

Mai Every, each. (MAY)

Mari Popular name derived from *mari* (ball). (MAH-REE)

Mariko Ball child. (MAH-REE-KO)

Masa Straightforward, honest. (MAH-SAH)

Masago Sand. (MAH-SAH-GO)

Matsu Derived from the root *matu* (pine), Matsu has the definition "pine tree." It is indicative of the parents' wish for their child to live a long life. (MAHT-SOO)

Matsuko Pine tree child. (MAHT-SOO-KO)

Matsuyo Pine tree generation. (MAHT-SOO-YO)

Michiko Beautiful, wise. The name is borne by the Japanese empress. (MEE-CHEE-KO)

Midori Derived from the Japanese *midori* (green). The name is borne by gifted violinist Midori Ito. (MEE-DOR-EE)

Mieko Bright. (MEE-EH-KO)

Mikazuki New moon. (MEE-KA-ZOO-KEE)

Miki Trunk of the family tree. Derived from *miki* (tree trunk). (MEE-KEE)

Mikie Generation tree trunk. (MEE-KEE-EH)

Mikiko Child of the tree trunk. (MEE-KEE-KO)

Mikka Derived from *mikka* (third day, three days). (MEEK-KA)

Minako Three seven child. (MEE-NAH-KO)

Minami South. Var: Miniami. (MEE-NAH-MEE)

Miné Peak, summit. (MEE-NEH)

Mineko Child of the summit. (MEE-NEH-KO)

Misao Fidelity, loyalty. (MEE-SAH-O)

Misoka Derived from *misoka* (the last day of the month). The name can mean "born on the last day of the month." (MEE-SO-KAH)

Mitsu Light. (MEET-SOO)

Mitsuko Child of the light. (MEET-SOO-KO)

Miyo Beautiful child. (MEE-YO)

Miyuki Silence of deep snow. Derived from the Japanese *yuki* (snow), the name can be indicative of a quiet, peaceful, and serene character. (MEE-YOO-KEE)

Mizuko Derived from *mizu* (water) and *ko* (child), the name can be indicative of a pure character. (MEE-ZOO-KO)

Mon Derived from the Japanese *mon* (gateway). (MON)

Mori Derived from the Japanese *mori* (wood, forest). (MO-REE)

Morie Tree branch of the forest. (MO-REE-EH)

Moriko Child of the forest. (MO-REE-KO)

Moriyo Generation forest. (MO-REE-YO)

Moto Derived from the Japanese *moto* (origin, source, fount). (MO-TŌ)

Motoko Child of the source. (MO-TŌ-KO)

Muika Derived from the Japanese *muika* (sixth day, six days), the name can be indicative of a child born on the sixth day of the week. (MOO-EE-KA)

Mura Derived from the Japanese *mura* (village). (MOO-RAH)

Murasaki Derived from the Japanese *murasaki* (the color purple). (MOOR-AH-SAH-KEE)

Nagisa The seashore. (NAH-GEE-SAH)

Nami Derived from the Japanese *nami* (surf, wave). Var: Namiko. (NAH-MEE)

Nao Right, honest. (NAH-O)

Nariko Gentle child. (NAH-REE-KO)

Natsu Born during the summer. Derived from the Japanese *natsu* (summer). (NAHT-SOO)

Natsuko Child of summer. (NAHT-SOO-KO)

Natsuyo Summer generation. (NAHT-SOO-YO)

Nishi Born in the west. Derived from the Japanese *nishi* (west). (NEE-SHEE)

Nishie West inlet. (NEE-SHEE-EH)

Nishiko Child of the west. (NEE-SHEE-KO)

Nishiyo West generation. (NEE-SHEE-YO)

Nyoko Gem. (NEE-YO-KO)

Rai Derived from the Japanese *rai-*, a prefix meaning "next." (RAH-EE)

Raiko Next child. (RAH-EE-KO)

Raku Derived from the Japanese *raku na* (easy, comfortable). (RAH-KOO)

Ran Popular name meaning "water lily." In Japan, the water lily is viewed as a symbol of purity. (RAHN)

Rei Derived from *rei* (thanks, appreciation, favor). (REH-EE)

Riku Derived from *riku* (land). (REE-KOO)

Rikuyo Generation of the land. (REE-KOO-YO)

ROKUKO Sixth born. Derived from the Japanese *roku* (six). (RO-KOO-KO)

SACHI Derived from the Japanese *sachi* (bliss). (SAH-CHEE)

SACHIKO Child of bliss. (SAH-CHEE-KO)

SAKAE Prosperity. (SAH-KAH-EH)

SAKURA Derived from the Japanese *sakura* (cherry, cherry blossom). The cherry blossom is a Japanese symbol of prosperity. (SAH-KUH-RAH)

SEIKO Derived from *seiko* (success, achievement). (SAY-KO)

SETSU Fidelity, loyalty, faithfulness. (SET-SOO)

SETSUKO Child of fidelity. (SET-SOO-KO)

SHINA Derived from the Japanese *shin* (faithful, loyal). (SHEE-NAH)

SHINAKO Faithful child. (SHEE-NAH-KO)

SHIZU Quiet, calm, clear. (SHEE-ZOO)

SHIZUE Quiet inlet. (SHEE-ZOO-EH)

SHIZUKO Quiet child. (SHEE-ZOO-KO)

SHIZUYO Quiet generation. (SHEE-ZOO-YO)

SUGI Derived from the Japanese *sugi* (cedar). The cedar tree is viewed as a symbol of morality. (SOO-GEE)

SUKI Derived from the Japanese *suki* (fond of). Var: Sukie. (SOO-KEE)

SUMIKO Derived from the Japanese *sumi* (corner; charcoal). (SOO-ME-KO)

SUZU Derived from *suzu* (bell). (SOO-ZOO)

SUZUKI Compound name composed from the elements *suzu* (bell) and *ki* (tree; yellow): hence, "yellow bell" or "bell tree." (SOO-ZOO-KEE)

SUZUME Derived from *suzume* (sparrow). (SOO-ZOO-MEE)

TAKARA Treasure, jewel. (TAH-KAH-RAH)

TAKEKO Derived from *take* (bamboo) and *ko* (child). Bamboo is seen as a symbol of resistance and strength; something unbending. (TAH-KEH-KO)

TAMA Derived from *tama* (ball, jewel). (TAH-MAH)

TAMAKO Jewel child. (TAH-MAH-KO)

TAMAYO Generation jewel. (TAH-MAH-YO)

TAMI People. (TAH-MEE)

TAMIE Tree branch people. (TAH-MEE-EH)

TAMIKO People child. (TAH-MEE-KO)

TANÉ Derived from the Japanese *tane* (a seed). (TAH-NEH)

TOOKA Derived from the Japanese *tooka* (tenth day, ten days). (TOO-OO-KAH)

TOOKAYO Tenth-day generation. (TOO-OO-KAH-YO)

TORI Derived from the Japanese *tori* (bird). (TŌ-REE)

TSUHGI Second-born child. (TSOO-GHEE)

TSURUKO Derived from *tsuru* (crane) and *ko* (child). The crane is viewed as a symbol of good luck and a long life. (TSOO-ROO-KO)

TUKIKO Derived from *tuki* (moon) and *ko* (child): hence, "child of the moon." (TOO-KEE-KO)

TUKIYO Moon generation. (TOO-KEE-YO)

UMÉ Derived from the Japanese *umé* (plum blossom). The name is indicative of wifely fidelity and devotion. (OO-MEH)

UMÉKI Derived from *umé* (plum blossom) and *ki* (tree): hence, "plum tree." (OO-MEH-KEE)

UMEKO Plum blossom child. (OO-MEH-KO)

UMIKO Derived from *umi* (the sea) and *ko* (child): hence, "child of the sea." (OO-MEE-KO)

UTA Derived from *uta* (song, poem). (OO-TAH)

UTAKO Child of the song. (OO-TAH-KO)

YOKKAKO Derived from *yokka* (fourth day, four days) and *ko* (child): hence, "child of the fourth day." (YOK-KAH-KO)

YOKO Four; positive; side. (YO-KO)

YOSHE Popular name meaning "a beauty, lovely." (YO-SHEH)

YOSHI Popular name meaning "good." (YO-SHEE)

YOSHIKO Good child. (YO-SHEE-KO)

YUKI Derived from *yuki* (snow). (YOO-KEE)

YUKIE Snow inlet, snow tree branch. (YOO-KEE-EH)

YUKIKO Snow child. (YOO-KEE-KO)

Chapter Seventeen

Jewish/Hebrew Names

THE STUDY of Jewish nomenclature is a fascinating one. The changes wrought upon Jewish names by so many different influences over the course of time can take one on a remarkable journey into European history. Often this bewildering array of social, political, and linguistic influences has altered many names until hardly a trace of their true forms can be found.

As surnames were being established in Europe from the 11th through the 16th centuries, Jewish people also began to add a second name to their first. Most often, patronymics and matronymics were used, as well as names indicating places of origin. To these were added names formed from abbreviations of words that reflected a special occasion in the life of the family, or names from a combination of abbreviated forms of the personal name and patronymic.

During this time, surnames were rarely fixed or hereditary and were not considered as important as the first. They merely helped to identify people having the same first name. For Ashkenazic Jews who were forced to live in special ghettos, this situation was actually desirable, for the ensuing governmental confusion it caused made it easier to avoid paying taxes and evade conscription into the army.

It wasn't until 1787, when Joseph II of Austria ordered all Jews to adopt fixed and hereditary surnames, that Jewish family names began to be regulated. The trend continued across Europe and ended with Russia mandating fixed surnames in 1845. In Germany and Austria, government officials forced those registering their names to pay. If a "good" name was desired, the payment was dear. Those who did not have the means of paying for a good name were given names such as Schmalz (grease) or Lugner (liar). In Hitlerian Germany it was decreed that all persons of Jewish birth, but having non-Jewish names, take the name Israel if a male and Sarah if female to identify themselves as Jews.

Early Jewish names were simply Hebrew names and remained so for many generations. However, after the destruction of the first temple and the Babylonian captivity, foreign influences began to be seen. Babylonian and Persian names were used, and soon Aramaic and Greek names were as well and actually predominated over Hebrew names during the Talmudic period.

The practice of having two personal names dates to several centuries before the destruction of the second temple. Originally, two Hebrew names were used. Soon, it was acceptable to use a Hebrew and an Aramaic name. Later, a Jewish and a non-Jewish name became popular as Greek influence grew and the Greek language began to be used by all. The Jewish name was used at home and between family and friends; the non-Jewish name was reserved for use when doing business or having contact with non-Jews. Many Hebrew names were Hellenized or Romanized, and in time, the non-Jewish name became the more important one.

This trend was not as significant among females. Aramaic names were common, as were some Greek and Latin names, but for the most part, the names stayed true to form. Because women were excluded from politics and business, there was little need to Hellenize or Romanize their Jewish names. The male name Yitzchak was Hellenized as Isaak and Isaakios, for example, but female names such as Martha and Sarah retained their true forms.

As Jewish people began to establish residences in many European countries, their names began to be influenced by local languages and trends such as nicknames and diminutive forms. They often adopted names common to the countries in which they resided or translated their Hebrew names into the language spoken in those countries.

In ancient times it was unheard-of to name a child after a living person. It was thought that a person's life essence would be transferred to the child and that the older person would die. Some also felt that the Angel of Death would make a mistake and take the child when it was time for the adult to die. And if the child was given the name of a deceased relative, it would interfere with the dead person's eternal rest.

In time, these beliefs fell to the wayside, and during the Talmudic period, it became commonplace to name the child for a relative or favored friend, living or dead. It came to be believed that this helped keep the memory of the deceased alive, and that it would keep the spirit alive of those still living. Among the more superstitious Ashkenazim, however, this practice is avoided for fear that the Angel of Death will make a mistake and take the life of the child.

The male child is named during the ritual of circumcision eight days after the birth. Until recently, no uniform practice of naming baby girls was established. Some named their daughters in a home ceremony; some in the synagogue on the first Sabbath the mother could be there following the birth; some in the synagogue when the father was called to the Torah. Lately, new naming and dedication ceremonies have come into being to welcome the baby girls into the Jewish faith with as much reverence as is done with a male child.

Nowadays, Jewish people in America tend to use the same names in popular usage throughout the country. However, many of those who have emotional or familial ties to Israel have shown interest in the types of names being used in that country today. In an effort to right the wrongs of centuries of persecution and prejudice, the Israeli government encouraged people to Hebraize their names or to give themselves both first and last Hebrew names. Foreign influences are now frowned upon and the Bible has become a prime source for names. Because of the relatively small number of female names in the Bible, place-names and the names of plants are often used, and the trend of making feminine forms from male names is popular. As in the United States, modern coinages are popular, but unlike many modern U.S. names, Israeli names have meanings expressive of the hopes and dreams and Zionist feelings of a newly liberated people.

Jewish/Hebrew Male Names

ABBA Aramaic name meaning "father." The name was borne by many Talmudic scholars. (AHB-BAH)

ABEL Derived from the Hebrew *hebel* (breath). Alternatively, some believe it is an Assyrian name meaning "meadow." The name is borne in the Old Testament by the second child of Adam and Eve. (Ā-BEL)

ABIEL My father is God. Abiel is borne in the Bible by the great-grandfather of King Saul. Var: Aviel. (AH-BĪ-EL)

ACHARON Last, latest. Acharon is traditionally bestowed upon the last son. (AH-CHAR-ON)

ACHAV Father's brother. The name is borne in the Old

Testament by a wicked king of Israel, the husband of Jezebel. Var: Ahab. (AH-CHAHV)

ACHAZYA God has grasped. The name is borne in the Old Testament by a king of Israel, a son of Ahab. Var: Achazia, Achaziah, Achazyahu, Ahaziah, Ahaziahu. (AH-CHA-ZĪ-AH)

ACHBAN Brother of an intelligent one. The name is borne in the Old Testament by a member of the tribe of Judah. (ACH-BAHN)

ACHER Hebrew name meaning "other." (AH-KER)

ACHIDA My brother is intelligent. (AH-KEE-DAH)

ACHIMELECH The king is my brother. The name is borne in the Old Testament by a priest who showed kindness to David and was thenceforth put to death by King Saul. Var: Ahimelech. (AH-KIM-MEH-LEK)

ACHISAR My brother is a prince. (AH-KEE-SAR)

ACHISHAR My brother is a song. Achishar is borne in the Old Testament by an officer who presided over the household of Solomon. Var: Ahishar. (AH-KEE-SHAR)

ACHIYA God is my brother. Var: Achiyahu, Ahia, Ahiah. (AH-KEE-YAH)

ADAEL Adorned by God, ornament of God. The name was borne by several Old Testament characters, including a leader of the tribe of Simeon. Var: Adiel. (AD-EE-EL)

ADAIAH Adorned by God, God's witness. The name was borne by a leader of the tribe of Benjamin. Var: Adaia, Adaya. (AH-DAY-Ī-AH)

ADAM Derived from the Hebrew *adama* (red earth). The name is borne in the Bible by the first man created by God. It was from his rib that Eve was supposedly formed. (AD-AM)

ADIN Beautiful, pleasant. Var: Aden. (Ā-DIN)

ADIR Noble, royal, majestic. (AH-DEER)

ADIV Pleasant, mild-mannered. (AH-DEEV)

ADLAI Aramaic name meaning "refuge of God, justice of the Lord." The name is borne in the Bible by the father of Shaphat, the overseer of King David's cattle. (ADD-LAY-Ī, ADD-LĪ)

ADMON Derived from the Hebrew *adama* (red earth). The name is borrowed from that of a type of red peony flower. (ADD-MON)

ADON Lord. (A-DŌN)

ADONIAH My Lord is Jehovah. The name is borne in the Bible by the fourth son of David. Var: Adonia, Adonijah, Adoniya, Adoniyahu. (ADD-O-NĪ-AH)

ADRIEL Flock of God. Some give it the alternative definition "God is my majesty." The name is borne in the Bible by the son-in-law of King Saul. (Ā-DREE-ELL)

AHARON The exalted one. The name is borne in the Bible by the elder brother of Moses and Miriam. In the Talmud, the name is borne by a 5th-century Babylonian scholar. Var: Aaron, Aron. (AHR-ON)

AKIVA Variant form of the Hebrew Yaakov, which is derived from *ya'aqob* (seizing by the heel, supplanting). The name was borne by several Talmudic scholars, including 1st-century Palestinian Akavya ben Mehalalel. Var: Akavia, Akaviah, Akavya, Akiba. Short: Kiba, Kiva. (AH-KEE-VAH)

ALITZ Joyful, lighthearted. Var: Aliz. (AH-LEETZ)

ALLON Oak tree. The name denotes a tree that served as a landmark near Zaanannim in biblical times. Var: Alon. (AL-LON)

AMARIAH Said of God. Amariah is borne in the Bible by a descendant of Aaron by Eleazar. He is thought to have been the last high priest of Eleazar's line. Var: Amaria, Amariahu, Amarya, Amaryahu. (AH-MAH-RĪ-AH)

AMASA Burden. The name is borne in the Bible by a nephew of King David. (AH-MAY-SAH)

AMASAI Burdensome. Amasai is borne by several Old Testament characters, including one of the priests appointed to proceed before the Ark with the blowing of trumpets while it was moved from the house of Obed-edom. (AH-MAY-SAH-EE)

AMASIAH Burden of God. The name is borne in the Bible by a captain in Jehoshaphat's army. Var: Amasia, Amasya. (AH-MAH-SĪ-AH)

AMIR Strong, powerful, mighty. (AH-MEER)

AMIRAM My nation is mighty. (AH-MEER-UM)

AMMIEL People of God. The name is borne by several Old Testament characters, including the father of Bathsheba. Var: Amiel. (AM-MEE-EL)

AMNON Faithful. The name Amnon was borne by the eldest son of King David. Var: Aminon. (AM-NON)

AMON Hebrew name meaning "hidden" or "builder." The name was borne by the fourteenth king of Judah. Var: Ammon. (Ā-MON)

Amos Borne, a burden. The name was borne by one of the twelve minor prophets, one of the first to have his prophecies recorded in writing. (Ā-MŌS)

Amoz Strong, powerful. The name is borne in the Bible by the father of Isaiah. Var: Amotz. (Ā-MAHZ)

Anaiah Jehovah has answered. Anaiah is borne in the Bible by a Jew who helped seal the covenant with Nehemiah. Var: Anaia, Anaya. (AH-NAH-Ī-AH)

Arach To prepare. The name is borne in the Talmud by the father of Elazar, a 1st-century Palestinian scholar. (ARE-OCK)

Ari Derived from the Hebrew *'arī* (lion). Var: Arie. (ARE-REE)

Ariel Derived from the Hebrew *'arī'ēl* (lion of God). In the Old Testament, the name is used as a symbolic name for Jerusalem. Var: Arel, Aryel, Aryell. (AR-REE-EL)

Arioch Lion-like; kingly. The name is borne in the Bible by a captain of Nebuchadnezzar's bodyguard. Var: Aryoch. (AR-EE-OK)

Arles Popular modern name derived from the Hebrew *eravon* (pledge, a promise to pay). Var: Arlee, Arleigh, Arley, Arlie, Arlis, Arliss, Arly. (AR-LZ)

Asa Aramaic name meaning "physician, to heal." The name was borne by the third king of Judah. (Ā-SAH)

Asaph Collector, gatherer. Asaph was one of the leaders in King David's choir. Var: Asaf, Asif, Asiph. (Ā-SAF)

Asher Popular name meaning "happy, blessed." It is borne in the Bible by Jacob's eighth son by Zilpah, his wife's maid. Var: Anschel, Anshel, Anshil (Yiddish). (ASH-ER)

Asriel Prince of God. (AS-REE-EL)

Ataiah The Lord is helper. It is borne in the Old Testament by a son of Uzziah of the tribe of Judah. Var: Ataya. (AH-TAH-Ī-AH)

Atzel Hebrew name meaning "noble" or "reserved, reserve." It is borne in the Bible by a descendant of King Saul. Var: Azel. (AT-ZULL)

Aviah My father is the Lord. The name is borne in the Bible by a son of Samuel. Var: Abia, Abiah, Abijah, Avia, Aviya. (AH-VĪ-AH)

Avikar My father is precious. (AH-VEE-KAR)

Aviram My father is mighty, father of height. The name is borne in the Old Testament by a conspirator who helped instigate a rebellion against Moses. Var: Abiram. (AH-VEE-RUM)

Avishai Aramaic name meaning "gift of God." It is borne in the Old Testament by the eldest son of David's sister Zeruiah. Var: Abishai, Avisha, Avshai. (AH-VEE-SHY)

Avital Father of dew. The name is borne in the Bible by one of David's six sons. Var: Abital, Avitul. (AH-VEE-TULL)

Aviur Father of fire. (AH-VEE-URR)

Aviv Spring. (AH-VEEV)

Avner Father of light, father is a lamp. The name was borne by a cousin of King Saul and commander in chief of his army. Var: Abner, Aviner. (AV-NUR)

Avraham Father of a multitude, father of many. The name is borne in the Bible by the first Hebrew, the patriarch of both the Arabs and the Hebrews. His original name was Avram, but upon accepting the one true God, added the Hebrew letter *H*, which is symbolic of God, thus changing it to Avraham. Var: Abraham (Ang.); Avrom, Avrum, Avrumke (Yiddish). Short: Bram. (Ā-VRA-HAM)

Avram Exalted father. It was the original name of Avraham. Var: Abram (Ang.). Short: Bram. (Ā-VRAM)

Az Strong, mighty. (AZ)

Azai Aramaic name meaning "strength." Var: Azzai. (AZ-ZĪ)

Azaniah Jehovah has given an ear, the hearing of God. Var: Azania, Azaniya, Azanyahu. (AZ-AH-NĪ-AH)

Azarael God is helper. It is borne in the Bible by several characters, including a temple musician during the reign of David. Var: Azareel, Azarel. (AZ-AH-RAY-EL)

Azariah Help of God. The name is borne in the Bible by a king of Judah. Var: Azaria, Azariahu, Azarya, Azaryahu. (AZ-AH-RĪ-AH)

Aziel God is my strength. (Ā-ZEE-EL)

Azrael Derived from the Hebrew *'azra'ēl* (help of God). According to ancient Jewish belief, Azrael is the name of the angel of God who parts the soul from the body at the time of death. Var: Azriel. (AZ-REE-ELL)

Bachir Eldest son. (BAH-SHEER)

Bachur Young man, youth. (BAH-SHOOR)

Barak Lightning, a flash of light. The name is borne in the Old Testament by the son of Abinoam who waged a successful war campaign against Jabin at the urging of the prophetess Deborah. (BAR-RAK)

BARTHOLOMEW From the Greek Bartholomaios, a patronymic meaning "son of Talmai." Talmai is an Aramaic name meaning "hill, mound, furrows." (BAR-THOL-O-MEW)

BARUCH Blessed. The name is borne in the Bible by the prophet Jeremiah's scribe. The apocryphal book of Baruch is attributed to him. (BAH-ROOK)

BECHER Hebrew name meaning "first-born, a youth." It is borne in the Bible by the second son of Benjamin. Var: Bechor. (BEE-CHER)

BEN Hebrew name meaning "son." The name is borne in the Bible by a priestly musician chosen by King David to serve before the Ark. (BEN)

BENAIAH Hebrew name meaning "God has built, built by Jehovah." The name was borne by a warrior and captain of King David's bodyguard who rose to the rank of commander in chief under King Solomon. Var: Benaya, Benayahu. (BEN-NAH-Ī-AH)

BINYAMIN Hebrew name meaning "son of the right hand." The name is borne in the Old Testament by the youngest of Jacob's twelve sons, the patriarch of the tribe of Benjamin. Var: Minyamin, Minyomei, Minyomi; Benjamin (Ang.). Short: Ben. (BIN-YAH-MIN)

BRAM Short form of Abraham (father of a multitude) and Abram (father is exalted). *See* AVRAHAM *and* AVRAM. (BRAM)

CHADLAI Aramaic name meaning "to cease, resting." The name was borne by the father of Amasa, a descendant of Ephraim. Var: Hadlai. (CHAD-LAH-Ī)

CHAGIAH Festival of God. The name is borne in the Bible by a Levite of the family of Merari. Var: Chagia, Chagiya, Haggiah, Hagia. (CHA-GĪ-AH)

CHAI Life. Var: Hai. (CHĪ)

CHALFON To change; to pass away. Var: Chalfan, Halfon, Halphon. (CHAL-FON)

CHALIL Flute. Var: Halil, Hallil. (CHA-LIL)

CHAM Warm, hot. The name Cham is borne in the Bible by the second son of Noah, one of the three progenitors of mankind after the Great Flood. Var: Ham. (CHAM)

CHANANIAH Popular Hebrew name meaning "the compassion of God, Jehovah has given." The name was borne by several Old Testament characters, including Shadrach, a young Hebrew captive who emerged from a blazing furnace unharmed. Var: Chanania, Chananya, Chananyahu, Chanina, Hanania, Hananiah. (CHA-NAH-NĪ-AH)

CHANIEL The grace of God. Var: Channiel, Haniel, Hanniel. (CHANE-EE-ELL)

CHANOCH Dedicated, initiated. The name Chanoch is borne in the Bible by the first-born son of Cain, after whom Cain founded and named a city. It is the first city mentioned in Scripture. Var: Hanoch; Enoch (Ang.). (CHAY-NOK)

CHASID Pious, devout, righteous. Var: Chasud. (CHA-SID)

CHASIEL Refuge of the Lord. Var: Hasiel. (CHA-SYELL)

CHASIN Strong, mighty. Var: Chason, Hasin, Hassin, Hason. (CHA-SIN)

CHAVIV Beloved. Var: Habib, Haviv. (CHA-VEEV)

CHAYIM Life. Chaim Weizmann (1874–1952) was Israel's first president in 1949. Var: Chaim, Chayyim, Chayym, Haim, Hayyim, Hayym. (CHĪ-YIM)

CHAZAIAH God has seen, Jehovah sees. Var: Chazaya, Hazaia, Hazaiah. (CHA-ZĪ-AH)

CHAZIEL Vision of God. Var: Haziel. (CHAY-ZEE-ELL)

CHEILEM Strength. Var: Chelem. (CHEL-LUM)

CHETZRON Enclosed, a settlement. The name is borne in the Bible by a son of Reuben. Var: Hezron. (CHEZ-RON)

CHIRAM Derived from the Hebrew *'ahīrām* (lofty, exalted, exalted brother). The name is borne in the Bible by a king of Tyre who entered into an allegiance with King David and later King Solomon. Var: Hiram. (CHĪ-REM)

CHIZKIAH Derived from the Hebrew *hizqīyāh* (Yahweh strengthens, God is my strength). The name is borne in the Bible by a king of Judah who reigned at the time of Isaiah. Var: Chizkia, Chizkiya, Chizkiyahu; Hezekiah (Ang.). (CHIZ-KĪ-AH)

CHONEN Gracious. (CHO-NUN)

CHOZAI Aramaic name meaning "prophet." Var: Hozai. (CHO-ZĪ)

CYRUS Derived from the Old Persian *kūrush* (sun?). The name was borne by Cyrus the Great, founder of the Persian Empire and liberator of the Jews from their Babylonian captivity. (SĪ-RUS)

DALFON Hebrew name meaning "raindrop." Var: Dalphon. (DAL-FON)

DAN Judge. The name is borne in the Old Testament by the fifth of Jacob's twelve sons. He was the progenitor of the tribe of Dan. The name is also used as a short form of Daniel (God is my judge). *See* DANIEL. Var: Dana. (DAN)

DANIEL Derived from the Hebrew *dānī'ēl* (God is my judge). The name is most famously borne by one of the major prophets. His faith in God kept him alive in a den of hungry lions. His story and prophecies are recorded in the Book of Daniel. Short: Dan. Pet: Danny. (DAN-YELL)

DARIUS Ancient name of uncertain meaning. It is thought to ultimately be derived from the Persian Daryavahush, the name of an ancient Persian king. The name takes the definition "king, kingly, one who is wealthy." (DAH-RĪ-US)

DATIEL Knowledge of Jehovah. (DAT-YELL)

DAVID Derived from the Hebrew *dāvīd* (beloved). The name is borne in the Bible by the eighth and youngest son of Jesse. He became the second and greatest of the Israelite kings, the successor of King Saul and the father of King Solomon. Var: Davyd. Short: Dave. Pet: Davey, Davi, Davy, Tavi. (DAY-VID)

DEKER To pierce. (DEH-KER)

DISHON To tread upon, to thresh. (DĪ-SHON)

DIVON To tread gently. (DĪ-VON)

DORON Derived from the Greek *dōron* (gift). (DOR-ON)

DOVID Yiddish form of David (beloved). *See* DAVID. Pet: Dudel. (DŌ-VID)

DURIEL God is my dwelling. (DUR-YELL)

EBEN Stone. Var: Eban, Even. (EH-BEN)

EBENEZER Derived from the Hebrew *eben-ha-'ēzer* (stone of help). Var: Evenezer. (EH-BEN-EE-ZER)

EDEN Derived from the Hebrew *'ēdhen* (delight). The Garden of Eden was the name of the paradise where Adam and Eve were created and first lived. Var: Edan. (EE-DUN)

EFRON A bird. Var: Ephron. (EE-FRON)

EHUD United. (Ā-HUDE)

EIFAH Darkness, gloom. The name is borne in the Bible by a grandson of Abraham. Var: Efa, Efah, Eifa, Epha, Ephah. (EE-FAH)

EILAM Eternal. Eilam is borne in the Old Testament by a grandson of Noah. Var: Elam. (EE-LAM)

EKER Root, an offspring. (EE-KER)

ELAN Tree. (EE-LUN)

ELAZAR Derived from the Hebrew *el'āzār* (God has helped). The name is borne in the Bible by several characters, including one of the two sons of Moses. Var: Eleazar, Eliezer; Lazer (Yiddish). Short: Lazar. (EL-Ā-ZAR)

ELI Derived from the Hebrew *'ēlī* (high, ascent). The name is borne in the Bible by a high priest of Israel at a time when the ark was at Shiloh. Var: Eili. (EE-LĪ)

ELIAKIM God will raise up, God will establish. It is borne in the Bible by several characters, including a son of Hilkiah who became governor of the palace of Hezekiah. Var: Elika, Elyakim, Elyakum. (EE-LĪ-AH-KIM)

ELIAZ My God is strong. (EE-LĪ-AZ)

ELIJAH Derived from the Hebrew *'ēlīyāhū* (Jehovah is God). The name was borne by a 9th-century B.C. prophet who, after many years of service, was taken up into heaven in a chariot of fire. Var: Elia. (EE-LĪ-JAH)

ELIMELECH My God is the King. The name was borne by the husband of Naomi and father-in-law of Ruth. (EE-LIM-MEH-LEK)

ELIRAN My God is song. Var: Eliron. (EE-LĪ-REN)

ELISHA Derived from the Hebrew *elīshā'* (God is salvation). The name was borne by the disciple and successor of Elijah. (EE-LĪ-SHA)

ELISHUA Derived from the Hebrew *elīshā'* (God is salvation). The name is borne in the Bible by a son of King David. (EE-LĪ-SHOO-AH)

ELIYAHU The Lord is my God. Short: Eliya. (EE-LĪ-YAH-HOO)

ELKANAH God created, God bought. The name is borne in the Bible by several characters, including the husband of Hannah and the father of Samuel. Var: Elkan, Elkin (Yiddish). (EL-KAY-NAH)

ELRAD God is the king. Var: Elrod. (ELL-RUD)

EMEK Valley. (EE-MEK)

ENOSH Man. Enosh was the name of a son of Seth. Var: Enos. (EE-NOSH)

EPHRAYIM Very fruitful. The name is borne in the Bible by the second son of Joseph and Asenath, progenitor of the tribe named after him. Var: Efraim, Efrayim, Efrem, Ephraim. (EE-FRAH-IM)

ERAN Watcher, awake. The name Eran is borne in the Bible by a grandson of Ephraim. (EE-RAHN)

Erel I will see God. (EE-REL)

Erez Cedar. (AIR-EZ)

Esau Derived from the Hebrew *'ēsāw* (hairy). The name is borne in the Bible by the elder twin son of Rebekah. He sold his birthright and later his covenant blessing to his brother Jacob. (EE-SAW)

Ethan Derived from the Hebrew *ēthān* (strength, firmness). Var: Eitan, Etan, Eytan. (EE-THUN)

Evron Jewish form of Ephrayim (very fruitful). *See* EPHRAYIM. (EV-RON)

Ezra Derived from the Hebrew *ezrā* (help). The name is borne in the Bible by a Hebrew prophet and religious reformer of the 5th century B.C. His story and prophecies are recorded in the Old Testament book of Ezra. (EZ-RA)

Ezri My help. (EZ-RĪ)

Faivish Yiddish form of Phoebus, a name derived from the Greek *phoibos* (bright one). Pet: Fayvel, Feivel, Feiwel. (FAY-VISH)

Gabriel Derived from the Hebrew *gavhri'ēl* (God is my strength). The name is borne in the Bible by an angel seen by Daniel in a vision, one of the seven archangels of God and the herald of Good News. Var: Gavrel, Gavriel. Short: Gabri, Gavri. Pet: Gabby, Gabe, Gabi. (GAY-BREE-ELL)

Gaddiel Fortune sent from God. The name is borne in the Bible by one of the twelve sent by Moses to scout the land. Var: Gadiel. (GAD-DEE-ELL)

Gamliel God is my reward. Var: Gamaliel. (GAM-LEE-ELL)

Gedaliah God is great, made great by Jehovah. The name Gedaliah is borne in the Bible by several characters. Var: Gedalia, Gedaliahu, Gedalya, Gedalyahu. (JED-AH-LĪ-AH)

Gefaniah The Lord's vineyard. Var: Gefania, Gefanya, Gephania, Gephaniah. (JEF-AH-NĪ-AH)

Geshem Shower, rain. (GEE-SHEM)

Gevariah The might of Jehovah. Var: Gevaria, Gevarya, Gevaryah, Gevaryahu. (GEV-AH-RĪ-AH)

Gidon Derived from the Hebrew *gidh'ōn* (hewer, mighty warrior). The name is borne in the Bible by an Israelite judge and leader in the defeat of the Midianites. Var: Gidoni; Gideon (Ang.). (GID-ON)

Gilad Hill of testimony. It is borrowed from that of a mountainous area east of Jordan. Var: Giladi; Gilead (Ang.). (GIL-AD)

Gilam Joy of a people. (GIL-LUM)

Gilon Joy. (GIL-ON)

Gomer Hebrew name used for both males and females meaning "complete, to end, vanishing." (GO-MER)

Guryon Lion. Var: Garon, Gorion, Gurion. (GOOR-EE-ON)

Hadriel Splendor of Jehovah. (HAD-REE-ELL)

Haskel Wisdom. Var: Chaskel, Haskell, Heskel. (HAS-KEL)

Hassan Derived from the Arabic *hasan* (beautiful, handsome, good). (HAHS-SAN)

Hevel Derived from the Hebrew *hebel* (breath, vapor). Abel is the Anglicized form of the name. (HEH-VEL)

Hirsh Popular Yiddish name derived from the German *hirsh* (deer). Var: Hersch, Hersh, Hertz, Herz, Hesh, Hirsch. Pet: Herschel, Hershel, Hertzel, Herzl, Heschel. (HURSH)

Hodiah Yahweh is my splendor. Var: Hodia, Hodiya. (HO-DĪ-AH)

Hoshama Heard of God, whom Jehovah hears. (HO-SHAH-MAH)

Hosheia Derived from the Hebrew *hōshēa'* (salvation). The name was borne by the first of the minor prophets, and the only one from the northern kingdom whose writings have been preserved. Var: Hosea (Ang.). (HO-SHE-AH)

Ikabod Derived from the Hebrew *ī-khābhōdh* (inglorious, without honor). Var: Ichabod, Ikavod. (IK-AH-BOD)

Ira Derived from the Hebrew *'īrā* (watchful). (Ī-RAH)

Isaac Anglicized form of Yitzchak (he will laugh). *See* YITZCHAK. Isaac was the son of Abraham and Sarah, and is considered the patriarch of the Hebrew people. Pet: Ike, Isa, Issa. (Ī-ZĀK)

Isaiah Derived from the Hebrew *yĕsha 'yah* (Yahweh is salvation). The name was borne by an 8th-century B.C. prophet considered to be the greatest of the three major prophets. Pet: Isa, Issa. (Ī-ZAY-AH)

Israel Derived from the Hebrew *yisrā'ēl* (contender with God). The name was bestowed upon Jacob after his struggle with the angel at Peniel. Israel is also the collective name of the twelve tribes descended from Jacob's twelve sons. (IZ-RAY-EL)

Jacob Anglicized form of Yaakov (seizing by the heel, supplanting). *See* YAAKOV. The name is borne in the

Bible by the younger twin brother of Esau. Jacob was the husband of Leah and Rachel and the father of twelve sons, who became the patriarchs of the twelve tribes of Israel. Pet: Jack, Jake. (JAY-KOB)

JARED Anglicized form of Yared (descendant). (JARE-ED)

JEREMIAH Anglicized form of the Hebrew Yirmeyahu (the Lord loosens, God will uplift). The name was borne by a minor prophet of the 7th and 6th centuries B.C. His prophecies and warnings of the future are recorded in the Old Testament book of Jeremiah. Pet: Jeremy. (JARE-EE-MĪ-AH)

JOHN Anglicized form of Yochanan, which is derived from the Hebrew *yehōhānān* (Yahweh is gracious). (JON)

JONATHAN Anglicized form of Yehonatan, which is derived from the Hebrew *yehōnāthān* (Yahweh has given). Short: Jon, Nathan. Pet: Jonnie, Jonny. (JON-AH-THUN)

JORDAN Anglicized form of Yarden (to flow down, descend). The name is that of the chief river of ancient Palestine. (JOR-DAN)

JOSEPH Anglicized form of Yosef, which is from the Hebrew *yōsēf* (may he add, God shall add). The name is borne in the Old Testament by a favorite son of Jacob and Rachel who was sold into slavery by his jealous brothers. Short: Joe. Pet: Joey. (JO-SEF, JO-ZEF)

JOSHUA Anglicized form of the Hebrew Yehoshua (God is salvation, Jehovah is help). The name is borne in the Bible by Moses' successor, who led the children of Israel into the Promised Land. Of all the Israelites born in Egypt, only Joshua and Caleb lived to occupy Canaan. His history is recorded in the Old Testament book of Joshua. Short: Josh. (JOSH-YOO-AH)

JOSIAH Anglicized form of the Hebrew Yoshiyah (the Lord supports, the Lord saves, the Lord heals). Josiah was a celebrated 7th-century B.C. king of Judah who led his people back to God. (JO-SĪ-AH)

KADMIEL God is the first, God is my east. The name was borne by the head of a Levite family who returned to Judah following the Babylonian exile. (KAD-MEE-EL)

KAHANA Aramaic name meaning "priest." (KAH-HAH-NAH)

KALEB Derived from the Hebrew *kālēb* (dog). The name, which is indicative of faithfulness, was borne by one of the twelve scouts sent by Moses to explore the Promised Land. He became a leader of Israel following Moses' death. Var: Kalev; Caleb (Ang.). (KAY-LEB)

KALIL Crown, wreath, garland. Var: Kailil. (KAY-LIL)

KAYAM Established. (KAY-YAM)

KEFIR A young lion, a lion cub. (KEE-FER)

KELAYA Aramaic name meaning "parched grain." (KEE-LAY-AH)

KEMUEL To stand up for God, helper of God. (KEH-MYOO-EL)

KENAN To acquire, to possess. The name is borne in the Bible by a son of Enosh. Var: Cainan. (KEE-NAN)

KEREM Vineyard. (KERR-REM)

KOLAIAH Voice of God. Var: Kolaia, Kolaya, Kolia, Koliya, Kolya. (KO-LAY-AH)

KONANIAH The establishment of Jehovah. Var: Konania, Konanya. (KO-NAH-NĪ-AH)

KOPPEL Yiddish pet form of Jacob, the Anglicized form of Yaakov (seizing by the heel). *See* YAAKOV. Var: Kapel. (KAH-PL)

KORESH To dig, to dig in the earth, farmer. The name is borne in the Bible by a Persian conqueror of Babylonia who was friendly toward the Jews. Var: Choreish, Choresh. (KOR-ESH)

LABAN Derived from the Hebrew *lābhān* (white). The name was borne by the father of Rachel and Leah. Var: Lavan. (LAY-BAHN)

LADAN A witness. (LAY-DAHN)

LAEL Belonging to Jehovah. (LAY-EL)

LAZER Yiddish form of Elazar (God has helped). *See* ELAZAR. (LAY-ZR)

LEV Hebrew name meaning "heart." It is also used as a short form of Levi (joining, adhesion). *See* LEVI. (LEEV)

LEVI Derived from the Hebrew *lēwī* (joining, adhesion). The name is borne in the Bible by the third son of Jacob and Leah. He was the progenitor of the tribe of Levi, which took on the priestly duties for the twelve tribes. Var: Lavi, Levai. Short: Lev. (LEE-VĪ)

LIAM My people, my nation. Var: Lyam. (LEE-UM)

LIRON My song, the song is mine. Var: Lyron. (LEE-RON)

MAASEIYA Creations of Jehovah, work of Jehovah. Var: Maaseiah, Masai. (MAY-AH-SĪ-AH)

MACCABEE Derived from the Aramaic *maqqābā* (hammer). The name originated from Maccabees, the surname of a family of Jewish patriots who led a successful revolt against the Syrians and henceforth ruled Palestine until 37 B.C. Var: Macabee, Makabi. (MAK-AH-BEE)

Machir Sold, merchandise. The name is borne in the Bible by a grandson of Jacob. (MAY-CHIR)

Malach Messenger, angel. (MAL-LAHK)

Malachi Derived from the Hebrew *mal'ākhī* (my messenger). The name was borne by a 5th-century B.C. prophet, the last of the Hebrew prophets. His prophecies of the coming Messiah and Judgment Day are recorded in the Old Testament book of Malachi. Var: Malachai, Malachy. (MAL-AH-KĪ)

Malkam Their king, God is their king. Var: Malcam, Malcham. (MAL-KAM)

Malki My king. (MAL-KĪ)

Malkiah Jehovah is my king, God is my king. Var: Malkia, Malkiya, Malkiyahu. (MAL-KĪ-AH)

Maluch Aramaic name meaning "king, ruler, reigning." (MAL-LUK)

Manasseh Popular Anglicized form of Menashe (who makes to forget). *See* MENASHE. Short: Mana. Pet: Mani. (MAH-NAHS-SEE)

Mani A pet form of any of the names beginning with the element *Man-*, Mani is also bestowed as an independent given name. Var: Manni, Manny, Mannye. (MAN-NEE)

Manoach Rest. The name is borne in the Old Testament by the father of Samson. Var: Manoa, Manoah. Pet: Mani. (MAH-NO-AHK)

Maon Dwelling, habitation. (MAY-ON)

Maresha Hilltop, summit. Maresha was the name of a son of Caleb. (MAH-REE-SHAH)

Mat Short form of any of the various names beginning with the element *Mat-*. Var: Matt. (MAT)

Mataniah Gift of God. Var: Matania, Matanya, Mattaniah. Short: Mat. (MAT-AH-NĪ-AH)

Matityah Derived from the Hebrew *mattīthyāh* (gift of God). Var: Matitia, Matitiah, Matityahu; Matthew (Ang.); Mattathias (Greek). Short: Mat, Matt, Matya. (MAT-I-TĪ-AH)

Matok Sweet. (MA-TOK)

Mattan Gift. Var: Matan, Matena, Maton, Mattun. Short: Mat. (MAT-TAN)

Meir Popular Hebrew name meaning "bright one, shining one." Var: Mayer, Meyer, Myer. (MY-URR)

Melech King, ruler. (MEE-LEK)

Menachem Popular Hebrew name meaning "comforter, comforting." The name is borne by Menahem Begin, prime minister of Israel (1977–83). Var: Menahem; Mendel (Yiddish). (MEN-AH-KEM)

Menashe Causing to forget. The name was borne by the eldest son of Joseph. Var: Menashi, Menashya; Manasseh (Ang.). (MEH-NAH-SHA)

Methushelach Derived from the Hebrew *methūshelach*, which possibly means "man who was sent, man of the dart, man of Shelah [a Babylonian god]." The name is borne in the Bible by the longest-living man. He is said to have died at the age of 969 years. Var: Methuselah, Metushelach. (MEH-THOO-SHA-LAHK)

Micha Derived from the Hebrew *mīkhāyah* (who is like God?). The name is borne in the Bible by several Old Testament characters, including an 8th-century B.C. prophet of Judah who predicted the destruction of the cities of Jerusalem and Samaria. His prophecies are found in the book of Micah. Var: Mica, Micah, Mika. (MĪ-KAH)

Michael Derived from the Hebrew *mīkhā'ēl* (who is like God?). The name is borne by one of the archangels, the one closest to God who has the responsibility of carrying out God's judgments. Michael is regarded as the leader of the heavenly host. Var: Michel, Mikel, Mychal. Short: Mica, Micah, Micha, Mikka. Pet: Micky, Miky. (MĪ-KAY-EL)

Midian Derived from the Hebrew *midhyān* (strife). The name was borne by the fourth son of Abraham by Keturah. (MID-EE-UN)

Moran Teacher, guide. (MOR-AN)

Mordechai Derived from the Hebrew *mordĕlhai*, which possibly means "a little man" or "worshiper of Marduk." The name is borne by the cousin and foster father of Queen Esther. He saved the Jews from the destruction planned by Haman, an event celebrated by the Jewish feast of Purim. Var: Mordecai; Mordche (Yiddish). Pet: Mordi; Motche (Yiddish). (MOR-DEH-KAY-Ī)

Mori My teacher, my guide. Var: Morie. (MOR-EE)

Moriel God is my teacher, Jehovah is my guide. (MOR-Ī-EL)

Mosha Salvation. (MO-SHA)

Moshe Derived from the Hebrew *mōsheh* (drawn out, drawn out of the water), which is thought to be from the Egyptian *mes*, *mesu* (son, child). The name was borne by the leader who brought the Israelites out of bondage in Egypt. He received the Ten Commandments on Mount Sinai and led his people to the borders of Canaan and the Promised Land. Moshe is one of the most popular of the Jewish names. Var: Moise, Mose, Moses, Moss, Moyse (Ang.). (MO-SHE)

NACHUM Derived from the Hebrew *nachūm* (comfort). The name is borne by a minor Hebrew prophet of the 7th century B.C. His prophecies are recorded in the Old Testament book of Nahum. Var: Nahum. (NAY-KAHM)

NADIR Oath. (NAY-DEER)

NAGID Ruler. (NAY-GEED, NAY-JEED)

NAHOR Aramaic name meaning "light, lamp." Var: Nahir, Nahur, Nehor. (NAY-HOR)

NAIM Sweet. (NAY-EEM)

NAT Short form of any of the names beginning with the element *Nat-*. (NAT)

NATHAN Derived from the Hebrew *nāthān* (gift). The name is borne in the Bible by a prophet who rebuked King David for the death of Uriah, which enabled the king to marry Bathsheba, Uriah's wife. Var: Natan. Short: Nat, Nate. (NAY-THUN)

NECHEMYA Derived from the Hebrew *nechemyāh* (comforted by the Lord, comfort of Jah). The name is borne in the Bible by a Hebrew leader of about the 5th century B.C. He was a patriot of the exile and governor of the city of Jerusalem, which he returned to physical and religious order. His story is told in the Old Testament book of Nehemiah. Var: Nechemia, Nechemiah, Nehemiah. (NEK-EH-MĪ-AH, NEE-AH-MĪ-AH)

NECHUM Derived from the Hebrew *nechum* (comfort). Var: Nehum. (NEE-KUM)

NEDAVIAH Moved of Jehovah, generosity of the Lord. Var: Nedabiah, Nedavia, Nedavya. Short: Ned. (NED-AH-VĪ-AH)

NETANIAH Gift of Jehovah. Var: Netania, Netanya, Nethaniah. (NEH-TAH-NĪ-AH)

NETHANEL Derived from the Hebrew *něthan'ēl* (gift of God). The name is borne in the Old Testament by the fourth son of Jesse. Var: Nathanael, Nathanel, Nathaniel, Nethanial. Short: Nat, Nate. (NEH-THAN-EL)

NIRAM Cultivated fields of the people. (NĪ-RUM)

NISAN Derived from *nīsān* (miracle). Nisan is the name of the seventh Jewish month, during which the Passover holiday occurs. Var: Nissan. (NEE-SAHN, NIS-SEN)

NOACH Derived from *nōach* (rest, comfort). Noach is the original Hebrew form of Noah, the one commanded by God to build the ark. *See* NOAH. (NO-UK)

NOADIAH Assembly of God, meeting with the Lord. Var: Noadia, Noadya. (NO-AH-DĪ-AH)

NOAH Derived from the Hebrew *nōach* (rest, comfort). The name is borne in the Bible by the patriarch commanded by God to build the ark, upon which he saved his family and two of every creature from the Great Flood. He is seen as the second progenitor of the human race. Noach is the original Hebrew form of the name. (NO-AH)

OBADIAH Derived from the Hebrew *'ōbhadhyāh* (servant of the Lord). The name is borne in the Bible by one of the minor Hebrew prophets. His prophecies are found in the book of Obadiah. Var: Ovadiah. (Ō-BAH-DĪ-AH)

OMAR Eloquent. The name Omar is borne in the Bible by the grandson of Esau. Var: Omer. (O-MAR)

OMRI Hebrew name of debated meaning. Some believe it means "servant of Jehovah." Others think it means "my sheaf." The name is borne in the Bible by a king of Israel (885–874 B.C.) who chose Samaria as his new capital city. (OM-RĪ)

ORAN Aramaic name meaning "light." (O-RAN)

OREN Hebrew name meaning "a pine tree, a cedar tree, an ash tree." Var: Orin, Orrin. (O-REN)

OREV Raven. (O-REV)

ORON Light. (O-RON)

OSHEA Helped by God, saved by God. Var: Oshaya. (O-SHE-AH)

OTHNIEL Lion of God, strength of God. The name is borne in the Bible by the first of the Hebrew judges. His wife Achsah, a daughter of Caleb, was given to him as a reward for his bravery in leading a successful expedition against Debir. Var: Otniel. (OTH-NEE-EL)

OVED Servant, serving. The name was borne by a son of Naomi. He was the father of Jesse and grandfather of King David. Var: Obed. (O-VED)

OZ Strength. The name Oz is also used as a short form of Ozni (hearing, my hearing). (ŌZ)

OZNI Hearing, my hearing. The name was borne by a grandson of Jacob. Short: Oz. (OZ-NĪ)

PAGIEL God allots, to pray to God. The name is borne in the Old Testament by a chief of the tribe of Asher. (PAY-JEE-EL)

PEDAHEL Redeemed of God. The name is borne in the Bible by a chief of the tribe of Naphtali. Var: Pedael. (PEH-DAH-EL)

PEDAT Redemption. (PEE-DAT, PEH-DAT)

PERACH Flower, blossom. Var: Perah. (PER-UK)

PERACHIAH Flower of Jehovah. Var: Perachia, Perachya. (PER-AH-KĪ-AH)

PERETZ Burst forth, breach. Var: Perez, Pharez. (PER-RETZ)

PETUEL Aramaic name meaning "vision of God." The name is borne in the Bible by the father of the prophet Joel. (PEH-TYOO-EL)

PINCHAS Hebrew name meaning "the mouth of a snake, mouth of brass." It may also be derived from the Egyptian *penechase* (Negro, dark-complexioned). The name is borne in the Bible by a grandson of Aaron, a high priest who became the chief adviser in the war with the Benjamites. Var: Phineas, Phinehas, Pinchos, Pinhas. (PIN-CHAS)

RAAMAH Thunder. Var: Raam. (RAY-AH-MAH)

RAAMIAH Hebrew name meaning "God's thunder." Var: Raamia, Raamya. (RAY-AH-MĪ-AH)

RAANAN Fresh, beautiful. Var: Ranan. (RAY-AH-NAN)

RACHAM Compassion, pity, mercy. Var: Raham. (RAY-KAHM)

RACHIM Aramaic name meaning "compassion." Var: Rahim. (RAY-KIM)

RACHMIEL Compassion of Jehovah, compassion from God. (RAYK-MEE-EL)

RAFA Heal. Var: Rapha (Ang.). (RAF-FAH)

RANEN To sing, to be joyful. Var: Ranon. (RA-NEN)

RAVIYA Hebrew name meaning "fourth, four." Var: Ravia. (RAH-VEE-YAH)

RAZIEL Aramaic name meaning "secret of Jehovah, God is my secret." (RA-ZEE-EL)

REPHAEL Derived from the Hebrew *refā'ēl* (God has healed). The name is borne by one of the seven archangels, the divine messenger mentioned in the Apocrypha. Var: Rafael, Raphael, Refael. Pet: Rafi, Refi. (REH-FAY-EL)

REPHAIAH Jehovah has healed. Var: Refaia, Refaya, Rephaia. (REH-FAY-AH)

RESHEPH Flame, fever, burning. The name is borne in the Bible by one of Ephraim's descendants. Var: Reshef. (REE-SHEF)

REUBEN Derived from the Hebrew *rĕūbēn* (behold, a son!). Reuben was the eldest son of Jacob and Leah, and patriarch of the tribe bearing his name. Var: Re'uven, Reuven, Ruben, Rubin. (ROO-BEN)

REUEL Hebrew name meaning "friend of God." Reuel is a name of Jethro, the father-in-law of Moses. Var: Ruel. (REE-OO-EL)

RISHON The first. (RIH-SHON)

RIVAI Strife, contention. (RIH-VĪ)

RON Hebrew name meaning "song, joy." Ron is also in use as a female name. (RON)

RONEL Song of Jehovah, joy of the Lord. (RON-EL)

RONI My song, my joy. Roni is also in use as a female name. (RON-EE)

ROSH Chief. (RŌSH)

ROZEN Ruler. (RŌ-ZEN)

SAAD Aramaic name meaning "help, support." (SAHD)

SAADIAH Aramaic name meaning "support of God, the help of God." Var: Saadia, Saadya, Saadyah. (SAH-DĪ-AH)

SACHAR A short form of Yisachar (there is reward), Sachar is also bestowed as an independent given name. *See* YISACHAR. (SAH-KAR, SAH-KER)

SALU Aramaic name meaning "basket." (SAH-LOO)

SAMAL Aramaic name meaning "symbol, sign." (SAH-MAHL)

SAMI Aramaic name meaning "high, exalted." (SAH-MEE)

SAMSON Derived from the Hebrew *shimshōn* (the sun). The name is borne in the Bible by an Israelite judge whose great strength stemmed from his long hair, which as a Nazarite he was forbidden to cut. He was treacherously betrayed to the Philistines by his mistress, Delilah. Samson and Delilah is a popular biblical story. Var: Sampson. (SAM-SUN)

SAMUEL Anglicized form of Shmuel (name of God, his name is God). The name is borne in the Bible by a Hebrew judge and prophet who anointed Saul as the first king of Israel. Short: Sam. Pet: Sammy, Samy. (SAM-YOO-EL)

SARAPH Derived from the Hebrew *sāraph* (to burn). The name is borne in the Bible by a descendant of Judah. Var: Saraf, Seraf, Seraph. (SAR-AF)

SAUL Derived from the Hebrew *sha'ūl* (asked for, asked of God). The name is borne in the Bible by the first Israelite king. Shaul is the original Hebrew form. (SOL)

SELIG Yiddish name meaning "happy." (SEE-lig)

SETH Anglicized form of Shet (appointed). It is borne in the Bible by the third son of Adam and Eve. (SETH)

SHACHAR Dawn, morning light. (SHAH-KAR)

SHACHOR Black. Var: Shahor. (SHAH-KOR)

SHADMON Farm. (SHAD-MON)

SHAFAN A badger, a coney (a type of rabbit). The name is borne in the Bible by a scribe of King Josiah. Var: Shaphan. (SHAY-FAN)

SHAFER Aramaic name meaning "good, handsome." (SHA-FER)

SHAI Aramaic name meaning "gift." Shai is also in use as a pet form of Isaiah (God is salvation). *See* ISAIAH. (SHY)

SHALEV Peaceful, calm, quiet. (SHAY-LEV)

SHALLUM Of debated meaning, some define Shallum as "retribution." Others think it means "whole." The name is borne in the Bible by many characters, including a son of King Josiah. Var: Shalem, Shalum. (SHAL-LUM)

SHALMAI Aramaic name meaning "peace." (SHAL-MĪ)

SHAMIR Aramaic and Hebrew name meaning "a sharp thorn, flint." According to Jewish legend, shamir was an extremely hard rock-like substance created at twilight on Sabbath Eve. Solomon used the shamir to cut the gigantic stones required for the building of the temple. Var: Shamur. (SHAY-MIR)

SHAMMAI Aramaic name meaning "name." Var: Shamai. (SHAM-MAY-Ī)

SHANI Scarlet, bright red. (SHA-NEE)

SHAUL Derived from the Hebrew *shā'ūl* (asked for, asked of God). The name was borne by the first Israelite king. Saul is the Anglicized form. (SHAY-OOL)

SHEFER Pleasant, nice, beautiful. (SHE-FER)

SHELESH Third-born child. (SHE-LESH)

SHEM Derived from the Hebrew *shēm* (name, renowned). The name is borne in the Bible by the eldest of Noah's three sons. They are considered the progenitors of the human race after the Great Flood. (SHEM)

SHEMAIAH Aramaic name meaning "whom Jehovah heard, heard of Jehovah." The name was borne by many biblical characters. Var: Shemaia, Shemaya. (SHEM-MI-AH)

SHEMARIAH Hebrew name meaning "whom Jehovah guards, protection of the Lord." Var: Shemaria, Shemarya, Shemaryahu, Shmarya; Shmerel (Yiddish). (SHEM-AH-RĪ-AH)

SHET Derived from the Hebrew *shēth* (appointed). The name is borne in the Bible by the third son of Adam and Eve, born after the death of Abel at the hands of his brother, Cain. Seth is the Anglicized form of the name. (SHET)

SHEVI Return. (SHEV-EE)

SHEVUEL Return to God. Var: Shvuel. (SHEV-YOO-EL)

SHILLEM Reward, recompense, requittal. It is borne in the Bible by the fourth son of Naphtali. Var: Shilem. (SHIL-LEM)

SHILOH Hebrew name of uncertain meaning. It is thought to mean "he who has been sent." The name is used in reference to the Messiah, the one to be sent by God. Var: Shilo. (SHY-LO)

SHIMON Derived from the Hebrew *shim'ōn* (heard). Var: Simeon, Simon (Ang.). (SHE-MONE)

SHIMRI My guard, my watcher. (SHIM-RĪ)

SHIMRON Guardian, watchman. (SHIM-RON)

SHIMSHON Derived from the Hebrew *shimshōn* (the sun). Shimshon is the original Hebrew form of Sampson. *See* SAMSON. (SHIM-SHON)

SHMUEL Derived from the Hebrew *shĕm'ūēl* (name of God, heard of God). Var: Shemuel; Samuel (Ang.). Pet: Shmelke, Shmiel, Shmulke (Yiddish). (SHMUL)

SHOMER A watchman, a guardian. (SHO-MER)

SHONI A change, a difference. (SHO-NĪ)

SHOVAI Aramaic name borrowed from that of a gem. (SHO-VĪ)

SHOVAL Hebrew name meaning "path." The name is borne in the Bible by the youngest son of Judah. (SHO-VAHL)

SOLOMON Derived from the Hebrew *shĕlōmōh* (peaceful). The name is borne in the Bible by the son and successor of King David, renowned for his wisdom and ability to communicate with animals. Var: Saloman, Salomon; Zalman, Zalmen, Zalmon, Zelman (Yiddish). Short: Sol. Pet: Solly; Zalkin (Yiddish). (SOL-O-MUN)

TABBAI Aramaic name meaning "good." (TAB-BĪ)

TALMAI Aramaic name meaning "hill, mound, furrows." The name is borne in the Bible by the father-in-law of King David. (TAHL-MĪ)

TALMI Hebrew name meaning "my hill, my furrow." (TAL-MĪ)

TAVAS Peacock. (TA-VAS)

TAVI Aramaic name meaning "good." Tavi is also in use as a pet form of David (beloved). *See* DAVID. (TAV-EE)

TAVOR Aramaic name meaning "misfortune." It is borrowed from that of a mountain in northern Israel. Var: Tabor. (TAY-VOR)

TERACH Wild goat. The name is borne in the Bible by the father of Abraham. Var: Tera, Terah. (TEE-RAHK)

TESHER Gift. (TEH-SHER)

THOMAS Derived from the Aramaic *tĕ'ōma* (a twin). Var: Tomas. Short: Thom, Tom. Pet: Tommy. (TOM-AHS)

TILON Small mound. (TĪ-LON)

TOMER Tall, statuesque. (TŌ-MER)

TOV Good. (TOVE)

TOVI My good. (TŌ-VĪ)

TOVIEL My Jehovah is gracious. (TŌ-VĪ-EL)

TOVIYA Goodness of God. (TŌ-VĪ-AH)

TUVIAH God is good. Var: Tobiah, Tobias, Tuvia, Tuviya. Pet: Toby. (TOO-VĪ-AH)

TZACH Clean, pure. Var: Tzachai. (ZAK)

TZACHAR White. (ZAK-KAR)

TZADIK Righteous, godly, just. Var: Tzadok, Zadik, Zadok. (ZAY-DIK)

TZADKIEL My righteousness is God. Var: Zadkiel. (ZAD-KEE-EL)

TZALMON Shady, darkness. Var: Zalmon. (ZAL-MON)

TZEDEKIAH Righteousness of Jehovah. The name is borne in the Bible by the last king of Judah (597–586 B.C.). He changed his name from Mattaniah after being appointed by the king of Babylonia, Nebuchadnezzar. Var: Tzidkiya, Zedekia, Zedikiah. (ZED-EE-KĪ-AH)

TZEPHANIAH Hidden by God, protected by God. Zephaniah was the name of a prophet who lived during the reign of King Josiah (640 B.C.). His prophecies are recorded in the Old Testament book of Zephaniah and warn of God's judgment against those who disobey God's laws. Var: Tzefanya, Zefania, Zefaniah, Zephania, Zephaniah. (ZEF-AH-NĪ-AH)

TZEVI Deer, gazelle. Var: Zevi. (ZEV-EE)

TZEVIEL Gazelle of the Lord. Var: Zeviel. (ZEV-EE-EL)

TZURIEL Jehovah is my rock, rock of God. Var: Zuriel. (ZUR-EE-EL)

URI Hebrew name meaning "my flame," which is derived from *ur* (flame). (YOO-RĪ)

URIAH Derived from the Hebrew *ūriyāh* (God is light, God is my flame). The name is borne in the Bible by Uriah the Hittite, the husband of the beautiful Bathsheba. After Uriah was put on the front lines of battle to ensure his death, King David married Bathsheba. Var: Uria, Uriya. (YOO-RĪ-AH)

URIEL Derived from the Hebrew *ūrī'ēl* (light of God). The name is borne by one of the seven archangels of God. (YOO-REE-EL)

UZIAH Jehovah is my strength. The name is borne in the Bible by a king of Judah. Var: Uzia, Uziya, Uzziah. (OO-ZĪ-AH)

UZIEL Strength of God. (OO-ZEE-EL)

YAAKOV Derived from the Hebrew *ya'aqob* (seizing by the heel, supplanting). Yaakov is the original Hebrew form of Jacob. The name is borne in the Bible by one of the twin sons of Isaac and Rebekah. Var: Yaaqov; Jacob (Ang.); Yankel (Yiddish). Pet: Yaki, Yuki; Jake (Ang.). (YAK-KOV)

YAAR Forest. (YAHR)

YAKAR Precious, cherished. Var: Yakir. (YAK-KAR)

YAKIM A short form of Yehoyakim (God will establish), Yakim is also popularly bestowed as an independent given name. *See* YEHOYAKIM. Var: Jakim. (YAK-KIM)

YAMIN Right hand. Var: Jamin. (YAH-MIN)

YANAI Aramaic name meaning "he will answer." It is borne in the Bible by the husband of Queen Salome. Var: Janai, Jannai, Yannai. Short: Yan, Yana. (YAN-NĪ)

YANOACH To rest. (YAH-NO-UK)

YARDEN To flow down, descend. Jordan is the Anglicized form of the name that belongs to the chief river of ancient Palestine. (YAR-DUN)

YARED To descend, descendant. The name is borne in the Bible by the grandfather of Methuselah. Var: Jared (Ang.). (YAR-RED)

YAREV He will quarrel, he will strive. Var: Yariv; Jareb, Jarib (Ang.). (YAR-REV)

YECHEZKEL Derived from the Hebrew *yechezq'ēl* (God strengthens). The name was borne by a 6th-century B.C. Hebrew prophet whose prophecies are recorded in the Old Testament book of Ezekiel. Var: Ezekiel (Ang.); Chaskel, Chatzkel, Keskel (Yiddish). (YEH-KEZ-KEL)

YEDIDIAH Beloved by Jehovah. At God's direction, Nathan bestowed this name upon the newly born Solomon as a symbol of divine favor. Var: Jedidia, Jedidiah, Yedidia, Yedidya. (YEH-DIH-DĪ-AH)

YEHOCHANAN Derived from the Hebrew *yehōchānān* (God is gracious). (YEH-HO-KAH-NAN)

YEHONATAN Derived from the Hebrew *yehōnāthān* (Yahweh has given). The name is borne in the Bible by the son of King Saul and close friend of David. Jonathan is the Anglicized form. Short: Yonatan. (YEH-HO-NAT-AN)

YEHOSHUA God is salvation. The name is borne in the Bible by the leader of the Israelites after the death of Moses. He led the children of Israel into the Promised Land. Joshua is the Anglicized form of the name. Short: Yeshua. (YEH-HO-SHOO-AH)

YEHOYAKIM God will establish. Var: Jehoiakim, Yehoiakim, Yoyakim; Joachim, Joakim (Ang.). Short: Akim, Yakim, Yokim. (YEH-HO-YAH-KIM)

YEHUDAH Praise. Judah is the popular Anglicized form of the name. It is borne in the Bible by the fourth son of Jacob and Leah. He was the patriarch of the successful tribe of Judah, the line from which King David descended. (YEH-HOO-DAH)

YERED Descend. Var: Jered. (YER-ED)

YERIEL Established by Jehovah, founded by God. Var: Jeriel. (YER-Ī-EL)

YESHAYAHU God is salvation. Isaiah is the Anglicized form of the name, which was borne by an 8th-century B.C. prophet, considered to be the greatest of the three major prophets. Short: Yeshaya. (YEH-SHA-YAH-HOO)

YIRMEYAHU The Lord loosens, God will uplift. The name is borne in the Bible by several characters, one of whom was a major prophet of the 6th and 7th centuries B.C. Jeremiah is the Anglicized form. (YIR-MEE-YAH-HOO)

YISHACHAR There is reward. In the Bible, Yishachar was the ninth son of Jacob and patriarch of one of the twelve tribes of Israel. Var: Yisaschar; Issachar (Ang.). Short: Sachar. (YISH-AH-KAR, YISH-AH-KER)

YISHMAEL God will hear. The name was borne by the son of Abraham and his concubine Hagar. After the birth of Isaac by Abraham's wife Sarah, Yishmael and Hagar were abandoned in the desert, where they were saved by God. Yishmael is considered to be the patriarch of the Arabs. Ishmael is the Anglicized form. (YISH-MAY-EL)

YISRAEL Derived from the Hebrew *yisrā'ēl* (contender with God), which is from the elements *sārāh* (to wrestle) and *ēl* (God). The name was bestowed upon Jacob, a son of Isaac, after his successful prayer-struggle with the angel at the river Jabbok. Var: Israel (Ang.); Isser, Issur, Isur (Yiddish). Pet: Issi (Yiddish). (YIZ-RAY-EL)

YITRO Hebrew name meaning "abundance, excellence." The name was borne by the father-in-law of Moses. Var: Yitran; Jethro (Ang.). (YIH-TRO)

YITZCHAK Popular name derived from the Hebrew *yitshāq* (laughter). Isaac is the Anglicized form of the name, which is borne in the Bible by the son of Abraham and Sarah. He is considered to be the patriarch of the Hebrews. Var: Yitzhak, Yizhak; Itzik (Yiddish). Pet: Zach. (YIT-ZAHK)

YOCHANAN Short form of Yehochanan (God is gracious). John is the Anglicized form of the name, which is borne in the Bible by the eldest son of Josiah. Var: Johanan, Yohanan. (YO-KAH-NAN)

YOEL Derived from the Hebrew *yō'ēl* (Jehovah is his God). The name is borne in the Bible by the second of the twelve minor prophets whose prophecies are recorded in the Old Testament book of Joel. Var: Joel (Ang.). (YOEL)

YONAH Derived from the Hebrew *yōnāh* (dove). The name was borne by a Hebrew prophet famous for being thrown overboard in a storm and being swallowed by a great fish for disobeying God. He was later deposited unharmed upon the shore. Var: Yona; Jona, Jonah (Ang.). (YO-NAH)

YONATAN Short form of Yehonatan (given by Jehovah), which is more popularly bestowed than the longer form. *See* YEHONATAN. Var: Jonathan (Ang.).

Short: Jon, Nathan, Yon. Pet: Jonnie, Jonny. (YO-NAH-TAN)

YOSEF Popular name derived from the Hebrew *yōsēf* (may he add, God shall add). The name is borne in the Bible by a favorite son of Jacob and Rachel. Joseph is the Anglicized form. Var: Yehosef, Yoseif, Yosifya. Pet: Seff, Sefi, Yosei, Yosi, Zif, Ziff; Yosel, Yossel, Yossil (Yiddish). (YO-SEF).

YOSHA Wisdom. (YO-SHA)

YUVAL Stream. Var: Jubal. (YOO-vul)

ZACH Hebrew name meaning "pure, clean, white." Zach is also used as a pet form of Yitzchak and Zachary. *See* YITZCHAK *and* ZECHARYA. (ZAK)

ZAHAVI Gold. (ZAY-HAH-VEE)

ZAHIR Bright, shining. Var: Zahur. (ZAY-HEER)

ZAKAI Pure, clean, innocent. Var: Zakkai. (ZAY-KĪ)

ZAKUR Male, masculine. Var: Zaccur. (ZAK-KUR)

ZAMIR Singing. (ZA-MEER)

ZAN Nourished, fed. Var: Zane. (ZAN)

ZAVAD Gift, a giving. Var: Zabad. (ZAY-VAD)

ZAVDIEL God is my gift, gift of God. Var: Zabdiel. (ZAV-DĪ-EL)

ZEBEDEE Gift of God. The name is borne in the New Testament by the father of the apostles James and John. (ZEH-BEH-DEE)

ZECHARYA Derived from the Hebrew *zĕcharyah* (remembrance of the Lord, God remembers). The name is borne in the Bible by one of the twelve minor prophets. Var: Zachariah, Zecharia, Zechariah; Zachary (Ang.); Zacharias (Greek). Short: Zach, Zack, Zak. Pet: Zachi, Zeke. (ZEK-AH-RĪ-AH)

ZEHARIAH Light of Jehovah. Var: Zeharia, Zeharya. (ZEH-HA-RĪ-AH)

ZEMARIAH Song, a melody. Var: Zemaria, Zemarya. (ZEH-MARE-REE-AH)

ZERACH Light, a lamp. The name is borne in the Bible by a son of Judah and Tamar. Var: Zerah. (ZEE-RAHK)

ZERACHIA The rising light of the Lord. Var: Zerachya. (ZER-AH-KĪ-AH)

ZEREM Stream. (ZER-EM)

ZERIKA Aramaic name meaning "sprinkling." (ZEE-RĪ-KAH)

ZEV Short form of any of the names beginning with the element *Zev-*. (ZEV)

ZEVACH Sacrifice. Var: Zevah. Short: Zev. (ZEV-UK)

ZEVACHIAH Hebrew name meaning "sacrifice of the Lord." Var: Zevachia, Zevachya. Short: Zev. (ZEV-AH-KĪ-AH)

ZEVADIAH God has bestowed. The name is borne in the Bible by the brother of Joab. Var: Zevadia, Zevadya. Short: Zev. (ZEV-AH-DĪ-AH)

ZEVID Gift, bestowal. (ZEV-ID)

ZEVULUN Dwelling, honorable dwelling. Var: Zebulon, Zebulun. Short: Zeb, Zev, Zevul. (ZEV-YOO-LUN)

ZIMRAN Celebrated, sacred. Zimran is borne in the Bible by a son of Abraham and Keturah. (ZIME-RAHN)

ZIMRI Praiseworthy. (ZIM-REE)

ZIV To shine. Var: Zivan, Zivi. (ZIV)

ZOMEIR One who prunes vines. Var: Zomer. (ZO-MIRE, ZO-MEER)

Jewish/Hebrew Female Names

ABIAH Jehovah is my father. The name is borne in the Bible by the mother of Hezekia. Var: Avia, Aviah, Aviya. (AH-BĪ-AH)

ABICHAYIL Father of might. The name is borne in the Old Testament by the sister-in-law of King David. Var: Abihail, Avichayil, Avihayil. (AB-EE-KALE)

ABIELA God is my father. Var: Abiela, Abiella, Aviela, Aviella. (AH-BĪ-EL-AH)

ABIGAYIL Derived from the Hebrew *abīgayil* (Father is rejoicing). The name is borne in the Bible by the wise and beautiful wife of Nabal, who later became the wife of King David. Var: Abigail, Avigayil. Short: Gail, Gayle. (AB-Ī-GALE)

ABIRA Strong. (AH-BĪ-RAH)

ABITAL Father of Dew. The name is borne in the Bible by one of King David's wives. Var: Avital. (AH-BĪ-TAHL)

ACHAVA Friendship. (AH-KAH-VAH)

ACHSAH Anklet. This Hebrew name is borne in the Bible by the only daughter of Caleb. Var: Achsa. (AHK-SAH)

ADAH Adornment. The name was borne by the wife of Lamech and mother of Jabal and Jubal. Var: Ada, Adda, Adaya. (Ā-DAH)

ADAMA Feminine form of Adam (man of the red earth), which is derived from the Hebrew *adama* (red earth). (AHD-AH-MAH)

ADARA Noble, exalted. (Ā-DAHR-AH)

ADENA Noble. Var: Adene, Adina. (Ā-DEE-NAH)

ADI Ornament. Var: Addie, Adie. (AD-EE)

ADIAH Ornament of Jehovah, ornament of the Lord. Var: Adia, Adiya. (AH-DĪ-AH)

ADIEL Ornament of God. Var: Adiella. (AD-EE-EL)

ADIRA Strong, mighty, powerful. (AH-DIR-AH)

AHAVAH Love. Var: Ahava, Ahavat. (AH-HAH-VAH)

AHUVAH Beloved. Var: Ahuva. (AH-HOO-VAH)

AHUVIAH Beloved of the Lord. Var: Ahuvia. (AH-HOO-VĪ-AH)

ALEI Leaf. (AH-LAY)

ALIMA Strong. (AH-LEE-MAH)

ALITZAH Happiness, joy, delight. Var: Aleeza, Aleezah, Alisa, Alitza, Aliza, Alizah. (AH-LEET-ZAH)

ALIYAH To ascend. Var: Aliya. (AH-LEE-YAH)

ALONA Oak, an oak tree. Var: Allona, Allonia, Alonia, Eilona. (AHL-LO-NAH)

AMANA Faithful. (AH-MAY-NAH)

AMANIAH Faithful to Jehovah. Var: Amania, Amanya. (AH-MAH-NĪ-AH).

AMIDAH Upright, standing. Var: Amida. Short: Ami. (AH-MEE-DAH)

AMIELA People of God. Var: Ammiela. Short: Ami. (AH-MEE-EL-LAH)

AMMA Servant. (AH-MAH)

ANINA Aramaic name meaning "answer my prayer." Var: Anena. (AH-NEE-NAH)

ANNA Anglicized form of the Hebrew Chaanach (gracious, full of grace, mercy). Var: Ana, Ann, Anne. Pet: Annie, Nan, Nanette. (AH-NAH, AN-NAH)

ARDAH Bronze. Var: Arda, Ardona, Ardonah. (AR-DAH)

ARELA Messenger, angel. Var: Arella. (AH-REL-LAH)

ARIA Feminine form of the Hebrew Ari (lion). (AR-EE-AH)

ARIELA Feminine form of the Hebrew Ariel (lion of God). Var: Ariella, Arielle. (AR-EE-EL-LAH)

ARIZA Cedar panels. The cedar tree, the national symbol of Lebanon, once grew in great forests, and highly prized carved panels were used to line the walls of King Solomon's palace and temple. After centuries of overharvesting, only a limited number of these trees remain in the Holy Land. (AH-REE-ZAH)

ASENATH Of debated etymology, some believe it to be an Aramaic name meaning "thornbush." Others think it is possibly an Egyptian name meaning "gift of the sun-god, gift of Isis." The name is borne in the Bible by the wife of Joseph and mother of Ephraim and Manasseh. Var: Asnat, Osnat. (AS-EH-NATH)

ASISA Juicy, ripe. (AH-SEE-SAH)

ASISYA The juice of Jehovah. Var: Asisia. (AH-SIS-EE-AH)

ASTERA A name derived from the Persian *stara* (star). Var: Asteria, Asteriya. Short: Asta. (AH-STER-AH, AS-TER-AH)

ASYA Action, performance, operation. Var: Asia, Assia. (AH-SEE-AH)

ATHALIAH Jehovah is exalted, the Lord is exalted. Var: Atalia, Ataliah, Atalya, Athalia. (AH-THA-LĪ-AH)

AVIVAH Springtime. Var: Abiba, Abibah, Abibi, Abibit, Aviva, Avivi, Avivit. (AH-VEE-VAH)

AVTALIA Lamb, fawn. Var: Avtalya. (AV-TAH-LĪ-AH)

AYALAH Deer, gazelle. Var: Ayala. (Ī-YAL-LAH)

AZIZAH Strong. Var: Aziza. (AH-ZEE-ZAH)

AZRIELA The Lord is my strength. (AZ-REE-EL-LAH)

BAKARA Visitation. (BAH-KAR-RAH)

BAKURA Ripe, a ripened fruit. Var: Bikura. (BAH-KUR-AH)

BARKAIT Morning star. Var: Barkat. (BAR-KATE)

BAT Daughter. Beth is the popular Anglicized form of the name. Var: Bet. (BAHT)

BAT-SHEBA Compound name composed of the elements *bat* (daughter) and Sheba (an oath): hence, "daughter of Sheva." The name is borne in the Bible by the beautiful wife of Uriah the Hittite. After King David placed her husband on the front lines of battle to ensure his death, the king married Bathsheba. She was the mother of Solomon. Var: Bathsheba, Batsheba, Bat-Sheva, Batsheva. (BAHT-SHE-BAH)

BATYA Daughter of God. Var: Basha; Peshe, Pessel (Yiddish). (BAHT-YAH)

BATZRA Fortress, fortification, enclosure. (BATZ-RAH)

BECHIRA The chosen one. (BEH-KIR-AH)

BERACHAH Blessing. Var: Beracha. Var: Berucha. (BEH-RAY-CHAH)

BERUCHIYA Hebrew name meaning "blessed of the Lord." Var: Beruchya. (BEH-ROO-CHĪ-YAH)

BETH Anglicized form of Bat (daughter). Beth is also used as a short form of the various names of which it is an element. (BETH)

BETHANY Derived from the Hebrew *bet t'eina* (house of figs). Bethany is the name of a small town on the eastern slope of the Mount of Olives. Short: Beth. (BETH-AH-NEE)

BETHEL Derived from the Hebrew *bēth'ēl* (house of God). The name is borrowed from that of an ancient and holy city south of Shiloh. (BETH-EL)

BETUEL Daughter of God. Var: Bethuel. Short: Bet, Beth. (BET-YOO-EL)

BETULAH Hebrew name meaning "maiden, young woman." Var: Bethula, Bethulah, Betula. (BEH-TYOO-LAH, BEH-TOO-LAH)

BEULAH Derived from the Hebrew *be'ūlāh* (married, possessed). Beulah was a name given to Palestine to acknowledge that God will be married to his people and their land. Var: Beula. (BYOO-LAH)

BINA Intelligence, understanding. Var: Bena. (BIN-AH)

BINYAMINA Feminine form of Binyamin (son of the right hand). *See* BINYAMIN (Male Names). Benjamina is the Anglicized form of the name. (BIN-YAH-MEE-NAH)

BIRA Fortress. Var: Biria, Biriya. (BEER-AH)

BRACHA Blessing. Var: Brocha. (BRA-KAH)

CARMA Aramaic and Hebrew name meaning "vineyard, orchard." Var: Karma. (KAR-MAH)

CARMANIA Aramaic and Hebrew name meaning "vineyard of the Lord." Var: Carmaniya. (KAR-MAH-NĪ-AH)

CARMEL Vineyard, orchard. Var: Carmela, Carmit, Karmel, Karmela, Karmit. (KAR-MEL)

CARMELI My vineyard, my orchard. Var: Karmeli. (KAR-MEL-LĪ)

CARMIYA Vineyard of Jehovah. Var: Carmia, Carmiela, Karmia, Karmiya. (KAR-MĪ-YAH)

CARNI Hebrew name meaning "my horn," derived from *carna* (horn). Var: Karni. (KAR-NĪ)

CARNIA Horn of Jehovah. Var: Carniya, Karnia, Karniya. (KAR-NĪ-AH)

CARNIELA Horn of the Lord. Var: Carniella, Karniela, Karniella. (KAR-NEE-EL-LAH)

CHAANACH Hebrew name meaning "grace, gracious, full of grace, mercy." The name, which is borne in the Bible by the mother of Samuel, is Anglicized as Anna. Var: Chana, Chanah, Hana, Hanna, Hannah; Ann, Anna (Ang.); Hende, Hendel, Hene, Heneh, Henna (Yiddish). Pet: Annie, Chani. (KAH-NAHK)

CHAFSIYA Free. Var: Chafshia, Hafshia. (KAF-SĪ-YAH).

CHAMANIA Sun, sunflower. Var: Chamaniya, Hamania, Hamaniya. (KAH-MAH-NĪ-AH)

CHANIA Encampment. Var: Chaniya, Hania, Haniya. (KAH-NĪ-AH)

CHANINA Gracious. Var: Hanina. (KAH-NĪ-NAH)

CHANIT Spear. Var: Chanita, Hanit, Hanita. (KAH-NIT)

CHANYA The grace of Jehovah. Var: Hanya. (KAHN-YAH)

CHARNA Yiddish name meaning "dark." (CHAR-NAH)

CHASHMONA Princess. Var: Chashmonit. (KASH-MO-NAH)

CHASIA Protected by the Lord. Var: Chasya, Hasia, Hasya. (KAH-SĪ-AH)

CHASIDA Righteous. Var: Hasida. (KAH-SEE-DAH)

CHASINA Aramaic name meaning "strong, mighty, a protection." Var: Hasina. (KAH-SEE-NAH)

CHAVA Hebrew name meaning "life." The name, Anglicized as Eve, is borne in the Bible by the first woman created by God, the "mother of all the living." Eve was the mother of three sons: Cain, Abel, and Seth. Var: Hava. (KAH-VAH)

CHAYA Alive, living. Var: Haya. (KAH-YAH)

CHAZONA A prophetess, a seer. (KAH-ZO-NAH)

CHEDRA Joy. Var: Hedra. (KED-RAH)

CHEFTZI-BA Hebrew name meaning "my delight is in her." The name is borne in the Bible by the wife of King Hezekiah. Var: Cheftzibah, Hefziba, Hefzibah, Hephziba, Hephzibah, Hepziba, Hepzibah. Pet: Hefzi, Hefzia, Hepzi, Hepzia. (KEFT-ZEE-BAH)

CHEFTZIYA God is my delight. (KEFT-ZĪ-YAH)

CHEIFA Harbor. Var: Chaifa, Haifa, Heifa. (KĪ-FAH)

CHEMDA Charm, attractiveness. Var: Hemda. (KEM-DAH)

CHEMDIAH God is my desire. Var: Chemdia, Chemdiya, Hemdia, Hemdiah. (KEM-DĪ-AH)

CHENIA Grace of the Lord. Var: Chenya, Henia, Henya. Short: Chen, Hen. (KEH-NĪ-AH)

CHERMONA Sacred mountain. Var: Hermona. (KER-MO-NAH)

CHIBA Love. Var: Hiba. (KEE-BAH)

CHULA Player of a musical instrument. (KOO-LAH)

CHULDA A weasel. The name is borne in the Bible by a prophetess, the wife of Shallum. Var: Hulda, Huldah. (KULL-DAH)

CHUMA Aramaic name meaning "warmth, heat." Var: Chumi, Huma, Humi. (KOO-MAH)

DALYA Branch, bough of a tree. Var: Dalia, Daliya. (DAL-YAH)

DANIAH Judgment of the Lord. Var: Dania, Daniya, Danya. (DAH-NĪ-AH)

DANIELA Feminine form of Daniel (God is my judge). *See* DANIEL (Male Names). Var: Daniele, Daniella, Danielle. (DAN-YELL-AH)

DATIAH The law of Jehovah. Var: Datia, Datiya, Datya. (DAH-TĪ-AH)

DAVIDA Feminine form of David (beloved). *See* DAVID (Male Names). Var: Davene, Davi, Davita. (DAY-VID-AH)

DELILAH Derived from the Hebrew *delīlāh* (delicate). Delilah was the name of the Philistine mistress of Samson who discovered the secret of his great strength. She treacherously betrayed him to the Philistines. Var: Delila. (DIH-LĪ-LAH)

DEVASHA Honey. Var: Devash. (DEH-VAH-SHA)

DEVORAH Derived from the Hebrew *devōrāh* (a bee). The name is borne in the Bible by Rebekah's nurse and by a great prophetess and judge who helped to organize an army and oversaw a decisive victory over the Canaanites. Var: Debera, Debora, Deborah, Debra, Devera, Devora, Devorit, Devra, Dvera, Dvora. Pet: Debbe, Debbi, Debbie, Debby, Debi, Devi. (DEV-OR-AH)

DIMONA South. (DIH-MO-NAH)

DINAH Derived from the Hebrew *dīnāh* (judged, vindicated). The name is borne in the Bible by a daughter of Jacob and Leah. Var: Deena, Deenah, Dena, Dina. (DĪ-NAH)

DINIA Judgment of Jehovah. Var: Dinya. (DĪ-NĪ-AH)

DIVONAH South. Var: Divona. (DIH-VO-NAH)

DOVEVA Graceful. Var: Dovevet, Dovit. Short: Dova. (DO-VEH-VAH)

DUMIA Silent. Var: Dumiya. (DOO-ME-AH)

EDIAH Adornment of Jehovah. Var: Edia, Ediya, Edya, Edyah. (EE-DĪ-AH)

EDNAH Derived from the Hebrew *'ēdnāh* (rejuvenation, delight). The name is found in the apocryphal book of Tobit, as the name of the mother of Sarah and stepmother of Tobias. Var: Edna. (ED-NAH)

EFAH Hebrew name meaning "darkness, gloom." The name is borne in the Bible by a concubine of Caleb. Var: Efa, Eifa, Eifah, Ephah. (EH-FAH)

EFRATA Fruitful. The name Efrata is borne in the Bible by the second wife of Caleb. It was also the ancient name of Bethlehem. Var: Efrat, Ephrat, Ephrata. (EH-FRAY-TAH)

EGLAH Heifer. The name is borne in the Old Testament by a wife of King David. Var: Egla. (EG-LAH)

EILAH Oak tree. Var: Ayla, Eila, Ela, Elah, Eyla. (Ī-LAH).

EILONA An oak tree. Var: Elona, Ilona. (Ī-LO-NAH)

ELAMA The Lord's people. (EL-AH-MAH)

ELIANA My Lord has answered. Var: Eliane, Elianna. (EL-LĪ-AH-NAH)

ELIAVAH My Lord is willing. Var: Eliava. (EL-LĪ-AH-VAH)

ELIEZRA My Lord is salvation. (EL-LEE-EEZ-RAH)

ELIORA My Lord is light. Var: Eleora. (EL-LĪ-OR-RAH, ELL-LEE-OR-RAH)

ELISABETH Anglicized form of Elisheva (God is my oath). Var: Elizabeth. Short: Beth, Elisa, Elise, Elissa. Pet: Ellie. (EE-LIZ-AH-BETH, EH-LIZ-AH-BETH)

ELISHEBA Derived from the Hebrew *elīsheba'* (God is my oath). The name, Anglicized as Elisabeth, is borne in the Bible by the wife of Aaron and sister-in-law of Moses. Var: Elisheva. Short: Elisa, Elise, Elissa, Eliza, Elize. Pet: Ellie. (EL-LĪ-SHE-BAH)

EMUNAH Faithful. Var: Emuna. (EH-MOO-NAH)

ERELA Angel, messenger. (EH-REL-LAH)

ESTHER Of debated origin and meaning, some believe it to be the Persian translation of the Hebrew name Hadassah (myrtle); others think it is derived from the Persian *stara* (star). It has also been suggested that it is derived from the Babylonian Ishtar, the name of a goddess of love and fertility. The name is borne in the Bible by the cousin and adopted daughter of Mordecai who became the queen of King Ahasuerus. Her story is told in the Old Testament book of Esther. Var: Ester. Pet: Essie. (EH-STER)

FEIGE Yiddish name derived from either *feigel* (bird) or *fayg* (fig). Var: Faga, Faiga, Feiga. (FĪ-GAH)

FEIGEL Yiddish name derived from the German *vogel* (bird). Var: Faigel. (FĪ-GEL)

FRAYDA Yiddish name meaning "joy." Var: Frayde, Freida, Freide. Pet: Fradel. (FRAY-DAH)

GAVRIELA Feminine form of Gavriel (God is my strength). *See* GABRIEL (Male Names). Var: Gabriela, Gabriele, Gabriella, Gavriella, Gavrielle; Gabrielle (Ang.). Pet: Gavi; Gabi (Ang.). (GAV-REE-ELL-LAH)

GAVRILA Strong. Var: Gavrilla. (GAH-VRIL-LAH, GAH-VREE-LAH)

GAYORA Valley of light. Short: Gay. (GAY-OR-AH)

GEFEN Vine. Var: Gafna, Gafnit, Geffen; Gaphna (Aramaic). (GEF-FEN)

GELILAH Rolling boundary, rolling hills. Var: Gelalia, Gelalya, Gelila, Gelilia, Geliliya. (GEH-LĪ-LAH)

GEONA Exaltation. Var: Geonit. (GEE-O-NAH)

GERUSHAH Exiled, sent away. Var: Gerusha. (GER-ROO-SHA)

GEVIRAH A queen, a lady. Var: Gevira. (GEH-VIR-RAH)

GIBORAH Strong. Var: Gibora. (GIB-OR-RAH)

GILADAH Feminine form of Gilad (hill of testimony). Var: Gilada. (GEE-LAH-DAH)

GILANAH Joy. Var: Gilana. (GEE-LAH-NAH)

GILIAH The joy of Jehovah. Var: Gilia, Giliya, Giliyah. (GEE-LĪ-AH, GIH-LĪ-AH)

GINA Garden. Var: Gena, Ginat. (GEE-NAH, JEE-NAH)

GITEL Yiddish name meaning "good." Var: Gitela, Gitele, Gittel. (GIH-TEL)

GIVOLA Bud. (GIH-VO-LAH)

GOLDA Derived from the English *gold* (gold, golden). The name was borne by Israeli Prime Minister Golda Meir (1898–1979). Pet: Goldie. (GOL-DAH)

GOZALA Hatchling, young bird. (GO-ZAH-LAH)

HADASSAH Hebrew name meaning "myrtle, a myrtle tree." In the Bible, Hadassah is the Hebrew name of Queen Esther. Var: Hadassa. Short: Hadas. Pet: Hada; Hodel (Yiddish). (HAH-DAHS-SAH)

HAGAR Believed to be derived from the Arabic *hajara* (to forsake, to emigrate). The name was borne by the concubine of Abraham and mother of Ishmael. After the birth of Isaac by Sarah, Hagar and Ishmael were abandoned in the desert, only to be rescued by God. Hagar is regarded as the matriarch of the Arab people, as her son Ishmael is venerated as the patriarch. (HAY-GAR)

HEDIAH Voice of Jehovah, echo of the Lord. Var: Hedia, Hedya. (HEH-DĪ-AH)

HINDA Yiddish name derived from the German *hinde* (hind, female red deer). Pet: Hindel, Hindelle. (HIN-DA)

IDRA Aramaic name meaning "fig tree." The fig tree, used as a symbol of learning, has been an important food source since before biblical times.The hopeful idea of peace and prosperity is summed up in the saying "everyone being able to sit under his own vine and fig tree." (IH-DRA)

IDRIYA A duck. Var: Idria. (IH-DREE-YAH)

ILANA Tree. Var: Ilanit. (IH-LAH-NAH)

ITIAH God is with me. Var: Itia, Itiya. (IH-TĪ-AH)

ITIEL God is with me. Var: Itil. (IH-TĪ-ELL)

JACOBA Feminine form of Jacob, which is the Anglicized form of Yaakov (seizing by the heel, supplanting). *See* JACOB (Male Names). (JAH-KOH-BAH)

Jaffe Derived from the Hebrew *yafe* (beautiful). (JAF-FEE)

Jemima Anglicized form of the Hebrew Yemima (dove). *See* YEMIMA. (JEH-MĪ-MAH)

Jerushah Anglicized form of Yerusha (possessed, a possession). *See* YERUSHA. Var: Jerusha. (JEH-ROO-SHA)

Jethra Feminine form of Jethro, which is the Anglicized form of Yitro (abundance, excellence). (JEH-THRA)

Jezebel Derived from the Hebrew *'īzebhel* (impure, wicked). The name is borne in the Bible by the wicked wife of King Ahab. Var: Izevel, Jezebela. (JEZ-EH-BELL)

Joela Feminine form of Joel, which is the Anglicized form of Yoel (Jehovah is his God). *See* YOEL (Male Names). Var: Joella, Joelle. (JO-ELL-LAH)

Johanna Anglicized form of Yochana, a feminine form of the Hebrew Yochanan (God is gracious). *See* YOCHANAN (Male Names). Var: Joanna. (JO-HAH-NAH)

Jordana Feminine form of Jordan, which is an Anglicized form of the Hebrew Yarden (flowing down, descending). *See* JORDAN (Male Names). Var: Jordena. Pet: Jordi, Jordie. (JOR-DĀ-NA, JOR-DAH-NAH)

Josefa Feminine form of Joseph, the Anglicized form of the Hebrew Yosef (he shall add, may God add). *See* JOSEPH (Male Names). Var: Josifa, Josipha. (JO-SEH-FAH)

Judith Anglicized form of Yehudit (he will be praised, from Judah). *See* YEHUDIT. Pet: Judi, Judy. (JOO-DITH)

Kadiah A pitcher. Var: Kadia, Kadya. (KAH-DĪ-AH)

Kama Ripened, mature. (KAH-MAH)

Kana Plant. (KAH-NAH)

Kanara A canary, a small songbird. Var: Kanarit. (KAH-NAR-AH)

Karmil Crimson, bright red. (KAR-MILL)

Kataniya Small. Var: Katania, Ketana. (KAH-TAH-NĪ-AH)

Kelila Crown, garland. Var: Kaile, Kaille, Kalia, Kayla, Kayle, Kyle, Kylia. (KEH-LIH-LAH)

Kerem Vineyard. The name Kerem is common to both females and males. (KEH-REM)

Keren A horn, an animal horn. Var: Keryn. (KEER-EN)

Keren-Hapuch Horn of eye paint, horn of antimony. A silvery dye made of antimony was used as a cosmetic during biblical times. It was often stored in a hollowed-out animal horn and applied to the lashes of women. The name is borne in the Bible by the youngest of Job's three daughters, born after his great affliction. Var: Keren-Happuch. Short: Keren. (KEER-EN-HAP-POOK)

Keshet Rainbow. (KEH-SHET)

Kessem Magic. (KES-SEM)

Ketifa To pluck, to pick. Var: Ketipha. (KEH-TEE-FAH)

Ketina Aramaic name meaning "a child, a youngster, a juvenile." (KEH-TEE-NAH)

Keturah Perfumed, incense. The name is borne in the Bible by the wife of Abraham. They were probably married after the death of Sarah. Keturah was the mother of several children, who were sent away into the east by their father. Sixteen progenitors of Arabian tribes are attributed to her. Var: Ketura. (KEH-TYOOR-AH)

Ketziah Hebrew name meaning "cassia," a type of cinnamon. The name is borne in the Bible by the second daughter of Job, born after his terrible affliction. Var: Ketzia, Kezia, Keziah. Pet: Kezi, Kezzi, Kezzie, Kezzy. (KET-ZĪ-AH, KET-ZEE-AH)

Kiriah Village. Var: Kiria, Kirya. (KIR-EE-AH)

Kitra Aramaic name meaning "crown." (KIH-TRAH)

Leah Derived from the Hebrew *lē'āh* (gazelle, wild cow) or from *lā'āh* (weary, to tire). The name is borne in the Bible by the eldest daughter of Laban, the first wife of Jacob. Though her sister Rachel was Jacob's favorite wife, she nevertheless bore him seven children. Var: Leia. Pet: Lea. (LEE-AH)

Leiana Combination name composed from Leia and Ana. *See* ANNA and LEAH. (LEE-AN-NAH)

Leilah A borrowing from the Arabic, Leilah is derived from *leila* (dark beauty, dark as night). Var: Laila, Leyla. (LAY-LAH)

Leili My night. Var: Laili, Lailie, Laylie, Leilie. (LAY-LEE)

Lena A short form of Magdalene (of Magdala), Lena is also bestowed as an independent given name. *See* MAGDALENE. (LEE-NAH)

Levana White. Var: Livana. (LEE-VAH-NAH)

Leviah Lioness of Jehovah. Var: Levia. (LEE-VĪ-AH).

Levona Frankincense. Var: Levonat. (LEH-VO-NAH)

LIBE Yiddish name derived from the German *liebe* (love). Var: Leeba, Liba, Libbe, Libbeh, Libi, Libke, Libkeh, Lipke, Lipkeh, Lube. (LEEB)

LILITH Old name derived from the Assyrian-Babylonian *lilītu* (of the night). In ancient Semitic folklore, Lilith was a vampire-like female demon who lived in desolate areas. In medieval Jewish folklore, she was both the first wife of Adam before Eve was created and a night witch who preyed upon sleeping infants. Var: Lillith. Pet: Lili, Lilli. (LIL-LITH)

LINIT To rest. (LIN-NIT)

LIOR My light. (LĪ-OR).

LIORA The light is mine. Var: Leora, Leorit, Liorit. (LĪ-OR-RAH)

LIVNA White. Var: Livnat, Livona. (LIV-NAH)

MAAYAN Mountain. Var: Mayana. (MAY-YAHN)

MAGDA A short form of Magdalene (of Magdala), Magda is also bestowed as an independent given name. *See* MAGDALENE. Short: Mag. Pet: Maggie. (MAG-DAH)

MAGDALENE Hebrew name meaning "of Magdala." Magdala was the name of a coastal town on the Sea of Galilee. In the New Testament, Mary Magdalene was the name of a woman Jesus cured of seven demons. Var: Madeena, Madelaine, Madeleine, Madelyn, Magdalen, Magdalena. Short: Lena, Mag, Magda. Pet: Maddie, Maggie. (MAG-DAH-LEEN)

MAHALIA Aramaic name meaning "marrow, fat." Var: Mehalia. (MAH-HAH-LEE-AH)

MAHIRA Energetic, lively. (MAH-HEER-AH)

MAKEDA Bowl, cup, vessel. (MAH-KEE-DAH)

MALKAH Queen. Var: Malka, Malkit. (MAHL-KAH)

MALKIAH A queen of Jehovah. Var: Malkia, Malkiya. (MAHL-KĪ-AH)

MALKOSHA Last rain. (MAHL-KO-SHA)

MARAH Hebrew name meaning "bitter." In the Bible, the name was taken by Naomi as an expression of her bitter grief at the death of her husband and two sons. Var: Mara. (MAR-AH)

MARGEA Peace. (MAHR-GEE-AH)

MARNINA Rejoice. Var: Marna. (MAHR-NĪ-NAH)

MARONA A flock of sheep. (MAH-RO-NAH)

MARTHA Derived from the Aramaic *mārthā* (lady, mistress). Var: Marthe. (MAR-THA)

MARY Popular Anglicized form of the Hebrew Miryam. *See* MIRYAM. (MARE-REE)

MATANA Gift. (MAH-TAH-NAH)

MAZHIRA Shining. (MAH-ZHEER-AH)

MECHOLA To dance. Var: Mahola. (MEH-KO-LAH)

MEDINA Derived from the Arabic *medinat* (city). The name is borrowed from that of a northwestern Saudi Arabian city which is the site of Muhammad's tomb. (MEH-DEE-NAH)

MEIRA Feminine form of Meir (light). Var: Meiri, Meirit. (MĪ-RAH)

MEIRONA Aramaic name meaning "sheep." Var: Merona. (MER-O-NAH, MĪ-RO-NAH)

MEONAH A dwelling, a resting place. Var: Meona. (MEE-O-NAH)

MEORAH Light. Var: Meora. (MEE-OR-AH)

MERAV Increase. The name was borne by the elder of King Saul's two daughters. Var: Meirav, Merab. (ME-RAV)

MERIMA Uplifted, exalted. Var: Meroma. (MER-EE-MAH)

MICHAELA Feminine form of Michael (who is like God?). *See* MICHAEL (Male Names). Var: Michaele. (MĪ-KAY-EL-AH)

MICHAL Short form of Michaela and Michael (who is like God?). The name is borne in the Bible by the younger of King Saul's two daughters. She became the wife of David and helped him escape from Saul, but later her father married her to another man. After David became king, he reclaimed her as his wife, but they eventually became alienated from one another. Var: Michala, Michalla, Michel. Short: Mica. (MĪ-KAHL)

MILCAH Queen, counsel. The name is borne in the Bible by the sister-in-law of Abraham. She was the wife of Nachor. Var: Milca, Milka, Milkah. (MIL-KAH)

MIRYAM Hebrew name of debated meaning. Many believe it to mean "sea of bitterness" or "sea of sorrow." However, some sources cite the alternative definitions of "rebellion," "wished-for child," and "mistress or lady of the sea." The name is borne in the Bible by the sister of Moses and Aaron. After the Exodus, she came to be known as a prophetess to the people. Var: Maryasha, Miriam; Mary (Ang.); Mishke (Yiddish). Short: Meri, Miri. Pet: Mimi, Minnie, Mira, Mirit, Mirra; Mirel, Mirele, Miril (Yiddish). (MIR-EE-AHM)

MORAN Teacher. Var: Moranit. (MO-RAN)

Morasha Legacy. (MOR-ASH-AH)

Moriya Teacher. The name is borrowed from that of a hill from which Abraham prepared to offer Isaac up as a sacrifice. It is a holy place now covered by the Muslim *Kubbet es-Sakhrah* (the Dome of the Rock). Var: Mariah, Moria, Moriah. (MOR-RĪ-AH)

Naamah Sweetness, beautiful. The name is borne in the Bible by the daughter of Lamech and Zillah and by one of the wives of King Solomon. Var: Naama, Naamana, Naami. (NAY-AH-MAH)

Naamiah Sweetness of Jehovah. Var: Naamia, Naamiya. (NAY-AH-MĪ-AH).

Naarah Girl, maiden. The name is borne in the Bible by the second of Ashur's two wives. Var: Naara. (NAY-AH-RAH)

Nadyan A pond. Since water is a precious commodity in arid climates, names such as Nadyan may have the implied meaning of preciousness. Var: Nadian. (NAD-EE-AN)

Nafshiya Friendship. (NAF-SHEE-AH)

Nagida Prosperous, successful. Var: Negida. (NAH-GEE-DAH)

Nahara Aramaic name which means "light." Var: Nehara, Nehora. (NAH-HAR-AH)

Naomi My joy, my delight. The name Naomi is borne in the Bible by the wife of Elimelech and mother of Mahlon and Chilion. Following the death of her husband and sons, she changed her name to Marah (bitterness) as an expression of her bitter sorrow and grief. Naomi was the mother-in-law of Ruth. Var: Naoma. (NAY-O-MEE)

Nasya Miracle of Jehovah. Var: Nasia. (NAH-SĪ-AH, NAH-SEE-AH)

Nataniah Gift of Jehovah. Var: Natania, Natanya, Nathania. (NAY-TAH-NĪ-AH)

Nataniela Feminine form of Nathaniel (gift of God). *See* NETHANEL (Male Names). Var: Nataniella, Natanielle, Nathaniella, Nathanielle, Netanela, Netaniela, Netaniella. (NAH-TAH-NEE-EL-LAH, NAH-TAN-EE-EL-LAH)

Nechama Comfort. Var: Nehama. Pet: Nachmi; Necha, Neche (Yiddish). (NEH-KAH-MAH)

Nechona Proper. (NEH-KO-NAH)

Nedaviah Generosity of Jehovah. Var: Nedavia, Nedavya. (NEH-DAH-VĪ-AH)

Nediva Noble, generous. (NEH-DIH-VAH)

Neima Strong. (NEE-MA)

Nemera Leopard. (NAH-MER-AH)

Nera Light, candle, lamp. (NEE-RAH)

Neriah Light of Jehovah, the lamp of God. Var: Neria, Neriya. (NEE-RĪ-AH)

Nesiah Miracle of Jehovah. Var: Nesia, Nessia, Nessiah, Nesya, Nisia, Nisiah, Nisya. (NEE-SĪ-AH)

Netana Gift. Var: Netina. (NEH-TAH-NAH)

Netaniah Gift of God. Var: Netania, Netanya, Nethania, Nethaniah. (NEH-TAN-Ī-AH)

Neviah Prophetess, seer into the future. Var: Nevia. (NEH-VĪ-AH)

Nima Hair. Var: Nema. (NIH-MAH)

Nissa To test. Var: Nisa. (NIS-SAH)

Niva Speech. Var: Neva. (NIH-VAH)

Nura Aramaic name meaning "light." (NOOR-AH)

Nurya Aramaic name meaning "light of the Lord." (NOOR-YAH)

Odelia Praising Jehovah, I praise God. Var: Odeleya. (O-DEH-LĪ-AH)

Odiya Song of God. (O-DĪ-AH)

Ohela Derived from the Hebrew *ohel* (tent). (O-HEL-AH)

Ophira Borrowed from the name of a region famous for its gold, hence the definition "gold." Jewish historian Flavius Josephus identified Ophira with the Malay Peninsula, but some believe it to have been somewhere in Yemen or Saudi Arabia. Var: Ofira. (O-FEER-AH)

Ophrah A fawn. The name is borne in the Bible by a descendant of Judah. Var: Afra, Afrat, Afrit, Aphra, Aphrat, Aphrit, Ofra, Ofrat, Ofrit, Ophra, Ophrat, Ophrit, Oprah. (AHF-RAH)

Orah Light. Var: Ora, Orit. (OR-AH)

Orpah A fawn, a forelock. The name Orpah is borne in the Bible by the daughter-in-law of Naomi and sister-in-law of Ruth. Var: Orpa. (OR-PAH)

Otzara Treasure, riches. Var: Ozara. (OT-ZAR-RAH)

Ozera Help, assistance, helper. (O-ZER-AH)

Paz Gold. Var: Paza, Pazit. (PAHZ, PAZ)

Paziah The gold of Jehovah. Var: Pazia, Pazit, Paziya, Pazya. (PAH-ZĪ-AH)

Peliah Miracle of God. Var: Pelia. (PEH-LĪ-AH)

Peninah Coral, a pearl, ruby. Var: Penina, Penini. Pet: Peni, Penie. (PEH-NIN-NAH)

Peniniya Hen, a female chicken. Var: Peninia. (PEH-NIH-NĪ-YAH, PEH-NIH-NEE-YAH)

Perach Blossom, bloom, flower. Var: Perah, Pericha, Pircha, Pirchia, Pirchit, Pirchiya, Pirha. (PER-AHK)

Pili Miraculous. (PIH-LEE)

Raanana Fresh, beautiful. Var: Ranana. (RAY-AH-NAH-NAH)

Rachav Broad, large. The name is borne in the Bible by a prostitute who hid Hebrew spies from the soldiers in Jericho. After the city of Jericho fell, Rachav and her entire family were spared and were assimilated into the tribes of Israel. Var: Rahab (Ang.). (RAH-KAHV)

Rachel Derived from the Hebrew *rāchēl* (ewe). The name is borne in the Bible by the younger daughter of Laban. Jacob had to toil for fourteen years as well as marry Rachel's older sister, Leah, before Laban would agree to let Jacob and Rachel marry. She was the mother of Joseph and Benjamin. Var: Rachaela, Rachaele, Rachela, Racheli, Rachelle, Rahel, Rahil, Rechel, Recheli; Raske, Rochel (Yiddish). (RAY-CHEL)

Rafya The healing of Jehovah. Var: Rafia, Raphia. (RAF-YAH, RAF-EE-AH)

Raisa Yiddish name meaning "rose." Var: Raise, Raissa, Raisse. Pet: Raisel, Raizel, Raizi. (RAY-EE-SAH, RAY-SAH)

Ranit Song, joy. Var: Ranita. (RAH-NIT)

Raya Friend. (RAY-YAH)

Rayna Song of the Lord. Var: Raina, Rana, Rane, Rania. (RAY-NAH)

Raziah Secret of Jehovah. Var: Razia, Raziya. (RAH-ZĪ-AH)

Raziela The Lord is my secret. (RAZ-Ī-EL-LAH)

Razili My secret. Var: Razilee. (RAZ-EE-LEE)

Rebekah Derived from the Hebrew *ribbqāh* (noose), which is from *rabak* (to bind, to tie). The name is borne in the Bible by the wife of Isaac and mother of his twin sons, Esau and Jacob. Rivka is the original Hebrew form. Var: Rebecca (Ang.). Pet: Beckie, Becky, Reba, Riki. (REH-BEH-KAH)

Reichana Sweet-smelling. Var: Rechana, Rehana. (REY-CHAH-NAH, REY-KAH-NAH)

Remaziah A sign from Jehovah. Var: Remazia, Remazya (REH-MAH-ZĪ-AH)

Renana Joy, song. Var: Renanit, Renina. (REH-NAN-AH, REH-NAH-NAH)

Rephaela Feminine form of Rephael (God has healed). See REPHAEL (Male Names). Var: Rafaela, Rafaele, Raphaela, Raphaele, Refaela. (REH-FAY-ELL-LAH)

Reuma Aramaic name meaning "antelope, exalted." The name is borne in the Bible by the concubine of Abraham's brother, Nachor. Var: Raomi. (REE-OO-MAH)

Revaya Satisfied, gratified, sated. Var: Revaia. (REH-VAY-YAH, REH-VAY-YAH)

Rinatya A song of Jehovah. Var: Renatia, Renatya, Rinatia. (RIH-NAH-TĪ-AH)

Rishona First, foremost. (RIH-SHO-NAH)

Ritzpah Hebrew name meaning "hot stone, a coal." The name was borne by a concubine of King Saul and mother of two of his sons. Var: Ritzpa, Rizpah. (RITZ-PAH)

Rivka Derived from the Hebrew *ribbqāh* (noose). Rivka is the original Hebrew form of Rebekah. *See* REBEKAH. Var: Rifka, Rifke, Rivca, Rivcka. Pet: Riki, Rivai, Rivi, Rivvy. (RIV-KAH)

Ron Song, joy. Var: Rona, Roni, Ronit. (RONE)

Roniya The song of Jevohah, joy of the Lord. Var: Ronela, Ronella, Ronia. (RO-NĪ-AH)

Rut Original Hebrew form of Ruth. *See* RUTH. Pet: Ruti. (ROOT)

Ruth Of uncertain etymology, most think it is derived from the Hebrew *ruth*, a possible contraction of *rē'uth* (companion, friend). The name is borne in the Bible by the Moabite wife of Mahlon and daughter-in-law of Naomi. After the death of her husband, father-in-law, and brother-in-law, Ruth returned to Bethlehem with Naomi, where she married Boaz and gave birth to Obed, the grandfather of David. Her story is told in the Old Testament book of Ruth. (ROOTH)

Salida A borrowing from the German, Salida is derived from *salida* (happiness, joy). Var: Selda, Selde, Zelda (Yiddish). (SAH-LEE-DAH)

Salome Derived from the Hebrew *shālōm* (peace). The name is borne in the New Testament by the mother of the apostles James and John. Shlomit is the original

Hebrew form. *See* SHLOMIT. (SAH-LO-MEE, SAH-LEH-MAY)

SAMIRA A borrowing from the Arabic, Samira is derived from *samīr* (companion in evening conversations). (SAH-MEER-AH)

SANSANA Hebrew name meaning "the inner structure of the palm leaf." (SAN-SAN-NAH)

SAPHIRA Sapphire. Var: Sapir, Sapira, Sapirit. (SAY-FEER-AH)

SARAH Derived from the Hebrew *sārāh* (princess). Sarah was the name of the half sister and wife of Abraham. Originally named Sarai, her name was changed to Sarah after Abraham was told of her pregnancy. Sarah was the mother of Isaac, the progenitor of the Hebrews. Var: Sara, Sareli, Sarene, Sari, Sarina, Sarit, Sarita, Sera, Zara; Sirel, Sorale, Sorali, Sura, Surah, Tzirel, Zirel (Yiddish). Pet: Sadie, Sadye, Saretta, Sarette. (SAR-RAH, SER-RAH)

SASONA Joy, bliss. (SAH-SOHN-NAH)

SEMEICHA Happy, joyful. Var: Semecha. (SEH-MEE-KAH)

SERACH Hebrew name meaning "abundance, excess." The name is borne in the Old Testament by the daughter of Asher. She supposedly showed Moses the resting place of Joseph in Egypt. Var: Serah. (SEE-RAHK)

SERAPHINA Derived from the Hebrew *sĕrāphīm* (burning ones, the angels surrounding the throne of God), which is from *sāraph* (to burn). Var: Serafina, Seraphine. (SER-RAH-FEE-NAH)

SHAANANA Calm, peaceful, tranquil. (SHAY-AH-NAH-NAH)

SHACHARIYA Dawn, morning. Var: Schacharia, Shacharit, Shacharita, Shaharit, Shaharita. (SHAK-AH-RĪ-AH)

SHALVAH Peace. Var: Shalva. (SHAHL-VAH)

SHALVIYA The peace of God. (SHAHL-VĪ-AH)

SHAMIRA Guardian, defender. (SHAY-MEER-AH)

SHAPIRA Aramaic name meaning "good." (SHAY-PEER-AH)

SHARON A plain, a flat area. In biblical times, Sharon was a fertile, coastal plain in Palestine where roses and oak trees grew in abundance. Var: Shaaron, Sharona, Sharoni, Sharonit, Sharyn, Sherran. (SHAR-RON)

SHEINA Popular Yiddish name meaning "beautiful." Var: Shaina, Shaine, Shana, Shayna, Shona, Shoni, Shonie. Pet: Shaindel, Shayndel, Sheindel. (SHAY-NAH)

SHEKEDA An almond tree. Var: Shekedia, Shekediya. (SHEH-KEH-DAH)

SHELAVYA To be joined together. Var: Shelavia. (SHEH-LAH-VĪ-AH)

SHELI Mine, belonging to me. Var: Shelli. (SHEL-LEE)

SHELIYA The Lord is mine. Var: Shelia. (SHEH-LĪ-AH, SHEH-LĪ-YAH)

SHEVA Hebrew name meaning "an oath." Var: Sheba. (SHE-VAH)

SHIFA Abundance, quantity. (SHI-FAH)

SHIFRAH Beautiful, good. Var: Schifra, Shifra. (SHI-FRAH)

SHIMONA Feminine form of Shimon (heard). *See* SHIMON (Male Names). Var: Simeona, Simona (Ang.). (SHI-MO-NAH)

SHIMRIAH Jehovah is protector, the Lord protects. Var: Shimra, Shimria, Shimrit, Shimriya. (SHIM-RĪ-AH)

SHIRAH A song, a melody. Var: Shira. (SHIR-RAH)

SHIRLI My song. Var: Shirlee. (SHIR-LĪ)

SHLOMIT Original Hebrew form of Salome, which is derived from *shālōm* (peace). *See* SALOME. Var: Shelomit, Shulamit, Shulamith. (SHLO-MIT)

SHOMERA Guard. Var: Shomria, Shomriah, Shomrit, Shomriya, Shomrona. (SHO-MER-AH)

SHOSHANNAH Derived from the Hebrew *shōshannāh* (a lily, a rose). Var: Shoshana, Shoshanah; Susannah, Susanne, Suzanne (Ang.). Short: Shoshan; Susan (Ang.). Pet: Su, Sue, Susie, Susy, Suzy, Suzette. (SHO-SHAH-NAH)

SHUALA Fox. (SHOO-AH-LAH)

SIVANA Derived from Sivan, the name of the ninth month of the Jewish calendar. (SĪ-VAH-NAH)

SOREKA Vine. (SO-REH-KAH)

TABITHA Derived from the Aramaic *tabhītha* (roe, gazelle). (TAB-IH-THA)

TALAL Dew, a covering of dew. Var: Talila. (TAH-LAL)

TALMA Hill, mound, furrow. (TAL-MAH)

TALYA Aramaic name meaning "lamb." Talya is also a Hebrew name derived from *tal* (dew). Var: Talia. (TAL-YAH)

TAMAH Wonder, amazement. Var: Tama. (TAY-MAH)

TAMAR Palm, a date palm. The name is borne in the Bible by a daughter-in-law of Judah and by a daughter of King David. Var: Tamara, Tamarah, Temara. (TAY-MAR)

TENUVAH Produce, fruit and vegetables. Var: Tenuva. (TEH-NOO-VAH)

TERIAH Fresh, new. Var: Tari, Taria, Teria. (TEH-REE-AH)

TESHUAH Salvation, deliverance. Var: Teshua. (TEH-SHOO-AH)

TESHURAH Gift, a giving. Var: Teshura. (TEH-SHOOR-AH)

TIFARA Beautiful, glorious. Var: Tiferet, Tiphara. (TIH-FAR-RAH)

TIRA Camp, encampment. (TIH-RAH)

TIRZAH Pleasantness, delight. The name is borne in the Bible by the youngest of Zelophehad's five daughters. Var: Thirza, Tirza. (TEER-zah)

TIVONA Lover of nature. Var: Tivoni. (TIH-VO-NAH)

TORI My turtledove. (TOH-REE)

TOVAH Good, pleasing. Var: Toba, Tobit, Tova, Tovat, Tovit. (TOH-VAH)

TZADIKA Pious, devout. Var: Zadika. (ZAH-DEE-KAH)

TZAFRA Morning. Var: Zafra. (ZAF-RAH)

TZAHALA Joy, happiness. Var: Zahala. (ZAH-HAH-LAH)

TZEFIRA Morning. Var: Zefira. (ZEH-FEER-AH)

TZEIRA Young, youthful. Var: Zeira. (ZIR-RAH)

TZEMICHA Flowering, blossoming. Var: Zemicha. (ZEH-MIH-KAH)

TZEVIYA Gazelle. Var: Tzevia. (ZEV-EE-AH)

TZILA Shadow, shade, gloom. Var: Zila. (ZIH-LAH)

TZILI My shadow. Var: Zili. (ZIH-LEE)

TZINA A protection, a shelter. Var: Zina. (ZIH-NAH)

TZIPIYA Hope. Var: Tzipia, Zipia. (ZIH-PEE-AH)

TZIPORAH A little bird, a female bird. It is borne in the Bible by the daughter of Reuel. She was the wife of Moses and mother of Gershom and Eliezer. Var: Cipora, Zipora, Ziporah, Zippora, Zipporah; Tzipeh, Tzippe, Zipeh (Yiddish). (ZIH-POR-AH)

TZIVYA Gazelle. The name is borne in the Old Testament by the mother of King Joash. Var: Civia, Tzivia, Zibiah, Zivia. (ZIV-YAH)

TZIYONA Derived from the Hebrew *tsīyōn* (a hill). The name, which is Anglicized as Zion, was in biblical times that of a Canaanite fortress captured by David, which then became known as the City of David. Later, it became the site on which the temple was built in Jerusalem. Zion is symbolic of Jewish national life. Var: Zeona, Ziona (Ang.). (ZĪ-YO-NAH)

TZOFI Scout. Var: Tzofit, Zofi, Zofit. (ZO-FEE)

TZOFIA A scout of Jehovah. Var: Tzofiya, Zofia. (ZO-FĪ-AH)

TZURIYA Jehovah is strength. Var: Tzuria, Zuria. (ZOO-RĪ-YAH)

UDIYA The fire of Jehovah. Var: Udia. (YOO-DĪ-AH)

URIELA The flame of Jehovah. Var: Uriella. (YOO-REE-EL-LAH)

USHRIYA Blessed of Jehovah. Var: Ushria. (YOO-SHRĪ-AH)

VASHTI Persian name meaning "beautiful." The name was borne by the queen of Ahasuerus who was deposed for refusing to appear at the king's summons. She was replaced by Esther. (VASH-TĪ)

YAARA Honeycomb. Var: Yaari, Yaarit, Yara. (YAY-AH-RAH)

YACHNE Yiddish form of Johanna (God is gracious). Var: Yachna. (YAHK-NEH)

YAEL Mountain goat. The name is borne in the Bible by the wife of Heber, the Kenite. After being defeated by Barak, the captain of the Canaanite army fled and sought refuge with the tribe of Heber. Yael invited him into her tent and killed him with a tent peg as he lay sleeping. Var: Yaala, Yaalat, Yaela, Yaella; Jael (Ang.). (YAY-EL)

YAKIRA Precious, dear. Var: Yekara, Yekarah. (YEH-KIH-RAH)

YARDENA Feminine form of Yarden (flowing down, descending). *See* YARDEN (Male Names). Var: Jardena (Ang.). (YAR-DEH-NAH)

YARDENIYA Garden of the Lord. Var: Jardenia, Yardenia. (YAR-DEH-NĪ-AH)

YASMIN Derived from the Arabic *yasmīn* (jasmine, a fragrant plant). Var: Jasmin, Jasmina, Jasmine, Yasmeen, Yasmina, Yasmine. (YAS-MIN, YAS-MINE)

YEHUDIT Hebrew name meaning "he will be praised." The name, Anglicized as Judith, was borne by one of the wives of Esau. Var: Yudit; Yutke (Yiddish). Pet: Yudi. (YEH-HOO-DIT)

YEMIMA Derived from *yemīmāh* (a dove). It is borne in the Bible by the first of Job's three daughters, born after his affliction. Var: Jemima. (YEH-MĪ-MAH)

YENTA Yiddish form of Henrietta, a feminine diminutive form of Henry (ruler of an enclosure, home ruler). *See* HENRY (English Names). Var: Yente, Yentel, Yentele, Yentil. (YEN-TAH)

YERUSHA Possessed, a possession. The name, Anglicized as Jerushah, was borne by the mother of King Jotham. (YEH-ROO-SHA)

YESHARA Straightforward, honest. (YEH-SHAR-RAH)

YOCHANA Feminine form of Yochanan (God is gracious). *See* YOCHANAN (Male Names). Var: Yochani. (YO-KAH-NAH)

YOCHEVED God's glory. The name, which is Anglicized as Jochebed, was borne by the mother of Miryam, Moses, and Aaron. Var: Yochebed. (YAH-KEH-VED)

YOELA The feminine form of Yoel (Jehovah is his God). *See* YOEL (Male Names). Var: Joela, Yoelit. (YO-ELL-LAH)

YOSEFA Feminine form of Yosef (he shall add, may God add). *See* YOSEF (Male Names). Var: Josefa, Josepha, Josifa, Josipha, Yoseifa, Yosepha, Yosipha. (YO-SEH-FAH, YO-SEH-FAH)

ZAHARA To shine. Var: Zahari, Zaharit. (ZAH-HAH-RAH, ZAH-HAH-RAH)

ZAKAH Pure, clear. Var: Zaka. (zah-kah)

ZAKIYA Pure, clear. Var: Zakia, Zakiah. (ZAH-KEE-AH)

ZAZA Movement. Var: Zazu. (ZAY-ZAH)

ZEHARA Brightness, light. Var: Zehorit. (ZEH-HAH-RAH, ZEH-HAH-RAH)

ZEHAVA Gold, golden. Var: Zahava, Zehovit, Zehuva, Zehuvit. (ZEH-HAH-VAH)

ZEHIRA Careful, cautious. (ZEH-HEER-AH)

ZELDA Yiddish name meaning "luck." Alternatively, Zelda is a short form of Grizelda, which is from the Germanic Griseldis, a name derived from *gries* (gravel, stone). Var: Selda. (ZEL-DAH)

ZEMIRA Song, melody. (ZEH-MY-RAH)

ZEMORAH Branch. Var: Zemora. (ZEH-MOR-RAH)

ZENANA A borrowing from the Persian, Zenana means "woman." Short: Zena, Zenia. (ZEH-NAN-AH)

ZENDA A borrowing from the Persian, Zenda means "sacred." (ZEN-DAH)

ZEVIDA Gift. Var: Zevuda. (ZEH-VEE-DAH, ZEH-VIH-DAH)

ZILPAH Of uncertain definition, some believe it has the meaning "a dropping." The name Zilpah is borne in the Bible by Leah's handmaid who was given to Jacob. She became the mother of Gad and Asher. Var: Zulpha, Zylpha. (ZIL-PAH)

ZIMRIAH Songfest. Var: Zimria, Zimriya. (ZIM-REE-AH)

ZIRAH Arena, ring. Var: Zira. (ZIR-AH)

CHAPTER EIGHTEEN

Korean Names

THE TRADITIONAL Korean system of naming is very old and based on clan genealogy. The family name dictates the length of a multigenerational cycle of names. To each child and paternal cousin of the same sex and generation, one of these names is added to another element, creating a unique, yet related, double name. In some families this element is given to all the children regardless of the sex of the child.

Female names are generally indicative of nature, goodness, or "feminine" qualities of grace and beauty. Male names often take the themes of strength, wisdom, and prosperity.

As families become smaller and people move to metropolitan areas or migrate abroad, the traditional way of naming with the genealogical name is becoming less common. In such instances, parents have been known to arbitrarily choose a favored name element and apply it to each of their children's names.

Korean Male Names

BAE Inspiration. (BEH)

CHIN HO Precious and goodness. (CHIN-HO)

CHUNG-HEE Righteous and pleasure. (CHUNG-HE)

CHUNG-HO Righteous and goodness. (CHUNG-HO)

CHUNG-SU Righteous and excellence; outstanding; long-life. (CHUNG-SOO)

DAE-HO Great and goodness. (DEH-HO)

DAE-HYUN Great and honor. (DEH-HYUN)

DAE-JUNG Great and righteous, honest.

DONG-MIN East and cleverness. (DŌNG-MIN)

DONG-SUN East and goodness. (DŌNG-SUN)

DUCK-YOUNG Virtue and prosperity; eternal. (DUK-YOUNG)

DU-HO Head and goodness. (DOO-HO)

HYO Familial duty. (HYO)

HYUN-KI Wisdom and energy, vigor. (HYUN-KEE)

HYUN-SHIK Wisdom and clear; honest. (HYUN-SHIK)

HYUN-SU Wisdom and outstanding; long-life. (HYUN-SOO)

IL-SUNG Superiority and achievement; sincere. (ILL-SUNG)

IN-HO Humanity and goodness. (IN-HO)

IN-SU Humanity and outstanding; long-life. (IN-SOO)

JAE-HWA Respect and beauty. (JEH-HWA)

JAE-SUN Respect and goodness. (JEH-SUN)

JIN-SANG Truth and benevolence; aid. (JIN-SAHNG)

JUNG HEE Righteous, honest and pleasure. (JUNG-HE)

JUNG-HWA Righteous, honest and beauty. (JUNG-WAH)

JUNG-SU Righteous, honest and beautiful. (JUNG-SOO)

KANG-DAE Strong and greatness. (KAHNG-DEH)

KI-HYUN Energy, vigor and wisdom.

KI-YOUNG Energy, vigor and prosperity, eternal.

KWAN Strong. (KWAHN)

KWANG HO Light and goodness. (KWAHNG-HO)

KWANG-SUN Light and goodness. (KWAHNG-SUN)

KYU BOK Standard and blessed. (KYOO-BOK)

KYU BONG Standard and eminence. (KYOO-BŌNG)

KYUNG Honored. (KEEUNG)

KYUNG-SAM Honored and achievement. (KEEUNG-SAHM)

MIN HO Cleverness and goodness. (MIN-HO)

MIN KI Cleverness and energy, vigor. (MIN-KEE)

MIN KYUNG Cleverness and honored. (MIN-KYUNG)

MUN-HEE Literate, educated and pleasure. (MUHN-HE)

MYUNG-DAE Brightness and greatness. (MYUNG-DEH)

MYUNG-KI Brightness and energy, vigor. (MYUNG-KEE)

NAM-KYU South and standard. (NAHM-KYU)

SAM YONG Achievement and prosperity; eternal. (SAM-YŌNG)

SANG KI Benevolence; aid and energy; vigor. (SAHNG-KEE)

SANG KYU Benevolence; aid and standard. (SAHNG-KYU)

SANG-MIN Benevolence; aid and cleverness. (SAHNG-MIN)

SHIN Faith, belief; trust. (SHIN)

SHIN-IL Faith, belief; trust and superiority. (SHIN-ILL)

SUK-CHUL Great, big and firmness. (SOK-CHULL)

TAE-HYUN Great and honor. (TEH-HYUN)

YONG-SOOK Prosperity; eternal and pure. (YŌNG-SOOK)

YONG-SUN Prosperity; eternal and goodness. (YŌNG-SUN)

YOUNG Prosperity; eternal. (YUNG)

YOUNG HO Prosperity; eternal and goodness. (YUNG-HO)

YOUNG IL Prosperity; eternal and superiority. (YUNG-ILL)

YOUNG JA Prosperity; eternal and attraction. (YUNG-JAH)

YOUNG JAE Prosperity; eternal and respect. (YUNG-JEH)

YOUNG MIN Prosperity; eternal and cleverness. (YUNG-MIN)

YOUNG-NAM Prosperity; eternal and south. (YUNG-NAHM)

YOUNG SOO Prosperity; excellence. (YUNG-SOO)

Korean Female Names

AE-CHA Love and daughter. (EH-CHAH)

AE-SOOK Love and purity. (EH-SOOK)

BONG-CHA Superior and daughter. (BŌNG-CHAH)

CHO-HEE Beautiful and pleasure. (CHO-HE)

CHUNG-AE Righteous and love. (CHUNG-EH)

CHUNG-CHA Righteous and daughter. (CHUNG-CHAH)

CHUN-HEI Justice and grace. (CHUN-HE)

EUN-AE Grace and love. (OON-EH)

EUN-HEE Grace and pleasure. (OON-HE)

EUN JUNG Grace and righteous, honor. (OON-JUNG)

EUN KYUNG Grace and honored. (OON-KYUNG)

EUN-MI Grace and beautiful. (OON-ME)

EUN SUN Grace and goodness. (OON-SUN)

HEA JUNG Grace and righteous. (HEH-JUNG)

HEA-WOO Grace and girl. (HEH-WOO)

HEE-YOUNG Pleasure and prosperity; eternal. (HE-YUNG)

HEI RYUNG Grace and brightness. (HEE-RYUNG)

HO-SOOK Goodness and purity. (HO-SOOK)

HWA-YOUNG Beauty and prosperity; eternal. (HWAH-YUNG)

HYE SU Grace and beautiful. (HE-SOO)

HYUN-AE Wise and love. (HYUN-EH)

HYUN JAE Wise and respect. (HYUN-JEH)

HYUN JUNG Wise and righteous. (HYUN-JUNG)

HYUN-OK Wise and jade, gem. (HYUN-Ō)

JAE-HWA Respect and beauty. (JEH-WAH)

JIN-AE Truth; treasure and love. (JIN-EH)

JIN-KYONG Truth; treasure and brightness. (JIN-KYŌNG)

KYUNG MI Honored and beautiful. (KYUNG-ME)

KYUNG-SOON Honored and mild, gentle. (KYUNG-SOON)

MI-CHA Beautiful and daughter. (ME-CHAH)

MI-HI Beautiful and joy. (ME-HE)

MI-KYONG Beautiful and brightness. (ME-KYŌNG)

MIN-HEE Cleverness and pleasure. (MIN-HE)

MIN-HO Cleverness and goodness. (MIN-HO)

MIN-JEE Cleverness and wisdom. (MIN-JEE)

MIN-JUNG Cleverness and righteous. (MIN-JUNG)

MI-SUN Beautiful and goodness. (ME-SUN)

MI-YOUNG Beautiful and prosperity; eternal. (ME-YUNG)

MUN-HEE Literate, educated and pleasure. (MUN-HE)

MYUNG-HEE Brightness and pleasure. (MYUNG-HE)

SANG-HEE benevolence, aid and pleasure. (SAHNG-HE)

SOO JIN Excellence and truth; treasure. (SOO-JIN)

SOOK-JOO Pure and jewel. (SOOK-JOO)

SOO MIN Excellence and cleverness. (SOO-MIN)

SOON-BOK Mild, gentle and blessed. (SOON-BOK)

SOO-YUN Excellence and lotus blossom. (SOO-YŪN)

SO-YOUNG Beautiful and prosperity; eternal. (SO-YUNG)

SUN HEE Goodness and pleasure. (SUN-HE)

SUN HI Goodness and joy. (SUN-HE)

SUN JUNG Goodness and righteous. (SUN-JUNG)

YOUNG-IL Prosperity; eternal and superiority. (YUNG-ILL)

YOUNG MI Prosperity; eternal and beautiful. (YUNG-ME)

YOUNG-SOON Prosperity; eternal and mild, gentle. (YUNG-SOON)

YUN HEE Lotus blossom and pleasure. (YUN-HE)

CHAPTER NINETEEN

Muslim/Arabic Names

ARABIC NAMES can be put into two general categories: pre-Islamic and post-Islamic. Pre-Islamic names were mainly influenced by nature, occupations, personal characteristics, and genealogy. Post-Islamic names were influenced by the Prophet Muḥammad, the catalyst for the beginning of a vast cultural transformation in the Arab world.

Pre-Islamic nature names such as the feminine Arwa (female mountain goat) and Randa (a sweet-smelling tree) and the masculine Fahd (panther) and Rabi (fragrant breeze) are still popular today.

While occupational names can still be found, they are not as common as the other types of names. Examples of occupational names are Rāwiya (storyteller) and Kateb (writer).

Personal characteristics, both positive and negative, form the basis for many names. Male names such as Tawīl (tall) and Saghir (short) and female names such as ʻAbla (having a fine, full figure), Najlā (having large, beautiful eyes), and Kalthūm (fat, plump cheeks) are examples.

Post-Islamic names were heavily influenced by the qualities espoused in Islam and by the Prophet Muḥammad. His suggestion that the best names were those derived from the ninety-nine qualities of God listed in the Koran, those formed from the root word *hamida* (praiseworthy, praise), and compound names beginning with *ʻAbd* (servant of), contributed greatly to the popularity of those names in the Arab world.

Names referring to the Prophet, his immediate family and friends, and his descendants are also common. In fact, the name Muḥammad, together with its five hundred variants, is the most common name in the world. Fātima (one who abstains from forbidden things), the name of one of the Prophet's daughters, is chosen by many parents for their daughters.

Islam recognizes both Judaism and Christianity, and many of the stories found in the Bible are also found in the Koran. Therefore, names such as Ibrāhīm, Yūsuf, and Maryam are popular, although more so among Christian Arabs.

Islamic doctrines of belief in one God, Allāh, following the path of Islam, purity of heart, benevolence to others, and the virtues of chastity and charity have also created many names for both males and females. For girls, Amīna (faithful), Fadīla (moral excellence), and Imān (faith, belief in God) are popular examples. Ahmad (more commendable) and Muḥammad (praiseworthy, the praised one) are among the most popular for boys. Many believe that angels pray in every house in which there is a Muḥammad or an Ahmad, which makes for an even greater incentive to choose these names for the newly born.

Converts to Islam usually change their name to that of an Islamic saint or to one of the names referring to the Prophet or his family. One of the most well known who has done so is Cassius Clay, who upon conversion, adopted the name of Muhammad Ali.

Although recent coinages often take the themes

found in pre-Islamic names, there is a strong pro-Islamic movement in the Arab world today which is certain to have an effect on the bestowal of names.

In many Muslim countries, births, deaths, and marriages were seldom registered, so last names were not needed. In place of surnames, terms such as *Bin* or *Ben* (son of) and *Binte* (daughter of) or *Abu* (father of) and *Um* (mother of) were often added to the given name, along with the name of the applicable family member. Tribal names or place-names were also added for identification.

In Persia, family names were required by law in 1926 and married women adopted their husband's chosen surname. In 1950 Moroccans were directed to adopt surnames derived from localities or occupations. It wasn't until 1960 that Tunis passed a law requiring families to adopt a permanent surname.

Unlike most European names, Arabic names consist mainly of vocabulary words that can easily be looked up in any Arabic dictionary. This helps a great deal in finding out what a name means and can also be a useful tool in creating your own Arabic or Muslim name.

Muslim/Arabic Male Names

'ABBĀS Derived from the Arabic *'abbās* (austere, stern), which is from *'abasa* (to look sternly at). Alternatively, 'Abbās is an appellation for the lion. The name was borne by the Prophet's uncle, 'Abbās ibn-'Abd-al-Muṭṭalib (c. 566–652). He was the ancestor of the Abbasid caliphs who reigned over the Islamic world from 750 to 1258. (AH-BAHS)

'ABD-AL-'ĀṬI Compound name composed of the Arabic elements *'abd* (servant of), *al* (the), and *'āṭi* (donor, giver): hence, "servant of the Giving One." Al-'Āṭi (the Giver) is an attribute of Allāh. Var: 'Abdel-'Āṭi. (AHBD-AHL-ATEE)

'ABD-AL-'AZĪZ Compounding of the elements *'abd* (servant of), *al* (the), and *'azīz* (powerful, mighty): hence, "servant of the Mighty One." Al-Azīz (the All-Powerful) is one of the ninety-nine attributes of Allāh. The name was borne by the founder and first king of Saudi Arabia, 'Abd-al-'Azīz II (c. 1880–1953). He undertook the conquest of Arabia in 1901 and extended his rule over most of the Arabian Peninsula during the next two decades. In 1934 his kingdom became known as Saudi Arabia. Var: Abdel-'Azīz, Abdul-Aziz. (AHBD-AHL-AH-ZEEZ)

'ABD-AL-FATTĀḤ Composed of the elements *'abd* (servant of), *al* (the), and *fattāḥ* (opener, in reference to the gates of sustenance and abundance). Al-Fattāḥ (the Opener) is an attribute of Allāh. Var: 'Abdel-Fattāḥ. (AHBD-AHL-FAH-TAH)

'ABD-AL-HĀDI Compound name composed of the elements *'abd* (servant of), *al* (the), and *hādi* (guide, leader). Al-Hādi (the Guide) is an attribute of Allāh. Var: 'Abdel-Hādi. (AHBD-AHL-HAH-DEE)

'ABD-AL-ḤAKĪM Compounding of the elements *'abd* (servant of), *al* (the), and *ḥakīm* (wise, intelligent, judicious): hence, "servant of the Wise One." Al-Ḥakīm (the Wise) is an attribute of Allāh. Var: Abdel-Ḥakīm. (AHBD-AHL-HAH-KEEM)

'ABD-AL-ḤALĪM Compound name composed of the elements *'abd* (servant of), *al* (the), and *ḥalīm* (patient, mild-mannered): hence, "servant of the Patient One." Al-Ḥalīm (the Patient) is an attribute of Allāh. Var: 'Abdel-Ḥalīm. (AHBD-AHL-HAH-LEEM)

'ABD-AL-ḤAMĪD Composed of the elements *'abd* (servant of), *al* (the), and *ḥamīd* (praiseworthy, commendable, laudable): hence, "servant of the Praiseworthy One." Al-Ḥamīd (the Praiseworthy) is an attribute of Allāh. The name was borne by a sultan of Turkey, Abdul Ḥamid II (1842–1918). Var: 'Abdel-Ḥamīd, 'Abd ul-Ḥamīd, Abdul-Ḥamīd. (AHBD-AHL-HAH-MEED)

'ABD-AL-JĀBIR Popular compound name composed of the elements *'abd* (servant of), *al* (the), and *jābir* (comforter), which is from *jabara* (to restore): hence, "servant of the Comforter." In the United States the name is most widely recognized as that of basketball star Kareem Abdul-Jabbar, formerly Lew Alcindor. Var: 'Abd-al-Jabbar, Abdul-Jabbar. (AHBD-AHL-JAH-BEER)

'ABD-AL-JAWWĀD Compounding of the elements *'abd* (servant of), *al* (the), and *jawwād* (generous, magnanimous). Al-Jawwād (the Magnanimous) is one of the attributes of Allāh. Var: 'Abdel-Gawwād. (AHBD-AHL-JAH-WAHD)

'ABD-AL-KARĪM Composed of the elements *'abd* (servant of), *al* (the), and *karīm* (generous): hence, "servant of the Generous One." Al-Karīm (the Generous) is one of the ninety-nine attributes of Allāh. The name was borne by a Moroccan leader of the Berbers, 'Abd-al-Karīm Al-Khaṭṭabi (1882–1963). He fought against the Spanish and then the French in the Rif region of Morocco from 1920 to 1926. Var: 'Abd-al-Krim, 'Abdel-Kerīm, Abd-el-Krim. (AHBD-AHL-KAH-REEM)

'ABD-ALLĀH Compound name composed of the elements *'abd* (servant of) and Allāh (God), which is derived from *al* (the) and *ilāh* (God). An ancient Arabic name, 'Abd-Allāh, along with its variants, is one of the most common names throughout the Islamic world. The name was borne by the Prophet's father, 'Abd-Allāh ibn-'Abd-al-Muttalib (c. 545–70), and more recently by Abdullah Ben Abdulazīz (b. 1924), crown prince of Saudi Arabia. Var: 'Abdalla, Abdulla, Abdullah. (AHB-DAHL-LAH)

'ABD-AL-LAṬĪF Compound name composed of the elements *'abd* (servant of), *al* (the), and *laṭīf* (kind, gentle): hence, "servant of the Kind One." Al-Laṭīf (the Kind) is one of the attributes of Allāh. Var: 'Abdel-Laṭīf, Abdullatif. (AHBD-AHL-LAH-TEEF)

'ABD-AL-MĀJID Compound name composed of the elements *'abd* (servant of), *al* (the), and *mājid* (glorious): hence, "servant of the Glorious One." The name was borne by a sultan of Turkey, Abdul-Medjid (1823–61), and more recently by Prince Abdul Majid Ben Abdulazīz (b. 1941), son of King 'Abd-al-'Azīz of Saudi Arabia. Var: Abdul Māgid, Abdul Majid, Abdul Medjid, Abdul Mejid. (AHBD-AL-MAH-JID)

'ABD-AL-MALIK Compounding of the elements *'abd* (servant of), *al* (the), and *malik* (king, sovereign). Al-Malik (the Sovereign) is one of the attributes of Allah. The name was borne by the fifth Umayyad caliph 'Abd-al-Malik ibn-Marwān (635–705). He was responsible for making Arabic the administrative language of the empire and for seeing many new cities into existence. Var: 'Abdel-Malik. (AHBD-AHL-MAL-IK)

'ABD-AL-MUḤSIN Derived from *'abd* (servant of), *al* (the), and *muḥsin* (charitable, generous): hence, "servant of the Charitable One." The name is borne by Prince Abdul Muhsen Ben Abdulazīz (b. 1927), governor of the Holy City of Medina in Saudi Arabia. Var: Abdul Muhsen. (AHBD-AHL-MOO-SIN)

'ABD-AL-MU'ṬI Compound name composed of the elements *'abd* (servant of), *al* (the), and *mu'ṭi* (donor, giver). Al-Mu'ti (the Donor) is one of the attributes of Allāh. Var: Abdel-Mu'ṭi. (AHBD-AHL-MOO-TEE)

'ABD-AL-QĀDIR Compounding of the elements *'abd* (servant of), *al* (the), and *qādir* (capable). Al-Qādir (the Capable) is one of the attributes of Allāh. The name was borne by 'Abd-al-Qādir Al Jazā'iri (1808–83), a leader of the Arab resistance during the French occupation of Algeria. Var: 'Abd-al-Qadir, Abd-al-Kadir, Abdel-'Ādir, Abdel-Kadir, Abd-el-Kadir, Abdulqader. (AHBD-AHL-KAH-DEER)

'ABD-AL-RAḤĪM Compound name composed of the elements *'abd* (servant of), *al* (the), and *raḥīm* (compassionate, sympathetic). Al-Raḥīm (the Compassionate) is one of the attributes of Allāh. Var: Abder Rahīm, Abdur Rahim. (AHBD-AHL-RAH-HEEM)

'ABD-AL-RAḤMĀN Derived from the elements *'abd* (servant of), *al* (the), and *raḥmān* (merciful). Al-Raḥmān (the All-Merciful) is an attribute of Allāh. The name was borne by the founder of the Umayyad dynasty in Spain, Al Raḥmān Al-Dākhil (d. 780) and by one of his successors, 'Abd-al-Raḥmān (891–961), under whose leadership Spain became a major Mediterranean power. The name is also borne by Prince Abdul Raḥmān Ben Abdulazīz (b. 1931), son of Saudi Arabian King 'Abd-al-Azīz. Var: Abd ar-Raḥmān, Abder Raḥmān, Abdul Raḥmān, Abdur Raḥmān. (AHBD-AHL-ROK-MAHN)

'ABD-AL-RA'ŪF Compound name composed of the Arabic elements *'abd* (servant of), *al* (the), and *ra'ūf* (compassionate, merciful): hence, "servant of the Compassionate One." Al-Ra'ūf (the Compassionate) is one of the ninety-nine attributes of Allāh. (AHBD-AHL-RAH-OOF)

'ABD-AL-RĀZIQ Composed of the elements *'abd* (servant of), *al* (the), and *rāziq* (provider). Al-Rāziq (the Provider) is one of the attributes of Allāh. Var: Abd-al-Razzāq, 'Abder-Razzā', 'Abder-Rāzi', Abdur Razzāq. (AHBD-AHL-RAH-ZEEK)

'ABD-AL-SALĀM Compounding of the elements *'abd* (servant of), *al* (the), and *salām* (peace). Al-Salām (the Peaceable) is an attribute of Allāh. The name is borne by Jordanian Prime Minister Abdel Salam Al-Majali. Var: Abdel Salam, Abd-es-Salām, Abdul Salam, Abdus Salam. (AHBD-AHL-SAH-LAHM)

'ABD-AL-WAHĀB Compound name composed of the elements *'abd* (servant of), *al* (the), and *wahāb* (giving). Al Wahāb (the Giver) is one of the attributes of Allāh. The name was borne by the founder of the fundamentalist Wahhabiyya religious movement, Muḥammad ibn-'Abd-al-Wahāb (1703–92). (AHBD-AHL-WAH-HAHB)

'ĀBID Derived from *'ābid* (server or worshiper of God), which is from *'abada* (to worship). Var: Abbud. (AH-BEED)

'ĀDIL Popular name derived from *'ādil* (just, fair), which is from *'adala* (to act justly, to be fair). Var: Adil. (AH-DEEL)

'ADNĀN Ancient Arabic name thought to be derived from *'adana* (to settle). The 'Adnāniyūn Arabs who lived in the northern area of the Arabian Peninsula are said to have been descended from 'Adnān, one of Ismā'īl's descendants. (ADD-NAN)

AḤMAD Highly popular name derived from *aḥmad* (more commendable), which is from *hamida* (to praise). The theologian Aḥmad ibn-Ḥanbal (780–855) was the founder of Hanbaliya, one of the four recognized schools of Islamic law. The name in its variant form of Ahmed is borne by Prince Ahmed Ben Abdulazīz of Saudi Arabia (b. 1941). Var: Ahmed. (AH-MAHD)

'ALĀ' Derived from *'alā'* (excellence, supremacy), which is from *'ala* (to ascend, to rise). 'Alā', a common element in many compound names, is also used as an independent given name. (AH-LA)

A'L AD-DĪN Compound name derived from the Arabic elements *a'lā* (height), *al* (the), and *dīn* (religion): hence, "height of the religion." The Anglicized form, Aladdin, was borne by the central character in one of the stories from *The Arabian Nights*. Var: Aladdin. (AHL-AH-DIN)

'ALI Derived from *'aliy*, *'ali* (sublime, exalted, elevated), which is from the verb *'alā* (to ascend, to rise). Al-'Aliy (the Sublime) is one of the attributes of Allāh. 'Ali ibn-Abi-Tālib (c. 600–61), a cousin of the Prophet and the husband of the Prophet's daughter Fātima, was the first male convert to Islam. He became the fourth rightly guided and last legitimate caliph. Var: Ali. (AH-LEE)

AMĪN Popular name derived from *amīn* (honest, honorable), which is from *amuna* (to be trustworthy or reliable). (AH-MEEN)

AMĪR Derived from the Arabic *amīr* (prince, emir), which is from the verb *amara* (to command, to rule). Amīr has been used as a title for a host of designations including rulers of provinces and caliphs. (AH-MEER)

AMJAD Derived from *amjad* (more glorious), which is from *majada* (to be praiseworthy). (AHM-JAHD)

'AMMĀR Derived from *'ammār* (long-lived), which is from *'amara* (to live long, to prosper). (AH-MAR)

'AMR Derived from *'amir* (thriving, flourishing), which is from the verb *'amara* (to live long, to prosper). The name was borne by 'Amr ibn-al-'Āṣ (d. 663), a statesman and military leader who took control of Egypt away from the Byzantines. (AH-MER)

ANWAR Derived from *anwar* (clearer, brighter). The name was borne by Egyptian President Anwar al-Sadāt (1918–81). He is remembered for establishing a peace accord with Israel at Camp David in 1977 and being awarded the 1978 Nobel Peace Prize for his efforts. However, the peace accord was rejected by most of the Arab states and led to his assassination in 1981 by a Muslim extremist group. (AHN-WAHR)

AS'AD Derived from *as'ad* (happier, luckier), which is from the verb *sa'ida* (to be happy, to be lucky). Var: Assa'd. (AH-SAHD)

ASHRAF Derived from *ashraf* (more honorable), which finds its root in the verb *sharafa* (to be honorable, noble, or distinguished). (ASH-RAF)

'ĀṢIM Derived from *'āṣim* (protector, guardian), which is from the verb *'aṣama* (to protect). (AH-SEEM)

'ĀṬIF Derived from *'aṭif* (sympathetic, compassionate), which is from *'aṭafa* (to sympathize). (AH-TEEF)

ATTIAH Arabic form of the Hebrew name Ataya (prepared, ready). (AH-TEE-AH)

AYMAN Derived from *ayman* (blessed, fortunate), which is from the verb *yamana* (to be fortunate). (Ā-MAHN)

'AZĪZ Derived from *'azīz* (powerful, mighty, beloved), which is from the verb *'azza* (to be powerful or to be cherished). Al-'Azīz (the All-Powerful) is one of the ninety-nine attributes of Allāh. The name was borne by the benevolent fifth Fatimid caliph of Egypt (955–96), Al-'Azīz. He is remembered for bringing peace and prosperity to his subjects, as well as for dedicating the Al-Azhar mosque to the teaching of Islam. (AH-ZEEZ)

BADR Derived from *badr* (full moon), which is from *badara* (to take by surprise). Badr is commonly used as both a male and a female name, and is borne by Prince Badr Ben Abdulazīz, son of Saudi Arabian King 'Abd-al-Azīz. (BAH-DER)

BADR-AL-DĪN Unusual but popular compound name composed of the elements *badr* (full moon), *al* (the), and *dīn* (religion). The name can allegorically describe one's life as being fully ruled by Islam. (BAH-DER-AHL-DIN)

BAHĀ' Derived from *bahā'* (magnificence, splendor), which is from *baha* (to be splendid or beautiful). The name was borne by Bahā' Ullāh (1817–92), the Persian founder of Bahaism, a religion that stresses universal brotherhood and social equality. (BAH-HAH)

Bahir Derived from the Arabic *bahir* (dazzling). (BAH-HEER)

Bahjat Derived from *bahja* (joy, delight), which is from the verb *bahija* (to be glad, to be happy). Var: Bahgat. (BAH-JAHT)

Bakr Derived from *bakr* (young camel). Bakr is a common name and was borne by Abu-Bakr al-Ṣiddīq (573–634), the father of ʻĀʻisha, a wife of Muḥammad. After the Prophet's death, Abu-Bakr became the first rightly guided caliph (632–34). Var: Bakor. (BAH-KER)

Bāsim Derived from *bāsim* (smiling), which is from the verb *basama* (to smile). Var: Bassam. (BAH-SIM, BAH-SEEM)

Dawūd Dawūd is the Arabic form of the Hebrew David, which is derived from *dāwīd* (beloved). (DAH-WUUD)

Ḍiyā' Derived from *ḍiyā'* (brightness, radiance), which is from *ḍā'* (to shine). Var: Ḍiya. (DEE-YAH)

Ḍiyā'-al-Dīn Compound name composed of the elements *ḍiyā'* (brightness), *al* (the), and *dīn* (religion, faith). Var: Ḍiya-al-Dīn. (DEE-YAH-AL-DIN)

Fādi Derived from *fādi* (redeemer, savior), which is from *fada* (to redeem). Al-Fādi (the Savior) is used by Arab Christians as an attribute of Jesus Christ. (FAH-DEE)

Fāḍil Popular name derived from *fāḍil* (generous), which is from *faḍala* (to surpass). Var: Fadil. (FAH-DIL, FAH-DEEL)

Faḍl Derived from *faḍl* (generosity, grace), which is from *faḍala* (to surpass). Var: Fadhl, Fadl. (FAH-DL)

Fahd Popular name derived from *fadh* (panther, leopard, lynx), which is symbolic of courage, strength, and fierceness. The name is borne by King Fahad Ben Abdulazīz (b. 1920), son of ʻAbd-al-Azīz, founder and first king of Saudi Arabia. King Fahad ascended to the throne in 1982, after the death of his half brother, King Khālid Ben Abdulazīz. (FAHD)

Fahīm Derived from *fahīm* (intelligent, learned), which is from *fahima* (to understand). (FAH-HEEM)

Fakhr Derived from *fakhr* (glory, pride), which is from *fakhara* (to be proud, to glorify). Var: Fakhir. (FAH-KER)

Fakhr-al-Dīn Compound name composed of the elements *fakhr* (glory, pride), *al* (the), and *dīn* (religion, faith). The name was borne by a Lebanese emir, Fakhr-al-Dīn II (1572–1635), who fought for independence from the Ottoman Empire. Var: Fakhir-al-Dīn, Fakhrid-Dīn. (FAH-KER-AHL-DIN)

Fakhri Derived from *fakhri* (meritorious), which is from *fakhara* (to be proud, to glorify). (FAH-KREE)

Faraj Derived from *faraj* (remedy), which is from *faraja* (to remedy, to cure or drive away). Var: Farag. (FAHR-RAJ)

Farīd Derived from *farīd* (unique), which is from the verb *farada* (to be unique). Farīd is a popular name throughout the Arab world. Var: Farid. (FAH-REED)

Farūq Derived from *farūq* (a person who distinguishes right from wrong and truth from falsehood), which is from the verb *faraqa* (to separate, to make a distinction). The name was borne by the last king of Egypt, King Farūq (1920–65). Despised as being a British puppet, he was deposed in 1952 by a military takeover and sent into exile. Var: Farū'. (FAH-RUUK)

Fatḥi Of debated origin, Fatḥi might be derived from *fātiḥ* (conqueror, victor), which is from the verb *fataḥa* (to conquer). Var: Fath'. (FAH-THEE)

Fawzi Derived from *fawz* (victory, achievement), which is from *fāza* (to achieve, to win). (FAW-ZEE)

Fāyiz Derived from *fā'iz* (victor, winner), which is from *Fāza* (to achieve, to win). (FAY-IZ, FĪ-IZ)

Fayṣal Derived from the Arabic *fayṣal* (a judge, a separator of right and wrong), which is from *faṣala* (to separate). The name was borne by a Saudi Arabian king, Fayṣal Ben Abdulazīz (1905–75), son of the founder of Saudi Arabia, King ʻAbd-al-Azīz. Var: Faiṣal, Faysal. (FĪ-SAHL)

Fikri Derived from *fikri* (intellectual), which is from the verb *fakara* (to meditate, to contemplate). (FIH-KREE)

Fu'ād Derived from *fu'ād* (heart). Var: Fouad. (FOO-AHD)

Ghālib Derived from *ghālib* (victor, conqueror), which is from the verb *ghalaba* (to defeat). Var: Ghalib. (GAH-LEEB)

Ghassān Old and popular name derived from *ghassān* (prime of youth). Besides being a personal name, it was borne by a northwestern Arabian tribe known as the Banu-Ghassān. Var: Ghassan. (GAH-SAHN)

Ghayth Derived from *ghayth* (rain), which is from *ghātha* (to rain, to sprinkle with rain). The name denotes preciousness, as water is a precious and prized commodity in the desert environment. Var: Ghaith. (GAYTH)

Gulzar Derived from the Persian *gulzār* (flourishing, blooming). (GUL-ZAHR)

Ḥabīb Derived from *ḥabīb* (beloved, dear), which is from *ḥabba* (to love, to hold dear). Var: Habib. (HAH-BEEB)

Hādi Derived from *hādi* (one who guides, a religious guide or leader), which is from *hadā* (to rightly guide). Alternatively, Hādi is a short form of *hādi'* (calm, quiet). (HAH-DEE)

Ḥāfiẓ Derived from *ḥāfiẓ* (guardian), which is from the verb *ḥafaẓa* (to guard). Var: Hafiz. (HAH-FIZ)

Ḥakīm Popular name derived from *ḥakīm* (judicious), which is from *ḥakama* (to pass judgment). Var: Hakeem. (HAH-KEEM)

Ḥāmid Derived from *ḥāmid* (praising, thankful). This is one of many names derived from the root *ḥamida* (to praise, to commend). Var: Hamid. (HAH-MID)

Ḥamza Old Arabic name derived from *ḥamuza* (to be strong). The name was borne by Muḥammad's uncle, an early convert to Islam, who was known for his strength and courage in battle. (HAHM-ZAH)

Hāni Derived from *hāni'* (happy, joyful), which is from *hani'a* (to be happy). (HAH-NEE)

Hanif Derived from *hanif* (true believer of Islam). Var: Hanef. (HAH-NIF)

Ḥārith Derived from *ḥaratha* (to be a good provider, to be capable). Var: Harith. (HAHR-ITH)

Harūn Derived from the Arabic *harūn* (exalted, lofty). The name was borne by the caliph of Baghdad Harūn al-Rashid (786–809), who was responsible for bringing in Hindu physicians to organize hospitals and medical schools in Baghdad. Var: Haroun. (HAH-ROON)

Ḥasan Very popular name derived from *ḥasan* (beautiful, handsome, good), which is from *ḥasuna* (to be good). The name was borne by the Prophet's grandson Al-Ḥasan (625–69), the son of Fātima bint-Muḥammad and 'Ali ibn-Abi-Ṭālib, the fourth rightly guided caliph. Al-Ḥasan, poisoned by one of his wives, is venerated as a martyr by the Shiites. Var: Hassan. (HAH-SAHN)

Hāshim Derived from *hāshim* (destroying, crushing), which is from *hashama* (to crush, to smash). The name was borne by a great-grandfather of Muḥammad, Hāshim ibn-'Abd-Manāf. Arab tradition relates that Hāshim, formerly known as 'Amr, brought some bread back from a trading trip, crushed it for his tribe, and thereafter was called Al-Hāshim (the Crusher). His descendants are known as Hashemites. (HAH-SHIM)

Ḥāsim Derived from *ḥāsim* (decisive), which is from *ḥasama* (to decide, to separate). (HAH-SIM)

Ḥātim Derived from *ḥātim* (determined), which is from *ḥatama* (to decide). Var: Hatim. (HAH-TIM)

Haytham Derived from *haytham* (young eagle). The name denotes pride. (HAY-THAM)

Ḥikmat Derived from *ḥikma* (wisdom), which is from *ḥakama* (to pass judgment). This is a name common to both males and females. (HIK-MAHT)

Hishām Derived from *hishām* (crushing), which is from *hashama* (to crush, to smash). The name was used to acknowledge the generosity of one who returned from a caravan trip with bread to share with the tribe, and now denotes generosity rather than the act of crushing bread. Var: Hisham. (HIH-SHAHM)

Ḥusayn Diminutive form of Ḥasan, which is derived from *ḥasan* (beautiful, handsome, good). Ḥusayn, one of the most popular Muslim names, was borne by Al-Ḥusayn (626–80), a son of the Prophet's daughter Fātima and 'Ali ibn-Abi-Ṭālib. Ḥusayn and his followers were massacred at Kerbelā' on October 10, 680, a day that is now celebrated as a Holy Day for the Shiites. The name is also borne by the king of Jordan, Ḥusayn ibn-Ṭalāl (b. 1935). He ascended to the throne in 1953 after the abdication of his father in 1952. Var: Ḥisein, Husain, Hussain, Hussein. (HOO-SANE)

Ḥusni Derived from *ḥusn* (excellence, beauty), which is from the verb *ḥasuna* (to be beautiful, to be good). The name is borne by the president of Egypt, Ḥusni Mubārak (b. 1928). (HUS-NEE)

Ibrāhīm Derived from the Hebrew Avraham (father of a multitude, father of many). Ibrāhīm was the father of Ishāq, whose descendants are the Jews, and Ismā'īl, whose descendants are the Arabs. Ibrāhīm and Ismā'īl built the sacred Kaaba temple at Mecca, which contains a black stone supposedly given to Ibrāhīm by the angel Gabriel. (IH-BRAH-HEEM)

Ihāb Derived from *ihāb* (gift, donation). The name is bestowed upon both males and females. (IH-HAHB)

Iḥsān Derived from *iḥsān* (charity), which is from *aḥsana* (to do good). This name is bestowed upon both girls and boys. Var: Ihsan. (IH-SAHN)

'Iṣām Derived from *'iṣām* (security, pledge), which is from *'aṣama* (to protect). Var: Isam. (IH-SAHM)

Ismā'īl Derived from the Hebrew *yishmā'ē'l* (God hears). The name was borne by the son of Abraham and his concubine Hagar. Victims of jealousy by Abraham's wife Sarah, Hagar and Ismā'īl were abandoned in the desert. God took pity on them, however, and uncovered a well, saving their lives. After Ismā'īl was grown, Abraham journeyed to see him, and together they built the sacred temple of Kaaba at Mecca. Ismā'īl is revered as the patriarch of the Arab people. Var: Isma'l. (IHS-MAY-ILL)

'IṢMAT Derived from *'iṣma* (safeguarding), which is from the verb *'aṣama* (to protect). The name is bestowed upon both males and females. (IHS-MAHT)

'IZZ-AL-DĪN Compound name derived from the elements *'izz* (power, glory), *al* (the), and *dīn* (religion): hence, "power of religion." Var: Izz-al-Din, 'Izz-ed-Dīn. (IZZ-AHL-DIN)

JĀBIR Popular name derived from *jābir* (comforter, bringer of consolation), which is from *jabara* (to restore). Var: Gābir, Jabbar. (JAH-BEER)

JABR Derived from *jabr* (consolation), which is from *jabara* (to restore). Var: Gabr. (JAHBR)

JA'FAR Derived from *ja'far* (stream). The name was borne by Ja'far ibn-Abi-Ṭālib (d. 629), heroic brother of the fourth rightly guided caliph, Ali ibn-Abi-Ṭālib. Ja'far is remembered for his valor in the Battle of Mota, where he was responsible for carrying the Muslim banner that proclaimed "Paradise!" Losing both of his hands in the battle, Ja'far kept the banner aloft by using his stumps until he was mortally wounded. Var: Ga'far. (JAH-FAR)

JALĀL Derived from *jalāl* (greatness), which is from *jalla* (to be great). Var: Galāl. (JAH-LAL)

JAMĀL Popular name derived from *jamāl* (beauty), which is from *jamula* (to be handsome or good-looking). The name was borne by the first Egyptian president, Jamāl 'Abd-al Nāṣir (1918–70). He took part in forming the Free-Officers' Group of nationalist army officers, who seized control of the government and deposed King Farouk in 1952. Nāṣir took the presidency in 1956 and led the country until his death in 1970. Var: Gamāl. (JAH-MAHL)

JAMĪL Derived from *jamīl* (beautiful, handsome), which is from *jamala* (to be beautiful). Var: Gamīl, Jamil. (JAH-MILL)

JAWDAT Derived from *jawda* (excellence, goodness), which is from the verb *jāda* (to be good, to become good). Var: Gawdat. (JAW-DAHT)

JINĀN Derived from *jinān* (garden, paradise). The name is bestowed upon both males and females. (JIH-NAHN)

KAMĀL Popular name derived from *kamāl* (perfection), which is from *kamula* (to be perfect or become perfect). (KAH-MAHL)

KĀMIL Popular name derived from *kāmil* (perfect), which is from the verb *kamula* (to be or become perfect). (KAH-MIL)

KARAM Derived from *karam* (generosity), which is from *karuma* (to be generous). (KAH-RAHM)

KARĪM Popular name derived from *karīm* (noble, generous), which is from *karuma* (to be noble, to be generous). The word *karīm* alternatively denotes jewels or precious stones, so the name Karīm can mean something precious or valuable. The name was adopted by basketball great Ferdinand Lewis Alcindor, Jr. He took the name Kareem Abdul-Jabbar. Var: Kareem. (KAH-REEM)

KATEB Old Arabic name meaning "writer." (KAH-TEB)

KHĀLID Widely popular name derived from *khālid* (eternal, undying), which is from *khalada* (to last forever, to be eternal). The name was borne by the Saudi Arabian king Khālid Ben Abdulazīz (1913–81), who took the crown in 1975 following the assassination of his brother Fayṣal. Var: Khaled. (KAH-LID)

KHALĪL From the Arabic *khalīl* (best friend). (KAH-LEEL)

KHAYRAT Derived from *khayra* (good deed). (KAY-RAHT)

KHAYRI From *khayri* (charitable, beneficent). (KAY-REE)

LAṬĪF Derived from *laṭīf* (kind, gentle). Al-Laṭīf (the Kind) is one of the ninety-nine attributes of Allāh. Var: Lateef, Latif. (LAH-TEEF)

MĀHIR Derived from *māhir* (skillful, competent), which is from *mahara* (to be skillful). Var: Mahir. (MAH-HEER)

MAḤMŪD Popular name derived from the Arabic *maḥmūd* (praiseworthy), which is from *ḥamida* (to praise). The name was borne by Maḥmūd of Ghazha (971–1030), a sultan of the small eastern Afghanistan state, who was the first Muslim conqueror of India. Although historians consider him to have been one of the greatest military leaders and sovereigns of all time, he was also probably one of the most heinous, plundering, destroying, and slaughtering with no mercy. Var: Mahmoud, Mahmud. (MAH-MOOD)

Majdi Popular name derived from *majdi* (laudable, commendable), which is from *majada* (to be glorious). (MAHJ-DEE)

Mājid Derived from *mājid* (glorious, illustrious), which is from *majada* (to be glorious). Var: Māgid. (MAH-JID)

Makram From *makram* (noble, generous), which is from *karuma* (to be noble, to be generous). (MAHK-RAHM)

Mamdūḥ Derived from *mamdūh* (praised), which is from *madaha* (to praise). (MAM-DUH)

Ma'mūn Derived from the Arabic *ma'mūn* (trustworthy, dependable), which is from *amuna* (to be dependable, to be faithful). The name was borne by Al-Ma'mūn (786–833), seventh Abbasid caliph and son of the great caliph Harūn al-Rashid of Baghdad. Al-Ma'mūn followed in his father's footsteps and established Dār Al-Hikma, the House of Wisdom, which was devoted to scholarly activities. (MAH-MUN)

Manāl Bestowed upon both males and females, this name is derived from *manāl* (attainment, achievement), which is from *nāla* (to obtain, to achieve). (MAH-NAHL)

Manār Bestowed upon both males and females, this name is derived from *manār* (lighthouse, beacon), from *nawara* (to illuminate). (MAH-NAHR)

Manṣūr From *manṣūr* (victorious), which is from *naṣara* (to assist, to render victorious). The name was borne by Al-Manṣūr Abu-Ja'far (712?–75), the second Abbasid caliph and founder of Baghdad. Var: Mansour, Mansur. (MAHN-SOOR)

Mas'ūd Derived from *mas'ūd* (lucky, fortunate), which is from *sa'ida* (to be lucky). Var: Mas'ud. (MAH-SOOD)

Māzin Of uncertain derivation, some believe it to be derived from the Arabic *muzn* (rain clouds). Var: Mazin. (MAH-ZIN)

Mousa Arabic form of Moses, which is derived from the Hebrew Mōsheh (drawn out of the water). *See* MOSHE (Jewish Names). (MOU-SA)

Mubārak Derived from *mubārak* (blessed, fortunate), which is from *bāraka* (to bless). (MOO-BAH-RAK)

Muḥammad Derived from the Arabic *muḥammad* (praiseworthy), which is from *ḥamida* (to praise). The name, one of the most popular in the Muslim world, was borne by the Arabic Prophet and founder of Islam, Muḥammad ibn-'Abd-Allāh ibn-'Abd-al-Muṭṭalib (570–632). After receiving his first revelation on Mount Hira in 610, he began denouncing the existing social and moral conditions. After twelve years of effort, and seeing only a small number of converts but much persecution, he and his followers traveled from Mecca to Yathrib (which he renamed Medina), a migration known today as the Hegira. He soon established himself as ruler of the city and began his conquest over the Jews, and eventually of Mecca. Muḥammad died in 632, seeing his religion of Islam become successfully established. Var: Mahomet, Mehmet, Miḥammad, Mohamet, Mohammad. (MOO-HAH-MED)

Muhannad From the Arabic *muhannad* (sword). (MOO-HAHN-NAHD)

Muḥsin Derived from *muḥsin* (charitable), which is from *ahsana* (to be charitable). (MOO-SIN)

Mukhtār Derived from *mukhtār* (chosen), which is from khāra (to choose). Var: Mukhtar. (MUK-TAHR)

Mun'im From the Arabic *mun'im* (benefactor), which is from *an'ama* (to bestow). (MOO-NIM)

Munīr Derived from *munīir* (luminous, shining), which is from *nawara* (to illuminate). (MOO-NEER)

Mus'ad Derived from *mus'ad* (lucky, fortunate), which is from the root *sa'ida* (to be lucky). The name is borne by Prince Musaed Ben Abdulazīz of Saudi Arabia. Var: Mis'id, Musaed. (MOO-SAHD)

Muṣṭafa Popular name derived from *mustafa* (chosen, selected). Al-Muṣṭafa (the Chosen) is a name for the Prophet Muḥammad. The name was also borne by Turkish General Muṣṭafa Kamāl (1881–1938). His military leadership led to the founding of the modern Turkish republic. Muṣṭafa Kamāl, also known as Kemal Atatürk, served as Turkey's first president. Var: Mustafa. (MOO-STAH-FAH)

Mu'taṣim Derived from *mu'taṣim* (seeking refuge, seeking refuge in God). (MOO-TAH-SIM)

Mu'tazz From *mu'tazz* (powerful), which is from *'azza* (to be powerful). (MOO-TAHZ)

Nabīl Popular name derived from *nabīl* (noble, honorable), which is from the verb *nabula* (to be noble). Var: Nabil. (NAH-BEEL)

Nadīm Derived from *nadīm* (drinking companion, friend), which is from *nādama* (to drink, to drink with someone). Var: Nadim. (NAH-DEEM)

Nādir Popular name derived from *nādir* (rare, precious), which is from *nadara* (to be rare). Var: Nadir. (NAH-DEER)

Nā'il From *nā'il* (attainer), which is from *nāla* (to attain). The name indicates a hope that the child will attain or achieve all of his desires. (NAH-ILL)

Na'īm Derived from *na'īm* (content, happy), which is from *na'ima* (to live comfortably, to be carefree). Var: Naeem. (NAH-EEM)

Nāji Derived from *nāji* (saved, rescued), which is from *naja* (to be saved). Var: Nāgi, Naji. (NAH-JEE)

Najīb Derived from the Arabic *najīb* (of noble descent, highborn, intelligent, distinguished), which is from *najuba* (to be of noble birth). The name was borne by Najīb 'Asūri (d. 1916), a Syro-Palestinian Christian who was cofounder of the League of the Arab Fatherland in Paris, a group that promoted the idea of an independent Arab empire. Var: Nagīb, Najib. (NAH-JEEB)

Nāṣir Derived from *nāṣir* (one who helps render victorious, supporter), which is from *naṣara* (to render victorious, to assist). (NAH-SIR)

Naṣr From the Arabic *naṣr* (victory). Var: Nasser. (NASR)

Nizār Popular name of uncertain derivation. (NIH-ZAHR)

Nūr Bestowed upon both males and females, Nūr is derived from *nūr* (light), which is from *nawara* (to illuminate). (NOOR)

Nūr-al-Dīn Compound name composed of the elements *nūr* (light), *al* (the), and *dīn* (religion): hence, "light of the religion." (NOOR-AHL-DIN)

Qādir Derived from *qadir* (capable). Al-Qādir (the Capable) is one of the ninety-nine attributes of Allāh. Var: Qadar. (KAH-DEER)

Qāsim Derived from *qāsim* (one who distributes among his people, i.e., food or material goods). Var: Qasim. (KAH-SIM)

Quṣay Ancient Arabic name derived from *qaṣiy* (distant), which is from the verb *qaṣa* (to be far away). Var: Qussay. (KYOO-SAY)

Rabi Old Arabic name denoting a fragrant, sweet-smelling breeze. (RAH-BEE)

Ra'd From *ra'd* (thunder). (RAHD)

Raḍwān Derived from *riḍwān* (pleasure), which is from *raḍiya* (to be satisfied). (RAHD-WAHN)

Ra'fat From the Arabic *ra'fah* (mercy), which has its root in the verb *ra'afa* (to be merciful). (RAH-FAHT)

Rafīq Popular name derived from *rafīq* (friend, companion), which is from *rāfaqa* (to be a friend). Alternatively, it can be derived from *rafīq* (gentle, kind), which is from *rafaqa* (to be gentle). Var: Rafi, Rafī', Rafiq. (RAH-FEEK)

Raghīd Derived from *raghīd* (carefree), which is from *raghuda* (to be carefree or without worry). Var: Raghid. (RAH-GEED)

Rajab Popular name borrowed from the name of the seventh month of the Arab calendar, one of the holy months. Its root is *rajaba* (to glorify). Var: Ragab. (RAH-JAHB)

Rashād Derived from *rashād* (good judgment), which is from *rashada* (to follow the right path). Var: Rashad. (RAH-SHAHD)

Rashīd Popular name derived from the Arabic *rashīd* (rightly guided), from the verb *rashada* (to follow the right course). Var: Rashid. (RAH-SHEED)

Ra'ūf Derived from the Arabic *ra'ūf* (compassionate, merciful), which is from the verb *ra'afa* (to be merciful). Al-Ra'ūf (the Compassionate) is one of the attributes of Allāh. (RAH-OOF)

Riḍa From the Arabic *riḍa* (contentment), which is from *raḍiya* (to be content). Var: Reda, Ridha. (REE-DAH)

Riḍa Siraj Compound name composed of the elements *riḍa* (contentment) and *siraj* (light, lamp): hence, "light of contentment." (REE-DAH-SIR-AHJ)

Riyāḍ Derived from *riyāḍ* (gardens). Var: Riyad, Riyadh. (REE-YAHD)

Ṣābir From *ṣābir* (enduring, patient), which is from *ṣabara* (to endure). Var: Sabir. (SAH-BEER)

Ṣabri Derived from *ṣabr* (patience, endurance), which is from *ṣabara* (to endure). (SAH-BREE)

Sa'd Derived from *sa'd* (good luck, good fortune), which is from *sa'ida* (to be lucky, to be happy). The name was borne by Sa'd ibn-Abi-Waqqāṣ, a cousin of Muḥammad and an early convert to Islam. He became a successful commander in chief of the military during the reign of the second rightly guided caliph, 'Umar ibn-al-Khaṭṭāb. (SAHD)

ṢAFĀ' A name bestowed upon both male and female children which is derived from the Arabic *safā'* (purity). (SAH-FAH)

ṢAFWAT Derived from *ṣafwah* (choice, select), which is from *ṣafa* (to be pure). (SAHF-WAHT)

SAGHIR Derived from *saghir* (short in stature). (SAH-GEER)

SA'ID Popular name derived from *sa'id* (lucky, happy), which is from *sa'ida* (to be lucky, to be happy). Var: Sa'ied. (SAH-EED)

ṢAKHR Derived from *ṣakhr* (solid rock). (SAHKR)

ṢALĀḤ Popular name derived from *ṣalāḥ* (righteousness), which is from *ṣaluḥa* (to be devout, to be righteous). Var: Saleh. (SAH-LAH)

ṢALĀḤ AL-DĪN Compound name composed of the elements *ṣalāḥ* (righteousness), *al* (the), and *dīn* (religion). The name was borne by Ṣalāḥ-ed-Dīn Yusuf ibn-Ayyub (1137–93), better known as Saladdin. He was an important military and political leader who overthrew the Fatimid dynasty in Egypt, becoming sultan in 1174 and founding his own Ayyubite dynasty. He then extended his reign over Syria, recaptured Jerusalem from the Crusaders, and was successful in repelling the invading forces of the Third Crusade. Var: Salah-ed-Dīn; Saladdin, Saladin (Ang.). (SAH-LAH-AHL-DIN)

SALĀMA Derived from *salāma* (safety, security), which is from *salima* (to be safe). (SAH-LAH-MAH)

ṢĀLIḤ Popular name derived from *ṣāliḥ* (virtuous, righteous), which is from *ṣaluḥa* (to be righteous). Var: Salih. (SAH-LIH)

SĀLIM From the Arabic *sālim* or *salīm* (secure). Var: Salīm. (SAH-LIM)

SALĪM Popular name derived from *salīm* (safe), which is from the root *salima* (to be safe). Var: Salim, Selīm. (SAH-LEEM)

SALMAN Derived from *salāma* (safety), which is from *salima* (to be safe). (SAHL-MAHN)

SĀMI Derived from the Arabic *sāmi* (elevated, exalted), which is from *sama* (to be elevated). (SAH-MEE)

SĀMIḤ Derived from the Arabic *sāmiḥ* or *samīḥ* (tolerant, forgiving), which is from the verb *samuḥa* (to be tolerant, to forgive). Var: Samīh. (SAH-MIH)

SĀMIR Derived from *sāmir* or *samīr* (a companion who joins in an evening conversation), which is from *samara* (to talk in the evening or night). Var: Samir, Samīr. (SAH-MEER)

SAYYID From *sayyid* (master, lord), which is from the verb *sāda* (to rule). (SAY-YID)

SHĀDI Derived from *shādi* (singer), which is from *shada* (to sing). Var: Shadi. (SHA-DEE)

SHAFĪQ Derived from *shafīq* (sympathetic, compassionate), which is from *shafaqa* (to sympathize). Var: Shafi, Shafī', Shafiq. (SHA-FEEK)

SHAKĪL Derived from *shakīl* (handsome, well-developed). Var: Shakil. (SHA-KEEL)

SHĀKIR Popular name derived from the Arabic *shākir* (thankful), which is from the verb *shakara* (to thank). Var: Shakir. (SHA-KEER)

SHAMĪM Bestowed upon both males and females, this name is from *shamīm* (fragrant). Var: Shamim. (SHA-MEEM)

SHARĪF Popular name derived from *sharīf* (honorable, eminent), which is from *sharafa* (to be distinguished). Besides being a personal name, Sharīf is used as a title bestowed upon the descendants of the Prophet. Var: Sharif, Sherif, Sherīf. (SHA-REEF)

SHUKRI Derived from *shukri* (thanks), which is from the verb *shakara* (to thank). The name was borne by the Syrian president Shukri Al-Quwatli (1891–1967), who formed the United Arab Republic in 1958 with the Egyptian president Jamāl 'Abd-al-Nāṣir. (SHOOK-REE)

SIRAJ Derived from *siraj* (light, lamp). (SIR-RAHJ).

SUHAYL Suhayl is the name referring to the second-brightest star in the southern skies, which is also known as Canopus. Var: Suhail. (SOO-HAIL)

SULAYMĀN Arabic form of Solomon, which is derived from the Hebrew *shĕlōmōh* (peaceful), a derivative of *shālōm* (peace). The name was borne by the Israelite king (c. 961–922 B.C.) who was noted for his great wisdom and ability to communicate with animals and birds. Var: Shelomon, Silimān, Sulaiman, Suleimān. (SOO-LAY-MAHN)

ṬĀHA Derived from the Arabic letters *t* and *h*, which are the opening letters of the twentieth sura in the Koran. Var: Taha. (TAH-HAH)

ṬĀHIR Popular name derived from the Arabic *ṭāhir* (pure, chaste), from the root *ṭahura* (to be pure, to be clean). Var: Tahir. (TAH-HEER)

TĀMIR Derived from *tāmir* (one who owns many dates). Var: Tamir. (TAH-MEER)

ṬĀRIQ Popular name derived from *ṭāriq* (one who knocks at the door), which is from *ṭaraqa* (to knock). Var: Tari, Tāri', Tarik, Tariq. (TAH-REEK)

TAWFĪQ Derived from *tawfiq* (good fortune), which is from *wafiqa* (to be successful). Var: Tawfī'. (TAW-FEEK)

TAWĪL From *tawīl* (tall). Var: Taweel. (TAH-WEEL)

'UMAR A name that dates back to pre-Islamic times yet remains a perennially popular name throughout the Arab world. It is derived from *'āmir* (flourishing, thriving), which is from *'amara* (to live long, to prosper). The name was borne by the second rightly guided caliph, 'Umar ibn-al-Khaṭṭāb (c. 581– 644). Var: Omar, Omer. (OO-MAHR)

'USĀMA Popular name derived from *'usāma* (lion). Var: Usamah. (OO-SAH-MAH)

'UTHMĀN Very popular name derived from *'uthmān* (baby bustard, a crane-like bird). The name was borne by 'Uthmān ibn-'Affān (c. 574–656), the third rightly guided caliph and husband of the Prophet's daughter Ruqayya. Var: Othman, Usman, 'Usmān, Uthman. (OOTH-MAHN)

WAHĪB Derived from *wahīb* (donor, one who gives), which is from *wahaba* (to give). Al-Wahīb (the Giver) is one of the attributes of Allāh. Var: Wahib. (WAH-HEEB)

WĀ'IL From the Arabic *wā'il* (one who reverts back to God). The name, which is borne by an important Arab tribe, is also bestowed as a first name.(WAH-ILL)

WAJĪH Derived from *wajīh* (distinguished), which is from *wajuha* (to be distinguished). Var: Wagīh. (WAH-JIH, WAH-JEE)

WALĪD Popular name derived from *walīd* (newborn), which is from *walada* (to give birth). The name was borne by Walīd I, Al-Walīd ibn-'Abd-al-Malik (d. 715), the strong Umayyad caliph whose military was responsible for conquering Spain. Var: Walid. (WAH-LEED)

WASĪM From the Arabic *wasīm* (handsome, good-looking), which is from the verb *wasama* (to distinguish). Var: Wasim. (WAH-SEEM)

YAḤYA Arabic form of John, which is derived from the Hebrew *yehōhānān* (Yahweh is gracious). Var: Yahya, Yiḥya. (YAH-YAH)

YA'QŪB Arabic form of Jacob, which is derived from the Hebrew *ja'aqob* (seizing by the heel, supplanting). *See* JACOB (Biblical Names). Var: Yaqoob, Yaqub. (YAH-KUB)

YASĪN Derived from the Arabic letters *y* and *s*, which are the opening letters of the thirty-sixth sura of the Koran. Var: Yasin. (YAH-SEEN)

YĀSIR Derived from *yāsir* (to be wealthy). The name is borne by Yāsir 'Arafāt (b. 1929), leader of the Palestine Liberation Organization and the new Palestinian government. Var: Yasir. (YAH-SIR)

YŪNIS Arabic form of Jonah, which is derived from the Hebrew *yōnāh* (a dove). *See* JONAH (Biblical Names). Var: Younis, Yunus. (YOO-NIS)

YUSHUA Arabic variant of Joshua, which is derived from the Hebrew *yehōshū'a* (help of Jehovah). *See* JOSHUA (Biblical Names). (YOO-SHOO-AH)

YŪSUF Arabic form of Joseph, which is derived from the Hebrew *yōsēph* (may he add). *See* JOSEPH (Biblical Names). Var: Youssef, Yousuf, Yūsif, Yusuf. (YOO-SUF)

ZAFAR Derived from *zafar* (victory), which is from *zafira* (to succeed). Var: Zafir. (ZAH-FAHR)

ZĀHIR Popular name derived from the Arabic *zāhir* (shining, flourishing), which is from *zahara* (to shine, to blossom). Var: Zahir. (ZAH-HEER)

ZAKARIYYA Arabic form of Zachariah, which is derived from the Hebrew *zĕharyah* (God remembers). Var: Zakaria. (ZAH-KAH-RĪ-YAH)

ZAKI Derived from *zakiy* (pure, virtuous), which is from *zaka* (to be pure). (ZAH-KEE)

ZAYD Ancient yet still popular name thought to be derived from the Arabic *zāda* (to increase, to become greater). The name was borne by the adopted son of the Prophet Muḥammad, Zayd ibn-Ḥāritha (d. 629), who as a child was sold into slavery to Khadīja, the Prophet's wife. After his adoption, he became an early convert to Islam and one of Muḥammad's strongest supporters. Var: Zaid, Zayed. (ZAH-EED)

ZIYA Derived from the Arabic *ziyā* (splendor, light). Var: Zia, Ziya. (ZEE-YAH)

ZIYĀD Derived from *ziyāda* (increase, growth), which is from *zada* (to increase). Var: Ziyad. (ZEE-YAHD)

ZUHAYR Popular name derived from the diminutive form of *zahr* (flowers, blossoms): hence, "little flowers." Var: Zuhair. (ZOO-HARE)

Muslim/Arabic Female Names

Abia Arabic name meaning "great." (AH-BEE-AH)

'Ābida Derived from the Arabic *'ābid* (worshiper), which is from *abada* (to worship). Var: Abida. (AH-BEE-DAH)

'Abīr Derived from *'abīr* (fragrance, aroma). (AH-BEER)

'Abla Derived from *'abla*, a word denoting a woman possessing a full figure, which is from *'abula* (to be big or full). Var: Ablah. (AH-BLAH)

Adara A name of Hebrew origin meaning "noble, exalted." It is derived from Adar, the name of the sixth month of the Jewish calendar. (AH-DAR-RAH)

'Adila Derived from *'ādil* (just, fair), which is from *adala* (to act justly). Var: Adila, Adilah. (AH-DEE-LAH)

Adiva Popular name derived from *adiva* (gracious, pleasant). (AH-DEE-VAH)

'Afāf Derived from the Arabic *'afāf* (chastity, virtuousness), which is from *'affa* (to refrain). Var: Afaf. (AH-FAHF)

'Afifa From *'afifa* (chaste), which is from the root *'affa* (to refrain). Var: Afifa, Afifah. (AH-FEE-FAH)

Afra Arabic form of the Hebrew Ofra (young deer, young mountain goat). (AH-FRAH)

Aḥlām Derived from *aḥlām* (dreams, visions), which is from *ḥalama* (to dream). Var: Ahlam. (AH-LAHM)

'Ā'isha One of the most popular names in the Arab world, 'Ā'isha is derived from *'ā'isha* (alive and well), which is from *'āsha* (to live). The name was borne by 'Ā'isha bint-Abi-Bakr (c. 613–78), daughter of the first guided caliph, Abu-Bakr al-Ṣiddīq, and Muḥammad's third and favorite wife. According to tradition, 'Ā'isha was only nine years old when Muḥammad married her. After Muḥammad's death, she strongly opposed 'Ali ibn-Abil Ṭālib, the fourth rightly guided caliph, and called on the Muslim community to depose him. In the Battle of the Camel in 656, 'Ā'isha led the rebel forces herself, but was defeated and sent back to Medina, where she devoted the rest of her life to religious studies. Var: Aisha, 'Āisha, Aishah, 'A'ishah. (AH-EE-SHA)

Akilah Derived from the Arabic *akila* (one who reasons, intelligent). (AH-KEE-LAH)

Alima A borrowing from the Hebrew, Alima means "strong." Var: Ahlima. (AH-LEE-MAH)

'Āliya Derived from *'āliya* (sublime, elevated), the root of which is *'alā* (to rise up). Var: Aliye, 'Alya. (AH-LEE-YAH)

Almira Popular name derived from the Arabic *almira* (princess, exalted one). (AHL-MEER-AH)

Altair Derived from *al ṭā'ir* (the bird). The name was assigned to the brightest star in the constellation Aquila. (AHL-TARE)

'Alyā' Derived from *'alyā'* (loftiness, sublimity), which is from *'alā* (to rise, to ascend). (AHL-YAH)

Amāl Bestowed upon both males and females, this name is derived from *amāl* (hope, expectation), which is from *amala* (to hope). Var: Amal, Amala. (AH-MAHL)

Amāni Popular name derived from *amāni* (desires, wishes), which is from *mana* (to desire). Var: Amani, Amany, Amāny. (AH-MAH-NEE)

Amīna Popular name derived from *amīn* (trustworthy, faithful), which is from *amuna* (to be faithful, to be reliable). Var: Amina, Aminah, Amine. (AH-MEE-NAH)

Āmina Derived from the Arabic *āmina* (peaceful, secure), which is from *amina* (to feel safe, to be safe). The name was borne by Āmina bint-Wahab (d. 576), the Prophet Muḥammad's mother. She belonged to the poor Beni-Zuhra clan of the Quraish tribe and died when Muḥammad was only six years old, leaving him to be raised by his grandfather and uncle. Var: Amna. (AH-MEE-NAH)

Amīra Feminine form of Amīr, which is derived from *amīr* (prince, emir), from the verb *amara* (to command, to rule). Var: Ameerah, Amira. Short: Meerah, Mira, Mīra. (AH-MEER-RAH)

Anisa Friendly, one who makes good company. Var: Anas. (AH-NEE-SAH)

Arub Old Arabic name meaning "a woman who is loving to her husband." (AH-RUB)

Arwa Popular name derived from *arwa* (female mountain goat). (AHR-WAH)

'Āsima Derived from *'āsim* (protector, guardian), which is from *'asama* (to protect). Var: Asima. (AH-SEE-MAH)

Asmā' Popular name throughout the Arab world. It is derived from the Arabic *asmā'* (prestige). The name was borne by a daughter of the first rightly guided caliph and father-in-law of Muḥammad, Abu-Bakr al-Ṣiddīq. Asmā' played an important part in helping Muḥammad and her father escape from Mecca in 622 and steadfastly refused to give their enemies any information regarding their whereabouts. (AHS-MAH)

'ĀTIFA Derived from *'ātif* (compassionate, sympathetic), which is from *'atafa* (to sympathize). Var: Atifa. (AH-TEE-FAH)

ATIYA Popular name meaning "gift." (AH-TEE-YAH)

'AWĀTIF From the Arabic *'awātif* (affection), which is from *'atafa* (to be fond of). Var: Awatif. (AH-WAH-TEEF)

'AYDA Derived from *'ā'ida* (benefit), which is from *'āda* (to return). (AH-EE-DAH)

AZHAR From the Arabic *zahr* (blossoms, flowers). (AH-ZAHR)

'AZĪZA Derived from *'azīza* (esteemed, precious, beloved). Var: Azizah. (AH-ZEE-ZAH)

'AZZA Of uncertain origin, 'Azza might be derived from the Arabic *'uzza* (female baby gazelle). Var: Azza. (AH-ZAH)

BADRIYYAH From the Arabic *badr* (full moon), which is from *badara* (to take by surprise). (BAH-DREE-YAH)

BAHĪJA Derived from *bahīja* (joyous, glad), which is from *bahija* (to be glad, to be happy). Var: Bahīga. (BAH-HEE-JAH)

BAHIRA From *bahir* (dazzling). (BAH-HEER-AH)

BANAN Derived from the Arabic *banan* (fingertips). (BAH-NAHN)

BANO Derived from the Persian *bāno* (lady, princess). (BAH-NO)

BARI'AH Derived from the Arabic *bari'a* (excelling). (BAH-REE-AH)

BASHIYRA Believed to be derived from the Arabic *bishr* (joy). (BAH-SHE-RAH)

BĀSIMA Popular name derived from *bāsim* (smiling), which is from *basama* (to smile). Var: Bāsimah. (BAH-SEE-MAH)

BASMA Derived from *basma* (a smile), which is from *basama* (to smile). (BAH-SMAH).

BIBI Derived from the Persian *bībī* (lady, mistress of the house). (BEE-BEE)

BUDŪR Derived from the Arabic *budūr* (full moons), which is from *badara* (to take by surprise). (BAH-DOOR)

BUTHAYNA Derived from *bathua* (flatland, easily worked land). Alternatively, some believe it means "beautiful of body." The name was borne by a cousin of Arab poet Jamīl ibn-Mu'ammar (d. 701), who was so in love with her that he devoted much of his poetry to her and even added her name to his, becoming known as Jamīl-Buthayna. Var: Busayna, Buthaynah. (BOO-THAY-NAH)

CANTARA Small bridge. (CAHN-TAH-RAH)

DALĀL Popular name derived from the Arabic *dalāl* (coquettishness), which is from *dalla* (to be coquettish). Var: Dhelal. (DAH-LAHL)

DĪMA Popular name derived from *dīma* (downpour, rain without thunder or lightning). Var: Dema. (DEE-MAH)

ḌIYĀ' Derived from *ḍiyā'* (brightness). (DEE-AH)

DU'Ā' Derived from the Arabic *du'ā'* (prayer), which is from *da'a* (to pray to God). (DOO-AH)

ḌUḤA From the Arabic *ḍuḥa* (forenoon, midmorning), which is from the root *ḍaḥa* (to become invisible). Var: Duha. (DOO-HAH)

FĀDIA Derived from *fādi* (REDEEMER, SAVIOR)

FAḌĪLA Popular name derived from the Arabic *faḍīla* (virtue, morality), which is from *faḍala* (to surpass). Var: Fadila, Fadilah. (FAH-DEE-LAH)

FAHĪMA Derived from *fahim* (intelligent), which is from *fahima* (to understand). Var: Fahima. (FAH-HEE-MAH)

FARDOOS Derived from the Arabic *firdaws* (paradise). (FAHR-DOOS)

FARĪDA Derived from *farīd* (unique), which is from *farada* (to be unique). Var: Faridah. (FAH-REE-DAH)

FARIHA From *fariha* (happy, joyful). Var: Farihah. (FAH-REE-HAH)

FATḤIYYA Derived from *fātiḥ* (conqueror), which is from *fataḥa* (to conquer). (FAH-THEE-YAH)

FĀṬIMA Popular name derived from the Arabic *fāṭima* (she who weans an infant; one who abstains from forbidden things), which is from the root *faṭama* (to wean; to abstain). The name was most famously borne by Fāṭima bint-Muḥammad (c. 606–32), the favorite daughter of the Prophet Muḥammad and his first wife, Khadīja. She was the wife of the fourth rightly guided caliph, 'Ali ibn-Abi-Ṭālib, and was the mother of Ḥasan, Ḥusayn, and Zaynab. Fāṭima was the progenitor of the

Fatimid dynasty. Var: Fatima, Fatimah, Fatma. (FAH-TEE-MAH)

Fātin Derived from *fātin* (charming, enchanting). The name is borne by Fātin Hamāma (b. 1932), Egyptian actress and ex-wife of Omar Sharif. Var: Fatin, Fatina, Fatinah. (FAH-TIN, FAH-TEEN)

Fawziyya From the Arabic *fawz* (triumph, achievement), which is from *fāza* (to achieve, to win). The name is borne by Princess Fawzia Ezzat, the wife of Prince Fawwaz Ben Abdulazīz of Saudi Arabia. (FAW-ZEE-YAH)

Fayrūz Derived from *fayrūz* (the turquoise stone). (FAY-ROOZ)

Fayza Derived from *fa'iz* (victor, winner), which is from *fāza* (to achieve, to win). Var: Faiza, Faizah. (FAY-ZAH)

Fiḍḍa Popular name derived from *fiḍḍa* (silver). Var: Fizza. (FIH-DAH)

Fikriyya Popular name derived from *fikri* (intellectual, meditative), which is from *fakara* (to meditate). (FIH-KREE-YAH)

Ghāda From the Arabic *ghāda* (a graceful girl or woman), which is from *ghayada* (to walk gracefully). Var: Ghada, Ghadah, Ghayda. (GAH-DAH)

Ghadīr Derived from the Arabic *ghadīr* (a brook, a stream). Water is a rare commodity in a desert environment; thus the name denotes preciousness. (GAH-DEER)

Ghaliya Derived from *ghaliya* (fragrant). Var: Ghaliyah. (GAH-LEE-YAH)

Ghufrān Popular name derived from *ghufrān* (forgiveness), which is from *ghafara* (to forgive). (GUH-FRAHN)

Ḥabība Derived from *ḥabīb* (beloved), which is from *ḥabba* (to love). Var: Habiba, Habibah, Haviva. (HAH-BEE-BAH)

Ḥādi' Derived from the Arabic *hādi'* (calm, serene), which is from the verb *hada'a* (to be calm). (HAH-DEE)

Hadīl Popular name derived from *hadīl* (the cooing of pigeons), which is from the verb *hadala* (to coo). Var: Hadil. (HAH-DEEL)

Hadya Derived from *hādi* (religious leader or guide), which is from *hadā* (to lead, to guide). Var: Hadiya. (HAHD-YAH)

Ḥafṣa Old name in common use since pre-Islamic times, which is of uncertain meaning. The name was borne by Ḥafṣa bint-'Umar (d. 665), daughter of the second rightly guided caliph, 'Umar ibn-al-Khaṭṭāb, and wife of Muḥammad. After Muḥammad's death, she was chosen to safeguard the sole written copy of the Koran, thus becoming known as Ḥāfiẓat Al-Qur'ān, the Koran Keeper. Var: Hafsah, Hafza. (HAHF-SAH)

Hājar Popular name thought to be derived from the Arabic *hajara* (to forsake, to emigrate). The name was borne by the Egyptian concubine of Ibrāhīm, given to him by his barren wife Sarah. Hājar bore Ibrāhīm a son, Ismā'īl. After Sarah finally conceived and gave birth to Isaac, she had Hājar and Ismā'īl abandoned in the desert. Tradition relates that in her desperate attempt to find water, she ran between the mounts Al-Safa and Al-Marwa near Mecca several times. God took pity on them and uncovered the well of Zamzam, saving their lives. To this day, part of the Muslim pilgrimage rites include walking the distance from Al-Safa to Al-Marwa seven times and drinking from the well of Zamzam. Hājar is revered as the "Mother of the Arabs." Var: Hāgir. (HAH-JAHR)

Hāla Old Arabic name derived from *hāla* (aureole, halo around the moon). Var: Hala, Halah. (HAH-LAH)

Halima Popular name derived from the Arabic *halima* (gentle, patient). Var: Halimah. (HAH-LEE-MAH)

Ḥāmida One of several popular names derived from the root *ḥamid* (thankful, praising), which is from *ḥamida* (to praise). Var: Hameedah, Hamida, Hamidah. (HAH-MEE-DAH)

Hanā' Derived from *hanā'* (happiness, bliss), which is from *hani'a* (to take pleasure in). Var: Hana. (HAH-NAH)

Ḥanān Derived from *ḥanān* (tenderness, mercy), which is from *ḥanna* (to feel compassion, to sympathize). Var: Hanan. (HAH-NAHN)

Haniyya Derived from *hāni'* (happy, pleased), which is from *hani'a* (to be happy). Var: Haniyyah. (HAH-NEE-YAH)

Hasna Old name derived from the Aramaic *chasna* (strong, powerful). (HAHS-NAH)

Hayat Arabic form of the Aramaic *chayuta* (life, livelihood). (HAY-YAHT, HĪ-YAHT)

Hayfā' Popular name derived from the Arabic *hayfā'* (slender, delicate). Var: Hayfa. (HAY-FAH, HĪ-FAH)

Hiba Derived from *hiba* (gift, donation), which is from *wahaba* (to give, to donate). (HI-BA)

Ḥikmat A popular name bestowed upon both females and males, Hikmat is derived from the Arabic *ḥikma* (wisdom), from *ḥakama* (to pass judgment). (HIK-MAHT)

Hind Very old yet still common Arabic name of uncertain origin and meaning. The name was borne by Hind bint-Abi-Umayya, a beautiful wife of the Prophet Muḥammad. (HIND)

Huda Popular name derived from *huda* (right guidance), which is from *hada* (to lead upon the right path). Var: Hoda. (HOO-DAH)

Hurriyyah Angel. (HOO-REE-YAH)

Ḥusn From the Arabic *ḥusn* (beauty, excellence), which is from *ḥasuna* (to be good, to be beautiful). Var: Husn. (HOOSN)

Ḥusniya Derived from *ḥusn* (beauty, excellence), which is from *ḥasuna* (to be good, to be beautiful). Var: Husniyah. (HOO-SNEE-YAH)

Ibtihaj Derived from *ibtihaj* (joy). (IB-TEE-HAHJ).

Ibtisām Derived from *ibtisām* (smiling), which is from the root *basama* (to smile). Var: Ebtissam, Ibtissam. Short: Essam, Issam. (IB-TIH-SAHM)

Ihāb Common to both males and females, Ihāb is derived from the Arabic *ihāb* (gift, donation), which is from *wahaba* (to give, to donate). (IH-HAHB)

Iḥsān Derived from *iḥsān* (charity), which is from *aḥsana* (to do good). Var: Ihsāna, Ihsanah. (IH-SAHN)

Imān Derived from the Arabic *imān* (faith, belief in God), which is from *āmana* (to believe). Imān is a popular name throughout the Muslim world. The name is borne by the Somali-born supermodel Iman. Var: Iman. (IH-MAHN)

In'ām Derived from the Arabic *in'ām* (benefaction, giving), which is from *an'ama* (to bestow). Var: Enam, Inam. (IH-NAHM)

Inas Derived from *inas* (sociability). (IH-NAHS)

Inaya From the Arabic *inaya* (to be solicitous, to be concerned). Var: Inayah. (IH-NAY-AH)

'Iṣmat A name common to both males and females which is derived from the Arabic *'iṣma* (safeguarding), which is from *'aṣama* (to guard, to protect). (ISS-MAHT)

Isrā' Derived from *isrā'* (nocturnal journey), which is from *sarā* (to travel at night). (IH-SRAH)

I'tidāl From the Arabic *i'tidāl* (moderation), which is from *'adala* (to be moderate). (IH-TIH-DAHL)

Izdihar Arabic name meaning "blossoming, flourishing," which is from the root *zahr* (flowers, blossoms). (IZ-DIH-HAHR)

Jala' Derived from the Arabic *jala'* (clarity, elucidation), which is from *jalla* (to be illustrious). (JAH-LAH)

Jalīla Derived from the Arabic *jalīla* (illustrious, exalted), which is from *jalla* (to be illustrious, to be great). Var: Galīla, Galilah, Jalilah. (JAH-LEE-LAH)

Jamīla Popular name derived from *jamīl* (beautiful, graceful), which is from *jamula* (to be beautiful). Var: Gamīla, Gamilah, Jamilah. (JAH-MEE-LAH)

Janan Derived from *janan* (heart, soul, spirit). (JAH-NAHN)

Jāthibiyya From the Arabic *jāthibiyya* (attractiveness, charm), which is from *jathaba* (to attract). Var: Gathbiyya, Gathbiyyah, Gathibiyya, Gathibiyyah, Gazbiyya, Gazbiyyah, Jāthbiyya, Jathbiyyah, Jathibiyyah. (JAH-THEE-BEE-YAH)

Jawāhir Derived from the Arabic *jawāhir* (jewels). Var: Gawāhir. (JAH-WAH-HEER)

Jinān A name commonly bestowed upon both male and female children which is derived from the Arabic *jinān* (garden, paradise). (JIH-NAHN)

Jumana Derived from the Arabic *jumana* (a pearl, a silver pearl). Var: Jumanah. (JOO-MAH-NAH)

Kalthūm Derived from *kalthūm* (one who has plump cheeks). Var: Kalsūm. (KAHL-THOOM)

Kāmila Popular name derived from the Arabic *kāmil* (perfect), which is from the verb *kamula* (to be perfect, to become perfect). Var: Kamila, Kamilah. (KAH-MEE-LAH)

Karīma A popular name throughout the Arabic world, Karīma is derived from *karīm* (generous, noble), which is from *karuma* (to be generous, to be noble). Var: Karima, Karimah. (KAH-REE-MAH)

Khadīja An old Arabic name popular throughout the Muslim world, Khadīja is derived from *khadīja* (premature baby). It was borne most famously by Khadīja bint-Khuwaylid (c. 555–619), the first wife of Muḥammad, and the mother of his children. She was a rich Meccan widow when Muḥammad came into her employ, and was about forty years old when they married in 595. Khadīja was a fervent, loyal supporter of Muḥammad, and the first convert to Islam. Var: Khadīga, Khadija. (KAH-DEE-JAH)

Khālida From the Arabic *khālid* (immortal, eternal), which is from *khalada* (to be immortal, to enjoy a long life). Var: Khalidah. (KAH-LEE-DAH)

Khalīla From *khalīl* (best friend, one who makes good company). Var: Khalilah. (KAH-LEE-LAH)

Kohinoor Derived from the Persian *kohinoor* (mountain of light). (KOH-HEE-NOOR)

Lamis Derived from *lamis* (soft to the touch). (LAH-MEES)

Lamyā' Derived from the Arabic *lamiā'* (having beautiful, dark lips). Var: Lama, Lamya. (LAHM-YAH)

Laṭīfa Popular name derived from *laṭīf* (gentle, kind). Var: Lateefah, Latifa, Latifah. (LAH-TEE-FAH)

Lawāḥiẓ From *lawāhiz* (glances), which is from *lahaza* (to look at). Var: Lawāhiz. (LAH-WAH-HIZ)

Layla Old Arabic name derived from *layla* (wine, alcohol). (LAY-LAH, LĪ-LAH)

Leila Derived from the Arabic *leila* (dark beauty, dark as night). Var: Laila, Lailah, Leela, Leilia, Lela, Leyla. (LAY-LAH, LEE-LAH)

Lilith Old name derived from the Assyrian-Babylonian *lilītu* (of the night). In ancient Semitic folklore, Lilith was a female demon who lived in desolate areas. In Jewish folklore, the name was borne by the first wife of Adam before Eve was created. (LIL-ITH)

Līna Derived from the Arabic *līna* (a palm tree). (LEE-NAH)

Lujayn Derived from *lujayn* (silver). (LOO-JANE)

Madīḥa From the Arabic *madīḥ* (praise, commendation), which is from *madaḥa* (to praise). Var: Madiha, Madihah. (MAH-DEE-HAH)

Maha Derived from the Arabic *maha* (wild cow). The name refers to large, luminous eyes. (MAH-HAH)

Maḥāsin Derived from *maḥāsin* (good qualities), which is from *ḥasuna* (to be good). (MAH-HAH-SEEN, MAH-HAH-SIN)

Malak Popular name derived from *malak* (angel). (MAH-LAHK)

Manāl Popular name bestowed upon both males and females which is derived from *manāl* (achievement, attainment). (MAH-NAHL)

Manār Commonly bestowed upon both males and females, this name is derived from *manār* (guiding light, beacon), which is from *nawara* (to illuminate). (MAH-NAHR)

Marwa Derived from the Arabic *marwa* (a fragrant plant; a type of flint-like rock). Al-Marwa is the name of one of the two mounts Hājar ran between in her search for water. *See* HĀJAR. (MAHR-WAH)

Maryam Arabic variant of the Hebrew Miryām, a name of disputed meaning. Some believe it to mean "sea of bitterness or sorrow." Others think it means "rebellion" or "wished-for child." Maryam is a popular name throughout the Arab world. (MAR-YAHM, MARE-EE-AHM)

Maysa Derived from *mayyas* (to walk with a proud, swinging gait), which is from *mayasa* (to swing from side to side, to walk proudly). Var: Ma'isah. (MAY-SAH)

Muḥayya From the Arabic *muḥayya* (face), which is from *hayya* (to greet). (MOO-HAY-YAH)

Muna From *muna* (wish, desire), which is from *maniya* (to desire). (MOO-NAH)

Nabiha Derived from *nabiha* (intelligent). Var: Nabihah. (NAH-BEE-HAH)

Nabīla Derived from the Arabic *nabīl* (noble, honorable), which is from nabula (to be noble). Var: Nabila, Nabilah. (NAH-BEE-LAH)

Nada Popular name derived from the Arabic *nada* (morning dew; generosity), which is from *nada* (to be moist with dew; to be generous). Both interpretations are popular. Var: Nadya. (NAH-DAH)

Nadida Derived from *nadida* (a peer, equal to another person). Var: Nadidah. (NAH-DEE-DAH)

Nādira From the Arabic *nādir* (rare, precious), which is from *nadara* (to be rare). Var: Nadira, Nadirah, Nadra, Nādra. (NAH-DEE-RAH)

Nahla Derived from *nahla* (a drink of water), which is from *nahala* (to quench one's thirst). (NAH-LAH)

Nā'ila Derived from *nā'il* (one who is successful in attaining one's desires), which is from *nāla* (to attain). The name was borne by a wife of the third rightly guided caliph, 'Uthmān ibn-'Affān. She is remembered for trying to save her husband's life by throwing herself in front of swords of a group of rebels who broke into their home to kill the caliph. It was to no avail; Nā'ila lost several fingers, and the caliph his life. Var: Nailah. (NAH-EE-LAH)

Na'īma Popular name derived from the Arabic *na'īm* (contented, happy), which is from *na'ima* (to live in comfort, to be worry-free). Var: Naeemah, Naimah, Na'īmah. (NAH-EE-MAH)

Najāt Derived from *najāh* (salvation, safety, escape), which is from *naja* (to be rescued, to escape from danger). Var: Nagāt, Najat. (NAH-JAHT)

Nājia From the Arabic *nāji* (saved), which is from *naja* (to be rescued, to escape from danger). Var: Nagia, Nāgia, Nagiah, Nagiya, Najia, Najiah, Nājiah, Najiya, Najiyah. (NAH-JEE-AH)

Najība Derived from the Arabic *najība* (of noble birth, distinguished), which is from *najuba* (to be of noble birth, to be distinguished). The word *najīb* also has the alternative definition of "smart, intelligent," so both interpretations of the same name are possible. Var: Nagība, Nagibah, Najibah. (NAH-JEE-BAH)

Najlā' From the Arabic *najlā'* (having large, beautiful eyes). Var: Nagla, Naglā, Najila, Najla, Najlaa, Najlah. (NAHJ-LAH)

Najwa Derived from *najwa* (confidential conversation, heart-to-heart talk), which is from *nāja* (to confide in). Var: Nagwa. (NAHJ-WAH)

Nasrīn Derived from the Persian *nasrīn* (wild rose). Var: Nasreen, Nasrin. (NAH-SREEN)

Nathifa Derived from the Arabic *nathifa* (clean, pure). Var: Nathifah, Natifa, Natifah. (NAH-THEE-FAH)

Nawāl Popular name derived from *nawāl* (gift, present, donation), which has its root in *nawala* (to bestow, to donate). (NAH-WAHL)

Nazihah Honest. (NAH-ZEE-HAH)

Nazira Derived from *nazira* (equal, the same as). Var: Nazirah. (NAH-ZIR-AH)

Nibāl Derived from the Arabic *nibāl* (arrows). Var: Nibal. (NIH-BAHL)

Nihāl Derived from the Arabic *nāhil* (one who has quenched his thirst). (NIH-HAHL)

Ni'mah Derived from the Arabic *ni'mah* (blessing, grace, favor), which is from *na'ima* (to live in comfort, to be worry-free). Var: Ni'mat. (NIH-MAH)

Ni'matu-Allāh Compound name composed of the elements *ni'mah* (blessing, grace, favor) and Allāh (God): hence, "the grace of God." (NIH-MAH-TOO-AHL-LAH)

Nudar From *nudar* (gold). (NOO-DAHR)

Nuha From *nuha* (intellect, mind). (NOO-HAH)

Nūr Commonly bestowed upon both males and females, this name is derived from *nūr* (light), which is from *nawara* (to illuminate, to light up). Var: Nura, Nuri. (NOOR)

Parvīn Derived from the Persian *parvīn* (the Pleiades, a cluster of stars in the constellation Taurus). Var: Parvin, Parwin. (PAHR-VEEN)

Rabāb Derived from the Arabic *rababah* (a stringed musical instrument). The name was borne by the wife of Muḥammad's grandson Husayn. She died in 681, a year after her husband and son were killed in the masssacre of Kerbelā'. Var: Rabab. (RAH-BAHB)

Rabi'ah Derived from *rabi'ah* (spring). Var: Rabiah. (RAH-BEE-AH)

Raghda Derived from the Arabic *raghīd* (carefree, happy), which is from *raghuda* (to enjoy a carefree life). (RAHG-DAH)

Ra'idah From *ra'idah* (leader). (RAH-EE-DAH)

Rajā' Popular name derived from the Arabic *raja'* (anticipation, hope), which is from *raja* (to anticipate). Var: Ragā', Raja. (RAH-JAH)

Rājya Derived from *rājya* (hopeful), which is from the root *raja* (to anticipate). Var: Ragya. (RAHJ-YAH)

Rana Popular name derived from the Arabic *rana* (a beautiful object which catches the eye), which is from *rana* (to gaze at, to look at). (RAH-NAH)

Randa Derived from *randa*, the name of a fragrant desert tree. (RAHN-DAH)

Ranya From the Arabic *ranya* (gazing at someone), which is from *rana* (to gaze at, to look at). Var: Raniyah. (RAHN-YAH)

Rasha Derived from *rasha* (a young gazelle). (RAH-SHA)

Rashīda Popular name derived from the Arabic *rashīd* (rightly guided, wise), which is from *rashada* (to follow the right course). Var: Rashida, Rashidah. (RAH-SHEE-DAH)

Rāwiya From *rāwiya* (narrator, storyteller), which is from the root *rawa* (to relate). Var: Rawiyah, Rawya. (RAH-WEE-YAH)

Rayya Derived from the Arabic *rayya* (sated with drink). (RAY-YAH)

Riḍa Derived from the Arabic *riḍa* (contentment, satisfaction), which is from *raḍiya* (to be content). Var: Radeya, Radeyah. (RIH-DAH, REE-DAH)

Rīm Derived from *rīm* (white antelope). Var: Rima. (REEM)

RUKAN Steady, confident. (ROO-KAHN)

RUQAYYA Popular name derived from the Arabic *ruqiy* (ascent, progress), which is from *raqiya* (to ascend, to rise up). The name was borne by Ruqayya bint-Muḥammad (d. 624), a daughter of the Prophet Muḥammad and Khadīja. She was married to the third rightly guided caliph 'Uthmān ibn-'Affān. Var: Ruqayah, Ruqayyah. (ROO-KAY-YAH)

RUWAYDAH Popular Arabic name meaning "walking gently, walking with grace." (ROO-WAY-DAH)

ṢABĀḤ Popular name derived from *ṣabāḥ* (morning), which is from *ṣabaḥa* (to happen in the morning). The name is borne by a famous Lebanese actress and singer. Var: Sabah. (SAH-BAH)

ṢABRIYYA Derived from *ṣabr* (patience, endurance), which is from *ṣabara* (to endure). Var: Sabira, Sabirah, Sabriyyah. (SAH-BREE-YAH)

ṢAFĀ' Popular name derived from the Arabic *safā'* (purity), which is from *safa* (to be pure, to be select). (SAH-FAH)

ṢAFIYYA Derived from *ṣafiyya* (confidant, best friend), which is from the verb *ṣafa* (to be pure, to be select). Var: Safiyyah. (SAH-FEE-YAH)

SAḤAR From the Arabic *saḥar* (dawn, sunrise, early morning). Var: Sahar. (SAH-HAR)

ṢĀLḤA Derived from the Arabic *ṣāliḥ* (virtuous, righteous), which is from *ṣaluḥa* (to be righteous). (SAHL-HAH)

SĀLIMA Popular name throughout the Arab world which is derived from the Arabic *sālima* (safe, healthy), from *salima* (to be unharmed). Var: Salimah, Salma. (SAH-LEE-MAH)

SALWA Derived from *salwa* (solace, consolation), which is from *sala* (to comfort, to distract). (SAHL-WAH)

SAMAR Derived from *samar* (intimate evening conversation), which is from *samara* (to talk in the evening, to talk at night). (SAH-MAHR)

SAMĪḤA Derived from *samīḥ* or *sāmiḥ* (generous, tolerant), which is from *samuḥa* (to be tolerant of). Var: Samihah. (SAH-MEE-HAH)

SAMĪRA Derived from *samīr* or *sāmir* (companion in evening conversations), which is from *samara* (to talk in the evening, to talk at night). Var: Samirah. (SAH-MEE-RAH)

SAMYA Derived from the Arabic *sāmi* (elevated, sublime), which is from *sama* (to rise up, to be elevated). Var: Samiyah. (SAM-YAH)

SANĀ' Popular name derived from the Arabic *sanā'* (radiance, brilliance), which is from *sana* (to gleam, to shine). Var: Sana. (SAH-NAH)

SANIYYA From *saniyya* (radiant, brilliant), which is from the root *sana* (to gleam, to shine). Var: Saniyyah. (SAH-NEE-YAH)

SĀRA Arabic form of the Hebrew Sarah, which is derived from *sārāh* (princess, noble). The name was borne by the wife of Abraham and mother of Isaac. Var: Sarah. (SAH-RAH)

SARĀB Derived from *sarāb* (mirage), which is from the verb *sariba* (to flow, to steal away). (SAH-RAHB)

SAWSAN Derived from the Arabic *sawsan* (lily of the valley). (SAW-SAHN)

SHADYA Derived from the Arabic *shādi* (singer), which is from the root *shada* (to sing). The name is borne by a famous Egyptian actress and singer. Var: Shadiya, Shadiyah. (SHA-DEE-YAH)

SHAFĪQA Derived from *shafiq* (sympathetic, compassionate), which is from *shafaqa* (to sympathize, to take pity on). Var: Shafī'a, Shafiqah. (SHA-FEE-KAH)

SHAHĪRA Derived from *shahīra* (well-known, famous), which is from *shuhira* (to be famous, to become well-known). Var: Shahirah. (SHA-HEE-RAH)

SHAHRAZĀD Compound name composed of the Persian elements *shahr* (city) and *zād* (person): hence, "city dweller, urbanite." The name is borne most famously by a character in *The Arabian Nights*, which is also known as *The Thousand and One Nights*. King Shahrayār, betrayed by his wife, vowed never to suffer the same fate again. He married a virgin each night and had her beheaded before dawn. After three years, Shahrazād begged her father to marry her to the king so she could try to end the bloodshed. After her marriage, she began to tell a fascinating story which lulled the king to sleep each night before he could give the order for her beheading. After a thousand and one nights, the king fell in love with Shahrazād and they lived happily ever after. Var: Shahrizād, Sheherazad, Sheherazade. (SHAH-RAH-ZAHD)

SHARĪFA Derived from *sharīf* (noble, distinguished), which is from the verb *sharafa* (to be distinguished, to be highborn). Var: Sharifah, Sherīfa, Sherifah. (SHA-REE-FAH)

SHATHA From the Arabic *shatha* (fragrance, perfume). (SHAH-THAH)

SHIRĪN Derived from the Persian *shirīn* (charming, sweet). Var: Shirin. (SHEER-EEN, SHEER-IN)

SHUKRIYYA Derived from the Arabic *shukri* (giving thanks, thanking), which is from *shakara* (to thank). Var: Shukriyyah. (SHOO-KREE-YAH)

SIHĀM Popular name derived from the Arabic *sihām* (arrows), which is from *sahama* (to cast, to draw). Var: Siham. (SEE-HAHM)

SUHA Derived from *suha* (a star). (SOO-HAH)

SUHĀD From the Arabic *suhād* (sleeplessness), which is from *sahida* (to be sleepless). (SOO-HAHD)

SUHAR From the Arabic *suhar* (sleeplessness), which is from *sahira* (to find no sleep). Var: Suhair, Suhayr. (SOO-HAR)

SUHAYLA A popular name throughout the Arab world, Suhayla is derived from the Arabic *suhayl* (Canopus, the second-brightest star in the southern skies). Var: Suhaila, Suhailah, Suhaylah. (SOO-HAY-LAH)

TAGHRĪD Derived from *taghrīd* (birdsong, the singing or warbling of birds), which is from *gharada* (to warble, to sing). (TAH-GREED)

ṬĀHIRA Derived from *ṭāhir* (pure, chaste), which is from *ṭahura* (to be pure, to be clean). Var: Tahira, Tahirah. (TAH-HEE-RAH)

TAḤIYYA Derived from the Arabic *taḥiyya* (greetings, salutation), which is from the root *ḥayya* (to greet). Var: Tahiyyah. (TAH-HEE-YAH)

TALIBA From *taliba* (seeker of knowledge). Var: Talibah. (TAH-LEE-BAH)

TAQIYYA Derived from the Arabic *tuqā* (piety, fear of God). Var: Takiyah, Takiyya, Takiyyah, Taqiyyah. (TAH-KEE-YAH)

ṬARŪB Derived from the Arabic *ṭarūb* (enthralled, merry), which is from *ṭariba* (to be moved with the joy of music, to be delighted or merry). Var: Tarub. (TAH-ROOB)

THANĀ' Derived from *thanā'* (praise, commendation), which is from *athna* (to praise, to commend). Var: Thana. (THAH-NAH)

THURAYYA From the Arabic *thurayya* (the Pleiades, stars in the constellation Taurus). Var: Surayya, Surayyah, Thurayyah. (THUR-RAY-YAH)

'UMAYMA Old yet perennially popular name derived from the Arabic *'umayma* (little mother). (OO-MAY-MAH)

'UM-KALTHŪM Compound name composed of the elements *'um* (mother) and *kalthūm* (one who has plump cheeks): hence, "mother of the one who has plump cheeks." The name was borne by one of the daughters of Khadīja and the Prophet Muḥammad, the wife of the third rightly guided caliph, 'Uthmān ibn-'Affān. She died in 630. Var: 'Um-Kalsūm. (OOM-KAHL-THOOM)

'UMNIYA Derived from *'umniya* (wish, desire), which is from the root *mana* (to desire, to wish for). (OOM-NEE-YAH)

WAFĀ' Popular name in the Muslim world derived from the Arabic *wafā'* (loyalty), which is from *wafa* (to fulfill a promise). Var: Wafa. (WAH-FAH)

WAFIYYA From *wafā'* (loyalty), which has its root in *wafa* (to fulfill a promise). Var: Wafiyyah. (WAH-FEE-YAH)

WAJĪHA Derived from the Arabic *wajīh* (distinguished, eminent), which is from *wajuha* (to be distinguished). Var: Wagiha, Wagīha, Wagihah, Wajiha, Wajihah. (WAH-JEE-HAH)

WALĪDA Derived from the Arabic *walīd* (a newborn), which is from *walada* (to give birth). Var: Walida, Walidah. (WAH-LEE-DAH)

WIDĀD Derived from *widād* (love, friendship), which is from *wadda* (to love, to be fond of). (WEE-DAHD)

YAMĪNA From *yamīna* (proper, of good morals). Var: Yaminah. (YAH-MEE-NAH)

YASMĪN Popular name derived from *yāsamīn* (jasmine, a fragrant plant). Var: Yasmīna, Yasminah. (YAHS-MEEN)

YUSRA Derived from *yusra* (prosperity, wealth), which is from *aysara* (to be wealthy, to become wealthy). Var: Yusriyya, Yusriyyah. (YOO-SRAH)

ZAFIRA From the Arabic *zafira* (to succeed). Var: Zafirah. (ZAH-FIR-AH, ZAH-FEE-RAH)

ZAHRA Derived from *zahra* (flower, blossom), which is from the root *zahara* (to blossom, to flower). Var: Zahirah, Zahrah, Zara, Zuhra. (ZAH-RAH)

ZAKIYYA Derived from the Arabic *zakiy* (pure, righteous), which is from *zaka* (to be pure, to be righteous). Var: Zakiyyah. (ZAH-KEE-YAH)

ZARINA Derived from the Persian *zarina* (golden, a golden chalice). (ZAH-RIH-NAH, ZAH-REE-NAH)

Zaynab Very popular name derived from the name of a fragrant plant. The name was borne by a daughter of Khadīja and the Prophet Muḥammad, by two of Muḥammad's wives, and by his granddaughter, the daughter of Fātima and 'Ali ibn-Abi-Tālib. Having witnessed the massacre of Kerbelā' in 680, she was exiled by the Umayyads to Egypt. Her courageous calls for revenge for the atrocity led to the Umayyad downfall. The Al-Sayyida Zaynab district in Cairo is named for her. Var: Zainab. (ZAY-NAHB)

Zubaidā Derived from the Arabic *zubaidā* (a marigold flower). The name was borne by Zubaidā (d. 831), wife of Harun al-Rashīd, the fifth Abbasid caliph. She is claimed to have been responsible for the building of the city of Tabriz in 806. Var: Zubaida, Zubaidah, Zubeda. (ZOO-BAY-DAH)

Chapter Twenty

Mythology and Astrology Names

Not only is mythology a collection of interesting stories about the pursuits and exploits of ancient gods, heroes and heroines, it is also an important means of seeing the foundations that different cultures developed upon.

In many European countries, names from mythology have become common to the pool of names in use. The Scandinavians have determinedly held on to their stock of names taken from popular gods and heroes, and Arthurian legend has given many names that remain popular to this day. The U.S. has its own body of legend and lore, but names from these are nearly all of European origin and have entered the name pool from other sources. Currently, there is a renewed interest in the bestowal of names from mythology, and many of these are of Greek and Roman origin.

Those interested in astrology are often searching for interesting names to use that reflect the birth signs of their children. If a child is born under a water sign, such as Pisces, "water" names such as Oceana, Marina, or Lake might be chosen. Earth signs might choose a name such as Terra. Other possibilities are the names of the archangels assigned to watch over those born under the different months, or perhaps names from birthstones or colors associated with the zodiac. A good astrological guide can be of great help and provide the inspiration for choosing a suitable name.

Mythology and Astrology Male Names

Acestes From Greek mythology, Acestes is a name borne by a Trojan king of the Sicilian settlement of Drepanum who was host to Aeneas and his shipmates during their voyage to Italy. (AH-SES-TEEZ)

Achates Derived from the Greek Achātēs (agate), a name borne by a loyal friend and companion of Aeneas, whose story is told in Virgil's *Aeneid*. (AH-KAY-TEEZ)

Achelous Derived from the Greek Achelōus, the ancient name of the Aspropotamo River in central Greece. In Greek mythology, Achelous was the name of a river-god, the oldest of the three thousand sons of Oceanus and Tethys. (AK-AH-LO-US)

Acheron Derived from the Greek *achos* (pain), Acheron (river of woe) is found in Greek mythology as the name of a river in Hades, across which Charon ferried the dead. (AK-EH-RUN)

ACHILLES Derived from Achilleus, an ancient name of unknown etymology borne in Greek mythology by the leader and warrior of the Trojan War. He was killed by the Trojan prince Paris with an arrow that struck his heel, his only vulnerable spot. Achilles is the hero of Homer's epic *Iliad*. (AH-KILL-EEZ)

ACTAEON Derived from the Greek Aktaiōn (an inhabitant of Acte, the ancient name of Attica). The name is borne in Greek mythology by the son of Aristaeus and Autonoë. While hunting one day, he chanced upon Artemis bathing in a stream. She thereupon transformed him into a stag and he was hunted down by his own dogs. (AK-TEE-UN)

ADAD From Assyro-Babylonian mythology, Adad was the god of storms, floods, and water. He represented both goodness and evil and could bring calming winds and gentle rain as well as violent storms and floods. (AH-DAHD)

ADAPA The name of a mortal who was created by the Assyro-Babylonian water-god Ea to rule over the human race. (AH-DAH-PAH)

ADONIS From Greek and Roman mythology, Adonis was a son of Cinyras, the king of Cyprus, and his daughter Myrrha. After Myrrha was transformed into a tree, Adonis was given to Persephone (Proserpina) to care for. It was decreed that he would spend four months in the underworld with Persephone, four months with Aphrodite (Venus), and four wherever he chose. He was killed by a wild boar while hunting and was transformed into the anemone flower by Aphrodite. His cult was widespread and the ceremonial festival of Adonia was held yearly after the harvest, in honor of his death and rebirth. (AH-DON-ISS)

AEACUS From the Greek Aiakos, a name of unknown origin and meaning borne in Greek mythology by a son of Zeus, a king of Aegina who became one of the three judges of the underworld after his death. (EE-AH-KUS)

AEGEUS From the Greek Aigeus, an evolution of Aegidius, which is derived from *aigis* (the goatskin shield of Zeus). The name is borne in Greek mythology by an Athenian king who drowned himself when he thought his son Theseus was dead. (EE-JEE-US)

AEGIS From the Greek *aigis* (the goatskin shield of Zeus, a protection). In Greek mythology, the aegis was the shield borne by Zeus and later by his daughter Athena. (EE-JIS)

AEGYPTUS From Greek mythology, Aegyptus was a king of Egypt whose fifty sons married the Danaides, the fifty daughters of his brother Danaus. (EE-GYP-TUS)

AEOLUS Derived from the Greek Aīolos (the changeable one). The name is borne in Greek mythology by the god of the winds. It was also borne by a king of Thessaly who was the legendary patriarch of the Aeolians. (EE-O-LUS, EE-AH-LUS)

AESON Of unknown etymology, Aeson was the name of a Thessalian prince, the father of Jason. In extreme old age, Aeson was transformed into a young man by the sorceress Medea. (EE-SON)

AGANJU From African mythology, Aganju is the name of the son and husband of the Yoruban earth-goddess Odudua. (AH-GAHN-JOO)

AINEIAS Derived from the Greek *ainein* (to praise). The name was borne in Greek mythology by the hero of Virgil's epic *Aeneid*. Aineias, the Trojan son of Anchises and Venus, wandered for years after escaping from the ruined city of Troy. Var: Aeneas. (IH-NEE-US)

AJAX Derived from the Greek Aias (alas). The name is borne in Greek mythology by two Greeks renowned for their valor and prowess. Ajax Telamon was a strong and brave warrior who led the Greeks in the Trojan War after Achilles withdrew. After Achilles returned, was killed, and his armor given to Odysseus, Ajax slew himself in a fit of jealousy. Ajax the Lesser, one of the swiftest runners in the Greek Army, was shipwrecked because he saved Cassandra from the altar of Athena. (Ā-JAX)

ALCYONEUS Derived from the Latin *alcyon* (a kingfisher, halcyon), which is from the Greek *alkyōn:* hence, "of or belonging to the halcyon." The name is borne in Greek mythology by one of the giants, a son of Uranus and Gaea. (AL-SĪ-AH-NEE-US)

ALPHEUS From the Greek Alpheiōs (the white or transparent thing). The name of the chief river of Peleponnesus, the manifestation of the Greek river-god who was the lover of the nymph Arethusa. (AL-FEE-US)

AMPHION Borne in Greek mythology by a son of Zeus and Antiope. A king of Thebes and husband of Viobe, he built a wall around his city by charming the stones into place with a lyre. (AM-FĪ-UN)

AMYCUS From the Greek Amykos, which is of uncertain derivation. It might be derived from the Latin *amicus* (loving, friendly, amicable). The name is borne in Greek mythology by a son of Poseidon who made all strangers box with him. Those who accepted the challenge were killed in the match; those who refused were drowned. Eventually, he was bested by Pollux, who boxed with him on behalf of the Argonauts. (AMEE-KUS)

ANAEL The name given to the archangel for those born under the astrological sign of Libra. (AH-NAY-EL)

ANCHISES Borne in Greek and Roman mythology by the father of Aeneas and Aphrodite. He was borne from the flames of Troy by Aeneas, but died when they reached Sicily. (AN-KĪ-SEES)

ANTAEUS Derived from the Greek Antaios, which is from *antaīos* (an adversary, one who is opposite). The name is borne in Greek mythology by a son of Poseidon and Gaea. A giant who forced all strangers to wrestle with him, he was beaten by Heracles, who realized that Antaeus was invincible as long as he was touching the earth. (AN-TEE-US)

APOLLO Derived from Apollōn, an ancient Greek name of unknown derivation. The name is borne in Greek mythology by the handsome son of Zeus and Leto and twin brother of the goddess Artemis. Apollo, one of the twelve major deities, was the god of music, poetry, prophecy, and medicine. (AH-PAHL-LO)

AQUILO Derived from the Latin *aquilo* (the swift flying thing, the north wind), Aquilo was the Roman mythical personification of the north wind. (AH-KWIH-LO)

ARCAS From Roman mythology, Arcas was a son of Jupiter and Callisto. The progenitor of the Arcadians, he was transformed after his death into the red star Arcturus to serve as guardian to his mother, who had been transformed into the Great Bear constellation. (AR-KUS)

ARES Borne in Greek mythology by a son of Zeus and Hera. One of the twelve major deities, Ares was the god of war and is equated with the Roman mythological god Mars. Var: Aries. (ERR-EEZ)

ARGUS From the Greek Argos, which is directly derived from *argos* (bright). The name is borne in Greek mythology by a giant with one hundred eyes who was ordered by Hera to watch the goddess Io after she transformed a maiden admired by Zeus into a heifer. After he was killed by Hermes, his eyes were put in the tail feathers of the peacock. (AHR-GUS)

ARIES Latin name meaning "the Ram." It is given to the first sign of the zodiac (March 21–April 20), ruled by the planet Mars. (ERR-EEZ, AHR-EEZ)

ARION A name found in Greek and Roman mythology as that of a horse endowed with speech and the special gift of prophecy. Arion was also the name of a celebrated musician, a player of the cithara who was rescued from drowning by dolphins. (AHR-EE-ON, AH-RĪ-UN)

ARISTAEUS Derived from the Greek *aristaīos* (one pertaining to a noble). The name is borne in Greek mythology by a son of Apollo and Cyrene, said to have taught men the skill of beekeeping and the treatment of milk, and to have been the first to plant olive trees. (AHR-IH-STĀ-US, ERR-IH-STĀ-US)

ARTHUR Of Celtic origin but of unknown meaning, Arthur was borne by the legendary British king. Leader of the knights of the Round Table, he was the son of Uther Pendragon and Igraine, and husband of Guinevere. (AHR-THUR)

ASARIEL Hebrew name meaning "prince of God" which is borne by the archangel who overlooks those born under the astrological sign of Pisces (February 20–March 20). (AH-SAH-REE-ELL)

ASCANIUS Borne in Roman mythology by a son of Aeneas and Creusa. (AS-KĀ-NEE-US)

ASHUR From Assyrian mythology, Ashur, the supreme deity of the Assyrian Empire, was the creator of all things, the ruler of the gods, and the god of war. (AH-SHOOR)

ASTRAEUS From the Greek *astraīa* (the starry one). The name is borne in Roman mythology by one of the Titans. Astraeus was the husband of Aurora and the father of the Winds. (AS-TREE-US)

ASTYANAX A Greek name meaning "king of the city," Astyanax is borne in Greek and Roman mythology by a son of Hector and Andromache. Upon the destruction of Troy, he was cast down from the city walls by Ulysses so he could not exact revenge. (AS-TĪ-AH-NAKS)

ATREUS From Greek mythology, Atreus was a son of Pelops and Ilippodamia, a king of Argos and Mycenae, whose sons were Agamemnon and Menelaus. (Ā-TROOS, Ā-TREE-US)

AURIEL Hebrew name meaning "lion of God" which is borne by the archangel who overlooks those born under the sign of Taurus (April 21–May 21). (OR-REE-ELL)

AZRAEL Derived from the Hebrew *'azra'ēl* (help of God). The name is borne by the archangel for the sign of Scorpio (October 24–November 22). In ancient Muslim and Jewish belief, Azrael was the angel who parted the soul from the body at the moment of death. Var: Azriel. (AZ-REE-ELL)

BACCHUS Derived from the Greek Bakchos, an ancient name of unknown derivation. The name is borne in Roman mythology by the god of wine, revelry, and poets. He is equated with the Greek mythological god Dionysus. (BAK-US)

BIRAL The name of the early legendary Australian hero who taught tribal lore and customs to his people in the northern part of the continent. (BEER-UL)

BISHAMON Japanese god of war and good luck and guardian of the north. Bishamon is also known as Tamon. (BIH-SHA-MON)

BRAHMA From the Sanskrit *brahman* (worship, prayer), Brahma is the Hindu supreme deity, the creator of the universe and the chief member of the trinity of Brahma, Vishnu, and Siva. (BRA-MAH)

BRAN Derived from the Gaelic *bran* (raven). The name is borne in Celtic mythology by Bran the Blessed, the brother of Branwen and Manawyddan. In revenge for the maltreatment of his sister by her husband, the Irish king, Bran attacked the island and was mortally wounded in the battle. (BRAN)

BRIAREUS Found in Greek and Roman mythology as the name of a hundred-armed giant, also commonly known as Aegaeon. The name is derived from the Greek Briarēos, which is from the root *briaros* (strong). (BRĪ-AHR-EE-US)

CADMUS Derived from the Greek Kādmos (one who excels). The name is borne in Greek and Roman mythology by a son of the Phoenician king Agenor and Telephassa, brother of Europa and husband of Harmonia. He was the founder of the Cadmea, the citadel of the Boetian tribes, and the inventor of alphabetic writing. Var: Kadmus. (KAD-MUS)

CAGN From African mythology, Cagn is the supreme god of the Bushmen, the creator of all living things whose dwelling place is known only to antelopes. (KAHGN)

CASSIEL The name given to the archangel who overlooks those born under the astrological sign of Capricorn (December 22–January 20). (KASS-EE-ELL)

CEPHEUS From Greek mythology, Cepheus was an Ethiopian king, the husband of Cassiopeia and father of Andromeda. He chained his daughter to a rock as a sacrifice to a threatening sea monster, but she was saved by Perseus. (SEE-FYOOS, SEE-FEE-US)

CREON Derived from the Greek *kreōn* (ruler, prince). The name is found in Greek mythology by a brother of Jocasta. Var: Kreon. (KREE-UN)

DANAUS From Greek mythology, Danaus was a king of Argos whose fifty daughters, the Danaides, married the fifty sons of Danaus' brother, Aegyptus. (DAN-EE-US)

EBISU From Japanese mythology, Ebisu, a god of labor and luck, is the son of Daikoku, a god of wealth and good luck. (EE-BIH-SOO)

ERYX From Greek mythology, Eryx was the name of a son of Aphrodite and Poseidon. (ERR-IX)

ETANA Borne in Assyro-Babylonian mythology by a mortal who was chosen by the gods to be the first ruler of mankind. (EH-TAH-NAH)

EVANDER From the Greek Evandros, which is derived from *andros* (manly). The name is borne in Roman mythology by the son of Hermes. The father of Roma, he founded a town called Pallanteum on the banks of the Tiber River which eventually became the city of Rome. Evander is credited with the introduction of the Greek alphabet and the pantheon of the Greek gods into Italy. (EE-VAN-DER)

GABRIEL Derived from the Hebrew *gavhrī'ēl* (God is my strength). The name is borne by the archangel who looks after those born under the astrological sign of Cancer (June 22–July 23). (GABE-REE-ELL)

GAWAIN Believed to be a derivative of the Welsh Gwalchmai, a compound name composed of the elements *gwalch* (a hawk) and *maedd* (a blow, a battle): hence, "battle hawk." The name is borne in Arthurian legend by a nephew of King Arthur. A knight of the Round Table, Gawain set off in search of the Holy Grail. (GAH-WIN, GUH-WANE)

GEIRROD Old name believed to be derived from the Germanic elements *ger* (spear, javelin) and *hruod* (fame): hence, "spear fame, famous with a spear." The name is borne in Norse mythology by a giant who made the mischievous god Loki lure Thor to his kingdom without his magical belt and hammer. (GARE-ROD)

GEMINI Latin name meaning "twins." It is the name of the third sign of the zodiac (May 22–June 21). (JEH-MIH-NĪ)

GENOS From Phoenician mythology, Genos and Genea were the first people to inhabit Phoenicia and the first to worship the sun. (JEE-NOS)

GERAINT Celtic name of uncertain derivation which is borne in Arthurian legend by a knight of the Round Table, the husband of Enid. (JUH-RAINT)

GUNNAR Derived from the Old Norse Gunnarr, which is from the word *gunnr* (war, strife, battle). The name Gunnar was borne by several interesting characters in Norse mythology, one of whom was the son of Giuki and Grimhild. He was the brother of Gudrun and the husband of Brynhild. (GOO-NAHR, GUN-NAR)

GUNTHER From the German Günther, a compound name composed from the Germanic elements *gund* (war, strife) and *har* (army): hence, "war army." The name is borne in the *Nibelungenlied* by a king of the Burgundians who was a brother of Kriemhild and the husband of Brunhild. (GOON-THER, GUN-THER)

HECTOR Derived from the Greek Hektōr (holding fast), which is from *echein* (to hold, to have). The name Hector is borne in the *Iliad* by a Trojan hero who was killed by Achilles to avenge the death of Patroclus, Priam's oldest son. (HEK-TER)

HERACLES Derived from the Greek Hērakleēs, a compound name composed of the name of the goddess Hera and *kleos* (glory): hence, "glory to Hera." The name is borne in Greek and Roman mythology by a son of Zeus and Alcmene who was renowned for his amazing feats of strength, including the twelve labors imposed on him. Hercules is the Latin form of the name. (HER-KYOO-LEEZ)

ICARUS From the Greek Ikaros, a name of uncertain derivation which is borne in Greek mythology by the son of Daedalus who escaped from Crete by flying with wings made by his father. He flew so high, however, that the sun's heat melted the wax by which the wings were fastened, and Icarus fell to his death in the sea, henceforth known as the Icarian Sea. (IK-AH-RUS)

ION From the Greek *iōn* (going). The name is borne in Greek mythology by a son of Apollo and Creusa who became the progenitor of the Ionians. (Ī-ON)

JANUS From the Latin *janus* (gate, arched passageway). The name is borne in Roman mythology by the god of beginnings and endings and guardian of doors and entryways. Janus, who was portrayed with two faces, one in front and one in back, gave his name to the month of January. (JĀ-NUS)

KANALOA The name of one of the major Hawaiian gods. (KAH-NAH-LO-AH)

KOMOKU From Japanese mythology, Komoku is the name of one of the Shi Tenno—guardians of the four major points of the compass and protectors against the entrance of demons. Komoku was the guardian of the south. (KO-MO-KOO)

LAKE Derived from *lake* (an inland body of water). The name may be bestowed upon those whose astrological signs are water signs. (LAKE)

LANCELOT French diminutive form of Lance, which is from the Old High German Lanzo, a name derived from *lant* (land). The name is found in Arthurian legend as that of the bravest and most celebrated of the knights of the Round Table. Sir Lancelot was the lover of King Arthur's wife, Guinevere, and the father of Sir Galahad. Var: Launcelot. (LANS-AH-LOT)

LEANDER From the Greek Leiandros, a name believed to be derived from the elements *leōn* (lion) and *andros* (man): hence, "lion man." The name is borne in Greek mythology by the young man who nightly swam the Hellespont River to visit his lover, Hero, in Sestos. (LEE-AN-DER)

LEO Latin name meaning "lion." Leo is the name of the fifth sign of the zodiac (July 24–August 23). (LEE-O)

LLOYD Derived from the Welsh *llwyd* (gray). The name is found in Celtic mythology as that of a friend of Gwawl. After Gwawl was rejected by Rhiannon in favor of Pryderi, Lloyd used his magic powers against Pryderi on behalf of Gwawl. (LOID)

MANU From Indian mythology, Manu, the survivor of the Deluge, became the progenitor of mankind and the giver of laws. (MAH-NOO)

MAUI From Hawaiian mythology, Maui is the name of the popular demigod whose special feats included the snaring of the sun so the days would be longer, and the discovery of fire. (MOU-EE)

MERLIN Derived from the Welsh Myrddin, which is believed to be derived from the Old Celtic Mori-dünon, a compound name composed of the elements *mori* (sea) and *dunom* (hill): hence, "sea hill." Myrddin was an early Celtic mythological hero who later became known as Merlin, a magician and helper of King Arthur in Arthurian legend. (MER-LIN)

MICHAEL Hebrew name derived from *mīkhā'ēl* (who is like God?). The name is borne by the archangel assigned to the astrological sign of Leo. (MĪ-KL)

NESTOR From the Greek Nēstor (the one going, the one departing). The name is borne in Greek mythology by a king of Pylos, an Argonaut who was the only one of the twelve sons of Neleus and Chloris not to be killed by Heracles. Nestor was famous for his wisdom and eloquence and is said to have lived through three generations of men. (NES-TER)

ODYSSEUS The name of the hero of the *Odyssey* who was a king of Ithaca and one of the Greek leaders of the Trojan War. The husband of Penelope and father of Telemachus, Odysseus wandered for ten years after the fall of Troy. Ulysses is the Latin form of the name, which is derived from the Greek root *dys* (hate). (O-DEE-SEE-US)

ORION From Greek and Roman mythology, Orion was a son of Poseidon. He loved the goddess Diana but was accidentally killed by her and thenceforth placed in the heavens as the constellation Orion. (O-RĪ-UN)

PARIS Borne in Greek legend by a son of Priam, the king of Troy, and Hecuba. Paris' kidnaping of Helen, the wife of Menelaus, set off the Trojan War. (PARE-ISS)

PERCIVAL From the Old French Perceval, which is believed to be composed of the elements *perce* (pierce) and *val* (valley): hence, "pierce valley." Percival was the name of the knight in Arthurian legend who saw the Holy Grail. (PER-SIH-VL)

PHILEMON Derived from the Greek *philēmōn* (affectionate). The name is found in Greek mythology as that of the husband of Baucis. A poor and elderly couple, Philemon and Baucis were the only ones hospitable to Zeus and Hermes. In reward, their lives were spared during a flood. (FIH-LEE-MUN)

PHOENIX From the Greek *phoinix* (phoenix, dark red). In Egyptian mythology, the phoenix was a beautiful, solitary bird that lived in the Arabian desert for five hundred or six hundred years before consuming itself in fire to rise anew to another extraordinarily long life. The phoenix is seen as a symbol of immortality. (FEE-NIX)

POLYNICES Borne in Greek legend by a son of Oedipus and brother of Eteocles. He was a member of the Seven against Thebes, an expedition of seven heroes formed to help Polynices regain his share of the throne of Thebes from his brother. (POL-LIH-NĪ-SEEZ)

PONTUS From Greek mythology, Pontus was an early god of the sea, a son of Uranus and Gaea. (PON-TUS)

QUIRINUS From Roman mythology, Quirinus was an early god of war who was later identified with Romulus. (KWIH-REE-NUS)

RAIDEN From Japanese mythology, Raiden was the name of the god of thunder. (RAY-DEN)

RAPHAEL Derived from the Hebrew *refā'ēl* (God has healed). The name is borne by the archangel assigned to the zodiacal signs of Gemini and Virgo. (RAH-FĀ-ELL, RAH-FEE-ELL)

REGIN Derived from the Old Norse *regn, ragn* (judgment, decision). In Norse legend, Regin, a very wise man, was appointed tutor and foster father of Sigurd. Var: Reagan, Regan. (REEG-UN)

SACHIEL Borne by the archangel that watches over those born under the sign of Sagittarius. (SA-CHEE-ELL)

SAMUEL Cognate of the Hebrew Shmuel, which is derived from *shĕmū'ēl* (name of God, his name is God). Samuel is the name of the archangel assigned to the zodiacal sign of Aries. (SAM-YOOL)

SIEGFRIED Compound name composed from the Germanic elements *segu* (power, victory) and *frid* (peace): hence, "powerful peace, victorious peace." The name was borne in Teutonic mythology by the heroic son of Siegmund and Sieglinde whose many feats and adventures are recorded in the *Nibelungenlied*. (SEEG-FREED)

SIEGMUND Germanic compound name composed from the elements *sig* (victory) and *mund* (hand, protection): hence, "victorious protection, hand of victory." The name is borne in Teutonic mythology by a king of the Netherlands, the husband of Sieglinde and father of Siegfried. (SEEG-MUND)

SIGMUND Derived from the Old Norse Sigmundr, a compound name composed of the Germanic elements *sig* (victory) and *mund* (hand, protection). Sigmund, a favored character and hero of Norse legend, was the father of Sinfiotli by his sister Signy. He was also the father of Sigurd, who was born after Sigmund died. (SIG-MUND)

SIGURD From the obsolete Old Norse Sigvörðr, a compound name composed of the elements *sigr* (victory, conquest) and *vörðr* (guardian): hence, "guardian of victory." The name is borne by several characters in Norse legend, including Sigurd Fafnirsbane, the slayer of the dragon Fafnir. (SIH-GERD)

TANE The name of the Polynesian sky-god, the father of all living creatures, who was the god of fertility and the protector of birds and the forests. He was primarily identified with fresh water and the sunlight. Kane is the Hawaiian form of the name. (TAH-NEH)

TELAMON From Greek mythology, Telamon was the name of a friend of Heracles. He was a son of Aeacus, a brother of Peleus, and the husband of Hesione. (TAL-AH-MON)

THESEUS Borne in Greek Legend by the main hero of Attica. Theseus was a son of Aegeus and is famed for his slaying of the Minotaur. (THEE-SYOOS, THEE-SEE-US)

THOR Derived from the Old Norse *Þórr* (thunder). The name is borne in Norse mythology by the son of Odin and Frigg. The god of thunder and strength, Thor was the husband of Sif and the father of Modi and Thrud. He also had a son, Magni, by the giantess Jarnsaxa, and was the possessor of three priceless objects: his hammer, Mjollnir, his strength-increasing belt, and his iron gauntlets. His principal role was to protect both Asgard and Midgard from attacks by giants. (THOR)

TIKI Maori and Marquesan name borne in Polynesian mythology by the first man or the god who created him. (TEE-KEE)

TRISTAN From the Old French Tristran, which is from the Celtic Drystan, a name derived from *drest* (riot, tumult). The name, which was altered in reference to the Latin *tristis* (sad), was borne in Celtic legend by a knight who freed Cornwall from a tribute of young men imposed by an Irish king. He was later sent to Ireland by King Mark of Cornwall to bring back Princess Iseult as the king's bride. On the return trip, Tristan and Iseult drank from a love potion intended for the king and fell in love. Tristan left to fight for King Howel of Brittany, and, seriously wounded, he sent for Iseult. She arrived too late and died from grief next to Tristan's deathbed. Var: Tristram. (TRIS-TUN)

TYDEUS From Greek legend, Tydeus, a son of Oeneus and the father of Diomedes, was one of the Seven against Thebes, an expedition of seven heroes formed to help Polynices regain his share of the throne of Thebes from his brother Eteocles. (TĪ-DYOOS, TĪ-DEE-US)

URIEL The name of the archangel assigned to the astrological sign Aquarius. It is derived from the Hebrew *ūrī'ēl* (light of God). (YOOR-EE-ELL, YOOR-EE-ULL)

UTHER A name of uncertain derivation borne in medieval legend by a king of Britain who was the father of King Arthur. (OO-THER)

VIDAR From the Old Norse Víðarr, a name of uncertain derivation. According to Norse mythology, Vidar was the son of Odin and the giantess Grid. He was the silent god, known for his great strength. At Ragnarok, he avenges Odin's death by killing the Fenris Wolf. (VID-DAHR)

ZETHUS From Greek mythology, Zethus was a son of Zeus and Antiope, a twin brother of Amphion and husband of the nymph Thebe. He was famed for building the great stone wall around the town of Thebes, which was named for his wife. (ZEE-THUS)

ZEUS Ancient name thought to be derived from the Indo-European root *deiwos* (a god). The name is borne in Greek mythology by the supreme god, the son of Cronus and Rhea, and husband of Hera. Zeus is equated with the Roman god Jupiter. (ZOOS)

Mythology and Astrology Female Names

ADITI From Indian mythology, Aditi was the mother of all the gods, the source of all things, the goddess of heaven, and an attendant of Indra. (AH-DEE-TEE)

ADMETE From Greek mythology, Admete was the daughter of Eurystheus. (AD-MEE-TEE)

ADONIA The Greek and Roman ceremonial festival celebrating the death and rebirth of Adonis, held following the annual harvest. (AH-DON-EE-AH, AH-DOE-NEE-AH)

ADRASTEA From Greek mythology, Adrastea was a nymph who cared for the infant Zeus on the island of Crete. (AH-DRAH-STĀ-AH)

AEGINA Borne in Greek mythology by a nymph who was the daughter of Asopus and Metope. She gave birth to Zeus' son Aeacus on the island bearing her name in the Aegean Sea off the southeast coast of Greece. (EE-JĪ-NAH)

AEGLE Borne in Greek mythology by one of the Hesperides, who were responsible for guarding the golden apples, as well as by a daughter of the sun and a daughter of Neaera and Jupiter. (EE-GL)

AETHRA From Greek mythology, the name Aethra was borne by one of the Oceanids who was the mother of the Hyades, and by the mother of Theseus. (EE-THRA)

AGLAIA Borne in Greek mythology by the youngest of the three Graces, who were daughters of Zeus and Eurynome. Aglaia represented brightness and splendor. (AH-GLĀ-AH)

AINO From Finnish mythology, Aino was the sister of Joukahainen. Her hand was promised in marriage to an old magician named Vainamoinen. In an effort to escape his advances, she fell into the sea and became a water spirit. (Ī-NO)

ALALA From Roman mythology, Alala was the sister of Mars, the god of war. The name has been bestowed as an astrological name upon female children born under Aries and Scorpio, signs ruled by the planet Mars. (AH-LAH-LAH)

ALCESTIS Borne in Greek mythology by the daughter of Pelias and wife of Admetus. She sacrificed herself so that Admetus could live. (AHL-SES-TIS)

Alima Astrological name for children born under the water signs of Cancer, Pisces, and Scorpio. (AH-LEE-MAH)

Althaea From the Greek *althaia* (healer). The name is borne in Greek mythology by the mother of Deianira, Meleager, and Tydeus. (AL-THEE-AH)

Amalthea From Greek mythology, Amalthea was the name of the mountain goat that nursed the infant Zeus. One of her horns became the Cornucopia, the Horn of Plenty. (AM-AHL-THEE-AH)

Amber The name of a honey-colored translucent fossil resin regarded as a gemstone of the astrological sign Leo. (AM-BER)

Amenti From Egyptian mythology, Amenti was a goddess of the west. She is depicted with a hawk or an ostrich plume on her head. Var: Ament, Iment. (AH-MEN-TEE)

Amethyst The name of a purple or violet type of quartz which is a gemstone of the astrological signs of Aries and Scorpio. (AM-EH-THIST)

Amymone The name of one of the Danaïds in Greek mythology. (AH-MĪ-MO-NEE)

Anahita Borne in Persian mythology by a goddess of rivers and water. (AH-NAH-HEE-TAH)

Andromeda Borne in Greek mythology by the daughter of Cassiopeia and the Ethiopian king Cephus. She was rescued from a sea monster by Perseus, who then married her. (AN-DRAH-MEH-DAH)

Anna From Roman mythology, Anna was the sister of Dido, the queen of Carthage. (AH-NAH, AN-NAH)

Anthea Derived from the Greek *antheios* (flowery). Anthea was a name of Hera, the queen of the gods, the goddess of women and marriage. (AN-THEE-AH)

Antigone From Greek mythology, Antigone was the daughter of Oedipus and Jocasta. In defiance of an edict of her uncle Creon, Antigone performed funeral rites for her brother and in consequence was put to death herself. (AN-TIH-GUH-NEE)

Aphrodite From Greek mythology, Aphrodite was one of the twelve major deities, the goddess of love and beauty. She is equated with the Roman goddess, Venus. (A-FRO-DĪ-TEE)

Arethusa From Greek mythology, Arethusa was a woodland nymph transformed into a stream by Artemis so that she could escape from the unwanted attentions of the river-god, Alpheus. (AIR-EH-THOO-SAH, AR-EH-THOO-SAH)

Ariadne Derived from the Greek elements *ari* (very, much) and *adnos* (holy). Ariadne (very holy one) is a name borne in Greek mythology by King Minos' daughter, who gave a ball of thread to Theseus which enabled him to escape from the labyrinth. (AIR-EE-AD-NEE, AR-EE-AD-NEE)

Artemis From Greek mythology, Artemis was the name of one of the twelve major deities, the goddess of the moon, hunting, and wild animals. She is equated with the Roman goddess Diana. (AR-TEH-MIS)

Asteria In Greek mythology, Asteria was the daughter of Coeus and Phoebe, and the mother of Hecate. She was transformed into a quail and jumped into the sea to escape from the attentions of Zeus, and thereby became the island of Ortygia, now known as Delos. (AH-STER-EE-AH)

Astraea Derived from the Greek *astraios* (starry). The name is borne in Greek mythology by the goddess of justice and innocence. She was the last deity to leave the earth after the Golden Age, thus becoming the constellation Virgo. Var: Astrea. (AS-TREE-AH)

Atalanta From Greek mythology, Atalanta was the name of a fleet-footed maiden who said she would marry the man who could defeat her in a footrace. All other contestants would be put to death. Hippomenes won by dropping three golden apples, which Atalanta stopped to pick up. Var: Atlanta, Atalante. (ATL-LAN-TAH)

Athene Ancient name of unknown etymology, Athene is the name borne in Greek mythology by the goddess of wisdom, skills, and warfare. She is equated to the Roman goddess Minerva. Var: Athena. (AH-THEE-NEE, AH-THEE-NAH)

Aurora Derived from the Latin *aurora* (dawn, daybreak). The name is borne in Roman mythology by the goddess of dawn. She is equated to the Greek goddess Eros. (O-ROR-AH, AH-ROR-AH)

Autonoë From Greek mythology, Autonoë was the daughter of Harmonia and Cadmus, mother of Actaeon, and wife of Aristaeus. (AH-TAH-NO-EE)

Avalon From the Middle Latin *Avallonis insula*, which is derived from the Welsh *ynys yr Afallon* (island of apples). From Celtic mythology, Avalon was an island paradise in the west, the home of fallen heroes where King Arthur was transported after his death. (AV-AH-LON)

Berecyntia A name of the Phrygian goddess of the earth and nature, Cybele. (BER-AH-SIN-TEE-AH)

Beryl The name of a type of gemstone assigned to the astrological sign of Gemini. Emerald and aquamarine are two types of beryl. (BEH-REL)

Branwen Derived from the Celtic elements *bran* (raven) and *gwen* (white, fair, blessed): hence, "blessed raven." The name is borne in Celtic mythology by the daughter of Llyr and sister of Bran and Manawyddan. Her marriage to the Irish king Matholwych temporarily united England and Ireland, but her mistreatment at the hands of her husband brought about war between the two islands. (BRAN-WEN)

Brigantia Believed to be derived from the Celtic element *brîgh* (strength). Brigantia was a goddess of springs and streams and a protector of the Brigantes, the largest tribe in ancient England. (BRIH-GAN-TEE-AH)

Brigit Believed to be derived from the Celtic element *brîgh* (strength). The name is borne in Irish mythology by a goddess of civilization, culture, the home, and fertility. (BRIJ-IT)

Briseis From Greek mythology, Briseis was the beautiful wife of King Mynes of Lyrnessus. She was given to Achilles as a prize of war and was captured by Agamemnon, thus invoking Achilles' wrath. (BRĪ-SEE-ISS)

Brynhild Compound name composed of the Old Norse elements *brynja* (armor) and *hildr* (battle, fight): hence, "battle armor, armored for fighting." In Norse mythology, she was a Valkyrie who was awakened from an enchanted sleep by Sigurd, with whom she fell deeply in love. Deceived by him into marrying Gunnar (so Sigurd could marry Gudrun), she eventually brought about Sigurd's death, then took her own life. (BRIN-HILD)

Camilla Derived from the Latin *camilla* (virgin of unblemished character). The name is borne in Roman mythology by a queen of the Volscians who fought in the army of the Trojan Aeneas. (KAH-MIL-LAH)

Castalia From Greek mythology, Castalia was the name of a nymph pursued by Apollo until she threw herself into a spring on Mount Parnassus. Afterward, the fountain became sacred to Apollo and the Muses. (KAH-STĀ-LEE-AH)

Ceres From the Sanskrit root *kri* (to cultivate) or *cri* (to ripen). The name is borne in Roman mythology by the daughter of Saturn and Ops. Ceres was the mother of Proserpine and goddess of agriculture. She is equated with the Greek goddess Demeter. (SIR-EEZ)

Chloris Derived from the Greek *chloros* (green, pale green). The name Chloris (the verdant one) is borne in Greek mythology by the goddess of vegetation. (KLOR-ISS)

Concordia From the Latin *concordia* (harmony, concord, union, unanimity). The name is borne in Roman mythology by the goddess of concord and harmony. (KON-KOR-DEE-AH)

Cressida Of unknown etymology. It was borne in medieval legend by a Trojan woman and daughter of the priest Calchus who defected to the Romans. Cressida later is unfaithful to her Trojan lover, Troilus, and leaves him for the Greek Diomedes. (KREH-SIH-DAH)

Cybele Borne by the Phrygian and Lydian goddess of nature and the earth. She is equated with the Greek goddess Rhea and the Roman goddess Ops. (SIH-BEH-LEE)

Cyrene From Greek mythology, Cyrene was a nymph of Thessaly and the mother of Aristaeus. Her name was given to an ancient Greek city in the province of Cyrenaica in Libya. (SĪ-REE-NEE)

Daisy The name of a flower assigned to the sign of Taurus. (DĀ-ZEE)

Danaë From the Greek Danae (the parched or dry one). In Greek mythology, Danaë was a daughter of Acrisius and mother of Perseus by Zeus, who visited her in the form of a golden shower when she was shut in a tower by her father. (DAN-AH-EE)

Danu From Celtic mythology, Danu was the mother of the deities of the Irish pantheon, the *Tuatha de Danann* (the people of Danu). She was representative of the earth, the mother of all things. Var: Dana. (DAN-OO)

Daphne Derived from the Greek *daphne* (a laurel or bay tree). The name is borne in Greek mythology by a nymph, the daughter of the river-god Peneus. She escaped from the attentions of Apollo by being transformed into a laurel tree. Var: Daphna, Daphney. (DAF-NEE)

Decembra Derived from the Latin *decem* (ten) and the Persian *bâr* (time, period): hence, "ten-time, ten-period." December was the tenth month of the year according to the ancient Roman calendar, which began in March. The name is bestowed upon those born in the month of December. (DEE-SEM-BRA)

Deianira From Greek mythology, Deianira was the daughter of Alathaea and Oeneus, the second wife of Heracles, whom she accidentally killed by giving him a cloak soaked with Nessus' blood. (DĀ-AH-NEER-AH)

Demeter Borne in Greek mythology by the daughter of Cronus and Rhea, the goddess of fertility, agriculture, and grain. She is equated with the Roman goddess Ceres. (DIH-MEE-TER)

DEVAKI Derived from the Sanskrit *devaki* (black). The name is borne in Indian mythology by the mother of Krishna. (DEH-VAH-KEE)

DEVI Derived from the Sanskrit *devi* (goddess). The name is borne in Indian mythology by a Hindu goddess, the consort of Shiva. She is seen as having both a mild and a fierce form. In her mild form she is known as Devi; in her fierce form she is called Kali. *See* KALI. (DEV-EE)

DIANA Derived from the Latin Diviana, which is from *divus* (divine). The name is borne in Roman mythology by the virgin goddess of the moon and of hunting. The daughter of Jupiter and Latona, and the sister of Apollo, Diana is equated with the Greek goddess Artemis. (DĪ-ANA)

DIONE Borne in Greek mythology by Titanus, a daughter of Oceanus and Tethys, mother of the goddess Aphrodite, and an early consort of Zeus before being replaced by Hera. (DĪ-AH-NEE)

DORIS Greek name meaning "Dorian woman." The Dorians, one of the four main tribes of ancient Greece, settled in the mountainous area also known as Doris. The name is borne in Greek mythology by a goddess of the sea and therefore has taken on the additional definition "of the sea." Var: Dorea, Doria, Dorice, Dorise, Dorisse, Dorris, Dorrise. (DOR-ISS)

EANNA From Assyro-Babylonian mythology, Eanna was the dwelling place of the supreme god, Anu. (EE-AH-NAH)

EARTHA A name that can be bestowed upon those borne under astrological signs having earth as their element: Capricorn, Taurus, and Virgo. (UR-THAH)

ECHO Derived from the Greek *echo* (a repercussion of sound, an echo). The name is borne in Greek mythology by a nymph whose unrequited love for Narcissus caused her to pine away until only her voice remained. (EH-KO)

EILEITHYIA From the Greek Eileithyia (she who has come). The name is borne in Greek mythology by the goddess of childbirth. Var: Ilithyia. (Ī-LEE-IH-THĪ-AH)

ELAINE Variant form of the Greek Helene, which is derived form the element *ēlē* (light, torch, bright). The name is borne by several characters in Arthurian legend, most notably by the mother of Galahad and by Elaine the Fair, whose love for Lancelot was unrequited. (EE-LANE)

ELEKTRA From the Greek Elektra (shining one), a name borne in Greek mythology by a daughter of Agamemnon and Clytemnestra. She persuaded her brother Orestes to kill their mother and their mother's lover in revenge for the murder of their father. Var: Electra. (IH-LEK-TRA)

EMERALD The name of a type of beryl, emerald is the gemstone for the signs of Cancer, Capricorn, Taurus, and Virgo. (EM-ER-LD)

ERINYES In Greek Mythology, the Erinyes were three female spirits known as the "mist walkers," who would punish those who committed crimes that went unavenged. Var: Erinys. (EE-RIN-E-EEZ)

EVADNE Derived from the Greek element *eu* (good, well): hence, "well-pleasing one." The name is borne in Greek mythology by the wife of Capaneus of Argos. After Capaneus was struck down by a thunderbolt while attempting to scale the walls of Thebes, a grief-stricken Evadne threw herself upon his funeral pyre. (EE-VAD-NEE)

FAUNA Believed to be derived from the Latin *faveo* (to favor, to promote or befriend). Fauna is borne in Roman mythology by the female counterpart of Faunus, a god of nature and the patron of farming, agriculture, and animals. Var: Fawna. (FAWN-NAH)

FLORA Derived from the Latin *floris* (a flower). The name is borne in Roman mythology by the goddess of flowers and spring. She is equated with the Greek goddess Chloris. (FLOR-AH)

FLORALIA The name of the ceremonial festival that was held each spring in honor of Flora, the Roman goddess of flowers and springtime. (FLOR-AH-LEE-AH)

FORTUNA Derived from the Latin *fortuna* (chance, fate, fortune). The name was borne by the Roman mythological goddess of fortune and happiness. (FOR-TYOO-NAH)

FREYA Feminine form of Frey (lord): hence, "lady, mistress, noblewoman." In Norse mythology, Freya was the goddess of fertility. A daughter of Njord and a sister of Frey, Freya was the most beautiful of the goddesses. She owned the Necklace of the Brísings, the Brísingamen. The day of the week Friday is derived from her name. Var: Freja, Freyja. (FRĀ-AH)

GALATEA From Greek mythology, Galatea was the name of a sea nymph, a daughter of Nereus and Doris, and the beloved of Acis. When he was killed by the giant Polyphemus, Galatea transformed Acis into the Acis River. The name was also that of a statue of a maiden to whom Aphrodite gave life, after its sculptor, Pygmalion, fell in love with it. (GAL-AH-TEE-AH)

GEMINA Derived from the Latin *gemini* (twins). The name is bestowed upon female children born under the third sign of the zodiac, Gemini. Var: Gemine, Geminia, Geminie, Gemma. (JEH-MINE-AH, JEH-MIH-NAH)

GENEA From Phoenician mythology, Genea and Genos were the first inhabitants of Phoenicia. (JEN-EE-AH)

GUINEVERE Derived from the Welsh Gwenhwyfar (fair lady), a compound name composed of the elements *gwyn, gwen* (white, fair, blessed) and *hwyfar* (smooth, soft). The name is borne in Arthurian legend by King Arthur's wife, who became the mistress of Sir Lancelot. Repentant for her unfaithfulness, Guinevere retired to the convent at Ambresbury. Var: Guinever, Gwenevere. (GWIN-EH-VEER)

HALCYON Derived from the Greek *alkyon* (kingfisher), which is from *hals* (sea). Halcyone was the name given to a legendary bird said to have a calming effect on the seas during the winter solstice. The name has taken on the descriptive definition of the word *halcyon* (calm, tranquil, happy). Var: Alcyone, Halcyone. (HAL-SEE-UN)

HARMONIA Derived from the Greek *harmos* (a fitting, harmony), the name Harmonia is borne in Greek mythology by the daughter of Aphrodite and Ares, and the wife of Cadmus. She was the personification of harmony and order. (HAR-MO-NEE-AH)

HATHOR Derived from the Egyptian Het-Hert (the house above). The name is borne in Egyptian mythology by the goddess of love, mirth, and happiness. She is often depicted with the head or ears of a cow. (HATH-OR)

HEBE Derived from the Greek *hebe* (youth). The name is borne in Greek mythology by the goddess of youth, the daughter of Zeus and Hera. She was cupbearer to the gods until replaced by Ganymede. (HEE-BEE)

HELENE Popular name derived from the root *ēlē* (light, torch). Helene is a name borne in Greek legend by the wife of the king of Sparta. Her abduction by the Trojan prince Paris sparked off the Trojan War. Var: Helen, Helena. (HELL-EEN)

HERMIONE Feminine form of Hermes, a name of uncertain etymology borne by the messenger god. The name Hermione is borne in Greek legend by the daughter of King Menelaus of Sparta and his wife, Helene of Troy. (HER-MĪ-AH-NEE)

HYACINTH Derived from the Greek *hyakinthos* (hyacinth, blue larkspur, bluebell, a blue gem). The name is borne in Greek mythology by a Spartan youth accidentally killed by Apollo in a game with the discus. A sorrowful Apollo caused to grow from Hyakinthos' blood a beautiful flower bearing on its petals the letters *AI, AI*, a Greek cry of lamentation. Var: Hyacinthe. (HĪ-AH-SINTH)

INANNA Borne in Assyro-Babylonian mythology by a goddess of war. She was also a goddess of the earth and sky, of the heavens, and of love. (IN-AN-NAH)

ISEULT Of debated origin and meaning, Iseult might be derived from the Old High German Isold, a compound name composed from the elements *is* (ice) and *waltan* (to rule): hence, "ruler of the ice." Alternatively, it could be a variant of the Welsh Esyllt (beautiful, fair). The name was borne in medieval legend by an Irish princess who was betrothed to King Mark of Cornwall. Through a magic potion, she became the beloved of Tristram, who was married to another Iseult. Var: Isolde, Isolt, Yseult, Ysolt. (IH-SOLT)

ISMENE Borne in Greek mythology by a daughter of Oedipus and Jocasta, and sister to Antigone, Eteocles, and Polynices. She refused to help Antigone perform funeral rites for Polynices for fear of what her uncle might do. (IS-MEE-NEE)

JASMINE The name of a beautiful, fragrant plant for the astrological sign of Gemini. Jasmine is derived from the Persian *yāsamīn*. Var: Jasmin, Jazmin, Jazmine. (JAZ-MIN)

JOCASTA From the Greek Iocaste, a name borne in Greek mythology by a queen who unwittingly married her own son, Oedipus, and killed herself when she found out. She was also the mother of Antigone, Eteocles, Ismene, and Polynices. (JO-KAS-TAH)

KALI From the Sanskrit *kali* (the black one). The name is borne in Indian mythology by the fierce aspect of the goddess Devi, the consort of Shiva. *See* DEVI. (KĀ-LEE)

KALLIOPE Compound name composed from the Greek elements *kallos* (beauty) and *ops* (voice). The name Kalliope (beautiful voice) is borne in Greek Mythology by the Muse of epic poetry and eloquence. She was the mother of Orpheus. Var: Calliope. Pet: Calli, Callie, Cally, Kalli, Kallie, Kally. (KAH-LĪ-AH-PEE)

KALLIRROE Compound name composed of the Greek elements *kallos* (beauty) and *roe* (stream): hence, "beautiful stream." The name is borne in Greek mythology by several characters, including the daughter of Achelous and second wife of Alcmaeon. She prayed that her two sons would grow to be men in one day to avenge their father's death, and Zeus granted her wish. Var: Callirhoe, Callirhoë, Calliroe, Calliroë, Callirrhoe, Callirrhoë, Callirroe, Callirroë. Pet: Calli, Callie, Cally, Kalli, Kallie, Kally. (KAL-LEE-RO)

Kallisto Derived from the Greek *kallos* (beauty). The name Kallisto (she that is most beautiful) is borne in Greek and Roman mythology by a nymph, a daughter of the Arcadian king Lycaon, and mother of Arcas. Beloved of Zeus, she was transformed into a she-bear by Hera and placed among the constellations. Var: Callisto, Callista, Calista, Kalista, Kallista. Pet: Calia, Calli, Callia, Callie, Cally, Kalia, Kalli, Kallia, Kallie, Kally. (KAH-LIS-TŌ)

Kynthia Derived from the Greek *kynthios* (from Kynthos, a mountain on the island of Delos). The name is found in Greek mythology as a name of Artemis, the goddess of the moon, hunting, and wild animals. Var: Cinthia, Cynthia. Pet: Cindy. (KIN-THEE-AH, SIN-THEE-AH)

Latona Borne in Roman mythology by a daughter of Phoebe and the Titan Coeus, and mother of Diana and Apollo. She is equated with the Greek Leto. (LAH-TŌ-NAH)

Lavinia Derived from the Latin Latium (an ancient country of Italy in which Rome was situated). The name Lavinia (of Latium) was borne in Roman mythology by the daughter of Latinus, the king of Latium. It was prophesied that Lavinia would marry a foreigner, and a battle was fought between Aeneas, Turnus, and the Rutulians. Aeneas was the victor and wed Lavinia, who produced a son, Iulus, the founder of the Roman race. (LAH-VIN-EE-AH)

Leda Borne in Greek mythology by the wife of the Spartan king Tyndareus. She was the mother of Clytemnestra and Castor, and after being visited by Zeus in the form of a swan, was the mother of the immortal children Helene and Pollux. (LEE-DAH)

Leto Borne in Greek mythology by a daughter of Phoebe and the Titan Coeus, and mother of Apollo and Artemis. She is equated with the Roman Latona. (LEE-TŌ)

Lissa From African mythology, Lissa was the mother goddess of the Dahoman tribe. She was the mother of the sun, the moon, and of Maou, the supreme god of all things. (LIS-SAH)

Lotus From the Greek *lotos*, which is from the Hebrew *lot* (lotus). From Greek legend, the lotus was a fruit that was supposed to induce forgetfulness and a dreamy state of languor. (LO-TUS)

Luna Directly derived from the Latin *luna* (the moon). She was the Roman mythological goddess of the moon and is equated with the Greek Selene. Luna can be used as an astrological name for those born under the sign of Cancer, which is ruled by the moon. (LOO-NAH)

Maia Borne in Greek mythology by the eldest and most beautiful of the Pleiades, a daughter of Atlas and mother of Hermes by Zeus. Maia is also borne in Roman mythology by an earth-goddess who is sometimes equated with the Greek Maia. The month of May is named in her honor. (MĀ-AH, MĪ-AH)

Marina Derived from *marina* (a small harbor), which is from the Latin *marinus* (of the sea). The name can be bestowed upon those whose astrological signs are water signs. (MAH-REE-NAH)

Maya From Indian mythology, Maya is a name of the goddess Devi, the consort of Shiva. (MĀ-YAH)

Medea Derived from the Greek Medeia (she of the wise or cunning plans). The name is borne in Greek mythology by a daughter of King Aeetes. A famous sorceress and lover of Jason the Argonaut, Medea assisted Jason in obtaining the Golden Fleece and then accompanied him to Greece. After Jason refused to marry her, she killed their children and the bride-to-be. She later married Aegeus, to whom she bore Medeus. (MEH-DEE-AH)

Minerva Believed to be derived from the Latin root *mens* (the mind, thought, intellect). Minerva is the name borne in Roman mythology by the goddess of wisdom, sense and reflection, the arts and sciences, technical skill and invention. She is equated with the Greek goddess Pallas Athene. (MIH-NER-VAH)

Morgan Derived from the Old French Morgain, which is believed to be from the Old Irish Morrigain (queen of the incubi, a sorceress), a name probably derived from *mar* (a nightmare, an evil spirit thought to produce nightmares) and *rigain* (queen). The name is borne in Arthurian legend by Morgan le Fay (Morgan the fairy), the evil half sister of King Arthur and mother of Gawain and Mordred. (MOR-GUN)

Neith Borne in Egyptian mythology by a goddess of the home, femininity, and the domestic arts. She was also a goddess of war and is often depicted carrying a shield and arrows or a bow and arrows. Var: Neit. (NEETH)

Nina Borne in Assyro-Babylonian mythology by a daughter of Ea, the god of water, wisdom, and technical skill. Nina was goddess of Nineva, the capital city of ancient Assyria. (NIH-NAH)

Niobe Borne in Greek mythology by a queen of Thebes, daughter of Tantalus and wife of Amphion. Continually weeping for her seven sons and seven daughters killed by Apollo and Diana, Niobe was turned into a stone from which tears continued to flow. (NĪ-AH-BEE)

Oceana Feminine form of Oceanus, a name derived from the Latin *oceanus* (ocean), which is from the Greek *okeanos* (ocean, the outer sea). Oceanus is a name borne in Greek mythology by a Titan who preceded Poseidon as god of the sea. He was married to his sister Tethys, and their children were the three thousand Oceanids. (O-SHE-AN-NAH)

Olympia Feminine form of the Greek Olympios (of Olympus, the mountain in northern Greece that was the home of the gods in Greek mythology). Olympia was the name of a plain in ancient Elis in western Peloponnesus which was sacred to the Greek gods. Olympia was considered the sanctuary of Zeus, and contained the Doric temples of Hera and Zeus, along with many other magnificent treasures and architectural structures. It was also the site of the ancient Olympic games. Var: Olimpia. Short: Pia. (O-LIM-PEE-AH)

Opal The name of the iridescent semiprecious stone used as the gemstone of the signs Libra and Aquarius. (O-PL)

Orithyia Derived from the Greek Oreithyia, a name borne in Greek mythology by a daughter of Erechtheus, king of Athens. She was the mother of Calais and Zetes, Argonauts who sailed with Jason in search of the Golden Fleece. (OR-RIH-THĪ-AH, OR-RITH-EE-AH)

Orthia Derived from the Greek *orthos* (straight, upright). The name is found in Greek mythology as a name of the goddess Artemis. *See* ARTEMIS. (OR-THĪ-AH)

Pallas Derived from the Greek *pallas* (maiden). The name is borne in Greek mythology by a daughter of Triton. She was a childhood playmate of the goddess Athene. After Athene accidentally killed her friend, she assumed the name Pallas and had a statue created of her (the Palladium), which stood in the temple of Vesta. Var: Pallus. (PAL-LUS)

Parthenope Borne in Greek mythology by a siren who, after her songs failed to lure Ulysses to shipwreck, threw herself into the sea out of grief. She was cast ashore where Naples later stood. (PAR-THEN-AH-PEE)

Pax Derived from the Latin *pax* (peace, the binding thing). The name is borne in Roman mythology by the goddess of peace. She is equated with the Greek goddess Irene. (PAX)

Pearl The name of a gem grown in certain mollusks and prized for their perfection. The pearl is a gemstone for the sign of Gemini. (PURL)

Penelope Derived from the Greek Penelope, a name borne in Greek mythology by Odysseus' wife, who, for twenty years, patiently awaited his return. The etymology of the name is debated. Some believe it is derived from the Greek *penelops* (a kind of duck), since Penelope was said to have been exposed to die as an infant and was fed and protected by a duck. Others think it might be from *pene* (thread on a bobbin) and give it the definition "weaver, worker of the loom," for Penelope spent her evenings weaving and unweaving while she waited for her husband to return. Pet: Pennie, Penny. (PEH-NEL-AH-PEE)

Persephone Borne in Greek mythology by the goddess of spring, a daughter of Zeus and Demeter. She was abducted by Hades and taken to the underworld to be his wife and queen. As a result of Demeter's grief at the loss of her daughter, Zeus decreed that Persephone could spend two-thirds of the year in the upperworld, and the remaining time in the underworld, thus dividing the year into the seasons of growth, harvest, and winter. She is equated with the Roman goddess Proserpina. (PER-SEF-AH-NEE)

Phaidra Greek name said to mean "bright one." It is borne in Greek mythology by a daughter of Pasiphaë and King Minos of Crete, sister of Ariadne and wife of Theseus. She killed herself after Hippolytus, her stepson, rejected her advances. Var: Phaedra. (FEE-DRA)

Phoebe Feminine form of the Greek Phoibos (bright one), which is derived from *phoibos* (bright). The name Phoebe is found in Greek mythology as a name of Artemis, the goddess of the moon. In poetry, Phoebe is the moon personified. (FEE-BEE)

Phoenix Derived from the Greek *phoinix* (dark red, blood-red). The phoenix was a mythical bird that lived for hundreds of years before consuming itself in fire and rising anew from the ashes to begin another long life. The bird is a symbol of immortality. (FEE-NIX)

Pirene Borne in Greek mythology by a daughter of the river-god, Achelous. After Artemis was accidentally killed by Pirene's son, Cenchrias, Pirene's bitter weeping transformed her into a fountain. (PĪ-REE-NEE)

Polyxena Compound name composed from the Greek elements *polys* (much, many) and *xenia* (hospitality): hence, "the very hospitable one." The name is borne in Greek mythology by a daughter of Priam and Hecuba. The beloved of Achilles, Polyxena was sacrificed at his tomb by his son Pyrrhus at the end of the Trojan War. (PAH-LIK-SEH-NEH)

Proserpine Borne in Roman mythology by a daughter of Ceres and Jupiter. While picking flowers, she was abducted and carried off to be the wife of Pluto and the queen of the underworld. Proserpine is equated with the Greek goddess Persephone. (PRO-SUR-PEH-NEH)

Psyche Derived from the Greek *psyche* (the soul). The name is borne in Roman mythology by a maiden who underwent many hardships due to Venus' jealousy of her beauty. Cupid was sent to make her fall in love with someone ugly, but fell in love with her himself and became her husband. She was granted immortality by Jupiter. (SĪ-KEE)

Pyrrha Derived from the Greek *pyrrhos* (red). The name is borne in Greek mythology by a daughter of Epimetheus and wife of Deucalion. She was a survivor of the great deluge. (PIR-AH)

Radha Derived from the Sanskrit *radha* (success). The name is borne in Indian mythology by a cowherd who became the consort of Krishna. (RAH-DAH)

Rhea Borne in Greek mythology by a fertility-goddess, the daughter of Uranus and Gaea, wife of Cronus, and mother of Zeus, Poseidon, Demeter, Hera, Hestia, and Hades. Rhea is equated with the Roman goddess Ops. (REE-AH)

Rhea Silvia From Roman mythology, Rhea Silvia was a daughter of Numitor, a vestal virgin who forsook her vows and became the mother, by Mars, of Romulus and Remus. (REE-AH-SIL-VEE-AH)

Rhiannon Welsh name believed to be derived from the Old Celtic Rigantona (great queen). The name is borne in Celtic mythology by a fertility-goddess, the wife of Pwyll and mother of Pryderi. Var: Rheannon. (REE-AN-NUN)

Roma Latin name of Rome, which is named in honor of the Roman mythological daughter of Evander, the protectress of the city. (RO-MAH)

Rose The name of a beautiful, fragrant flower which is the flower for the astrological sign Libra. (ROZE)

Ruby The name of a deep red variety of corundum which is the gemstone of the sign of Leo. (ROO-BEE)

Salus Derived from the Latin *salus* (safety, well-being, health). The name is borne in Roman mythology by the goddess of health and welfare. She was the personification of safety. (SĀ-LUS)

Selene Derived from the Greek *selēnē* (the moon). The name is borne in Greek mythology by the goddess of the moon who was the daughter of Hyperion and Theia, and the sister of Helios and Eos. She was associated with Artemis and equated with the Roman goddesses Diana and Luna. Var: Selena. (SIH-LEE-NEE)

Semele From Greek mythology, Semele is the name of a daughter of Cadmus and Harmonia. The mother, by Zeus, of Dionysius, Semele asked to see Zeus in true form. Her request granted, she was instantly consumed in his lightning and carried away to the heavens. In Roman mythology, Semele was the mother of Bacchus by Jupiter. (SEM-EH-LEE)

Sesheta From Egyptian mythology, Sesheta was a goddess of the stars and the patroness of literature, writing, and the recording of historical events. She is identified by the carrying of a star and crescent, and the wearing of two plumes upon her head. Var: Seshat. (SEH-SHA-TAH)

Sibyl Derived from the Latin Sibylla (a fortune-teller, a prophetess), from the Greek Sibylla, which, according to old etymology, is a corruption of *Lios Boyle* (Jove's counsel, Zeus' counsel). The sibyls, women of ancient Greece and Rome, were the mouthpieces of the ancient oracles and seers into the future. In the Middle Ages, they were thought to be receptors of divine revelation; thus Sibyl came into use as a given name. Var: Sibylla, Sybil, Sybilla. (SIH-BL)

Sif Derived from the Old Norse *sifr* (kindred, relationship). In Norse mythology, Sif is a golden-haired fertility-goddess who was the wife of Thor and the mother of Thrud. She was also considered to be the goddess of agriculture, and her emblem was a ripened ear of corn. Var: Siv. (SIF)

Signy Derived from an Old Norse compound name made up from the elements *sigr* (victory) and *ný* (new): hence, "new victory." The name is borne in Norse mythology by the twin sister of Sigmund, the wife of the detestable Siggeir, with whom she had two sons. Signy was also the mother of Sinfiotli, the result of an incestuous relationship with Sigmund. Var: Signe, Signi. (SIG-NEE)

Sri Derived from the Hindi *sri* (glorious), which is from the Sanskrit *śri* (luster, beauty, majesty, prosperity). In Indian mythology, Sri was the name given to the goddess Lakshmi when she became the wife of Ramachandra. Var: Shree. (SHREE)

Terra Derived from *terra* (the earth). The name is often bestowed upon those whose astrological sign is an earth sign. (TARE-UH)

Tethys The daughter of Uranus and wife of Oceanus, Tethys was the mother of Electra, Aphrodite, and Doris. (TEE-THIS)

Thaleia Derived from the Greek *thallein* (to flourish, to bloom). The name is borne in Greek mythology by the Muse of comedy and pastoral poetry. Var: Thalia. (THA-LĪ-AH, THĀ-LEE-AH)

THEIA Derived from the Greek *theos* (God), Theia (divine one) was a name borne in Greek mythology by the wife of Hyperion and mother of Eos, Helios, and Selene. Var: Thia. (THEE-AH, THĪ-AH)

THEMIS Derived from the Greek *thema* (the law, what is laid down, justice). The name is borne in Greek mythology by the goddess of justice and prophecy, a Titan who was the daughter of Uranus and Gaea. She is depicted holding a scale for weighing opposite claims, or sometimes a cornucopia. (THEE-MIS)

TYCHE Believed to be derived from the Greek *teuchein* (to prepare). The name is borne in Greek mythology by the goddess of chance and fortune. (TĪ-KEE)

UMA Derived from the Sanskrit *uma* (flax, turmeric). The name is borne in Indian mythology as a name of the goddess Parvati in the aspect of a representation of light. (OO-MAH)

URANIA Derived from the Greek *ourania* (the heavenly one). The name is borne in Greek mythology by the Muse of astronomy. Var: Ourania, Uranie. (YOO-RĀ-NEE-AH)

VENUS From the Latin *venus* (the loved one, beloved), which is thought to be from the Indo-European root *wenos* (desire). The name is borne in Roman mythology by the goddess of love, beauty, and the springtime. She is equated with the Greek goddess Aphrodite. The planet Venus rules the zodiacal signs of Taurus and Libra. (VEE-NUS)

VESTA Derived from the Greek Estia (she that dwells or tarries), which is thought to be from the Sanskrit root *vas* (to dwell or tarry). The name is borne in Roman mythology by the goddess of the hearth and fire. In ancient Rome, Vesta's sacred fire was tended by priestesses known as vestal virgins. She is equated with the Greek goddess Hestia. (VES-TAH)

VICTORIA Directly derived from the Latin *victoria* (victory). The name is found in Roman mythology as the personification of victory. Pet: Tori, Torie, Vicki, Vicky. (VIK-TOR-EE-AH)

XANTHO Derived from the Greek *xanthos* (yellow, golden). The name Xantho (golden-haired one) is borne in Greek mythology by a sea nymph, a daughter of Nereus and Doris. (ZAN-THO)

XILONEN Borne in Aztec mythology by a beautiful goddess who took the form of newly formed green corn. (ZIL-O-NEN)

ZARYA Borne in Slavic mythology by a water priestess, a goddess and protectress of warriors. Var: Zorya. (ZAHR-YA)

CHAPTER TWENTY-ONE

North American Indian Names

FROM COLONIAL times until the late nineteenth century, vast cultural differences, prejudice, and differing views over the meaning of landownership caused tremendous friction and a series of wars between Native Americans on the one hand and settlers and the U.S. government on the other. In 1887 the Dawes General Allotment Act, which broke up 86 million acres of tribal lands, was aimed at forcing Native Americans into assimilating themselves into the dominant Anglo society. Boarding schools were established, and when children came of school age, they were taken from their parents and the reservations and forced to conform to Anglo standards. The children were given Anglo names, taught English, and forbidden to speak in their native tongues. Upon graduation, they were ill-fitted for either the Indian or the Anglo world.

Today, as tribal elders grow older, an urgency is felt in many of the Indian nations, as oftentimes it is only the very oldest of their members who still remember the native language and culture. Unless the languages, tribal stories, and myths are put into written form and taught to the youngsters, knowledge of the ancient ways will die with the elders.

As each tribe is a unique cultural group with its own social customs, traditional naming practices and ceremonies often vary greatly from one tribe to another. Common to many, however, is the practice of bestowing names during important times in a person's life. Birth, childhood, puberty, adulthood, an event marking an important achievement, change of rank—all can precipitate the bestowal of a name. Names influenced by nature are very common, as are those describing a particular feat or personal characteristic.

Native Americans were obligated to assume fixed and hereditary surnames. Anglo names, often both first and last names, were assigned to children in the Indian boarding schools. Many adults assumed Anglo first names and used their native names, or an English translation of them, as their surnames, which they then passed on to their children. Although the majority of Native Americans nowadays have Anglo names, the current trend is toward the bestowal of native names upon the children.

Native American Male Names

Abomazine Keeper of the ceremonial fire. Abnaki. Var: Bombazine. (AH-BOM-AH-ZEEN)

Adits'aii One who hears and understands. Navajo. The name was borne by the great tribal chairman Henry Chee Dodge (1860–1947). He was appointed tribal chief in 1884, and in 1923 became the first chairman of the Navajo Tribal Council. (AD-ITS-AY)

Adoeete Kiowa name derived from *ado* (tree) and *e-et* (big, large, great). The name was borne by a Kiowa chief (c. 1847–1929) who was responsible for raiding parties against white and Indian travelers on the Texas Plains. He was captured, imprisoned, and later pardoned. He eventually did an about-face by converting to Christianity, settling down, and running a supply train for many years. He was known to whites as Big Tree. Var: Adoette, Adooeette. (AD-O-EET)

Ahusaka Strikes his wings. Winnebago. (AH-HOO-SAH-KAH)

Aihits Palojami Fair land. Nez Percé. (AY-HITS-PAL-O-JAM-EE)

Akecheta Warrior. Sioux. (AH-KECH-TAH)

Alahmoot Elm limb. Nez Percé. (AL-AH-MOOT)

Aleekchea'ahoosh Many achievements. Crow. (AH-LEEK-CHEE-AH-AH-HOOSH)

Alikkees Hair cut short. Nez Percé. (AL-IK-KEES)

Allahkoliken Buck antlers. Nez Percé. (AL-LAH-KO-LIK-EN)

Angpetu Tokecha Other day. Sioux. The name was borne by John Otherday (1801–71), a Wahpeton missionary and interpreter known for his friendship with the whites. (ANG-PEH-TOO-TŌ-KECH-AH)

Annawon Commander, chief. Algonquian. The name was borne by a Wampanoag sachem who became war captain to Metacom. Var: Annawan. (AN-NAH-WAHN)

Apash Wyakaikt Flint necklace. Nez Percé. (AH-PASH-WĪ-AH-KAH-IKT)

A'piatan Wooden lance. Kiowa. The name was borne by the last principal chief of the tribe (c. 1860–1931). He is remembered for being an active and respected chief. Var: Ahpeatone, Ahpiatom, Apiatan. (AH-PEE-AH-TAN)

Appanoose A chief when a child. Sauk. (AP-PAH-NOOS)

Arapoosh Sour belly. Crow. The name was borne by a chief of the River Sioux (c. 1790–1834) who was said to have great spirit power. Var: Arrapooish. (AR-AH-POOSH, AIR-RAH-POOSH)

Ar-ke-kee-tah An Oto name, Ar-ke-kee-tah (stay by it) was borne by a chief from whom the Kansas town of Oketo was named. (AR-KEH-KEE-TAH)

Arre-catte-waho Omaha name derived from *arre-catta* (elk) and *waho* (big): hence, "big elk." (AR-REH-KAT-TAH-WAH-HO)

Ashishishe The crow. Crow. Var: Shishi'esh. (AH-SHE-SHE-SHEH)

Ashkii Dighin Holy boy. Navajo. (ASH-KEE-EE-DIG-HIN)

Atagulkalu Leaning wood. Cherokee. Atagulkalu was a prominent Cherokee leader (c.1700–78) who was taken to England in 1730 by Sir Alexander Cumming. He became a commissioned officer for the English. Later, however, during the Revolutionary War, he offered a regiment of five hundred warriors to fight for the Americans. Var: Attakullakulla. (AT-AH-GUL-KAH-LOO)

Atsidi Smith, ironworker. Navajo. Atsidi Sani (c. 1830–70) was a famous Navajo medicine man who introduced silversmithing to his people, which he learned from Nakai Tsosi, a Mexican ironsmith. (AT-SEE-DEE)

Bemidji River crossing a lake. Ojibway. (BE-MEED-JEE)

Beshiltheeni Knife maker, metalworker. Navajo. (BEH-SHIL-THEE-NEE)

Bisahalani The orator. Navajo. (BIH-SAH-AH-LAN-EE)

Bugonegijig Opening in the sky. Chippewa. Var: Bagwunagijik. (BUG-O-NEG-EE-JIG)

Canowicakte Kills in the woods. Sioux. (KAN-O-WEE-CAK-TEH)

Cashesegra Big tracks. Osage. Var: Koshisigré. (CAH-SHEH-SEG-RAH)

Cetanwakuwa Charging hawk. Sioux. (SET-AN-WAH-KOO-WAH)

Chapowits Plenty coyotes. Nez Percé. (CHAP-O-WITZ)

Chaska First-born son. Sioux. (CHASKA)

Chea Sequah Red bird. Cherokee. (CHEE-AH-SEH-KWAH)

Cheauka Clay. Hopi. (CHEE-AU-KAH)

Chebona Bula Laughing boy. Creek. (CHEH-BO-NAH-BOO-LAH)

Chitto Recklessly brave. Creek. The name was borne by Chitto Harjo (Crazy Snake), the leader of the Snake Uprising in Oklahoma in 1901. He is known for creating the Snake Government, a system parallel to the U.S. government. It was continued pressure against the Snake Government that led to the uprising. (CHIT-TŌ)

Chuslum Bull. Nez Percé. (CHUH-SLUHM)

Chuslum Moxmox Yellow bull. Nez Percé. (CHUH-SLUHM-MOX-MOX)

Cochise Hardwood. Apache. The name was borne by the leader (1812–74) of the Chiricahua Apache. They lived in peaceful coexistence with whites for nearly ten years, until the peace was destroyed in 1861 when Lieutenant George Bascom refused to believe that Cochise had not kidnaped a white child. Ensuing bloodshed between the two groups was great. In 1872 peace was restored when the Chiricahua were guaranteed their own reservation in the Chiricahua Mountains. (KO-CHEES)

Coowescoowe The egret. Cherokee. (KOO-WEH-SKOO-WEH)

Dadgayadoh The boys betting. Seneca. (DAD-GAY-AH-DŌ)

Dakota Derived from *dakóta* (to be thought of as friends, allies). This is the Siouan name for the group of Native American tribes better known as Sioux, a name from the Ojibway which ironically has the meaning "enemy, snake." (DAH-KO-TAH)

Degataga Standing together. Cherokee. (DEH-GAH-TAH-GAH)

Dekanawida Iroquois name borne by a great leader and prophet who founded the League of the Iroquois with Hiawatha. The name means "two rivers flowing together." Var: Deganawidah. (DEH-KAN-AH-WEE-DAH)

Diwali The bowl. Cherokee. (DIH-WAH-LEE)

Dohásan Little bluff. Kiowa. The name was borne by an important leader (c. 1805–66) who is remembered for having established peace between the Kiowa and the Osage, and for building the tribe back up to importance. He was forced to agree to the Treaty of the Little Arkansas, which placed his people on a reservation in the Oklahoma panhandle. Var: Dohosan. (DO-HAH-SAHN)

Doháte Bluff. Kiowa. (DO-HAH-TEH)

Ealahweemah About sleep. Nez Percé. (EE-AH-LAH-WEE-MAH)

Ealaothek Kaunis Flying birds lighting on the earth. Nez Percé. (EE-AH-LAH-OT-HEK-KAH-OO-NIS)

Ealaot Wadass Common earth. Nez Percé. (EE-AH-LAH-OT-WAH-DASS)

Eapalekthiloom Cloud piler, pile of clouds, piling clouds. Nez Percé. The name was borne by a Nez Percé chief known to whites as Cloud Piler. (EE-AH-PAH-LEK-THEE-LOOM)

Edensaw Derived from the Tlingit *edensaw* (glacier). The name was borne by Charles Edensaw (1839–1924), a preeminent carver and artist of the Haida people. (ED-EN-SAW)

Elaskolatat Animal entering a hole. Nez Percé. (EL-AS-KO-LAH-TAT)

Enapay Goes forth bravely. Sioux. (EN-AH-PAY)

Eskaminzim Big mouth. Apache. (ES-KAH-MIN-ZIM)

Espowyes Light in the mountain. Nez Percé. (ES-POW-YES)

E-ya-no-sa Big both ways. Sioux. The name was traditionally borne by those of great stature. (EE-YAH-NO-SAH)

Galegina Cherokee name derived from *ga-le-he-noh* (male deer, stag). The name was borne by Buck Watie (1803–39), the brother of Stand Watie. He was a distinguished chief of the Cherokees in Georgia. Later in life he discarded his native name and became known as Elias Boudinot, after a French benefactor. He was the first editor of the *Cherokee Phoenix* newspaper and was murdered because of his support of the removal of the Cherokee people to Indian Territory. Var: Ga-la-ge-noh. (GAL-EH-GEE-NAH)

Ganeodiyo Derived from the Iroquoian *ganio'dai-io* (beautiful lake). This was the native name of Handsome Lake (c. 1735–1815), a Seneca leader and prophet who was the half brother of Cornplanter. *See* GYANTWAKA. He taught *Gai'wiio* (the Good Word) to his people, a message of returning to the traditional customs and beliefs of the Iroquois. Var: Ganyodaiyo, Kaniatario. (GAN-EE-O-DEE-YO)

Ganun'dalegi Cherokee name derived from *gahna tahltlegi* (one who follows the ridge). The name was borne by John, the son of Nunna Hidihi, Major Ridge. They were members of the doomed Treaty Party, which believed the Cherokee would get a better deal if they compromised with the United States government. The

Ridge Treaty was never to be, and the members were forced to sign the treaty of New Echota, a travesty in which the Cherokee people were forced to trade their prosperous farms and lands in Georgia for desolate land in Indian Territory. (GAN-UN-DAH-LEG-EE)

GARAKONTHIE Iroquois name derived from *gara kontie* (moving sun). (GAR-AH-KON-THEE)

GAWASOWANEH Big snow snake. Iroquois. (GAH-WAH-SO-WAH-NEH)

GAYNWAWPIAHSIKA The leader. Shawnee. Short: Gaynwah. (GANE-WAW-PEE-AH-SEE-KAH)

GAYTAHKIPIAHSIKAH Wild cat. Shawnee. (GAY-TAH-KEE-PEE-AH-SEE-KAH)

GELELEMEND The leader. Delaware. (GEL-EL-EH-MEND)

GOMDA Wind. Kiowa. (GOM-DAH)

GOSAWYIENNIGHT Bull bait. Nez Percé. (GOS-AW-YEE-EN-NITE)

GOYATHLAY One who yawns. Apache. The name was borne by the Chiricahua warrior and leader Geronimo (1829–1909). He led many of his people into Mexico to evade the forced removal of the Chiricahua from Apache Pass to the San Carlos Reservation. He was captured and returned, but wanting no part of farming and not content with reservation life, spent many years raiding both Mexicans and whites. His name became a battle cry, still in use today. (GOY-ATH-LAY)

GU'ATON-BIAN Big ribs. Kiowa. Gu'aton-bian was the childhood name of Chief Satanta. *See* SET-TAINTE. (GOO-AH-TON-BEE-AN)

GUIPAGHO Lone wolf. Kiowa. (GOO-EE-PAG-HO)

GYANTWAKA Iroquois name derived from *gaiant-wa'ka* (by what one plants, the planter). The name was borne by Cornplanter, a Seneca chief who sided with the British during the American Revolution and with the Americans during the War of 1812. The Cornplanter Reservation in Pennsylvania was named in his honor. (GĪ-AN-TWAK-AH)

HACHE-HI Wolf. Arapaho. (HACH-HI, HACH-EH-HI)

HADAWA'KO Shaking snow. Iroquois. (HAD-AWA-KO)

HAHTALEKIN Red echo. Nez Percé. (HAH-TAL-EH-KIN)

HAKADAH The last one. Sioux. (HAK-AH-DAH)

HALLALHOTSOOT From the Salish, Hallalhotsoot (the Talker) was the name of a leader of the Nez Percé who was nicknamed the Lawyer (c. 1795–1876). (HAL-LAL-HOT-SOOT)

HALLUTEEN Big belly. Nez Percé. (HAL-LOO-TEEN)

HALPUTTA HADJO Crazy alligator. Seminole. (HAL-PUT-TAH-HAD-JO)

HASHKEH NAABAH The angry warrior. Navajo. (HASH-KEH-NAH-AB-AH)

HASSE OLA Creek name derived from *háshay* (sun) and *ola* (rising): hence, "rising sun." (HAS-SEH-O-LAH)

HATCHOOTUCKNEE The snapping turtle. Choctaw. (HATCH-OO-TUK-NEE)

HEINMOT Thunder. Nez Percé. (HEE-IN-MOT)

HEINMOT ILPPILP Nez Percé name derived from the elements *heinmot* (thunder) and *ilppilp* (red): hence, "red thunder." (HEE-IN-MOT-IL-PILP)

HEINMOT TOOYALAKEKT Thunder traveling to loftier mountain heights. Nez Percé. (HEE-IN-MOT-TOO-YAL-AH-KEKT)

HEINMOT TOSINLIKT Bunched lightning. Nez Percé. (HEE-IN-MOT-TOS-IN-LIKT)

HEMATUTE HIKAITH Thunder eyes. Nez Percé. (HEM-AH-TOO-TEH-HIH-KAH-ITH)

HEMENE Wolf. Nez Percé. (HEM-EN-EH)

HEMENE ILPPILP Nez Percé name derived from the elements *hemene* (wolf) and *ilppilp* (red): hence, "red wolf." (HEM-EN-EH-ILP-PILP)

HEMENE ISTOOPTOOPNIN Sheared wolf. Nez Percé. (HEM-EN-EH-ISS-TOOP-TOOP-NIN)

HEMENE MOXMOX Nez Percé name derived from *hemene* (wolf) and *moxmox* (yellow). (HEM-EN-EH-MOX-MOX)

HIAWATHA Derived from the Iroquoian Haio-hwa'tha (he makes rivers). The name was borne by the famous Mohawk-born cofounder of the League of the Iroquois. Hiawatha was a skilled diplomat and orator responsible for bringing the message of peace and unity to the tribes. He is the subject of Henry Wadsworth Longfellow's epic poem *Hiawatha*. (HĪ-A-WAH-THA)

HIMSLEHKIN Raw. Nez Percé. (HIM-SLEH-KIN)

HINMATON YALATKIT Rolling thunder in the heights. Nez Percé. The name was borne by Chief Joseph (c. 1832–1904), one of the greatest Native American military leaders. He was a passive and diplomatic chief whose people were grossly taken advantage of and forced into a state of war with the United States government. It was upon his surrender that he uttered the famous words "From where the sun now stands, I will fight no more forever." (HIN-MAH-TON-YAL-AT-KIT)

HIYATOMMON Shouter, crier, whooper. Nez Percé. (HI-YAH-TOM-MON)

HOHANONIVAH Shield. Cheyenne. (HO-HAN-O-NEEV-AH)

HOHOTS Bear. Nez Percé. (HO-HOTS)

HOHOTS ILPPILP Nez Percé name derived from *hohots* (bear) and *ilppilp* (red). The name was borne by a famous Nez Percé chief known as Red Bear. (HO-HOTS-ILP-PILP)

HOHOTS TAMALWEYAT Grizzly bear ruler, grizzly bear lawgiver. Nez Percé. (HO-HOTS-TAM-AL-WEH-YAT)

HOLATA Alligator. Seminole. (HO-LAH-TAH)

HOSA Young crow. Arapaho. (HO-SAH)

HOTHLEPOYA Crazy war hunter. Creek. (HOTH-LEH-POY-AH)

HOWI Turtledove. Miwok. (HOW-EE)

HOYOUWERLIKT Good necklace. Nez Percé. (HO-YO-OO-WER-LIKT)

HUAN-TOA War lance. Kiowa. (HOO-AN-TŌ-AH)

HUHUEWAHEHLE Good child. Creek. (HOO-HOO-EH-WAH-HEH-LEH)

HULA Eagle. Osage. (HOO-LAH)

HUSISHUSIS KUTE Bald head. Nez Percé. (HOO-SIS-HOO-SIS-KOO-TEH)

HUSIS MOXMOX Yellow head. Nez Percé. (HOO-SIS-MOX-MOX)

HUYA-NA Little eagle. Sioux. (HOO-YAH-NAH)

INEN TOXXOUKE My echo. Nez Percé. (IN-EN-TOX-XO-OO-KEH)

INKPADUTA Derived from the Siouan *inka* (point) and *duta* (scarlet, red). (INK-PAH-DOO-TAH)

IPPAKNESS WAYHAYKEN Looking glass around neck. Nez Percé. The name was borne by a Nez Percé chief who refused to settle on the reservation. (IP-PAK-NESS-WAY-HAY-KEN)

IRATEBA Beautiful bird. Mohave. Var: Arateva, Yaratev. (IR-AH-TEH-BAH)

IROMAGAJA Derived from the Siouan *ite amaraju-lit* (face raining). It was borne by a Hunkpapa Sioux chief who was one of the leading warriors in the Battle of the Little Bighorn. Var: Iromagaju. (IR-O-MAH-GAH-JAH)

ISHI'EYO NISSI Two moons. Cheyenne. The name was borne by two important chiefs. The elder Two Moon led Cheyenne warriors in the 1866 attack on Fort Phil Kearney and later joined with the Sioux in an attempt to close all westward passages. The younger Two Moon, a nephew of the elder, led his forces in the Battle of the Little Bighorn. In the aftermath, he led his people to Fort Keogh and surrendered to General Miles. He then served as a United States Army scout. He became chief of the Northern Cheyenne on the reservation and died in 1917. Var: Ishaynishus. (ISHI-EH-YO-NIS-SEE)

ISHNA WITCA Lone man. Sioux. (ISH-NAH-WIT-KAH)

ITZÁ-CHÛ Apache name derived from the elements *itzá* (hawk) and *chû* (great): hence, "great hawk, eagle." (IT-ZAH-CHOO)

JLIN LITZÓQUE Derived from the Apache elements *jlin* (horse) and *litzóque* (yellow): hence, "yellow horse." (JLIN-LIT-ZO-KAY)

KAHATUNKA Crow, raven. Osage. Var: Ca-xe Tonkah. (KAH-AH-TUN-KAH)

KAHGEGWAGEBOW Ojibwa name derived from *kagige-gabo* (he who stands forever). The name was borne by one of the first Native American writers to have his work widely read by whites. He was also known as George Copway (c. 1818–63). (KAH-GEG-WAG-EH-BOW)

KANGI Crow, raven. Sioux. Var: Kangee. (KAN-GEE)

KANGI SUNKA Crow dog. Sioux. The name was borne by Crow Dog (c. 1835–1910), a Brûlé chief who murdered Spotted Tail. A believer in the Ghost Dance religion and the resurrection of the dead warriors, he led his people into the Badlands, joining with Sitting Bull, Big Foot, and Two Strike to dance and await salvation from the whites. (KAN-GEE-SUN-KAH)

KAWA Great. Apache. (KAH-WAH)

KEINTIKEAD White shield. Kiowa. (KEH-IN-TIH-KEH-AD)

KELE Sparrow hawk. Hopi. Var: Kelle. (KE-LEH)

KÉNAKUK Putting his foot down. Kickapoo. (KEN-AH-KUK)

KEOKUK Sauk name derived from Kiyo'kaga (one who moves about alert). The name was borne by a well-known Sauk leader and rival of Black Hawk. Whereas Black Hawk is remembered for his honor and his efforts to create a confederation of tribes to stand up to white expansion, Keokuk is by and large remembered for his vanity and willingness to be bought off by trinkets. (KEE-O-KUK)

Kikikwawason Flash in the sky. Cree. (KIH-KIK-WAH-WAH-SON)

Kilchii Red boy. Navajo. (KIL-CHEE-EE)

Kiliahote Let's kindle a fire. Choctaw. (KIL-EE-AH-HO-TEH)

Kitstsui Shamkin Metal shirt. Nez Percé. (KITS-TSOO-EE-SHAM-KIN)

Kiyiyah Howling wolf. Nez Percé. (KEE-YEE-YAH)

Kiyo'kaya One who moves about warily, he who is alert. Sauk. (KEE-YO-KAY-AH)

Klah Left-handed. Navajo. (KLAH)

Kohana Swift. Sioux. (KO-HAH-NAH)

Koi Panther. Choctaw. (KO-EE)

Konieschguanokee Maker of daylight. Delaware. (KO-NEE-ESK-GOO-AH-NO-KEE)

Konish Autassin Wounded buzzard. Nez Percé. (KO-NISH-AH-OO-TAS-SIN)

Koolkool Snehee Red owl. Nez Percé. (KOOL-KOOL-SNEH-HEE)

Koopnee Broken, broke. Nez Percé. (KOOP-NEE)

Kulakinah Male deer, stag. Cherokee. Var: Kilakina, Kullageenah. (KOO-LAH-KEE-NAH)

Lahpatupt Twice-broken bone. Nez Percé. (LAH-PAT-UPT)

Lahpeealoot Geese three times alighting in water. Nez Percé. (LAH-PEE-AH-LOOT)

Lakochets Kunnin Rattle blanket. Nez Percé. (LAH-KO-CHETS-KUN-NIN)

Lallo Little boy. Kiowa. This was the native name of the exceptional Indian painter Spencer Asah (c. 1908–54). (LAL-LO)

Lauliwásikau Shawnee name derived from *lalawe' thika* (rattle). It was the original name of Tenskwa'tawa, the twin brother of Tecumseh. *See* TENSKWÁTAWA. (LAH-OO-LEE-WAH-SEE-KAH-OO)

Len Flute. Hopi. (LEN)

Lepeet Hessemdooks Two moons. Nez Percé. (LEH-PEET-HES-SEM-DOOKS)

Letalesha Old knife. Pawnee. (LEH-TAL-ESHA)

Liwanu Bear growling. Miwok. (LIH-WAH-NOO)

Lumhe Chati Red eagle. Creek. (LOO-MHE-CHA-TEE)

Mahaska Derived from *mew-hu-she-kaw* (white cloud). The name was borne by a distinguished Iowa chief. The town of White Cloud, Kansas, is named in his honor. Var: Mahushkah, Mohaska, Mohoska. (MAH-HAS-KAH)

Mahkah Earth. Sioux. (MAH-KAH)

Mahpee Sky. Sioux. (MAH-PEE)

Makataimeshekiakiak Sauk name derived from *makatawi-mishi-kaka* (big black chest), which makes reference to the black sparrow hawk. The name was borne by the chief known to whites as Black Hawk (1767–1838). He is known for his efforts to create a vast confederation of tribes that would be able to withstand white advancements into their territory. The Black Hawk Purchase of 1832, in which their lands were ceded, was in retaliation for the Indian attacks. (MAH-KAH-TAH-EE-MEH-SHEH-KEE-AH-KEE-AHK)

Makhpia-Luta Red cloud. Sioux. The name was borne by a chief (1822–1909) of the Oglala Sioux. He is remembered for being a strong, intelligent leader who for many years successfully defended his tribe's last and best hunting grounds from white expansion. He refused to sign a peace treaty in 1868 until all troops had withdrawn and all forts had been abandoned. Var: Makhpfya-Luta, Makhpia-Sha. (MAHK-PEE-AH-LOO-TAH)

Makya Eagle hunter. Hopi. (MAHK-YAH)

Mammedaty Walking above. Kiowa. (MAM-MEH-DA-TEE)

Manishee Cannot walk. Oglala Sioux. (MAN-EE-SHE)

Mankato Blue earth. Sioux. Var: Mah-e-ca-te, Mahecate, Mon-eca-to, Monecato. (MAN-KAY-TO)

Maqui-banasha Young bear. Mesquakie. (MAH-KEE-BAN-ASH-AH)

Mashema Elk horns. Kickapoo. The name was borne by a minor chief who fought at the Battle of Tippecanoe. Var: Mashumah. (MAH-SHE-MAH)

Maspera Mohe Water elk, moose. Sioux. (MAS-PER-AH-MO-HE)

Mato Bear. Mandan. (MAH-TŌ)

Matohinsda Bear shedding his hair. Sioux. Derived via the Mandan *mato* (bear). (MAH-TŌ-HINS-DAH)

Matoskah White bear. Sioux. Derived from the Mandan *mato* (bear) and the Sioux *skah* (white). (MAH-TŌ-SKAH)

Mato Tope Derived from the Mandan *mato* (bear) and *tope* (four): hence, "four bears." The name was borne by two chiefs of the Mandan tribe who were father and son. The elder Mato Tope died in a calamitous smallpox epidemic in which only thirty-one of the sixteen hundred Mandan survived. The son survived, becoming chief and unifying what was left of his tribe with other groups in the area. (MAH-TŌ-TŌ-PEH)

MATO WATAKPE Charging bear. Sioux. Derived from the Mandan *mato* (bear). (MAH-TŌ-WAH-TAK-PEE)

MENEWA Great warrior. Creek. Var: Menawa. (MEN-EH-WAH)

MICANOPY Seminole name derived from *micco* (chief) and *nopi* (head): hence, "head chief." The name was borne by a Seminole chief under whose leadership the tribe became prosperous and employed runaway slaves as workers. He refused to sign a treaty in which the tribes were to cede their lands in exchange for new homes with the Creek Nation in Indian Territory, and led the ambush upon Major Francis Dade that precipitated the Seminole Wars. (MIH-CAN-O-PEE)

MICCO Chief. Seminole. (MIK-KO)

MIKASI Coyote. Omaha. (MIH-KAH-SEE)

MINCO Chief. Choctaw. (MIN-KO)

MISU Rippling water. Miwok. (MIH-SOO)

MI'TSU Grizzly bear. Osage. (MIH-TSOO)

MOHE The elk. Cheyenne. (MO-HEE)

MOOTSKA Point of yucca. Hopi. Var: Mootzka. (MOOT-SKA)

MOTSQUEH Chipmunk. Nez Percé. (MOT-SKOO-EH)

NAKAI Mexican. Navajo. (NA-KAH-EE)

NAPE-ZI Yellow hand. Cheyenne. (NAH-PEH-ZEE)

NASHASHUK Thundering. Sauk. (NAH-SHA-SHUK)

NASHEAKUSH Sauk name borne by a son of Chief Black Hawk and Asshewequa (Singing Bird). (NAH-SHE-AH-KUSH)

NASHOBA Wolf. Choctaw. Var: Neshoba. (NAH-SHO-BAH)

NASOMSEE Sauk name borne by a son of Chief Black Hawk and Asshewequa (Singing Bird). (NAH-SOM-SEE)

NENNEN CHEKOOSTIN Black raven. Nez Percé. (NEN-NEN-CHEH-KOOS-TIN)

NETOTWEPTUS Three feathers. Nez Percé. (NEH-TOT-WEP-TUS)

NINASTOKO Mountain chief. Blackfoot. (NIN-AS-TŌ-KO).

NITOH MAHKWI Lone wolf. Blackfoot. The name was borne by artist Hart Merriam Schultz (1882–1970), also known as Lone Wolf Shultz. He was a gifted painter of both watercolors and oils and a talented sculptor. (NIH-TŌ-MAHK-WEE)

NOCONA The camper, the wanderer. Comanche. Var: Nokoni. (NO-KO-NAH)

NOKOSI Bear. Seminole. (NO-KO-SEE)

NO-PA-WALLA Thunder fear. Osage. The name was borne by a chief who was one of the signers of the Drum Creek Treaty. No-Pa-Walla, or Napawalla, reportedly a very large man, had a Kansas town named in his honor, but the town's name was later changed to Oxford. Var: Napawalla, Nepawalla, Nopawalla. (NO-PAH-WAL-LAH)

NUNNA HIDIHI Cherokee name derived from *nungno huttarhee* (man on the mountaintop). The name was borne by Major Ridge (c. 1770–1839). A prosperous farmer and Speaker of the Cherokee Council, he realized the problems of incoming settlers onto Cherokee land. He formed the Treaty Party with his son John and his nephew Elias Boudinot, believing that only through compromise and accommodation would the Cherokee people be treated fairly by the United States government. The Cherokee Council disagreed and the Ridge Treaty was never to be. The Cherokee were forced to accept the terms of the Treaty of New Echota, which took their prosperous farms and lands in return for desolate land in Indian Territory. (NUN-NAH-HIH-DEE-HEE)

ODAKOTA Derived from the Siouan *dakóta* (to be thought of as friends, allies). *See* DAKOTA. (O-DAH-KO-TAH)

OGALEESHA Red shirt. Sioux. (O-GAL-EE-SHA)

OHANZEE Shadow. Sioux. (O-HAN-ZEE)

OHITEKAH Brave. Sioux. (O-HIH-TEH-KAH)

OHIYESA Sioux name borne by Charles Alexander Eastman (1858–1939), a Santee Sioux physician and author. He established thirty-two Indian YMCA groups across the country and helped to found the Boy Scouts and the Campfire Girls. Ohiyesa means "the winner." (O-HIH-YEH-SAH)

OH-TO-AH-NE-SO-TO-WHO Seven bulls. Osage. The name was borne by a signer of the Little River Treaty in 1865. (OH-TŌ-AH-NEE-SO-TŌ-HOO)

OKEMOS Little chief. Ojibway. (O-KEH-MOS)

Onacona White owl. Cherokee. Var: Oukounaka. (ON-AH-KO-NAH)

Ongwaterohiathe He lightens the sky for us. Iroquois. (ONG-WAH-TER-O-HI-AH-THE)

Onwarenhiiaki Tree cutter. Mohawk. (ON-WAR-EN-HEE-EE-AH-KEE)

Oqwa Pi Red cloud. Tewa. The name was borne by Abel Sánchez (c. 1900–71), an important Pueblo artist whose genre was watercolor painting. (OK-WAH-PEE)

Osceola Creek name derived from *asi* (black drink) and *yaholo* (crier, holloer): hence, "black drink crier." The name was borne by the Creek leader of the Seminole who fled to Seminole country with his mother following the Creek War of 1813. When slave catchers seized one of his wives with the permission of General Wiley Thompson, Osceola vowed revenge, thus touching off the Second Seminole War. (OS-SEE-O-LAH)

Ossiolachih Singing eagle. Creek. (OSS-SEE-O-LAH-CHIH)

Otee Emathla He makes sense. Seminole. (O-TEE-EM-AHTH-LAH)

Otetiani He is prepared. Iroquois. (O-TET-EE-AN-EE)

Otskai Going out. Nez Percé. (OT-SKAH-EE)

Otstotpoo Fire body. Nez Percé. (OT-STOT-POO)

Ouray The arrow. Ute. The name was borne by a peaceful chief of the Uncompaghre Ute. He is remembered for his ability to get along with both his tribe and whites, his work in securing a good settlement for his tribe, and his willingness to compromise. (OW-RAY)

Pahkatos Five wounds. Nez Percé. (PAH-KAH-TOS)

Pahkatos Qohqoh Five ravens. Nez Percé. (PAH-KAH-TOS-KO-KO)

Pahkowyalkelaked Turning around five times, five suns turning, the turning of five snows. Nez Percé. (PAH-KO-WĪ-AHL-KEH-LAH-KED)

Passaconaway Pennacook name derived from *papisse-conwa* (bear cub). The name was borne by an important Pennacook chief who was known as being a powerful medicine man and skillful military leader. (PAS-SAH-KON-AH-WAY)

Pawhuska White hair. Osage. The name was borne by a well-known Osage leader. He got his name from an incident in which he grabbed the wig from General St. Claire during battle. St. Claire escaped, but from then on Pawhuska wore the wig for luck and strength in battle. Var: Pahhuska, Pahuska, Pauhuska. (PAW-HUS-KAH)

Pawishik He who shakes something off himself. Fox. The name makes reference to an aroused bear. Var: Poweshiek. (PAH-WIH-SHIK)

Peopeo Bird. Nez Percé. (PAY-O-PAY-O)

Peopeo Hihhih White bird. Nez Percé. (PAY-O-PAY-O-HIH-HIH)

Peopeo Ipsewahk Lone bird. Nez Percé. (PAY-O-PAY-O-IP-SEH-WAHK)

Peopeo Kiskiok Hihih White goose, white bird. Nez Percé. The name was borne by a respected chief and medicine man. (PAY-O-PAY-O-KIS-KEE-OK-HIH-HIH)

Peopeo Moxmox Yellow bird. Nez Percé. The name was borne by a noted chief of the Walla Wallas who was murdered by troops while being held as an unarmed hostage. (PAY-O-PAY-O-MOX-MOX)

Peopeo Tholekt Bird alighting. Nez Percé. (PAY-O-PAY-O-THO-LEKT)

Petalésharo Man chief, chief of men. Pawnee. Petalésharo was the name of a chief known for putting a stop to the Sacrifice to the Morning Star. Var: Pitalésharu, Pitarésharu. (PEH-TAH-LEH-SHAR-O)

Peta Nocona Lone camper. Comanche. The name was borne by a chief who is most remembered for his many raids on the southwestern plains. He was responsible for raiding Fort Parker and the kidnaping of nine-year-old Cynthia Ann Parker. Their eventual marriage seems to have been a love match, for he married no other. Twenty-four years later, a group of Texas Rangers invaded the camp while the men were away, capturing Cynthia. She was returned to her parents and imprisoned in their home after trying to escape. Peta Nocona and Cynthia were never to see each other again. Peta Nocona died a year later from an infected wound, and Cynthia four years later, supposedly from a broken heart. (PEH-TAH-NO-KO-NAH)

Pezi Grass. Sioux. (PEH-ZEE)

Pizí Man who goes in the middle. Sioux. (PIH-ZEE)

Pocano Coming of the spirits. Pueblo. (PO-CAN-O)

Podaladalte Snake head. Kiowa. (PO-DAL-AH-DAL-TEH)

Pohd-lohk Old wolf. Kiowa. (PŌD-LŌK)

Po-na-kah-ko-wah Falling leaf. Delaware. Fall Leaf, a Delaware chief, was employed as a scout by Major John Sedgwick. After successfully guiding John Frémont to California, Fall Leaf found some gold in Colorado, touching off the Pikes Peak gold rush in 1859. (PO-NAH-KAH-KO-WAH)

POWESHIEK Fox name derived from *pawishik* (he who shakes something off himself), a name that makes reference to an aroused bear. Poweshiek (c. 1813–45) was the name of a chief of the Bear clan who fought with Black Hawk at the beginning of the Black Hawk War. He is remembered for his honor and integrity, and for working for the betterment of his tribe in trying times. Var: Pawishik. (PO-WEH-SHEE-EK)

POWHATAN Algonquian name derived from *pauwauatan* (hill of the powwow). It was borne by the father of Pocahontas. A powerful ruling chief of the Powhatan Confederacy in Virginia, Powhatan was responsible for enlarging the confederacy from six tribes to thirty, numbering some nine thousand people. (POW-HAT-AN)

QOHQOH ILPPILP Red raven. Nez Percé. (KO-KO-ILP-PILP)

QUANAH Comanche name derived from *kwaina* (sweet-smelling, fragrant). The name was borne by Quanah Parker, the son of Peta Nocona and Cynthia Ann Parker. He became chief of the Quahadi Comanche after the death of his father and for many years refused to accept the terms of the Medicine Lodge Treaty of 1867. He finally surrendered in 1876 and became a successful farmer and a judge of the Court of Indian Affairs. (KWAN-NAH)

QUED KOI Painted robe. Kiowa. Qued Koi was the native name of Stephen Mopope (1898–1974), a Kiowa painter and dancer. (KWED-KO-EE)

QUELATIKAN The blue horn. Salish. (KWEL-AT-IH-KAN)

QUNNOUNE High, tall, lifted up, lofty. Narragansett. (KWUN-NO-OON)

SAGOYEWÁTHA He causes them to be awake. Iroquois. (SAG-O-YEH-WAH-THA)

SAHKONTEIC White eagle. Nez Percé. (SAH-KON-TEH-IK)

SAKARISSA Spear dagger. Tuscarora. Sakarissa was the name of an important chief who worked tirelessly for his people. He was one of the founders of the Tuscarora Congregational Church. Var: Sagarissa, Sequareesa. (SAK-AH-RIS-SAH)

SAKURUTA The coming sun. Pawnee. (SAK-OO-ROO-TAH)

SAMOSET Derived from the Algonquian *osamoset* (he walks over much). The name was often bestowed upon those who took long journeys. Samoset (c. 1590–1653) is famous for being the first person to greet the Pilgrims upon their arrival in the New World. Var: Samaset. (SAM-O-SET)

SANI Old. Navajo. (SAH-NEE)

SARPSIS ILPPILP Red moccasin tops. Nez Percé. (SARP-SIS-ILP-PILP)

SASSACUS Pequot name derived from the Massachuset *sassakusu* (wild or fierce man). The name was borne by the last chief of the doomed Pequot tribe. In 1634 he surrendered all of his tribal lands in exchange for a plantation and peace for his people, a move that caused Uncas, his son-in-law, and several followers to form the Mohegan Nation. Sassacus continued fighting, and in 1637 almost all of his entire tribe was killed. The few survivors were assimilated into neighboring tribes. (SAS-A-KUS)

SASTARETSI The rat. Tionantati. Sastaretsi was a by-name of Chief Adario (c. 1650–1701) of the Tionantati. (SAS-TAR-ET-SEE)

SAUTS Bat. Cheyenne. (SAUTS)

SEEYAKOON ILPPILP Red spy. Nez Percé. (SEE-YAH-KOON-ILP-PILP)

SEQUOYAH Derived from the Cherokee *tsikwaya* (sparrow, principal bird). The name was borne by the inventor of the Cherokee Syllabary. He and his daughter, Ahyoka, spent years developing the system, beginning first with pictures for all the words. At one point, he was accused of practicing witchcraft and all of his pictures were burned. He persevered, and in place of the impractical pictures, developed a syllabary of eighty-six characters. His tribe became the first north of Mexico to have its own system of written communication. He died in Mexico, seeking the "lost Cherokee." (SEH-KOY-YAH)

SETANGYA Kiowa name derived from *set-angia* (sitting bear). The name was borne by the war chief, also known as Satank (c. 1810–71), who was a signer of the Medicine Lodge Treaty of 1867, but continued to participate in raiding parties. After attacking the Warren wagon train in Texas, he and other participants were arrested. On his way to trial, he sang his death song and attacked a guard, resulting in his shooting death. (SEH-TAHN-GAH)

SETIMKIA Charging bear. Kiowa. (SEH-TIM-KEE-AH)

SET-TAINTE Kiowa name derived from *set* (bear), *tain* (white), and *te* (person). It was borne by the great chief Satanta (1830–78), who was one of the signers of the Medicine Lodge Treaty of 1867. In spite of the treaty, raids continued to take place and he was captured and put in prison. He is acknowledged as one of his tribe's greatest war chiefs. Var: Satanta. (SET-TANE-TEH)

SHAPPA Red thunder. Sioux. (SHAP-PAH)

SHATEYARONYAH Two equal clouds. Huron. (SHA-TEH-YAH-RO-NĪ-AH)

SHONKAH SABE Derived from the Osage *shonka* (dog, horse) and *sabe* (black): hence, "black dog, black horse." Because horses were not native to this continent, the Native Americans did not have a word for them. They often called them walking dogs, in contrast to their real dogs, which were usually running around. (SHON-KAH-SAH-BEH)

SIKWAJI Derived from the Cherokee *tsikwaya* (sparrow, principal bird). (SIK-WAH-JEE)

SINTE GLESKA Spotted tail. Sioux. Var: Sinte Galeska. (SIN-TEH-GLES-KAH)

SINTE MAZA Iron tail. Sioux. (SIN-TEH-MAH-ZAH)

SKENANDOA Derived from the Iroquois *skennon'do* (deer). (SKEH-NAN-DŌ-AH)

SKIRIKI Coyote. Pawnee. (SKEER-EE-KEE)

SLEM-HAK-KAH Derived from the Kalispel *slum-xi-ki* (bear claw). (SLEM-HAK-KAH)

SPEMICALAWBA Derived from the Shawnee *spumuk* (high) and *alaba* (horn): hence, "high horn." The name was borne by a prominent Shawnee chief, the nephew of Tecumseh. He was captured as a child by General James Logan, who raised and educated him. He returned to his people and tried to keep the peace at a time when Tecumseh was trying to unite the Indians against the settlers. Var: Spamagelabe. (SPEM-EE-CAL-AW-BAH)

SULKTALTHSCOSUM Half sun, piece split from the sun. Salish. Var: Sulktashkosha. (SULK-TALTH-SKO-SUM)

SWATANEY Derived from the Iroquois *onkhiswathetani* (our enlightener). Var: Swateny. (SWA-TAN-EE)

TÁB-BE-BO Sun man. Paiute. Táb-be-bo (c. 1810–70) was an important medicine man and the father of Wovoka, the founder of the Ghost Dance religion. (TAB-BEH-BO)

TADI Wind. Omaha. (TAD-EE)

TAG-HEE Chief. Bannock. Tag-hee (c. 1825–71) was a Bannock chief remembered for seeking peaceful solutions to the troubles between his tribe and the whites. Var: Taighe, Taihee, Tyhee, Tyee. (TAG-HEE)

TAHATAN Hawk. Sioux. (TAH-HAH-TAN)

TA-HE-GAXE Buck making horns. Osage. The name describes a deer scraping velvet from his antlers. (TAH-HEE-GAX-EH)

TAHETON Crow. Sioux. (TAH-HEE-TON)

TAHOMA Water's edge. Navajo. Alternatively, Tahoma is a Pacific Northwest Indian name meaning "snowy peak," the native name of Mount Rainier in Washington State, and the name from which the Washington city of Tacoma is derived. Var: Tohoma. (TAH-HO-MAH)

TAIMAH Thunderclap. Fox. Var: Taima, Taiomah, Tama, Tamah. (TAH-EE-MAH)

TAKLISHIM Apache name borne by the father of Geronimo. It means "the gray one." (TAK-LISH-IM)

TAKODA Sioux name derived from *dakóta* (to be thought of as friends, allies). *See* DAKOTA. (TAH-KO-DAH)

TALOF HARJO Crazy bear. Creek. Talof Harjo was the last chief of the Creek Nation before it became a part of the state of Oklahoma. He was known to whites as Pleasant Porter (1840–1907) and is remembered for his leadership abilities and his efforts to get the best deal for his tribe at a time when their land was being encroached upon by settlers and divided by the railroad. (TAH-LOF-HAR-JO)

TAMELA PASHME Dull knife. Sioux. Dull Knife (c. 1810–83) was a Northern Cheyenne and coleader with Little Wolf of the 1,500-mile journey of about three hundred exiled Northern Cheyenne back to their homeland in 1878. After months of hardship, eventual imprisonment, death, and escape, they were finally given their own reservation in the Rosebud Valley. (TAM-EH-LAH-PASH-MEE)

TAMMANY The affable. Delaware. Var: Tamanend. (TAM-MAH-NEE)

TARHE The tree. Wyandot. (TAR-HEE)

TASHUNKA Horse. Sioux. Var: Tasunke. (TAH-SHUN-KAH)

TASHUNKA WITCO Crazy horse. Sioux. The name was borne most notably by the warrior Crazy Horse (c. 1841–77). He is known for having possessed great Spirit Power and for being an accomplished military leader and one of the Sioux's most fearless and daring warriors. He is responsible for annihilating Custer at Little Bighorn and is supposedly buried at Wounded Knee. (TAH-SHUN-KAH-WIT-KO)

TASI NAGI Yellow robe. Sioux. Var: Tashinagi. (TAH-SEE-NAG-EE)

TATANKA IYOTANKA Sitting bull. Sioux. Tatanka Iyotanka was borne by several people, most notably a Hunkpapa medicine man and a well-known Oglala leader. The former (1834–90) was head of the Strong Hearts, a warrior society active in the Plains Indian wars and many other battles including the Battle of the Little Bighorn. The latter, sometimes called Sitting Bull the Minor (1841–76), was at first friendly to the whites, becoming fluent in English and learning to read and write. His attitude changed, however, after the outrage at Sand Creek in 1864. He fought under Little Wound for the next three years, avenging the deaths at Sand Creek. Seeing the desperate situation on the reserves, he abandoned the fight and enrolled in the Red Cloud Agency to work for better supplies and living conditions. (TAH-TAHN-KAH-Ī-YO-TAHN-KAH).

TATANK'AMIMI Walking buffalo. Sioux. (TAH-TAHNK-AH-MEE-MEE)

TATANKA PSICA Jumping bull. Sioux. (TAH-TAHN-KAH-PSEE-KAH)

TATANKA PTECILA Short bull. Sioux. (TAH-TAHN-KAH-PTEH-SEE-LAH)

TATONGA Derived from the Siouan *ta-to-ga* (big deer, buck). (TAH-TAHN-GAH)

TAWA The sun. Hopi. (TAH-WAH)

TAWAGAHE Town builder. Osage. (TAH-WAH-GAH-HEE)

TAWANIMA How the sun is measured. Hopi. The name was borne by Louis Tawanima (c. 1879–1969), one of the first Native Americans to participate in the Olympic Games. He won a silver medal for the 10,000-meter run in the 1912 Olympics. Var: Tewanima. (TAH-WAH-NEE-MAH)

TAWAQUAPTEWA Sun in the horizon. Hopi. The name was borne by a leader (c. 1882–1960) who was initially friendly to the whites. In 1906 he was forced to go to the Riverside Indian School in California for four years, during which time an effort was made by his rival to usurp his position as chief. His village, Oraibi, is the oldest continuously inhabited village in the United States. Var: Tewaquoptiwa. (TAH-WAH-KWAP-TEH-WAH)

TECUMSEH Goes through one place to another. Shawnee. The name makes reference to a shooting star. Tecumseh (1768–1813) was a Shawnee chief known for his attempt to create an Indian confederacy to deal with the United States as an equal. He believed that all the land belonged to all the Indians, and one tribe could not sell any of it unless all the tribes agreed. His dream was lost with his death at the Battle of the Thames in 1813. (TEH-KUM-SEH)

TEKONSHA Little caribou. Algonquian. (TEH-KON-SHA)

TENDOY The climber. Bannock. The name was borne by a chief (c. 1834–1907) remembered for remaining at peace with the whites, a strategy that maintained a trading relationship with them and kept his village fairly prosperous. Var: Tendoi. (TEN-DOI)

TENE-ANGOP'TE The kicking bird. Kiowa. (TEH-NEH-AN-GOP-TEH)

TENSKWÁTAWA Derived from the Shawnee *tenskwátawaskwate* (door) and *thénui* (to be open): hence, "the open door." The name was borne by the twin brother of Tecumseh. Known by whites as the Shawnee Prophet (1768–1837), he was a visionary and preached a message of returning to the lifestyle of their forefathers and rejecting all things white. He often tailored his speeches to his brother's efforts by preaching a system of common ownership of land by all tribes. After the Battle of Tippecanoe, he lost his prestige as a prophet and moved to Canada. (TEN-SKWA-TAH-WAH)

THAONAWYUTHE Chain breaker. Seneca. It was borne by an important chief known as Blacksnake (1760–1859). He is known for keeping the Seneca people united and for keeping their religion, *Gaiwiio*, alive in the critical and uneasy times following the American Revolution. Var: Thaowayuths. (THA-O-NAH-WĪ-OOTH-EH)

THAYENDANÉGEA Derived from the Iroquois *thayeñdane-ke* (he places two bets). The name was borne by a Mohawk chief who was also known as Joseph Brant (1742–1807). He supported the British during the American Revolution, an act that split the Iroquois League. (THAY-EN-DAH-NEHG-EE-AH)

TOH YAH Walking by the river. Navajo. Toh Yah was the native name of gifted artist Gerald Nailor (1917–52). (TŌ-YAH)

TOKALA Fox. Sioux. (TŌ-KAH-LAH)

TOMOCHICHI The one who causes to fly up. Creek. The name was borne by a chief (c. 1650–1739) who, with his wife Scenanki and several others, sailed to England with Ogelthorpe in 1734. It was a result of this journey that the Creek Nation became trading partners with white traders, a prosperous move for both. Var: Tomo-chee-chee. (TŌ-MO-CHEE-CHEE)

TOOHULHULSOTE Sound. Nez Percé. Toohulhulsote was a strong, determined chief who refused to sign the Treaty of 1863. He and several other Nez Percé leaders would not go to the reservation area and kept their people on their ancient tribal lands. This led to trouble in 1877 when the United States government pressed compliance with the treaty. Toohulhulsote was jailed, eventually released, and fought in the Nez Percé War. He was killed in the final battle at Bear Paw in Montana in 1877. Var: Toohoolhoolzote. (TOO-HOOL-HOOL-ZO-TEH)

TOOP'WEETS Rock. Ute. This name, which denotes strength, was traditionally bestowed upon a person of stoic, strong character. (TOOP-WEETS)

TSATOKE Kiowa name derived from *tsa-tokee* (hunting horse). Var: Tsa-Ta-Ke. (TSAH-TŌ-KEE)

TSELA Stars lying down. Navajo. (TSEH-LAH)

TSEN T'AINTE White horse. Kiowa. (TSEN-TAIN-TEH)

TSÍYI Canoe. Cherokee. (TSEE-YEE)

TSÍYU-GUNSÍNI Dragging canoe. Cherokee. The name was borne by the son (c. 1730–92) of Chief Attakullakulla. He was a leader who strongly opposed white expansion into Indian lands, and the selling of all of Kentucky and part of Tennessee. He sided with the British during the Revolutionary War. (TSEE-YOO-GUN-SEE-NEE)

TSOAI Rock tree. Kiowa. The name Tsoai is the native name of Devil's Tower in Wyoming. (TSO-AH-EE)

TSOTOHAH Red bluff. Kiowa. (TSO-TŌ-HAH)

UNÁDUTI Derived from the Cherokee *unádena* (woolly) and *duti* (head): hence, "woolly head." The name was often used to denote a person of African-Native American ancestry. (UN-AH-DOO-TEE)

UN'KAS The fox. Mohegan. Var: Uncas, Wonkas. (UN-KAS)

WABANAQUOT Chippewa name derived from *waban* (white) and *aquot* (cloud): hence, "white cloud." (WAH-BAN-AH-KWOT)

WABAUNSEE Dawn of day, daybreak. Potawatomi. The name was borne by a Potawatomi chief after whom Wabaunsee County in Kansas is named. He is remembered for his fierceness and courage in battle. Var: Wahbon-seh. (WAH-BAUN-SEE)

WABONISHI He lives through the winter. Potawatomi. (WAH-BON-ISH-EE)

WAHCHUMYUS Rainbow. Nez Percé. The name was borne by a warrior who claimed to get his power and strength from the air and the rainbow. (WAH-CHUM-YUS)

WAHNAHTAH Derived from the Sioux *wanata* (he who rushes on). Var: Wahnaataa. (WAH-NAH-TAH)

WAHOTKONK Black eagle. Kiowa. (WAH-HOT-KONK)

WAHSHEHAH Fat on skin. Osage. Wahshehah (1860–1932) was the name borne by an Osage leader and representative to the United States government. He was known to whites as Bacon Rind. (WAH-SHE-HAH)

WAHTSAKE Eagle. Osage. (WAHT-SAH-KEH)

WAKARA *See* WALKARA.

WAKOYANTANKE Big thunder. Sioux. (WAH-KO-YAN-TAHN-KEH)

WAKUNTCHAPINKA Good thunder. Winnebago. The name was borne by a leader of the Winnebago who supported the Anglo position and took the whites' side in the Black Hawk War in 1832; even so, his people were relocated to a reservation in South Dakota, where they endured terrible conditions. (WAH-KUNT-CHA-PEEN-KAH)

WALKARA Yellow. Ute. The name was borne by a chief who was known to whites as Walker (c. 1808–55). He is remembered for successfully stealing over three thousand horses from the Mexicans in 1840. He was friendly with Brigham Young, and for a while there was peace. Upon his death, his two wives and two captive Indian children were killed and buried with him. This was the last recorded instance of this Ute custom. Var: Wakara, Walka-ra. (WAHL-KAR-AH)

WAMBLEESKA White eagle. Sioux. (WAM-BLEE-SKA)

WANEKIA One who makes life. Paiute. It was one of the names of Wovoka (the Cutter). *See* WOVOKA. (WAN-EH-KEE-AH)

WANETA Derived from the Siouan *wanata* (he who rushes on, the charger). The name was borne by a chief (c. 1795–1848) who fought bravely with the British army in the War of 1812. He was commissioned a captain and remained allied to the British for the next eight years. He then aligned himself with the Americans and was a signer of the Treaty of Prairie du Chien in 1825. (WAN-EE-TAH)

WÁNIG SUCHKA Red bird. Winnebago. (WAH-NIG-SUCH-KAH)

WANONCE Point of attack. Sioux. (WAH-NON-SEH)

WAPASHA Derived from the Siouan *wape* (leaf) and *sha* (red): hence, "red leaf." The name Wapasha was borne by a number of Sioux chiefs who were known for keeping their tribe at peace, even when they were forced into reservation living. Var: Wabasha, Wapusha. (WAH-PAH-SHA)

WASECHUN-TASHUNKA Siouan name borne by an Oglala Sioux chief known as American Horse. He was the son of Sitting Bear. (WAH-SEH-CHUN-TAH-SHUN-KAH)

WASHAKIE Shoshoni name derived from *wus'sik-he* (a gourd rattle). The name was borne by a Shoshoni chief (1804–1900) remembered for his benevolence toward the settlers and his strong stand against his tribe's traditional enemies, the Blackfoot, the Cheyenne, and the Sioux. Var: Wa'sha-kie. (WAH-SHA-KEE)

WASONAUNEQUA Yellow hair. Chippewa. (WAH-SON-AH-UN-EH-KWAH)

WASSAJA Signaling. Yavapai. Var: Wasagah. (WAS-SAH-JAH)

WATHOHUCK Bright path. Sauk. The name was borne by Jim Thorpe (1888–1953), one of the greatest American athletes. He won both the pentathlon and the decathlon at the 1912 Olympics, something never done before or since. In 1920 he helped organize the American Professional Football Association. In 1955 the National Football League established the Jim Thorpe Memorial Trophy in his honor. (WAH-THO-HUK)

WATTAN Black. Arapaho. Var: Waatina. (WAT-TAN)

WAUNAKEE He has peace. Algonquian. (WAH-UN-AH-KEE)

WAYA Wolf. Cherokee. (WAY-AH)

WICAHPI ISNALA Lone star. Sioux. (WIH-KAH-PEE-ISS-NAH-LAH)

WILHAUTYAH Wind blowing, blowing wind. Nez Percé. (WIL-HAH-OO-TĪ-YAH)

WINNEMUCCA Paiute name borne by a chief, known to Anglos as Captain Truckee, who guided Captain John Frémont across the mountains and into California. The name is thought to be derived from a time when Frémont observed the chief wearing only one moccasin (one muck). (WIN-NEH-MUK-KAH)

WONAH'ILAYHUNKA War chief. Winnebago. (WO-NAH-IL-AY-HUN-KAH)

WOVOKA Paiute name borne by the leader of the Ghost Dance religion. He possessed a mystical nature, and during the solar eclipse of January 1, 1888, he fell ill with fever, subsequently experiencing a profound vision. He saw the whites disappearing, the resurrection of all dead natives, and the land returning to the stewardship of the Native American. The new religion unsettled the Anglos and they actively campaigned against it, culminating in the tragic massacre at Wounded Knee. Wovoka was crushed by the tragedy that had grown out of a peaceful religion. In grief, he retired to the Walker River Reservation. Var: Wo-vo'ka. (WO-VO-KAH)

WUSÁMEQUIN Yellow feather. Algonquian. Var: Ousamequin. (WOO-SAH-MEH-KWIN)

WYANDANCH The wise speaker. Montauk. The name was borne by the last major Native American leader on Long Island (1600–59). Var: Wiantance. (WĪ-AN-DANCH)

YAHOLO Crier, holloer. Creek. (YAH-HO-LO)

YOOMTIS KUNNIN Grizzly bear blanket. Nez Percé. (YOOM-TIS-KUN-NIN)

YOUKIOMA Almost perfect. Hopi. Var: Youkeoma, Yukeoma, Yukioma. (YO-OO-KEE-O-MAH)

ZIPKIYAH Big bow. Kiowa. Var: Zipko-eete, Zipkoheta. (ZIP-KĪ-YAH)

ZITKADUTA Red bird. Sioux. (ZIT-KAH-DOO-TAH)

ZOTOM The biter. Kiowa. (ZO-TOM)

ZYA TIMENNA No heart. Nez Percé. (ZĪ-AH-TIH-MEN-NAH)

Native American Female Names

ABEDABUN Peep of day, dawn. Chippewa. (AH-BEH-DAH-BUN)

ABEQUA She stays home. Chippewa. Var: Abeque. (AH-BEH-KWA)

ABEY Leaf. Omaha. (AH-BAY)

ABEYTU Green leaf. Omaha. Derived from the root *abey* (leaf). (AH-BAY-TOO)

ABEYTZI Yellow leaf. Omaha. Derived from the root *abey* (leaf). Var: Abetzi. (AH-BAYT-ZEE)

ACADIA Derived from the Micmac *acada* (village, place of plenty). (AH-KADE-EE-AH)

Adoeete Kiowa name derived from *ado* (tree) and *e-et* (big, large): hence, "big tree." Adoeete is also used as a male name and was borne by Chief Big Tree. *See* ADOEETE (Male Names). Var: Adoette, Adooeette. (AD-O-EE-TEH)

Adsila Blossom. Cherokee. (AD-SIL-AH)

Ahawhypersie Crow name of uncertain meaning. (AH-HAW-HI-PER-SEE-EH)

Ahawi Deer. Cherokee. (AH-HAH-WEE)

Ah-Yoka She who brought happiness. Cherokee. The name was borne by the daughter of Sequoyah, author of the Cherokee Syllabary. Var: Ahyoka. (AH-YO-KAH)

Aleshanee She plays all of the time. Coos. (AH-LEH-SHAN-EE)

Altsoba All are at war. Navajo. (ALT-SO-BAH)

Ama Water. Cherokee. (AH-MAH)

Amkima Kiowa name of uncertain meaning. (AM-KEE-MAH)

Anaba She returns from war. Navajo. (AN-AH-BAH)

Anamosa White fawn. Sauk. (AN-AH-MO-SAH)

Angpetu Day, radiant. Sioux. Var: Anpaytoo, Anpetu. (ANG-PEH-TOO)

Anna Mother. Algonquin. (AH-NAH)

Asshewequa Singing bird. Sauk. The name was borne by the wife of Chief Black Hawk. (AS-SHEH-WEH-KAH)

Aungattay Standing in the track. Kiowa. (AUN-GAT-TAY)

Awanatu Turtle. Miwok. Var: Awanata. (AH-WAH-NAH-TOO)

Awinita Young deer. Cherokee. Var: Awenita. (AH-WIN-EE-TAH)

Ayasha Little one. Cherokee. Var: Ayashe. (AH-YAH-SHA)

Boinaiv Grass maiden. Shoshoni. Boinaiv was the childhood name of Sacajawea, the Shoshoni interpreter and intermediary who accompanied the Lewis and Clark Expedition. *See* SACAJAWEA. (BO-IN-AH-IV)

Byhalia White oaks standing. Choctaw. (BĪ-HAL-EE-AH)

Caneadea Where the heavens rest upon the earth, horizon. Iroquois. It was from this that the country of Canada got its name. Var: Canada, Kanáda. (KAN-EE-AH-DEE-AH)

Chapa A beaver. Sioux. (CHAP-AH)

Chapawee Active like a beaver, industrious. Sioux. Derived from *chapa* (a beaver). (CHAP-AH-WEE).

Che-cho-ter Morning dawn. Seminole. The name was borne by a wife of Osceola and the mother of his four children. Because Che-cho-ter was part African, she was taken into slavery, an act that prompted Osceola to vow revenge and touched off the Second Seminole War. (CHE-CHO-TER)

Cheyenne A name given to a tribe of Algonquian Indians by the Sioux, derived from *shaiyena* (unintelligible speakers). (SHĪ-ENN, SHĪ-AN)

Chula Fox. Muskogean. (CHOO-LAH)

Chumani Dewdrops. Sioux. (CHOO-MAH-NEE)

Coahoma Red panther. Choctaw. (KO-AH-HO-MAH)

Dabuda Wide hips. Washo. The name was borne by the basket designer and weaver Datsolalee (c. 1835–1925). (DAH-BOO-DAH)

Dezba Going to war. Navajo. (DEZ-BAH)

Doli Bluebird. Navajo. (DŌ-LEE)

Donoma The sun is there. Omaha. (DŌ-NO-MAH)

Dowanhowee Singing voice. Sioux. (DŌ-WAN-HO-WEE)

Ehawee She is laughing. Sioux. (EE-HAH-WEE)

Ethete Good. Arapaho. (ETH-EH-TEH)

Eyota Greatest. Sioux. (EE-YO-TAH)

Galilani Amiable, friendly, attractive. Cherokee. (GAL-IH-LAN-EE)

Genesee Beautiful valley. Iroquois. (GEN-EH-SEE)

Gennisheyo Shining, beautiful valley. Iroquois. Var: Geneseo. (GEN-NIH-SHE-YO)

Hachi Stream. Seminole. (HA-CHEE)

Haiwee Dove. Shoshone. (HAH-EE-WEE)

Hantaywee Cedar maid. Sioux. (HAN-TAY-WEE)

Hialeah Seminole-Creek nâme derived from *haiyakpo hili* (pretty prairie). The name was given to a city in southeast Florida. (HĪ-AH-LEE-AH)

Hiawassee Derived from the Cherokee *ayuhwasi* (meadow). (HĪ-AH-WAS-SEE)

Hinookmahiwi-Kilinaka Fleecy cloud floating into place. Winnebago. (HIH-NOOK-MAH-EE-WEE-KIL-EE-NAH-KAH)

Honovi Strong deer. Hopi. (HON-O-VEE)

Huyana Falling rain. Miwok. (HOO-YANA)

Immokalee Tumbling water. Cherokee. (IM-MO-KAH-LEE)

Inola Black fox. Cherokee. (IN-O-LAH)

Inshtatheumba Bright eyes. Omaha. Var: Inshta Theaumba. (INSH-TAH-THEE-OOM-BAH)

Isi Deer. Choctaw. (IS-EE)

Itinsa Waterfall. Tlingit. (IH-TIN-SAH)

Kaemoxmith Yakima name of uncertain meaning. (KAH-EE-MOX-MITH)

Kai Willow tree. Navajo. (KAH-EE)

Kaitchkma-Winema The strong-hearted woman. Modoc. (KAH-ITCH-KMA-WIN-EH-MAH)

Kanestie Head of navigation. Seneca. (KAN-ES-TEE)

Karneetsa Beneath the Robes. Spokane. (KAR-NEET-SAH)

Kau-au-ointy The cry of the goose. Kiowa. (KAU-AU-OIN-TEE)

Kaya My elder sister. Hopi. (KAY-AH)

Keahdinekeah Throwing it down. Kiowa. (KE-AH-DIN-EH-KE-AH)

Keezheekoni Fire briskly burning. Chippewa. (KEE-ZHEE-KO-NEE)

Kéhachiwinga Wolf's mountain home maker. Winnebago. The name was borne by Mountain Wolf Woman, the subject of an autobiography in 1958 of the same name. (KE-HACH-IH-WIN-GAH)

Kewanee Prairie hen. Potawatomi. Var: Kewaunee. (KE-WAN-EE)

Khapkhaponimi Bark scraping. Cayuse. (KAP-KAP-O-NEE-MEE)

Kimama Butterfly. Shoshone. (KEE-MAH-MAH)

Kimi Secret. Algonquin. (KIM-MEE)

Kimimela Butterfly. Sioux. (KIM-MEE-MEH-LAH)

Kinta Beaver. Choctaw. (KIN-TAH)

Kiwidinok Woman of the wind. Chippewa. (KIH-WIH-DIN-OK)

Knasgowa Heron. Cherokee. (KNAS-GOW-AH)

Koko Night. Blackfoot. (KO-KO)

Kooskooskia Clear water. Nez Percé. (KOOS-KOOS-KEE-AH)

Kwanita Zuni variant of the Spanish Juanita, which is a diminutive form of Juan (God is gracious). *See* JUANITA (Spanish Names). (KWAN-EE-TAH)

Len-ag-see Shawnee name borne by the wife of Chief Blackhoof. Var: Lenexa. (LEN-AG-SEE)

Litonya Hummingbird darting. Miwok. (LIH-TON-YAH)

Magaskawee Swan maiden. Sioux. (MAG-AS-KAH-WEE)

Mahaska White cloud. Iowa. (MAH-HAS-KAH)

Mahwah Beautiful. Algonquian. (MAH-WAH)

Maka Earth. Sioux. (MAH-KAH)

Makawee Motherly, generous, abundant. Sioux. Var: Macawi. (MAH-KAH-WEE)

Mamakiaeh Curly hair. Cheyenne. (MAH-MAH-KEE-AH-EH)

Mansi Plucked flower. Hopi. (MAN-SEE)

Manwangopath Sweet breeze. Miami. (MAHN-WAHN-GO-PATH)

Mapiya Sky, heavenly. Sioux. (MAH-PEE-YAH)

Mataoaka She plays with things. Pamunkey. Var: Matoax, Matowaka. (MAH-TAH-O-AH-KAH)

Menasha Island. Algonquian. (MEN-ASH-AH)

Meoquanee Clothed in red. Chippewa. (ME-O-KWAH-NEE)

Migisi Eagle. Chippewa. (MIH-GEE-SEE)

Mimiteh New moon. Blackfoot. (MIH-MIH-TEH)

Mi-na First-born daughter. Sioux. (MIH-NAH)

Minnehaha Laughing water. Dakota. The name was borne by the maiden who was loved by Hiawatha. (MIN-NEH-HAH-HAH)

Minneokadawin Empties into water. Sioux. (MIN-NEH-O-KAD-AH-WIN)

Misae White sun. Osage. (MIH-SAH-EH, MIH-SAY)

Mitena Born during the new moon. Omaha. (MIH-TEN-AH)

Momone Heather flower. Montauk. The name was borne by the daughter of Chief Wyandach. (MO-MO-NEH)

Moneka Derived from the Siouan *mon-in-ka* (earth, soil). Var: Moneca. (MON-EH-KAH)

Moweaqua Wolf woman. Potawatomi. (MO-WEE-AH-KWAH)

Mutsiawotan Ahki Fine shield woman. Blackfoot. The name was borne by the mother of artist Lone Wolf Schultz. *See* NITOH MAHKWI (Male Names). (MOOT-SEE-AH-WO-TAN-AH-KEE)

Nahimana Mystic. Sioux. (NA-HEE-MAH-NAH)

Nalín Derived from the Apache *nalín* (maiden, young woman). (NAH-LIN)

Nampeyo Snake girl. Tewa. Nampeyo was a celebrated Hopi potter (1859–1942) who resurrected her tribe's ancient forms and designs of ceramic ware. Var: Nampayo, Nampayu. (NAM-PAY-YO)

Nanye-hi One who goes about. Cherokee. The name was borne by the well-loved Nancy Ward (c. 1738–1824). As a youth she bore the nickname Tsistunagiska (Wild Rose) because of her beautiful complexion and pretty looks. Her courage during the 1755 Battle of Taliwa, in which her husband, Kingfisher, was killed, earned her the title Ghighau (Beloved Woman), which gave her a lifetime voice in council meetings and the power to pardon condemned captives. She is remembered for being an active voice for peace and friendship. (NAN-YEH-HEE)

Nascha Owl. Navajo. (NAS-CHA)

Natane Daughter. Arapaho. (NAH-TAN-EH)

Nauasia Sauk name borne by a daughter of Black Hawk and Asshewequa. (NAU-AH-SEE-AH)

Necedah Yellow. Winnebago. (NEH-SEH-DAH)

Neche Friend. Ojibway. (NEH-CHE)

Neenah Running water. Winnebago. (NEE-NAH)

Nekoma Grandmother. Chippewa. (NEH-KO-MAH)

Niabi Fawn, young deer. Osage. (NEE-AB-EE)

Ninovan Our home. Cheyenne. (NIN-O-VAN)

Nita Bear. Choctaw. (NEE-TAH)

Nonooktowa The strange child. Modoc. (NO-NOOK-TŌ-WAH)

Odina Mountain. Algonquian. (O-DEE-NAH)

Oheo Beautiful. Iroquois. (O-HEE-O)

Ojinjintka Rose. Sioux. (O-JIN-JINT-KAH)

Olathe Beautiful. Shawnee. The name was bestowed upon the county seat of Johnson County, Kansas, by Dr. John T. Barton after his Shawnee interpreter Dave Daugherty declared the area "Olathe!" (O-LATH)

Omemee Pigeon, dove. Ojibway. (O-MEH-MEE)

Ominotago Pleasant voice. Chippewa. (O-MIN-O-TAH-GO)

Onaiwah Awake. Ojibway. (ON-AH-EE-WAH)

Oniatario Sparkling or beautiful water, fine lake. Iroquois. It was from this that the smallest of the Great Lakes and the Canadian province received their names. Var: Ontario. (ON-EE-AH-TAR-EE-O)

Opa Owl. Choctaw. (O-PAH)

Oskaloosa A name of questionable origin and meaning, of which the translation "last of the beautiful" has come to be accepted. Some believe the name was borne by one of the wives of Mahaska; others think that Oskaloosa was a wife of Osceola. (OS-KAH-LOO-SAH)

Osyka Eagle. Choctaw. (OS-Ī-KAH)

Pala Water. Luiseño. (PAH-LAH)

Pana Partridge. Cahokia. (PAH-NAH)

Panola Cotton. Choctaw. (PAH-NO-LAH)

Papina A vine growing on an oak tree. Miwok. (PAH-PEE-NAH)

Peta Golden eagle. Blackfoot. (PEH-TAH)

Ping-jarje Derived from the Apache *ping* (deer) and *jarje* (small): hence, "small deer." (PING-JAR-JEH)

Pinquana Sweet-smelling. Shoshoni. (PIN-KWAN-NAH)

Pocahontas Derived from the Algonquian *pocahántesu* (she is playful). The name was borne by the daughter (1595?–1617) of Powhatan. After Captain John Smith of Jamestown was captured and sentenced to death, Pocahontas successfully argued for his release. Five years later, she was taken hostage by the Jamestown settlers, who held her for ransom. She enjoyed Jamestown and married John Rolfe, with whom she had one son. Pocahontas died four years later in England due to a shipboard smallpox epidemic. It was because of her marriage that her father kept the peace between his tribe and the white colonists for as long as he lived. (PO-KAH-HON-TAS)

POSALA Farewell to spring flower. Miwok. (PO-SAH-LAH)

PTAYSANWEE White buffalo. Sioux. (PTAY-SAN-WEE)

QUAH AH White coral beads. Pueblo. The name was borne by Tonita Peña (1895–1949), a Pueblo painter who was the first to break away from the traditional restrictions put on women, and paint as she wished. She was commissioned to produce many murals throughout Arizona and New Mexico. (KWAH-AH)

RANT-CHE-WAI-ME Female flying pigeon. Iowa. The name was borne by the youngest and favorite wife of Mahaska the Elder (Old White Cloud). (RANT-CHEH-WAY-MEE)

RU-TAN-YE-WEE-MA Strutting pigeon. Iowa. The name was borne by a wife of Mahaska (White Cloud), son of Mahaska the Elder. (ROO-TAN-YEH-WEE-MAH)

SACAJAWEA Of debated origin and meaning, some think Sacajawea, or Sacagawea, is from the Hidatsa *tsakakawía* (bird woman). Others think it might mean "boat traveler." The name was borne by a young Shoshoni woman whose childhood name was Boinaiv (grass maiden). She was captured by Crow warriors as an adolescent and sold to Toussaint Charbonneau, a French-Canadian fur trader who was hired as a guide for Lewis and Clark. Sacajawea and her newborn son accompanied them, and she proved to be an invaluable interpreter and intermediary. Var: Sacagawea. (SAK-AH-JAH- WEE-AH)

SAHKYO Mink. Navajo. (SAHK-YO)

SAHPOOLY Owl. Kiowa. (SAH-POO-LEE)

SALALI Squirrel. Cherokee. (SAL-AL-EE)

SANUYE Red cloud coming with sundown. Miwok. (SAN-OO-YEH)

SASSACUS Pequot name of uncertain meaning. (SASS-AH-KUS)

SAWNI Echo. Seminole. Var: Suwanee. (SAW-NEE)

SCENANKI Creek name of uncertain meaning borne by the wife of Tomochichi. She sailed to England in 1734 with her husband and several other Creeks with James Oglethorpe, a move that led to commercial trade between the Creek Nation and white traders. (SKEN-AN-KEE)

SHANINGO Beautiful one. Algonquian. Var: Shenango. (SHAN-IN-GO)

SHAWNEE Derived from the Algonquian tribal name Shawunogi (southerners), which is from *shawun* (south) and *ogi* (people). (SHAW-NEE)

SHEAUGA Raccoon. Iroquois. (SHE-AU-GAH)

SHENANDOAH Derived from the Algonquian *schind-han-do-wi,* the literal translation of which has been thought to be "spruce stream," "great plains," or "beautiful daughter of the stars." The name of a river and valley in the Blue Ridge Mountains of northern Virginia, Shenandoah was popularized as a given name by the folk song "Shenandoah." (SHEN-AN-DO-AH)

SHONAK Place of the spring. Pima. (SHO-NAK)

SIBETA Pulling white sucker fish from under a rock. Miwok. (SIH-BEH-TAH)

SILPE Flathead name of uncertain meaning. (SIL-PEH)

SIMI Valley of the wind. Chumash. (SEE-MEE)

SINOPA Kit fox. Blackfoot. (SIN-O-PAH)

SITALA Good memory. Miwok. (SEE-TAH-LAH)

SNANA Jingles. Sioux. (SNAH-NAH)

SOYALA Time of the winter solstice. Hopi. (O-YAH-LAH)

SULETU To fly around. Miwok. (SOO-LEH-TOO)

TADEWI Wind. Omaha. (TAH-DEH-WEE)

TAHCAWIN The doe. Sioux. The name Tahcawin was borne by a niece of Sitting Bull. (TAH-KAH-WIN)

TAIMA Thunderclap. Fox. Var: Taimah, Taiomah. (TAH-EE-MAH)

TAINI Coming new moon. Omaha. Var: Tainee. (TAH-EE-NEE)

TAKALA Corn tassel. Hopi. Var: Takalah. (TAH-KAH-LAH)

TAKAYREN Noise in the house. Tlingit. This was used primarily as a child's name. (TAH-KAY-REN)

TALISE Beautiful water. Creek. (TAH-LEES)

TALULA Jumping water, leaping water. Choctaw. The name was borne by actress Tallulah Bankhead (1903–

68). Var: Tallula, Tallulah, Talulah, Talulla, Talullah. (TAH-LOO-LAH)

TALUTAH Scarlet. Sioux. (TAH-LOO-TAH)

TAMA Beautiful. Fox. The name was borne by a wife of Chief Poweshiek. (TAH-MAH)

TASINA SAPEWIN Black blanket. Oglala. The name was borne by the wife of Crazy Horse. (TAH-SEE-NAH-SAP-EH-WIN)

TAYANITA Young beaver. Cherokee. (TAY-AH-NEE-TAH)

TCU MANA Snake girl. Hopi. (TKOO-MAH-NAH)

TEKAHIONWAKE Double wampum. Mohawk. Tekahionwake was the native name of Canadian poet Emily Pauline Johnson (1861–1913), the daughter of Mohawk Chief Henry Martin Johnson and Emily S. Howells, an Englishwoman. (TEH-KAH-HĪ-ON-WAH-KEH)

THOCMETONY Shell flower. Paiute. The name was borne by Sarah Winnemucca, granddaughter of the elder Chief Winnemucca. She is remembered for her tireless work promoting better conditions for the Paiute. Var: Tocmetone. (THOK-MEH-TON-EE)

TIVA Dance. Hopi. (TIH-VAH)

TOCMETONE *See* THOCMETONY.

TSISTUNAGISKA Wild rose. Cherokee. Tsistunagiska was a nickname of Nancy Ward during her youth, reportedly because of the beautiful and delicate texture of her skin. *See* NANYE-HI. (TSIS-TUN-AH-GIS-KAH)

TSOMAH Yellow hair. Kiowa. (TSO-MAH)

TSULA Fox. Cherokee. (TSOO-LAH)

TULA Peak. Choctaw. (TOO-LAH)

TUSA Prairie dog. Zuni. (TOO-SAH)

TUWA Earth. Hopi. (TOO-WAH)

UNA Remember. Hopi. (OO-NAH)

WACHIWI Dancing girl. Sioux. (WAH-CHEE-WEE)

WAHCHINTONKA Patient. Sioux. (WAH-CHIN-TOHN-KAH)

WAIPSHWA Rock carrier. Wanapum. (WAIP-SHWA)

WAPIN' Daybreak, dawn. Potawatomi. (WAH-PIN)

WASHTA Good. Sioux. (WASH-TAH)

WASULA Hair storm. Sioux. (WAH-SOO-LAH)

WATSEKA Woman, pretty woman. Potawatomi. (WAT-SEH-KAH)

WAUNA Snow geese calling as they fly. Miwok. (WAH-OO-NAH)

WAYLAHSKISE Graceful one. Shawnee. (WAY-LAH-SKEE-SEH)

WAYNOKA Sweet water. Cheyenne. (WAY-NO-KAH)

WEAYAYA Setting sun, sunset. Sioux. (WEE-AH-YAH-YAH)

WEEKO Pretty girl. Sioux. (WEE-KO)

WEETAMOO Sweetheart. Pocasset. The name was borne by a leader (c. 1650–76) of a small Pocasset tribe in Rhode Island. The wife of Wamsutta and the sister-in-law of Metacom, she is remembered for being a capable, concerned leader. She was hostile toward the whites and fought with Metacom during King Philip's War. Var: Weetamoe, Weetamore, Wetamoo, Wetemoo. (WEE-TAH-MOO)

WEHINAHPAY Rising sun. Sioux. (WEH-HIN-AH-PAY)

WICAHPI Star. Sioux. Var: Wicapi. (WIH-KAH-PEE)

WICAHPI ISNALA Long star. Sioux. Var: Wicapi Isnala. (WIH-KAH-PEE-ISS-NAH-LAH)

WICAHPI WAKAN Holy star. Sioux. Var: Wicapi Wakan. (WIH-KAH-PEE-WAH-KAN)

WIHAKAYDA Youngest daughter. Sioux. (WEE-HAH-KAY-DAH)

WINNE-COMAC Pleasant land. Algonquian. (WIN-NEH-KO-MAC)

WINONA First-born daughter, eldest daughter. Sioux. Var: Wenona. (WIH-NO-NAH)

WITASHNAH Virginal, untouched. Sioux. (WIH-TASH-NAH)

WIYAKA-WASTEWIN Pretty plume. Sioux. The name was borne by one of the wives of the Hunkpapa Sioux leader Sitting Bull. *See* TATANKA IYOTANKA (Male Names). (WIH-YAH-KAH-WAS-TEH-WIN)

WYOME Large plain. Algonquian. It is from this that the state of Wyoming got its name. (WĪ-O-MEH)

YANAHA She meets the enemy. Navajo. (YAH-NAH-HA)

ZIHNA Spinning. Hopi. (ZIH-NAH)

ZIRACUNY Water monster. Kiowa. (ZIR-AH-KOO-NEE)

Zitkala Bird. Sioux. (ZIT-KAH-LAH)

Zitkala-sa Red bird. Yankton Sioux. The name was borne by an Indian reformer and writer whose Anglo name was Gertrude Simmons Bonnin (1875–1938). She is known for her tireless efforts to improve the conditions of Native Americans and to reform United States Indian policy. She founded the Council of American Indians in 1926. (ZIT-KAH-LAH-SAH)

Zonta Trustworthy. Sioux. (ZON-TAH)

Zuzela Sioux name borne by one of the many wives of Sitting Bull. *See* TATANKA IYOTANKA (Male Names). (ZOO-ZEH-LAH)

CHAPTER TWENTY-TWO

Polish Names

AFTER BEING introduced to Christianity in 966, Poland today remains 95 percent Roman Catholic. Thus, it is not unexpected to see that many popular names are taken from the Bible or from beloved saints of the church, in addition to traditional Polish names and those taken from popular kings and queens. Diminutive forms of names are quite popular, and most children are addressed by a diminutive or nickname rather than their formal first name.

German domination in World War II also influenced the bestowal of names in Poland. During the occupation, many German names were given to Polish children. However, after the end of the war, anti-German sentiment was high and those with German surnames hastened to change them. German names in general became greatly disfavored.

The first surnames in Poland started out as appellations used by the wealthy to connect themselves with their estates. The suffix *-ski* or *-chi* was added to the name to indicate nobility. By the 16th century, 75 percent of the nobility possessed surnames having this termination. Polish kings often granted the right to use the suffix as a reward for those showing honorable or valorous service. In time, the lower classes began applying the suffix to personal names, and it came to be thought of as meaning "son of." The terminations *-ak*, *-ck*, *-czak*, *-czek*, *-czyk*, and *-yk* are diminutives. Women's surnames end in *-a*.

Many Polish immigrants to the United States added the termination *-ski* to their surnames, in the hope of achieving prestige among fellow immigrants who knew nothing of their family background.

Polish Male Names

AARON Derived from the Hebrew *aharōn* (the exalted one). The name is borne in the Bible by the older brother of Moses. Var: Aron. (AH-RON)

ABRAHAM Derived from the Hebrew Avraham (father of many, father of a multitude). The name is borne in the Bible by the first patriarch and ancestor of the Hebrews and the Arabs. (AH-BRAH-HAHM).

ADAM Derived from the Hebrew *adama* (red earth). The name is borne in the Bible by the first man created by God. According to biblical tradition, it was from Adam's rib that the first woman, Eve, was formed. (AH-DAHM)

ADOLF A borrowing from the German, Adolf is composed from the Old High German elements *adal* (noble) and *wolf* (wolf): hence, "noble wolf." (AH-DOLF)

ADRIAN A borrowing from the English, Adrian is derived from the Latin Adriānus (man from the city of Adria) and Hadriānus (man from the city of Hadria). (AH-DREE-AHN)

ALBERT Derived from the Old High German Adalbrecht, a compound name composed from the elements *adal* (noble) and *beraht* (bright, famous). Var: Albrecht, Elbert. (AHL-BERT)

ALBIN From the Latin Albinus (white), which is derived from *albus* (white). (AHL-BIN)

ALEKSANDER Popular name derived from the Greek Alexandros, a compound name composed of the elements *alexein* (to defend) and *andros* (man). The name was borne by several early saints and martyrs which helped to establish the name's popularity. Pet: Olech, Olek, Oleś (AH-LEHK-SAHN-DER)

ALEKSY Polish cognate of Alexius, a name derived from the Greek *alexein* (to defend, to help). (AH-LEHK-SEE)

ALFONS Polish form of Alphonse (noble and ready), a derivative of the Old German Adalfuns, a compound name composed of the elements *adal* (noble) and *funs* (ready, eager, prompt, apt). (AHL-FONS)

ALFRED A borrowing from the English, Alfred is derived from the Old English Ælfred, a compound name composed of the elements *ælf* (elf) and *ræd* (counsel). Elves were considered to be supernatural beings often having the ability to see into the future; thus the name took on the additional meaning "wise counsel." (AHL-FRED)

ALOJZY Polish cognate of Aloysius, a Latinized form of Aloys, a Provençal cognate of Louis (famous in war), which is from the Old High German Hluodowig, a compounding of the elements *hluod* (famous) and *wīg* (war, strife). (AH-LO-ZYEE)

AMBROŻY Polish cognate of the Greek Ambrosios, a name derived from *ambrosios* (immortal). The name was borne by a 4th-century saint who was bishop of Milan. He is considered to be one of the four great Latin doctors of the Christian Church. Short: Mroż. Pet: Mrożek. (AHM-BRO-ZHEE)

ANATOL Polish form of the Greek Anatolios, a name derived from *anatolē* (sunrise, daybreak, dawn). (AH-NAH-TOL)

ANDRZEJ Polish cognate of the Greek Andreas, a name derived from *andreios* (manly), which is from *anēr* (man). The name was borne by one of the Twelve Apostles of Christ, which originally induced the name's popularity. (AHN-ZHAY)

ANIOL Polish cognate of Angel, which is from the Latin *angelus* (divine messenger, angel), a derivative of the Greek *angelos* (messenger). (AHN-YOL)

ANTONI Polish form of Anthony, which is from the old Roman family name Antonius, which is of uncertain origin and meaning. A popular name throughout Europe, Anthony has been borne by many saints, the most notable being Anthony of Padua (1195–1231). Var: Antonin, Antoniy. (AHN-TO-NEE)

ANZELM Polish form of the Germanic Anselme (divine protection), a compound name composed of the elements *ansi* (divinity, a god) and *helm* (helmet, protection). (AHN-ZELM)

APOLINARY Polish form of the Italian Apollinare (of Apollo), a derivative of Apollo, the name of the mythological god of music, poetry, prophecy, and medicine. (AH-PO-LEE-NAH-REE)

APOLONIUSZ Polish form of the Latin Apollonius (of Apollo), a name derived from Apollo, the name of the mythological god of music, poetry, prophecy, and medicine. (AH-PO-LO-NEE-OOSH)

ARTUR Polish form of Arthur, a name of Celtic origin but of unknown meaning. The name was borne by the legendary British King Arthur, leader of the knights of the Round Table, who was supposed to have lived in the 5th or 6th century. The name gained popularity from the great body of Arthurian legend that has remained of interest over the centuries. (AHR-TOOR)

AUGUST A borrowing from the Latin, August is directly derived from *augustus* (august, consecrated by the augurs, great). (AH-OO-GOOST)

AUGUSTYN Derived from the Latin Augustinus, a diminutive form of Augustus, which is from *augustus* (great, consecrated by the augurs). The name was borne by St. Augustine (354–430), an early church father who was born in Numidia and became the bishop of Hippo in northern Africa. (AH-OO-GOO-STEEN)

AURELI Derived from the Latin Aurēlius, an old Roman family name derived from *aurum* (gold). Var: Aurek. (OW-REH-LEE)

BABTYSTA Polish cognate of the French Baptiste (baptist), which is derived from the Ecclesiastic Late Latin *baptista* (a baptist, one who baptizes). The name is traditionally bestowed in honor of John the Baptist, the forerunner and cousin of Christ. (BAB-TEE-STAH)

BARNABY Polish form of Barnabas, which is derived from the Aramaic *barnebhū'āh* (son of exhortation). The name is borne in the Bible by the Christian apostle and missionary companion of Paul. Var: Barnaba. (BAHR-NAH-BEE)

Bartłomiej Polish cognate of the Latin Bartholomaeus, which is from the Aramaic Bartholomaios (son of Talmai). Talmai is an Aramaic name meaning "hill, mound, furrows." The name is borne in the Bible by one of the Twelve Apostles of Christ. (BAHR-TOL-O-MEW)

Bazyli Polish form of the Latin Basilius (kingly, royal) and the Greek Basileios (kingly, royal), which are derived from *basileus* (king). The name was borne by a 4th-century Greek theologian known as St. Basil the Great (c. 330–79). A bishop of Caesarea, he is considered to be one of the fathers of the Eastern Church. (BAH-ZEE-LEE)

Benedykt Polish form of Benedict, which is from the Latin Benedictus (blessed), a name derived from *benedicere* (to speak well of, to bless). The name was borne by St. Benedict (c. 480–543), an Italian monk and founder of the Benedictine Order. He was responsible for the building of the great monastery at Monte Cassino, which remains the spiritual center of the Benedictines. Var: Bendek. Pet: Benek. (BEN-EH-DEEKT)

Beniamin Polish form of Benjamin, which is derived from the Hebrew *binyāmin* (son of the right hand, favorite son). The name is borne in the Bible by the youngest son of Jacob and Rachel, founder of one of the twelve tribes of Israel. (BEHN-YAH-MEEN)

Bernard Derived from the Old High German Berinhard, a compound name composed from the elements *bero* (bear) and *hart* (bold, strong, hearty): hence, "bold or strong as a bear." The name was borne by St. Bernard of Menthon (923–1008), a French monk who founded hospices in the Swiss Alps, and by St. Bernard of Clairvaux (1090–1163), another French monk, who founded the Cistercian Order. Var: Bernadyn. (BARE-NAHRD)

Białas Derived from *biało* (white, in white), Białas takes the definition "white-haired boy." Var: Biały. (BYAH-WAHS)

Błażej Polish form of the French Blaise, which is a name of uncertain etymology. Some believe it is derived from the Latin Blaesus, which is from *blaesus* (deformed, stuttering). The name was borne by a 4th- century martyr who is the patron saint of wool workers. (BLAH-ZHAY)

Bogdan Popular compound name composed of the Slavonic elements *bog* (God) and *dan* (gift): hence, "God's gift." Var: Bohdan. Pet: Bodek, Bodzio. (BOG-DAHN)

Boguchwał Compound name composed of the elements *bog* (God) and *chwała* (praise, laud, glory): hence, "God's glory." Var: Bogufał. (BO-GOO-MEERSH)

Bogumierz Compound name composed from the Slavonic elements *bog* (God) and *meri* (great, famous): hence, "God is great." (BO-GOO-MEERSH)

Bogumil Compound name composed of the Slavonic elements *bog* (God) and *mil* (love, grace, favor): hence, "God's love." (BO-GOO-MEEL)

Bogusław Compound name composed of the Slavonic elements *bog* (God) and *slav* (glory): hence, "God's glory." Pet: Bogusz, Bohusz. (BO-GOO-SWAHV)

Bolesław Compound name composed of the Slavonic elements *bole* (large, great) and *slav* (glory): hence, "great glory." (BO-LEH-SWAHV)

Bonifacy From the Italian Bonifacio, which is from the Late Latin Bonifatius, a compound name composed from the elements *bonum* (good, profit, bonus) and *fatum* (fate): hence, "of good fate, auspicious." (BO-NEE-FAH-SEE)

Borys From the Russian Boris, a name of debated origin. Some believe it is derived from the Slavonic *bor* (battle, fight). Others think it originated from the Tartar Bogoris (small). (BOR-EES)

Borysław Compound name composed from the Slavonic elements *bor* (battle, fight) and *slav* (glory): hence, "battle glory, glory in battle." (BOR-EE-SWAHV)

Bożydar Compound name composed of the elements *boży* (of God, divine) and *dar* (gift): hence, "divine gift, a gift of God." (BO-ZHEE-DAHR)

Bratumił Compound name composed of the Slavonic elements *brat* (brother) and *mil* (love, grace, favor): hence, "brotherly love." (BRAH-TOO-MEW)

Bronisław Compound name composed of the Slavonic elements *bron* (armor, protection) and *slav* (glory): hence, "glorious protection." (BRO-NEE-SWAHV)

Brunon Derived from the Germanic *brun* (brown). (BROO-NON)

Budzisław Compound name composed of the Slavonic elements *budit* (to awaken, to stir) and *slav* (glory): hence, "awakening glory." Pet: Budzisz, Budzyk. (BOOD-ZIH-SWAHV)

Cecyl From the Latin Caecilius, an old Roman family name derived from *caecus* (blind, dim-sighted). The name was borne by a 3rd-century saint and companion of St. Cyprian. (SEH-SIL)

Cezar From the Latin Caesar, a name of uncertain etymology. Some believe Caesar to be derived from *caedo* (to cut); others think it is from *caesius* (blue-gray). Another suggestion is that it is derived from *caesaries* (hairy). The name was borne by Gaius Julius Caesar (100?–44 B.C.), the Roman general and statesman who was dictator of the Roman Empire from 49 to 44 B.C. Caesar was subsequently used as the imperial title of the emperor of Rome. Var: Cesary, Cezary. (SEH-ZAHR)

CHWALIBOG Compound name composed of the Polish elements *chwała* (praise, laud, glory) and *bog* (God): hence, "praise God, glory to God." (SHWAH-LEE-BOG)

CYPRIAN From the Latin Cyprius, which is derived from the Greek Kyprios (from Cyprus, a Cypriot). The name was borne by St. Cyprian, a 3rd-century bishop of Carthage who was martyred in 258. (SEE-PREE-AHN)

CYRYL From the Late Latin Cyrillus, a derivative of the Greek Kyrillos (lordly), which is derived from *kyrios* (a lord). The name was borne by St. Cyril (827–69), a Greek missionary to the Slavs, to whom the Cyrillic alphabet is attributed. Pet: Cyrek. (SIR-IL)

CZCIBOR Compound name composed from the Slavonic elements *chest* (honor) and *borit* (to fight): hence, "to fight with honor." Var: Cibor, Ścibor. (CHEE-ZIH-BOR)

CZESŁAW Popular compound name composed from the Slavonic elements *chest* (honor) and *slav* (glory): hence, "honor and glory." Pet: Czech, Czesiek. (CHEHZ-WAHV)

DAMIAN From the Greek Damianos, which is thought to be derived from *damān* (to tame). The name was borne by the brother of Kosmas, both of whom were martyred in 303 under Diocletian. A cult arose about them, spreading across Europe and receiving much attention, when the brothers' relics were supposedly found in Milan by St. Ambrose. (DAH-MEE-AHN)

DAN Borne in the Bible by the fifth son of Jacob from whom one of the twelve tribes of Israel descended. Dan (he judged) is derived from the Hebrew *dān* (a judge). (DAHN)

DANIEL Derived from the Hebrew *dāni'ēl* (God is my judge). The name is borne in the Bible by a Hebrew prophet whose faith kept him alive in a den of lions. Daniel and the Lions' Den was a favorite story during the Middle Ages, which helped to promote the use of the name throughout Europe. (DAHN-YEL)

DARIUSZ Polish form of Darius, an old Latin name derived from the Greek Dareios, which is of uncertain origin and meaning. It is thought to ultimately be derived from Darayavahush, the name of an ancient Persian king. Var: Darjusz. (DAH-REE-OOSH)

DAWID Polish form of David, which is derived from the Hebrew *dāvīd* (beloved). It is borne in the Bible by the second and greatest of the Israelite kings. (DAH-VEED)

DEMETRJUSZ Derived from the Greek Demetrios (of Demeter). Demeter is an ancient name of unknown etymology borne by the mythological goddess of agriculture and fertility. Var: Dymitr. (DEH-MEE-TREE-OOSH)

DEZYDERY Derived from the Late Latin Dēsīderius, which is from *dēsīderium* (longing). (DEH-ZEE-DEH-REE)

DIONIZY Polish form of the Greek Dionysios (of Dionysos). Dionysos is an ancient name of unknown etymology borne by the mythological god of wine and revelry. (DEE-O-NEE-ZEE)

DOBIESŁAW Compound name composed of the elements *dobi* (to strive, to seek for) and *slav* (glory): hence, "striving for glory." (DŌ-BEE-SWAHV)

DOBROMIERZ Compound name composed of the Slavonic elements *dobro* (good, kind) and *meri* (great, famous): hence, "good and famous." (DŌ-BRO-MEERSH)

DOBROMIL Compounding of the Slavonic elements *dobro* (good, kind) and *mil* (love, grace, favor). (DŌ-BRO-MEEL)

DOBROSŁAW Compound name composed of the elements *dobro* (good, kind) and *slav* (glory). (DŌ-BRO-SWAHV)

DOBRY Derived from the Polish *dobro* (good, kind). (DŌ-BREE)

DOMINIK Derived from the Latin Dominicus (belonging to a lord), which is from *dominus* (a lord, a master). (DŌ-MEE-NEEK)

DONAT From the Late Latin Dōnātus (given by God), which is derived from *donare* (to give, to donate). (DŌ-NAHT)

DOREK Polish cognate of Derek (ruler of the people), which is derived from a short form of the obsolete Germanic Thiudoreiks, a compounding of the elements *thiuda* (folk) and *reiks* (ruler, leader, king). (DŌ-REK)

EDGAR A borrowing from the English, Edgar is from the Old English Eadgar (spear of prosperity), a compounding of the elements *ēad* (prosperity, fortune, riches) and *gar* (a spear). (ED-GAHR)

EDMUND A borrowing from the English, Edmund is from the Old English Eadmund (wealthy protection), a compounding of the elements *ēad* (prosperity, fortune, riches) and *mund* (hand, protection). The name was borne by a 9th-century East Anglian king killed by invading Danes for refusing to share his Christian kingdom with them. He was revered as a martyr, and his cult quickly spread to the Continent. (ED-MOOND)

EDWARD A borrowing from the English, Edward is from the Old English Eadweard (wealthy guardian), a compounding of the elements *ēad* (prosperity, fortune, riches) and *weard* (guardian, protector). Var: Eduard. (ED-WAHRD)

EGIDIUSZ Derived from the Latin Aegidius (shield bearer), which is from *aegis*, *aigis* (the goatskin shield of Zeus, a protection). The aegis was the shield carried by Zeus, Athena, and occasionally Apollo. Pet: Idzi. (EGG-EE-DOOSH)

ELJASZ Polish form of the Greek Elias, which is a cognate of the Hebrew Eliyahu, a derivative of *'ēlīyāhū* (Jehovah is God). (EHL-YAHSH)

EMANUEL Derived from the Greek Emmanouēl, which is from the Hebrew *'immānūēl* (God with us). In the Bible, Emmanuel is the name of the promised Messiah. (EE-MAH-NOO-EL)

EMIL Derived from the Latin Aemilius, an old Roman family name probably derived from *aemulus* (emulating, trying to equal or excel, rival). Var: Emilian. (EE-MEEL)

ERNEST Cognate of the German Ernst, which is from the Old High German Ernost and Ernust, names derived from *ernust* (earnest, resolute). (ER-NEHST)

ERYK Polish cognate of the Scandinavian Erik (eternal ruler), a compound name composed of the Old Norse elements *ei* (ever, always) and *ríkr* (ruler). (EH-REEK)

EUFEMIUSZ Masculine form of Eufemia (fair speech, of good voice). *See* EUFEMIA (Female Names). (EH-OO-FEH-MEE-OOSH)

EUGENIUSZ Derived from the Greek Eugenios, which is from *eugenes* (well-born). (EH-OO-JEN-EE-OOSH)

EUSTACHY Polish form of the Greek Eustachius (steadfast), a compound name composed of the elements *eu* (well, good, happy) and *stēnai* (to stand). (EH-OO-STAH-KEE)

EWALD A borrowing from the German, Ewald (lawful rule) is a compound name composed of the elements *ēo* (law, right) and *wald* (rule). (EH-WAHLD)

FABIAN Derived from the Latin Fabianus (of Fabius), which is from the old Roman family name Fabius, a derivative of the Latin *faba* (a bean). (FAH-BEE-AHN)

FELICJAN From the Italian Feliciano (lucky), which is from the Latin Feliciānus, a derivative of Felicius. The names have their root in the Latin *felix* (lucky). (FEH-LEE-SYAHN)

FELIKS Polish cognate of Felix, a name derived directly from the Latin *felix* (lucky). (FEH-LEEKS)

FERDYNAND From the Spanish Ferdinando, which is of uncertain etymology. It is thought to be of Germanic origin composed from the elements *frithu* (peace), *fardi* (journey), or *ferchvus* (youth, life) and *nanths* (courage), *nanthi* (venture, risk), or *nand* (ready, prepared). (FEHR-DEE-NAHND)

FIDELIS Late Latin name derived directly from *fidēlis* (faithful, trusty, sincere). (FEE-DEH-LEES)

FILIP From the Latin Philippus, a derivative of the Greek Philippos (lover of horses), a compounding of the elements *philos* (loving) and *hippos* (a horse). The name is borne in the Bible by one of the Twelve Apostles of Christ. Short: Fil. (FEE-LEEP)

FLAWIUSZ Polish form of Flavius, a Latin name that originated as a Roman family name derived from *flāvus* (fair, blond, golden, tawny). (FLAH-VEE-OOSH)

FLORENTYN From the Latin Florentīnus, an elaboration of Florens, which is derived from *florens* (to blossom, to flourish). (FLOR-EN-TEEN)

FLORIAN From the Latin Flōriānus, an elaboration of Flōrus, an old Roman family name derived from *flōs* (a flower). The name is borne by the patron saint of Poland, a Roman military officer who was martyred under Diocletian. (FLOR-EE-AHN)

FRANCISZK Derived from the Middle Latin Franciscus (a Frenchman), which is from Francus (a Frank, a freeman), a name that has its root in the Old French *franc* (free). Var: Francizek. (FRAHN-SEE-SHEK)

FRYDERYK Polish cognate of the German Friedrich (peace ruler), which is from the obsolete Fridurih, a compound name composed from the elements *frid* (peace) and *rik* (ruler, king). Short: Fredek. (FREE-DEH-REEK)

GABRIEL From the Hebrew Gavriel, which is derived from *gavhrī'ēl* (God is my strength). The name is borne in the Bible by one of the seven archangels, the herald of Good News who appeared to Mary to announce her pregnancy and the impending birth of the Christ child. Var: Gabrjel. Pet: Gabryś, Gabrysz. (GAH-BREE-EL)

GERARD Derived from the Old High German Gerhart (spear strength, brave with a spear), a compound name composed of the elements *ger* (a spear) and *hart* (hearty, brave, strong). (GEHR-AHRD)

GERIK From the English Gerrick, which originated as a pet form of Gerard (spear strength, brave with a spear). *See* GERARD. (GEH-RIK)

GERWAZY Polish cognate of Gervaise, a name of uncertain etymology. Most likely, it is a derivative of the Old German Gervas, the first element of which is *ger* (a spear), and the second of which is believed to be from the Celtic *vass* (servant): hence, "servant of the spear, warrior." (GEHR-VAH-ZEE)

GRZEGORZ From the Late Latin Gregorius, a cognate of the Greek Grēgorios (vigilant, a watchman), which is derived from the verb *egeirein* (to awaken). The name was borne by several early saints and popes. In 1582 Pope Gregory XIII introduced the Gregorian calendar, a corrected form of the Julian calendar which is now used in most countries of the world. (GZEH-GORSH)

GUSTAW From the German Gustav and the Swedish Gustaf, names of debated origin. Some believe they are derived from the Germanic Gotzstaf (divine staff), a compounding of the elements *gott* (God) and *staf* (staff). Others feel they are derived from the Old Norse elements *Gautr* (the tribal name of the Goths) and *stafr* (staff): hence, "staff of the Goths." (GOO-STAHV)

GWIDO From the Italian Guido, which is derived from *guido* (a leader, a guide). Var: Gwidon. (GWEE-DŌ)

HENRYK Polish form of the German Heinrich, a name derived from the Old High German Haganrih (ruler of an enclosure), a compound name composed of the elements *hag* (an enclosure, a hedging-in) and *rihhi* (ruler), and from the Old High German Heimerich (home ruler), a compounding of the elements *heim* (home, estate) and *rik* (ruler, king). (HEN-RIK)

HERMAN From the German Hermann, a name derived from the Old High German Hariman (army man, soldier), a compounding of the elements *hari* (army) and *man* (man). (HER-MAHN)

HIERONIM Derived from the Greek Hieronymos (holy name), a compound name composed of the elements *hieros* (holy) and *onyma* (name). (HYEER-O-NEEM)

HILARY Derived from the Latin Hilarius (cheerful), which is from *hilaris* (cheerful, glad). (HEE-LAHR-EE)

HIPOLIT Derived from the Greek Hippolytus (freer of horses), a compound name composed of the elements *hippos* (a horse) and *lyein* (to free, to loosen). (HEE-PO-LEET)

HUBERT Derived from the Old High German Huguberht (bright in heart and spirit), a compounding of the elements *hugu* (heart, mind, spirit) and *beraht* (bright, famous). (HYOO-BERT)

HUGO A borrowing from the German, Hugo is derived from the Old High German *hugu* (heart, mind, spirit). (HYOO-GO)

HUMPHREY A borrowing from the English, Humphrey is derived from the Germanic Hunfrid (warrior of peace), a compound name composed of the elements *hun* (strength, warrior) and *frid* (peace). (HYUM-FREE)

IGNACY From the Latin Ignatius, which is derived from Egnatius, an old Roman family name of uncertain etymology. Some believe it to be of Etruscan origin. Others derive it from the Latin *ignis* (fire). The name was borne by several saints, including St. Ignatius of Loyola (1491–1556), a Spanish priest and founder of the Society of Jesus—the Jesuits. Pet: Ignacek, Nacek. (EEG-NAH-SEE)

IGOR A borrowing from the Russian, Igor is a variant of Ivor, a name introduced by the Scandinavians, which is derived from the Old Norse elements*ýr* (yew, bow) and *herr* (army, warrior): hence, "an archer." (EE-GOR)

INNOCENTY From the Latin Innocent, a name borne by thirteen popes, which is derived from *innocens* (innocent). (EE-NO-KEN-TEE)

IVAN Polish cognate of John (God is gracious), which is derived from the Middle Latin Johannes, an evolution of the Ecclesiastic Late Latin Joannes. Joannes is from the Greek Iōannes, a derivative of the Hebrew *yōhānān*, a contraction of *yehōhānān* (Yahweh is gracious). Var: Evan, Iwan. (EE-VAHN)

IWO Polish cognate of Yves, a French name derived from the Germanic *iv* (yew). (EE-VO)

IZAAK Polish cognate of Isaac, which is from the Hebrew Yitzchak (he will laugh), a derivative of *yitshāq* (laughter). The name is borne in the Bible by one of the three sons of Abraham and Sarah, the father of Esau and Jacob. Var: Izak. (EE-ZAHK)

IZAJASZ Polish cognate of Isaiah, which is from the Ecclesiastic Late Latin Isaias and the Ecclesiastic Greek Ēsaias, names from the Hebrew Yeshayahu, a derivative of *yĕsha'yah* (God is salvation). The name is borne in the Bible by an 8th-century B.C. Hebrew prophet whose teachings are found in the Book of Isaiah. (EE-ZHASH)

IZYDOR Derived from the Greek Isidōros, a compound name composed of Isis (the name of an Egyptian goddess) and the Greek *dōron* (gift): hence, "gift of Isis." (EE-ZEE-DOR)

JACEK A pet form of Jacenty (hyacinth), Jacek is also popularly bestowed as an independent given name. *See* JACENTY. Pet: Jach, Jack. (YAH-SEK)

JACENTY Polish cognate of the Greek Hyakinthos (hyacinth, bluebell, a blue or purple gem). The name is borne in Greek mythology by a Spartan youth who was accidentally killed by Apollo in a game with the discus. A sorrowful Apollo caused to grow from Hyakinthos' blood a beautiful flower bearing on its petals the letters *AI*, *AI*, a Greek cry of lamentation. Pet: Jacek, Jach, Jack. (YAH-SEN-TEE)

JACH Pet form of any of the various names beginning with the element *Ja-*. Var: Jack. (YAHK)

JAKÓB Polish cognate of Jacob, which is from the Ecclesiastic Late Latin Iacomus and Iacobus, derivatives of the Greek Iakōbos, which is from the Hebrew Yaakov, a name derived from *ya'aqob* (supplanting, seizing by the heel). Var: Jakub. Pet: Kuba, Kubú. (YAH-KOB)

JAN Polish form of John (God is gracious). *See* IVAN. Pet: Janek, Janik, Janko, Janusz. (YAHN)

JANUARIUS A borrowing from the Latin, *Januarius* (of Janus) is the name of the first month of the year. The month is named after Janus, the double-faced Roman mythological god in charge of guarding portals, and the patron of beginnings and endings. Var: Janiusz, Janiuszek. Pet: Jarek. (YAH-NOO-AH-REE-OOS)

JAREK Pet form of any of the various Polish names beginning with the Slavonic element *jaro* (spring). (YAH-REK)

JAROGNIEW Compound name composed of the Slavonic elements *jaro* (spring) and *gniew* (anger): hence, "spring anger, new anger." Pet: Jarek. (YAHR-OG-NYOO)

JAROMIERZ Compound name composed of the Slavonic elements *jaro* (spring) and *meri* (great, famous): hence, "famous spring." Pet: Jarek. (YAHR-O-MYERZ)

JAROMIŁ Compound name composed of the Slavonic elements *jaro* (spring) and *milo* (love, grace, favor): hence, "lover of spring." Pet: Jarek. (JAH-RO-MEEL)

JAROPELK Compound name composed of the Slavonic elements *jaro* (spring) and *polk* (people, folk, tribe): hence, "spring people." Pet: Jarek. (YAHR-O-PELK)

JAROSŁAW Compound name composed of the Slavonic elements *jaro* (spring) and *slav* (glory): hence, "spring glory, glory in spring." Pet: Jarek. (YAHR-O-SWAHV)

JAZON Polish cognate of Jason, which is from the Latin and Greek Iāson (healer), a derivative of *iasthai* (to heal). (YAH-ZON)

JĘDREJ Polish cognate of Andrew, which is from the Greek Andreas, a derivative of *andreios* (manly). Pet: Jedrik. (YED-REE)

JERZY Polish cognate of George, which is from the Greek Geōrgios, a derivative of *geōrgos* (earthworker, farmer). Pet: Jurek. (YER-ZEE)

JOACHIM Derived from the Hebrew Jehoiakim, which is from Yehoyakim (God will establish). Jehoiakim is borne in the Bible by a king of Judah who was defeated by the Babylonians under King Nebuchadnezzar. In medieval Christian tradition, Joachim was the name assigned to the father of the Virgin Mary, as Anne was assigned to her mother. (YAH-KEEM)

JONASZ From the Ecclesiastic Late Latin Jonas, which is from the Greek Īonas, a derivative of the Hebrew *yōnāh* (a dove). The name is borne in the Bible by a Hebrew prophet who fell overboard during a storm because he had disobeyed God. He was swallowed by a whale, but three days later was cast upon the shore unharmed. (YO-NAHSH)

JONATAN From the Hebrew Yonatan, a short form of Yehonatan, which is derived from *yehōnātān* (Yahweh has given, God has given). The name is borne in the Bible by the eldest son of King Saul and a close friend of David's. (YO-NAH-TAHN)

JÓZEF Derived from the Ecclesiastic Late Latin Joseph and the Ecclesiastic Greek Iōsēph, which are from the Hebrew Yosef, a name derived from *yōsēf* (may he add, God shall add). The name is borne in the Bible by the favorite son of Jacob, by the husband of the Virgin Mary, and by Joseph of Arimathea, a rich Jew who, according to medieval legend, brought the Holy Grail to Britain. Var: Josef, Josep, Yusef. (YO-ZEF)

JULIAN From the Latin Julianus, which is a derivative of Julius, an old Roman family name thought to be derived from Iulus (the first down on the chin, downy-bearded). Because a person just beginning to develop facial hair is young, "youth" became an accepted meaning of the name. (YOO-LEE-AHN)

JULIUSZ Polish form of Julius, an old Roman family name thought to be derived from Iulus (the first down on the chin, downy-bearded, youth). (YOO-LEE-OSH)

JUSTYN Polish cognate of Justin, which is from the Latin Justīnus, a name derived from *justus* (lawful, right, just). (YOO-STEEN)

KAJETAN Polish form of Gaetano, a name derived from the name of the Italian city of Gaeta, which was originally known as Caieta. The name is of uncertain derivation. (KAH-YAH-TAHN)

KAROL Polish cognate of Charles, which is derived from the Germanic *karl* (full-grown, a man). The name is borne by Karol Wojtyla (b. 1920), the Polish-born Pope John Paul II. Pet: Karolek. (KAH-ROL)

KASIMIERZ Compound name composed of the elements *kazi´* (to destroy, to corrupt) and *meri* (great, famous):

hence, "famous destroyer." The name was borne by several Polish kings. Var: Casimir. Pet: Mirek. (KAH-SEE-MEERSH)

KASPER Polish form of Gaspar, a name of uncertain etymology, which, along with Balthasar and Melchior, was assigned to the Three Wise Men, who brought gifts to the Christ child. The names are not found in the Bible and are thought to have been fixed in the 11th century. Gaspar might have been derived from the Persian *genashber* (treasure master), which is in keeping with his role of the bringer of precious gifts. (KAH-SPEHR)

KLAUDIUSZ From the Latin Claudius, an old Roman family name derived from *claudus* (lame). (KLAU-DY-OOSH)

KLEMENS From the Late Latin Clēmens, which is derived from *clemens* (mild, gentle, merciful). Pet: Klimek. (KLEH-MEHNS)

KONRAD A borrowing from the German, Konrad is from the Old High German Kuonrat, a compound name composed of the elements *kuon* (bold, wise) and *rat* (counsel): hence, "wise counsel." Pet: Kurt. (KON-RAHD)

KONSTANTYN Polish form of Constantine, which is from the Latin Constantinus, a derivative of *constans* (steadfast, constant). The name was borne by Constantine the Great (280?–337), the first emperor of Rome to be converted to Christianity. Var: Konstancji, Konstanty. (KON-STAHN-TEEN)

KORNEL From the Latin Cornelius, an old Roman family name of uncertain etymology. Some believe it is derived from *cornu* (horn). Var: Korneli, Korneliusz. Pet: Kornek, Kornelek. (KOR-NEHL)

KOSMY Polish form of the Greek Kosmas, a name derived from *kosmos* (universe, order, harmony). (KOS-MEE)

KRYSTYN A popular name in Poland, Krystyn is derived from the Ecclesiastic Late Latin *Christianus*, which is from the Greek *Christianos* (a Christian, a follower of Christ). Var: Krystian. (KREES-TEEN)

KRZYSZTOF Polish cognate of Christopher (bearing Christ), which is from the Ecclesiastic Late Latin Christophorus and the Ecclesiastic Greek Christophoros, a compound name composed from the elements *Christos* (Christ) and *pherein* (to bear). The name was borne by St. Christopher, a 3rd-century Christian martyr of Asia Minor who is the patron saint of travelers. (KREES-TOF)

KSAWERY Polish cognate of Xavier, which represents the transferred use of the Spanish surname derived from the place-name Xavier in Navarre. The name, which is believed to be derived from the Basque Etcheberria (the new house), was borne by St. Francis Xavier (1506–52), a Spanish missionary of Japan and the East Indies and the patron saint of missionaries in foreign lands. (KSAH-VER-EE)

KWIATOSŁAW Compound name composed of the Slavonic elements *kviat* (flower) and *slav* (glory): hence, "glorious flower." (KVEE-AH-TO-SWAHV)

KWINTYN Polish cognate of the French Quentin, which is from the Latin Quentīnus, a derivative of the Roman name Quintus, which is directly derived from *quintus* (the fifth). The name was originally bestowed by Romans upon the fifth-born male child. (KVEEN-TEEN)

LAURENCJUSZ From the Latin Laurentius (man from Laurentum), which is from Laurentum, the name of a town in Latium, which is probably derived from *laurus* (laurel). Var: Laiurenty, Lawrenty, Wawrzyniec. (LAH-OO-REHN-SYOOSH)

ŁAZARZ From the Ecclesiastic Late Latin Lazarus, which is from the Ecclesiastic Greek Lazaros, a name derived from the Hebrew *el'āzār* (God has helped). The name is borne in the Bible by Martha's brother whom Christ raised from the dead. (LAH-ZARZH)

LECH Ancient name of uncertain derivation borne by the legendary founder of the Polish race. His brothers Czech and Rus were the patriarchs of the Czechs and the Russians. The name Lech, which has come to be defined as "a Pole," is borne by the Polish president Lech Wałęsa (b. 1943). Lech is also used as a short form of Lechosław (glory of the Poles). *See* LECHOSŁAW. Pet: Leszek. (LEK)

LECHOSŁAW Compound name composed of Lech (a Pole) and the Slavonic element *slav* (glory): hence, "glory of the Poles." Var: Lesław. Short: Lech. (LEK-O-SWAHV)

LEON A variant of the Late Latin Leo, a name derived from *leo* (lion). (LEH-ŌN)

LEW Polish form of the Russian Lev, a name directly derived from *lev* (lion). (LEW)

LIUZ Derived from the Latin Lucius, a name derived from the root *lux* (light). (LEE-OOZ)

LUBOMIERZ Compound name composed of the Slavonic elements *lub* (love) and *meri* (great, famous): hence, "great love." Var: Lubomir. (LOO-BO-MEERSH)

LUBOMIŁ Compound name composed of the Slavonic elements *lub* (love) and *mil* (grace, favor): hence, "lover of grace." (LOO-BO-MEW)

LUBOSŁAW Compound name composed of the Slavonic elements *lub* (love) and *slav* (glory): hence, "lover of glory." (LOO-BO-SWAHV)

Lucas A borrowing from the Latin, Lucas is a derivative of Lucius, a name derived from the root *lux* (light). (LOO-KAHS)

Lucjan Polish form of Lucien, which is from the Latin Luciānus (of Lucius), a derivative of Lucius, which has its root in *lux* (light). (LOO-SYAHN)

Lucjusz Polish cognate of Lucius, a Latin name derived from *lux* (light). The name was borne by three popes. (LOO-SYOOSH)

Ludomierz Compound name composed of the Slavonic elements *lud* (people, folk, tribe) and *meri* (great, famous): hence, "famous people." (LOO-DŌ-MEE-ERZ)

Ludosław Compound name composed of the Slavonic elements *lud* (people, folk, tribe) and *slav* (glory): hence, "glorious people." Var: Lutosław. (LOO-DO-SWAHV)

Ludwik Polish form of Ludwig (famous in war), a German name derived from the obsolete Hluodowig, a compound name composed of the elements *hluod* (famous) and *wīg* (war, strife). (LOOD-VEEK)

Maciej Polish form of Matthew, which is from the Ecclesiastic Late Latin Matthaeus, a derivative of the Ecclesiastic Greek Matthaios and Matthias, contractions of Mattathias. The name has its root in the Hebrew Matityah, which is derived from *mattīthyāh* (gift of God). The name is borne in the Bible by one of the four evangelists, the author of the first Gospel, Matthew. Pet: Maciek. (MAH-CHEE)

Makary From the Greek Makarios, which is derived from *makaros* (blessed). (MAH-KAH-REE)

Makimus From the Latin Maximus, which is derived directly from *maximus* (greatest). (MAH-KEE-MOOS)

Maksymilian Polish form of Maximilian, a name that arose as a blending of the Latin names Maximus and Aemiliānus by the Emperor Friedrich III, who bestowed it upon his first-born son, Maximilian I (1459–1519), in honor of the two famous Roman generals. Maximus is derived from the Latin *maximus* (greatest), but the etymology of Aemiliānus is uncertain. It is thought to be from the Latin *aemulus* (emulating, trying to equal or excel, rival). Short: Maksym. (MAH-KSEE-MEE-LEE-AHN)

Marceli From the Latin Marcellīnus, a diminutive variant of Marcus, which is of uncertain derivation. Most believe it has its root in Mars, the name of the Roman mythological god of war. Others, however, think it is from *mas* (manly) or from the Greek *malakoz* (soft, tender). Var: Marcel, Marcely. (MAHR-SEL-EE)

Marcin Polish form of Martin, which is from the Latin Martinus, a derivative of Mars, the name of the Roman mythological god of war. Pet: Marcinek. (MAHR-SEEN)

Marek Polish cognate of Marcus, a Latin name of uncertain derivation. Most believe it has its root in Mars, the name of the Roman mythological god of war. Others, however, think it is from *mas* (manly) or from the Greek *malakoz* (soft, tender). The name is borne in the Bible by one of the four evangelists, the author of the second Gospel, Mark. (MAH-REK)

Marian From the Latin Mariānus (of Marius), which is from Marius, a derivative of Mars, the name of the Roman mythological god of war. As a result of similarity of form, the name eventually became associated with Maria, the name of the Blessed Virgin, and was often bestowed in her honor. (MAH-REE-AHN)

Mateusz Derived from the Ecclesiastic Late Latin Matthaeus, a derivative of the Ecclesiastic Greek Matthaios and Matthias, which are contractions of Mattathias. The name is derived from the Hebrew Matityah, which has its root in *mattīthyāh* (gift of God). The name is borne in the Bible by one of the four evangelists, the author of the first Gospel, Matthew. Pet: Matus, Matusek, Matuszek, Matys, Matysek. (MAH-TAY-ŌSH)

Matjasz Polish form of the Ecclesiastic Greek Matthias, which is derived from the Hebrew *mattīthyāh* (gift of God). The name is borne in the Bible by the apostle chosen by lot to replace Judas Iscariot. (MAH-TEE-AHSH)

Maurycy Polish cognate of Maurice, which is from the Latin Mauritius (Moorish), a derivative of Maurus (a Moor). The name also came to mean "dark" or "swarthy" in reference to the coloring of the Moors. Short: Maury. (MAH-OO-REE-SEE)

Melchior A name that, along with Gaspar and Balthasar, was assigned to the Three Wise Men, who brought gifts to the Christ child. The names are not found in the Bible and are thought to have been fixed in the 11th century. Melchior is believed to be derived from the Persian elements *melk* (a king) and *quart* (city): hence, "city of the king." (MEHL-KEE-OR)

Michal Derived from the Hebrew Michael, a derivative of *mīkhā'ēl* (who is like God?). The name is borne in the Bible by the archangel closest to God, the one responsible for carrying out God's judgments. Considered the leader of the heavenly host, Michael is regarded as the patron of soldiers. Var: Michel. (MEE-HAHL)

Mieczysław Compound name, the first element of which is of uncertain derivation. Some believe it to be from *miecz* (sword), the Old Polish *miecz* (man, father), or *mieszka* (bear). The second element is the Slavonic *slav* (glory). The name was borne by two early kings of Poland. Var: Masław. Pet: Mieszko, Mietek. (MEES-CHEE-SWAHV)

MIKOLAJ Polish form of Nicholas (victory of the people), which is from the Greek Nikolaos, a compound name composed of the elements *nikē* (victory) and *laos* (the people). Var: Mikolai. Pet: Mikulášek, Mikuš. (MEE-KO-LĪ)

MILOSŁAW Compound name composed of the Slavonic element *mil* (grace, favor, love) and *slav* (glory): hence, "lover of glory." Pet: Milek, Miłosz. (MEE-LO-SWAHV)

MIRON Polish form of the Greek Myron, a name derived from *myron* (myrrh, a fragrant resin used in making incense and perfume). The name is said to have been taken up by early Christians because of the gift of myrrh made to the Christ child by the Wise Men. (MEE-RON)

MIROSŁAW Compound name composed of the Slavonic elements *meri* (great, famous) and *slav* (glory): hence, "great glory." Var: Mirosławy. Pet: Mirek. (MEE-RO-SWAHV)

MOJŻESZ Polish form of the Ecclesiastic Greek Mōsēs, which is from the Hebrew Moshe, a derivative of *mōsheh* (drawn out of the water) and the Egyptian *mes*, *mesu* (son, child). The name is borne in the Bible by the leader who brought the Israelites out of bondage in Egypt. He received the Ten Commandments on Mount Sinai and led his people to the borders of Canaan and the Promised Land. (MO-ZHESH)

NAPOLEON Compound name derived from the Greek *neapolis* (new city) and the Latin *leōn* (lion): hence, "lion of the new city." The name was borne by the military leader and emperor of France Napoléon Bonaparte (1769–1821). (NAH-PO-LEH-ŌN)

NATHAN Derived from the Hebrew Natan, which is from *nāthān* (gift). The name is borne in the Bible by a prophet who rebuked King David for the death of Uriah. Var: Natan. (NAH-TAHN)

NATHANIEL From the Ecclesiastic Late Latin and Ecclesiastic Greek Nathanaēl, a derivative of the Hebrew Netanel, which is from *n'than'ēl* (gift of God). The name is borne in the Bible by one of the disciples of Christ, more commonly known as Bartholomew. Var: Nataniel, Nathanial. (NAH-TAHN-YEL)

NESTOR A borrowing from the Greek, Nestor is derived from *nēstor* (the one going or departing). *See* NESTOR (Mythology and Astrology Names). (NEH-STOR)

NIKODEM From the Greek Nikodemos, a compound name composed of the elements *nikē* (victory) and *demos* (people): hence, "victory of the people." (NEE-KO-DEEM)

NOE Polish cognate of Noah, a derivative of the Hebrew Noach, which is derived from *nōah* (rest, comfort, quiet). The name is borne in the Bible by the patriarch who built the ark to save his family and two of every creature from the waters of the Great Flood. (NO-EH)

NOEL A borrowing from the French, Noel is from the Old French Nouel (natal, Christmas). *See* NOËL (French Names). The name is commonly bestowed upon children born during the Christmas season. (NO-EL)

OKTAWJAN Polish cognate of the Latin Octavius, which is derived from *octavus* (eighth). (OK-TAH-VYAHN)

OLAF A borrowing from the Scandinavians, Olaf is derived from the Old Norse Anlaff (ancestor's relic), a compounding of the elements *anu* (ancestor) and *laf* (what is remaining, what is left of his forefathers, relic). (O-LAHF)

OLIWJER Polish cognate of the French Olivier, which is generally considered to be from the Old French *olivier* (olive tree). Some believe it is of Germanic origin, however, and is thus probably from the Middle Low German Alfihar (elf army), a compound name composed of the elements *alf* (elf) and *hari* (army). (O-LIV-YER)

OSMAN Polish form of the Scandinavian Åsmund (God is protector), a compounding of the Old Norse elements *áss* (God) and *mundr* (protector). (OS-MAHN)

OTTO A borrowing from the German, Otto originated as a short form of any of the various Germanic names containing the element *od*, *ot* (wealth, riches, prosperity). Var: Otton. (O-TŌ)

PATRYK Polish cognate of Patrick, which is from the Latin *patricius* (a patrician, a nobleman). Var: Patrycy. (PAH-TREEK)

PAULOS A borrowing from the Greek, Paulos is derived from the Latin *paulus* (small). *See* PAWEL. (PAH-OO-LOS)

PAWEL Polish cognate of Paul, which is from the Latin Paulus, which originated as a Roman family name derived from *paulus* (small). The name was adopted in the Bible by Saul of Tarsus, a Jewish Roman citizen who was converted to Christianity by a vision of Christ. Paul and Peter are regarded as cofounders of the Christian Church. Var: Pawl. Pet: Inek, Pawelek. (PAH-VEL)

PIOTR Polish cognate of Peter, which is derived from the Ecclesiastic Latin Petrus and the Greek Petros, names derived from *petrus* (a rock) and *petros* (a stone). The name is borne in the Bible by one of the Twelve Apostles of Christ. Peter is considered to have been the first pope and cofounder, with Paul, of the Christian Church. Pet: Pietrek, Piotrek. (PEE-O-TR)

PIUS A borrowing from the Latin, Pius is directly derived from *pius* (pious, devout). The name was borne by twelve popes. (PEE-OOS)

PLACYD Polish form of Placido, which is from the Latin Placidus, a direct derivation of *placidus* (gentle, quiet, calm, placid). (PLAH-SEED)

PROKOP From the Greek Prokopios (progressive), a compound name composed of the elements *pro* (before) and *kopios* (in great abundance, copious). The name was borne by a 4th-century Greek saint, the first to be martyred in Palestine under the reign of Diocletian. (PRO-KOP)

PRYM Polish form of the Italian Primo, which is derived from the Latin *primus* (first). (PREEM)

PRZBYSŁAW Compound name composed of the Slavonic elements *pribit* (to help, to be present) and *slav* (glory): hence, "helper of glory." (PZHEE-BEE-SWAHV)

RACŁAW A contracted form of Radosław (glad for glory). *See* RADOSŁAW. (RAH-SWAHV)

RADOSŁAW Compound name composed of the Slavonic elements *rad* (glad) and *slav* (glory): hence, "glad for glory." Pet: Slawek. (RAH-DŌ-SWAHV)

RAFAŁ Polish form of Raphael, which is from the Hebrew Refael, a derivative of *refā'ēl* (God has healed). (RAH-FAHL)

RAJMUND Polish form of the French Raymond, which is an evolution of the Old Norman French Raimund, a derivative of the Germanic Raginmund, which is a compound name composed of the elements *ragin* (advice, counsel) and *mund* (hand, protection): hence, "wise protection." (RĪ-MOOND)

REMIGIUSZ Polish form of the Latin Rēmigius, a name derived from *rēmēx* (a rower, an oarsman). (REH-MEE-GEE-OOSH)

RENARD A borrowing from the French, Renard is derived from the Old High German Reginhart (strong advice, strong judgment), a compounding of the elements *ragin* (advice, judgment, counsel) and *hard* (strong, brave, hearty). (REH-NAHRD)

RENAT Polish form of the Italian Renato (reborn), which is from the Late Latin Renātus, a direct derivative of the Latin *renātus* (reborn, born again). The name was traditionally bestowed as a baptismal name in celebration of spiritual rebirth. (REH-NAHT)

ROBERT Derived from the Old High German Hruodperht (bright with fame), a compound name composed of the elements *hruod* (fame) and *beraht* (bright). (RO-BEHRT)

RODERYK From the Middle Latin Rodericus, which is derived from the Old High German Hrodrich (famous ruler), a compound name composed from the elements *hruod* (fame) and *rik* (king, ruler). (RO-DEH-REEK)

ROMAN From the Latin Rōmānus (a Roman), which is from Roma, the Italian name of Rome, the capital city of Italy. (RO-MAHN)

ROŚCISŁAW Compound name composed of the Slavonic elements *rosts* (usurp, seize, appropriate) and *slav* (glory): hence, "seizer of glory." (ROSH-SEE-SWAHV)

RUDOLF A borrowing from the German, Rudolf is an evolution of the Old High German Hrodulf (famous wolf), a compounding of the elements *hruod* (fame) and *wulf* (wolf). (ROO-DOLF)

RUFIN From the Latin family name Rufinus, which is derived from Rufus (red, ruddy), a name that originated as a nickname for one with red hair or a ruddy complexion. (ROO-FEEN)

RYSZARD Polish cognate of Richard (brave ruler), which is from the Old High German Richart, a compounding of the elements *rik, rīc* (ruler, king) and *hard* (strong, brave, hearty). (REE-SHARD)

SATURNIN From the Italian Saturnino, which is from the Latin Sāturninus (of or belonging to Saturn, a Saturnian), a derivative of Saturnus, a name borne in Roman mythology by the most ancient king of Latium, who came to Italy during the reign of Janus and then became honored as the god of agriculture, vegetation, and civilization. (SAH-TOOR-NEEN)

SEBASTJAN Derived from the Greek Sebastianos (a man of Sebastia, a town in Asia Minor). The name was borne by a 3rd-century Christian soldier of Rome, martyred under Diocletian by the arrows of his fellow soldiers. (SEH-BAHS-TYAHN)

SERAFIN Derived from the Ecclesiastic Late Latin Seraphim (burning ones, the angels surrounding the throne of God), which is from the Hebrew *śerāphīm* (seraphim, angels), a derivative of *sāraph* (to burn). (SEHR-AH-FEEN)

SERJIUSZ From the Latin Sergius, an old Roman family name of uncertain etymology. (SEHR-YOOSH)

SEWERYN Polish form of the Italian Severino, which is from the Latin Sevērīnus, a Latin family name derived from the old Roman family name Sevērus, a direct derivation of *sevērus* (severe, stern, serious). (SEH-VEH-REEN)

SŁAWOMIERZ Compound name composed of the Slavonic elements *slav* (glory) and *meri* (great, famous): hence, "great glory, glory is great." (SWAH-VO-MEERSH)

SOBIESŁAW Compound name composed of the Slavonic elements *sobi* (to usurp, to overtake) and *slav* (glory): hence, "usurper of glory." (SO-BEE-EH-SWAHV)

STANISŁAW Compound name composed of the Slavonic elements *stan* (government) and *slav* (glory): hence, "glorious government." The name was borne by the last Polish king, Stanislav II Poniatowski. He ruled from 1764 to 1795. Var: Stanislav. Pet: Stach, Stas, Stasio. (STAH-NEE-SWAHV)

STEFAN From the Latin Stephanus, which is from the Greek Stephanos, a derivative of *stephanos* (a crown, a garland). The name was borne by St. Stephen, the first Christian martyr who was one of the seven chosen to assist the Twelve Apostles. Var: Szczepan. (STEH-FAHN)

ŚWIĘTOMIERZ Compound name composed of the Slavonic elements *svyanto* (bright, holy) and *meri* (great, famous): hence, "holy and famous." (SHVEE-EH-TŌ-MEE-ERZ)

ŚWIĘTOPEŁK Compound name composed of the Slavonic elements *svyanto* (bright, holy) and *polk* (people, folk, race): hence, "holy people." (SHVEE-EH-TŌ-PELK)

ŚWIĘTOSŁAW Compound name composed of the Slavonic elements *svyanto* (bright, holy) and *slav* (glory): hence, "holy glory." (SHVEE-EH-TŌ-SWAHV)

SYLWESTER From the Latin Silvester, which is from *silvester* (of a wood or forest), a derivative of *silva* (a wood). The name was borne by three popes, the first of whom is said to have baptized Constantine and cured him of leprosy. Var: Siłvester. (SEEL-VES-TER)

SYMEON Ecclesiastic Late Latin name derived from the Hebrew *shim'ōn* (heard). The name is borne in the Bible by the second son of Jacob and Leah, the founder of one of the twelve tribes of Israel. (SEE-MEE-ŌN)

SZCZĘSNY Direct derivative of the Polish *szczęsny* (fortunate, propitious, lucky). (SH-CHEZ-NEE)

SZYMON Polish form of Simon, which is from the Ecclesiastic Greek Simōn, a derivative of the Hebrew *shim'ōn* (heard). The name is borne in the Bible by two of the Twelve Apostles and a brother of Jesus, as well as several other New Testament characters. (SHEE-MON)

TADEUSZ Derived from the Ecclesiastic Late Latin Thaddeus, which is from the Greek Thaddaios, a name of uncertain derivation. Some believe it a variant of Theodōros (God's gift). Others feel it is from an Aramaic word meaning "praised." The name is borne by the Polish prime minister, Tadeusz Mazowiecki (b. 1927). (TAH-DAY-OOSH)

TEODOR Polish cognate of Theodore, which is from the Greek Theodōros (God's gift), a compounding of the elements *theos* (God) and *dōron* (gift). Var: Fedor, Feodor. Pet: Teos, Tolek. (TAY-O-DOR)

TEOFIL Polish form of the Greek Theophilos (lover of God, beloved of God), a compound name composed of the elements *theos* (God) and *philos* (loving). (TAY-O-FEEL)

TOMASZ From the Ecclesiastic Greek Thōmas, which is derived from the Aramaic *tĕōma* (a twin). The name is borne in the Bible by an apostle who doubted the resurrection of Christ. Pet: Tomcio, Tomek. (TŌ-MAHSH)

TYMOTEUSZ Polish form of Timothy, which is from the Latin Timotheus, a derivative of the Greek Timotheos, a compound name composed of the elements *timē* (honor, respect) and *theos* (God). The name is borne in the Bible by a disciple, helper, and companion of the apostle Paul. Pet: Tomek, Tymek, Tymon. (TEE-MO-TAY-OOSH)

ULISSES Polish form of the Latin Ulysses, a cognate of the Greek Odysseus (hater), which is from the root *dys* (hate). The name is borne in mythology by a king of Ithaca who was a Greek leader of the Trojan War and the hero of the *Odyssey*. (OO-LEE-SEHS)

ULRYK From the German Ulrich (wealthy ruler, king of prosperity), which is from the Old High German Udalrich, a compounding of the elements *uodal* (riches, prosperity, wealth) and *rik* (king, ruler). (OOL-REEK)

URBAN From the Latin Urbānus (city dweller, urban), which is derived from *urbs* (a city). The name was borne by several saints and popes. (OOR-BAHN)

URJASZ Polish form of Uriah, which is from the Hebrew *ūrīyāh* (God is light). The name is borne in the Bible by a Hittite military leader whose wife King David desired and made pregnant. Uriah was put on the front lines of battle to ensure his death so that David could marry Bathsheba. (OOR-YAHSH)

VALENTYN Polish form of Valentine, which is from the Latin Valentīnus, a derivative of *valens* (to be healthy, strong). Var: Walenty, Walentyn. (VAH-LEN-TEEN)

VIKTOR Derived from the Latin Victor, a direct derivation of *victor* (conqueror, winner). Var: Wiktor. (VEEK-TOR)

VINCENTY Polish form of Vincent (conquering), which is from the Late Latin Vincentius, a derivative of *vincere* (to conquer). Var: Wicent, Wicenty, Wincenty. Pet: Wicek, Wicus. (VEEN-SEN-TEE)

WALDEMAR Germanic compound name composed of the elements *wald* (rule) and *mari, meri* (famous): hence, "famous ruler." (VAHL-DEH-MAHR)

WALERIAN From the Latin Valerianus (of Valerius), which is from Valerius, an old Roman family name believed to be derived from *valere* (to be strong). Var: Waleran. (VAH-LAY-REE-AHN)

WALTER Derived from the Old Norman French Waltier, which is from the Germanic Waldhere, a compound name composed of the elements *wald* (ruler) and *heri* (army): hence, "ruler of an army." (VAHL-TER)

WENCZESŁAW Compound name composed of the elements *Wend,* a term denoting a member of the old Slavic people who now live in an enclave south of Berlin, and *slav* (glory): hence, "glory of the Wends." Var: Wacław, Wieńczysław. (VEN-CHEH-SWAHV)

WIELISŁAW Compound name composed of the Slavonic elements *vele* (great) and *slav* (glory): hence, "great glory, glory is great." Var: Wiesław. Pet: Wiesiek, Wiesiulek. (VEE-EH-LEE-SWAHV)

WILHELM A borrowing from the German, Wilhelm is from the Old High German Willehelm (resolute protector), a compound name composed of the elements *willeo* (will, resolution) and *helm* (helmet, protection). Pet: Wilek, Wilus. (VEEL-HELM)

WIT From the Latin Vita, which is derived from *vita* (life). (VEET)

WŁADYSŁAW Popular compound name composed of the Slavonic elements *volod* (rule) and *slav* (glory): hence, "glorious rule." The name was borne by four Polish kings. Var: Włodzisław. (VLAH-DEE-SWAHV)

WŁODZIMIERZ Polish form of Vladimir (famous ruler), a compound name composed of the Slavonic elements *volod* (rule) and *meri* (great, famous). (VWODE-ZEE-MEE-ERZ)

WOJCIECH Popular name composed of the Slavonic elements *voi* (soldier, warrior) and *tech* (consolation, comfort, solace): hence, "soldier of consolation." Pet: Wojteczek, Wojtek. (VOY-CHEK)

ZACHARJASZ Polish form of Zachariah, which is from the Ecclesiastic Late Latin and Ecclesiastic Greek Zacharias, a name derived from the Hebrew *zĕharyah* (God remembers). The name is borne in the Bible by the father of John the Baptist. (ZAH-HAHR-YAHSH)

ZAREK Greek pet form of Belshazzar, from the Hebrew *bēlshatstsar,* which is from the Babylonian Ibelsharra-usur (may Bel protect the king). The name is borne in the Bible by the last king of Babylon, who was forewarned of defeat by the handwriting on the wall of his dining hall. (ZAH-REK)

ZBIGNIEW Popular compound name composed of the elements *zbit* (to do away with, to be rid of) and *gniew* (anger): hence, "to do away with anger." Pet: Zbyszko. (ZBEEG-NYEHV)

ZDZISŁAW Compound name composed of the Slavonic elements *zde* (here, present) and *slav* (glory): hence, "glory is here." Pet: Zdzich, Zdziech, Zdziesz, Zdzieszko, Zdziś, Zdzisiek. (ZDEE-ZIH-SWAHV)

ZENON A borrowing from the Greek, Zenon is derived from Zenoe, a name believed to be derived from Zeus, the name of the supreme deity in Greek mythology. (ZEE-NON)

ZIVEN From the Czech Živan (vigorous, alive), which is derived from the Slavonic *zhiv* (living). Var: Zivon. Short: Ziv. (ZEE-VEHN)

ZYGMUNT Polish cognate of the Germanic Sigmund (victorious protection), a compound name composed of the elements *sig* (victory) and *mund* (hand, protection). (ZEEG-MOONT)

Polish Female Names

ADELA Short form of any of the various Germanic names containing the element *adal* (noble). (AH-DEH-LAH)

ADELAJDA Polish form of Adelaide (nobility), which is derived from the German Adelheid, a compound name composed of the elements *adal* (noble) and *heit* (kind, sort). Short: Adela. (AH-DEH-LAY-DAH)

ADELINA A borrowing from the French, Adelina (little noble one) is a diminutive form of Adèle, which is a short form of any of the Germanic names containing the element *adal* (noble). (AH-DEH-LEE-NAH)

AGATA Polish form of the Greek Agathē, a name derived from *agathos* (good, kind). The name was borne by a famous 3rd-century saint. *See* AGATA (Italian Names). (AH-GAH-TAH)

Agnieszka Polish form of Agnes, which is a popular name throughout Europe. The name, which is derived from the Greek Hagnē, is from *hagnos* (chaste, pure, sacred). It was borne by a thirteen-year-old Roman martyred for her Christian beliefs during the reign of the Roman emperor Diocletian. *See* AGNESE (Italian Names). (AHG-NEE-ESH-KAH)

Alberta Feminine form of Albert, which is derived from the Old High German Adalbrecht, a compound name composed from the elements *adal* (noble) and *beraht* (bright). (AHL-BEHR-TAH)

Albinka Derived from the Latin Albina, a feminine form of Albinus, which is derived from *albus* (white). (AHL-BEEN-KAH)

Aldona Feminine form of Aldo, an Italian name derived from the Germanic *ald* (old) or from *adal* (noble). (AHL-DŌ-NAH)

Aleksandra Feminine form of Aleksander (defender or helper of mankind), which is derived from the Greek Alexandros, a compound name composed from the elements *alexein* (to defend) and *andros* (man). (AH-LEK-SAHN-DRAH)

Alicja Polish form of Alicia, which is a Latinate form of Alice (nobility). This name evolved through a series of variants of the Germanic Adalheidis, a compound name composed of the elements *adal* (noble) and *heid* (kind, sort). Adalheidis was contracted to Adalheid, which the French changed to Adélaïde, then contracted to Adaliz, and contracted yet again to Aaliz and Aliz. The English then changed the spelling to Aeleis, Alys, and eventually to Alice. Pet: Ala, Alinka. (AH-LEE-SYAH)

Alina A borrowing from the German, Alina is believed to be a Latinate form of Aline, a contracted form of Adelina (little noble one). *See* ADELINA. (AH-LEE-NAH)

Alka A pet form of Adelajda (noble one), Alka is also bestowed as an independent given name. *See* ADELAJDA. (AHL-KAH)

Altea From the Latin Althaea, which is from the Greek Althaia (healer), a name derived from *althainein* (to heal). (AHL-TAY-AH)

Amalia A borrowing from the German, Amalia is the Latin form of Amal, a name derived from *amal* (work). Var: Amalja, Amelia, Amelja. (AH-MAH-LEE-AH)

Anastazja From the Russian Anastasia, which is a feminine form of the Greek Anastasios (of the resurrection). The name was borne by a 4th-century saint and martyr of Dalmatia. Pet: Nastka, Nastusia. (AH-NAH-STAH-ZYAH)

Andżelika Polish form of the English Angelica, a name derived from *angelic* (heavenly, like an angel), which is derived from the Latin *angelicus* (angelic) and the Greek *angelikos* (angelic). (AHN-JAY-LEE-KAH)

Aniela Polish form of Angela, a Latinate form of the name Angel, which is ultimately derived from the Greek *angelos* (messenger of God). Pet: Ania. (AH-NEE-EH-LAH)

Anna A popular name throughout Europe, Anna is the Latinate form of Anne, which is a cognate of the Hebrew Hannah, a name derived from *hannāh, chaanach* (grace, gracious, mercy). In medieval Christian tradition, Anne was the name assigned to the mother of the Virgin Mary, as Joachim was assigned to her father. Var: Ania. Pet: Anka, Anula, Anusia. (AH-NAH)

Antonina Feminine form of Antony, which is derived from Antonius, an old Roman family name of uncertain origin and meaning. Some believe it to have originally been an Etruscan name. "Priceless" and "of inestimable worth" are popular folk definitions. (AHN-TŌ-NEE-NAH)

Antuaneta Polish form of the French Antoinette, a feminine diminutive form of Antoine, which is a cognate of Anthony. The name is derived from the old Roman family name Antonius, which is of uncertain origin and meaning. (AHN-TOO-AH-NEH-TAH)

Augusta Feminine form of Augustus, a Latin name derived from *augustus* (consecrated by the augurs, great, venerable). (AH-OO-GOO-STAH)

Aurelia A borrowing from the Italian, Aurelia is the feminine form of the Latin Aurēlius (golden), which is derived from *aurum* (gold). (AH-OO-RAY-LEE-AH)

Barbara A borrowing from the Latin, Barbara (foreign woman) is derived from *barbarus* (foreign, strange), a term applied to non-Romans or those deemed to be uncivilized. Pet: Basa, Basha, Basia. (BAHR-BAHR-AH)

Beatrix Derived from the Latin *beatrix* (she who makes happy, she who brings happiness), which is from *beātus* (happy, blessed). (BEH-AH-TREEKS)

Benedykta Feminine form of Benedykt, which is the Polish form of Benedict, a name derived from the Latin *benedictus* (blessed). (BEH-NEH-DEEK-TAH)

Berta A borrowing from the German, Berta is derived from *beraht* (bright, famous). (BEHR-TAH)

BOGDANA Feminine form of Bogdan, a compound name composed of the Slavonic elements *bog* (God) and *dan* (gift): hence, "God's gift." Var: Bohdana. Short: Bogna, Dana. (BOG-DAH-NAH)

BOGUMIŁA Feminine form of Bogumił (grace of God), a compound name composed of the elements *bog* (God) and *mil* (grace, favor, thanks). (BO-GOO-MEE-LAH)

BOGUSŁAWA Feminine form of Bogusław (glory of God), a compound name composed of the Slavonic elements *bog* (God) and *slav* (glory). (BO-GOO-SWAH-VAH)

BOLESŁAWA Feminine form of Bolesław (strong glory), a compound name composed of the Slavonic elements *bole* (strong, large) and *slav* (glory). (BO-LEH-SWAH-VAH)

BONA A borrowing from the Italian, Bona is derived from the Latin *bona* (good, fair). The name was taken to Poland in the 16th century by Bona Sforza, the Italian wife of King Sigismund I of Poland. (BO-NAH)

BRONISŁAWA Feminine form of Bronisław (armor glory), a compound name composed of the Slavonic elements *bron* (armor, protection) and *slav* (glory). The name was borne by the Blessed Bronislava (d. 1259). Pet: Bronya. (BRO-NEE-SWAH-VAH)

BRYGID Polish form of the old Irish name Bríghid, which is believed to be derived from the Gaelic *brígh* (strength). The name was made popular in Europe by the fame of St. Birgitta (1302–73), the patron saint of Sweden. A noblewoman and mother of eight children, she founded the Order of the Brigittines after her husband's death, and traveled to Rome, where she attempted to reform religious life. Var: Brygida, Brygita. Pet: Zytka. (BREE-GEED)

CECILIA A popular name throughout Europe, Cecilia is a feminine form of Cecil, which is derived from Caecilius, an old Roman family name which has its root in the Latin *caecus* (blind, dim-sighted). The name was borne by a 3rd-century Christian who founded a church in the Trastevere section of Rome. During the 6th century, a story of her life was written and she was henceforth venerated as a martyr. She is regarded as the patron saint of musicians. Var: Cecylja. Short: Celja. (SEH-SEE-LEE-AH)

CELESTYNA From the French Celestine (celestial), an elaboration of Céleste, which is derived from *céleste* (celestial). Var: Celestyn. (SEH-LEH-STEE-NAH)

CELINA Derived from the Greek Selene, which is from the Greek *selēnē* (the moon). Pet: Cela, Celek, Cesia. (SEH-LEE-NAH)

DANA Feminine form of the Hebrew Dan (he judged), a name borne in the Bible by one of Jacob's sons from whom the twelve tribes of Israel descended. Alternatively, Dana is used as a short form of Bogdana (God's gift). *See* BOGDANA. (DAH-NAH)

DANICA A name common to the Eastern Europeans derived from an old Slavonic element meaning "morning star." Var: Danika. (DAH-NEE-KAH)

DANIELA Feminine form of Daniel, which is derived from the Hebrew *dānī'ēl* (God is my judge). *See* Daniel (Biblical Names). (DAH-NEE-EH-LAH)

DANUTA Of uncertain derivation, some believe it is an elaboration of Dana or derived from the Latin Donata (given, given by God). (DAH-NOO-TAH)

DARIA Feminine form of Darius, an old Latin name derived from the Greek Dareios, which is of uncertain origin and meaning. It is thought to ultimately be derived from Darayavahush, the name of an ancient Persian king. (DAH-REE-AH)

DEBORA Derived from the Hebrew *devōrāh* (a bee, a swarm of bees). The name is borne in the Bible by a prophetess and judge who led the Israelites to victory over the Canaanites. (DEH-BOR-AH)

DELFINA From the Latin Delphina (woman from Delphi). Alternatively, Delfina may be derived from the name of the delphinium flower, which is from the Greek *delphin* (a dolphin). (DEHL-FEE-NAH)

DELJA A short form of Kordelja (daughter of the sea), Delja is also bestowed as an independent given name. *See* KORDELJA. (DEHL-YAH)

DIANA Derived from the Latin Diviana, which is from *divus* (divine). The name is borne in Roman mythology by the virgin goddess of the moon and of hunting. Var: Djana. (DEE-AH-NAH)

DOMINIKA Feminine form of Dominik, which is from the Latin Dominicus (belonging to a lord), a name derived from *dominus* (a master, a lord). (DO-MEE-NEE-KAH)

DORA A borrowing from the Greek, Dora is derived from *doron* (gift). Alternatively, it is used as a short form of Dorota (gift of God). *See* DOROTA. (DOR-AH)

DOROTA Polish cognate of Dorothea (gift of God), a compound name composed from the Greek elements *doron* (gift) and *theos* (God). Short: Dora. (DOR-O-TAH)

EDYTA Polish form of the English Edith, which is derived from the Old English Eadgyth, a compound name composed of the elements *ēad* (riches, prosperity) and *gyð* (war, strife): hence, "riches of war." (EH-DEE-TAH)

ELEONORA Latinate form of Eleanor, a derivative of Alienor, a Provençal form of the Greek Helenē, which is derived from the element *ēlē* (light, torch, bright). (EH-LEH-O-NOR-AH)

ELŻBIETA Polish form of Elizabeth, a name derived from the Hebrew *elīsheba'* (God is my oath). The name is borne in the Bible by a kinswoman of the Virgin Mary, the mother of John the Baptist. Pet: Ela, Eliza. (ELZH-BEE-EH-TAH)

EMILIA Derived from the Latin Aemilia, which is from Aemilius, an old Roman family name probably derived from *aemulus* (emulating, trying to equal or excel, rival). Var: Emilja. (EH-MEE-LEE-AH)

EMMA Variant of the Germanic Erma, a name that originated as a short form of any of the various names containing the element *erm(en)* or *irm(en)* (strength). (EHM-MAH)

ESTERA Polish form of Esther, a popular name of debated origin and meaning. Some believe it to be the Persian translation of the Hebrew name Hadassah (myrtle). Others think it is derived from the Persian *stara* (star). It has also been suggested that it derives from the Babylonian Ishtar (the name of the goddess of love and fertility). The name was borne in the Bible by the Jewish wife of the Persian king Ahasuerus. (EHS-TEHR-AH)

ETEL Polish form of the English Ethel (noble), a name that originated as a short form of any of the various Old English compound names containing the element *æthel* (noble). (EH-TEL)

EUDORA A borrowing from the Greek, Eudora is a compound name composed of the elements *eu* (well, good, happy) and *doron* (gift): hence, "good gift." The name was borne in Greek mythology by one of the Nereids, the fifty sea-nymph daughters of Nereus. Short: Dora, Euda. (EH-OO-DOR-AH)

EUFEMIA A borrowing from the Italian, Eufemia is derived from the Greek Euphemia, a compound name composed from the elements *eu* (well, good, happy) and *pheme* (voice): hence, "of good voice, fair speech." The name was borne by a young virgin martyr of the ancient Greek city of Chalcedon, who so courageously withstood her torture that her fame spread both East and West. (EH-OO-FEH-MEE-AH)

EUFENJA Derived from the Greek Euphenia (sweet voice, musical), which is from *euphonia* (sweet-voiced, of good voice). (EH-OO-FEHN-YAH)

EUGENIA A borrowing from the Greek, Eugenia is a feminine form of Eugenios, which is derived from *eugenēs* (well-born). Var: Eugenja. (EH-OO-JEN-EE-AH)

EULALJA Polish form of the Greek Eulalia, a compound name composed from the elements *eu* (well, good, fair, happy) and the verb *lalein* (to talk): hence, "fair of speech." (EH-OO-LAHL-YAH)

EUZEBIA Feminine form of Euzebio, which is from the Greek Eusebios, a derivative of *eusebes* (pious, devout). (EH-OO-ZEH-BEE-AH)

EWA Polish form of Eva, a name derived from the Hebrew Chava (life). The name is borne in the Bible by the first woman, "the mother of all the living." Pet: Ewka, Ewusia. (Ā-VAH)

EWANGELINA Polish form of the French Evangeline (bringer of good news), a derivative of the Ecclesiastic Late Latin *evangelium* (good news), which is from the Greek *euangelos* (bringing good news). (Ā-VAHN-JEH-LEE-NAH)

EWELINA Elaborated form of Ewa (life). *See* EWA. (EH-VAH-LEE-NAH)

FAUSTYNA From the Italian Faustina, an elaboration of Fausta (lucky), a name derived from *fauste* (lucky, favorably, fortunately). (FAH-OO-STEE-NAH)

FEBE Polish form of the Greek Phoebe, a feminine form of Phoibos (bright one), which is derived from *phoibos* (bright). The name is found in Greek mythology as a name of Artemis, the goddess of the moon. (FEH-BEH)

FELICIA Feminine form of Feliks (happy, lucky), which is the Polish form of Felix, a Latin name directly derived from *felix* (happy, lucky). Var: Felcia, Felicja, Felicya. Short: Fela. Pet: Felka. (FEH-LEE-SEE-AH)

FELICYTA Polish form of Felicity, which is from the Late Latin Felicitas, a direct derivative of *felicitas* (happiness, felicity, good fortune). (FEH-LEE-SEE-TAH)

FIDELJA From the Latin Fidelia, a name derived from *fidelis* (faithful, trusty). (FEE-DEHL-YAH)

FILIPA Polish form of the Greek Philippa, a feminine form of Philippos, a compound name composed from the elements *philos* (loving) and *hippos* (a horse): hence, "lover of horses." (FEE-LEE-PAH)

FILIPINA Elaboration of Filipa (lover of horses). *See* FILIPA. (FEE-LEE-PEE-NAH)

FILOMENA Derived from the Greek Philomena (lover of strength), a compound name composed from the elements *philos* (loving) and *menos* (strength). (FEE-LO-MEH-NAH)

Florens Polish form of Florence, a medieval English form of the Latin Florentia, a name derived from *florens* (blooming, flourishing, prosperous). The name was made popular by Florence Nightingale (1820–1910), a nurse in the Crimean War who is regarded as the founder of modern nursing. (FLO-RENS)

Florentyna From the Italian Florentina, which is derived from Florentinus, a derivative of *florens* (blooming, flourishing, prosperous). (FLO-REN-TEE-NAH)

Franciszka Polish form of the Italian Francesca, the feminine form of Francesco, the Italian cognate of Francis, which is from the Middle Latin Franciscus, a derivative of Francus (a Frank, a freeman). Short: Fraka, Frania. (FRAHN-SEESH-KAH)

Fryderyka Feminine form of Fryderyk (peaceful ruler), which is derived from the Germanic Friedrich, a compound name composed of the elements *frithu* (peace) and *rik* (king, ruler). (FREE-DEH-REE-KAH)

Gabriela A borrowing from the Italian, Gabriela is the feminine form of Gabriel, a name derived from the Hebrew *gavhri'ēl* (God is my strength). Pet: Gabrysia. (GAH-BREE-EH-LAH)

Gertruda Derived from the Old High German Geretrudis (spear maiden, spear strength), a compound name composed of the elements *gēr* (spear) and *trut* (dear, maiden) or *þruþ* (strength). Var: Giertruda. Short: Truda. Pet: Trudka. (GEHR-TROO-DAH)

Gizela Polish form of Giselle, a name of Germanic origin derived from *gisil* (pledge). (GEE-ZEH-LAH)

Gracja Polish cognate of the Italian Grazia (grace, favor), which is derived from the Latin *gratia* (grace, favor, thanks). Var: Grażyna. (GRAH-SYAH)

Hanka Feminine form of the Germanic Hanke, which is a pet form of Johan (God is gracious). *See* JOHN (English Names). (HAHN-KAH)

Hanna A popular name throughout Europe, Hanna is derived from the Hebrew *chaanach*, *hannāh* (grace, gracious, mercy). The name is borne in the Bible by the mother of the prophet Samuel. (HAH-NAH)

Helena A borrowing from the English, Helena is from the Greek Helene, a name derived from the root *ēlē* (light, torch, bright). The name is borne in Greek legend by the wife of King Menelaus of Sparta. Her abduction by the Trojan prince Paris sparked off the Trojan War. The name became popular throughout the Christian world due to the fame of St. Helena (248–327), the mother of Constantine the Great. Her influence led to the toleration of Christianity, and she is credited with finding the True Cross buried in a hillock close to Calvary. Var: Halina. (HEH-LEH-NAH)

Henrieta From the French Henriette, a feminine diminutive form of Henri, the French cognate of Heinrich, a German name derived from the Old High German Haganrih (ruler of an enclosure, home ruler), a compound name composed from the elements *hag* (an enclosure, a hedging-in) and *rihhi* (ruler), and from the Old High German Heimerich (home ruler), a compound name composed from the elements *heim* (home) and *rik* (ruler, king). (HEHN-REE-EH-TAH)

Henryka Feminine form of Henryk, which is the Polish form of Heinrich (ruler of an enclosure, home ruler). *See* HENRIETA. Short: Henka. (HEHN-REE-KAH)

Hilaria Taken from the Latin, Hilaria is derived from *hilaris* (cheerful, noisy, merry). (HEE-LAH-REE-AH)

Honorata Feminine form of the Latin Honoratus, which is derived from *honoratus* (honored, respected). (HON-O-RAH-TAH)

Hortensia A borrowing from the Latin, Hortensia is a feminine form of the old Roman family name Hortensius (gardener), which is derived from *hortensius* (of a gardener), a derivation of *hortus* (a garden). Var: Hortenspa, Hortenzja. (HOR-TEHN-SEE-AH)

Inga A borrowing from the Scandinavians, Inga is a short form of any of the various names of Old Norse origin that contain the name of the Indo-European fertility god Ing as a first element. (EEN-GAH)

Irena From the Greek Eirēnē, an evolution of the older Eirene, which is from *eirēnē* (peace). The name is borne in Greek mythology by the goddess of peace. (EE-REH-NAH)

Iwona Polish feminine form of the Germanic Ivon (archer), which is derived from the element *iv* (yew). (EE-VO-NAH)

Izabella Derived from Isabella, a Spanish form of Elizabeth, which is derived from the Hebrew *elisheba'* (God is my oath). Var: Izabel, Izabela. Short: Iza. (EE-ZAH-BEH-LAH)

Jadwiga Popular Polish cognate of Hedwig (war), a compound name composed from the Germanic elements *hada* (contention) and *wīg* (war, strife). The name was borne by St. Jadwiga (c. 1174–1243), the Moravian wife of the duke of Silesia, and by the Blessed Jadwiga (1371–99), the wife of Władysław Jagiełła, grand duke of Lithuania. Both women did a great deal to promote

Christianity in Poland. Short: Wiga. Pet: Wisa. (YAHD-VEE-GAH)

JANA Feminine form of Jan, which is the Polish form of John (God is gracious). *See* IVAN (Male Names). Pet: Janecska, Janka, Jasia. (YAH-NAH)

JANINA Polish form of the French Jeannine, which is a feminine form of Jean (God is gracious). *See* IVAN (Male Names). Pet: Janka, Janki. (YAH-NEE-NAH)

JOANNA Middle Latin feminine form of Joannes (God is gracious), a name derived from the Greek Ioannes, which is from the Hebrew *yehōhānān* (Yahweh is gracious). Pet: Joanka, Joanny. (YO-HAHN-NAH)

JOLANTA Polish form of the Italian Jolanda, which is from the French Yolande (violet), a name derived from the Latin *viola* (violet). Short: Jola. (YO-LAHN-TAH)

JÓZEFA Feminine form of Józef, which is derived from the Hebrew *yosef* (God will add, God will increase). (YO-ZEH-FAH)

JÓZEFINA Polish form of the French Josephine, a feminine form of Joseph, which is derived from the Hebrew *yosef* (God will add, God will increase). (YO-ZEH-FEE-NAH)

JUDYTA Polish form of Judith, an English cognate of the Hebrew Jehudith and Yehudit, which are feminine forms of Jehuda and Yehudhah. These names, Anglicized as Judah, mean "he will be praised." Because Judah was also the name of a kingdom in ancient Palestine, the name can also mean "from Judah." (YOO-DEE-TAH)

JULIA Feminine form of the Latin Julius, an old Roman family name thought to be derived from Iulus (the first down on the chin, downy-bearded). Because a person just beginning to develop facial hair is young, the definition of this name and its related forms has evolved to "youth." Var: Julja. Pet: Julita. (YOO-LEE-AH)

JULJANA Polish form of Juliana, the Latin feminine form of Julianus, which is from the old Roman family name Julius, believed to be derived from Iulus (the first down on the chin, downy-bearded). *See* JULIA. (YOOL-YAH-NAH)

JUSTYNA Feminine form of Justyn, which is from the Latin Justinus, a name derived from *justus* (rightful, proper, just). (YOO-STEE-NAH)

KAMILLA Polish form of Camilla, which is derived from the Latin *camilla* (virgin of unblemished character). The name is borne in Roman mythology by a queen of the Volscians who fought in the army of the Trojan Aeneas. Var: Kamilka. Short: Mila, Milla. (KAH-MEE-LAH)

KARIN A borrowing from the Scandinavians, Karin is a Swedish form of Katherine, which is from the Greek Aikaterinē, a name derived from *katharos* (pure, unsullied). (KAH-REEN)

KAROLIN Polish form of Caroline, a feminine form of the Latin Carolus, which is a cognate of Charles (full-grown, a man). Var: Karolina. (KAH-RO-LEEN)

KATARZYNA Polish cognate of Katherine, which is from the Greek Aikaterinē, a name derived from *katharos* (pure, unsullied). Pet: Kasia, Kasienka, Kasin, Kaska, Kassia. (KAH-TAHR-ZEE-NAH)

KATRINE A borrowing from the German, Katrine is a cognate of Katherine (pure, unsullied). *See* KATARZYNA. Var: Katrin. Pet: Kati. (KAH-TREEN)

KATYA A borrowing from the Russian, Katya is a pet form of Yekatarina, the Russian cognate of Katherine (pure, unsullied). *See* KATARZYNA. (KAH-TYAH)

KAZIMIERA Feminine form of Kazimierz, a compound name composed of the elements *kazic* (to corrupt, to destroy) and *meri* (great, famous): hence, "great destroyer." Short: Kazi, Kazia. (KAH-ZEE-MEE-EH-RAH)

KLARA Polish form of Clara, which is derived from the Latin *clārus* (bright, clear, famous). (KLAH-RAH)

KLARYBEL Polish form of the English Clarabelle, a combination name composed of the names Clara (bright, clear, famous) and Belle (beautiful). (KLAH-REE-BEL)

KLARYSA Elaboration of Klara, a name derived from the Latin *clārus* (bright, clear, famous). (KLAH-REE-SAH)

KLAUDIA Derived from the Latin Claudius, an old Roman family name, which is from *claudus* (lame, halting). Var: Klaudja. (KLAH-OO-DEE-AH)

KLEMENTYNA Feminine form of Klement, the Polish form of Clement, which is from the Latin *clemens* (mild, gentle). (KLEH-MEHN-TEE-NAH)

KONSTANCJA Polish form of the French Constantia, a derivative of the Latin *constans* (standing together, constancy). (KON-STAHN-SYAH)

KORA A borrowing from the Greek, Kora is derived from *korē* (maiden), a name found in Greek mythology as a name of Persephone. (KO-RAH)

KORDELJA Polish cognate of Cordelia, a name of uncertain origin. It is thought to be from the Celtic name Creiryddlydd (daughter of the sea). The name is borne in Shakespeare's *King Lear* as the name of Lear's youngest daughter, the only one who was faithful to him. (KOR-DEHL-YAH)

Kornelja Polish cognate of the Latin Cornelia, the feminine form of Cornelius, an old Roman family name of unknown etymology. Some believe it to be derived from the Latin *cornu* (horn). (KOR-NEHL-YAH)

Krystjana Polish cognate of the Greek Christiana, a feminine form of Christiano (a Christian), which is derived from *christianos* (a follower of Christ, a Christian). Short: Krysta. Pet: Krystka. (KREES-TYAH-NAH)

Krystyna Polish form of Christina, a name derived from the Greek *christianos* (a follower of Christ, a Christian). The name is borne by Krystyna Danuta Chojnowska-Listkiewicz (b. 1936), the first woman to sail solo around the world (1976–1978). Var: Krystyn. Short: Krysta, Krysia. Pet: Krystka, Krystynka. (KREES-TEE-NAH)

Laura A borrowing from the Italian, Laura (crown of laurel) is derived from the Latin *laurus* (laurel, an evergreen shrub or tree, the leaves of which were woven into wreaths by the ancient Greeks to crown victors in various contests). (LAH-OO-RAH)

Laurinda Elaboration of Laura (crown of laurel). *See* LAURA. (LAH-OO-REEN-DAH)

Lechsinska A name of uncertain derivation, borne in Polish legend by a woodland spirit. (LEK-SEEN-SKAH)

Lena Short form of any of the various names containing or ending in the element *lena*. (LEH-NAH)

Leokadia Polish form of the Spanish Leocadia, a name of uncertain derivation. Some suggest that it is from the Greek *leukas, leukos* (light, bright, clear). Another suggestion is that it is from the Latin *leo* (a lion). (LEH-O-KAH-DEE-AH)

Letycja Polish form of Letitia, which is derived from the Latin *laetitia* (gladness, happiness, joy). (LEH-TEE-SYAH)

Lidia Polish form of Lydia (woman from Lydia, an ancient kingdom in western Asia Minor), a name of Greek origin. (LEE-DEE-AH)

Lilianna Latinate form of the English Lilian, which is an evolution of the older Lilion, a name derived from the Latin *lilium* (lily). Var: Liljana. (LEE-LEE-AH-NAH)

Łucja Polish form of the Italian Lucia, a feminine form of Lucius, which is derived from the Latin *lux* (light). The name was borne by St. Lucia of Syracuse, a 4th-century martyr whose popularity during the Middle Ages led to widespread use of the name. (LOO-SYAH)

Lucyna Elaboration of Łucja (light). *See* ŁUCJA. (LOO-SEE-NAH)

Ludmiła Compound name composed of the Slavonic elements *lud* (people, tribe) and *mil* (grace, favor, love): hence, "people's love" or "love of people." Short: Mila. (LOOD-MEE-LAH)

Ludwika Feminine form of Ludwik (famous warrior), a Germanic compound name composed of the elements *hluod* (fame) and *wīg* (warrior). Var: Lodoiska, Lucwika. Short: Ludka. Pet: Iza, Lilka. (LOOD-VEE-KAH)

Luisa A borrowing from the German, Luisa is a cognate of Lucja (light). *See* ŁUCJA. (LOO-EE-SAH)

Magdalena Derived from the Ecclesiastic Greek Magdalene (of Magdala, a town on the Sea of Galilee). The name is borne in the Bible by Mary Magdalene, a woman Christ cured of seven demons. Var: Magdelina. Short: Madde. Pet: Madzia, Magdosia, Magdusia. (MAHG-DAH-LEH-NAH)

Małgorzata Polish cognate of the Greek Margarītēs, which is derived from *margaron* (a pearl). Pet: Gosia, Małgosia. (MAHL-GOR-ZAH-TAH)

Marcela From the Latin Marcellus, a diminutive form of Marcus, which is of uncertain derivation. Most believe it has its root in Mars, the name of the Roman mythological god of war, and thus give it the definition "war-like." Others, however, think it is from *mas* (manly) or from the Greek *malakoz* (soft, tender). (MAHR-SEH-LAH)

Marcelina Diminutive form of Marcela. *See* MARCELA. (MAHR-SEH-LEE-NAH)

Margarita A borrowing from the Spanish, Margarita is a cognate of Margaret (a pearl), which is ultimately derived from the Greek *margaron* (a pearl). Var: Margisia. Short: Gita, Rita. (MAHR-GAH-REE-TAH)

Maria Latin form of Mary, which is derived from the Hebrew Miryam (sea of bitterness or sorrow). There is much debate over the meaning of the name, however. While "sea of bitterness/sea of sorrow" seems to be the most probable, some sources give the alternative definitions of "rebellion," "wished-for child," and "mistress or lady of the sea." Maria, a popular name throughout Europe and the Christian world, is usually bestowed in honor of the Virgin Mary, the mother of Jesus Christ. Var: Marja. Pet: Macia, Mani, Mania, Manka, Marika, Marusia, Maryla, Maryli, Marysi, Marysia, Marzena, Masia. (MAH-REE-AH)

Marianna Feminine form of Marian, which is from the Latin Marianus, a derivative of Marius (of Mars), which is from Mars, the name of the Roman mythological god of war. Early Christians believed the name to be derived from Maria, thus increasing the name's popularity throughout Europe. Var: Marjanna. (MAH-REE-AH-NAH)

MARIA-RUTH Combination name composed of the names Maria and Ruth. *See* MARIA *and* RUTH. (MAH-REE-AH-ROOT)

MARIA-TERESA Combination name composed of the names Maria and Teresa. *See* MARIA *and* TERESA. (MAH-REE-AH-TEH-REH-ZAH)

MARION Borrowed from the French, Marion is a diminutive form of Maria. *See* MARIA. (MAH-REE-ON)

MARTA Polish cognate of Martha, which is derived from the Aramaic *mārthā* (lady, mistress). The name is borne in the Bible by the sister of Lazarus and Mary of Bethany. (MAHR-TAH)

MATYLDA Polish cognate of Matilda, which is from the Old High German Mahthilde, a compound name composed of the elements *maht* (might, power) and *hiltia* (battle): hence, "powerful in battle." (MAH-TEEL-DAH)

MELANIA Latin name derived from *melaina* (dark, black). The name was made popular through its association with two 5th-century Roman saints, a grandmother and granddaughter, remembered for their piety and good works for the poor. Short: Ela, Mela. Pet: Melcia, Melka. (MEH-LAH-NEE-AH)

MELISA Derived from the Greek *melissa* (a bee). The 16th-century Italian poet Ariosto used the name for the good fairy who protected Bradamante and helped Ruggero escape from Atlante upon the hippogriff, in the poem *Orlando Furioso*. (MEH-LEE-SAH)

MICHALINA Feminine form of Michal, the Polish cognate of Michael, which is derived from the Hebrew *mikha'el* (who is like God?). Var: Michalin. Pet: Misia. (MEE-CHAH-LEE-NAH)

MILOSŁAWA Feminine form of Milosław, a compound name composed from the Slavonic elements *mil* (grace, favor, love) and *slav* (glory): hence, "love of glory." (MEE-LO-SWAH-VAH)

MINA From the German Mine, a short form of Wilhelmina (resolute protector), a feminine form of Wilhelm, which is composed of the elements *willeo* (will, desire, resolution) and *helm* (helmet, protection). Pet: Minka. (MEE-NAH)

MIRANDA A borrowing from the English, Miranda is a name coined by Shakespeare for the heroine of his play *The Tempest*. The name is derived from the Latin *mirandus* (wonderful, to be admired). (MEE-RAHN-DAH)

MIROSŁAWA Compound name composed of the Slavonic elements *meri* (great, famous) and *slav* (glory): hence, "great glory." Short: Mira. Pet: Mirka. (MEE-RO-SWAH-VAH)

MONIKA Polish form of Monica, an ancient name of uncertain etymology. Monica was the mother of St. Augustine. She was born in Numidia, an ancient country in northern Africa, and thus the name might be of African origin. However, Monica is said to have been a citizen of Carthage, a city founded by the Phoenicians. Therefore, her name could be of Phoenician origin. Alternatively, some believe it to be from the Latin *moneo* (to advise). (MO-NEE-KAH)

MORELA Derived from the Polish *morela* (apricot). (MO-REH-LAH)

NADZIEJA Polish cognate of the Russian Nadezhda (hope), a direct derivative of the vocabulary word. Short: Nadzia, Natia. Pet: Nata, Natka. (NAHD-ZEE-EH-YAH)

NATALIA Latin name derived from *diēs nātālis* (natal day, Christmas). The name is often bestowed upon children born on Christmas Day. (NAH-TAH-LEE-AH)

NATIA A short form of Nadzieja (hope), Natia is also bestowed as an independent given name. Short: Nata. Pet: Natka. (NAH-TEE-AH)

OFELJA Polish form of Ophelia, a name believed to have been coined by Sannazzaro in 1504 for the name of a character in his pastoral *Arcadia*. He is thought to have taken it from the Greek *ophelia* (help, succor). Shakespeare also used the name for the daughter of Polonius in *Hamlet*, which no doubt contributed to its common use. (O-FEHL-YAH)

OKTAWJA Polish form of Octavia, which is a cognate of the Italian Ottavia, a feminine form of Octavius, which is derived from the Latin *octavus* (eighth). (OK-TAV-YAH)

OLESIA Feminine form of Oleś, a pet form of Aleksander (defender or helper of mankind). *See* ALEKSANDRA. Short: Ola. (O-LEH-SEE-AH)

OLGA A borrowing from the Russian, Olga is a feminine form of Oleg (hearty, happy, blessed, holy), which is derived from the Scandinavian Helge, a name derived from the Old Norse *heilagr* (prosperous, successful, blessed, holy). (OL-GAH)

OLIMPIA A borrowing from the Italian, Olimpia is derived from the Greek Olympia, which is a feminine form of Olympios (of Olympus). Olympus is a mountain in northern Greece which was the home of the gods in Greek mythology. Short: Pia. (O-LEEM-PEE-AH)

OLIWJA Polish form of Olive, which is an evolution of the older and now obsolete Oliva, a name taken from the Latin *oliva* (a tree of the olive family, a branch from which is a symbol of peace). (O-LEEV-YAH)

OTYLIA Derived from the French Ottilie, a derivative of Odile, which is from the Germanic Odila, a name derived from the element *od* (prosperity, riches, fortune). (O-TEE-LEE-AH)

PAULA Feminine form of Paul, which is derived from Paulus, a name that originated as a Roman surname from the Latin *paulus* (small). Var: Pola. (PAH-OO-LAH)

PAULINA From the Latin Paulina, a feminine form of the Late Latin Paulinus, a derivative of the Roman family name Paulus, which is from *paulus* (small). (PAH-OO-LEE-NAH)

PELAGIA Feminine form of the Greek Pelagios (sea dweller), which is derived from *pelagos* (the open sea). Short: Pela. (PEH-LAH-GEE-AH)

PENELOPA Derived from the Greek Penelope, a name in Greek mythology borne by Odysseus' wife, who, for twenty years, patiently awaited his return. The etymology of the name is debated. Some believe it is derived from the Greek *penelops* (a kind of duck), since Penelope was said to have been exposed to die as an infant and was fed and protected by a duck. Others think it is derived from *pene* (thread on the bobbin) and give it the definition "weaver, worker of the loom," for Penelope is said to have spent most of her time weaving and unweaving while awaiting Odysseus' return. Short: Lopa, Pela. Pet: Pelcia. (PEN-EH-LO-PAH)

PETRONELA From the Latin Petronilla, a feminine diminutive form of Petronius, a Roman family name of uncertain derivation. Some believe it to be derived from the Latin *petra* (a rock) or the Greek *petros* (a stone). Short: Ela, Nela, Petra. Pet: Nelka. (PEH-TRO-NEH-LAH)

PHILLIS Polish form of the Greek Phyllis, a name derived from *phyllon* (a leaf). The name was borne in Greek mythology by a girl who hanged herself for love and was then transformed into an almond tree. (FEE-LEES)

PIA A short form of Olimpia (of Olympos), Pia is also commonly bestowed as an independent given name. *See* OLIMPIA. (PEE-AH)

PRISCYLLA Diminutive form of the Latin Prisca, a feminine form of Priscus, which is a Roman surname derived from *priscus* (ancient, primitive). (PREE-SEEL-LAH)

RACHEL From the Ecclesiastic Late Latin and the Ecclesiastic Greek Rhachēl, which is derived from the Hebrew *rāchēl* (ewe). The name was borne in the Bible by the younger of the two wives of Jacob. She was the mother of Joseph and Benjamin. Var: Rachela, Rahel. (RAH-HEL)

RADOSŁAWA Compound name composed of the Slavonic elements *rad* (glad) and *slav* (glory): hence, "glad for glory." Short: Rada. (RAH-DO-SWAH-VAH)

REA A borrowing from the Greek, Rea is derived from the Greek *rhoia* (flowing). (RAY-AH)

REBEKA Polish form of Rebecca, which is from the Ecclesiastic Late Latin and the Ecclesiastic Greek Rhebekka, a name derived from the Hebrew *ribbqāh* (noose), from *rabak* (to bind, to tie). The name is borne in the Bible by the wife of Isaac and mother of Jacob and Esau. (REH-BEH-KAH)

REGINY From Regina (queen), an Italian name derived from the Latin *regina* (a queen). (REH-GEE-NEE)

RENATA From the Late Latin Renatus (reborn), which is derived from *renascor* (to be born again, to grow or rise again). The name was a common baptismal name signifying spiritual rebirth. (REH-NAH-TAH)

RITA A short form of Margarita (a pearl), Rita is also bestowed as an independent given name. *See* MARGARITA. (REE-TAH)

RODA Polish form of the English Rhoda, which is from the Latin Rhode and the Greek Rhode, names derived from the Greek *rhodon* (a rose). (RO-DAH)

ROKSANA Polish form of the Greek Roxane, which is believed to be derived from the Persian Roschana (dawn of day). The name was borne by the Bactrian wife of Alexander the Great, which seems to substantiate the name's roots. (ROK-SAH-NAH)

ROMANA Feminine form of Roman, which is from the Late Latin Romanus (a Roman, an inhabitant of Roma). (RO-MAH-NAH)

ROSABELLA A borrowing from the Italian, Rosabella is a combination name composed of the name Rosa (rose) and *bella* (beautiful): hence, "beautiful rose." (RO-SAH-BEH-LAH)

ROŚCISŁAWA Feminine form of Rościsław (glory in conquest), a compound name composed of the Slavonic elements *rosts* (to usurp, to take over) and *slav* (glory). (RO-SIH-SWAH-VAH)

RÓŻA Polish cognate of Rosa (a rose), which is derived directly from the Latin *rosa* (a rose). Var: Róży. Pet: Różyczka. (RO-ZHA)

ROZALIA From the Latin *rosalia* (an annual ceremony of hanging garlands of roses on tombs), which is derived from *rosa* (a rose). Var: Rozalja. (RO-ZAH-LEE-AH)

RUTH Of uncertain etymology, some believe it to be derived from the Hebrew *ruth,* a possible contraction of *rē'uth* (companion, friend). The name is borne in the Bible by a Moabite woman who was devoted to her mother-in-law. Her story is told in the Book of Ruth. Var: Rut. (ROOT)

RYSZARDA Feminine form of Ryszard, the Polish cognate of Richard, which is from the Old High German Richart, a compound name composed from the elements *rik* (king) and *harthuz* (strong): hence, "strong king." (REE-SHAR-DAH)

SABINA From the Latin Sabina (Sabine woman). The Sabines were an ancient tribe that lived in the Apennines of central Italy. They were conquered by the Romans in the 3rd century B.C. Var: Sabiny. (SAH-BEE-NAH)

SALOMEA From the Greek Salōmē, which is from the Hebrew *shālōm* (peace). The name is borne in the Bible by one of the three women who followed Jesus in Galilee and cared for his needs. She was present at the crucifixion and later was witness to the empty tomb. (SAH-LO-MEH-AH)

SARA Derived from the Hebrew *sārāh* (princess). The name is borne in the Bible by the wife of the patriarch Abraham and mother of Isaac. (SAH-RAH)

SEREFINA Derived from the Hebrew *šeāphim* (burning ones), a name used in the Bible for the heavenly, winged angels surrounding the throne of God. (SEH-REH-FEE-NAH)

SEWERYNA From the Italian Severina (severe, strict, stern), a name derived from the Latin family name Sevērinus, which is from the old Roman family name Sevērus, a direct derivation of *sevērus* (severe, strict, stern). (SEH-VEH-REE-NAH)

SIBILIA From the Latin Sibylla (a prophetess, a fortuneteller), which is from the Greek Sibylla. The sibyls, women of ancient Greece and Rome, were mouthpieces of the ancient oracles and seers into the future. In the Middle Ages they were believed to be receptors of divine revelation; thus Sibyl was accepted as a given name. (SEE-BEE-LEE-AH)

SOFRONJA Polish form of Sophronia, which is derived from the Greek *sophia* (wisdom, skill). (SO-FRON-YAH)

STANISŁAWA Feminine form of Stanisław, a popular compound name composed from the Slavonic elements *stan* (government) and *slav* (glory): hence, "glorious government." (STAH-NEE-SWAH-VAH)

STEFANIA A borrowing from the Italian, Stefania is a feminine form of Stefano, which is derived from the Latin *stephanos* (a crown, a garland). (STEH-FAH-NEE-AH)

SYLWIA Derived from the Latin Silvia, a feminine form of Silvius, which is derived from *silva* (wood). Var: Sylwja. (SEEL-VEE-AH)

TADEA Feminine form of Tadeusz, the Polish cognate of Thaddeus, which is an Ecclesiastic Late Latin form of the Greek Thaddaios, a name of uncertain derivation. *See* TADEUSZ (Male Names). (TAH-DEH-AH)

TAMARY Polish form of Tamara, the Russian cognate of the Hebrew Tamar (date palm, palm tree). The name Tamar is borne in the Bible by the daughter-in-law of Judah, the mother of his twin sons, and by a daughter of King David. (TAH-MAH-REE)

TEKLA From the Greek Thekla, which is a derivative of Theokleia (divine glory), a compound name composed of the elements *theos* (God) and *kleia* (glory). The name was borne by the first virgin martyr, who is said to have been a disciple of St. Paul. Pet: Tekli. (TEH-KLAH)

TEODORA From the Greek Theodōra (gift of God), a compound name composed of the elements *theos* (God) and *dōron* (a gift). Pet: Teda, Teodory. (TEH-O-DOR-AH)

TEODOZJI Polish form of Theodosia, which is the feminine form of the Latin Theodosius and the Greek Theodosios, compound names composed from the Greek elements *theos* (God) and *dōsis* (a gift, a giving): hence, "God-given, a gift of God." (TEH-O-DOZH-YEE)

TERESA Of uncertain etymology, Teresa is generally believed to be derived from the Greek *therizein* (to reap, to gather in). The first known bearer of the name was the Spanish wife of St. Paulinus, a 5th-century Roman bishop of Nola. Teresa was not used outside the Iberian Peninsula until the 16th century, when the fame of St. Teresa of Avila (1515–82) made the name popular among Roman Catholics throughout Europe. Pet: Zyta. (TEH-REH-ZAH)

THEOFILA Feminine form of Teofilo (beloved of God), which is a cognate of the Greek Theophilos, a compound name composed of the elements *theos* (God) and *philos* (loving). (TEH-O-FEE-LAH)

TOMAZJA Feminine form of Tomasz, the Polish form of Thomas, which is derived from the Aramaic *t'ōma* (a twin). *See* TOMASZ (Male Names). (TŌ-MAHZ-YAH)

TRUDA A short form of Gertruda (spear strength), Truda is also bestowed as an independent given name. *See* GERTRUDA. Pet: Trudka. (TROO-DAH)

ULRYKA Polish form of the German Ulrike, a feminine form of Ulrich (noble ruler), which is a compound name composed of the elements *uodal* (prosperity, riches, fortune) and *rik* (king, ruler). (OOL-REE-KAH)

URANJA Polish form of the Greek Urania, which is derived from Ourania (the heavenly one). The name is borne in Greek mythology by the Muse of astronomy. (OOR-AH-NYAH)

URSZULA From the Latin Ursula, a diminutive form of *ursa* (she-bear). The name was borne by a legendary Christian British princess who is said to have been martyred in the 4th century along with eleven thousand virgins by the Huns at Cologne. Var: Urszuli. (OOR-SHOO-LAH)

VALESKA Contraction of the Slavonic Vladislavka, a compound name composed of the elements *vlad* (power, rule) and *slav* (glory): hence, "ruling glory" or "glorious ruler." (VAH-LEH-SKAH)

WALENTYA Feminine form of Walenty, the Polish cognate of Valentine, which is derived from the Latin *valens* (healthy, strong). (VAH-LEN-TEE-AH)

WANDA Of uncertain etymology, Wanda is generally believed to be of Germanic origin, perhaps from *vond* (wand, stem, young tree) or from *Wend,* a term denoting a member of the old Slavic people who lived in an enclave south of Berlin. The name was used in 1883 by author Ouida, who chose it for the heroine of her novel *Wanda.* Var: Vanda, Wandy. (VAHN-DAH)

WERONIKIA Polish form of Veronica, a name of debated origin and meaning. Some believe it to be derived from the Late Latin *veraiconica*, the word given to a piece of cloth or garment with a representation of the face of Christ on it. *Veraiconica* is composed from the elements *verus* (true) and *iconicus* (of or belonging to an image). Alternatively, some believe Veronica to be a variant form of Berenice, a derivative of the Greek Berenikē, which is a variant of the older Pherenikē, a compound name composed from the elements *pherein* (to bring) and *nikē* (victory). (VEH-RO-NEE-KEE-AH)

WIKTORIA Popular name derived from the Latin *victoria* (victory). Var: Wikitoria, Wiktorja. Pet: Wicia, Wikta, Wisia. (VEEK-TOR-EE-AH)

WIOLETTA Polish form of the Old French Violette, a diminutive form of *viole*, which is derived from the Latin *viola* (violet). (VEE-O-LEH-TAH)

WLADYSŁAWA Feminine form of Wladysław, a compound name composed from the Slavonic elements *vlad* (rule) and *slav* (glory): hence, "ruling glory" or "glorious ruler." (VLAH-DEE-SWAH-VAH)

ŻANETA Polish form of the French Jeannette, a diminutive form of Jeanne, which is the feminine form of Jean (God is gracious). Jean is the French form of John, which is derived from the Hebrew *yehōhānān* (Yahweh is gracious). (ZHAH-NEH-TAH)

ZEFIRYN Derived from the Greek Zephyra (like the zephyr), the feminine form of Zephyrus, which is derived from the Greek *zephyros* (the west wind). The name Zephyrus is borne in Greek mythology by the god of the west wind. (ZEH-FEE-REEN)

ZENOBJA From the Greek Zenobia, the feminine form of Zenobios, a compound name composed of the elements *zēn* (of Zeus) and *bios* (life): hence, "the life of Zeus." The name was borne by a 3rd-century queen of Palmyra noted for her beauty and intelligence, as well as her ruthlessness with her foes. (ZEH-NO-BYAH)

ŻERALDINA Polish form of the German Geraldine, a feminine form of Gerald (to rule with a spear), which is an evolution of the obsolete Gerwald, a compound name composed of the elements *ger* (spear) and *wald* (might, power, rule). (ZHARE-AHL-DEE-NAH)

ZOE A borrowing from the Greek, Zoe is derived from *zōē* (life). (ZO-EH, ZO-EE)

ZOFIA Polish form of the Greek Sophia, a name directly derived from *sophia* (wisdom, skill). Var: Zofja. (ZO-FEE-AH)

ŻULJETA Polish form of the French Juliette, which is a diminutive form of Julie (youth; downy-bearded). *See* JULIA. (ZHOOL-YEH-TAH)

ZUZANNA Polish form of Susannah, which is from the Hebrew Shoshana, a derivative of *shōshannāh* (a lily, a rose). The name is borne in the Bible by a woman falsely accused of adultery. Her story is told in the apocryphal book of Susannah and the Elders. Var: Zuzanny. (ZOO-ZAH-NAH)

CHAPTER TWENTY-THREE

Polynesian Names

REPORTS OF the idyllic, carefree lifestyle of Polynesia eventually prompted missionary groups to travel to the islands. Finding the relaxed, uninhibited lifestyle heathenish, they attempted to impose a completely new social order and set about turning the Polynesians away from their native religions, ceremonies, dances, and other customs which had been the basis of their way of life for thousands of years.

Today, although the majority of the people are now Christian, they have successfully revived many of their native traditions and island culture thrives once again. This mix of Christianity and traditional beliefs is reflected in the types of names found in Polynesia. Nature and aspects of daily living form the basis for most native names. Since many of these names are used for both males and females, several have been separated simply according to traditional Western thoughts of masculinity and femininity. Also in common use are island forms of Bible names. As in Hawaii, these names are altered to fit in with the sounds and alphabets of the Polynesian languages.

Polynesian Male Names

AFA A hurricane; a wonder maker. (AH-FAH)

AFI Fire. (AH-FEE)

AFU Red-hot, roasting. (AH-FOO)

AHIO A waterspout, a whirlwind. (AH-HEE-O)

AHOHAKO The stormy day. (AH-HO-HAH-KO)

AHOMANA The day of thunder, day of wonders. (AH-HO-MAH-NAH)

AISAKE Polynesian form of Isaac (he will laugh). *See* ISAAC (Biblical Names). Var: Aisek, Isake, Waisake. (Ā-EE-SAH-KEY)

AISEA Polynesian form of Isaiah (God is salvation). *See* ISAIAH (Biblical Names). Var: Isaia, Iseias, Waisea. (Ā-EE-SAY-AH)

AKOLO A town fence. (AH-KO-LO)

ALEKI Polynesian form of Alex (defender, helper). *See* ALEX (English Names). Var: Eliki. (AH-LAY-KEE)

ALIPATE Polynesian form of Albert (bright through nobility). *See* ALBERT (English Names). Var: Albet, Alpert. (AH-LEE-PAH-TAY)

ANITELU Polynesian form of Andrew (manly). *See* ANDREW (Biblical Names). (AH-NEE-TAY-LOO)

ANITONI Polynesian form of Anthony. *See* ANTHONY (English Names). (AH-NEE-TŌ-NEE)

ANUI The big outrigger canoe. (AH-NOO-EE)

ELONI Polynesian form of Aaron (the exalted one). *See* AARON (Biblical Names). Var: Eroni. (Ā-LO-NEE)

Emosi Polynesian form of Amos (born). *See* AMOS (Biblical Names). Var: Amus, Hemos. (Ā-MO-SEE)

Fainga To wrestle, to contend with. (FAH-EEN-GAH)

Faipa To prepare the fishhook for fishing. (FAH-EE-PAH)

Fale House. (FAH-LAY)

Faleaka A house made from the aka plant. (FAH-LAY-AH-KAH)

Fangaloka The seashore being pounded by waves. (FAHN-GAH-LO-KAH)

Fangatua To wrestle. (FAHN-GAH-TOO-AH)

Fau To build; the hau tree. (FAH-OO)

Fauiki Small hau trees. (FAH-OO-EE-KEE)

Fautave Tall hau trees. (FAH-OO-TAH-VAY)

Feilo To know one another. (FAY-EE-LO)

Fekitoa The meeting of two brave men. (FAY-KEE-TŌ-AH)

Feleti Polynesian form of Fred (peace). *See* FRED (English Names). Var: Fereti. (FEH-LEH-TEE)

Felipe Polynesian form of Philip (lover of horses). *See* PHILIP (English Names). (FEE-LEE-PEH)

Filimoeika An enemy of the shark. (FEE-LEE-MO-Ā-EE-KAH)

Folau A voyage, a voyager, to sail. (FO-LAH-OO)

Fuanilevu The great. (FOO-AH-NEE-LAY-VOO)

Fuikefu The grass loincloth used when fishing. (FOO-EE-KAY-FOO)

Fuleheu A bird. (FOO-LAY-HAY-OO)

Hafoka To appear to be big, to look great. (HAH-FO-KAH)

Halapolo The road where the chili peppers grow. (HAH-LAH-PO-LO)

Halatoa The grove of toa trees, the road by the toa trees. (HAH-LAH-TŌ-AH)

Hale Polynesian form of Harry (home ruler, ruler of an enclosure). *See* HARRY (English Names). (HAH-LAY)

Havea Chief. (HAH-VAY-AH)

Hifo A sacrifice. (HEE-FO)

Hikila To raise the sail. (HEE-KEE-LAH)

Hoani Bird of the gods. (HO-AH-NEE)

Hola To flee, to run away. (HO-LAH)

Holisi To put reeds on a house. (HO-LEE-SEE)

Hotaia That is mine. (HO-TAH-EE-AH)

Huakava A kava drink. Kava is made from the roots of the kava plant. (HOO-AH-KAH-VAH)

Ikale An eagle. (EE-KAH-LAY)

Ikamalohi A strong fish. (EE-KAH-MAH-LO-HEE)

Ikani Polynesian form of Egan (little fiery one). *See* EGAN (Irish Names). (EE-KAH-NEE)

Inoke Polynesian form of Enoch (dedicated). *See* ENOCH (Biblical Names). (IH-NO-KEE)

Iongi Young. (EE-ŌN-GEE)

Isikeli Polynesian form of Ezekiel (God strengthens). *See* EZEKIEL (Biblical Names). (EE-SEE-KAY-LEE)

Isileli Polynesian form of Israel (contender with God). *See* ISRAEL (Biblical Names). (EE-SEE-LAY-LEE)

Kaho An arrow, a reed. (KAH-HO)

Kaihau Supreme ruler. (KAH-EE-HAH-OO)

Kailahi To eat a great deal. (KAH-EE-LAH-HEE)

Kakau To swim. (KAH-KAH-OO)

Kalani A gallon. (KAH-LAH-NEE)

Kalikau Athletic, powerful, robust. (KAH-LEE-KAH-OO)

Kapa Iron; to besiege. (KAH-PAH)

Katoa All, the whole thing. (KAH-TŌ-AH)

Kaufana A bow (for arrows). (KAH-OO-FAH-NAH)

Kaumavae Those that have separated. (KAH-OO-MAH-VAH-Ā)

Kefu Yellow-haired. (KAY-FOO)

Kelepi Polynesian form of Caleb (dog; faithful). *See* CALEB (Biblical Names). (KAY-LAY-PEE)

Kolomalu A place of refuge. (KO-LO-MAH-LOO)

Kulikefu The yellow dog. (KOO-LEE-KAY-FOO)

Kunei He is there. (KOO-NAY-EE)

Lafi To hide, a child nestling against its mother. (LAH-FEE)

Lagi Heaven. (LAH-GEE)

Langilea Thunder, the voice of the sky. (LAHN-GEE-LAY-AH)

Langiloa A dark, stormy sky. (LAHN-GEE-LO-AH)

Latavao To like to stay in the bush. (LAH-TAH-VAH-O)

Latuhilangi Latu of the sky, chief of the sky. (LAH-TOO-HEE-LAHN-GEE)

Lauaki The supreme, the highest. (LAH-OO-AH-KEE)

Leni Presently, now. (LAY-NEE)

Leo To watch, to guard. (LAY-O)

Leokau To watch without moving. (LAY-O-KAH-OO)

Leopolo To guard the polo tree. (LAY-O-PO-LO)

Lepolo Beautiful. A name borrowed from that of a plant. (LAY-PO-LO)

Limu Seaweed. (LEE-MOO)

Lisiate Polynesian form of Richard (brave king). *See* RICHARD (English Names). (LEE-SEE-AH-TAY)

Lopeti Polynesian form of Robert (bright with fame). *See* ROBERT (English Names). (LO-PAY-TEE)

Lou A leaf. (LO-OO)

Lu The leaves of the taro plant. (LOO)

Maake Polynesian form of Mark (war-like). *See* MARK (English Names). (MAH-AH-KAY)

Maana For him. (MAH-AH-NAH)

Maasi March. (MAH-AH-SEE)

Mafi A conqueror. (MAH-FEE)

Mafileokaveka The good-looking conqueror. (MAH-FEE-LAY-O-KAH-VAY-KAH)

Mafitea A conqueror with fair skin. (MAH-FEE-TAY-AH)

Mafiuliuli Dark conqueror. (MAH-FEE-OO-LEE-OO-LEE)

Makalohi Slate. (MAH-KAH-LO-HEE)

Makanesi Polynesian name for Mackenzie (son of Coinneach). *See* COINNEACH (Irish Names). (MAH-KAH-NAY-SEE)

Malo Victor. (MAH-LO)

Malu A gentle wind, a calm wind. (MAH-LOO)

Manase Polynesian form of Manasseh (causing to forget). *See* MANASSEH (Biblical Names). (MAH-NAH-SAY)

Manu Bird, animal; bird of the night. (MAH-NOO)

Manuetoafa A bird of the desert. (MAH-NOO-Ā-TŌ-AH-FAH)

Manutapu Sacred bird. (MAH-NOO-TAH-POO)

Manutea White bird. (MAH-NOO-TEH-AH)

Matafeo The edge of the coral. (MAH-TAH-FAY-O)

Mataio Polynesian form of Matthew (gift of God). *See* MATTHEW (Biblical Names). Var: Matai. (MAH-TAH-YO)

Mateni Polynesian form of Martin (war-like). *See* MARTIN (English Names). (MAH-TEH-NEE)

Matolo Scraped. (MAH-TŌ-LO)

Moko Bent. (MO-KO)

Mosese Polynesian form of Moses (drawn out of the water). *See* MOSES (Biblical Names). (MO-SAY-SAY)

Mounga Mountain. (MO-OON-GAH)

Mua First, chief. (MOO-AH)

Muamoholeva The handsome chief. (MOO-AH-MO-HO-LAY-VAH)

Natane Polynesian form of Nathan (gift). *See* NATHAN (Biblical Names). (NAH-TAH-NEH)

Nauleo A good watcher. (NAH-OO-LAY-O)

Niutei A very long coconut tree. (NEE-OO-TAY-EE)

Osileani To speak for the last time. (O-SEE-LAY-AH-NEE)

Palaki Black. (PAH-LAH-KEE)

Palauni Brown. (PAH-LAH-OO-NEE)

Palefu Black. (PAH-LAY-FOO)

Peleki Polynesian form of Blake (black, dark-complexioned; pale, wan). *See* BLAKE (English Names). (PAY-LAY-KEE)

Pesekava A kava song. Kava is a traditional drink made from the roots of the kava plant. (PAY-SAY-KAH-VAH)

Pita Polynesian form of Peter (a rock). *See* PETER (Biblical Names). (PEE-TAH)

Posoa A night of flirting at the fence. (PO-SO-AH)

Puakaeafe A thousand pigs. (POO-AH-KAH-Ā-AH-FAY)

Puakatau A boar. (POO-AH-KAH-TAH-OO)

Pulikeka Handsome. (POO-LEE-KAY-KAH)

Rahiti The sunrise. (RAH-HEE-TEE)

Samani Salmon. (SAH-MAH-NEE)

Samisoni Polynesian form of Samson (sun). *See* SAMSON (Biblical Names). (SAH-MEE-SO-NEE)

Saula Polynesian form of Saul (asked). *See* SAUL (Biblical Names). (SAH-OO-LAH)

Selemaea Polynesian form of Jeremiah (the Lord loosens). *See* JEREMIAH (Biblical Names). Var: Seremaia. (SAY-LAY-MAH-Ā-AH)

Semi Polynesian form of Shem (reputation). *See* SHEM (Biblical Names). (SAY-MEE)

Semisi Polynesian form of James (seizing by the heel, supplanting). *See* JAMES (English Names). Var: Semesa. (SAY-MEE-SEE)

Sese Polynesian form of Francis (a freeman, a Frenchman). *See* FRANCIS (English Names). (SAY-SAY)

Siaki Polynesian form of Jack (God is gracious). *See* JACK (English Names). (SEE-AH-KEE)

Siaosi Polynesian form of George (earthworker, farmer). *See* GEORGE (English Names). (SEE-AH-O-SEE)

Simi Polynesian form of Jim (supplanting, seizing by the heel). *See* JAMES (English Names). (SEE-MEE)

Sione Polynesian form of John (God is gracious). *See* JOHN (English Names). Var: Soane, Sone. (SEE-O-NEE)

Siua To fish in the ocean. Siua is also used as the Polynesian form of Joshua (God is salvation). *See* JOSHUA (Biblical Names). (SEE-OO-AH)

Sosaia Polynesian form of Josiah (the Lord supports). *See* JOSIAH (Biblical Names). Var: Siosaia. (SO-SAH-EE-AH)

Taha The number one. (TAH-HAH)

Tahi The sea. (TAH-HEE)

Tanafa To beat the drum. (TAH-NAH-FAH)

Tanaki To count something, to collect. (TAH-NAH-KEE)

Tangaloa The large gut. (TAHN-GAH-LO-AH)

Tapunui The sacred head. (TAH-POO-NOO-EE)

Tava Borrowed from that of a type of fruit-bearing tree. (TAH-VAH)

Teo Polynesian form of Theodore (God's gift). *See* THEODORE (English Names). (TAY-O)

Temaru Majestic sunrise. (TEH-MAH-ROO)

Temoe The sunrise. (TEH-MO-EE)

Tevita Polynesian form of David (beloved). *See* DAVID (Biblical Names). (TAY-VEE-TAH)

Toa Courage, bravery. (TŌ-AH)

Toafo Wilderness. (TŌ-AH-FO)

Uata Polynesian form of Walter (ruler of an army). *See* WALTER (English Names). Var: Uate. (OO-AH-TAH)

Uhila Lightning. (OO-HEE-LAH)

Vaea King of the ocean. (VAH-EH-AH)

Vala A loincloth. (VAH-LAH)

Valu Eight. Valu is also the name of a type of fish. (VAH-LOO)

Vea A chief. (VAY-AH)

Veamalohi A strong chief. (VAY-AH-MAH-LO-HEE)

Veatama The child who is a chief. (VAY-AH-TAH-MAH)

Viliami Polynesian form of William (resolute protector). *See* WILLIAM (English Names). (VEE-LEE-AH-MEE)

Polynesian Female Names

Afei To wrap around the body. (AH-FAY-EE)

Afuvale A mulberry tree with too many shoots. (AH-FOO-VAH-LAY)

Ahauano Many people. (AH-HAH-OO-AH-NO)

Ahia Temptation. (AH-HEE-AH)

Aholelei The suitable day. (AH-HO-LAY-LAY-EE)

Aholo The day of plenty. (AH-HO-LO)

Ahopomee The day of the night dance. (AH-HO-PO-MAY-Ā)

Ailine Polynesian form of Irene (peace). *See* IRENE (English Names). Var: Elina. (AH-EE-LEE-NAY)

AKANESI Polynesian form of Agnes (pure, chaste, holy). *See* AGNES (English Names). (AH-KAH-NAY-SEE)

ALAME A flower garland. (AH-LAH-MAY)

ALOFA Love. (AH-LO-FAH)

ALISI Polynesian form of Alice (noble one). *See* ALICE (English Names). (AH-LEE-SEE)

ANA A cave. Ana is also used as the Polynesian form of Anna (gracious, mercy). *See* ANNA (English Names). (AH-NAH)

ANAMALIA Polynesian form of Anna Maria. *See* ANNA *and* MARIA (English Names). (AH-NAH-MAH-LEE-AH)

ANE Polynesian form of Anne (gracious, mercy). *See* ANNE (English Names). (AH-NAY)

ANUATA Shadow woman of the night. (AH-NOO-AH-TAH)

ASENAHANA A beautiful red berry. (AH-SAY-NAH-HAH-NAH)

ETINI White flowers on the path. (EH-TEE-NEE)

ELILI The periwinkle. (AY-LEE-LEE)

FA'AFETAI Thanks. (FAH-AH-FEH-TAH-EE)

FA'ANUI Woman of the valley. (FAH-AH-NOO-EE)

FAIVA Entertainment, a game. (FAH-EE-VAH)

FAKAPELEA A pet. (FAH-KAH-PAY-LEE-AH)

FALAKIKA My mat. (FAH-LAH-KEE-KAH)

FANUA Land. (FAH-NOO-AH)

FATUIMOANA The hala garlands threaded to take to the ocean fishing. (FAH-TOO-EE-MO-AH-NAH)

FELENI Friend, friendly. (FEH-LEH-NEE)

FETUU A star. (FAY-TOO-OO)

FIELIKI Wishing to be washed with oil and water like a newborn baby. (FEE-Ā-LEE-KEE)

FIAFIA Happy. (FEE-AH-FEE-AH)

FIHAKI To mix the flowers in a garland. (FEE-HAH-KEE)

FILIA To chose from many. (FEE-LEE-AH)

FINEEVA A woman who is always talking. (FEE-NAY-Ā-VAH)

FINEONGO The beautiful woman, the much-talked-about woman. (FEE-NAY-ŌN-GO)

FIPE Polynesian form of Phoebe (bright one). *See* PHOEBE (English Names). (FEE-PEH)

FISI A bud, a blossom. (FEE-SEE)

FUSI Bananas. (FOO-SEE)

FUSILEKA The banana plant. (FOO-SEE-LAY-KAH)

HALAPUA The road near the pua trees. (HAH-LAH-POO-AH)

HERENUI The love of gods. (HEH-REH-NOO-EE)

HIKULEO An echo. (HEE-KOO-LAY-O)

HINATEA Girl of the goddess. (HEE-NAH-TAY-AH)

HIVA A song, to sing. (HEE-VAH)

HULUAVA A lighthouse at the passage for vessels. (HOO-LOO-AH-VAH)

IRIATA The skin of the clouds. (IR-EE-AH-TAH)

KAKALA A garland, a fragrant flower. (KAH-KAH-LAH)

KALI A wooden pillow. (KAH-LEE)

KALILEA Speaking pillow. (KAH-LEE-LAY-AH)

KAMI To love, to be enamored of. (KAH-MEE)

KETI Polynesian form of Kate (pure, unsullied). *See* KATE (English Names). (KAY-TEE)

KULUKULUTEA The white fruit dove. (KOO-LOO-KOO-LOO-TAY-AH)

LANGIKULA The red sunset. (LAHN-GEE-KOO-LAH)

LEALIKI The voice of the waves on the shore. (LAY-AH-LEE-KEE)

LEISI Lace. (LAY-EE-SEE)

LESIELI Polynesian form of Rachel (ewe). *See* RACHEL (Biblical Names). (LAY-SEE-Ā-LEE)

LIA Polynesian form of Leah (to weary, to tire). *See* LEAH (Biblical Names). (LEE-AH)

LOSA Polynesian form of Rosa (a rose). *See* ROSA (Spanish names). Var: Lose. (LO-SAH)

LOSAKI To gather together. (LO-SAH-KEE)

LOSANA Polynesian form of Rosanna. *See* ROSE-ANNE (English Names). (LO-SAH-NAH)

LUPE The fruit pigeon. (LOO-PAY)

LUSEANE Polynesian form of the name Lucy Anne. *See* ANNE *and* LUCY (English Names). (LOO-SAY-AH-NAY)

Lute Polynesian form of Ruth (companion). *See* RUTH (Biblical Names). (LOO-TAY)

Maata Polynesian form of Martha (lady, mistress). See MARTHA (Biblical Names). (MAH-AH-TAH)

Mahanga Twins. (MAH-HAHN-GAH)

Maili To blow gently, a gentle breeze. (MAH-EE-LEE)

Makelesi Polynesian form of Margaret (a pearl). *See* MARGARET (English Names). (MAH-KEH-LAY-SEE)

Malama To shine, to shimmer. (MAH-LAH-MAH)

Malie Pleasing, fortunate. (MAH-LEE-Ā)

Malieta Polynesian form of Marietta (little Maria). *See* MARIETTE (American Names). (MAH-LEE-EH-TAH)

Matelita Polynesian form of Matilda (mighty in battle). *See* MATILDA (English Names). (MAH-TEH-LEE-TAH)

Mele Polynesian form of Mary. *See* MARY (English Names). (MEH-LEH)

Meleane Polynesian form of Mary Anne. *See* MARIANNE (English Names). (MEH-LEH-AH-NEH)

Meleseini Polynesian form of Mary Jane. *See* JANE *and* MARY (English Names). (MEH-LEH-SEH-EE-NEE)

Meliame Polynesian form of Miriam (sea of bitterness or sorrow). *See* MIRIAM (Biblical Names). (MEH-LEE-AH-MEH)

Nanise Polynesian form of Nancy (gracious, mercy). *See* NANCY (English Names). (NAH-NEE-SAY)

Nukuluve Land of the dove. (NOO-KOO-LOO-VAY)

Nunia A chief woman. (NOO-NEE-AH)

Ofa Love, affection. (O-FAH)

Poli Polynesian form of Polly, a pet form of Margaret (a pearl). *See* MARGARET (English Names). (PO-LEE)

Pua Borrowed from that of a flowering tree. (POO-AH)

Pulupaki A fragrant garland of flowers. (POO-LOO-PAH-KEE)

Ra'inui Sky without clouds. (RAH-EE-NOO-EE)

Reva Red flag. (REH-VAH)

Salote Polynesian form of Charlotte (full-grown, a woman). *See* CHARLOTTE (French Names). (SAH-LO-TAY)

Seini Polynesian form of Jane (God is gracious). *See* JANE (English Names). (SAY-EE-NEE)

Sela Polynesian form of Sarah (princess). *See* SARAH (Biblical Names). (SAY-LAH)

Seli Polynesian form of Shirley. *See* SHIRLEY (English Names). (SEH-LEE)

Sisilia Polynesian form of Cecilia (blind, dim-sighted). *See* CECILIA (English Names). (SEE-SEE-LEE-AH)

Taulaki To wash off, to clean the hair; to wait. (TAH-OO-LAH-KEE)

Tohuia A beautiful, fragrant flower. (TŌ-HOO-EE-AH)

Tua The back; outside. (TOO-AH)

Tualau The first; to talk outside. (TOO-AH-LAH-OO)

Uinise Polynesian form of Eunice (fair victory). *See* EUNICE (English Names). (OO-EE-NEE-SAY)

Uluaki First. (OO-LOO-AH-KEE)

Vailea The speaking water. (VAH-EE-LAY-AH)

Vana A sea urchin. (VAH-NAH)

Vika Polynesian form of Victoria (victory). *See* VICTORIA (English Names). (VEE-KAH)

Vikaheilala Victoria of the heilala tree. (VEE-KAH-HAY-EE-LAH-LAH)

CHAPTER TWENTY-FOUR

Portuguese Names

NINETY-SEVEN percent of the population of Portugal is Roman Catholic and this directly influences the bestowal of names. As in other Catholic countries, many names are chosen from those of popular saints and Bible characters. By far the most popular name for females is Maria. Among males, João and José are popular.

Family names first developed as early as the 11th century among wealthy landowners and noblemen. Quite often they referred to themselves by using the names of their estates. Surnames became hereditary in the 15th century, and fixed in the 16th century. The majority of the names are patronymics, but some families derive their names from the names of trees, and a few are derived from nicknames based on physical characteristics.

Portuguese Male Names

ADÃO Portuguese cognate of Adam, a name derived from the Hebrew *adama* (red earth). The name is borne in the Bible by the first man created by God. (AH-DOW)

ADRIÃO Portuguese cognate of Adrian, a name derived from the Latin Adriānus (man from the city of Adria) and Hadriānus (man from the city of Hadria). (AHD-REE-OW)

AGOSTINHO Derived from the Latin Augustinus, a diminutive form of Augustus (great, venerable). *See* AUGUSTO. (AH-GO-STEE-NO)

ALBANO Derived from the Latin Albanus (from the Italian city of Alba). The name might have its root in the Latin *albus* (white). (AHL-BAH-NO)

ALBERTO Portuguese form of Albert (nobly bright), a name derived from the Old High German Adalbrecht, a compounding of the elements *adal* (noble) and *beraht* (bright, famous). (AHL-BARE-TŌ)

ALEXIO Derived from the Greek Alexios, which is derived from the verb *alexein* (to defend, to help): hence, "defender or helper." Var: Aleixo. (AH-LESH-EE-O)

ALFONSO Portuguese cognate of the French Alphonse (noble and ready), a name derived from the Old German Adalfuns, a compounding of the elements *adal* (noble) and *funs* (ready, prompt, apt). The name was borne by six kings of Portugal. Var: Affonso, Afonso. (AHL-FAHN-SO)

ALFREDO Portuguese cognate of Alfred (elf counsel), a name derived from the Old English Ælfred, a compounding of the elements *ælf* (elf) and *ræd* (counsel). Elves were considered to be supernatural beings having special powers of seeing into the future; thus the name took on the meaning "wise counsel." (AHL-FRĀ-DŌ)

ALVARO Portuguese cognate of the English Alvar (elfin army), a name derived from the Old English Ælfhere, a compounding of the elements *ælf* (elf) and *here* (army). (AHL-VAH-RO)

AMERICO Portuguese cognate of Amerigo, an Italian variant of Enrico (ruler of an enclosure, home ruler). *See* HENRIQUE. (AH-MAY-REE-KO)

ANDRE Portuguese cognate of the Greek Andreas, a name derived from *andreios* (manly). (AHN-DRAY)

ANGELO Derived from the Latin *angelus* (divine messenger, angel), which is from the Greek *angelos* (messenger). (AHN-ZHEH-LO)

ANTONIO Derived from the Latin Antōnius, an old Roman family name of unknown etymology. "Priceless" and "of inestimable worth" are popular folk definitions of the name. Short: Tonio. (AHN-TŌ-NEE-O)

ARMANDO Portuguese cognate of the German Hermann (soldier, warrior), which is from the Old High German Hariman, a compounding of the elements *heri* (army) and *man* (man). (AHR-MAHN-DŌ)

ARNALDO Portuguese cognate of Arnold (powerful as an eagle), a name derived from the Germanic Arnwald, a compounding of the elements *arn* (eagle) and *wald* (power, strength). (AHR-NAHL-DŌ)

AUGUSTO Derived from the Latin Augustus, which is derived from *augustus* (great, venerable, consecrated by the augurs). (OW-GOO-STO)

BAPTISTA Ecclesiastic Late Latin name derived from *baptista* (a baptist, one who baptizes). The name was traditionally bestowed in honor of John the Baptist, a kinsman and forerunner of Christ. (BAHP-TEES-TAH)

BARTHOLOMÃO Derived from the Late Latin Bartholomaeus and the Greek Bartholomaios (son of Talmai). Talmai is an Aramaic name meaning "hill, mound, furrows." Var: Bartolomeu. (BAHR-TŌ-LŌ-MOW)

BASTIÃO A short form of Sebastião (man from Sebastia), Bastiao is also bestowed as an independent given name. *See* SEBASTIÃO. (BAHS-TEE-OW)

BATHASAR Portuguese cognate of Balthasar, a name assigned to one of the Three Wise Men, who brought gifts to the Christ child. Some believe the name to be derived from the Chaldean Belshazzar (Bel's prince) or from the Persian Beltshazzar (prince of splendor). Others think the name might simply have been an invention with an Eastern sound to it. Var: Baltasar. (BAH-TAH-ZAHR)

BENEDICTO Derived from the Latin Benedictus, which is from *benedictus* (blessed). Var: Benedito. Short: Bento. (BEH-NEH-DEEK-TŌ)

BENJAMINHO Portuguese cognate of Benjamin, which is from the Hebrew Binyamin, a name derived from *binyāmīn* (son of the right hand). (BEH-ZHAH-MEE-NO)

BENTO A short form of Benedicto (blessed), Bento is also bestowed as an independent given name. *See* BENEDICTO. (BEN-TŌ)

BERNARDO From the Old High German Berinhard (strong as a bear), a compound name composed from the elements *bern* (bear) and *hard* (hearty, strong, brave). Var: Bernaldo, Bernardim. Pet: Bernardino. (BEHR-NAHR-DŌ)

BERTRÃO Portuguese cognate of Bertram, a name derived from the Old High German Berahtram (bright raven), a compound name composed of the elements *beraht* (bright, famous) and *hraban* (raven). (BEHR-TROW)

BOAVENTURA Portuguese form of the Italian Bonaventura, a compounding of the elements *bona* (good, fair) and *ventura* (luck, fortune). (BO-AH-VANE-TOO-RAH)

BRAZ Portuguese cognate of the French Blaise, a name of uncertain etymology. Some believe it is from the Latin Blaesus, which is from *blaesus* (deformed, stuttering). (BRAHSH)

CARLOS Portuguese cognate of Charles, which is from the Germanic *karl* (full-grown, a man). The name was borne by the Portuguese king Carlos I (1863–1908). Pet: Carlito, Carlitos. (KAHR-LOS)

CHRISTIANO Derived from the Latin *christiānus* (a Christian, a follower of Christ), which is from the Greek *christianos* (a Christian). Var: Cristiano. (SHREES-TEE-AH-NO)

CHRISTÔVÃO Portuguese cognate of Christopher (bearing Christ), a name derived from the Greek Christophoros, which is composed of the elements *Christos* (Christ) and *pherein* (to bear). Var: Cristóvão. (SHREE-STO-VOW)

CLEMENTE From the Late Latin Clēmens, which is derived from *clemens* (mild, gentle, merciful). (KLEH-MEN-TAY)

CYRILO Derived from the Late Latin Cyrillus, which is from the Greek Kyrillos (lordly), a derivative of *kyrios* (a lord). (SEE-REE-LO)

DAMIÃO Derived from the Greek Damianos, which is thought to be from *damān* (to tame). (DAH-ME-OW)

DANIEL Derived from the Hebrew *dāni'ēl* (God is my judge). (DAHN-EE-EHL)

David Derived from the Hebrew *dāvīd* (beloved). (DAH-VEED)

Demetrio Derived from the Greek Dēmētrios (of Demeter), which is from Demeter, the Greek mythological goddess of agriculture and fertility. (DEH-MEY-TREE-O)

Denis A borrowing from the French, Denis is from the Greek Dionysios (of Dionysos, the mythological god of wine and revelry). The name was borne by one king of Portugal. Var: Dinis. (DEH-NEES)

Diago Portuguese form of Diego, a Spanish diminutive form of Jaime, which is a cognate of James (supplanting, seizing by the heel). *See* JAIME. Var: Diogo. (DEE-AH-GO)

Dionysio Portuguese cognate of the Greek Dionysios (of Dionysos, the mythological god of wine and revelry). Var: Dionisio. (DEE-O-NEE-SEE-O)

Domingos Portuguese form of the Latin Dominicus (belonging to a lord), which is from *dominus* (a master, a lord). (DŌ-MEEN-GŌS)

Donato From the Late Latin Dōnāyus (given by God), which is derived from *donare* (to give, to donate). (DŌ-NAH-TŌ)

Duarte Portuguese form of Duardo, a short form of Eduardo (wealthy protector). *See* EDUARDO. Duarte is also bestowed as an independent given name. The name was borne by the Portuguese king Duarte I (1391–1438). (DOO-AHR-CHEE)

Edmundo Cognate of Edmund (wealthy protection), a name derived from the Old English Ēadmund, a compounding of the elements *ēad* (prosperity, riches, fortune) and *mund* (hand, protection). (EHD-MOON-DŌ)

Eduardo Portuguese cognate of Edward (wealthy protector), which is from the Old English Ēadweard, a compound name composed of the elements *ēad* (prosperity, riches, fortune) and *weard* (guardian, protector). Short: Duarte. (EH-DOO-AHR-DŌ)

Emilio Derived from the Latin Aemilius, an old Roman family name probably derived from *aemulus* (emulating, trying to equal or excel, rival). (Ā-MEE-LEE-O)

Estevão Portuguese cognate of Stephen, which is from the Greek Stephanos, a name derived from *stephanos* (a crown, a garland). (EH-STEH-VOW)

Fabião Portuguese cognate of Fabio, which is from Fabius, an old Roman family name derived from the Latin *faba* (a bean). (FAH-BEE-OW)

Fausto Derived from the Latin Faustus, which is from *fauste* (propitious, lucky, fortunate). (FAU-STO)

Felippe From the Latin Philippus (lover of horses), a derivative of the Greek Philippos, which is a compounding of the elements *philos* (loving) and *hippos* (horse). Var: Felipe, Felpinho. (FEH-LEEP-PEE)

Feliz Portuguese cognate of the Latin Felix, a name derived from *felix* (lucky, happy). (FEH-LEESH)

Fernando From the Spanish Ferdinando, a name of uncertain origin and meaning. It is thought to be of Germanic origin composed from the elements *frithu* (peace), *fardi* (journey), or *ferchvus* (youth, life) and *nanths* (courage), *nanthi* (venture, risk), or *nand* (ready, prepared). Var: Ferdinand, Fernão. (FEHR-NAHN-DŌ)

Flavio Derived from the Latin Flavius, which originated as an old Roman family name derived from *flāvus* (fair, blond, golden, tawny). (FLAH-VEE-O)

Francisco From the Middle Latin Franciscus (a Frenchman), which is from Francus (a Frank, a freeman), the root of which is the Old French *franc* (free). Var: Francisquinho. (FRAHN-SEES-KO)

Frederico Portuguese cognate of the Gemanic Friedrich, which is from the obsolete Fridurih, a compounding of the elements *frid* (peace) and *rik* (ruler, king). (FREH-DEH-REE-KO)

Gabrielo Portuguese cognate of Gabriel, which is from the Hebrew *gavhrī'ēl* (God is my strength). (GAH-BREE-EH-LO)

Germano Portuguese cognate of the German Hermann (soldier, warrior), which is from the Old High German Hariman, a compounding of the elements *hari* (army) and *man* (man). (ZHEHR-MAH-NO)

Gervasio Portuguese cognate of Gervaise, which is likely a derivative of the Old German Gervas, the first element of which is *ger* (a spear) and the second of which is believed to be from the Celtic vass (servant): hence, "servant of the spear." (ZEHR-VAHZ-EE-O)

Gilberto Portuguese cognate of the French Gilbert, an evolution of the Old French Guillebert, a derivative of the Old High German Gisilberht, which is composed of the elements *gisil* (pledge) and *beraht* (bright, famous). Short: Gil. (GEEL-BEHR-TŌ)

Gonçalo Portuguese form of the Spanish Gonzalo, a name derived from the Old German Gundisalvis (war combat). (GŌN-SAH-LO)

Gregorio Derived from the Latin Gregorius, a cognate of the Greek Grēgorios (vigilant, a watchman), which is derived from the verb *egeirein* (to awaken). (GREH-GOR-EE-O)

GUALTER Portuguese cognate of Walter, a name derived from the Frankish Waldhere (ruler of the army), a compounding of the elements *waldan* (to rule) and *heri, hari* (army). Var: Gualterio. (GWAL-TER)

GUILHERMO Portuguese cognate of William (resolute protector), a name derived from the Old Norman French Willaume, which is from the Old High German Willehelm, a compounding of the elements *willeo* (will) and *helm* (helmet, protection). Var: Guilherme. (GEHR-MO)

HEITOR Portuguese cognate of the Greek Hektor (steadfast, holding fast), a name derived from *echein* (to hold, to have). (EE-TOR)

HENRIQUE Cognate of Henry, which is from the German Heinrich (ruler of an enclosure, home ruler). The name is derived from the Old High German Haganrih, a compounding of the elements *hag* (an enclosure, a hedging-in) and *rihhi* (ruler), and from the Old High German Heimerich, a compound name composed of the elements *heim* (home, an estate) and *rik* (ruler, king). Var: Enrique. (EHN-REE-KAY)

HERBERTO Portuguese cognate of Herbert, which is from the Old English Herebeorht (bright army). *See* HERBERT (English Names). Var: Heriberto. (HARE-BARE-TŌ)

HERCULANO Derived from Hercules, the Latin form of the Greek Hērakleēs, a compound name composed from Hēra (the name of the mythological queen of the gods) and *kleos* (glory): hence, "glory of Hera, divine glory." (EHR-KOO-LAH-NO)

HIERONIMO Derived from the Greek Hieronymos (holy name), a compounding of the elements *hieros* (holy) and *onyma* (name). Var: Jeronimo. (Ā´RO-NEE-MO)

HILARIO Derived from the Latin Hilarius, which is from *hilaris* (cheerful, glad). (EE-LAHR-EE-O)

HORACIO Derived from the Latin Horatius, an old Roman family name of unknown etymology. There are some who believe it to be derived from the Latin *hora* (hour, time, period). (O-RAHS-EE-O)

HUBERTO Portuguese cognate of Hubert, a name derived from the Old High German Huguberht (bright in spirit), a compounding of the elements *hugu* (heart, mind, spirit) and *beraht* (bright, famous). (OO-BEHR-TO)

HUGO A borrowing from the German, Hugo is derived from the Old High German *hugu* (heart, mind, spirit). (OO-GO)

INÁCIO From the Latin Ignatius, a derivative of Egnatius, an old Roman family name of uncertain etymology. Some believe it to be of Etruscan origin. Others derive it from the Latin *ignis* (fire). The name was borne by several saints, including St. Ignatius of Loyola (1491–1556), a Spanish priest and founder of the Society of Jesus—the Jesuits. (EE-NAH-SEE-O)

ISIDORO From the Greek Isidōros (gift of Isis), a compound name composed of Isis, the name of an Egyptian goddess, and the Greek *dōron* (gift). (EE-SEE-DŌ-RO)

JACINTO Derived from the Greek Hyakinthos (hyacinth). (ZHAH-SEEN-TŌ)

JAIME Portuguese cognate of James, a name derived from the Ecclesiastic Late Latin Iacomus, an evolution of Iacobus, which is derived from the Greek Iakōbos. Iakōbos is from the Hebrew Yaakov, a derivative of *ya'aqob* (seizing by the heel, supplanting). Var: Jayme. (ZHAY-MEE)

JANUARIO Derived from the Latin *Januarius* (of Janus), the name of the first month of the year. It is derived from Janus, the name of the double-faced Roman mythological god in charge of guarding portals, and the patron of beginnings and endings. (ZHAH-NOO-AHR-EE-O)

JAVIER Derived from the surname Xavier, which is from the place-name Xavier in Navarre. The name, which is believed to be derived from the Basque Etcheberria (the new house), was originally bestowed in honor of St. Francis Xavier (1506—52), a Spanish missionary to Japan and the East Indies and the patron saint of missionaries in foreign lands.

JESÚS Portuguese form of Jesus, a name derived from the Ecclesiastic Late Latin Iesus and the Ecclesiastic Greek Iēsous, which are from the Hebrew *yēshū'a*, a contraction of *yehōshū'a* (Jehovah is help, God is salvation). The name is borne in the Bible by the Son of God and the Virgin Mary, the long-awaited Messiah who came to bring eternal life to all who accepted him as savior. The name, bestowed in honor of Christ, is often chosen by parents seeking to bring their child under the special protection of the Son of God. (ZHAY-ZOOSH)

JOÃNICO Portuguese form of John (God is gracious). *See* JOHN. Var: João, Joãozinho. (ZHO-AH-NEE-KO)

JOAQUIM Derived from the Hebrew Jeohiakim, which is from Yehoyakim (God will establish, God gives strength). In medieval Christian tradition, Joachim was the name assigned to the father of the Virgin Mary, as Anne was assigned to her mother. (ZHO-AH-KEEM)

JOHN Derived from the Middle Latin Johannes (God is gracious), an evolution of the Ecclesiastic Late Latin Joannes and the Ecclesiastic Greek Iōannes, derivatives of the Hebrew Yehanan, a short form of Yehohanan, which is from *yehōhānān* (Yahweh is gracious). The name was borne by six kings of Portugal. (ZHŌN)

JORDÃO Portuguese cognate of Jordan, a name derived from the Hebrew Yarden (to flow down, to descend). The name was originally used in the Middle Ages for a child baptized in holy water that was said to be from the river Jordan, the river in which Jesus was baptized by John the Baptist. (ZHŌR-DOW)

JORGE Portuguese cognate of George, which is from the Greek Geōrgios, a derivative of *geōrgos* (earthworker, farmer), which is composed of the elements *gē* (earth) and *ergein* (to work). Var: Jorgezinho. (ZHŌR-ZHEE)

JOSÉ Portuguese cognate of Joseph, an Ecclesiastic Late Latin form of the Greek Iōsēph, which is from the Hebrew Yosef, a derivative of *yōsēf* (may he add, God shall add). Var: Jozé. (ZHŌ-ZEE)

JULIÃO Portuguese form of Julian, which is from the Latin Julianus, a derivative of Julius (the first down on the chin, downy-bearded, youth). *See* JULIO. (ZHOO-LEE-OW)

JULIO Portuguese form of Julius, an old Roman family name thought to be derived from Iulus (the first down on the chin, downy-bearded). Because a person just beginning to develop facial hair is young, "youth" became an accepted definition of the name. (ZHOO-LEE-O)

LADISLÃO Portuguese cognate of the Slavonic Vladislav (glorious rule), a compound name composed of the elements *volod* (rule) and *slav* (glory). (LAH-DEE-SLOW)

LAURENCHO Portuguese cognate of Laurence, which is from the Latin Laurentius (man from Laurentum). Laurentum, the name of a town in Latium, is probably derived from *laurus* (laurel). Var: Laudalino, Lorenco, Lourenco. (LAH-REHN-SHO)

LEÃO Derived from the Latin *leo* (lion). (LAY-O)

LEONARDO From the Old High German Lewenhart, a compound name composed from the elements *lewo* (lion) and *hart* (strong, brave, hearty): hence, "strong as a lion, lion-hearted." (LAY-O-NAHR-DO)

LIBERATO Derived from the Latin Liberatus (he who has been liberated). (LEE-BEH-RAH-TŌ)

LUCIO Portuguese cognate of Lucius, which is from the root *lux* (light). (LOO-SEE-O)

LUIS Cognate of the French Louis (famous in war), a derivative of the Old French Loeis, which is from the Old High German Hluodowig, a compounding of the elements *hluod* (famous) and *wīg* (war, strife). The name was borne by the Portuguese king Luis I (1838–89). Var: Luiz. (LOO-EESH)

MANUEL Derived from the Greek Emmanouēl, which is from the Hebrew *'immānūēl* (God is with us). In the Bible Emmanuel is the name of the promised Messiah. The name was borne by two kings of Portugal. Var: Manoel. (MAH-NOO-EL)

MARCOS Derived from the Latin Marcus, a name of uncertain derivation. Most believe it has its root in Mars, the name of the Roman mythological god of war. Others, however, think it is from *mas* (manly) or from the Greek *malakoz* (soft, tender). Var: Marco. (MAHR-KOSH)

MARIO Derived from the Latin Marius, an old Roman family name of uncertain derivation. Some believe it has its root in Mars, the name of the Roman mythological god of war, but others think it might be from *mas* (manly) or from the Greek *malakoz* (soft, tender). (MAH-REE-O)

MARTINHO From the Latin Martinus (war-like), a derivative of Mars, the name of the Roman mythological god of war. Var: Martin. (MAHR-TEE-NO)

MATTEUS Derived from the Ecclesiastic Late Latin Matthaeus and the Ecclesiastic Greek Matthaios and Matthias, contractions of Mattathias. The name has its root in the Hebrew Matityah, which is derived from *mattīthyāh* (gift of God). Var: Mateus. (MAH-TAY-OOS)

MAURICIO Derived from the Latin Mauritius (Moorish), a derivative of Maurus (a Moor). The Moors were a Muslim people of mixed Arab and Berber descent; thus the name came to mean "dark" or "swarthy" in reference to their coloring. (MAH-REE-SEE-O)

MAXIMILIAO Portuguese cognate of Maximilian, a blending of the Latin names Maximus and Aemiliānus used by Friedrich III, who bestowed it upon his first-born son, Maximilian I (1459–1519) in honor of two famous Roman generals. Maximus is derived from the Latin *maximus* (greatest), but the etymology of Aemiliānus is uncertain. Some believe it to be from the Latin *aemulus* (emulating, trying to equal or excel, rival). (MAHKS-EE-MEE-LEE-AH-O)

MAXIMINO Derived from the Latin Maximus, a name directly derived from the vocabulary word meaning "greatest." (MAH-ZEE-MEE-NO)

MIGUEL Portuguese cognate of Michael, a derivative of the Hebrew *mīkhā'ēl* (who is like God?). (MEE-GWELL)

MOISES Portuguese cognate of Moses, an Ecclesiastic Greek name derived from the Hebrew Moshe, which is from *mōsheh* (drawn out, drawn out of the water) and the Egyptian *mes, mesu* (son, child). (MO-EE-ZEHSH)

NICOLAIO Portuguese cognate of Nicholas (victory of the people), a name derived from the Greek Nikolaos, which is composed of the elements *nikē* (victory) and *laos* (the people). Var: Nicolau. (NEE-KO-LAH-EE-O)

OLIVIÊROS Portuguese cognate of the French Olivier, a name derived from the Old French *olivier* (olive tree). However, some believe it to be Germanic in origin and derived from the Middle Low German Alfihar (elf army), a compounding of the elements *alf* (elf) and *hari* (army). Var: Oliverio. (O-LEE-VYEH-RŌSH)

OSVALDO Portuguese form of Oswald, which is from the Old English Osweald, a compound name composed of the elements *os* (a god) and *weald* (power): hence, "divine power." (OS-VAHL-DŌ)

OTHÃO Portuguese cognate of Othello (rich). (O-TOW)

OTAVIO Portuguese form of Octavius, which is derived from the Latin *octavus* (eighth). (O-TAH-VEE-O)

PASCOAL From the Late Latin Paschālis (of Easter), a derivative of Pascha (Easter), which is from the Hebrew *pesach, pesah* (Passover). The name is often bestowed upon children born during the Easter season. (PAHS-KO-AHL)

PATRICIO Derived from the Latin *patricius* (a patrician, an aristocrat). (PAH-TREE-SEE-O)

PAULO Derived from the Latin Paulus, a Roman family name derived from *paulus* (small). (PAH-OO-LO)

PEDRO Portuguese form of Peter, which is from the Ecclesiastic Late Latin Petrus and the Ecclesiastic Greek Petros, names derived from the vocabulary words *petra* (a rock) and *petros* (a stone). The name was borne by five Portuguese kings. Var: Pedrinho. (PEH-dro)

PLACIDO Derived from the Late Latin Placidus, a direct derivation of *placidus* (gentle, quiet, calm, placid). (PLAH-SEE-DŌ)

RAFAEL Derived from the Ecclesiastic Late Latin Raphael and the Ecclesiastic Greek Rhaphēl, which are from the Hebrew Refael, a name derived from *refā'ēl* (God has healed). (RAH-FĪ-EL)

RAIMUNDO From the Old French Raimund, a name derived from the Germanic Raginmund, a compound name composed of the elements *ragin* (advice, counsel) and *mund* (hand, protection): hence, "wise protection." (RĪ-MOON-DŌ)

REINALDO From the Old High German Raganald and Raginold, compound names composed from the elements *ragna, ragina* (advice, counsel) and *wald* (ruler): hence, "ruler of judgment." (RAY-NAHL-DŌ)

REMIGIO Portuguese form of the French Rémy, which is from the Latin Rēmigius, a name derived from *rēmigis* (oarsman). (REH-MEE-ZHEE-O)

RENATO From the Late Latin Renātus, which is a direct derivative of *renātus* (reborn, born again). (REH-NAH-TŌ)

RICARDO Portuguese cognate of Richard (brave ruler), which is from the Old High German Richart, a compound name composed of the elements *rik* (king, ruler) and *hart* (hearty, brave, strong). (REE-KAHR-DŌ)

ROBERTO Portuguese form of Robert (bright with fame), which is derived from the Old High German Hruodperht, a compound name composed of the elements *hruod* (fame) and *beraht* (bright). (RO-BEHR-TŌ)

RODRIGO Portuguese cognate of Roderick (famous ruler), a name derived from the Middle Latin Rodericus, which is from the Old High German Hrodrich, a compounding of the elements *hruod* (fame) and *rik* (ruler). Short: Rui. (RO-DREE-GO)

ROGERIO Portuguese cognate of Roger (spear fame), a name derived from the Old High German Hrodger, a compounding of the elements *hruod* (fame) and *ger* (a spear). (RO-ZHEH-REE-O)

ROLANDO Derived from the French Roland, which is from the Old High German Hruodland, a compounding of the elements *hruod* (fame) and *land* (land): hence, "fame of the land, famous land." Var: Roldao. (RO-LAHN-DŌ)

ROMAO Derived from the Latin Romanus (a Roman), which is from Roma, the Italian name of the capital city of Italy. (RO-MAH-O)

SALOMÃO Portuguese cognate of Solomon, an Ecclesiastic Greek name derived from the Hebrew *shᵉlōmōh* (peaceful), which is from *shālōm* (peace). (SAH-LO-MOW)

SAMSÃO Portuguese cognate of Samson, a name derived from the Ecclesiastic Greek Sampsōn, which is from the Hebrew *shimshōn* (sun). (SAHM-SOW)

SEBASTIÃO From the Latin Sebastiānus, a derivative of the Greek Sebastianos (a man of Sebastia, a town in Asia Minor). Short: Bastião. (SEH-BAHS-TEE-OW)

SERAFIM From the Ecclesiastic Late Latin *seraphim* (burning ones, the angels surrounding the throne of God), which is from the Hebrew *šerāphīm*, a word believed to be derived from *sāraph* (to burn). (SEHR-AH-FEEM)

SILVINO From the Latin Silvānus (of the woods), which is derived from *silva* (a wood). Silvanus was a Roman mythological god of the woods and fields. (SEEL-VEE-NO)

SILVIO Derived from the Latin *silva* (a forest, a wood). (SEEL-VEE-O)

SIMÃO Portuguese form of Simon, an Ecclesiastic Greek form of the Hebrew Shimon, which is derived from *shim'ōn* (heard). (SEE-MOW)

STANISLÃO Portuguese form of the Slavonic Stanislav (glorious government), a compounding of the elements *stan* (government) and *slav* (glory). Var: Estanislau. (STAH-NEES-LOW)

TADEU Portuguese cognate of Thaddeus, an Ecclesiastic Late Latin name derived from the Ecclesiastic Greek Thaddaios, which is of uncertain derivation. Some believe it to be a variant of Theodōros (God's gift). Others feel it is from an Aramaic word meaning "praised." (TAH-DAYOO)

THEOBALDO Derived from the Old German Theudobald and Theodblad, compound names composed of the elements *thiuda* (folk, people) and *bald* (brave, bold): hence, "brave people." (TEH-O-BAHL-DŌ)

THEODORICO Portuguese cognate of Theodoric (ruler of the people), which is from the Late Latin Theodoricus, a derivative of the Germanic Thiudoreiks, which is composed of the elements *thiuda* (folk, people) and *rik* (ruler, king). Var: Teodorico. (TEH-O-DŌ-REE-KO)

THEODORO Portuguese cognate of Theodore (God's gift). The name is derived from the Greek Theodōros, a compounding of the elements *theos* (God) and *dōron* (gift). Var: Teodoro. (TEH-O-DŌ-RO)

THEODOSIO Derived from the Greek Theodosios, a compound name composed of the elements *theos* (God) and *dosis* (a gift, a giving): hence, "a gift of God, God-given." Var: Teodosio. (TEH-O-DŌ-SEE-O)

THEOFHILO Derived from the Greek Theophilos (beloved of God, lover of God), a compounding of the elements *theos* (God) and *philos* (loving). Var: Teofilo. (TEH-O-FEE-LO)

TIMOTEO From the Latin Timotheus, a derivative of the Greek Timotheos, a compound name derived from the elements *timē* (honor, respect) and *theos* (GOD). (TEE-MO-TAY-O)

TOMÁS Portuguese form of Thomas, an Ecclesiastic Greek name derived from the Aramaic *tě'ōma* (a twin). Var: Tomáz. (TŌ-MAHSH)

TONIO A short form of Antonio, the Portuguese cognate of Anthony, Tonio is also bestowed as an independent given name. *See* ANTONIO. (TŌ-NEE-O)

TRISTÃO Portuguese form of Tristan, which is from the Gaelic Drystan, a name derived from *drest* (tumult, riot). *See* TRISTRAM (English Names). (TREEST-OW)

VINCENTE From the Late Latin Vincentius (conquering), which is derived from *vincere* (to conquer). (VEEN-KEN-TEE)

ZACHARIAS Ecclesiastic Greek name derived from the Hebrew *zeharyah* (God remembers, remembrance of the Lord). (ZASH-AH-REE-AHSH)

ZACHEO Portuguese form of Zacchaeus, a derivative of the Ecclesiastic Greek Zacharias (remembrance of the Lord). *See* ZACHARIAS. (ZASH-EH-O)

Portuguese Female Names

ADELA From the French Adèle, a short form of any of the various names containing the Germanic element *adal* (noble). Dim: Adelina. (AH-DEH-LAH)

ADELINA A diminutive form of Adela (noble), Adelina is commonly bestowed as an independent given name. (AH-DEH-LEE-NAH)

ADRIANA Feminine form of Adrián (man from the city of Adria, man from the city of Hadria). (AH-DREE-AH-NAH)

AGOSTINHA Feminine form of Agostinho, the Portuguese cognate of the Latin Augustinus, which is a diminutive form of Augustus (great, venerable). (AH-GO-STEEN-AH)

AGUEDA Derived from the Portuguese *agueda* (pure). (AH-GOO-EH-DAH)

ALBERTINA Feminine form of Alberto (noble, bright). *See* ALBERTO (Male Names). (AHL-BER-TEE-NAH)

Amélia Derived from the German Amalia, a name derived from *amal* (work). Alternatively, Amelia may be a variant of the Latin Aemilia, a feminine form of Aemiliūs, an old Roman family name probably derived from *aemulus* (emulating, trying to equal or excel, rival). (AH-MAY-LEE-AH)

Ana The Portuguese cognate of Anna, a name derived from the Hebrew Hannah, which is from *hannāh*, *chaanach* (gracious, full of grace, mercy). In medieval Christian tradition, Anne was the name assigned to the mother of the Virgin Mary, as Joachim was assigned to her father. (AH-NAH)

Anamaria Popular combination name made up of the names Ana (gracious, full of grace) and Maria. *See* ANA *and* MARIA. (AH-NAH-MAH-REE-AH)

Angela Derived from the Latin *angelus* (angel, messenger of God, guiding spirit), which is from the Greek *angelos* (messenger, messenger of God). (AHN-ZHEH-LAH)

Angelina Diminutive form of Angela (angel, messenger of God, guiding spirit). *See* ANGELA. (AHN-ZHEH-LEE-NAH)

Assuncão Derived from the Portuguese *assuncão* (assumption). The name makes reference to the assumption of the Virgin Mary to heaven following her death. (AH-SOON-KOW)

Bárbara Derived from the Latin *barbarus* (foreign, strange), Bárbara has the definition "foreign woman." (BAHR-BAHR-AH)

Beatrix Latin name derived from *beatrix* (she who makes happy, she who brings happiness). The variant form Beatrice was borne by one queen of Portugal. Var: Beatrice, Beatriz. (BAY-AH-TREES)

Benedicta Feminine form of Benedicto, which is derived from the Latin *benedictus* (blessed). (BEH-NEH-DEEK-TAH)

Bianca A borrowing from the Italian, Bianca is derived from *bianca* (white, fair). (BEE-AHN-KAH)

Brites Portuguese cognate of the Irish Bríghid, which is believed to be derived from the Gaelic *brígh* (strength). *See* BRIGIDA (Italian Names). (BREE-TESH)

Caridade Derived from the Portuguese *caridade* (charity). (KAH-REE-DAH-JEE)

Carla Popular feminine form of Carlos, a cognate of Charles (full-grown, a man). (KAR-LAH)

Carlota Portuguese form of the French Charlotte, a feminine form of Charlot, which is a diminutive form of Charles (full-grown, a man). (KAHR-LO-TAH)

Carmen Portuguese cognate of Carmel (vineyard, orchard), which is from the Hebrew. Mount Carmel is a mountain in northwestern Israel which was inhabited in early Christian times by a group of hermits who later became Carmelite monks in the Order of Our Lady of Mount Carmel. The name is usually bestowed in reference to the Virgin Mary, "Our Lady of Carmel." Var: Carma. (KAR-MEHN)

Carolina Feminine form of Carolus, which is a cognate of Charles (full-grown, a man). *See* CARLOS (Male Names). Var: Caralina. (KAHR-O-LEE-NAH)

Catherine Derived from the Greek Aikaterinē, which is from *katharos* (pure, unsullied). Var: Catarina. (KAH-TEH-REE-NEE)

Cecília Derived from the Latin Caecilius, an old Roman family name derived from *caecus* (blind, dimsighted). (SAY-SEE-LEE-AH)

Célia Derived from the Latin Caelia, a feminine form of Caelius, an old Roman family name thought to be derived from *caelum* (heaven). (SAY-LEE-AH)

Christinha Portuguese form of Christine, a derivative of the Ecclesiastic Late Latin *christiānus*, which is from the Greek *christianos* (a Christian, a follower of Christ). Var: Cristina. (SHREE-STEEN-AH)

Conceição Portuguese cognate of the Spanish Concepción, a name derived from the Latin *conceptio* (conception). The name, bestowed in honor of the Virgin Mary, is in reference to her sinlessness from the moment of conception. Var: Conceisão. (KŌN-SEH-EE-SOW)

Constancia Portuguese cognate of the French Constantia, which is derived from the Latin *constans* (standing together, constancy). (KŌN-STAHN-SEE-AH)

Daniela Feminine form of Daniel (God is my judge). *See* DANIEL (Male Names). (DAH-NEE-EH-LAH)

Deolinda Compound name composed of the elements *deo* (God) and *linda* (beautiful, pretty): hence, "beautiful God." (DEH-O-LEEN-DAH)

Diamantina Derived from the Portuguese *diamante* (diamond). (DEE-AH-MAHN-TEE-NAH)

Diana Derived from the Latin Diviana, which is from *divus* (divine). (DEE-AH-NAH)

Dolores Derived from *dolores* (sorrows, suffering). The name, bestowed in honor of the Virgin Mary, makes reference to the seven sorrows of Mary in her relationship with her son. Short: Dores. (DŌ-LO-RESH)

EDUARDA Feminine form of Eduardo (wealthy protector), a cognate of the English Edward. *See* EDUARDO (Male Names). (EH-DOO-AHR-DAH)

ELIANA Derived from the Late Latin Aeliāna, the feminine form of the Latin family name Aeliānus (of the sun), which is derived from the Greek *hēlios* (sun). (EH-LEE-AH-NAH)

ELIZABETA Popular name derived from the Hebrew *elīsheba'* (God is my oath). The name is borne in the Bible by a kinswoman of the Virgin Mary and mother of John the Baptist. Var: Elzira. Short: Lizete. (EH-LEE-ZAH-BEH-TAH)

ELVIRA Portuguese and Spanish name of uncertain etymology. Some believe it to be of Gothic origin. "Amiable" and "friendly" are popular folk definitions of the name. (EHL-VEE-RAH)

EMILIA From the Latin Aemilia, which is from Aemilius, an old Roman family name probably derived from *aemulus* (trying to equal or excel, rival). Var: Emiliana. (Ā-MEE-LEE-AH)

ESTEPHANIA Feminine form of Estevão, the Portuguese cognate of Stephen (a crown, a garland). *See* ESTEVÃO (Male Names). (EH-STEH-FAH-NEE-AH)

EUFEMIA A borrowing from the Italian, Eufemia is derived from the Greek Euphēmia, a compound name composed of the elements *eu* (good, well, fair) and *phēmē* (voice): hence, "of fair voice." (EH-OO-FEH-MEE-AH)

EUGÊNIA Feminine form of Eugênio, the Portuguese cognate of Eugene, which is from the Latin Eugenius and the Greek Eugenios, names derived from *eugenēs* (wellborn, noble). (ĀFOO-ZHAY-NEE-AH)

EVA Derived from the Hebrew Chava, which is from *hawwāh* (life). The name is borne in the Bible by the first woman, "the mother of all the living." She is said to have been formed from Adam's rib. (EH-VAH)

FATIMA Derived from the Arabic *fātima* (she who weans an infant; one who abstains from forbidden things). The name is that of a town in Portugal where the Virgin Mary appeared to three young children in 1917. It is usually in the honor of Our Lady of Fatima, the Virgin Mary, that the name is bestowed. (FAH-TEE-MAH)

FELIPA Feminine form of Felippe, the Portuguese cognate of Philip (lover of horses). *See* FELIPPE (Male Names). (FEH-LEE-PAH)

FERNANDA Feminine form of Fernando, a name of uncertain origin and meaning. *See* FERNANDO. (FEHR-NAHN-DAH)

FORTUNATA Feminine form of the Late Latin Fortūnātus, a direct derivation of *fortūnātus* (fortunate, prosperous, lucky). (FOR-TOO-NAH-TAH)

FRANCISCA Feminine form of Francisco (a Frenchman). *See* FRANCISCO (Male Names). (FRAHN-SEESH-KAH)

FRANCISCA-JOSEPHA Popular combination name composed of the names Francisca (a Frenchwoman) and Josepha (he shall add). *See* FRANCISCA *and* JOSEPHA. (FRAHN-SEESH-KAH-ZHO-ZEH-FAH)

FREDERICA Feminine form of Frederico (peace ruler). *See* FREDERICO (Male Names). (FREH-DEH-REE-KAH)

GABRIELA Feminine form of Gabrielo, which is derived from the Hebrew *gavhrī'ēl* (God is my strength). (GAH-BREE-ELL-LAH)

GENOVEVA Derived from the Gaulish Genovefa, a name with Celtic roots but the meaning of which is uncertain. The first element is believed to be from *genos* (race, people, tribe); the second is possibly from an element meaning "woman." (ZHEH-NO-VEH-VAH)

GEORGETA Derived from the French Georgette, a feminine diminutive form of George, which is from the Greek Geōrgios, a derivative of *geōrgos* (earthworker, farmer). (ZHEH-OR-ZHEH-TAH)

GILBERTA Feminine form of Gilberto (bright pledge). *See* GILBERTO (Male Names). (ZHEEL-BEHR-TAH)

GLORIA Latin name derived from *glōria* (glory). (GLOR-EE-AH)

GRACA Derived from the Portuguese *graca* (graceful, elegance or beauty of form). Var: Graça, Gracinha. (GRAH-KAH)

HELENA Derived from the Greek Helenē, which is from the element *ēlē* (light, torch, bright). (EH-LEH-NAH)

HENRIQUETA Feminine form of Henrique (ruler of an enclosure, home ruler), the Portuguese cognate of Henry. *See* HENRIQUE (Male Names). (EHN-REE-KWEH-TAH)

HILARIÃO Feminine form of Hilario, a name derived from the Latin *hilaris* (cheerful, glad). (EE-LAH-REE-OW)

HORACIA Feminine form of Horacio, a name of unknown etymology. *See* HORACIO (Male Names). (OR-AH-SEE-AH)

Inez Portuguese form of Agnes, a name derived from the Greek Hagnē, which is from *hagnos* (chaste, pure, sacred). *See* AGNESE (Italian Names). Var: Inaz, Inês. (EE-NEHZ)

Isabela Variant form of Elizabeth, which is derived from the Hebrew *elīsheba'* (God is my oath). The name was borne by three queens of Portugal. Var: Isabel, Isabelinha. (EE-SAH-BEH-LAH)

Isabela Rosa Popular combination name composed of the names Isabela (God is my oath) and Rosa (a Rose). *See* ISABELA *and* ROSA. (EE-SAH-BEH-LAH-RO-ZAH)

Jacinta From the Latin *hyacinthus* (hyacinth), which is derived from the Greek *hyakinthos* (wild hyacinth, blue larkspur, a blue gem). (ZHAH-SEEN-TAH)

Joana From the Middle Latin Johanna, a feminine form of Johannes (God is gracious). Var: Joaniniha, Johannina, Jovanna. (ZHO-AH-NAH)

Joquina Feminine form of Joaquim (God will establish, God gives strength). *See* JOAQUIM (Male Names). (ZHO-KWEE-NAH)

Josepha Feminine form of Joseph, which is ultimately derived from the Hebrew *yōsēf* (he shall add, God will add). *See* JOSÉ (Male Names). Josepha is also used as a popular element in combination names. Var: Josefa. (ZHO-ZEH-FAH)

Josephina From the French Joséphine, a feminine form of Joseph (he shall add, God will add). Var: Josefina. (ZHO-ZEH-FEE-NAH)

Julia Feminine form of the Latin Julius, an old Roman family name thought to be derived from Iulus (the first down on the chin, downy-bearded, youth). (ZHOO-LEE-AH)

Juliana Latin feminine form of Julianus, from the old Roman family name Julius, which is believed to be derived from Iulus (downy-bearded, youth). Short: Liana. (ZHOO-LEE-AH-NAH)

Laurenza Feminine form of Laurencho (man from Laurentum). *See* LAURENCHO (Male Names). Var: Laudalina, Laurençya, Laurinda. (LAH-OO-REHN-ZHAH)

Leonor Portuguese form of Eleanor, a name derived from Alienor, a Provençal form of the Greek Helenē, which is derived from the element *ēlē* (light, torch, bright). The name was borne by the wife of King John II and mother of King Manuel I. (LEH-O-NOR)

Leticia Derived from the Latin *laetitia* (gladness, happiness, joy). (LAY-TEE-SEE-AH)

Liberada Feminine form of Liberato, a name derived from the Latin Liberatus (he who has been liberated). The name was borne by a mystical saint of Portugal who grew a beard to maintain her vow of virginity. (LEE-BEH-RAH-DAH)

Lúcia Feminine form of the Latin Lucius, which is derived from *lux* (light). (LOO-SHEE-AH)

Lucinda Elaborated form of Lúcia (light). Lucinda originated as a literary name in Cervantes' *Don Quixote* (1605). (LOO-SEEN-DAH)

Luísa Feminine form of Luis (famous in war), the Portuguese cognate of Louis. *See* LUIS (Male Names). Var: Luíza, Luizinha. (LOO-EE-SAH)

Magdalena Derived from the Ecclesiastic Greek Magdalēnē (of Magdala, a town near the Sea of Galilee). Var: Madalena. (MAH-DAH-LAY-NAH)

Manuela Feminine form of Manuel (God with us). *See* MANUEL (Male Names). (MAHN-WAY-LAH)

Margarita Derived from the Greek Margarītēs, which is from *margaron* (a pearl). Var: Margareda, Margarida, Mariquinhas, Mariquita. Short: Rita. Pet: Guidinha. (MAHR-GAH-REE-TAH)

Maria A highly popular name, Maria is the Latin form of Mary, which is derived from the Hebrew Miryām, which is of debated meaning. Many believe it to mean "sea of bitterness" or "sea of sorrow." However, some sources cite the alternative definitions of "rebellion," "wished-for child," and "mistress or lady of the sea." The name, borne in the Bible by the virgin mother of Jesus, has become one of the most enduringly popular names in the Christian world. It is usually bestowed in reverence for the Virgin Mary and to bring the child under the special protection of the Mother of God. In Portugal the name was borne by two queens, the last being Maria II (1819–53), the mother of eleven children, including Pedro V (1837–61) and Luis I (1838–89). (MAH-REE-AH)

Maria Amelia Popular combination name composed of the names Maria and Amelia. *See* AMELIA *and* MARIA. (MAH-REE-AH-AH-MEH-LEE-AH)

Maria da Assuncão Combination name composed of the names Maria and Assuncão. *See* MARIA *and* ASSUNCÃO. The name makes reference to the assumption of the Virgin Mary to heaven following her death. (MAH-REE-AH-DAH-AH-SOON-KOW)

Maria da Gloria Combination name composed of the names Maria and Gloria. *See* GLORIA *and* MARIA. (MAH-REE-AH-DAH-GLOR-EE-AH)

Maria das Neves Combination name composed of the names Maria and Neves. The name is bestowed in honor of the Virgin Mary, "Maria of Snows," which is in reference to the miracle in Rome of unmelted snow during hot weather. *See* MARIA *and* NEVES. (MAH-REE-AH-DAHSH-NEH-VESH)

Maria Josepha Combination name composed of the names Maria and Josepha. The name is bestowed in honor of the mother and foster father of Christ. *See* JOSEPHA *and* MARIA. (MAH-REE-AH-ZHO-ZEH-FAH)

Mariana Feminine form of the Latin Mariānus, a derivative of Marius, which is an old Roman family name of uncertain derivation. Some believe the name has its root in Mars, the Roman mythological god of war, but others think it is derived from the Latin *mas* (manly). Early Christians associated the name with Maran, the Latin name of the Virgin Mary. (MAH-REE-AH-NAH)

Mariana Victoria Combination name composed of the names Maria and Victoria (victory). *See* MARIA *and* VICTORIA. The name was borne by Mariana Victoria of Spain (1718–81), a queen of Portugal. (MAH-REE-AH-NAH-VEEK-TOR-EE-AH)

Maria Pia Combination name composed of the names Maria and Pia. *See* MARIA *and* PIA. The name was borne by the wife of King Luis I (1838–89). (MAH-REE-AH-PEE-AH)

Marta Portuguese form of Martha, an Aramaic name derived from *mārthā* (lady, mistress). The name is borne in the Bible by the sister of Lazarus and Mary of Bethany. (MAHR-TAH)

Miguela Feminine form of Miguel, a cognate of Michael (who is like God?). *See* MIGUEL (Male Names). (MEE-GWEL-AH)

Monica Ancient name of uncertain etymology. *See* MONICA (Greek Names). (MO-NEE-KAH)

Natalia Latin name derived from *diēs nātālis* (natal day, Christmas). Natalia is traditionally bestowed upon children born on Christmas Day. (NAH-TAH-LEE-AH)

Neves Derived from the Portuguese *neves* (snows). The name makes reference to a title of the Virgin Mary, "*Maria das Neves*" (Maria of Snows). (NAY-VESH)

Olimpia Derived from the Greek Olympia, a feminine form of Olympios (of Olympus). Olympus is a mountain in northern Greece which was the home of the gods in Greek mythology. Short: Pia. (O-LEEM-PEE-AH)

Olivia Derived from the Latin *oliva* (a tree of the olive family). A branch from the olive tree has long been regarded as a symbol of peace. (O-LEE-VEE-AH)

Patricia Feminine form of Patrick, which is derived from the Latin *patricius* (a patrician). (PAH-TREE-SHA)

Paula Feminine form of Paulo, the Portuguese cognate of Paul (small). *See* PAULO (Male Names). (POW-LAH)

Pia A short form of Olimpia (of Olympus), Pia is also popularly bestowed as an independent given name. (PEE-AH)

Roberta Feminine form of Roberto (bright with fame). *See* ROBERTO (Male Names). (RO-BEHR-TAH)

Rosa Popular name derived from *rosa* (a rose). Rosa is also used as a common name element in combination names, and as a short form of those names. (RO-ZAH)

Rosalina Portuguese form of Rosalinda, an evolution of the Germanic Roslindis, which is a compound name composed from the elements *hrôs* (fame) and *lind* (gentle, tender, soft). (RO-ZAH-LEE-NAH)

Roseta Diminutive form of Rosa (a rose). (RO-ZEH-TAH)

Sabina Latin name meaning "Sabine woman." The Sabines were an ancient tribe living in central Italy who were conquered by the Romans in 3 B.C. (SAH-BEE-NAH)

Salomão Portuguese cognate of Salome, an Ecclesiastic Greek name derived from the Hebrew *shālōm* (peace). Salome was the name of the daughter of Herodias whose dancing so pleased Herod that he granted her request for the head of John the Baptist. In spite of its history, the name remains popular in many countries. Var: Salamão. (SAH-LO-MOW)

Sara Derived from the Hebrew *sārāh* (princess). (SAHR-AH)

Silvia Derived from the Latin *silva* (a wood). (SEEL-VEE-AH)

Tatiana Borrowed from the Russian, Tatiana is a feminine form of Tatiānus, which is believed to be derived from Tatius, a name of uncertain origin which was borne by a king of the Sabines who ruled jointly with Romulus. (TAH-TEE-AH-NAH)

Teresa Of uncertain etymology, Teresa is generally believed to be derived from the Greek *therizein* (to reap, to gather in) and thus takes the definition of "harvester." The first known bearer of the name was the Spanish wife of St. Paulinus, a 5th-century Roman bishop of Nola. Teresa was not used outside the Iberian Peninsula until the 16th century, when the fame of St. Teresa of Avila (1515–82) made the name popular among Roman

Catholics throughout Europe. Var: Tereza, Theresa. (TEH-REH-ZAH)

URSULA Middle Latin diminutive form of *ursa* (she-bear). The name was borne by a legendary 4th-century saint, a Christian British princess said to have been martyred along with eleven thousand virgins by the Huns at Cologne. The story was very popular in the Middle Ages, which helped establish the name throughout Europe. (OOR-SOO-LAH)

VICTORIA Derived from the Latin *victoria* (victory). (VEEK-TOR-EE-AH)

VIDONIA Latin name derived from *vinea* (a vine, a branch). (VEE-DŌ-NEE-AH)

VIOLANTE Derived from the French Violette, a diminutive form of Viole, which is from the Latin *viola* (a violet). (VEE-O-LAHN-TEE)

ZENAIDE Greek name meaning "pertaining to Zeus," which is derived from *zēn* (of Zeus). Zeus was the supreme deity of the ancient Greeks. (ZEH-NAH-EE-DEE)

CHAPTER TWENTY-FIVE

Romanian Names

THE MODERN country of Romania originated when the kingdom of Dacia became a Roman province in the 2nd century. At this time, the Rumanian language was born out of a mix of Vulgar Latin and native tongues.

Following the departure of the legionnaires, the area was invaded by various Germanic and Slavic tribes, the Bulgarians, and the Magyars. All levels of society were affected as people began to trade and intermarry.

The Romanian names found today are the legacy of these different cultural groups. German names, Hungarian names, and names of Latin and Slavic origin are quite common. As in other countries with a Catholic tradition, many names are taken from those of popular saints and historical figures. Also popular are borrowings from other countries, in particular, those from the former Communist bloc.

Romanian Male Names

ADRIAN From the Latin Adriānus (man from the city of Adria) and Hadriānus (man from the city of Hadria). The name was borne by several popes of the Catholic Church, which helped spread its use across Europe. (AHD-REE-AHN)

ALEXANDRU Derived from the Greek Alexandros (defender or helper of mankind), a compounding of the elements *alexein* (to defend, to help) and *andros* (man). Short: Sandru. (AH-LEHK-SAHN-DRU)

ANATOLIE Derived from the Greek Anatolios, a derivative of *anatolē* (sunrise, daybreak, dawn). (AH-NAH-TŌ-LEE)

ANDREI Romanian cognate of Andrew, which is from the Greek Andreas, a name derived from *andreios* (manly), which is from the root *anēr* (man). Pet: Dela. (AHN-DREE)

ANTON Romanian form of Anthony, which is from the old Roman family name Antonius, a name of uncertain origin and meaning. (AHN-TOHN)

BELA A borrowing from the Hungarian, Bela is believed to be the Magyar form of Albert (nobly bright), which is derived from the Old High German Adalbrecht, a compound name composed of the elements *adal* (noble) and *beraht* (bright, famous). (BEH-LAH)

BENEDIKTE Derived from the Latin Benedictus (blessed), which is from *benedicere* (to speak well of, to bless). (BEH-NEH-DEEK-TEH)

BORIS A borrowing from the Russian, Boris is derived from *boris* (fight). (BO-REES)

CAROL Romanian form of Charles (full-grown, a man). The name is derived from the Germanic *karl* (full-grown, a man) and has been borne by two Romanian kings, Carol I (1839–1914) and Carol II (1893–1953). (KAH-REL)

CRISTOFOR From the Ecclesiastic Late Latin Christophorus, which is derived from the Ecclesiastic Greek Christophoros, a compound name composed from the elements *Christos* (Christ) and *pherein* (to bear): hence, "bearing Christ." The name was borne by St. Christopher, a 3rd-century Christian martyr who is the patron saint of travelers. (KREE-STO-FOR)

DANIEL Derived from the Hebrew *dānī'ēl* (God is my judge). Var: Danila. Short: Dan. (DAHN-YEL)

DEMETRI Derived from the Greek Demetrios (of Demeter). Demeter is an ancient name of unknown etymology borne in Greek mythology by the goddess of agriculture and fertility. Var: Dimitru. (DEH-MEH-TREE)

DOMINIK From the Latin Dominicus (belonging to a lord), which is derived from *dominus* (a lord, a master). (DAH-MEE-NEEK)

EMIL A borrowing from the German, Emil is from the Latin Aemilius, an old Roman family name of uncertain derivation. Some believe it to be from the Latin *aemulus* (emulating, trying to equal or excel, rival). (EE-MEEL)

FELIX Derived from the Latin *felix* (lucky, happy). Felix was the name of four popes and several early saints. (FEH-LEEKS)

FERDINAND From the Spanish Ferdinando, which is of uncertain origin and meaning. It is thought to be of Germanic origin composed from the elements *frithu* (peace), *fardi* (journey), or *ferchvus* (youth, life) and *nanths* (courage), *nanthi* (venture, risk), or *nand* (ready, prepared). The name was borne by King Ferdinand I (1865–1927), who ruled from 1914 to 1927. (FEHR-DEE-NAHND)

FRANTISEK Derived from the Middle Latin Franciscus (a Frenchman), which is from Francus (a Frank, a freeman), which has its root in the Old French *franc* (free). (FRAHN-TEE-SEK)

GABRIEL From the Hebrew Gavriel, which is derived from *gavhrī'ēl* (God is my strength). Pet: Gabi. (GAH-BREE-EL)

GHEORGHE Romanian form of George (earthworker, farmer). The name is from the Greek Georgios, which is derived from *geōrgos*, a compounding of the elements *gē* (earth) and *ergein* (to work). Var: Iorghu, Iorgu. (GHEE-OR-GHEE)

IOAN Romanian form of John (God's gracious gift), a name derived from the Middle Latin Johannes, which is from the Ecclesiastic Late Latin Joannes, from the Ecclesiastic Greek Iōannes, a derivative of the Hebrew Yehanan, a short form of Yehohanan, which is from *yehōhānān* (Yahweh is gracious). The name, the most enduringly popular of the biblical names, is borne in the Bible by several important characters. Many saints, twenty-three popes, and many kings across Europe carried the name, which was first used in the Eastern Church. The variant form Ion is borne by Ion Iliescu, the Romanian president. Var: Ion. Pet: Iancu, Ionel. (YO-AHN)

IOSIF Romanian cognate of Joseph, which is from the Ecclesiastic Greek Iōsēph, a derivative of the Hebrew Yosef, which is from *yōsēf* (may he add). Var: Yousef. (YO-SEEF)

IULIAN From the Latin Julianus, which is a derivative of Julius, an old Roman family name thought to be derived from Iulus (the first down on the chin, downy-bearded, youth). (YOO-LEE-UN)

IVAN Borrowed from the Russian, Ivan is a cognate of John (God is gracious), which is from the Ecclesiastic Late Latin Joannes and the Ecclesiastic Greek Iōannes, derivatives of the Hebrew *yōhānān*, a contraction of *yehōhānān*, (Yahweh is gracious). (EE-VAHN)

MARTIN Derived from the Latin Martīnus (war-like), a derivative of Mars, the name of the Roman mythological god of war. (MAHR-TEEN)

MICHAEL Derivative of the Hebrew *mīkhā'ēl* (who is like God?). King Michael (b. 1921) was Romania's last king. He ruled from 1940 to 1947 before the downfall of the monarchy. Mihai and Mihail are common Romanian cognates of Michael. (MEE-KEHL)

MIHAI Romanian form of Michael (who is like God?). *See* MICHAEL. Var: Mihail, Mihas. (MEE-HI)

NICHOLAS From the Old French Nicolas, which is from the Latin Nicolaus, a derivative of the Greek Nikolaos (victory of the people), a compound name composed of the elements *nikē* (victory) and *laos* (the people). Nicolae is a popular Romanian form of the name. (NEE-KO-LAHS)

NICOLAE Romanian cognate of Nicholas (victory of the people). *See* NICHOLAS. Short: Nic, Nicu. (NEE-KO-LAY)

PETAR Romanian form of Peter, which is derived from the Ecclesiastic Late Latin Petrus and the Greek Petros, names derived from *petrus* (a rock) and *petros* (a stone). The variant form Petre is borne by Prime Minister Petre Roman. Var: Petre, Petru. (PEH-TAHR)

Robert Derived from the Old High German Hruodperht (bright with fame), a compound name composed of the elements *hruod* (fame) and *beraht* (bright). Pet: Robin. (RO-BEHRT)

Robin Originally a pet form of Robert (bright with fame), Robin is now commonly bestowed as an independent given name. *See* ROBERT. (RO-BEEN)

Simu Romanian cognate of Simon, which is from the Hebrew Shimon, a derivative of *shim'on* (heard). (SEE-MOO)

Stanislav A name of Slavonic origin, Stanislav is composed of the elements *stan* (government) and *slav* (glory): hence, "government is glory." (STAH-NEE-SLAHV)

Stefan From the Latin Stephanus, which is from the Greek Stephanos, a derivative of *stephanos* (a crown, a garland). (STEH-FAHN)

Toma Romanian form of Thomas, which is from the Ecclesiastic Greek Thōmas, a derivative of the Aramaic *tě'ōma* (a twin). (TŌ-MAH)

Valeriu From the Latin Valerius, an old Roman family name believed to be derived from *valere* (to be strong). (VAH-LAY-REE-OO)

Vasile Romanian cognate of the Latin Basilius and the Greek Basileios (kingly, royal), names derived from *basileus* (king). (VAH-SEE-LEH)

Victor Derived from the Latin *victor* (conqueror, winner). (VEEK-TOR)

Vilhelm Romanian cognate of William (resolute protector). The name is from the Old Norman French Willaume, which is derived from the Old High German Willehelm, a compound name composed from the elements *willeo* (will, determination) and *helm* (protection, helmet). (VEEL-HELM)

Vladimir Compound name composed from the Slavonic elements *volod* (rule) and *meri* (great, famous): hence, "famous ruler." Short: Vlad. (VLAH-DEE-MEER)

Romanian Female Names

Alexandra Feminine form of Alexandru, the Romanian cognate of Alexander (defender or helper of mankind), a compound name composed of the Greek elements *alexein* (to defend, to help) and *andros* (man, mankind). Short: Alexa, Sandra. (AH-LEHK-SAHN-DRAH)

Alicia Latinate form of Alice (truthful, noble), which developed as a variant of Adelaide, a contracted form of the Old High German Adalheidis (noble one), a compounding of the elements *adal* (noble) and *heid* (kind, sort). Var: Elica. (AH-LEE-SEE-AH)

Ana Romanian form of Anna, which is from the Hebrew Hannah, a derivative of *hannāh, chaanach* (grace, gracious, mercy). Pet: Anica, Anicuta. (AH-NAH)

Angelika A borrowing from the German, Angelika is derived from the Latin *angelicus* and the Greek *angelikos* (angelic, heavenly). (AHN-ZEH-LEE-KAH, AHN-ZHEH-LEE-KAH)

Antanasia Romanian form of Anastasia, which is derived from the Greek *anastasis* (resurrection). Var: Atanasia. (AHN-TAHN-AHS-SYAH)

Beatrix Derived from the Latin *beatrix* (she who makes happy, she who brings happiness). (BEH-AH-TREEKS)

Bianca Borrowed from the Italian, Bianca is derived from *bianca* (white, fair). (BEE-AHN-KAH)

Brigita Romanian form of Birgitta, which is derived from the Gaelic Bríghid, a name thought to be derived from *brígh* (strength). (BREE-GEE-TAH)

Daniela Feminine form of Daniel (God is my judge). *See* DANIEL (Male Names). (DAHN-YEH-LAH)

Dorota Romanian form of the Greek Dorothea (gift of God), a compound name composed of the elements *dōron* (gift) and *theos* (God). (DOR-O-TAH)

Ecaterina Romanian cognate of the Greek Aikaterinē, a name derived from *katharos* (pure, unsullied). Var: Catelina, Caterina, Ekaterina. (EH-KAH-TAH-REE-NAH)

Elena A popular name, Elena is the Romanian cognate of the Greek Helenē, which is derived from the element *ēlē* (light, torch, bright). Pet: Elenuta. (EH-LEH-NAH)

Elisabeta Romanian form of Elizabeth, which is derived from the Hebrew *elīsheba'* (God is my oath). Var: Elizabeta. Short: Elisa, Eliza. Pet: Beti. (EH-LEE-SAH-BEH-TAH)

ILEANA Romanian cognate of the Latin Aeliāna, which is the feminine form of the Latin family name Aeliānus (of the sun), which is derived from the Greek *hēlios* (sun). (EE-LEE-AH-NAH)

IOANA A popular name, Ioana is the feminine form of Ioan, the Romanian cognate of John (God is gracious). *See* IOAN (Male Names). (YO-AH-NAH)

IOLANDA Romanian cognate of Yolanda, a name of uncertain etymology. Some believe it to be a derivative of Violante (violet), a medieval French name derived from the Latin Viola (violet). (YO-LAHN-DAH)

IRINA A popular name in Romania, Irina is a cognate of the Greek Eirēnē, which is derived from *eirēnē*(peace). Pet: Irini. (EE-REE-NAH)

IULIA Romanian cognate of Julia, the feminine form of Julian, which is from Julianus, a Latin family name believed to be derived from Iulus (the first down on the chin, downy-bearded). Because a person just beginning to develop facial hair is young, "youth" became an accepted definition of the name. (YOO-LEE-AH)

IZABELA Romanian cognate of Isabela, which is a variant form of Elizabeth (God is my oath). *See* ELISABETA. (EE-zah-BEH-lah)

LUCIA A borrowing from the Italian, Lucia is a feminine form of Lucius, which is derived from the Latin *lux* (light). (LOO-SEE-AH)

MAGDA A short form of Magdalena (of Magdala), Magda is also bestowed as an independent given name. *See* MAGDALENA. (MAHG-DAH)

MAGDALENA Latinate form of Magdalene, from the Ecclesiastic Greek Magdalēnē (of Magdala). Mary Magdalene was the name of a woman Christ cured of seven demons. Short: Magda. (MAHG-DAH-LEH-NAH)

MARGARITA Romanian cognate of Margaret, which is from the Greek Margaritēs, a name derived from *margaron* (a pearl). (MAHR-GAH-REE-TAH)

MARIA Latin form of Mary, which is derived from the Hebrew Miryām, a name of debated meaning. While "sea of bitterness, sea of sorrow," seems to be the most probable, some sources cite the alternative definitions of "rebellion," "wished-for child," and "mistress or lady of the sea." Var: Marie. Pet: Marica, Maricara, Marika. (MAH-REE-AH)

MARIE A borrowing from the French, Marie is a cognate of Maria. *See* MARIA. (MAH-REE)

MARTINA Feminine form of Martin (war-like), which is from the Latin Martīnus, a derivative of Mars, the name of the Roman mythological god of war. (MAHR-TEE-NAH)

NADIA Derived from the Russian Nadya, which is from the Russian word meaning "hope." The name is borne by gold medal gymnast Nadia Comaneci (b. 1961). (NAH-DEE-AH)

NATHALIE A borrowing from the French, Nathalie is from the Latin Natalia, a name derived from *diēs nātālis* (natal day, Christmas). The name is often bestowed upon children born on Christmas Day. (NAH-THAH-LEE, NAH-TAH-LEE)

OLGA A borrowing from the Russian, Olga is the feminine form of Oleg (holy), which is from Helgi, a Scandinavian name derived from the Old Norse *heill* (hale, hearty; blessed, holy). (OL-GAH)

REVEKA Romanian cognate of the Ecclesiastic Late Latin and Ecclesiastic Greek Rhebekka, which is derived from the Hebrew *ribbqāh* (noose), from *rabak* (to bind, to tie). (REH-VEH-KAH)

SOPHIE Derived from the Greek Sophia, which is derived from *sophia* (wisdom, skill). Sophie, a popular name among European nobility, is borne by a daughter (b. 1957) of Michael I and Anne of Bourbon-Parma. (SO-FEE)

SUZANA Romanian form of Susannah, which is from the Hebrew Shoshana, a derivative of *shōshannāh* (a lily, a rose). (SOO-ZAH-NAH)

TATIANA Feminine form of the Latin Tatiānus, a derivative of the old Roman family name Tatius, which is of uncertain origin. (TAH-TYAH-NAH)

TEREZA Romanian cognate of Theresa, a name of uncertain etymology. It is generally believed to be derived from the Greek *therizein* (to reap, to gather in) and has taken the definition "harvester, gatherer." *See* THERESA (English Names). Pet: Zizi. (TEH-REH-ZAH)

VIORICA Romanian form of the German Friederike, a feminine form of Friedrich (ruler of peace), a compounding of the elements *frid* (peace) and *rik* (king, ruler). (FEE-O-REE-KAH)

CHAPTER TWENTY-SIX

Russian Names

FROM MEDIEVAL times through the introduction of communism in 1917, the Orthodox Church has had a great influence on Russian society, and through it, a great number of names of Greek, Latin, and Hebrew origin have entered popular usage. The Russian Revolution of 1917 brought many social changes, and the bestowal of names was affected as well. Favored names of saints were discouraged, and parents were urged to choose names suggestive of the new way of things. In spite of this, certain traditional names remained popular.

Today, Russians use three names: a given name, a patronymic, and a surname. The patronymic was originally used only by princes and the nobility. Now it is common to all the people. When a person reaches the age of sixteen, he or she is regarded as entering into adulthood. It is at this time that a person is addressed formally by his or her given name and patronymic, much as the titles Ms., Miss, Mrs., and Mr. are used in the United States as a sign of respect. The patronymic consists of the father's given name to which the ending *-ovich* (son of) is added for a male, and *-ovna* or *-evna* (daughter of) for a female.

Russian surnames developed around the 15th century, in much the same way as other European surnames. Many are derived from place-names, nicknames, and occupational names. Others are taken from nature, as in the names of animals, birds, and landscape features. There are also the common patronymical surnames. The majority of surnames end in the terminations *-ev*, *-ov*, or *-in*. Other terminations include *-sky*, *-ik*, *-oy*, *-ich*, and *-ovich*.

Upon marriage, a couple may either retain their individual surnames or share one of the names. If both individual names are kept, the parents decide which name their children will have.

Russian names are remarkable for their many pet forms and diminutives, which are commonly used in everyday speech in place of the formal given name.

Russian Male Names

ABRAM A borrowing from the Hebrew, Abram is a variant form of Avram (father is exalted), the original name of the biblical patriarch Abraham. Var: Avraam, Avram, Avramij. Pet: Abrasha. (AH-BRAHM)

ADRIAN From the Latin Adriānus (man from the city of Adria) and Hadriānus (man from the city of Hadria). Pet: Adja, Adrik, Adya. (AHD-REE-AHN)

ADYA Common pet form of various names beginning with the letter A. Var: Adja. (AHD-YAH)

AFANASI Derived from the Greek Athanasios, which

is from *athanasia* (immortality, eternal existence). The name was borne by St. Athanasius (297–373), an Alexandrian theologian venerated in the Eastern Church. Var: Afanasii, Afanassij. Pet: Afon, Afonja, Afonya, Fanja, Fanya, Fonja, Fonya. (AH-FAH-NAH-SEE)

AGAFON Derived from the Greek *agathos* (good, kind, honorable). (AH-GAH-FONE)

AKIM Russian form of Joachim, a cognate of the Hebrew Jehoiakim, which is from Yehoyakim (God will establish). In medieval Christian tradition, the name was assigned to the father of the Virgin Mary, as Anne was assigned to her mother. Var: Ioakim, Yakim. Pet: Iov, Kima. (AH-KIM)

ALEK A short form of Aleksandr and Aleksei, Alek is also bestowed as an independent given name. *See* ALEKSANDR *and* ALEKSEI. Var: Aleks, Alik. (AH-LEEK)

ALEKSANDR Derived from the Greek Alexandros, a compounding of the elements *alexein* (to defend, to help) and *andros* (man): hence, "defender or helper of mankind." Pet: Alek, Aleks, Alik, Sanya, Sasha, Shura. (AH-LEK-SAHN-DER)

ALEKSEI Derived from the Greek Alexios (defender, helper), a name derived from the verb *alexein* (to defend, to help). Var: Aleksije. Pet: Alek, Aleks, Alësha, Alik, Lëlja, Lëlya, Lënja, Lënya, Lësha. (AH-LEK-SAY)

AMBROSSIJ Derived from the Greek Ambrosios, a name derived from *ambrosios* (immortal). The name was borne by a 4th-century saint who was bishop of Milan and is considered to be one of the four great Latin doctors of the church. (AHM-BRO-SEE)

ANATOLI Derived from the Greek Anatolios, a derivative of *anatolē* (sunrise, daybreak, dawn). The name was borne by St. Anatolius, bishop of Constantinople from 449 to 458. His leadership had a great influence on the Eastern Church. Var: Anatolii. Pet: Tólja, Tólya, Tósha, Túlja, Túlya. (AH-NAH-TŌ-LEE)

ANDREI Russian form of Andrew, a cognate of the Greek Andreas, a name derived from *andreios* (manly). The name is borne in the Bible by one of the Twelve Apostles of Christ. Pet: Adja, Adya, Andrjusha, Andryusha. (AHN-DREE)

ANIKITA Derived from the Greek Aniketos (unconquered), a compound name composed of the elements *a* (not) and *nikān* (to conquer). The short form Nikita is now in more common use. Short: Nikita. (AH-NIH-KEE-TAH)

ANISIM Derived from the Greek Onesimos (useful, profitable). The name, which was used as a common slave name in ancient times, was borne by a runaway slave converted to Christianity by St. Paul. Var: Onisim. Pet: Nika, Sima. (AH-NEE-SEEM)

ANTON Russian cognate of Anthony, a name derived from the Latin Antonius, an old Roman family name of uncertain origin and meaning. "Priceless" and "of inestimable worth" are popular folk definitions given to the name. Var: Antoni. Pet: Antosha, Tosha. (AHN-TAHN)

APOLLON Derived from the Greek Apollōn, an ancient name of unknown etymology borne in Greek mythology by the god of music, poetry, prophecy, and medicine. The name is indicative of physical perfection. Var: Apolloni. Pet: Apolja, Apollosha, Apolyn, Polja, Polya. (AH-PAH-LONE)

ARKADI Derived from the Greek Arkadios (of Arcadia, an ancient pastoral region in Peloponnesus). The name was borne by a 4th-century missionary bishop venerated in the Eastern Church. Pet: Ardik, Arik, Arkasha. (AHR-KAH-DEE)

ARKHIP Derived from the Greek Arkhippos (ruler of horses), a compounding of the elements *arkhē* (rule) and *hippos* (horse). The name was borne by St. Arkhippos, one of the earliest Christian converts. Pet: Khipa. (AHR-KHEEP)

ARMAN From the German Hermann, which is from the Old High German Hariman, a compound name composed from the elements *heri* (army) and *man* (man): hence, "soldier, warrior." (AHR-MAHN)

ARSENI Derived from the Greek Arsenios (male, virile, masculine). Pet: Arsen, Arshya, Arsja, Senya. (AHR-SEE-NEE)

ARTEMI Derived from the Greek Artemios (of Artemis, the Greek mythological goddess of the moon, hunting, and wild animals). The name was borne by St. Artemius (d. 363), an important official who served under Constantine the Great. Var: Artëm. Pet: Tëma. (AHR-TEH-MEE)

AVEL Russian cognate of Abel, a derivative of the Hebrew *hebel* (breath). The name is borne in the Bible by the second son of Adam and Eve. Abel was the first murder victim, killed in a jealous rage by his elder brother, Cain. Var: Awel. (AH-VIL)

AVGUSTIN Russian cognate of Augustine, a derivative of the Latin Augustinus, a diminutive form of Augustus, which is from *augustus* (great, venerable). The name was borne by St. Augustine (354–430), an early church father who was born in Numidia and became the bishop of Hippo in northern Africa. Var: Avgust. (AHV-GOO-STEEN)

Bogdan Compound name derived from the Slavonic elements *bog* (God) and *dan* (gift): hence, "God's gift." Var: Bohdan. Pet: Danja, Danya. (BOG-DAHN)

Boris Russian name of debated origin. Some believe it is derived from the Slavonic *bor* (battle, fight). Others think it originated from the Tartar Bogoris (small). Pet: Boba, Borinka, Borja, Borka, Borya, Busja, Busya. (BOR-EES)

Borislav Compound name composed from the Slavonic elements *bor* (battle, fight) and *slav* (glory): hence, "battle glory, glory in battle." Pet: Slava. (BOR-EE-SLAV)

Damian Derived from the Greek Damianos, an ancient name believed to be derived from *damān* (to tame). (DAHM-EE-YAHN)

Dan Hebrew name meaning "judge." The name is borne in the Bible by the fifth of Jacob's twelve sons, the progenitor of the tribe of Dan. (DAHN)

Daniel Derived from the Hebrew *dānī'ēl* (God is my judge). The name is borne in the Bible by a Hebrew prophet whose faith kept him alive in a den of lions. Var: Danil, Danila. Pet: Danja, Danya. (DAHN-YEEL)

Danya Pet form of any of the various names beginning with the letter *D*. Var: Danja. (DAHN-YAH)

David Derived from the Hebrew *dāvīd* (beloved). The name is borne in the Bible by the second and greatest of the Israelite kings. Var: Daveed. Pet: Danja, Danya, Dodya. (DAH-VEED)

Denis A popular name, Denis is the Russian cognate of the Greek Dionysios (of Dionysos). Dionysos is an ancient name of unknown etymology borne by the Greek mythological god of wine and revelry. Var: Dionisij. Pet: Denya. (DEH-NEES)

Dmitri Derived from the Greek Demetrios (of Demeter). Demeter is an ancient name of unknown etymology borne by the Greek mythological goddess of agriculture and fertility. Var: Dimitri, Dimitrij. Pet: Dima, Mitya. (DIH-MEE-TREE)

Dominik Derived from the Latin Dominicus (of or belonging to a lord), which is from *dominus* (a lord, a master). (DOM-IH-NEEK)

Eelia Russian cognate of the Hebrew Eliyahu, a derivative of *'ēlīyāhū* (Jehovah is God). The name is borne in the Bible by one of the earliest of the Hebrew prophets. Pet: Eelusha. (EEL-EE-YAH)

Eesaia Russian cognate of Isaiah, a name derived from the Hebrew *y̆sha'yah* (God is salvation). The name is borne in the Bible by a Hebrew prophet of the 8th century B.C. His prophecies are found in the Old Testament book of Isaiah. (EE-SĪ-AH)

Efrem Derived from the Hebrew Efrayim (fruitful). The name is borne in the Bible by the second son of Joseph, a son of Jacob. Pet: Efrasha, Rema. (YEH-FREHM)

Egor Russian cognate of Ivor (archer, bow warrior), a name introduced by the Scandinavians and derived from the Old Norse elements*ýr* (yew, bow) and *herr* (army, warrior). Pet: Egorka, Egunya, Gora, Gorya. (EE-GUR)

Evfimi Russian cognate of the Greek Euphemios (fair speech, fair of voice), a compound name composed of the elements *eu* (well, good, happy) and *pheme* (voice). Short: Efim. (YEH-FEE-MEE)

Evgeni Russian cognate of the Greek Eugenios, a name derived from *eugenēs* (well-born, noble). The name was borne by four popes and several early saints. Var: Jevginij. Pet: Geka, Genya, Gesha, Zheka, Zhenya. (YEV-GEH-NEE)

Fabiyan From the Latin Fabianus (of Fabius), which is derived from the old Roman family name Fabius, a derivative of the Latin *faba* (a bean). Pet: Fabi. (FAH-BEE-UN)

Feliks Derived from the Latin *felix* (happy, lucky). (FAY-LEEKS)

Filip Russian cognate of Philip (lover of horses), which is derived from the Greek elements *philos* (loving) and *hippos* (a horse). (FEE-LEEP)

Foka Derived from the Greek Phocas (from Phocaea, an ancient Ionian city in western Asia Minor). (FO-KAH)

Gavriil Russian form of Gabriel, a cognate of the Hebrew Gavriel, which is derived from *gavhrī'ēl* (God is my strength). The name is borne in the Bible by one of the seven archangels, the herald of Good News who appeared to Mary to announce her pregnancy and the impending birth of the Christ child. Var: Gavrila. Pet: Ganya, Gavrya. (GAV-REEL)

Gennadi Derived from *Januārius*, the Latin name of January, the first month of the year, which is dedicated to Janus, an ancient sun-god. Pet: Gena, Genya. (GEH-NAH-DEE)

Georgi Derived from the Greek Geōrgios, a derivative of *geōrgos* (earthworker, farmer), which is composed of the elements *gē* (earth) and *ergein* (to work). Pet: Gorya, Gosha, Gunya, Jura, Zhora, Zhorzh, Zhura. (GYOR-GEE)

GERMAN Russian cognate of the German Hermann (army man, soldier), a name derived from the Old High German Hariman, a compounding of the elements *hari, heri* (army) and *man* (man). Pet: Gera, Gesha. (GEHR-MAHN)

GRIGORI From the Greek Grēgorios (vigilant, a watchman), which is derived from the verb *egeirein* (to awaken). The name was borne by several early saints and popes. In 1582 Pope Gregory XIII introduced the Gregorian calendar, a corrected form of the Julian calendar which is now used in most countries of the world. Var: Grigorij. Short: Grigor. Pet: Grinya, Grisha. (GREE-GOR-EE)

IAKOV From the Greek Iakobos, which is from the Hebrew *ya'aqob* (seizing by the heel, supplanting). It is a cognate of Jacob, a name borne in the Bible by a son of Isaac and patriarch of the founders of the twelve tribes of Israel. (YAH-KOV)

IEREMIYA From the Ecclesiastic Greek Hieremias, a name derived from the Hebrew *yirmeyāh* (the Lord loosens, the Lord will uplift). Ieremiya is a cognate of Jeremiah. Var: Eremei, Ieremija. (YER-EE-MEE-YAH)

IGNATI Derived from the Greek Ignatios, a cognate of the Latin Ignatius, which is from Egnatius, an old Roman family name of uncertain etymology. Some believe it to be of Etruscan origin. Others derive it from the Latin *ignis* (fire). Short: Ignat. Pet: Ignasha. (EEG-NAH-TEE)

IGOR Variant form of Ivor (bow warrior, an archer), a name introduced to Russia by the Scandinavians, which is composed of the elements *ýr* (yew, bow) and *herr* (army, warrior). Pet: Gorik, Gosha, Iga. (EE-GUR)

ILLARION Derived from the Greek Hilarion, a derivative of the Latin Hilarius (cheerful), which is from *hilaris* (cheerful, glad). Pet: Iarya. (EE-LAHR-EE-OWN)

INNOKENTI Derived from Innocent, which is from the Latin *innocens* (innocent). Pet: Kenya, Kesha. (EE-NO-KANE-TEE).

IOSEPH Derived from the Ecclesiastic Greek Iōsēph, a cognate of the Hebrew Yosef, which is from *yōsēf* (may he add, God shall add). The name is borne in the Bible by the favorite son of Jacob and by the husband of the Virgin Mary. Var: Iosif, Osip. Pet: Osya. (EE-O-SEEF)

IPPOLIT Derived from the Greek Hippolytus (freer or loosener of horses), which is derived from the elements *hippos* (horse) and *lyein* (to free, to loosen). Pet: Polya. (EE-PAH-LIT)

ISAAK Russian cognate of Isaac, a derivative of the Hebrew Yitzchak (he will laugh), which is from *yitshāq* (laughter). The name is borne in the Bible by one of the three sons of Abraham and Sarah, the father of Esau and Jacob. Var: Eisaak, Isak. (EE-SAHK)

ISIDOR Derived from the Greek Isidoros (gift of Isis, divine gift), a compound name composed of Isis, the name of the Egyptian goddess of fertility, and *dōron* (gift). Var: Eesidor. Short: Sidor. (EE-SEE-DOR)

ISRAIL Russian cognate of Israel, the Anglicized form of the Hebrew Yisrael, which is from *yisrā'ēl* (wrestler of God). In the biblical Old Testament, the name was given to Jacob after he wrestled with an angel of God. (EE-ZRĪ-EEL)

IVAN A popular name, Ivan is the Russian cognate of John (God is gracious), which is from the Ecclesiastic Late Latin Joannes and the Ecclesiastic Greek Iōannes, derivatives of the Hebrew *yōhānān*, a contraction of *yehōhānān* (Yahweh is gracious). Var: Ioann. Pet: Vanya. (EE-VAHN)

JEREMIJA Russian cognate of Jeremiah, which is from the Hebrew Yirmeyahu, a name derived from *yirmeyāh* (the Lord loosens, God will uplift). The name is borne in the Bible by a 5th- or 6th-century B.C. Hebrew prophet whose story and prophecies are recorded in the Old Testament book of Jeremiah. Var: Jeremej. (YEHR-IH-MEE-YAH)

JESEKIJEL Russian cognate of Ezekiel, a name derived from the Hebrew *yehezq'ēl* (God strengthens). The name is borne in the Bible by a Hebrew prophet of the 6th century B.C. His prophecies are recorded in the Old Testament book of Ezekiel. (YEH-ZEE-KEEL)

JEVSTACHI Russian cognate of the Greek Eustakhios, a compound name composed of the elements *eu* (well, good) and *stachys* (grapes): hence, "fruitful, fair harvest." (YEHV-STAH-HEE)

KARL Russian cognate of the German Karl (a man, freeman, peasant). (KARL)

KASSIAN From the Latin Cassiānus, a name derived from Cassius, an old Roman family name of uncertain meaning. It is possibly derived from the Latin *cassus* (hollow, empty). Var: Kas'yan. Pet: Kasya. (KAH-SEE-AHN)

KHARALAMM Derived from the Greek Charalampios, a compounding of the elements *kara* (joy) and *lampās* (a torch). Var: Kharalample. (HAR-LAHM)

KIRILL Derived from the Greek Kyrillos (lordly), which is from *kyrios* (a lord). The name was borne by a

9th-century Greek prelate and missionary to the Slavs, to whom the Cyrillic alphabet is attributed. Var: Kiríla. Pet: Kíra. (KEE-RIL)

KLIMENT Derived from the Greek Klemenis, which is from the Latin Clemens (mild, gentle, merciful), a direct derivation from the vocabulary word of the same definition. Var: Klimenti. Short: Klim. Pet: Klima. (KLEE-MEE-YEHNT)

KONDRATI Derived from the German Konrad, a name derived from the Old High German Kuonrat (wise counsel), which is a compounding of the elements *kuon* (bold, wise) and *rat* (counsel). Var: Kondrat. Pet: Kondrasha. (KAHN-DRAH-TEE)

KONSTANTIN Derived from the Latin Constantinus, which is from *constans* (steadfast, constant). The name was borne by Constantine the Great (280?–337), the first emperor of Rome to be converted to Christianity. Pet: Kostya. (KAHN-STAHN-TEEN)

KOSMA From the Greek Kosmas, a name derived from *kosmos* (universe, order, harmony). Var: Kavzma, Kozma, Kuzma. Pet: Kuzya. (KAHZ-MAH)

LEONGARD Russian cognate of the German Leonhard, a name derived from the Old High German Lewenhart, a compounding of the elements *lewo* (lion) and *hart* (strong, brave, hearty): hence, "brave as a lion, lion-hearted." (LAY-O-NAHRD)

MAKARI Derived from the Greek Makarios, which is from *makaros* (blessed). Var: Makár. (MAH-KAH-REE)

MAKSIM A short form of Maksimilian, Maksim is also bestowed as an independent given name. Short: Maks, Sima. (MAHK-SEEM)

MAKSIMILIAN Russian form of Maximilian, a name that arose as a blending of the Latin names Maximus and Aemiliānus by the Emperor Friedrich III, who bestowed it upon his first-born son, Maximilian I (1459–1519), in honor of two famous Roman generals. Maximus is derived from the Latin *maximus* (greatest), but the etymology of Aemiliānus is uncertain. It is thought to be from the Latin *aemulus* (emulating, trying to equal or excel, rival). Short: Maks, Maksim, Sima. (MAHK-SEE-MIL-EE-AHN)

MARK Cognate of the Latin Marcus, a name of debated origin and meaning. Most believe it has its root in Mars, the name of the Roman mythological god of war, and thus give it the meaning "war-like." Others think it might be from *mas* (manly) or from the Greek *malakoz* (soft, tender). The name is borne in the Bible by one of the four evangelists, the author of the second Gospel, Mark. (MARK)

MARTIN From the Latin Martinus (of Mars, war-like), a derivative of Mars, the name of the Roman mythological god of war. (MAHR-TIN)

MATVEI Russian cognate of Matthew, a derivative of the Ecclesiastic Late Latin Matthaeus, a cognate of the Ecclesiastic Greek Matthaios and Matthias, which are contractions of Mattathias. The name is derived from the Hebrew Matityah, which has its root in *mattīthyāh* (gift of God). The name is borne in the Bible by one of the four evangelists, the author of the first Gospel, Matthew. Var: Matfei. Pet: Motya. (MAHT-VEE)

MEFODI Derived from the Greek Methodios (fellow traveler), a compounding of the elements *meta* (with) and *hodos* (road, path). The name was borne by the evangelist St. Methodius (d. 885), the first translator of the Bible into the Slavonic language. Var: Mefodya. (MEH-FO-DEE)

MIKHAIL Russian cognate of Michael, a name derived from the Hebrew *mīkhā'ēl* (who is like God?). The name is borne in the Bible by the archangel closest to God, the one responsible for carrying out God's judgments. Considered the leader of the heavenly host, Michael is regarded as the patron of soldiers. Pet: Michej, Mika, Minya, Misha. (MEE-HI-EEL)

MIRON Russian form of the Greek Myron, a name derived from *myron* (myrrh, a fragrant resin used in making incense and perfume). The name was borne by a Greek sculptor of the 5th century B.C. and is said to have been taken up by early Christians because of the gift of myrrh made to the Christ child by the Three Wise Men. Pet: Mirosha, Ronya. (MEE-RONE)

MOISSE Russian form of Moses, an Ecclesiastic Greek name derived from the Hebrew *mōsheh* (drawn out of the water) and from the Egyptian *mes, mesu* (child, son). The name is borne in the Bible by the leader who brought the Israelites out of bondage in Egypt and received the Ten Commandments on Mount Sinai. (MOY-SAY)

MORIZ Derived from the Greek Moris, a cognate of the Latin Maurus (a Moor). The Moors were a Muslim people of mixed Arab and Berber descent; thus the name came to mean "dark" or "swarthy" in reference to their coloring. (MOR-ISS)

MSTISLAV Russian cognate of the Polish Mieczysław, a compound name of uncertain derivation. Some believe it to be either from *miecz* (sword), the Old Polish *miecz* (man, father), or *mieszka* (bear). The second element is the Slavonic *slav* (glory). Pet: Slava. (MIS-TEE-SLAV)

NATANIEL Derived from the Ecclesiastic Greek Nathanaēl, a derivative of the Hebrew Netanel, which is from *nĕthan'ēl* (gift of God). The name is borne in the Bible by one of the disciples of Christ, more commonly known as Bartholomew. (NAH-TAHN-YEL)

NIKITA Cognate of the Greek Aniketos (unconquered), a compounding of the elements *a* (not) and *nikān* (to conquer). The name was borne by Russian premier Nikita Khrushchev (1894–1971). Var: Mikita. Pet: Nika. (NEE-KEE-TAH)

NIKODIM From the Greek Nikodemos, a compound name composed of the elements *nikē* (victory) and *demos* (people): hence, "victory of the people." Pet: Dima, Nika. (NEE-KO-DEEM)

NIKOLAI Russian cognate of the Greek Nikolaos, a compounding of the elements *nikē* (victory) and *laos* (the people): hence, "victory of the people." The name was borne by St. Nikolaos, a 4th-century bishop of Myra who is regarded as the patron saint of Greece and Russia and of children, sailors, and wolves. It was also borne by Nikolai Aleksandrovich (1868–1918), the last czar of Russia. Pet: Koka, Kolya, Nika, Nil, Nilya. (NEE-KO-LĪ)

NIL A pet form of Nikolai (victory of the people), Nil is also bestowed as an independent given name. Pet: Nilya. (NEEL)

NOE Russian cognate of Noah, which is from the Hebrew Noach, a derivative of *nōah* (rest, comfort, quiet). The name is borne in the Bible by the patriarch who built the ark to save his family and two of every creature from the Great Flood. (NOY)

OLEG Popular Russian name meaning "holy." (AH-LEG)

PAVEL Russian cognate of Paul, which is from the Latin Paulus, a Roman family name derived from *paulus* (small). The name was adopted in the Bible by a Jew and Roman citizen, Saul of Tarsus, who was converted to Christianity by a vision of Christ. St. Paul and St. Peter are regarded as the cofounders of the Christian Church. Pet: Panya, Pasha, Pava, Pusha. (PAH-VEEL)

PIJ Russian cognate of the Latin Pius, a direct derivative of *pius* (pious, devout, obedient). (PEE)

PIOTR Russian cognate of Peter, a name derived from the Ecclesiastic Late Latin Petrus (a rock) and the Ecclesiastic Greek Petros (a stone). The name is borne in the Bible by one of the Twelve Apostles of Christ. A cofounder of the Christian Church, St. Peter is also regarded as the first pope. Var: Petr, Pyotr. Pet: Petenka, Petya. (PEE-O-TER)

PROKHOP Russian form of the Greek Prokopios (progressive), a compound name composed of the elements *pro* (before) and *kopios* (in great abundance, copious). The name was borne by a 4th-century Greek saint, the first to be martyred in Palestine under the reign of Diocletian. Var: Prokopi. Pet: Pronya, Prosha. (PRO-KOPE)

PROKHOR Derived from the Greek Prŏchoros (leader of the dance), a compounding of the elements *pro* (before) and *choros* (dance, a band of dancers or singers). (PRO-HOR)

ROBERT A borrowing from the Europeans, Robert is derived from the Old High German Hruodperht (bright with fame), a compounding of the elements *hruod* (fame) and *beraht* (bright). Var: Robertas. (RO-BERT)

SACHARIJA Russian form of the Ecclesiastic Greek Zacharias (remembrance of the Lord), a name derived from the Hebrew *zeharyah* (God remembers). Var: Zakhari. Short: Sachar, Zakhar. (ZAH-HAH-REE-AH)

SASHA A pet form of Aleksandr (defender or helper of mankind), Sasha is also popularly bestowed as an independent given name. *See* ALEKSANDR. (SAH-SHA)

SAVVEL Russian form of Saul, a cognate of the Hebrew Shaul, which is derived from *shā'ūl* (asked of, borrowed). The name is borne in the Bible by the first king of Israel, appointed by the prophet Samuel, and by Saul of Tarsus, who later became the apostle Paul. Var: Savel, Saveli. Pet: Sava. (SAH-VEL)

SERAFIM Derived from the Ecclesiastic Late Latin *seraphim* (burning ones, the angels surrounding the throne of God), which is from the Hebrew *sĕrāphīm*, a word believed to be derived from *sāraph* (to burn). Pet: Sima. (SARE-AH-FEEM)

SERGEI Popular name derived from the Greek Sergios, which is from the Latin Sergius, an old Roman family name of uncertain etymology. Var: Serguei. Pet: Serezha, Serzh. (SARE-GAY)

SEVASTIAN From the Greek Sebastianos (man of Sebastia). Sebastia was the name of Samaria after the time of Herod the Great (73?–4 B.C.). Var: Sevastyan. Pet: Seva, Sevastyasha. (SEH-VAH-STEE-AHN)

SIMA Pet form of any of the various names containing the element *sim* or *fim*. (SEE-MAH)

SIMEON Cognate of the Hebrew Shimon, a derivative of *shim'ōn* (heard). The name is borne in the Bible by one of the Twelve Apostles and a brother of Jesus, as well as several other New Testament characters. (SIM-EE-OWN)

Spiridon Derived from the Greek Spiridon, a name of debated derivation. Some believe it is derived from the Greek *spyrīz* (a round basket). Others think it is a diminutive form of the Latin *spiritus* (spirit, soul). The name was borne by a 4th-century Cypriot saint who was a hermit before becoming a bishop and playing a major role at the Nicene Council in 325. Pet: Spira, Spiridosha, Spirya. (SPEER-EE-DŌNE)

Stanislav Compound name composed of the Slavonic elements *stan* (government) and *slav* (glory): hence, "glorious government." Var: Stanislov. Pet: Slava, Slavik, Stas, Stasi. (STAHN-EE-SLAHV)

Stefan From the Greek Stephanos, a derivative of *stephanos* (a crown, a garland, that which surrounds). The name is borne in the Bible by the first Christian martyr, who was one of the seven chosen to assist the Twelve Apostles. Var: Stepan. Pet: Stenya, Stepa. (STEH-FAHN)

Svjatopolk Compound name composed of the Slavonic elements *svyanto* (bright, holy) and *polk* (people, folk, race): hence, "holy people." (SVYAH-TAH-POLK)

Svjatoslav Compound name composed of the Slavonic elements *svyanto* (bright, holy) and *slav* (glory): hence, "holy glory." Pet: Slava. (SVYAH-TAH-SLAHV)

Thaddej Derived from the Greek Thaddaios, a name of uncertain derivation. Some believe it to be a variant of Theodōros (God's gift). Others feel it is from an Aramaic word meaning "praised." The name is found in the Bible as a name of one of the Twelve Apostles of Christ. (FAH-DEE)

Timofei Russian form of Timothy, which is a cognate of the Greek Timotheos (honor God, respect God), a compounding of the elements *timē* (honor, respect) and *theos* (God). The name is borne in the Bible by a disciple and companion of the apostle Paul. (TEE-MO-FEE)

Valentin Russian form of Valentine, which is from the Latin Valentīnus, a derivative of *valens* (to be healthy, to be strong). Pet: Valja, Valya. (VAH-LEN-TEEN)

Valeri Derived from the Latin Valerius, an old Roman family name believed to be from *valere* (to be strong). Pet: Lera, Valja, Valya. (VAH-LARE-EE)

Valerian From the Latin Valerianus (of Valerius), which is from Valerius, an old Roman family name believed to be derived from *valere* (to be strong). Var: Valer'jan, Valer'yan. Pet: Valja, Valya. (VAH-LARE-EE-AHN)

Vasili Derived from the Greek Basileois (king). The name was borne by a 4th-century Greek theologian known as St. Basil the Great (c. 330–79). A bishop of Caesarea, he is regarded as one of the fathers of the Eastern Church. Pet: Vasja, Vasya. (VAH-SEE-LEE)

Veniamin Russian cognate of Benjamin, a name derived from the Hebrew *benyāmīn* (son of the right hand). The name is borne in the Bible by the youngest of Jacob's twelve sons. Pet: Venja, Venya. (VEE-NYAH-MEEN)

Vikenti Russian cognate of Vincent, which is from the Late Latin Vincentius (conquering), the root of which is *vincere* (to conquer). Pet: Kesha, Vika, Vikesha. (VEE-KEN-TEE)

Viktor Derived from the Latin Victor, a direct derivation of *victor* (conqueror, winner). Pet: Vika, Vitja, Vitya. (VEEK-TOR)

Vitali Russian cognate of the Italian Vitale, which is from *vitalis* (vital, life-giving), the root of which is *vita* (life). Var: Vitalii, Vitalij. Pet: Talik, Vitja, Vitya. (VEE-TAH-LEE)

Vladimir Popular compound name composed of the Slavonic elements *volod* (rule) and *meri* (great, famous): hence, "famous ruler." Pet: Dima, Vladja, Vladya, Volja, Volodja, Volodya, Volya, Vova. (VLAH-DEE-MIR)

Vladislav Compound name composed of the Slavonic elements *volod* (rule) and *slav* (glory): hence, "glorious rule." (VLAH-DEE-SLAHV)

Vladja Pet form of any of the various names containing the element *vlad*. Var: Vladya. (VLAHD-YAH)

Zinovi Derived from the Greek Zenobios (the life of Zeus), a compound name composed of the elements *zēn* (of Zeus) and *bios* (life). Pet: Zinok. (ZEE-NO-VEE)

Zivon Derived from the Greek *zōē* (life). Var: Ziven. (ZEE-VON)

Russian Female Names

ADELAÏDE Variant form of the German Adalheid (noble one), a compound name composed of the elements *adal* (noble) and *heid* (kind, sort). Var: Adelaida. Pet: Ada. (AH-DAH-LAY-DAH)

AGAFIYA Derived from the Greek *agathos* (good, kind). Var: Agafia, Agapiya, Aglaida, Aglaya. Pet: Agasha, Ganya, Gasha, Glasha. (AH-GAH-FEE-YAH)

AGNESSA Russian form of Agnes, a cognate of the Greek Hagnē, which is derived from *hagnos* (chaste, pure, sacred). The name was borne by a thirteen-year-old Roman martyred for her Christian beliefs during the reign of the Roman emperor Diocletian. Var: Agnesija. Pet: Agniya, Agnya, Gusya, Nyusha. (AHG-NES-SAH)

AGRAFENA Russian form of the Latin Agrippina, a name of uncertain etymology borne by Agrippina the Younger (A.D. 15?–59), the mother of Nero. Some believe it to mean "born feet-first." Var: Agrippina. Pet: Fenya, Grunja, Grunya, Gruscha, Gruschka, Grusha, Ina, Pina. (AH-GRAH-FEE-YEH-NAH)

AKULINA Derived from the Late Latin Aquilina, a diminutive form of *aquila* (eagle). Var: Akilina, Akulnia. Pet: Akulya, Kilya, Kulya, Lina. (AH-KOO-LEE-NAH)

ALBINA Feminine form of Albin, a derivative of the Latin Albinus, which is from *albus* (white). (AHL-BEE-NAH)

ALEKSANDRA Russian cognate of Alexandra, the feminine form of the Greek Alexandros (defender or helper of mankind), a compounding of the elements *alexein* (to defend, to help) and *andros* (man). Pet: Alya, Ksana, Sandra, Sanya, Sasha, Shura. (AH-LEHK-SAHN-DRAH)

ALINA A borrowing from the German, Alina is believed to be a Latinate form of Aline, a contraction of Adelina (little noble one), which is a diminutive form of Adelaide. *See* ADELAÏDE. Pet: Alya, Lina. (AH-LEE-NAH)

AMALIYA Derived from the German Amalia (industrious), which is from the element *amal* (work). Var: Amaliji. (AH-MAHL-EE-AH)

ANASTASIYA Feminine form of the Greek Anastasios (of the resurrection), a derivative of *anastasis* (resurrection). The name was borne by a daughter of Czar Nicholas II. She was supposedly murdered by the Bolsheviks along with the rest of her family in 1918. However, there is some speculation that she survived the attack. Var: Anastasia, Nastassja. Pet: Asya, Nastenka, Nastya, Stasya, Tasya. (AH-NAH-STAH-SEE-AH)

ANGELA Latinate form of Angel (messenger of God, guiding spirit), which is from the Greek *angelos* (messenger). Var: Anzhela. Pet: Gelya. (AHN-ZEHL-AH)

ANGELICA Derived from the Latin *angelicus* and the Greek *angelikos* (angelic, like an angel). Var: Anjelika, Anzhelika. Pet: Gelya, Lika. (AHN-ZEH-LEE-KAH)

ANGELINA Diminutive form of Angela, a name derived from the Ecclesiastic Late Latin *angelus* (angel, messenger of God), which is from the Greek *angelos* (a messenger). Pet: Lina. (AHN-ZEH-LEE-NAH)

ANNA Derived from the Hebrew Hannah, which is from *hannāh, chaanach* (gracious, full of grace, mercy). Medieval Christian tradition assigned the name to the mother of the Virgin Mary, as Joachim was assigned to her father. Pet: Anežka, Anninka, Annjuscha, Annusia, Nina. (AHN-NAH)

ANTONINA Feminine form of Anthony, which is from Antonius, an old Roman family name of uncertain origin and meaning. Some believe it to have originally been an Etruscan name. (AHN-TŌ-NEE-NAH). Short: Nina.

DARIYA Feminine form of Darius, a cognate of the Greek Dareios, which is an ancient name of uncertain origin. It is thought to ultimately be derived from Darayavahush, the name of an ancient Persian king. Dariya is one of the most popular names in Russia today, and Dasha is the favored pet form. Var: Darya. Pet: Danya, Dasha. (DAH-REE-AH)

DIANA Derived from the Latin Diviana, which is from *divus* (divine). The name is borne in Roman mythology by the virgin goddess of the moon and of hunting. (DEE-AH-NAH)

DINA A short or pet form of various names containing the element *din*, Dina is also bestowed as an independent given name. (DEE-NAH)

DOMINIKA Feminine form of Dominik, which is from the Latin Dominicus (belonging to a Lord), a name derived from *dominus* (a lord, a master). Pet: Minka, Nika. (DŌ-MIH-NEE-KAH)

DORA A borrowing from the Greek, Dora is derived from *dōron* (gift). (DŌ-RAH)

DUSCHA Derived from the Russian *duscha* (happy). Pet: Dusa, Duschinka, Dusica. (DYOO-SHA)

EKATERINA From the Greek Aikaterinē, a popular name derived from *katharos* (pure, unsullied). The name was borne by Ekaterina Alekseevna (1684–1727), known as Catherine I, the wife of Peter the Great, and by Catherine II, Ekaterina Alekseevna (1729–96), the German-born empress of Russia, known as Catherine the Great. Var: Katerina. Pet: Katya, Ketti, Ketya, Kitti, Koka. (YEH-KAH-TEH-REE-NAH)

ELENA Popular name derived from the Greek Helenē, a name derived from the element *ēlē* (light, torch, bright). Var: Alena, Alyena, Elina, Yelena. Pet: Elya, Leka, Lelya, Lena, Lilya, Nelli, Nelya. (YEH-LEH-NAH)

ELIZABETA Derived from the Hebrew *elisheba'* (God is my oath). The name is borne in the Bible by a kinswoman of the Virgin Mary, the mother of John the Baptist. Var: Lizabeta. Short: Eliza, Liza, Lizabeta. Pet: Eliya, Elisif, Lilya, Lisilka. (YEH-LEE-ZAH-BEH-TAH)

ELLA Originated as a short form of any of the various names containing the Germanic element *ali* (foreign, other). It is now often associated with Ellen (light) and its variant forms. (EL-LAH)

ELVIRA A borrowing from the Spanish, Elvira is a name of uncertain etymology. Some believe it to be of Gothic origin. "Amiable" and "friendly" are popular folk definitions of the name. (EL-VEE-RAH)

EVA Latinate form of Eve, a derivative of the Hebrew Chava, which is from *hawwah* (life). The name is borne in the Bible by the first woman, "the mother of all the living." She is said to have been created from one of Adam's ribs. Var: Evva, Jevva. (YEH-VAH)

EVDOKIYA Russian cognate of the Greek Eudosia (good, gift), a name derived from the elements *eu* (good, well) and *dōsis* (a giving, a gift). Var: Avdota, Eudokhia, Eudokia. Pet: Avdosha, Avdunya, Avdusya, Dotya, Dunya, Dusha, Dusya. (YEV-DŌ-KEE-YAH)

EVELINA Elaborated form of Eva (life). *See* EVA. (YEV-EH-LEE-NAH)

EVFEMIYA Russian cognate of the Greek Eufēmia, a compound name composed of the elements *eu* (good, well, fair) and *phēmē* (voice): hence, "fair of voice, fair speech." Var: Jevfimija. (YEV-FEE-MEE-YAH)

EVGENIYA Russian cognate of the Greek Eugenia, a feminine form of Eugenios (well-born, noble), which is from *eugenēs* (well-born). Var: Evgenia, Jevginnia. Pet: Geka, Genya, Zheka, Zhenya. (YEV-GAY-NEE-AH)

EVLALIYA Russian cognate of the Greek Eulalia, a compound name composed of the elements *eu* (good, well, fair) and *lalein* (to talk): hence, "well-spoken." Var: Jevlalija. (YEV-LAH-LEE-AH)

FEDOSYA Russian cognate of the Greek Theodosia (a gift of God, God-given), a feminine form of Theodosis, which is a compounding of the elements *theos* (God) and *dosis* (a gift, a giving). Pet: Fesya. (FEH-DŌ-SEE-YAH)

FEODORIYA Russian cognate of the Greek Theodora (God's gift), a feminine form of Theodoros, which is a compounding of the elements *theos* (God) and *dōron* (gift). Pet: Fenya. (FEE-AH-DOR-EE-AH)

FILIKITATA Russian cognate of the Italian Felicitas, a name derived from the Latin *fēlīcitas* (happiness, felicity, good fortune). (FEE-LEE-KEE-TAH-TAH)

GALINA Of uncertain derivation, Galina might be from Gallien, the name given to the land of Gaul. Pet: Gala, Galya, Lina. (GAH-LEE-NAH)

GEORGINA Feminine form of Georgi (earthworker, farmer), a cognate of the Greek Geōrgios, which is composed of the elements *gē* (earth) and *ergein* (to work). Pet: Gina. (ZHOR-ZHEE-NAH)

GJUZEL Russian form of the German Giselle (a pledge), a name derived from *gisil* (to owe, a pledge, a mutual obligation). It was a common practice in the early Middle Ages for rival factions to offer a person, often a child, to each other as a pledge of peace. (ZHYOO-ZEL)

IDA A borrowing from the German, Ida is derived from the element *īd* (work, labor). The name is also used as a pet form of Zinaida (of Zeus). (EE-DAH)

INESSA Russian form of Agnes, a cognate of the Greek Hagnē, which is derived from *hagnos* (chaste, pure, sacred). (EE-NES-SAH)

INGA A borrowing from the Scandinavians, Inga was originally a short form of the various names containing *Ing(e)* as a first element. It is now commonly bestowed as an independent given name. In Norse mythology, Ing was a name of the fertility god Frey. (EEN-GAH)

IRENE Derived from the Greek Eirēnē, which is directly from *eirēnē* (peace). The name is very popular throughout Russia. Var: Irena, Irina. (EE-REE-NAH)

IVANNA Popular feminine form of Ivan, a Russian cognate of John (God is gracious). *See* IVAN (Male Names). (EE-VAH-NAH)

KHRISTINA Derived from the Ecclesiastic Late Latin *christiānus*, which is from the Greek *christianos* (a Christian, a follower of Christ). Short: Khristya, Kristya, Tina. (KREE-STEE-NAH)

KIRA Feminine form of the Greek Kyros, a name thought to be derived from *kyrios* (a lord) or from the Persian *khur* (the sun). (KEE-RAH)

KLARA Cognate of Clara, a name derived from the Latin *clārus* (bright, clear, famous). Pet: Lara. (KLAH-RAH)

KLAVDIYA Russian cognate of Claudia, a feminine form of the Latin Claudius, which is an old Roman family name derived from *claudus* (lame). Pet: Klanya, Klasha, Klava, Klavdya. (KLAHV-DEE-YAH)

KLEMENTINA Russian cognate of Clementine, a feminine diminutive form of Clement, which is derived from the Latin *clemens* (mild, gentle, merciful). Pet: Klima. (KLEM-EN-TEE-NAH)

LARA A pet form of Klara and Larisa, Lara is also bestowed as an independent given name. *See* KLARA *and* LARISA. (LAH-RAH)

LARISA Of uncertain derivation, some believe it to be derived from the name of an ancient city of Thessaly; others feel it is derived from the Latin *hilaris* (cheerful). Pet: Lara, Risa. (LAH-REE-SAH)

LIA A short form of the various names containing *lia* as an element, Lia is also bestowed as an independent given name. Var: Liya. (LEE-AH)

LIDIYA Russian cognate of the Greek Lydia (woman from Lydia), a name derived from the name of an ancient kingdom in western Asia Minor. Var: Lidia. Pet: Lida. (LEE-DEE-YAH)

LILIYA Derived from the Latin *lilium* (lily). Var: Lilia. Pet: Lia, Liya. (LEE-LEE-AH)

LIZA A short form of Elizabeta (God is my oath), Liza is popularly bestowed as an independent given name. *See* ELIZABETA. (LEE-ZAH)

LUDMILA Compound name composed of the Slavonic elements *lud* (people, tribe) and *mil* (grace, favor, love): hence, "people's love" or "love of people." Var: Lyudmila. Pet: Lyuda, Lyuka, Lyusya, Mika, Mila. (LOOD-MEE-LAH)

LUIZA Popular feminine form of Louis (famous in war), a name derived from the Old French Loeis, which is from the Old High German Hluodowig, a compounding of the elements *hluod* (famous) and *wīg* (war, strife). (LWEE-ZAH)

MADINA Russian form of the Greek Magdalēnē (of Magdala, a town near the Sea of Galilee). The name is borne in the Bible by Mary Magdalene, a woman from whom Christ exorcised seven demons. She became a devoted follower and was the first to see Christ after he arose from the dead. (MAH-DEE-NAH)

MAIYA Russian form of Maia, the name of a Greek fertility goddess, the daughter of Atlas and Pleione, and mother of Hermes (Mercury) by Zeus. The name is thought to be derived from the root *māi* (great). Var: Maya. (MY-YAH)

MARGARETE Russian form of Margaret, a cognate of the Greek Margarītēs, which is from *margaron* (a pearl). Var: Margarita. Short: Rita. Pet: Margo, Margosha. (MAHR-GAH-REET)

MARIANNA Feminine form of the Latin Mariānus, a derivative of Marius, which is an old Roman family name of uncertain derivation. Some believe the name has its root in Mars, the Roman mythological god of war, but others think it might be derived from the Latin *mas* (manly). Early Christians associated the name with Maria, the Latin name of the Virgin Mary; thus it enjoyed widespread use. Var: Maryana. Pet: Maryasha. (MAHR-EE-AH-NAH)

MARINA Of debated origin and meaning, some believe it to be derived from the Latin Marius (of Mars, the Roman mythological god of war). Others think Marina is derived from the Latin *marinus* (of the sea). (MAH-REE-NAH)

MARIYA Russian form of Mary, a name derived from the Hebrew Miryām, which is of debated meaning. Many believe it to mean "sea of bitterness" or "sea of sorrow." However, some sources cite the alternative definitions of "rebellion," "wished-for child," and "mistress or lady of the sea." The name, borne in the Bible by the virgin mother of Jesus, has become one of the most enduringly popular names in the Christian world. Var: Mar'ya. Pet: Manya, Mara, Marisha, Masha, Meri, Munya, Mura, Musya. (MAH-REE-YAH)

MARTA Russian form of Martha, a name derived from the Aramaic *mārthā* (lady, mistress). The name is borne in the Bible by the sister of Lazarus and Mary of Bethany. Var: Marfa. Pet: Muta. (MAHR-TAH)

MATRIONA Derived from the Latin *matrona* (a married woman or widow, a matron), which is from *mater* (mother). Var: Matrena. Pet: Matresha, Matyusha, Motrya, Motya. (MAH-TREE-O-NAH)

MELANIYA Derived from the Greek Melaina, which is from the root *melas* (black, dark). The name was made popular throughout Europe through its association with two 5th-century Roman saints, a grandmother and granddaughter remembered for their piety and good works for the poor. Var: Malan'ya. Pet: Malasha, Milya. (MEE-LAH-NEE-YAH)

NADEZHDA Popular name derived from the Russian vocabulary word meaning "hope." Var: Nadejda. Pet: Nadya. (NAH-DEE-EHZH-DAH)

NADYA The pet form of Nadezhda (hope), Nadya is also popularly bestowed as an independent given name. (NAH-DYAH)

NATALIYA A popular borrowing from the Latin, Natalia is a name derived from *diēs nātālis* (natal day, Christmas). It has been traditionally bestowed upon children born on Christmas Day. Var: Natalia, Natalie, Nataly, Natalya, Natella. Pet: Nata, Natascha, Nataschenka, Natasha, Talya, Tasha, Tasya, Tata, Tusya. (NAH-TAH-LEE-AH)

NATASHA A popular pet form of Natalia (natal day, Christmas), Natasha is also popularly bestowed as an independent given name. *See* NATALIYA. Var: Natascha. Pet: Nataschenka, Tasha, Tasya, Tata, Tusya. (NAH-TAH-SHA)

NELLI A pet form of Elena (light) and Ninel, Nelli is also bestowed as an independent given name. *See* ELENA *and* NINEL. (NEH-LEE)

NIKA A short form of Veronika, Nika is also bestowed as an independent given name. *See* VERONICA. (NEE-KAH)

NINA A diminutive form of Anna (gracious, full of grace, mercy), Nina is also bestowed as an independent given name. *See* ANNA. (NEE-NAH)

NINEL A name from the Soviet era, Ninel is an anagram of Lenin, the surname of Vladimir Ilyich Lenin (1870–1924), the Russian leader of the Communist Revolution of 1917 and premier of the U.S.S.R. The name is now falling out of favor, as with many Soviet-era names. Pet: Nelli, Nelya. (NIH-NEL)

OKSANA Popular name of Hebrew origin meaning "praise be to God." The name is borne by Ukranian Olympic gold medal figure skater Oksana Baiul. (OK-SAH-NAH)

OLGA Feminine form of Oleg (holy), a name derived from the Scandinavian Helgi, which has its root in the Old Norse *heill* (hale, hearty; blessed, holy). Var: Elga, Helga. Pet: Lelya, Lyalya, Lyusha, Lyusya, Olesya, Olya. (OL-GAH)

OLIMPIADA Derived from the Greek Olympia, a feminine form of Olympios (of Olympus). Olympus is the name of a mountain in northern Greece which was the home of the gods in Greek mythology. Short: Ada. Pet: Lipa. (O-LIM-PEE-AH-DAH)

PARASKEVA Derived from the Greek *Paraskewe* (Good Friday, the Day of Preparation), a combining of the elements *para* (beyond) and *skewē* (gear, implements). The name was traditionally bestowed upon children born on Good Friday, the Friday before Easter. Var: Praskovya. Pet: Pascha. (PAH-RAH-SKYEH-VAH)

PELAGIYA Feminine form of the Greek Pelagios (of or belonging to the sea), a name derived from *pelagos* (the sea). Var: Pelageya. Pet: Palasha, Polya. (PEE-LAH-GEE-YAH)

POLINA Feminine form of Paul, which is from Paulus, an old Roman family name derived from *paulus* (small). Pet: Lina, Polya. (PAH-LEE-NAH)

RENATA Feminine form of the Late Latin Renātus (reborn), which is derived from *renascor* (to be born again). The name is a traditional baptismal name. Short: Rena. Pet: Nata. (REH-NAH-TAH)

ROKSANA From the Greek Roxanē, which is believed to be derived from the Persian Roschana (dawn of day). The name was borne by the Bactrian wife of Alexander the Great, which seems to substantiate the name's roots. Short: Ksana. (ROKS-AH-NAH)

ROZA Russian cognate of Rosa, a name derived from the Latin *rosa* (a rose, red). Pet: Rozi. (RO-ZAH)

RUBINA Variant of Rufina, a name derived from the Latin *rufus* (reddish, red). The name originated in Italy as a nickname for a person with red hair. (ROO-BEE-NAH)

SASHA A pet form of Aleksandra (defender or helper of mankind), Sasha is also bestowed as an independent given name. *See* ALEKSANDRA. (SAH-SHA)

SERAFIMA Derived from the Hebrew *sĕrāphīm* (burning ones), which is from *sāraph* (to burn). The name is used in the Bible for the heavenly winged angels surrounding the throne of God. Short: Fima. Pet: Sima. (SARE-AH-FEE-MAH)

SHANNA Russian form of the Hebrew Shoshana, a derivative of *shōshannāh* (a lily, a rose). Var: Zhanna. (ZHAH-NAH)

SOFIYA Popular Russian cognate of Sophia, a Greek name derived from *sophia* (wisdom, skill). Var: Sofya. Pet: Sofa, Sofi, Sonya. (SO-FEE-YAH)

SONYA A popular pet form of Sofiya (wisdom, skill), Sonya is also bestowed as an independent given name. *See* SOFIYA. (SONE-YAH)

STEPHANIA A feminine form of the Greek Stephanos (a crown, a garland). *See* STEFAN (Male Names). Var: Stefanida, Stefanya, Stepanida. Pet: Pany, Stesha. (STYEH-PAH-NEE-DAH)

SVETLANA Popular Russian name meaning "star." Var: Swetlana. Pet: Lana, Sveta. (SVEHT-LAH-NAH)

TAISIYA Believed to be a Russian form of the Greek Thais, which is of uncertain derivation. "Bond" is a popular folk definition. The name was borne by a 4th-century B.C. courtesan who accompanied Alexander the Great on his Asiatic campaign. Pet: Tasya, Taya. (TAY-EE-SEE-YAH)

TAMARA Russian cognate of the Hebrew Tamar (a date palm, a palm tree). Var: Tamary. Short: Mara, Tama. Pet: Toma. (TAH-MAH-RAH)

TANYA A pet form of Tatiana, a name ultimately of uncertain origin, Tanya is also bestowed as an independent given name. *See* TATIANA. (TAHN-YAH)

TASHA Pet form of Natalia and Tatiana. *See* NATALIA *and* TATIANA. (TAH-SHA)

TATIANA A popular Russian name, Tatiana is the feminine form of the Latin Tatiānus, a derivative of the old Roman family name Tatius, which is of uncertain origin. The name Tatius was borne by a king of the Sabines who ruled jointly with Romulus. Var: Tatyana. Pet: Tanya, Tasha, Tata, Tusya. (TAH-TEE-AH-NAH)

TEKLA Russian form of the Greek Thekla, a derivative of Theokleia (divine glory). The name, which is a compounding of the elements *theos* (God) and *kleia* (glory), was borne by the first virgin martyr, who is said to have been a disciple of St. Paul. Var: Fekla, Tjokle. (TEH-KLAH)

URSULA A borrowing from the Middle Latin, Ursula is a diminutive form of the Latin *ursa* (a she-bear). (OOR-SYOO-LAH)

VALENTINA Feminine form of Valentin, the Russian cognate of Valentine, which is from the Latin Valentīnus, a derivative of *valens* (to be healthy, to be strong). Pet: Tina, Valya. (VAH-LEN-TEE-NAH)

VALERIYA Russian cognate of the French Valerie, which is from the Latin Valerius, an old Roman family name derived from *valere* (to be strong, healthy). Pet: Lera, Valya. (VAH-LARE-EE-YAH)

VARVARA Russian cognate of Barbara (foreign woman), a name derived from the Latin *barbarus* (foreign, strange). Pet: Varya, Vava. (VAHR-VAHR-AH)

VASILISA Feminine form of Vasili, the Russian cognate of the Greek Basileois (king). *See* VASILI (Male Names). Pet: Vasya. (VAS-EE-LEE-SAH)

VERA Popular name derived from the Russian *vjera* (faith). Pet: Verochka. (VEER-AH)

VERONICA Of debated origin and meaning, some believe it to be derived from the Late Latin *veraiconica*, the word given to a piece of cloth or garment with a representation of the face of Christ on it. *Veraiconica* is composed from the elements *verus* (true) and *iconicus* (of or belonging to an image). Alternatively, Veronica is thought to be a variant form of the Greek Berenikē (bringer of victory), a compound name composed of the elements *pherein* (to bring) and *nikē* (victory). Var: Veronika. Pet: Nika. (VER-O-NEE-KAH)

VICTORIYA Derived from the Latin *victoria* (victory). Var: Viktoria. Pet: Vika, Vitya, Tora. (VEEK-TOR-EE-AH)

VIOLETTA From the Old French *violette*, a diminutive form of *viole*, which is derived from the Latin *viola* (a violet). (VEE-O-LEH-TAH)

VITA Common name derived from the Latin *vita* (life). (VEE-TAH)

YULIYA Russian cognate of Julia, a feminine form of Julius, an old Roman family name thought to be derived from Iulus (the first down on the chin, downy-bearded). Because a person just beginning to develop facial hair is young, "youth" has become an accepted definition of the name and its related forms. Var: Iuliya, Youlia, Yulia. Pet: Yulya. (YOO-LEE-AH)

ZANETA Russian cognate of Janet, a diminutive form of Jane, which is a feminine form of John (God is gracious). *See* IVAN (Male Names). (ZHA-NEH-TAH)

ZINA A short form of Zinaida (of or pertaining to Zeus) and Zinobiya (the life of Zeus), Zina is also bestowed as an independent given name. *See* ZINAIDA *and* ZINOBIYA. (ZEE-NAH)

ZINAIDA Derived from the Greek Zenaide (of or pertaining to Zeus), a name derived from *zēn* (of Zeus). *See* ZENAIDE (Portuguese Names). Pet: Ida, Zina. (ZEE-NAH-EE-DAH)

ZINOBIYA Russian cognate of the Greek Zenobia, the feminine form of Zenobios (the life of Zeus). The name is a compounding of the elements *zēn* (of Zeus) and *bios* (life). Var: Zinobia. Pet: Zina, Zoya. (ZEE-NO-VEE-AH)

ZOYA Derived from the Greek *zōē* (life). Pet: Zoyecha, Zoyenka. (ZOY-YAH)

Chapter Twenty-seven

Scandinavian Names

Naming traditions in Scandinavia vary from region to region, but they all bear a common cultural heritage starting with the emigration of Germanic barbarians from western Asia in the early Middle Ages. Religion at this time was pagan and polytheistic, taking a gloomy view of the world and man's role in it. This helped to create a fierce race of people. They lived in a male-dominated society which took great pleasure in excess. They had an eager sense of adventure, which found them discovering new places overseas and raiding and settling neighboring lands. Siring a large number of children was seen as a symbol of one's virility and unfortunately went hand in hand with the commonly practiced barbaric act of infanticide.

By the beginning of the early Middle Ages, the people had divided into many different groups, such as the Scandinavians, Goths, Vandals, and Dutch. Their language changed as well, dividing into the modern languages of Danish, Icelandic, Norwegian, and Swedish. Dutch, the language of the Netherlands, is rooted in West Germanic, the branch that also produced the English and German languages.

As Christianity supplanted the old religion, many of the old gods were forgotten. Nevertheless, it is becoming as popular to give children names from Norse mythology or those with a strong Nordic flavor as it is to give them saints' names.

Before the nineteenth century, people in Denmark were only known by one name. In 1828 the government directed people to give their children a family name as well as a Christian name at baptism. Usually the chosen name was the father's name with either *-sen* (son of) or *-datter* (daughter of) added. A law passed in the 1860s made the family name hereditary. In 1904 the government reduced the charges for registering names in order to encourage people to adopt family names other than the *-sen* or *-datter* patronymics.

In Holland the Dutch long used generational-changing patronymics. The names became permanent and hereditary for the upper and middle classes in the thirteenth and fourteenth centuries. Not until the seventeenth century did the names become fixed for the lower-middle and lower classes.

The system of naming children in Iceland is an old one sanctioned by law. Babies are given a first name followed by the father's last name in the genitive case with an ending of *-son* (son of) or *-dottir* (daughter of). Women do not adopt their husband's surname upon marriage, but the title Fru is used to indicate marital status.

Hereditary family names began in urban Norway in the sixteenth century, but it wasn't until late in the nineteenth century that permanent family names became fixed throughout Norway. People who lived in the country had three names: a first name, a patronymic, and a "farm" name. The given names were handed down in a fixed order. The first-born son was given the name of the paternal grandfather; the first-born daughter was named for her paternal grandmother. The second son was given the maternal grandfather's name, and the second daughter was given the name of the maternal grandmother. Subsequent children were named for other family members.

The Swedish naming system consisted of a given name and the father's given name to which *-son* (son of) or *-dotter* (daughter of) was added. In 1901 the Swedish government passed a law fixing the family names into hereditary names instead of allowing them to change with each generation.

Many Scandinavian personal names have their roots in the old Germanic language. Most of these names are compound names composed of two separate elements. As the language died out, the names lost their meanings. Opposing name elements were used to create new names with contradictory meanings or meanings that made no sense. The female Friedelinde, which is composed of the elements *frid* (peace) and *lind* (weak, soft, tender), is an example. Dead languages of the Old West Norse and Old East Norse also form the basis of many of the names. Because of the region's shared history, similar societies, and language roots, many personal names are common throughout Scandinavia and the Netherlands.

Scandinavian Male Names

ÅKE Danish name of disputed origin and meaning, some relate it to the Germanic Anicho, which is derived from the element *ano* (ancestor). Others associate it with the Latin Achatius (agate) or Acacius (blameless). Var: Åge. (OAK)

AKSEL Danish derivative of the Hebrew Absalom, which is from *'abshālōm* (the father is peace). Absalom is borne in the Bible by the third son of King David. He rebelled against his father and was eventually killed when he was caught by the hair in an oak tree as he fled. Var: Axel. Pet: Acke. (EK-SEL, AK-SEL)

ALARIK Derived from the Germanic Alaric, which is composed of the elements *ala* (all) and *rik* (ruler, king): hence, "ruler of all." (EL-AH-RIK, AL-AH-RIK)

ALBERT A borrowing from the French, Albert (bright through nobility) is derived from the Old High German Adalbrecht, a compounding of the elements *adal* (noble, nobility) and *beraht* (bright). Albert Mecklenburg was the name of the puppet king of Sweden in 1364. (EL-BER, AL-BER)

ALEXANDER From the Greek Alexandrōs (defender or helper of mankind), a compound name composed of the elements *alexein* (to defend, to help) and *andros* (man, mankind). The fame of Alexander the Great (356–323 B.C.), king of Macedonia, and several early saints and martyrs helped popularize the name throughout Europe. (EL-EK-SAHN-DER, AL-EK-SAHN-DER)

ALGOT Derived from the obsolete Alfgautr, which is composed of the elements *alfr* (elf) and *Gautr*, a Gothic tribal name. (EL-GO, AL-GO)

ALOYSIUS Of uncertain origin, Aloysius is believed to be a Latinate form of the Old French Loeis (famous in war). The popularity of St. Aloysius of Gonzaga (1568–91), patron saint of boys and girls, led to common use of the name. (AL-O-EE-SEE-US)

ALVIS Of uncertain meaning borne in Norse mythology by a dwarf who fell in love with Thor's daughter, the giantess Thrud. (AL-VIS)

ÅMUND Derived from an Old Norse name composed of the elements *ag* (awe, fear; edge, point) and *mundr* (protector). Var: Amund. (AH-MUND, AH-MOON)

ANDERS Scandinavian cognate of Andrew, which is from the Greek Andreas, a derivative of *andreios* (manly). The popularity of St. Andrew, one of the Twelve Apostles, led to the name and its cognates being firmly established throughout Europe. Cognate: Andries (Dutch). Short: Dries (Dutch). (AN-DERS)

ANDOR From an Old Norse name composed of the elements *arn* (eagle) and Þorr (Thor, the name of the god of thunder). (AN-DOR)

ANKER Derived from *annkarl* (harvester), which is composed of the elements *ann* (harvest) and *karl* (peasant). Alternatively, some believe it is derived from the elements *arn* (eagle) and *karl* (peasant). (AN-KER)

ANNAR The second. The name is borne in Norse mythology by the second husband of Nótt (Night) and father of Jörð (Earth). (AN-NAR)

ANTON Scandinavian cognate of Anthony, which is derived from the Latin Antōnius, an old Roman family name of uncertain origin. Anthony the Great (c. 251–c. 356), an Egyptian hermit and founder of Christian monasticism, was one of several saints of this name. The fame of Anton van Leeuwenhoek (1632–1723), Dutch businessman and amateur scientist who pioneered microscopy and discovered protozoa and bacteria, led to the popularity of Anton as a given name. Cognate: Antonius (Dutch). Short: Teunis (Dutch); Tönjes, Tönnies (Frisian). (AN-TOHN)

ARE From the Old Norse name Ari, a short form of any of the various names containing the element *arn* (eagle). (AR-EH)

ARNBJÖRN Swedish name derived from the Old Norse elements *arn* (eagle) and *björn* (bear). Var: Armbjörn. Cognate: Arnbjørn (Norwegian). (ARN-BYORN, ARN-BYUR)

ARNE A short form of any of the names containing the element *arn* (eagle), it is commonly used as an independent given name. Var: Aren. (ARN-EH, ARN)

ARVID Derived from the Old Norse Arnviðr, a compound name composed of the elements *arn* (eagle) and *viðr* (wood, tree): hence, "eagle tree." (AR-VID)

ÅSMUND From the Old Norse Ásmundr, a name composed of the elements *áss* (god) and *mundr* (protector): hence, "God is protector." (ŌS-MOOND)

BALDER Prince, ruler, lord. In Norse mythology, Balder was the handsome son of Odin and Frigg. He was considered to be the wisest, most gentle, and fairest-spoken of the gods. He was accidentally slain by his blind brother Hoder. (BALL-DER)

BAREND Transferred use of the Germanic surname Bahrend (firm bear), which is used primarily in the Netherlands. (BAH-REN)

BARTHOLOMEUS Dutch form of Bartholomew, which is ultimately derived from the Greek Bartholomaios (son of Talmai). Talmai is an Aramaic name meaning "hill, mound, furrows." The name is borne in the Bible by one of the Twelve Apostles of Christ. Var: Bartel. (BAR-TOL-O-MAY-OOS)

BECK Transferred use of the surname meaning "dweller near the brook." (BEK)

BENEDIKT From the Latin Benedictus (blessed). St. Benedict of Nursii (c. 480–c. 543) was an Italian monk who founded the great monastery and the Benedictine Order in Monte Cassino, Italy. Pet: Bendt, Bent (Danish); Bengt (Swedish). (BEN-EH-DEEKT)

BERG Derived from *berg* (mountain). (BAIRG)

BERNT Scandinavian short form of Bernard (bold as a bear), which is derived from the Old High German Berinhard, a compounding of the elements *bero* (bear) and *hard* (bold, strong, hardy). (BERNT, BĀRNT)

BERT Originally a short form of Robert (bright through fame), Bert is now also bestowed as an independent given name. *See* ROBERT. (BERT)

BERTIL Scandinavian name derived from a Germanic pet form of names containing the element *beraht* (bright, famous). Var: Bertel. (BER-TEEL)

BIRGER Swedish name of Old Norse origin thought to be a derivative of *biarga* (to help). In common use since the Viking age, the name was borne by Birger Jarl, the greatest Swedish statesman of the Middle Ages and the founder of Stockholm. Var: Birghir, Börje, Byrghir, Byrgir. Cognate: Børge (Danish, Norwegian); Børre (Norwegian). Pet: Bigge, Birre. (BEER-GER)

BJÖRN Swedish name derived from the Old Norse *björn* (bear). It is also used as a short form of any of the various names containing the element *björn*. In use since Viking times, the name got a boost in popularity in recent years due to the fame of Swedish tennis star Björn Borg (b. 1956). Cognate: Bjarne, Bjørn (Norwegian). (BYURN, BYORN)

BO Derived from the Old Norse *búa* (to live, dwell, to have a household). Bo originated as a nickname for a householder. Pet: Bosse (Swedish). (BO)

BOYE Dutch name of uncertain and disputed origin. Some believe it to be a cognate of the English *boy* (lad, youth), from the Middle English *boie* (boy, knave, servant). Cognate: Boje (Frisian). (BOY-YEH)

BRODER From the Old Norse word *bróðir* (brother). This name was traditionally bestowed upon younger sons. Cognate: Bror (Swedish). Pet: Brolle (Swedish). (BRO-DER)

CANUTE Anglicized form of Knut, a name derived from the Old Norse Knútr (knot). *See* KNUT. The name was borne by the Danish king Knut (994–1035), known in the English-speaking world as Canute the Great. He was the first Danish king of England and also ruled Denmark and Norway. (KAH-NOOT)

CARL Derived from the Old English *carl* (freeman, peasant) or the Old Norse *karl* (man, freeman, peasant). The name Carl was borne by ten kings of Sweden, the latest being the popular Carl XVI Gustav (b. 1946). (KARL)

CAROLUS Latinate form of Charles, which is derived from the Old English *ceorl* (freeman, peasant) or the Old

Norse and Germanic *karl* (man, freeman, peasant). (KARL-US)

CASPAR Dutch form of Gaspar, which, along with Balthasar and Melchior, was assigned to the Three Wise Men, who brought gifts to the Christ child. The names are not found in the Bible and are thought to have been fixed in the 11th century. Of uncertain etymology, Gaspar might have been derived from the Persian *genashber* (treasure master), which is in keeping with his role of the bringer of precious gifts. Var: Casper, Kaspar, Kasper. Cognate: Jesper (Danish). (KAS-PAR)

CHRISTIAN Derived from the Latin *christiānus* (a Christian, a follower of Christ). The name was borne by ten kings of Denmark, which helped bring great popularity to the name. Cognate: Kristen (Danish); Christer (Danish, Swedish); Kerstan (Dutch); Krister, Kristian (Norwegian, Swedish). Short: Kris, Krist. Pet: Kit (Dutch). (KREES-CHEN)

CHRISTOPHER Derived from the Ecclesiastic Greek Christophoros, which is composed of the elements *Christos* (Christ) and *pherein* (to bear): hence, "bearing Christ." The name was borne by three kings of Denmark. Cognate: Kristofel, Kristofer (Dutch, Swedish). Short: Toff, Toffel (Dutch, Swedish). (KREES-TŌ-FER)

CLAUS Short form of Nicolaus (victory of the people), which is from the Greek Nikolaos, a compounding of the elements *nikē* (victory) and *laos* (the people). Claus is often bestowed as an independent given name. Var: Klaas, Klasse, Klaus (Dutch); Klaes (Frisian). (KLAUS)

CORNELIS Dutch form of the Latin Cornelius, an old Roman family name of uncertain origin and meaning. It is possibly a derivation of the Latin *cornu* (horn). Short: Cor, Niels. Pet: Cees, Kees. (KOR-NEE-LIS)

DAG Derived from the Old Norse *dagr* (day). The name is borne in Norse mythology by the son of Nótt (Night) and Dellingr (Dayspring). His duty was to drive his horse Skinfaxi (Shiningmare) around the earth once every twenty-four hours, illuminating the earth with the light from the horse's hair. (DAG)

DANA Derived from the Old Norse Danr (a Dane, one from Denmark). Var: Dane. (DANE-AH)

DANIEL Derived from the Hebrew *dāni'ēl* (God is my judge). The name is borne in the Bible by a Hebrew prophet whose faith kept him alive in a den of lions. Daniel and the Lions' Den was a favorite story during the Middle Ages, which led to popular use of the name throughout Europe. (DAN-YELL)

DAVID From the Hebrew *dāvīd* (beloved). The name David is borne in the Bible by the greatest of the Israelite kings. (DAY-VID)

DELLINGER Derived from the Old Norse Dellingr (Dayspring). The name is borne in Norse mythology by the god of dawn, the third husband of Nótt (Night) and father of Dagr (Day). (DELL-ING-ER)

DIEDERIK Dutch form of Dietrich, a German variant of Derek, which in turn is a short form of Theodoric (ruler of the people). Theodoric is from the obsolete Gothic Thiudoreiks, a compound name composed of the elements *thiuda* (folk, people) and *reiks* (ruler, leader, king). Var: Didhrikr, Didrik. Short: Dierk. Pet: Tiede. (DEE-DER-RIK)

DIERK A short form of Dietrich (ruler of the people), Dierk is also bestowed as an independent given name. *See* DIEDERIK. (DYURK, DEERK)

DIRK Flemish and Dutch cognate of the German Derek, a short form of Theodoric, which is from the obsolete Gothic Thiudoreiks, a compounding of the elements *thiuda* (folk, people) and *reiks* (ruler, king, leader). The name is often mistakenly thought to be from the Scottish word *dirk* (dagger, small sword). (DIRK)

EDMOND From the Old English Ēadmund, a compound name composed of the elements *ēad* (riches, wealth, prosperity) and *mund* (hand, protection): hence, "wealthy protector." (ED-MOON, ĀD-MOON)

EDVARD From the Old English Ēadward, a compound name composed of the elements *ēad* (riches, wealth, prosperity) and *weard* (guardian, protector): hence, "wealthy guardian." Cognate: Eduard (Dutch). (ED-VAR, ĀD-VAR)

EDZARD Frisian form of the Germanic Eckhard, a name composed from the elements *eg, ek* (edge, point) and *hard* (hardy, brave, strong). (ED-ZAHRD, ĀD-ZAR)

EGIL Derived from the Old Norse element *eg* (edge, point of a sword). (EH-GL)

EILERT Derivative of the Germanic Eckhard, which is composed of the elements *eg, ek* (edge, point) and *hard* (hardy, brave, strong). (Ī-LERT)

EILIF Norwegian name derived from the Old Norse elements *ei* (always, ever) and *lífr* (alive): hence, "immortal." Var: Eiliv. (Ī-LIF)

EINAR Scandinavian name composed of the Old Norse elements *einn* (one, alone) and *herr* (army, warrior): hence, "lone warrior." In Norse legend, the *einherjar* were the Heroes, the eminent warriors who were sent to Valhalla upon their deaths. (Ī-NAR)

ELOF Swedish name derived from the Old Norse Einlāfr, which is composed of the elements *einn* (one, alone) and *lāfr* (descendant, heir): hence, "lone descendant." Var: Elov. Cognate: Eluf (Danish). Pet: Loffe (Swedish). (Ī-LOF)

EMANUEL Derived from the Greek Emmanouēl, which is from the Hebrew *'immānūēl* (God is with us). This was the byname of Jesus Christ, as prophesied by Isaiah. (IH-MAN-YOOL)

EMIL Germanic name commonly used throughout Scandinavia and the Netherlands. It is a cognate of the French Émile, which is from the old Roman family name Aemilius, a name believed to be derived from the Latin *aemulus* (emulating, trying to equal or excel, rival). (EE-MIL)

ERIK A name that has remained popular since the Viking age. Erik is derived from the Old Norse Eirìkr (ever powerful, eternal ruler), a compounding of the elements *ei* (ever, always) and *ríkr* (ruler, king). The name has been borne by twelve kings of Denmark, Norway, and Sweden, which helped to keep the name in common use. Var: Eirik, Eric. Cognate: Jerk, Jerker (Swedish). (ERR-RIK)

ERLEND Derived from the Old Norse *örlendr* (foreigner, stranger). Var: Erland. (ERR-LEN, ERR-LEND)

ESBJÖRN Old Norse name that has remained in popular use. It is derived from the elements *áss* (god, divinity) and *björn* (bear): hence, "divine bear." Cognate: Esben, Esbern (Danish); Asbjørn, Esbjørn (Norwegian). Pet: Ebbe. (ESS-BYORN, ESS-BYURN)

ESKEL Of Old Norse derivation, Eskel is composed of the elements *áss* (god, divinity) and *ketill* (sacrificial cauldron). Var: Eskil. (ESS-KEL)

EVERHART Dutch name derived from the Old High German Eburhart, a compound name composed of the elements *ebur* (wild boar) and *harto* (strong, hearty). Var: Evert. (EV-ER-HAHR)

EWOULD Dutch form of the Germanic Ewald, a compound name composed of the elements *ēo* (law, right) and *wald* (rule): hence, "lawful rule." (EE-WOOL)

EYULF Norwegian name derived from the elements *anja* (luck) and *úlfr* (wolf). Henrik Ibsen's play *Little Eyolf* (1894) helped popularize the name. Var: Eyolf. (Ī-ULF)

EYVIND Old Norse name composed of the elements *ey* (island) and *Vind* (the name of an old Slavic people now known as Wend): hence, "island of the Wend." The name was borne by poet Eyvind Finnsson, author of "Hákonarmál," an ode to King Haakon the Good (c. 946–61). (Ī-VIN)

FAAS Dutch and Flemish form of Fastred (resolute counsel), a name derived from the Old German elements *fast* (firm, resolute) and *red* (advice, counsel). (FAHS)

FEEL Dutch cognate of Felix, a Latin name derived from *felix* (lucky, happy). (FEEL)

FENRIS Ancient name of uncertain meaning borne in Norse mythology by the son of Loki and the giantess Angrboda. He took the shape of an enormous wolf and became very threatening to the gods, being responsible for biting off the hand of the god Tyr. (FEN-RIS)

FILIP Derived from the Greek Philippos (lover of horses), which is composed of the elements *philos* (loving) and *hippos* (a horse). The name, which has remained popular since classical times, was borne by one of the Twelve Apostles of Christ and several other Christian saints. (FIL-IP)

FINN Derived from the Old Norse Finnr (a Finn, one from Finland). Var: Finnur. (FIN)

FISKE Swedish name derived from *fiske* (fish). The name originated as a byname for a fisherman, thus taking the definition "a fisherman." Var: Fisk. (FISK)

FLEMMING A very popular name in Denmark, Flemming is derived from the Middle Dutch Vlaming (Flemish, a native of Flanders). (FLEM-MING)

FLORIS Dutch cognate of the Latin Florentia (a blooming), which is derived from *florens* (blossoming, flourishing). (FLO-RIS)

FOLKE Derived from the Old Norse *folk* (people, tribe). Var: Folki. (FOLK)

FOLKVAR Derivation of the Old Norse Folkvarðr (guard of the people), a compound name composed of the elements *folk* (people, tribe) and *varðr* (guard). Var: Falkor. (FOLK-VAHR)

FREDERIK From the Germanic Friedrich (peaceful ruler), which is composed of the elements *frid* (peace) and *rik* (ruler, king). A popular name throughout Scandinavia and the Netherlands, it has been borne by nine kings of Denmark and one of Sweden. Cognate: Frerik (Dutch); Fredrik (Swedish). Pet: Freek (Dutch). (FREED-EH-RIK)

FREY Lord, he who is foremost. According to Norse mythology, the fertility-god Frey was the son of Njörðr and brother to Freya. The most handsome of the gods, his duties were to see to the fruitfulness of the earth and to the good fortunes of men. Early in the Viking age, the cult of Frey was quite popular, and many place-names and given names were formed from his name and his byname, Ing. (FRAY)

FRITJOF Derived from the Old Norse Friðþjófr (peace thief), which is composed of the elements *friðr* (peace) and *þjófr* (thief). Var: Fridtjof, Fridtjov, Fritjov. (FRIT-YOF)

FRODE Derived from the Old Norse *fróðr* (knowing, wise, learned). (FRO-DEH)

FRODI The name of the legendary Danish king who proclaimed universal peace throughout his empire. The armistice lasted for thirty years and is known as the Peace of Frodi. He is known in Norse mythology as the son of the god Frey and the mortal Freygerda. (FRO-DEE)

GARTH Popular name derived from the Old Norse *garðr* (yard, enclosure). The name originally denoted one who lived beside an enclosure. (GARTH)

GEORGE Derived from the Greek Geōrgios (earthworker, farmer), which is from the elements *gē* (earth) and *ergein* (to work). Cognate: Georg (Danish, Swedish); Joris (Dutch, Frisian); Göran, Jöran, Örjan (Swedish). (GEE-ORG)

GERARD Derived from the Germanic Gerhart (brave with the spear), a name composed of the Old High German elements *ger* (a spear, a javelin) and *hart* (hearty, brave, strong). Cognate: Geeraard, Geerd, Geert, Gert (Dutch, Flemish); Garrit, Gerrit (Frisian); Gerhard (Norwegian, Swedish). (GARE-RARD)

GERLACH Dutch cognate of Gerlaich, an old Germanic name composed of the elements *ger* (a spear, a javelin) and *laich* (play, sport). The name was borne by St. Gerlach, a 12th-century saint who lived as a hermit near Valkenberg. (GARE-LAHK)

GEROLT Dutch cognate of Gerald, from the obsolete Old High German Gerwald, a name composed of the elements *ger* (a spear, a javelin) and *wald* (rule): hence, "rule with a spear." Cognate: Gerold (Danish). (GARE-OLT)

GILLIS Derivative of the Old French Gilles, which is from the Latin Aegidius, a name derived from *aegis* (the goatskin shield of Zeus, a protection). (GIL-LEES)

GJORD Swedish contracted form of the Old Norse Guðfriðr (god of peace), a compound name composed of the elements *guð* (god) and *friðr* (peace). Cognate: Gjurd. (YORD, YURD)

GODFRIED Derived from the Old Norse Guðfriðr (god of peace), which is composed of the elements *guð* (god) and *friðr* (peace). (GOD-FREED)

GREGOR Derived from the Greek Grēgorios (vigilant, watchful), which is from *egeirein* (to awaken). The name was borne by several early saints and popes. Cognate: Gregers (Danish, Norwegian); Joris (Dutch, Frisian); Greger (Swedish). (GREE-GOR)

GUNNAR Derived from the Old Norse Gunnarr, which is from *gunnr* (war, strife, battle). Alternatively, some believe it is of Germanic origin, a cognate of Günther (war army). *See* GÜNTHER (German Names). The name Gunnar was borne by several interesting characters in Norse mythology, one of whom was the brother of Gudrunand, husband of Brynhild. Var: Gunder (Danish). (GOO-NAR)

GUSTAV Derived from the Old Norse elements *Gautr* (the tribal name of the Goths) and *stafr* (staff): hence, "staff of the Goths." The name has been borne by six kings of Sweden, the last being King Gustav VI Adolph (1882–1973). Cognate: Gustaof (Danish); Gustaaf (Dutch); Gösta, Gustaf (Swedish). Pet: Staaf (Dutch). (GOO-STAHF)

GYLFI Ancient name of uncertain meaning borne in Norse mythology by the legendary king of Sweden who visited Asgard in disguise and questioned the three supreme gods to elicit all the mythological information. (GIL-FEE)

HAAKON From the Old Norse Hákon, which is derived from the elements *há* (high, chosen) and *konr* (son, descendant). Haakon is an ancient name that remains popular to this day. Haakon Magnus is the name of the son of King Harald V and Queen Sonja of Norway. Cognate: Hagen, Hakon (Danish); Håkon (Norwegian); Håkan (Swedish). (HAH-KEN, HO-KEN)

HALDOR Derived from the Old Norse elements *hallr* (rock) and Þórr (Thor): hence, "Thor's rock." Var: Halldor. Short: Halle. (HAHL-DOR)

HALFDAN Derived from the Old Norse Hálfdanr, a compound name composed of the elements *hálfr* (half) and *Danr* (a Dane): hence, "half Dane." The name was originally a byname of someone who was half Danish and is borne by many characters in Nordic legend. Var: Halvdan. (HAHLF-DAHN)

HALLE A short form of any of the names containing the element *hallr* (rock), Halle is also in use as a pet form of Harald (leader of the army). *See* HARALD. (HAL-LEH)

Halsten Swedish name composed of the Old Norse elements *hallr* (rock) and *stein* (stone). Var: Hallstein, Hallsten. Short: Halle. (HAHL-STEHN)

Halvard Derived from the Old Norse Halvarðr, a compounding of the elements *hallr* (rock) and *varðr* (guardian, defender): hence, "defender of the rock." Cognate: Hallvard, Hallvor, Halvor (Norwegian); Halvar (Swedish). (HAHL-VAR)

Hamund Ancient name of uncertain meaning borne in Norse mythology by the son of Sigmund and Borghild of Bralund. (HAH-MOOND)

Hannes A short form of Johannes (God is gracious), Hannes is also bestowed as an independent given name. *See* JOHANNES. (HAH-NESS)

Harald From the Old Norse Haraldr, a name believed to be derived from the older Germanic name Hariwald (ruler of the army), a compounding of the elements *hari* (army) and *wald* (rule). Harald, a popular name since the early Viking age, was borne by four kings and many princes of Norway, the earliest being King Harald Fairhair (d. 936?), the latest being King Harald V (b. 1937). Var: Arild. Pet: Halle, Harry. (HAHR-ALD)

Harbert Dutch cognate of the English Herbert and the Germanic Harbrecht. Herbert is from the Old English Herebeorht, a compounding of the elements *here* (army) and *beorht* (bright, fair). Harbrecht is derived from the elements *hari* (army) and *beraht* (bright). (HAHR-BERT)

Haward From the Old Norse Havarðr, a compound name composed of the elements *hā* (high) and *varðr* (guardian, defender). (HAH-WAHRD)

Heimdall Given the definition "the white god," Heimdall is from the Old Norse Heimdallr. The name is borne in Norse mythology by the son of Odin and the nine Wave Maidens. He disguised himself and had illicit affairs with three mortal women, founding the classes of the serfs and thralls, peasants and karls, and warriors and jarls. His duty was to guard the rainbow bridge, Bifrost. (HIME-DAHL)

Helgi Derived from the Old Norse *heilagr* (successful), which is from *heill* (hale, hearty, happy). The name is borne by many characters in Norse legend and remains popular to this day. Var: Helge, Helje. (HEL-GEE)

Hendrik From the Germanic Heinrich (home ruler, ruler of an enclosure), which is derived from the obsolete Old High German names Haganrih and Heimerich. *See* HEINRICH (German Names). The variant form Henrik was borne by Henrik Ibsen (1828–1906), the Norwegian poet and playwright whose works include *Peer Gynt*. Var: Henerik, Henrik. Pet: Harry; Henning (Danish). (HEN-RIK)

Henning A pet form of Hendrik (home ruler, ruler of an enclosure) and Johannes (God is gracious), Henning is also in use as an independent given name. *See* HENDRIK *and* JOHANNES. (HEN-NING)

Herleif Derived from the obsolete Old Norse Herleifr, a compound name composed of the elements *herr* (army) and *leifr* (heir, descendant; beloved). Var: Härlief, Herlof, Herluf. (HAHR-LEEF)

Hermod Derived from the Old Norse Hermóðr, an ancient name borne in Norse mythology by the son of Odin and Frigg. His duty was to welcome the fallen heroes and warriors to Valhalla. (HER-MOD)

Hjalmar Popular since the Viking ages, Hjalmar is composed of the Old Norse elements *hjalmr* (helmet, protection) and *herr* (army, warrior): hence, "warrior's helmet." Cognate: Hjälmar (Swedish). (HYALL-MAR)

Hoder Derived from the Old Norse Höðr, a name borne in Norse mythology by a blind god who accidentally killed his much-loved brother, Balder. Var: Hodur. (HO-DER)

Hoenir Ancient name borne in Norse mythology by the son of Bor and Bestla and brother of Odin. He gave humanity the gifts of understanding, motion, and the senses. Var: Honir. (HO-NEER)

Hubert From the Old High German Huguberht (bright in mind and spirit), a compound name composed of the elements *hugu* (mind, heart, spirit) and *beraht* (bright, famous). The name was borne by St. Hubert, an 8th-century bishop of Maastrict in the Netherlands who is regarded as the patron saint of hunters. Var: Hubertus, Hubrecht (Dutch). Pet: Huib, Huub (Dutch). (HYOO-BERT)

Hugo Germanic name in common use throughout Scandinavia and the Netherlands. It is derived from *hugu* (mind, heart, spirit). The name was borne by Huig de Greet (1583–1645), also known as Hugo Grotius, a great Dutch scholar and statesman. Cognate: Huig (Dutch). (HYOO-GOO)

Ignaas Dutch cognate of the Latin Ignatius, which is thought to be derived from the element *ignis* (fire). (EEG-NAHS)

Inge He who is foremost, lord. Short form of any of the names beginning with the element *Ing(e)*, which is a byname of the fertility-god Frey in Norse mythology. Inge is commonly bestowed as an independent given name and has been borne by four kings of Norway and Sweden. (ING-A)

INGMAR Popular name derived from Ing, a byname of the mythological fertility-god, and the Old Norse *mærr* (famous): hence, "famous Ing." The name is borne by Swedish film director Ingmar Bergman (b. 1918). Var: Ingemar. Short: Inge. (ING-MAR)

INGVAR Popular name derived from Ing, a byname of the mythological fertility-god, and the Old Norse *arr* (warrior). Var: Yngvar, Yngve. (ING-VAR)

ISAK Swedish cognate of Isaac, which is from the Ecclesiastic Greek Isaak, a derivative of the Hebrew Yitzchak (he will laugh), which has its root in *yitshāq* (laughter). The name is borne in the Bible by one of the three patriarchs, the son of Abraham and Sarah and father of Jacob and Esau. (EE-SAHK)

IVAR Old but perennially popular name composed from the Old Norse elements *ýr* (yew, bow) and *herr* (warriors, army): hence, "bow warriors, archers." Ivar the Boneless, a son of Ragnar Shaggybritches, invaded East Anglia in revenge for his father's death, thus laying the foundation of the Danelaw in England. Var: Iver (Danish). (EE-VAHR)

JACOB Derived from the Greek Iakōbos, a name derived from the Hebrew Yaakov, which is from *ja'aqob* (seizing by the heel, supplanting). The name is borne in the Bible by a son of Isaac who is said to have grabbed his twin brother Esau's heel upon birth, causing Jacob to be born first. Var: Jakob. Pet: Cobus, Coos, Jaap (Dutch). (YAH-KOOB)

JARL Nobleman. Jarl is borne in Norse mythology by the son, through illicit union, of Heimdall and the mortal Modir. Jarl and his wife Erna became the progenitors of the warrior and ruling classes. (YARL)

JEREMIAS A borrowing from the Latin, Jeremias is from the Ecclesiastic Greek Hieremias, which is from the Hebrew Yirmeyahu, a name derived from *yirmeyāh* (the Lord loosens, God will uplift). The name is borne in the Bible by a 6th- or 7th-century B.C. Hebrew prophet whose story and prophecies are recorded in the Old Testament book of Jeremiah. (YER-EH-MĪ-AHS)

JEROEN Dutch cognate of Jerome, which is derived from the Latin Hieronymus and the Greek Hierōnymos, both of which are composed of the elements *hieros* (holy) and *onyma* (name): hence, "holy name." The name was borne by an Italian monk, born Eusebius Hieronymus Sophronius, who was the author of the Vulgate, the Latin version of the Bible which was the authorized version of the Roman Catholic Church. (YER-O-EN)

JOAKIM Derived from the Hebrew Yehoyakim (God will establish). The name is borne in the Bible by a king of Judah who was defeated by the Babylonians under King Nebuchadnezzar. In medieval Christian tradition, Joachim was the name assigned to the father of the Virgin Mary, as Anne was assigned to her mother. Cognate: Jockum (Danish); Jokum (Danish, Norwegian). Pet: Kim. (YO-AH-KEEM)

JOHANNES Middle Latin name popular throughout Scandinavia and the Netherlands. It is derived from the Ecclesiastic Greek Iōannes, which is from the Hebrew Yehanan, a short form of Yehohanan, which is from *yehōhānān* (Yahweh is gracious). Johannes (John) and all its cognates and variants are one of the most popular and enduring of the biblical names. Cognate: Jan, Jens, Johan, Jon, Jöns. Pet: Joop (Dutch); Janne, Jösse (Swedish). (YO-HAH-NESS)

JOOST Dutch form of the name Justus, which is from the Latin *justus* (lawful, just, proper). Var: Just. (YOOST)

JORDAAN Dutch form of Jordan, a name derived from the Hebrew Yarden (to flow down, descend). The name was originally used in the Middle Ages for a child baptized in holy water that was said to be from the river Jordan. Pet: Joord. (YOR-DAHN)

JØRGEN Danish cognate of George, a cognate of the Greek Georgios, which is derived from *geōrgos* (earthworker, farmer), a compounding of the elements *gē* (earth) and *ergein* (to work). Cognate: Jörgen (Swedish). Short: Jørn (Danish). (YER-GUHN)

JOSEF Derived from the Hebrew Yosef via the Ecclesiastic Greek Iōsēph. Yosef is from *yōsēf* (may he add). The name is borne in the Bible by several favored characters, thus keeping the name popular. Pet: Joop (Dutch). (YO-SEF)

JOZUA Dutch cognate of Joshua, a derivative of the Hebrew Yehoshua, which is from *yehōshū'a* (Jehovah is help, God is salvation). The name is borne in the Bible by Moses' successor, who led the children of Israel into the Promised Land. (YO-ZHOO-AH)

KAI Popular Scandinavian name of uncertain origin and meaning. Cognate: Kaj (Danish). (KĪ)

KARI From the Old Norse *kári* (gust of wind; curly-haired). According to Norse mythology, Kari, the son of the giant Gymir, ruled the wind and air. In more modern times, Kari came to be a byname for someone with curly hair. Var: Kåre. (KAH-REH)

KARL From the Old Norse and Germanic *karl* (freeman, peasant). According to Norse mythology, Karl was the son of the god Heimdall and the mortal Amma. Karl and his wife Snor were the progenitors of the class of peasants and yeomen, also known as karls. Karl has been a perennially popular name throughout Scandinavia and the German-speaking world. Cognate: Karel (Dutch). Pet: Kalle (Swedish). (KARL)

KENNET Scandinavian cognate of Kenneth, which is derived from the Scottish Gaelic Caioneach (handsome, comely). Var: Kent. (KANE-NET)

KETTIL Swedish name derived from the Old Norse *ketill* (sacrificial cauldron). Cognate: Keld, Kjeld, Kjell (Danish); Kjetil (Norwegian). (KAY-TIL)

KLEMENS Danish and Swedish cognate of Clement, which is from the Latin Clemens, a derivative of the vocabulary word *clemens* (gentle, merciful, lenient). (KLAY-MENS)

KNUT From the Old Norse Knútr (knot). Knut was the name of a Danish king (944–1035) who ruled over Denmark, Holland, and England. King Knut IV (d. 1086), great-nephew of Knut the Great, was responsible for founding churches throughout Denmark. After his death at the hands of resentful nobles, he was canonized and became the patron saint of Denmark. Var: Knud; Canute (Ang.). (K-NOOT)

KONRAD A borrowing from the German, Konrad is derived from the Old High German Kuonrat (wise counsel), a compounding of the elements *kuon* (bold, wise) and *rat* (counsel). Cognate: Koenraad (Dutch). Short: Koen, Kort. (KONE-RAHD)

KONSTANTIN Scandinavian cognate of Constantine (resolute), which is from the Latin Constantinus, a derivative of *constans* (standing together, resolute, constant). Constantine the Great (280–337) was the first Christian emperor of Rome. Var: Konstanz (Dutch). (KONE-STAHN-TIN)

KONUR A name of uncertain meaning. According to Norse mythology, Konur was the youngest son of Jarl and Erna, the progenitors of the ruling and warrior classes. Little is known about him, other than that he was exceedingly remarkable. He was as strong as eight men, could speak with animals, calm stormy seas, and ease troubled hearts. He or one of his descendants is said to have been the first king of Denmark. (KONE-UR)

KORT A contracted form of the Dutch Koenraad (wise counsel), Kort is also commonly bestowed as an independent given name. *See* KONRAD. (KORT)

KRISTOFFER From the Ecclesiastic Greek Christophoros, a compound name composed of the elements *Christos* (Christ) and *pherein* (to bear). The name was borne by a 3rd-century saint, the patron of travelers, which gave rise to the saying "St. Christopher protect us." (KREES-TOH-FUR)

LAMBERT Germanic name in common use in the Netherlands. Lambert is composed of the elements *land* (land) and *beraht* (bright, famous): hence, "famous land." During the Middle Ages, the name was bestowed in honor of St. Lambert, a 7th-century bishop of Maastricht. Var: Lammert. (LAM-BERT)

LARS Very popular Scandinavian cognate of Laurence (man from Laurentum). *See* LORENS. (LARZ)

LEIF From the Old Norse Leifr, which is directly derived from *leifr* (what is remaining, relic), from the verb *lev* (to leave). Over time, *leif* or *laf* became confused with the Germanic *leib* or *lip* (love) and is now often thought to mean "beloved." The name was borne by Leif Ericsson, a Norwegian explorer and adventurer who discovered North America around A.D. 1000. He was the son of Eric the Red. Var: Leiv. (LAYF)

LENNART Cognate of Leonard, which is from the Old High German Lewenhart (brave as a lion, lion-hearted), a compound name composed of the elements *lewo* (lion) and *hart* (strong, brave, hearty). Cognate: Leonhard (Danish). Pet: Lelle, Lenne, Nenne. (LEN-NERT)

LIF Derived from the Old Norse *lifr* (life). According to Norse mythology, Lif was the name of the sole man to survive Ragnarok and become the father of humanity thereafter. His wife, Lifthrasir, was the only woman to survive. (LEEF)

LODEWIJK Dutch cognate of the Germanic Ludwig (famous in war), which is derived from the elements *hluod* (famous) and *wīg* (war, strife). (LO-DAH-WEEK)

LODUR Ancient name of uncertain meaning. According to Norse mythology, Lodur was a son of Bor and Bestla and a brother to Odin and Hoenir. His contributions to humanity were blood and bodily color. He was also known as Vé. (LO-DER)

LORENS Scandinavian cognate of Laurence, which is from the Latin Laurentius (man from Laurentum). Laurentum, the name of a town in Latium, is thought to be derived from *laurus* (laurel). Cognate: Larse, Laurans, Laurens (Norwegian); Lars (Norwegian, Swedish). Pet: Lauri. (LORENZ)

LUCAS A borrowing from the Latin, Lucas is thought to be a derivative of Lucius, the root of which is *lux* (light). Alternatively, some believe the name is derived from the Ecclesiastic Greek Loukas, a contraction of Loukanos (man from Lucania). (LOO-KAS)

LUDGER Dutch cognate of the Germanic Leutgar (people's spear), which is composed of *leut* (people) and *gar* (a spear, a javelin). (LOOD-GER)

LUDOVIC Derived from the Germanic Ludwig (famous in war), a compound name composed of the elements *hluod* (famous) and *wīg* (war, strife). The name was borne by Ludovic Holberg (1684–1754), an author and playwright who is claimed by both Norway and Denmark. Cognate: Lodewijk (Dutch). (LOO-DO-VEEK, LOO-DO-VIK)

MAARTEN Dutch cognate of the Latin Martinus (of Mars, war-like), which is derived from Mars, the name of the Roman mythological god of war. The name became popular in the Middle Ages due in part to the fame of the German theologian Martin Luther (1483–1546). Cognate: Martijn (Dutch); Morten (Norwegian); Mårten (Swedish). (MAHR-TEN)

MAGNI Derived from the Old Norse *megin* (might), this name has been given the definition "colossal might." According to Norse mythology, Magni was the son of Thor and the giantess Jarnsaxa. He rescued his father during Thor's duel with the giant Hrungnir. (MAG-NEH, MAG-NEE)

MAGNUS Derived from the Latin *magnus* (great, large). The name has been borne by seven kings of Norway and three kings of Sweden. Cognate: Mogens (Danish); Måns (Swedish). (MAG-NES)

MANFRED Derived from the old Germanic name Maginfred (mighty peace), which is composed of the elements *magin* (might) and *frid* (peace). (MAN-FRED)

MARCUS A borrowing from the Latin, Marcus is of uncertain derivation. Most believe it has its root in Mars, the name of the Roman mythological god of war, and thus give it the meaning "war-like." Others think it is from *mas* (manly) or the Greek *malakoz* (soft, tender). (MAHR-KUS)

MATHIAS A borrowing from the Greek, Mathias is a contraction of Mattathias, a name derived from the Hebrew Matityah, which is from *mattīthyāh* (gift of God). The name is borne in the Bible by one of the four evangelists, the author of the first Gospel, Matthew. Cognate: Mathies, Matthews (Danish); Matheu, Matthijs (Dutch); Matthies (Frisian); Matteus (Swedish). Short: Mads (Danish); Thijs (Dutch); Mats (Norwegian, Swedish). (MAH-THĪ-US, MAH-THEE-US)

MAURITS Scandinavian cognate of Maurice, which is derived from the Late Latin Maurus (a Moor, of Moorish lineage). Maurice of Nassau (1567–1625) was a Dutch statesman and military leader. Var: Maurids, Morets. (MORE-RITZ)

MICHAEL Derived from the Hebrew *mīkhā'ēl* (who is like God?). The name is borne in the Bible by the archangel closest to God, the one responsible for carrying out God's judgments. He is regarded as the patron of the Christian warrior. The name has been borne by many saints and is popular throughout Europe. Cognate: Mikkel (Danish, Norwegian); Michiel (Dutch); Mikael, Mikel (Swedish). Pet: Micheltje (Dutch); Mikas (Swedish). (MĪ-KL, MIH-KL, MEE-CHEL)

NATANAEL From the Ecclesiastic Late Latin and Ecclesiastic Greek Nathanaēl, a derivative of the Hebrew Netanel, which is from *nĕthan'ēl* (gift of God). The name is borne in the Bible by one of the disciples of Christ, more commonly known as Bartholomew. (NAH-TAH-NALE)

NIELS A Danish form of Nicholas (victory of the people) and a Dutch short form of Cornelis (horn), Niels is also bestowed as an independent given name. *See* CORNELIS *and* NIKOLAUS. (NEELZ)

NIKOLAUS Derived from the Greek Nikolaos (victory of the people), a compounding of the elements *nikē* (victory) and *laos* (the people). The name was borne by St. Nicholas, a 4th-century bishop of Myra about whom many legends have grown. He is known to children as the bringer of gifts on Christmas. Cognate: Niels (Danish); Nicolaus, Niklaas (Danish, Dutch); Niklas, Nils (Danish, Swedish); Nels (Norwegian, Swedish); Nicklas (Swedish). Short: Claus, Klaas, Klasse (Dutch); Klaus (Danish); Klaes (Frisian); Nisse (Swedish). (NIH-KO-LAHS)

NJORD Derived from the Old Norse Njörðr (north). According to Norse mythology, Njord was one of the Vanir race of gods. He was a god of the sea, the father of Frey and Freya, and the husband of Nerthus the giantess Skadi, and the patron of fishermen and sailors. Var: Njorth. (NYORD)

ODIN Derived from the Old Norse Othinn, which is of uncertain meaning. In Norse mythology, Odin was the chief deity and god of art and culture, and of war and the dead. He was the husband of Fjorgyn, Frigg, and Rind, and had ten sons, including Thor and Balder. According to Norse folklore, Odin gave people soul and life and received the fallen heroes and warriors in his hall, Valhalla. (O-DIN)

ODUR Derived from the Old Norse Óðr, which is of uncertain meaning. According to Norse mythology, Odur, the first husband of Freya, was accustomed to going away for long periods of time, leaving Freya to weep for his return. (O-DER)

OLAF Derived from the Old Norse Anlaff (ancestor's relic), which is composed of the elements *anu* (ancestor) and *laf* (what is remaining, what is left of his forefathers, relic). The name has been in constant use since the Viking age and was borne by St. Olaf, king of Norway (995–1030), who helped spread the Christian religion throughout his realm. He is now regarded as the patron saint of Norway. Cognate: Olav, Ole (Danish, Norwegian); Ola (Norwegian, Swedish); Olof, Olov, Oluf (Swedish). (O-LEF, O-LAHF)

OSKAR Scandinavian cognate of Oscar (spear of the gods), which is from the Old English Osgar, a compounding of the elements *os* (a god) and *gar* (spear). The name was borne by two kings of Sweden, the latest being Oscar II (1829–1907). (AHS-KER, O-SKER)

PAUL From the Latin Paulus, which is derived from *paulus* (small). It is a popular name throughout Europe, due to St. Paul, author of several of the epistles in the New Testament and one of the Twelve Apostles. St. Paul and St. Peter are regarded as cofounders of the Christian Church. Cognate: Poul (Danish); Pal (Norwegian); Pal, Pål, Påvel (Swedish). (POWL, PAHL)

PETER From the Ecclesiastic Late Latin Petrus and the Greek Petros, names derived from the vocabulary words *petra* (a rock) and *petros* (a stone). The name is borne in the Bible by one of the Twelve Apostles of Christ. Peter is considered to have been the first pope and cofounder of the Christian Church. Cognate: Peder, Per (Danish, Norwegian, Swedish); Pieter, Pietr (Dutch); Petter (Norwegian, Swedish); Pär (Swedish). Short: Piet (Dutch); Pelle (Swedish). (PEE-TER, PEE-DER)

RAGNAR In common use since the Viking age, Ragnar (warrior of judgment) is composed of the elements *ragn* (judgment, decision) and *hari* (warrior, army). Ragnar Shaggybritches was a Danish warrior who was put to death by King Ælle of Northumbria. His fierce sons avenged his death by invading East Anglia and bringing it under Danish rule, thus laying the foundation of Danelaw in England. Var: Regner. (RAG-NAHR)

RAGNVALD Derived from the Old Norse Rögnvaldr, a compound name composed of the elements *ragn* (advice, judgment, decision) and *valdr* (power, ruler): hence, "powerful judgment." (RAGN-VALT)

REGIN Derived from the Old Norse element *ragn* (advice, judgment, decision). According to Norse mythology, Regin, a very wise man, was the appointed tutor and foster father of Sigurd. (REE-GHIN)

REINE Originally a short form of any of the names containing the element *Rein-*, which is derived from the Old Norse *ragn* (advice, judgment, decision) or the Germanic *ragina* (judgment, counsel). Reine is now often bestowed as an independent given name. (RINE)

RIKARD From the Old High German Richart (brave ruler), a compound name composed of the elements *rik* (ruler, king) and *hart* (hearty, brave, strong). Cognate: Riikard, Rijkert (Dutch). Short: Riik (Dutch). (RIH-KAR, REE-KAR)

ROALD A Norwegian name derived from the Old Norse elements *hróðr* (famous) and *valdr* (ruler, king): hence, "famous ruler." In 1911 Norwegian explorer Roald Amundsen (1872–1928) was the first person to reach the south pole. (RO-AHL)

ROBERT A borrowing from the French, Robert is from the Old High German Hruodperaht, a compounding of the elements *hruod* (fame) and *beraht* (bright): hence, "bright with fame." Robert is a perennially popular name throughout Europe. Short: Bert, Rob. (RO-BERT)

ROGIER Dutch cognate of Roger (famous spear), a name derived from the Old High German Hruodger, which is composed of the elements *hruod* (fame) and *ger* (spear). Cognate: Rutger (Dutch); Hrodgjer, Raadgjer (Norwegian). (RO-JARE)

ROLAND A borrowing from the French, Roland is in common use throughout Scandinavia and the Netherlands. It is derived from the Old High German Hruodland (famous land), a compounding of the elements *hruod* (fame) and *land* (land). (RO-LAN)

RUDOLF Derived from the obsolete Old High German Hrothwulf (famous wolf), a compound name composed of the elements *hruod* (fame) and *wulf* (wolf). Cognate: Rodolf, Roelof (Dutch); Rolfr, Ruodulf (Norwegian); Rolf (Swedish). Short: Ruud (Dutch). (ROO-DOLF)

RUNE Derived from the Old Norse element *rún* (rune, secret lore). (ROON-EH)

RURIK Scandinavian cognate of Roderick (famous king), a name derived from the obsolete Old High German Hruoderich, a compounding of the elements *hruod* (fame) and *rik* (ruler, king). Cognate: Hrorek, Rothrekr (Norwegian). Short: Roar, Roth. (ROO-RIK)

RUUD A short form of Rudolf (famous wolf), Ruud is also bestowed as an independent given name. The name is borne by Ruud Lubbers, prime minister of the Netherlands. (ROOD)

SEBASTIAN Derived from the Greek Sebastianos (a man from Sebastia, a town in Asia Minor). The name was borne by a 3rd-century Christian soldier of Rome martyred by the arrows of his fellow soldiers. He was a popular subject of medieval painters, which led to the spread of his name across Europe. Cognate: Sebastiaan (Dutch). Short: Baste (Dutch). (SEH-BAHS-CHEN, SEH-BAHS-CHAHN)

SERVAAS Derived from the Late Latin Servatius, which is from *servātus* (saved, redeemed). The name is used primarily by the Dutch. (SER-VAHS)

SIGBJÖRN Swedish name derived from the Old Norse elements *sigr* (victory, conquest) and *björn* (bear): hence, "victory bear." Cognate: Sigbjørn (Norwegian). Pet: Sikke (Frisian); Sigge (Swedish). (SIG-BYORN, SEEG-BYORN)

SIGGE Pet form of any of the names beginning with the element *Sig-*. (SIG-AH, SEEG-AH)

SIGMUND Derived from the Old Norse Sigmundr (victorious protection), which is composed of the Germanic elements *sig* (conquest, victory) and *mund* (hand, protection). Sigmund was a favored character and hero of Norse legend. Pet: Sikke (Frisian); Sigge (Swedish). (SIG-MUN, SEEG-MUN)

SIGURD From the obsolete Old Norse Sigvörðr (guardian of victory), a compounding of the elements *sigr* (victory, conquest) and *vörðr* (guardian). A popular name since the Viking age, Sigurd is borne by several characters in Norse legend. In particular was Sigurd Fafnirsbane, the slayer of the dragon Fafnir. Cognate: Sjurd (Norwegian). Pet: Sikke (Frisian); Sigge (Swedish). (SIH-GER, SEE-GER)

SIKKE Frisian pet form of any of the names beginning with the element *Sig-*. (SIK-AH, SEEK-AH)

SIMON Derived from the Ecclesiastic Greek Simōn and Seimōn, which are from the Hebrew Shimon, a derivative of *shim'ōn* (heard). The name is borne in the Bible by two of the Twelve Apostles and a brother of Jesus. Cognate: Siemen (Dutch). (SĪ-MUN)

SOREN Danish name possibly derived from the old Roman family name Sevērinus, which is from *sevērus* (apart). Var: Sören, Søren. (SORE-UN)

STEINAR Popular name derived from the Old Norse elements *steinn* (stone) and *hari* (warrior): hence, "stone warrior." Short: Stein. (STĪ-NAHR)

STEN Swedish short form of any of the names containing the Old Norse element *steinn* (stone). It is now commonly bestowed as an independent given name. Var: Steen (Danish); Stein (Norwegian). (STEN, STEEN, STINE)

STEPHAN Derived from the Greek Stephanos, a direct derivative of *stephanos* (a crown, a garland). St. Stephen was one of the seven chosen to help the Twelve Apostles and was the first Christian martyr. Cognate: Steven (Dutch); Stephen (Scandinavian); Stefan, Steffan (Swedish). (STEH-FEN)

STIAN Contracted form of the Old Norse Stígandr (wanderer), which is derived from the root *stig* (step, mounting upward). *Stígandr* was originally used to denote a wanderer or one who journeyed about. In use throughout Scandinavia, Stian is especially popular in Norway. (STEE-AN)

STIG A short form of the Old Norse Stígandr (wanderer), which is derived from the universal root *stig* (step, mounting upward), Stig is now popularly bestowed as an independent given name. Cognate: Styge, Stygge (Danish). (STEEG)

STURE Derived from the Swedish verb *stura* (to be contrary, impudent, self-willed). This was originally a medieval byname for someone who was impudent or stuck-up, but it has since lost its unsavory attributes and is a common given name. (STOOR-EH)

SVEINN Old Norse name meaning "strong youth," which is derived from the root *svinn* (strong, able, wise). According to Norse mythology, Sveinn was a son of Jarl and Erna, the progenitors of the ruling class. Cognate: Svend (Danish, Swedish); Svein, Sven (Norwegian); Svends (Swedish). (SVANE, SVEN)

SWAIN Old Viking name derived from the root *svinn* (strong, able, wise). Swain Forkbeard became the first Danish king of England after he drove out King Ethelred in 1013. (SVANE)

TAIT Derived from the Old Norse *teitr* (cheerful). Var: Tate, Teit. (TITE, TATE)

THEODOOR Dutch cognate of Theodore (gift of God), which is from the Greek Theodōros, a compound name composed of the elements *theos* (God) and *dōron* (gift). Cognate: Theodrekr (Norwegian); Teodor (Swedish). (THEE-O-DORE)

THIASSI Ancient name of uncertain meaning borne in Norse mythology by one of the most formidable of the giants. He was responsible for kidnaping Idun and her apples of immortality. Var: Thiazi, Thjazi. (THEE-YAH-SEH)

THOMAS A borrowing from the Ecclesiastic Greek, Thomas is derived from the Arabic *tĕōma* (a twin). The name was borne by one of the Twelve Apostles of Christ, irreverently nicknamed "doubting Thomas" because he doubted Christ's resurrection. Cognate: Thomaas

(Dutch); Tomas (Norwegian, Swedish). Short: Maas (Dutch); Tom (Norwegian, Swedish). (TŌ-MAS)

THOR Derived from the Old Norse *þórr* (thunder). The name is borne in Norse mythology by the god of strength and thunder, the son of Odin and Frigg. He owned three priceless objects: his hammer, Mjollnir, his strength-increasing belt, and his iron gauntlets. His principal role was to protect both Asgard and Midgard from attacks by giants. Var: Tor. (THOR)

THORER Old Viking name still in common use. It is derived from the obsolete Þórrir (Thor's warrior), a compound name composed of the elements Þórr (Thor) and *verr* (man, warrior). According to Norse legend, Thorer was the son of Viking and the brother of Thorsten. Var: Tore, Torer, Ture. (THOR-EH)

THORSTEIN Used primarily in Denmark and Sweden, Thorstein is an old Viking name derived from the Old Norse elements Þórr (Thor) and *steinn* (stone): hence, "Thor's stone." According to Norse legend, Thorstein was one of the elder sons of the hero Viking. Var: Thorsteinn, Thorsten, Torsten. Cognate: Torstein (Norwegian). Short: Stein, Steinn, Sten. (THOR-STINE)

THORVALDR Old Viking name composed of the Old Norse elements Þórr (Thor) and *valdr* (ruler): hence, "Thor's rule." Var: Thorvald, Thorwald, Torvald. Short: Tove, Tuve. (THOR-VAHL-DER)

TORBJÖRN Swedish name composed of the Old Norse elements Þórr (Thor) and *björn* (bear): hence, "Thor's bear." Cognate: Thorbjørn (Norwegian). (TOR-BYORN)

TORD Contracted form of the Old Norse Þorfriðr (peace of Thor), a compounding of the elements Þórr (Thor) and *friðr* (peace). (TORD)

TORGER Swedish name composed of the Old Norse elements Þórr (Thor) and *guirr* (spear): hence, "Thor's spear." Cognate: Terje, Torgeir (Norwegian). (TOR-GER)

TORKEL Swedish contracted form of the obsolete Old Norse Þorketill (Thor's cauldron), a compound name composed of the elements Þórr (Thor) and *ketill* (sacrificial cauldron). Var: Thorkel, Torkil. Cognate: Torkild (Danish); Torkjell (Norwegian). (TOR-KUL, TOR-KELL)

TOROLF Old Viking name meaning "Thor's wolf" which continues to be in common use in Denmark and Sweden. It is derived from the popular Old Norse elements Þórr (Thor) and *úlfr* (wolf). Cognate: Thorolf (Danish); Torolv, Torulfr (Norwegian). Short: Tolv (Norwegian). (TOR-OLF)

TOVE Swedish short form of Thorvaldr (Thor's rule), now in common use as an independent given name for both males and females. *See* THORVALDR. Var: Tuve. (TŌ-VEH)

TROND From Trøndelag. It was originally used as a byname for someone who came from Trøndelag, an area in central Norway. (TROND, TRON)

TYCHO Derived from the Greek Tychōn (hitting the mark). St. Tychon was a 5th-century bishop of Amathus in Cyprus who is known for suppressing the cult of Aphrodite. In Scandinavia the name was borne by the Danish astronomer Tycho Brahe (1545–1601). Cognate: Tyge (Danish); Tyko (Swedish). (TOO-KO)

TYR Borne by the oldest of all the Gothonic gods. His name is thought to be derived from the ancient Indo-European Djevs (Sky Father, the Shining One). He was considered to be the most daring and courageous of the gods in Norse mythology. (TIR)

ULF Derived from the popular Old Norse element *úlfr* (wolf). This form of the name is found mainly in Denmark and Sweden. Cognate: Ulv (Norwegian). (ULF)

ULL Thought to be derived from the Gothic *wulþus* (glory). According to Norse mythology, Ull was the god of winter, hunting, archery, and skiing. The aurora borealis was thought to be Ull putting on a display. He was also known as Ullr, Uller, and Volder. (ULL)

ULRIK Derived from the old Germanic name Udalrich (noble ruler), a compound name composed of the elements *uodal* (nobility, prosperity, fortune) and *rik* (ruler, power). (ULL-RIK)

URBAN Derived from the Latin *urbanus* (from the city, city dweller). Urban was the name of a pope (1042–99), which led to the name traveling to other languages. In Scandinavia the name is found primarily in Denmark and Sweden. (OOR-BAHN)

VALDEMAR Derivative of an old German name composed of the elements *wald* (ruler, power) and *mari* (famous). Valdemar was the name of four kings of Denmark. At one point, Swedes were sent to Russia to provide protection from warring clans, and Valdemar was then used as a cognate of Vladimir, a name of Slavonic origin and composed of synonymous elements. *See* VLADIMIR (Russian Names). Var: Waldemar, Woldemar. (VAHL-DEH-MAHR)

VALENTIN Derived from the Latin Valentinus, which is from *valens* (to be strong, healthy). St. Valentine was a 3rd-century Christian Roman martyred under Diocletian. His feast day coincides with that of an ancient pagan festival marking the beginning of spring. (VAH-LEN-TIN)

VÁLI Ancient name of uncertain meaning. According to Norse mythology, Váli was a son of Odin and Rind. He was known to be brave in battle and a good shot. His main function seems to have been to avenge Balder's death by killing Hodur. Váli was also one of the few to survive Ragnarok. Var: Áli. (VAL-LEH)

VIDAR Derived from the Old Norse Víðarr, an ancient name of uncertain meaning. According to Norse mythology, Vidar was the son of Odin and the giantess Grid. He was the silent god, known for his great strength. At Ragnarok, he avenged Odin's death by killing the Fenris Wolf. (VEE-DAHR)

VIDKUN Derived from the obsolete Víðkunnr, which is composed of the Old Norse elements *víðr* (wide) and *kunnr* (wise, experienced). It has fallen out of favor due to the infamy of Vidkun Quisling, the Norwegian politician who betrayed his country to the Nazis and became its puppet ruler. (VEED-KOON, VID-KOON)

VIKTOR Derived from the Latin *victor* (conqueror, winner). The name, a favorite of early Christians, was often bestowed in honor of Christ's victory over death. (VEEK-TOR)

VINCENT Derived from the Late Latin Vincentius, a name derived from *vincens* (conquering). The name was borne by St. Vincent de Paul, a 17th-century French priest who is remembered for his charitable works for the needy. (VEEN-SENT)

VON Derived from the Old Norse *ván* (hope). According to Norse mythology, Ván (hope) and Víl (despair) were the two rivers that flowed from the mouth of the slain Fenris Wolf. (VON)

WALTER Derived from the obsolete Frankish Waldhere (ruler of the army), a compound name composed of the elements *waldan* (to rule) and *hari, heri* (army). Var: Valter. Cognate: Wolter, Wouter (Dutch); Valter (Swedish). Short: Wout (Dutch). (WAHL-TER, VAHL-TER)

WERNER Used throughout Scandinavia and the Netherlands, Werner is derived from the old Germanic Warenheri (protecting army), a compounding of the elements *ware* (protector, defender) and *heri* (army). Var: Verner. Pet: Wessel (Dutch, Frisian). (WER-NER, VER-NER)

WILFRED Derived from the Old English Wilfrith (a desire for peace), which is composed of the elements *willa* (a wish, a will, a desire) and *frith* (peace). The name was brought back to Scandinavia by the Vikings. (WIL-FRED, VIL-FRED)

WILLEM From the Old Norman French Willaume (resolute protector), a derivative of the Old High German Willehelm, a compounding of the elements *willeo* (will, resolution) and *helm* (helmet, protection). The name was borne by three kings of the Netherlands. Var: Vilhelm. (WEEL-HELM, VEEL-HELM)

YMIR Ancient name of uncertain meaning. According to Norse mythology, Ymir was a primeval giant—the first living creature. It was from his slain body that his grandsons, the gods Odin, Vili, and Ve, created the world. (EE-MEER)

ZWI Dutch cognate of the Hebrew Zvi, which is derived from *tzevi* (deer, gazelle). (ZWEE)

Scandinavian Female Names

AALT Dutch contracted form of Adalheidis (noble one). *See* ADALHEIDIS. Pet: Aaltje. (AHLT)

ABELONE Danish form of Apollonia, the feminine form of Apollonios (of Apollo), a derivative of Apollo, the name of the Greek mythological sun-god. St. Apollonia was an elderly deaconess martyred at Alexandria under the emperor Decius in the 3rd century. Var: Abellona. Short: Lone. (AH-BEH-LO-NEH)

ADALHEIDIS Medieval Germanic name composed of the elements *adal* (noble) and *heid* (kind, sort): hence, "noble one." Var: Adalheid, Adelheid, Aleida, Alida. Pet: Elke. (AH-DAL-HIDE-ISS)

AGATA From the Greek Agathē, a derivative of *agathos* (good, kind). The name was popularized by the fame of a 3rd-century saint and martyr. *See* AGATA (Italian Names). Cognate: Ågot (Norwegian); Agda (Swedish). (AH-GAH-TAH)

AGNA Swedish pet form of Agneta (chaste, pure), which is often bestowed as an independent given name. *See* AGNES. (AHG-NAH)

AGNES Derived from the Greek Hagnē, which is from *hagnos* (chaste, pure, sacred). The name was borne by a thirteen-year-old Roman martyred for her Christian beliefs during the reign of Diocletian. Her fame in the Middle Ages helped bring about the additional meaning of "holy" to the name. Cognate: Agnethe (Scandinavian); Agneta (Swedish). Short: Neta (Swedish). Pet: Agna (Swedish). (AHG-NES)

ALEXANDRA Feminine form of Alexander (defender or helper of mankind), which is derived from the Greek Alexandros, a compounding of the elements *alexein* (to defend, to help) and *andros* (man). The name was made popular, in part, by Queen Alexandra, the Danish wife of Edward VIII. (AH-LEX-AN-DRAH)

ALICIA Latinate form of Alice (truthful, noble), which developed as a variant of the Middle English Alys, via the Old French Aliz, from Adaliz, a variant of Adelaïde, which in turn is a contracted form of the Old High German Adalheidis (noble one). *See* ADALHEIDIS. (AH-LEE-SEE-AH, AH-LEE-SHA)

AMALIA Popular Latinized form of the Germanic Amal, a derivative of *amal* (work). Traditionally, Amal was the first element in various compound names. (AH-MAHL-EE-AH, AH-MAHL-YA)

AMMA Grandmother. In Norse mythology, Amma was a mortal, the wife of Afi and mother of Karl by an illicit union with the god Heimdall. Karl and his wife were the progenitors of the peasant class. (AH-MA)

ANITRA Literary coinage by Norwegian playwright and poet Henrik Ibsen (1828–1906). Anitra was the name given to the Eastern princess in his work *Peer Gynt*. It is now commonly used throughout Scandinavia. (AH-NEE-TRA)

ANNA Derived from the Hebrew Hannah (gracious, full of grace), which is from *hannāh*, *chaanach* (grace, gracious, mercy). Anna is popularly used throughout Scandinavia. Var: Ann, Anne. Pet: Anke, Anki, Anneka, Anneke, Antje (Dutch); Annika (Swedish). (AH-NAH)

ANNALINA Combination name composed of Anna (gracious, full of grace) and the Latinate second element *-lina*. *See* ANNA. (AH-NAH-LEE-NAH)

ANNELIESE Combination name composed of Anne (gracious, full of grace) and Liese (God is my oath). *See* ANNA *and* ELISABET. Var: Annaliese, Annalise, Annelise. Short: Liese, Lise. Pet: Anneli. (AH-NAH-LEES-EH)

ANNETTE A borrowing from the French, Annette is a pet form of Anne (gracious, full of grace) in common use throughout Scandinavia. *See* ANNA. Cognate: Anette (Norwegian). (AH-NET, AH-NET-TEH)

ANNFRID Norwegian name derived from the Old Norse Arnfríðr (beautiful eagle), a compound name composed of the elements *arn* (eagle) and *fríðr* (beautiful, fair). (AHN-FREED, AHN-FRID)

ANTONIA A borrowing from the Latin, Antonia is the feminine form of Antōnius, an old Roman family name of uncertain origin and meaning. Some believe it to have originally been an Etruscan name. "Priceless" and "inestimable worth" are modern definitions ascribed to the name. (AHN-TŌ-NEE-AH)

ARNA Derived from the Old Norse *arn* (eagle). (AR-NA)

ÅSA Pet form of any of the various Old Norse names containing the element *áss* (god). Var: Åse. (AW-SAH)

ASLAUG Compound name composed of the Old Norse elements *áss* (god) and *laug* (consecrated, dedicated): hence, "consecrated to God." In Norse mythology, Aslaug was the daughter of Sigurd and Brynhild. Orphaned at the age of three, she led a Cinderella type of existence with an old peasant couple until she was rescued by her future husband, Ragnar Lodbrog, son of King Sigurd Ring of Denmark. Cognate: Asløg (Danish); Åslaug (Norwegian); Aslög (Swedish). Short: Åsa, Åse. (AHS-LAUG)

ÅSTA Scandinavian name derived from the Old Norse Ásta, a derivative of *ást* (love). (AW-STA)

ASTRID In popular use since the Viking age, Astrid (beautiful goddess) is derived from the Old Norse elements *áss* (god) and *fríðr* (beautiful, fair). Short: Asta. Pet: Sassa (Swedish). (AH-STREE, AH-STREED)

AUD Derived from the Old Norse *auðr* (riches, prosperity, happiness). Aud the Deepminded was the widow of Olaf the White, Viking king of Dublin. She helped Christianize Irish immigrants in Iceland. In Norse mythology, Aud (Auðr) was the son of Nótt (Night) and Naglfari (Darkling). Auðr, with the substantive definition of "waste," was in this instance defined as "Space." (AUD)

AUDHILD From the Old Norse Auðhildr (battle riches), a compound name composed of the elements *auðr* (riches, prosperity) and *hildr* (battle). (AUD-HIL, AUD-HILD)

AUDNY Derived from the Old Norse element *auðr* (riches, prosperity). (AUD-NEE)

BARBRO Swedish form of Barbara (foreign woman), which is from the Latin *barbarus* (foreign, strange), a term applied to non-Romans or those deemed to be uncivilized. (BAHR-BRO)

BEATRIX From the Latin *beatrix* (she who makes happy, she who brings happiness). The name is borne by the Queen of the Netherlands (b. 1938), the daughter of Queen Juliana and Prince Bernhard. Queen Beatrix is the last in a line of queens of the Netherlands which has spanned a hundred years; she has three sons. (BE-AH-TREEX)

BENEDIKTA Feminine form of Benedikt, which is from the Latin Benedictus (blessed), a name derived from *benedicere* (to speak well of, to bless). The name is borne by Benedikte Astrid Ingeborg Ingrid (b. 1944), second daughter of King Frederik IX of Denmark (1899–1972). Var: Benedikte. Short: Bente. (BEN-EH-DEEK-TAH)

BENTE A short form of Benedikta (blessed), Bente is also popularly bestowed as an independent given name. *See* BENEDIKTA. (BEN-TEH)

BIRGIT Scandinavian form of the Irish Gaelic Bríghid, which is derived from the Gaelic *brígh* (strength). A common name throughout Scandinavia, it owes its immense popularity to St. Birgitta (1302–73), patron saint of Sweden. A noblewoman and mother of eight children, she founded the Brigittine Order of nuns after her husband's death and traveled to Rome, where she attempted to reform religious life. Var: Berit, Birgitta, Birgitte, Birte, Birthe, Brita, Britt, Britta. Short: Gitta, Gitte. (BEER-GEET)

BODIL Scandinavian (mainly Danish) name of debated derivation. Some believe it is from the Old Norse Bóthildr (compensation for battle), which is composed of the elements *bót* (remedy, compensation) and *hildr* (battle). Others feel it is from the obsolete Boðvildr, which is from *boð* (battle) and *hildr* (battle). Var: Botilda, Bothild. (BO-DEEL)

BORGHILD Especially common in Norway, Borghild is derived from the Old Norse Borghildr (fortified for battle), a compounding of the elements *borg* (fortification) and *hildr* (battle). According to Norse legend, Borghild of Bralund was the wife of Sigmund and mother of Hamond and Helgi. (BORG-HEEL)

BORGNY Derived from the Old Norse element *borg* (fortification) and *ný* (new): hence, "newly fortified." (BORG-NEE)

BRYNHILD A name that dates back to the Viking age and beyond. It is derived from Brynhildr (armored for battle), a compounding of the elements *brynja* (armor) and *hildr* (battle). In Norse mythology, she was a Valkyrie who was awakened from an enchanted sleep by Sigurd, with whom she fell deeply in love. Deceived by him into marrying Gunnar, she eventually brought about Sigurd's death, then took her own life. (BRIN-HEEL)

CARINA Derived from the Latin *carina* (a keel of a ship). Carina is the name of a southern constellation which contains the star Canopus, the second brightest in the southern skies. Var: Karina. (KAH-REE-NAH)

CAROL A short form of Caroline (a freeman, peasant), Carol is also bestowed as an independent given name. *See* CAROLINE. (KARE-OL)

CAROLINE Dutch feminine form of Karel, a cognate of Karl, which is derived from the Old Norse and Germanic *karl* (man, freeman, peasant). The name was borne by two queens of Denmark, which led to its popular usage. Short: Carol. (KARE-O-LEE-NAH)

CECILIA From the Latin Caecilia, a feminine form of Caecilius, an old Roman family name that has its root in the Latin *caecus* (blind, dim-sighted). Cecilia is a common name throughout Scandinavia due to the fame of a 3rd-century Christian who founded a church in the Trastevere section of Rome. During the 6th century, a story of her life was written and she was henceforth venerated as a martyr. She is regarded as the patron saint of musicians. Cognate: Silja (Finnish). Short: Celia. Pet: Sissel. (SEH-SEE-LEE-AH)

CELIA A short form of Cecilia (blind, dim-sighted), Celia is also commonly bestowed as an independent given name. *See* CECILIA. (SEE-LEE-AH)

CHARLOTTA Latinate form of the French Charlotte, a feminine diminutive form of Charles (full-grown, a man). The name has been borne by a queen of the Netherlands, which helped to popularize its use. (SHAR-LO-TAH)

CHRISTA Latinate short form of Christina (a Christian), which is popular throughout Scandinavia. *See* CHRISTINA. (KREES-TAH)

CHRISTINA Derived from the Latin Christiāna, which is from *christiānus*, a derivative of the Greek *christianos* (a Christian, a follower of Christ). This is a common name throughout Scandinavia, its popularity in the past due, in part, to Queen Christina of Sweden (1626–89). Var: Cristina. Short: Christa, Stina, Tina. (KREES-TEE-NAH)

CORNELIA Latin feminine form of Cornelius, an old Roman family name of unknown origin and meaning. Cornelia was the name of the mother of Tiberius and Gaius Gracchus, Roman statesmen and social reformers in the 2nd century B.C. Pet: Cokkie, Nelleke (Dutch); Nellie (Scandinavian). (KOR-NEE-LEE-AH)

DAGMAR Mainly Danish name of uncertain and debated derivation. Some believe it to be derived from the Old Scandinavian elements *dag* (day) and *mār* (maid).

Others think it is from the Germanic *dag* (day) and *mar* (splendid). (DAG-MAHR)

DAGNA Derived from the Old Norse elements *dagr* (day) and *ny´* (new): hence, "new day." Var: Dagne, Dagny. (DAG-NEH)

DANIA Feminine form of Daniel, which is from the Hebrew *dānī'ēl* (God is my judge). *See* DANIEL (Male Names). (DAN-EE-AH)

DISA Latinized short form of any of the various female names of Old Norse origin that contain the element *dís* (goddess). (DEESA)

DOROTHEA A borrowing from the Greek, Dorothea (gift of God) is composed of the elements *dōron* (gift) and *theos* (God). Queen Dorothea of Brandenburg (1430–95) was the wife of the Danish king Christian I. The name was also borne by the poet Dorothe Engelbretsdatter (1634–1716), the first poet to receive a poet's stipend from the king. Cognate: Dorete, Dorte, Dorthe (Danish). Pet: Doortje (Dutch). (DOR-O-THEE-AH)

EBBA A borrowing from the German, Ebba is a feminine contracted form of the Old High German Eburhart (strong as a wild boar), a compounding of the elements *ebur* (wild boar) and *harto* (strong). Var: Ebbe. (EH-BAH)

EDDA Attributed to the *Prose Edda* and the *Poetic Edda*, collections of poetry, myths, and stories of Norse mythology written by Snorri Sturluson early in the 13th century. Some believe Edda to be the possessive case of Oddi, the place where the author lived. Others believe it to mean "grandmother" or "great-grandmother," due to the way in which it occurs in several poems. According to legend, Edda was an old woman, and through an illicit union with the god Heimdallr, became the mother of Thrall, who was progenitor of the serf class. (EH-DAH)

EDITH A borrowing from the English, Edith is derived from the Old English Ēadgyð (prosperous in war), a compound name composed from the elements *ēad* (prosperity, fortune, riches) and *gyð* (war, strife). The name is common throughout Scandinavia. (EE-DITH)

EINMYRIA Of uncertain meaning borne in Norse mythology by one of the two daughters of Loki, the trickster god. Little is known of her other than her name and that of her sister, Eisa. (ĪN-MEE-REE-AH)

EIRA Of uncertain meaning borne in Norse mythology by the goddess of medicine. By Norse tradition, only women practiced the healing arts. Var: Eir, Eyra. (Ī-RAH)

EISA Of uncertain meaning borne in Norse mythology by one of the two daughters of Loki and his first wife, Glut. Her sister was Einmyria. (Ī-SAH)

ELISABET Derived from the Hebrew *elīsheba* (God is my oath). The name is borne in the Bible by the mother of John the Baptist. Var: Eliesabet. Short: Elsa, Else, Liese, Lis, Lisa, Lisabet, Lisbet. Pet: Ailsa, Betje. (EH-LEES-AH-BET)

ELKE Dutch pet form of Adelheid (noble one), commonly bestowed as an independent given name. *See* ADALHEIDIS. (ELL-KEH, ELL-KEE)

ELLI Old age. The name is borne in Norse mythology by an old woman from Utgard, with whom Thor unsuccessfully wrestled. The giant Utgard-Loki later told Thor that he never had a chance because Elli was really Old Age in disguise, and no one can be victorious over old age. (ELL-LEE)

ELSA Short form of Elisabet (God is my oath). Commonly bestowed as an independent given name, Elsa is readily associated with the lioness named Elsa in the movie *Born Free*. *See* ELISABET. Var: Else. (ELL-SAH)

ERIKA Feminine form of Erik, which is from the Old Norse Eirìkr. The actual origin of the name is debated. Most believe it to be composed of the Old Norse elements *ei* (ever, always) and *ríkr* (ruler): hence, "eternal ruler." There are some, however, who think it comes to the Old Norse via the Germanic *ehre* (honor) and the Proto-Germanic *rīk* (king): hence, "honorable ruler." Var: Erica. (EH-REE-KAH).

ERNA Capable. According to Norse mythology, Erna was the wife of Jarl, the son of the god Heimdallr and the mortal Modir. Jarl and Erna became the progenitors of the noble and warrior classes. Their youngest son, Konur, or one of his descendants, became the first king of Denmark. (ER-NAH)

ESTER Scandinavian form of Esther, a name of debated etymology. Some believe it to be the Persian translation of the Hebrew Hadassah (myrtle); others think it is derived from the Persian *stara* (star). It has also been suggested that it derives from the Babylonian Ishtar, a goddess of love and fertility. The name is borne in the Bible by the Jewish wife of the Persian king Ahasuerus. (ESS-TER)

EVA Latinate form of Eve commonly used throughout Scandinavia. It is derived from the Hebrew Chava, which is from *hawwāh* (life). The name is borne in the Bible by the first woman created by God. (EE-VAH, EH-VAH)

FENIA Of uncertain meaning borne in Norse mythology by a giantess who was enslaved with Menia by Frodi. They had the task of grinding out gold, peace, and fair fortune for King Frodi at a mill called Grotti. Var: Fenja. (FEN-EE-AH, FEEN-EE-AH)

FREYA Feminine form of Frey (lord, he who is foremost), Freya has the definition "lady, mistress, noblewoman." In Norse mythology, Freya was the goddess of fertility. A daughter of Njord and a sister of Frey, Freya was the most beautiful of the goddesses. She owned the Necklace of the Brísings, the Brísingamen. Var: Freja, Freyja, Fröja. (FREY-AH)

FRIGG Beloved. The name is borne in Norse mythology by one of the oldest of the female deities. She was the daughter of the Sky Father and Nótt (Night), wife of Odin, mother of the gods, the supreme goddess, the earth mother, and the principal goddess of fertility and love. The race of gods and goddesses called the Æsir came from the union of Frigg and Odin. She was also known as Jörð (Earth), Fjörgyn, Frigga, Nerthus, and Wode. Her name is derived from the verb *frjá* (to love). Var: Frigga. (FRIG, FREEG)

FULLA Of uncertain meaning borne in Norse mythology by a fertility-goddess who acted as Frigg's attendant and messenger and who was the keeper of Frigg's ashwood casket. (FOO-LAH)

GALA Scandinavian name derived from the Old French *gale* (enjoyment, pleasure) via the Middle Dutch *wale* (riches, wealth). (GAH-LAH)

GEFJUN Ancient name believed to be connected with the verb *gefa* (to give) and the Gothic *gabei* (riches): hence, "bestower of wealth." According to Norse mythology, Gefjun was an attendant of Frigg. She slept with the legendary king of Sweden, Gylfi, and was thus allowed to claim as much of his nation as she could plow within a twenty-four-hour period. She harnessed four giant oxen to a huge plow and gouged out a great tract of land, which she towed out to sea to become Zealand. The hole in Sweden soon filled with water to become Lake Mälaren. Var: Gefion, Gefjon. (GEF-YOON)

GEORGINA Latinate feminine form of George, which is from the Greek *geōrgos* (earthworker, farmer), a compounding of the elements *gē* (earth) and *ergein* (to work). Originally an English name, Georgina has been borrowed by many European countries, including those of Scandinavia. (GEE-YOR-GEE-NAH)

GERD Derived from the Old Norse Gerðr (guarded, protected). The name is borne in Norse mythology by an exceptionally beautiful giantess who was the wife of Frey. She was regarded as a minor fertility-goddess. Var: Gerda. Cognate: Gärd (Swedish). (GEERD)

GERSEMI Gem, jewel, treasure. In Norse mythology, Gersemi was one of the two daughters of Freya and Od. According to legend, they were so beautiful that all precious stones (gems) have taken their names from them. Gersemi is also known as Hnoss and Gem. (GEER-SEE-ME)

GISELA Dutch cognate of the Germanic Giselle, which is derived from *gisil* (pledge). (GEE-SEHL-AH)

GISLAUG Norwegian name derived from the Old Norse elements *gisil* (hostage) and *laug* (consecrated): hence, "consecrated hostage." Cognate: Gislög (Swedish). (GEES-LAUG)

GRATIA Dutch cognate of the English Grace, which is from *grace* (elegance or beauty of form, favor, kindness, mercy). (GRAH-TEE-AH)

GRIET Dutch pet form of Margaret (a pearl), which is now used as an independent given name. *See* MARGARET. Var: Greet, Gret. Pet: Greetje, Gretje. (GREET)

GUDRUN Old Norse name of debated definition. Some believe it to be derived from *guð* (a god) and *rūn* (secret lore): hence, "secret lore of the gods." Alternatively, it might be derived from Guthrūn, which is from *guthr* (war, battle) and *runa* (close friend): hence, "a friend of war." In Norse mythology, Gudrun was the daughter of Gjuki, the Nikelung king, and sister of Gunnar. She was responsible for luring Sigurd away from Brynhild and marrying him, which brought about his destruction. Pet: Guro (Norwegian). (GUD-RUN)

GULL Pet form of any of the names of Old Norse origin that contain the first element *Guð-* (a god) or *gull* (gold). It is often used in the creation of compound names such as Gull-Lis. (GULL)

GUNILLA Swedish form of Gunnhild (battle maid) that has been in use since the 16th century. Gunilla Bielke (1568–97) was the wife of King Johan III of Sweden. Short: Gun. (GUN-EE-LAH, GOON-EE-LAH)

GUNN Short form of any of the Old Norse names that contain the first element *Gunnr-* (war, strife, battle). Var: Gun. (GUN, GOON)

GUNNBORG Derived from the Old Norse elements *gunnr* (war, strife, battle) and *borg* (fortification). Var: Gunborg. Short: Gun, Gunn. (GUN-BOR, GUN-BORG, GOON-BOR, GOON-BORG)

GUNNHILD From an Old Norse compound name meaning "battle maid" which contains the elements *gunnr* (war, strife, battle) and *hildr* (battle). The name was popular in the Viking age and is attributed to several women in Norse mythology, one being the wife of Asmund, the son of the Norwegian king Svipdag. Another, Queen Gunhild, was the wife of King Sweyn Forkbeard of Denmark and the mother of Canute the Great. Var: Gunhild. Short: Gun, Gunn. (GUN-HIL, GUN-HILD, GOON-HIL, GOON-HILD)

GUNNLOD From the Old Norse Gunnlöð, which is derived from the element *gunnr* (war, strife, battle). According to Norse mythology, Gunnlod was the giantess daughter of Suttung. She was seduced by Odin so he could gain the mead of poetry. As a result, she became the mother of the god Bragi. (GUN-LOD, GOON-LOD)

GUNNVOR Derived from the Old Norse elements *gunnr* (war, strife, battle) and *vor* (cautious, wary): hence, "cautious in battle." Var: Gunver, Gunvor. Short: Gun, Gunn. (GUN-VOR, GOON-VOR)

HANNA Scandinavian form of Hannah, which is from the Hebrew *hannāh*, *chaanach* (gracious, full of grace, mercy). The name is borne in the Bible by the mother of the prophet Samuel. Var: Hanne. (HAH-NAH)

HANSINE Danish feminine form of Hans, a contracted form of Johannes, which is ultimately from the Hebrew *yehōhānān* (Yahweh is gracious). *See* JOHANNES (Male Names). (HAHN-SEE-NEH)

HEDDA Pet form of Hedvig, the Scandinavian form of the German Hedwig (war). Hedda is often bestowed as an independent given name. *See* HEDVIG. (HED-DAH)

HEDVIG Popular Scandinavian form of the German Hedwig, a compounding of the elements *hadu* (contention) and *wīg* (war, strife). The name is borne by the central character in Henrik Ibsen's play *The Wild Duck*. Pet: Hedda. (HED-VEEG, HED-VIG)

HELENA Latinate form of Helen, from the Greek Helenē, which is derived from *ēlē* (light, torch, bright). The name was made popular by the story of Helen of Troy, the famous beauty whose capture by the Trojan prince Paris sparked off the Trojan War. Short: Elna (Danish); Lene, Nel (Dutch); Lena (Dutch, Scandinavian). (HEL-LEN-AH)

HELGE Derived from the Old Norse *heilagr* (prosperous, successful), which is from *heill* (hale, hearty, happy). The word *heill* later developed the meaning "blessed, holy." Var: Helga. Pet: Hella. (HEL-GEH)

HENDRIKA Feminine form of Hendrik (home ruler, ruler of an enclosure). *See* HENDRIK (Male Names). Var: Henrika. Pet: Hen, Henie, Hennie, Henny. (HEN-REE-KAH)

HERLINDIS Dutch name of Germanic origin composed of the elements *heri* (army) and *lind* (gentle, soft, tender): hence, "gentle army." The name was made popular, in part, by St. Herlindis (d. 745), the first abbess of Aldeneyck on the Meuse. (HER-LEEN-DIS)

HILD Derived from the Old Norse *hildr* (battle). In Norse mythology, Hild was a Valkyrie who conveyed fallen warriors to Valhalla. Warfare was often called Hild's Game. Var: Hilda, Hilde, Hildur. Pet: Helle. (HILD, HIL)

HILDA A Latinized short form of any of the female compound names containing the element *hildr* (battle), Hilda is now commonly used as an independent given name. (HIL-DAH)

HILDEGARD From an old Germanic compound name composed of the elements *hild* (battle) and *gard* (to enclose, to protect): hence, "battle protector." Hildegard was the name of the second wife of Charlemagne. Short: Hilda, Hilde. (HIL-DEH-GAHR)

HILLEVI Danish form of the Germanic Heilwig (safe in battle), a compounding of the elements *heil* (safe, whole, hearty) and *wīg* (war). (HIL-LEE-VEE)

HJÖRDIS From the Old Norse Hjardis (goddess of the sword), a compound name composed of the elements *hjarr* (sword) and *dīs* (goddess). In Norse mythology, Hjördis was the second wife of the unfortunate Sigmund and mother of Sigurd Fafnirsbane. After Sigmund's death, Hjördis married Alf, the king of Denmark. (HYOR-DIS)

HLÍN Ancient name of uncertain meaning borne in Norse mythology by one of Frigg's attendants, the goddess of consolation who relieved grief and heard the prayers of mortals. (HLEEN)

HULDA 18th-century Swedish name derived from *huld* (sweet, lovable, endearing). The name is now common throughout Scandinavia. (HUL-DAH)

IDONY Popular medieval name derived from the Old Norse Iðunnr, which is thought to be derived from the element *ið* (again). In Norse mythology, Idony was the name of the wife of Bragi. It was her responsibility to guard the ashwood casket that held the gods' apples of immortality. She is regarded as the goddess of spring and eternal youth; thus the name takes the additional definition of "renewal, rejuvenation." Var: Idonea, Idun. (EE-DOON-NEE)

INGA-LIESE Popular combination name composed of the names Inga (Ing) and Liese (God is my oath). *See* INGE *and* ELISABET. (EEN-GAH-LEE-SEH)

INGE A short form of any of the names that contain *Ing(e)* as a first element, Inge is now commonly bestowed as an independent given name. In Norse mythology, Ing (lord, he who is foremost) is a byname of the fertility-god Frey. Var: Inga. (EEN-GEH)

INGEBORG Old Norse compound name composed of the name Ing and *borg* (fortification): hence, "fortification of Ing, Ing's protection." The name is borne by several characters in Norse legend and mythology, as well as by a 13th-century queen of Denmark. Short: Inge. (EEN-GEH-BOR, EEN-GAH-BORG)

INGEGERD Derived from the Old Norse Ingegarðr, a compound name composed of the name of the fertility-god Ing and *garðr* (enclosure, stronghold, fortress): hence, "Ing's fortress." Cognate: Ingjerd (Norwegian); Ingegärd (Swedish). Short: Inge; Inger (Swedish). (EEN-GEH-GER, EEN-GEH-GERD)

INGRID From an Old Norse compound name composed of Ing (a byname of the fertility-god Frey) and *friðr* (fair, beautiful): hence, "beautiful Ing." Frey is said to have been the most handsome of the gods in Norse mythology. The name Ingrid has become extremely popular, due in part to the affection bestowed upon Ingrid, the queen mother of Denmark, and the fame of the Swedish film actress Ingrid Bergman (1915–82). Short: Inger (Swedish). (EEN-GRID)

IRENA Latinate form of Irene, which is from the Greek Eirēnē, a derivative of *eirēnē* (peace). (Ī-REE-NAH)

IRIS From the Greek *iris* (rainbow). The name is borne in Greek mythology by the goddess of the rainbow, a messenger of the gods. Iris is a popular name in the Netherlands. (Ī-RIS)

JANITA Feminine diminutive form of Jan (God is gracious). *See* JOHANNES (Male Names). Pet: Jaantje, Jans, Jansje. (YAH-NEE-TAH)

JANNA Dutch contracted form of Johanna (God is gracious). *See* JOHANNA. (YAH-NAH)

JANNE Danish and Norwegian contraction of Johanna (God is gracious), which is commonly bestowed as an independent given name. *See* JOHANNA. (YAH-NEH)

JANNIKE Scandinavian form of the French Jeannique, a diminutive form of Jeanne, a feminine form of Jean (God is gracious). *See* JOHANNES (Male Names). (YAHN-NEE-KEH)

JÁRNSAXA Ancient name of unknown meaning borne in Norse mythology by the giantess mother of Magni (colossal might) and Modi (fierce courage). Var: Iarnsaxa. (YAHRN-SAX-AH)

JENSINE Feminine form of Jens (God is gracious). *See* JOHANNES (Male Names). (YEN-SEE-NEH, YEN-SEEN)

JETTE Modern name derived from the black lignite of the same name which is used in jewelry making. (YEH-TEH, YUH-TEH)

JOHANNA A Latinate feminine form of Johannes (God is gracious), the name Johanna is common to many European countries, including Scandinavia and the Netherlands. Johannes is ultimately derived from the Hebrew *yehōhānān* (Yahweh is gracious). Short: Jonna (Danish); Janne (Danish, Norwegian); Janna (Dutch). Pet: Jans, Jaantje, Jansje. (YO-HAH-NAH)

JONNA Danish contracted form of Johanna (God is gracious). *See* JOHANNA. (YON-NAH)

JOSEFA Feminine form of Joseph in common use in Scandinavia. The name is derived from the Hebrew Yosef, which is from *yōsēf* (God will add, God will increase). (YO-SEH-FAH)

JUDITH From the Ecclesiastic Greek Ioudith, which is from the Hebrew Jehudith and Yehudit, feminine forms of Jehuda and Yehūdāh. These names, Anglicized as Judah, mean "he will be praised." Because Judah was also the name of a kingdom in ancient Palestine, the name can also mean "from Judah." Pet: Jutka, Jytte (Danish); Jutte, Juut, Juute (Dutch). (YOO-DITH, YOO-DEETH)

JULIANA Feminine form of Julian, from the Latin Julianus, a derivative of Julius (downy-bearded, youth). The name is common throughout Scandinavia and the Netherlands, getting a boost in popularity from Queen Juliana of the Netherlands, who abdicated in 1980 in favor of her daughter, Beatrix. (YOO-LEE-AHN-NAH)

KAREN Danish form of Katherine, a cognate of the Greek Aikaterinē, which is from *katharos* (pure, unsullied). Var: Karan, Karin. (KARE-UN, KAR-UN)

KARITA Scandinavian form of Charity, a name derived from the Latin *caritas* (esteem, affection), which has its root in *carus* (dear, valued, loved). Short: Kari. (KAR-EE-TAH)

KARLA Feminine form of Karl, which is from the Old Norse and Germanic *karl* (man, freeman, peasant). (KAR-LAH)

KAROLINA Latinate feminine form of Karl, which is from the Old Norse and Germanic *karl* (man, freeman, peasant). Var: Karoline (Danish). (KAR-O-LEE-NA, KAR-O-LINE-AH)

KATHERINE Scandinavian form of the Greek Aikaterinē, a name derived from *katharos* (pure, unsullied). The name in its variant form Catherine has been borne by several queens of Sweden. Cognate: Katrine (Danish); Katrien, Katrijn, Katryn (Dutch); Catherine, Katarina (Swedish). Short: Trine (Danish); Tryn (Dutch); Kata (Swedish). Pet: Kaatje (Norwegian); Kajsa, Kaysa (Swedish). (KATH-EH-REE-NEH, KATH-EH-RIN)

KELDA Derived from the Old Norse *kildr* (a spring). Var: Kilde. (KEL-DAH)

KLARA Scandinavian form of Clara, which is derived from the Latin *clarus* (bright, clear, famous). Pet: Klaartje (Dutch). (KLAHR-AH)

KRISTINA Scandinavian (mainly Swedish) form of Christina, which is from Christiana, the Late Latin feminine form of Christiānus, which in turn is derived from the Greek *christianos* (a follower of Christ, a Christian). The name was borne by Queen Kristina (1626–89), who succeeded her father, Gustavus Adolphus, to the Swedish throne in 1632. Cognate: Kirsten (Danish, Norwegian); Kerstin (Swedish). Pet: Stinne (Danish); Kicki (Swedish). (KRIS-TEE-NAH)

KUNIGONDE Dutch cognate of the Germanic Kunigunde (brave in battle), a compound name composed of the elements *kuoni* (brave) and *gund* (battle, strife). Var: Cunegonde. (KOO-NEE-GOND)

LAILA Popular throughout Scandinavia and the Netherlands, Laila is an ancient name believed to be derived from the Arabic *leila* (night, dark beauty) or the Persian *leila* (dark-haired). (LAH-EE-LAH, LAY-LAH)

LAUFEIA Leafy Island. The name is borne in Norse mythology by the giantess wife of Fárbauti and mother of the mischievous god Loki. She is also known as Laufey and Nál. Var: Laufey. (LAU-FEE-EH)

LENA A short form of any of the various names ending in *-lena*. Lena is also commonly bestowed as an independent given name. Var: Lene. (LEE-NAH)

LIDWINA Feminine form of the Germanic Lidwin (friend of the people), a compounding of the elements *liut* (folk, people) and *win* (friend). The name was often bestowed in honor of the Blessed Lidwina of Schiedam (1380–1433), who was an invalid and mystic. (LID-WEE-NAH, LEED-WEE-NAH)

LIFTHRASIR She who holds fast to life, desiring life. According to Norse mythology, Lifthrasir and her husband Lif (life) were the sole mortal survivors of Ragnarok at a place called Hoddmimir's Holt. She is considered to be the mother of humanity after all perished at Ragnarok. The name is derived from the Old Norse *lifr* (life). (LIF-THRA-SEER, LEEF-THRA-SEER)

LINNÉA Popular name originally bestowed in honor of the Swedish botanist Karl von Linné (1707–78), who gave his name to the Linnaean system of classifying plants and animals and to a type of flower (linnaea). Var: Linnaea, Linnea. Short: Nea. (LIN-NĀ-AH)

LIS Short form of Elisabet (God is my oath), which is used as a common element in combination names such as Anne-Lis and Lis-Ann. (LEES)

LISA A short form of Elisabet (God is my oath) and Lisabet, Lisa is also popularly bestowed as an independent given name. *See* ELISABET *and* LISABET. (LEE-SAH)

LISABET A short form of Elisabet (God is my oath), Lisabet is commonly used as an independent given name. *See* ELISABET. Var: Lisbet. Short: Bette, Lis, Lisa. (LEE-SAH-BET)

LIV Popular name derived from the Old Norse *lifr* (life). (LIV, LEEV)

LOFN Borne in Norse mythology by a minor goddess, an attendant of Frigg. Her duties were to ease the path of love and to win permission for mortals to marry. Her name is derived from the Old Norse *lof* (permission, leave), ostensibly because she permits the lovers to win each other, and that permission is called "leave." (LOFN)

LONE A short form of Abelone (of Apollo) and Magdelone (of Magdala), Lone is also in common use as an independent given name. *See* ABELONE *and* MAGDALENA. (LO-NEH)

LORELEI Derived from Lurlei, the name of the rock "ambush cliff," which is derived from the Middle High German *luren* (to watch) and *lei* (a cliff, a rock). The name was altered to Lorelei by C. Brentano, a German poet. In German legend, Lorelei was a beautiful siren who sat upon a rock in the Rhine and lured sailors to shipwreck and death. (LOR-EH-LĪ)

LOUISE Feminine form of Louis (famous in war), which is ultimately from the old Germanic Hluodowig, a compounding of the elements *hluod* (famous) and *wīg* (war, strife). The name was borne by several queens of Sweden, Denmark, and Norway. Var: Louisa, Lovisa, Lovise. Short: Lova. (LOO-EE-SEH)

LUDOVICA Feminine form of Ludovic (famous in war), which is from the Middle Latin Ludovicus, a derivative of the Germanic Hluodowig, a compounding of the elements *hluod* (famous) and *wīg* (war, strife). (LOO-DO-VEE-KAH)

MAGDALENA Latinate form of Magdalene, from the Ecclesiastic Greek Magdalēnē (of Magdala). Mary

Magdalene was the name of a woman Christ cured of seven demons. Cognate: Magdalone, Malene (Danish). Short: Lone, Magda. (MAG-DAH-LEE-NAH)

Mai A pet form of Maria and Margit (a pearl), Mai is now commonly used as an independent given name and is a popular element in combination names such as Anne-Mai and Mai-Lis. Var: Maj (Swedish). (MĪ)

Maja Scandinavian form of Maia, the name of a Greek fertility-goddess, the daughter of Atlas and Pleione, and mother of Hermes (Mercury) by Zeus. The name is thought to be derived from the root *māi* (great). Additionally, Maja is a Swedish pet form of Maria. *See* MARIA. (MAH-YAH)

Margaret From the Greek Margaritēs, which is derived from *margaron* (a pearl). The name was borne by several saints as well as the powerful Queen Margareta (1353–1412), the daughter of King Waldemar IV of Denmark, wife of Haakon VI of Norway, and mother of Olaf V. She ruled Denmark, Norway, and Sweden. The popular Queen Margrethe II of Denmark (b. 1940) is one of the three reigning queens of Europe today, and the name is often bestowed in her honor. Cognate: Margarete, Margarethe, Margrethe (Danish); Margriet (Dutch); Margareta, Margaretha, Margit (Scandinavian). Short: Grete, Merete (Danish); Greet, Gret, Griet (Dutch); Marit (Norwegian, Swedish); Greta, Maj (Swedish). Pet: Meta, Mette (Danish, Swedish); Greetje, Gretja, Grietje (Dutch). (MAH-GAH-RET)

Maria Latin form of Mary, which is derived from the Hebrew Miryām (sea of bitterness, sea of sorrow). There is much debate over the meaning of this name. While "sea of bitterness" or "sea of sorrow" seems to be the most probable, some sources give the alternative definitions of "rebellion," "wished-for child," and "mistress or lady of the sea." Maria is a popular name throughout Europe and the Christian world and is commonly bestowed in honor of Mary, the mother of Jesus. Pet: Mia (Danish, Swedish); Marieke, Maryk, Mieke, Miep (Dutch); Maj, Maja (Swedish). (MAH-REE-AH)

Marna Swedish form of Marina, which is from the Latin *marinus* (of the sea, marine), the root of which is *mare* (the sea). (MAR-NAH)

Märta Danish contraction of Märeta, an obsolete form of Merete, which is a short form of Margarete (a pearl). *See* MARGARET. (MAR-TAH)

Martha Derived from the Aramaic Mārthā (lady, mistress). The name is borne in the Bible by the sister of Lazarus and Mary of Bethany. Var: Marta, Marte, Marthe. (MAR-THAH)

Martina Feminine form of Martin, from the Latin Martīnus, which is derived from Mars, the name of the Roman mythological god of war. The name is popular throughout Europe. Pet: Maartje (Dutch). (MAR-TEE-NAH)

Matilda Scandinavian form of the Old High German Mahthilda, which is derived from *maht* (power, might) and *hiltia* (battle). Cognate: Matilde (Danish). Short: Tilda; Tilde (Danish). (MAH-TEEL-DAH)

Melanie Variant of the Latin Melania, which is derived from the Greek *melas* (black, dark): hence, "dark-skinned." This name is in use primarily in the Netherlands. (MEH-LAH-NEE)

Menia Of unknown meaning borne in Norse mythology by a giantess who was enslaved with Fenia by Frodi. They had the task of grinding out gold, peace, and fair fortune for King Frodi at a mill called Grotti. Var: Menja. (MEHN-YAH)

Mia Danish and Swedish pet form of Maria, which is also commonly bestowed as an independent given name. *See* MARIA. (MEE-AH)

Mikaela Swedish feminine form of Michael, a name derived from the Hebrew *mīkhā'ēl* (who is like God?). *See* MICHAEL (Male Names). (MEE-KAH-EE-LAH, MIH-KAY-LAH)

Mina Short form of any of the names containing the element *mina* or *mine*. Var: Mine. (MEE-NAH)

Monika Scandinavian form of Monica, a name of uncertain origin and meaning. *See* MONICA (English Names). Short: Mona. (MO-NEE-KAH)

Nanna From Norse mythology, Nanna was the wife of Balder. Her chief duty was to accompany her husband to Hel. The name is a derivative of the Old Norse *nenna* (the brave, the persevering) or from the Gothic *nanþjan* (daring). (NAN-NAH)

Nel Dutch short form of Cornelia (horn), which is also bestowed as an independent given name. Pet: Nelleke. (NEL)

Nerthus Given the definition "mother earth," Nerthus is a byname of the Norse mythological goddess Frigg. She is one of the oldest known goddesses worshiped in Europe. *See* FRIGG. (NER-THUS)

Nilsine Swedish feminine form of Nils, a diminutive of Niklas (victory of the people). *See* NIKOLAUS (Male Names). (NIL-SEE-NEH, NIL-SEEN)

Nora A borrowing from the English, Nora originated as a short form of names such as Eleanora (light, torch, bright). Nora is now commonly bestowed as an independent given name. The name is borne by the heroine of Henrik Ibsen's play *A Doll's House.* (NOR-AH)

ODA Norwegian short form of names starting with the element *Aud-* or *Odd-* (point, the point of a weapon). (OO-DAH)

ODD Derived from the Old Norse Oddr, which is derived from *oddr* (point, the point of a weapon). (ODD)

ODDRUN Derived from the Old Norse Oddrún, which is composed of the elements *oddr* (point, the point of a weapon) and *run* (secret lore). The name is borne in Norse mythology by the unrequited love of Gunnar. Her story is told in the "Lament of Oddrun," the Oddrúnargrátr. Short: Oda. (ODD-RUN)

ODDVEIG A name that dates back to the Viking age and is composed of the Old Norse elements *oddr* (point, point of a weapon) and *veig* (woman): hence, "spear woman." Short: Oda. (ODD-VAYG, ODD-VAY)

OLA Norwegian name thought to be a feminine form of Olaf (ancestor's relic). *See* OLAF (Male Names). (OO-LAH)

OLAUG Of Old Norse origin composed of the elements *oo* (ancestor, ancestral) and *laug* (consecrated, dedicated): hence, "dedicated to the ancestors." (OO-LAUG)

OLGA A variant form of the Scandinavian Helge, which has its root in the Old Norse *heilagr* (prosperous, successful), which is from *heill* (hale, hearty, happy). The word *heill* later developed the meaning "blessed, holy." (OL-GAH)

PETRA Derived from the Latin *petra* (rock). (PEH-TRAH).

PETRINE Feminine form of Pet, a short form of Peter (a rock, a stone). *See* PETER (Male Names). (PEH-TREEN, PEH-TREE-NEH)

PETRONILLA A borrowing from the Latin, Petronilla is a feminine diminutive form of the Roman family name Petrōnius, which is of uncertain derivation. The name Petronilla was borne by a 1st-century martyr, and early Christians came to associate it with Peter (a rock). *See* PETER (Male Names). Cognate: Pernille (Danish); Pernilla (Swedish). Short: Nille (Danish). Pet: Pella. (PEH-TRO-NEE-LAH)

PIA Common Scandinavian name derived from the Latin *pius* (pious, devout, affectionate). (PEE-AH)

QUENBY A borrowing from the English, Quenby is derived from the Old English *cwēn* (queen) and *by* (settlement): hence, "queen's settlement." (KWEN-BE)

RAE Popular Scandinavian name meaning "doe, a female deer." (RAY)

RAGNA Old Norse name derived from the element *regin* (advice, counsel, decision). It is also used as a common element in compound names. (RAH-NAH)

RAGNBORG Derived from the Old Norse elements *regin* (advice, counsel, decision) and *borg* (fortification). Cognate: Ramborg (Swedish). (RAHN-BORG)

RAGNHILD Derived from the Old Norse elements *regin* (advice, counsel, decision) and *hildr* (battle): hence, "battle decision." Var: Ragnild. (RAHN-HIL, RAHN-HEEL)

RAKEL Scandinavian cognate of Rachel, a derivative of the Ecclesiastic Greek Rhachēl, which is from the Hebrew *rāhēl* (ewe). The name is borne in the Bible by the younger of the two wives of Jacob. (RAH-KEL)

RÁN Ancient name of uncertain meaning borne in Norse mythology by the goddess of the sea. She used a net to haul men off the decks of ships to their deaths beneath the sea. She was the wife of Aegir and the mother of nine beautiful daughters who were known as the Wave Maidens. Var: Ran. (RON)

RANVEIG Norwegian name composed of the elements *ran* (house) and *veig* (woman): hence, "housewife." Var: Rønnaug. (RON-VAYG, RON-VAY)

REBECKA From the Ecclesiastic Greek Rhebekka, which is derived from the Hebrew *ribbqāh* (noose), from *rabak* (to bind, to tie). The name is borne in the Bible by the wife of Isaac and mother of Esau and Jacob. Cognate: Rebekka (Danish, Norwegian). (REH-BEH-KAH)

RIGBORG Danish cognate of the Old High German Richborg, a compound name composed of the elements *rīc* (power, strength) and *borg* (fortification). (REE-BORG, REE-BOR)

RIGMOR Scandinavian form of an Old High German compound name composed of the elements *rīc* (power, strength) and *muot* (spirit, courage). (REE-MOR)

RINDA Derived from the Old Norse Rindr, an ancient name of uncertain meaning. It is borne in Norse mythology by the third wife of Odin and the mother of Váli. There is some confusion between her and the mortal Rind, a daughter of King Billing of Russia, who rejected Odin's attempt to seduce her. Var: Rind. (REEN-DAH)

RITA Scandinavian short form of Margarita (a pearl), which is now commonly bestowed as an independent given name. (REE-TAH)

RONA Norwegian name meaning "mighty power." (RO-NAH)

ROSEMARIE Popular name taken from the herb rosemary. It is derived from the Latin *ros marinus* (dew of the sea). Alternatively, the name can also be taken as a combination of the names Rose and Mary. (ROZE-MAH-REE)

RUNA Derived from the Old Norse Rúna, which is from *rún* (secret lore). (ROO-NAH)

RUT Scandinavian form of Ruth, which is derived from the Hebrew *rūth* (companion). The name is borne in the Bible by a Moabite woman who was devoted to her mother-in-law, Naomi. (ROOT)

SAGA Derived from the Old Norse Sága, a name of uncertain meaning. It is borne in Norse mythology by a goddess who was a mistress of Odin. He visited her at her hall for a daily drink. Var: Sága. (SAH-GAH)

SANNA Originally a short form of Susanna (a lily), Sanna is often bestowed as an independent given name, possibly favored because of its closeness to the adjective *sann* (true). (SAH-NAH)

SARA Variant of Sarah, which is derived from the Hebrew *sārāh* (princess). Sarah was the biblical wife of the patriarch Abraham and mother of Isaac. Pet: Sassa (Swedish). (SAH-RAH)

SASKIA Dutch name of uncertain meaning. It was borne by the wife of the Dutch painter Rembrandt van Rijn (1606–69). (SAS-KEE-AH, SAS-KEE-AH)

SIBYLLA A variant of Sybil, Sibylla is from the Latin and Greek words *sibylla* (prophetess, fortune-teller). The sibyls, women of ancient Greece and Rome, were mouthpieces of the ancient oracles and seers into the future. In the Middle Ages, they were believed to be receptors of divine revelation. Var: Sibella, Sibilla. (SIH-BEE-LAH)

SIF Kindred, relationship. The name is borne in Norse mythology by a golden-haired fertility-goddess who was the wife of Thor and mother of Thrud. She was also considered to be the goddess of agriculture, her emblem being ripened corn. Var: Siv. (SEEF)

SIGNY From an Old Norse compound name composed of the elements *sigr* (victory) and *ný* (new): hence, "new victory." The name is borne in Norse mythology by the twin sister of Sigmund and the wife of the detestable Siggeir, with whom she had two sons. Var: Signe, Signi. (SEEG-NEE, SIG-NEE)

SIGRID From an Old Norse compound name composed of the elements *sigr* (victory) and *fríðr* (fair, beautiful). Sigrid the Haughty was the wife of Sweyn Forkbeard and the stepmother of Canute the Great. Pet: Siri. (SEEG-REED, SIG-RID)

SIGRUN From an Old Norse compound name composed of *sigr* (victory) and *rūn* (secret lore). The name is borne in Norse mythology by the Valkyrie daughter of King Hogni. (SEEG-RUN)

SIGYN Derived from an Old Norse name composed of the element *sigr* (victory). The name is borne in Norse mythology by the all-faithful third wife of the malevolent Loki, and mother of Narve and Vali. (SEEG-EEN)

SILJA A borrowing from the Finnish, Silja is a cognate of Cecilia (blind, dim-sighted). The name is in common use in Scandinavia. (SIL-YAH)

SIXTEN Mainly Swedish name derived from the obsolete Old Norse Sigsteinn (victory stone), a compounding of the elements *sigr* (victory) and *steinn* (stone). (SEEX-TEN)

SJÖFN From the Old Norse *sjafni* (love). The name is borne in Norse mythology by an attendant of Frigg, a goddess whose duty was to kindle love between men and women. (SYOH-FN)

SOFIA Norwegian and Swedish cognate of Sophia, which is from the Greek *sophia* (wisdom, skill). Eight queens of Scandinavia and the Netherlands have borne the name, which is a favorite of royal families. Cognate: Sofie (Danish, Dutch). Pet: Saffi. (SO-FEE-AH)

SOLVEIG Norwegian name composed of the Old Norse elements *salr* (house, hall) and *veig* (strength): hence, "house of strength." Solveig is the name of the heroine in Henrik Ibsen's *Peer Gynt*. Cognate: Solvej (Danish); Solvig (Swedish). (SOL-VAYG, SOL-VAY)

SONJE Scandinavian cognate of Sonya, a Russian pet form of Sofya (wisdom, skill). *See* SOFIA. Sonja is the name of the wife of King Harald V of Norway and mother of Crown Prince Haakon Magnus and Princess Martha Louise. Var: Sonja. (SONE-YAH)

STELLA A borrowing from the Latin, Stella is derived directly from *stella* (STAR). (STEH-LAH)

SUNNIVA Scandinavian form of Sunngifu, an Old English name composed of the elements *sunne* (sun) and *gifu* (gift): hence, "a gift of the sun." The name was borne by St. Sunniva, a legendary 10th-century British maiden who was shipwrecked off the Norwegian coast and murdered after she made it to shore. Cognate: Synnøve (Danish, Norwegian); Synnöve (Swedish). (SOO-NEE-VAH)

SUSANNA Derivative of the Hebrew Shoshana, which is derived from *shōshannāh* (a lily, a rose). Short: Sanna. (SOO-SAH-NAH)

SVANHILD Scandinavian form of Swanhild, an old Saxon name composed of the elements *swan* (swan) and *hild* (battle): hence, "battle swan." The name is borne in Norse mythology by the daughter of Sigurd and Gudrun. (SVAN-HIL)

SVANNI Slender. The name is borne in Norse mythology by one of the daughters of Karl and Snor. Her name was characteristic of the attribute she represented for the peasant class. (SVAN-NEE)

SVEA 19th-century Swedish coinage formed from Svearike, the former name of Sweden. The first element of the name is uncertain, but the second is derived from the Old Norse *riki* (kingdom). Svea is often bestowed as a patriotic gesture. (SVEE-AH)

SYLVIA Popular Scandinavian form of the Latin Silvia (of the woods or forest), a name derived from *silva* (a forest, a wood). (SEEL-VEE-AH)

TEKLA Scandinavian form of the Greek Thekla, which is a compound name composed of the elements *theos* (God) and *kleos* (glory, fame). (TEH-KLAH)

TEODORA Feminine form of Theodore (God's gift), which is derived from the Greek elements *theos* (God) and *dōron* (gift). (TEE-O-DOR-AH)

THORA Feminine form of Thor, the name of the Norse mythological god of strength and thunder, which is derived from the Old Norse *þórr* (thunder). Thora has been a common name since the Viking age. In Norse mythology, Thora is the daughter of Hakon and wife of a Danish king named Elf, with whom Gudrun took refuge for seven years. (THOR-AH)

TILDA A short form of Matilda (powerful in battle), Tilda is also bestowed as an independent given name. *See* MATILDA. Var: Tilde. (TEEL-DAH)

TINA A very popular short form of Cristina (a follower of Christ, a Christian), Tina is also bestowed as an independent name. *See* CHRISTINA. (TEE-NAH)

TORA Latinate short form of any of the names containing the element *tor*, from the Old Norse *Þórr* (thunder). (TOR-AH)

TORBORG Modern variant of an Old Norse name derived from Thor, the mythological god of thunder and strength, and *borg* (fortification): hence, "Thor's hall." Cognate: Torbjørg (Norwegian); Thorborg (Scandinavian). Short: Tora. (TOR-BOR)

TORDIS Derived from an Old Norse compound name composed of the name of the god Thor and *dís* (goddess): hence, "Thor's goddess." (TOR-DEES)

TORUNN Derived from the Old Norse Þórunnr, a compound name composed of the elements Þórr (Thor) and *unnr* (love): hence, "loved by Thor." (TOR-UN)

TOVA Swedish form of Tōfa, an Old Norse name that originated as a short form of Þórfríðr (beautiful Thor), a compounding of the elements Þórr (Thor) and *fríðr* (fair, beautiful). Cognate: Tove (Danish, Norwegian). (TŌ-VAH)

TURID Derived from the Old Norse Þórfríðr (beautiful Thor), a compounding of the elements Þórr (Thor) and *fríðr* (fair, beautiful). (TOOR-EED)

ULLA Derived from the Old Norse *ullr* (will, determination). Alternatively, Ulla has been used as a short form of Ulrika (noble ruler). *See* ULRIKA. (OO-LAH)

ULRIKA Latinate form of Ulrike, the feminine form of Ulrich, which is derived from the Old Germanic elements *uodal* (nobility, prosperity, fortune) and *rīc* (ruler, power): hence, "noble ruler." The name was borne by two queens of Sweden, Ulrika Eleonora of Denmark, the wife of Carl XI, and their daughter of the same name. Short: Ulla. (OOL-REE-KAH)

UNN Derived from the Old Norse element *unnr* (love). (UN)

URSULA Middle Latin name which is a diminutive form of *ursa* (she-bear). The name has been popular in Scandinavia and the Netherlands, possibly due to the veneration of St. Ursula, a 4th-century Christian martyred, reportedly with eleven thousand virgins, by the Huns at Cologne. (OOR-SOO-LAH)

VANJA Scandinavian form of Vanya, a Russian pet form of Ivan, which is a cognate of John (God is gracious). Although it is used as a male name in Russia, in Scandinavia it is bestowed upon female children. (VAHN-YAH)

VÁRA Of uncertain meaning borne in Norse mythology by an attendant of Frigg. Vara's duties were to see to the keeping of oaths, pledges, and vows, the punishment of those who would break them, and the rewarding of those who kept them. Var: Vár. (VAR-AH)

VEGA A popular Swedish borrowing from the Latin, Vega (star) is the name of a very bright star in the constellation Lyra. (VAY-GAH)

VERA From the Russian Vjera (faith), which coincides with the Latin word *vera* (truth), which is derived from *vērus* (true). (VEER-AH)

VERONIKA Scandinavian form of Veronica, a name of debated etymology, which was supposedly the name of the woman who wiped the bleeding face of Jesus on the way to Calvary. *See* VERONICA (English Names). (VEH-RON-EE-KAH)

VICTORIA Popular name directly derived from the Latin *victoria* (victory). Victoria of Baden (1862–1930) was the wife of the Swedish king Gustav V. More recently, the Swedish heir to the throne is Crown Princess Victoria (b. 1977), the elder daughter of King Carl Gustav and Queen Silvia. (VEEK-TOR-EE-AH)

VIGDIS Old Norse name composed of the elements *víg* (war) and *dís* (goddess): hence, "goddess of war." (VEE-DEES)

VIOLA Directly derived from the Latin *viola* (violet). The name was used by Shakespeare in his play *Twelfth Night*. (VEE-O-LAH)

VIRGINIA Latinate feminine form of Virginius (spring-like, flourishing), an old Roman family name, which has its root in the Latin *ver* (spring). (VEER-GEE-NEE-AH)

VITA Danish name derived from the Latin *vita* (life). (VEE-TAH)

VIVIEN Derived from the Latin Vivianus, which is from *vivus* (alive). According to Arthurian legend, Vivien was the name of the Lady of the Lake, an enchantress and mistress of Merlin. Var: Vivianne, Vivienne. Short: Viv, Vivi. (VEE-VEE-EN)

VOR Borne in Norse mythology by one of Frigg's attendants. According to the Eddas, the name means "faith," but it is more likely to be derived from the adjective *varr* (wary, attentive). Vor is said to have been wise and prudent and to have had full knowledge of the future. (VOR)

WIBEKE Originally a pet form of the medieval Wibe, which is a contraction of the Germanic Wigburg, itself composed of *wīg* (war) and *burg* (castle, fortress). Wibeke is now bestowed as an independent given name. Cognate: Wiebke (Danish, Norwegian); Viveca, Viveka, Vivica (Swedish). (VEE-BEH-KEH)

WIGBURG Used primarily in the Netherlands, Wigburg is an old Germanic name composed of the elements *wīg* (war) and *burg* (castle, fortress). (VEE-BUR)

WILHELMINA Feminine form of the Germanic Wilhelm (resolute protector), a compounding of the elements *willeo* (will, desire) and *helm* (helmet, protection). The name, used primarily in the Netherlands, is often bestowed in honor of Queen Wilhelmina of the Netherlands, who ruled from 1890 to 1948. She was well liked and revered as the mother of her people. Cognate: Vilhelmine (Danish, Norwegian); Vilhelmina (Swedish). Short: Mine (Danish, Norwegian); Mina, Wilna (Dutch); Mina (Swedish). (WEEL-HEL-MEE-NAH, VEEL-HEL-MEE-NAH)

YVETTE A borrowing from the French, Yvette is a pet form of Yvonne, a feminine form of Yvon and Yves, which are of Germanic origin and derived from the element *iv* (yew). Yvette is commonly bestowed as an independent given name. (EE-VET)

YVONNE Feminine form of the French Yvon and Yves, names of Germanic origin derived from the element *iv* (yew). The wood from the yew tree was used in the making of bows and arrows; thus the name has the definition "archer." Pet: Yvette. (EE-VON, EE-VON-EH)

Chapter Twenty-Eight

Scottish Names

Scotland is divided into three physical regions: the Highlands, the Southern Uplands, and the Central Lowlands, where two-thirds of the population live.

Many traditional Scottish names come from the Feen, the heroic Celtic ancestors of the Scots race whose fantastic exploits form the basis of many legends and myths. English and Norman names are also widely used, though more so in the Lowlands than in the Highlands, where Scots Gaelic is still widely spoken and cultural pride is strong.

Surnames developed in the Scottish Lowlands after the Norman Conquest, as they did in England. But, being some distance from the Norman seat of power, they came about more slowly and were not hereditary for some time.

In the Highlands the clan was the source of power and protection. When people joined a clan, they added the clan surname to their own, even if there was no familial relationship. The surname usually consisted of the name of the chieftain to which was prefixed the word *mac* (son).

Thus, though Lowland surnames developed as patronymics and matronymics, and from occupational names, locales, or personal characteristics, the majority of Highland surnames are patronymics and did not become hereditary until the 18th century.

Scottish Male Names

Adaidh Gaelic form of Adie, which is a pet form of Adam (red earth). *See* ADAM *and* ÀDHAMH. (AID-EE)

Adam Derived from the Hebrew *adama* (red earth). The name is borne in the Bible by the first man created by God. According to tradition, it was from Adam's rib that the first woman, Eve, was formed. The Gaelic form of Adam is Àdhamh. Pet: Adie. (AD-AM)

Ádhamh Scottish Gaelic form of Adam, a name derived from the Hebrew *adama* (red earth). Pet: Adaidh. (AD-AHM)

Ádhamhnán Diminutive form of Ádhamh, the Gaelic form of Adam: hence, "little Adam." (AD-AHM-NAN)

Aidan A borrowing from the Irish, Aidan is an Anglicized form of the Gaelic Aodán, which is a diminutive form of Aodh (fire). Var: Edan. (AY-DUN)

Ailbeart Scottish Gaelic form of Albert (bright through nobility). *See* ALBERT. (AYL-BERT)

Ailean Scottish Gaelic form of Alan, which is a Celtic name of uncertain derivation. *See* ALAN. (AYL-EEN)

Ailpean Very old name in common use in Scotland since history first began to be recorded there. It is of unknown etymology, perhaps of Pictish origin. Var: Ailpein, Alpine. (AYL-PEEN)

Aindrea Scottish Gaelic form of Andrew (manly). *See* ANDREW. Var: Anndra. (AYN-DRAH)

Ainsley Transferred use of the Scottish surname taken from the place-name Ainsley, which is derived from the name element Æne's or Ægen's and the Old English *lēah* (woods, clearing, meadow). (AYNZ-LEE)

Alan Old name of Breton origin but of uncertain meaning. Some believe it to mean "handsome." Others promote the possibility that it is from a Celtic word meaning "rock." Alan was brought to England by the Normans during the Conquest. It was borne by Alan, earl of Brittany and a companion of William the Conqueror. The Gaelic form is Ailean. Var: Allan, Allen. (AL-UN)

Alasdair Scottish Gaelic form of Alexander (defender of mankind). *See* ALEXANDER. Var: Alastair, Alaster, Alisdair, Alistair, Alister, Allaster. Pet: Aly. (AL-ISS-TER)

Albert Derived from the Old High German Adalbrecht, a compound name composed of the elements *adal* (noble) and *beraht* (bright). (AL-BERT)

Alex A short form of Alexander (defender of mankind), Alex and its variants are also bestowed as independent given names. The Gaelic form is Ailig. *See* ALEXANDER. Var: Alec, Alick. (AL-EK)

Alexander Derived from the Greek Alexandros (defender or helper of mankind), a compound name composed from the elements *alexein* (to defend) and *andros* (man): hence, "defender of mankind." Alexander was borne by several early saints and martyrs, which helped to establish the name's popularity throughout Europe. In Scotland the name has been borne by three kings. The Gaelic form of Alexander is Alasdair. Short: Alec, Alex, Alick. Pet: Sandy. (AL-EX-ZAN-DER)

Alpin Anglicized form of Ailpein, an old Scottish name of unknown etymology. Var: Alpine. (AL-PIN)

Amhlaidh Scottish Gaelic form of Olaf (ancestor's relic), which was introduced into the area by the Vikings and Scandinavian immigrants. Olaf is a compound name composed of the Old Norse elements *anu* (ancestor) and *laf* (what is remaining, what is left of a forefather, relic). *See* OLAF (Scandinavian Names). The name has been Anglicized as Aulay. Var: Amhladh. (AU-LAY)

Andra Scottish form of Andrew (manly) common to the Lowlands. *See* ANDREW. (AN-DRAH)

Andrew A borrowing from the English, Andrew is a cognate of the Greek Andreas, a derivative of *andreios* (manly), which is from *aner* (man). The name was borne by one of the Twelve Apostles of Christ, which originally induced the name's popularity. It is currently borne by Prince Andrew, the duke of York (b. 1960), a son of Queen Elizabeth and Prince Philip. Andra is a popular Lowland form of the name, and Anndra and Aindrea are Gaelic forms. Short: Drew. Pet: Andy. (AN-DREW)

Angus Popular Anglicized form of Aonghus and Aonghas, Celtic names derived from the element *aon* (one, choice, preeminent). *See* AONGHUS. The name was borne in Celtic mythology by the god of love. Short: Gus. Pet: Angie. (ANG-GUSS)

Aodán Diminutive form of the Gaelic Aodh (fire). The name is Anglicized as Aidan and Edan. (AY-DAN)

Aodh Derived from the name of the Celtic god of the sun, Aodh (fire). It is a very old name that has been in common use in Scotland since history first began to be recorded there. The name continues to be commonly bestowed and is often Anglicized as Hugh and Eugene. (AYD)

Aodhagán Diminutive form of Aodh (fire). Iagan and Egan are Anglicized spellings of Aodhagán. (AYD-AH-GAN)

Aonghas Popular name derived from the Gaelic *aon* (one, choice, preeminent). The name has been Anglicized as Angus. Var: Aonghus. (ANG-GUS)

Arailt Scottish Gaelic form of Harold (leader of the army). *See* HAROLD. (AAR-ILT)

Archibald Of Germanic origin, Archibald is a compound name composed of the elements *ercan* (genuine, authentic) and *bald* (bold, brave). The name was introduced to the British Isles by the Normans. It has also been used as the English equivalent of Gillespie (bishop's servant). *See* GILLESPIE. Pet: Archie, Archy, Baldie; Eairrdsidh, Eairdsidh (Gaelic). (ARCHI-BALD)

Art Derived from the Gaelic *art* (bear). Alternatively, Art is in use as a short form of Arthur, a Celtic name of unknown meaning. *See* ARTHUR. Pet: Artan (of the Gaelic Art). (ART)

Artair Scottish Gaelic form of Arthur, a Celtic name of unknown meaning. *See* ARTHUR. Short: Art. (AR-TARE)

Arthur Of Celtic origin but of unknown meaning. The name was borne by the legendary British King Arthur, leader of the knights of the Round Table, who was supposed to have lived in the 5th or 6th century. The name gained popularity from the great body of Arthurian legend that has continued to remain of interest over the centuries. Artair is the Scottish Gaelic form of Arthur. Short: Art. (AR-THUR)

Augustus A borrowing of the Latin Augustas, which is derived from *augustus* (great, august, consecrated by the augurs). Short: Gus. (AW-GUS-TUS)

AULAY Anglicized form of Amhlaidh, the Scottish Gaelic cognate of Olaf (ancestor's relic). *See* AMHLAIDH. (AW-LAY)

BAIRD Derived from the Gaelic *bard* (a poet, an ancient Celtic poet and singer of epic poems). Var: Bard. (BAIRD)

BARCLAY Transferred use of the surname found as de Berchelai (from Berkeley) in 1086. Berkeley, a place-name in Gloucestershire, a southwestern English county, is derived from the Old English elements *beorc* (birch) and *lēah* (wood, clearing, meadow). The name was taken to Scotland in 1165 by William de Berchelai, chamberlain of Scotland and patriarch of the powerful Scottish Barclays. (BAR-KLAY)

BEAN Anglicized form of the Gaelic Beathan, which is derived from *beatha* (life). (BEEN)

BEARNARD Scottish Gaelic form of Bernard (bold or strong as a bear). *See* BERNARD. (BAIR-NARD)

BEATHAN Derived from the Scottish Gaelic *beatha* (life). The name is Anglicized as both Bean and Benjamin. (BEE-THUN)

BENEDICT Derived from the Latin Benedictus (blessed), which is from *benedicere* (to speak well of, to bless). *See* BENEDICT (English Names). The Scottish Gaelic form of Benedict is Benneit. Short: Ben. (BEN-EH-DIKT)

BENJAMIN Derived from the Hebrew *binyāmīn* (son of the right hand, favorite son). Benjamin is used in the Highlands as an Anglicized form of Beathan (life). Short: Ben. Pet: Benji, Benny. (BEN-JAH-MIN)

BENNEIT Scottish Gaelic form of Benedict (blessed). *See* BENEDICT. (BEN-ET)

BERNARD Derived from the Old High German Berinhard, a compound name composed of the elements *bern* (bear)and *hart* (bold, strong, hearty). *See* BERNARD (English Names). The Scottish Gaelic form of the name is Bearnard. (BER-NARD)

BHALTAIR Scottish Gaelic form of Walter (ruler of an army), which is of Germanic origin. *See* WALTER. Var: Bhàtair. (BAHL-TARE)

BLAIR Transferred use of the Scottish surname derived from place-names containing the Gaelic element *blár* (plain, level field). Blair therefore takes the definition "dweller on the plain or level field." (BLARE)

BOYD Transferred use of the surname derived from the Gaelic Mac Giolla Buidhe (son of the one with yellow hair). (BOID)

BRIAN A borrowing from the Irish, Brian is of uncertain etymology. It is generally thought to be of Celtic origin, but its meaning is disputed. Some believe it to be derived from the root *bri* (force, strength), *brigh* (courage, valor), or *bruaich* (a hill, steep, high). Var: Bryan. (BRĪ-UN)

BROC Derived from the Old English *brocc* (badger). (BROK)

BRODIE Transferred use of the surname meaning "from Brodie." Brodie is a place-name believed to be derived from the Gaelic *broth* (a ditch). Var: Brody. (BRO-DEE)

BRUCE Transferred use of the surname originating from the French Brieuse (a locality in France) and introduced by the Normans. The name was firmly established in Scotland by Robert de Bruce (1274–1329), a Norman who ruled the country as Robert I from 1306 to 1329. (BROOS)

BUCHANAN Transferred use of the surname meaning "belonging to Buchanan [Scotland]." It is believed to ultimately be a Pictish name with no connection to the Welsh *bychan* (small) or the Gaelic *bothan* (a hut), as many supposed. Short: Buck. (BYOO-KAN-NUN)

CAILEAN Gaelic form of the Late Latin Columba (dove). St. Columba (521–97) was an Irish missionary of great influence in both Ireland and Scotland. He founded several monastery schools in Ireland before traveling with twelve companions to the isle of Iona, the base from which he worked to convert the Scottish inhabitants to Christianity. Cailean is Anglicized as Colin. (KAY-LIN)

CALUM Popular Scottish Gaelic form of the Late Latin Columba (dove), the name borne by the Irish saint (521–97) who worked to convert Scotland to Christianity. *See* CAILEAN. Pet: Caley, Cally. (KAL-UM)

CAMERON Transferred use of the Scottish surname originating from the Gaelic nickname *cam sròn* (crooked nose). The name is borne by a famous Highland clan. Short: Cam. Pet: Camey. (KAM-ER-ON)

CAMPBELL Transferred use of the surname originating from the Gaelic nickname *cam béul* (crooked mouth). The name is borne by a famous Highland clan. Short: Cam. Pet: Camey. (KAMBL)

CANICE A borrowing from the Irish, Canice is an Anglicized form of the Gaelic Coinneach (handsome, comely). (KAN-EESS)

CHARLES A popular name throughout Europe and Great Britain, Charles is derived from the Germanic *karl* (full-grown, a man), which is a cognate of the Old

English *ceorl* (a man, a freeman, a peasant). It is a royal name and was introduced to the British Isles by Mary, Queen of Scots (1542–87), who bestowed it upon her son Charles James (1566–1625). His son and grandson both ruled as King Charles. The name was also borne by Bonnie Prince Charlie, the leader of the 1745 rebellion and pretender to the throne. Pet: Charlie. (CHARLZ)

CHRIS A short form of Christopher (bearing Christ), Chris is also bestowed as an independent given name. *See* CHRISTOPHER. (KRIS)

CHRISTOPHER Evolution of the Middle English Christofre, which is from the Late Latin Christophorus, a derivative of the Ecclesiastic Greek Christophoros, a compound name composed from the elements *Christos* (Christ) and *pherein* (to bear): hence, "bearing Christ." Short: Chris. Pet: Christie, Christy. (KRIS-TŌ-FER)

CLEMENT Derived from the Latin Clemens, which is directly derived from *clemens* (gentle, mild, merciful). The Gaelic form of Clement is Cliamain. (KLEM-ENT)

CLIAMAIN Scottish Gaelic form of Clement (gentle, mild, merciful). *See* CLEMENT. (KLĪ-MAIN)

COINNEACH Popular name derived from an old Gaelic nickname meaning "handsome, comely." The name is Anglicized as Canice and Kenneth. (KON-YAHK)

CÒISEAM Scottish Gaelic form of Constantine (steadfast, constant). *See* CONSTANTINE. (KOY-SEM)

COLIN A popular name, Colin is the Anglicized form of the Gaelic Cailean (dove). *See* CAILEAN. (KOL-IN)

CONALL Popular name derived from the Celtic element *conn* (strength; wisdom; high) or from *con* (wolf, dog). Var: Comhnall, Connell, Connull. (KON-NUL)

CONSTANTINE Derived from the Late Latin Constantinus, a derivative of Constans (steadfast, constant). The name, borne by three Scottish kings, is used to Anglicize the Gaelic Conn. Còiseam is the Gaelic form of Constantine. (KON-STAN-TEEN)

CORMAG Scottish Gaelic form of the Irish Cormac, a popular name of debated origin. Some believe it to mean "raven"; others derive it from the element *corb* (defilement) and *mac* (son). Another proposal is that it is from the element *corb* (a chariot, a charioteer) and *mac* (son). (KOR-MAG)

CRAIG Transferred use of the Scottish surname derived from the Gaelic *creag* (rugged rocks, crag): hence, "dweller by the crag." Var: Craigg. (KRAIG)

CREIGHTON Transferred use of the Scottish surname, which originally indicated a person from Crichton, a town in southeastern Scotland that derives its name from the Gaelic *crìoch* (border, boundary) and the Middle English *tune* (settlement, village, town). (KRAY-TUN)

CRISDEAN Derived from the Gaelic *Crìosd* (Christ). The name is seen as equivalent to the English Christopher (bearing Christ). (KREES-DEEN)

CUITHBEART Scottish Gaelic form of Cuthbert (well-known, famous). *See* CUTHBERT. Var: Cuithbrig. (KOOTH-BERT)

CÚMHAIGE A compound name composed of the Gaelic elements *cu* (hound) and *magh* (a plain): hence, "hound of the plain." The name is Anglicized as Quentin. (COO-EE)

CUTHBERT Compound name composed of the Old English elements *cūð, cuth* (known) and *beraht* (bright, famous). The name was borne by a 7th-century saint from Lindisfarne. Pet: Cuddy. (KUTH-BERT)

DÀIBHIDH Scottish Gaelic form of David (beloved). *See* DAVID. (DAY-VID)

DÀNIEL Scottish Gaelic form of Daniel, which is derived from the Hebrew *dāni'ēl* (God is my judge). Short: Dan. (DAN-YELL)

DARACH Anglicized form of the Gaelic Dubhdarach, a compound name composed of the elements *dubh* (black, dark) and *dair* (oak): hence, "dark oak." (DAHR-RAH)

DAVID Derived from the Hebrew *dāwīd* (beloved). It is borne in the Bible by the second and greatest of the Israelite kings. In the British Isles, the name was borne by St. David (also known as St. Dewi), a 6th-century Welsh bishop who is the patron saint of Wales, and by David I (c. 1084–1153), a king of Scotland who ruled from 1124 to 1153. The Scottish Gaelic form of David is Dàibhidh. Short: Dave. Pet: Davey, Davi, Dewy. (DAY-VID)

DEÒRSA Scottish Gaelic form of George (worker of the earth, farmer). *See* GEORGE. (DEER-SAH)

DIARMAD A Gaelic name of uncertain derivation, Diarmad is thought to be from the elements *dí* (without) and *airmit* (injunction): hence, "freeman." Diarmad is Anglicized as Dermid, Dermot, and Diarmid. (DĪ-AR-MAHD)

DOLAIDH Gaelic form of Dolly, which is a pet form of Donald (world ruler). *See* DONALD. (DŌ-LAY)

DOMHNALL Gaelic name thought to be derived from the primitive Celtic Dubno-walos, from *dubno* (world) and *walos* (mighty, ruler). The name is Anglicized as Donald. *See* DONALD. (DON-AHL)

DON Variant of the Scottish Donn as well as a short form of Donald. *See* DONALD *and* DONN. (DON)

DONALD A very popular name, Donald is the Anglicized form of the Gaelic Domhnall (world ruler). *See* DOMHNALL. Short: Don. Pet: Dolly (Gaelic Dolaidh); Donnie, Donny (Gaelic Donaidh, Donnaidh). (DON-ULD)

DONN A borrowing from the Irish, Donn is derived from the Gaelic *don* (brown, brown-haired). Var: Don. (DON)

DONNCHADH Gaelic name composed of Old Celtic elements *donn* (brown) and *chadh* (warrior). The name is Anglicized as Duncan. *See* DUNCAN. (DONN-KUH)

DOUGAL Anglicized form of the Gaelic Dubhghall and Dùghall, names meaning "dark-haired stranger." *See* DUBHGHALL. Var: Dugald, Dugal. Pet: Dougie. (DOOGL)

DOUGLAS Transferred use of the surname derived from the Gaelic elements *dubh* (black, dark) and *glas* (blue, green, gray; stream). Dubhglas was a common Celtic river name, and the surname might have originated to denote one who lived near the river. Short: Doug. Pet: Dougie, Duggie. (DUG-LAHS)

DREW Originally a short form of Andrew (manly), Drew is commonly used as an independent given name. *See* ANDREW. (DROO)

DUBHGHALL Compound name composed of the Gaelic elements *dubh* (dark, black) and *gall* (stranger): hence, "dark-haired stranger." The name is Anglicized as Dougal. Var: Dùghall. (DOOGL)

DÙBHGHLAS Gaelic compound name composed of the elements *dubh* (black, dark) and *glas* (blue, green, gray; stream). The name gave rise to the surname Douglas, the name of a powerful Scottish clan. (DOOG-LAHS)

DUFF Transferred use of the surname, which arose from a nickname for someone with dark hair or skin. The name is derived from the Gaelic element *dubh* (dark, black). (DUFF)

DUNCAN Anglicized form of the Gaelic Donnchadh (brown warrior). *See* DONNCHADH. The name was borne by a 7th-century saint who was abbot of the monastery on the isle of Iona. Pet: Dunky. (DUN-KUN)

EACHANN Compound name derived from the Gaelic elements *each* (horse) and *donn* (brown): hence, "brown horse." The name is Anglicized as Hector. (EE-KUN)

EAIRRDSIDH Gaelic form of Archie, which is a pet form of Archibald (genuinely bold, genuinely brave). *See* ARCHIBALD. Var: Eairrsidh. (AIR-CHEE)

EALLAIR Evolution of the Gaelic Ceallair, which originated as a nickname for one who worked as a steward in a monastery. The name is derived from the Latin *cellarius*, which is from *cella* (cellar, storeroom). The name is Anglicized as Ellar. (EEL-LER)

EANRAIG Scottish Gaelic form of Henry (ruler of an enclosure, home ruler), a name introduced to the British Isles by the Normans. *See* HENRY. (ANE-RAY)

EDMUND Derived from the Old English Eadmund (wealthy protection), a name composed of the elements *ēad* (prosperity, riches, fortune) and *mund* (hand, protection). The name was borne by a 9th-century East Anglian king killed by invading Danes for refusing to share his Christian kingdom with them. The Scottish Gaelic form is Eumann. Short: Ed. Pet: Eddie, Eddy. (ED-MUND)

EDWARD Derived from the Old English Eadweard, a compound name composed of the elements *ēad* (riches, prosperity, fortune) and *weard* (guardian, protector). Edward is a royal name, having been borne by three Anglo-Saxon kings and eight kings of England, as well as by the youngest son of Queen Elizabeth II, Prince Edward (b. 1964). Short: Ed, Ned, Ted. Pet: Eddie, Eddy. (ED-WARD)

EIDEARD Scottish Gaelic form of Edward (wealthy guardian). *See* EDWARD. Var: Eudard. (Ī-DERD)

ELLAR Anglicized form of Eallair, a Gaelic name derived from Ceallair (worker in a cellar). *See* EALLAIR. (EL-LAR)

ELLIOT Transferred use of the surname originating as a diminutive form of the Old French Élie, a cognate of the Hebrew Elijah (Jehovah is God). *See* ELIJAH (Biblical Names). Var: Elliott. (EL-LEE-UT)

EÓGHAN Ancient name thought to be derived from *êoghunn* (youth). Euan, Ewan, Evan, and Hugh are Anglicized forms. Var: Eòghann. (EH-VAHN)

EÒIN Gaelic form of John (God is gracious). *See* JOHN. (EE-UN)

ERIC Derived from the Old Norse Eiríkr, a compound name composed of the elements *ei* (ever, always) and *ríkr* (ruler). The name was introduced to the British Isles before the Norman Conquest by Viking invaders and subsequent Scandinavian settlers. (ERR-IK)

ERROL Of debated etymology. Some believe Errol is from a Scottish place-name of uncertain origin. Others think it is derived from the Latin *errare* (to wander). Var: Erroll. (AIR-L)

ERSKINE Transferred use of the Scottish surname derived from a place-name of uncertain meaning. One possibility is that it is derived from the Gaelic *aird sgainne* (height of the cleft). (ER-SKIN)

EUAN Anglicized form of the Gaelic Eóghan (youth). *See* EÓGHAN. (YOO-UN)

EUGENE A borrowing from the French, Eugene is derived from the Latin Eugenius, which is from *eugenēs* (well-born, noble). *See* EUGÈNE (French Names). Short: Gene. (YOO-JEEN)

EUMANN Scottish Gaelic form of Edmund (wealthy protection). *See* EDMUND. (YOO-MUN)

EUNAN Anglicized form of Ádhamhnán, a Gaelic name of debated meaning. *See* ÁDHAMHNÁN. The name was borne by the 7th-century St. Eunan, a biographer of St. Columba and an abbot of the monastery founded by the revered saint on the isle of Iona. (YOO-NUN)

EVAN Anglicized form of the Gaelic Eóghan (youth). *See* EÓGHAN. (EH-VUN)

EVANDER Derived from the Greek Euandros, a compound name composed of the elements *eu* (good, well) and *andros* (man). The name is used to Anglicize the Gaelic Ìomhair (archer). *See* ÌOMHAIR. (EE-VAN-DER)

EWAN Anglicized form of the Gaelic Eóghan (youth). *See* EÓGHAN. Var: Ewen. (YOO-AN)

EWART Transferred use of the surname derived from Ewe-herd, an occupational name composed of the Old English elements *ewe* (ewe, female sheep) and *heorde* (herd): hence, "shepherd." The surname was alternatively derived from the Old English *æwweard* (a priest), which is composed of the elements *æw* (divine law, religion) and *weard* (guardian, protection). (YOO-ART)

FARQUHAR Anglicized form of the Gaelic Fearchar (dear man). *See* FEARCHAR. (FAHR-KWAR)

FEARCHAR Compound name composed of the Gaelic elements *fear* (man) and *char* (dear). Fearchar is Anglicized as Farquhar. (FAHR-KAHR)

FEARGHAS Compound name composed from the Gaelic *fear* (man) and *ghas*, *gus* (valor, strength). The name is Anglicized as Fergus. (FER-GUS)

FERDINAND From the Spanish Ferdinando, a name of uncertain origin and meaning. It is thought to be of Germanic origin composed from the elements *frithu* (peace), *fardi* (journey), or *ferchvus* (youth, life) and *nanths* (courage), *nanthi* (venture, risk), or *nand* (ready, prepared). The name Ferdinand is used to Anglicize the Gaelic Fearadhach (manly). (FER-DIH-NAND)

FERGUS Typical Scottish name which is the Anglicized form of the Gaelic Fearghas, a compound name composed of the elements *fear* (man) and *ghas* (valor, strength): hence, "man of valor or strength." Pet: Fergie. (FER-GUS)

FIFE Transferred use of the surname originating from the place-name Fife, a region in eastern Scotland. Fife is thought to be named for Fib, a legendary Pictish hero who was one of the seven sons of Craithne. Var: Fyfe. (FIFE)

FILIB Gaelic form of Philip (lover of horses), a name introduced from England. *See* PHILIP. (FIL-IB)

FINGALL Anglicized form of Fionnghall, a compound name composed of the Gaelic elements *fionn* (white, fair) and *gal* (a stranger): hence, "fair-haired stranger." The name originated as a nickname for Norse immigrants. Var: Fingal. (FINGL)

FINLAY Anglicized form of Fionnlagh and Fionnla, compound names composed of the Gaelic elements *fionn* (white, fair) and *laogh* (warrior, calf): hence, "fair-haired warrior." Var: Finley. (FIN-LAY)

FIONNLAGH Compound name composed of the Gaelic elements *fionn* (white, fair) and *laogh* (warrior, calf): hence, "white warrior, fair-haired warrior," a byname for Viking invaders. Var: Fionnla. (FEE-ON-LAY)

FORBES Transferred use of the surname thought to be derived from the Old Gaelic *forba* (a field). (FORBZ)

FRANCIS From Franceis, an Old French form of the Italian Francisco, which is from the Middle Latin Franciscus (a Frenchman). Franciscus is derived from Francus (a Frank, a freeman), which has its root in the Old French *franc* (free). The Scottish Gaelic form of the name is Frang. Short: Frank. Pet: Frankie. (FRAN-SIS)

FRANG Gaelic form of Francis (a Frenchman). *See* FRANCIS. Pet: Frangag. (FRANG)

FRASER Transferred use of the surname, which is a corruption of the earlier Frisell (a Frisian). Var: Frazer. (FRAZE-ER)

FULTON Transferred use of the surname originating from the old place-name Fultone, which is of uncertain meaning. Some believe it to be derived from the Old English elements *fugel* (fowl) and *tūn* (town, enclosure, settlement, village): hence, "the fowl enclosure" or more simply "a chicken coop." (FUL-TUN)

GAVIN Of uncertain etymology, some believe Gavin to be from the obsolete Gwalchmai, a Gaelic name derived from the elements *gwalch* (a hawk) and *maedd* (a blow, battle). In Arthurian legend, Gavin is a byname for Sir Gawain, a knight of the Round Table and nephew of King Arthur. The name, which died out at the end of the Middle Ages, remained viable in Scotland until its revival elsewhere in the British Isles in the 20th century. (GAV-IN)

GENE Short form of Eugene (well-born, noble), Gene is also occasionally bestowed as an independent given name. (JEEN)

GEORGE From the French Georges, the root of which is the Greek Geōrgios, a name derived from *geōrgos* (earthworker, farmer), which is composed of the elements *gē* (earth) and *ergein* (to work). The name George was uncommon in the British Isles until the Hanoverian George became king in 1714. The use of the name by the four succeeding kings firmly established its use and popularity. Seòras and Deòrsa are Scottish Gaelic forms of George. Pet: Geordie. (JORJ)

GIBIDH Gaelic form of Gibby, which is a pet form of Gilbert (famous pledge), a name introduced by the Normans. *See* GILBERT. (GIH-BEE)

GILBERT From the Old French Guillebert, a derivative of the Old High German Gisilberht, which is composed from the elements *gisil* (pledge) and *beraht* (bright, famous). The name was introduced by the Normans and became very popular, resulting in the formation of several surnames. Gilleabart is the Gaelic form of Gilbert. Pet: Gibby. (GIL-BERT)

GILCHRIST Anglicized form of the Gaelic Giolla Chríost, a combination name composed of the elements *giolla* (servant of) and *Chríost* (Christ): hence, "servant of Christ." Short: Chris, Gil. Pet: Gilly. (GIL-KRIST)

GILLANDERS Derived from the Gaelic Gille Ainndreis and Gille Anndrais (servant of St. Andrew). (GIL-AN-DERZ)

GILLEABART Scottish Gaelic form of Gilbert (famous pledge). *See* GILBERT. Pet: Gibidh. (GIL-BERT)

GILLEONAN Derived from the Gaelic Gille Adhamhnain (servant of St. Adomnan). (GIL-O-NAN)

GILLESPIE Derived from the Gaelic Gille Easbaig (servant of the bishop). The name is Anglicized as Archibald. (GIL-ESS-PEE)

GILLIES Derived from the Gaelic Gille Ìosa (servant of Jesus). (GIL-EEZ)

GILROY Transferred use of the surname derived from the Gaelic Gill Ruaidh (servant of the red-haired lad). (GIL-ROY)

GLADSTONE Transferred use of the surname derived from a place-name composed of the Old English elements *glæd* (kite) and *stān* (rock, stone). (GLAD-STONE)

GLENN Derived from the Gaelic *gleann* (mountain valley, a narrow, secluded valley). It is unclear whether the surname or the given name came first. Var: Glen. (GLEN)

GODFREY From the Old French Godefrei (peace of God), which is derived from the Germanic Godafrid, a compound name composed from the elements *god* (God) and *frid* (peace). The name was introduced to the British Isles by the Normans and became very popular in the Middle Ages, giving rise to several surnames. Goiridh and Goraidh are Gaelic forms of the name. (GOD-FREE)

GOIRIDH Scottish Gaelic form of Godfrey (peace of God). *See* GODFREY. Var: Goraidh. (GOY-REE)

GORDON Transferred use of the Scottish surname believed to have originated from the place-name Gordon in Berwickshire. The place-name is of uncertain etymology. The use of Gordon as a given name dates to the 19th century, when it was bestowed in honor of the popular British general Charles Gordon (1833–85), called Chinese Gordon from his service in China, Egypt, and Sudan. (GOR-DON)

GRAHAM Transferred use of the surname originating from the place-name Grantham in Lincolnshire. The first element is uncertain, but the second is from the Old English *ham* (home, dwelling, manor). The name was taken to Scotland in the 12th century by William de Graham, a Norman and founder of the famous Scottish clan. Var: Graeme, Grahame. (GRAY-AM)

GRANT Transferred use of the Scottish surname derived from the Anglo-French *graund, graunt* (great) and the Old French *grand, grant* (great). The name originated as a nickname for a large or tall person. (GRANT)

GREG Short form of both Gregor and Gregory (vigilant), Greg is also occasionally bestowed as an independent given name. *See* GREGOR *and* GREGORY. Var: Gregg, Greig. (GREG)

GREGOR Short form of Gregory (vigilant), Gregor is now used as an independent given name. Griogair is the Gaelic form. *See* GREGORY. Short: Greg, Gregg, Greig. (GREG-OR)

GREGORY From the Late Latin Gregorius, a cognate of the Greek Grēgorios (vigilant, a watchman), which is derived from the verb *egeirein* (to awaken). Short: Greg, Gregg, Greig. (GREG-OR-EE)

GRIOGAIR Scottish Gaelic form of Gregory (vigilant, a watchman). The name is often Anglicized as Gregor. Var: Griogal. Short: Grieg. (GREE-GER)

HAMILTON Transferred use of the surname taken from the name of a no-longer-existing English town. The name is derived from the Old English elements *hamel* (blunt) and *dun* (hill). (HAMML-TUN)

HAMISH Gaelic form of James and Jacob (supplanter). *See* JACOB *and* JAMES. (HAY-MISH)

HARAL Scottish Gaelic form of Harold (leader of the army). *See* HAROLD. Var: Arailt. (HAR-AL)

HAROLD A borrowing from the English, Harold is derived from the obsolete Old English Hereweald (leader of the army), a compound name composed of the elements *heri* (army) and *weald* (ruler, power, control). The name, which fell from use in the Middle Ages, was revived in the 19th century. Arailt and Haral are Scottish Gaelic forms of Harold. (HARLD)

HARRY A pet form of Henry (ruler of an enclosure, home ruler), Harry is also bestowed as an independent given name. *See* HENRY. (HAA-REE)

HECTOR From the Greek Hektōr, which is derived from the verb *ekhein* (to restrain). The name is used to Anglicize the Gaelic Eachann (brown horse). (HEK-TOR)

HENRY From the French Henri, from the German Heinrich, which is from the Old High German Haganrih (ruler of an enclosure), a compound name composed from the elements *hag* (an enclosure, a hedging-in) and *rihhi* (ruler), and from the Old High German Heimerich (home ruler), a compound name composed from the elements *heim* (home) and *rik* (ruler, king). The name, introduced to the British Isles by the Normans and borne by eight English kings, took the English vernacular form Harry until the 17th century, when Henry became popular and Harry was used as a pet form. Pet: Harry. (HEN-REE)

HUGH From the Old French Hue, which is from the Old High German Hugo, a derivative of *hugu* (heart, mind, spirit). Hugh is used to Anglicize Aodh, Eóghan, and Ùisdean. Pet: Hewie, Hughie. (HYOO)

IAGAN Variant spelling of Aodhagán (little fire), a diminutive form of Aodh (fire). Var: Egan. (EE-GAN)

IAIN Scottish Gaelic form of Ian, which is a Scottish form of John (God is gracious). *See* JOHN. (EE-AN)

IAN Popular Scottish form of John (God is gracious). *See* JOHN. The Gaelic form is Iain. (EE-AN)

INNES Transferred use of the surname derived from the name of a barony in the former county of Moray in northeastern Scotland. Innes is derived from the Gaelic *innis* (island). (IN-NES)

ÌOMHAIR Scottish Gaelic form of Ivor, a Scottish variant of the Scandinavian Ivar, a compound name composed of the Old Norse elements *ýr* (yew, bow) and *herr* (warrior, army): hence, "archer, bow warrior." Var: Ìmhear, Ìomhar. (YO-MER)

IÒSEPH Gaelic form of Joseph (may he add). *See* JOSEPH. Pet: Seòsaidh. (YO-SEF)

IRVING Transferred use of the surname, which arose from an old parish in Ayrshire and an old parish in Dumfriesshire. The name of the town in Ayrshire is thought to be derived from the name of the river, which is from the Gaelic *iar* (west) and *abhuinn* (river). Var: Irvin, Irvine. (ER-VING)

IVOR Scottish form of Ivar, a name introduced by Scandinavian settlers. It is derived from the Old Norse elements *ýr* (yew, bow) and *herr* (warrior, army): hence, "archer, bow warrior." Ìmhear, Ìomhair, and Ìomhar are Gaelic forms of the name. (Ī-VOR)

JACK Originally a pet form of John (God is gracious), Jack is now often bestowed as an independent given name. It evolved from the Middle English Jackin, which evolved from Jankin, a diminutive form of Jehan and Jan, Middle English forms of John. *See* JOHN. Var: Jock. Pet: Jackie, Jacky. (JAK)

JACOB From the Ecclesiastic Late Latin Iacobus, which is from the Greek Iakōbos, a name derived from the Hebrew Yaakov, which is from *ya'aqob* (seizing by the heel, supplanting). Pet: Jake. (JAY-KOB)

JAMES From the Ecclesiastic Late Latin Iacomus, an evolution of Iacobus, which is ultimately from the Hebrew Yaakov (seizing by the heel, supplanting). *See* JACOB. The name, which is borne in the Bible by a brother of Jesus, has long been in use in Scotland and is, in particular, associated with the royal House of Stuart. James I (1394–1437) enthusiastically ruled Scotland from 1424 to 1437. James VI (1566–1625), the son of Mary Stuart, became king in 1567 and succeeded to the English throne in 1603 as James I and henceforth ruled Scotland, England, and Ireland. His grandson James II (1633–1701), a Roman Catholic, ruled from 1685 until 1688, when he was deposed in favor of his Protestant daughter, Mary. The name then became a national symbol of Catholicism and Highland opposition to the

English throne. Séamus is the Gaelic form. Pet: Jamie, Jimmie, Jimmy. (JAYMZ)

JESSE Derived from the Hebrew Yishai, which is from *yīshai* (gift, wealthy). Short: Jess. (JES-SEE)

JOCK Scottish variant of Jack, which is a pet form of John (God is gracious). Jock is also bestowed as an independent given name. *See* JOHN. Seoc is the Gaelic form. Pet: Jockan, Jockie, Jocky. (JOK)

JOE A short form of Joseph (may he add), Joe is also occasionally bestowed as an independent given name. *See* JOSEPH. (JO)

JOHN The most enduring of all the biblical names, John is derived from the Middle Latin Johannes, which is from the Ecclesiastic Late Latin Joannes, from the Ecclesiastic Greek Iōannes, a derivative of the Hebrew Yehanan, a short form of Yehohanan, which is from *yehōhānān* (Yahweh is gracious). First used by the Eastern Church, John was brought to the British Isles after the First Crusade and was quickly established. Pet: Jack, Jock, Johnnie, Johnny. (JON)

JON Short form of Jonathan (God has given), Jon is also bestowed as an independent given name, usually as a variant of John (God is gracious). *See* JOHN *and* JONATHAN. (JON)

JONATHAN From the Hebrew Yonatan, a short form of Yehonatan, which is derived from *yehōnātān* (Yahweh has given). Var: Johnathan, Jonathon. Short: Jon. (JON-AH-THAN)

JOSEPH A borrowing from the Ecclesiastic Late Latin, Joseph is from the Ecclesiastic Greek Iōsēph, which is from the Hebrew Yosef, a name derived from *yōsēf* (may he add). The name is borne in the Bible by the favorite son of Jacob, by the husband of the Virgin Mary, and by Joseph of Arimathea, a rich Jew who, according to medieval legend, brought the Holy Grail to Britain. The Gaelic form is Iòseph. Short: Joe. Pet: Josie. (JO-SEF)

KEIR Derived from the Celtic *keir* (of dark complexion, swarthy). Alternatively, Keir represents the transferred use of the surname originating from a place-name in Stirlingshire, which is believed to be derived from the Gaelic *cathair* (a fort) or the Welsh *caer* (a fort). (KEER)

KEITH Transferred use of the Scottish surname originating from several place-names, which are of uncertain derivation. Keith might be formed from a Gaelic root meaning "the wind" or "wood." The use of Keith as a given name dates to the 19th century. (KEETH)

KENNEDY Transferred use of the surname derived from the Irish Ceinneidigh, a compound name composed of the elements *ceann* (head, chief, leader) and *eidigh* (ugly): hence, "ugly head" or "ugly chief." (KEN-NEH-DEE)

KENNETH Anglicized form of the Gaelic Cinaed and Cionaed (born of fire) and Coinneach and Caioneach (comely, handsome). The name, borne by Cinaed, Kenneth I MacAlpin (d. 860), the first king of Scotland, has continued to be popular in Scotland and all of the English-speaking world. Short: Ken. Pet: Kenny. (KEN-NETH)

KESTER Scottish Gaelic form of Christopher (bearing Christ). *See* CHRISTOPHER. (KES-TER)

KIERAN A borrowing from the Irish, Kieran is the Irish form of the Gaelic Ciarán (little dark one), which is from *ciar* (black, dark), a word meaning "dark-haired" or "black-haired" when applied to humans. St. Kiaran was the patron saint of the Scots who first came from Ireland. His name is often found in the variant form Queran. Var: Ceiran, Kiaran, Queran. (KEER-AN)

KIPP Transferred use of the surname derived from the Northern English *kip* (a pointed hill). (KIP)

KIRK Transferred use of the surname derived from the Old Norse *kirkja* (church), which was originally used for one who resided by a church: hence, "dweller by the church." (KIRK)

KYLE Transferred use of the surname originating from the region of the same name in southwestern Scotland. Kyle, a topographical term referring to a narrow, straight, channel, is derived from the Gaelic *caol* (narrow, a sound, a strait).

LABHRAINN Scottish Gaelic form of Laurence (man from Laurentum). *See* LAURENCE. (LAH-REN)

LACHLAN Derived from the Gaelic *laochail* (war-like), which is from the root *laoch* (war, strife). Alternatively, it may be from the Irish Lochlainn (Lakeland, Fiordland), a name that originated from the name the Irish used for the native home of the Norse invaders. Var: Lachann, Lachlann. Pet: Lachie. (LAAK-LAN)

LARRY A pet form of Laurence (man from Laurentum), Larry is also bestowed as an independent given name. *See* LAURENCE. (LA-REE)

LAURENCE From the Latin Laurentius (from Laurentum), which is from Laurentum, the name of a town in Latium that is probably derived from *laurus* (laurel). Labhrainn is the Gaelic form of the name. Pet: Larry. (LOR-ENS)

LENNOX Transferred use of the surname derived from a place-name in Dumbarton. The name is believed to be derived from the Gaelic *leamhanach* (elm trees). Var: Lennex, Lenox. Short: Len. Pet: Lenny. (LEN-NEX)

LESLIE Transferred use of the Scottish surname taken from Lesslyn, a place-name in Aberdeenshire. The name might be derived from the Gaelic elements *lios* (enclosure, garden, fort) and *chuillinn* (a holly tree) or *liath* (gray): hence, "garden of hollies" or "the gray fort." The name, borne by a Scottish clan, was not in common use as a personal name until late in the 19th century. Short: Les. (LES-LEE)

LEWIS Variant of Louis, a borrowing from the French which evolved from the Old French Loeis, a name derived from the Old High German Hluodowig, a compound name composed of the elements *hluod* (famous) and *wīg* (war, strife): hence, "famous in war." Lewis had the alternative role of Anglicizing the Gaelic Lughaidh, an ancient name of uncertain derivation. Luthais is the Gaelic form. Short: Lew. Pet: Lewie. (LOO-ISS)

LINDSAY Transferred use of the surname de Lindsay, meaning "from Lindsay," a part of the county of Lincolnshire in northeastern England. Lindsay is derived from Lincoln, a shortened form of Lindum Colonia, the first part of which is thought to be from the Welsh *llyn* (lake), and the second from the Latin *colonia* (settlement, colony). The name is bestowed upon both males and females in Scotland. (LIND-ZEE)

LOGAN Transferred use of the Irish surname, which is from the Gaelic *lagan* (a little hollow): hence, "dweller near the little hollow." (LO-GUN)

LUTHAIS Gaelic form of Lewis (famous warrior). *See* LEWIS. (LOO-EE)

MAC Derived from the Gaelic *mac* (son of), a common first element in Scottish and Irish surnames. Var: Mack. (MAK)

MAGNUS A borrowing from the Latin, Magnus is derived from *magnus* (great). The name was brought to the British Isles by the Scandinavians during the Middle Ages. Mànus is the Gaelic form. (MAG-NUS)

MALCOLM Derived from the Gaelic Maolcolm (servant of St. Columba), a compound name composed of the elements *maol* (servant, votary) and Colm (Columba). St. Columba (521–97) was an Irish missionary who played a major role in converting Scotland and northern England to Christianity. (MAL-KUM)

MÀNUS Gaelic form of Magnus (great). *See* MAGNUS. (MAN-US)

MARC A short form of Marcus, Marc is also bestowed as an independent given name. *See* MARCUS. (MARK)

MARCUS A borrowing from the Latin, Marcus is of uncertain derivation. Most believe it has its root in Mars, the name of the Roman mythological god of war, and is therefore given the meaning "war-like." Others think it is from *mas* (manly) or the Greek *malakoz* (soft, tender). Short: Marc. (MAR-KUS)

MÀRTAINN Gaelic form of Martin (war-like). *See* MARTIN. (MAHR-TANE)

MARTIN From the Latin Martinus, a derivative of Mars, the name of the Roman mythological god of war. Màrtainn is the Gaelic form. (MAHR-TIN)

MATA Gaelic form of Matthew (gift of God). *See* MATTHEW. (MA-TA)

MATTHEW Evolution of the Middle English Matheu, which is from the Ecclesiastic Late Latin Matthaeus, a derivative of the Ecclesiastic Greek Matthaios and Matthias, contractions of Mattathias. The name is derived from the Hebrew Matityah, which has its root in *mattūthyāh* (gift of God). Mata is the Gaelic form. Short: Matt. (MATH-YOO)

MICHAEL A borrowing from the Ecclesiastic Late Latin, Greek, and Hebrew, Michael is derived from the Hebrew *mīkhā'ēl* (who is like God?). The name is borne in the Bible by the archangel closest to God, who is responsible for carrying out God's judgments. Considered the leader of the heavenly host, Michael is regarded as the patron saint of soldiers. Micheil is the Gaelic form. Short: Mick, Mike. Pet: Micky, Mikey. (MĪ-KL)

MICHEIL Gaelic form of Michael (who is like God?). *See* MICHAEL. (MĪ-KEL)

MONRO Transferred use of the surname derived from the Gaelic elements *moine* (a morass, a marsh) and *ruadh* (red): hence, "dweller at the red morass." Var: Monroe, Munroe. (MON-RO)

MUIR Transferred use of the Scottish surname meaning "dweller near the moor." It is derived from the Old English and Old Norse *mór* (moor, heath). (MYOOR)

MUIREADHACH Compound name composed of the Gaelic elements *muir* (sea) and *adhach* (happy, fortunate, lucky), with the definition "mariner, seaman." Murdoch is the Scottish and Irish form of the name. (MYOOR-DAHK)

MUNGO Possibly derived from the Welsh *mwyn* (kind, gentle). (MUN-GO)

MURCHADH Derived from the obsolete Celtic Moricatu-s, a compound name composed from the elements *mor* (sea) and *cath* (warrior, war). Murchadh is a popular name and is Anglicized as Murphy in Scotland and Murrough in Ireland. Var: Muireach. (MUR-AHK)

Murdoch Introduced by the Irish, Murdoch is from the Gaelic Muireadhach (mariner). *See* MUIREADHACH. Short: Murdo. (MUR-DOK)

Murphy Popular name, Murphy is the Anglicized form of the Gaelic Murchadh (sea warrior). *See* MURCHADH. (MUR-FEE)

Neacal Gaelic form of Nicholas (victory of the people). *See* NICHOLAS. (NEEKL)

Neil Anglicized form of the Gaelic Niall, a name of debated meaning. *See* NIALL. Var: Neal, Neill, Niel, Niell. (NEEL)

Niall A borrowing from the Irish, Niall is a very old yet still popular Gaelic name of debated meaning. Some believe it is derived from *niadh* (a champion). Others think it is from *néall* (cloud). Neil and its variants are Anglicized forms of the name. (NĪ-AHL)

Nicholas From the Old French Nicolas, which is from the Latin Nicolaus, a derivative of the Greek Nikolaos, a compound name composed of the elements *nikē* (victory) and *laos* (the people). The name was borne by St. Nicholas, a 4th-century bishop of Myra who is regarded as the patron saint of Russia and Greece, and of children, sailors, and wolves. St. Nicholas is known to children as Father Christmas, the bringer of gifts at Christmastime. Var: Nicolas. Short: Nicol. Pet: Nick, Nicky. (NIH-KO-LAS)

Norman From the Old French Normant, derived from the Frankish *nortman*, which is composed of the elements *nort* (north) and *man* (man): hence, "northman, Norseman." The name originally was used to identify a member of the group of Scandinavians who occupied Normandy in the 10th century, and later, the native inhabitants of Normandy. Norman has a cognate in the Germanic Nordman, a compound name composed of the elements *nord* (north) and *man* (man), and it is this form that was used in Britain before the Norman invasion. Tòrmod is the Gaelic form. (NOR-MAN)

Oilbhries Gaelic form of Oliver, a name of debated meaning. *See* OLIVER. (OY-LEH-REE)

Olghar Gaelic form of Oliver. *See* OLIVER. (OHL-VER)

Oliver Derived from the French Olivier, which is generally considered to be from the Old French *olivier* (olive tree). Some believe it is of Germanic origin, however, and is thus probably from the Middle Low German Alfihar, a compound name composed of the elements *alf* (elf) and *hari* (army): hence, "elf army." Oilbhries and Olghar are Gaelic forms of the name. Pet: Ollie. (O-LIH-VER)

Oscar From the Old English Osgar, a compound name composed of the elements *os* (a god) and *gar* (spear). Alternatively, there is an Irish Oscar, which is derived from the Gaelic elements *os* (a deer) and *cara* (friend): hence, "a friend of deer." Both names were introduced to Scotland. Var: Osgar. (OS-CAR)

Pàdraig Common Gaelic form of Patrick (a patrician). *See* PATRICK. Var: Padraic, Pàdruig. Pet: Pàidean. (PA-DREEG)

Pàl Gaelic form of Paul (small). *See* PAUL. Var: Pòl. (PAHL)

Parlan Scottish Gaelic form of the biblical Bartholomew (son of Talmai). *See* BARTHOLOMEW (English Names). (PAR-LAN)

Patrick Derived from the Latin *patricius* (a patrician). The name was adopted by St. Patrick (c. 385–461), a missionary to and patron saint of Ireland. He was a Christian Briton and a Roman citizen whose original name was Sucat. Padraic, Pàdraig, and Pàdruig are common Gaelic forms of Patrick. Short: Pat. Pet: Pate, Patie. (PAT-RIK)

Paul From the Latin Paulus, which originated as a Roman family name derived from *paulus* (small). The name was adopted in the Bible by Saul of Tarsus, a Jewish Roman citizen who was converted to Christianity by a vision of Christ. Paul and St. Peter are regarded as cofounders of the Christian Church. Pàl and Pòl are Gaelic forms. (PAHL)

Peader Popular Gaelic form of Peter (a rock, a stone). *See* PETER. Pet: Peidearan. (PEE-DER)

Peter From the Ecclesiastic Late Latin Petrus and the Greek Petros, names derived from *petra* (a rock) and *petros* (a stone). The name is borne in the Bible by one of the Twelve Apostles of Christ. Peter is considered to have been the first pope and cofounder, with Paul, of the Christian Church. Peader is the Gaelic form used in Scotland. (PEE-TER)

Philip From the Latin Philippus, a derivative of the Greek Philippos, which is composed from the elements *philos* (loving) and *hippos* (horse): hence, "lover of horses." The name is borne in the Bible by one of the Twelve Apostles of Christ. Filib is the Gaelic form. *See* PHILIP (English Names). (FIL-IP)

Quentin A borrowing from the French, Quentin is from the Latin Quentīnus, a derivative of the Roman personal name Quintus, which is from *quintus* (the fifth). The name was normally bestowed by the Romans upon the fifth-born male child, a custom the French and English adopted. Quentin is used to Anglicize the Gaelic

Cúmhaighe (hound of the plain). *See* CÚMHAIGHE. (KWIN-TIN)

RAGHNALL Gaelic name derived from the Scandinavian Rögnvaldr (powerful judgment), a compound name composed from the Old Norse elements *regin* (advice, decision, judgment) and *valdr* (ruler, power, might). The name was also derived from the Germanic Raganald, a compound name, introduced by the Anglo-Normans, composed from the Old High German elements *ragin* (advice, judgment, counsel) and *wald* (ruler). Reginald and Ronald are English forms. (RAHN-ALL)

RAIBEART Gaelic form of Robert (bright fame). *See* ROBERT. Short: Rab. Pet: Rabbie. (RAY-BERT)

RAMSEY Transferred use of the surname originating from several different place-names. It is derived from the name Hræm's Island, which is from the Old English elements *hræm(n)* (raven) and *ég, íg* (island); from Ram's Island, which is from the Old English *ramm* (a ram) and *ég, íg* (island); or from Ramm's Island, which derives its name from the Old Norse elements *rammr* (strong) and *ey* (island). Var: Ramsay. (RAM-ZEE)

RANULF Scottish form of Randolf (shield wolf). The name, introduced by the Scandinavians, is derived from the Old Norse Randulfr, a compound name composed from the elements *rand, rönd* (the edge or rim of a shield) and *ulfr* (wolf). (RAN-NULF)

RAONULL Gaelic name derived from Rögnvaldr, a compound name, introduced by Scandinavian settlers, composed from the Old Norse elements *regin, rögn* (advice, judgment, decision) and *valdr* (ruler, power). The name is Anglicized as Ranald and Ronald. (RAHN-UL)

READ Transferred use of the surname originating as a nickname for a person with red hair or a ruddy complexion. The name is derived from the Old English *réad* (red). Reid is the Scottish form. (REED)

REID Transferred use of the surname originating as a nickname for a person with red hair or a ruddy complexion. The name is derived from the Scottish *reid* (red). (REED)

RICHARD A borrowing from the Old French, Richard is derived from the Old High German Richart, a compound name composed from the elements *rīc, rik* (power, ruler) and *hard* (strong, brave, hearty): hence, "brave ruler." Ruiseart is a Gaelic form. *See* RICHARD (English Names). Short: Rich, Rick. Pet: Richie, Ricky. (RIH-CHARD)

ROBERT Introduced to the British Isles by the Normans, Robert is derived from the Old High German Hruodperht, a compound name composed of the elements *hruod* (fame) and *perht* (bright). The name was borne by Robert I (d. 1035), the duke of Normandy and father of William the Conqueror, and by three kings of Scotland. Short: Rab, Robb. Pet: Rabbie, Robbie. (RO-BERT)

RODDY A pet form of Roderick (famous king), Roddy is also bestowed as an independent given name. *See* RODERICK. (RAHD-DEE)

RODERICK From the Middle Latin Rodericus, which is derived from the Old High German Hrodrich, a compound name composed from the elements *hruod* (fame) and *rik* (ruler, king): hence, "famous king." The name was introduced to the British Isles by the Scandinavians and later by the Normans, but fell out of use in the Middle Ages until it was revived in the 19th century. In Scotland, Roderick is used to Anglicize Rory and the Gaelic Ruaidhrí and Ruairidh (red, ruddy). Pet: Roddy. (RAH-DEH-RIK)

RONALD Introduced to Scotland by Scandinavian settlers in the form of Rögnvaldr (ruler of decision, judgment power), a compound name composed of the Old Norse elements *regin, rögn* (advice, judgment, decision) and *valdr* (ruler, power). Ronald and its variant Ranald continue to be very popular names in Scotland. Var: Ranald. Short: Ran, Ron. Pet: Ronny. (RAN-ALD)

RORY A borrowing from the Irish, Rory is an Irish form of the Gaelic Ruairidh and Ruairí, names derived from *rua* (red, ruddy). Roderick and Roger are names used to Anglicize Rory. (ROR-REE)

ROSS Transferred use of the surname derived from the Gaelic *ros* (a promontory or peninsula): hence, "dweller on the promontory or peninsula." Alternatively, the name originated as a nickname for a person with red hair and in this case is derived from the Middle English *rous(e)* (red, rust-colored). (ROSS)

ROY Transferred use of the surname originating as a descriptive nickname for a person with red hair or a ruddy complexion. It is derived from the Gaelic *ruadh* (red). (ROI)

RUARAIDH Derived from the Gaelic *rua* (red, ruddy). Ruaraidh has been Anglicized as Roderick and Rory. Var: Ruaidhrí, Ruairi, Ruairidh. (RUR-REE)

RUISEART Gaelic form of Richard (brave ruler). *See* RICHARD. (ROO-ISH-ART)

SACHAIRI Gaelic form of Zachary (God remembers). *See* ZACHARY. (SAY-KARE-REE)

SANDAIDH Gaelic form of Sandy, which is a pet form of Alexander (defender or helper of mankind). *See* ALEXANDER. (SAN-DEE)

SANDY A pet form of Alexander (defender or helper of mankind), Sandy is also bestowed as an independent given name. Sandaidh is the Gaelic form. Var: Sawney. (SAN-DEE)

SCOTT Transferred use of the surname derived from the Old English *Scottas*, originally "an Irishman," and later, "a Gael from Scotland, a Scotchman." Pet: Scotty. (SKOT)

SEAGHAN From the Irish Gaelic Seaghán, a variant of Eóin, which is the Gaelic form of John (God is gracious). Shane is the Anglicized form. *See* JOHN. (SHANE)

SÉAMUS Gaelic form of James (seizing by the heel, supplanting). Pet: Simidh. *See* JAMES. (SHAY-MUS)

SEOC Gaelic form of Jock, which is a variant form of Jack, itself a pet form of John (God is gracious). *See* JOHN. Pet: Seocan. (SHOK)

SETH Ecclesiastic Late Latin form of the Ecclesiastic Greek Sēth, a name from the Hebrew Shet, which is derived from *sheth* (appointed). (SEETH)

SHANE Anglicized form of Seaghan, a variant of Eóin, which is the Gaelic form of John (God is gracious). *See* JOHN. (SHANE)

SHAW Transferred use of the surname derived from the Middle English *schagh, schaw(e), shaw(e)* (a wood or grove): hence, "dweller at a wood or grove." Alternatively, the Highland surname Shaw is an Anglicized form of Schethoch (son of the wolf), which is derived from the Old Gaelic *si thech* (a wolf). (SHAW)

SÌM Gaelic form of Simon (heard). *See* SIMON. (SIME)

SIMIDH Pet form of Séamus, the Gaelic form of James (seizing by the heel, supplanting). *See* JAMES. Simidh is the Gaelic equivalent of Jimmy. (SIM-MEE)

SIMON A borrowing from the Ecclesiastic Late Latin, Simon is from the Greek Simōn and Seimōn, which are from the Hebrew Shimon, a derivative of *shim'ōn* (heard). Sìm is a Gaelic form. *See* SIMON (English Names). (SĪ-mun)

SINCLAIR Transferred use of the surname originating from the place-name St. Clair in Normandy. *See* CLAIRE (French Female Names). (SEEN-KLARE)

SOMERLED From the Gaelic *Somhairle*, which is derived from the Old Norse *Sumarliði* (Viking, mariner, sailor). The name originated as a term used to denote Viking raiders who came during the summer months. (SUM-MER-LED)

SORLEY A borrowing from the Irish, Sorley is the Irish equivalent of Somerled (Viking, summer wanderer, mariner). The names are derived from the Gaelic *Somhairle*, which is from the Old Norse *Sumarliði* (Viking, mariner, sailor). (SOR-LEE)

STEAPHAN Gaelic form of Stephen (a crown, a garland). *See* STEPHEN. (STEE-FEN)

STEPHEN From the Latin Stephanus, which is from the Greek Stephanos, a derivative of *stephanos* (a crown, a garland). (STEE-VEN)

STEWART Transferred use of the surname originating as an occupational name derived from the Old English *stiward, stiweard* (steward, keeper of the animal enclosure), a position that in many cases was hereditary, especially among noble or royal households. The name, in its French form of Stuart, is borne by the Scottish royal family who are said to be descended from a line of stewards from Brittany before the Conquest. It was taken to Scotland by Mary Stuart, Queen of Scots, who was raised in France. Var: Stuart. Short: Stew, Stu. (STYOO-ART)

TADHG A borrowing from the Irish, Tadhg is an old Gaelic name meaning "a poet." It has been Anglicized as Thaddeus and Timothy. Var: Taogh, Teague. (TAYG)

TEÀRLACH Gaelic form of Charles (full-grown, a man). *See* CHARLES. Var: Tearlach. (CHAIR-LACH)

THADDEUS Ecclesiastic Late Latin form of the Ecclesiastic Greek Thaddaios, a name of uncertain derivation. Some believe it to be a variant of Theodōros (God's gift). Others feel it is from an Aramaic word meaning "praised." The name is used to Anglicize the Gaelic Tadhg (a poet). (THAD-DEE-US)

THOMAS From the Ecclesiastic Greek Thōmas, which is derived from the Aramaic *tĕōma* (a twin). The name is borne in the Bible by an apostle who doubted the resurrection of Christ. It is from him that the expression "doubting Thomas" came into being. Tòmas is the Gaelic form. Short: Tam, Tom. Pet: Tommy. (TAH-MUS)

TIMOTHY From the Greek Timotheos (honor God), a compound name composed of the elements *timē* (honor, respect) and *theos* (God). The name is used to Anglicize the Gaelic Tadhg (a poet). *See* TIMOTHY (English Names). Short: Tim. Pet: Timmy. (TIM-AH-THEE)

TODD Transferred use of the surname derived from the Middle and dialectal English *tod, todde* (a fox). (TOD)

TOIRDHEALBHACH A borrowing from the Irish, Toirdhealbhach means "shaped like Thor," the Norse god of thunder and strength. The name has been Anglicized as Turlough and Terence. (TUR-EE-AHL-VAH)

Tòmas Gaelic form of Thomas (a twin). *See* THOMAS. Var: Tòmag. Pet: Tòmachan. (TO-MAHS)

Tòrmod Gaelic form of Norman (northman). *See* NORMAN. Var: Tormod. (TOR-MOD)

Uilleam Gaelic form of William (resolute protector). *See* WILLIAM. Var: Uilliam. Pet: Uilleachan, Uillidh. (WIL-LEM)

Virgil From the Latin Vergilius, an old Roman family name of uncertain derivation. Some believe it might be from *ver* (spring) and have the definition "youthful, flourishing." (VER-JIL)

Walter Introduced to the British Isles by the Normans, Walter is from the Old Norman French Waltier, which is from the Germanic Waldheri, a compound name composed from the elements *wald* (rule) and *heri* (army): hence, "ruler of an army." Bhaltair and Bhàtair are Gaelic forms of the name. Short: Walt. Pet: Wally. (WAHL-TER)

William From the Old Norman French Willaume, which is derived from the Old High German Willehelm, a compound name composed from the elements *willeo* (will, determination) and *helm* (protection, helmet): hence, "resolute protector." Uilleam and Uilliam are Gaelic forms of the name in common use in Scotland. Short: Will. Pet: Willy. (WIL-YUM)

Zachary Cognate of the Ecclesiastic Late Latin and Ecclesiastic Greek Zacharias, which is from the Hebrew Zecharya, a derivative of *ẑeharyah* (God remembers, memory). Sachairi is the Gaelic form. Short: Zack, Zak. (ZAK-AH-REE)

Scottish Female Names

Agnes Popular name derived from the Greek Hagnē, which is from *hagnos* (chaste, pure). Agnes has also been used to Anglicize the Gaelic name Ùna. *See* ÙNA. Pet: Aggie. (AG-NES)

Aileen Variant of the name Eileen, which is used to Anglicize Eibhlín, the Gaelic form of Evelyn. Evelyn is an English variant of Aveline, a French diminutive form of the Germanic Avila, which is thought to be a Latinate form of Aveza, a name ultimately of uncertain meaning. Var: Alina, Aline, Eileen. Pet: Ailie. (Ā-LEEN)

Ailie Anglicized spelling of Eilidh, a Gaelic form of Ellie, which is a pet form of any of the various names beginning with the element *El-*. Ailie is also used as a pet form of Aileen. *See* AILEEN *and* EILIDH. Var: Aili. (Ā-LEE)

Ailsa A borrowing from the Scottish place-name Ailsa Craig, a small yet tall craggy island off the Ayrshire Coast. The islet derives its name from the Old Norse Alfsigesey (island of Alfsigr). Alfsigr is an obsolete compound name composed of the Old Norse elements *aelf* (elf) and *sígr* (victory). Alternatively, Ailsa is used to Anglicize Ealasaid, the Scottish Gaelic form of Elizabeth. (AIL-SA)

Aimili Gaelic form of Amelia, which is an English variant of the Germanic Amalia, a name derived from *amal* (work). (AIM-EE-LEE)

Aingealag Gaelic form of the English Angelica, a derivative of *angelic* (heavenly, like an angel), which is from the Latin *angelicus* and the Greek *angelikos* (angelic). (AIN-JEH-LAH)

Ainslee Transferred use of the Scottish surname taken from the place-name Ainsley, which is derived from the name element *Æne's* or *Ægen's* and the Old English *lēah* (wood, clearing, meadow, enclosure). Var: Ainslie. (AINZ-LEE)

Alana Feminine form of Alan, which is an old name of Breton origin but of uncertain meaning. Some believe it to mean "handsome." Others promote the possibility that it is from a Celtic word meaning "rock." Var: Alane, Alanna, Alannah, Alanne, Allana, Alline, Allyne, Alayne. Short: Lana, Lane, Lanna, Lannah. (AH-LAN-NAH)

Alexandra Popular name derived from the Greek Alexandros (helper or defender of mankind), a compound name composed of the elements *alexein* (to defend, to help) and *andros* (man). The name was introduced late in the 19th century through the fame of Queen Alexandra, the Danish wife of Edward VII. Pet: Sandy, Lexy. (ALEK-SAN-DRAH)

Alexina Feminine form of Alex, which is a short form of Alexander (defender or helper of mankind). *See* ALEXANDRA. (ALEKS-EE-NAH)

Alickina Feminine form of Alick, a variant of Alex, which is a short form of Alexander (defender or helper of mankind). *See* ALEXANDRA. Short: Kina. (AL-IH-KEE-NAH)

ALISON Popular medieval Norman diminutive form of Alice (nobility) which survived in Scotland and was revived elsewhere in the English-speaking world in the 20th century. *See* ALICE (English Names). Pet: Allie. (AL-IH-SON)

AMELIA A borrowing from the English, Amelia is a variant of the Germanic Amalia, a name derived from *amal* (work). (AH-MEEL-YAH)

ANGELA A borrowing from the English, Angela is a Latinate form of Angel, which is a direct derivative of *angel* (guiding spirit, messenger of God), which is ultimately derived from the Greek *angelos* (messenger, messenger of God). Alternatively, Angela is used as a contracted form of Angelica (angelic). *See* ANGELICA. Pet: Angie. (AN-JEH-LAH)

ANGELICA A borrowing from the English, Angelica is from *angelic* (heavenly, like an angel), which is derived from the Latin *angelicus* and the Greek *angelikos* (angelic). Pet: Angie. (AN-JEH-LEE-KAH)

ANGIE Originally a short form of Angela and Angelica, Angie is also bestowed as an independent given name. *See* ANGELA *and* ANGELICA. (AN-JEE)

ANGUSINA Feminine form of Angus, the Anglicized form of the Gaelic Aonghus and Aonghas, both of which are derived from the element *aon* (one, choice, preeminent). (AIN-GUH-SEE-NAH)

ANNA A Latinate form of Anne (gracious, full of grace), Anna is a common name throughout Scotland. Annag is the Gaelic form. *See* ANNE. (AN-NAH)

ANNABEL A name of uncertain etymology which has been in common use in Scotland since the 12th century. Some believe it to be an old Norman name derived from the element *arn* (eagle) or *arin* (a hearth). Others think it a variant of Amabel, an Old French name derived from the Latin *amābilis* (lovable) or from the Gaelic Ainè (joy). Its use in the English-speaking world was reinforced by the names Anna and Belle and is often taken as a combination of such. Alternatively, Annabel has been used to Anglicize Barabel, the Gaelic form of Barbara (foreign woman). Var: Annabella, Annabelle. (AN-NAH-BEL)

ANNAG Scottish Gaelic form of Anna (gracious, full of grace). *See* ANNE. (AN-NAH)

ANNE A borrowing from the French, Anne is derived from the Hebrew Hannah, which is from *chaanach, hannāh* (gracious, full of grace). Annag and Annot are Gaelic forms of the name. Var: Anna, Annag, Annot. (AN-NAH)

ANNELLA Popular elaboration of Anne (gracious, full of grace). *See* ANNE. (AN-NEL-LAH)

ANNIS Vernacular form of Agnes (pure, chaste), which arose in the Middle Ages. *See* AGNES. Var: Annice, Annys. (AN-NIS)

ANNOT Scottish form of Anne (gracious, full of grace). *See* ANNE. (AN-NOT)

ARABELLA Old name of uncertain etymology. Some believe it to be a Norman name derived from the element *arn* (eagle) or *arin* (a hearth). Others think it a variant of Annabel, another name of debated origin and meaning. *See* ANNABEL. Var: Arabel, Arabell, Orabel. (AIR-RAH-BEL-LAH)

AUDREY A borrowing from the English, Audrey is derived from the Old English Æðelþryð, Æthelthryth, a compound name composed of the elements *æðel, æthel* (noble) and *þryð, thryth* (might, strength): hence, "noble strength." Var: Audra. Pet: Audie. (AUD-REE)

BARABAL Scottish Gaelic form of Barbara (foreign woman), a borrowing from the Latin, which is derived from *barbarus* (foreign, strange), a term applied to non-Romans or those deemed to be uncivilized. Barabal has been Anglicized as Annabel. *See* ANNABEL. (BAHR-AH-BAHL)

BEARNAS Scottish Gaelic form of Berenice (bringer of victory), which is derived from the Greek Berenikē, a variant of the older Pherenikē, a compound name composed of the elements *pherein* (to bring) and *nikē* (victory). Alternatively, Bearnas is used as a feminine form of Bearnard, the Scottish form of Bernard (bold or strong as a bear). *See* BERNARD (Male Names). (BEAR-NUS)

BEATHAG Feminine form of Beathan (life), which is derived from the Gaelic *beatha* (life, livelihood; welcome, salutation). Beathag has been Anglicized as Sophia (wisdom). (BEE-THA)

BEITIDH Scottish Gaelic form of Betsy and Betty, pet forms of Elizabeth (God is my oath), which are also in common use as independent given names. (BEH-TEE)

BEITIRIS Scottish Gaelic form of Beatrix (bringer of blessings and joy), which is from the Latin *beatrix* (she who makes happy, she who brings happiness), a derivative of *beātus* (happy, blessed). (BEE-TIH-RIS)

BHICTORIA Scottish form of Victoria, which is derived from the Latin *victoria* (victory). Victoria was brought to the British Isles in the 19th century, when Edward, duke of Kent, married the German Maria Louisa Victoria of Saxe-Coburg (1786–1861). Their daughter, the future Queen Victoria (1819–1901), was christened

Alexandrine Victoria, furthering the use of the name. (VEEK-TOR-EE-AH)

BONNIE Derived from the Lowland Scotch *bonnie* (beautiful, good-natured, and cheerful). The use of Bonnie as a given name in Scotland is very recent and most likely due to influences from Margaret Mitchell's novel *Gone with the Wind* (1936). Var: Bonny. (BON-NEE)

BRENDA Of uncertain origin and meaning, Brenda is thought to be a Celtic name derived from *brandr* (the blade of a sword). Alternatively, it might be a feminine form of the obsolete Brandolf (sword wolf). (BREN-DAH)

BRIDE A borrowing from the Irish, Bride is the Anglicized form of the Gaelic Bríd, a contracted form of Brighid, a name of disputed etymology Anglicized as Bridget. *See* BRIGHID. (BRIDE)

BRIDGET Anglicized form of the Gaelic Brighid, a name of disputed etymology. *See* BRIGHID. Var: Brigit. (BRID-JET)

BRIGHID Of disputed etymology, Brighid was the name borne by an ancient Celtic goddess of wisdom, skill, song, and poetry. Some believe the name to be derived from the Celtic element Brîgh (strength). Others link the name to *breosaighead* (fire arrow) and to an ancient tribe called the Brigantes, who lived in northern England. The name was Anglicized as Bridget. Var: Bride, Bridget, Brigit. (BRIJ-ID)

CAIRISTÌONA Scottish Gaelic form of Christina (Christian, a follower of Christ). *See* CHRISTINA. Var: Cairistìne. Pet: Stìneag. (KARE-IH-STYO-NAH)

CÁIT A short form of Caitrìona, Cáit is also bestowed as an independent given name and corresponds to the English Kate. *See* CAITRÌONA. (KATE)

CAITIR Derivative of Caitrìona (pure, unsullied), the Gaelic form of Katherine. *See* CAITRÌONA. The name has been Anglicized as Clarissa (bright, clear, famous). (KAY-TR)

CAITRÌONA Gaelic cognate of Katherine, which is from the Greek Aikaterinē, a name derived from *katharos* (pure, unsullied). The name is Anglicized as Catriona and Catrina. Var: Caitriana, Catrina, Catriona. Short: Cáit, Ceit. Pet: Ceiteag, Tríona. (KAY-TREE-O-NAH)

CALUMINA Feminine form of Calum, which is the Scottish Gaelic cognate of the Late Latin Columba (dove). *See* CALUM (Male Names). Var: Calaminag. Short: Mina. (KAL-UM-EE-NAH)

CATRIONA Anglicized form of Caitrìona, the Gaelic cognate of Katherine (pure, unsullied). *See* CAITRÌONA. Var: Catrina. (KAT-REE-O-NAH)

CECILY A borrowing from the English, Cecily is a variant form of Cecilia, a feminine form of Cecil, which is derived from the Latin Caecilius, an old Roman family name, which has its root in the Latin *caecus* (blind, dim-sighted). *See* CECILIA (English Names). (SEH-SIL-LEE)

CEIT Short form of Caitrìona, the Gaelic form of Katherine (pure, unsullied). Ceit corresponds to the English Kate. *See* CAITRÌONA *and* KATHERINE. (KATE)

CEITEAG Pet form of Caitrìona, the Gaelic form of Katherine (pure, unsullied). Ceiteag corresponds to the English Katie. *See* CAITRÌONA *and* KATHERINE. (KAY-TEE)

CHARLOTTE A borrowing from the English, Charlotte is a feminine diminutive form of Charles (full-grown, a man). *See* CHARLES (Male Names). Teàrlag is the Gaelic form. (SHAR-LOT)

CHRISTINA A borrowing from the English, Christina is from the Latin Christiāna, which is from *christiānus*, a derivative of the Greek *christianos* (a Christian, a follower of Christ). Christina was not in common use in the British Isles before the 19th century. Var: Christine; Cairistìne, Cairistìona (Gaelic). Short: Ina. Pet: Chirsty, Chrissie, Kirstie; Ciorsdan, Ciorstag, Ciorstaidh, Criosaidh, Curstaidh, Stìneag (Gaelic). (KRIS-TEE-NAH)

CHRISTY A pet form of Christina and Christine, Christy is also bestowed as an independent given name. *See* CHRISTINA. (KRIS-TEE)

CIORSTAIDH Scottish Gaelic form of Kirstie, a pet form of the Scandinavian Kirsten, which is a cognate of Christine (a Christian, a follower of Christ). Var: Ciorstag, Curstaidh, Curstag. (KEERS-TEE)

CLARA A borrowing from the English, Clara is derived from the Latin *clārus* (bright, clear, famous). The name is also used as an equivalent of the Gaelic Sorcha (brightness). Var: Clare. Pet: Clarrie. (KLAR-AH)

CLARISSA A borrowing from the English, Clarissa is an elaboration of Clara (bright, clear, famous). *See* CLARA. The name is also used to Anglicize Caitir, a variant of Caitrìona, which is the Gaelic form of Katherine (pure, unsullied). *See* CAITRÌONA *and* KATHERINE. Var: Clarisa. (KLAH-RIH-SAH)

CRIOSAIDH Gaelic form of Chrissie, a pet form of Christina and Christine (a Christian). *See* CHRISTINA. (KRIS-SEE)

Davida Feminine form of David, which is derived from the Hebrew *dāwīd* (beloved). *See* DAVID (Male Names). Var: Davina, Davinia. (DAH-VEE-DAH)

Deòiridh Derived from the Scottish Gaelic *deòiridh* (pilgrim). The name has been Anglicized as Dorcas (gazelle). (DOR-EE)

Deònaid Vernacular form of Seònaid, which is the Gaelic form of Janet (God is gracious). *See* SEÒNAID. (DEH-NADE)

Devorgilla Anglicized form of the Gaelic Diorbhail (true oath, true testimony). *See* DIORBHAIL. (DEH-VOR-GIL-LAH)

Diana A borrowing from the English, Diana is derived from the Latin Diviana, which is from *divus* (divine). The name is borne in Roman mythology by the virgin goddess of the moon and of hunting. It received a boost in popularity after Prince Charles married Lady Diana Spencer. Short: Di. (DI-AN-NAH)

Dina A short form of Murdina (sea warrior) and Rodina (famous king), Dina is also bestowed as an independent given name. *See* MURDAG *and* RHODA. (DĪNA)

Diorbhail Derived from the obsolete Diorbhorguil (true oath, true testimony), which is from Dearbhforgail, a compound name composed of the Gaelic elements *dearbh* (an oath, testimony) and *fior-glan* (true). The name was Anglicized as Devorgilla and Dorothy. (DER-VIL)

Donalda Feminine form of Donald, which is an Anglicized form of the Gaelic Domhnall (world ruler). *See* DOMHNALL (Male Names). Var: Donella, Dolanna, Dolena, Dolina. Short: Donna, Ina, Lena, Lina. (DON-AL-DAH)

Donnag Feminine diminutive form of Donald, an Anglicized form of the Gaelic Domhnall (world ruler). *See* DOMHNALL (Male Names) *and* DONALDA. Short: Donna. Pet: Doileag, Dolag, Dollag. (DON-NAH)

Dorcas A borrowing from the English, Dorcas is derived from the Greek *dorkas* (a gazelle, a doe). The name, popular among 16th-century Puritans, has been used to Anglicize the Gaelic Deòiridh (pilgrim). *See* DEÒIRIDH. (DOR-KAHS)

Dorothy A borrowing from the English, Dorothy is derived from the Greek Dōrothea, a compound name composed from the elements *dōron* (gift) and *theos* (God): hence, "gift of God." Dorothy has also been used to Anglicize the Gaelic Diorbhail (true oath, true testimony). *See* DIORBHAIL. (DOR-O-THEE)

Ealasaid Scottish Gaelic cognate of Elizabeth, which is derived from the Hebrew *elīsheba'* (God is my oath). *See* ELIZABETH. (EE-LEH-SAH)

Eamhair Gaelic cognate of the Irish Emer, which is of uncertain meaning. The name was borne in Irish legend by the wife of Cuchulainn, said to be blessed with beauty, fairness in voice, wisdom, and skill in needlework. Var: Éimhear. (EM-MER)

Edmée Scottish variant of the French Esmée, a name derived from *esmé* (loved), the past participle of the verb *esmer* (to love, value, esteem). Var: Edmé. (ED-MAY)

Effie Anglicized form of the Gaelic Oighrig, a name of debated derivation. *See* OIGHRIG. (EH-FEE)

Eibhlín Gaelic form of Evelyn, which is an English variant of Aveline, a French diminutive form of the Germanic Avila, which is thought to be a Latinate form of Aveza, a name ultimately of uncertain meaning. Eileen is the Anglicized spelling. (EHV-LIN)

Eileen Anglicized spelling of Eibhlín, the Gaelic form of Evelyn. *See* EIBHLÍN. Var: Aileen, Alina, Aline. Pet: Ailie, Eilie. (I-LEEN)

Eilidh Gaelic form of Ellie, which is a pet form of any of the various names beginning with the element *El-*. The name has been Anglicized as Ailie and Helen. (EL-LEE)

Elizabeth A borrowing from the English, Elizabeth is derived from the Hebrew *elīsheba'* (God is my oath). The name is borne in the Bible by the mother of John the Baptist who was a kinswoman of the Virgin Mary. The name was borne by Queen Elizabeth I (1533–1603) and continues to be a popular name from its association with the queen mother (b. 1900), the former Elizabeth Bowes-Lyon, and her daughter Queen Elizabeth II (b. 1926). Var: Elspeth. Pet: Elsie, Elspie. (EE-LIZ-AH-BETH)

Erica Feminine form of Eric, which is derived from the Old Norse Eirìkr, a compound name composed of the elements *ei* (ever, always) and *rīkr* (ruler): hence, "eternal ruler." Erica is also used in Scotland to Anglicize the Gaelic Oighrig. *See* OIGHRIG. (ER-IH-KAH)

Erskina Feminine form of Erskine, a Scottish surname originating from a place-name of uncertain meaning. Some believe it to be derived from the Gaelic *aird sgainne* (height of the cleft). (ER-SKEE-NAH)

Eubh Scottish Gaelic cognate of Eve (life). *See* EVE. Var: Eubha. (E-VAH)

Euna Anglicized form of the Gaelic Ùna, a name of debated meaning. *See* ÙNA. (YOO-NAH)

EVE Derived from the Hebrew Chava (life), which is from *hawwāh* (life). The name is borne in the Bible by the first woman, "the mother of all the living." Eubh and Eubha are the Gaelic forms. Var: Eva. (EEV)

FINELLA Anglicized form of the Gaelic Fionnaghuala (white shoulders). *See* FIONNAGHUALA. Var: Fenella, Finola, Fionola. (FIN-NEL-LAH)

FIONA Popular name derived from the Gaelic *fionn* (white, fair, clear, transparent). (FEE-O-NAH)

FIONNAGHUALA Scottish Gaelic form of the Irish Gaelic Fionnguala, a compound name composed of the elements *fionn* (white, fair) and *guala* (shoulder): hence, "white shoulders." The name has been Anglicized as Flora (a flower). Finella and its variants are Anglicized spellings. *See* FINELLA. Var: Fenella, Finella, Finola, Fionnaghal, Fionnala, Fionnauala, Fionnghala, Fionnghuala, Fionnuala, Fionola. Short: Nuala. (FIH-NEL-LAH)

FLORA Used in Scotland as an Anglicized form of the Gaelic Fionnaghuala (white shoulders). *See* FIONNAGHUALA. Flora is derived from the Latin *floris* (a flower). The name was borne by Flora Macdonald (1722–90), a daughter of Ranald Macdonald of Milton. It was she who helped Bonnie Prince Charlie disguise himself as a woman and escape to the island of Skye after his defeat at Culloden in 1746. Pet: Florrie; Flòraigh (Gaelic). (FLOR-AH)

FRANCES A borrowing from the English, Frances is a French feminine form of Franceis (a Frank, from the Frankish Empire). *See* FRANCES (English Names). Fràngag is the Gaelic form. (FRAN-SES)

FRÀNGAG Scottish Gaelic cognate of Frances (from France). *See* FRANCES. (FRAN-SAS)

FREDA A short form of Winifred (blessed peace), Freda is also used as an independent given name. *See* WINIFRED. (FREE-DAH)

FREYA Brought to Scotland by the Norsemen, Freya (lady, mistress, noblewoman) is believed to be derived from the Germanic *frouwa* (lady, mistress). The name is borne in Norse mythology by the goddess of fertility. *See* FREYA (Scandinavian Names). (FRAY-AH)

GAIL A borrowing from the English, Gail was originally a short form of the biblical Abigail (father of exaltation). It is now in common use as an independent given name. *See* ABIGAIL (English Names). (GALE)

GAVINA Feminine form of Gavin (battle hawk). *See* GAVIN (Male Names). Var: Gavenia. (GAH-VEE-NAH)

GEORGINA Feminine form of George, which is ultimately derived from the Greek *geōrgos* (farmer, husbandman, earthworker). The name originated in Scotland in the 18th century and is now employed in other European countries and throughout the English-speaking world. Short: Ina. (JOR-JEE-NAH)

GLENNA Feminine form of Glenn, a name derived from the Gaelic *gleann* (mountain valley, a narrow, secluded valley). (GLEN-NAH)

GORDONA Feminine form of Gordon, which is of uncertain etymology. *See* GORDON (Male Names). Var: Gordana, Gordania. (GOR-DAH-NAH)

GORMLAITH Derived from the obsolete Gormfhlait, a compound name composed of the Gaelic elements *gorm* (blue, green) and *fhlaith* (lady, princess): hence, "blue lady." The name was borne by the wife of Irish King Brian Boru. Var: Gormla, Gormelia. (GORM-LAH)

GRACE A borrowing from the English, Grace is inspired by *grace* (elegance or beauty of form, favor, kindness, mercy), which is derived from the Latin *gratia* (favor, thanks). The name was made popular by 17th-century Puritans, who bestowed it in reference to God's favor and love toward mankind. Pet: Gracie. (GRACE)

GREER Transferred use of the Scottish surname originating in the Middle Ages from a contraction of Gregor, a cognate of the Latin *gregorius* (watchful, vigilant). Var: Grier. (GREER)

HARRIET A borrowing from the English, Harriet is an English form of the French Henriette, a feminine diminutive of Henri, which is derived from the German Heinrich (ruler of an estate, home ruler). *See* HENRY (Male Names). In Scotland, Harriet was also used to Anglicize the Gaelic Oighrig. *See* OIGHRIG. Var: Harriette. Pet: Hattie. (HAR-REE-ET)

HEATHER A borrowing from the English, Heather is derived from the name of the plant, common to the British Isles, which has scale-like leaves and small, purplish-pink flowers. The word is derived from the Old English *haddyr* (heather, plants of the heath family). (HEH-THER)

HELEN A borrowing from the English, Helen is a cognate of the Greek Helenē, which is derived from the root *ēlē* (light). The name has also been used in Scotland to Anglicize the Gaelic Eilidh. *See* EILIDH. (HEL-LEN)

HENRIETTA A borrowing from the English, Henrietta is derived from the French Henriette, a feminine diminutive form of Henri (ruler of an enclosure, home ruler). *See* HENRY (Male Names). The name has also been used in

Scotland to Anglicize the Gaelic Oighrig. *See* OIGHRIG. Pet: Hattie, Hettie. (HEN-REE-EH-TAH)

HUGHINA Feminine form of Hugh, a name used to Anglicize the Gaelic names Aodh, Ùisdean, and Eódhnag. Hugh is derived from the Old French Hue, which is from the Old High German Hugo, a derivative of *hugu* (heart, mind, spirit). (HYOO-EE-NAH)

INNES Transferred use of the surname (Mac) Innes, which originated from the Gaelic MacAonghuis (son of Angus). Angus is the Anglicized form of the Gaelic Aonghus and Aonghas, which are derived from the element *aon* (one, choice, preeminence). (IN-NES)

IONA Taken from the name of a small island in the Hebrides, a group of islands off the west coast of Scotland. Iona was the island upon which St. Columba founded a monastery which he used as a base while working to convert the Scottish people to Christianity. The derivation of the name is uncertain. Some believe it to be a misspelling of Ioua, an older name for the island. The Gaelic name for the island is I, from the Old Norse *ey* (island). Thus, it stands to reason that the name is derived from this root. (I-O-NAH)

ISABEL A borrowing from the English, Isabel is derived from Isabella, a name that originated as a Spanish variant of Elizabeth (God is my oath). *See* ELIZABETH. Var: Isbel, Isobel; Iseabail, Ishbel (Gaelic). (IS-AH-BEL)

ISEABAIL Scottish Gaelic form of Isabel (God is my oath). *See* ISABEL. Var: Ishbel. Pet: Beileag. (IS-EH-BEL)

ISLA Modern coinage derived from the pronunciation of Islay, which is the name of a Scottish island. (I-LAY)

JAMESINA Feminine form of James (supplanting, seizing by the heel). *See* JAMES (Male Names). Pet: Jamie. (JAY-MEH-SEE-NAH)

JAN Feminine form of John (God is gracious). *See* John (Male Names). Alternatively, Jan is used as a short form of any of the various names beginning with the element *Jan-*. (JAN)

JANE A borrowing from the English, Jane is a cognate of the French Jehanne and Jeanne, which are feminine forms of Jean, a cognate of John (God is gracious). *See* JOHN (Male Names). Sìne and Siubhan are the Gaelic cognates of Jane. (JANE)

JANET Diminutive form of Jane, which is a feminine form of John (God is gracious). *See* JOHN (Male Names). Though the name fell out of favor toward the end of the Middle Ages until its revival in the 19th century, Janet remained in common and popular use in Scotland. The Gaelic form is Seònaid. (JAN-NET)

JEAN A borrowing from the English, Jean is a cognate of the French Jeanne, a feminine form of Jean, which is a cognate of John (God is gracious). *See* JOHN (Male Names). Sìne is the Gaelic cognate. Pet: Jeanie, Jeannie, Jessie. (JEEN)

JEANIE A pet form of Jean (God is gracious), Jeanie is also bestowed as an independent given name. *See* JEAN. Sìneag and Sìonag are Gaelic forms. Var: Jeannie. (JEE-NEE)

JENNIFER Cornish derivation of Guinevere, which is from the Welsh Gwenhwyfar (fair lady), a compound name composed from the elements *gwen, gwyn* (white, fair, blessed) and *hwyfar* (smooth, soft). *See* Guinevere (English Names). Pet: Jenna, Jenny. (JEN-NIH-FER)

JENNY A pet form of Jennifer, and in the Middle Ages of Jean, Jenny is also bestowed as an independent given name. *See* JENNIFER. Var: Jenna. (JEN-NEE)

JESSICA Of uncertain derivation and meaning, Jessica can be an elaboration of Jessie, which was originally a pet form of Janet and Jean. Alternatively, it can be interpreted as an elaborated feminine form of Jesse, which is derived from the Hebrew *yīshai* (gift). Pet: Jessie. (JES-SIH-KAH)

JESSIE Used as a Scottish pet form of Jean, a short form of Jessica, and a feminine form of Jesse, which is derived from the Hebrew *yīshai* (gift). The Gaelic form of Jessie is Teasag. Short: Jess. (JES-SEE)

JOAN A borrowing from the English, Joan is a contracted form of the French Johanne, a feminine form of John (God is gracious). *See* JOAN (English Names). The Scottish Gaelic form of Joan is Seonag. (JONE)

JUDITH A borrowing from the English, Judith is a cognate of the Hebrew Jehudith and Yehudit (he will be praised). *See* JUDITH (English Names). Judith has also been used in Scotland as an Anglicized form of Siobhán and Siubhan. Pet: Judi, Judie, Judy. (JOO-DITH)

KATE A short form of Katherine (pure, unsullied) and its variants, Kate is also bestowed as an independent given name. *See* KATHERINE. Cáit and Ceit are Gaelic forms. Pet: Katie. (KATE)

KATHERINE A borrowing from the English, Katherine is a cognate of the Greek Aikaterinē, which is derived from *katharos* (pure, unsullied). The name was borne by the first wife of Henry VIII, Katherine of Aragon (1485–1536). Catriona and Caitrìona are Scottish cognates of Katherine. *See* CAITRÌONA. Var: Catharine, Catherine, Cathryn, Katharine, Kathryn. Short: Cath, Kate, Kath. Pet: Cathy, Kathy, Katie. (KATH-EH-RIN)

KEITHA Feminine form of Keith, which represents the transferred use of the Scottish surname originating from several place-names of uncertain derivation. Keith might be formed from a Gaelic root meaning "the wind" or "wood." The use of Keith as a given name dates to the 19th century. (KEE-THA)

KENNA Feminine form of Kenneth, which is the Anglicized form of the Gaelic Cinaed, Cionaed (born of fire), and Caioneach, Coinneach (comely, handsome). *See* KENNETH (Male Names). Var: Kenina. (KEN-NAH)

KIRSTIE A pet form of Kirstin (a Christian), Kirstie is also in common use as an independent given name. *See* KIRSTIN. The Gaelic forms of Kirstie are Ciorstiadh, Ciorstag, Curstag, and Curstaidh. Var: Chirsty, Kirsty. (KEER-STEE)

KIRSTIN Scottish form of the Scandinavian Kirsten, a cognate of Christine (a Christian). *See* CHRISTINA. Pet: Kirstie, Kirsty. (KEER-STIN)

LACHINA Feminine form of Lachlan and Lachann (land of the lochs), which are derived from Lochlann, a name that originated as a term referring to migrant Norwegians who came from the "land of the lochs." (LAH-KEE-NAH)

LAURA A borrowing from the English, Laura is derived from the Latin *laurus* (laurel, an evergreen shrub or tree whose leaves were woven into wreaths by the ancient Greeks to crown victors in various contests). Originally an Italian name, Laura came into use in the British Isles in the 19th century. Pet: Laurie. (LOR-RAH)

LEAGSAIDH Scottish Gaelic form of Lexy, which is a pet form of Alexandra (defender or helper of mankind). *See* ALEXANDRA. (LEKS-EE)

LENA A short form of any of the various names ending in *-lena*, the name is also bestowed as an independent given name. (LEE-NAH)

LESLIE Transferred use of the surname originating in Scotland from the place-name Lesslyn, which is said to be derived from *less lea* (smaller meadow, smaller clearing). (LEZ-LEE)

LEXINE Elaborated form of Lexy, which is a pet form of Alexandra (defender or helper of mankind). *See* ALEXANDRA. (LEKS-EEN)

LEXY A pet form of Alexandra (defender or helper of mankind), Lexy is also bestowed as an independent given name. *See* ALEXANDRA. (LEKS-EE)

LINA Short form of any of the various names ending in *-lina*. (LĪ-NAH)

LINDSAY Transferred use of the old Scottish surname de Lindsay, meaning "from Lindsay," a part of the county of Lincolnshire in northeastern England. Lindsay is derived from Lincoln, a shortened form of Lindum Colonia, the first part of which is thought to be from the Welsh *llyn* (lake) and the second from the Latin *colonia* (settlement, colony). Lindsay is bestowed as both a male and a female name in Scotland. Var: Lynsey. Pet: Lindie. (LIND-ZAY)

LINDSEY Taken from the old surname Lindesie, meaning "from Lindsey." In this instance, Lindsey is derived from the Old English elements *lind* (the linden tree) and *ey* (wetland). Var: Lynsey. Pet: Lindie. (LIND-ZEE)

LIÙSAIDH Scottish Gaelic form of Louisa (famous in war) and Lucy (light). *See* LOUISA *and* LUCY. (LWEE-SAH)

LORI A short form of Lorraine, Lori is also bestowed as an independent given name. *See* LORRAINE. Var: Lorri. (LOR-EE)

LORNA 19th-century coinage of English novelist R. D. Blackmore (1825–1900), borne by the heroine of his book *Lorna Doone* (1869). The name is believed to be taken from the Scottish place-name Lorne, the Gaelic form of which is Latharna. (LOR-NAH)

LORRAINE Transferred use of the surname originating from the name of a province in eastern France which is derived from the Latin Lotharingia (territory of the people of Lothar). Lothar (famous army), of Germanic origin, is derived from the elements *hluod* (famous) and *hari*, *heri* (army). Var: Lorane. Short: Lori, Lorri. (LOR-RANE)

LOUISA A borrowing from the English, Louisa is a feminine form of Louis (famous in war), which is from the Germanic Hluodowig, a compound name composed from the elements *hluod* (famous) and *wīg* (war, strife). The Gaelic form of Louisa is Liùsaidh. (LOO-EE-SAH)

LUCY A borrowing from the English, Lucy is a cognate of Lucia, which is derived from the Latin *lux* (light). The Gaelic form of Lucy is Liùsaidh. (LOO-SEE)

MAGAIDH Gaelic form of Maggie, which is a pet form of Margaret (a pearl). *See* MARGARET. (MAG-EE)

MAGGIE A pet form of Margaret (a pearl), Maggie is also bestowed as an independent given name. *See* MARGARET. The Gaelic form of Maggie is Magaidh. (MAG-EE)

MAIDIE Originally a pet name for a young woman, Maidie is derived from *maid* (a young unmarried woman), from the Middle English *maide*, a contraction of *maiden*, which is derived from the Old English *mægden* (a maid, a virgin). (MAY-DEE)

MAIREAD Scottish Gaelic form of Margaret (a pearl). *See* MARGARET. Mairead is Anglicized as Maretta. Var: Maighread. Pet: Magaidh, Maisie, Peigi. (MAY-RED)

MÀIRI Scottish Gaelic form of Mary. *See* MARY. In Scotland, Moire is the form reserved to indicate the Virgin Mary. Var: Màili. Pet: Màireag. (MAY-REE)

MALAMHÌN Derived from the Gaelic *mala mhìn* (smooth brow). The name is Anglicized as Malvina, a name coined by Scottish poet James Macpherson (1736–96) from the Gaelic form. (MAL-A-VIN)

MALCOLMINA Feminine form of Malcolm, the Anglicized form of the Gaelic Maolcolm (servant of Columba), which is derived from the elements *maol* (servant of) and Colm (Columba). St. Columba (521–97) was an Irish missionary who played a major role in converting Scotland to Christianity. Var: Malina. (MAL-KO-MEE-NAH)

MALVINA Coinage by Scottish poet James Macpherson (1736–96) from the Gaelic Malamhìn, a name derived from *mala mhìn* (smooth brow). (MAL-VEE-NAH)

MARCELLA Cognate of the French Marcelle, a feminine form of Marcel, which is from the Latin Marcellus, a diminutive form of Marcus, which is of uncertain derivation. *See* MARCUS (Male Names). The Gaelic form of Marcella is Marsaili. *See* MARSAILI. (MAR-SEH-LAH)

MARETTA Anglicized form of Mairead, a Scottish Gaelic form of Margaret (a pearl). *See* MAIREAD *and* MARGARET. Short: Etta. (MAH-REH-TAH)

MARGARET A borrowing from the English, Margaret is from the Greek *margarītēs*, which is derived from *margaron* (a pearl). The name, popular in Scotland, was borne by the daughter of Edmund Ironside of England who became the wife of King Malcolm Canmore, and by Margaret Tudor (1489–1541), sister of Henry VIII. The wife of James IV of Scotland, she ruled as regent after his death. Màiread, Màireag, and Maighread are Gaelic forms of the name. Pet: Maggie, Mai, Maisie, May. (MAR-GAH-RET)

MARGERY Variant form of Margaret (a pearl), which originated in the Middle Ages. *See* MARGARET. The Gaelic form of Margery is Marsail. (MAR-JER-REE)

MARINA Of debated origin and meaning, some believe it to be derived from the Latin Marius (of Mars, the Roman mythological god of war). Others think Marina is derived from the Latin *marinus* (of the sea). The name has been used in Scotland as an Anglicized form of Màiri, the Gaelic form of Mary. (MAH-REE-NAH)

MARION A borrowing from the French, Marion is a diminutive form of Marie, a cognate of Mary. The name has been in common use in the British Isles since the Middle Ages, and in Scotland it has been used to Anglicize the Gaelic Muireall (sea bright). *See* MUIREALL. (MARE-EE-ON)

MARSAILI Scottish Gaelic form of Margery, which is a variant of Margaret (a pearl) originating in the Middle Ages, and of Marcella, a name borrowed from the French. *See* MARCELLA *and* MARGARET. Var: Marsail. (MAR-SAY-LEE)

MARTHA Derived from the Aramaic Mārthā (lady, mistress). The Gaelic form of Martha is Moireach. (MAR-THA)

MARY Anglicized form of Maria, which is derived from the Hebrew Miryām (sea of bitterness, sea of sorrow). There is much debate over the meaning of this name. While "sea of bitterness or sorrow" seems to be the most probable, some sources give the alternative definitions of "rebellion," "wished-for child," and "mistress or lady of the sea." The name, borne in the Bible by the virgin mother of Jesus, has become one of the most enduringly popular names in the Christian world. The Gaelic form of Mary is Màiri or Màili, with the name Moire reserved to indicate the Blessed Virgin. (MARE-EE)

MAURA A name of Celtic origin perhaps derived from *mohr* (great). Alternatively, Maura is a feminine form of the Latin Maurus (dark-skinned), which is derived from the Greek *mauritius* (of Moorish lineage). (MOR-RAH)

MAUREEN A borrowing from the Irish, Maureen is an Anglicized form of Máirín, a pet form of Máire, which is the Irish cognate of Mary. *See* MARY. The name is now common throughout the British Isles. Var: Maurene, Maurine. (MOR-REEN)

MINA A short form of Calumina and Normina, Mina is also occasionally bestowed as an independent given name. *See* CALUMINA *and* NORMINA. (MEE-NAH)

MÓR Derived from the Gaelic *mór* (great, large). In Scotland the name has been Anglicized as Sarah (princess). Pet: Mórag, Morag, Moreen. (MOR)

MORAINN Scottish Gaelic cognate of the Irish Muireann, a compound name composed of the elements *muir* (sea) and *fionn* (white, fair, clear): hence, "fair seas." Alternatively, some believe the name means "very hairy" or "long-haired" and derive it from the elements *mór* (more, great) and *fionnach* (hairy). Var: Morann. (MOR-AIN)

Muireall A compound name composed of the Gaelic elements *muir* (sea) and *geal* (bright, fair): hence, "bright seas, fair one of the sea." Muireall has been Anglicized as Marion. (MYOOR-EE-AHL)

Murdag Feminine form of Murchadh, an evolution of Muireadhach (sea warrior), which is derived from the element *muir* (sea). Var: Murdann, Murdina. Short: Dina, Ina. (MOOR-DAH)

Myrna A borrowing from the Irish, Myrna is an Anglicized form of the Gaelic Muirne (beloved, affection). Var: Morna. (MUR-NAH)

Nan Originally a pet form or an anagram of Ann (gracious, full of grace). Nan is now generally used as a short form of Nancy, which also originated as a pet form of Ann, but is now regarded as an independent given name. Pet: Nanny; Nandag (Gaelic). (NAN)

Neilina Feminine form of Neil, which is the Anglicized form of the Gaelic Niall, which is of disputed meaning. Some believe it is derived from *niadh* (a champion); others think it is from *néall* (cloud). (NEEL-EE-NAH)

Netta Feminine form of Neil, the Anglicized form of the Gaelic Niall, which is derived from *niadh* (champion) or *néall* (cloud). (NEH-TAH)

Nora Scottish feminine form of Norman (Norseman, man from the north), which is from the Germanic Nordman, a compound name composed of the elements *nord* (north) and *man* (man). *See* NORMAN (Male Names). Var: Norah. (NOR-AH)

Normina Feminine form of Norman (Norseman, man from the north), which is from the Germanic Nordman, a compound name composed of the elements *nord* (north) and *man* (man). *See* NORMAN (Male Names). Short: Mina. (NOR-MEE-NAH)

Oighrig Of uncertain derivation, some think it to be an evolution of the older Aithbhreac (new speckled one). Others believe it is a cognate of Euphemia (fair speech), which is from the Greek Euphēmia, a compound name composed of the elements *eu* (good, fair, well) and *phēmē* (voice). Oighrig has been Anglicized as Africa, Effie, Efric, Erica, Euphemia, Harriet, and Henrietta. Var: Eirie, Eithrig. (EF-RIK)

Patricia Feminine form of Patrick, which is from the Latin *patricius* (a patrician, an aristocrat). The name became popular after its association with Princess Victoria Patricia Helena Elizabeth (b. 1886), who was known as Princess Patricia. (PAH-TREESH-AH)

Peigi Gaelic form of Peggy, a pet form of Margaret (a pearl) modeled after Meggie. It is now occasionally bestowed as an independent given name. *See* MARGARET. (PEG-GEE)

Rachel From the Ecclesiastic Late Latin and the Ecclesiastic Greek Rhachēl, which is derived from the Hebrew *rāhēl* (ewe). Raonaid is the Gaelic form of the name, which is also used in Scotland to Anglicize the Gaelic Raghnaid (counsel in battle). *See* RAGHNAID. (RAY-CHEL)

Raghnaid Derived from the Old Norse Ragnhildr, a compound name composed of the elements *regin* (advice, counsel, decision) and *hildr* (battle). The name is Anglicized as Rachel (ewe). (RAYG-NAH)

Raonaid Gaelic form of Rachel (ewe). *See* RACHEL. (RAH-NAH)

Rebecca From the Ecclesiastic Late Latin and Ecclesiastic Greek Rhebekka, which is derived from the Hebrew *ribbqāh* (noose), from *rabak* (to bind, to tie). The name, borne in the Bible by the wife of Isaac and mother of Jacob and Esau, was not used in the British Isles until after the Reformation in the 16th century. In Scotland the name has been used to Anglicize the Gaelic Beathag (life). *See* BEATHAG. (REH-BEH-KAH)

Rhoda Feminine form of Roderick (famous king), which is derived from the Germanic elements *hruod* (fame) and *rik* (king, ruler). *See* RODERICK (Male Names). Var: Rodina. Short: Dina. (RO-DAH)

Robina Feminine form of Robin, which originated as a pet form of Robert (bright fame) but which is now considered to be an independent given name derived from the name of the bird. *See* ROBERT (Male Names). Var: Robena. (RO-BEE-NAH)

Rona Of uncertain derivation, Rona can be a feminine form of Ronald (wise ruler, powerful ruler) or a borrowing of the name of a Hebridean island. The name is believed to have been coined in Scotland in the late 19th century. Var: Rhona. (RO-NAH)

Ronalda Feminine form of Ronald, a name introduced to Scotland by Scandinavian settlers in the form of Rögnvaldr, a compound name composed of the Old Norse elements *rögn, regin* (advice, judgment, decision) and *valdr* (ruler, power): hence, "ruler of decision, judgment power." (RAH-NAHL-DAH)

Rowena Of uncertain origin and meaning, Rowena is thought to be derived from the obsolete Old English Hrothwina, Hrōðwyn, a compound name composed of the elements *hroth, hrōð* (fame) and *wine* (friend) or *wynn* (bliss, joy). Alternatively, it might be a derivative of the Cymric Rhonwen, which is composed from the elements *rhon* (spear, lance) and *gwen, gwyn* (white, fair, blessed). (RO-WEE-NAH)

SANDY A pet form of Alexandra (defender or helper of mankind) and its short form Saundra, Sandy is also occasionally bestowed as an independent given name. *See* ALEXANDRA. (SAN-DEE)

SAUNDRA A Scottish short form of Alexandra (defender or helper of mankind), Saundra is commonly bestowed as an independent given name. *See* ALEXANDRA. Pet: Sandy. (SAUN-DRAH)

SENGA Scottish coinage formed either by spelling Agnes backward or as a derivative of the Gaelic *seang* (slender, lanky). *See* AGNES. (SEN-GAH)

SEONA Anglicized form of Seònaid, the Gaelic form of Janet, which is a diminutive form of Jane (God is gracious). *See* JANET. Var: Shona. (SHO-NAH)

SEONAG Scottish Gaelic form of Joan, a feminine form of John (God is gracious). *See* JOAN. (SHO-NAH)

SEÒNAID Scottish Gaelic form of Janet, a diminutive form of Jane, which is a feminine cognate of Jean, itself a cognate of John (God is gracious). *See* JANE *and* JANET. Seònaid is Anglicized as Seona and Shona. Var: Deònaid. (SHO-NAH)

SEÒRDAG Feminine form of Seòras, the Scottish Gaelic cognate of George (farmer, earthworker). *See* GEORGE (Male Names). (SHOR-DAH)

SHEENA Anglicized form of Sìne, the Scottish Gaelic form of Jane, which is a feminine form of John (God is gracious). *See* JANE. The name is borne by the popular Scottish singer and actress Sheena Easton. (SHEE-NAH)

SÌNE Scottish Gaelic form of Jane (God is gracious). *See* JANE. The name is Anglicized as Sheena. Pet: Sineag. (SHEE-NAH)

SIUBHAN Cognate of the Irish Siobhán, which is a Gaelic form of Jane (God is gracious). *See* SIOBHÁN (Irish Names). (SHEH-VON)

SIÙSAN Gaelic form of Susan (lily, rose). *See* SUSAN. Var: Siùsaidh. (SOO-SAN)

SOPHIA Derived from the Greek *sophia* (wisdom, skill), this name has been in use in England since the 17th century, when it was bestowed upon the infant daughter of James I in 1607. The name is also used in Scotland to Anglicize the Gaelic name Beathag (life). Pet: Sophie. (SO-FEE-AH)

SORCHA Early Celtic name meaning "bright" which is common to both Scotland and Ireland. It has been Anglicized as both Sarah (princess) and Clara (famous, clear, bright). (SOR-AH)

SUSAN Anglicized form of the French Susanne, a cognate of the Ecclesiastic Late Latin Susanna, which is derived from the Hebrew *shōshannāh* (lily, rose). The Gaelic form of Susan is Siùsan. Var: Suzan. Short: Sue. Pet: Susie, Suzie, Suzy. (SOO-ZAN)

SUSANNAH Derived from the Hebrew Shoshana, which is from *shōshannāh* (a lily, a rose). Var: Susan, Susanna, Suzan, Suzanna, Suzannah. Short: Sue. Pet: Susie, Suzie, Suzy. (SOO-SAN-NAH)

TARA A borrowing from the Irish, Tara is the transferred use of a place-name belonging to a hill in central Ireland which was an ancient seat of kingship. *See* TARA (Irish Names). (TAR-AH)

TEASAG Scottish Gaelic form of Jessie, which is a pet form of Jean, a short form of Jessica, and a feminine form of Jesse. *See* JESSICA. (CHES-SAH)

TRÍONA Short form of Caitrìona, which is the Gaelic form of Katherine (pure, unsullied). Tríona is also bestowed as an independent given name. Var: Triona. (TREE-O-NAH)

ÙNA Of debated derivation and meaning, most believe it is derived from the Gaelic *úna* (dearth, famine, hunger), but others derive it from *uan* (lamb). The name has been Anglicized as Euna, Agnes, and Winifred. (YOO-NAH)

VICTORIA Derived from the Latin *victoria* (victory). The name was generally unknown in the British Isles until the 19th century, when Edward, duke of Kent, married the German Maria Louisa Victoria of Saxe-Coburg (1786–1861). Their daughter, the future Queen Victoria (1819–1901), was christened Alexandrina Victoria, thus furthering recognition of the name. The Gaelic form is Bhictoria. Pet: Tori, Torie, Tory, Vicki, Vickie, Vicky. (VIK-TOR-EE-AH)

WINIFRED From the Welsh Gwenfrewi, which is derived from the elements *gwen, gwyn* (white, fair, blessed) and *frewi* (reconciliation, peace): hence, "blessed peace." Alternatively, the name may be derived from the Old English Wynnfrið, a compound name composed of the elements *wynn* (joy, bliss) and *frið, frith* (peace): hence, "joyful peace." The name has been used to Anglicize the Gaelic Ùna. *See* ÙNA. Short: Freda, Win. Pet: Winnie. (WIN-IH-FRED)

CHAPTER TWENTY-NINE

Southeast Asian Names

LIKE MANY immigrant groups before them, many recent immigrants from Southeast Asia have adopted the practice of taking an "American" name to use in addition to their native name. Thus today, babies born in America to Vietnamese parents are often given an American name in conjunction with a Vietnamese name.

The Vietnamese use three names. The surname is written first, followed by a middle name and an individual name. Girls are generally given pretty, flowery names and names indicative of morality and respect. Boys' names often represent intelligence and strength of character.

Much of Cambodia's culture was borrowed from India in the 1st century A.D., when the kingdom of Funan was founded. Today, nearly 90 percent of Cambodians are Buddhists, and religion is one of the main sources of personal names. Early epithets of the Buddha, and words representing qualities highly regarded in Buddhism, such as morality and good conduct, are commonly incorporated into Cambodian names. Nature is another popular theme on which to base a child's name.

Southeast Asian Male Names

AN Peace, amity, security. Vietnam. (AHN)

AN TOAN Secure, safe. Vietnam. (AHN-TWAN)

ARAN Forest. Thailand. (AH-RAHN)

ARUN The sun. Cambodia, Thailand. Var: Aroon. (AH-ROON)

BAY Vietnamese name meaning "seventh." It is indicative of a child born during the seventh month of the year, the seventh day of the week, or of a seventh child. (BY)

BINH Piece, part, portion. Vietnam. (BUN)

BOUREY Country. Cambodia. (BOO-REE)

BUU Principal, leader. Vietnam. (BOO)

CADAO A folk song. Vietnam. (KAH-YOW)

Can Derived from the Vietnamese *can* (to concern, advise, interest). (GUN)

Cham Industrious, a hard worker. Vietnam. (CHAM)

Chan True, correct. Vietnam. (CHAN)

Chankrisna Cambodian name borrowed from that of a type of tree. (CHEN-KREES-NEH)

Chau A pearl, something precious. Vietnam (CHAH-OO)

Chet Brother. Thailand. (CHET)

Chim Bird. Vietnam. (JIM)

Chong Duy Vietnamese name possibly meaning "to eat like a bird." (CHONG-YEE)

Dan Yes. Vietnam. (YUN)

Dang Merit, worthiness; to have the heart to do something. Vietnam. (YAHNG)

Dara Stars. Cambodia. (DEH-REH)

Dieu Hien Vietnamese name possibly meaning "bright red amaryllis." (DEE-O-HEEN)

Dinh Summit, peak, crest. Vietnam. (DIN)

Dinh Hoa Vietnamese combination name meaning "summit, peak, crest" and "flower." (DIN-HWA)

Dong East. Vietnam. (DŌNG)

Du To play, to amuse oneself; to flatter; elm. Vietnam. (YOO)

Duc Moral, ethical, virtuous. Vietnam. (DUCK) Var: Duy. (YOO-EE)

Hai The sea, the ocean. Vietnam. (HI) Var: Han. (HAHN)

Hao Ngoc Jade. Vietnam. (HWA-N-GOK)

Hau To long for, desire. Vietnam. (HOW)

Hien To be mild, sweet, good-natured. Vietnam. (HEENG)

Hieu Respect, regard, admiration. Vietnam. (HYOO)

Hoa Flower. Vietnam. (HWA)

Hoang Finished, completed. Vietnam. (HWANG)

Hoc Study. Vietnam. (HWOK)

Hung Brave, heroic. Vietnam. (HUNG)

Huy Sunlight, to be radiant, beautiful. Vietnam. (HWEE)

Hy Hope, wish. Vietnam. (HEE)

Kama Love. Thailand. (KAH-MAH)

Khang To be strong, healthy. Vietnam. (KHANG)

Khuong To help, assist. Vietnam. (KOONG)

Kim Gold, metal; needle. Vietnam. (KIM)

Kim Hu Metal jar, golden jar. Vietnam. (KIM-HWU)

Kiri Mountain, peak. Cambodia. (KEE-REE)

Lan Unicorn. Vietnam. (LAHN)

Lap Independent, self-reliant. Vietnam. (LAHP)

Liem To be honest. Vietnam. (LIM)

Loc Luck, to be blessed. Vietnam. (LOWK)

Long Hair; dragon. Vietnam. (LOWNG)

Luong Big bamboo. Vietnam. (LOONG)

Man Keen, quick-minded, sharp. Vietnam. (MUN)

Minh Bright, clear, light. Vietnam. (MIN)

Moc Van Many risings of the sun and moon. Vietnam. (MOHK-VAHN)

Munny Wise, intelligent. Cambodia. (MOH-NEE)

Nam South. Vietnam. (NAHM)

Ngai Herb. Vietnam. (N-GAHEE)

Nghi Suspected. Vietnam. (N-GHEE)

Nghia Eternity, forever. Vietnam. (N-GHEE-AH)

Ngoc Anh Jade flower. Vietnam. (N-GOK-AHN)

Nhean Intuitive, knowledgeable. Cambodia. (NEE-AHN)

Nien Year. Vietnam. (NEE-EN)

Niran Eternal. Thailand. (NEE-RUN)

Phirun Rain. Cambodia. (FEE-RUM)

Phuoc Good. Vietnam. (FOOK)

Pich Diamond. Cambodia. (PEECH)

Pin Loyal, faithful. Vietnam. (PEEN)

Quang Thieu To be bright and young. Vietnam. (KWANG-THEE-OO)

Quan Van Civilian, official. Vietnam. (KWANG-VUN)

Rithisak Powerful. Cambodia. (REETH-EE-SAK)

Sahn To compare; to brim over. Vietnam. (SAHN)

Sakngea Dignitary, statesman. Cambodia. (SAK-N-GHEE-Ā)

So Number; first-born. Vietnam. (SO)

Son Mountain. Vietnam. (SUN)

Sopheara Handsome. Cambodia. (SO-PEER-AH)

Sovann Gold. Cambodia. (SO-VEN)

Tai Talent, gifted. Vietnam. (TY)

Tam Eight. Vietnam. (TAHM)

Tan New. Vietnam. (TAHN)

Tang Thuy Deep water. Vietnam. (TANG-TOO-EE)

Tanh Characteristic, manner. Vietnam. (TAN)

Thai Many, several. Vietnam. (TY)

Thang Victory. Vietnam. (TUNG)

Thanh Finish, completion, end; brilliant. Vietnam. (TAHN)

Tho To live long. Vietnam. (TAH)

Thong To be intelligent. Vietnam. (TŌNG)

Thu Autumn, fall. Vietnam. (TŌ)

Thuc Aware, alert. Vietnam. (TOKE)

Thuong To chase. Vietnam. (TOONG)

Thuy Gentle. Vietnam. (TOO-EE)

Tien To be first. Vietnam. (TING)

Tiet Season, festival. Vietnam. (TATE)

Tin Think, meditate, reason. Vietnam. (THUN)

Tong Fragrant, redolent. Vietnam. (TAHM)

Trai Oyster, pearl. Vietnam. (TRY)

Tu Four. Vietnam. (TOO)

Tuan Without complications, uneventful. Vietnam. (TUNG)

Tung Composure, calmness, dignity, stateliness. Vietnam. (TŌNG)

Tu'ong All, every. Vietnam. (TWUNG)

Tuyen Angel. Vietnam. (TOOING)

Van Appearance, looks. Vietnam. (VAN)

Veasna Fortunately. Cambodia. (VEH-EH-SNEH)

Viet Destroy. Vietnam. (VEE-ET)

Vui To be joyful, merry, to be amused. Vietnam. (VOO-EE)

Yen Calm, peaceful; a swallow. Vietnam. (ING)

Southeast Asian Female Names

Ai Beloved, cherished. Vietnam. (Ī)

Am Lunar, of the moon. Vietnam. (AHM)

An Peace, security, safety. Vietnam. (AHN)

Bich Jewelry, jade jewelry. Vietnam. (BIT)

Boupha Flower-like. Cambodia. (BO-FA)

Bua Amulet, a charm. Vietnam. (BOO-AH)

Cai Female. Vietnam. (KAH-EE)

Cam Sweet, an orange. Vietnam. (KAM)

Chan Cambodian name borrowed from that of a type of fragrant tree. (CHAN)

Channary A moon-faced girl. Cambodia. (CHAN-NAH-REE)

Chantou Flower. Cambodia. (CHAN-TAU)

Chantrea The moon, the light of the moon. Cambodia. (CHAN-THEE-Ā)

Chau Pearl, something precious. Vietnam. (CHOW)

Chi Twig. Vietnam. (CHEE)

Dara Stars. Cambodia. (DAH-RAH)

Diet Destroy, conquer. Vietnam. (YEE-ET)

Dieu-Kiem To search for love, seeker of love. Vietnam. (YOO-KEE-EM)

Ha River. Vietnam. (HA)

Hang Angel in the full moon. Vietnam. (HAHNG)

Hanh Moral, ethical, faithful. Vietnam. (HAHN)

Hoa Peace, amity; a flower, a blossom. Vietnam. (HWAH)

Hong Pink. Vietnam. (HAH-ONG)

Hue Conventional, out-dated, old-fashioned. Vietnam. (HWAY)

Huong Flower, blossom; fragrance. Vietnam. (HOONG)

Huynh Golden, yellow. Vietnam. (HWEHN)

Kalliyan Best, superior. Cambodia. (KELL-LEE-ENN)

KANNITHA Angels. Cambodia. (KEN-NEE-THA)

KANYA Young lady. Thailand. (KAHN-YAH)

KIEU To be graceful, to be beautiful; arrogant. It is borne by famous actress Chinh Kieu. Vietnam. (KEE-OO)

KIM Needle; metal, gold. Vietnam. (KEEM)

KOLAB A rose. Cambodia. (KOE-LAB)

KUNTHEA Fragrant. Cambodia. (KUNN-THEE-EH)

LAN Vietnamese name borrowed from that of a type of flower. (LAHN)

LANG Flower. Vietnam. (LANG)

LE A pear. Vietnam. (LAY)

LIEN Lotus; chain, link. Vietnam. (LEEN)

LUAN To discuss, to consider. Vietnam. (LUN)

MAI A flower. Vietnam. (MY)

MAI LY A plum flower, a plum blossom. Vietnam. (MY-LEE)

MALI Flower. Thailand. (MAH-LEE)

MIEU Salt. Vietnam. (MEE-OO)

MLISS Cambodian name borrowed from that of a type of flower. (MLEES)

MY Pretty, beautiful. Vietnam. (MEE)

MY-KHANH Beautiful stone, attractive jewelry. Vietnam. (MEE-KAHN)

NGOC Jade. Vietnam. (N-GOWK)

NGUYET Moon. Vietnam. (NOO-ET)

NU Girl. Vietnam. (NOO)

PHEAKKLEY Faithfulness, loyalty. Cambodia. (FAK-KLEH)

QUYEN Bird. Vietnam. (KWEN)

SOPHEARY Beautiful, lovely, attractive. Cambodia. (SO-FEAR-EE)

SOPORTEVY Angelic, beautiful and angelic. Cambodia. (SO-PER-TEH-VEE)

SUMALI Beautiful flower. Thailand. Var: Sumalee. (SOO-MAH-LEE)

SUNEE Good. Thailand. (SOO-NEE)

SUONG Fog. Vietnam. (SOO-AHNG)

SUVATTANA Heaven, of heaven. Thailand. (SOO-VAHT-TAH-NAH)

TAM Heart. Vietnam. (TAHM)

TAO Apple. Vietnam. (TOW)

TEVY Angel. Cambodia. (TEH-VEE)

THAO Respect, courtesy, honorable. Vietnam. (TAH-O)

THE Promised. Vietnam. (TĀ)

THU Autumn, fall. Vietnam. Var: Tu. (TOO)

THUY Gentle. Vietnam. (TOO-EE)

TRANG Intelligent, knowledgeable; beautiful. Vietnam. (DRANG, TRANG)

TRINH Virgin. Vietnam. (DJIN)

TRUC Wish, desire. Vietnam. (DJUKE)

TUYET Snow. Vietnam. (TOO-ET)

UT Last. Vietnam. (OP)

VANNA Golden. Cambodia. (VAH-NAH)

VEATA The wind. Cambodia. (VEH-EH-TEH)

VINH Bay, gulf. Vietnam. (VUN)

XUAN Spring. Vietnam. (ZHWUNG)

Chapter Thirty

Spanish Names

After eight hundred years of Arab-Christian-Jewish civilization in Spain, during which time the Christians increasingly asserted control, the "saving" of Spain was completed when the fifteenth-century Catholic monarchs Isabella and Ferdinand united their kingdoms of Castile and Aragon and set about destroying the Moors and expelling all Jews who refused to convert to Catholicism.

What followed was the Spanish Inquisition: the government search for those who falsely claimed to have converted to Catholicism. This brought about extreme measures of "proving" one's Catholicism to his community. The remarkable contributions the Jews and Muslims had made to Spanish society were lost or abandoned through the inquisition process, which made it heresy to have anything to do with those peoples and their religions.

This had a marked impact on the bestowal of names. No longer were Jewish, Muslim, or Arabic names used. Instead, at baptism, the infant was welcomed into the church community and was given a name chosen from the Catholic Calendar of Saints or from among five thousand names in the Roman Martyrology.

Surnames had become fixed and hereditary in Spain by the fifteenth century. Before this, it was customary to have a given name to which was added the father's name in the genitive case. The son of Fernando González, for example, would be Juan Fernández.

In the last two centuries, it has been the custom to take both the father's and the mother's last names. The father's surname comes first, followed by a *y* or a hyphen, then the mother's surname. It is the father's surname that descends to the children. For example, if María Gómez y García marries José Ramírez y Martínez, her name would become María Gómez de Ramírez. Their son Julio would be Julio Ramírez y Gómez.

By far the most popular baptismal name for girls is María. It is so common that other qualities or names referring to the Virgin Mary are added to create names such as María de los Dolores (Mary of Sorrows). Also popular are names that refer to festivals, objects, or events associated with the church and the adoration of the Virgin Mary, or names that refer to an abstract concept in the life of Jesus or Mary. Originally, these names, such as Asunción (ascension), Concepción (conception), Presentación (presentation), and Rosario (rosary), were borne by both males and females. Now, however, they are used far more often for girls than boys.

The use of diminutives, pet forms of names, and nicknames is common throughout the Spanish-speaking world. The suffixes *-ito* and *-ita* or *-cito* and *-cita* can be added to almost any name to create a diminutive. For example, Carmela becomes Carmelita, Carmen becomes Carmencita, and Pepe, a pet form of José, becomes Pepito.

Among the most popular female names are María, Guadalupe, Margarita, Juanita, Rosa, and Francisca. For males, José, Juan, Manuel, Jesús, and Luis are among the names chosen most often.

Spanish Male Names

AARÓN Derived from the Hebrew *aharōn* (the exalted one). The name is borne in the Bible by the elder brother of Moses. Var: Arón, Arrón, Erón. (AH-ROAN)

ABÁN From Persian mythology, Abán is the name of the Muse of liberal arts and mechanics. (AH-BAHN)

ABDÉNAGO From Abednego (servant of the god Nego), the Aramaic name of one of three companions who were cast into a blazing furnace for refusing to pray to a foreign god. Miraculously, they emerged from the furnace unharmed. Var: Abdeniago, Abedmago, Adbonego. (AHB-DAY-NAH-GO)

ABDÍAS Hebrew name meaning "slave of God." The name was borne by an ancient prophet who foretold the destruction of Edom in 900 B.C. (AHB-DEE-AHS)

ABDIEL Hebrew name meaning "servant of God." It is borne in the Bible by a prophet who withstood Satan. (AHB-DEEL)

ABEJUNDIO Derived from *abejuno* (of a bee, relating to a bee), which is from *abeja* (a bee). (AH-BAY-HOON-DEE-O)

ABEL Derived from the Hebrew *hebel* (breath). The name is borne in the Bible by the second son of Adam and Eve. He was killed by his elder brother, Cain, in a fit of jealous rage. Var: Abiel, Avel. (AH-BELL)

ABELARDO Cognate of the French Adelard, a derivative of the Old High German Adalhard (noble and strong), which is composed from the elements *adal* (noble) and *hard* (brave, strong, hardy). Var: Abalardo, Abedardo, Abelada, Ablardo, Alvelardo, Avelardo, Ebelardo, Evalardo. Dim: Beluch, Lalo. (AH-BAY-LAHR-DŌ)

ABRAHAM Derived from the Hebrew Avraham (father of many, father of a multitude). The name is borne in the Bible by the first patriarch and ancestor of the Arabs and the Jews. Var: Aberhán, Abraam, Abraán, Abrahán, Abram, Abrán, Avrán, Ibrahim. Dim: Brancho. (AH-BRAH-AHM)

ABSALÓN Derived from the Hebrew Absalom (the father is peace). The name is borne in the Bible by the third and favorite son of David. (AHB-SAH-LOAN)

ABUNDIO Derived from the Latin Abundius (of plenty), which has its root in *abundans* (abundant, copious, plenty). Var: Abondio, Aboundio, Abundo, Avundio. Dim: Abunito. (AH-BOON-DEE-O)

ACACIO Derived from the Greek Acacios, which probably has its root in *akakia* (acacia tree, a thorny tree). Var: Ecasio. (AH-KAH-SEE-O)

ACIANO Borrowed from the name of the blue bottleflower. (AH-SEE-AH-NO)

ACILINO Derived from the Latin *aquila* (eagle). Var: Acilnio, Ancilino. (AH-SEE-LEE-NO)

ADALBERTO Derived from the German Adalbert (nobly bright), a compound name composed of the elements *adal* (noble) and *beraht* (bright). Var: Adalverto, Adelberto, Edilberto. Short: Adal. Pet: Beto. (AH-DAHL-BARE-TŌ)

ADÁN Spanish form of Adam, a name derived from the Hebrew *adama* (red earth). Var: Adame, Adana. (AH-DAHN)

ADELMO Of Germanic origin meaning "noble protector." Dim: Delma, Delmo. (AH-DELL-MO)

ADEMAR Of Germanic origin meaning "famous in battle." (AH-DAY-MAR)

ADOLFO Derived from the Germanic Adolf (noble wolf), an evolution of the Old High German Adulf, which is a compounding of the elements *adal* (noble) and *wulf* (wolf). Var: Adalfo, Adulfo. Dim: Dolfito, Dolfo, Fito, Fonso. (AH-DOLE-FO)

ADONÍAS Derived from the Hebrew Adonijah (Jehovah is lord). Var: Adonaicio, Adonais, Adonaiso. Dim: Adona. (AH-DŌ-NEE-AHS)

ADONÍS Derived from the Greek Adōnis, a name of unknown etymology borne in Greek mythology by a handsome young man loved by Aphrodite; hence its accepted translation of "handsome, very good-looking." Short: Adón. (AH-DŌ-NEES)

ADRIÁN Derived from the Latin Adriānus (man from the city of Adria) and Hadriānus (man from the city of Hadria). Var: Adriano, Adrín. (AH-DREE-AHN)

ADULIO Of Latin origin meaning "excessive desire to please." Var: Adolio. (AH-DYOO-LEE-O)

AEMILIANO Derived from the Latin Aemilianus (of Aemilius), which is from Aemilius, an old Roman family name thought to be derived from *aemulus* (rival, trying to equal or excel, emulating). (AH-MEE-LEE-AH-NO)

AEMILIO From the Latin Aemilius, an old Roman family name thought to be derived from *aemulus* (rival, trying to equal or excel, emulating). Var: Emilio. (AH-MEE-LEE-O)

ALADINO Muslim name of Arabic origin. It is derived from A'l ad-Dīn (height of the religion), a compounding of the elements *a'lā* (height), *al* (the), and *dīn* (religion). (AH-LAH-DEE-NO)

ALAMAR Muslim name of Arabic origin meaning "golden, coated in gold." Var: Alamaro. (AH-LAH-MAR)

ALANO Spanish cognate of Alan, a Celtic name of uncertain derivation. (AH-LAH-NO)

ALARICO Derived from Alaric, a variant form of the German Adalrich (noble ruler), which is composed of the elements *adal* (noble) and *rik* (ruler, king). Short: Rico. (AH-LAH-REE-CO)

ALBANO Derived from the Latin Albanus (from the Italian city of Alba). Some believe it has its root in *albus* (white). (AHL-BAH-NO)

ALBERTO Spanish form of Albert (nobly bright), derived from the Old High German Adalbrecht, which is composed of the elements *adal* (noble) and *beraht* (bright, famous). Var: Albarto, Alberdo, Alverto, Eliberto. Dim: Aber, Aberto. (AHL-BARE-TŌ)

ALDO Germanic name derived from the element *adal* (noble) or *waldan* (to rule). (AHL-DŌ)

ALEJANDRO Popular Spanish form of Alexander (defender or helper of mankind), a cognate of the Greek Alexandros, which is composed from the elements *alexein* (to defend, to help) and *andros* (man). Var: Alajandro, Aldjandro, Alefandro, Alegandro, Alejandor, Alisondro, Alizando, Alizondo, Allesandro, Alyandro, Elesandro, Elijandro, Elisandre, Elisandro, Elisondro, Elissandro, Elixandro, Elizandro. Short: Lejandro. Dim: Alacio, Alasio, Alazio, Alecio, Aleco, Alejho, Alejo, Alejos, Alejoz, Alendro, Jeandro. (AHL-LAH-HAHN-DRO)

ALFONSO Spanish cognate of the French Alphonse (noble and ready), a name derived from the Old German Adulfuns, a compounding of the elements *adal* (noble) and *funs* (ready, prompt, apt). The name was borne by the patron saint of Mallorca and Palma. Var: Affonso, Alefonso, Alfanso, Alfonzo, Alifonso, Alifonzo, Alonso, Alphons, Elifonso. Dim: Foncho, Fonso, Loncho, Poncho, Ponso. (AHL-FONE-SO)

ALFREDO Spanish cognate of Alfred (elf counsel), a name derived from the Old English Ælfred, a compounding of the elements *ælf* (elf) and *ræd* (counsel). Elves were considered to be supernatural beings having special powers of seeing into the future; thus the name took on the meaning "wise counsel." Var: Alfedo, Alferdo, Alfrado, Alfredus, Alfrido, Elfridio. (AHL-FRAY-DŌ)

ALICIO Derived from the Greek Alexios (defender, helper), which is from the verb *alexein* (to defend, to help). Var: Elicio. Pet: Chichi. (AH-LEE-SEE-O)

ALOISIO Spanish form of Aloysius, a Latinized form of Aloys, which is a Provençal cognate of Louis (famous in war). Louis is from the Old High German Hluodowig, a compounding of the elements *hluod* (famous) and *wīg* (war, strife). The name was borne by St. Aloysius Gonzaga, a patron saint of young people. Var: Aloiza, Alouiso, Alouso, Aloyisious. (AH-LOW-EE-SEE-O)

ÁLVARO Spanish cognate of the English Alvar (elfin army), a name derived from the Old English Ælfhere, a compounding of the elements *ælf* (elf) and *here* (army). Var: Albar, Álbaro, Alvarso, Alverio. (AHL-BAH-RO)

AMADEO Derived from the Latin Amadeus, a compound name composed of the elements *ama* (love) and *deus* (God): hence, "love of God." Var: Amades, Amadís, Amedes. (AH-MAH-DAY-O)

AMBROSIO From the Late Latin Ambrosius, which is from the Greek Ambrosios, a name derived from *ambrosios* (immortal). The name was borne by a 4th-century saint who was bishop of Milan and is considered to be one of the four great Latin doctors of the church. Var: Ambarosio, Ambersio, Amborsio, Ambrasio, Ambraso, Ambriosio, Ambrocio, Ambronso, Ambros, Ambroseno, Ambrozio, Embrocio. Pet: Bocho. (AHM-BRO-SEE-O)

AMÉRICO Spanish cognate of Amerigo, an Italian variant of Enrico (ruler of an enclosure, home ruler). *See* ENRIQUE. Dim: Merco, Mimeco. (AH-MAY-REE-CO)

AMÓS Hebrew name derived from *'āmōs* (borne, to be burdened). The name is borne in the Bible by an 8th-century B.C. Hebrew prophet whose prophecies are recorded in the Old Testament book of Amos. (AH-MOHS)

ANACLETO Derived from the Greek Anaklētos (called forth, invoked), a name that originated as a divine appellation. Var: Anaclito, Anicleto, Enicleto. Short: Cleto. (AH-NAH-KLEH-TŌ)

ANASTACIO Spanish cognate of the Greek Anastasios (of the resurrection), a name derived from *anastasis* (resurrection). Var: Anaslacio, Anassasio, Anastaceo, Anastación, Anastanio, Anastano, Anastas, Anastasa, Anastasi, Anastasio, Anastecio, Anastesio, Anostasio. (AH-NAH-STAH-CEE-O)

ANATOLIO Spanish cognate of the Greek Anatolios, a name derived from *anatolē* (sunrise, daybreak, dawn). Var: Anastolio, Antolín. (AH-NAH-TŌ-LEE-O)

ANDRÉS Spanish form of Andrew, a cognate of the Greek Andreas, which is derived from *andreios* (manly). The name is borne in the Bible by one of the Twelve Apostles, a brother of Peter. It was he who brought the boy with the basket of loaves and fishes to see Jesus, whereupon the miracle of feeding the five thousand was performed. Var: Andero, Andrean, Andreo, Andreón, Andrez. Dim: Andi, Andresito. (AHN-DRAYS)

ANGEL Popular name derived from the Latin *angelus* (divine messenger, angel). Var: Angelo, Angelmo, Anjelo. (AHN-HELL)

ANSELMO Of Germanic origin, Anselmo (divine helmet, divine protection) is from the elements *ansi* (divinity, a god) and *helm* (helmet, protection). Var: Amselmo, Ancelemo, Ancelmo, Anselino, Anselm, Anzelmo, Enselmo. Short: Selmo. Pet: Chemo, Semo. (AHN-SELL-MO)

ANTONIO Derived from the Latin Antōnius, an old Roman family name of unknown etymology. "Priceless" and "of inestimable worth" are popular folk definitions of the name. Var: Andón, Antoneo, Antonino, Antonión, Antonius. Dim: Antoñito. Pet: Anto, Antolín, Antón, Nico, Nino, Toni, Tonico, Tonio, Tono, Tony, Toñico, Toñin, Toño, Tuco, Tuncho. (AHN-TŌ-NEE-O)

APOLONIO Derived from the Greek Apollōn (of Apollo). Apollo is the name of the Greek mythological god of music, poetry, prophecy, and medicine. Var: Apalonio, Aplonio, Apolanio, Apolionio, Apollonio, Apoloneo, Apolonís, Apolono, Appalonio, Appoliano, Appolinario, Appollanio, Appollonia, Appolonio. (AH-PO-LOW-NEE-O)

AQUILES Spanish form of Achilles, a cognate of Achilleus, which is of unknown etymology. The name is borne in Greek mythology by a leader and warrior of the Trojan War. He was killed by an arrow that struck his only vulnerable spot, his heel. Var: Aquileo, Aquilo. Short: Quilo. (AH-KEY-LACE)

AQUILINO From the Latin Aquilinus (of Aquila), which is from Aquila, a name directly derived from *aquila* (eagle). Var: Aguijuna. (AH-KEE-LEE-NO)

ARCADIO Derived from the Greek Arkadios (of Arcadia, an ancient pastoral region in Peloponnesus). Var: Alcadio, Alcalio, Alcardio, Alcedio, Arcadie, Arcadro, Arkadi. Short: Cadio. (AHR-CAH-DEE-O)

ARISTEO From the Greek Aristides, a name derived from *aristos* (best). Var: Aresteo, Aristedes, Aristelo, Aristes, Aristides, Aristio, Aristo, Eristeo. (AH-REES-TAY-O)

ARMANDO Spanish cognate of the German Hermann (soldier, warrior), which is from the Old High German Hariman, a compounding of the elements *heri* (army) and *man* (man). Var: Armondo, Armundo, Aromando, Ermando, Harmando. Short: Mando. (AHR-MAHN-DŌ)

ARNO Germanic name derived from the element *arn* (eagle). Var: Arnel. (AHR-NO)

ARNOLDO Spanish cognate of Arnold (powerful as an eagle), a name derived from the Germanic Arnwald, a compounding of the elements *arn* (eagle) and *wald* (power, strength). Var: Armaldo, Arnaldo, Arnuldo, Ornaldo. (AHR-NOL-DŌ)

ARNULFO Of Germanic origin composed from the elements *arn* (eagle) and *wulf* (wolf). Var: Arnulf, Arnulpho, Ernolfo. Short: Nuflo, Nulfo. (ARE-NULL-FO)

ARQUÍMEDES Derived from the Greek Archimedes, a compound name composed of the elements *archi* (chief, first, head) and *mēdesthai* (to ponder, to meditate upon): hence, "to first think about or meditate upon." Var: Achimedes, Arquimedes, Arquímedis. (ARE-KEE-MAY-DEES)

ARSENIO Derived from the Greek Arsenios (male, virile, masculine). Var: Arcenio, Arsanio, Arsemio, Eresenio. (ARE-SAY-NEE-O)

ARTEMIO Derived from the Greek Artemios (of Artemis, the Greek mythological goddess of the moon, hunting, and wild animals). Var: Artemiro, Artenio, Artimeo, Ertimio, Hortemio, Ortemio, Ortimio. (ARE-TAY-MEE-O)

ARTURO Spanish cognate of Arthur, a name of Celtic origin but of unknown meaning. *See* ARTHUR (English Names). Var: Alturo, Artero, Arthuro, Auturo, Orturo. Pet: Pituro, Turi, Turín, Turis. (ARE-TOO-RO)

ASUNCIÓN Derived from the Spanish *asunción* (assumption). The name, bestowed upon both males and females, is used in reference to the Assumption, the taking of the body and soul of the Virgin Mary into heaven after her death. Var: Ascención, Ascenciono, Ascentio, Ascinción, Ascunsión, Asecenciano, Asención, Assensión, Assentión, Assumpción. Short: Acencio, Asencio, Aucencio, Cención, Censión, Sención. Pet: Chencho, Chica. (AH-SOON-SEE-OWN)

ATANASIO Cognate of the Greek Athanasios, which is from the Greek *athanasia* (immortality). Var: Atamasio, Atanacio, Atanaseo, Atanocio, Atanosio, Atansio,

Athanasio, Atonacio, Atonasio. Short: Tanacio, Tenasio. (AH-TAH-NAH-SEE-O)

ATREO Derived from the Greek Atreus, a name of uncertain derivation. The name is borne in Greek mythology by a son of Pelops and Ilippodamia. Atreus was a king of Argos and Mycenae and father of Agamemnon and Menelaus. The tragic fate of the family was the basis for many classical tragedies. (AH-TRAY-O)

AUGUSTINO Derived from the Latin Augustinus, a diminutive form of Augustus, which is from *augustus* (great, venerable, consecrated by the augurs). Var: Agusdín, Agustico, Agustín, Agustino, Agustón, Agutín, Augostino, Augusdín, Augustín. Pet: Asta, Cacho, Chucho, Tin, Tincho, Tino, Tinuch, Tito. (AH-GOOS-TEE-NO)

AUGUSTO Derived from the Latin Augustus, which is derived from *augustus* (great, venerable, consecrated by the augurs). Var: Agusdo, Agusteo, Agusto, Augusdro, Austeo, Aygusta. Pet: Asta, Tino, Tincho, Tito. (AH-GOOS-TŌ)

AURELIO Derived from the Latin Aurēlius, an old Roman family name derived from *aurum* (gold). Var: Anrelio, Anreliono, Arelio, Auraliano, Aurelaino, Aureleo, Aurrelio. (OW-RAY-LEE-O)

AUREO Derived from the Latin Aureus, which is from *aurum* (gold). The name was borne by a 9th-century Muslim denounced for abandoning Islam in favor of Christianity. (OW-RAY-O)

AVELLINO Borrowed from the city of Avellino (place of hazelnut trees). It is derived from *avellanos* (hazelnut trees). Var: Abelino, Avalino, Aveleno, Avelín, Avelino. (AH-BAY-YEE-NO)

BALDOMERO Spanish form of the Germanic Waldemar, a compound name composed of the elements *wald* (ruler, power) and *mari* (famous). *See* VALDEMAR (Scandinavian Names). Var: Baldamar, Baldamero, Baldamiro, Baldemar, Baldemero, Baldimar, Baldimero, Baldomer, Baltimero, Baltomero, Valdamar, Valdamero, Valdemar, Valdemaro, Valdemero, Valdmar. (BALL-DŌ-MAY-RO)

BALTASAR Spanish cognate of Balthasar, a name assigned to one of the Three Wise Men, who brought gifts to the Christ child. Some believe the name to be derived from the Chaldean Beltshazzar (prince of splendor). Others think the name might simply have been an invention with an Eastern sound to it. Var: Baldazar, Baltaras, Baltarsar, Baltassar, Baltazán, Baltazar, Baltesar, Baltezar, Baltosar, Baltozar, Valtazar, Valtesar. Short: Balto. (BALL-TA-SAHR)

BAPTISTA Ecclesiastic Late Latin name derived from *baptista* (a baptist, one who baptizes). The name was traditionally bestowed in honor of John the Baptist, a kinsman and forerunner of Jesus Christ. Var: Baptisto, Battista, Bautista. Pet: Baucha. (BAP-TEE-STA)

BARNABUS Spanish form of Barnebas, a name derived from the Aramaic *barnebhū'āh* (son of exhortation). It is borne in the Bible by an apostle and missionary companion of Paul. Var: Barnaba, Barnabé. (BAR-NAH-BUS)

BARTOLOMÉ Spanish form of Bartholomew, a cognate of the Late Latin Bartholomaeus and the Greek Bartholomaios (hill of Talmai). Talmai is an Aramaic name meaning "hill, mound, furrows." The name is borne in the Bible by one of the Twelve Apostles of Christ. Var: Bartalo, Bartelo, Bartelomeo, Bartholo, Bartilo, Bartolamé, Bartoli, Bartollo, Bartolo, Bartolomeo, Bartolomí, Bartoloneo. Short: Barto, Tola, Toli. (BAR-TŌ-LOW-MAY)

BASILIO Derived from the Greek Basileois (kingly). Var: Bacilio, Bacillio, Bacilo, Basileo, Basillio, Basilo, Bassilleo, Bassillio, Bazilio, Vacilio, Vasilio. Pet: Bacho, Chilo. (BAH-SEE-LEE-O)

BAUDILIO Derived from the Latin Baudelius, a name believed to have its root in the Celtic language with the definition "victory." The name was borne by a 3rd- or 4th-century saint and missionary who helped spread the Christian religion throughout France. Var: Baudelio, Baudilión, Baudillo. (BOUGH-DEE-LEE-O)

BENEDICTO Derived from the Latin Benedictus, which is from *benedictus* (blessed). The name was borne by St. Benedict of Nursii (c. 480–543), an Italian monk and founder of the Benedictine Order at Monte Cassino. Var: Bendito, Benedetto, Benedictae, Benedito, Benito. Pet: Beni, Bento. (BAY-NAY-DEEK-TŌ)

BENJAMÍN From the Hebrew Binyamin, a name derived from *binyāmīn* (son of the right hand). The name is borne in the Bible by the youngest of Jacob's twelve sons, the progenitor of the tribe of Benjamin. Var: Beniamín, Benjamé, Benjammén, Benjemín, Venjamín. Pet: Benja, Chelín, Min, Mincho, Mino. (BEHN-HAH-MEEN)

BERILO Spanish form of Beryl, a name borrowed from that of the pale green gemstone. Beryl is derived from the Greek *bēryllos* (sea-green gem). Var: Barilio. (BAY-REE-LOW)

BERNARDO From the Old High German Berinhard (strong as a bear), a compound name composed from the elements *bern* (bear) and *hard* (hearty, strong, brave). The name was borne by St. Bernard of Clairvaux (1090?–1153), a French monk who founded sixty-eight

Cistercian monasteries and led the Knights of the Temple against the Turks. Var: Benardo, Bernandino, Bernardus, Venardo, Vernardino, Vernardo. Pet: Beño, Berno, Dino, Nado, Nardo. (BARE-NAR-DŌ)

BERTO Short form of any of the names ending in this element. Var: Beto. (BARE-TŌ)

BLASIO Spanish cognate of the French Blaise, a name of uncertain etymology. Some believe it is derived from the Latin Blaesus, which is from *blaesus* (deformed, stuttering). The name was borne by a 4th-century martyr and patron saint of wool workers. Var: Blas, Blasius, Blassio. (BLAH-SEE-O)

BONAVENTURA A borrowing from the Italian, Bonaventura is a compounding of the elements *bona* (good, fair) and *ventura* (luck, fortune): hence, "good luck, fair fortune." Var: Bonavendura, Bonavento, Bonoventura. Short: Ventura. (BO-NAH-BANE-TOOR-AH)

BONIFACIO Derived from the Late Latin Bonifatius (of good fate, auspicious), a compounding of the elements *bonum* (good) and *fatum* (fate). Var: Bonafatio, Bonaficio, Bonefacio, Bonifazio, Bonificio, Bonofacio. (BO-NEE-FAH-SEE-O)

CALIXTO Masculine Spanish form of the Greek Kallistō (she that is most beautiful), a name derived from the element *kallos* (beauty, beautiful): hence, "handsome, he that is most handsome." Var: Calesto, Calexto, Calistaro, Calisto, Callixto. Short: Cali. (CAH-LEEKS-TŌ)

CALVINO Spanish form of Calvin, a name derived from the French surname Cauvin, a derivative of the Latin *calvinus* (little bald one), which has its root in *calvus* (bald). The name was borne by Jean Calvin (1509–64), a French Protestant reformer and promoter of the Calvinist doctrine. (CALL-BEE-NO)

CAMILO A masculine Spanish form of the Latin Camilla, a name derived from *camilla* (virgin of unblemished character, pure, chaste). The name was borne by the founder of the Camellian Order of the Fathers of Good Death. Camilo José Cela of Spain was the 1989 Nobel Prize winner for literature. Var: Camillo. Short: Milo. Dim: Camito. Pet: Milico. (CAH-MEE-LOW)

CANDELARIO Derived from the Spanish *candelario* (candle, wax candle). The name is in reference to the Catholic feast day during which many candles are lit in commemoration of the Holy Family's visit to the temple. Var: Andelario, Candalario, Candelareo, Candeleno, Candelerio, Candilario, Candolario, Escandelario. Short: Canda, Candeda, Candelas. (CAHN-DAY-LAH-REE-O)

CARLOS Spanish cognate of Charles, which is from the Germanic *karl* (full-grown, a man). The name was borne by four kings of Spain. Short: Lito, Litos. Dim: Carlito, Carlitos. Pet: Carlucho. (CAR-LOHS)

CASIMIRO Spanish cognate of the Polish Kazimierz (famous destroyer), a compounding of the elements *kazić* (to destroy, to corrupt) and *meri* (great, famous). Var: Casemiera, Casemiro, Casimaro, Casimeiro, Casimere, Casimero, Casimiera, Casimir. Pet: Cachi, Cashi. (CAH-SEE-MEE-RO)

CAYETANO Derived from the Latin Gaetano (of Gaeta), a name derived from the name of the city of Gaeta, which was originally called Caieta. The name is of uncertain derivation. Var: Ayetano, Cagetano, Caietano, Caitano, Caiteno, Cajatano, Cajetano, Cajetón, Cajitano, Gaetán, Gaietano, Gayetano, Quetano. Short: Tano. (KYE-YEA-TAH-NO)

CECILIO From the Latin Caecilius, an old Roman family name derived from *caecus* (blind, dim-sighted). The name was borne by a 3rd-century saint who was a friend and companion of St. Cyprian. Var: Caecilio, Cecilo, Cesilio, Cicilio. Short: Celio, Cilio. (SAY-SEE-LEE-O)

CELESTINO Derived from the Latin Caelius (belonging to heaven), an old Roman family name derived from *caelum* (heaven). The name was borne by a famous antagonist of the doctrine that man is born without original sin. Var: Alestino, Calestino, Celestín, Selestino, Selistino. (SAY-LAY-STEE-NO)

CELIO Masculine form of Celia, a name derived from the Latin Caelius (belonging to heaven), an old Roman family name derived from *caelum* (heaven). Pet: Celín, Chelo, Lino. (SAY-LEO)

CÉSAR Derived from the Latin Caesar, a name of uncertain etymology. Some believe Caesar to be derived from *caedo* (to cut); others think it to be from *caesius* (blue-gray). Another suggestion is that it is derived from *caesaries* (hairy, with abundant hair). *See* CESARE (Italian Names). Var: Ceasario, Cesareo, Cesares, Cesaro, Cézar, Cezario, Ceserio, Cizario, Sésar, Sesareo, Sesario, Sezaro. Dim: Sarito. Pet: Chayo, Checha. (SAY-SAHR)

CIPRIANO Derived from the Latin Cypriānus (a Cyprian), a name that originally referred to a person from the island of Cyprus. Var: Cipiano, Ciprano, Ciprián, Cypriano, Siprián, Sipriano. Short: Cip, Sipio. Pet: Chano, Cippie. (SEE-PREE-AH-NO)

Cirilo Spanish form of Cyril, a cognate of the Late Latin Cyrillus, which is from the Greek Kyrillos (lordly), a derivative of *kyrios* (a lord). Var: Cerilo, Cirileo, Cyrillo, Sirilio. Pet: Lilo. (SEE-REE-LO)

Claudio From the Latin Claudius, an old Roman family name derived from *claudus* (lame). The name is listed forty-four times in the *Dictionary of Saints*. Var: Cladio, Claudicio, Clavio, Glaudio. Dim: Claudino. Pet: Cloyo. (KLAU-DEE-O)

Cleandro Of Greek origin derived from the elements *kleo* (fame, glory) and *andros* (man): hence, "man of glory." Var: Cleanto. (CLAY-AHN-DRO)

Clemente Derived from the Late Latin Clēmens, which is from *clemens* (mild, gentle, merciful). The name is found forty-five times in the *Dictionary of Saints* and was borne by six popes. Var: Clemen, Clementio, Clemento, Clemons, Climente. Short: Cleme, Te. Dim: Clementino. Pet: Tente. (CLAY-MEN-TAY)

Conrado Spanish cognate of the German Konrad (wise counsel), a name derived from the Old High German Kuonrat, which is composed of the elements *kuon* (bold, wise) and *rat* (counsel). Var: Conradio, Conrod, Conrodo, Conrrado. (CONE-RAH-DŌ)

Cornelio Derived from the Latin Cornelius, an old Roman family name of uncertain etymology. Some believe it is derived from *cornu* (horn). Var: Cornello, Cornilio. Short: Nelo. (COR-NAY-LEE-O)

Crisanto Derived from the Greek *chrysanthemon* (golden flower). The name was borne by eight saints, one of which was buried alive for his work in helping to spread Christianity. Var: Cresanto, Crisento, Crizanto, Crysanto. (KREE-SAHN-TŌ)

Crisóforo Spanish form of Christopher (bearing Christ), a name derived from the Greek Christophoros, which is composed of the elements *Christos* (Christ) and *pherein* (to bear). Var: Cresáforo, Crisófero. (KREE-SO-FOR-RO)

Cristián Spanish form of Christian, a name derived from the Latin *christiānus*, which is from the Greek *christianos* (a Christian, a follower of Christ). Var: Christino, Cristiano, Cristino. (KREES-TEE-AHN)

Cristo Derived from the Greek *christos* (the anointed), which is from *chriein* (to anoint). Christos is the name given to Jesus of Nazareth (c. 4 B.C.–c. A.D. 29), regarded by Christians to be the fulfillment of the Messianic prophecy in the biblical Old Testament and the founder of the Christian religion. Var: Christos, Cristón. (KREES-TŌ)

Cristóbal Spanish variant of Crisóforo, which is a cognate of Christopher (bearing Christ). *See* CRISÓFORO. Var: Christóbal, Christóval, Cristóval. Short: Chris, Cris, Tobal. Dim: Tobalito. (KREES-TŌ-BALL)

Cruz Derived from the Spanish *cruz* (cross, crucifix), which is from the Latin *crux*. The cross, a Roman instrument of torture, is symbolic of Christ, who was nailed to a cross and left to die. (KRUCE)

Damario Masculine Spanish form of the Greek Damaris, a name derived from *damān* (to tame). Var: Damaro. (DAH-MAH-REE-O)

Dámaso From the Greek Damasus, a name believed to be derived from *damān* (to tame). The name was borne by a 4th-century pope. Var: Damacio, Damas, Damasiano, Dámazo, Damisio, Demasio, Domasio, Dómaso. (DAH-MAH-SO)

Damián Derived from the Greek Damianos, an ancient name believed to be derived from *damān* (to tame): hence, "tame, gentle." Var: Damiano. (DAH-MEE-AHN)

Daniel Hebrew name derived from *dāni'ēl* (God is my judge). The name is borne in the Bible by a Hebrew prophet whose faith kept him alive in a den of lions. Var: Danialo, Danilo, Donelo. Short: Dani, Nelo, Nilo. (DAHN-YELL)

Darío From the Greek Dareios, an old name of uncertain derivation. Some believe it to be derived from Darayavahush, the name of an ancient Persian king. Var: Daréo. Short: Darí. Pet: Dayo. (DAHR-REE-O)

David Hebrew name derived from *dāwīd* (beloved). It is borne in the Bible by the second and greatest of the Israelite kings, known for slaughtering the giant Goliath with his slingshot when but a lad. Var: Dabid. (DAH-BEED)

Decio Derived from the Latin *decius* (tenth). (DAY-SEE-O)

Delgadino Derived from the Spanish *delgado* (slim, slender). (DELL-GAH-DEE-NO)

Demetrio Derived from the Greek Demetrios (of Demeter). Demeter is an ancient name of unknown etymology borne by the Greek mythological goddess of agriculture and fertility. The name is listed in the *Dictionary of Saints* fifty-three times. Var: Demeterio, Demetre, Demetreo, Dimitreo, Dimitrio. (DAY-MAY-TREE-O)

Democles Derived from the Greek Damoklēs (glory of the people), a compound name composed of the elements *dēmos* (people, population) and *kleos* (fame, glory). The name was borne by a courtier of ancient

Syracuse. He was given a lesson on the perils of being a king when he was seated at a banquet with a sword suspended by a single hair above his head. It is from this story that the expression "the sword of Damocles" came. Var: Damaclo. (DAY-MO-CLAYS)

DIEGO A pet form of Jaime, the Spanish cognate of James, Diego is also popularly bestowed as an independent given name. *See* JAIME. (DEE-Ā-GO)

DIONISIO Derived from the Greek Dionysios (of Dionysos). Dionysos, the name of the Greek mythological god of wine and revelry, is of unknown etymology. Var: Deonysio, Dionisis. Pet: Chonicho, Nicho. (DEE-O-NEE-SEE-O)

DOMINGO Spanish cognate of Dominic (belonging to the Lord), a derivative of the Latin Dominicus, which is from *dominus* (a lord, a master). The name was borne by St. Dominic (1170–1221), a Spanish priest and founder of the Dominican Order. Var: Domenico, Dominego, Dominigue. Pet: Chomín, Chumín, Mingo. (DŌ-MEEN-GO)

DONACIANO Spanish form of Donatus, a name derived from the Latin *donatus* (given), the past participle of *donare* (to give, to donate). The name was borne by a 4th-century bishop of Casae Nigrae who founded a North African Christian sect which held rigorous views concerning purity and sanctity. Var: Donacio, Donatiano, Donotiano. Pet: Chano. (DŌ-NAH-SEE-AH-NO)

DONALDO Spanish form of Donald, an English cognate of the Gaelic Domhnall (world ruler). *See* DONALD (English Names). (DŌ-NAHL-DŌ)

EBERARDO Spanish form of the French Evrard (strong as a wild boar). *See* EVRARD (French Names). Var: Averando, Eberedo, Evelardo, Everado, Everando, Everardo. Pet: Lalo. (Ā-BAY-RAHR-DŌ)

EDMUNDO Spanish form of Edmund (wealthy protection), a name derived from the Old English Ēadmund, which is a compounding of the elements *ēad* (prosperity, riches, fortune) and *mund* (hand, protection). Var: Admundo. Short: Mundo. (AID-MOON-DŌ)

EDUARDO Spanish cognate of Edward (wealthy protector), a name derived from the Old English Eadweard, which is a compounding of the elements *ēad* (prosperity, riches, fortune) and *weard* (guardian, protector).Var: Eduarelo, Edrardo, Eudardo. Short: Duardo. Pet: Guayo. (Ā-DWAHR-DŌ)

EFRAÍN Spanish form of Ephraim, a name derived from the Hebrew *ephrayim* (very fruitful). The name is borne in the Bible by the second son of Joseph by Asenath. He is the traditional ancestor of the tribe of Ephraim. Var: Efraém, Efraén, Efraine, Efrén, Ephraín, Ifraín. Short: Efra. (Ā-FRAH-EEN)

ELEÁZAR Spanish form of Lazarus, a derivative of the Ecclesiastic Greek Lazaros, which is from the Hebrew *el'āzār* (God has helped). The name is borne in the Bible by the brother of Mary and Martha. He was raised from the dead by Jesus. Var: Aliásar, Elaízar, Elazar, Eleásar, Eleázor, Eleózar, Elízar. (Ā-LEE-AH-ZAR)

ELÍAS Variant of Elijah, a name derived from the Hebrew Eliyahu, which is from *'ēlīyāhū* (Jehovah is God). Var: Eliaz. Pet: Lincha. (Ā-LEE-AHS)

ELISEO Spanish cognate of Elisha, a Hebrew name derived from *elīshā'* (God is salvation). The name is borne in the Bible by a prophet appointed by God to be Elijah's successor. Var: Elesio, Elisaeo, Elisio, Elizeo. Pet: Cheo, Cheyo, Licha. (Ā-LEE-SAY-O)

EMILIO Derived from the Latin Aemilius, an old Roman family name probably derived from *aemulus* (rival, trying to equal or excel, emulating). There are some who think Emilio is of Germanic origin and derive it from the element *amal* (work). Var: Aemilio, Emelio, Emielo, Emileo, Emiliano, Hemilio, Imelio. Short: Melo, Milo. Pet: Llillo, Miyo. (Ā-MEE-LEE-O)

ENRIQUE Popular Spanish form of Henry, a cognate of the German Heinrich (ruler of an enclosure, home ruler). *See* HEINRICH (German Names). Var: Anrique, Enrigque, Enrigue, Enriques, Enrrique, Henrico, Henriko, Inriques. Pet: Kiko, Quique. (ENN-REE-KAY)

EPIFANIO Derived from the Ecclesiastic Late Latin *epiphania*, which is from the Greek *epiphaneia* (appearance, manifestation). The name is indicative of the Epiphany, a Christian festival that commemorates three events: the visit of the Magi, the baptism of Jesus, and Jesus' first public miracle, which took place at Cana. Var: Epefanio, Epfanio, Ephifanio, Epifán, Epifaneo, Epiphanio. Short: Pifano. (Ā-PEE-FAH-NEE-O)

ERASMO From the Greek Erasmios (lovely), a name derived from the verb *eran* (to love). Var: Erasmun, Erazmo, Eresmo, Erusmo, Irasmo. (Ā-RAHS-MO)

ERASTO Derived from the Greek Erastos (beloved), which is from the verb *eran* (to love). Var: Herasto. (Ā-RAHS-TŌ)

ERNESTO Spanish form of the German Ernst, a name derived from the Old High German Ernust and Ernost (earnest, resolute). Var: Arnesto, Ernestor, Erneterio. Pet: Ernio, Necho. (AIR-NAY-STO)

ESTANISLAO Spanish form of Stanislaus, a Slavonic name derived from the elements *stan* (government) and *slav* (glory): hence, "glorious government." Var: Adislado, Adislao, Adisteo, Estaneslado, Estanilao, Estanislado, Estanislano, Estanistav, Taneslado, Tanislado. Short: Lao. Pet: Lalo, Chelago. (Ā-STAHN-EES-LAH-O)

ESTEBAN Spanish cognate of Stephen, which is from the Latin Stephanus, a derivative of the Greek Stephanos, which has its root in *stephanos* (a crown, a garland, that which adorns the head). The name is borne in the Bible by St. Stephen, the first Christian martyr, who was one of the seven chosen to assist the Twelve Apostles. Var: Astevan, Estaván, Esteben, Estefan, Estefon, Estiban, Estifan, Estovan, Istevan. Short: Teb. (Ā-STAY-BAHN)

ESTUARDO Spanish cognate of Stuart (a steward, a keeper of the animal enclosure). *See* STUART (English Names). (Ā-STOO-ARE-DŌ)

EUGENIO Spanish form of Eugene, a cognate of the Greek Eugenios, which is derived from *eugenēs* (well-born, noble). The name, which was borne by four popes, is listed fifty-four times in the *Dictionary of Saints*. Var: Ahenio, Eginio, Ejinio, Euginio, Eujenio, Eujinio, Ugenio. Short: Genio, Geño. Pet: Cheno. (Ā-OO-HAY-NEE-O)

EURICO Spanish cognate of Erik, a name derived from the Old Norse Eirikr (eternal ruler), a compounding of the elements *ei* (ever, always) and *rīkr* (ruler, king). However, there are some who believe the name comes to the Old Norse via the Germanic *ehre* (honor) and *rīk* (king): hence, "honorable king." The name Euric was borne by the Visigothic leader who initiated the conquest of Spain in the 5th century. Var: Eurique. (Ā-OO-REE-KO)

EUSEBIO Derived from Eusebios, a Late Greek name composed of the elements *eu* (well, good) and *sebein* (to worship, to venerate): hence, "pious, devout." Var: Eucebio, Euesebio, Eusabio, Eusevio, Eusibio, Euzebio, Usebio, Usibio. Pet: Chebo, Shebo. (Ā-OO-SAY-BEE-O)

EVARISTO Of Greek origin, Evaristo is derived from the element *eu* (well, good). The name was borne by the fourth pope following St. Peter. Var: Averisto, Ebaristo, Evarisdo, Everisto. (Ā-BAH-REE-STO)

EZEQUÍAS Spanish cognate of Hezekiah, a Hebrew name derived from *ḥizqīyāh* (God strengthens). The name is borne in the Bible by a king of Judah who ruled in the time of Isaiah. He was noted for his leadership abilities. Var: Esequíez, Ezequíos. Pet: Checo. (Ā-ZAY-KEE-AHS)

EZEQUIEL Spanish form of Ezekiel, which is derived from the Greek Iezekiēl, a name derived from the Hebrew *yeḥezq'ēl* (God strengthens). The name is borne in the Bible by a 6th-century B.C. Hebrew prophet. His prophecies are found in the Old Testament book of Ezekiel. Var: Esekial, Esequiel, Esequio, Esiquio, Esquio, Eusequio, Exiquio, Ezcquio, Ezechiel, Ezechio, Ezekiel, Ezekio, Ezequio, Eziekel, Eziqulo, Hesiqio, Hesiquio, Hexiquio, Isiquiel, Izechiel. Short: Quiel, Sequiel, Ziek. Pet: Chaco, Checo, Chequil, Chequelo. (Ā-ZAY-KEE-ELL)

FABIÁN From the Latin Fabianus (of Fabius), which is derived from the old Roman family name Fabius, a derivative of *faba* (a bean). Var: Fabiano, Fabién, Fabio, Favián. (FAH-BEE-AHN)

FAUSTINO Derived from the Latin Faustus (bringer of good luck), which is from *fauste* (propitious, lucky, fortunate). Var: Fastino, Faustano, Fausteno, Faustín, Fausto, Faustulo, Fauztino, Festo. (FOUSE-TEE-NO)

FEDERICO Spanish form of Frederick, a name derived from the German Friedrich (ruler of peace). *See* FRIEDRICH (German Names). Var: Federigo, Federío, Fredericlo, Fredico, Fredrico, Friderico. Short: Fede, Lico, Rico. (FAY-DAY-REE-KO)

FELIPO Spanish form of the Latin Philippus, a derivative of the Greek Philippos (lover of horses), which is composed of the elements *philos* (loving) and *hippos* (horse). The name, borne by five Spanish kings, is borne by Spanish Prime Minister Felipe González Márquez, and by Prince Felipe (b. 1968), the youngest child of King Juan Carlos. Var: Felip, Felipe, Felippe, Felippo, Filip, Filipe, Filipo, Filippe, Phillippo. Short: Felo, Lipe, Lipo. Pet: Felichi. (FAY-LEE-PO)

FÉLIX A borrowing from the Latin, Félix is directly derived from *felix* (lucky, happy). Var: Félex, Felixiano, Felizano, Feliziano. (FAY-LEEKS)

FERDINANDO Spanish name of uncertain origin and meaning. It is thought to be of Germanic origin composed from the elements *frithu* (peace), *fardi* (journey), or *ferchvus* (youth, life) and *nanths* (courage), *nanthi* (venture, risk), or *nand* (ready, prepared). Var: Ferando, Ferdenando, Ferdino, Fernandeo. Short: Ferdi, Ferni, Nando, Nano. (FARE-NAHN-DŌ)

FIDEL Derived from the Latin *fidelis* (faithful, trusty). The name is borne by Cuban leader Fidel Castro. He seized power in 1959 following the flight of former president and dictator Fulgencio Batista. Var: Fedelio, Fedil, Fidal, Fidelio, Fidélix. Pet: Fido, Fidolo. (FEE-DELL)

Filadelfo Derived from the Latin Philadelphus (brotherly love). Var: Filadelfio. (FEE-LAH-DEL-FO)

Filemón Spanish cognate of Philemon, which is derived from the Greek *philēmōn* (affectionate). Var: Felemón, Felimón. (FEE-LAY-MOAN)

Filiberto Spanish form of Philibert, a name derived from the Germanic Filaberht (very bright, very famous), which is composed of the elements *fila* (much) and *beraht* (bright, famous). Var: Feliberto, Fileberto. Short: Berto. (FEE-LEE-BARE-TŌ)

Florencio Spanish cognate of Florence, a name derived from the Latin Florentia (a blooming), which is from *florens* (blooming, flourishing, prosperous). Var: Felorencio, Floranzio, Florenso, Florentián, Florentías, Florentino, Florenzio, Florenzo. (FLOR-REN-SEE-O)

Fortunato Derived from the Late Latin Fortūnātus, which is from *fortūnātus* (fortunate, prosperous, lucky). The name is found sixty-nine times in the *Dictionary of Saints*. Var: Fortunado. (FORE-TOO-NAH-DŌ)

Fortuno Derived from the Latin *fortuna* (chance, fate, fortune). Var: Fortunio. Short: Tino, Tuni. (FOR-TOO-NO)

Francisco Popular name derived from the Middle Latin Franciscus (a Frenchman), which is from Francus (a Frank, a freeman), the root of which is the Old French *franc* (free). The name was borne by Francisco Pizarro (1470?–1541), a Spanish explorer and conqueror of Peru. Var: Francesco, Franciscis, Francisko, Fransico, Fransisco, Franzisko. Short: Chisco, Cisco, Frisco. Pet: Chicho, Chilo, Chito, Chuco, Francho, Pacho, Paco, Panchio, Pancho, Pancholo, Panzo, Paquín, Paquito, Quito. (FRAHN-SEES-KO)

Gabriel Hebrew name derived from *gavhrī'ēl* (God is my strength). The name is borne in the Bible by one of the seven archangels of God, the herald of Good News who appeared to Mary to announce her pregnancy and the impending birth of the Christ child. Var: Gabián, Gabiel, Gabirel, Gabreil, Gabrial. Short: Gabe, Riel. Pet: Chela, Gaby, Lelo. (GAH-BREE-ELL)

Galeno Derived from Galenus, a surname believed to be derived from the Greek *galēnē* (calm). The name was borne by Claudius Galenus (c. 130–200), a Greek physician and writer on medicine and philosophy to whom the system of medical practice Galenism is attributed. Var: Galieno, Gallieno. (GAH-LAY-NO)

García Transferred use of the common Spanish surname. It is a very old name of uncertain etymology; some think it might mean "fox." Var: Garcisa. (GAHR-SEE-AH)

Gaspar One of the three names assigned to the biblical Three Wise Men (the Magi), who brought gifts to the Christ child. The names are not found in the Bible and are thought to have been fixed in the 11th century. Of uncertain etymology, Gaspar might have been derived from the Persian *genashber* (treasure master), which is in keeping with his role of the bringer of precious gifts. Var: Caspar, Casparo, Gazpar. (GAHS-PAR)

Gastón A borrowing from the French, Gaston is an evolution of Gascon, a name of uncertain etymology. *See* GASTON (French Names). (GAHS-TONE)

Gedeón Spanish form of Gideon, a Hebrew name derived from *gidh'ōn* (hewer). The name is borne in the Bible by the fifth recorded judge of Israel and a leader in the defeat of the Midianites. (HAY-DAY-OWN)

Gemino Derived from the Latin *gemini* (twins), the name given to the third sign of the zodiac and to a constellation found between Taurus and Cancer. Var: Geminiano. (HAY-MEE-NO)

Génaro Derived from the Latin *Januarius* (the month of Janus). Janus is the name of the Roman mythological god of portals and patron of beginnings and endings. He has two faces, one in the front and one in the back of his head. Var: Énaro, Enereo, Genareo, Génarro, Géniro, Génnaro, Gínaro, Jénaro, Jenerio, Jénero. (HAY-NAH-RO)

Geraldo Derived from the Germanic Gerwald, a compound name composed from the elements *ger* (a spear) and *wald* (rule): hence, "spear ruler, to rule with a spear." Var: Gerado, Herrado, Jeraldo. (HAY-RAHL-DŌ, JER-RAHL-DŌ)

Gerardo Spanish form of Gerard, a name derived from the Old High German Gerhart (spear strength, brave with the spear), which is composed from the elements *ger* (a spear) and *hart* (hearty, brave, strong). Var: Gehardo, Gerrado, Herardo, Jerado, Xerardo. (HAY-RAHR-DŌ, JER-RAHR-DŌ)

Germán Spanish cognate of the German Hermann (soldier, warrior), a name derived from the Old High German Hariman, which is a compounding of the elements *hari* (army) and *man* (man). (HAIR-MAHN)

Gervasio Spanish form of Gervaise, a name of uncertain etymology. Most think it is a derivative of the Old German Gervas, the first element of which is *ger* (a spear) and the second of which is believed to be from the Celtic *vass* (servant): hence, "servant of the spear." Var: Gervacio, Gervasius, Jervaso. (HARE-BAH-SEE-O)

Gilberto Spanish cognate of the French Gilbert, an evolution of the Old French Guillebert, which is derived from the Old High German Gisilberht. The name is composed from the elements *gisil* (pledge) and *beraht* (bright, famous). Var: Gelberto, Geliberto, Gilbero, Gilbirto, Gilverto, Guiberto, Hilberto, Hillberto, Hilverto, Ilberto, Jilberto. Short: Berto, Gil. Pet: Beto, Gillio, Gilito, Xil. (HEEL-BARE-TŌ)

GREGORIO Derived from the Latin Gregorius, a cognate of the Greek Grēgorios (vigilant, a watchman), which is derived from the verb *egeirein* (to awaken). The name was borne by several early saints and many popes. In 1582 Pope Gregory XIII introduced the Gregorian calendar, a corrected form of the Julian calendar which is now used in most countries of the world. Var: Gregerio, Gregorica, Gregrio, Grejori. Short: Gorio, Grega. Dim: Gregorito. Pet: Gollo, Golo, Goyito, Goyo. (GRAY-GO-REE-O)

GUIDO Derived from *guida* (guide, a leader). (GHEE-DŌ)

GUILLERMO One of the most popular Spanish names, Guillermo is a cognate of William (resolute protector), a name derived from the Old Norman French Willaume, which is from the Old High German Willehelm, a compounding of the elements *willeo* (will, determination) and *helm* (helmet, protection). Var: Giermo, Gigermo, Gijermo, Gillermo, Gillirmo, Giyermo, Guermillo, Guiermo, Guilermón, Guillelmo, Guillermino, Guirmo, Gullermo, Quillermo. Short: Guille, Guillo, Llermo. Pet: Memo. (GHEE-YARE-MO)

HÉCTOR Derived from the Latin Hector (steadfast), a cognate of the Greek Hektōr (holding fast), which is from *echein* (to hold, to have). Var: Éctor, Hécktor. Pet: Éto, Heco, Tito. (AYK-TOR)

HELIO Derived from the Greek *hēlios* (the sun). Var: Elio. (AY-LEE-O)

HERÁCLIO Derived from the Greek Hērakleēs, a compound name composed from Hēra (the name of the mythological queen of the gods) and *kleos* (glory): hence, "glory of Hera, divine glory." The name is borne in Greek and Roman mythology by the son of Zeus and Alemene, renowned for his amazing strength. Var: Erácleo, Eraclio, Ereclio, Herclio, Heroclio. (AIR-A-KLEE-O)

HERBERTO Spanish cognate of Herbert, a name derived from the Old English Herebeorht (bright army), which is composed from the elements *here* (army) and *beorht* (bright, fair, white). Var: Eliberto, Ereberto, Eriberto, Eriverto, Heriberio, Heriberto. Short: Berto, Heri. (AIR-BARE-TŌ)

HERCULANO Derived from Hercules, the Latin form of the Greek Hērakleēs (divine glory, glory of Hera). *See* HERÁCLIO. Var: Arculano, Erculano, Herculeno. (AIR-KOO-LAH-NO)

HERMÁN From the German Hermann (soldier, warrior), a name derived from the elements *heri* (army) and *man* (man). Var: Arminio, Herminio, Hermino. Pet: Hermio. (AIR-MAHN)

HILARIO Derived from the Latin Hilarius, which is from *hilaris* (cheerful, glad). The name was borne by a 4th-century saint who fought against Arianism. Var: Helario, Hilarión, Hilarrio, Hilorio, Ilario, Illario, Ilaro. Pet: Lalo. (EE-LAH-REE-O)

HOMERO From the Greek Homeros, a name derived from *homēros* (a pledge, a hostage; blind). The name was borne by the 9th-century B.C. Greek epic poet who wrote the *Odyssey*. Var: Omero. (O-MAY-RO)

HORATIO Derived from the Latin Horatius, an old Roman family name of uncertain derivation. Some think it is derived from the Latin *hora* (hour, time, period). Var: Horacio, Oracio, Orasio. Pet: Lacho, Racho. (O-RAH-SEE-O)

IGNACIO From the Latin Ignatius, a derivative of Egnatius, an old Roman family name of uncertain etymology. Some believe it to be of Etruscan origin. Others derive it from the Latin *ignis* (fire). The name was borne by several saints, including St. Ignatius Loyola (1491–1556), a Spanish priest and founder of the Society of Jesus—the Jesuits. Var: Egnacio, Hignacio, Ignacius, Ignasio, Ignatio, Ignazio, Ignocio, Ingnacio, Ygnasio, Ygnocio. Short: Nas. Pet: Nacho. (EEG-NAH-SEE-O)

INDALECIO Popular name derived from the Greek Indaletios (of or like a teacher). Var: Andalecio, Andalusio, Andelesio, Andolesio, Endalesio, Endelesio, Indalesio, Indalisio, Indelesio, Yndalecio, Yndalesio. Pet: Lecho. (EEN-DAH-LAY-SEE-O)

INOCENCIO Spanish cognate of Innocent, a name derived from the Latin *innocens* (innocent). The name was borne by thirteen popes and is found in the *Dictionary of Saints* twenty-seven times. It was originally bestowed in reference to the slaughter of innocent male children by order of Herod in his quest to kill the Christ child. Var: Enesenico, Enicencio, Enocencio, Incencio, Incención, Innocencio, Innocención, Innocensio, Innocentio, Ynocencio, Ynocensio, Ynocente. Short: Sencio. Pet: Chencho, Chente. (EE-NO-SANE-SEE-O)

ISAAC Derived from the Hebrew Yitzchak (he will laugh), which is from *yitshāq* (laughter). The name is borne in the Bible by one of the three patriarchs, the son of Abraham and Sarah, and father of Esau and Jacob. Var: Isaak, Isaco, Izaac, Ysaac, Ysaach, Yssac. Pet: Caco. (EE-SOCK)

ISANDRO Derived from the Greek Lysandros (freer of mankind, liberator), a name composed from the elements *lysis* (freeing, loosening) and *andros* (man). (EE-SAHN-DRO)

ISIDORO Popular name derived from the Greek Isidoros (gift of Isis, divine gift), a compounding of Isis, the name of the Egyptian goddess of fertility, and *dōron* (gift). The name was borne by an 11th-century saint and patron of Madrid. Var: Ecedro, Ecidro, Esidor, Esidore, Esidoro, Esidro, Hisidro, Icidro, Iscidro, Isedro, Isidro, Isodoro, Izidro, Ysidor, Ysidoro, Ysidro. Short: Cedro, Chidro, Cidro, Sidro. Pet: Ishico. (EE-SEE-DOR-O)

ISMAEL Derived from the Hebrew *yishmā'ē'l* (God hears). The name is borne in the Bible by the son of Abraham and his concubine Hagar. Ismael is the patriarch of the Arabs. Var: Esmael, Isamel, Ishmael, Ismeal, Ysmael. Dim: Melito. (EES-MAH-ELL).

ISRAEL Derived from the Hebrew *yisrā'ēl* (contender with God). In the Bible the name was bestowed upon Jacob after wrestling with the archangel Michael. Var: Isareal, Israil, Isreal, Ysrael. Short: Isra, Israh. (EES-RAH-ELL)

JACIÁN Spanish form of Jason, a cognate of the Greek Iāson, which is derived from *iāson* (healer). The name is borne in Greek mythology by a prince who led the Argonauts in the quest to find the Golden Fleece. (HAH-SEE-AHN)

JACINTO Derived from the Greek Hyakinthos (hyacinth). The name is borne in Greek mythology by a youth who was loved, yet accidentally slain, by Apollo. (HAH-SEEN-TŌ)

JAIME Spanish cognate of James, a name derived from the Ecclesiastic Late Latin Iacomus, an evolution of Iacobus, which is derived from the Greek Iakōbos. Iakōbos is from the Hebrew Yaakov, a derivative of *ya'aqob* (seizing by the heel, supplanting). Var: Haime, Xaime. Dim: Jaimito, Mito. Pet: Chago, Diego. (HI-MAY)

JAVIER Derived from the surname Xavier, which is from the place-name Xavier in Navarre. The name, which is believed to be derived from the Basque Etcheberria (the new house), was originally bestowed in honor of St. Francis Xavier (1506–52), a Spanish missionary to Japan and the East Indies and the patron saint of missionaries in foreign lands. Var: Javeir, Jevier, Xabier, Xaverio, Zavier. (HAH-BEE-AIR)

JEREMÍAS Ecclesiastic Late Latin cognate of the Ecclesiastic Greek Hieremias, which is from the Hebrew Yirmeyahu, a name derived from *yirmeyāh* (the Lord loosens, God will uplift). The name is borne in the Bible by a 6th- or 7th-century B.C. Hebrew prophet whose story and prophecies are recorded in the Old Testament book of Jeremiah. Var: Jeremío. (HAY-RAY-MEE-AHS)

JERÓNIMO Derived from the Greek Hieronymos (holy name), a compounding of the elements *hieros* (holy) and *onyma* (name). The name was borne by St. Jerome (340–420), born Eusebius Hieronymus Sophronius in Pannonia, an ancient Roman province in central Europe. A monk and church scholar, he was the author of the Vulgate (the translation of the Bible into Latin) and is regarded as one of the doctors of the church. Var: Gerómino, Gerómnimo, Gerónemo, Gerónimo, Herónimo, Herónomo, Hierónymo, Jeránimo, Jerímino, Jerónemo, Jerónino, Jirónimo, Xerónimo. Short: Xerón. Pet: Chombo. (HAY-RO-NEE-MO)

JESÚS Derived from the Ecclesiastic Late Latin Iesus, which is from the Ecclesiastic Greek Iēsous, a name derived from the Hebrew *yēshū'a*, a contraction of *yehōshū'a* (help of Jehovah, God is salvation). The name, an equivalent of Joshua, is bestowed in honor of Jesus Christ (c. 4 B.C.–c. A.D. 29), the founder of the Christian religion and son of God and the Virgin Mary, regarded by Christians to be the promised Messiah. Unlike most Christians, who decline to use the name Jesus out of respect, Christians in the Spanish-speaking world commonly bestow it to bring the bearer under the special protection of the son of God. Var: Hesús, Jechú, Jessús, Jesú, Jesuso, Jezús. Pet: Chuchín, Chuchita, Chucho, Chus, Chusita. (HAY-SOOS).

JOAQUÍN Derived from the Hebrew Jehoiakim, which is from Yehoyakim (God will establish, God gives strength). In medieval Christian tradition, the name was assigned to the father of the Virgin Mary, as Anne was assigned to her mother. Var: Joachín, Joachino, Joakín, Jocquín, Juaquín, Juaquino, Quaquín, Yoaquín. Short: Juacho, Quin. Pet: Chachín, Quincho, Quino. (HWA-KEEN)

JORGE Spanish cognate of George, which is from the Greek Geōrgios, a derivative of *geōrgos* (earthworker, farmer). Var: Jorje, Xorge. Pet: Coque. (HOR-HAY)

JOSÉ Spanish form of Joseph, an Ecclesiastic Late Latin form of the Greek Iōsēph, which is from the Hebrew Yosef, a derivative of *yōsēf* (may he add, God shall add). The name is borne in the Bible by a favorite son of Jacob and Rachel, by the husband of the Virgin Mary, and by Joseph of Arimathea, a rich Jew and secret follower of Jesus who helped take Jesus' body from the cross to prepare it for burial. Pet: Pepe, Pepito. (HO-SAY)

JUAN Highly popular Spanish cognate of John (God is gracious). The name is ultimately derived from the Hebrew Yehanan, a short form of Yehohanan, which is from *yehōhānān* (Yahweh is gracious). The name, borne in the Bible by a kinsman and forerunner of Jesus, John the Baptist, is borne by Spanish King Juan Carlos (b. 1938). Var: Juann. Dim: Juancito, Juanito. Pet: Chan, Chano, Juancho, Yoni. (HWAHN)

JULIO Spanish form of Julius, an old Roman family name thought to be derived from Iulus (the first down on the chin, downy-bearded). Because a person just beginning to develop facial hair is young, "youth" became an accepted definition. The name is listed 198 times in the *Dictionary of Saints* and is recently borne by popular singer Julio Iglesias (b. 1943). Var: Gulianno, Juelio, Julián, Juliano, Yulius. Short: Ulio. Dim: Julito. (HOO-LEE-O)

JUSTINO Derived from the Latin Justinus, which is derived from *justus* (just, right, proper). Var: Gustino, Justano, Justeno. Short: Tino. Pet: Tuto. (HOOS-TEE-NO)

LADISLAO Spanish cognate of the Slavonic Vladislav (glorious rule), a compound name composed of the elements *volod* (rule) and *slav* (glory). Var: Ladaslao, Ladeslao, Ladislad, Ladislado, Ladislau, Ladislaus, Ladislo, Ladislos. Short: Ladis. Pet: Lalo. (LAH-DEES-LAH-O)

LÁZARO Spanish form of Lazarus, a cognate of the Greek Lazaros, which is derived from the Hebrew *el'āzār* (God has helped). The name is borne in the Bible by a brother of Martha and Mary of Bethany, miraculously raised from the dead by Christ. Var: Laízar, Laízaro, Lasario, Lásaro, Lassaro, Laszio. Pet: Lacho. (LAH-ZAH-RO)

LEANDRO Derived from the Greek Leander (lion man), a compound name composed from the elements *leōn* (lion) and *andros* (man). Var: Leando, Leandrón, Liandro. (LAY-AHN-DRO)

LEÓN A borrowing from the Latin, León is derived from *leo* (lion). Var: Lionzo. (LAY-OWN)

LEONARDO Derived from the Old High German Lewenhart, a compound name composed from the elements *lewo* (lion) and *hart* (strong, brave, hearty): hence, "strong as a lion, brave as a lion." Var: Leanard, Leanardo, Leinardo, Lenardo, Lionardo. Short: Nardo. Pet: Nado. (LAY-O-NAHR-DŌ)

LEONCIO Derived from the Latin *leo* (lion). Var: Leonicio, Leonso, Leonzo, Lionisio. Pet: Loncho. (LAY-OWN-SEE-O)

LIBERATO Derived from the Latin Liberatus (he who has been liberated), which is directly derived from *liberatus* (set free, released). Var: Liberao, Liberto, Librao. (LEE-BAY-RAH-TŌ)

LISANDRO Derived from the Greek Lysandros (liberator), a compound name composed from the elements *lysis* (freeing, loosening) and *andros* (man). Var: Lesandro. Pet: Chando, Licho. (LEE-SAHN-DRO)

LORENZO Spanish cognate of Laurence, a name derived from the Latin Laurentius (man from Laurentum). Laurentum, the name of a town in Latium, is probably derived from *laurus* (laurel). The name, listed thirty-two times in the *Dictionary of Saints*, was borne by St. Laurence the Deacon, who was martyred in Rome in 258. Ordered to hand over the church's treasures, he brought forth the sick and poor. Var: Larenzo, Lorenjio, Lorenjo, Lorenso, Lorenzio. Pet: Chencho, Lencho. (LOW-REN-ZO)

LUCAS Ecclesiastic Late Latin name thought to be a derivative of Lucius, which is from the root *lux* (light). Alternatively, some believe the name is derived from the Ecclesiastic Greek Loukas, a contraction of Loukanos (man from Lucania). The name is borne in the Bible by one of the four evangelists. A physician, he worked with Paul and authored the Gospel of Luke and the Acts of the Apostles. Var: Luciano, Luciliano, Lucino, Lucio. Pet: Chano, Lucho. (LOO-KAHS)

LUIS Cognate of the French Louis (famous in war), a derivative of the Old French Loeis, which is from the Old High German Hluodowig, a compounding of the elements *hluod* (famous) and *wīg* (war, strife). (LOO-EES)

MACARIO Spanish cognate of the Greek Makarios, a name derived from *makaros* (blessed). The name was borne by seventy-three saints. Var: Macareo, Macarro, Maccario, Mackario, Marcario, Mecario. (MAH-KAH-REE-O)

MALAQUÍAS Spanish form of Malachi, a Hebrew name derived from *mal'ākhī* (my messenger). The name is borne in the Bible by a 5th-century B.C. prophet. His prophecies are found in the Old Testament book of Malachi. Var: Maloquías. (MAH-LAH-KEE-AHS)

MANASÉS Derived from the Hebrew Manasseh, which is from *m'nasseh* (causing to forget). The name is borne in the Bible by the elder son of Joseph and Asenath. He was the progenitor of the tribe of Manasseh. Var: Manasio. (MAH-NAH-SASE)

MANUEL Highly popular name derived from the Greek Emmanouēl, which is from the Hebrew *'immānūēl* (God is with us). In the Bible, Emmanuel is the name of the promised Messiah. Var: Emanuel, Emanuelo, Emmanuel, Mannuel, Manuelo. Pet: Manny, Mano, Manolo, Nelo. (MAHN-WELL)

MARCOS Derived from the Latin Marcus, a name of uncertain derivation. Most believe it has its root in Mars, the name of the Roman mythological god of war. Others, however, think it might be from *mas* (manly) or from the Greek *malakoz* (soft, tender). The name is borne in the Bible by one of the four evangelists, the author of the second Gospel, Mark. Var: Marcano, Marco, Marko. Dim: Marcolino. (MAR-KOZE)

MARTÍN From the Latin Martinus (war-like), a derivative of Mars, the name of the Roman mythological god of war. The name was borne by many saints, including St. Martin I (d. 655), a pope who was martyred under the Byzantine emperor Constans II. Var: Martino. Short: Marto, Tin, Tino. (MAR-TEEN)

MATEO Spanish form of Matthew, a derivative of the Ecclesiastic Late Latin Matthaeus and the Ecclesiastic Greek Matthaios and Matthias, contractions of Mattathias. The name has its root in the Hebrew Matityah, which is derived from *mattīthyāh* (gift of God). The name is borne in the Bible by one of the four evangelists, the author of the first Gospel, Matthew. Var: Matejo, Matheo, Matteo, Mattheo. Short: Teo. Pet: Matty. (MAH-TAY-O)

MATÍAS Spanish cognate of the Greek Matthias (gift of God). *See* MATEO. The name is borne in the Bible by the one chosen by lot to replace Judas as one of the Twelve Apostles. Var: Mathías, Mathios, Matíos, Mattáes, Mattías. (MAH-TEE-AHS)

MAURICIO Derived from the Latin Mauritius (Moorish), a derivative of Maurus (a Moor). The Moors were a Muslim people of mixed Arab and Berber descent; thus the name came to mean "dark" or "swarthy" in reference to their coloring. Var: Maricio, Maurecio, Maurisio, Mauritio, Maurizio. Pet: Richo. (MAU-REE-SEE-O)

MAXIMIANO Latin name meaning "son of Maximus." Maximus is directly derived from the vocabulary word meaning "greatest." Var: Masimiano, Maxsimiano, Miximino. (MAHKS-EE-MEE-AH-NO)

MAXIMILIANO Spanish form of Maximilian, a blending of the Latin names Maximus and Aemiliānus used by Emperor Friedrich III, who bestowed it upon his first-born son, Maximilian I (1459–1519), in honor of two famous Roman generals. Maximus is derived from the Latin *maximus* (greatest), but the etymology of Aemiliānus is uncertain. Some believe it to be from the Latin *aemulus* (emulating, trying to equal or excel, rival). Var: Mascimilián, Mascimiliano, Miximilianus, Maximillano. Pet: Chilano, Mancho. (MAHKS-EE-MEE-LEE-AH-NO)

MÁXIMO From the Latin Maximus, a name directly derived from the vocabulary word meaning "greatest." Var: Máscimo, Másimio, Máxcimo, Méssimo. (MAHKS-EE-MO)

MELESIO Derived from the Greek Meletios (careful, attentive). Var: Malecio, Malesio, Melacio, Melecio, Melicio, Melesios, Meletio, Melezio, Meliseo, Milesio. Short: Mesio. (MAY-LAY-SEE-O)

MIGUEL Spanish cognate of Michael, a Hebrew name derived from *mīkhā'ēl* (who is like God?). The name is borne in the Bible by the archangel closest to God, the one responsible for carrying out God's judgments. Considered the leader of the heavenly host, Michael is regarded as the patron of soldiers. Var: Migel, Migueo. Pet: Mico. (MEE-GELL)

MODESTO Derived from the Latin *modestus* (modest, keeping due measure). The name is listed twenty times in the *Dictionary of Saints*. Var: Madesto, Medesto. Pet: Mota. (MO-DASE-TŌ)

MOISÉS Spanish form of Moses, an Ecclesiastic Greek name derived from the Hebrew Moshe, which is from *mōsheh* (drawn out, drawn out of the water) and the Egyptian *mes, mesu* (son, child). The name is borne in the Bible by the leader who brought the Israelites out of bondage in Egypt. He received the Ten Commandments on Mount Sinai and led his people to the borders of Canaan and the Promised Land. Var: Moesés, Moicés, Moisís, Moysés, Moysís, Mozés. Short: Moisá, Mos. Pet: Monchi. (MOY-SASE)

NAPOLEÓN Compound name composed from the Greek elements *neapolis* (new city) and *leōn* (lion): hence, "lion of the new city." Var: Napalión, Napolián, Neapoleón. (NAH-PO-LAY-OWN)

NAZARIO Derived from the Ecclesiastic Late Latin *Nazaraeus*, which is from the Ecclesiastic Greek *Nazaraios*, a word derived from the Hebrew *nāzir* (separate, consecrated). The word refers to a Nazarite, a person who voluntarily submitted to strict religious vows, hence the definition "consecrated to God." Var: Nasareo, Nasario, Nasarrio, Nassario, Nazareo, Nazaro, Nazarro. Short: Nazor. (NAH-ZAH-REE-O)

NÉSTOR Derived from the Greek Nēstor, a direct borrowing from the vocabulary word meaning "the one going or departing." Var: Nester, Nestereo, Nesterio, Nestore, Néstorio. (NASE-TOR)

NICANDRO Derived from the Greek Nikander, a compound name composed from the elements *nikē* (victory) and *andros* (man): hence, "man of victory." The name was borne by a 3rd-century Egyptian physician martyred for caring for the persecuted Christians. Var: Nicandreo. (NEE-KAHN-DRO)

NICOLÁS Spanish form of Nicholas (victory of the people), a name derived from the Greek Nikolaos, which is composed of the elements *nikē* (victory) and *laos* (the people). The name was borne by St. Nicholas, a 4th-century bishop of Myra, who is regarded as the patron saint of Greece, Russia, children, sailors, and wolves. Var: Nicalous, Nickolás, Nicolao, Nicolio, Nicolós, Nikolaus. Short: Cola, Colás, Nico. Pet: Colacho, Culacho, Lacho. (NEE-CO-LAHS)

NICOMEDES A borrowing from the Greek, Nicomedes is a compound name composed from the elements *nike* (victory) and *mēdesthai* (to ponder, to meditate upon): hence, "to ponder victory." Var: Necomedes, Necomedez, Nicomedeo, Nicomedis, Nicomedo. Short: Nico. (NEE-CO-MAY-DAYS)

NUNCIO Derived from the Latin *nuntius* (messenger, announcer). Var: Nunciano, Nunzio. (NOON-SEE-O)

OCTAVIO From the Latin Octavius, which is derived from *octavus* (eighth). The name was borne by several saints, one of which, a 5th-century African, led a hermit-like existence in an elm tree. Var: Actaviano, Actavio, Octavianno, Octavino, Octavión, Octovio. (OAK-TAH-BEE-O)

PACIANO From the Latin Pacianus (peaceful), which is derived from *pax* (peace). (PAH-SEE-AH-NO)

PACÍFICO Derived from the Latin Pacificus (pacify, to make peaceful or calm), which is from *pax* (peace). Pet: Paco. (PAH-SEE-FEE-KO)

PASQUAL From the Late Latin *Paschālis* (of Easter), a derivative of *Pascha* (Easter), which is from the Hebrew *pesach* (Passover). The name is traditionally bestowed upon children born during the Passover and Easter season. Var: Pascalo, Pascualo, Pascuelo, Pasqualo, Pasquel, Pazcual, Pazqual. Short: Pasco. Pet: Paco. (PAHS-KWALL)

PATRICIO Derived from the Latin *patricius* (a patrician, an aristocrat). Var: Patrico, Patrizio. Pet: Pachi, Richi, Ticho. (PAH-TREE-SEE-O)

PAULO From the Latin Paulus, a Roman family name derived from *paulus* (small). The name was adopted in the Bible by Saul of Tarsus, who was converted to Christianity by a vision of Christ. Paul and St. Peter are regarded as cofounders of the Christian Church. Var: Pablo, Paublo, Pavlo. Short: Lino. Dim: Pablino, Paulino, Polín. Pet: Pauli. (POW-LO)

PEDRO Spanish cognate of Peter, a name derived from the Latin *petra* (a rock) and the Greek *petros* (a stone). The name is borne in the Bible by one of the Twelve Apostles of Christ. Peter is considered to have been the first pope and cofounder of the Christian Church with Paul. Pet: Pedrín, Pedruco, Peyo. (PAY-DRO)

PLÁCIDO Derived from the Latin *placidus* (placid, tranquil, quiet, calm). Var: Plácedo, Placijo, Plásido. Short: Plasio. (PLAH-SEE-DŌ)

PROCOPIO Derived from the Greek Prokopios (progressive), a compound name composed of the elements *pro* (before) and *kopios* (in great abundance, copious). Var: Procobio, Procopo, Prokopio. (PRO-KO-PEE-O)

PRÓSPERO Derived from the Spanish *próspero* (prosperous, successful, happy). (PROSE-PAY-RO)

QUINTO Derived from the Latin *quintus* (fifth). The name was borne by forty-two saints. Var: Quinino, Quintin, Quintón. (KEEN-TŌ)

RAFAEL Spanish cognate of the Hebrew Refael, a derivative of *refāēl* (God has healed). The name is borne in the Bible by an archangel and messenger of God mentioned in the apocryphal books of Enoch and Tobit. Var: Rafaelo, Rafeal, Rafel, Raffael, Raphel. Dim: Rafito. Pet: Fallo, Falo, Felio, Rafi, Rafo. (RAH-FAH-ELL)

RAIMUNDO From the Old Norman French Raimund, a derivative of the Frankish Raginmund, which is a compounding of the elements *ragin* (counsel, advice) and *mund* (hand, protection): hence, "wise protection." Var: Raimondo, Ramón, Ramondo, Ramone, Ramundo, Raymón, Reymondo. Short: Monchi, Mundo. (RYE-MOON-DŌ)

RAÚL Spanish cognate of Ralph (wolf counsel). *See* RALPH (English Names). Var: Raol, Raoul, Raulio. Pet: Rulo. (RAH-OOL)

REINALDO Spanish cognate of Reynold (ruler with counsel), a variant form of Reginald. *See* REGINALD (English Names). Var: Rainaldo, Ranaldo, Raynaldo, Renaldo, Reynaldo, Rinaldo. Short: Naldo. (RAY-NAHL-DŌ)

RENATO Derived from the Late Latin Renātus (reborn, born again). The name is a common baptismal name, bestowed in reference to spiritual rebirth. Var: Renan. (RAY-NAH-TŌ)

René A borrowing from the French, René is derived from the Late Latin Renātus (reborn, born again). (RAY-NAY)

Reubén Derived from the Hebrew *rĕūbēn* (behold, a son!). The name is borne in the Bible by the first-born son of Jacob and Leah. He was the patriarch of one of the twelve tribes of Israel. Var: Rubén. (ROO-BANE)

Ricardo Spanish cognate of Richard (brave ruler), which is from the Old High German Richart, a compound name composed of the elements *rik* (king) and *hart* (hearty, brave, strong). Var: Recardo, Recaredo, Ricardio, Ricarrdo, Riccardo, Richardo. Short: Cardo. Pet: Ricky, Rico. (REE-KAR-DŌ)

Rico A common pet form of several names, including Ricardo. (REE-KO)

Roberto Spanish form of Robert (bright with fame), which is derived from the Old High German Hruodperht, a compounding of the elements *hruod* (fame) and *beraht* (bright). Var: Raberto, Roverto. Short: Berto. Pet: Beto, Tito. (RO-BARE-TŌ)

Rodrigo Spanish cognate of Roderick (famous ruler), a name derived from the Middle Latin Rodericus, which is from the Old High German Hrodrich, a compounding of the elements *hruod* (fame) and *rik* (ruler). Var: Rodrego. Pet: Gigo. (RO-DREE-GO)

Rolando Derived from the French Roland, which is from the Old High German Hruodland, a compounding of the elements *hruod* (fame) and *land* (land): hence, "fame of the land." Var: Orlando, Orlondo, Raldán, Rolán, Roldán, Roldón. Short: Lando, Olo. (RO-LAHN-DŌ)

Román Derived from the Latin Romanus (a Roman), which is from Roma, the Italian name of the capital city of Italy. Pet: Mancho. (RO-MAHN)

Salomón Spanish cognate of Solomon, an Ecclesiastic Greek name derived from the Hebrew *shĕlōmōh* (peaceful), which is from *shālōm* (peace). The name is borne in the Bible by the son and successor of King David, noted for his great wisdom and ability to communicate with animals. Var: Salamón, Salomán. Short: Mon. (SAH-LOW-MOAN)

Salvador Derived from *salvador* (savior, rescuer, deliverer). The name is bestowed in reference to Jesus Christ as the savior of mankind. Var: Salavador, Salbador, Salvado, Salvadore, Salvadro, Salvarado, Salvator, Salvodor. Pet: Chavo. (SAHL-BAH-DOR)

Samuel Derived from the Hebrew Shmuel, which is from *shĕmūʾēl* (name of God, his name is God). The name is borne in the Bible by a Hebrew judge and prophet who anointed Saul as the first king of Israel. Var: Samuelo. Pet: Sami. (SAHM-WELL)

Sancho Derived from the Latin *sanctius* (sacred). Var: Sanctio, Sanctos, Santón. (SAHN-CHO)

Santiago Compound name composed from *san* (saint) and Diego (James): hence, "St. James." Var: Antiago, Sandiago, Sandiego, Saniago, Santago, Santeago, Santiaco, Santiego, Santigo, Santiogo. Short: Tago. Pet: Chago, Chano, Vego. (SAHN-TEE-AH-GO)

Saúl Cognate of the Hebrew Shaul, which is from *shāūl* (asked of, borrowed). The name is borne in the Bible by the first king of Israel. Var: Saulo. (SAH-OOL)

Seferino Derived from the Latin *zephyrus*, which is from the Greek *zephyros* (the west wind, a soft, gentle breeze). Var: Ceferino, Ceferín, Sebarino, Sefarino, Sefereno, Seferín, Sepherino, Sephirino, Zefarino, Zeferín, Zepherino. Short: Cefero, Fino, Sef. (SAY-FAY-REE-NO)

Serafín From the Ecclesiastic Late Latin *seraphim* (burning ones, the angels surrounding the throne of God), which is from the Hebrew *śĕrāphīm*, a word believed to be derived from *sāraph* (to burn). Var: Cerafino, Cerefino, Serafino, Seraphín, Serefino. (SAY-RAH-FEEN)

Sergio From the Latin Sergius, an old Roman family name of uncertain etymology. Var: Cergio, Sergeo, Serjio, Zergio. Pet: Checho, Checo. (SARE-HEE-O)

Servacio Derived from the Latin Servatius (to save, to preserve). (SARE-BAH-SEE-O)

Sevastián From the Latin Sebastiānus, a derivative of the Greek Sebastianos (a man of Sebastia, a town in Asia Minor). The name was borne by a 3rd-century Christian soldier of Rome (d. 288?) martyred under Diocletian by the arrows of his fellow soldiers. Var: Savastián, Sebastaín, Sebastiano, Sebastién, Sebastín, Sebastión. Short: Bastián, Tan. Pet: Tano. (SAY-BAH-STEE-AHN)

Severo From the old Roman family name Sevērus, which is from *sevērus* (strict, stern, severe). Var: Cevero, Saverio, Savero, Severano, Severeano, Severiano, Severino, Siverio, Sivero. Dim: Severito. (SAY-BAY-RO)

Silvano From the Latin Silvānus (of the woods), which is derived from *silva* (a wood, a forest). Var: Silbanio, Silván, Silvanio, Silviano. (SEEL-BAH-NO)

TEODORO Spanish cognate of Theodore (God's gift). The name is derived from the Greek Theodōros, a compounding of the elements *theos* (God) and *dōron* (gift). The name is listed 146 times in the *Dictionary of Saints*. Var: Deodoro, Teadoro, Teodario, Teodero, Teodorio, Teodro. (TAY-O-DŌ-RO)

TEÓFILO Derived from the Greek Theophilos (beloved of God), a compounding of the elements *theos* (God) and *philos* (loving). The name is borne in the Bible by the person to whom the Gospel of Luke and the Acts of the Apostles are addressed. Var: Teófel, Teófelo, Teófil, Teofilio, Teófolo, Teóphilo. Short: Filo. (TAY-O-FEE-LO)

TIMOTEO Derived from the Greek Timotheos (honor God, respect God), a compound name composed from the elements *timē* (honor, respect) and *theos* (God). The name is borne in the Bible by a disciple and companion of the Apostle Paul. Var: Timateo, Timeteo, Tomoteo. Short: Timo. Pet: Teyo. (TEE-MO-TAY-O)

TITO Spanish form of the Greek Titos, an ancient name of uncertain derivation. Some believe it to be from the Greek *tīo* (to honor). In the Bible, Titus was a missionary friend of St. Paul to whom the epistle Titus is addressed. Alternatively, Tito is a short form of various names, such as Augustino. (TEE-TŌ)

TOMÁS Spanish form of Thomas, an Ecclesiastic Greek name derived from the Aramaic *tĕōma* (a twin). The name is borne in the Bible by an apostle who doubted the resurrection of Christ. It is from him that the term "doubting Thomas" arises. Var: Tamás, Tamascio, Tomaso, Tomaz, Tomazcio. Dim: Tomito. Pet: Tomi. (TŌ-MAHS)

URBANO Derived from the Latin Urbānus (city dweller, urban). The name was borne by eight popes and thirty saints. Var: Urvano. (OOR-BAH-NO)

VALENTÍN Derived from the Latin Valentīnus, a derivative of *valens* (to be healthy, to be strong). The name was borne by fifty-one saints, including the 3rd-century Roman saint and martyr whose feast day, February 14, coincides with that of a pagan festival marking the beginning of spring. Var: Balente, Balentin, Balentino, Balento, Valentén, Valentío, Valentón. Short: Tin, Tino. (BAHL-ENN-TEEN)

VALERIO Derived from the Latin Valerius, an old Roman family name believed to be derived from *valere* (to be strong). Var: Balerio, Baleriano. (BAH-LAIR-EE-O)

VENCESLAO Spanish form of Wenceslaus, a Slavonic name composed from the elements *Wend*, a term denoting a member of the old Slavic people who now live in an ancient enclave south of Berlin, and *slav* (glory): hence, "glory of the Wends." Var: Benceslado, Benceslao, Vanceslao, Veceslado, Vencelado, Vencelas, Venselado, Venseslado. Short: Bences, Benses, Vences. Pet: Chelao, Chelo. (BANE-SASE-LAH-O)

VENTURO Derived from the Spanish *ventura* (good fortune). Var: Benturo, Ventureno, Venturio. (BANE-TOO-RO)

VÍCTOR A borrowing from the Latin, Víctor is from *victor* (conqueror, winner, victor). The name is listed 230 times in the *Dictionary of Saints*. Var: Bíctar, Bíctor. Short: Victo. Pet: Torico, Vicho, Vico, Vito. (BEAK-TOR)

VIDAL Derived from the Latin *vitalis* (vital, full of life, vigor), which is from *vita* (life). Var: Bidal, Vidalo, Videl, Videlio. (BEE-DOLL)

VINCENTIO Spanish cognate of Vincent (conquering), which is from the Late Latin Vincentius, a derivative of *vincere* (to conquer). Var: Besento, Bisente, Vencente, Vensento, Vicencio, Vicensio, Vicente, Vincenzio. Pet: Chenche, Chente, Chicho, Tente, Viche. (BEAN-SANE-TEE-O)

ZACARÍAS Spanish cognate of the Ecclesiastic Greek Zacharias (remembrance of the Lord), which is derived from the Hebrew *zĕcharyah* (God remembers). The name is borne in the Bible by the husband of Elizabeth and father of John the Baptist. Var: Zacaríaz, Zacarío, Zacaríos, Zacaríus, Zacarrías. (ZAH-KAH-REE-AHS)

ZENOBIO Spanish cognate of the Greek Zenobios (the life of Zeus), a compound name composed from the elements *zēn* (of Zeus) and *bios* (life). Var: Cenobio, Cenovio, Senobio, Senovio, Zenovio. (ZAY-NO-BEE-O)

ZENÓN Spanish cognate of the Greek Zenon, a name believed to be derived from Zeus, the name of the supreme deity in Greek mythology. Var: Cenón, Senón, Zinón. (ZAY-NONE)

Spanish Female Names

Aarona Feminine form of Aarón (the exalted one). *See* AARÓN (Male Names). Var: Arona, Aronida, Arrona. (AH-ROAN-NAH)

Abegaíl From the Hebrew Avigayil, which is derived from *avīgayil* (father of exaltation, father is rejoicing). The name was borne in the Bible by one of the wives of King David. Var: Abigael, Avigail. (AH-BEE-GAH-EEL)

Abila Derived from the Latin Abella (the beautiful), which is from *bella* (beautiful). Var: Abiliana, Abilica. (AH-BEE-LAH)

Adanelia Combination name composed from the male Adán (Adam) and Helia (the sun). (AH-DAH-NAY-LEE-AH)

Adela From the French Adèle, a short form of any of the various names containing the Germanic element *adal* (noble). Var: Adelea, Adeliza, Adella. Short: Dela. Pet: Adi, Adita, Lela. (AH-DAY-LAH)

Adelaida From the French Adélaïde, a name derived from the German Adelheid (noble one), a compounding of the elements *adal* (noble) and *heid* (kind, sort). Var: Adaelaida, Adalaida, Adelada, Adeladia, Adelaidae, Adelaya, Adelayda, Adelayde, Adeleida, Adeleide, Adelicia, Aleyda. Short: Layda. Pet: Lala. (AH-DAY-LIE-DAH)

Adelina A diminutive form of Adela (noble), Adelina is popularly bestowed as an independent given name. *See* ADELA. Var: Adalena, Adalilia, Adalina, Adelaina, Adelena, Adeliana, Adelinda, Adelinia, Adilina, Audella, Audilia. (AH-DAY-LEE-NAH)

Adina Derived from the Hebrew Adah (ornament, adornment). The name is borne in the Bible by the wife of Esau. (AH-DEE-NAH)

Adriana Feminine form of Adrián (man from the city of Adria, man from the city of Hadria). *See* ADRIÁN (Male Names). Var: Adrana, Adreana. (AHD-REE-AH-NAH)

Ágata Derived from the Greek Agathē, which is from *agathos* (good, kind). The name was borne by a 3rd-century Roman martyr and saint. *See* AGATA (Italian Names). (AH-GAH-TAH)

Agraciana Spanish name meaning "to pardon, to forgive." (AH-GRAH-TSEE-AHN-NAH)

Aída Of uncertain derivation popularized after Verdi used it for the name of the central character in his opera *Aida* (1871). Var: Ayda. (AH-EE-DAH)

Aislara Derived from the Spanish *aislar* (to isolate, to separate). The name is indicative of a person who keeps to herself. (AY-SLAR-RAH)

Albina From the Latin Albinus, which is from Albus, an old Roman family name derived from *albus* (white). Var: Albinia, Alveena, Alvena, Alvienta, Alvinda, Elbina. (AHL-BEE-NAH)

Alegra Derived from the Latin *allegra* (merry, cheerful, happy). Var: Elegria. (AH-LAY-GRAH)

Alejandra Feminine form of Alejandro (defender or helper of mankind). *See* ALEJANDRO (Male Names). Var: Alehandra, Alejadra, Alejanda, Alhandra, Dejandra, Elejandra, Elesandra, Elisandrah, Elissandra, Elizandra, Elizanda. Short: Asandra, Sandara, Sandra, Sandrah, Saundra, Xandra, Zandra. (AH-LAY-HAHN-DRA)

Alicia Latinate form of the French and English Alice (noble one). *See* ALICE (French Names). Var: Alcia, Aliccia, Alis, Alisa, Alisha, Alisia, Aliza, Alyssa. Short: Licia. Pet: Chita, Licha. (AH-LEE-SEE-AH)

Alma Derived from the Spanish *alma* (soul). (AHL-MAH)

Altagracia Compound name composed from the Spanish elements *alta* (tall) and *gracias* (grace, favor, thanks): hence, "high grace." The name is bestowed in honor of the Virgin Mary, "the Lady of High Grace." Var: Alagracia, Allagracia, Altagratia, Altagratiae, Altagrazia. Short: Alta. (AHL-TAH-GRAH-TSEE-AH)

Alvera Feminine form of Álvaro (elf army). *See* ÁLVARO (Male Names). Var: Alviria, Alvra. (AHL-BER-AH)

Amada Derived from the Latin *amada* (to love). Var: Amadia, Amadida, Amata. (AH-MAH-DAH)

Amalia A borrowing from the German, Amalia is derived from the element *amal* (work): hence, "industrious." Var: Amaelia, Amelia, Amila, Amilia, Emala, Emalia. Short: Mela, Meli. Dim: Amalita, Amelida, Amelina, Ameline, Lita, Melita. Pet: Lila, Maya, Meya. (AH-MAH-LEE-AH)

Amanda Popular name derived from the Latin *amanda* (lovable, worthy to be loved). The name originated as a literary coinage of English playwright Colley Cibber (1671–1757). Var: Amenda. Short: Manda. Dim: Ammendina, Mandita. Pet: Mandi. (AH-MAHN-DA)

AMORA Derived from the Spanish *amor* (love). (AH-MOR-RAH)

ANA Spanish form of Anna, which is from the Hebrew Hannah, a name derived from *hannāh, chanaach* (gracious, full of grace, mercy). During medieval Christian times, Anna was the name assigned to the mother of the Virgin Mary, as Joachim was assigned to her father. Var: Anica, Anina, Anissa, Anizia. Dim: Aneta, Anetta, Anita, Anitta, Nanita, Nita. Pet: Nana. (AH-NAH)

ANABEL Combination name composed from Ana and Belia. *See* ANA *and* BELIA. Var: Anabelia, Anavel, Anavelia, Anival, Anvela. (AH-NAH-BELL)

ANALILIA Combination name composed from the names Ana and Lilia. *See* ANA *and* LILIA. (AH-NAH-LEE-LEE-AH)

ANAROSA Combination name composed from the names Ana and Rosa. *See* ANA *and* ROSA. (AH-NAH-RO-SAH)

ANASTASIA Popular name derived from the Greek *anastasis* (of the resurrection). Var: Anassacia, Anastasa, Anastatia, Anastia, Anatascia, Anestania, Anistazia, Annastasia. Short: Anasta. (AH-NAH-STAH-SEE-AH)

ANATOLIA Feminine form of Anatolio (sunrise, daybreak, dawn). *See* ANATOLIO (Male Names). Var: Anstolia, Antalina. (AH-NAH-TŌ-LEE-AH)

ANDRÍA Feminine form of Andrés (manly): hence, "womanly." *See* ANDRÉS (Male Names). Var: Andreina, Andrella, Andrianna. Dim: Andreita, Andreitta, Andrellita. (AHN-DREE-AH)

ANGELA Popular name derived from the Spanish *ángel*, which is from the Latin *angelus* (divine messenger, messenger of God). The name has its root in the Greek *angelos* (a messenger). Var: Angeliata, Angélica, Angella. Dim: Angalina, Angalita, Angelena, Angelida, Angelina, Anhelita, Anjelita, Lina. Pet: Angie, Nina. (AHN-HEL-LAH)

ANTOINETTA From the French Antoinette, a feminine diminutive form of Antoine, the French cognate of Anthony. (AHN-TWAH-NEH-TAH)

ANTONIA Feminine form of Antonio, a name of uncertain derivation. *See* ANTONIO (Male Names). Var: Andona, Andonia, Antania, Antionia, Antoliana, Antoliona. Short: Tonia. (AHN-TŌ-NEE-AH)

ANUNCIACIÓN Spanish name meaning "to announce." The name is bestowed in reference to the Annunciation, the time when the angel Gabriel told Mary of her pregnancy and the impending birth of the Christ child. Var: Annuciana, Anunziata. (AH-NOON-SEE-AH-SEE-OWN)

APARICIÓN Derived from the Spanish *aparición* (apparition). The name is in reference to Christ's appearance to his apostles after the resurrection. (AH-PAH-REE-SEE-OWN)

APOLONIA Feminine form of Apolonio (of Apollo). *See* APOLONIO (Male Names). The name was borne by a 3rd-century martyr of Alexandria whose teeth are said to have been pulled out with pincers. She is called upon by those suffering from dental problems. Var: Afolonia, Apalaria, Apalina, Apilinaria, Apolina, Apolinairia, Apolinia, Apolonica, Apolonoa, Appalenia, Appolinina, Appollonia, Appolonia, Epelonia, Epolonia, Opalinaria, Papolonia, Pollinaria. Short: Apolia, Palinaria, Pelonia, Pelonoia, Polania, Poliana. (AH-PO-LO-NEE-AH)

AQUILINA Feminine form of Aquilino (of Aquila), a name that has its root in the Latin *aquila* (eagle). (AH-KEE-LEE-NAH)

ARIELA Feminine form of the Hebrew Ariel (lion of God). (AY-REE-AY-LAH)

ASELA Derived from the Latin Asella, a name believed to be derived from Asinus (little burro). Var: Acela, Asael, Asalia, Azela, Azelia. Dim: Aselina, Azelina. (AH-SELL-AH)

ASUNCIÓN Derived from the Spanish *asunción* (assumption). The name is bestowed in reference to the assumption of Mary to heaven following her death. Var: Ascensiana, Ascenssia, Assunta, Asunsia. Pet: Chica, Choncha. (AH-SOON-SEE-OWN)

ATHANASIA Derived from the Greek *athanasia* (immortality, without death). The name is bestowed in reference to spiritual immortality. Var: Atanecia, Atenacia, Athanesia. Short: Atancia, Stanacia, Stanasia. (AH-THA-NAS-EE-AH)

AURELIA Feminine form of Aurelio (gold). *See* AURELIO (Male Names). Var: Aralia, Arella, Arrelia, Auralia, Auraliano, Aureana, Aurelina, Aurielia, Aurlia. (OW-RAY-LEE-O)

AVELLINA Feminine form of Avellino (place of hazelnut trees). *See* AVELLINO (Male Names). Var: Abelena, Abelia, Abelina, Abelinda, Avelina, Avelia, Avelinda. Short: Lina. (AH-BAY-YEE-NAH)

AZUCENA Derived from the Spanish *azucena* (a lily, white lily). The lily has long been regarded as a symbol of purity and perfection. Var: Asucena, Asusena, Asuzena, Auscena, Azusena, Azuzena. (AH-ZOO-SAY-NAH)

BÁRBARA Derived from the Latin *barbarus* (foreign, strange), Bárbara has the definition "foreign woman." Var: Bábara, Bábarra, Bárbera, Barbiano, Barbra, Bárvara, Várvara, Várvera. Short: Bar, Bara. Dim: Barbarina, Barbina. (BAR-BAH-RAH)

BEATRIX A borrowing from the Latin, Beatrix (she who brings happiness and joy) is derived from *beātus* (happy, blessed). Var: Baetriz, Beadriz, Beatrex, Beatrez, Beatrica, Beatricia, Beatrís, Beatriz, Beatrize, Biatrís, Biatriz, Veatrés, Veatrís, Veatriz. Pet: Beti, Bita, Ticha, Tichi. (BAY-AH-TREEX)

BELIA Derived from the Spanish *bella* (beautiful). Var: Beliano. (BAY-LEE-AH)

BELIAROSA Combination name composed from the names Belia and Rosa: hence, "beautiful rose." (BAY-LEE-AH-RO-SAH)

BETSABÉ Derived from the Hebrew Bathsheba (daughter of Sheba, daughter of the oath). The name is borne in the Bible by the beautiful wife of Uriah. She was married to King David after he ensured Uriah's death in battle. Var: Bethsabeé, Bethzabé, Betzabé. Pet: Betsy. (BATE-SAH-BAY)

BLANCA Derived from the Spanish *blanca* (white). Var: Bleanca. (BLAHN-KAH)

BONA Derived from the Latin *bona* (good). Dim: Bonita. (BO-NAH)

CABALINA Derived from the Latin Caballinus (belonging to a horse), which is from *caballa* (horse). (KAH-BAH-LEE-NAH)

CALIOPA Derived from the Greek Kalliope (beautiful voice), a compounding of the elements *kallos* (beauty, beautiful) and *ops* (voice). The name is borne in Greek mythology by the Muse of epic poetry and eloquence. (KAH-LEE-O-PAH)

CAMELIA Derived from the Latin *camilla* (virgin of unblemished character). Var: Camelea. Short: Melia, Mila. Dim: Camelina, Camelita. (KAH-MAY-LEE-AH)

CANDELARIA Feminine form of Candelario (candle, wax candle). *See* CANDELARIO (Male Names). Var: Candeleria, Candeleva, Candelona, Candeloria, Candeluria, Kandelaria. Short: Canda. Dim: Candelina. Pet: Calala, Candi. (KAN-DAH-LAH-REE-AH)

CAPARINA Borrowed from the name of a type of butterfly. (KAH-PAH-REE-NAH)

CARIDAD Derived from the Spanish *caridad* (charity). The name was borne by one of the three daughters of St. Sophia, all of whom were martyred in the second century. (KAH-REE-DAHD)

CARINA Derived from the Spanish *cariño* (affection, love). Var: Cariana, Carima, Carimira, Carimisa, Kerina. (KAH-REE-NAH)

CARISA Spanish form of the Italian Carissa, an elaborated form of Cara (beloved, dear). Var: Caríssima. (CAH-REE-SAH)

CARLOTTA Popular feminine form of Carlos, the Spanish cognate of Charles (full-grown, a man). *See* CARLOS (Male Names). Var: Carlata, Carloda, Carlona, Carlonina, Carlota, Carolata, Carrlota. Dim: Carlina. (KAR-LŌT-TAH)

CARMEN Spanish cognate of the Hebrew Carmel (vineyard, orchard). Mount Carmel is a mountain in northwestern Israel which was inhabited in early Christian times by a group of hermits who later became Carmelite monks in the Order of Our Lady of Mount Carmel. The name is bestowed in honor of the Virgin Mary, "Our Lady of Mount Carmel." Var: Carimila, Carma, Carman, Camele, Carmelinda, Carmenia, Carmenza, Carmeta, Carmilla. Short: Lita, Mela. Dim: Camucha, Carmelina, Carmelita, Carmencha, Carmenchita, Carmita, Melita. Pet: Chita. (KAHR-MEHN)

CAROLINA Feminine form of the Latin Carolus, which is a cognate of Charles (full-grown, a man). *See* CARLOS (Male Names). Var: Caralino, Caroliana. Short: Caro, Ina, Lina, Liana. Pet: Cayoya. (KAHR-O-LEE-NAH)

CASSANDRA Derived from the Greek Kassandra, a name of uncertain etymology borne in Greek mythology by the daughter of Priana and Hecuba. *See* KASSANDRA (Greek Names). Var: Casandra, Cassaundra, Kasandra. (KAH-SAHN-DRAH)

CATHERINA Spanish cognate of the Greek Aikaterinē, a name derived from *katharos* (pure, unsullied). Var: Atarina, Catalina, Catania, Catareno, Catariana, Catarrine, Catelena, Catelina, Cathalina, Catharina, Cathelina, Cathrina, Katalina, Katriona. Short: Calina, Cata, Catina, Rina, Trina. Dim: Catocha, Catuca, Catucha. (CAH-TAH-REE-NAH)

CECILIA Feminine form of Cecilio (blind, dimsighted). *See* CECILIO (Male Names). The name is borne by the patron saint of musicians. Var: Ceceilia, Ceciela, Celicia, Celilia, Cisilia, Secilia, Sisilia. (SAY-SEE-LEE-AH)

Celadonia Derived from the Greek *celedonus* (a swallow). Var: Celadina, Celedaria, Celida, Seldona, Selodona, Zeledonia. Short: Cela. (SAY-LAH-DŌ-NEE-AH)

Celestina Feminine form of Celestino (belonging to heaven). *See* CELESTINO (Male Names). Var: Celestria, Salastina, Selestena. Short: Celia. (SAY-LAY-STEE-NAH)

Celia Derived from the Latin Caelia, a feminine form of Caelius, an old Roman family name thought to be derived from *caelum* (heaven). Alternatively, Celia is used as a short form of Celestina, a name derived from the same root. (SAY-LEE-AH)

Cipriana Feminine form of Cipriano (a Cyprian, from Cyprus). Var: Cipriona, Cyprana, Sipriana, Zipriana. Dim: Ciprianita, Siprianita. (SEE-PREE-AH-NAH)

Clara Derived from the Latin *clārus* (bright, clear, famous). The name was borne by St. Clare of Assisi (c. 1193–1253), an Italian nun and founder of the order of the Poor Clares. Var: Claira, Clarisa, Clarisia, Clarra, Clarrisa. Pet: Clarita. (KLAH-RAH)

Clemencia Feminine form of Clemente (mild, gentle, merciful). *See* CLEMENTE (Male Names). Var: Clemcia, Clemecencia, Clemenia, Clemenisa, Clementia, Clementiana, Clemenzia. Short: Clema, Tina. Pet: Clemchita, Lencha, Mencha. (CLAY-MEN-SEE-AH)

Concepción Derived from the Spanish *concepción* (conception). The name is in reference to the sinlessness of the Virgin Mary from the moment of her conception. Var: Concepián, Concepsión, Conscenciana. Pet: Chona, Choncha, Chonchita, Chonita, Concha. (CONE-SAPE-SEE-OWN)

Conseja Derived from the Spanish *consejo* (advice, counsel). The name is in reference to the Virgin Mary, "*Nuestra Señora del Bueno Consejo*" (Our Lady of Good Counsel). (CONE-SAY-HA)

Consuelo Popular name derived from the Spanish *consuelo* (consolation). (CONE-SWAY-LOW)

Corazón Derived from the Spanish *corazón* (heart). The name is in reference to the Sacred Heart of Jesus. (KOR-AH-ZONE)

Crescensia Feminine form of Crescencio, a name derived from the Latin *crescentianus* (to grow). Var: Crecenciana, Crecentiana, Cresancia, Crescecia, Crescendia, Crescensiana, Cresecenciana, Crescinia, Cresencia, Cresensiana. Pet: Checha. (CRAY-SEN-SEE-AH)

Cristina Feminine form of Cristián (a Christian, a follower of Christ). *See* CRISTIÁN (Male Names). The name is borne by the youngest daughter (b. 1965) of King Juan Carlos I. Var: Crestena, Cristinea, Kristina. Short: Ina, Tina. Pet: Nina. (KREES-TEE-NAH)

Cruza Feminine form of Cruz, which is derived from the Spanish *cruz* (cross, crucifix). The cross is symbolic of Christ, who was put to death on one. Var: Crucida, Crucila, Cruzelia. Dim: Crusita, Cruzesita. Pet: Cucha. (CROO-ZAH)

Dahlia Borrowed from the name of a popular Mexican flower named after Swedish botanist Anders Dahl (1759–89). Var: Dalia, Daliala. (DAH-LEE-AH)

Damiana Feminine form of Damián (tame, gentle). *See* DAMIÁN (Male Names). Var: Damina. (DAH-MEE-AH-NAH)

Danniela Feminine form of Daniel (God is my judge). *See* DANIEL (Male Names). Var: Danelya, Donelia, Donilia. (DON-YELL-AH)

Davida Feminine form of David (beloved). *See* DAVID (Male Names). Var: Daviana. (DAH-BEED-AH)

Débora Derived from the Hebrew *devōrāh* (a bee). The name is borne in the Bible by a prophetess and judge who led the Israelites to victory over the Canaanites. Var: Déborah, Débbora, Déborah, Deboricia, Debrah. Pet: Debby. (DAY-BO-RAH)

Delfina From the Latin Delphīna (woman from Delphi). Alternatively, Delfina may be derived from the name of the delphinium flower, which is from the Greek *delphin* (dolphin). Var: Dalfina. Dim: Finita. (DELL-FEE-NAH)

Delicia A borrowing from the Latin, Delicia means "that which causes pleasure, delicious." Var: Deliciano, Delisa, Delissa, Delyssa. (DAY-LEE-SEE-AH)

Destina Derived from the Spanish *destino* (destiny). (DAY-STEE-NAH)

Deyanira Derived from the Greek Dejanira (he who kills forcefully). The name is borne in Greek mythology by the wife of Heracles. Var: Dellanira, Denanira, Dianira. Short: Nira. (DAY-YAH-NEE-RAH)

Diana Derived from the Latin Diviana (divine). Var: Dianna. (DEE-AH-NAH)

Dina Derived from the Hebrew *dīnāh* (judged). The name is borne in the Bible by a daughter of Jacob. (DEE-NAH)

Dionisa Feminine form of Dionisio (of Dionysos). Var: Dianisia, Dionisea, Dionizsia, Dyonicia. (DEE-O-NEE-SAH)

Dolores Derived from the Spanish *dolores* (sorrows, aches). The name, bestowed in honor of the Virgin Mary, "*María de los Dolores*" (Mary of the Sorrows), makes reference to the seven sorrows of Mary in her relationship with her son. Var: Dalores, Doleriana, Dolora, Doloris. Dim: Dolorcita, Dolorita, Doloritta, Lola, Loli, Lolica, Lolicia, Lolita. (DŌ-LOW-RAZE)

Dorolinda Combination name composed from Dorotea and Linda. *See* DOROTEA *and* LINDA. (DOR-O-LEEN-DAH)

Dorotea From the Greek Dōrothea (gift of God), a compounding of the elements *dōron* (gift) and *theos* (God). Var: Darotea, Derotea, Dorelia, Dores, Doreta, Doretea, Doretha, Doria, Doriciana, Dorotia, Dorotiana. Short: Dori. Dim: Dorita. Pet: Lola, Teya. (DOR-O-TAY-AH)

Dulce Derived from the Latin Dulcia, which is from *dulcis* (sweet, agreeable). The name makes reference to "*dulce nombre de María*" (the sweet name of Mary). Var: Dulcina, Dulcinea, Dulcinia. (DOOL-SAY)

Edelmira Derived from the Germanic Adelmar (of noble race), a compounding of the elements *adal* (noble) and *mar* (race, people, tribe). Var: Almira, Delmira, Edelmera, Edelmida, Eldimira. (Ā-DELL-MEE-RAH)

Edenia Spanish form of Eden, which is derived from the Hebrew *'ēdhen* (delight). In the Bible the garden of Eden is the place Adam and Eve first lived. The word denotes a paradise. (Ā-DAY-NEE-AH)

Electa Feminine form of the Latin Electus (choosing, choice, selection). (Ā-LAKE-TAH)

Electra Derived from the Greek Ēlektra (the shining one), which is from *ēlektōr* (shining). The name is borne in Greek mythology by a sister of Orestes who sought vengeance for the murder of their father. Var: Alectra. (Ā-LAKE-TRAH)

Elena Spanish form of Helen, which is a cognate of the Greek Helenē, a name derived from *ēlē* (light). The name is borne by the eldest daughter (b. 1963) of King Juan Carlos I. Var: Alena, Elaina, Elenina, Elina, Ileana, Ilene, Iliana. Short: Lena, Lina. Pet: Leni, Nelida, Nelly, Nena, Nina. (Ā-LAY-NAH)

Eleonor A borrowing from the English, Eleonor is derived from Alienor, a Provençal form of the Greek Helenē (light, torch, bright). Var: Eleonara, Eleonora, Eleonore, Elianora. Short: Nora. (Ā-LAY-O-NOR)

Eleuthera Derived from the Greek *eleutheria* (liberty, freedom). Var: Elesteria, Elestheria, Eleutnera, Eulateria, Eulenteria, Eulesteria. (Ā-LAY-YOO-THAY-RAH)

Elisabeth Derived from the Hebrew *elīsheba'* (God is my oath). The name is borne in the Bible by the mother of John the Baptist. Var: Elezabeth, Elisabet, Elixabet, Elixabeth, Elizabet, Elizabetha, Elizabetta, Elsabet, Lizebeth. Short: Elesia, Elissa, Eliza, Elliza, Elsa, Elsi, Isa, Lisa, Lisbet, Liseta, Liza, Lizbet. Pet: Besi, Beti, Betsi, Licha. (Ā-LEE-SAH-BET)

Elissa A short form of Elisabeth (God is my oath), Elissa is also bestowed as an independent given name. *See* ELISABETH. (Ā-LEE-SAH)

Eloisa Spanish form of the French Éloise, a name of uncertain origin and meaning. *See* ÉLOISE (French Names). Var: Elaisa, Eleosa, Eloesa, Eloisea, Eloiza, Elosa, Eloysa, Eloysae, Eloyza, Eluysa, Elysa. Pet: Licha. (Ā-LOW-EE-SAH)

Elvira Of uncertain derivation, most believe it to be of Germanic origin and give it the definition "amiable, friendly." Var: Albira, Alvirra, Elberia, Elbiera, Elevira, Elveira, Elvera, Elveria, Elvirea, Elviria, Elvirra, Ilvira. Dim: Vivita. Pet: Evia, Vila. (ELL-BEE-RAH)

Emalinda Combination name composed from Emma and Linda. *See* EMMA *and* LINDA. (Ā-MAH-LEEN-DAH)

Emelia Derived from the Latin Aemilia, the feminine form of Aemiliūs, an old Roman family name believed to be derived from *aemulus* (emulating, trying to equal or excel, rival). Var: Emilla, Hemelia, Milana, Miliana. Short: Lina, Mila. Dim: Emelina, Imilina. Pet: Lila, Mila, Mimila. (Ā-MAY-LEE-AH)

Emelinda Combination name composed from Emelia and Linda. *See* EMELIA *and* LINDA. (Ā-MAY-LEEN-DAH)

Emerenciana Derived from the Latin Emerentius (worthy, worthy of merit or respect), which is from *ēmereo* (to deserve well of a person, to earn). Var: Emencia, Emenziana, Emeranciana, Emeronsia, Emrenciona, Merensiana, Ermencia, Merenza. (Ā-MAY-REN-SEE-AH-NAH)

Emma A borrowing from the German, Emma is a variant form of Erma, a short form of various names, many now obsolete, which begin with the element *Erm(en)*, *Irm(en)* (strength). Dim: Emmaline. (Ā-MAH)

Encarnación Derived from the Spanish *encarnación* (incarnation). The name is in reference to Christ, the second person of the Trinity, who is the human incarnation of God. Var: Carnación, Ecarnación, Encancaión, Encarencia, Encarnasción, Incarnación. Pet: Canacho, Caña, Chonita, Encaña. (ENN-KAR-NAH-SEE-OWN)

ENEIDA Feminine form of Eneas, a cognate of the Greek Aineias, which is derived from *ainein* (to praise). Var: Enereida, Enerida. (Ā-NAY-DAH)

ENFIANIA A borrowing from the Latin, Enfiania has the definition "to have faith." (ENN-FEE-AH-NEE-AH)

ENGRACIA Derived from the Latin *in gratia* (in the Lord's grace). Var: Engrahia, Eugracia. (ENN-GRAH-SEE-AH)

ENRIQUA Feminine form of Enrique, the popular Spanish form of Henry. *See* ENRIQUE (Male Names). Var: Anniqueta, Endrigueta, Endriqueta, Enregueta, Enrequeta, Enrequette, Enrica, Enriceta, Enricetta, Enrigua, Enrigueta, Enriguetta, Enriquela, Enriqueta, Enriquetta, Enriquita, Henerequeta, Henrequeta, Henrequetta, Henrigueta, Henriqua, Henriquetta. Short: Queta, Riqueta. Dim: Quetita. (ENN-REE-KAH)

EPIFANIA Derived from the Greek *epiphaneia* (manifestation, appearance). The name refers to the Epiphany, the yearly Christian festival commemorating the visit of the Three Wise Men, the baptism of Jesus, and the miracle at Cana. Var: Epefina, Epephania, Epfifania, Ephefania, Ephiphania, Epifaina, Epifina, Epifinia. Short: Pifania. (Ā-PEE-FAH-NEE-AH)

ERÉNDIRA Aztec name meaning "the one who smiles." Var: Erendina, Hirendina. (Ā-RAIN-DEE-RAH)

ERNESTA Feminine form of Ernesto (earnest). *See* ERNESTO (Male Names). Var: Erestina, Ernessina, Ernestia, Ernestica, Ernistina, Hernesta, Hernestina, Hernistina, Irnestina. Short: Erna, Ina, Irnia, Tina. Dim: Titina. (AIR-NAY-STAH)

ESENIA Derived from the Latin *Esseni* (an Essene, one belonging to the Essenes, an ancient Jewish brotherhood of ascetics and mytics). (Ā-SAY-NEE-AH)

ESMERALDA Derived from the Spanish *esmeralda* (emerald). Var: Esmarada, Esmeraldina, Esmeranda, Esmerelda, Ezmeralda, Ismaerelda, Ismaralda, Ismeralda. (ACE-MAY-RALL-DAH)

ESPERANZA Derived from the Spanish *esperanza* (hope, expectation). Var: Esparansa, Esparanza, Esperansa, Esperensa, Esperenza, Esperonza, Espiranza, Espransa, Espranza, Sperancia, Speranza. Short: Pera. Pet: Lancha, Pelancha, Pelanchita, Perita. (ACE-PAY-RAHN-ZAH)

ESPIRIDIANA Feminine form of Espiridión, a cognate of the Greek Spiridion (basket maker), which is from *spīra* (coil, wreath, a twisting). Var: Esperia, Esperirina, Espiriona, Spiriona. Short: Spriana.(ACE-PEE-REE-DEE-AH-NAH)

ESTEBANA Feminine form of Esteban, which is the Spanish cognate of Stephen (wreath, garland). *See* ESTEBAN (Male Names). Var: Estafania, Estafina, Estefana, Estefania, Estevana, Estiphana, Stefana, Stephona, Stifana. Short: Fana, Stefa. Dim: Estefanita. (Ā-STAY-BAH-NAH)

ESTELLA Derived from the Latin *stella* (a star). Var: Estela, Estelae, Estell, Estellia, Estilla. Short: Tela. Dim: Estelita, Telita. Pet: Neta. (ACE-TAY-LAH)

ESTER Spanish cognate of Esther, a name of debated origin and meaning. *See* ESTHER (English Names). Var: Estaer, Estar, Esteranza, Esterlisa, Esterra, Estoria. Dim: Esterlita. (ACE-TARE).

EUFEMIA Derived from the Greek Euphēmia (of fine voice), a compound name composed from the elements *eu* (good, well, fine) and *phēmē* (voice). Var: Eufamia, Eufenia, Eufimia, Eufinia, Euphania, Euphenia, Ufemia, Ufenia. Short: Femia. (Ā-OO-FAY-MEE-AH).

EUGENIA Feminine form of Eugenio (well-born, noble). *See* EUGENIO (Male Names). The name was borne by St. Eugenia of Alexandria, who disguised herself as a man and joined a monastery. Var: Egenia, Eugina, Eujina. Pet: Cenia, Queña. (Ā-OO-HAY-NEE-AH).

EULALIA A borrowing from the Greek, Eulalia (well-spoken) is composed from the elements *eu* (well, good, fair) and *lalein* (to talk). The name was borne by a twelve-year-old Spanish martyr (d. 304?) who was burned to death because she refused to renounce her faith. Var: Aualia, Auyela, Ayalia, Elulalia, Eralia, Erlalia, Erulalia, Eulahia, Eulaia, Eulila, Eulilia, Evlalia, Hulalia. Short: Eulia, Lalia, Ulia. Dim: Layita. Pet: Lalie, Lalo, Laya. (Ā-OO-LAH-LEE-AH)

EUNICE Derived from the Greek Eunikē, a compound name composed from the elements *eu* (good, well, fair) and *nikē* (victory): hence, "fair victory." The name is borne in the Bible by the understanding mother of Timothy. Var: Eunecia, Euniza, Eunizia. (Ā-OO-NEE-SAY)

EUTROPIA A borrowing from the Greek, Eutropia is composed from the elements *eu* (good, well, fair) and *tropis* (the lees of wine). (Ā-OO-TRO-PEE-AH)

EVA Spanish form of Eve, a cognate of the Hebrew Chava, which is derived from *hawwāh* (life). The name is borne in the Bible by the first woman created by God, "the mother of all the living." Var: Ava. Dim: Evita. (Ā-BAH)

EVANGELINA Derived from the Latin *evangelium* (Good News, the Gospel). The name is in reference to the four evangelists Matthew, Mark, Luke, and John. Var: Abanagelina, Ebangelina, Elvanelia, Engelina,

Evagelina, Evanagelina, Evangela, Evangeline, Evangelintina, Evangelista, Evangilina, Evanjelina, Evengelina, Ivangelina. (Ā-BAHN-HAY-LEE-NAH)

EVELLIA From the Greek Euellia, a name derived from the element *eu* (well, good, fair). Var: Ebilia, Eubelia, Evelalia. (Ā-BAY-LEE-AH)

FABIOLA Derived from the Latin Fabius, an old Roman family name derived from *faba* (a bean). Var: Fabola. Pet: Faby. (FAH-BEE-O-LAH)

FAUSTINA Feminine form of Faustino (bringer of good luck). *See* FAUSTINO (Male Names). Var: Faustia, Faustiana. Pet: Fata. (FOWS-TEE-NAH)

FEBE Derived from the Greek Phoebe, which is derived from *phoibos* (bright). (FAY-BEE)

FELIPA Feminine form of Felipo, the Spanish cognate of Phillip (lover of horses). *See* FELIPO (Male Names). Var: Filipia, Filippa. Dim: Felepita. (FAY-LEE-PAH)

FELIXA Feminine form of Félix, which is from the Latin *felix* (happy, lucky). Var: Felecia, Felia, Felica, Felicanna, Feliciania, Felicianna, Felicina, Felisa, Felixia, Felizia. (FAY-LEEK-SAH)

FIDELA Feminine form of Fidel (faithful, trusty). *See* FIDEL (Male Names). Var: Fedila, Fideila, Fidelia. Pet: Lela. (FEE-DAY-LAH)

FILOMENA Derived from the Greek Philomena, a compound name composed of the elements *philos* (loving) and *menos* (strength): hence, "lover of strength." Var: Felmina, Felomela, Filamena, Filomana. Short: Felma, Mena. Pet: Menalia. (FEE-LOW-MAY-NAH)

FLORENCIA Derived from the Latin Florentia (a blooming), which is from *florens* (blooming, flourishing, prosperous). Var: Floralia, Florenca, Florentia, Floria, Florincia. Dim: Florencita, Florita. Pet: Coya. (FLO-REN-SEE-AH)

FRANCISCA Feminine form of Francisco (a Frenchman). *See* FRANCISCO (Male Names). Var: Franasca, Francasca, Francesia, Francica, Franciskita, Franciszka, Franisca. Pet: Chichicha. (FRAHN-SEES-KAH)

FUENSANTA Compound name composed from the Latin elements *fons* (fount) and *sanctus* (holy): hence, "holy fount." The name is bestowed in honor of the Virgin Mary, "*Nuestra Señora de la Fuensanta*" (Our Lady of the Holy Fount). Short: Fuenta. (FWEHN-SAHN-TAH)

GABRIELA Feminine form of Gabriel (God is my strength). *See* GABRIEL (Male Names). Var: Gabella, Gabrela, Gabrieala, Gebriela, Graviella. Pet: Chela, Gaby. (GAH-BREE-Ā-LAH)

GENAIDA Derived from the Greek *genēs* (born). (HAY-NIGH-DAH)

GENEROSA Derived from the Spanish *generoso* (generous). (HAY-NAY-RO-SAH)

GENOVEVA Derived from the Gaulish Genovefa, a name with Celtic roots but the meaning of which is uncertain. The first element is believed to be from *genos* (race, people, tribe); the second is possibly from an element meaning "woman." The name and its many variants are very popular. Var: Genavera, Genaveva, Genaviva, Genefeva, Genevie, Genevine, Geneviva, Genevive, Genieve, Geniveve, Genofefa, Genofeva, Genovefa, Genovena, Genovesa, Genovia, Genoviera, Genoviva, Genovova, Genufia, Ginoveva, Guineveva, Jeaneva, Jenefeva, Jeneiveves, Jeneva, Jenevieve, Jenovefa, Jenoveva. Short: Genona, Genora, Geva, Veva. Dim: Genovita. (HAY-NO-BAY-BAH)

GODELIVA Spanish form of the English Godiva (God's gift). *See* GODIVA (English Names). Var: Godeleva, Godelva, Goldevia. (GO-DAY-LEE-BAH)

GRACIELA Derived from the Latin *gratia* (agreeableness, pleasantness). The name is in reference to the grace of God. Var: Gracela, Gracella, Gracensia, Gracielia, Graciella, Gracielle, Gracilla, Grasiela, Graziana, Graziela, Graziella. Dim: Chelita. Pet: Cheya, Chita. Dim: Chelita. (GRAH-SEE-Ā-LAH)

GRISELDA A borrowing from the German, Griselda is derived from Griseldis, which is from the element *gries* (gravel, stone, gray). The name was borne by a medieval woman whose husband continually tested her devotion and loyalty. Var: Chrisela, Chriselda, Criselda, Criszelda, Crizelda, Grisalda, Griscelda, Grizelda. Pet: Chela. (GREE-SALE-DAH)

GUADALUPE Spanish name meaning "valley of the wolf." Var: Guadaloupa, Guadaloupe, Guadalupana, Guadalupi, Guadelupe, Guadilupa, Guadolupa, Guadolupe, Quadalupe. Short: Guada, Lupe. Dim: Lopita, Lupeta, Lupina, Lupita. (GWAH-DAH-LOO-PAY)

GUILLERMINA Feminine form of Guillermo, the Spanish cognate of William. *See* GUILLERMO (Male Names). Var: Gellermina, Gerolmina, Gillermina, Guilermina, Guilleriminia. Short: Guilla, Mina. Pet: Nina. (GHEE-YARE-MEE-NAH)

HAIDEE Of Greek origin meaning "calm, tranquil." Var: Jaide. (Ā-DAY)

HEIDI A borrowing from the German, Heidi originated as a pet form of Adalheid (noble one). *See* HEIDI (German Names). (HI-DEE)

Herminia Feminine form of Herminio (soldier). *See* HERMÁN (Male Names). Var: Ereminia, Erminia, Herimia, Hermena, Hermensia, Hermilina, Herminnia, Herminea. Short: Mina, Minia. Dim: Hermita, Minita. Pet: Mimi, Nina. (AIR-MEE-NEE-AH)

Hersilia Greek name meaning "tender, delicate." It is borne in Greek legend by a beautiful Sabine woman who was abducted by Romulus. Var: Ercilia, Ersila, Erzelia, Erzilia, Hercilia, Irsilia. (AIR-SEE-LEE-AH)

Honoria Derived from the Latin *honor* (esteem, integrity, dignity). The name is listed fifty-one times in the *Dictionary of Saints*. (O-NO-REE-AH)

Hortencia Derived from the Latin Hortensia, a feminine form of the old Roman family name Hortensius (gardener), which is derived from *hortensius* (belonging to a gardener), a derivative of *hortus* (a garden). Var: Artencia, Hartencia, Hartensia, Hartinsia, Hortecia, Hortenia, Hortenxia, Hortinzia. Pet: Chencha, Tencha. (OR-TANE-SEE-AH)

Ida A borrowing from the German, Ida is derived from the element *īd* (work, labor). "Diligent" and "industrious" are popular definitions of the name. (EE-DAH)

Idalia Greek name meaning "I see the sun." It might be derived from the ancient place-name Idalia, a place consecrated to Venus, the goddess of love. Var: Hidalia, Idalea, Idalina. (EE-DAH-LEE-AH)

Idolina Derived from the Latin *idolum* (idol, image, likeness). Var: Hidolina, Indolina. (EE-DŌ-LEE-NAH)

Idonia Derived from the Latin Idoneus (of good disposition). (EE-DŌ-NEE-AH)

Ifigenia Derived from the Greek Iphigeneia (of royal birth). Var: Efenia, Effigenia, Efigencia, Efigeneia, Efigenia, Efignia, Epigenia, Eufigenia, Feginia, Figenia. Pet: Effa. (EE-FAY-HAY-NEE-AH)

Imelda Derived from the Germanic Irmenhild, a compound name composed of the elements *irmen* (entire, all) and *hild* (battle): hence, "entire battle." Var: Amelda, Himelda, Imaelde, Imela, Imelde, Ymelda. Short: Mela. (EE-MELL-DAH)

Indiana Derived from the Late Latin Indianus (of India), which has its root in the Latin India (India, the East Indies). Var: Idiana. (EEN-DEE-AH-NAH)

Inés Popular Spanish form of Agnes, a name derived from the Greek Hagnē, which is from *hagnos* (chaste, pure, sacred). *See* AGNESE (Italian Names). Var: Agnese, Agnete, Einés, Enés, Innez, Ynéss, Ynez. Dim: Agnesita. (EE-NAYS)

Irene Derived from the Greek Eirēnē (peace). The name is listed twenty-one times in the *Dictionary of Saints*. Var: Hirena, Ireane, Irenia, Ireniz, Ireña, Irina, Irinia, Yrena, Yrene, Yrenia, Yrinea. (EE-RAY-NAY)

Isabela Variant form of Elisabeth, which is derived from the Hebrew *elīsheba'* (God is my oath). The name was borne by two queens of Spain, including Isabella I of Castile (1474–1504). She married Ferdinand of Aragon and joined their states into the country of Spain in 1469. Var: Esabela, Esabella, Esebella, Esibell, Isabell, Isabella, Isabelle, Isebela, Issabel, Issabela, Issabelle, Izabel, Izabela, Sabela, Ysabel, Yzabel, Yzabela. Short: Isa, Issa, Iza, Yssa, Yza. Dim: Belicia, Belita. Pet: Chabica, Chavelle, Chela. (EE-SAH-BELL-AH)

Jacaranda Tupi-Guarani name meaning "strong odor." The name is borrowed from that of a tropical tree which has fine leaves and large clusters of lavender flowers. (HAH-CAH-RAHN-DAH)

Jazmín Derived from the Arabic *yāsmīn* (jasmine), the name of a fragrant plant with flowers used in perfumes and teas. Var: Yazmin. (HAHS-MEEN)

Jemsa Derived from the Spanish *gema* (gem, precious stone). (HEM-SAH)

Josefa Feminine form of Joseph (may he add, God shall add). *See* JOSÉ (Male Names). Var: Hosefina, Hosephina, Josefana, Josefenia, Josefenna, Josefina, Joseifa, Josepa, Josepha, Josephae, Josephina, Joseva, Josevia, Josifina, Jozefa, Jozefina. Short: Fina, Sefa. Dim: Josefita. Pet: Chefa, Chefina, Chepa, Chepina, Chepita, Chofa, Pepa, Pepina. (HOE-SAY-FA)

Juana Popular feminine form of Juan, the Spanish cognate of John (God is gracious). *See* JUAN (Male Names). Var: Juanna, Yuana. Dim: Janina, Joanita, Juanita. (HWAHN-AH)

Julia Feminine form of Julio (the first down on the chin, downy-bearded, youth). *See* JULIO (Male Names). Var: Guillia, Huliana, Julea, Juleana, Juliena. Short: Lián, Liana, Lyana. Dim: Julianita, Julieta, Julina. Pet: Chula. (HOO-LEE-AH)

Larrina Feminine form of the Italian Larino, a name believed to be derived from the Latin *laurus* (laurel). Var: Larina. (LAH-REE-NA)

Laura A borrowing from the Italian, Laura is derived from *laurus* (laurel). The name was borne by a 9th-century nun and saint of Cordova, martyred in boiling pitch by the Moors. Var: Larela, Laryssa, Laurantina, Laureana, Laurela, Lora, Loraida. (LAH-OO-RAH)

Laurentia Feminine form of Lorenzo, the Spanish cognate of Laurence (man from Laurentum). *See* LORENZO (Male Names). Var: Larensa, Laurentena, Lorezza. (LAH-REHN-CHEE-AH)

Lavinia Old Latin name believed to be a feminine form of Latinus (from Latium, the area surrounding and including ancient Rome). The name is borne in Roman mythology by a daughter of King Latinus. She was the last wife of Aeneas and was considered to be the mother of the Roman people. Var: Levina, Livinia, Lavina, Luvena, Luvenia. (LAH-BEE-NEE-AH)

Leah A borrowing from the Hebrew, Leah is derived from *lā'āh* (weary, to tire). The name is borne in the Bible by the eldest daughter of Laban and the first of Jacob's four wives. Var: Lea, Lía. (LAY-AH)

Leda A borrowing from the Greek, Leda is an ancient name of uncertain derivation. It is borne in Greek mythology by the mother of Clytemnestra, Helenē of Troy, Castor, and Pollux. Var: Laida, Layda, Ledia, Lediana, Leida, Leidia, Lyda. (LAY-DAH)

Leila A borrowing from the Arabic, Leila means "dark beauty, dark as night." Var: Laila, Layla, Leilani, Leillia, Leyla. (LAY-EE-LAH)

Leocadia Derived from the Greek Eleokadia (splendid brightness), which is from *ēlē* (light, torch, bright). Var: Eleocaida, Elocadia, Lacadia, Leokadia, Liocadia. (LEE-O-KAY-DEE-AH)

Leonarda Feminine form of Leonardo (strong as a lion, brave as a lion). *See* LEONARDO (Male Names). Var: Lenadra, Leonada, Leonaida, Leonorda. (LAY-O-NAR-DAH)

Leoncia Feminine form of Leoncio, a name derived from the Latin *leo* (lion). Var: Lencia, Leonisia, Lianicia. (LAY-OWN-SEE-AH)

Leonor Variant form of Eleanor, a cognate of the Greek Helenē (light, torch, bright). Alternatively, some believe this name to be a feminine form of Leonard, which is derived from the Old High German Lewenhart (brave as a lion). Var: Leonara, Leonora, Lionora, Lioria. Short: Nora. Dim: Norita. Pet: Nelida, Nola, Nony. (LAY-O-NOR)

Leticia Derived from the Latin *laetitia* (gladness, happiness). Var: Alaticia, Eleticia, Eletisia, Laeticia, Laititia, Laticia, Leatitia, Letecea, Letisia, Letizia, Letticia, Liticia. Pet: Lettie, Lety, Licha, Ticha. (LAY-TEE-SEE-AH)

Liberada Derived from the Latin Liberatus (he has been liberated). Var: Elibrada, Libera, Liberasta, Liberda, Libirada, Librara, Livrada. Short: Libra, Livra. Dim: Libertina, Libranita. (LEE-BAY-RAH-DAH)

Libia Derived from the Latin Libya (from Libya, a country in northern Africa). Var: Livia, Lyvia. (LEE-BEE-AH)

Lidia Spanish form of the Greek Lydia (woman from Lydia, an ancient kingdom in western Asia Minor). Var: Leydia, Lidda, Litia. (LEE-DAH)

Lilia Spanish form of Lillian, which is derived from the Latin *lilium* (lily). The lily is regarded as a symbol of purity and innocence. Var: Liela, Lili, Liliosa. (LEE-LEE-AH)

Linda Derived from the Spanish *linda* (beautiful, pretty). Var: Lynda. (LEEN-DAH)

Lorena Spanish form of the French Lorraine (territory of the people of Lothar). *See* LORRAINE (French Names). Var: Lorenya. (LOW-RAY-NAH)

Lourdes Transferred use of a Basque place-name meaning "craggy slope." Lourdes, a town in southwestern France, was popularized as a given name after St. Bernadette experienced visions of the Virgin Mary there in 1858. Var: Lordes, Lurdes. (LURE-DAYS)

Lucía Feminine form of the Latin Lucius, which is derived from *lux* (light). The name was borne by 4th-century martyr St. Lucia of Syracuse. Var: Luci, Lucila, Lucilda, Lucy, Lusila. Pet: Chia, Chila. (LOO-SEE-AH)

Lucinda Elaborated form of Lucía (light). Lucinda originated as a literary name in Cervantes' *Don Quixote* (1605). Var: Lucenda, Lucinida, Luscienda, Luscinda, Lusinda. Short: Chinda. (LOO-SEEN-DAH)

Luisa Feminine form of Luis (famous in war). *See* LUIS (Male Names). (LOO-EE-SAH)

Luminosa Latin name meaning "luminous, brilliant." Var: Lumina. (LOO-MEE-NO-SAH)

Luz Derived from the Spanish *luz* (light). The name is bestowed in reference to the Virgin Mary, "*Nuestra Señora de la Luz*" (Our Lady of Light). Var: Lucila, Lucelida, Lusa, Luzana. Dim: Lucecita. Pet: Chitta, Lucha. (LOOSE)

Lyndia Combination name composed from Lidia and Linda. *See* LIDIA *and* LINDA. (LEEN-DEE-AH)

Macaria Feminine form of Macario (blessed). *See* MACARIO (Male Names). Var: Macarisa, Macarria. (MAH-KAH-REE-AH)

Magdalena Derived from the Ecclesiastic Greek Magdalēnē (of Magdala, a town near the Sea of Galilee). The name is borne in the Bible by Mary Magdalene, a woman Christ cured of seven demons. Var: Madalina,

Madela, Madelina, Madeline, Madina, Magadalena, Magadelana, Magdalina, Magdelana, Magdlena. Short: Lena, Mada, Maga, Malena, Nena. (MAHG-DAH-LANE-NAH)

MANUELA Feminine form of Manuel (God with us). *See* MANUEL (Male Names). Var: Ammanuela, Emmanuela, Mannela, Manuella, Manula. Dim: Manuelitta, Melita. Pet: Chema, Nelia. (MAHN-WELL-LAH)

MARANELA Combination name composed of María and Nela. *See* MARÍA *and* NELA. (MAH-RAH-NAY-LAH)

MARAVILLA Derived from the Latin Mirabilia, which is from *mīrābilis* (wonderful, marvelous, extraordinary). Var: Marivel, Marivella, Marvella. (MAH-RAH-BEE-YAH)

MARCELINA From the Italian Marcella, a feminine form of the Latin Marcellus, a diminutive form of Marcus, which is of uncertain derivation. *See* MARCOS (Male Names). Var: Marcellena, Marcelliana, Marcellonia, Maresila, Maricana, Marsalina. (MAR-SAY-LEE-NAH)

MARCIA Feminine form of the Latin Marcius, a variant of Marcus, which is of uncertain derivation. *See* MARCOS (Male Names). Var: Marzima. Pet: Chicha. (MAR-SEE-AH)

MARCIANA Feminine form of the Latin Marcianus (of Marcius), which is from Marcius, a name of uncertain derivation. *See* MARCOS (Male Names). Var: Marsiana, Marziana. (MAR-SEE-AH-NAH)

MARGARITA Spanish form of Margaret, a cognate of the Greek Margarītēs, which is derived from *margaron* (a pearl). Var: Magarita, Margaita, Margareta, Margaritta, Margirita, Margita, Marguerida, Marguerit, Marguerita. Short: Ita, Rita. Pet: Magi, Mago, Margó, Meta, Tita. (MAR-GAH-REE-TA)

MARÍA The most popular of Spanish names, María is the Latinate form of Mary, which is from the Hebrew Miryām, a name of debated meaning. Many believe it to mean "sea of bitterness" or "sea of sorrow." However, some sources cite the alternative definitions of "rebellion," "wished-for child," and "mistress or lady of the sea." The name is bestowed in honor of the virgin mother of Christ. Because María is so popular, it is often bestowed in the form of a combination name to distinguish among individuals. It is not uncommon to have several Marías in the same family. Var: Mareano, Mariae, Marián. Short: Ría. Pet: Chepa, Chulia, Malia, Malita, Marí, Marica, Marichu, Mariquilla, Marucha. (MAH-REE-AH)

MARÍA AMELIA Combination name composed from María and Amelia. *See* AMALIA *and* MARÍA. The name was borne by a queen of Spain and other members of Spanish royalty. (MAH-REE-AH-AH-MAY-LEE-AH)

MARÍA ANTOINETTA Popular combination name. It was borne by several members of Spanish royalty, which could have contributed to its popularity. *See* ANTOINETTA *and* MARÍA. (MAH-REE-AH-AHN-TWAH-NAY-TAH)

MARÍADELA Compound name composed of María and Adela. *See* ADELA *and* MARÍA. Var: Mariadel. (MAH-REE-AH-DAY-LAH)

MARÍA DEL PILAR Combination name referring to the miracle of the Virgin Mary appearing to Santiago over a marble pillar. The name was borne by at least two members of Spanish royalty. *See* MARÍA *and* PILAR. (MAH-REE-AH-DALE-PEE-LAR)

MARIAELENA Compound name composed of María and Elena. *See* ELENA *and* MARÍA. (MAH-REE-AH-LAY-NAH)

MARÍA JOSEPHA Popular combination name bestowed in honor of the Virgin Mary and her husband, Joseph. *See* JOSEFA *and* MARÍA. (MAH-REE-AH-YO-SEF-AH)

MARIANA Feminine form of the Latin Mariānus, a derivative of the old family name Marius, which is of uncertain derivation. Some believe the name has its root in Mars, the Roman mythological god of war, but others think it is derived from the Latin *mas* (manly). Early Christians associated the name with Maran, the Latin name of the Virgin Mary; it thus enjoyed widespread use. (MAH-REE-AH-NAH)

MARIBEL Compound name composed from María and the French *belle* (beautiful): hence, "beautiful María." (MAH-REE-BELL)

MARINA Feminine form of Marino, a name derived from the Latin Marinus (a mariner, a man of the sea). Var: Marima. Short: Ina, Mina. (MAH-REE-NAH)

MARISA Compound name composed from María and Luisa. *See* LUISA *and* MARÍA. Var: Maricia, Marissa, Mariza, Marrisa. (MAR-REE-SAH)

MARISOL Popular compound name composed from María and Soledad. *See* MARÍA *and* SOLEDAD. Var: Marizol. (MAH-REE-SOLE)

MARISTELA Compound name composed from María and Estela. *See* ESTELLA *and* MARÍA. (MAH-REE-STAY-LAH)

Marta Spanish form of Martha, an Aramaic name derived from *mārthā* (lady, mistress). The name is borne in the Bible by a friend and follower of Jesus, a sister of Lazarus and Mary of Bethany. Var: Martia. Dim: Martila, Martina. (MAR-TAH)

Maximilla Feminine form of Maximiliano. *See* MAXIMILIANO (Male Names). Var: Maxismilla. (MAHKS-EE-MEE-LAH)

Maya Derived from Maia, the name of the Greek mythological goddess of increase. Alternatively, Maya is used as a pet form of Amalia (industrious, hardworking). *See* AMALIA. Dim: Mayanita. (MY-YAH)

Melissa A borrowing from the Greek, Melissa is directly derived from *melissa* (a bee). Var: Malisa, Malissa, Melisa, Meliza, Melizza, Milissa. (MAY-LEE-SAH)

Mercedes Derived from the Spanish *merced* (mercy). The name is bestowed in honor of the Virgin Mary, *"Nuestra Señora de las Mercedes"* (Our Lady of Mercy). Var: Marceda, Marcedes, Mercedas, Mercedez, Mersedes. Dim: Mechita. Pet: Mecha, Meche. (MARE-SAY-DAYS)

Mersera Compound name composed from Mercedes and Sara. *See* MERCEDES *and* SARA. (MARE-SAY-RAH)

Miguela Feminine form of Miguel, the Spanish cognate of Michael (who is like God?). *See* MIGUEL (Male Names). Var: Macaela, Macaliana, Micaela, Micaella, Micaila, Micalea, Micalla, Migela, Miguaela, Mikaela, Miqaela, Miquaela, Miquela, Miquella. Short: Cailas, Quela. Pet: Mime. (MEE-GELL-LAH)

Milagros Derived from the Spanish *milagro* (miracle, wonder). The name is bestowed in honor of the Virgin Mary, *"Nuestra Señora de los Milagros"* (Our Lady of Miracles). Pet: Mili. (MEE-LAH-GROSS)

Milena Compound name composed from Milagros and Elena. *See* ELENA *and* MILAGROS. (MEE-LAY-NAH)

Miranda Coined by Shakespeare for the heroine of *The Tempest*. It is derived from the Latin *mirandus* (wonderful, to be admired). (MEE-RAHN-DAH)

Natalia From the Latin Natalia, a name derived from *diēs nātālis* (natal day, Christmas). The name is traditionally bestowed upon children born on Christmas Day. Var: Natalina, Nathalia. Dim: Talia. (NAH-TAH-LEE-AH)

Nela A short form of names such as Daniela and Petronella. Nela is also bestowed as an independent given name and is used as an element in combination names. (NEH-LAH)

Nereida Derived from the Greek *nereid* (sea nymph). In Greek mythology, the Nereids were fifty sea-nymph daughters of Nereus. Var: Nireida. (NAY-RAY-DAH)

Nevara Derived from the Spanish *nevar* (to snow). The name is indicative of purity. (NAY-BAH-RAH)

Nieves Derived from the Spanish *nieves* (snows). The name is bestowed in honor of the Virgin Mary, *"Nuestra Señora de las Nieves"* (Our Lady of Snows), in reference to a miracle of unmelted snow in hot weather. Var: Neaves, Neives, Nievas, Nievez, Nievis. (NEE-Ā-BAYS)

Nina Short or pet form of several names, including Cristina. (NEE-NAH)

Noemí Spanish form of the Hebrew Naomi, a name derived from *nāomī* (my delight). The name is borne in the Bible by the mother-in-law of Ruth. Var: Naiomá, Naiomí, Neomí, Noehmí, Noemá, Noemé, Noemíe. Pet: Mimi. (NO-AY-MEE)

Octavia Feminine form of the Latin Octāvius, an old Roman family name derived from *octāvus* (eighth). Var: Octaviacia, Octiana, Octoviana, Otavita, Ottava, Ottaviana. (OAK-TAH-BEE-AH)

Odilia Popular name, Odilia is a Spanish cognate of the German Otthild (prosperous in war), a compound name composed from the elements *od* (riches, prosperity, fortune) and *hild* (battle, war). Var: Eodelia, Eudalia, Eudella, Eudlia, Eudolia, Eudelia, Odalia, Odelea, Odelia, Odella, Odolia, Othelia, Othilia, Otilda, Ottiliana, Ottilla, Ottillia, Otylia, Udelia, Udilia, Uidalia. Short: Tila, Tilla. Pet: Tilde. (O-DEE-LEE-AH)

Olimpia Derived from the Greek Olympia, a feminine form of Olympios (of Olympus). Olympus is a mountain in northern Greece which was regarded as the home of the gods in Greek mythology. (O-LEEM-PEE-AH)

Ovelia Spanish form of the Greek Ophelia (a help, a helper). Var: Availia, Ovalia, Ovellia, Ubelia, Uvelia. (O-BAY-LEE-AH)

Paciencia Directly derived from *paciencia* (patience). Var: Pasencia. Pet: Pacis. (PAH-SEE-ENN-SEE-AH)

Pacífica Derived from the Latin Pacificus (pacify, to make peace), which is from the root *pax* (peace). Var: Pacificia, Pasifica. (PAH-SEE-FEE-CAH)

Paloma Derived from the Spanish *paloma* (dove, pigeon). The dove has long been regarded as a symbol of peace. (PAH-LOW-MAH)

Paola Feminine form of Paulo (small). *See* PAULO (Male Names). Var: Pala, Paulana, Paviana. Dim: Pauleta. (POW-LAH).

Pascuala Feminine form of Pasqual (Easter, Passover). *See* PASQUAL (Male Names). The name is traditionally bestowed upon children born during the Easter or Passover season. Var: Paschala, Pascula, Pasculia, Pasqualia, Pasquelina, Pasqula. (PAHS-KWALL-LAH)

Patricia Derived from the Latin *patricius* (a patrician, an aristocrat). Var: Patriciana, Patrisa, Patrisia, Petricia. Short: Pat, Tricia. Pet: Pati. (PAH-TREE-SEE-AH)

Pefilia Derived from the Spanish *perfilar* (to silhouette, to outline). (PAY-FEE-LEE-AH)

Pentea Borrowed from the name of a flower that belongs to the orchid family. (PANE-TAY-AH)

Perpetua Latin name derived from *perpetuus* (continuous, uninterrupted, perpetual). (PARE-PAY-TOO-AH)

Petronilla Feminine form of Petronilo, which is from the Latin Petronius, an old Roman family name derived from *petra* (a rock, a stone). Var: Petrainla, Petranilla, Petrinila, Petromila, Petronia, Petronella. (PAY-TRO-NEE-LAH)

Piedad Derived from the Spanish *piedad* (piety). The name is bestowed in honor of the Virgin Mary, *"Nuestra Señora de la Piedad"* (Our Lady of Piety). Var: Piedá, Piedada, Pietá. Pet: Picho. (PEE-AY-DAHD)

Pilar Derived from the Spanish *pilar* (pillar, column). The name, bestowed in honor of the Virgin Mary, makes reference to her miraculous appearance to Santiago over a marble pillar. Var: Pelar, Peleria, Piliar, Pillar. Dim: Piluca, Pilucha. Pet: Pili. (PEE-LAHR)

Preciosa Derived from the Spanish *precioso* (precious, valuable). The name makes reference to the precious blood of Christ. Var: Precisia. (PRAY-SEE-O-SAH)

Presencia Derived from the Spanish *presencia* (presence, figure). The name makes reference to the presence of God in all things and the presence of Christ in the Eucharist. (PRAY-SANE-SEE-AH)

Presentación Derived from the Spanish *presentación* (presentation). The name makes reference to the presentation of Jesus in the temple when he was a youngster. Var: Presentatiana. (PRAY-SANE-TAH-SEE-OWN)

Prisciliana Spanish form of Priscilla, a Latin diminutive form of Prisca, which is from Priscus, an old Roman family name meaning "old, ancient." Var: Brisciliana, Brisiliana, Precileana, Presiliana, Prisciana, Prisiliana. (PREE-SEE-LEE-AH-NAH)

Prudencia Derived from the Spanish *prudencia* (prudence, discretion). Var: Prudenciana, Prudintia. Dim: Pensita. (PROO-DANE-SEE-AH)

Purificación Derived from the Spanish *purificación* (purification). The name makes reference to the ritual purification of Mary forty days after the birth of the Christ child. Var: Puresa, Purificasión. Short: Puro. (POO-REE-FEE-KAH-SEE-OWN)

Rafaela Feminine form of Rafael (God has healed). *See* RAFAEL (Male Names). Var: Raefaela, Rafaelia, Rafaila, Rafala, Rafalla, Rafeala, Rafela, Rafelia, Rafiela. Dim: Rafaelina, Rafaelita. (RAH-FAH-ELL-LAH)

Ramona Feminine form of Ramón (wise protection). *See* RAIMUNDO (Male Names). Var: Ramana, Ramina, Ramiona, Ramonelia, Ramonia. Short: Mona. (RAH-MO-NAH)

Raquel Spanish form of Rachel, a cognate of the Ecclesiastic Late Latin and Ecclesiastic Greek Rhachēl, which is derived from the Hebrew *rāhēl* (ewe). The name is borne in the Bible by the younger of Jacob's wives. She was the mother of Joseph and Benjamin. Var: Racaela, Racquel, Raechel, Raquia, Requel. Short: Quela. Dim: Quelita, Rachelina. (RAH-KELL)

Rebeca Spanish form of Rebecca, a cognate of the Ecclesiastic Late Latin and Ecclesiastic Greek Rhebekka, which is derived from the Hebrew *ribbqāh* (noose). The name is borne in the Bible by the wife of Isaac and mother of Jacob and Esau. Var: Rabecca, Rebbeca, Rebbecca, Rebekah, Reveca. Dim: Bequi, Bequita. (RAY-BAY-KAH)

Ricarda Feminine form of Ricardo, the Spanish cognate of Richard (strong king). *See* RICARDO (Male Names). Var: Recharda. Short: Rica, Ricia. (REE-KAR-DAH)

Rita A short form of Margarita (a pearl), Rita is also popularly bestowed as an independent given name. *See* MARGARITA. Var: Reita, Rida, Ritae. (REE-TAH)

Rosa Derived from the Spanish *rosa* (rose). The rose is symbolic of the Virgin Mary. Var: Rozella. Dim: Chalina, Roseta, Rosetta, Rosita. (RO-SAH)

Rosabel Compound name composed from Rosa and *bella* (beautiful): hence, "beautiful rose." (RO-SAH-BELL)

Rosalia Derived from the Latin *rosalia* (the annual Roman ceremony of hanging garlands of roses on tombs). Var: Rosaelia, Rosailia, Rosalá, Rosalya, Rosela. Short: Lía. Pet: Chala, Chalina. (RO-SAH-LEE-AH)

Rosalinda Introduced to Spain by Goth invaders, Rosalinda evolves from the Germanic Roslindis, a compound name composed from the elements *hrôs* (fame) and *lind* (gentle, tender, soft). Folk etymology now attributes the name to the elements *rosa* (rose) and *linda* (pretty). Var: Roslinda. (RO-SAH-LEEN-DAH)

Rosana Compound name composed from Rosa and Ana. *See* ANA *and* ROSA. Var: Rosaana, Rosania, Rosanna, Rozanna. (RO-SAH-NAH)

Sabina Latin name meaning "Sabine woman." The Sabines were an ancient tribe living in central Italy who were conquered by the Romans in 3 B.C. Var: Sabena, Sabiana, Sabinta, Sebrina, Suvina, Zabina, Zabriana, Zabrina. (SAH-BEE-NAH)

Samjuana Compound name composed from Samuel (his name is God) and Juana (God is gracious). *See* JUAN *and* SAMUEL (Male Names). (SAM-HWAHN-NAH)

Sanjuana Compound name composed from *san* (saint) and Juana (God is gracious). *See* JUAN (Male Names). Var: Sanjana, Sanjuna. (SAHN-HWAHN-NAH)

Santana Compound name composed from the elements *san* (saint) and Ana. *See* ANA. (SAHN-TAH-NAH)

Sara Derived from the Hebrew *sārāh* (princess). The name is borne in the Bible by the wife of Abraham and mother of Isaac. Var: Saara, Sahra, Sarea, Sarra, Sarrah, Sera, Serah, Serra, Zahara, Zara, Zayra, Zera. Dim: Charita, Saraita, Sarita. Pet: Chara. (SAH-RAH)

Seferina Feminine form of Seferino (zephyr, the west wind). *See* SEFERINO (Male Names). Var: Cefariana, Cefeorina, Cefernia, Safarena, Saferina, Safira, Sarafina, Sefelina, Seferana, Seforina, Sefrenia, Sefriana, Sefrinia, Sephania, Sepharina, Serafana, Serafena, Serafina, Sypherina, Zaferina, Zefarana, Zefenira, Zeferna, Zepherena. Short: Cefia, Rina, Sefia, Sera, Zefia, Zephia. (SAY-FAY-REE-NO)

Simplicia Feminine form of the Latin Simplicius, which is from *simplex* (simple, single). Var: Semplicia, Simpilia, Simplicitas, Siplicia. (SEEM-PLEE-SEE-AH)

Socorra Derived from the Spanish *socorro* (help, aid, assistance). The name is bestowed in honor of the Virgin Mary, "*Nuestra Señora del Perpetuo Socorro*" (Our Lady of Perpetual Help). Var: Secora, Socaria, Soccora, Sucorra. (SO-KO-RAH)

Sofía Derived from the Greek Sophia, which is directly derived from *sophia* (wisdom, skill). The name, listed eighteen times in the *Dictionary of Saints*, was borne by St. Sophia, a woman martyred along with her three daughters. Var: Safía, Sofí, Sofina, Zofía. (SO-FEE-AH)

Soledad Derived from the Spanish *soledad* (solitude). The name is bestowed in honor of the Virgin Mary, "*Nuestra Señora de la Soledad*" (Our Lady of Solitude). Var: Saledá, Saledad, Soladá, Soletá, Solitá. (SO-LAY-DAHD)

Susana Derived from the Hebrew Shoshana, which is from *shōshannāh* (a lily, a rose). The name is borne in the Bible by a woman falsely accused of adultery. Her story is told in the apocryphal book of Susannah and the Elders. Var: Sussana, Suzanea, Suzanna, Zuzana, Zuzanna. Short: Susa, Suse. Pet: Susi, Susy, Suzy. (SOO-SAH-NAH)

Teodora Feminine form of Teodoro (God's gift). *See* TEODORO (Male Names). Var: Teodara, Tiodora, Tiodoria. Short: Dora. (TAY-O-DOR-AH)

Teresa Generally believed to be derived from the Greek *therizein* (to reap, to gather in). The first known bearer of the name was the Spanish wife of St. Paulinus, a 5th-century Roman bishop of Nola. Teresa was not used outside the Iberian Peninsula until the 16th century, when the Spanish mystic St. Teresa of Avila (1515–82) made the name popular among Roman Catholics throughout Europe. Var: Terasa, Teresia, Tereza, Terezia, Terusa, Therese, Theresia, Tresa. Short: Tera. Dim: Teresita. Pet: Tea, Techa, Tessa. (TAY-RAY-SAH)

Tomasa Feminine form of Tomás (a twin). *See* TOMÁS (Male Names). Var: Tamasa, Tomana, Tomasena, Tomasila, Tomasina, Tomaza, Tomeseta. Dim: Tomasita. (TŌ-MAHS-AH)

Tresiliana Derived from the Spanish *tres* (three), Tresiliana has the definition "third-born child." (TRAY-SEE-LEE-AH-NAH)

Tulia Feminine form of Tulio, a name derived from the Latin Tullius, an old Roman family name of uncertain derivation. Var: Tulenia, Tuliana. (TOO-LEE-AH)

Úrsula Diminutive form of the Latin *ursa* (she-bear): hence, "little she-bear." Var: Orsinia, Órsula, Úrsala, Úrsela, Urselia, Ursuela, Ursulina, Úrzula. (OOR-SOO-LAH)

Vandelia Borrowed from the name of a popular flowering plant. Var: Bandelia. (BAHN-DAY-LEE-AH)

Veneranda Derived from the Spanish *venerando* (venerable, worthy of respect). Var: Benaranda, Beneranda. (BAY-NAH-RAHN-DAH)

VERÓNICA Of debated origin and meaning. *See* VERONICA (Italian Names). The name was supposedly borne by the woman who helped Christ on his way to Calvary, wiping his face with her veil, which was left with an imprint of it. Var: Varónica. (BAY-RO-NEE-KAH)

VICTORIA Derived from the Latin *victoria* (victory). Var: Bictoria, Bitoria, Bitriana, Victariana, Victorana, Viktoriana. Pet: Bique, Lina, Tolita, Toya. (BEEK-TOR-EE-AH)

VINCENTA Feminine form of Vincentio (conquering). *See* VINCENTIO (Male Names). Var: Becentia, Bicentu, Bisenta, Bizenta, Vecenta, Vicentia, Vicienta, Vincencia, Vincentia, Vincienta, Visenta. Pet: Chenta. (BEE-SANE-TAH)

VIVIÁN Derived from the Latin Vivianus, which is from *vivus* (alive). The name was borne by St. Perpetua, born Vivia Perpetua, a Roman matron who was martyred for her beliefs. Var: Bibiana, Bibián, Bibianna, Bivián, Biviana, Veviana, Vibiena, Vivia, Viviana, Vivianna, Vivina. Short: Biana, Viana. Dim: Bianilla. Pet: Bibi, Vivi. (BEE-BEE-AHN)

YOLANDA Of uncertain etymology, some believe it to be a derivative of Violante (violet), a medieval French name derived from the Latin Viola (violet). Var: Iolanda, Jolanda, Yolonda. Short: Yola. Pet: Yoli, Yolie. (YO-LAHN-DAH)

ZENAIDA Greek name meaning "pertaining to Zeus," which is from *zēn* (of Zeus). The name is borne in Greek mythology by a daughter of Zeus. Zeneida is also the name given to two types of wild doves found from the southern United States to South America; thus the name is beginning to be used in reference to the doves. Var: Cenaida, Cenaide, Cenanida, Sanaida, Seneida, Seniada, Sinayda, Xenaida, Zeneida. Short: Naida. (ZAY-NAY-DAH)

ZOÉ Derived from the Greek *zōē* (life). (ZO-Ā)

ZOILA Feminine form of the Greek Zoilo, which is derived from *zōē* (life). Var: Soilla, Zaila, Zalia, Ziola, Zolla, Zoyla. Pet: Chola. (ZOY-LAH)

ZORAIDA Of Arabic origin meaning "captivating woman." The name was popularized in the 19th century by Donizetti's opera *Zoraida di Granata* (1822). Var: Saraida, Soraida, Soraita, Zaraida, Zarida, Zeraida, Zorida. (ZO-RYE-DAH)

ZULEICA Derived from the Arabic *zuleika* (fair). Var: Zulaica. (ZOO-LAY-KAH)

Chapter Thirty-One

Welsh Names

The Norman invasion of 1066, which brought such profound change to the English, also had a great affect on the Welsh. Adventurous Norman lords, called "marcher lords," began to conquer areas in central and southern Wales. By the end of the reign of King Henry I, the southern Welsh were thoroughly subdued, leading to the intermixing of the population and culture. Over time, the Welsh language was suppressed and its use discouraged. As a result, Norman and English names nearly superseded Welsh names. Eventually, few traditional Welsh names survived.

In the 1960s, *Cymdeithas yr Iaith Gymraeg* (the Welsh Language Society), pressed for recognition of the language, which led to the adoption of the 1967 Welsh Language Act. This in turn spurred a modern effort to teach the language in schools, and to promote Welsh culture and a sense of Welsh identity. In response, names are being revived from traditional Welsh poetry, legends, ancient princes and heroes, and are once again being proudly bestowed upon the children of Wales.

Welsh Male Names

Adda Welsh form of Adam, which is derived from the Hebrew *adama* (red earth). (AD-DAH)

Aed Welsh form of the Scottish and Irish Aodh (fire), which is directly derived from the Gaelic *aodh*. In Celtic mythology, Aodh is the name of the ancient sun-god. (AYD)

Aeddon Elaboration of Aed (fire). *See* AED. (AYD-UN)

Alun Welsh form of Alan, a Celtic name of Breton origin but of uncertain meaning. Some believe it to mean "handsome." Others promote the possibility that it is from a Celtic word meaning "rock." The name was brought to the British Isles by the Normans during the Conquest. Var: Alyn. (AL-IN)

Alwyn A borrowing from the English, Alwyn is a variant form of Alvin (friend of the elves). Alvin is derived from the Old English Alfwine, a compound name composed of the elements *ælf* (elf) and *wine* (friend). Var: Aylwin. (AL-WIN)

Andras Welsh form of Andrew (manly). *See* ANDREW. (AN-DRAS)

Andrew English cognate of the Greek Andreas, a derivative of *andreios* (manly) which has its root in *anēr* (man). The name is borne in the Bible by one of the Twelve Apostles of Christ, which originally induced the name's popularity. Contemporaneously, the name is borne by Prince Andrew, the duke of York (b. 1960), the son of Queen Elizabeth II and Prince Philip. (AN-DREW)

ANEIRIN Evolution of Neirin, an old name of uncertain derivation. Some believe it to be derived from the Gaelic *nár* (noble, modest). Another source gives the definition "man of excellence." Var: Aneurin. Pet: Nye. (AN-Ī-RIN)

ARIAN Derived from the Welsh *arian* (silver). (AR-EE-AN)

ART Derived from the Gaelic *art* (bear). Art is also used as a short form of Arthur, a Celtic name of unknown meaning. *See* ARTHUR. (ART)

ARTHUR Of Celtic origin but of unknown meaning. The name was borne by the legendary British King Arthur, leader of the knights of the Round Table, who supposedly lived in the 5th or 6th century. The name gained popularity from the great body of Arthurian legend that has remained of interest over the centuries. Var: Arthwr. Short: Art. (AR-THER)

AUSTIN A borrowing from the English, Austin is a contracted form of Augustine, an English cognate of the Latin Augustinus, a diminutive form of Augustus, which is derived from *augustus* (great, venerable, consecrated by the augurs). Awstin is the Welsh form. Var: Austen. (AU-STIN)

AWSTIN Welsh form of Austin (great, venerable). *See* AUSTIN. Short: Awst. (AWS-STIN)

BARRIS Transferred use of the surname that originated as ab Harris (son of Harris). Harris originated as a patronymic meaning "son of Harry" or "son of Henry," both names meaning "home ruler." *See* HARRY *and* HENRY (English Names).

BERWYN Compound name composed of the Welsh elements *barr* (head) and *gwyn* (white, fair, blessed): hence, "fair-haired, white-headed." (BARE-WIN)

BEVIN Transferred use of the surname that originated as ab Iefan (son of Iefan). *See* IEFAN. Var: Bevan. (BEH-VIN)

BLEDDYN Ancient compound name composed of *blaidd* (wolf; hero) and the suffix *-yn*. (BLETH-IN)

BRAN Popular name derived from *brân* (raven). The name is borne in Welsh mythology by the Blessed Bran, the brother of Branwen and Manawyddan. His sister's marriage to King Matholwych of Ireland temporarily united the two islands. But her mistreatment at the hands of her husband prompted an attack of revenge by Bran—an attack during which he was mortally wounded. (BRAN)

BRIAN Borrowed from the Irish, Brian is of uncertain etymology. It is generally thought to be of Celtic origin, but its meaning is disputed. *See* BRIAN (Irish Names). Var: Brien, Bryan. (BRI-UN)

BRODERICK Transferred use of the surname that originated as ab Roderick (son of Roderick). *See* RODERICK. (BRAH-DER-RICK)

BRYCHAN Derived from an old Welsh word meaning "speckled." (BRI-CHAN)

BRYN Popular name derived from the Welsh *bryn* (hill). Alternatively, Bryn is used as a short form of Brynmor (great hill). *See* BRYNMOR. (BRIN)

BRYNMOR Compound name composed of the Welsh elements *bryn* (hill) and *mawr* (great, large): hence, "great hill." Short: Bryn. (BRIN-MOR)

CADELL Derived from the Old Welsh elements *cad*, *cath* (war, battle, defense) and the diminutive suffix *-ell*: hence, "small battle." The name was borne by a 12th-century saint. Originally a fierce and renowned warrior, he recovered from wounds he received in battle, repented, and journeyed to the Holy Land, where he became a monk. (KADDL)

CADMAN Derived from the Old Welsh elements *cad*, *cath* (war, battle, defense). Var: Cadmon, Caedman, Caedmon. (KAD-MAHN)

CADOGAN Anglicized form of Cadwgawn (battle glory, battle of distinction). *See* CADWGAWN. (KAH-DUG-GAN)

CADWALLON Compound name composed of the Welsh elements *cad*, *cath* (war, battle, defense) and *wallon* (arranger, scatterer): hence, "battle arranger." Var: Cadwallen. (KAD-WO-LUN)

CADWGAWN Compound name composed of the Old Welsh elements *cad*, *cath* (war, battle, defense) and *gwogawn* (honor, valor, glory): hence, "glorious battle." Cadogan is the Anglicized form. Var: Cadwgan. (KAH-DOO-GUN)

CAERWYN Compound name composed of the elements *caer* (fort, fortress) and *gwyn* (white, fair, blessed): hence, "white fortress." Var: Carwyn. (KIR-WIN)

CARADOC Ancient name derived from the elements *cāra* (beloved). Var: Caradog, Caradwg. (KAH-RAH-DOK)

CAREY A borrowing from the Irish and the English, Carey represents the transferred use of a surname. The Irish form is from the surname Ó Ciardha (descendant of the dark one), which is derived from the Gaelic *ciar* (black, dark). The English surname originated from a place-name derived from an old Celtic river name of uncertain meaning. It has been suggested that it is from the Gaelic *caraich* (to move, to stir) or *caraidh* (movement). Var: Cary. (KER-REE)

Charles A popular name throughout Europe and Great Britain, Charles is derived from the Germanic *karl* (full-grown, a man), which is a cognate of the English *ceorl* (a man, freeman, peasant). It is a royal name, being borne by ten kings of France as well as by kings of Hungary, Naples, Sardinia, and Württemberg. It was introduced to Great Britain by Mary, Queen of Scots (1542–87), who bestowed it upon her son, Charles James (1566–1625). His son and grandson both ruled as King Charles, furthering the name's popularity. Currently, the name is borne by Prince Charles, the duke of Wales (b. 1948) and heir to the British throne. Siarl is a popular Welsh form of the name. Pet: Charlie. (CHARLZ)

Cledwyn Compound name composed of the elements *caled* (hard, rough) and *gwyn* (white, fair, blessed). (KLED-WIN)

Cyndeyrn Welsh form of the Scottish Kantigern (head chief), a name derived from the Celtic elements *can* (head) and *tighearn* (chief, king, ruler). The name was borne by a Christian apostle, the patron of Glasgow who was driven out of Scotland by pagan persecutors. He fled to Wales, where he founded the Church of Llandwy. (KUN-DAIRN)

Cyril A borrowing from the English, Cyril is from the Late Latin Cyrillus, a derivative of the Greek Kyrillos (lordly), which is from *kyrios* (a lord). *See* CYRIL (English Names). (SIR-EL)

Cystenian Welsh form of Constantine, a name derived from the Late Latin Constantīnus, which is from *constans* (constant, steadfast). The name was borne by Constantine the Great (280?–337), the first emperor of Rome to be converted to Christianity. (KUH-STEN-YEN)

Dafydd Welsh form of David (beloved). *See* DAVID. Var: Dafod, Dawfydd. (DAY-VITH)

Dai Derived from the Celtic *dei* (to shine). Alternatively, Dai is used as a pet form of David (beloved). *See* DAVID. (DIE)

Daniel Derived from the Hebrew *dānī'ēl* (God is my judge). The name is borne in the Bible by a Hebrew prophet whose faith kept him alive in a den of hungry lions. Daniel and the Lions' Den was a favorite story during the Middle Ages, which helped to promote the use of the name throughout Europe and the British Isles. Deiniol is the Welsh cognate. Short: Dan. (DAN-YEL)

David Derived from the Hebrew *dāvīd* (beloved). It is borne in the Bible by the second and greatest of the Israelite kings. In Wales the name was borne by St. David (also known as St. Dewi), a 5th-century Welsh bishop who is the patron saint of Wales. Dafydd and Dewi are Welsh forms of the name. Pet: Dai. (DAY-VID)

Deiniol Welsh form of Daniel (God is my judge). *See* DANIEL. (DIN-YOLE)

Dewi Welsh form of David (beloved) that evolved from the earlier form of Dewydd. *See* DAVID. The name was borne by the 5th-century St. Dewi (also known as St. David), the patron saint of Wales. Var: Dewey. Short: Dew. (DEH-WEE)

Dilwyn Compound name composed of the Welsh elements *dilys* (genuine, steadfast, true) and *gwyn* (white, fair, blessed): hence, "blessed truth." Var: Dillwyn. (DIL-WIN)

Drystan Variant form of Tristan (sad). *See* TRISTAN. (DRIS-TUN)

Dylan Of uncertain derivation, some believe it to be from an Old Celtic element meaning "sea." The name is borne in Welsh mythology by the brother of the hero Llew Llaw Gyffes. More recently, the name received a boost in popularity through the fame of Welsh poet Dylan Thomas (1914–53). (DIL-LUN)

Einion Derived from the Welsh *einion* (anvil). Pet: Einwys. (Ī N-EE-ON)

Emlyn Common Welsh name of uncertain origin and meaning. (EM-LIN)

Emrys Welsh form of Ambrose, an Old French name derived from the Latin Ambrosius, which is from the Greek Ambrosios, a direct derivation from *ambrosios* (immortal). The name was borne by St. Ambrose, a 4th-century bishop of Milan, who is considered to be one of the four great Latin doctors of the church. (EM-RISS)

Emyr Derived from *emyr* (ruler, king). (EM-MER)

Eoghan A borrowing from the Scotch and Irish. Eoghan is an ancient name of uncertain derivation. Most believe it is from *êoghunn* (youth). (EH-VAHN)

Evan Anglicized form of Iefan, the Welsh cognate of John (God is gracious). *See* JOHN. Var: Ifan. (EH-VAN)

Folant Welsh form of Valentine, which is from the Latin Valentīnus, a derivative of *valens* (to be healthy, strong). St. Valentine was a 3rd-century Roman martyr whose feast day, February 14, coincides with that of a pagan festival marking the beginning of spring. (FO-LAN)

Gareth Celtic name of uncertain meaning. Because its pet form Gary is identical in form with the English

Gary (spear of battle), many now equate the two names as equal, but they are not. *See* GARY (English Names). The name is borne in Arthurian legend by the lover of Eluned. Pet: Gary. (GARE-ETH)

GARTH A borrowing from the English, Garth represents the transferred use of the surname derived from the Middle English *garth* (an enclosed yard or garden). The name originated as an occupational name for a person in charge of a garden or an enclosed yard or paddock. (GARTH)

GARY A pet form of Gareth, Gary is also commonly bestowed as an independent given name. *See* GARETH. (GARE-EE)

GAVIN A borrowing from the Scottish, Gavin is a name of uncertain etymology. Some believe it is from Gwalchmai, a Gaelic name derived from the elements *gwalch* (a hawk) and *maedd* (a blow, battle). In Arthurian legend, Gavin is a byname for Sir Gawain, a knight of the Round Table and nephew of King Arthur. (GAV-IN)

GEOFFREY A borrowing from the English, Geoffrey is derived from the Middle English Geffrey, which is from the Old French Geoffroi, a name thought to have evolved from several different Germanic names. Gaufrid, of the elements *govja* (a district) and *frithu* (peace), Walahfrid, from *valha* (traveler) and *frithu* (peace), and Gisfrid, from the elements *gis* (pledge) and *frithu* (peace), are thought to be the root names. The name was borne by Geoffrey of Monmouth (c. 1100–54), a Welsh bishop, historical chronicler, and preserver of Arthurian legend. Sieffre is a common Welsh form of Geoffrey. (JOF-FREE, JEF-FREE)

GEORGE A borrowing from the English, George is a cognate of the Greek Georgios, which is derived from *geōrgos* (earthworker, farmer), a compounding of the elements *gē* (earth) and *ergein* (to work). The name was uncommon to the British Isles until the Hanoverian George became king in 1714. The use of the name by the four succeeding kings firmly established its use and popularity. Siôr is theWelsh form of the name. (JORJ)

GERAINT Ancient yet still popular name of uncertain origin. Geraint is borne in Arthurian legend by a knight of the Round Table. Having won Enid's hand at a tournament, he became hopelessly infatuated with her and, finally, wrongly accused her of infidelity. Enid proved her loyalty to Geraint by being submissive and obedient. (GER-ĪNT)

GERALLT Welsh form of Gerald (spear ruler), a Germanic name composed of the elements *gēr* (spear) and *wald* (rule). (JER-ULT)

GETHIN Modern variant of the old nickname Cethin (dark, swarthy). Var: Gethen. (GETH-IN)

GLADUS Welsh cognate of the Latin Claudius, an old Roman family name derived from *claudus* (lame). (GLAD-US)

GLYN Modern name derived from *glyn* (valley, glen). Glyn is also used as a short form of Glyndwr (valley of water). *See* GLYNDŴR. Var: Glynn, Glynne. (GLIN)

GLYNDŴR Transferred use of the surname originating as a place-name. The name is composed of the elements *glyn* (valley, glen) and *dŵ* (water): hence, "valley of water." Short: Glyn. (GLIN-DOOER)

GREGORY A borrowing from the English, Gregory is from the Late Latin Gregorius, a cognate of the Greek Grēgorios (vigilant, watchful), which is from the verb *egeirein* (to awaken). Grigor is the Welsh form of the name. *See* GREGORY (English Names). (GREG-OR-EE)

GRIFFIN Evolved from Griffinus, a Latinate form of Griffith used in the Middle Ages. *See* GRIFFITH. Short: Griff. (GRIF-FIN)

GRIFFITH Of debated origin, some believe it to be an Anglicized form of Gruffudd, the Welsh form of the Roman Rufus (red, ruddy). Others derive the name from the Old Welsh Grippiud (prince). Short: Griff. (GRIF-FITH)

GRIGOR Welsh form of Gregory (watchful). *See* GREGORY. (GRĪ-GOR)

GRUFFUDD Welsh form of the Roman Rufus (red, ruddy). The name was borne by Gruffudd ap Llywelyn, the 11th-century ruler who successfully united all the kingdoms of Wales. Var: Griffudd, Gruffydd. Pet: Guto, Gutun, Gutyn. (GREE-FEETH)

GWALCHMAI Compound name composed of the elements *gwalch* (hawk) and *mai* (plain) or *maedd* (a blow, battle). The name is borne in Arthurian legend by a nephew of King Arthur, his most distinguished and celebrated knight. (GWAHL-KMĪ)

GWALLTER Welsh form of Walter (ruler of an army). *See* WALTER. (GWAHL-TER)

GWILYM Welsh cognate of William (resolute protector). *See* WILLIAM. (GWIL-UM)

GWYN Popular name derived from *gwyn* (white, fair, blessed). Var: Gwynn, Gwynne. (GWIN)

GWYNEDD Derived from the element *gwyn* (white, fair, blessed). Gwynedd was originally the name of a medieval region of northern Wales. (GWIN-NETH)

GWYNFOR Modern name composed of the elements *gwyn* (white, fair, blessed) and a variant form of *mawr* (great, large). (GWIN-VOR)

GWYTHYR Welsh form of Victor (conqueror, winner). *See* VICTOR. Var: Gwydyr. (GWĪ-THER, GWIH-THER)

HEDDWYN Modern compound name composed of the elements *hedd* (peace) and *gwyn* (white, fair, blessed): hence, "blessed peace." (HED-WIN)

HILARY A borrowing from the English, Hilary is from the Latin Hilarius (cheerful), which is from *hilaris* (cheerful, glad). Ilar is the Welsh form of the name. (HIL-AH-REE)

HOPKIN Transferred use of the surname, which arose in the Middle Ages from the personal name Hob, a pet form of Robert (bright fame). Var: Hopcyn. (HOP-KIN)

HOWELL Anglicized form of Hywel (eminent, prominent, conspicuous). *See* HYWEL. (HOW-EL)

HUGH A borrowing from the English, Hugh is from the Old French Hue, which is from the Old High German Hugo, a derivative of *hugu* (heart, mind, spirit). The Welsh form of the name is Huw. (HEW)

HUMPHREY A borrowing from the English, Humphrey represents the transferred use of the surname, which originated from the Germanic Hunfrid (warrior of peace), a compound name composed from the elements *hun* (strength, warrior) and *frid* (peace). The name was brought to England by the Normans and replaced the earlier Hunfrith, which was composed from the Old Norse *húnn* (bear cub) and the Old English *frith* (peace). Wmffre is the Welsh form. (HUM-FREE)

HUW Welsh form of Hugh (heart, mind, spirit). *See* HUGH. (HEW)

HYWEL Derived from *hywel* (eminent, prominent, conspicuous). The name is Anglicized as Howell. Var: Hywell. (HOW-EL)

IAGO Welsh form of James, which is ultimately derived from the Hebrew *ya'aqob* (supplanting, seizing by the heel). *See* JAMES (English Names). (EE-AH-GO)

IAON Welsh cognate of John (God is gracious). *See* JOHN. (EE-OO-AN)

IDRIS Compound name composed of the elements *iud* (lord) and *rīs* (ardent, impulsive). The name was common during the Middle Ages but died out until its revival in the 20th century. (ID-RISS)

IEFAN Welsh cognate of John (God is gracious), which is an evolution of the earlier Ieuan. *See* JOHN. Iefan is Anglicized as Evan. Var: Ifan. (Ī-VAHN)

IESTYN Welsh form of Justin (lawful, right, just). *See* JUSTIN (English Names). (YES-TIN)

IEUAN Original Welsh form of John (God is gracious). The name gave rise to the variant forms Iefan and Ifan. *See* IEFAN *and* JOHN. (YĪ-YAN)

IFOR Ancient yet still common name of uncertain derivation. It has been Anglicized as Ivor (archer), a name of Scandinavian origin. *See* IVOR. (Ī-VOR)

ILLTUD Compound name composed of the elements *il* (multitude) and *tud* (land, people): hence, "land of the multitude." Var: Illtyd. (IHL-TID)

IORWERTH Popular compound name composed of *iōr* (lord) and a variant form of *berth* (handsome). The name has been Anglicized as Edward. Var: Yorath. Pet: Iolo, Iolyn. (YOR-WAIRTH)

ISLWYN Transferred use of a Welsh place-name composed of the elements *is* (below) and *llwyn* (grove). (ISS-LOO-WIN)

IVOR Derived from the Scandinavian Ivar (bow warrior, archer), a compound name composed of the Old Norse elements*ýr* (yew, bow) and *herr* (army, warrior). The name was introduced to England by Ivar the Boneless, who invaded East Anglia in retaliation for the death of his father. The name is used in Wales to Anglicize Ifor, an ancient name of uncertain derivation. (Ī-VOR)

JENKIN Transferred use of the surname originating from Jankin, a medieval pet form of Jan, a variant of John (God is gracious). *See* JOHN. The Welsh form of Jenkin is Siencyn. (JEN-KIN)

JOHN A borrowing from the English, John is the most enduring of all the biblical names. It is derived from the Middle Latin Johannes, which is from the Ecclesiastic Late Latin Joannes, from the Ecclesiastic Greek Iōannes, a derivative of the Hebrew Yehanan, a short form of Yehohanan, which is from *yehōhānān* (Yahweh is gracious). Iefan, Ifan, Ieuan, and Siôn are Welsh forms of the name. Evan is a popular Anglicized form of the Welsh cognates. (JON)

KENDALL Used as both a masculine and a feminine name in Wales, Kendall is the transferred use of the surname, which arose from the place-name Kendal in Westmorland, northwestern England. The town, which is in the valley of the river Kent, derives its name from the name of the river and *dale* (valley): hence, "valley of the river Kent." Another source for the surname is the place-name Kendale in Humberside, northeastern England. In this case, the name is derived from the Old Norse element *keld* (spring) and the Old English *dale* (valley): hence, "valley of the spring." Var: Kendal. (KEN-DL)

LEWIS A borrowing from the English, Lewis is from the French Louis, a derivative of the Old French Loeis, which is from the Old High German Hluodowig (famous warrior), a compound name composed of the elements *hluod* (famous) and *wīg* (war, strife). The name has been used in Wales to Anglicize the name Llewelyn. *See* Llewelyn. Short: Lew. Pet: Lewie. (LOO-ISS)

LLEU Derived from the element *lleu* (bright, shining). The name is borne in Welsh mythology by the popular hero Lleu Llaw Gyffes, the brother of Dylan and son of Aranrhod and her brother Gwydion. (HLOO)

LLEW Derived from *llew* (lion). The name is also used as a short form of Llewelyn. *See* LLEWELYN. The name is borne in Welsh legend by the brother-in-law of King Arthur and father of the famous knight Gwalchmai. (HLEW)

LLEWELYN Ancient name of uncertain etymology, some think it is derived from the Old Celtic Lugobelinos (the bright one, the shining one). Others think it might be from Llewel (lion-like), which is derived from *llew* (lion). Another suggestion is that it is ultimately derived from the Latin Lucius, which is from the root *lux* (light). The name was borne by Prince Llewelyn the Great of Wales (1173–1240) and by his grandson, the last native prince of Wales, Llewelyn ap Gruffyd, who died in 1282 at Piercefield. Short: Llew, Lyn. Pet: Llelo. (HLEH-WEL-LIN)

LLOYD Anglicized form of the Welsh Llwyd (gray, gray-haired), which is directly derived from *llwyd* (gray). (LOID)

LLWYD A direct derivation of *llwyd* (gray), Llwyd originated as a nickname for a person with gray hair. Lloyd is the Anglicized form. (HLOO-ID)

LUC Welsh cognate of Luke (light). *See* LUKE (English Names). (LUKE)

MABON From the Old Celtic element *mab* (son). (MAB-BUN)

MAURICE A borrowing from the English, Maurice is from the Late Latin Mauritius (Moorish), which is derived from *maurus* (a Moor). *See* MAURICE (English Names). Meurig and Meuriz are Welsh forms. (MOR-RISS, MOR-REES)

MEIC Short form of Meical, the Welsh cognate of Michael (who is like God?). Meic corresponds to the English Mike. *See* MICHAEL. (MIKE)

MEICAL Welsh cognate of Michael (who is like God?). *See* MICHAEL. Short: Meic. (MĪ-KL, MEE-KL)

MEILYR Derived from the obsolete Old Celtic Maglorīx, a compound name composed of the elements *maglos* (chief) and *rīx* (ruler): hence, "chief ruler." (MĪ-LER)

MEIRION Welsh form of the Latin Mariānus, a derivative of Marius, which is an old Roman family name of uncertain derivation. Some believe the name has its root in Mars, the Roman mythological god of war, but others think it is derived from the Latin *mas* (manly). Early Christians associated the name with the Virgin Mary, and it thus enjoyed widespread use. (MEER-EE-ON)

MERFYN Popular name derived from the Old Welsh elements *mer* (marrow, brains) or *môr* (sea) and *myn* (eminent, prominent, high, hill): hence, "sea hill, eminent marrow." The name is Anglicized as Mervyn. (MER-VIN)

MERLIN Derived from the Welsh Myrddin, which is believed to be derived from the Primitive Celtic elements *mer, mori* (sea) and *dunom* (hill, fortress), therefore meaning "sea hill" or "sea fortress." Myrddin was an early Celtic mythological hero who was later found as a magician and helper of King Arthur in Arthurian legend. Var: Merlyn. (MER-LIN)

MERVYN Anglicized form of Merfyn (sea hill, eminent marrow). *See* MERFYN. Var: Mervin, Merwin, Merwyn. (MER-VIN)

MEURIZ Welsh form of Maurice (dark, swarthy). *See* MAURICE. Var: Meurig. (MĪ-RIZ)

MICHAEL Derivative of the Hebrew *mīkhā'ēl* (who is like God?). The name is borne in the Bible by the archangel closest to God, the one responsible for carrying out God's judgments. Considered the leader of the heavenly host, Michael is regarded as the patron of soldiers. The name, one of the most successful of the biblical names, has cognates in many languages and is in popular use throughout Europe and abroad. Meical and Mihangel are Welsh forms of the name. Short: Mike. (MĪ-KL)

MIHANGEL Welsh form of Michael (who is like God?). *See* MICHAEL. (MĪ-AH-GEL)

MORGAN From the Old Welsh Morcant, a compound name thought to be composed of the elements *môr* (sea) and *cant* (circle, completion) or *can* (white, bright). (MOR-GUN)

MORYS Welsh cognate of Maurice (a Moor). *See* MAURICE (English Names). (MOR-EES)

Mostyn Transferred use of the Welsh place-name derived from the Old English elements *mos* (moss) and *tūn* (town, settlement, village, enclosure). (MOSS-TIN)

Owain A popular name of uncertain derivation, some believe it to be from the Welsh *oen* (lamb). Others feel it is from the Gaelic *êoghunn* (youth), and yet another suggestion is that it is the Welsh form of the Latin Eugenius (well-born, noble). The name was borne by Owain Glyndŵr, last of the Welsh fighting patriots (14th–15th century). Var: Owen. (O-WEN)

Padrig Welsh cognate of Patrick, which is derived from the Latin *patricius* (a patrician). Pet: Paddy. (PAH-DRIG)

Pawl Welsh cognate of Paul, which is derived from the Latin *paulus* (small). (PAUL)

Pedr Welsh cognate of Peter (rock). *See* PETER. (PEE-DR)

Peter From the Ecclesiastic Late Latin Petrus and the Ecclesiastic Greek Petros, names derived from the vocabulary words *petra* (a rock) and *petros* (a stone). The name is borne in the Bible by one of the Twelve Apostles of Christ. Peter is considered to have been the first pope and cofounder of the Christian Church with Paul. Pedr is the Welsh cognate of the name. Short: Pete. (PEE-TER)

Pewlin Welsh form of the Latin Paulīnus, a derivative of Paulus, a name that originated as an old Roman family name from *paulus* (small). *See* PAUL (English Names). Var: Peulan. (PEW-LIN)

Pryderi Old Welsh name meaning "caring for, concern." (PRIH-DARE-EE)

Pyrs Welsh cognate of Pierce, a name that originated as a variant of Peter (a rock). *See* PIERCE (English Names). (PEERSS)

Rees Anglicized form of Rhys (ardor). *See* RHYS. (REESS)

Reynold A borrowing from the English, Reynold is a variant form of Reginald, a derivative of the Middle Latin Reginaldus, which is from the Old High German Raganald and Raginold, compound names composed from the elements *ragin* (advice, judgment, counsel) and *wald* (ruler). Rheinallt is the Welsh form of the name. (RENLD)

Rheinallt Welsh cognate of Reynold (judgment ruler). *See* REYNOLD. (RENLD)

Rhisiart Welsh cognate of Richard (brave ruler). *See* RICHARD. (RIH-SHERD)

Rhodri Compound name composed from the Old Welsh *rhod* (wheel) and *rhi* (ruler, king). (ROD-REE)

Rhys Popular name derived from the element *rhys* (ardor), which was borne by several Welsh rulers. Rees is the Anglicized form of the name. (REES)

Richard A borrowing from the English and the French, Richard is from the Old High German Richart, a compound name composed of the elements *rīc*, *rik* (power, ruler) and *hard* (strong, brave, hearty): hence, "brave ruler." *See* RICHARD (English Names). Rhisiart is the Welsh cognate. (RICH-ERD)

Roderick From the Middle Latin Rodericus, which is derived from the Old High German Hrodrich (famous ruler), a compound name composed from the elements *hruod* (fame) and *rik* (king, ruler). The name has been used to Anglicize the Welsh Rhydderch (reddish-brown, rust-colored). Short: Rod. (ROD-EH-RIK)

Rolant Welsh form of the French Roland, a name derived from the Old High German Hruodland (famous land), a compound name composed from the elements *hruod* (fame) and *land* (land). The name was introduced to the British Isles by the Normans. (RO-LAND)

Samuel Ecclesiastic Late Latin form of the Ecclesiastic Greek Samouel, which is from the Hebrew Shmuel, a name derived from *shĕmū'ēl* (name of God, his name is God). The name is borne in the Bible by a Hebrew judge and prophet who anointed Saul as the first king of Israel. Sawyl is the Welsh form of the name. Short: Sam. (SAM-YOOL)

Sawyl Welsh form of Samuel (name of God, his name is God), which evolved from the earlier Safwyl. *See* SAMUEL. (SAW-EL)

Siarl Welsh cognate of Charles (full-grown, a man). *See* CHARLES. (SHARL)

Siencyn Welsh form of Jenkin (God is gracious). *See* JENKIN. (SHANE-KIN)

Siôn Popular Welsh cognate of John (God is gracious). *See* JOHN. Pet: Sionym. (SHON)

Siôr Welsh form of George (earthworker, farmer). *See* GEORGE. Pet: Siors, Siorys. (SHOR)

Steffan Welsh cognate of Stephen (a crown, a garland). *See* STEPHEN. (STEV-VAHN)

Stephen A borrowing from the English, Stephen is from the Latin Stephanus, a derivative of *stephanos* (a crown, a garland). The name was borne by St. Stephen. The first Christian martyr, he was one of the seven chosen to assist the Twelve Apostles. Steffan is the popular Welsh form of the name. (STEE-VEN)

STUART A borrowing from the English and the Scotch, Stuart represents the transferred use of the surname, which is the French form of the English Stewart. This surname originated as an occupational name derived from the Old English *stiward, stiweard* (steward, keeper of the animal enclosure), a position that was in many cases a hereditary one, especially among noble or royal households. *See* STUART (English Names). Var: Stewart. (STYOO-ART)

TALFRYN Compound name composed of the Welsh element *tal* (high) and a variant form of *bryn* (hill): hence, "high hill." (TAL-VRIN)

TALIESIN Compound name composed of the Welsh elements *tâl* (brow) and *ìesin* (shining, radiant): hence, "radiant brow." The name was borne by a famous 6th-century Welsh poet. (TAL-EH-SIN)

TEWDWR Welsh form of Theodore (God's gift). *See* THEODORE. (THYOO-DYOOR)

THEODORE A borrowing from the English, Theodore is from the Latin Theodorus, which is from the Greek Theodōros (God's gift), a compound name composed of the elements *theos* (God) and *dōron* (gift). Tewdwr is the Welsh form of the name. Short: Theo. Pet: Ted, Teddy. (THEE-O-DORE)

THOMAS From the Ecclesiastic Greek Thōmas, which is derived from the Aramaic *t'ōma* (a twin). The name is borne in the Bible by an apostle who doubted the resurrection of Christ. It is from him that the expression "doubting Thomas" came into being. The Welsh cognate of Thomas is Tomos. (TOM-US)

TIMOTHY A borrowing from the English, Timothy is derived from the French Timothée, which is from the Latin Timotheus, a derivative of the Greek Timotheos (honor God), a compounding of the elements *timē* (honor, respect) and *theos* (God). The name, not used in the British Isles before the Reformation, is borne by Welsh-born actor Timothy Dalton. (TĬM-O-THEE)

TOMOS Welsh form of Thomas (a twin). *See* THOMAS. (TOM-US)

TRAHAEARN Common Welsh name formed by adding the intensive prefix *tra-* to *haearn* (iron): hence, "iron-like." The name is Anglicized as Traherne. (TRA-HERN)

TRAHERNE Anglicized form of the Welsh Trahaearn (like iron, strong as iron). Var: Trahern. (TRA-HERN)

TREFOR Transferred use of the surname originating from a place-name composed of the elements *tref* (settlement, village) and *fôr*, a variant form of *mawr* (large): hence, "dweller at the large village." Var: Trevor. Short: Tref, Trev. (TREH-VER)

TRISTAN From the Old French Tristran, which is from the Celtic Drystan, a name derived from *drest* (tumult, riot). The name, which was altered in reference to the Latin *tristis* (sad), was borne in Celtic legend by a knight who freed Cornwall from a tribute of young men imposed by an Irish king. He was later sent to Ireland by King Mark of Cornwall to bring back Princess Iseult as the king's bride. On the return voyage, both Tristan and Iseult drank from a love potion intended for the king, and became lovers. Tristan left to fight for King Howel of Brittany and, seriously wounded in battle, sent for Iseult. She arrived too late and died from grief next to Tristan's deathbed. The tale was the subject of many popular tragedies during the Middle Ages. Var: Tristram, Trystan, Trystram. (TRIS-TUN)

TUDOR Anglicized form of Tudur (ruler of the people). *See* TUDUR. (TOO-DOR)

TUDUR Derived from the Old Celtic Teutorix, a compound name derived from the elements *teut* (people, tribe) and *rīx* (ruler, king): hence, "ruler of the people." Tudor is the Anglicized spelling. Var: Tudyr. (TID-DEER)

URIEN A common name of uncertain derivation, some believe it might be composed of the Primitive Celtic elements *ōrbo* (privileged) and *gen* (birth): hence, "of privileged birth." Others suggest that the name was left from the time of Roman occupation and believe it is a derivative of the Latin Uranius, which is from the root *ouranos* (heavenly). (YOO-RĪ-UN)

VAUGHN Transferred use of the surname originating as a nickname and derived from a variant form of *bychan* (small). (VON)

VICTOR A borrowing from the English, Victor originates from the Latin *victor* (conqueror, winner, victor). *See* VICTOR (English Names). Gwythyr and Gwydyr are Welsh forms of the name. (VIK-TOR)

WALTER A borrowing from the English, Walter is a name introduced by the Normans. It is from the Old Norman French Waltier, which is from the Germanic Waldhere, a compound name composed from the elements *wald* (ruler) and *heri* (army): hence, "ruler of an army." Gwallter is the Welsh form. (WAL-TER)

WILLIAM A borrowing from the English, William is from the Old Norman French Willaume, which is from the Old High German Willehelm, a compound name composed from the elements *willeo* (will, determination) and *helm* (protection, helmet): hence, "resolute protector." *See* WILLIAM (English Names). Gwilym is the native Welsh form. (WILL-YUM)

WMFFRE Welsh form of Humphrey (warrior of peace). *See* HUMPHREY. (HUM-FREE)

WYN Common name derived from the element *gwyn* (white, fair, blessed) which first arose as a nickname for someone with a very pale complexion or very pale hair. Var: Wynn, Wynne. (WIN)

YNYR Of uncertain derivation, some think it is a Welsh form of the Latin Honōrius (honorable) which arose during the time of Roman occupation. (UN-UR)

YORATH Anglicized form of Iorwerth (handsome lord). *See* IORWERTH. (YAW-RATH).

Welsh Female Names

AERON Derived from Agrona, the name of the Celtic mythological goddess of battle and slaughter. The name is derived from the Welsh *aer* (battle). (AY-RON)

AERONWEN Compound name composed of the Welsh name Aeron (battle) and *gwen* (white, fair, blessed). *See* AERON. (AY-RON-WEN)

AERONWY Derived from the Welsh Aeron (battle). *See* AERON. (AY-RON-EE)

AGNES A popular name throughout Europe and the British Isles, Agnes is derived from the Greek Hagnē, which is from *hagnos* (chaste, pure, sacred). The name was borne by a thirteen-year-old Roman martyred for her Christian beliefs during the reign of Diocletian. Nest and Nesta are Welsh forms of the name. (AG-NESS)

ALMEDHA Anglicized form of Elined (shapely), a name derived from *llun* (a shape or form). Elined, a daughter of Brychan, was martyred on the hill of Penginger and was canonized as St. Almedha. (AL-MEE-DAH)

ANGHARAD Derived from *angharz* (undisgraced, free from shame). The name is borne in Welsh mythology by a maiden who gave blood from her own veins to heal a lady who could only be cured with the blood of a virgin of unblemished character. Angharad has been Anglicized as Anne (gracious, full of grace). Var: Anarawd, Angharawd. (ANG-HAHR-ROD)

ANNA Latinate form of Anne (gracious, full of grace) which is common throughout the British Isles. *See* ANNE. (AHN-NAH)

ANNE A borrowing from the English and the French, Anne is a cognate of the Hebrew Hannah (gracious, full of grace), which is from *hannāh, chaanach* (grace, gracious, mercy). In medieval Christian tradition, Anne was the name assigned to the mother of the Virgin Mary, as Joachim was assigned to her father. The name has remained popular in Britain and is borne by Princess Anne (b. 1950), daughter of Queen Elizabeth II and Prince Philip. Var: Ann, Anna. Pet: Annie. (AN)

ANNWYL Derived from the Welsh *annwyl* (beloved). Var: Anwyl. Short: Ann. (AN-WIL)

ARANRHOD Compound name composed of the Celtic elements *aran* (round, humped) and *rhod* (wheel). The name is borne in Welsh mythology by the sister of Gwydion and the mother of Dylan and the hero Lleu Llaw Gyffes. (AR-AN-ROD)

ARIANA Popular name derived from the Welsh element *arian* (silver). (AR-EE-AN-NAH)

ARIANRHOD Compound name composed of the Welsh elements *arian* (silver) and *rhod* (silver): hence, "silver wheel." (AR-EE-AN-ROD)

ARIANWEN Compound name composed of the element *arian* (silver) and *gwen* (white, fair, blessed): hence, "silver woman." (AR-EE-AN-WEN)

ARTHES Derived from the Gaelic *art* (bear). (AHR-THUS)

BETH Short form of Elizabeth (God is my oath), which is also popularly bestowed as an independent given name. Var: Bethan. (BETH)

BETHAN Popular Welsh form of Beth, a short form of Elizabeth (God is my oath). *See* ELIZABETH. (BETH-UN)

BETRYS Welsh cognate of Beatrix, a name derived from the Latin *beatrix* (she who makes happy, she who brings happiness), which is from *beātus* (happy, blessed). Var: Bettrys. (BET-RISS)

BLODEUWEDD Derived from the obsolete Blodeuedd (flower face), which is from *blawd* (flowers). The name is found in Welsh legend as the name of a woman conjured up from flowers to be the wife of the hero Lleu Llaw

Gyffes. She was transformed into an owl after she had her husband killed. Var: Blodwedd. (BLOD-WED)

BLODWEN Derived from *blodeuyn* (white flowers). (BLOD-WEN)

BRANWEN Compound name composed from the elements *brân* (raven) and *gwen* (white, fair, blessed). The name Branwen is borne in Welsh mythology by the sister of Bran, the daughter of Iweridd and Llyr, a Celtic god of the sea. Her marriage to King Matholwych of Ireland united Britain and Ireland until the king's abuse of Branwen prompted Bran's attack on the island. (BRAN-WEN)

BRIALLEN Derived from the Welsh *briallen* (primrose). Var: Briallan, Briallon. (BREE-AH-THEN)

CAINWEN Old name derived from the Welsh elements *cain* (fair, lovely; jewels, treasures) and *gwen* (white, fair, blessed): hence, "blessed fair one." Var: Ceinwen, Kayne, Keyne. (KANE-WEN)

CARYS Derived from the Welsh *caru* (love) and the suffix *-ys*. (KARE-ISS)

CATHWG Welsh form of Katherine, a cognate of the Greek Aikaterinē, which is from *katharos* (pure, unsullied). (KATH-EE)

CATRIN Welsh form of Katherine (pure, unsullied). *See* CATHWG. (KAT-RIN)

CERIDWEN Compound name derived from the Welsh elements *cerdd* (poetry) and *gwen* (white, fair, blessed): hence, "blessed poetry, fair poet." The name is borne in Celtic mythology by the goddess of poetry. Var: Ceridwyn. Short: Ceri. (KEH-RID-WEN)

CORDELIA Of uncertain origin, Cordelia is thought to be from the Celtic name Creirdyddlydd (jewel of the sea). Short: Delia. Pet: Cordi, Cori, Corri. (KOR-DEE-LEE-AH)

CREIRDYDDLYDD Compound name composed of the Welsh elements *creir* (a token, a jewel, a sacred object) and *llud* (sea): hence, "token of the sea, jewel of the sea." (KREE-DUTH-ITH)

CREIRWY Derived from the Welsh *creir* (a token, a jewel, a sacred article upon which an oath is taken). The name is borne in Welsh mythology by a daughter of Llyr. (KREE-REE)

DELWYN Compound name composed of the Welsh elements *del* (pretty, neat) and *gwen, gwyn* (white, fair, blessed): hence, "pretty and blessed." (DEL-WIN)

DELYTH Derived from the Welsh element *del* (pretty, neat) and the suffix *-yth*. (DEL-ITH)

DIANA A borrowing from the English, Diana is derived from the Latin Diviana, which is from *divus* (divine). The name is borne in Roman mythology by the virgin goddess of the moon and of hunting. In the British Isles, the name received a boost in popularity due to Diana, the princess of Wales. (DI-AN-NAH)

DILWEN Compound name composed of the elements *dilys* (genuine, steadfast, true) and *gwen* (white, fair, blessed): hence, "genuine and blessed." (DIL-WEN)

DILYS Directly derived from the Welsh *dilys* (genuine, steadfast, true). (DIL-ISS)

DWYNWEN Compound name composed from the Welsh elements *dwyn* (wave) and *gwen, gwyn* (white, fair, blessed): hence, "white wave." (DIN-WEN)

EIBHLÍN A borrowing from the Irish, Eibhlín is the Gaelic form of Evelyn, which is an English variant of Aveline, a French diminutive form of the Germanic Avila, which is thought to be a Latinate form of Aveza, a name ultimately of uncertain meaning. Eileen is the Anglicized spelling. (Ī-LEEN)

EIDDWEN Compound name composed of the elements *eiddun* (desirous, fond) and *gwen* (white, fair, blessed). (ĪTH-WEN)

EILEEN English variant of the French Aveline, used to Anglicize Eibhlín, the Gaelic form of Evelyn, which also has the same roots. *See* EIBHLÍN. Var: Aileen. (Ī-LEEN)

EIRA Derived directly from the Welsh *eira* (snow). (Ī-RAH)

EIRWEN Modern coinage formed by combining the name Eira (snow) and the element *gwen* (white, fair, blessed): hence, "white snow, blessed snow." (Ī-RWEN)

ELEN Derived from *elin* (nymph). Alternatively, some use Elen as a Welsh form of the English Ellen and Helen (light). Var: Elin, Ellin. (EL-EN)

ELERI Of unknown etymology, the name Eleri is found in Welsh legend as the daughter of the 5th-century chief Brychan. (EL-EH-REE)

ELISA Short form of Elizabeth (God is my oath), Elisa is also bestowed as an independent given name. *See* ELIZABETH. (EH-LEE-SAH)

ELIZABETH Derived from the Hebrew *elīsheba'* (God is my oath). The name is borne in the Bible by a kinswoman of the Virgin Mary and mother of John the Baptist. In the British Isles, the name has remained popular by its association with the queen mother (b. 1900), the former Elizabeth Bowes-Lyon, and her daughter

Queen Elizabeth II (b. 1926). Var: Elisabeth. Short: Beth, Elisa; Bethan (Welsh). (EE-LIZ-AH-BETH)

ELLEN A borrowing from the English, Ellen originated as a variant of Helen, but is now commonly viewed as a variant of Eleanor. Both names, however, are from the same Greek root, *ēlē* (light, torch, bright). Var: Elen. (EL-LUN)

ELUNED Popular elaboration of Luned (shape, form). *See* LUNED. Var: Eiluned. (EL-LEE-NED)

ENFYS Directly derived from *enfys* (rainbow). (EN-VIS)

ENID Of uncertain derivation, Enid is a Celtic name borne in Arthurian legend by the wife of Geraint. After being accused of infidelity by her jealous husband, Enid regained Geraint's trust by being submissive, obedient, and loyal. (EN-NID, EE-NID)

EOGHANIA Feminine form of Eoghan (youth, young warrior). *See* EOGHAN (Male Names). The name is Anglicized as Eugenia (well-born). (EH-VAN-YAH)

ERMIN Derived from the Latin Erminia (lordly), a feminine form of the German Hermann (soldier), a compound name composed of the elements *hari* (army) and *man* (man). (ER-MIN)

ESYLLT Popular Welsh name meaning "beautiful, fair." The name is also used as a variant of Isolde, a name of uncertain derivation. *See* ISOLDE. The name is borne in medieval legend by an Irish princess who was betrothed to King Mark of Cornwall. Through a magic potion, she became the beloved of Tristram, who was married to another Isolde. Var: Iseult, Isolde, Yseult, Ysolt. (EE-SOLD)

FFRAID Welsh cognate of Bridget, the Anglicized form of the Gaelic Bríghid, which is believed to be derived from *brîgh* (strength). *See* BRÍGHID (Irish Names). (FRADE)

GAENOR Welsh form of Gaynor, which is a medieval form of the English Guinevere and the Welsh Gwenhwyfar. (GAY-NOR)

GLENDA Derived from the Welsh *glân* (clean, pure, holy) and *da* (good), elements that represent desirable attributes. (GLEN-DAH)

GLENYS Derived from the Welsh *glân* (clean, pure, holy) and the suffix *-ys*. Var: Glenice, Glenis, Glynis. (GLEN-ISS)

GORAWEN Derived from the Welsh *gorawen* (joy). (GOR-AH-WEN)

GWANWYN Derived from the Welsh *gwanwyn* (spring). (GWAHN-WIN)

GWEN Derived from *gwen*, the feminine form of *gwyn* (white, fair, blessed). When employed as an element in compound names, the element *gwen* also represents the poetical definition of a woman. Alternatively, Gwen is used as a short form of any of the various names containing *gwen* as an element. (GWEN)

GWENDA Compound name composed of the elements *gwen* (white, fair, blessed) and *da* (good). Short: Gwen. (GWEN-DAH)

GWENDOLEN Compound name composed of the elements *gwen* (white, fair, blessed) and *dolen* (bow, ring). The name is borne in Welsh mythology by the wife of King Locrine. After her husband left her for the German princess Estrildis, Gwendolen has Estrilda and her daughter drowned. Var: Gwendolin, Gwendoline, Gwendolyn, Wendolen, Wendolyn. Short: Gwen. Pet: Wendy. (GWEN-DŌ-LEN)

GWENEAL Compound name composed of the elements *gwen* (white, fair, blessed) and *angel* (angel): hence, "white angel, blessed angel." (GWIN-EE-UL)

GWENFREWI Compound name composed of the elements *gwen* (white, fair, blessed) and *frewi* (reconciliation, peace). The name was borne by a 7th-century Welsh saint who was martyred after rejecting the attentions of a prince named Caradoc. A well sprung up from the place of her martyrdom which is said to have miraculous healing properties, and the surrounding stones are marked with red veins said to represent the blood of the saint. (GWEN-FROO-EE)

GWENHWYFAR Compound name composed of the Welsh elements *gwen* (white, fair, blessed) and *hwyfar* (smooth, soft): hence, "fair lady." The name is Anglicized as Guinevere. *See* GUINEVERE. Var: Gwynhwyfar. Short: Gwen. (GWEN-HI-VAR)

GWENLLIAN Compound name composed of the elements *gwen* (white, fair, blessed) and *llian* (linen) or *lliant* (flood, flow). Short: Gwen. (GWEN-THEE-UN)

GWERFUL Compound name composed of the elements *gwair* (circle, ring) and *ful*, a mutation of *mul* (modest, shy): hence, "completely shy." Var: Gweirful, Gwerfyl. (GWARE-VUL)

GWLADUS Old name of uncertain derivation, perhaps a Welsh feminine form of the Latin Claudius, an old Roman family name derived from *claudus* (lame). Var: Gladys, Gwladys. (GWLAD-US)

GWYNETH Feminine form of Gwynedd, a derivative of *gwyn* (white, fair, blessed). The name Gwynedd originated as a place-name in northern Wales. Var: Gwenyth, Gyneth. (GWEN-ETH)

HELEDD Ancient yet still common Celtic name of uncertain derivation. Var: Hyledd. (HEE-LID)

HELEN A borrowing from the English, Helen is a cognate of the Greek Helenē, which is derived from the root *ēlē* (light, torch, bright). *See* HELENE (Mythology and Astrology Names). (HEL-UN)

ISOLDE Of debated origin and meaning, Isolde may be derived from the Old High German Isold, a name composed of the elements *is* (ice) and *waltan* (to rule): hence, "ruler of the ice." Alternatively, it is also used as a variant of the Welsh Esyllt (beautiful, fair) and is often used in English versions of tales from Welsh legend. *See* ESYLLT. (IH-SOLD)

JANE A borrowing from the English, Jane is a cognate of the French Jehanne and Jeanne, feminine forms of Jean, which is the French cognate of John (God is gracious). *See* JOHN (Male Names). Siân is the Welsh form of the name. *See* SIÂN. (JANE)

JANET A borrowing from the English, Janet is a diminutive form of Jane (God is gracious) which arose in the Middle Ages. Sioned is the popular Welsh form. (JAN-ET)

KENDALL Transferred use of the surname derived from the place-name Kendal in northwestern England. The town, which is in the valley of the river Kent, derives its name from the name of the river and *dale* (valley): hence, "dweller in the valley of the river Kent." Another source for the surname is the place-name Kendale in Humberside, northeastern England. In this case, the name is derived from the Old Norse *keld* (spring) and the Old English *dale* (valley): hence, "dweller in the valley of the spring." Alternatively, Kendall is used as an Anglicized feminine form of Cynddelw, an old Welsh male name of uncertain derivation. Var: Kendal, Kendell. (KEN-DL)

LLEULU Welsh form of Lucia, a feminine form of Lucius, which is derived from the Latin *lux* (light). The name was borne by St. Lucia of Syracuse, a 4th-century martyr whose popularity during the Middle Ages led to widespread use of the name. (HLYOO-LOO)

LUNED Popular name derived from the Welsh *llun* (shape, form). Var: Eiluned, Eluned, Linet, Lunette. (LOO-NED)

MALLT Welsh form of Maud (powerful in battle). *See* MAUD. (MAHLD)

MARGARET A borrowing from the English and the Scotch, Margaret is from the Greek Margarītēs, which is derived from *margaron* (a pearl). *See* MARGARET (English Names). Marged and Mererid are Welsh forms. *See* MARGED. Pet: Margie, Meggie. (MAR-GAH-RET)

MARGED Welsh form of Margaret (a pearl). *See* MARGARET. Var: Mared. Pet: Meaghan, Meg, Megan, Meghan. (MAHR-GET)

MARI A Welsh form of Mary, Mair is an evolution of the older Meir. *See* MARY. Var: Mair. (MARE-EE)

MARTHA Derived from the Aramaic Mārthā (lady, mistress). The name is borne in the Bible by the sister of Lazarus and Mary of Bethany. (MAR-THA)

MAUD Anglicized Norman contraction of Mathilda (powerful in battle) in use since the Middle Ages. Mathilda is derived from the Old High German Mahthilda, a compound name composed of the elements *maht* (might, power) and *hiltia* (battle). Maud and Matilda were both brought to the British Isles by the Normans during the Conquest. The Welsh form is Mallt. (MAUD, MOD)

MEGAN Pet form of Marged, which is a Welsh cognate of Margaret (a pearl). Megan is also commonly bestowed as an independent given name. *See* MARGARET. Var: Meaghan, Meghan. Short: Meg. (MEH-GAN)

MEINWEN Compound name composed of the Welsh elements *main* (slender) and *gwen* (white, fair, blessed): hence, "slender fair one, slender woman." (MINE-WEN)

MEIRIONA Feminine form of Meirion, the Welsh cognate of the Latin Mariānus, which is a derivative of Marius, an old Roman family name of uncertain derivation. Some believe it has its root in Mars, the Roman mythological god of war, but others think it is derived from the Latin *mas* (manly). Early Christians associated the name with Maria, the virgin mother, and thus the name enjoyed widespread use. (MEER-EE-O-NAH)

MEIRIONWEN Compound name composed of the name Meiriona and the Welsh element *gwen* (white, fair, blessed). *See* MEIRIONA. (MEER-EE-ON-WEN)

MEREDITH Modern form of the Old Welsh Maredudd and Meredudd, which are of uncertain derivation. Some believe *iudd* (lord) is the second element. (MEH-REH-DITH)

MERERID Welsh form of Margaret (a pearl). *See* MARGARET. (MEH-REH-RID)

MORGAN Modern form of Morcant, an ancient name of uncertain and debated derivation. Some believe the first element is derived from the Welsh *môr* (sea) and thus define the name as "lady of the sea." Others derive the second element from the Celtic *cant* (circle, completion). The name is borne in Arthurian legend by

Morgan le Fay, the sorceress and stepsister of King Arthur and mother of Modred and Gawain. Var: Morgana. (MOR-GUN)

MORGWEN Compound name believed to be composed of the elements *môr* (sea) and *gwen* (white, fair, blessed): hence, "fair seas, lady of the sea." (MOR-GWEN)

MORWENNA Old name of uncertain and debated derivation. Some believe it to be from *morwyn* (maiden). Others think it derives from the elements *môr* (sea) and *gwen* (white, fair, blessed): hence, "white seas, blessed seas." (MOR-WEN-NAH)

MYFANWY An old name of debated meaning, some believe it is from My-manwy (my fine one, rare one). Others think it is translated as "child of the water." Var: Myvanwy. Short: Myff. (MUH-VAN-WEE)

MYRDDIN Derived from the Primitive Celtic elements *mori* (sea) and *dunom* (hill, fortress): hence, "sea hill, fortress by the sea." (MUR-THIN)

NERYS Modern coinage believed to be derived from the Welsh *nér* (lord) and the popular suffix *-ys*. (NER-ISS)

NEST Welsh cognate of Agnes (pure, chaste). *See* AGNES. Var: Nesta. (NEST)

OLWEN Compound name composed of the elements *ôl* (footprint, track) and *gwen* (white, fair, blessed): hence, "white footprint." The name is borne in Welsh mythology by a maiden from whom flowers sprung up behind as she walked. (AHL-WEN)

OWENA Feminine form of Owen, an old name of uncertain and debated origin. *See* OWEN (Male Names). (O-EN-AH)

RHIANNON Ancient Celtic name of uncertain derivation. Some believe it to be derived from the Old Celtic Rigantona (great queen). The name, which is borne in Celtic mythology by a goddess of fertility, was not in use as a given name until the 20th century. The song "Rhiannon" by the rock group Fleetwood Mac popularized the name throughout Great Britain and abroad. (REE-AN-NUN)

RHIANWEN An old name, the first element of which is of uncertain derivation. The second element is believed to be derived from *gwen* (white, fair, blessed). It is often given the definition "fair maiden." (REE-AN-WEN)

RHONWEN Compound name composed of the elements *rhon* (lance) or *rhawn* (hair) and *gwen* (white, fair, blessed): hence, "fair-haired or blessed lance." (RON-WEN)

RHOSYN Derived from the Welsh *rhosyn* (a rose). (HRO-SUN)

SABRINA Of uncertain etymology, Sabrina is believed to be of Celtic origin, as it is borne in Celtic mythology by an illegitimate daughter of the Welsh King Locrine. The child was ordered drowned by the king's wife Gwendolen, thus giving her name to the river in which the foul deed took place. Latin writings of the 1st century list the river's name as Sabrina. It is now known as the river Severn. (SAH-BREE-NAH)

SEREN Derived from the Welsh *seren* (star). (SEH-REN)

SHAN Anglicized form of Siân, the Welsh cognate of Jane (God is gracious). *See* JANE *and* SIÂN. (SHAN)

SHANEE Anglicized form of Siani, the pet form of Siân, which is the Welsh cognate of Jane (God is gracious). *See* JANE. (SHAN-EE)

SIÂN Welsh cognate of Jane (God is gracious). *See* JANE. Shan is an Anglicized form. Pet: Siani. (SHAN)

SIANI Pet form of Siân (God is gracious). *See* SIÂN. Shanee is the Anglicized form of Siani. (SHAN-EE)

SIONED Welsh form of Janet, which is a diminutive form of Jane (God is gracious). The name Janet arose in the Middle Ages. *See* JANE. (SHAN-ED)

TEGWEN Compound name composed of the elements *teg* (fair, lovely) and *gwen* (white, fair, blessed): hence, "lovely maiden." (TEG-WEN)

TELERI Elaboration of Eleri, an ancient name of unknown origin and meaning. *See* ELERI. (TEL-EH-REE)

TIRION Directly derived from *tirion* (gentle, kind). (TEER-EE-ON)

WENDY A modern pet form of Gwendolen (white-browed), Wendy is also bestowed as an independent given name. *See* GWENDOLEN; *see also* WENDY (English Names). (WEN-DEE)

WINIFRED Anglicized form of the Welsh Gwenfrewi (blessed peace). Short: Freda, Win. Pet: Winnie. (WIN-IH-FRED)

Bibliography

Arnold-Baker, C. *Dictionary of Dates*. 4th Ed. E. P. Dutton, New York, 1954.

Arthur, William. *An Etymological Dictionary of Family and Christian Names*. Sheldon, Blakeman & Co., New York, 1857.

Attwater, Donald. *Martyrs: From St. Stephen to John Tung*. Sheed & Ward, New York, 1957.

Benson, Morton. *Dictionary of Russian Personal Names*. Univ. of Penn. Press, Philadelphia, 1964.

Beyer, Harald. *A History of Norwegian Literature*. New York Univ. Press, 1956.

The Book of Saints: A Dictionary of Servants of God Canonised by the Catholic Church. Compiled by the Benedictine Monks of St. Augustine's Abbey, Ramsgate. Macmillan & Co., New York, 1944.

Branston, Brian. *Gods of the North*. Vanguard Press, New York, 1955.

Brown, Peter. *The Cult of the Saints: Its Rise and Function in Latin Christianity*. Univ. of Chicago Press, Chicago, 1981.

Bryant, T. A. *Today's Dictionary of the Bible*. Bethany House Publishers, Minneapolis, 1982.

Canesso, Claudia. *Cambodia*. Chelsea House Publishers, New York, 1989.

Chuks-Orti, Ogonna. *Names from Africa*. Johnson Publishing Co., Chicago, 1972.

Dockstader, Frederick J. *Great North American Indians*. Van Nostrand Reinhold, New York, 1977.

Ewen, C. L'Estrange. *A History of Surnames of the British Isles*. Genealogical Publishing Co., Baltimore, 1968.

Famous Indians: A Collection of Short Biographies. U.S. Government Printing Office, 1966.

Fox, Edward W. *Atlas of European History*. Oxford Univ. Press, New York, 1957.

Freeman, William. *Dictionary of Fictional Characters*. Boston, 1963.

Gifford, Edward Winslow. *Tongan Society*. Bulletin 61. Bernice P. Bishop Museum.

Hamilton, E. N. *Bible Names*. John Howell, San Francisco, 1940.

Hanks, Patrick, and Flavia Hodges. *A Dictionary of First Names*. London, 1992.

Harrison, Henry. *Surnames of the United Kingdom*. Genealogical Publishing Co., Baltimore, 1969.

Hitchcock, H. R. *An English-Hawaiian Dictionary*. Charles E. Tuttle Co., Tokyo, 1968.

Ka'ano'i, Patrick, and Robert Lokomaika'iokalani Snakenberg. *The Hawaiian Name Book*. Bess Press, Inc., Honolulu, Hawaii, 1988.

Kaganoff, Benzion C. *A Dictionary of Jewish Names and Their History*. Schocken Books, New York, 1977.

Kennedy, Hugh. *The Prophet and the Age of the Caliphates*. Longman Publishing Group, White Plains, New York, 1986.

Lannoy, Richard. *The Speaking Tree*. Oxford Univ. Press, New York, 1971.

Larousse World Mythology. W. H. Smith Publishers, Inc., New York, 1989.

Lê-bá-Khanh, and Lê-bá-Kong. *Vietnamese-English Dictionary*. Frederick Ungar Publishing Co., New York, 1955.

The Lion Encyclopedia of the Bible. Lion Publishing Co., Totowa, New Jersey, 1978.

Lunt, W. E. *History of England*. Harper & Brothers, New York, 1945.

MacAlpine, Neil. *Pronouncing Gaelic-English Dictionary*. Neil Gairm Publications, Glasgow, 1975.

MacLysaght, Edward. *The Surnames of Ireland*. Irish Academic Press, Dublin, 1985.

Madubuike, Ihechukwu. *A Handbook of African Names*. Three Continents Press, Washington, 1976.

Miller, G. M. *BBC Pronouncing Dictionary of British Names*. Oxford Univ. Press, London, 1971.

Morris, Jan. *Wales*. Oxford Univ. Press, Oxford, 1982.

Munch, Peter Andreas. *Norse Mythology*. Singing Tree Press, Detroit, 1968.

The New American Bible. Catholic Book Publishing Co., New York, 1970.

The New Combined Bible Dictionary and Concordance. Baker Book House, Grand Rapids, Mich., 1965.

O'Corráin, Donnchadh, and Fidelma Maguire. *Gaelic Personal Names*. Dublin, 1981.

Perrott, D. V. *Concise Swahili and English Dictionary*. NTC Publishing Group, Chicago, 1992.

Puckett, Newbell Niles. *Black Names in America*. G. K. Hall & Co., Boston, 1975.

Pukui, Mary Kawena, and Samuel H. Elbert. *New Pocket Hawaiian Dictionary*. Univ. of Hawaii Press, Honolulu, 1992.

Reaney, P. H. *A Dictionary of British Surnames*. Routledge & Kegan Paul, London, 1958.

Reaney, P. H. *The Origin of English Place-Names*. Routledge & Kegan Paul, Ltd., London, 1960.

Rodinson, Maxine. *The Arabs*. Univ. of Chicago Press, Chicago, 1981.

Rossi, Carlo. *Portuguese: The Language of Brazil*. Holt, Rinehart & Winston, Inc., New York, 1945.

Simpson, D. P. *Cassell's New Latin Dictionary*, Funk and Wagnalls, New York, 1968.

Smith, Eldson C. *American Surnames*. Chilton Book Co., Philadelphia, 1969.

Smith, Elsdon C. *New Dictionary of American Family Names*. Harper & Row, New York, 1973.

Smith, Elsdon C. *Treasury of Name Lore*. Harper & Row, New York, 1967.

Smout, T. C. *A History of the Scottish People 1560–1830*. Charles Scribner's Sons, New York, 1969.

Stewart, George R. *American Given Names*. Oxford Univ. Press, New York, 1979.

Stewart, Julia. *African Names*. Carol Publishing Group, New York, 1993.

Thomas, Henry. *Biographical Encyclopedia of Philosophy*. Doubleday & Co. Inc., Garden City, N. Y., 1965.

Verma, G. *100 Great Indians Through the Ages*. Great Indian Publishers, New Delhi and GIP Books, Campbell, Calif., 1992.

Williamson, David. *Debrett's Kings and Queens of Europe*. Salem House, Topsfield, Mass., 1988.

Withycombe, E. G. *The Oxford Dictionary of English Christian Names*. Clarendon Press, Oxford, 1977.

Woods, Richard. *Hispanic First Names*. Greenwood Press, Westport, Conn., 1984.

Woulfe, Patrick. *Irish Names and Surnames*. Irish Genealogical Foundation, Kansas City, Mo., 1992.

Yonge, Charlotte M. *History of Christian Names*. Macmillan & Co., London, 1884.

Index